# The American Constitution

*M. Wayne Holsinger*

*1971*

MC GRAW-HILL SERIES IN POLITICAL SCIENCE

ADRIAN · *State and Local Governments*

ADRIAN AND PRESS · *Governing Urban America*

BONE · *American Politics and the Party System*

CHRISTENSON AND MC WILLIAMS · *Voice of the People: Readings in Public Opinion and Propaganda*

GERBERDING · *United States Foreign Policy*

HARMON · *Political Thought: From Plato to the Present*

MC CLOSKY AND TURNER · *The Soviet Dictatorship*

MILLETT · *Government and Public Administration*

MILLETT · *Management in the Public Service*

NEUMANN · *European Government*

PIERSON AND GIL · *Governments of Latin America*

POOL · *Contemporary Political Science: Toward Empirical Theory*

POWELL AND PARKER · *Major Aspects of American Government*

PRITCHETT · *The American Constitution*

PRITCHETT · *American Constitutional Issues*

SCHUMAN · *International Politics*

TURNER · *Politics in the United States: Readings in Political Parties and Pressure Groups*

VANDENBOSCH AND HOGAN · *Toward World Order*

WILSON · *Police Administration*

# The American Constitution

Second Edition

**C. HERMAN PRITCHETT**

PROFESSOR OF POLITICAL SCIENCE
UNIVERSITY OF CHICAGO

McGRAW-HILL BOOK COMPANY

NEW YORK   ST. LOUIS   SAN FRANCISCO   TORONTO
LONDON   SYDNEY

*The American Constitution*

*Library of Congress Catalog Card Number: 68–16490*

50876

234567890   MAMM   754321069

for Jeanie and Philip

. . . the theory that the Constitution is a written document is a legal fiction. The idea that it can be understood by a study of its language and the history of its past development is equally mythical. It is what the Government and the people who count in public affairs recognize and respect as such, what they think it is. More than this. It is not merely what it has been, or what it is today. It is always becoming something else and those who criticize it and the acts done under it, as well as those who praise, help to make it what it will be tomorrow.

Charles A. Beard and William Beard,
*The American Leviathan*, p. 39.

# *Preface to the Second Edition*

The nine years that have elapsed since the first edition of this volume appeared have been years of unprecedented activity in constitutional interpretation. In no comparable period, even during what was then thought to be the "constitutional revolution" which terminated the Supreme Court's battle with the New Deal in 1937, has the Court developed so much new constitutional doctrine in so many important fields or dealt simultaneously with so many controversial issues. Even more significant, never before has the Court so consistently taken an activist stance which so often challenges important conservative interests, institutions, and philosophies. Some of the same people who used to regard the Court as "the sheet anchor of the Republic" because of its defense of the *status quo* now want to "impeach Earl Warren" or "curb the Court" because of its defense of civil liberties.

It is the intention of this edition to place these recent constitutional interpretations in the perspective of the older body of doctrine out of which they developed, and to explain the conflicting positions taken by the justices as they have wrestled with these difficult issues. It is inevitable that a judicial body which is expected to referee basic value conflicts in our society will not enjoy universal popularity. The umpire must expect some booing from the stands. But it is possible to hope that an understanding of the Court's role and its reasoning will promote agreement that the Court is performing responsibly a function of the highest importance for a free and demo-

cratic society. As *The New York Times* said editorially on October 5, 1953, the day that Chief Justice Warren took his seat on the Court:

> Liberty under the law is one of the noblest of human concepts. But how much liberty and how much law?
>
> If nine men, or five men out of nine, had to give the final answer, we could well despair, just as we might well despair if the perpetuation of this republic depended on the election or re-election every four years of a supreme genius as President. But the nine men, however detached, however scrupulously impartial, are part of the world in which they live and move. We do not vote for them or against them, and would not want to, but all honest thought has some influence upon them. They are, at their best, America thinking, just as the President, a general, a manufacturer, a labor leader, a professional man, may be America acting. We may well feel a sense of reverence as the Court walks in—not solely for nine men brought to this place in part by chance as well as by achievement and ability, but for the function they perform. They are a substitute for force—the best yet invented.
>
> The Court resumes. When its entrance is announced we can arise with alacrity, for here in this room, where orders are sometimes given that no other power can contravene, is a symbol of our civilization and our freedom.

In the preparation of this second edition, the author has had the advantage of a careful review and critique of the first edition by Professor Robert A. Horn of Stanford University, to whom grateful acknowledgment is made.

C. HERMAN PRITCHETT

# Preface to the First Edition

The Constitution of the United States of America, drafted between May 14 and September 17, 1787, by fifty-five men meeting in the city of Philadelphia, and made effective on June 21, 1788, by the vote of nine state ratifying conventions, is now the oldest and preeminently the most successful written constitution in the modern history of man. The attention devoted to the American Constitution has been fully in proportion to the status it has achieved. It has attracted praise of outrageous extravagance—"the most wonderful work ever struck off at a given time by the brain and purpose of man," said William Gladstone. It has supplied a symbol of national unity sorely needed in a pageantless republic.

The Constitution has in fact been all things to all men. Conservatives have hailed its effectiveness as a guarantee of vested rights. Liberals have held it in high esteem for its protection of civil liberties. All interests, all shades of opinion, have acknowledged its prestige by seeking to prove their causes to be in support of, or at least not incompatible with, the Constitution.

There is legitimate ground for disagreement as to what the Constitution means or authorizes. For the document ratified in 1788—the parchment sheets preserved in a national shrine in the Archives in Washington—is not really the Constitution. Adding the twenty-two amendments which had been adopted up to 1958 does not markedly change the situation. All this language has had to be given life and meaning by the events that have

occurred since 1788. In a real sense America's history is the American Constitution.

Congress re-creates the Constitution every time it passes a law or holds a hearing. The President construes the Constitution whenever he makes a decision, issues an executive order, or signs a bill into law. The Constitution of the United States is the body of practice built up during past decades by the executive departments. It is manifested in the historic crises that have been met—Lincoln facing the disintegration of the Union, Roosevelt facing the collapse of the national economy. It is discoverable equally at lower levels, in the routines and the customs of public life, in what Justice Holmes called the inarticulate major premises of a nation and a people.

Since all this is true, it follows that one of the best avenues to an understanding of the Constitution is through the history of American constitutional crises and practices as they have unfolded—in other words, through constitutional history. The several excellent American constitutional histories available do in fact convey an incomparably valuable sense of the Constitution as a living and changing force, and reveal the influence which the document, as popularly understood, has had upon the stream of American history.

However, there are other paths to constitutional understanding than through constitutional history, which has its dilemmas and its shortcomings. The stream of history, like the stream of consciousness, is disorganized and chaotic. Action is going on in many rings simultaneously. The constitutional historian has to cover so wide a field, deal with such a wide range of sources of constitutional interpretation, that he must impose strict standards of selection and arbitrarily rearrange sequences of action. The historian cannot re-create history and often cannot even explain it.

This book employs a different approach—that of constitutional law. Approaching the Constitution through the discipline and tradition of law presents its own problems, but in several respects they appear less difficult than those of the historian. The range and the source of the data are more restricted. By definition, one is concerned only with the controversies about the Constitution which have occurred in a legal context or which have employed legal arguments. By "legal context" is meant primarily proceedings in the law courts. Interpretation of the Constitution has been at issue in tens of thousands of the suits filed in American federal and state courts since 1789. A fraction of 1 per cent of this number has risen to the level of the United States Supreme Court for final decision, but in that handful are rulings of the most profound significance for the American nation. The great prestige of this Court is in fact based on its accepted position as ultimate judicial interpreter of the Constitution.

One who uses the decisions of the Supreme Court as material for his understanding of the American Constitution has many advantages over the historian. He need not dredge for his data in brittle newspapers and dusty

documents. He finds the *United States Reports* neatly shelved in every law library, together with an extraordinary array of commentary, analysis, and cross referencing. The judgment of the Court is set forth in reasoned opinions which vary greatly in quality, but which at their best may be gems of forensic skill and occasionally even noble literature. With only fourteen Chief Justices and eighty-two associate justices on the Court since 1789, the impact of individual judicial minds upon constitutional development becomes interestingly visible.

It is true that interpretation of the Constitution is actually performed by the Supreme Court only when, if, and insofar as it is necessary in order to dispose of a specific dispute which is before the Court. Thus some important constitutional issues may long remain judicially unsettled, because no case is ever successfully raised involving them. The justices, moreover, officially know only so much of the background of the problem as is presented in the briefs, and may thus lack something of a full understanding of the issues. In contrast with the full-bodied, imperative manner in which constitutional issues force themselves on the attention of Congress or the President, or are seized and exploited by them, the Court's handling of constitutional problems may at times seem rather academic and sterile.

Nevertheless, it is largely because of its judicial techniques and its degree of detachment from political battles that the Supreme Court enjoys such prestige and acceptance as ultimate arbiter of the Constitution. The political branches of the government may dispute, or on occasion, override the judicial interpretation, but in the great majority of cases the Constitution, as Charles Evans Hughes sagely observed, means what the Supreme Court says it means.

This book, then, is an exposition of what the Supreme Court has said the American Constitution means. The approach is analytical. Part 1 centers on the document itself—its background, adoption, and process of subsequent development. Parts 2 through 5 deal with the structure and powers of the institutions which make up the federal system. Parts 6 and 7 are concerned with constitutional limitations on national and state powers. For each problem of constitutional interpretation some sense of the historical development is sought to be conveyed, and on those problems where little in the way of judicial opinion is available, executive or legislative practice may be noted to fill the gap.

The author is deeply indebted to Robert A. Horn of Stanford University, who has read the entire manuscript; his profound knowledge has prevented numerous errors of fact and judgment. Robert K. Carr of Dartmouth College was kind enough to give his comments on the chapter dealing with congressional investigations. Walter Murphy, now of Princeton University, as the author's research assistant wrote the first drafts of Chapters 5, 6, and 33. James Holton checked the quotations and prepared the table of cases. The manuscript was typed by Jean Pritchett, Avis Coates, and Carol Lerner, and

funds for stenographic and research assistance were supplied by the Social Science Division of the University of Chicago.

The author's deepest obligation is to Leonard D. White, for over thirty years teacher, colleague, and friend, without whose aid and example this work would never have been written.

C. HERMAN PRITCHETT

# Contents

*Preface to the Second Edition*    *vii*

*Preface to the First Edition*    *ix*

### PART ONE    THE DOCUMENT

1    THE PRECONSTITUTIONAL PERIOD    3

  *Political Unification and the Revolution    4*
  *The Political Theory of the Revolutionary Period    8*
  *The Post-Revolutionary Experience    10*
  *The Movement for a New Constitution    13*

2    THE CONSTITUTIONAL CONVENTION    16

  *Membership and Procedure    16*
  *The Major Decisions    19*
  *Ratification of the Constitution    28*

3    AMENDMENT OF THE CONSTITUTION    32

  *The Development of Article V    33*
  *Use of the Amending Power    34*

*The "Political" Character of the Amending Process    35*
*The Proposing of Amendments    36*
*The Ratification of Amendments    39*
*Appraisal of the Amending Process    40*

4    INTERPRETATION OF THE CONSTITUTION    44

*Approaches to Constitutional Meaning    45*
*The Personal Factor in Judicial Interpretation    50*


PART TWO    THE UNION


5    NATION AND STATE    63

*The Nature of the Union    64*
*National Supremacy    69*
*Admission of New States    77*
*Obligations of the National Government to the States    80*
*Representation in State Legislatures    84*
*Control over Territories    93*


6    INTERSTATE RELATIONS    98

*Interstate Privileges and Immunities    98*
*Full Faith and Credit    100*
*Rendition    106*
*Interstate Compacts    107*
*Disputes between States    109*


PART THREE    THE JUDICIARY


7    JUDICIAL POWER AND ORGANIZATION    115

*Federal Judicial Power    116*
*Legislative Structuring of the Court System    122*
*The Lower Federal Courts    125*
*The Supreme Court    127*
*Specialized and Legislative Courts    132*
*Staffing the Federal Judiciary    135*
*Judicial Tenure and Compensation    137*

8    JURISDICTION OF THE FEDERAL COURTS   *141*

  *Federal Judicial Power: Subject Matter   142*
  *Federal Judicial Power: Parties   144*
  *Federal-State Court Relations: Concurrency of Jurisdiction   151*
  *Federal-State Court Relations: Conflicts of Jurisdiction   153*


9    JUDICIAL REVIEW   *158*

  *The Prehistory of Judicial Review   160*
  *The Establishment of Judicial Review   163*
  *Judicial Self-restraint: Justiciable Questions   167*
  *Judicial Self-restraint: Separation of Powers   174*


PART FOUR    THE LEGISLATURE


10    MEMBERSHIP   *181*

  *The Senate   181*
  *Apportionment of Representatives   182*
  *Districting for the House   183*
  *Terms   188*
  *Qualifications   188*
  *Expulsion and Censure   190*
  *The Filling of Vacancies   191*
  *Privileges and Immunities of Members   192*


11    LEGISLATIVE POWERS AND PROCEDURE   *195*

  *Principles of Legislative Power   196*
  *Delegation of Legislative Power   198*
  *The Impeachment Power   203*
  *The Power of Administrative Supervision   205*
  *Legislative Procedure   209*


12    THE INVESTIGATORY POWER   *214*

  *The Constitutional Basis   215*
  *The Legislative Contempt Power   217*
  *Constitutional Defenses for Witnesses   218*
  *Contempt after Watkins   222*

*Contempt after Braden    227*
*The Dilemma of Judicial Control    230*


13    TAXATION AND FISCAL POWERS    233

*Specific Limitations on the Taxing Power    234*
*Taxation for Nonrevenue Purposes    237*
*Intergovernmental Tax Immunity    240*
*The Power to Spend    245*
*Borrowing and Monetary Powers    248*


14    THE COMMERCE POWER    252

*Gibbons* v. *Ogden    253*
*Interstate and Intrastate Commerce    255*
*The Power to "Regulate"    259*
*The Concept of "Effect upon Commerce"    263*
*The Commerce Power after 1937    269*


15    THE COMMERCE POWER AND THE STATES    281

*The Exclusiveness Issue    281*
*State Regulation and Commerce    287*
*State Taxation and the Imports-Exports Clause    294*
*State Taxation and Commerce    296*


PART FIVE      THE EXECUTIVE


16    QUALIFICATIONS AND ELECTION    307

*Qualifications    308*
*Presidential Election and the Constitution    309*
*Electoral College Problems    312*
*Proposals for Electoral Reform    315*
*Term and Tenure    320*
*Succession    321*
*Presidential Inability    324*


17    EXECUTIVE POWERS IN GENERAL    329

*The President and Lawmaking    329*
*Theories of Executive Power    333*

*The Power of Appointment  341*
*The Power of Removal  344*
*The Power to Pardon  348*

18    CONTROL OF FOREIGN RELATIONS  *353*

*The Nature of Federal Power  354*
*The Role of the President  356*
*Congress and Foreign Relations  360*
*Constitutional Aspects of the Treaty Power  362*
*The Bricker Amendment  364*
*Control over Passports  366*

19    THE PRESIDENT AS COMMANDER IN CHIEF  *372*

*The State of War  373*
*The President and the Armed Forces  378*
*The President and Martial Law  379*
*The President and Military Justice  382*
*The President and the Home Front  388*


PART SIX    FIRST AMENDMENT FREEDOMS

20    CONSTITUTIONAL BASIS FOR PROTECTION
OF INDIVIDUAL RIGHTS  *395*

*The Bill of Rights  396*
*Civil Rights Problems to the Civil War  398*
*Drafting of the Fourteenth Amendment  404*

21    THE JUDICIAL APPROACH TO CIVIL LIBERTIES  *412*

*History and the First Amendment  413*
*The Clear and Present Danger Test  415*
*Legislative Reasonableness  419*
*Preferred Position  420*
*The Absolutist-Literalist Position  423*
*Balancing  426*
*The Two-level Theory  428*
*Appraisal  429*

22    FREEDOM OF THE PRESS  *431*

*The Right to Publish  431*
*Freedom of Circulation: Handbills  436*

*Freedom of Circulation: The Post Office*   437
*Free Press and Fair Trial*   442

23   RESTRAINT OF SPEECH AND ASSEMBLY   *451*

*Speech in the Public Forum*   452
*"Pure Speech" versus "Speech Plus"*   454
*Face-to-face Communication*   455
*Meetings in the Public Forum*   456
*Picketing in Labor Disputes*   459
*Public Demonstrations*   463
*Non-public Forum Problems*   470

24   PUNISHMENT OF SPEECH AND ASSEMBLY   *474*

*Breach of the Peace: The Three-stage Analysis*   475
*The Expectation of Violence*   478
*Trespass and Sit-ins*   481
*The Constitutional Challenge of Direct Action*   485

25   OBSCENITY   *490*

*Legal Tests for Obscenity*   491
*The Two-level Theory*   493
*Hard-core Pornography*   496
*The Fourth Test: Pandering*   497
*Objectivity and Standards*   500
*The Techniques of Morals Censorship: Books*   503
*The Techniques of Morals Censorship: Movies*   505

26   LIBEL   *509*

*Seditious Libel*   510
*Libel of Public Officials*   512
*Private Defamation*   515
*Group Libel*   518

27   FREEDOM OF ASSOCIATION   *521*

*The Communist Party and Guilt by Association*   523
*The Smith Act*   526
*The Internal Security Act of 1950*   533
*The Public Service and Subversion*   536
*The Status of the Communist Party and Its Members*   545
*The NAACP and the Ku Klux Klan*   547

28    RELIGIOUS FREEDOM AND ESTABLISHMENT    *552*

      *Free Exercise of Religion    554*
      *Establishment of Religion    567*


PART SEVEN    DUE PROCESS AND EQUAL PROTECTION


29    DUE PROCESS STANDARDS    *587*

      *Due Process and Legislation    588*
      *Due Process in Judicial Proceedings    589*


30    CRIMINAL PROSECUTIONS    *598*

      *Crimes against the United States    599*
      *Criminal Procedure in the Original Constitution    601*
      *Unreasonable Searches and Seizures    603*
      *Self-incrimination    616*
      *Coerced Confessions    623*
      *The Right to Counsel    625*
      *Indictment by Grand Jury    633*
      *Trial by Jury    633*
      *The Sixth Amendment    638*
      *Due Process, Fair Trial, and Equal Protection    641*
      *Double Jeopardy    645*
      *Excessive Bail    649*
      *Cruel and Unusual Punishment    650*
      *Conclusion    651*


31    SUBSTANTIVE DUE PROCESS    *656*

      *Procedure into Substance    656*
      *The Police Power: Health, Morals, and Safety    660*
      *Economic Regulation    668*
      *Substantive Due Process and the Right to Privacy    684*


32    CONTRACTS, EMINENT DOMAIN, AND TAXATION    *689*

      *The Protection of Contracts    689*
      *Eminent Domain    697*
      *Due Process in Taxation    701*

33    EQUAL PROTECTION OF THE LAWS    708

    *The Original Understanding    709*
    *Racial Equality in Commerce    714*
    *Geographical Segregation    715*
    *Segregation in Public Transportation    717*
    *Segregation in Education    720*
    *Enforcement of the* Brown *Decision    725*
    *State Miscegenation Laws    730*
    *State Action    732*
    *Federal Protection of Civil Rights    738*


34    THE FRANCHISE    745

    *Constitutional Foundation of the Right to Vote    745*
    *State Limitations on the Franchise    747*
    *The Constitutional Status of Primary Elections    750*
    *Federal Protection of Voting Rights    753*


35    CITIZENSHIP, NATURALIZATION, AND IMMIGRATION    759

    *Citizenship    759*
    *Naturalization    761*
    *Denaturalization    763*
    *Expatriation    765*
    *Exclusion of Aliens    769*
    *Control of Aliens and Deportation    774*


**APPENDIXES**

CONSTITUTION OF THE UNITED STATES OF AMERICA    *781*

MEMBERS OF THE UNITED STATES SUPREME COURT
1789–1968    *796*

*Index of Cases    799*
*Subject Index    827*

# Part 1

## The document

# 1

## The preconstitutional period

"By constitution," wrote Lord Bolingbroke in 1733, "we mean, whenever we speak with propriety and exactness, that assemblage of laws, institutions and customs, derived from certain fixed principles of reason, directed to certain fixed objects of public good, that compose the general system, according to which the community hath agreed to be governed." In making this definition Bolingbroke was naturally thinking mainly of the English constitution, but in fact his statement accorded with the traditional understanding which, as McIlwain says, applied the term "constitution" to the "substantive principles to be deduced from a nation's actual institutions and their development."

The latter part of the eighteenth century, however, brought a new concept of "constitution" into existence. The French and American Revolutions introduced as an essential governmental instrument the written constitution. The general system under which the community agreed to be governed was not, under the new regime, to be left to evolution and deduction. The "laws, institutions and customs" were not to be a heterogeneous assemblage. The fixed principles of reason, the fixed objects of the public good, were to be stated specifically in a formal basic document.

To one accustomed to the older view of constitutions, this was a disturbing departure. The Englishman Arthur Young, writing in 1792, spoke with contempt of the French idea of a constitution—"a new term they have

adopted; and which they use as if a constitution was a pudding to be made by a receipt [i.e., recipe]." To an Englishman it was obvious that a constitution could not be made; it had to grow.

Actually, of course, constitutions can combine both qualities. The American Constitution was made in the summer of 1787 and has been growing ever since. English experience has demonstrated that a democratic political system can develop and individual liberties be protected as well with a traditional unwritten constitution as with the newfangled recipe type of constitution. We have even come to see that there may be actually little difference between written and unwritten constitutions—the written one is constantly being reinterpreted and revised by practice and unwritten custom, while the principles of the unwritten constitution are constantly being reduced to writing in statutes, judicial decisions, and constitutional commentaries.

In the eighteenth century, however, it was not possible to be so broad-minded on this matter. Tom Paine replied to English attacks on the new form of constitution by denying that the English type was a constitution at all. "The continual use of the word 'constitution' in the English parliament shows there is none," he said, "and that the whole is merely a form of government without a constitution, and constituting itself with what power it pleases." A constitution to Paine could not be "the act of a government, but of a people constituting a government. . . . A constitution is a thing *antecedent* to a government; and a government is only the creature of a constitution." Unquestionably Paine stated the dominant American position, and we need to review briefly the American political experience and political theory which produced this attitude and, ultimately, the American Constitution.

## POLITICAL UNIFICATION AND THE REVOLUTION

The political unification necessary for adoption of the American Constitution was the product of the American Revolution. The thirteen American Colonies, though at first greatly diverse in status and character, had ultimately become in most cases royal provinces, administered by a governor named by the king. All had popularly elected legislatures, the same heritage of the common law, and much the same judicial organization and procedure. There were, however, substantial geographical, economic, and political barriers among the Colonies, and it took grave events to bring them together into the loosest sort of joint endeavor.

The thirteen Colonies were strung out for over a thousand miles along the Atlantic Ocean from Maine (then part of Massachusetts) to Georgia, and extended inland only to the Appalachians. The only satisfactory transportation was by water. There were no decent roads, and travel by land for

any distance had to be by horseback. The Colonies traded extensively with England but very little with each other.

What finally brought the Colonies together was a common and increasingly intense dislike of British rule. It should have been clear from a very early period that Britain would encounter grave difficulties in maintaining controls over these vigorous and rapidly growing communities. The three thousand miles of ocean intervening would have made the task difficult enough, but it was even more complicated by the kind of people who settled the Colonies. They were predominantly Englishmen and, for a time, continued to think of themselves as such. But they were also merchant adventurers, religious dissenters, indentured servants, convicts, political refugees —and such a group was bound to contain a high proportion of persons who would resent the exercise of distant authority. Within twenty-five years of the landing of the Pilgrims, Massachusetts was in trouble with the English government. She adopted her own criminal code, established an independent church, passed harsh laws for the suppression of heresy, treated members of the Church of England with intolerance, coined her own money, issued writs in the name of the Commonwealth instead of the king, resisted all attempts to appeal from colonial to English courts, and evaded as far as possible every effort at interference on the part of the king's government. Finally in 1684 royal exasperation led to annulment of the corporation's charter, which was replaced in 1691 by one imposing greater control on the Colony.

In general, the British constitution succeeded in developing ways of adjusting minor conflicts with the Colonies. There was a rough distribution of powers, under which Parliament dealt with imperial affairs and left each colony to make its own laws on such local matters as inheritance, relations of master and servant, health, education, and criminal punishment. Acts passed by colonial legislatures could be vetoed by the governor and "disallowed" by the Privy Council in London. Judicial decisions were also subject to appeal to the Privy Council, and some 265 such appeals were heard between 1680 and 1780. The principal weapon of the colonial legislatures against the royal governors was the power of the purse.

The French and Indian wars demonstrated the looseness of English control over the Colonies. The necessity of calling on each colony separately for its quota of troops or funds, which might or might not be readily forthcoming, convinced some Englishmen that a plan of colonial union should be devised to deal with instances of common danger. The British government inspired a congress of delegates from seven colonies which met at Albany in 1754 to discuss a proposal for colonial union drafted by Benjamin Franklin. The so-called "Albany Plan" provided for a grand council composed of delegates chosen by the assembly of each colony, to meet under a president-general appointed by the Crown. This body would have power

to carry on wars in which the Colonies were involved, and to raise troops and collect taxes for this purpose. Each colony, however, would exercise control over its purely internal affairs. The plan was rejected both by the Crown, which was unwilling to admit such a degree of local autonomy, and by the mutually jealous Colonies. But it is noteworthy as the first effort in the experience of the American Colonies to develop a basis for joint action and a plan of central-local distribution of powers.

The conclusion of the French and Indian wars in 1763 brought disturbing evidence that the English government intended to tighten up the system of colonial administration. It had been irritated by the halfhearted cooperation of American legislatures in wartime measures, and was particularly annoyed at colonial traders who had conducted illicit commerce with French and Spanish possessions while England was at war with those countries. To enforce the ban on smuggling, the English made use of writs of assistance, which, unlike ordinary search warrants, were general warrants enabling officers to enter and search almost at will.

In 1764 Parliament passed the Stamp Act as a revenue measure. Americans had been accustomed to paying taxes on commercial transactions, but this was a direct tax, the levying of which had long been regarded as belonging exclusively to the colonial legislatures. The Stamp Act was immediately denounced in America as taxation without representation, and the protests led to convening of the Stamp Act Congress in New York in October, 1765. In the resolutions adopted there, the delegates, acknowledging their allegiance to the Crown, claimed all the rights and privileges of British subjects, one of which, they contended, was that no taxes be imposed on them without their consent. Since their geographical situation precluded representation in the House of Commons, they were in reality contending that no taxes could be levied on the Colonies except by their own legislatures. The protests were weighed in Parliament, and Franklin was even called before the bar of the House to explain the American attitude. The Stamp Act was repealed, but Parliament rejected the American legal arguments. Instead it asserted its complete supremacy and its power to bind the Colonies "in all cases whatsoever."

Worse vexations than the Stamp Act were in store as the English government continued to act on this theory. In 1767 taxation on specific articles of import was levied to supply funds for colonial administration and defense, a scheme which would relieve the royal governors from depending on the legislatures for funds. The tax on tea led to the Boston Tea Party in 1773, for which Britain retaliated by blockading the port, suspending the Colony's charter, and resorting to military rule with the quartering of troops in private homes.

The beginning of a system of intercolonial organization was brought into existence by these disputes, as Virginia in the early seventies suggested extension of the Massachusetts system of Committees of Correspondence.

Virginia also was responsible for convening the First Continental Congress in Philadelphia in September, 1774. Delegates were selected in a variety of extralegal ways, the Committees of Correspondence playing a large part. The Congress was a completely irregular body representing dissatisfied elements, but on the whole the instructions of the delegates were not revolutionary. Most of those present wanted to restore normal relations with London and stay within the Empire, but without recognizing the authority asserted by Parliament.

A revised version of Franklin's Albany Plan of Union was presented to the Congress by Joseph Galloway, but it proved too conservative for the delegates. Franklin himself opposed the Plan, feeling that any closer union with the corrupt British government would be undesirable. The report finally accepted by the Congress declared that the Colonies were "entitled to a free and exclusive power of legislation in their several provincial legislatures . . . in all cases of taxation and internal polity, subject only to the negative of their sovereign, in such manner as has been heretofore used and accustomed." It promised consent to the operation of acts of Parliament for the bona fide regulation of external commerce to promote the advantage of the whole empire, but "excluding every idea of taxation, internal or external, for raising a revenue on the subjects in America, without their consent."

The American consensus at this point appeared to be a willingness to acknowledge the sovereignty of the king over the Colonies, but a denial of the authority of the British Parliament to legislate for them. The British government dispatched a reply to the Congress which was intended to be conciliatory, but which did not yield on the key claim of parliamentary power. In any case, it came too late. Military preparations were under way on both sides, and before the Second Continental Congress met in May, 1775, the Battle of Lexington had occurred. Congress thus found itself suddenly busy with the task of managing a military operation. Articles of war had to be adopted; an army had to be organized, equipped, and financed. The Congress continued for a time to profess loyalty to the king, and explained the developing armed clashes as resistance to his ministers. Even after Bunker Hill, when the king proclaimed the Americans as rebels, the general presumption was that reconciliation with England would eventually be effected.

But gradually sentiment swung toward a permanent separation. Tom Paine's pamphlet, *Common Sense*, published early in 1776, said that "reconciliation is . . . a fallacious dream." By May of that year the Continental Congress was advising the Colonies to suppress every exercise of royal authority and take over powers of government under authority of their people. On June 7, Richard Henry Lee, on the instructions of the temporary government of Virginia, presented a resolution in the Congress declaring that all the Colonies were free and independent states. The formal declaration was drafted by Thomas Jefferson, and was proclaimed by the Congress

on July 4—a noble and impassioned statement of the Colonies' grievances and the political theory on which they based the rightness of their claim to independence.

### THE POLITICAL THEORY OF THE
### REVOLUTIONARY PERIOD

The Declaration of Independence has been generally regarded as the cornerstone of American ideas about government and the preeminent statement of American political theory. The basic conceptions had obviously come from Locke, but the doctrines were sharpened and intensified by the experience of resistance to British rule. These principles were so much a part of American thinking that the Declaration referred to them as "self-evident." In addition to the Declaration, the state constitutions adopted between 1776 and 1780 abound in statements of the current political theory.

The first principle of the political thought of the time was that men are by nature endowed with certain inalienable rights. This conception posited the existence of a state of nature antedating the establishment of civil government. In this primeval condition all men were free, in the sense that they were subject to no one, and equal in the right to rule themselves. A body of natural rights belonged to them as men, including the right to "life, liberty, and the pursuit of happiness." These rights not only antedated the existence of government; they were superior to it in authority. As John Dickinson expressed it, "Our liberties do not come from charters; for these are only the declaration of preexisting rights. They do not depend on parchments or seals; but come from the King of Kings and Lord of all the earth."

The exercise of coercive power by governments over men born free and equal could be justified only by the consent of the governed. The process as hypothesized by the Massachusetts Bill of Rights was that "the body politic is formed by a voluntary association of individuals: it is a social compact by which the whole people covenants with each citizen, and each citizen with the whole people, that all shall be governed by certain laws for the common good." The exact nature of the contract on which government was based, or the circumstances under which it was entered into, were little discussed, but the concept was given a sense of reality by the numerous written compacts which had figured in American development, especially the Mayflower Compact of 1620 and the colonial charters. The slogan "no taxation without representation" was a particular application of the consent theory, with deep roots in English constitutional history.

Government is created by contract to serve the welfare of the people. To quote again the Massachusetts document, the end of government is "to secure the existence of the body politic, to protect it, and to furnish the individuals who compose it with the power of enjoying in safety and tranquillity their natural rights, and the blessings of life." A government which

fails to serve the ends for which it was set up has breached the contract under which it was established and forfeited the loyalty of its citizens. Thus the right of revolution, obviously fundamental to legitimizing the American action, was defended. The Declaration of Independence stated the case as follows: "Whenever any form of government becomes destructive of these ends, it is the right of the people to alter or to abolish it, and to institute new government, laying its foundation on such principles and organizing its powers in such form, as to them shall seem most likely to effect their safety and happiness."

These democratic principles were not necessarily incompatible with the institution of monarchy. Before the actual outbreak of hostilities, in fact, there was widespread support for monarchy and the hereditary principle. John Adams, and even Samuel Adams, pointed out the strong features of the British system. Tom Paine's bitter attack in *Common Sense* marked the turn against monarchical government. "Of more worth is one honest man to society, and in the sight of God, than all the crowned ruffians that ever lived," he wrote.

The consequences of these basic political ideas quickly became visible in the constitutions adopted by the new states. Because of the contract theory, there was a widespread insistence that the constitutions be adopted by conventions especially charged with that duty, instead of by the regular legislatures, and that the draft constitutions be submitted to the voters for approval. Nine of the twelve constitutions adopted by 1778 were drawn up by this method.

Governmental power was limited in several ways. The royal governors had been the symbol of tyranny, and so the executive office in the new constitutions was deliberately weakened, while the legislature, symbol of resistance to foreign rule, was strengthened. In eight states the governor was chosen by the legislature, he had only a one-year term in ten states, his appointing power was generally limited, and he had the veto power in only three states. The one-year rule was common for all officials, not only for governors; as John Adams said, "Where annual elections end, there tyranny begins."

The separation of powers doctrine was also vigorously professed, though the imbalance between the legislature and executive was rather inconsistent with this theory. The Massachusetts formulation earned fame by its doctrinaire quality: "In the government of this commonwealth, the legislative department shall never exercise the executive and judicial powers, or either of them: the executive shall never exercise the legislative and judicial powers, or either of them: the judicial shall never exercise the legislative and executive powers, or either of them: to the end it may be a government of laws and not of men." Other restrictions were sought to be achieved by clear subordination of the military to the civil power, by decentralization of governmental functions, and by bills of rights which forbade governmental

interference in certain fields of individual activity. Eight states had such bills of rights, their principles derived largely from the English common law as expounded by Blackstone.

The democratic theory professed in the new constitutions was not consistently practiced, however. Under the colonial government the lower classes had been rather generally excluded from political life. The Revolutionary movement for a time gave promise of bringing the back-country folk and the unfranchised workers into the stream of politics, but actually the circle of power-holders was little changed in the new state governments. Property and religious qualifications for officeholding were general. Indeed, property, religious, and racial limitations were seemingly not regarded as inconsistent with the rights of man or the principles of political philosophy so eloquently stated in the Declaration of Independence.

## THE POST–REVOLUTIONARY EXPERIENCE

The Continental Congress met in session after session from May, 1775, until March 1781, when the Articles of Confederation became effective. It performed the functions of a *de facto* government—raising, directing, and financing armies, sending and receiving diplomatic agents, entering into treaties with foreign countries. Whether it had any legal power to perform these actions is another question. The people of the states did not conceive that they had surrendered any of their rights to the Congress, and no state government felt bound by its decisions. Delegates to the Congress, once the states were set up, were appointed by the state legislatures and subject to their instructions.

It was generally agreed that something more effective in the way of intercolonial organization was required. Franklin, author of the Albany Plan in 1754, drew on it in presenting a new proposal of union to the Congress in July, 1775, but no action was taken. Then on June 7, 1776, after Lee had moved his resolution in favor of a declaration of independence, he offered a second one proposing a permanent confederation. A committee, which was appointed on June 12 with John Dickinson as chairman, went to work with Franklin's draft as a basis. The committee's major difficulties had to do with whether the states would be represented equally or in proportion to population, how contributions to the general treasury would be apportioned, and what disposition would be made of the claims several states were making to lands stretching back into the interior of the country. The Articles were not adopted and sent to the states until November, 1777. Ratification by every state was required to make them binding. The twelfth state signed in February, 1779, but Maryland was adamant, and did not agree until March 1, 1781, at which time the Articles came into effect.

The framework of government set up by the Articles was quite unlike that of the states. Virtually all functions were concentrated in a single legislative

chamber, called a Congress. There was no second branch of the legislature and no separation of executive from legislative powers. Congress was to appoint such committees and civil officers as might be needed to carry on executive work, and it could provide courts only for the limited purposes of dealing with disputes between states and captures and felonies on the high seas.

The authority of Congress did not rest on the people, but on the state legislatures which had created it. Each state legislature chose and paid its delegates to Congress, and each state had one vote. A two-thirds vote of the state delegations was required for the adoption of important measures, and amendments to the Articles required the unanimous consent of the states.

The Articles did specify certain rules of interstate comity to which the states were pledged. But the essential powers necessary to an effective central government were denied to the Confederation. Congress could not levy taxes; it could only make a "requisition" on each state for its share of the estimated monetary needs of the union. Congress could not regulate interstate commerce; and although it could make commercial treaties with foreign nations, the states felt free to retaliate against countries which discriminated against their trade. Finally, Congress could not act directly on the citizens; it had to depend on the state governments for the execution of its measures. The Confederation could scarcely be called a government. As the Articles truthfully stated, it was a league of friendship entered into by sovereign states.

As for organizational arrangements, certain executive officers were immediately established. In fact, a secretary for foreign affairs, responsible to the Congress, had been created before the Articles were finally ratified, and also the offices of superintendent of finance and secretary at war. Congress chose a presiding officer with the title of president. A federal prize court had been created in 1780, and it was continued and regularized after the adoption of the Articles. The provision of the Articles for adjudicating disputes between states involved a much more cumbersome arrangement. States in dispute might by joint consent, through the Congress as intermediary, choose commissioners to decide the dispute.

In spite of its limited authority over internal affairs, the Confederation did achieve some successes. The Bank of North America was chartered by Congress in 1781, though the fact that the Articles gave no authority to grant charters of incorporation led the bank to secure a new charter from Pennsylvania. Preparations for the government of the new lands to the west led to adoption of the famous Northwest Ordinance of 1787, applying to the area between the Ohio and the Mississippi. The ordinance provided for the eventual division of this land into from three to five states. In the meantime the territory was to be governed directly by officials chosen by Congress.

In other areas Congress was less successful at temporizing solutions for

the problems of the Confederation. Attempts to negotiate commercial treaties with England, France, and Spain failed, in part at least because of doubt whether the states would feel bound by any such treaties. As for internal trade, the rivalries of the states led to various forms of discriminatory taxation. The situation of New Jersey, whose goods came in through New York on one side and Philadelphia on the other, led to Madison's famous comparison of the state to a cask tapped at both ends.

The public finances were very nearly hopeless. During the first two years under the Articles, Congress requisitioned 10 million dollars from the states and received less than 1.5 million dollars. There were no funds to pay interest on the debt, which actually rose after the war was over. Redemption of the worthless Continental currency was impossible. Speculators bought at a heavy discount the certificates of indebtedness issued during hostilities to pay for necessary supplies. Robert Morris, superintendent of finance, resigned in 1786, not wishing, he said, to be a "minister of injustice."

With Congress incapable of dealing with the economic ills of the country, pressure fell on the state legislatures. The most widespread demand was for relief from the burden of debts incurred during the Revolutionary inflation, by state issuance of legal tender paper and by various forms of moratoria on payment of debts. The paper money forces got a majority for their inflationary program in seven state legislatures. When these forces were defeated in Massachusetts, farmers under the lead of Daniel Shays resorted to violence, breaking up court sessions trying debt cases and attempting to seize arms from the government arsenal at Springfield.

Shays' Rebellion was most effective in convincing the conservative and the propertied that there were serious defects in the government both of the states and the Confederation. The Revolutionary enthusiasm for the legislature as the dominant branch of the government had diminished. Now responsible citizens were looking for some way of checking legislatures which, as Madison said, were drawing all power into their "impetuous vortex." In most states the governor was still too weak for this purpose. Here and there were the beginnings of a system of judicial review of legislation. But the only effective control over state radicalism appeared to be a strengthening of the central government. In a paper written in the spring of 1787 Madison, concerned about the absence of any "guarantee to the States of their constitutions and laws against internal violence," thought that establishing central government control over "the internal vicissitudes of State policy, and the aggressions of interested majorities on the rights of minorities and of individuals" would have a "happy effect."

Perhaps under the pressures that were developing, the Confederation, given the time, might by firm assertion, ingenious argument, and common consent have come to assume more of the stature of a real government. There were some tendencies in this direction. James Wilson sought to defend the chartering of the Bank of North America on the ground that any power

which could be exercised only on a national scale must belong to the Congress, no matter what the Articles said. Hamilton in the case of *Rutgers* v. *Waddington* (1784) argued that an act of the New York legislature was void, among other reasons, because contrary to the Articles. John Jay in a report to Congress in 1786 argued that treaties were binding on state legislatures, and most of the states seemed to agree. But the weakness of the Confederation, and the urgency of the times, called not for ingenious construction of the Articles, but radical reconstruction of the governmental system.

### THE MOVEMENT FOR A NEW CONSTITUTION

There were stirrings toward improvement of the Articles before they were even officially in force. The three main weaknesses—lack of authority to raise revenue, to regulate commerce, or to exercise general coercive powers— were obvious to all. Article 13 provided that "Every State shall abide by the determinations of the United States in Congress assembled, on all questions which by this Confederation are submitted to them." Some argued that this article implied powers of enforcement against the states, and Congress studied the problem interminably through committees but characteristically never reached any decision.

If Congress was to have no coercive power over the states with respect to revenues, an alternative was to permit Congress to levy taxes directly. A month before the Articles became effective, Congress sent to the states an amendment permitting it to levy a duty of 5 per cent ad valorem on all imports. Amendment of the Articles required unanimous vote, and this proposal failed when Rhode Island rejected it in 1782. A revised revenue amendment which sought to meet Rhode Island's objection got the approval of only two states in three years. When a committee of Congress reported in 1786 that the lack of a general revenue was placing the very existence of the union in jeopardy, and that the states must permit the establishment of a revenue system, New York wrecked agreement by its lone veto.

As for the commerce power, vulnerable New Jersey pressed for central regulatory power from the beginning, but unsuccessfully. Foreign discrimination against American commerce led Congress to submit a commerce amendment to the states in 1784, which failed, as did later proposals to the same end.

This continuing demonstration of what a Virginia delegate to Congress called the "imbecillity" of the Confederation could lead only to the breaking up of the union, or its reconstitution under a stronger government. There was considerable speculation about and support for the first alternative from 1783 on. The conflicting interests and conditions of the different sections were stressed. The advantages of a connection with the Southern states were widely questioned in the North. Dr. Benjamin Rush of Philadelphia reported that "some of our enlightened men . . . have secretly proposed an Eastern,

Middle and Southern Confederacy, to be united by an alliance offensive and defensive. These Confederacies, they say, will be united by nature, by interests, and by manners, and consequently they will be safe, agreeable, and durable."

It was the other alternative which won out, however. In 1782 Hamilton had prevailed on the New York legislature to request that Congress call a general convention, and Massachusetts took similar action in 1785. These efforts failed. What did happen in 1785 was a meeting of representatives from Virginia and Maryland at Washington's home at Mount Vernon, for the purpose of discussing joint problems of navigation on Chesapeake Bay and the Potomac. Ignoring a provision in the Articles which required congressional consent to all agreements between states, they developed a plan for uniform import duties, regulations of commerce, and currency in the two states.

When the Maryland legislature accepted these proposals in December, 1785, it suggested that Pennsylvania and Delaware be invited to join in the plan. In Virginia, Madison saw the possibility of using this initiative to get a general meeting on commercial problems, which the Virginia assembly proposed should meet at Annapolis in September, 1786. Nine states appointed delegates to go to Annapolis, but only five were present at the opening session. They waited three weeks for more delegates and then adjourned. But a report was drafted and sent to every state legislature and to Congress, suggesting that the states designate commissioners to meet in Philadelphia in May, 1787, "to take into consideration the situation of the United States, to devise such further provisions as shall appear to them necessary to render the Constitution of the Federal Government adequate to the exigencies of the Union."

All the states complied except Rhode Island, though New Hampshire delayed until June, after the Convention had assembled. Congress at first ignored the project, but in February, 1787, recommended a convention at the time and place already set, to meet for the "sole and express purpose of revising the Articles of Confederation," and of reporting to the Congress such alterations as would "render the federal constitution adequate to the exigencies of government, and the preservation of the union." Thus the official status of the Philadelphia Convention was merely that of a body advisory to Congress.

### SELECTED REFERENCES

ANDREWS, CHARLES M., *The Colonial Period of American History*. New Haven, Conn.: Yale University Press, 1934.

BECKER, CARL L., *The Declaration of Independence: A Study in the History of Political Ideas*. New York: Alfred A. Knopf, Inc., 1942.

BURNETT, EDMUND C., *The Continental Congress*. New York: The Macmillan Company, 1941.

HARTZ, LOUIS, *The Liberal Tradition in America*. New York: Harcourt, Brace & World, Inc., 1955.

HOCKETT, HOMER C., *The Constitutional History of the United States, 1776–1826*, chaps. 1–10. New York: The Macmillan Company, 1939.

JAMESON, J. FRANKLIN, *The American Revolution Considered as a Social Movement*. Boston: Beacon Press, 1956.

JENSEN, MERRILL, *The Articles of Confederation*. Madison, Wis.: The University of Wisconsin Press, 1940.

————, *The New Nation: A History of the United States during the Confederation, 1781–1789*. New York: Alfred A. Knopf, Inc., 1950.

KELLY, ALFRED H., and WINFRED A. HARBISON, *The American Constitution: Its Origins and Development*, chaps. 1–4. New York: W. W. Norton & Company, Inc., 1963 (third edition).

MC ILWAIN, CHARLES H., *The American Revolution: A Constitutional Interpretation*. New York: The Macmillan Company, 1923.

————, *Constitutionalism Ancient and Modern*, chap. 1. Ithaca, N.Y.: Cornell University Press, 1940.

MC LAUGHLIN, ANDREW C., *The Confederation and the Constitution, 1783–1789*. New York: Collier Books, a division of Crowell-Collier Publishing Co., 1962.

————, *A Constitutional History of the United States*, chaps. 1–13. New York: Appleton-Century-Crofts, Inc., 1935.

MERRIAM, CHARLES E., *A History of American Political Theories*, chaps. 1–3. New York: The Macmillan Company, 1903, 1924.

MILLER, JOHN C., *Origins of the American Revolution*. Boston: Little, Brown and Company, 1943.

MITCHELL, BROADUS, and LOUISE MITCHELL, *A Biography of the Constitution of the United States*, chap. 1. Fair Lawn, N.J.: Oxford University Press, 1964.

MORGAN, EDMUND S., *The Birth of the Republic*. Chicago: The University of Chicago Press, 1956.

NEVINS, ALLAN, *The American States during and after the Revolution, 1775–1789*. New York: The Macmillan Company, 1924.

ROSSITER, CLINTON, *Seedtime of the Republic: The Origin of the American Tradition of Political Liberty*. New York: Harcourt, Brace & World, Inc., 1953.

SWISHER, CARL B., *American Constitutional Development*, chap. 1. Boston: Houghton Mifflin Company, 1954 (second edition).

WORMUTH, FRANCIS D., *The Origins of Modern Constitutionalism*. New York: Harper & Row, Publishers, Incorporated, 1949.

# 2

## The constitutional convention

The Convention was scheduled to meet at the State House in Philadelphia on May 14, 1787, but on that day representatives from only two states, Virginia and Pennsylvania, were present. On succeeding days additional delegates appeared, but it was not until May 25 that a majority of the states were represented. The Convention then organized, with Washington the unanimous choice as presiding officer. The Convention met in its first regular session on Monday, May 28, and continued its deliberations until the completed document was ready for signature on September 17.

### MEMBERSHIP AND PROCEDURE

The session of May 28 was attended by twenty-nine delegates from seven states. Some seventy-four delegates were appointed, but only fifty-five of them ever attended the sessions. Every state except Rhode Island was eventually represented, New Hampshire's delegates being the last to arrive, on July 23. By any standards, in any country, these men would have been judged a notable assemblage. The French chargé wrote that "if all the delegates named for this Philadelphia Convention are present, one will never have seen, even in Europe, an assembly more respectable for talents, knowledge, disinterestedness and patriotism than those who will compose it."

The fifty-five delegates were comparatively young men, only twelve being over fifty-four years of age, while six were under thirty-one. About half were college graduates. They were almost without exception men of substance and status in the new country—lawyers, physicians, planters, merchants. Most of them had risked their necks in prominent military or civilian posts during the Revolution. But the fact that only eight of the fifty-six signers of the Declaration of Independence were in the Constitutional Convention is evidence that making a constitution enlisted different talents than making a revolution. Of course Jefferson and Paine were in Europe, but Patrick Henry "smelled a rat" and stayed at home, and such Revolutionary figures as Richard Henry Lee, Sam Adams, and John Hancock were also missing.

Among the Convention's leaders, some few stand out and deserve brief mention here. The two figures with greatest prestige were Washington and Franklin. When Washington resigned his commission in December, 1783, he told Congress he was taking his leave "of all the employments of public life." Though the difficulties of the new nation affected him deeply, and he was firmly convinced that a stronger government was required, he resisted efforts to enlist his services in the political arena. In August, 1786, he wrote to John Jay: "Having happily assisted in bringing the ship into port, and having been fairly discharged; it is not my business to embark again on a sea of troubles." But in March, 1787, the call of duty overrode all other considerations, and he accepted designation as a delegate from Virginia. He feared that if he did not attend, it would be taken as an indication that he had lost faith in a republican form of government. He participated seldom in debates, but there can be no doubt that his influence and endorsement were essential to the adoption of the Constitution.

Franklin, by then eighty-one years old and suffering from the gout, was nearing the end of his glorious career, and was unable to take an active part in debate. But he was, after Washington, the most influential American of his time, and his talents as a peacemaker helped the Convention ease past several danger points.

The men generally ranked as exercising the greatest influence in the decisions of the Convention are Gouverneur Morris and James Wilson of Pennsylvania, James Madison of Virginia, and Roger Sherman of Connecticut. Morris made 173 speeches, Wilson 168, Madison 161, and Sherman 138. Virginia was also ably represented by George Mason and Edmund Randolph, as was Massachusetts with Elbridge Gerry and Rufus King, and South Carolina with John Rutledge and Charles Pinckney. Oliver Ellsworth of Connecticut, Alexander Hamilton from New York, John Dickinson of Delaware, and William Paterson of New Jersey must also be ranked among the leaders.

Under the Convention's rules as adopted on May 28 and 29, the deliberations were to be completely secret, and they were kept so for thirty years afterward. The official journal was confined to the formal motions made and the ayes and noes. But Madison throughout the proceedings sat with his

back to Washington, facing the other members, and writing down what went on in his own version of shorthand. He did this with the silent approval of the Convention. The members trusted him and helped him fill out his reports from their own notes or memories. Madison's notes provide the principal information as to the proceedings of the Convention.[1]

Edmund Randolph started off the work of the body by presenting for the Virginia delegation a series of resolutions, largely drafted by Madison, providing for a new national government. The Convention turned itself into a committee of the whole and for three weeks mulled over the Virginia proposals, as well as a more limited plan placed before the committee by New Jersey. The New Jersey proposal was defeated on June 19. The members then reverted from committee status and, as a convention, began to go over again the various features of the Virginia Plan. One month of discussion produced agreement on a substantial number of points, so that on July 23 the Convention voted to set up a committee of detail which would draft a constitution embodying the principles agreed upon. The members of this committee were Gorham of Massachusetts, Ellsworth, Wilson, Randolph, and Rutledge. This group, however, did more than redraft the Convention's resolutions into documentary form. It expanded some of the resolutions, and developed some entirely new provisions. The resulting document was presented to the Convention on August 6, and was the subject of further extended discussion. On September 8 a committee was appointed "to revise the stile of and arrange the articles which had been agreed to by the House"; it consisted of Johnson of Connecticut, Hamilton, Gouverneur Morris, Madison, and King. Morris actually did the bulk of the work for the committee of style, and was responsible for much of the phrasing of the final document.

On September 17, when the Constitution was ready for signing, forty-two delegates were present. Some had departed because they disagreed with the Convention's work. Yates and Lansing of New York had left in the midst of the proceedings, and for the last two months of the Convention Hamilton was thus the sole representative from New York. Although he spoke often, he declined to take the responsibility of casting New York's vote, which was consequently never recorded during the latter part of the proceedings. Others had departed, not because they disagreed with the Convention's results, but because of pressure of other business or because they felt all the important issues had been decided.

Of the forty-two delegates present on September 17, three declined to sign—Mason, Gerry, and Randolph, all of whom had played important parts in the drafting process. Madison records that while the last of the other thirty-nine delegates were still signing the document,

[1] All the statements at the Convention quoted in this chapter come from Madison's notes, as printed in Max Farrand (ed.), *The Records of the Federal Convention of 1787* (New Haven, Conn.: Yale University Press, 1937).

. . . Doctr. Franklin looking towards the Presidents Chair, at the back of which a rising sun happened to be painted, observed to a few members near him, that Painters had found it difficult to distinguish in their art a rising from a setting sun. I have, said he, often and often in the course of the Session, and the vicissitudes of my hopes and fears as to its issue, looked at that behind the President without being able to tell whether it was rising or setting: But now at length I have the happiness to know that it is a rising and not a setting Sun.

## THE MAJOR DECISIONS

The various provisions of the Constitution on which the sun had thus arisen will be the subject of examination and comment at appropriate points throughout this volume. Here an attempt will be made only to place the major decisions of the Convention in their setting, outlining the considerations that were effective in the adoption of these provisions and the alternatives which were discussed and discarded.

A NEW CONSTITUTION    The Convention almost immediately on assembling proceeded to disregard the instructions it had received from Congress to confine its efforts to revising the Articles of Confederation. Because of the suspicions of the state legislatures, which tended to represent the small farmers and debtors, toward the proposal to hold a convention, the supporters of the movement had felt it necessary to play down the real purposes of the call. They had seen the Annapolis meeting of 1786 break up in failure when all but five states were frightened off by talk of strengthening the central government. Consequently, Alexander Hamilton drafted the call for the 1787 meeting in terms merely of revising the Articles, with any changes proposed having to go back to the states for decision as to their adoption.

But once the delegates met, it was obvious that the goals they had in mind required scrapping the Articles. It was too apparent to them that the Confederation, with its powerless Congress, could not provide what they felt the country needed—security for business development, protection against competitive state taxation, the assurance of a sound currency, encouragement and protection of foreign trade, safety against foreign countries and Indians on the frontier. Thus the Virginia resolutions, which ignored the Articles, were accepted unanimously as the basis for the initial discussions. It was only after the demand of the small states for equal representation in the Senate had been defeated that some delegates began to suggest that the Convention was contravening its instructions. Lansing of New York said his state "would never have concurred in sending deputies to the convention, if she had supposed the deliberations were to turn on a consolidation of the States, and a National Government." Paterson, presenting the New Jersey Plan, limited to revision of the Articles, added: "If the con-

federacy was radically wrong, let us return to our States, and obtain larger powers, not assume them of ourselves." But when only three states supported the New Jersey Plan, the die was irrevocably cast for a new Constitution.

A NATIONAL GOVERNMENT    The decision to set up a national government and the decision to draft a new Constitution were two sides of the same coin. It was because the delegates believed a strong central government essential that they could not be content with a patching job on the Articles. The two most eloquent defenses of a national government in the Convention were those of Hamilton and Madison on June 18 and June 19. Hamilton objected to both the Paterson and the Randolph plans. Believing that the British government was the best in the world, he wanted to go as far in that direction as possible, with an executive and an upper chamber both serving for life. "It seemed to be admitted," he said, "that no good [Executive] could be established on Republican principles."

Madison's was a more moderate exposition of the differences between a federal and a national plan. The New Jersey Plan, he said, would correct none of the evils which had brought the delegates together. Would it prevent state violations of the laws of nations and of treaties? Would it prevent encroachments on federal authority? Would it prevent trespass of the states on each other? Would it secure the internal tranquillity of the states (mentioning particularly Shays' Rebellion)? Would it secure the Union against the influence of foreign powers over its members?

Acceptance of the national principle was settled by the vote of June 19. This meant that the government would operate directly upon the people, in contrast with the Confederation, which operated only on the states. It meant that the central government would have power to collect its own taxes, to make laws and enforce them in its own courts. Over each citizen there would be two governments, national and state, both derived from the people, to both of which their citizens would owe obedience.

A SEPARATION OF POWERS    Under the Articles the only governmental institution was Congress, but with a national government there was a necessity of adding executive and judicial instruments, and of relating them all to each other. Montesquieu's work on the separation of powers was known in America at that time and was occasionally quoted by Madison and others, but it probably was not too influential on the decisions of the delegates. The allocation of powers to three separate branches, and the division of authority so that each could impose some limits on actions of the other two, were established not to fit any theoretical models but to handle the very practical problems the Convention faced.

The Founding Fathers were still so close to George III that dread of a strong executive was very real. Their experience with state legislatures had led them to fear the domination of an overweening Congress. Their experi-

ence with paper money democracy as practiced in some states left them wary of putting too much power in the hands of the people. The system of checks and balances, then, was to blunt the drive of popular emotions—to provide, in Madison's words, by a "distribution and organization" of governmental powers "better guards than are found in any other popular government against interested combinations of a majority against the rights of a minority."

A BICAMERAL LEGISLATURE     There was little doubt in the minds of the delegates that, if a national government was to be established, it must have a two-house legislature. This was the practice in England and in almost all of the states. The New Jersey Plan for revising the Articles retained a Congress of a single house, but after it was defeated there was no further consideration of a unicameral plan. The two-house legislature of course made possible the compromise between large and small states without which probably no Constitution could have been adopted.

It was generally accepted from the beginning that the House of Representatives would be elected by the people, and that membership would be proportionate to population. Much more difficult was the composition and basis of selection of the Senate. The Randolph plan contemplated that the Senate would be elected by the House from persons nominated by the state legislatures, and that the basis of representation should be the same in both houses. The first feature of this proposal, which would have made the Senate subservient to the House, never got much support. The general sentiment was for election of the Senate by the state legislatures.

The basis of representation in the Senate was the rock on which the Convention almost foundered. The big states wanted representation by population. But in the Congress under the Confederation, and in the Convention itself, each state had one vote, and the small states would not agree to a plan which did not preserve their status in some way. On June 9 Paterson said of the proportional proposal that New Jersey "will never confederate on the plan before the Committee. She would be swallowed up. He had rather submit to a monarch, to a despot, than to such a fate." Wilson was quickly on his feet to reply that if the small states would not confederate on the proportional plan, Pennsylvania would not confederate on any other. On June 11, just after adopting proportional representation for the House by a vote of nine to two, the committee of the whole accepted the same rule for the Senate by a vote of six to five. It was this defeat for the small states which triggered the presentation of the New Jersey Plan.

The committee's decision was reconsidered by the Convention, and on June 29 proportional representation in the House was reaffirmed, but only by a vote of six to four, with Maryland divided. Ellsworth then proposed that each state have one vote in the Senate, saying that such a variation in the representation of the two houses would be an appropriate recognition of the

fact that we were "partly national; partly federal." On July 2 the Convention split five to five on this issue, with Georgia divided. A committee was set up to work over the July 4 holiday for a solution to this impasse. At Franklin's suggestion they proposed equal state representation in the Senate, but the House was to have the sole right to originate all money bills, which the Senate could accept or reject, but not modify.

This compromise was bitterly attacked by some members from the large states, including Madison, Wilson, and Gouverneur Morris. The success of the Convention seemed again in grave danger, and it was at this point that Yates and Lansing of New York went home. However, the crisis passed and the Convention held together. The big states made alternative suggestions— that the Senate representation be on the basis of state wealth, or that the states be divided into three classes on the basis of population, giving the classes one, two, and three senators respectively. But these were futile. On July 16 equal representation in the Senate was adopted by a five to four vote, with Massachusetts divided and New York not voting. Madison records that the next morning the large states held an indignation meeting to discuss what could be done, but that "the time was wasted in vague conversation." And so the issue was settled.

POWERS OF CONGRESS    The original Virginia Plan proposed to grant Congress its powers under four heads: (1) the same legislative rights vested in Congress by the Confederation; (2) the right "to legislate in all cases to which the separate States are incompetent, or in which the harmony of the United States may be interrupted by the exercise of individual Legislation"; (3) "to negative all laws passed by the several States, contravening in the opinion of the National Legislature the articles of Union"; and (4) "to call forth the force of the Union agst. any member of the Union failing to fulfill its duty under the articles thereof."

This last heading was dropped on May 31 at Madison's suggestion; he was afraid that "the use of force agst. a State, would look more like a declaration of war, than an infliction of punishment, and would probably be considered by the party attacked as a dissolution of all previous compacts by which it might be bound."

The power to negative state laws was eliminated by the Convention on July 17, in spite of the strong protests of Madison, who thought "the propensity of the States to pursue their particular interests in opposition to the general interest . . . will continue to disturb the system, unless effectually controuled." But Gouverneur Morris believed that such a power would "disgust all the States." Besides, "a law that ought to be negatived will be set aside in the Judiciary Departmt." Following the defeat of this plan for a legislative veto of state laws, Luther Martin proposed what ultimately became the supremacy clause of Article VI, which the delegates adopted unanimously as a preferable method of asserting national control over state action.

The second heading of Randolph's proposal was subjected to considerable revision on July 17. Several delegates had earlier objected to the vagueness of the term "incompetent," and wished a more "exact enumeration" of powers, but this was not attempted by the committee of the whole. On July 17 Sherman tried to sharpen up the language by provisions which would give Congress power "to make laws binding on the people of the United States in all cases which may concern the common interests of the Union; but not to interfere with the Government of the individual States in any matters of internal police which respect the Govt. of such States only, and wherein the General welfare of the U. States is not concerned."

Gouverneur Morris thought this left too much power with the states; "the internal police . . . ought to be infringed in many cases, as in the case of paper money & other tricks by which Citizens of other States may be affected." Finally the following language was adopted by a vote of eight to two: "to legislate in all cases for the general interests of the Union, and also in those to which the States are separately incompetent, or in which the harmony of the U. States may be interrupted by the exercise of individual Legislation."

The committee of detail eliminated this provision entirely, in favor of a long list of specific powers which it felt Congress might want to exercise. The list started out with the power to tax and to regulate commerce, included fifteen other grants, and wound up with the sweeping authority "to make all laws that shall be necessary and proper for carrying into execution the foregoing powers, and all other powers vested, by this Constitution, in the government of the United States." The Convention accepted the enumeration approach and went to work on this list, adding or revising some powers, and dropping others. The result was to spell out in detail, rather than to grant by broad generalizations, those powers the absence of which in the Confederation had made the movement for a new Constitution necessary.

LIMITATIONS ON THE POWERS OF CONGRESS    The general emphasis of the Convention was on assuring that Congress had enough powers to remedy the defects of the Confederation. But conflicting sectional interests led the delegates to insist on inserting certain prohibitions on national power. The slave interest was the one which most feared discriminatory action by the new government. A majority of the Convention was opposed to "this infernal trafic," as Mason called it, but North Carolina, South Carolina, and Georgia would have refused to join the Union if the slave trade had been prohibited. The committee of detail reported a provision that no tax or duty should be laid "on the migration or importation of such persons as the several States shall think proper to admit; nor shall such migration or importation be prohibited." Opposition to this formula was intense. Apart from the moral issue, the fact that other imports would be taxed whereas slaves would not amounted, as Wilson charged, to a bounty on slaves. Ultimately, on August 25 agreement was reached on a provision that the importation of slaves

would not be prohibited before 1808, and permitting a limited power of taxation on imports of slaves.

The prohibition on the power of Congress to levy direct taxes except on an apportionment basis also represented the efforts of the slavery supporters to assure that internal taxes based specifically on slaves could not be adopted. The prohibition of taxes on exports derived, not from the slave interest as such, but from the different character of the economy of the eight Northern and five Southern states. The latter, being engaged primarily in the production of agricultural commodities for which the principal market was foreign, feared that a Northern-dominated Congress would adopt export taxes falling most heavily on their trade.

LIMITATIONS ON THE POWERS OF THE STATES    The supremacy clause was relied on to prevent state legislation contrary to the national Constitution, laws, or treaties, but there were certain specific subjects on which the delegates felt so strongly that they banned state legislation in forthright language. The sharpest feeling was against state paper money and debtor relief laws. Mercer was the only delegate who ever confessed that he was "a friend to paper money," and he warned it was impolitic "to excite the opposition of all those who were friends to paper money." Gorham likewise wondered how wise it was to line up all the paper money addicts against the Constitution. But Ellsworth replied that this was a "favorable moment to shut and bar the door against paper money."

So the Convention voted to forbid the states to coin money, to print money, or to require anything but gold and silver coin to be accepted in the payment of debts. Then, taking account of the state laws which had been passed to relieve debtors of their business obligations, language forbidding the states to pass any law impairing the obligation of contracts was added with little discussion. Gerry's effort to extend the same prohibition to Congress failed.

THE PRESIDENTIAL OFFICE    The Virginia Plan contemplated a national executive to be named by electors chosen by Congress. In the debate which began on June 1, Randolph proposed an executive council of three men, contending that "unity in the Executive magistracy" would be "the foetus of monarchy." Wilson replied that unity in the executive would be "the best safeguard against tyranny." Gerry thought that in military matters a plural executive would be "a general with three heads." The inconvenience and impracticability of Randolph's proposal was plain, and a single executive was approved on June 4 by a vote of seven to three.

Although this issue was decided early, the method of election and term of the executive were not. These two problems were closely related. If the executive was to be chosen by Congress, then a fairly long term with no re-eligibility was favored, in order to reduce the possibility of intrigue with

Congress for a second term. If the President was to be chosen in some other fashion, then re-eligibility was not objectionable and a shorter term became possible. The Convention considered many proposals, changed its mind repeatedly, and did not finally resolve the issue until almost the end of its sessions. Wilson said that the question of how to elect the President was "the most difficult of all on which we have had to decide."

The discussions are too complex to follow closely. The committee of the whole left Randolph's plan for election by Congress unchanged. Wilson's alternate proposal that the people elect electors who in turn would elect the President was defeated eight to two on June 2. The Convention was not too comfortable with its decision for congressional election, however, and on July 17 Gouverneur Morris again proposed popular election of presidential electors. The people would not fail to elect a man of "continental reputation," he thought, whereas legislative choice would be "the work of intrigue, of cabal, and of faction." But Pinckney thought the people would be led "by a few active & designing men," and Mason added that "it would be as unnatural to refer the choice of a proper character for chief Magistrate to the people, as it would, to refer a trial of colours to a blind man."

The elector plan failed, and the Convention then reaffirmed legislative election unanimously. Yet two days later Morris was again preaching the need "that the Executive Magistrate should be the guardian of the people, even of the lower classes, agst. Legislative tyranny, against the Great & the wealthy who in the course of things will necessarily compose—the Legislative body." This time Madison joined in urging that the executive should be independent of the legislature, and supported the elector plan. The Convention then switched to electors, but contrary to Wilson's proposal, provided for their choice by the state legislatures, and shortened the term to six years.

This decision led to some dispute over the number of electors to be allotted to the respective states. Then on July 24 Houston from Georgia complained that capable men would be unwilling to come in from the more distant states just to ballot for President, and so the Convention flopped back to the original scheme of legislative election. This change, it was argued, made it necessary to reinstate the ban on re-eligibility, which had been dropped in the meantime, or to lengthen the term to protect the President against congressional domination. The Convention was heckled by suggestions for increasing the tenure to eight, eleven, or fifteen years. King, with tongue in cheek, suggested twenty years—"the medium life of princes." Gerry ejaculated, "We seem to be entirely at a loss on this head," and then added to the confusion by suggesting that the governors of the states select the President, or that the state legislatures do the electing. Dickinson capped this by proposing that the people of each state elect "its best citizen," and that Congress then choose among the thirteen candidates.

Afraid of election by Congress, but unable to agree on a plan of election by the people, the Convention sent to the committee of detail its decision for

congressional election for a seven-year term, with no re-eligibility. But how would Congress vote for President? If the two houses voted separately, they might never agree on a candidate. If they voted jointly, the big states could name the President. Joint election was adopted on August 24 by a seven to four vote, and an effort to provide that the votes would be cast by states, each state having one vote, failed by six to five. At this point Morris again urged popular election of electors, and lost by only one vote, six to five. The matter was so completely in dispute that it was turned over to a committee of eleven members, one of whom was Morris.

At long last Morris succeeded. The report of the committee proposed that the states appoint electors equaling in number the senators and representatives from the state. These electors were to meet in the respective states and ballot for two persons, one of whom could not be an inhabitant of the same state with themselves. The ballots would be sent to the capital and counted in the Senate. If one candidate received the votes of a majority of the electors, he was elected President. The runner-up was Vice President, an office which this committee invented. If no candidate received a majority, or if two candidates were tied, then the Senate would choose the President from among the five highest candidates. The term was reduced to four years.

This complicated electoral plan, it was generally believed, would enable the large states in effect to "nominate" the leading candidates, none of whom would normally have a majority. Then the small states with their equal votes in the Senate would have a considerable voice in the final selection. This feature was a calculated bid to win the votes of the small states, though Morris sought to rationalize Senate election by arguing that "fewer could then, say to the President, you owe your appointment to us." But Wilson pointed out in rebuttal that the Senate had to approve presidential appointments, and that a President named by the Senate would feel obligated to that body, to the point that the Senate would actually take over the appointing power. The plan would have "a dangerous tendency to aristocracy." And so in a final flurry of voting on September 6 the Convention adopted Sherman's suggestion of choice by the House, but with the members from each state having one vote, thus preserving the principle of state equality that election by the Senate would have provided. Only Delaware voted no.

THE VICE PRESIDENCY    As just noted, the committee of eleven invented the vice presidency at a late stage in the Convention. The report of the committee of detail on August 6 had provided for the president of the Senate to exercise the powers and duties of the President in case of removal, death, resignation, or disability. The committee of eleven proposed that the Vice President be available for this purpose, and also made him ex officio president of the Senate. This latter arrangement caused a debate on September 7. Gerry and Mason thought this was an improper mixture of legislative and

executive. But Sherman pointed out that "if the vice-President were not to be President of the Senate, he would be without employment."

THE JUDICIARY    There was universal agreement on the need for a national judiciary, the absence of which was one of the weaknesses of the Confederation. Even the New Jersey Plan of revising the Articles called for the creation of a federal supreme tribunal. The Virginia Plan, however, provided for inferior tribunals as well as for a Supreme Court. On June 5 the proposal for inferior courts was attacked by Rutledge, who contended that the state courts should hear all cases in the first instance; the right of appeal to the Supreme Court would be sufficient to protect national rights and provide uniformity of judgments. But Madison argued that there should be "an effective Judiciary establishment commensurate to the legislative authority. . . . A Government without a proper Executive & Judiciary would be the mere trunk of a body without arms or legs to act or move." A compromise was then voted under which the national legislature was empowered to institute inferior tribunals, and this was adopted by a vote of eight to two.

The Randolph proposal that judges, like the President, be elected by Congress was soon eliminated. On June 5 Wilson argued for appointment by the President. "A principal reason for unity in the Executive was that officers might be appointed by a single, responsible person." Madison inclined toward appointment by the Senate, as the more stable and independent branch of the legislature. Franklin entertained the gathering with a Scotch plan "in which the nomination proceeded from the Lawyers, who always selected the ablest of the profession in order to get rid of him, and share his practice among themselves."

On July 18 Gorham's proposal for executive appointment, by and with the advice and consent of the Senate, was rejected by a tie vote. Senate appointment was reaffirmed on July 21, and the matter went to the committee of detail in this posture. In its report, the general appointing power was given to the President, but the appointment of justices and ambassadors remained with the Senate. It was the committee of eleven, reporting on September 4, which gave the appointment of Supreme Court justices to the President, with Senate advice and consent. This formula was accepted by the Convention on September 7, through Wilson objected that blending a branch of the legislature with the executive in appointments would destroy executive responsibility. Gouverneur Morris replied "that as the President was to nominate, there would be responsibility, and as the Senate was to concur, there would be security." There was never any disagreement that judicial tenure should be during good behavior.

THE FAILURE TO INCLUDE A BILL OF RIGHTS    The Convention adopted several provisions aimed to protect individuals against unjust punishment or

government reprisal. The committee of detail worked out the treason provision, and it was subjected to intensive discussion on August 20. The Convention also adopted a prohibition on bills of attainder and ex post facto laws, guaranteed a jury trial on criminal charges, and provided that the privilege of the writ of habeas corpus could not be suspended except in cases of rebellion or invasion.

These provisions were not thought sufficient by some delegates. On September 12 Mason expressed his disappointment that the constitutional plan had not "been prefaced with a Bill of Rights," but the attempt which he and Gerry made to get a committee appointed to prepare such a document was defeated ten to zero. Sherman's reason was that "the State Declarations of Rights are not repealed by this Constitution; and being in force are sufficient." Perhaps a more pressing reason was that the delegates had been at the job for three and a half months, and wanted to get home.

### RATIFICATION OF THE CONSTITUTION

The Virginia Plan called for ratification of the new Constitution by special conventions popularly elected for that purpose. The Convention agreed on July 23 by a vote of nine to one, and on August 31 added the provision bringing the Constitution into operation by the favorable vote of nine state conventions. Madison thought from the beginning that ratification by conventions rather than by state legislatures was essential. The theoretical reasons were that the new government must derive its authority directly from the people. There were also some practical considerations which were frankly stated. Thus on July 23 Randolph warned of "the local demogagues who will be degraded by [the Constitution] from the importance they now hold," and who would spare no effort to defeat the proposal. "It is of great importance therefore that the consideration of this subject should be transferred from the Legislatures where this class of men, have their full influence to a field in which their efforts can be less mischievous." Others were more diplomatic in referring to the conventions as "more likely to be composed of the ablest men in the States."

Abandonment of the rule of unanimity in adoption of the Constitution was obviously necessitated by Rhode Island's refusal even to attend the Convention. The delegates also contemplated that resistance might be expected from other states. Gorham said that "the present advantage which N. York seems to be so much attached to, of taxing her neighbours [by the regulation of her trade], makes it very probable, that she will be of the number." On August 30 Carroll argued that unanimity was "necessary to dissolve the existing confederacy which had been unanimously established," but Butler "revolted at the idea, that one or two States should restrain the rest from consulting their safety." Nine was finally fixed as the number of states necessary for ratification because, as Mason said, this "had been re-

quired in all great cases under the Confederation" and was therefore "familiar to the people."

The forces favorable to adoption of the Constitution sought to get the conventions elected as promptly as possible, before the opposition had a chance to organize. Unquestionably many farmers and backwoodsmen, who would have tended to oppose the Constitution, were neutralized in this way. About three-fourths of the male white citizens over twenty-one failed to vote in the elections for convention delegates, Charles A. Beard contends, either on account of their indifference or their disfranchisement by property qualifications. He thinks it is probable that a majority of the voters in at least six states opposed ratification. His thesis that the Constitution was adopted primarily by the manufacturing, trade, shipping, and creditor interests in the country, and that the small farming and debtor interests were largely opposed to the Constitution, has been vigorously challenged by more recent studies. It now appears quite probable that class distinctions at the time were much less significant, that property qualifications for voting excluded few from the polls, and that the Constitution was adopted by people who were primarily middle-class property owners, including farmers.

Whatever the bases of the alignments, the political campaign over ratification was intense and bitter. One of its legacies was the most famous commentary on American government, *The Federalist*. These essays were newspaper articles written to influence the vote in the doubtful state of New York by Madison, Hamilton, and John Jay. Although their discussions of the proposed Constitution may not have had great influence at the time, they have been widely accepted as authoritative guides to constitutional interpretation.

The first state convention to ratify the Constitution was that of Delaware on December 7, 1787, which was less than three months after the document was signed. Pennsylvania ratified five days later. New Jersey (December 19), Georgia (January 2), Connecticut (January 9), Massachusetts (February 6), Maryland (April 23), and South Carolina (May 23) followed. New Hampshire was the ninth state, and its ratification on June 21, 1788, brought the Constitution into effect. However, without New York and Virginia the union could not have succeeded. Virginia came in by a narrow margin on June 25, and New York followed on July 26, though an attempt to attach conditions to its ratification almost succeeded. North Carolina finally ratified on November 21, 1789, and Rhode Island held out until May 29, 1790.

The absence of a bill of rights provoked the most widespread criticism in the ratifying conventions, and in Massachusetts, New York, and Virginia the promise that a bill of rights would be added was instrumental in securing the votes needed for ratification. Several of the state conventions submitted lists of proposed amendments to the new Constitution at the time they ratified, and there was a general agreement that addition of a bill of rights to

the Constitution through the amending process would be a first order of business.

The motive force for putting the new government in operation was supplied by the Continental Congress. On September 13, 1788, it adopted a resolution designating "the present seat of Congress," which was New York, as the site of the new government. The resolution also fixed the first Wednesday of January, 1789, as the day for choosing presidential electors, the first Wednesday of February for the meeting of electors, and the first Wednesday of March, which fell on March 4, for the opening session of the new Congress. Various delays kept Congress from convening on that day, however, and it was not until April 30, 1789, that George Washington was inaugurated as the first President of the United States.

The framing of the American Constitution has been the subject of never-ending controversy. Some have seen the Founders as little short of demigods; for others they were a "reform caucus" of practical politicians. Was the Constitution a democratic or an aristocratic instrument? Were its drafters conservatives or liberals? Was the document more concerned with establishing the powers of the new government or the limitations on those powers?

There is room for such disagreement, because the basic truth about the Constitution is that it was the product of compromise. The men who met in Philadelphia in the summer of 1787 were generally of the opinion that government is a "necessary evil"; they were jealous of individual rights and had strong loyalties to their states. But experience with the Articles had demonstrated that a weak government could not provide the security and prosperity they wanted, and the amazing thing is how unanimous the Convention was in seeing the need for a central "government of powers." As Martin Diamond has said: "This was the great and novel idea which came from the Convention: a large, powerful republic with a competent national government regulated under a wise Constitution." [2]

### SELECTED REFERENCES

BEARD, CHARLES A., *An Economic Interpretation of the Constitution of the United States*. New York: The Macmillan Company, 1913, 1935.

BOWEN, CATHERINE DRINKER, *Miracle at Philadelphia*. Boston: Little, Brown and Company, 1966.

BRANT, IRVING, *James Madison: Father of the Constitution, 1787–1800*. Indianapolis: The Bobbs-Merrill Company, Inc., 1950.

BROWN, ROBERT E., *Charles Beard and the Constitution: A Critical Analysis of "An Economic Interpretation of the Constitution."* Princeton, N.J.: Princeton University Press, 1956.

[2] "What the Framers Meant by Federalism," in Robert A. Goldwin (ed.), *A Nation of States* (Chicago: Rand McNally & Company, 1963), p. 37.

————, *Reinterpretation of the Formation of the American Constitution.* Boston: Boston University Press, 1963.

DIAMOND, MARTIN, "The Federalist's View of Federalism," in George C. S. Benson et al., *Essays in Federalism.* Claremont, Calif.: Claremont Men's College, 1961.

ELLIOT, JONATHAN (ed.), *The Debates in the Several State Conventions in the Adoption of the Federal Constitution,* 5 vols. Washington: Taylor & Maury, 1854 (second edition).

FARRAND, MAX, *The Framing of the Constitution of the United States.* New Haven, Conn.: Yale University Press, 1913.

———— (ed.), *The Records of the Federal Convention of 1787,* 4 vols. New Haven, Conn.: Yale University Press, 1911, 1937.

*The Federalist* (Henry Cabot Lodge, ed.). New York: G. P. Putnam's Sons, 1904.

HOLCOMBE, ARTHUR N., *The Constitutional System.* Chicago: Scott, Foresman and Company, 1964.

KELLY, ALFRED H., and WINFRED A. HARBISON, *The American Constitution: Its Origins and Development,* chaps. 5, 6. New York: W. W. Norton & Company, Inc., 1963 (third edition).

MAIN, JACKSON TURNER, *The Antifederalists: Critics of the Constitution, 1781–1788.* Chapel Hill, N.C.: The University of North Carolina Press, 1961.

MC DONALD, FORREST, *We the People: The Economic Origins of the Constitution.* Chicago: The University of Chicago Press, 1958.

MC LAUGHLIN, ANDREW C., *A Constitutional History of the United States,* chaps. 14, 15. New York: Appleton-Century-Crofts, Inc., 1935.

MITCHELL, BROADUS, and LOUISE MITCHELL, *A Biography of the Constitution of the United States,* chaps. 2–4. Fair Lawn, N.J.: Oxford University Press, 1964.

ROCHE, JOHN P., "The Founding Fathers: A Reform Caucus in Action," in *Shadow and Substance,* pp. 91–126. New York: The Macmillan Company, 1964. Also 55 *American Political Science Review* 799–816 (1961).

ROSSITER, CLINTON, *1787: The Grand Convention.* New York: The Macmillan Company, 1966.

SMITH, DAVID G., *The Convention and the Constitution: The Political Ideas of the Founding Fathers.* New York: St. Martin's Press, Inc., 1965.

SOLBERG, WINTON U. (ed.), *The Federal Convention and the Formation of the Union of the American States.* New York: The Liberal Arts Press, Inc., 1958.

SUTHERLAND, ARTHUR B., *Constitutionalism in America.* Waltham, Mass.: Blaisdell Publishing Company, 1965.

SWISHER, CARL B., *American Constitutional Development,* chap. 2. Boston: Houghton Mifflin Company, 1954 (second edition).

VAN DOREN, CARL, *The Great Rehearsal: The Story of the Making and Ratifying of the Constitution of the United States.* New York: The Viking Press, Inc., 1948.

WARREN, CHARLES, *The Making of the Constitution.* Boston: Little, Brown and Company, 1928.

WRIGHT, BENJAMIN F., *Consensus and Continuity, 1776–1787.* Boston: Boston University Press, 1958.

# 3

## Amendment of the constitution

The United States thus launched its experiment in building a federal government on the basis of a written document which has conditioned the entire development of American governmental experience since 1789. Public policy has been continuously subject to the test of constitutionality. Much of the rhetoric of public debate has been in terms of invoking the support of the document for proposals favored, and throwing doubt on the constitutional legitimacy of actions opposed.

A perennial problem of American politics has been the meaning of the American Constitution. As years and decades have passed, changes have occurred in the physical world. Technical discoveries or inventions have affected the life of the country. Population has multiplied. The political party has undergone a transformation from a despised source of faction to an indispensable instrument of representative government. Public agencies have taken over responsibilities undreamed of in the eighteenth century. Standards of public morality have changed. How is a government of continental proportions and world-wide responsibilities, with a peacetime budget of well over 100 billion dollars, to be accommodated within the confines of a document drafted a century and three-quarters earlier for a handful of people in thirteen isolated states along the Atlantic seaboard?

One answer is that the framers of the Constitution were wise enough to avoid the evil of too great specificity in drafting key provisions of the

document. Their general intent was to stick to fundamentals and leave implementation to subsequent legislative decision. Thus no departmental organization of the executive branch was written into the Constitution. The question of a system of lower courts was left to Congress, as was the matter of presidential succession beyond the Vice President, and the time, place, and manner of electing representatives and senators. The powers given to the President and to Congress were typically stated in fairly broad language. Although there was a spelling out in Article I, section 8, of congressional authority in a number of areas, the section wound up with what was called "the sweeping clause," conferring on Congress the power "to make all laws which shall be necessary and proper for carrying into execution the foregoing powers, and all other powers vested by this Constitution in the government of the United States, or in any department or officer thereof."

Nevertheless, no amount of drafting skill could be expected to eliminate the necessity of revision and development to adapt the Constitution to the unforeseen and the unforeseeable. This adaptation has taken two forms—constitutional amendment and constitutional interpretation.

### THE DEVELOPMENT OF ARTICLE V

Formal provision for revision of the Constitution through amendment was made by Article V. The original Virginia Plan had provided for amendments, and added that "the assent of the National Legislature ought not to be required thereto." On June 11 Mason urged the necessity of an amending clause, saying: "The plan now to be formed will certainly be defective, as the Confederation has been found on trial to be. Amendments therefore will be necessary, and it will be better to provide for them, in an easy, regular and Constitutional way than to trust to chance and violence." The reason for excluding Congress from the process as he saw it was that "they may abuse their power, and refuse their consent on that very account."

The committee of detail later produced a revised plan for amendments which also eliminated Congress. On the application of the legislatures of two-thirds of the states, Congress would be required to call a convention for amendment of the Constitution. This plan was adopted on August 30, but by September 10 the Convention was quite unhappy about it. Madison said the language was too vague. Hamilton said there must be an easier way of securing amendments. The states would never "apply for alterations but with a view to increase their own powers." Congress would be "most sensible to the necessity of amendments," Hamilton thought, and should be able to initiate the process.

The Convention then began to rewrite the amending provision on the floor, with Madison putting the various suggestions into the form finally adopted. Legislatures of two-thirds of the states could still request Congress to call a convention, but Congress itself by a two-thirds vote in each house

could propose amendments to the states. Amendments initiated in either fashion would have to be ratified either by the legislatures or special conventions in three-fourths of the states, according to the mode of ratification specified by Congress.

Rutledge then objected that "he never could agree to give a power by which the articles relating to slaves might be altered by the States not interested in that property and prejudiced against it." Consequently a proviso was added protecting the clauses pertaining to slavery from amendment until the year 1808. Then on September 15 Sherman had a last-minute fear "that three fourths of the States might be brought to do things fatal to particular States, as abolishing them altogether or depriving them of their equality in the Senate." He wanted another proviso that no state should by amendment "be affected in its internal police, or deprived of its equal suffrage in the Senate." Madison warned that if the Convention once began with these "special provisos," every state would insist on some for its boundaries or exports. However, "the circulating murmurs of the small States" led Gouverneur Morris to propose adding the proviso protecting equality in the Senate, and it was agreed to unanimously. Thus Article V was completed.

### USE OF THE AMENDING POWER

The presence of the amending clause was one of the factors which led Jefferson, originally inclined to oppose the Constitution, to decide in its favor. Since 1789 the procedures of Article V have been utilized to add twenty-five amendments to the Constitution. The first ten of these amendments were drafted to meet the widespread protests against the absence of a bill of rights in the original Constitution. To fill this gap, twelve amendments were proposed by the First Congress on September 25, 1789. The first two failed of ratification, but acceptance of the remaining ten was completed on December 15, 1791. The substance of these and subsequent amendments will be discussed at appropriate points throughout this volume. Here we are interested only in the chronology and general circumstances of adoption.

The Eleventh Amendment was adopted in 1795, its purpose being to override the Supreme Court's holding in *Chisholm* v. *Georgia* (1793) which allowed federal courts to accept jurisdiction of a suit against a state by a citizen of another state. The Twelfth Amendment, ratified in 1804, was intended to prevent a repetition of the confusion attendant on the presidential election of 1800, when Jefferson and Burr received an equal number of electoral votes. As the candidates for President and Vice President of the same party, they were supported by all the party's electors, but under the original language of Article II, there was no separate designation of votes for these two offices. Thus the election had to be decided by the House, where the Federalists were tempted to vote for Burr to spite Jefferson. The Twelfth Amendment requires electors to vote for the two offices separately.

The Thirteenth, Fourteenth, and Fifteenth Amendments were adopted

as a result of the Civil War. The Thirteenth Amendment, which abolished slavery, was ratified in 1865. The Fourteenth, the longest of the lot and too complex to summarize at this point, aimed to protect the rights of the newly freed Negroes. It also dealt with certain political problems which were an aftermath of the War. When it appeared that the Fourteenth Amendment would not secure the right to vote for Negroes, the Fifteenth Amendment, ratified in 1870, was adopted specifically guaranteeing the right to vote against denial or abridgement on the basis of race or color.

The next two amendments reflected the progressive political philosophy of the first part of the twentieth century. The Sixteenth, ratified in 1913, reversed another Supreme Court decision, *Pollock* v. *Farmers' Loan & Trust Co.* (1895), and authorized the federal government to levy taxes on incomes. The Seventeenth Amendment, ratified two months later, provided for direct popular election of senators.

The Eighteenth Amendment, which became effective in 1919, was the controversial prohibition amendment. Suffrage for women was guaranteed in 1920 by the Nineteenth Amendment. The Twentieth Amendment, ratified in 1933, fixed the date for convening the regular annual session of Congress on January 3, and the beginning of presidential terms on January 20. In addition, it sought to clarify certain points with respect to presidential succession. The Twenty-first Amendment, also adopted in 1933, repealed the Eighteenth, but did give the states full powers to prohibit the transportation, importation, or use of intoxicating liquor.

The Twenty-second Amendment, ratified in 1951, limits a President to two terms in office. The Twenty-third (1961) permits residents of the District of Columbia to vote for President and gives the District three electoral votes. The Twenty-fourth (1964) forbids the states to use the poll tax as a voting requirement in federal elections. The Twenty-fifth (1967) provides for the appointment of a new Vice President when the original occupant of that office has succeeded to the Presidency, and authorizes the Vice President to act as President if the President is incapacitated.

Only five amendments have been proposed by Congress which have failed of ratification. Two of these came from the First Congress, as already noted. The most recent was the child labor amendment, proposed in 1924 to give Congress authority to regulate or prohibit child labor, which had been denied by Supreme Court decisions in 1918 and 1922.[1]

### THE "POLITICAL" CHARACTER OF THE AMENDING PROCESS

The Supreme Court has generally regarded the amending process as almost entirely a concern of Congress, subject to very little in the way of judicial supervision or control. For example, after the Civil War the states which had attempted to secede and which had not been readmitted to the full en-

[1] *Hammer* v. *Dagenhart* (1918); *Bailey* v. *Drexel Furniture Co.* (1922).

joyment of the privileges of states, were required by Congress to ratify the Fourteenth and Fifteenth Amendments as a condition to their readmission. The Supreme Court refused to question this requirement.[2]

Until 1939, however, the Court was willing to pass on procedural problems pertaining to the adoption of amendments. In the *National Prohibition Cases* (1920), it ruled that the two-thirds vote in each house required to propose an amendment means two-thirds of the members present—assuming the presence of a quorum—and not a vote of two-thirds of the entire membership. In *Leser* v. *Garnett* (1922), the validity of the Nineteenth Amendment was attacked on the ground that the ratifying resolutions in two states were adopted in violation of those states' rules of legislative procedure. But the Court regarded official notice of ratification from the states to the United States Secretary of State as conclusive upon him, and held that his certification was conclusive on the courts.

The Eighteenth Amendment was the first to specify a period of years—in this case, seven—within which ratification had to be effected. In *Dillon* v. *Gloss* (1921) the Court ruled that there was no doubt about the power of Congress to fix a definite period for ratification, "within reasonable limits," and it agreed seven years was reasonable. The implication of this ruling seemed to be that an amendment could not be ratified when it had been before the country for more than a "reasonable" time. Consequently, when the child labor amendment, which Congress had proposed in 1924, with no time limit specified, was ratified by Kansas and Kentucky in 1937, efforts were made to get a judicial ruling that because of the lapse of time the amendment was no longer open for ratification.

In *Coleman* v. *Miller* (1939), however, the Court refused to take responsibility for deciding what was a "reasonable" period for ratification. That was an essentially political question, which Congress would have to determine. Four members of the Court went further to hold that the Court's assertion in *Dillon* v. *Gloss* that amendments must be ratified within a reasonable period was entirely unauthorized, and nothing more than an "admonition to the Congress in the nature of an advisory opinion." Their view was that the entire process of amendment was political and "not subject to judicial guidance, control or interference at any point." Even the majority decision, it should be noted, left open the possibility of only a bare minimum of judicial control over the amending process, and it is significant to note that the Court has not dealt with an amending clause problem since *Coleman* v. *Miller*.

### THE PROPOSING OF AMENDMENTS

Of the two methods which Article V provides for proposing amendments—by a two-thirds majority of each house of Congress, or by a convention

[2] *White* v. *Hart* (1872).

summoned by Congress at the request of the legislatures of two-thirds of the states—only the former has been employed. On numerous occasions state legislatures have petitioned Congress to call a convention, but always unsuccessfully. In the early part of this century some thirty-one states, meeting the two-thirds requirement at that time, submitted petitions for an amendment to provide for direct election of senators. Congress failed to call a convention, but eventually proposed the amendment itself.

In 1962 the Council of State Governments asked state legislatures to petition for a convention to adopt a package of three "states' rights" amendments, but the number responding fell far short of the required two-thirds. In 1964 the council began a new convention campaign after the Supreme Court ruled in *Reynolds* v. *Sims* that members of both houses in the state legislatures must be elected from equal population districts. The council asked the states to petition for a convention to propose an amendment which would permit one house to be apportioned on some basis other than population, provided the people of the state approved in a referendum vote. By the end of 1965 some twenty-eight state legislatures had passed various resolutions to this effect, six short of the two-thirds requirement of thirty-four.

In the meantime a national organization had been formed and had hired a California public relations firm to promote support for a similar amendment sponsored by Senator Dirksen. After this amendment was defeated in the Senate in 1966, the committee and its public relations agent, with Senator Dirksen's assistance, began to lobby selected state legislatures in an effort to get the remaining state votes needed to request Congress to call a convention. By early 1967 four more states had adopted resolutions, only two short of the number required.

This campaign concentrated new attention on the many uncertainties surrounding the convention device. If two-thirds of the legislatures submit petitions, must they be in identical language, and must they be received within a limited time period? May Congress refuse to act on the petitions? If Congress does refuse, can the courts force Congress to act? If a convention is called, how are the delegates chosen, and what are the voting rules in the convention? Can a convention be prevented from going beyond the subject for which it was convened, as the Constitutional Convention did in 1787?

These unknowns are so serious that it would be well for Congress to adopt general implementing legislation before it is faced with a valid convention call. A bill for this purpose was submitted by Senator Ervin in August, 1967 (S. 2307). It requires petitions to be directed to the Speaker of the House and the President of the Senate, who are to tabulate the number of petitions and give them full publicity. Applications are to be valid for six years, unless rescinded sooner by the state. When the two houses of Congress determine that the requisite number of petitions has been received, it is the "duty" of each house to agree to a concurrent resolution setting up the convention.

The Ervin bill would give each state as many delegates as it has representatives in Congress, their election or appointment to be controlled by state law. Each state would have one vote in the convention, and amendments would be adopted by a simple majority vote. This is a throwback to the 1787 Convention which is clearly unacceptable, for it would permit amendments to be proposed by spokesmen for a minority of the population from the twenty-six least populous states. Finally, the Ervin bill has several provisions guaranteeing that the convention will not be permitted to propose amendments on any subject other than those specified in the petitions.

The principal support for the convention device has come from interests sponsoring proposals which could not gain congressional approval. It is an alternative attractive to manipulators of opinion who find it more congenial to work in the recesses of fifty state legislatures than in the glare of the congressional spotlight. The national interest in the amending process is best protected by leaving the responsibility for proposing amendments in the hands of Congress.

Under the convention formula, Congress would lose its role in the proposing of amendments, but would retain control over the amending procedure by specifying convention powers and voting arrangements. The Council of State Governments in its 1962 program sought to make it possible to eliminate Congress completely from the amending process. The council would have abolished the convention method, substituting for it a plan whereby the legislatures of two-thirds of the states could propose an amendment by adopting identical texts. A measure thus proposed would go automatically before the states for ratification by three-fourths of their legislatures. This astonishing proposal for returning the United States to the condition of a confederation was immediately and almost without discussion accepted by twelve state legislatures, but as soon as the intent of the plan was understood, the movement collapsed.[3]

It is settled that the President plays no official role in the proposing of amendments, in spite of the provision in Article I, section 7, that "every order, resolution, or vote to which the concurrence of the Senate and House of Representatives may be necessary . . . shall be presented to the President." Presumably the reason is that proposing an amendment is not an exercise of ordinary legislative power.[4] Another factor is that, since proposed amendments must be passed by a two-thirds vote of each house and since that is the margin necessary to override a presidential veto, no purpose would normally be served by presidential participation in proposing amend-

[3] See Charles L. Black, Jr., "The Proposed Amendment of Article V: A Threatened Disaster," 72 *Yale Law Journal* 957–966 (1963); Symposium, "Constitutional Amendments Proposed by the Council of State Governments," 39 *Notre Dame Lawyer* 625–679 (1964); "Amending the Constitution to Strengthen the States in the Federal System," 36 *State Government* 10–15 (1963).

[4] See *Hollingsworth* v. *Virginia* (1798); *Hawke* v. *Smith* (1920).

ments. The Ervin bill provides for calling a constitutional convention by concurrent resolution of the two houses, thus excluding the President from participation. However, the Ervin bill itself would be subject to presidential veto, which would give the President an opportunity to influence its provisions.

The fact that the President does not pass on proposals for amendment of course constitutes no reason why he should not interest himself in proposed amendments. When the Bricker Amendment limiting the treaty power was before Congress, President Eisenhower's vigorous opposition was criticized by Senator Bricker on the ground that the President should have no concern with the amending process, but the President was fully justified in defending executive prerogatives in the field of foreign relations against attack by constitutional amendment.

## THE RATIFICATION OF AMENDMENTS

The ratification of all the amendments to the Constitution except one has been by vote of three-fourths of the state legislatures. Only in the case of the Twenty-first Amendment, which repealed the Eighteenth, did Congress require the use of state conventions. The reason for this exception was the fear in Congress that the overrepresentation in the state legislatures of rural areas, which tended to be "dry," might imperil adoption of the amendment, whereas conventions would more equitably represent the views of the urban areas. The 1962 Council of State Governments' proposal would have deprived Congress of its authority to select the state convention mode of ratification.

Notification of state ratification is transmitted by the states to the head of the General Services Administration in Washington. His action in proclaiming the adoption of an amendment when he has received official notices from the required number of states is purely ministerial; the amendment is brought into effect by the ratifying action of the necessary states and on the day when the required number of ratifications is reached.[5] However, the Eighteenth Amendment had an unusual provision postponing its effectiveness for one year after ratification was completed.

Since the Supreme Court has announced that it will not pass on the reasonableness of the period during which an amendment remains before the states for ratification, it seems desirable for Congress to state such time limits in the amendment itself, and this is now generally done. The child labor amendment, proposed in 1924 with no time limit, might technically be regarded as still open for ratification. In fact, however, Congress now has

[5] This responsibility was transferred from the Secretary of State in 1950. When the Twenty-fifth Amendment became effective in 1967, President Johnson staged a "signing" ceremony in the White House, but his signature was simply as a witness for the General Services Administrator.

by judicial construction the power which that amendment was intended to give, so it is clearly a dead letter.

A state which has refused to ratify a proposed amendment may later change its mind and vote favorably. In *Coleman* v. *Miller* the Supreme Court said such action should be regarded as a political matter with the ultimate authority of decision in Congress. However, it has been thought that an affirmative vote on ratification cannot be subsequently withdrawn, even though the amendment has not been proclaimed in effect. Ohio and New Jersey attempted to withdraw their approval of the Fourteenth Amendment before its ratification had been announced. After some uncertainty, the Secretary of State disregarded the withdrawal votes and proclaimed the amendment in effect. Congress supported this decision by adopting a concurrent resolution to the same effect. Since the votes of these two states were essential to the ratification of the Fourteenth Amendment, some of its critics have contended that it is not a valid part of the Constitution. The Ervin bill would permit states to rescind ratification of a proposed amendment provided the ratifications of three-fourths of the states had not yet been secured.

States cannot make ratification depend upon a popular referendum vote. The Ohio supreme court upheld the right of opponents of prohibition to invoke a referendum on the action of the state legislature in ratifying the Eighteenth Amendment, on the ground that, when Article V referred to "legislatures," it meant the general legislative power of the state. The Supreme Court, however, reversed this interpretation, holding that in 1787 the term "legislature" meant only the representative lawmaking body.[6] Similarly, a provision of the Tennessee constitution forbidding a legislative vote on an amendment unless the legislature had been elected after the amendment was submitted, was held invalid in *Leser* v. *Garnett* (1922). Finally, it should be noted that a state governor has no power to veto a legislative ratifying resolution, his position being the same as that of the President in the proposing of amendments.

### APPRAISAL OF THE AMENDING PROCESS

Perhaps the most striking fact about the amending process is the infrequency with which it has been used. Excluding the initial ten amendments, which must be considered practically part of the original Constitution, amendments have been adopted at a rate of less than one per decade. Following the Civil War amendments, there was a period of over forty years during which the Constitution appeared unamendable. This was an era of agrarian discontent, industrial unrest, and growing interest in political and economic

[6] *Hawke* v. *Smith* (1920). Of course *Coleman* v. *Miller* (1939) casts doubt on the continuing validity of these earlier judicial pronouncements on the amending procedure.

reforms. The conservatism of the Supreme Court, symbolized by its invalidation of the income tax in 1895, made constitutional amendment seem a necessary step toward achieving liberal legislative goals.

Under these circumstances there was much talk about the necessity of easing the amending process. For example, Senator La Follette in 1912 urged an amendment under which Congress would be compelled to propose amendments on application of the legislatures of ten states or by popular majority vote in ten states. Then ratification would be by majority of the electors voting in the majority of the states, provided they constituted a majority of the total vote cast in the country on the proposal.

In 1913, however, the long liberal campaign for the income tax and direct election of senators succeeded, and the women's suffrage amendment followed shortly thereafter. Also, adoption of the Eighteenth Amendment revealed the possibility of a small but dedicated pressure group exploiting the amending machinery successfully. With six amendments added to the Constitution between 1913 and 1933, the amending process no longer seemed so formidable. Moreover, the liberalization of the Supreme Court's views by President Franklin Roosevelt's appointments substantially eliminated liberal interest in further amendments.

After the 1930s, pressure for amendments to the Constitution came almost entirely from conservative and reactionary political quarters. Interest of conservatives in the amending process was motivated by their loss of influence in all three branches of the government. The increase in executive power and congressional expenditures, the acceptance of new welfare functions internally and new responsibilities internationally by the federal government, and the reduced role of the states were all trends which stimulated the resistance of various conservative groups. Lacking the power to block these developments through the normal political processes, they fell back on the device of constitutional amendment, but here they were scarcely more successful. The only amendment actually secured by these interests was the Twenty-second, adopted in 1951. This limitation of the President to two terms was initially proposed as a Republican measure after their party had suffered four defeats at the hands of President Roosevelt, but was subsequently supported by conservatives of both parties who feared strong executive leadership. Ironically, the first President to feel the effects of the amendment was a Republican, President Eisenhower, who criticized the limitation as unwise.

The best known of the measures unsuccessfully pressed during the 1940s and 1950s was the Bricker Amendment. This proposal represented an effort by isolationists, largely Republicans, to limit the treaty-making power and the President's authority to enter into executive agreements. Somewhat modified in form, it came within one vote of securing the necessary two-thirds Senate majority in 1955.

Another goal persistently sought by constitutional amendment has been

reform of the system for electing the President. The various plans proposed during the 1950s were sponsored by conservatives of both parties, and had the common feature of attempting to reduce the present preponderant influence of the large industrial states with their heavy labor and minority group electorates.[7]

Frustrated in their efforts to amend the Constitution, conservatives reacted in the same fashion as the radicals of the Progressive era, by seeking to make the Constitution easier to amend. The proposals of the Council of State Governments, as already noted, sought to provide an alternative which would eliminate Congress entirely and open the way to amendment by the state legislatures, where conservatives hoped they would have more influence than in Congress.

The adoption of three amendments in six years—the Twenty-third, Twenty-fourth, and Twenty-fifth—is evidence that the amending machinery is not hard to operate if there is a genuine consensus on the need, and may even lead to some concern that amendments are too easy to achieve. The Twenty-fourth Amendment has been criticized because the same goal could almost certainly have been secured by statute. It is of prime importance that the Constitution retain its brevity and be limited to basic structural arrangements and the protection of individual liberties. It would be disastrous if it became, through the amending power, a vehicle by which pressure groups and crackpots could impose their nostrums on the nation.

## SELECTED REFERENCES

BIRCHFIELD, CYRIL F., *Problems Relating to a Federal Constitutional Convention,* U.S. House of Representatives, Committee on the Judiciary, 85th Cong., 1st sess., 1957. Washington: Government Printing Office, 1957.

BONFIELD, ARTHUR EARL, "Proposing Constitutional Amendments by Convention: Some Problems," 39 *Notre Dame Lawyer* 659–679 (1964).

*The Constitution of the United States of America: Analysis and Interpretation,* Sen. Doc. no. 39, 88th Cong., pp. 797–803. Washington: Government Printing Office, 1964.

ELLIOTT, WILLIAM Y., *The Need for Constitutional Reform: A Program for National Security.* New York: McGraw-Hill Book Company, 1935.

GRAHAM, FRED P., "The Role of the States in Proposing Constitutional Amendments," 49 *American Bar Association Journal* 1175–1183 (1963).

HAZLITT, HENRY, *A New Constitution Now.* New York: McGraw-Hill Book Company, 1942.

HEHMEYER, ALEXANDER, *Time for Change: A Proposal for a Second Constitutional Convention.* New York: Holt, Rinehart and Winston, Inc., 1943.

[7] See the more detailed discussion in Chap. 16.

JOHNSTON, FELTON M., and RICHARD D. HUPMAN, "Proposed Amendments to the Constitution of the United States, Introduced in Congress from . . . December 6, 1926, to January 3, 1957." Sen. Doc. no. 65, 85th Cong., 1st sess. Washington: Government Printing Office, 1957.

Note, "Proposing Amendments to the U.S. Constitution by Convention," 70 *Harvard Law Review* 1067–1076 (1957).

OBERST, PAUL, "The Genesis of the Three States-rights Amendments of 1963," 39 *Notre Dame Lawyer* 644–658 (1964).

ORFIELD, LESTER B., *The Amending of the Federal Constitution.* Ann Arbor, Mich.: The University of Michigan Press, 1942.

ROVERE, RICHARD A., *The Eisenhower Years: Affairs of State,* chap. 26. New York: Farrar, Straus & Giroux, 1956.

SORENSON, THEODORE C., "The Quiet Campaign to Rewrite the Constitution," 50 *Saturday Review* 17–20 (July 15, 1967).

VOSE, CLEMENT E., "Conservatism by Amendment," 46 *The Yale Review* 176–190 (1957).

# 4

## Interpretation of the constitution

More gradual but more continuous than the amending process in adapting the Constitution to changing conditions is the device of constitutional interpretation. In fact, it has been the possibility of modification of constitutional meanings over the years to meet new times and new necessities which has permitted resort to formal amendment to be relatively infrequent.

The process of constitutional adaptation is one which goes on at many levels and in many contexts. There are adaptations which develop on an entirely unplanned basis in the form of usages or customs or methods of procedure or institutions. Perhaps the most striking example in American history is the prompt development after 1789 of a party system, for which the framers had not planned, and which in fact they had taken some pains to try to prevent. The development of committees in Congress, the tradition against a third term, the use of executive agreements instead of treaties, the rule that representatives must be residents of the districts they represent in Congress—these and many other customs and usages represented evolutionary adjustments of the constitutional system to practical problems with which it was confronted.

A much more intentional and sophisticated type of constitutional interpretation goes on in the decision making of the executive and legislative branches. President Truman's decision to seize the steel mills in 1952, or President Roosevelt's destroyers-for-bases deal with Britain in 1940, were

consciously based on theories of executive power under the Constitution. Likewise when Congress is considering legislation of a novel character, it is sure to hear many speeches defending or attacking the constitutionality of the proposal.

The most highly rationalized type of constitutional interpretation is no doubt that engaged in by judges, and particularly by the Supreme Court of the United States, which is the focus of this volume. Wherever the process of constitutional interpretation goes on, it is guided by some more or less articulate theory of the meaning of the Constitution. But in the 180 years during which the American nation has sought to relate the words of the written document to the diversity of its economic interests, political strivings, and moral goals, every conceivable rationalization has been developed for demonstrating that the policy preferences of the interpreter are in accord with the "true meaning" of the Constitution. The major theories of constitutional interpretation deserve brief consideration.

## APPROACHES TO CONSTITUTIONAL MEANING

THE INTENTION OF THE FRAMERS    One widely supported proposition is that the meaning of the Constitution should be determined by reference to the intention of the men who made it. It seems natural and logical that in the famous case of *Marbury* v. *Madison* (1803), where the issue was whether the judiciary had authority to invalidate acts of Congress, Chief Justice Marshall should have asked about "the intention of those who gave this power." But it is significant that, 165 years later, scholars are still disputing as to whether Marshall's conclusions about the intent of the framers on this important issue were supported by the evidence.

Consider the difficulties in using the test of intent. Who were the men who made the Constitution? Fifty-five delegates were present at one or more sessions of the Convention, but some took little or no part in the proceedings. Some propositions on which they voted were carried by a narrow majority. What was said, and the reasons given for votes cast, are known almost entirely through the necessarily incomplete notes which Madison took. On no issues did all members speak; on few did a majority speak. Many decisions must have been compromises which fully pleased no one. The language finally adopted was at times deliberately chosen to bridge over differences of opinion. Gouverneur Morris, the draftsman of the Constitution, confessed that he found it necessary "to select phrases which, expressing my own notions, would not alarm the others or shock their self love." Two of the influential members of the Convention—Hamilton and Randolph—differed within two years after it went into effect on the fundamental issue of strict or loose construction of congressional powers.

If the intention of the fifty-five men at Philadelphia cannot be discovered with assurance, what chance is there of determining the intention of the

delegates to the state ratifying conventions whose votes put the Constitution into operation? Yet surely they are also entitled to rate as men who made the Constitution. The records of the speeches made in the state conventions are quite incomplete, and offer no basis for establishing the existence of any consensus on interpretation of the many indefinite phrases of the Constitution.

The ultimate in uncertainty is reached if we seek to discover the intention of the people who elected the members of the state conventions. But were they not also participants, in fact perhaps the most essential participants of all, in the "original and supreme will" which Marshall declared to have organized the government and assigned to the different departments their respective powers? Only a minority of the adult males participated in the election of delegates to the state conventions. In New York the majority of voters were against ratification, yet the delegates they elected ultimately voed for ratification. Where is the intention of the framers to be discovered in this situation?

The same problems are presented by amendments to the Constitution. What did the members of Congress who drafted the First Amendment in 1789 or the Fourteenth Amendment in 1866 intend by such broad phrases as "freedom of speech" or "equal protection of the laws"? Historical data can throw some light on the purposes behind such language, but all too often "intention of the framers" has been a rhetorical device employed by partisans to read their own policy preferences into the Constitution.

Justice Brennan had something useful to say about intentions of the framers in *School District of Abington Township* v. *Schempp* (1963), where the Court had to decide whether the saying of prayers and reading of the Bible in public schools constituted an establishment of religion contrary to the First Amendment. Justice Brennan thought "a too literal quest for the advice of the Founding Fathers" on this issue would be "futile and misdirected." The history was "ambiguous," the structure of American education has greatly changed since 1791, and we are a vastly more diverse people religiously than were our forefathers. Consequently, Brennan believed that, instead of looking for the intent of the framers, it would be more fruitful to inquire whether the practices challenged in the *Schempp* case threatened those consequences of interdependence between religion and the state "which the Framers deeply feared."

Where the Supreme Court has used history to support its conclusions, it has often been very bad history. Historian Alfred H. Kelly has noted two techniques used by the Court. One is the "creation of history a priori by . . . 'judicial fiat' or 'authoritative revelation.' " He suggests that several of Marshall's most notable opinions involve the creation of history by judicial fiat, with little if any inquiry into "actual history."

A second method is what Kelly calls "law-office history," that is, extended essays in constitutional history usually written for the purpose of justifying

the reversal of precedent by proving that the precedent itself was contrary to the original intention of the Constitution. Nineteenth-century illustrations of law-office history are Chief Justice Taney's essay in the *Dred Scott* case on the Negro's role in early America, designed to prove that the Constitution was a "white man's document," and Chief Justice Fuller's essays in the *Income Tax Cases*, designed to break down the established precedents that income taxes were not direct taxes. The activist Court of the 1950s and 1960s also used the historical essay to justify departures from established doctrines in several fields.[1]

THE MEANING OF THE WORDS     There is a second theory of constitutional interpretation which also employs the historical approach but for a different purpose. This is the method of interpretation on the basis of the meaning of the words at the time they were used. W. W. Crosskey's reinterpretation of the Constitution is based on this method.[2] On the flyleaf of his first volume he offers as his touchstone this quotation from Justice Holmes: "We ask, not what this man meant, but what those words would mean in the mouth of a normal speaker of English, using them in the circumstances in which they were used." As employed by Crosskey, this method of research in word usage during the era of constitutional formulation yielded a "specialized dictionary," on the basis of which he radically revised the meaning of many of the key provisions in the Constitution.

The search for original word meanings, like that for intent of the framers, assumes the binding nature of the obligations imposed by the decisions of 1787 on subsequent generations. Both approaches have the value, necessary to all law, of seeking to preserve some sense of stability and continuity in the agreements and understandings on which legitimate governmental power is based. In searching for the original meaning of the words, however, the second approach employs somewhat narrower lexicographic skills as opposed to the social history on which the first method relies. It is more closely confined by the document itself and is more closely related to the processes by which the written instruments of private law are construed.

The objections to these two methods of constitutional interpretation are likewise somewhat similar. Original meaning may be as difficult to establish as original intent. Crosskey's work is sufficient confirmation of this point. The original word meanings which his laborious research in the written materials of the time purports to establish can perhaps legitimately be challenged only on the basis of equally laborious research which reaches other conclusions. But certainly observers who have not done this research

[1] Alfred H. Kelly, "Clio and the Court: An Illicit Love Affair," in Philip B. Kurland (ed.), *The Supreme Court Review: 1965* (Chicago: The University of Chicago Press, 1965), pp. 119–158.
[2] W. W. Crosskey, *Politics and the Constitution in the History of the United States* (Chicago: The University of Chicago Press, 1953).

are entitled to express reservations about the validity of conclusions attributing original meaning to words, which differ so markedly from the meanings accepted for those words only a few years after adoption of the Constitution by responsible jurists and statesmen, many of whom had themselves been active in the drafting and adoption of the Constitution.

Perhaps the most serious objection to both methods, however, is the extent to which they propose to make a nation the prisoner of its past, and reject any method of constitutional development save constitutional amendment. Both reject the legitimacy of change by consensus or usage. Both deny the possibility that evolution in moral standards or political ideology can be given effect in the Constitution without changing its language.

LOGICAL REASONING    Logical analysis is an alternative to the historical methods of determining constitutional meaning, and particularly worthy of note because of the extensive use made of it by Chief Justice Marshall in his great decisions. The method is most aptly demonstrated by reference again to *Marbury* v. *Madison*. There Marshall cites no judicial decisions to support his arguments. While referring to "original intention," he makes no effort to quote contemporaneous evidence or opinion. His argument is primarily an exercise in logic. "It seems only necessary to recognize certain principles," he says, "supposed to have been long and well established, to decide it." The major principle is that the Constitution is the supreme law of the land. The Supreme Court has taken an oath to uphold the Constitution. The conclusion logically follows that when an act of Congress conflicts with the superior law, the Supreme Court cannot enforce it but must declare it null and void.

This position has been so long accepted that the logic supporting it may seem unassailable. Yet is it not equally logical to argue that, since the Constitution is the supreme law of the land, and since the President has taken an oath to support the Constitution, he cannot enforce a decision of the Supreme Court which conflicts with the Constitution, but must declare it null and void.

The problem is simply not one to which logic can guarantee a correct answer. The fallacy of the logical form may be made clearer by stating a part of Marshall's argument as a syllogism.

> Major premise: A law repugnant to the Constitution is void.
> Minor premise: This law is repugnant to the Constitution.
> Conclusion: This law is void.

Assuming the validity of the major premise, the soundness of the conclusion depends upon whether the minor premise is *factually* true. But logic cannot tell us whether a particular law is repugnant to the Constitution. That is a matter of informed opinion and judgment. This explains why Justice Holmes said, in one of the most famous passages in his lectures on *The Common Law:* "The life of the law has not been logic: it has been experience. The

felt necessities of the time, the prevalent moral and political theories, intui-
tions of public policy, avowed or unconscious, even the prejudices which
judges share with their fellow-men, have had a good deal more to do than
the syllogism in determining the rules by which men should be governed." [3]

Another device often employed in Supreme Court decisions is to test a
constitutional argument "by pushing it to its logical conclusion." Obviously
there is some utility in examining the soundness of a proposed decision by
considering its logically possible implications, so long as these implications
are not treated as inevitable consequents of the ruling. But all too often the
purpose of this technique is to demonstrate that if the Court accepts the
constitutionality of a particular legislative or executive action, which may
seem comparatively mild and reasonable, there will be no logical stopping
place at which the Court could forbid extensions of the same principle until
a clearly unconstitutional result had been reached. Consequently it is
claimed that the Court must forbid even the initial steps down the road
toward an unconstitutional terminus. Thomas Reed Powell called this
method "the parade of the imaginary horribles."

THE EXPERIENTIAL APPROACH    Historical evidence as to the intent of the
framers, textual analysis of the language of the Constitution, and application of the rules of logical thinking all have a useful place, but neither alone
nor in combination can they supply the key to constitutional interpretation.
There is a further factor, which Holmes designated as "experience." The
experiential approach is one which treats the Constitution more as a political
than a legal document. It considers current understandings as relevant as the
debates of the Constitutional Convention. It frankly recognizes that interpretation of the Constitution will and must be influenced by present-day
values and by the sum total of American experience.

The intention of the framers is surely part of that experience, but so are
the breadlines of 1933 and the sit-ins of the 1960s. The meaning of the words
as originally used is a relevant datum, but so also is the language of each
presidential message to Congress. One may invoke logic and technical rules
of construction, but one may also invoke such intangibles as "the spirit of
the Constitution." The goal of constitutional interpretation, it may be suggested, is the achieving of consensus as to the *current meaning* of the document framed in 1787, a meaning which makes it possible to deal rationally
with current necessities and acknowledge the lessons of experience while
still recognizing guidelines derived from the written document and the
philosophy of limited governmental power which it sought to express.

This approach recognizes the right of each generation to adapt the Constitution to its own needs, to the extent that such adaptations are reconcilable
with the language of the Constitution. Naturally, the provision that the

[3] Mark DeWolfe Howe (ed.), *The Common Law* (Cambridge, Mass.: The
Belknap Press, Harvard University Press, 1963), p. 5.

President shall have a four-year term cannot be reinterpreted to justify a five-year term. But the meaning of the clause giving Congress the authority to regulate commerce among the states or forbidding cruel and unusual punishment may legitimately change over a period of time. Marshall was defending this notion of a flexible Constitution when he said in *McCulloch v. Maryland:* "We must never forget, that it is a constitution we are expounding," one which is "intended to endure for ages to come, and consequently, to be adapted to the various crises of human affairs." Holmes put the conception of the "living" Constitution into eloquent language when he wrote, in the case of *Missouri v. Holland* (1920):

> When we are dealing with words that also are a constituent act, like the Constitution of the United States, we must realize that they have called into life a being the development of which could not have been foreseen completely by the most gifted of its begetters. It was enough for them to realize or to hope that they had created an organism; it has taken a century and has cost their successors much sweat and blood to prove that they created a nation. The case before us must be considered in the light of our whole experience and not merely in that of what was said a hundred years ago.

The experiential approach is profoundly disturbing to those who demand of the Constitution that it supply the certainty of absolutes and rigid guarantees against change. Instead of providing a single right answer, it permits a number of right answers, from among which choices must be made by the political process. It is a profound mistake, however, to think that the range of choice is left unlimited by this freedom. Not everything that the public may currently want to do is necessarily constitutional. The distinctive feature of the experiential approach is that decisions on constitutional allowability are made with full recognition of the need for the adjustments and expansions inevitable in a dynamic society. The constitutional system is not regarded as separate from the political system, but a necessary part of it, performing the vital function of giving order and structure to the inevitable processes of change.

### THE PERSONAL FACTOR IN JUDICIAL INTERPRETATION

When we say that the Supreme Court has made a decision, we actually mean that the nine justices who compose the Court at a particular point in history have made the decision. Often, in fact, it is a decision made by only five members of the Court, with which the remaining four disagree. These justices are men—men of varying abilities, backgrounds, and political preferences—who have been fortuitously elevated to the highest judicial body by the process of presidential selection. How the Constitution will be interpreted by these men depends in part upon what kind of men they are and how the world looks to them.

This has not always been understood. During considerable periods of American history there has been a popular impression that when men were appointed to the Supreme Court, they somehow became depersonalized and disembodied of all ordinary prejudices and passions. In the rarefied atmosphere of their chambers they were presumed to be at work discovering the law by the exercise of pure reason. This myth has typically been strongest during periods when the Court was under conservative domination, and it served the purpose of convincing the public that judicial protection of property or the thwarting of regulatory legislation was not an expression of the personal preferences of the justices but a voicing of the authentic commands of the Constitution. This myth, however, was finally and irretrievably destroyed in the years from 1935 to 1937, when it became all too apparent that the doctrine which the Supreme Court majority was expounding was their personal laissez-faire economic beliefs. As Max Lerner said, the public learned then "that judicial decisions are not babies brought by constitutional storks."

It is an equally grave error, however, to jump to the conclusion that Supreme Court justices typically determine the meaning of the Constitution merely by consulting their personal preferences. There is an institutional ethos about the Court which cannot fail to have a restraining effect upon the most opinionated justice. One of these institutional factors, for example, is *stare decisis*, the rule of precedent. The individual judge may think that a particular precedent is wrong or outmoded. If so, he may follow his personal preference and state his reasons for voting to overrule the earlier holding. He is free to do that. But he is not free to ignore the precedents, to act as though they did not exist. He has free choice, but only among limited alternatives and after he has satisfied himself that he has met the obligations of consistency and respect for settled principles which his responsibility to the Court imposes upon him. His private views as an individual help to form and may be incorporated into his public views as a justice, but they are not the same thing.

From 1789 to 1968 the Supreme Court had fourteen Chief Justices and eighty-six associate justices. Biographies of the more important of these men provide excellent insights into the characteristic processes of judicial review as well as their own particular problems and contributions. Here it is possible to note only the principal judicial personalities and the major historical influences associated with the Court's power to interpret the American Constitution.

THE PRE-MARSHALL COURT    The first decade of the Court's history was singularly unimpressive. President Washington's appointees were uniformly Federalists, and the entire judiciary quickly developed a definite partisan tone. John Jay, the first Chief Justice, spent one year in England on a diplomatic mission and ran twice for Governor of New York while on the bench.

After he succeeded the second time, he resigned the chief justiceship in 1795. John Rutledge, another original appointee, failed to attend a session of the Court during its first two years. Appointed Chief Justice to succeed Jay, he served for four months before the Senate refused him confirmation, and then went insane.

Oliver Ellsworth, the next Chief Justice, resigned in 1800. James Wilson, also a member of the original Court, was an able lawyer but also a land speculator who narrowly avoided imprisonment for debt. Samuel Chase, appointed in 1795, dominated the Court in the latter part of this period. He was blatant in giving effect to his Federalist views from the bench, and in 1800 a term of the Court could not be held because he was absent electioneering for Adams. When the Jeffersonians came into power, he was impeached, but escaped conviction.

Though the Court had comparatively little business during these years, it did make some significant decisions. For one thing, it declined to advise President Washington on some legal questions in the field of foreign relations which he submitted to the Court and thereby established a precedent against giving "advisory opinions." Also the Court strongly supported federal authority against the states in two important decisions. *Ware* v. *Hylton* (1796) held the treaty of peace with Britain to override a Virginia law on the sensitive issue of debts owed by Americans to British subjects. The decision in *Chisholm* v. *Georgia* (1793) asserted that states could be sued in federal courts by citizens of other states, a holding so bitterly resented by the states that the Eleventh Amendment was quickly adopted to void it.

THE MARSHALL COURT    One month before Thomas Jefferson's inauguration in 1801, John Marshall was appointed Chief Justice by the outgoing Federalist administration. For the next thirty-five years he dominated the Court and did more than any other man in Supreme Court history to determine the character of the federal constitutional system. It was Marshall who in *Marbury* v. *Madison* (1803) successfully asserted the Court's power to declare acts of Congress unconstitutional. It was Marshall who in *McCulloch* v. *Maryland* (1819) established the broad authority of Congress to achieve national purposes under the "necessary and proper" clause and other broad grants of constitutional power. It was Marshall who in *Gibbons* v. *Ogden* (1824) first construed the commerce clause and struck down state regulation of commerce. It was Marshall who in *Dartmouth College* v. *Woodward* (1819) expanded the coverage of the contract clause and encouraged the judicial protection of vested rights which was to be a theme of great significance throughout much of the Court's history. It was Marshall who by his courage, his convictions, and his intellectual vigor raised the Supreme Court from a third-rate status to a position of equality with President and Congress.

The Federalist dominance in membership was soon lost on the Marshall

Court as new appointments were made by Republican Presidents, but with few exceptions these colleagues were no match for Marshall. One exception was the able and much underrated William Johnson, whose disagreements with Marshall made him the first great dissenter. Another was the scholarly Joseph Story, nominally a Republican but actually closely attuned to Marshall's views. Thus Marshall was able to direct the Court for more than three decades toward his twin goals—strengthening the powers of the federal government and protecting the rights of private property.

THE TANEY COURT    Roger B. Taney, Democrat from Maryland, was appointed Chief Justice by President Jackson in 1836. Taney's Jacksonian democracy was in marked contrast with Marshall's federalism. States' rights and state police powers were emphasized more on the Court and central authority less. Property rights retained their influence with the Court, but it was agrarian property—land and slaves—rather than the commercial-creditor classes which now won judicial favor.

During his first twenty years on the Court, Taney's attachment to the economic interests of the South and West made him look like an economic liberal. But this same attachment led to the fatal *Dred Scott* decision in 1857, which permanently blackened Taney's reputation. No less intent than Marshall in his determination to preserve the prerogatives of judicial review and control, Taney's great talents were spent in his latter years in a lost and unworthy cause. He died in 1864, an embittered man who had lived too long.

THE POST-CIVIL WAR COURT    The next three Chief Justices—Salmon P. Chase, Morrison R. Waite, and Melville W. Fuller—fell far short of the stature of Marshall and Taney, and failed to mold the Court in their own image. The *Dred Scott* decision had plunged the Court to its lowest depths. Congress revealed its contempt for the Court by changing its size three times in seven years for obvious political purposes. When the Court showed signs of declaring some of the Reconstruction legislation unconstitutional in 1868, Congress brusquely withdrew the Court's jurisdiction to decide the case.

With no strong leadership, the intellectual quality of the Court for the first time was to be found in its associate justices—men like Samuel Miller of Iowa (1862–1890), Stephen J. Field of California (1863–1897), Joseph P. Bradley of New Jersey (1870–1892), and John M. Harlan of Kentucky (1877–1911). Gradually the Court regained its prestige by reestablishing contact with the dominant trends of the times. The postwar period was one of raw and rapid industrial expansion. A continent was being harnessed with railroads, resources were being exploited, great fortunes built. At first the Court was reluctant to legitimize the economic freedom which the burgeoning corporations demanded. In the *Slaughter-House Cases* (1873)

and in *Munn* v. *Illinois* (1877) it declined to use the newly adopted Fourteenth Amendment to strike down state regulatory legislation.

But eventually the pressures were too strong to resist. The due process clause, interpreted by the Court as valueless to protect the civil rights of Negroes, was readily adapted to protect the property rights of corporations. The high point in the Court's dedication to the new capitalism came in 1895, with no less than three significant decisions. One declared the income tax unconstitutional. Another held that the sugar trust did not violate the Sherman Act. The third upheld the jailing of the Socialist leader, Eugene V. Debs, for violating a federal court injunction against a strike by the railway workers' union.

THE HOLMES DECADES    Fuller was Chief Justice until his death in 1910, and was succeeded by Edward D. White of Louisiana. In 1921 former President William Howard Taft took the post and held it until 1930. The most influential and distinguished member of the Court during these years, however, was Associate Justice Oliver Wendell Holmes. Appointed by President Theodore Roosevelt in 1902 from the highest court of Massachusetts, he steadily grew in stature and reputation until his resignation in 1932 at the age of ninety-one.

His character and intellectual alignments defy any brief summary. The public knew him as the great dissenter, and thought of him as a liberal because his dissents were often protests against the denial of civil liberties or the judicial invalidation of liberal legislation. But these protests were less an expression of political liberalism than of a philosophy of limited judicial review which insisted that judges should not substitute their views for those of legislators so long as the legislative policy remained within the bounds of reason.

Holmes's colleagues were generally reluctant to accept such limitations on judicial power. In *Lochner* v. *New York* (1905) the Court struck down a ten-hour law for bakers against Holmes's warning that "the Fourteenth Amendment does not enact Mr. Herbert Spencer's Social Statics." But his position was gradually strengthened in the country and on the Court, as by the appointment of Charles Evans Hughes in 1910, fresh from his work as a reform Governor of New York. Hughes left the Court in 1916 to run for President, but that same year President Wilson named to the Court an ardent progressive, Louis D. Brandeis, and got him confirmed in spite of the opposition of the organized bar and big business.

The phrase, "Holmes and Brandeis dissenting," quickly became a part of American folklore as these two men, though proceeding from differing premises, joined in case after case to protest the Court's policies. In 1925 the duo became a trio as President Coolidge named his liberal Attorney General, Harlan F. Stone, to the Court. In their dissenting opinions they mapped out an alternative to the doctrinaire conservatism of the Court

majority which, if adopted in time, would have averted the crisis into which the Court was heading.

THE HUGHES COURT AND THE NEW DEAL    Hughes returned to the Court in 1931 as Chief Justice. A much more flexible man than Taft, he had the responsibility of guiding the Court in its review of the constitutional aspects of the new and experimental legislation enacted by the New Deal to combat the Great Depression. On the Court he headed, Brandeis and Stone had been joined by Benjamin N. Cardozo, appointed in 1932 to fill the Holmes vacancy. These three justices could generally be counted on to uphold the New Deal, but they were offset by four conservative justices—Willis Van Devanter, appointed by Taft in 1910; James C. McReynolds, named by Wilson in 1914; and two Harding appointees of 1922, George Sutherland and Pierce Butler. The balance of power on the Court thus rested with the Chief Justice himself and with the ninth member, Owen J. Roberts, appointed by Hoover in 1930.

The initial tests of 1934 seemed to suggest that the Court would accept the new legislative trends by a vote of five to four, but this forecast soon proved mistaken. In 1935 and 1936 the Court invalidated a series of important federal and state regulatory laws, usually by a vote of five to four or six or three, depending upon whether Roberts alone, or Roberts and Hughes, voted with the conservative block. After his electoral triumph in 1936 President Roosevelt, who had had no Court vacancies to fill during his first term, undertook to eliminate this judicial barrier to reform by a proposal to increase the Court's size to fifteen justices.

Juggling the size of the Court was no longer so acceptable as it had been in the 1860s, however, and the Court-packing plan was defeated in Congress. However, in several key cases in the spring of 1937 Roberts swung over to the liberal side, giving the administration some five to four victories. At the end of the term Van Devanter retired, and President Roosevelt had his opportunity to begin remaking the Court.

THE RECENT COURT    Between 1937 and 1943 President Roosevelt appointed eight members to the Court (one position being filled twice) and elevated Harlan Stone to the chief justiceship. All these appointees were economic liberals, and there ceased to be any danger of judicial invalidation of regulatory legislation affecting property. The characteristic problem of the Roosevelt Court dealt rather with civil liberty, and the justices, in spite of their basic libertarian leanings, quickly found themselves more divided than ever, but now over the nature of their judicial responsibility for the protection of libertarian goals. Justices Hugo Black, William O. Douglas, Frank Murphy, and Wiley Rutledge were a cohesive group as firmly committed to the use of judicial power to protect civil liberties from legislative infringement as the anti-New Deal conservatives had been in the protection of eco-

nomic freedom a decade earlier. Justice Felix Frankfurter, on the other hand, argued that the Holmes tradition called for judicial restraint in both areas.

The libertarian temper of the Roosevelt Court was substantially diluted by President Truman's four appointments. Chief Justice Fred Vinson replaced Stone on the latter's death in 1946. Both Rutledge and Murphy died in the summer of 1949, thus leaving only Black and Douglas in the Court's activist bloc. The most difficult problems of the Vinson Court were those generated by the cold war against communism. In its most celebrated decision, it upheld the Smith Act convictions of the leaders of the American Communist Party in *Dennis* v. *United States* (1951), with Black and Douglas dissenting, and it was careful to refrain from interfering with the "Red" hunts of congressional investigating committees.

On Vinson's death in 1953, President Eisenhower named Earl Warren of California to be Chief Justice. In the first term under his leadership the Court unanimously declared unconstitutional racial segregation in the public schools, boldly overturning the doctrine of "separate but equal" which had been used to justify segregation for almost sixty years.

President Eisenhower had the opportunity to make four additional appointments—John M. Harlan, grandson of the earlier Harlan, replacing Jackson; William J. Brennan, Jr., replacing Minton; Charles E. Whittaker, replacing Reed; and Potter Stewart, replacing Burton. With the appointment of Brennan, a liberal Catholic Democrat, a new four-judge activist bloc developed on the Court, as Brennan voted rather consistently with Warren, Black, and Douglas. The other new members of the Court, however, tended to look to Justice Frankfurter for intellectual leadership, and particularly after 1957 there were a series of five to four defeats for the activist bloc.

President Kennedy made two appointments to the Court in 1962. Whittaker's place was taken by Byron R. White, forty-four-year-old ex-Rhodes scholar and famous football player who had been Deputy Attorney General in the Kennedy administration. When Justice Frankfurter retired because of illness, his seat was filled by Arthur J. Goldberg, dynamic general counsel for the AFL–CIO. The Court's balance was swung sharply toward the liberal side by these appointments, as was immediately evidenced by dramatic decisions dealing with such controversial matters as legislative reapportionment, prayer and Bible reading in the public schools, and increased procedural protections in criminal prosecutions.

In 1965 President Johnson asked Justice Goldberg to become United States Ambassador to the United Nations, and to fill the vacancy the President named one of his close advisers, Abe Fortas, member of a prominent Washington law firm who in 1963 had argued the famous case of *Gideon* v. *Wainwright* before the Court. Justice Clark retired in 1967 to avoid any conflict of interest after his son, Ramsey, was named Attorney General. To his place President Johnson appointed Solicitor General and former court of

appeals judge Thurgood Marshall, the Court's first Negro and the man who as chief counsel for the NAACP had argued the school desegregation case, *Brown* v. *Board of Education* (1954), before the Court.

The Warren Court was one of the most controversial in Supreme Court history. Its decisions defending minority rights and civil liberties made the impeachment of Earl Warren a favorite demand of the radical right. The attacks on the Warren Court came from three principal quarters—from Southern opponents of the desegregation decision; from those who contended that the Court had handicapped the fight against Communist subversion by its limitations on congressional investigatory power and insistence on the procedural rights of "political offenders"; and from those who maintained that the Court had infringed state authority over a wide range of activities, including economic regulation, procedure in criminal cases, religious observances in the public schools, and legislative apportionment.

The states' case against the Court on all issues except segregation was summed up in 1958 in a highly unusual document issued by the Conference of Chief Justices of the states.[4] While critical of the Court for some of its specific decisions, the report did not stop there but went on to suggest that the Court had assumed "primarily legislative powers" and had come to exercise a dominance of authority incompatible with a system of checks and balances and a distribution of authority between national and state governments. The conference did not propose any curbing of the Court's authority, but asked only that the Court use its great powers with more self-restraint.

In Congress the assault on the Court reached a climax in the closing days of the 1958 session, when a series of measures intended to curb or reverse the Court were narrowly defeated.[5] The Court soon thereafter withdrew from some of the positions which had led to congressional anger, particularly with respect to judicial control over congressional investigating committees.

Then in 1962 the Court again stirred up a storm by declaring unconstitutional religious observances in the public schools (*Engel* v. *Vitale*) and opening up state legislative-apportionment practices to judicial review and control (*Baker* v. *Carr*). However, efforts to reverse the Court's rulings by constitutional amendments failed, and in the legislative-apportionment field the Court proceeded to carry through a political revolution by requiring the long underrepresented urban and suburban areas to be given their proper weight in state legislatures.

The failure of each of these efforts at Court curbing is full of significance for an understanding of the place of the Supreme Court in the American governmental system. The Court is at once a representative and a nonrepresentative institution, an instrument both of justice and of politics. It is in-

[4] Reprinted in C. Herman Pritchett, *Congress versus the Supreme Court: 1957–1960* (Minneapolis: The University of Minnesota Press, 1961), pp. 141–159.
[5] *Ibid.*; see also Walter F. Murphy, *Congress and the Court* (Chicago: The University of Chicago Press, 1962).

evitable that Congress and the President will concern themselves with the Court's decisions, but the interest must be expressed in a way that will not damage the essential values of the judicial institution.

Opposition to limitations on the Court's historic powers does not stem from the assumption that the Court never makes mistakes. Nor can it be contended that the Court should not be subjected to criticism. All honest thought should have an impact on the justices. But what does protect the Court is the widespread public recognition that it constitutes one of the vital balances in the governmental system, with unique qualifications for defining and defending the basic liberating principles of the American Constitution. "Our constitutional ideal of equal justice under law is thus made a living truth." [6]

In summary, the American constitutional system is one in which important policy questions are frequently cast in the form of a lawsuit and brought to the Supreme Court for decision. The Court is basically a public law court, and its highest public law function is to determine the current meaning of the Constitution when that is necessary to settle a judicial controversy that comes before it. In the search for current meanings the justices inevitably consult their own policy preferences, but the institutional setting is one which forces responsibility upon them and requires them to meet high standards of consistency and logic. Theirs is the difficult task of moving with the times, yet without departing from constitutional fundamentals or impairing that popular expectation of judicial stability which is so necessary an asset to the moral authority of the Court.

With this insight into the nature of the judicial obligation, we turn to examine under six general headings the powers and limitations of the American Constitution as judicially interpreted.

## SELECTED REFERENCES

ANDERSON, WILLIAM, "The Intention of the Framers: A Note on Constitutional Interpretation," 49 *American Political Science Review* 340–352 (June, 1955).

BAKER, LEONARD, *Back to Back: The Duel Between FDR and the Supreme Court.* New York: The Macmillan Company, 1967.

BEVERIDGE, ALBERT J., *The Life of John Marshall,* 4 vols. Boston: Houghton Mifflin Company, 1916.

BOWEN, CATHERINE DRINKER, *Yankee from Olympus: Justice Holmes and His Family.* Boston: Little, Brown and Company, 1944.

CROSSKEY, WILLIAM W., *Politics and the Constitution in the History of the United States,* chap. 1. Chicago: The University of Chicago Press, 1953.

[6] *Cooper* v. *Aaron* (1958).

CURTIS, CHARLES P., JR., *Lions under the Throne*. Boston: Houghton Mifflin Company, 1947.

DUNHAM, ALLISON, and PHILIP B. KURLAND, *Mr. Justice*. Chicago: The University of Chicago Press, 1956.

EWING, CORTEZ A. M., *The Judges of the Supreme Court, 1789–1937*. Minneapolis: The University of Minnesota Press, 1938.

FAIRMAN, CHARLES, *Mr. Justice Miller and the Supreme Court, 1862–1890*. Cambridge, Mass.: Harvard University Press, 1939.

FRANK, JOHN P., *Marble Palace: The Supreme Court in American Life*. New York: Alfred A. Knopf, Inc., 1958.

———, *The Warren Court*. New York: The Macmillan Company, 1964.

FRANKFURTER, FELIX, *Mr. Justice Holmes and the Supreme Court*. Cambridge, Mass.: Harvard University Press, 1938.

FREUND, PAUL A., *On Understanding the Supreme Court*. Boston: Little, Brown and Company, 1949.

HAINES, CHARLES GROVE, *The Role of the Supreme Court in American Government and Politics, 1789–1835*. Berkeley, Calif.: University of California Press, 1944.

———, and FOSTER H. SHERWOOD, *The Role of the Supreme Court in American Government and Politics, 1835–1864*. Berkeley, Calif.: University of California Press, 1957.

HOWE, MARK DE WOLFE, *Justice Oliver Wendell Holmes*, 2 vols. Cambridge, Mass.: Harvard University Press, 1957, 1963.

KING, WILLARD L., *Melville Weston Fuller: Chief Justice of the United States, 1888–1910*. Chicago: The University of Chicago Press, 1967.

LERNER, MAX, "The Supreme Court and American Capitalism," in Robert G. McCloskey (ed.), *Essays in Constitutional Law*, chap. 4. New York: Alfred A. Knopf, Inc., 1957.

LEUCHTENBURG, WILLIAM E., "The Origins of Franklin D. Roosevelt's 'Court-packing' Plan," in Philip B. Kurland (ed.), *The Supreme Court Review: 1966*, pp. 347–400. Chicago: The University of Chicago Press, 1966.

LEVI, EDWARD H., *An Introduction to Legal Reasoning*. Chicago: The University of Chicago Press, 1949.

MASON, ALPHEUS T., *Brandeis: A Free Man's Life*. New York: The Viking Press, Inc., 1946.

———, *Harlan Fiske Stone: Pillar of the Law*. New York: The Viking Press, Inc., 1956.

———, *The Supreme Court from Taft to Warren*. Baton Rouge, La.: Louisiana State University Press, 1958.

MORGAN, DONALD G., *Congress and the Constitution*. Cambridge, Mass.: The Belknap Press, Harvard University Press, 1966.

POWELL, THOMAS REED, "The Logic and Rhetoric of Constitutional Law," in Robert G. McCloskey (ed.), *Essays in Constitutional Law*, chap. 3. New York: Alfred A. Knopf, Inc., 1957.

PRITCHETT, C. HERMAN, *Civil Liberties and the Vinson Court*. Chicago: The University of Chicago Press, 1954.

———, *The Political Offender and the Warren Court*. Boston: Boston University Press, 1958.

————, *The Roosevelt Court: A Study in Judicial Politics and Values, 1937–1947.* New York: The Macmillan Company, 1948.

PUSEY, MERLO J., *Charles Evans Hughes,* 2 vols. New York: The Macmillan Company, 1951.

RODELL, FRED, *Nine Men: A Political History of the Supreme Court from 1790 to 1955.* New York: Random House, Inc., 1955.

SCHMIDHAUSER, JOHN R., *The Supreme Court: Its Politics, Personalities, and Procedures.* New York: Holt, Rinehart and Winston, Inc., 1960.

SCHUBERT, GLENDON, *The Judicial Mind: Attitudes and Ideologies of Supreme Court Justices, 1946–1963.* Evanston, Ill.: Northwestern University Press, 1965.

SWISHER, CARL B., *Roger B. Taney.* New York: The Macmillan Company, 1936.

————, *Stephen J. Field: Craftsman of the Law.* Washington, D.C.: The Brookings Institution, 1930.

THOMAS, HELEN SHIRLEY, *Felix Frankfurter: Scholar on the Bench.* Baltimore: The Johns Hopkins Press, 1960.

WARREN, CHARLES, *The Supreme Court in United States History,* 2 vols. Boston: Little, Brown and Company, 1947 (revised edition).

# Part 2

## The union

# 5

## Nation and state

One of the serious reservations which the framers had in setting up a new Constitution was whether a large country would be a threat to the freedom of its citizens. The delegates who opposed the Virginia Plan for a strong central government had a picture in their minds, drawn in part at least from the experience of the Greek city-states, of the "small republic" as the ideal form of government. Roger Sherman put it this way: "The people are more happy in small than large States."

The problem was that small republics were too weak, standing alone, to protect their independence and their economies, and so they had to associate in some common organization for mutual protection. But Sherman and other supporters of the New Jersey Plan believed that a confederation limited to the functions of keeping the peace among the states and defending them against foreign enemies was all that was needed.

It was James Madison's role to answer the small republic argument. He contended that, from antiquity to the current American states, small republics had been beset by conflicts between classes which were fatal to liberty. A large republic would be preferable, for there, he argued, liberty would be protected by "the great variety of interests, parties, and sects which it embraces." An "extended republic of the United States" would be divided into many groups, no single one amounting to a majority. Only as smaller groups

voluntarily associated could majorities be formed, a process which would force each group to moderate its position and protect the liberties of all.

The Convention was persuaded by Madison's argument and even more by realization that their goals of security, peace, and economic development could be achieved only through a strong central government. But the Founders' insistence on also preserving the states as strong organs of local government forced them to invent a federal system.

We now think of the threefold distinction among the confederal, federal, and unitary forms of government as self-evident. But in 1787 only two forms, the confederal and the national (unitary), were recognized. The opening words of the resolution proposing the Virginia Plan stated these two alternatives: a "merely federal" union or "a National Government." "Merely federal" meant a confederation such as was then in existence. It was because this "merely federal" plan had failed that the Virginia delegation proposed a truly "national" government. But what actually emerged from the Convention was the blueprint for a large republic intended to achieve both liberty and security by a division of responsibilities and functions which has come to be considered the true form of federalism.

The Constitution, it should be noted, does not use the term "federalism." Because of the vague theoretical origins of American federalism, disagreement over the nature of the Union was almost inevitable. The existence of sharply divisive sectional interests led to the exploitation of these disagreements for intensely practical purposes. Regional differences were compounded by localistic patriotism and hope of economic gain. Where such animus is present in constitutional issues, judicial decisions are not likely to be accepted as final. During the first half of the nineteenth century these controversies were fostered by all the resources of the political process, and ultimately had to be resolved by a bitter civil war. Only after the nature of the Union had been determined by the arbitrament of arms was it possible for the courts to continue with adjudication of the lesser but continuing problems of adjustment in the federal system.

## THE NATURE OF THE UNION

A COMPACT OF STATES OR OF PEOPLE?    The prevailing political philosophy of the eighteenth century, as we have seen, stressed contract as the basis of governmental authority. The Constitution was such a contract, but who were the parties to it—the states or the people of the United States? The language of the Constitution could be cited to support both views. Article VII provides that approval by conventions in nine states "shall be sufficient for the establishment of this Constitution *between the states* so ratifying the same." [1] On the other hand, the Preamble to the Constitution declares that it is "the people of the United States" who "do ordain and establish this

[1] Italics supplied.

Constitution," and conventions rather than state legislatures were chosen as the instruments of ratification precisely to emphasize the popular base of the contract. Again, it could be pointed out that, although the Articles of Confederation had specifically provided that the states were sovereign, the Constitution was discreetly silent on the location of sovereignty.

Discussions during the ratification campaign did little to clear up these ambiguities. Madison in No. 39 of *The Federalist* contended that the "people" of the Preamble were not the people of the nation but the people of the several states. Ratification, he said, "is to be given by the people not as individuals composing one entire nation, but as composing the distinct and independent states to which they respectively belong." But although Madison considered ratification to be a federal, and not a national, act, he did not concede that this status made the Constitution any the less binding on the states which ratified. When New York proposed to ratify on condition that a bill of rights be added, and claimed the right to withdraw if the addition was not made within a stipulated time, Madison replied that "any condition whatever must vitiate the ratification," adding that "the Constitution requires an adoption in toto and forever." Likewise in the Virginia convention Mason, who opposed ratification, declared that the Constitution "will be paramount to everything. After having once consented to it, we cannot recede from it."

INTERPOSITION    After the establishment of the new government, the first significant theoretical attack on the authority of the national government came in the form of the famous Kentucky and Virginia Resolutions against the Alien and Sedition Acts. The first paragraph of the Kentucky Resolutions, which Jefferson drafted, reads:

> Resolved, That the several states composing the United States of America are not united on the principle of unlimited submission to their general government; but that, by compact, under the style and title of a Constitution for the United States, and of amendments thereto, they constituted a general government for special purposes, delegated to that government certain definite powers, reserving, each state to itself, the residuary mass of right to their own self-government; and that whensoever the general government assumed undelegated powers, its acts are unauthoritative, void, and of no force; that to this compact each state acceded as a state, and is an integral party; that this government, created by this compact, was not made the exclusive or final judge of the extent of the powers delegated to itself, since that would have made its discretion, and not the Constitution, the measure of its powers; but that, as in all other cases of compact among parties having no common Judge, *each party has an equal right to judge for itself, as well of infractions as of the mode and measure of redress.*

In a second set of resolutions passed in 1799, the Kentucky legislature proclaimed: "That a Nullification, by those sovereignties, of all unauthorized

acts done under color of that instrument, is the rightful remedy." Madison, who drafted the Virginia Resolutions, contributed the concept of "interposition" to American constitutional history in the third paragraph of those resolutions, when he concluded "that, in case of a deliberate, palpable, and dangerous exercise of other powers, not granted by the said compact, the states, who are parties thereto, have the right, and are in duty bound, to interpose, for arresting the progress of the evil, and for maintaining within their respective limits, the authorities, rights, and liberties, appertaining to them."

It is puzzling to know just how seriously to take this language about nullification and interposition. Certainly Madison and Jefferson were deadly serious in their belief that the Federalist Congress had passed legislation prohibited by the Constitution, and in wanting to organize resistance to it. But both sets of resolutions were vague as to how such resistance was to be carried out. Interposition, it was suggested, might take several forms. One was to call for the submission to the states of an amendment to the Constitution authorizing the alleged improper assertion of federal power. If such an amendment failed of ratification by three-fourths of the states, then the action would be nullified as an act of usurpation not warranted by the Constitution.

Did Madison and Jefferson mean, beyond this, to claim that the Union was a system of fully sovereign states, a confederation from which each state could retire at any time? Did they mean that refusal to be bound by any objectionable act of Congress was within the rights of the states, and that an attempt to enforce the act on a state would justify its secession? It seems highly unlikely. While they referred to the states as sovereign, they also conceded that the national government was sovereign. Acceptance of the divisibility of sovereignty was common at that time. Thirty years later, Madison sought to restate his meaning:

> Were this a mere league, each of the parties would have an equal right to expound it; and of course, there would be as much right in one to insist on the bargain, as in another to renounce it. But the Union of the States is, according to the Virginia doctrine in 98–99, a *Constitutional Union;* and the right to judge *in the last resort,* concerning usurpations of power, affecting the validity of the Union, referred by that doctrine to the parties to the compact. On recurring to original principles, and to extreme cases, a single State might indeed be so oppressed as to be justified in shaking off the yoke; so might a single county of a State be, under an extremity of oppression. But until such justifications can be pleaded, the compact is obligatory in both cases.

The Kentucky and Virginia Resolutions were circulated among the other states, and they elicited responses from at least seven, mostly in the Federalist Northeast, upholding the concept of federal supremacy and denying the right of a state to nullify federal law. Jefferson's victory over the Federal-

ists in the election of 1800, due in no small part to popular resentment over the Alien and Sedition Acts, terminated this episode. But within a decade the New England states were themselves to enunciate extreme states' rights doctrine, under the pressure of the severe economic hardships they experienced as a result of President Jefferson's embargo policy. This sectional disaffection was increased by the strains of the War of 1812, during which the New England states sometimes refused to cooperate with American military operations and continued considerable trade with Britain. The Hartford Convention of 1814–1815, in which this movement culminated, recommended to the legislatures of the states represented that they pass measures to protect their citizens from the operation of unconstitutional national acts. But before the resolutions even got to Washington, the war was over, the complaints were forgotten, and the only result of the Convention was to annihilate the Federalist party.

NULLIFICATION    Not until 1828 was there a real elaboration of a theory of resistance to national authority. It originated with John C. Calhoun, as a rationalization of Southern opposition to the constant increase in tariff rates between 1816 and 1828. Calhoun was alarmed at the open talk of secession in the South, and offered the doctrine of nullification as a substitute, contending that his plan was a logical extension of the Virginia and Kentucky Resolutions.

Calhoun held that the Constitution was a compact formed by "sovereign and independent communities." The national government was not a party to the compact but an emanation from it, "a joint commission, appointed to superintend and administer the interests in which all are jointly concerned, but having, beyond its proper sphere, no more power than if it did not exist." It would be "monstrous" to claim that the agent could finally determine its powers "as against the principals, much less to use force against them." He thought, however, that mere recognition of the right of interposition would probably "supersede the necessity of its exercise, by impressing on the movements of the Government that moderation and justice so essential to harmony and peace, in a country of such vast extent and diversity of interests as ours." [2]

After President Jackson's denunciation of nullification in 1830, South Carolina was convinced of the necessity of action. In 1832 a state convention passed an "Ordinance of Nullification" declaring the federal tariff acts of 1828 and 1832 "null, void, and no law, nor binding upon this State, its officers or citizens." Federal agents were forbidden to collect the tariff in South Carolina. Appeal to the Supreme Court was denied, and if the federal government used force in any way to coerce citizens of the state into obedience to the nullified laws, the state would consider itself absolved from

[2] Richard K. Crallé (ed.), *The Works of John C. Calhoun* (New York: D. Appleton & Company, Inc., 1859), vol. 6, pp. 59–94.

all political connection with the other states and would proceed to organize an independent government.

President Jackson immediately challenged this action, saying that the power of nullification was "incompatible with the existence of the Union, contradicted expressly by the letter of the Constitution, unauthorized by its spirit, inconsistent with every principle on which it was founded, and destructive of the great object for which it was formed." He sent a warship and seven revenue cutters into Charleston Harbor to enforce the tariff, and requested Congress to pass a "Force Bill" enabling him to enforce federal law by use of the military. While Calhoun delayed the bill in the Senate, Henry Clay promoted enactment of a compromise tariff bill with lowered rates. Both bills were enacted on the same day. Thus mollified, the South Carolina convention withdrew its nullification ordinance, but to show that there had been no retreat on the principle, took the formal step of nullifying the Force Bill.

Failure was thus the uniform result for all three of these efforts to assert that the Constitution was only a compact among the several states, which left them with sovereignty unimpaired and free to meet federal coercion by interposing their own authority. One more test of the nature of the Union was to come, the supreme test of secession and civil war over the issue of slavery.

SECESSION    In the years preceding the Civil War, with the controversies over slavery and the tariff going on around them, Southern statesmen shifted their ground from the right of nullification to secession as the means to preserve their economic life and social institutions. Jefferson Davis pointed to the reservations which Virginia, New York, and Rhode Island had made in ratifying the Constitution, wherein they asserted that the powers granted to the federal government might be reassumed by the people in case of oppression, and concluded: "The right of the people of the several States to resume the powers delegated by them to the common agency, was not left without positive and ample assertion, even at a period when it had never been denied." [3]

For Calhoun, secession was justified as a final remedy to preserve a state's rights. According to his theory, after a state had interposed its authority to prevent federal action, the federal government could appeal to the amending process. If three-fourths of the states upheld the federal claim, the matter was settled as far as those states were concerned. But the dissenting state was not obliged to acquiesce in all instances.

> That a State, as a party to the constitutional compact, has the right to secede,—acting in the same capacity in which it ratified the constitution,

[3] Jefferson Davis, *The Rise and Fall of the Confederate Government* (New York: D. Appleton & Company, Inc., 1881), vol. 1, p. 173.

—cannot, with any show of reason, be denied by any one who regards the constitution as a compact,—if a power should be inserted by the amending power, which would radically change the character of the constitution, or the nature of the system.[4]

Lincoln's decision to use force to keep the Southern states in the Union and the victory of the North in the Civil War closed the debate over the legality of secession. The final decision was rendered at Appomattox Courthouse. After the war, the Supreme Court tidied up a bit in *Texas* v. *White* (1869). The case hinged on the question whether or not Texas had ever left the Union, and the Court held:

> When, therefore, Texas became one of the United States, she entered into an indissoluble relation. . . . The act which consummated her admission into the Union was something more than a compact; it was the incorporation of a new member into the political body. And it was final. The union between Texas and the other States was as complete, as perpetual, and as indissoluble as the union between the original States.

Chief Justice Chase summed up the principle involved: "The Constitution, in all its provisions, looks to an indestructible Union, composed of indestructible States."

## NATIONAL SUPREMACY

DIVISION OF POWERS    In essence, American federalism is a form of political organization in which the exercise of power is divided between two levels of government, each having the use of those powers as a matter of right, and each acting on the same citizen body. The appropriate division of powers between these two levels was one of the major concerns of the Constitutional Convention, and the pattern of allocation which emerged was fairly complex, as the following summary indicates:

*1. Exclusively national powers*    Since a nation obviously must speak with one voice in foreign relations, the power to declare war and make treaties was allocated to the national government. For different but equally obvious reasons, a uniform monetary system was essential, which necessitated central control of the power to coin money.

*2. Exclusively state powers*    Since the federal government was one of delegated powers, obviously any powers not delegated to it remained with the states. Rather than leave this matter to inference, however, the Tenth Amendment spelled it out: "The powers not delegated to the United States by the Constitution, nor prohibited by it to the States, are reserved to the States respectively, or to the people." There has been much misunderstanding about this amendment, and it has often been viewed as the principal

[4] *Ibid.*, p. 301.

guarantor of the rights of the states. Actually it adds nothing new to the Constitution, being simply declaratory of the relation between the national government and the states.[5]

*3. Concurrent powers*   The Constitution expressly gives to the national government such important powers as levying taxes and regulating commerce, but it makes no effort to prohibit the states from also exercising such authority within their own borders.

*4. Powers prohibited to the national government*   According to the principle that the national government is one of delegated powers, which was accepted by the framers though not spelled out until the Tenth Amendment was added, the national government has no authority to exercise powers not authorized by the Constitution. It was this argument, we have seen, which was used at the Convention to deny the necessity for a protective bill of rights. However, the framers did include in the original Constitution a few express prohibitions on federal power, such as those against the levying of direct taxes or suspending the writ of habeas corpus. When the Bill of Rights was added, the extensive prohibitions of the first eight amendments were incorporated in this group.

*5. Powers prohibited to the states*   In Article I, section 10, a group of activities is forbidden to the States. The purpose of these prohibitions is primarily to enforce the exclusive nature of national control over foreign relations, the monetary system, and foreign commerce. A further prohibition, which does not fall in any of these three categories, is on any law impairing the obligation of contracts.

*6. Powers prohibited to both the nation and the states*   Certain prohibitions on the states in Article I, section 10, are also imposed on the national government by the preceding section. These include the ban on passing bills of attainder and ex post facto laws, and granting titles of nobility.

LEGISLATIVE SUPREMACY   With this rather elaborate division of functions and powers between the two levels of government, disputes are bound to occur. The Constitution supplies a principle for settling them in the "supremacy clause" of Article VI: "This Constitution, and the laws of the United States which shall be made in pursuance thereof; and all treaties made, or which shall be made, under the authority of the United States,

---

[5] Walter Berns, "The Meaning of the Tenth Amendment," in Robert A. Goldwin (ed.), *A Nation of States* (Chicago: Rand McNally & Company, 1963), pp. 126–148. Justice Frankfurter once referred to the Tenth Amendment as an "empty hobgoblin." See Walter F. Murphy, *Elements of Judicial Strategy* (Chicago: The University of Chicago Press, 1964), p. 51.

shall be the supreme law of the land; and the judges in every state shall be bound thereby, any thing in the Constitution or laws of any state to the contrary notwithstanding."

The effectiveness of this section was early demonstrated in the case of *McCulloch* v. *Maryland* (1819). In 1818 the Maryland Legislature levied a tax on the politically unpopular Bank of the United States, which had been chartered by the federal government. The cashier of the Baltimore branch of the Bank refused to pay the tax and was convicted of violating the law by the state courts. The Supreme Court unanimously upheld the Bank's position, Chief Justice Marshall basing his opinion squarely on the supremacy clause. "If any one proposition could command the universal assent of mankind," he wrote, "we might expect it would be this: that the government of the Union, though limited in its powers, is supreme within its sphere of action." Consequently, no state had any power "to retard, impede, burden, or in any manner control, the operations of the constitutional laws enacted by congress."

When Congress enters a field in which it is authorized to act, then, its legislation supersedes all incompatible state regulations. In practical terms, however, the question whether Congress has preempted a given area is a difficult one, since federal statutes seldom state whether all local rules on the matter are suspended. It falls ultimately to the Supreme Court to determine the relation of federal and state statutes. In *Pennsylvania* v. *Nelson* (1956), Chief Justice Warren attempted to codify the tests which the Court has used to guide such decisions. First, is the scheme of federal regulation so pervasive as to make it a reasonable inference that Congress has left no room for the states? Second, do the federal statutes touch a field in which the interest of the national government is so dominant that it must be assumed to preclude state action on the same subject? Third, does enforcement of the state act present a serious danger of conflict with the administration of the federal program?

In the *Nelson* case, a conviction for violation of the Pennsylvania sedition act had been reversed by the state supreme court on the ground that a federal sedition act (the Smith Act of 1940) had occupied the field and superseded the state law. The United States Supreme Court agreed. Using the three criteria just suggested, Warren concluded that Congress had taken over the entire task of protecting the country from seditious conduct when it passed the Smith Act, even though no express intention to exclude the states was stated in that statute. Three dissenting justices did not agree that the federal government's interest in protection against sedition was more dominant than that of the states. Since Congress had not forbidden the states to legislate in this area, they thought the courts should not.

Following the *Nelson* decision Congress considered a bill reversing the Court's interpretation and permitting the states to enforce their own sedition laws, as well as a much more far-reaching measure providing that no

federal law should be deemed to exclude similar state laws unless Congress so specified or unless there was a "direct and positive conflict" between state and federal law.[6] The Department of Justice warned that adoption of this latter bill would cause immense confusion in the regulation of interstate commerce, where the preemption doctrine has been perhaps most widely applied. The Senate defeated both proposals in 1958 by a one-vote margin, thus preserving for the judiciary its delicate task of "balancing the national interests with the local interests and, if possible, . . . reconciling them by allowing the two statutes to mesh and function together."[7]

DUAL FEDERALISM    Congressional supremacy, thus established under Marshall, had to face a different kind of challenge from the Taney Court, grounded on the Tenth Amendment. Under the influence of Taney's states' rights constitutional theories, the Supreme Court on many occasions took its legal bearings more from this amendment than from the national supremacy clause. Espousing a doctrine called "dual federalism," the Court assumed that the two levels of government were coequal sovereignties, each supreme within its own sphere. Thus the fact that certain powers had been reserved to the states constituted a limit on the authority specifically delegated to the national government.

From 1890 to 1937 the Court with its laissez-faire philosophy found it convenient to use the Taney doctrine. On the one hand the federal government was restricted from enacting economic regulation by "invisible radiations" from the Tenth Amendment, and on the other hand the states were barred from interference with the workings of the economic system by the due process clause of the Fourteenth Amendment.

The theory of dual federalism received its clearest statement in *Hammer* v. *Dagenhart* (1918). By a five to four vote, the Court here invalidated a congressional statute restricting the transportation in interstate commerce of goods produced by child labor. For the majority, Justice Day wrote: "The grant of authority over a purely federal matter was not intended to destroy the local power always existing and carefully reserved to the States in the Tenth Amendment." He went on to say that in interpreting the Constitution it should never be forgotten that "the powers not expressly delegated to the National Government are reserved" to the states and the people by the Tenth Amendment.

To arrive at this conclusion Justice Day had to misquote the amendment; the term "expressly" does not appear in its text. He had to ignore judicial precedent; Marshall in *McCulloch* v. *Maryland* had held that the omission

---

[6] See C. Herman Pritchett, *Congress versus the Supreme Court: 1957–1960* (Minneapolis: The University of Minnesota Press, 1961), chap. 6.

[7] William O. Douglas, *We the Judges* (Garden City, N.Y.: Doubleday & Company, Inc., 1956), p. 233. The Supreme Court substantially relaxed its *Nelson* holding in *Uphaus* v. *Wyman* (1959).

of the word "expressly" had left the question whether a particular power had been delegated to the national government to be answered by a "fair construction of the whole instrument." Justice Day had also to assume a position which was historically inaccurate; when the Tenth Amendment was under consideration in the First Congress the anti-Federalists had tried to insert the word "expressly," but had been voted down. In any case, the commerce power had been expressly delegated to Congress. These errors did not go unchallenged. Speaking for the four dissenters Justice Holmes declared: "I should have thought that the most conspicuous decisions of this Court had made it clear that the power to regulate commerce and other constitutional powers could not be cut down or qualified by the fact that it might interfere with the carrying out of the domestic policy of any State."

Much of the struggle in the middle 1930s between the conservative members of the Supreme Court and President Roosevelt may be seen as a clash between Taney's dual federalism and the older national supremacy of Marshall. In the end it was the interpretation of Marshall and Roosevelt which prevailed. In a series of cases culminating in *United States* v. *Darby Lumber Co.* (1941), the reconstituted and rejuvenated Supreme Court upheld a number of federal laws which directly affected local policies. In the *Darby* opinion Justice Stone wrote that the Tenth Amendment "states but a truism that all is retained which has not been surrendered. There is nothing in the history of its adoption to suggest that it was more than declaratory of the relationship between the national and state governments as it had been established by the Constitution before the amendment." The *Darby* decision specifically overruled *Hammer* v. *Dagenhart*.

JUDICIAL SUPREMACY     Implementing the principle of national supremacy requires that the Supreme Court have authority to review the decisions of state courts. The Judiciary Act of 1789, in section 25, provided for such review of final judgments or decrees "in the highest court of law or equity of a State in which a decision in the suit could be had," in three classes of cases: (1) where the validity of a federal law or treaty was "drawn in question," and the decision was against its validity; (2) where a state statute was questioned as "repugnant to the constitution, treaties or laws of the United States," and the decision was in favor of its validity; and (3) where the construction of the federal Constitution, treaty, or statute was drawn in question, and the decision was against the title, right, privilege, or exemption claimed. These categories were all based on the principle that if the Constitution and laws of the United States were to be observed, the Supreme Court would have to have an opportunity to review decisions of state courts which ruled adversely on asserted federal rights.

The Supreme Court's power of review over state supreme court decisions was not established without incident. In *Fairfax's Devisee* v. *Hunter's Lessee* (1813) the Supreme Court (John Marshall not sitting because his brother

was involved in the litigation) reversed a decision of the Virginia high court regarding the land rights of British subjects who were protected under the Jay Treaty. Virginia refused to acquiesce in the decision; the state court argued that although a state was bound to respect the Constitution, laws, and treaties of the United States as supreme, it was obliged to follow only its own interpretations, not those of a federal court. Because the courts of the United States represented one sovereignty, they could not review decisions of state courts, which belonged to another sovereignty.

Consequently the Supreme Court's order was returned unobeyed. The Court in *Martin* v. *Hunter's Lessee* (1816) strongly reaffirmed its right to review state decisions. Justice Story answered Virginia's argument with the statement that the Constitution was not ordained by the states, but by the "people of the United States," and these people could invest the national government with whatever powers they thought proper. "The courts of the United States can, without question, revise the proceedings of the executive and legislative authorities of the States. . . . Surely, the exercise of the same right over judicial tribunals is not a higher or more dangerous act of sovereign power."

The second Supreme Court order bypassed the Virginia supreme court and was directed to the court in which the case had originated. There the mandate was obeyed. Charles Warren, the historian of the Court, has termed Story's opinion in this case as having been ever since "the keystone of the whole arch of Federal judicial power." [8] However, the states' rights forces were not easily daunted, and they returned to the attack in *Cohens* v. *Virginia* (1821). Congress had passed an act authorizing the District of Columbia to conduct lotteries to finance civic improvements. The state of Virginia, which had a law forbidding lotteries, arrested and convicted two persons for selling the Washington tickets within its domain. After conviction, the defendants appealed to the Supreme Court. The Virginia Legislature was highly incensed at this reiteration of federal appellate jurisdiction over state courts, and denied the existence of any such authority. The argument for the state was that the Supreme Court could not exercise appellate powers over a state court decision to which a state was a party, since the Constitution placed all cases in which a state was a party within the Supreme Court's *original* jurisdiction. Counsel argued that the power of the federal judiciary was either exclusive or concurrent, but not paramount. Where it was concurrent, "whichsoever judiciary gets possession of the case [first], should proceed to final judgment, from which there should be no appeal."

Again the Supreme Court rejected the anarchic principles of this contention. Marshall held that where a state had obtained a judgment against an individual and in so doing had overruled a defense set up under the Constitution or laws of the United States, it was the undeniable right of the

---

[8] Charles Warren, *The Supreme Court in United States History* (Boston: Little, Brown and Company, rev. ed., 1947), vol. 1, p. 449.

Supreme Court to review the decision. Then the Court examined the merits of the case and decided against the defendants on the ground that Congress had not intended the lottery tickets to be sold outside the District of Columbia. Many Viriginia officials and newspapers were enraged at the assertion of federal jurisdiction, but because of the decision on the merits they were left with no order to disobey or resist.

NULLIFICATION AND THE COURTS    The right to review and reverse judgments of state courts and to review state legislative or executive action through Supreme Court reexamination of state or lower federal court orders has been challenged from time to time by the theory of nullification. Rather surprisingly, the principal episodes of this kind occurred in the Northern states. The first controversy, *United States* v. *Peters* (1809), concerned the decision of a lower federal court in Pennsylvania on a claim growing out of a prize case from the Revolutionary War. The state Legislature defied the court's judgment and declared it to be in violation of the Eleventh Amendment. In the Supreme Court's decision Marshall made short shrift of the state's claim to interfere with the actions of a federal court, saying: "If the legislatures of the several States may, at will, annul the judgments of the courts of the United States, and destroy the rights acquired under those judgments, the constitution itself becomes a solemn mockery; and the nation is deprived of the means of enforcing its laws by the instrumentality of its own tribunals."

The reply of the Pennsylvania Legislature was to enact defiant resolutions expressly denying the authority of the Supreme Court to sit in judgment on rights of the state. The Governor announced that he would prevent the enforcement of the Court's decree and the federal marshal attempting to carry out the Court's order was met by state troops. A federal grand jury indicted the commanding officer of the state militia, and he was later convicted of resisting the laws of the United States. While the officer's fate was pending, the Governor appealed to President Madison for assistance in resisting the Court. Madison, author of the Virginia Resolutions ten years earlier, replied that not only could he not render such assistance, but that it was his positive duty to aid the Supreme Court in executing its decree. The state militia was then withdrawn, the Court's decree was carried out, and the sentence of the commanding general of the state militia was remitted by Madison.

After the incident, Pennsylvania called for a constitutional amendment to establish an impartial tribunal to hear disputes between the states and the federal government. Among the states returning unfavorable replies were Kentucky and Virginia. The Virginia answer declared that the Supreme Court of the United States was fully capable of performing the function in question.

Shortly before the Civil War, nullification reappeared in the North. In

Wisconsin, Sherman M. Booth, a Milwaukee newspaper editor, helped rescue an escaped slave from a deputy federal marshal. Booth was arrested by federal authorities, and since there were no federal prisons in the area, he was placed in a local jail to await trial. A judge of the Wisconsin supreme court issued a writ of habeas corpus and declared the federal Fugitive Slave Law unconstitutional. The federal marshal appealed to the entire state supreme court against the obvious irregularity of a state judge issuing orders to federal officials. But the Wisconsin supreme court upheld the judge both on the issuance of the writ and the unconstitutionality of the law. The marshal then appealed to the United States Supreme Court. But before that Court could hear the case, Booth was convicted in federal district court and sentenced to a fine of $1,000 and a month in prison. Once again Booth applied to the Wisconsin supreme court for habeas corpus and once again that court issued the writ, freeing Booth.

In *Ableman* v. *Booth* (1859) Chief Justice Taney voiced the unanimous opinion of the Supreme Court that Wisconsin "has reversed and annulled the provisions of the Constitution itself, and the [Judiciary] act of Congress of 1789, and made the superior and appellant tribunal the inferior and subordinate." If Wisconsin could so control the actions of federal agencies within that state, so could every other state. The language of Article VI was "too plain to admit of doubt or to need comment." The decisions of federal courts were "as far beyond the reach of the judicial process issued by a State judge or a State Court, as if the line of division was traced by landmarks and monuments visible to the eye." In closing his opinion, Taney, himself a firm believer in states' rights, affirmed that "no power is more clearly conferred by the Constitution and laws of the United States, than the power of this court to decide, ultimately and finally, all cases arising under such Constitution and laws."

After a delay of several months, federal officials rearrested Booth, this time lodging him in the federal building in Milwaukee. The Attorney General faced something of a dilemma. While wishing to maintain federal supremacy, he had to commit the politically unpopular act of upholding in Wisconsin the Fugitive Slave Law. The prisoner further complicated the situation by refusing to pay his fine or to ask for a presidential pardon. The affair was fortuitously resolved by an abolitionist mob which freed Booth.

In 1956 the dust was blown off the doctrines of interposition and nullification, as they were invoked by several Southern states in protest against the Supreme Court's decision invalidating racial segregation in the schools.[9] In its act of nullification the state of Alabama laid down the basic premise of its action:

> WHEREAS the states, being the parties to the constitutional compact, it follows of necessity that there can be no tribunal above their authority to decide, in the last resort, whether the compact made by them be vio-

[9] *Brown* v. *Board of Education of Topeka* (1954).

lated; and, consequently, they must decide themselves, in the last resort, such questions as may be of sufficient magnitude to require their interposition.

On these grounds the Legislature of Alabama declared, "The decisions and orders of the Supreme Court of the United States relating to the separation of races in the public schools are, as a matter of right, null, void, and of no effect; and . . . as a matter of right, this State is not bound to abide thereby." [10]

All such actions and arguments are condemned by their opposition to the mainstream of American history and constitutional development. In the 1958 Little Rock case, *Cooper* v. *Aaron*, the Supreme Court disposed sharply and decisively of the contention that the Governor and Legislature of Arkansas were not bound by the Court's 1954 decision declaring segregated schools unconstitutional. Later, in *Bush* v. *Orleans School Board* (1960) the Court quoted with approval the terse comment of a federal district court: "The conclusion is clear that interposition is not a *constitutional* doctrine. If taken seriously, it is illegal defiance of constitutional authority."

### ADMISSION OF NEW STATES

With the migration to the territory between the Appalachians and the Mississippi, it was apparent even before the Constitutional Convention that new states might well be formed in the area. The claims of certain states to western territory had been ceded to the general government when the Articles of Confederation were adopted, with the understanding that Congress would eventually organize the territory into states and admit them to the Union. By the Northwest Ordinance of 1787, the Confederation Congress provided that the Northwest Territory was to be divided into not less than three nor more than five states, and that 60,000 inhabitants would be requisite for admission of a state.

Article IV, section 3, provides for the admission of new states into the Union by Congress. The only stated limitations on congressional discretion are that "no new state shall be formed or erected within the jurisdiction of any other state; nor any state be formed by the junction of two or more states, or parts of states, without the consent of the legislatures of the states concerned as well as of the Congress."

Thirty-five new states were admitted to the Union between 1791 and 1912. Five were carved out of the territory of older states—Vermont, Kentucky, Tennessee, Maine, and West Virginia. In the first four cases the legislature of the older state gave its consent. But West Virginia was formed from the western counties of Virginia during the Civil War when Virginia was in military opposition to the Union. In this situation consent was given by a

[10] Act no. 42, Special Session 1956, Alabama, reprinted in 1 *Race Relations Law Reporter* 437 (1956).

rump legislature from the area convened especially for this purpose. After the war, Virginia formally consented to the dismemberment.

Of the remaining thirty states, all but two went through a probationary status as organized territories before they were admitted as states. The exceptions were Texas, which upon its admission in 1845 was an independent republic, and California, which was formed out of a region ceded by Mexico in 1848.

The normal procedure by which a territory becomes a state calls for Congress to pass an enabling act allowing the territorial government to convene a popular convention to propose a state constitution. If the voters ratify this constitution, it is submitted to Congress for approval. Congress then may pass a resolution admitting the new state. A statehood resolution, like other legislation, is subject to presidential veto, but unlike other statutes, once adopted it is irrepealable.

Congress may grant or withhold statehood for any reasons it chooses. Before the Civil War the primary motive in admission was to maintain a balance between slave and free states. Nevada was admitted, in spite of its sparse population, to provide a necessary ratifying vote for the Thirteenth Amendment. Hawaii and Alaska were strong candidates for admission from at least 1944, when the platforms of both political parties recommended statehood, but various political considerations delayed favorable action by Congress. Alaska finally won admission in 1958, and Hawaii in 1959.

Under the Northwest Ordinance of 1787 new states were to be admitted "on an equal footing with the original states, in all respects whatever." Consequently it is surprising that the Constitutional Convention of the same year voted, nine states to two, against placing a similar equal status provision in Article IV. However, this omission has had no practical effect, for the principle of equality is a fundamental part of American constitutional law. Thus the joint resolution admitting Texas in 1845 specified that Texas "shall be admitted into the Union . . . on an equal footing with the existing States."

The Supreme Court has on many occasions recognized equality of status as an inherent attribute of the federal Union. *Coyle* v. *Smith* (1911) supplies the best illustration of its position. Under the enabling act admitting Oklahoma as a state, Congress had specified that the capital should be located at Guthrie for at least seven years. After four years, the Oklahoma Legislature ordered the capital moved to Oklahoma City. The Supreme Court held that the state was not bound by the congressional limitation, reasoning as follows:

> The power is to admit "new States into *this* Union." "This Union" was and is a union of States, equal in power, dignity and authority, each competent to exert that residuum of sovereignty not delegated to the United States by the Constitution itself. To maintain otherwise would be to say that the Union, through the power of Congress to admit new

States, might come to be a union of States unequal in power, as including States whose powers were restricted only by the Constitution, with others whose powers had been further restricted by an act of Congress accepted as a condition of admission.

Another illustration of the ineffectiveness of preadmission restrictions after admission was supplied by the experience of Arizona, which proposed a state constitution providing for the recall of elected officials, including judges. President Taft objected to this feature, and vetoed the resolution of admission. Arizona then amended her constitution to eliminate this provision, and was then admitted. Shortly thereafter Arizona, secure in her statehood, put recall of judges back into her constitution.

However, preadmission conditions which are not construed to affect equality of political power can be enforced after admission. In *Stearns* v. *Minnesota* (1900), the Supreme Court upheld an agreement imposed upon Minnesota prior to admission which limited the state's right to tax lands held by the United States at the time of admission, which had subsequently been granted to a railroad. The Court said that "a mere agreement in reference to property involves no question of equality of status, but only of the power of a state to deal with the nation . . . in reference to such property."

Another application of the equal footing doctrine, this time to the disadvantage of a state, came in the case of *United States* v. *Texas* (1950). In 1947 the Court had ruled in a case involving California tideland oil that the soil beneath the 3-mile marginal belt along the Atlantic Ocean had not belonged to the original states and, consequently, that the states later admitted to the Union did not own the 3-mile belt along their coasts either.[11] But Texas had been an independent nation prior to admission, and was conceded to have owned its coastal belt of land during that period. The Supreme Court held, however, that Texas had surrendered its dominion and sovereignty over its coastal shelf when it entered the Union on terms of equality with the existing states.

Congress subsequently reversed the effect of this holding by passing the Submerged Lands Act of 1953 which ceded to the states ownership of land and resources under adjoining seas to a distance of 3 miles from shore or to the state's "historic boundaries." The Supreme Court then interpreted this statute to grant Florida and Texas jurisdiction 10 miles into the Gulf, since their historic boundaries were 3 marine leagues, whereas the other Gulf states have only 3 miles.[12] To this extent the equal footing rule has been disregarded by Congress and the Court.

[11] *United States* v. *California* (1947); *United States* v. *Louisiana* (1950).

[12] *United States* v. *States of Louisiana, Texas, Mississippi, Alabama, and Florida* (1960). In *United States* v. *Louisiana* (1967) the Court held that Texas could not claim that for purposes of the three-leagues provision its coastline extended to the seaward edge of artificial jetties constructed by Texas in the Gulf of Mexico after the admission of Texas to the Union in 1845.

## OBLIGATIONS OF THE NATIONAL GOVERNMENT
## TO THE STATES

There are several obligations which the Constitution imposes upon the national government with respect to the states. Under Article V no state may be denied equal representation in the Senate without its consent. Again, the government must respect the territorial integrity of the existing states in the formation of new states, as noted in the preceding section. In addition there are three other obligations, all appearing in Article IV, section 4, which deserve more extended treatment.

GUARANTEE AGAINST INVASION AND DOMESTIC VIOLENCE    The protection against foreign invasion is simply a corollary of national self-defense. While no court could order the President to fulfill this obligation, it is inconceivable that any Chief Executive would deliberately violate the provision. During the War of 1812 and the Civil War, of course, it was for a time beyond the power of the federal government to repel invasions.

Article IV, section 4, goes on to provide that, on application of a state legislature, or of the governor if the legislature cannot be convened, the United States shall guarantee a state against "domestic violence." A statute adopted by Congress in 1795 spelling out this obligation uses the term "insurrection" rather than domestic violence. On at least 16 occasions states have sought federal assistance in suppressing domestic violence. The most recent was the Detroit riots in the summer of 1967, in connection with which Governor Romney charged President Johnson with delaying the dispatch of troops for political reasons. Afterward Attorney General Clark sought to clarify the situation for the future by specifying what the states must do before the President can act. First, the governor must make a finding that "serious domestic violence" exists, which cannot be brought under control by law enforcement resources available to him. The legislature or governor must then request the President to employ the armed forces to bring the violence under control.

A request from the state legislature or governor is not necessary, however, where domestic violence threatens the enforcement of national laws. Article I, section 8, authorizes Congress to provide for calling forth the militia to execute the laws of the Union, suppress insurrections, and repel invasions. In 1792 Congress adopted legislation which, as revised in 1795, provided:

> That whenever the laws of the United States shall be opposed, or the execution thereof obstructed, in any state, by combinations too powerful to be suppressed by the ordinary course of judicial proceedings, or by the powers vested in the marshals by this act, it shall be lawful for the President of the United States, to call forth the militia of such state, or of any other state or states, as may be necessary to suppress such combinations, and to cause the laws to be duly executed.[13]

[13] 1 Stat. 424 (1795).

An important presidential use of troops to enforce national laws occurred in Chicago in 1894. A strike by the railwaymen's union against the Pullman Company had spread to trains using Pullman equipment, causing an almost complete stoppage on the railroads operating out of Chicago. The federal district attorney in Chicago obtained an injunction against Eugene Debs, the leader of the union, and other labor officials, forbidding them to hinder the mails or interstate commerce in any way. When the injunction went unheeded and violence increased, the federal marshal informed the United States Attorney General that an emergency existed with which he was unable to cope. President Cleveland then ordered federal troops into the city to restore order and assist in getting the trains running. This action was not taken in pursuance of a request by the state executive. In fact, Governor Altgeld strongly protested Cleveland's order.

Debs and the other leaders were arrested for contempt of court in disobeying the injunction, and received sentences of from three to six months. The Supreme Court refused to issue a writ of habeas corpus, upholding the presidential action in a unanimous opinion with these words:

> The entire strength of the nation may be used to enforce in any part of the land the full and free exercise of all national powers and the security of all rights entrusted by the Constitution to its care. The strong arm of the national Government may be put forth to brush away all obstructions to the freedom of interstate commerce or the transportation of the mails. If the emergency arises, the army of the Nation, and all its militia, are at the service of the Nation to compel obedience to its laws.[14]

In 1957 President Eisenhower found it necessary to use federal troops to control violence in Little Rock, Arkansas, and enforce court orders seeking to accomplish gradual desegregation of the local high school. Again in 1962 federal troops had to be used to quell violence arising out of a school integration controversy. The University of Mississippi had been ordered by the federal courts to admit James H. Meredith as its first Negro student. The order was resisted, and both the Governor and Lieutenant Governor were found guilty of contempt. On September 30 President Kennedy issued a proclamation calling on Mississippi citizens to cease interfering with the court ruling, and an executive order authorizing the Secretary of Defense to use troops to enforce the Meredith order. Some four hundred federal marshals were sent to Mississippi to escort Meredith onto the campus, along with state police. The police failed to act when violence began, and the marshals, under siege, had to defend themselves with tear gas until the federalized National Guard arrived. Federal troops appeared early on October 1, reaching a total of 16,000, and brought the area under control. Two persons were killed during the night of rioting. Meredith was enrolled and attended classes on October 1, accompanied by United States marshals.[15]

---

[14] *In re Debs* (1895).

[15] On the general subject of civil disorder, see "Riot Control and the Use of Federal Troops," 81 *Harvard Law Review* 638–652 (1968).

In March, 1965, Alabama state troops on the order of Governor George Wallace halted a voting rights march which Martin Luther King was attempting to lead from Selma to Montgomery. A federal district judge enjoined state officials from interfering with the march. Governor Wallace then sent a telegram to President Johnson requesting that he provide "sufficient federal civil authorities or officers" to guarantee the safety of the marchers and citizens along the route, alleging that his state could not afford the cost of mobilizing the National Guard. President Johnson complied, but expressed regret that "the Governor and the legislature of a sovereign state [should] decline to exercise their responsibility and . . . request that duty be assumed by the Federal Government." [16]

In 1964, however, Attorney General Kennedy refused the request of the NAACP to use federal forces for preventive police action in Mississippi to deal with violence and conspiracy which it was alleged were obstructing the execution of federal civil rights laws. The Attorney General contended that this was a local law-enforcement matter to which federal authority did not extend.[17]

GUARANTEE OF A REPUBLICAN FORM OF GOVERNMENT    Article IV, section 4, provides that "The United States shall guarantee to every State in this Union a republican form of government." This is the only limitation in the Constitution on the internal governmental organization of a state. No definition is provided of a republican form of government, but the language may be interpreted as requiring a form somewhere between a monarchy or oligarchy on the one hand, and a pure or direct democracy on the other.

In designating the "United States" as responsible for this guarantee, the Constitution does not specify which branch has the responsibility for its enforcement. The Supreme Court, however, has ruled on several occasions against judicial enforcement of the clause. The first occasion was in the case of *Luther* v. *Borden* (1849). In 1841 Rhode Island was still operating largely under the system of government established by a charter from Charles II which made no provision for amendment. Dissident groups, protesting mainly against the limits on suffrage, combined to form a popular convention which drafted a new constitution. Elections were held the following year, and Thomas Dorr was elected Governor. All the while the old charter government continued to operate and was attempting to put down what it regarded as a rebellion. When one of its agents tried to arrest a Dorr supporter, he was sued for trespass, and one of the issues at the trial was whether the charter government was "republican" under the terms of the Constitution.

Chief Justice Taney for the Supreme Court denied that a court possessed the machinery either to hold a plebiscite or to interrogate enough witnesses

[16] *Ibid.*, March 26, 1965, p. 532.
[17] *The New York Times*, July 1, 1964.

to determine which government had the support of a majority of the people. This was a purely political decision which had to be made by Congress. Taney wrote:

> Under this article of the constitution it rests with congress to decide what government is the established one in a State. For as the United States guarantee to each State a republican government, congress must necessarily decide what government is established in the State before it can determine whether it is republican or not. And when the senators and representatives of a State are admitted into the councils of the Union, the authority of the government under which they are appointed, as well as its republican character, is recognized by the proper constitutional authority. And its decision is binding on every other department of the government, and could not be questioned in a judicial tribunal.

In this case no representatives had been elected from Rhode Island while the dispute was in progress, so there had been no congressional contest over seating. But the constitutional guarantee against domestic violence had been invoked. The President had recognized one of the contending governors as the legitimate executive authority of the state, and had taken steps to call out the militia to support his authority, should that be necessary. The announcement of this presidential determination had in fact been responsible for terminating Dorr's rebellion against the charter government. After the President had made such a decision, Taney continued,

> . . . is a circuit court of the United States authorized to inquire whether his decision was right? Could the court, while the parties were actually contending in arms for the possession of the government, call witnesses before it, and inquire which party represented a majority of the people? . . . If the judicial power extends so far, the guarantee contained in the constitution of the United States is a guarantee of anarchy, and not of order.

The Supreme Court had occasion to reiterate that the republican form of government guarantee is judicially nonenforceable in a 1912 case where it was alleged that the insertion in the Oregon constitution of a provision for direct legislation by way of the initiative and referendum deprived the state of a republican form of government. The Court's reply was that, in the absence of any determination on this point by the political departments of the federal government, it would refuse to consider such charges.[18] More recently, the Court dealt with the republican form of government provision in connection with the problem of apportionment and representation in state legislatures, to which we now turn.

---

[18] *Pacific States Telephone & Telegraph Co.* v. *Oregon* (1912). After three civil rights murders in Mississippi in 1964, the NAACP urged President Johnson to take over the administration of the state on the ground that for nearly a century Mississippi had failed to maintain a republican form of government. *The New York Times,* June 27, 1964.

## REPRESENTATION IN STATE LEGISLATURES

Until 1962 the states were free from any federal constitutional controls over apportionment and districting in their legislatures, and they followed a great variety of representation practices. David and Eisenberg divided the states into four general classes on the basis of their representation arrangements: [19]

> **1.**   Sixteen states had an equivalent of the "federal" plan, in which one house (like the United States Senate) had a fixed apportionment of representation among fixed districts with no regard for population, while the other house was apportioned more or less on the basis of population. In seven of these states, counties were treated exactly like states in the federal union, each county having at least one representative in the lower house and equal representation with other counties in the upper house. Towns were represented in the lower houses of Vermont and Connecticut.
>
> **2.**   In nine states, the constitution provided for a straight population basis of representation in one house and some kind of qualified population standard in the other house. Some of these states were close to the federal pattern. In California, the requirement that no county have more than one state senator limited Los Angeles County, with a population of over six million, to a single member in the state Senate.
>
> **3.**   In sixteen states, population was the principal criterion for both houses, but was qualified in one way or another for both.
>
> **4.**   In the final group of nine states, population was the constitutional criterion for representation in the entire legislature.

In the nineteenth century these provisions for representation of each county or town and the various departures from population representation did not result in great inequalities of election districts. But as large urban centers developed in the present century, they were increasingly under-represented. Moreover, in rurally controlled legislatures the power-holders took steps to protect their position, either by writing new restrictions on population representation into the constitution or by failing to redistrict when such action would have given additional representatives to urban areas.

It was a situation of this latter sort with which the Supreme Court was confronted in the famous 1962 case of *Baker* v. *Carr*. The constitution of Tennessee provided for ninety-nine members of the House and thirty-three members of the Senate, and directed the Legislature to allocate, at least every ten years, the senators and representatives among the several counties or districts "according to the number of qualified voters in each." Despite these mandatory requirements, no reapportionment had been made since

---

[19] Paul T. David and Ralph Eisenberg, *State Legislative Redistricting* (Chicago: Public Administration Service, 1962), pp. 8–10.

1901. During the period between 1901 and 1950, the population grew from 2,021,000 to 3,292,000, but the growth was very uneven among counties. Thus 37 per cent of the voting population could control twenty of the thirty-three members of the Senate, while 40 per cent of the voters could control sixty-three of the ninety-nine members of the House.

In 1959 suit was brought in federal district court by certain citizens of Tennessee against state election officials under the Civil Rights Act of 1871, alleging deprivation of federal constitutional rights. The principal obstacle to success in their suit was that in *Colegrove* v. *Green* (1946) the Supreme Court had declined to rule on a similar claim made against congressional districts in Illinois, where likewise a failure since 1901 to obey the constitutional mandate to redistrict every ten years had resulted in population inequalities as great as nine to one. The Court, speaking through Justice Frankfurter, had held in a four to three decision that these election controversies constituted a political thicket which judges must avoid.[20]

In *Baker* v. *Carr*, however, the Court reversed the *Colegrove* rule and held the Tennessee complaint to be justiciable. Justice Brennan asserted two main grounds for refusing to follow *Colegrove*. First, Frankfurter's position on justiciability had been supported by only three of the seven participating justices. Justice Rutledge, who supplied the fourth vote, actually agreed with the three dissenters that the issue was justiciable, and only voted as he did because he felt that it would be unwise to upset the Illinois arrangements so soon before the congressional elections of 1946.

Second, Brennan traced the "political question" doctrine, on which Frankfurter had relied, all the way back to *Luther* v. *Borden* to demonstrate that it did not cover the Tennessee type of election controversy. A true political question, from his view, was presented only where there was a separation of powers issue at stake. A political question was one that the courts should avoid out of deference to the President or Congress, as in *Luther* v. *Borden*. Since there was no such conflict here, the question was justiciable.

Justice Frankfurter, dissenting along with Harlan, argued on the contrary that the significant factors in past judicial refusals to get involved in political questions were these:

> . . . the caution not to undertake decision where standards meet for judicial judgment are lacking, the reluctance to interfere with matters of state government in the absence of an unquestionable and effectively enforceable mandate, the unwillingness to make courts arbiters of the broad issues of political organization historically committed to other institutions and for whose adjustment the judicial process is ill-adapted.

The Tennessee case, Frankfurter felt, fell squarely in this tradition of controversies that do not lend themselves to judicial standards or judicial remedies.

---

[20] For a fuller treatment of *Colegrove* v. *Green*, see Chap. 10.

Justice Frankfurter made specific use of the republican guarantee clause in his argument, saying: "The present case involves all of the elements that have made the Guarantee Clause cases non-justiciable. It is, in effect, a Guarantee Clause claim masquerading under a different label."

Legislative apportionment, Frankfurter continued, was a political problem bound to prove vastly embarrassing to courts if they got involved in it. There are no standards for decision except political preferences and competing political philosophies, while "in every strand of this complicated, intricate web of values meet the contending forces of partisan politics." This was the political thicket which the Court majority would require the federal district courts to enter, he warned, with no standards or constitutional principles to guide them, no indication of what kind of remedies they could formulate to correct legislative apportionments.

Justice Brennan, however, assumed that the Court would be equal to developing remedies when the need arose. None were required here, since the Court merely held that the complaint against Tennessee's legislative districts should not have been dismissed. This ruling opened the gates to a flood of suits.

The first one to reach the Court was *Gray* v. *Sanders* (1963), involving not a state legislature but rather the Georgia county-unit system of primary elections to statewide offices. This system was deliberately designed to give control of the electoral process to rural minorities. The 8 largest counties had six unit votes each; the next 30 had four unit votes each; and the remaining 121 counties each had two unit votes. The candidate for nomination who received the most popular votes in a primary was awarded the unit votes for that county. Fulton County, containing the city of Atlanta, with a population of over a half million, comprising 14.11 per cent of the state's total population, cast 1.46 per cent of the total of 410 unit votes. The smallest county in the state, Echols County, with a population of less than 2,000, cast 0.48 per cent of the total unit vote. Put another way, one unit vote in Echols County represented 938 residents, and in Fulton County 92,721 residents.

The Supreme Court, with only Justice Harlan dissenting, invalidated the county-unit plan on the ground that no preferred class of voters is permissible under the Constitution and by American traditions. Every voter is equal to every other voter in his state: "The conception of political equality from the Declaration of Independence, to Lincoln's Gettysburg address, to the Fifteenth, Seventeenth, and Nineteenth Amendments can mean only one thing—one person, one vote." Applying this conception to the present case, the Court concluded:

> Once the geographical unit for which a representative is to be chosen is designated, all who participate in the election are to have an equal vote—whatever their race, whatever their sex, whatever their occupation, whatever their income, and wherever their home may be in that

geographical unit. This is required by the Equal Protection Clause of the Fourteenth Amendment.

While *Gray* v. *Sanders* was a voting case, not an apportionment case, the standard of "one person, one vote" had obvious relevance for legislative districting. However, there were many who expected that the Court would apply this rule to only one house of bicameral state legislatures, leaving room for other principles in the makeup of the second house. But on June 15, 1964, in *Reynolds* v. *Sims* and fourteen companion cases the Supreme Court confounded these expectations and made "one man, one vote" the constitutional rule for both houses. The legislatures of all fifteen states under review were declared unconstitutional by the Court, with varying majorities of from six to eight justices, because of substantial violations of the one-man, one-vote standard.

Chief Justice Warren wrote the opinion of the Court in all of these cases. He started with "the basic standard of equality among voters," as established in *Gray* v. *Sanders* and supported by general principles of representative government, majority rule, and equal protection of the laws. Representative government, the Chief Justice said, "is in essence self-government through the medium of elected representatives of the people, and each and every citizen has an inalienable right to full and effective participation in the political processes of his State's legislative bodies." He rejected any sophisticated notions about representation. "Legislators represent people, not trees or acres. Legislators are elected by voters, not farms or cities or economic interests."

The principle of representative government is majority rule, Warren went on. It is logical and reasonable "that a majority of the people of a State could elect a majority of that State's legislature. To conclude differently, and to sanction minority control of state legislative bodies, would appear to deny majority rights in a way that far surpasses any possible denial of minority rights that might otherwise be thought to result." The Chief Justice was of course not insensitive to minority rights, but he thought that "our constitutional system amply provides for the protection of minorities by means other than giving them majority control of state legislatures."

The principle of equality Warren believed to be essential to both representative government and majority rule. No one would argue that some voters could vote two, five, or ten times for state legislators, or that votes of certain citizens should be given a weight of two, five, or ten times that of voters in other areas. But this is what happens when legislative districting schemes "give the same number of representatives to unequal numbers of constituents. . . . To the extent that a citizen's right to vote is debased, he is that much less a citizen."

The Supreme Court firmly rejected the idea that the rule of equality might be applied to only one house of a bicameral legislature. The right to equal representation in one house, Warren said, "would amount to little if States

could effectively submerge the equal-population principle in the apportionment of seats in the other house." The two houses might compromise on some issues, but "in all too many cases the more probable result would be frustration of the majority will through minority veto in the house not apportioned on a population basis."

The Court rejected any analogy between state legislatures and the Congress, where the Senate represents states and the House population. Warren found the federal analogy "inapposite and irrelevant to state legislative and districting schemes," little more than an "after-the-fact rationalization offered in defense of maladjusted state apportionment arrangements."

The system of representation in the federal Congress, the Chief Justice noted, was the fruit of a compromise between the larger and smaller states which averted a deadlock in the Constitutional Convention. It arose from "unique historical circumstances . . . based on the consideration that in establishing our type of federalism a group of formerly independent states bound themselves together under one national government." At the heart of the federal system remains the concept of "separate and distinct entities which have delegated some, but not all, of their formerly held powers to the single national government." In contrast, "political subdivisions of states— counties, cities, or whatever—never were and never have been considered as sovereign entities," but only as "subordinate governmental instrumentalities created by the State to assist in the carrying out of state governmental functions."

Another objection which the Court had to meet was that the value of bicameral legislatures would be destroyed if both houses had the same representation base. But one of the principal purposes of a two-house system, to prevent precipitate action and to insure deliberation in consideration of legislative measures, is not affected at all by the Court's ruling. Moreover, it is still possible for different constituencies to be represented in the two houses. As the Chief Justice said:

> One body could be composed of single-member districts while the other could have at least some multimember districts. The length of terms of the legislators in the separate bodies could differ. The numerical size of the two bodies could be made to differ, even significantly, and the geographical size of districts from which legislators are elected could also be made to differ. And apportionment in one house could be arranged so as to balance off minor inequities in the representation of certain areas in the other house.

The Court made it clear that it did not mean to impose impractically strict requirements. What was required of each state was that it make "an honest and good faith effort to construct districts, in both houses of its legislature, as nearly of equal population as is practicable." Mathematical exactness was not intended. Further, the states might use political subdivision lines in drawing districts, "so long as the resulting apportionment was one based substantially on population and the equal-population prin-

ciple was not diluted in any significant way." In fact, "a State can rationally consider according political subdivisions some independent representation in at least one body of the state legislature, as long as the basic standard of equality of population among districts is maintained." In general, "so long as the divergences from a strict population standard are based on legitimate considerations incident to the effectuation of a rational state policy, some deviations from the equal-population principle are constitutionally permissible." But "neither history alone, nor economic or other sorts of group interests," nor considerations of area alone, "are permissible factors in attempting to justify disparities from population-based representation."

Justices Stewart and Clark, who had been part of the majorities in *Baker* and *Gray,* dissented. For Justice Stewart the holding that both houses of a bicameral state legislature must be apportioned on a population basis represented "the uncritical, simplistic, and heavy-handed application of sixth-grade arithmetic." The true view of representative theory was that it must accommodate "the interests and aspirations of diverse groups of people, without subjecting any group or class to absolute domination by a geographically concentrated or highly organized majority. Representative government is a process of accommodating group interests through democratic institutional arrangements." Toward this end population factors have often been "to some degree . . . subordinated . . . to achieve the important goal of ensuring a fair, effective, and balanced representation of the regional, social, and economic interests within a State."

Justice Stewart believed that any plan which "reasonably achieves" such balanced representation of interests "without sacrificing the principle of effective majority rule" could not be considered unconstitutional. He concluded:

> I think that the Equal Protection Clause demands but two basic attributes of any plan of state legislative apportionment. First, it demands that, in the light of the state's own characteristics and needs, the plan must be a rational one. Secondly, it demands that a plan must be such as not to permit the systematic frustration of the will of a majority of the electorate of the State.

On this latter point, Stewart suggested that a liberal arrangement for use of the initiative and referendum in approving or reviewing apportionment plans should be regarded as an acceptable guarantee against frustration of the basic principle of majority rule.

Application of this twofold test led Stewart and Clark to uphold the legislative apportionments of New York, Colorado, Illinois, and Michigan, all of which were condemned by the Court majority as violative of one man, one vote. In addition, Stewart alone would have approved the Ohio apportionment. The Stewart-Clark standard gave the same result as one man, one vote in the ten other states which the Court considered in the spring of 1964.[21]

[21] In four of these cases, however, Justice Stewart voted to remand for further proceedings.

The other dissenter, Justice Harlan, continued the vehement opposition he had expressed in *Baker* and *Gray*. The bulk of his opinion was devoted to two points. The first was the inapplicability of the equal protection clause to representation matters. He contended that section 2 of the Fourteenth Amendment, authorizing Congress to reduce the representation in the House of states which deny or abridge the right to vote, was the sole remedy intended for representation errors, and that there was no thought when the amendment was adopted of controlling the elective franchise by section 1. Bringing state legislative apportionment under the purview of the equal protection clause, he charged, "amounts to nothing less than an exercise of the amending power by this Court." [22]

Harlan's second major point was that giving courts the "blanket authority and the constitutional duty to supervise apportionment" was an "intolerable and inappropriate interference . . . with the independent legislatures of the States." Since he first registered his opposition to such judicial involvement in the *Baker* case, there had been two years of experience with court-threatened or court-ordered reapportionments, and Harlan recounted a number of these instances. He concluded: "They present a jarring picture of courts threatening to take action in an area which they have no business entering, inevitably on the basis of political judgments which they are incompetent to make. They show legislatures of the State meeting in haste and deliberating and deciding in haste to avoid the threat of judicial interference."

The process which Justice Harlan described of course continued with even greater vigor after the *Reynolds* decision, but not all judgments on its success are as harsh as his. Although no detailed account can be attempted here, within two years after *Reynolds* the great majority of state legislatures had been reapportioned on something close to a one-man, one-vote basis, sometimes by uncoerced legislative action, sometimes by legislatures acting under court orders, and in a few instances by direct court action.

The Supreme Court's decisions in *Baker* v. *Carr* and subsequent cases were surprisingly popular, considering the drastic remedies they imposed, and the opposition was never able to organize effective resistance in Congress. The principal effort was the Dirksen Amendment, offered in 1965 and 1966. It would have required one house of a bicameral state legislature to be apportioned on the basis of population, but would have permitted the other house to be apportioned "among the people on the bases of population, geography, and political subdivisions in order to insure effective representation in the State's legislature of the various groups and interests making up the electorate." The Dirksen Amendment was defeated in the Senate in

[22] Justice Harlan's position on this issue is effectively rebutted by William W. Van Alstyne, "The Fourteenth Amendment, the 'Right' to Vote, and the Understanding of the Thirty-ninth Congress," in Philip B. Kurland (ed.), *The Supreme Court Review: 1965* (Chicago: The University of Chicago Press, 1965), pp. 33–86.

1965, when it failed by seven votes to get the two-thirds majority needed, and it lost again in the 1966 session by the same margin.

It remains for the future to determine how much further the Supreme Court may be drawn into the task of supervising state legislative districting to enforce the rule of equal protection.[23] Districts can be roughly equal in population, yet gerrymandered so as to produce grossly unfair electoral results. The Court has not yet indicated whether one man, one vote requires it to deal with this problem, though if the gerrymandering had a racial basis it would undoubtedly do so.[24] In *Fortson* v. *Dorsey* (1965) the Court declined to invalidate a Georgia multimember constituency apportionment scheme, alleged to have been adopted for the purpose of minimizing the strength of racial and political minorities in large urban counties, on the ground that these allegations had not been proved. Again, in *Burns* v. *Richardson* (1966) the Court held that multimember constituencies in Hawaii would not be invalidated unless it could be proved that they effected an invidious result. The Court here reiterated that legislative reapportionment was primarily a matter for legislative determination, with the courts intervening only after the legislatures, given adequate opportunity, had failed to reapportion according to constitutional requisites.[25]

[23] In *Scott* v. *Germano* (1965) the Court, announcing a policy of encouraging state action in apportionment matters, directed the federal district court to vacate its reapportionment decree for Illinois and fix a time limit for state agencies to establish a valid plan to be utilized in the next election. In *Swann* v. *Adams* (1967) the Court reversed a Florida apportionment where there were variations of 30 per cent among Senate districts and 40 per cent among House districts, on the ground that both the state and federal district court had failed "to articulate acceptable reasons for the variations." A Texas reapportionment statute was invalidated in *Kilgarlin* v. *Hill* (1967).

Supervision of reapportionment continued to be an active concern of the Court during the 1967–1968 term. In *Rockefeller* v. *Wells* (1967) the Court affirmed a lower court ruling that New York's congressional districts must be reapportioned before the 1968 election, and in *Lucas* v. *Rhodes* (1967) the Court summarily reversed a lower court decision which had upheld Ohio's 1964 congressional redistricting law. Congressional redistricting in Florida and Massachusetts was affirmed in *Kirk* v. *Gong* (1968) and *Dinis* v. *Volpe* (1968).

[24] In *Sims* v. *Baggett* (1965) a federal district court rejected an Alabama House reapportionment, because of systematic and intentional dilution of Negro voting power.

[25] In *Avery* v. *Midland County* (1968) the Court applied the rule of one-man, one-vote to local governments, holding that where county, city, or town governments elect their representatives from single-member districts, the districts must be substantially equal in population. The vote was 5 to 3, with Justice White writing the majority opinion. In this county there were five county commissioners, only one of whom was elected from the city of Midland, which had 95 per cent of the county's population. Justice Harlan, dissenting, said: "I continue to think that these adventures of the Court in the realm of political science are beyond its constitutional powers." In an earlier case, *Sailors* v. *Board of Education of Kent County* (1967), the Court held that the functions of a county board of education were essentially administrative rather than legislative and that consequently there was no constitutional objection to a system whereby each local school board, regardless of population in its area, had one vote on the county board. See also *Dusch* v. *Davis* (1967).

In *Fortson* v. *Morris* (1966) the Court declined by a vote of five to four to apply the rule of one man, one vote to a disputed election for governor in Georgia. The state constitution provided that in case no candidate received a majority in the gubernatorial election, the state Legislature should make the choice from between the two highest candidates. In the 1966 election the Republican, Callaway, led his Democratic opponent, Maddox, by 1,850 votes, but secured only 47 per cent of the total vote, because of a third candidate.

The federal district court held that legislative election of the governor would violate the reasoning of the Georgia county-unit case, *Gray* v. *Sanders,* and this position was supported by four members of the Supreme Court, including Justice Douglas, who wrote the *Gray* opinion. However, Justice Black for the majority ruled that *Gray* was only a "voting case," and had no relation to how a state should elect its governors.

Justice Fortas for the dissenters argued that *Fortson* was also a voting case and that under *Gray* v. *Sanders,* "the Equal Protection Clause is violated when persons are elected to statewide office on a basis other than their receiving more votes than their rivals." Interestingly enough, Fortas connected the voting rights cases with the republican form of government provision: "They represent . . . an acknowledgement that the Republican form of government guaranteed by the Constitution, read in light of the General Welfare Clause, the guaranties of equal protection of the laws and the privileges and immunities of citizens of the United States, requires something more than an adherence to form." This is the closest the Court has come to judicial interpretation and enforcement of the republican form of government guarantee.

A representation issue of a quite different sort from the apportionment problems previously discussed was presented in *Bond* v. *Floyd* (1966). Julian Bond, a Negro and an official of the Student Nonviolent Coordinating Committee, was twice denied the seat to which he had been elected in the Georgia Legislature, because of statements he had made seeming to support SNCC opposition to the war in Vietnam and opposition to the draft. Bond was prepared to take the required oath to support the federal and state constitutions, and he met the other stated qualifications, but the Legislature excluded him on the ground that his remarks showed he could not take the oath "in good faith."

The Supreme Court unanimously held that Bond was entitled to his seat, relying primarily on First Amendment grounds. The oath requirement, said Chief Justice Warren,

> . . . does not authorize a majority of state legislators to test the sincerity with which another duly elected legislator can swear to uphold the Constitution. Such a power could be utilized to restrict the right of legislators to dissent from national or state policy or that of a majority of their colleagues under the guise of judging their loyalty to the Constitution.

The state agreed that Bond's statements would not have violated the law if made by a private citizen, but contended that a stricter standard could be applied to legislators. Warren rejoined: "The manifest function of the First Amendment in a representative government requires that legislators be given the widest latitude to express their views on issues of policy."

## CONTROL OVER TERRITORIES

Jefferson's doubts about the authority of the federal government to acquire new territory are well known. In making the Louisiana Purchase he felt he had been justified in seizing the opportunity to protect American rights to the Mississippi waterway, but for future defense of the Constitution he requested Congress to propose a formal amendment. No such action has ever been taken, and few have thought this course necessary. John Marshall supplied the constitutional justification for the acquisition of new domain when he held in 1828: "The Constitution confers absolutely upon the government of the Union, the powers of making war, and of making treaties; consequently, that government possesses the power of acquiring territory, either by conquest or by treaty." [26]

Marshall might reasonably have construed at least two other provisions of the Constitution as conferring the right to increase the territory of the United States: the power of Congress to admit new states and to govern territory. There is also the fact that the United States as a sovereign nation has the same rights under international law to obtain new land as any other nation.[27] The Supreme Court has long treated the matter as completely closed.

In contrast, the power of Congress to "dispose" of territory is explicitly written into the Constitution.[28] With the possible exception of the Webster-Ashburton Treaty, this power has been exercised only in the granting of independence to the Philippine Islands and in minor leasing alterations with Panama in the Canal Zone area.

Article IV, section 3, gives Congress power to "make all needful rules and regulations" respecting territories of the United States. This is a plenary grant of authority, and in its exercise Congress may act with full national and local sovereignty.[29] Congressional power is not wholly unlimited, however. In *The Insular Cases* (1901)[30] a badly divided Supreme Court made a distinction between territories which were "incorporated" and those which were "unincorporated." In the former, which are supposedly destined for statehood, Congress must accord all the rights and privileges of the Constitution except those clearly applicable only to state citizens, such as par-

---

[26] *American Insurance Co.* v. *Canter* (1828).
[27] See *Jones* v. *United States* (1890).
[28] Art. IV, sec. 3.
[29] *First National Bank* v. *Yankton County* (1880); *Simms* v. *Simms* (1899).
[30] *DeLima* v. *Bidwell* (1901); *Downes* v. *Bidwell* (1901).

ticipation in a national election. In the "unincorporated" areas, however, it is mandatory only that "fundamental" rights be guaranteed. Since the admission of Alaska and Hawaii as states, there are no longer any "incorporated" territories.

The District of Columbia has a distinctive and unique status. By Article I, section 8, Congress has power of "exclusive legislation" in the District. Though the District was allowed home rule prior to 1874, it was thereafter completely deprived of any right to control its own affairs. To all intents and purposes it was governed by the House and Senate committees on the District of Columbia, with three presidentially appointed commissioners administering the local government.

A long succession of efforts to restore to the District's residents, a majority of whom are Negroes, the right to elect their own governmental officials failed in Congress; but in 1967 President Johnson effectively bypassed Southern and conservative opposition by presenting to Congress a reorganization plan giving the District at least the structure of representative government in lieu of outright home rule. This plan, which Congress approved in August, 1967, authorized the President to appoint a commissioner as chief executive of the District and a nine-member city council. President Johnson appointed a Negro to the post of commissioner and five Negroes to the council.

Surprisingly, the House followed up this move in September, 1967, by voting 324 to 3 to give District residents the right to elect their school board, and began consideration of a constitutional amendment providing full representation (one representative and two senators) for the District in Congress. The Twenty-third Amendment, adopted in 1961, had already granted voters of the District the right to vote in presidential elections. It now seems only a matter of time before the District will become a fully self-governing unit. A large federal subsidy to the District will always be necessary because of the great amount of tax-exempt federal property there, which will ensure some continuing congressional responsibility for District affairs.

Puerto Rico is in a category by itself. In 1950 Congress proposed through Public Law 600 a "compact" between Puerto Rico and the United States whereby Puerto Rico would adopt a constitution acceptable to Congress, and would then assume a "Commonwealth" status. Only two advance restrictions were placed on this constitution: that it provide for a republican form of government and that it contain a bill of rights. This compact arrangement was approved by referendum vote, and a constitution was subsequently drafted. With only minor changes Congress gave its consent to this document as the fundamental law of Puerto Rico.

The constitution is much like that of the United States, providing for popular elections, separation of powers, a bicameral legislature, judicial review, and an enumeration of certain guaranteed rights, including a maximum working day of no more than eight hours unless overtime pay is given.

Two of the more interesting stipulations are abolition of capital punishment and provision for jury decisions by a majority of nine rather than by unanimous vote.

Most federal laws do not apply in Puerto Rico, but Congress can pass legislation specifically applicable there. Puerto Ricans do not pay federal income tax, and Congress has given the island certain tax advantages. Puerto Ricans are of course American citizens and can move freely between Puerto Rico and the United States.

Under this Commonwealth status, control over Puerto Rico's foreign policy remains with the United States. In addition to conforming to the Puerto Rican constitution, local legislation must also conform to the terms of Public Law 600, the law approving the Puerto Rican constitution, and the applicable provisions of the United States Constitution. Appellate jurisdiction over the decisions of the Puerto Rican supreme court is exercised by the Court of Appeals for the First Circuit in cases involving the writ of habeas corpus or questions of federal law. It is very probable that island court determinations of local law will be treated as final.

Theoretically, Congress could at any time revoke the compact entered into with Puerto Rico and resume direct rule over the island, but such action is most unlikely. In a 1967 referendum 60.5 per cent of Puerto Ricans voting favored a continuation of commonwealth status, but there was a surprisingly large vote (39 per cent) for statehood, a status which would give full representation in Congress but make Puerto Ricans liable for federal income tax. There is also fairly strong sentiment for independence among intellectuals and radicals, who boycotted the referendum.

There are certain other territories in the possession of the United States. The Virgin Islands and Guam have a large measure of self-government, though their governors are appointed from Washington. Their residents have full rights of American citizenship. The residents of Samoa, however, are classed as American "nationals," a condition less than full citizenship but involving allegiance to the United States and the obligation of protection by the American government. Certain former Japanese islands in the Pacific—the Marianas, Marshalls, and Carolines—are held by the United States under the supervision of the United Nations. The Panama Canal Zone is a strip of land on either side of the Canal which the United States controls under treaty with Panama.

## SELECTED REFERENCES

ANDERSON, WILLIAM A., *The Nations and the States: Rivals or Partners?* Minneapolis: The University of Minnesota Press, 1955.

AUERBACH, CARL A., "The Reapportionment Cases: One Person, One Vote—One

Vote, One Value," in Philip B. Kurland (ed.), *The Supreme Court Review: 1964*, pp. 1–88. Chicago: The University of Chicago Press, 1964.

BAKER, GORDON E., *The Reapportionment Revolution*. New York: Random House, Inc., 1966.

BOYD, WILLIAM J. D., *Changing Patterns of Apportionment*. New York: National Municipal League, 1965.

Commission on Intergovernmental Relations, *Report to the President*. Washington: Government Printing Office, 1955.

*The Constitution of the United States of America: Analysis and Interpretation*, Sen. Doc. no. 39, 88th Cong., pp. 787–796. Washington: Government Printing Office, 1964.

CORWIN, EDWARD S., *The Commerce Power versus States Rights*, chap. 5. Princeton, N.J.: Princeton University Press, 1936.

——, "The Passing of Dual Federalism," in Robert G. McCloskey (ed.), *Essays in Constitutional Law*, pp. 185–210. New York: Alfred A. Knopf, Inc., 1957.

CROSSKEY, WILLIAM W., *Politics and the Constitution in the History of the United States*, chaps. 23, 24. Chicago: The University of Chicago Press, 1953.

ELAZAR, DANIEL J., *American Federalism: A View from the States*. New York: Thomas Y. Crowell Company, 1966.

GOLDWIN, ROBERT A. (ed.), *A Nation of States: Essays on the American Federal System*. Chicago: Rand McNally & Company, 1963.

——, *Representation and Misrepresentation*. Chicago: Rand McNally & Company, 1968.

GRODZINS, MORTON, *The American System: A New View of Government in the United States*. Chicago: Rand McNally & Company, 1966.

HANSON, ROYCE, *The Political Thicket: Reapportionment and Constitutional Democracy*. Englewood Cliffs, N.J.: Prentice-Hall, Inc., 1966.

"Interposition vs. Judicial Power," 1 *Race Relations Law Reporter* 465–499 (April, 1956).

JEWELL, MALCOLM E. (ed.), *The Politics of Reapportionment*. New York: The Atherton Press, 1962.

KELLY, ALFRED H., and WINFRED A. HARBISON, *The American Constitution: Its Origins and Development*, chaps. 12, 14–16. New York: W. W. Norton & Company, Inc., 1963 (third edition).
1957.

KILPATRICK, JAMES J., *The Sovereign States*. Chicago: Henry Regnery Company,

MACMAHON, ARTHUR W. (ed.), *Federalism, Mature and Emergent*. Garden City, N.Y.: Doubleday & Company, Inc., 1955.

MAGRUDER, CALVERT, "The Commonwealth Status of Puerto Rico," 15 *University of Pittsburgh Law Review* 1–33 (Fall, 1953).

MC CLOSKEY, ROBERT G., "The Reapportionment Case," 76 *Harvard Law Review* 54–74 (1962).

MC KAY, ROBERT B., *Reapportionment: The Law and Politics of Equal Representation*. New York: The Twentieth Century Fund, 1965.

NEAL, PHIL C., "Baker v. Carr: Politics in Search of Law," in Philip B. Kurland (ed.), *The Supreme Court Review: 1962*, pp. 252–327. Chicago: The University of Chicago Press, 1962.

PRITCHETT, C. HERMAN, "Equal Protection and the Urban Majority," 58 *American Political Science Review* 869–875 (1964).

RICH, BENNETT M., *The Presidents and Civil Disorder.* Washington, D.C.: The Brookings Institution, 1941.

RIKER, WILLIAM H., *Federalism: Origin, Operation, Significance.* Boston: Little, Brown and Company, 1964.

SCHMIDHAUSER, JOHN R., *The Supreme Court as Final Arbiter in Federal-State Relations, 1789–1957.* Chapel Hill, N.C.: The University of North Carolina Press, 1958.

SCHUBERT, GLENDON, *Reapportionment.* New York: Charles Scribner's Sons, 1965.

SHAPIRO, MARTIN, *Law and Politics in the Supreme Court,* chap. 5. New York: The Free Press of Glencoe, 1964.

WHEARE, KENNETH C., *Federal Government.* Fair Lawn, N.J.: Oxford University Press, 1964 (fourth edition).

WHITE, LEONARD D., *The States and the Nation.* Baton Rouge, La.: Louisiana State University Press, 1953.

# 6

## Interstate relations

Federalism is characterized not only by the vertical relationships between nation and state examined in the preceding chapter, but also by horizontal contacts between state and state. The Constitution foresaw five kinds of interstate problems and adopted language for handling them.

### INTERSTATE PRIVILEGES AND IMMUNITIES

Article IV, section 2, provides: "The citizens of each state shall be entitled to all privileges and immunities of citizens in the several states." There is no definition of the privileges and immunities to which citizens in the several states are entitled. Neither is it made clear whether the citizen is entitled to these privileges in his own state, or when he is temporarily in other states, or both. Nor is any test of state citizenship suggested.

The idea for this provision clearly came from the Articles of Confederation, which guaranteed to "the free inhabitants of each of these states, . . . all privileges and immunities of free citizens in the several states." But in the Articles there was the additional and somewhat more specific provision: "The people of each state shall have free ingress and regress to and from any other state, and shall enjoy therein all the privileges of trade and commerce, subject to the same duties, impositions and restrictions as the inhabitants thereof respectively." The records of the Convention throw no

light on what was intended by the clause that was written into the Constitution, nor does there appear to have been any significant discussion of it during the ratification campaign. Thus it was left to judicial construction to determine its meaning.

The earliest effort at interpretation was that of Justice Bushrod Washington, sitting in federal circuit court in the case of *Corfield* v. *Coryell* (1823). A New Jersey statute prohibited any person who was not an actual inhabitant or resident of New Jersey from gathering oysters in the state. Was this statute in conflict with Article IV, section 2? Washington decided that it was not. The privileges and immunities which the Constitution protects, said Washington, are those "which are, in their nature, fundamental; which belong, of right, to the citizens of all free governments." The justice thought it would "be more tedious than difficult" to enumerate these rights, but then risked tedium by suggesting quite a list, including the right of a citizen of one state to pass through, or reside in, other states for purposes of trade or profession; the right to institute and maintain court actions; exemption from higher taxes than are paid by other citizens of the state; and the elective franchise, as regulated by the laws of the state in which it is exercised.

The effect of the privileges and immunities clause, then, is to forbid any state to discriminate against citizens of other states in favor of its own citizens with respect to these "fundamental" rights. As Justice Miller said in the *Slaughter-House Cases* (1873), the purpose of the clause was "to declare to the several States, that whatever these rights, as you grant or establish them to your own citizens, or as you limit or qualify, or impose restrictions on their exercise, the same, neither more nor less, shall be the measure of the rights of citizens of other States within your jurisdiction."

However, Article IV, section 2, does not preclude a state from treating out-of-state citizens differently when there are acceptable reasons why the two groups should be placed on different footings. Technical requirements for access to the courts may be somewhat different for out-of-state than for local citizens.[1] The right to engage in normal businesses is protected, but the practice of certain professions connected with the public interest, such as medicine or law, can be restricted by individual states, and persons who pursue these professions must prove to the state government competence in their fields.

In addition, some public rights do not accrue to a citizen who moves across a state line. For example, a state can limit the right to vote to its own citizens. The privilege of sharing in the use of public property may be denied to nonresidents, as in *Corfield* v. *Coryell*, or offered at a higher rate than that charged local citizens. Thus tuition in state universities is usually lower for state citizens than for outsiders. Wildlife was once considered to be part of the public trust administered by the state for all of its citizens,[2] but more

---

[1] *Ward* v. *Maryland* (1871); *Miles* v. *Illinois Central Rr.* (1942).
[2] *Geer* v. *Connecticut* (1896).

recently the ownership doctrine has been labeled as a mere "fiction expressive in legal shorthand of the importance to its people that a State have power to preserve and regulate the exploitation of an important resource." [3] This power of regulation must not be exercised unfairly where the differentiation rests solely on out-of-state citizenship. Higher fees for hunting or fishing in the case of outsiders can be justified on the ground that local citizens pay additional taxes which are used in part for the upkeep of the public domain, or the state may show that there is an added cost in enforcing its police regulations against people who live outside the state.

*Toomer* v. *Witsell* (1948) furnishes an interesting illustration of this problem. South Carolina had undertaken to conserve the shrimp in the marginal sea off its coasts by imposing a licensing fee of $2,500 on out-of-state trawlers, while the fee for its own citizens was only $25. The Supreme Court found this to be a clear violation of the privileges and immunities clause. The Court also rejected the contention that free-swimming fish within the 3-mile limit might be considered as state property and as such subject to whatever regulations South Carolina might impose. Commercial shrimping was held to be one of the "common callings" which were protected by Article IV, section 2. Similarly an Alaska statute imposing a $50 licensing fee for nonresident commercial fishermen compared with $5 for local citizens, was held to be unjustified in *Mullaney* v. *Anderson* (1952).

In *New York* v. *O'Neill* (1959) a rather burdensome law was upheld because it was not discriminatory. Some forty-two states, including Florida, had adopted a uniform reciprocal state law to secure the attendance of witnesses in criminal proceedings. A citizen of Illinois, while attending a convention in Florida, was summoned to appear at a hearing for determination as to whether he should be surrendered to a New York officer and taken to New York, at that state's expense, where his testimony was wanted in a court proceeding. Two dissenting justices thought this was an interference with a privilege of national citizenship of free ingress and egress, but the Court supported the law as a useful example of "free-willed collaboration of independent states."

### FULL FAITH AND CREDIT

Article IV, section 1, commands that each state accord full faith and credit to three types of official acts of sister states: public records, statutes, and court decisions. Congress is given power to issue uniform regulations for authentication of the legal papers which deserve such recognition, and to determine the precise effect to be given such documents. Even without this explicit requirement some obligation of the sort would have existed under the doctrine of comity in international law. As a demonstration of friendship, nations customarily recognize as valid the public proceedings of other coun-

[3] *Toomer* v. *Witsell* (1948).

tries, provided there is no contrary local policy. The Constitution, however, removes the matter of faith and credit from considerations of mutual courtesy and amity and makes it a legal duty enforceable in federal courts.

JUDICIAL PROCEEDINGS    Under authority of the full faith and credit clause Congress passed legislation in 1790 and 1804, providing a simple method of authentication and commanding that judicial proceedings and public records be given the same effect in every court that they had in the court which issued them. Because of these explicit provisions the matter of according full faith and credit to judicial acts is relatively uncomplicated, except in divorce cases, which are considered below. In 1813 a young attorney named Francis Scott Key argued before the  Supreme Court that the obligation imposed by Article IV had been met when a state merely received a sister-state judgment as evidence and weighed it with the other evidence in the case. The Court, however, rejected this contention and held that a judgment conclusive in one state must be recognized as final in all others.[4]

This conclusiveness is not automatic. A person who has secured a court order in one state and wishes to have it enforced against a person who has since gone to another state must bring a new legal action in the latter state. In this action the court will accept the original decree, examine it, and if it finds the order to be properly authenticated, will issue an enforcement order of its own. This must be done even if the public policy of the second state would not have permitted such a decision had the case originated there. The defendant may appear in court and contest the order. He may not, however, reargue the merits of the case. The only valid line of attack open to him is the claim that the court where the original decree was handed down did not have proper jurisdiction over either the parties or the subject matter involved in the dispute.

A second situation in which the full faith and credit clause applies to judicial proceedings occurs where a judgment of a court in one state is offered *in defense* against a new proceeding in another state growing out of the same facts that were involved in the original suit. An illustration would be supplied where a decree of divorce granted in one state was offered as a bar to a divorce suit by the other party to the marriage in a second state. Because of the lenient divorce laws in some states, particularly Nevada and Florida, a major problem has arisen as to whether other states are required to give full faith and credit to these "quickie" divorces.

Historically a divorce suit has been treated as an action *in rem*, that is, a proceeding against the marriage status. A court must have jurisdiction over the marriage status in order to grant a divorce decree, and the test of jurisdiction has been domicile. Where both parties were domiciled in the same state, there could of course be no question about the jurisdiction of courts in that state. The full faith and credit problem arose where the hus-

[4] *Mills* v. *Duryee* (1813).

band and wife were domiciled in different states, and where the plaintiff brought the divorce suit in the state of his or her domicile. What is the obligation of courts in the state of the defendant's domicile, or courts in states other than the two states of domicile, to recognize the validity of such a divorce?

The rule prevailing up to 1906 is illustrated by the case of *Atherton* v. *Atherton* (1901), which held that, where husband and wife are domiciled in different states, a decree granted in either state is to be given full faith and credit. The virtue of the *Atherton* doctrine was its certainty. A divorce granted in a state where the plaintiff was domiciled was valid in all states, even if the defendant had no personal service (i.e., notice of the suit) and was not represented in court. The objection to the *Atherton* doctrine was that it permitted ex parte divorces, that is, divorces in which only one party to the marriage was in court. Justice Jackson once said that to him the notion of an ex parte divorce was as perverse and unrealistic as ex parte marriage.[5]

In *Haddock* v. *Haddock* (1906) the Supreme Court upset the certainty of *Atherton*. A husband, having transferred his residence from New York to Connecticut, brought suit for divorce there against his wife who had remained in New York. The Supreme Court held this suit to be one *in personam*, i.e., against the wife rather than against the marriage status, and consequently personal service or her voluntary appearance in court was required. Since neither had been had, the decree was ineffective as to the wife in the state of her domicile. Nevertheless, the Court held that a state had the inherent power to determine the marital status of its own citizens, and consequently ruled that the husband's divorce was effective in his home state. The result of this holding was that the Haddocks, when both were in Connecticut, were divorced; when both were in New York, were married; and when the husband was in Connecticut and the wife in New York, he was legally single and she was still married. A later comment by Justice Jackson also seems appropriate to this situation: "If there is one thing that the people are entitled to expect from their lawmakers, it is rules of law that will enable individuals to tell whether they are married and, if so, to whom." [6]

Fortunately much of the confusion inherent in this situation was eliminated by the sensible action of most of the states in recognizing out-of-state divorces as a matter of comity. Moreover, for a considerable period there appeared to be no disposition to question the power of each state to determine for itself what should constitute domicile for divorce purposes. In 1942, however, the lax Nevada domicile requirement of only six weeks was responsible for the case of *Williams* v. *North Carolina*. Two residents of North Carolina, which has relatively rigid divorce laws, went to Nevada, lived in a tourist court for six weeks, shed their respective spouses, married each other, and then returned to North Carolina. That state refused to recog-

---

[5] *Rice* v. *Rice* (1949).
[6] *Estin* v. *Estin* (1948).

nize the validity of the Nevada divorce, and brought bigamy charges against the couple. They were convicted on the ground that the Nevada divorce had no effect in North Carolina because adequate notice of the proceedings had not been given to the North Carolina spouses, under the *Haddock* doctrine.

A divided Supreme Court reversed this finding by overruling *Haddock* v. *Haddock.* The majority was disturbed about the possibility that a person could be "a bigamist for living in one state with the only one with whom the other state would permit him lawfully to live." The *Williams* decision held that the "substituted service" here employed met the requirements of due process. The divorce decree was thus "wholly effective" in Nevada to change the marital status of the two couples, and the full faith and credit clause required other states to recognize this change, even though it might conflict with their public policy. "Such is part of the price of our federal system," said Justice Douglas.

The state court conviction had not been based on a contention that there was no bona fide domicile in Nevada, and consequently the Supreme Court had no occasion to examine this issue in the first *Williams* decision. However, North Carolina, rebuffed in its first attempt, brought another bigamy prosecution (in spite of the fact that one of the home-staying spouses had died and the other had remarried), this time alleging that the Nevada domicile was a sham, and consequently that North Carolina was under no obligation to recognize the decrees. In this second proceeding, *Williams* v. *North Carolina* (1945), the Supreme Court, still divided, upheld the right of North Carolina courts to decide for themselves, before recognizing the validity of an out-of-state divorce, whether residents of the state had established a bona fide domicile outside the state.

For the majority, Justice Frankfurter contended that "the decree of divorce is a conclusive adjudication of everything except the jurisdictional facts upon which it is founded, and domicil is a jurisdictional fact. To permit the necessary finding of domicil by one State to foreclose all States in the protection of their social institutions would be intolerable." Justice Rutledge, one of three dissenters, rejoined: "I do not believe the Constitution has thus confided to the caprice of juries the faith and credit due the laws and judgments of sister states. . . . Were all judgments given the same infirmity, the full faith and credit clause would be only a dead constitutional letter."

Subsequent to the second *Williams* decision, the Court sought to restore some measure of stability to the situation by holding that if the question of bona fide residence was specifically argued in a court of one state, in a case where both parties to the marriage were before the court or represented by counsel, an assertion of jurisdiction by that court would not be reexamined in any court of another state.[7]

The net result of the *Williams* decisions is a recognition of the right of

[7] *Sherrer* v. *Sherrer* (1948); *Coe* v. *Coe* (1948).

any actual domiciliary state to grant ex parte divorces to which other states must accord full faith and credit. The Court, however, in its post-*Williams* phase has drawn back from some of the consequences of ex parte divorces, particularly as they affect property rights of the parties, alimony payments, or custody of children. In *Estin* v. *Estin* (1948), the wife received a separation order on grounds of desertion and an alimony award in New York. The next year the husband moved to Nevada and brought suit for divorce. The spouse was notified by constructive service, but entered no appearance, and Estin received an absolute divorce with no provision for alimony, though the Nevada court had been advised of the New York decree. When his ex-wife sued him in New York for nonpayment of alimony, Estin appeared and set up his Nevada decree as a defense. The New York courts admitted that Estin was a bona fide resident of Nevada, but held that the New York support order had survived the Nevada decree.

The Supreme Court, through Justice Douglas, agreed, on the ground that the divorce was "divisible"—effective as to marital status but ineffective on the issue of alimony. The New York judgment was a property interest created in a proceeding in which both parties participated. This property was an intangible, over which a court could have jurisdiction only by control over the owner. The debtor's state of domicile had no power to determine the personal rights of the creditor in the intangible unless the creditor had been personally served or appeared in the proceeding. As a matter of public policy, New York had a concern that the abandoned spouse not be left impoverished and perhaps become a public charge.

Justice Jackson, protesting this "Solomon-like conclusion," did not see how it could be *full* faith and credit to hold the Nevada decree half good and half bad. "It is good to free the husband from the marriage; it is not good to free him from its incidental obligations." But the Court has found the concept of divisible divorce decrees to be a useful one, and has continued to employ it for the purpose of achieving what it regards as desirable public policies.[8]

Thus the present situation is that an ex parte divorce, founded upon acquisition of domicile by one spouse in the state granting the divorce, effectively terminates the marital status of both parties in the domiciliary state and probably in all other states. However, such a divorce, though protecting against possible prosecutions for bigamy, does not necessarily alter rights as to property, alimony, or custody of children in the domiciliary state of a spouse who was not served personally and did not appear in court.

STATE LEGISLATION    The matter of the extrastate effect of state statutes has been less satisfactorily resolved than that of judgments or records. Not until 1948 did Congress legislate with respect to the full faith and credit

---

[8] See *Rice* v. *Rice* (1949); *Vanderbilt* v. *Vanderbilt* (1957); *Simons* v. *Miami Beach First National Bank* (1965).

to be given to state statutes, and this legislation has as yet had little impact. In general, no state is obliged to enforce the criminal laws of another state.[9] For other types of statutes, the general principle is that the full faith and credit clause does not abolish the dominance of local policy over the rules of comity. Thus the effect of the *Dred Scott* decision was that Scott, though he had become a free man during his residence in Illinois, where slavery did not exist, on his return to Missouri became subject to its local policy as stated in its laws and judicial decisions, and so reverted to slave status.[10]

Problems as to the extrastate effect of a state statute customarily arise when a statute of one state is set up as a defense to a suit brought under the statute of another state, or where a foreign statute is set up as a defense to a suit or proceeding under a local statute. The Supreme Court's practice in handling such conflicts was well summed up by Justice Stone in *Alaska Packers Association* v. *Industrial Accident Commission* (1935): "The conflict is to be resolved, not by giving automatic effect to the full faith and credit clause, compelling the courts of each state to subordinate its own statutes to those of the other, but by appraising the governmental interests of each jurisdiction, and turning the scale of decision according to their weight."

Cases involving the full faith and credit to be accorded statutes have arisen in three principal fields: commercial law, insurance, and workmen's compensation. A few examples from this third area will amply serve for illustrative purposes. Numerous states provide an "exclusive" statutory remedy in industrial accidents. But what happens if a workman employed under a contract entered into in such a state is injured in another state which has its own laws on the subject? Each state has an interest in the enforcement of its own public policy. In 1932 the Court ruled that the exclusive contract was entitled to be enforced if the state where the injury actually occurred had no other relationship to the parties.[11] But in 1939 the Court permitted the law of the "place of injury" state to prevail in *Pacific Employers Insurance Co.* v. *Industrial Accident Commission.* There a resident of Massachusetts normally employed in that state by a Massachusetts corporation was injured while working temporarily in California. The Massachusetts compensation act purported to provide an exclusive remedy for industrial accidents, even those occurring outside its borders, but California also had a compensation act fixing liability on employers regardless of any contract, rule, or regulation, and the California courts enforced it strictly. The Supreme Court held the exclusive requirement of the Massachusetts law was obnoxious to California policy, and would not be enforced.[12]

[9] *Huntington* v. *Attrill* (1892).
[10] *Dred Scott* v. *Sandford* (1857).
[11] *Bradford Electric Light Co.* v. *Clapper* (1932).
[12] See also *Carroll* v. *Lanza* (1955); *Crider* v. *Zurich Ins. Co.* (1965).

### RENDITION

The obvious gap in federalism caused by the fact that full faith and credit is never given by one state to another state's criminal laws is to a great extent closed by the obligation imposed by the command of Article IV, section 2, that: "A person charged in any state with treason, felony, or other crime, who shall flee from justice, and be found in another state, shall on demand of the executive authority of the state from which he fled, be delivered up, to be removed to the state having jurisdiction of the crime." Edmund Randolph, the first Attorney General of the United States, offered the opinion that this part of the Constitution was not self-executing. Accordingly, Congress in 1793 passed a statute affirming the obligation of a governor to surrender a fugitive from another state.

Under international law there is no right on the part of one nation to demand the return of a fugitive unless there is a treaty between the two countries providing for extradition. It is usual in such treaties for the crimes for which extradition can be requested to be specifically listed. Political offenses (that is, those against a particular government or governing group rather than against the state itself) are almost universally nonextraditable; nor will a nation usually extradite its own citizens. Moreover, a person extradited under a treaty arrangement can be tried only for the crime which was alleged in the request for surrender. If other charges are to be pressed against the prisoner, he must first be allowed to return to the country to which he had fled.

The Constitution states no such restrictions. It simply specifies that "fugitives" from justice shall be turned over to the demanding executive authority. The question whether certain crimes were excluded from rendition was raised on the very eve of the Civil War in *Kentucky* v. *Dennison* (1861). William Lago, a free Negro, had been indicted in Kentucky for assisting a slave to escape. To avoid trial Lago fled across the border to Ohio, and the Governor of Kentucky presented a request for Lago's return. Dennison, the Governor of Ohio, refused to comply on the ground that the crime in question was one which the Constitution had not meant to include.

Kentucky brought suit in the Supreme Court for a writ of mandamus to compel Dennison to perform his duty. The contention was that the Constitution had superseded the usual rules of comity which would have existed between independent nations and had imposed a "perfect obligation," leaving the states no discretion in the matter of rendition. Ohio answered by claiming that the Supreme Court had no jurisdiction to hear the case, since neither the federal government nor any of its branches could legally coerce the executive of a state or impose any duty upon him. Each state could determine with finality its obligations in regard to the return of fugitives.

The Supreme Court was aware of the political situation in March, 1861, and realized that a direct order to the Governor of Ohio would probably

be disobeyed. The tactics adopted by Chief Justice Taney were, first, to reject absolutely the contention that certain crimes were outside the purview of Article IV. Neither could Taney see any doubt that it was the duty of the Governor of Ohio to return the fugitive. The Governor could look no further than to see whether the fugitive had been charged with a crime in the regular course of judicial proceedings. His was a ministerial act which admitted of no discretion.

Then, having firmly established what was the law in the case, Taney began to extricate the Court from the position of having to issue an order which would be ignored. Whether the Court, Taney hedged, could command Governor Dennison to perform this function was an entirely different question. The statute of 1793 had not provided any means to compel the execution of the duty of rendition; nor could the federal government constitutionally coerce a state official. "Indeed, such a power would place every State under the control and dominion of the General Government." Although this is dubious doctrine so far as general nation-state relations are concerned, the rule of the *Dennison* case has been respected subsequently in rendition matters.

The refusal of a state to return a fugitive has at times met a counterattack less civilized than a lawsuit. In 1887 the Governor of Kentucky requested the Governor of West Virginia to return an accused murderer. When there was delay in granting the request, Kentucky sent an armed group across the border and forcibly brought the accused back for trial. In *Mahon* v. *Justice* (1888) the Supreme Court admitted that the abduction was a lawless act whose perpetrators West Virginia might punish if it ever caught them or if it could persuade Kentucky to extradite them. But the Court held that the jurisdiction of the Kentucky courts to try the prisoner was unaffected by the manner in which he had been brought to the bar of justice.

It should be emphasized that although governors occasionally refuse to return a fugitive, orderly rendition is the normal course of events. To eliminate serious breaches of justice Congress in 1934 exercised its power under the commerce clause to make it a federal offense for anyone to cross a state line fleeing from justice or for anyone to help another to do so. Since this act provides that the fugitive must be tried in the federal district court in the state from which he fled, the prisoner is readily available to local officials if the federal government does not complete its prosecution. Moreover, since 1936 over forty states have adopted a uniform criminal extradition act.

## INTERSTATE COMPACTS

In recent years there have been numerous protests against the centralizing tendencies of the federal government. One means to avoid concentration of power in Washington and to permit state handling of problems which ex-

tend beyond the borders of a single state has been the interstate compact. Initially this method was used to solve relatively minor issues, such as marking disputed land or water boundaries. In the twentieth century, however, the device has been more fully exploited. Compacts between states have regulated such diverse matters as conservation of natural resources in gas, oil, water, and timber; civil defense coordination for possible emergencies; mutual sharing of water power of large rivers; water and air pollution control; development of interstate metropolitan areas and interstate facilities such as bridges and harbors; regulation of ocean fisheries; and interstate programs of graduate and professional education.

Perhaps the most famous interstate compact has been that between New York and New Jersey which established the Port of New York Authority to develop and operate harbor and transportation facilities in the bistate area. In 1953 the same states signed another important compact regulating labor practices in the New York port area. Because of the evidence of crime and racketeering along the waterfront, the states agreed on a comprehensive set of regulations for licensing and employment on the docks. To enforce the terms of the agreement, the compact set up a two-man waterfront commission, with one member from each state. No person can work as a stevedore or longshoreman in the port area without securing a license from the commission.

Truly sovereign states would be at liberty to make treaties at will, but the Constitution imposes definite limitations on the states in this respect. Article I, section 10, clause 1, provides: "No state shall enter into any treaty, alliance, or confederation . . ." while the third clause of the same section stipulates that: "No state shall, without the consent of Congress . . . enter into any agreement or compact with another state, or with a foreign power." Obviously the justification for the interstate compact must be found in the uncertain distinction between "treaty" and "agreement or compact." Presumably this distinction is a political question for Congress to determine in giving its consent.

Although congressional consent to interstate compacts is required, there is no set formula as to when and how that approval should be registered. The assent may be given before or after the agreement; it may be explicit, implicit, or tacit.[13] Nor is there any form in which Congress must cast its approval. It may be done by specific statute, by a joint resolution, by ratification of a state constitution which contains such a compact, or by means of a compact between Congress and the states involved.[14] Congress may even extend blanket approval to future agreements in certain specified areas.

No case has arisen in which a compact has been held unconstitutional by the Supreme Court. Still there can be no doubt that interstate agreements must conform to the Constitution; otherwise the combined action of

[13] *Virginia* v. *Tennessee* (1893).
[14] *Burton's Lessee* v. *Williams* (1818).

two states and a congressional majority could amend the Constitution. The presidential veto is an added safety device to that supplied by the courts. On two occasions Franklin D. Roosevelt refused to approve congressional legislation which would have consented to state agreements, once when he thought that the advance approval was too broad, and again when he considered that federal jurisdiction was being infringed.

Once a state has formally ratified a compact and the approval of Congress has been obtained, the agreement is binding on the state and all its officers—executive, legislative, and judicial. A state cannot unilaterally declare that a compact is in violation of its constitution and use this as a basis for withdrawal.[15]


### DISPUTES BETWEEN STATES

There are, in general, three methods open to a nation in settling disputes with its neighbors: war, diplomacy, or submission of the controversy to some form of judicial determination. Under the Constitution only the last two methods are open to American states. Interstate diplomacy might terminate in an informal agreement between governors or in a full-fledged compact requiring the consent of Congress. Litigation between states is handled exclusively by the Supreme Court under its original jurisdiction, according to Article III, section 2, of the Constitution.

The Articles of Confederation made Congress the tribunal of last resort for interstate disputes and laid down elaborate provisions for the selection of a panel of impartial arbiters to hear the controversies. The Constitutional Convention discussed a similar proposal which would have given jurisdiction over territorial and jurisdictional disputes to the Senate, but finally decided that the scope of the federal judicial power would render this grant unnecessary.

The first question which the Supreme Court must answer in hearing a dispute between states is whether or not the matter is properly a controversy between states. This matter is not always so simple as it might appear at first glance. After the Civil War, Louisiana defaulted on certain state bonds and under the Eleventh Amendment she could not be sued without her consent by citizens of other states. A group of bondholders from New Hampshire tried to evade this provision by nominally transferring their holdings to New Hampshire and having that state bring suit against Louisiana for payment. The Court viewed this as a mere subterfuge and refused to decide the case.[16] However, some twenty years later South Dakota bondholders gave their state government full title to some North Carolina securities on which that state had defaulted. In this case the Supreme Court by a five to four vote held that there was an actual controversy between states and

[15] *West Virginia ex rel. Dyer* v. *Sims* (1951).
[16] *New Hampshire* v. *Louisiana* (1883).

that its jurisdiction had been properly invoked. Judgment was given in favor of South Dakota.[17]

On the whole, in controversies between states the Supreme Court has strictly applied its usual standards of what constitutes sufficient injury to bring about a real "case or controversy." [18] It has refused to entertain suits where a state has sought to enjoin other states from forbidding the importation of prison-made goods or levying inheritance taxes on intangibles held by its citizens in another state.[19] On several occasions, the Court has gone out of its judicial way to discourage litigation and to suggest that the disputing states settle their controversies by negotiation or compact.[20] On the other hand, the Court has accepted cases where serious and irreparable injury was allegedly threatened by such hazards as sewage pollution of large rivers or by the diversion of vitally necessary water from interstate streams. The Court has extended its jurisdiction to disputes such as those involving state boundaries, where it might have claimed that the issue was "political" rather than legal.[21]

Once a case between two states has been accepted by the Court, the next problems which arise are what law should be applied and what procedure the Court should follow. Generally the law of the case is decided on principles of international law modified by the exigencies of a federal system. In *Kansas* v. *Colorado* (1907) Justice Brewer noted that federal law, state law, and international law would be employed as the situation might demand. He also suggested that in judging interstate conflicts the Court had been in effect "building up what may not improperly be called interstate common law."

Where the factual issues involved in these disputes are complicated, the Court frequently appoints a "special master," usually a member of the Supreme Court bar, to act as a fact finder. He may have the right to summon witnesses and take depositions. After the findings of the master are filed, the Court will allow the parties to the case to submit exceptions and will hear argument on the objections. It is not unusual, however, for the master's report as filed to be adopted by the Court in its final decree.

There always exists, potentially at least, the problem of what the Supreme Court might do if one of the states chose to ignore or disobey the judgment. The nearest this question came to a practical answer was in the historic Virginia–West Virginia dispute. As part of the terms of its becoming a separate state during the Civil War, West Virginia had agreed to assume its just share of the Virginia state debt and the compact had been duly ratified by

---

[17] *South Dakota* v. *North Carolina* (1904).
[18] See discussion of the "case or controversy" requirement in Chap. 7.
[19] *Alabama* v. *Arizona* (1934); *Massachusetts* v. *Missouri* (1939).
[20] *Washington* v. *Oregon* (1909); *Minnesota* v. *Wisconsin* (1920); *New York* v. *New Jersey* (1921).
[21] See discussion of the "political question" doctrine in Chap. 9.

Congress. In 1907, after four decades of negotiation had yielded no monetary results, Virginia brought suit for collection. The litigation continued to 1915, when the Supreme Court affirmed the report of its special master and fixed the amount of West Virginia's liability. However, West Virginia still made no motion to pay.

The matter came to a head in 1918. Chief Justice White spoke for a unanimous Court and warned West Virginia:

> That judicial power essentially involves the right to enforce the results of its exertion is elementary. . . . And that this applies to the exertion of such power in controversies between States as the result of the exercise of original jurisdiction conferred upon this court by the Constitution is therefore certain.[22]

The Chief Justice asserted that it was patent from the wording of the legislative and judicial articles in the Constitution and from the limitations placed thereby on the states, that the federal government had the power to enforce a court decision against a recalcitrant state. There were two general remedies available. First, Congress could legislate. Second, further court action was possible. Precisely what course of compulsion could or would be pursued was not indicated. The case was postponed for reargument on the judicial remedies which should be invoked and to allow time for congressional action or further opportunity for peaceful settlement. Before the case was reopened, the West Virginia Legislature appropriated the money to meet the obligation.

What action the Court could have taken to force West Virginia to comply with the money judgment is uncertain. Undoubtedly some sort of compulsory writ would have been issued, with the Court depending either on West Virginia's respect for law for obedience, or possibly on assistance from the federal executive in the execution of the writ.

In a different type of problem, but one also involving West Virginia, that state tried to withdraw from a compact which had been approved by Congress. The state supreme court had ruled that the compact violated the state constitution and was therefore void. Though this was not a suit between states, six states filed briefs as *amici curiae* contending that West Virginia had no right to withdraw on these grounds, once Congress had consented to the compact. In *West Virginia ex rel. Dyer* v. *Sims* (1951), the Supreme Court concurred, Justice Frankfurter writing:

> It requires no elaborate argument to reject the suggestion that an agreement solemnly entered into between States by those who alone have political authority to speak for a State can be unilaterally nullified, or given final meaning by an organ of one of the contracting States. A State cannot be its own judge in a controversy with a sister State.

[22] *Virginia* v. *West Virginia* (1918).

## SELECTED REFERENCES

BARTON, WELDON V., *Interstate Compacts in the Political Process*. Chapel Hill, N.C.: University of North Carolina Press, 1967.

*The Constitution of the United States of America: Analysis and Interpretation*, Sen. Doc. no. 39, 88th Cong., pp. 739–786. Washington: Government Printing Office, 1964.

Council of State Governments, *The Book of the States*. Chicago: Council of State Governments (biennial).

FRANKFURTER, FELIX, and JAMES M. LANDIS, "The Compact Clause of the Constitution—A Study in Interstate Adjustments," 34 *Yale Law Journal* 685–758 (1925).

JACKSON, ROBERT H., *Full Faith and Credit: The Lawyer's Clause of the Constitution*. New York: Columbia University Press, 1945.

LEACH, RICHARD H., and REDDING S. SUGG, JR., *The Administration of Interstate Compacts*. Baton Rouge, La.: Louisiana State University Press, 1959.

MARTIN, ROSCOE C., *The Cities and the Federal System*. New York: The Atherton Press, 1965.

THURSBY, VINCENT, *Interstate Cooperation: A Study of the Interstate Compact*. Washington, D.C.: Public Affairs Press, 1953.

TRELEASE, FRANK J., "Arizona v. California: Allocation of Water Resources to People, States, and Nation," in Philip B. Kurland (ed.), *The Supreme Court Review: 1963*, pp. 158–205. Chicago: The University of Chicago Press, 1963.

# Part 3

## The judiciary

# 7

## Judicial power and organization

The federal judiciary, asserted Alexander Hamilton in No. 78 of *The Federalist*, is "beyond comparison the weakest of the three departments of power." He went on:

> The judiciary, from the nature of its functions, will always be the least dangerous to the political rights of the Constitution, because it will be least in a capacity to annoy or injure them. The Executive not only dispenses the honours, but holds the sword of the community. The legislature not only commands the purse, but prescribes the rules by which the duties and rights of every citizen are to be regulated. The judiciary, on the contrary, has no influence over either the sword or the purse; no direction either of the strength or of the wealth of the society; and can take no active resolution whatever. It may truly be said to have neither force nor will, but merely judgment.

This appraisal of the comparative power positions of the three branches seems accurate enough 180 years later. Nevertheless, for present purposes it is "judgment" rather than "force" or "will" that is most important. Since this is a study of the meaning of the American Constitution as judicially determined, it is appropriate that a survey of the three departments of government begin, not with Article I, which creates and empowers the Congress, nor with Article II, which establishes the executive, but with Article III, which pertains to the judiciary. An understanding of judicial power and

organization and the conditions under which constitutional controversies are decided by the federal courts, which it is the purpose of this section to supply, is required both for itself and for the background it provides to the discussions in the subsequent sections of this volume.

## FEDERAL JUDICIAL POWER

Article III begins with this sentence: "The judicial power of the United States shall be vested in one supreme court, and in such inferior courts as the Congress may, from time to time, ordain and establish." This language tells who is to exercise the federal judicial power, but it does not define that power. In practice, the judicial power exercised by the federal courts is an amalgam of constitutional authority, legislative authorization and interpretation, traditional forms, and prudential practice. The federal courts behave as they do partly under the directives of the Constitution and Congress, and partly because they stand in the time-honored tradition of the English common-law and equity courts. In addition, their development has been shaped by the overriding necessity of accommodation to a federal system with a dual structure of courts, which continually creates problems of adjustment and division of responsibilities.

POWER TO DECIDE CASES AND CONTROVERSIES    The basic power of the federal courts, as indicated in Article III, section 2, is to decide "cases" and "controversies." This authorization has been interpreted to foreclose the handling of any case by the federal courts unless it meets four tests: (1) it must involve *adverse parties* (2) who have a substantial *legal interest* (3) in a controversy growing out of a *real set of facts* (4) which admits of an *enforceable determination* of the legal rights of the parties. As Chief Justice Hughes said in *Aetna Life Insurance Co.* v. *Haworth* (1937): "A justiciable controversy is . . . distinguished from a difference or dispute of a hypothetical or abstract character. . . . The controversy must be definite and concrete, touching the legal relations of parties having adverse legal interests. . . . It must be a real and substantial controversy admitting of specific relief through a decree of conclusive character." These conditions are so well understood that they customarily raise no difficulties, but we shall see in Chapter 9 that they do impose limitations of real importance on judicial review.

The power of the federal courts to enforce their decisions is likewise normally taken for granted, but in fact the courts have no enforcement machinery at their direct disposal except for a few marshals. The judiciary must look to the executive and Congress for help in case of any real resistance to its orders. Whether apocryphal or not, Andrew Jackson's comment, "John Marshall has made his decision, now let him enforce it," reveals the hollowness of the Supreme Court's authority unless it is sustained by the support of its governmental colleagues and the backing of public opinion.

The matter of the enforceability of judicial decisions was most strikingly raised by the Supreme Court's 1954 ruling on the constitutionality of racial segregation in the public schools.[1] Recognizing the bitterness of the resistance which this ruling would evoke, the Court authorized a pattern of compliance which could be varied in character and speed to meet local conditions. When in 1957, in spite of these ameliorative efforts, mob violence and official state obstruction frustrated enforcement of the court order in Little Rock, Arkansas, President Eisenhower promptly made it clear that the entire compulsive power of the government was available to enforce the judicial decree, stating: "Failure to act in such a case would be tantamount to acquiescence in anarchy and the dissolution of the Union."

THE CONTEMPT POWER    In order to carry out their primary function of making binding decisions in cases or controversies, the federal courts possess certain auxiliary sanctions. First is the power to punish for contempt of their authority. The origin of the contempt power was in England, where disobedience of court orders was regarded as contempt of the king himself. Presumably the courts of the United States would have enjoyed similar power without specific legislation, but in fact the Judiciary Act of 1789 did confer power "to punish by fine or imprisonment, at the discretion of said courts, all contempts of authority in any cause or hearing before the same."

Contempts may be either civil or criminal. A civil contempt consists in the refusal of a person to obey a court order, and the purpose of the sanction is to preserve and enforce the rights of the parties in the proceeding. Civil contempt may be purged by obedience to the court order. In a criminal contempt, however, the purpose of the punishment is to vindicate the authority of the court. The act of contempt has been completed, and the guilty person cannot purge himself of contempt by subsequent action. The same conduct may amount to both civil and criminal contempt, and the court may impose both coercive and punitive measures in the same proceeding.[2]

The judicial power to punish for contempt has often been a source of serious concern. It was historically a summary power, i.e., exercised by the judge without jury or other procedural protections. Moreover, as developed in England it applied to contempts committed out of court as well as those in the presence of the court. American experience has resulted in limiting the contempt power in both respects.[3] A congressional act of 1831 confined its exercise to misbehavior in the presence of the court "or so near thereto as to obstruct the administration of justice," and to disobedience to lawful writs or orders of the court.

As for summary punishment for contempt, it is now authorized by the federal rules of criminal procedure only when the judge certifies that he

[1] *Brown* v. *Board of Education* (1954).
[2] *United States* v. *United Mine Workers* (1947).
[3] On the problem of out-of-court contempt by newspapers in commenting on judicial proceedings, see Chap. 22.

saw or heard the conduct constituting the contempt. The discretion which a judge exercises in summarily punishing contempts occurring in his presence is seldom challenged successfully on appeal, but it did happen in *In re McConnell* (1962), where counsel for one of the parties had been held in contempt for insisting on asking questions which the judge had barred. The Supreme Court, observing that "a vigorous, independent bar" was as necessary in our system of justice as an independent judiciary, reversed the conviction.[4]

All other contempts can be prosecuted only after notice, with representation by counsel, trial by jury if provided for by act of Congress, and—where the contempt involved disrespect to or criticism of the judge—trial before a different judge. This latter requirement was at issue in *Sacher* v. *United States* (1952), involving the contempt of court sentences passed on the lawyers for the defendants in the 1949 Smith Act prosecution of eleven Communist Party leaders.[5] The nine months' trial of the case was among the most turbulent and hectic in American court annals. The five principal defense lawyers carried on a running battle with Judge Medina which appeared "wilfully obstructive" of the conduct of the trial. The trial judge was convinced that the lawyers had deliberately badgered and insulted him throughout the long months of the trial. On many occasions he warned counsel that their conduct was contemptuous, but in order not to delay the trial or deprive defendants of counsel, he did not cite them for contempt until after the jury had brought in its verdict and been discharged. Immediately thereafter he asked the lawyers to stand up, read them a small portion of a lengthy "contempt certificate" he had prepared, found them all guilty of contempt, and sentenced them to prison.

The Supreme Court majority upheld Medina's procedure, on the ground that he himself had heard and seen the contempt.[6] But Justice Frankfurter, dissenting along with Black and Douglas, contended that this rule "merely permits summary punishment" of contempts committed in the presence of the court; it does not command it. The power of summary punishment is

---

[4] Another example is *Harris* v. *United States* (1965), where a witness had refused to answer questions before a grand jury on the ground of self-incrimination, and had then been brought before a judge, granted immunity, and asked the same questions. When he again refused to answer, the judge acted summarily under Rule 42(a) to hold him in contempt for conduct which he had seen and heard. The Supreme Court held that this was not the kind of situation which the federal rules had in mind when authorizing summary punishment for contempt in the presence of the judge. Here the contempt, if any, had occurred before the grand jury, and the appearance before the judge was only ancillary. In these circumstances the Court, overruling *Brown* v. *United States* (1959), held that the normal procedure of trial for contempt after notice and hearing was required.

[5] *Dennis* v. *United States* (1951). See Chap. 27.

[6] The decision in *Ungar* v. *Sarafite* (1964) was to the same effect. But *Offutt* v. *United States* (1954) held that the trial judge was so "personally embroiled" with the witness whom he held in contempt that the contempt should have been tried before a different judge.

subject to "the inherent limitation that the power shall be fairly used" for the purpose for which it is conferred.

> Among the restrictions to be implied, as a matter of course, are two basic principles of our law—that no judge should sit in a case in which he is personally involved and that no criminal punishment should be meted out except upon notice and due hearing, unless overriding necessity precludes such indispensable safeguards for assuring fairness and affording the feeling that fairness has been done.

Historically there has been no jury trial in contempt cases. The explanation has been that a judge's authority would be seriously compromised if he had to depend upon a jury verdict for defense of his position against contemptuous assaults. However, Congress can if it wishes require trial by jury in the federal courts for contempts, and it has done so in several statutes.[7] This issue was debated when the Civil Rights Act of 1957 was under consideration in Congress, and a compromise provision was included under which any person accused in a criminal contempt proceeding of violating an injunction issued to protect voting rights was entitled to a trial by jury if the penalty imposed on conviction by the judge was a fine in excess of $300 or imprisonment for more than forty-five days.[8]

In recent years some justices of the Supreme Court have contended that criminal contempt proceedings are so similar to ordinary criminal trials that all the constitutional protections of criminal trials—principally indictment by grand jury and trial by jury—must be accorded. In *Green* v. *United States* (1958) two of the eleven Communist Party leaders convicted under the Smith Act in 1951 failed to appear in court for sentencing and went into hiding. When they voluntarily surrendered five years later, they were charged with criminal contempt for violating the surrender order, tried without a jury, convicted, and sentenced to three years' imprisonment in addition to their earlier sentence.

Such a long sentence as punishment for contempt was unprecedented, and three members of the Court—Black, Warren, and Douglas—protested that severe punishment under summary conditions, where the same "functionary" lays down the law, prosecutes, sits in judgment on his own charges, and punishes as he sees fit, amounted to "autocratic omnipotence." Justice Black thought that "there is no justification in history, in necessity, or most important in the Constitution for trying those charged with violating a court's decree in a manner wholly different from those accused of disobeying any other mandate of the state."

This argument was continued in *United States* v. *Barnett* (1964), a pro-

---

[7] The Clayton Act of 1914, 38 Stat. 738–740, requires a jury trial in contempt proceedings arising out of disobedience to federal court orders, provided the conduct complained of also constitutes a criminal offense under federal or state laws.

[8] 71 Stat. 634, 638 (1957). A similar provision is in the Civil Rights Act of 1964, 78 Stat. 241, 268 (1964).

ceeding which grew out of the effort of the state of Mississippi to prevent the enrollment of a Negro student, James Meredith, in the state university. The Governor and Lieutenant Governor of the state were found by the federal court of appeals to have disobeyed its order not to interfere with Meredith's admission, and were held in civil contempt. However, the court of appeals was evenly divided on whether the officials were entitled to a jury trial on a criminal contempt charge, and certified the question to the Supreme Court. A five-judge majority upheld the time-honored practice of summary trial for contempt. However, Justice Goldberg in dissent endeavored to prove that summary convictions had been accepted in the past only because the penalties imposed had been "minor" or "trivial." A rather delphic footnote in Justice Clark's opinion for the Court indicated that one or more members of the majority also accepted this view.[9]

Two years later, in *Cheff* v. *Schnackenberg* (1966), the Court definitely adopted this view. The majority again denied that a criminal contempt proceeding was a criminal prosecution within the meaning of the Bill of Rights guarantee of trial by jury, but in an exercise of its supervisory power over federal courts, it ruled that sentences exceeding six months for criminal contempt could not be imposed without a jury trial.[10]

At the same time, limitations were placed on punishment for civil contempt in *Shillitani* v. *United States* (1966) and *Pappadio* v. *United States* (1966). Here witnesses before a grand jury investigating possible violations of federal narcotics laws refused to answer questions, even after being granted immunity. A federal court imposed two-year sentences of contempt but gave the witnesses the unqualified right to be released if and when they obeyed the order to testify. The Court held that the conditional nature of the sentences rendered each of the actions a civil contempt proceeding for which indictment and jury trial were not constitutionally required. However, since the term of the grand jury which had demanded the testimony had expired, imprisonment would no longer serve any useful coercive purpose, and so the Court vacated the contempt judgments.

POWER TO ISSUE WRITS     The Judiciary Act of 1789, in section 14, gave all courts of the United States power "to issue writs of *scire facias, habeas corpus,* and all other writs not specially provided for by statute, which may be necessary for the exercise of their respective jurisdictions, and agreeable to the principles and usages of law." In addition, the Supreme Court was authorized to issue writs of mandamus "in cases warranted by the principles

[9] See Shelton Tefft, "United States v. Barnett: ' 'Twas A Famous Victory,' " in Philip B. Kurland (ed.), *The Supreme Court Review: 1964* (Chicago: The University of Chicago Press, 1964), pp. 123, 133.
[10] The Supreme Court granted certiorari in *Bloom* v. *Illinois* (1967) to consider whether state court judges can impose long prison terms for criminal contempt without granting jury trials.

and usages of law, to any courts appointed, or persons holding office, under the authority of the United States." It was this provision which was to be held unconstitutional in *Marbury* v. *Madison* (1803).

The writ of habeas corpus, though mentioned in Article I, section 9, is issued only in accordance with statutory authorization. The historic purpose of the writ had been to challenge detention by executive authorities without judicial trial, and up to 1867 it was not available against any sentence imposed by a court of competent jurisdiction. But in that year Congress gave federal courts a broad authorization to issue writs of habeas corpus to prisoners in custody "in violation of the constitution or of any treaty or law of the United States."

Similarly the equity power to issue writs of injunction is dependent upon congressional authorization and subject to congressional limitation. In the original act of 1789, Congress provided that no equity suit should be maintained where there was an adequate remedy at law. In 1793 it passed the first of a long series of statutes limiting the power of federal courts to issue injunctions against state courts or state officers. In 1867 the federal courts were forbidden to enjoin the collection of federal taxes. The Norris–La Guardia Act of 1932 restrained the use of injunctions in labor disputes.[11] Under the Emergency Price Control Act of 1942, the Emergency Court of Appeals was the only court permitted to enjoin price control orders or regulations, and it was limited to permanent injunctions. It could not issue temporary restraining orders or interlocutory decrees. Chief Justice Stone, in upholding this limitation, said that there "is nothing in the Constitution which requires Congress to confer equity jurisdiction on any particular inferior federal court." [12]

OTHER JUDICIAL POWERS    Federal courts possess the power of making rules governing their process and practice, but this too is derived from statutes. The process acts of 1789 and 1792 were upheld by Chief Justice Marshall in *Wayman* v. *Southard* (1825). Although he regarded the rule-making power as essentially legislative in nature, he thought that Congress could delegate to courts the power to "fill up the details."

The federal courts have full authority to appoint special aides required for the performance of their duties, such as masters in chancery, referees, or auditors. Insolvent enterprises which come under judicial control are normally administered by court-appointed officers. In particularly complex cases a court may appoint aides to take testimony and to make findings and recommendations.

Attorneys are officers of the courts, which have inherent power over their admission to practice and disbarment, subject to any general statutory

[11] The act was held constitutional in *Lauf* v. *E. G. Shinner & Co.* (1938).
[12] *Lockerty* v. *Phillips* (1943).

qualifications that may be imposed. These powers, however, cannot be used, in Chief Justice Taney's words, in an "arbitrary and despotic" manner.[13] The Test Oath Act of 1862 sought to exclude former Confederates from the practice of law in the federal courts, but the Supreme Court in *Ex parte Garland* (1867) held it unconstitutional as a bill of attainder.

The Supreme Court upheld the Illinois supreme court in denying admission to the bar to a conscientious objector in *In re Summers* (1945), but in *Konigsberg* v. *State Bar of California* (1957) it reversed a denial of admission on character grounds involving alleged connections with the Communist Party.[14] The California bar then gave the applicant another hearing and again refused him admission, this time specifically on the ground that his refusal to answer questions concerning possible Communist Party membership had obstructed a full investigation into his qualifications. The Court upheld this action in 1961 by a five to four vote, concluding that a committee can require a bar applicant "to provide unprivileged answers to questions having a substantial relevance to his qualifications." [15]

### LEGISLATIVE STRUCTURING OF THE COURT SYSTEM

It took congressional action to turn the bare outlines of Article III into a functioning judicial establishment. The First Congress set up the organization and defined the jurisdiction of the federal judicial system by the famous Judiciary Act of 1789. This act was the result of protracted debate during the summer of 1789 between Federalists seeking a strong and complete system of federal courts, and anti-Federalists intent on keeping the judicial establishment within the narrowest possible bounds. The Federalists won a limited victory, the statute providing for two judicial levels—district courts in every state and three circuit courts—below the Supreme Court. The circuit courts had no separate judiciary, however. They were to be staffed by the six Supreme Court justices, who would ride circuit between sessions, plus the district judge in whose district the circuit court was sitting.

The act gave to the district and circuit courts jurisdiction in admiralty and in suits between citizens of different states. It conferred little of the potentially broad jurisdiction allowed by the Constitution over cases arising under the Constitution, laws, or treaties, awarding only jurisdiction over a small number of federal crimes, plus penalties and forfeitures made under the laws of the United States. The state courts were allowed to retain jurisdiction concurrent with that of the federal courts in suits between citizens of different states and in numerous types of cases involving the enforcement of federal laws. It was not until 1875 that Congress gave the federal courts the

---

[13] *Ex parte Secombe* (1857).
[14] The same position was taken in *Schware* v. *New Mexico Board of Bar Examiners* (1957).
[15] The Court reached the same result in *In re Anastaplo* (1961).

full range of jurisdiction they were capable of exercising under the Constitution.

The act of 1789 also provided for the appointment in each district of a marshal to execute the orders of the court, and of an attorney for the United States to prosecute criminal cases and civil actions in which the United States was a party. Finally, the act set up the office of Attorney General of the United States, whose duty it was "to prosecute and conduct all suits in the Supreme Court in which the United States shall be concerned, and to give his advice and opinion upon questions of law when required by the President of the United States, or when requested by the heads of any of the departments." The Attorney General was not given any supervisory responsibility over the district attorneys, and the Department of Justice was not created until 1870.

The Judiciary Act of 1789 has been generally hailed as an outstanding piece of legislation, but there were weaknesses in it. The role of the federal court system was limited because the Supreme Court could meet only in the capital, access to which was made difficult by poor transportation; the federal trial courts could meet only at one or at most two places in each state, and had limited jurisdiction. Thus the new system of courts was remote and expensive. From 1789 to 1801 only three cases were appealed from state courts to the Supreme Court. Riding circuit over abominable roads was a judge-killing assignment for the high court's members. Moreover, sitting in circuit courts meant that they reviewed their own decisions when cases were appealed to the Supreme Court.

After their defeat by Jefferson in 1800, the Federalists passed the Judiciary Act of 1801, which terminated circuit riding by the justices. The six-member Court was to be reduced to five when the next vacancy occurred, to avoid tie votes and to give incoming President Jefferson one less vacancy to fill. More district courts were created, and the old circuit court system was abolished in favor of six new courts with increased jurisdiction, manned by resident circuit judges. The fact that all these new judgeships were filled by the outgoing Federalist administration led the Jeffersonians to attack the "midnight judges bill" as judicial jobbery, and it was promptly repealed.

Instead, the Jeffersonians adopted a new act in 1802 providing for six circuits, composed of one Supreme Court justice and one district judge, but allowing the circuit courts to be held by a single judge, a practice that became increasingly common. This act again tied the size of the Supreme Court to the number of circuits, and as the country expanded and more circuits were added, the size of the Supreme Court had to be increased. A seventh member was added in 1807, and in 1837 the size went to nine. A tenth justice was added for a tenth circuit in 1864. President Johnson's difficulties with Congress led it to adopt an act in 1866 reducing the Court to seven, as vacancies occurred, and reorganizing the circuits into nine. Actually, the number of justices did not go below eight. By an act of 1869 the size of the

Court was again increased to nine. This statute also drastically curtailed the circuit-riding responsibilities of the justices, but the postwar development of judicial business and the territorial expansion of the country left the pressure on the Court as heavy as ever. By 1890 it had 1,800 cases on its docket.

The problem of the circuit courts also continued unabated. A panel of circuit judges had been provided by the 1869 act, but the number was quite inadequate. By the 1880s, eight-ninths of the litigation in the circuit courts was disposed of by single judges, usually district judges. Cases which came to the circuit courts on appeal from the districts were thus customarily heard by the same judge who had decided the case in the district court.

A remedy was finally found for the Supreme Court's problem in the Circuit Courts of Appeals Act of 1891. A new level of intermediate appellate courts was established, consisting of a court of appeals for each of the nine circuits and the District of Columbia. The old district and circuit courts were retained, but except for certain categories of direct appeal to the Supreme Court, their decisions were routed to the new courts of appeals for final disposition. As a gesture to tradition, the circuit duty of Supreme Court justices was not eliminated, but little was expected of them. The Supreme Court immediately felt the benefits of the act as the flood of litigation it had been receiving was shunted to the circuit courts of appeals. The one obvious error in the 1891 statute was the retention of the circuit courts, which were finally abolished by statute in 1911, through a merger of their jurisdiction with that of the district courts. Thus the present organization of the federal court system was achieved.

Keeping the Supreme Court's business under control required further legislation. Principally the problem was that in a considerable number of situations there was a statutory right of appeal from lower federal courts and from state supreme courts to the Supreme Court. A 1916 act seeking to give the Supreme Court greater discretionary review did not go far enough. With Taft's appointment as Chief Justice in 1921, he took the lead in urging an extension of the discretionary principle, and the Court itself developed a bill which was adopted as the Judiciary Act of 1925.

This act was based on the proposition that the Supreme Court's time had to be conserved for handling issues of national significance. Litigation which did not meet this test was to be left to state courts of last resort and to the circuit courts of appeals. To achieve these purposes, most decisions of the circuit courts of appeals were made reviewable in the Supreme Court only by the writ of certiorari, which the Court granted or denied in its own discretion. Again, cases which previously could be appealed directly from district courts to the Supreme Court were now, with some important exceptions, directed instead to the circuit courts of appeals. Finally, the act confined to two classes the cases which could as a matter of right be taken from the state courts to the Supreme Court: (1) where the validity of a state statute

was challenged on federal constitutional grounds and its validity sustained; and (2) where a federal statute or treaty was invoked and its validity denied by a state court.

The size of the Court, which had been stabilized at nine since 1869, again became an issue in 1937 with President Roosevelt's proposal that Congress authorize appointment of one new justice for each sitting justice who remained on the Court after reaching the age of seventy, to a maximum limit of fifteen justices. The plan was generally disliked even by those who disapproved of what the Court had been doing, and it was defeated in Congress. The episode led to a subsequent effort by the organized bar to freeze the size of the Supreme Court at nine justices by an amendment to the Constitution. The proposal passed the Senate in 1954, but failed in the House.

## THE LOWER FEDERAL COURTS

THE DISTRICT COURTS    The district courts are the trial courts of the federal system. Cases are heard by a single judge, with participation of a jury when appropriate. There are currently ninety-four district courts, including those located in Puerto Rico, the Canal Zone, Guam, and the Virgin Islands. Each state has at least one federal district court, and some have as many as four. The number of judges per district ranges from one to a high of eighteen in the southern district of New York, which covers New York City. In 1966 there were over three hundred district judgeships.

About one-third of all the civil suits tried in the district courts involve the government as a party, either as plaintiff or defendant. As for private civil suits, there are three main heads of jurisdiction: (1) federal questions, covering all cases in law and equity arising under the Constitution, laws, and treaties of the United States; (2) diversity of citizenship; and (3) admiralty. In addition, federal courts in the District of Columbia, the Canal Zone, Guam, and the Virgin Islands have general local jurisdiction and law-enforcement responsibilities.

The diversity of citizenship cases are by far the most numerous single category of civil cases in the federal courts. The theory of the Constitution in opening the federal courts to suits involving citizens of different states was that the state courts might well be biased against out-of-state litigants, whereas the federal courts would provide a neutral tribunal for all parties. The anti-Federalists opposed giving such jurisdiction to the federal courts, and periodically there have been efforts to abolish it. The present-day objections to diversity jurisdiction are that it congests the federal courts with a tremendous number of cases growing out of essentially local issues which federal judges must determine according to state law. While in 1789 there might have been prejudice in state courts against outsiders, it is argued that this possibility is no longer important. These arguments have not prevailed,

but in 1958 Congress did limit access to the federal courts in diversity cases by various restrictions.[16]

The federal district courts also deal with a heavy load of criminal prosecutions. Criminal cases begun in 1965 totaled over 33,000, including prosecutions for violation of the immigration laws, fraud, transportation of stolen automobiles, and violations of the narcotics, liquor, migratory bird, selective service, white slave, and food and drug laws.

THREE-JUDGE DISTRICT COURTS    There are certain situations where a district court consisting of three district or court of appeals judges must be impaneled. A three-judge trial court was first authorized by Congress in the expediting act of 1903 which empowered the Attorney General, in any proceeding brought by the United States under the Sherman Act or the Interstate Commerce Act which "in his opinion, . . . is of general public importance," to file a certificate to that effect with the court where the case was docketed. Thereupon the case was to be given precedence and assigned to a panel of three judges, from whose decision appeal lay directly to the Supreme Court.

A second occasion for use of this device was provided by the Supreme Court's ruling in 1908 that lower federal courts could enjoin state officers from enforcing state statutes on the ground of their unconstitutionality.[17] Congress was alarmed over the prospect of a single federal judge enjoining a state legislative program, and in the Mann-Elkins Act of 1910 and the Judicial Code of 1911, provided that a three-judge court would have to be convened to pass on the constitutionality of state legislation before injunctions could be issued.

The Mann-Elkins Act also created a five-judge Commerce Court which was to hear all appeals of Interstate Commerce Commission cases. In 1913 this court was abolished and injunctions against ICC orders were required to be heard by a three-judge district court. Later statutes set up the same arrangements for certain other federal administrative agencies. In 1937 Congress provided that no interlocutory or permanent injunction against enforcement of an act of Congress on the ground of its alleged unconstitutionality could be issued except by a three-judge court.

Because appeal from decisions of a three-judge district court is directly to the Supreme Court and is a matter of right, the Court has tended to interpret strictly the various statutes providing for three-judge courts.[18] In

[16] The Jurisdiction Act of 1958, 72 Stat. 415, provided that the amount involved in a diversity suit must be at least $10,000, and barred removal to federal courts from state courts of cases arising under state workmen's compensation laws.

[17] *Ex parte Young* ( 1908 ).

[18] *Phillips* v. *United States* (1941); *Swift & Co.* v. *Wickham* (1965). See David P. Currie, "The Three-judge District Court in Constitutional Litigation," 32 *University of Chicago Law Review* 1–79 (1964); also "The Three-judge District Court," 77 *Harvard Law Review* 299–317 ( 1963).

1950 Congress abolished the three-judge provision for all federal agencies except the ICC. On the other hand, the civil rights era brought many challenges to the constitutionality of state action which had to be tried before three-judge courts. For example, *Baker v. Carr, Reynolds v. Sims,* and most of the other attacks on state legislative apportionment in the 1960s were heard by three-judge courts.

THE FEDERAL COURTS OF APPEALS    The courts of appeals, created by Congress in 1891, and known until 1948 as circuit courts of appeals, constitute the second level of the federal judiciary. Their purpose is primarily to relieve the Supreme Court by hearing appeals from decisions of the district courts, and in practice they are the courts of last resort for the great majority of all federal cases. For judicial purposes the country is divided into ten numbered circuits; an eleventh court of appeals sits in the District of Columbia. Members of the Supreme Court are assigned as supervising justices for each of the circuits. There are from three to nine circuit judges in each circuit, and a total of eighty (in 1966) for the eleven courts. A panel of three normally sits on a case.

All final decisions and some intermediate orders of the district courts are subject to review by the courts of appeals. In 1965, 6,700 appeals were taken to the circuit courts, and 5,500 of these were from the district courts. The balance were appeals from federal administrative boards and commissions, such as the Tax Court, the National Labor Relations Board, the Federal Communications Commission, and so on. Trials in the courts of appeals are conducted on the basis of the record made in the original proceeding before the district court or administrative agency. New evidence may not be presented.

### THE SUPREME COURT

The Supreme Court is composed of the Chief Justice of the United States and eight associate justices. The Court meets annually in October for its regular term and remains in session, though with periodic recesses, until the following June. The Chief Justice may call the Court into session for special terms during the summer, as was done in 1958 to dispose of the Little Rock segregation controversy [19] and in 1942 to review the death sentences imposed on eight Germans who had come to the United States by submarine on a sabotage mission.[20] The Court formerly sat in the old Senate chamber in the basement of the Capitol, but it now occupies a palace of dazzling white marble so elegant that, when it was completed in 1935, one justice suggested that the members of the Court should ride in on elephants.

[19] *Cooper v. Aaron* (1958).
[20] *Ex parte Quirin* (1942).

THE COURT'S OPERATION    The Court sits for four hours daily, Monday through Thursday, in an impressive high-ceilinged courtroom, with enormous pillars and red velvet hangings. The justices meet in the robing room behind the drapes shortly before ten o'clock. By tradition, each justice shakes hands with every one of his colleagues. Promptly at ten the court crier smashes his gavel, spectators rise, the velvet curtains part, and the justices come through to take their places behind the long bench.

During its public sessions the Court hears oral arguments in scheduled cases and announces its decisions. For every case on the docket, the record of the proceedings in the lower courts and briefs stating the arguments for each side are filed with the Court. The justices study these materials before the case comes up for hearing. The time for oral argument is strictly limited; except in the most important cases, counsel for each side will have one hour or less to address the Court. When the time is up, a red light goes on at the lectern where the counsel stands facing the court, and he must stop immediately. Legend has it that Chief Justice Hughes once called time on a lawyer in the middle of the word "if."

Counsel seldom have an opportunity to make their arguments without interruption. The justices frequently break in with questions, comments, or requests for clarification. From the questions asked, it is often possible to predict how the individual justices are likely to vote in deciding the case. Probably their minds are not often changed by the oral argument, but it does give counsel a chance to emphasize what they feel are the main points for their side.

On Friday of each week when the Court has been sitting, the justices meet in conference to decide the cases heard that week. These proceedings are absolutely secret. No one other than the justices is present. The Chief Justice presents each case which is ready for decision, making such comments and offering such views as he chooses. Discussion then goes down the table, each associate justice speaking in order of seniority. When all have given their views on the case, voting begins. Now the order is reversed, the most junior justice voting first and the Chief Justice last. This procedure maximizes the role of the Chief Justice, since he has a chance to formulate the issues initially and to break the tie if his colleagues are evenly divided.

Following the vote, the Chief Justice assigns the writing of the "opinion of the Court" to himself or one of the associate justices. However, if there is a divided vote and the Chief Justice is in the minority, then the senior associate justice who voted in the majority controls the assigning of the opinion of the Court. Drafts of opinions are circulated among the justices, and the author may revise the final draft on the basis of comments by his colleagues.

In the early years of the Court, it was customary for all justices to give their opinions seriatim in a case, and there was no single opinion of the Court. However, when Marshall became Chief Justice, he saw that the

Court would be more influential if it spoke with a single voice, and so he himself wrote the opinion of the Court in almost all important cases.

Justices were still free to write concurring or dissenting opinions, but there was a tendency for them to go along with the opinion of the Court unless their disagreement was sharp. The fame of Justices Holmes and Brandeis as dissenters was based on the quality rather than the quantity of their dissents. However, the Supreme Court's struggle with the New Deal caused dissents to become more frequent, and since the 1943 term non-unanimous opinions have outnumbered the unanimous opinions. Concurring opinions are written by justices who agree with the result reached by the Court but not entirely with the reasons given in the opinion of the Court. The number of concurring opinions written by Supreme Court justices has also increased markedly in the past three decades.

The Court's decisions, formerly announced only on Mondays, since 1965 may be given at the beginning of any session. The author of the opinion of the Court summarizes the main points of his ruling in a few minutes. Dissenters may also outline their disagreement if they wish. No advance notice is ever given as to when a decision in a particular case will be ready, and the opinions are distributed to newsmen only after the decision has been announced from the bench. In the printing operation, each opinion is divided among several printers so they will not know what case they are working on.

The role of the Chief Justice is extremely important, for he can develop a substantial position of leadership on the Court. His formal authority stems primarily from his role as presiding officer at Court sessions and in the conference, and from his power to assign the writing of opinions. But he is also the symbolic head of the Court and the highest officer of the government after the President and Vice President, and if he has the necessary skill, he can use his position to guide the decision-making process toward consensus and keep discussion from bogging down in quibbling and personalities.

ORIGINAL JURISDICTION    The Supreme Court is primarily an appellate court, but the Constitution does define two categories of cases which can be heard in the Court's original jurisdiction, i.e., without prior consideration by any other court. These are cases in which a state is a party, and those affecting ambassadors, public ministers, and consuls. This grant of original jurisdiction is self-executing and requires no legislation to make it effective. Since it flows directly from the Constitution, Congress can neither restrict it nor enlarge it. This latter point was decided in the case of *Marbury* v. *Madison* (1803), where the Court held a provision of the Judiciary Act of 1789 unconstitutional on the ground that it sought to add to the Supreme Court's original jurisdiction the power of issuing writs of mandamus.

Congress can, however, adopt legislation implementing the constitutional language on original jurisdiction. Thus Congress has provided that the Supreme Court shall have "original and exclusive" jurisdiction of all controversies between two or more states, whereas other cases in which a state is a party can be heard either by the Supreme Court or lower federal courts. Because of such arrangements for concurrent jurisdiction, the Supreme Court generally does not need to accept a suit invoking its original jurisdiction unless it feels there is a good reason why it should. As the Court stated in an 1895 case, its original jurisdiction "is limited and manifestly to be sparingly exercised, and should not be expanded by construction." [21]

APPELLATE JURISDICTION    All the remaining business of the Supreme Court comes to it in its appellate jurisdiction, which it exercises, as the Constitution says, "with such exceptions, and under such regulations as the Congress shall make." It might have been argued that the Court's appellate jurisdiction, like its original jurisdiction, flowed directly from the Constitution, and did not require legislative authorization. However, the fact is that the Judiciary Act of 1789 did legislate on the subject of appellate jurisdiction, and in 1796 the Court agreed that without a statute prescribing a rule for appellate proceedings, the Court could not assume jurisdiction.[22] In 1810 Marshall held that an affirmative statutory bestowal of appellate jurisdiction implied a denial of jurisdiction not granted.[23]

The consequences of this judicial surrender of control over appellate jurisdiction to Congress were dramatically demonstrated in the post-Civil War case of *Ex parte McCardle* (1869). Stringent Reconstruction measures establishing military rule over the South were enacted by Congress. A Mississippi editor, McCardle, held for trial before a military commission authorized by these acts, petitioned for a writ of habeas corpus under a statute passed in 1867 which gave federal judges power to grant habeas corpus to any person restrained in violation of the federal Constitution or laws, and provided for appeal to the Supreme Court in such cases. McCardle was denied the writ and appealed to the Supreme Court.

That Court had just declared Lincoln's wartime use of military commissions unconstitutional in *Ex parte Milligan* (1866), and Congress feared that it would use the *McCardle* appeal to invalidate the Reconstruction legislation. Consequently in March, 1868, the Radical Republicans rushed through Congress, and repassed over the President's veto, a statute repealing the act of 1867 so far as it granted appeals to the Supreme Court, and withdrawing "any such jurisdiction by said Supreme Court, on appeals which have been, or may hereafter be taken." The Court, which had already heard argument on the *McCardle* case when this act was passed, felt constrained to rule that

[21] *California* v. *Southern Pacific Co.* (1895).
[22] *Wiscart* v. *Dauchy* (1796).
[23] *Durousseau* v. *United States* (1810).

its authority to render a decision had been abrogated. Congress had withdrawn the Court's jurisdiction in the clearest possible fashion. "Without jurisdiction the court cannot proceed at all in any cause. Jurisdiction is power to declare the law, and when it ceases to exist, the only function remaining to the court is that of announcing the fact and dismissing the cause."

Under the *McCardle* principle, then, it would be constitutionally possible for Congress to abolish the appellate jurisdiction entirely and leave the Supreme Court with only the handful of cases that can be brought in its original jurisdiction. It is highly unlikely that anything approaching this will ever happen, but in 1957 Senator Jenner sought reprisal against the Court's decisions in certain national security cases by introducing legislation withdrawing the Court's appellate jurisdiction in five specific areas, including cases involving the investigatory power of Congress. It was widely recognized that adoption of such legislation would be subversive of the whole concept of the rule of law, and his proposal, as modified by Senator Butler, was defeated in the Senate in August, 1958, by a vote of forty-nine to forty-one.[24]

METHODS OF REVIEW    Except in the limited classes of cases where there is an appeal to the Supreme Court as of right, review is sought by filing with the Court a petition for writ of certiorari to a state supreme court or federal court of appeals.[25] This writ, if granted, directs the lower court to send up the record in the case for review so that the decision may be made "more certain." During the 1965–1966 term the Court acted on 2,362 petitions for certiorari, of which 1,314 were *in forma pauperis* (i.e., without prepayment of costs) mostly originating with convicts in state or federal prisons. During that term the Court granted 12.8 per cent of the regular petitions for certiorari, but only 3.4 per cent of those *in forma pauperis*.

Certiorari petitions, including pertinent portions of the record, petitioner's brief, and opposing response, are circulated among all members of the Court. There can be oral argument on granting petitions, but normally this

[24] See C. Herman Pritchett, *Congress versus the Supreme Court: 1957–1960* (Minneapolis: The University of Minnesota Press, 1961), chap. 3; Walter F. Murphy, *Congress and the Court* (Chicago: The University of Chicago Press, 1962). Leonard G. Ratner, in "Congressional Power over the Appellate Jurisdiction of the Supreme Court," 109 *University of Pennsylvania Law Review* 157–202 (1960), argues that congressional power over the Court's appellate jurisdiction could not extend to depriving the Court of all appellate jurisdiction, and that its use must be consistent with exercise of "the essential functions of the Supreme Court under this Constitution." In *Glidden* v. *Zdanok* (1962), Justice Douglas said: "There is a serious question whether the McCardle case could command a majority view today."

[25] Certiorari may be sought to review a federal district court decision while the case is still pending in the court of appeals, but the Supreme Court will grant the writ in these circumstances only if the case is of such "imperative public importance" as to require immediate settlement. See *Aaron* v. *Cooper* (1958) and *Youngstown Sheet & Tube Co.* v. *Sawyer* (1952).

does not happen. Petitions are granted on the affirmative vote of four justices. The rule of four was adopted when the Judiciary Act of 1925 was passed, to reassure Congress that access to the Court by the discretionary writ of certiorari would not be refused too easily.

Review of the flood of certiorari petitions imposes a heavy burden on the justices. The Court's Rule 19 states that review on certiorari "will be granted only where there are special and important reasons therefor." Among the circumstances cited in the rule as justifying the grant of certiorari are the following: where two courts of appeals have rendered conflicting decisions; where a state court or a federal court of appeals has decided an important question of federal law on which the Supreme Court has never passed, or in such a way as to conflict with applicable decisions of the Court; or where a federal court has so far departed from the accepted canons of judicial proceedings as to call for exercise of the Supreme Court's power of supervision.

Usually the Court announces no reason for denial of certiorari. Many petitions, particularly those *in forma pauperis*, are wholly without merit and ought never to have been filed. When the Court does state a reason, often it is a technical one—for example, that the federal question is not properly presented, or was not passed on below. But some denials are clearly for policy reasons. As Justice Frankfurter said in *Maryland* v. *Baltimore Radio Show* (1950):

> A decision may satisfy all . . . technical requirements and yet may commend itself for review to fewer than four members of the Court. Pertinent considerations of judicial policy here come into play. A case may raise an important question but the record may be cloudy. It may be desirable to have different aspects of an issue further illumined by the lower courts. Wise adjudication has its own time for ripening.

The denial of a writ leaves the decision of the lower court in effect, but it has no other legal significance. It does not mean necessarily that the Supreme Court approves of the decision below, and is in no sense an affirmance of the decree. However, this is a point which is difficult to get across to the public. Denials of certiorari are often cited as precedents, and it must be admitted that in practice they may have such effect, particularly since decisions are reversed in a very high proportion of the cases in which certiorari is granted.

## SPECIALIZED AND LEGISLATIVE COURTS

In addition to the regular federal courts, Congress has from time to time set up courts for the performance of specialized functions. The oldest of the specialized courts is the Court of Claims, created in 1855, whose function is to try claims against the government. Other specialized courts are the Customs Court, which sits in New York, and the Court of Customs and

Patent Appeals. A Commerce Court to review decisions of the ICC was created in 1910, but had an unhappy history and was abolished in 1913. The Emergency Court of Appeals was set up during World War II to try certain suits under the price control statutes. It was staffed by judges from the regular federal courts and was authorized to sit anywhere in the United States. The so-called Tax Court, which reviews tax decisions by the Bureau of Internal Revenue, is legally not a court at all, but a part of the executive branch. Decisions of the Customs Court are appealed to the Court of Customs and Patent Appeals. Cases from all the other specialized courts go to the Supreme Court on writ of certiorari or certification of questions.

The reason for these specialized courts is primarily to permit certain difficult classes of litigation to be handled by judges who have particular competence in the field. In the case of the Emergency Court of Appeals, it was feared that the wartime program of price control would break down if every federal and state judge in the country could issue injunctions against price control orders, so this power was centralized in a single specialized court.

Congress provides a system of courts for the District of Columbia and for other territories under United States control. For this purpose Congress does not have to rely upon Article III. It is given complete authority to legislate for the District of Columbia by Article I, section 8, and has power to "make all needful rules and regulations" respecting territories of the United States under Article IV, section 3. Courts created by Congress under its authority to legislate for the District or the territories have consequently been called "legislative" courts, in contrast with the "constitutional" courts authorized by Article III.

The practical significance of this distinction is that Congress need not observe the provisions of Article III so far as appointments to and jurisdiction of the legislative courts are concerned. This point has been clear since *American Insurance Co.* v. *Canter* (1828). Congress had created an admiralty court for the territory of Florida, the judges of which were limited to four-year terms of office. This court could have been held unconstitutional because the judges did not enjoy tenure for good behavior. Instead Marshall ruled that the provisions of Article III did not apply to this court, since it was created under congressional power to legislate for the territories. It followed that the judges of a legislative court could not only be given term appointments, but could also be removed by the President, their salaries could be reduced while they were in office, and they could be given jurisdiction other than that specified in Article III.

The test of a legislative court laid down in the *Canter* case was clear enough; it was a geographical test, location in a territory. The same test made the courts of the District of Columbia legislative courts, and the Supreme Court in *Ex parte Bakelite Corp.* (1929) and *Williams* v. *United States* (1933) held that the Court of Customs and Patent Appeals and the Court

of Claims were neither confined in jurisdiction nor protected in independence by Article III, but that both had been created by virtue of substantive powers possessed by Congress under Article I. Consequently Congress could give the District of Columbia courts nonjudicial functions such as revisionary powers over grants of patents and rates fixed by the local public utility commission. There was a conceptual hitch, however. Legislative courts had been regarded as exercising no part of the "judicial power of the United States," since they were not created under Article III, whereas the Supreme Court could exercise nothing but "judicial power." How was it possible, then, for the Supreme Court to hear appeals from legislative courts?

When this point was first raised, the Supreme Court concluded that it was not possible. In *Gordon v. United States* (1864), Chief Justice Taney ruled that Court of Claims decisions, which were in effect only advisory to the Secretary of the Treasury, could not be reviewed by the Supreme Court. Congress then amended the law to give finality to judgments of the Court of Claims, and on that basis the Court accepted appeals from it.[26] The same thing happened with the revisory power of courts of the District of Columbia over the Federal Radio Commission.[27] Thus the Court developed the rule that in proceedings before a legislative court which are judicial in nature and admit of a final judgment, the Supreme Court will accept appellate jurisdiction—an arrangement which Corwin calls a "workable anomaly."

It was made somewhat less anomalous but somewhat more confusing in 1933 when the Court suddenly decided that the courts of the District of Columbia were *both* legislative and constitutional courts.[28] As regards their organization and the tenure and compensation of their judges, they were constitutional courts controlled by Article III, but as regards their jurisdiction and powers they were both legislative and constitutional courts, and so could be vested with nonjudicial powers while sharing the judicial power of the United States.

The difficulties of this dual status were only partially resolved by the decision in *Glidden Co. v. Zdanok* (1962). Congress had sought to clear up the status of the Court of Claims in 1953 by legislation flatly declaring it to have been established under Article III,[29] and it did the same thing for the Court of Customs and Patent Appeals in 1958.[30] The validity of this legislation came into question when judges of these two courts were assigned temporarily by the Chief Justice to sit in regular federal courts which were short of judges because of disability or disqualification. The contention in *Glidden* was that they were not Article III judges, and so could not sit in Article III courts.

[26] *DeGroot v. United States* (1867).
[27] *Federal Radio Commission v. General Electric Co.* (1930).
[28] *O'Donoghue v. United States* (1933).
[29] 67 Stat. 226 (1953).
[30] 72 Stat. 848 (1958).

By a five to two vote the Supreme Court upheld the Article III status of these judges, but the majority was split as to the reasons. Three justices held that the two courts were now Article III courts because Congress had said so, and they overruled *Bakelite* and *Williams* which had said they were not. The other two justices in the majority said the two courts had become Article III courts because Congress had withdrawn questionable jurisdiction from those courts since the *Bakelite* and *Williams* decisions, which they would not overrule. The two dissenters, Douglas and Black, thought that these two specialized courts were still performing legislative and executive functions, that *Bakelite* and *Williams* were still the law, and that it was as improper for their judges to be assigned to sit in a regular federal court as it would be for a member of the Interstate Commerce Commission to sit there.

There appears to be something about the legislative court concept which breeds confusion. It might be better if Marshall had never invented it.

### STAFFING THE FEDERAL JUDICIARY

The appointment of federal judges is frankly and entirely a political process. With few exceptions the President limits his choice to members of his own party. During the eight most recent presidential terms, from 1933 to 1965, there were only two exceptions to this rule in Supreme Court appointments —President Truman's appointment of Republican Harold Burton, with whom he had been associated in the Senate, and President Eisenhower's naming of Democrat William Brennan, Jr. In the lower federal courts, during the present century over 90 per cent of all judicial appointments have gone to members of the President's party. For example, President Eisenhower appointed 158 Republicans and 12 Democrats to the district and appeals courts. President Kennedy named 113 Democrats, 10 Republicans, and 1 Liberal.[31]

District judgeships are filled primarily on the recommendation of the state party organization and the senator from the state, if there is one of the President's party. The nominees thus suggested are given a thorough check by the Department of Justice, the FBI, and the American Bar Association's committee on the federal judiciary. Of the 228 district judges appointed by Eisenhower and Kennedy, 124 were practicing lawyers at the time of appointment, while 53 were state judges, 24 were lawyers in government positions, and 20 held other government or political positions.

For appointments to the federal courts of appeals, again the recommendations of the appropriate senators and state party organizations are of primary importance. Since the appellate circuits cover more than one state,

---

[31] These and subsequent data are taken from Sheldon Goldman, "Characteristics of Eisenhower and Kennedy Appointees to the Lower Federal Courts," 18 *Western Political Quarterly* 755–762 (1965).

vacancies must be allocated to the various states on some basis satisfactory to the party organizations. Positions on the courts of appeals are much more likely to go to men with previous judicial experience than in the case of district judgeships. Among the sixty-six appellate judges named by Eisenhower and Kennedy, thirty-five were either state or federal district judges at the time of their appointment, while seventeen were in private law practice, seven were government lawyers, and three were in other government positions.

Vacancies on the Supreme Court present major policy problems for the President. He receives suggestions from many sources and particularly from his Attorney General, but he makes his own decisions, and often he has his own ideas on the subject, either as to specific candidates or as to the qualifications he wants. Presidents are usually interested in the political viewpoint of a possible nominee and the line he is likely to take in deciding cases. Of course, predicting the future decisions of a man to be placed in a lifetime position on the bench is risky business. Theodore Roosevelt was unusually careful in picking men who could be expected to vote right on the big issues, and he was very angry when Justice Oliver Wendell Holmes, soon after his appointment to the Court, disappointed his expectations in an important antitrust case. President Taft felt that the most significant thing he had done during his administration was to appoint six justices who shared his conservative views. "And I have said to them," Taft chuckled to newspapermen when his term was expiring, "'Damn you, if any of you die, I'll disown you.'" [32]

The Senate must confirm all judicial appointees, and this gives senators their control over judicial selections. If the President should name a man who is opposed by the senator from the state concerned, the senator has only to notify the Senate that the nominee is "personally obnoxious" to him, and the rule of "senatorial courtesy" will ensure his rejection. Occasionally the Senate declines to confirm a nominee for the lower federal courts on other grounds. In 1965 an interesting case occurred when Senate concern about the obvious unfitness of a nominee sponsored by Senator Edward Kennedy led to withdrawal of the nomination.

For Supreme Court appointments the Senate confirmation stage affords an opportunity to consider the political views of the nominee. Perhaps the most famous instance was the violent opposition to Louis D. Brandeis when he was nominated by President Wilson in 1916. Brandeis was attacked by conservatives because of his alleged lack of judicial temperament, but won confirmation on a straight party vote. Charles Evans Hughes was also unsuccessfully opposed in 1931, some liberal Democrats and agrarian Republicans picturing him as a "corporation lawyer." The nomination of John J. Parker was actually defeated in 1930—the only instance of this sort in the

[32] Henry F. Pringle, *The Life and Times of William Howard Taft* (New York: Holt, Rinehart and Winston, Inc., 1939), p. 854.

present century—because of allegations that he was antilabor and anti-Negro. His distinguished career on a federal appeals court subsequently made it appear that he would have been more liberal than the justice who got the position, Owen J. Roberts.

While judicial appointments go almost entirely to members of the party in power, the character of American parties guarantees that the appointees will represent various shades of opinion on political issues. President Eisenhower's four Republican appointees to the Court could be categorized as one liberal (Warren), two moderates (Harlan and Stewart), and one conservative (Whittaker). He also appointed Brennan, a liberal Democrat. On the other hand, President Kennedy, under pressure from conservative Southern Democratic senators, named several segregationist judges in Southern states.

It is sometimes argued that only men with previous judicial experience should be given federal judicial appointments. In fact, this already happens frequently. Almost 30 per cent of the district judges named by Eisenhower and Kennedy had had prior judicial experience, while 60 per cent of their appointees to the courts of appeals were former judges.

It would be unfortunate, however, if presidential freedom of selection were limited by a judicial experience requirement, particularly at the Supreme Court level. The major questions with which the Supreme Court deals require political judgment more than technical proficiency in private law. If judicial experience had been a prerequisite in the past, many of the greatest Supreme Court justices would have been ineligible for appointment, including Marshall, Story, Taney, Miller, Bradley, Hughes (at his first appointment), Brandeis, Stone, Black, Frankfurter, and Warren.[33] In spite of all criticisms, it should be recognized that the present system of selecting judges has resulted in a federal bench of high prestige, a very satisfactory level of ability, and unquestioned honesty.

## JUDICIAL TENURE AND COMPENSATION

Appointment of federal judges for "good behavior" is one of the great pillars of judicial independence. A federal judge can be removed from office only by conviction on impeachment. Only one Supreme Court justice has ever been subjected to impeachment proceedings, Samuel Chase, whose judicial conduct was marked by gross and violent Federalist partisanship. In 1804 the triumphant Jeffersonians sought his removal by impeachment, but failed to secure a conviction. They were successful, however, in impeaching and con-

[33] Justice Frankfurter himself, after a detailed study of this problem in 1957, concluded: "One is entitled to say without qualification that the correlation between prior judicial experience and fitness for the functions of the Supreme Court is zero." "The Supreme Court in the Mirror of Justices," 105 *University of Pennsylvania Law Review* 781 (1957).

victing a district judge, John Pickering, who was a Federalist but also apparently insane. Only seven other federal judges have been impeached, three successfully, and in no case were any partisan political motives involved.

Whether Congress can effect the removal of a judge from office by abolishing his position is a disputed question. As already noted, the Jeffersonians in 1802 repealed the statute of 1801 which created sixteen new circuit judgeships for the Federalists to fill. The intent of the 1802 act was to oust the judges who had been appointed to these posts, and the Jeffersonian theory was that they had ceased to be judges when their offices were abolished. Congress took steps to prevent any of the ousted judges from bringing suit by passing a second statute limiting the Supreme Court to one term annually, and postponing the next term for fourteen months. By that time the controversy had died down, and the Court was able to avoid a decision on the question.[34] On two subsequent occasions when Congress has abolished federal courts, it has provided for the transfer of their judges to other courts, and this seems to be the more correct constitutional practice.

Congress on occasion creates "temporary" district judgeships, but appointees to these positions have full lifetime tenure. The purpose of a temporary judgeship is temporarily to increase the manpower in a district without increasing the number of authorized judgeships. The next vacancy that occurs after a temporary judgeship has been provided for cannot be filled, thus reducing the judges in the district to the authorized number.

Congress is of course free to encourage the resignation of federal judges by attractive retirement arrangements. The absence or inadequacy of retirement allowances has in the past been responsible for some judges retaining their posts long after they were physically or mentally incapacitated for the work. When Justice Grier had become senile in 1870, a committee of his colleagues, headed by Justice Field, finally waited on him and suggested that he retire. Twenty-six years later Field himself became mentally incompetent. His worried colleagues deputed Justice Harlan to approach Field and ask him if he could recall the course of action he had suggested to Grier. Field finally got the point and, momentarily recovering his acuteness, burst out: "Yes! And a dirtier day's work I never did in my life!" His colleagues then abandoned their efforts, but within a few months Field submitted his resignation.[35]

The age of Supreme Court justices was one of the key issues in President Roosevelt's 1937 "Court-packing" plan. As an aftermath of this controversy, Congress passed a liberalized retirement act which permits federal justices to retire after seventy on full pay without resigning, remaining thereafter subject to recall for further judicial duty in the lower courts.

[34] *Stuart* v. *Laird* (1803).
[35] Carl B. Swisher, *Stephen J. Field* (Washington, D.C.: The Brookings Institution, 1930), p. 444.

The provision that a judge's compensation may not be reduced while he is in office is a subsidiary support for judicial independence.[36] The only federal legislation which has ever been challenged on this score was the federal income tax as applied to judges. In 1920 the Supreme Court in *Evans* v. *Gore* adopted the ridiculous proposition that a federal judge could not be assessed income tax because it would amount to an unconstitutional reduction of his salary. Justices Holmes and Brandeis dissented, Holmes saying that judges were not "a privileged class, free from bearing their share of the cost of the institutions upon which their well-being if not their life depends."

The Court persisted, and in 1925 compounded its error when in *Miles* v. *Graham* it ruled that a judge appointed after the effective date of the tax was also entitled to the immunity. Congress overrode this decision by express legislation, and in 1939 a more sensible Court reopened the matter and overruled *Evans* v. *Gore,* Justice Frankfurter saying in *O'Malley* v. *Woodrough:* "To suggest that [the tax] makes inroads upon the independence of judges . . . is to trivialize the great historic experience on which the framers based the safeguards of Article III."

The immunity of judges from liability for damages for acts committed within their judicial jurisdiction was firmly established at common law, and the Supreme Court recognized this doctrine in *Bradley* v. *Fisher* (1871). This immunity applies even when the judge is accused of acting maliciously or corruptly. The doctrine is not "for the protection of a malicious or corrupt judge, but for the benefit of the public, whose interest it is that the judges should be at liberty to exercise their functions with independence, and without fear of consequences." [37]

### SELECTED REFERENCES

ABRAHAM, HENRY J., *The Judicial Process.* Fair Lawn, N.J.: Oxford University Press, 1962.

CLAYTON, JAMES E., *The Making of Justice: The Supreme Court in Action.* New York: E. P. Dutton & Co., Inc., 1964.

[36] Traditionally, the Chief Justice of the United States has been paid the same amount as the Vice President and the Speaker of the House, with the associate justices receiving $500 less than the Chief Justice. This arrangement was thought to symbolize the equality of the three branches of government. In a 1964 government salary bill Congress voted a $7,500 increase for its own members and for the federal judiciary. However, in an unprecedented action Congress limited the increase for the Supreme Court's members to $4,500, in effect assessing a penalty of $3,000 against each justice to express disapproval of some of the Court's decisions.

[37] In *Pierson* v. *Ray* (1967) the Court held that the Civil Rights Act of 1871, making liable "any person" who under "color of law" deprives another person of his civil rights, did not abolish the immunity of judges for acts within their judicial role.

*The Constitution of the United States of America: Analysis and Interpretation,* Sen. Doc. no. 39, 88th Cong., pp. 563–596. Washington: Government Printing Office, 1964.

DANELSKI, DAVID J., *A Supreme Court Justice Is Appointed.* New York: Random House, Inc., 1964.

FRANK, JOHN P., *Marble Palace: The Supreme Court in American Life.* New York: Alfred A. Knopf, Inc., 1958.

FRANKFURTER, FELIX, and JAMES M. LANDIS, *The Business of the Supreme Court: A Study in the Federal Judicial System.* New York: The Macmillan Company, 1928.

GOLDFARB, RONALD L., *The Contempt Power.* New York: Columbia University Press, 1963.

GROSSMAN, JOEL B., *Lawyers and Judges: The American Bar Association and the Politics of Judicial Selection.* New York: John Wiley & Sons, Inc., 1965.

HARRIS, JOSEPH P., *The Advice and Consent of the Senate.* Berkeley, Calif.: University of California Press, 1953.

HARRIS, ROBERT J., *The Judicial Power of the United States.* Baton Rouge, La.: Louisiana State University Press, 1940.

HART, HENRY M., JR., and HERBERT WECHSLER, *The Federal Courts and the Federal System,* chaps. 1, 3. Brooklyn, N.Y.: The Foundation Press, Inc., 1953.

HUGHES, CHARLES EVANS, *The Supreme Court of the United States.* New York: Columbia University Press, 1928.

JACOB, HERBERT, *Justice in America: Courts, Lawyers, and the Judicial Process.* Boston: Little, Brown and Company, 1965.

LEWIS, ANTHONY, *Gideon's Trumpet.* New York: Random House, Inc., 1964.

PELTASON, JACK W., *Federal Courts and the Political Process.* Garden City, N.Y.: Doubleday & Company, Inc., 1955.

SCHMIDHAUSER, JOHN R., *The Supreme Court: Its Politics, Personalities, and Procedures.* New York: Holt, Rinehart and Winston, Inc., 1960.

# 8

## Jurisdiction of the federal courts

Article III, section 1, provides that the "judicial power of the United States shall be vested in one Supreme Court, and in such inferior courts as the Congress may from time to time ordain and establish." As we know, the Constitution thus left undecided the basic question as to whether there would be a system of lower federal courts, but the First Congress proceeded to create a complete hierarchy of courts.

The "judicial power" is defined in Article III, section 2, which sets out the various classes of cases and controversies over which the federal courts can be given jurisdiction. "Jurisdiction" in the judicial sense means the power of a court to hear (or try) a case. A court may exercise judicial power only within its authorized jurisdiction. The terms "judicial power" and "jurisdiction" are often used synonymously. However, so far as the federal courts are concerned, it is necessary to distinguish between "the judicial power of the United States" and "the jurisdiction of the federal courts," because, in spite of the word "shall," the judicial power of the United States is not automatically vested in the lower federal courts by Article III.

These courts are creatures of Congress. It could have failed to establish them in the first place, and presumably it could abolish them if it chose to do so.[1] Consequently Congress has assumed from the beginning that it can

---

[1] However, as we saw in the preceding chapter, it is not clear that Congress could abolish the positions of sitting judges.

control the jurisdiction of the lower federal courts, and the Supreme Court has acquiesced in this position in a long series of decisions.[2] The Judiciary Act of 1789 conferred jurisdiction on the lower federal courts, but not all the jurisdiction they were capable of receiving under the federal judicial power.

The situation, then, is that for the lower federal courts to have jurisdiction of a case or controversy, (1) it must be one which the Constitution has defined as within the judicial power of the United States, and (2) an act of Congress must have conferred jurisdiction over such cases on the courts. For example, the Constitution extends federal judicial power to controversies between citizens of different states, but Congress has given the federal courts jurisdiction of such cases only if the amount in controversy exceeds $10,000. The jurisdiction of the Supreme Court is a special problem which was discussed in Chapter 7.

### FEDERAL JUDICIAL POWER: SUBJECT MATTER

The judicial power of the United States is defined by Article III on two different bases—subject matter and nature of the parties involved. The subject-matter classifications are (1) all cases in law and equity arising under the Constitution; (2) all cases in law and equity arising under "the laws of the United States"; (3) all cases in law and equity arising under treaties made under the authority of the United States; and (4) all cases of admiralty and maritime jurisdiction. The federal judicial power extends to any case falling in these four fields, regardless of who the parties to the controversy may be.

THE CONSTITUTION AS A SOURCE OF JUDICIAL POWER    Cases "arising under this Constitution" are those in which an interpretation or application of the Constitution is necessary in order to arrive at a decision. They usually arise when an individual challenges the enforcement against himself of federal or state legislation or executive action, which he asserts to be in violation of federal constitutional provisions. Suits raising a constitutional issue may be filed in the federal courts, or if filed in state courts are subject to review by the Supreme Court after they have progressed through the highest state court to which appeal is possible.[3] The most striking aspect of the American judicial system is the power of courts, both federal and state, to strike down legislation, both federal and state, on the ground of its conflict with the Con-

---

[2] *Turner* v. *Bank of North America* (1799); *United States* v. *Hudson and Goodwin* (1812); *Cary* v. *Curtis* (1845); *Shelden* v. *Sill* (1850).

[3] The case of *Thompson* v. *City of Louisville* (1960) went directly from the Louisville police court to the Supreme Court; it involved two fines of $10 each, and police-court fines of less than $20 on a single charge were not appealable to any other Kentucky court.

stitution. This power of judicial review is so significant that it is reserved for treatment in the following chapter.

LAWS AND TREATIES AS SOURCES OF JUDICIAL POWER    The "laws of the United States" referred to in Article III are statutes passed by Congress. At first there was some contention that the phrase also covered federal common law. It was asserted that a new political system must carry over and enforce, until revised or repealed, the customary law previously prevailing, which in this case was the English common law. The Supreme Court, however, took the general position that "courts which are created by written law, and whose jurisdiction is defined by written law, cannot transcend that jurisdiction." [4] In 1812 it specifically ruled that there was no common law of crimes enforceable by the federal courts.[5]

Under Article VI, "all treaties made, or which shall be made, under the authority of the United States" share with the Constitution and the laws of the United States the status of the "supreme law of the land." A treaty which is self-executing—i.e., which operates of itself, without the aid of any legislative enforcement—thus has the status of municipal law and is directly enforceable by the courts. This distinctive feature of the American Constitution resulted from experience under the Articles, when the fulfillment of treaties entered into by Congress was dependent on the action of state legislatures. Laws and treaties are of course subordinate to the Constitution, but as to each other are on the same level of authority. Thus in the case of a conflict between a law and a treaty, the later one in point of time will be enforced by the courts.[6]

Issues arising under the Constitution, laws, or treaties of the United States are referred to generally as "federal questions." A plaintiff seeking to bring a case in the federal courts on one of these grounds must set forth on the face of his complaint a substantial claim as to the federal question involved. The mere allegation that such a question is present will not suffice; its presence must be clearly shown. The right or immunity created by the Constitution, laws, or treaties must be such that it will be supported if they are given one construction or defeated if given another. The question alleged to exist must not be insubstantial, or have been so conclusively settled as to foreclose the issue entirely.

ADMIRALTY AND MARITIME JURISDICTION    Under the Articles, decisions of state admiralty courts could be taken to an admiralty court of appeals set up by the Congress. The Constitution, in pursuance of its goal of promoting uniform regulation of commerce, provided for admiralty and maritime jurisdiction in the federal courts. The Judiciary Act of 1789 vested this

[4] *Ex parte Bollman* ( 1807 ).
[5] *United States* v. *Hudson and Goodwin* ( 1812 ).
[6] *Head Money Cases* ( 1884 ).

jurisdiction exclusively in the federal district courts, although parties were enabled to avail themselves of common-law remedies in the state courts.

In England admiralty jurisdiction, which dealt with local shipping, harbor, and fishing regulations, extended inland only as far as the ebb and flow of the tide. In a small country like England where practically all navigable streams are tidal, this was an adequate definition, but it did not prove so in the United States. It was gradually expanded until a congressional act of 1845 extended admiralty jurisdiction to all the navigable waters of the country. The Supreme Court upheld this law in the case of *The Genesee Chief* (1852).

Admiralty and maritime jurisdiction covers two general classes of cases. The first relates to acts committed on the high seas or other navigable waters, and includes prize and forfeiture cases as well as torts, injuries, and crimes. Locality is the determining circumstance in this class of jurisdiction. The second category relates to contracts and transactions connected with shipping, including seamen's suits for wages, litigation over marine insurance policies, and the like.

The general principle of exclusiveness of federal admiralty jurisdiction does not prevent the states from retaining their general or political powers of law enforcement on navigable waters, as was established in 1818 when the Supreme Court invalidated a federal court conviction for a murder committed in Boston Harbor.[7] Moreover, the states may create rights by law which are enforceable in federal admiralty proceedings. The law administered by the federal courts in admiralty cases, as Corwin says, is "an amalgam of the general maritime law insofar as it is acceptable to the courts, modifications of that law by Congressional enactments, the common law of torts and contracts as modified by State or National legislation, and international prize law."[8]

## FEDERAL JUDICIAL POWER: PARTIES

Apart from the four subject-matter classifications, federal judicial power is defined in terms of parties. Article III extends federal power to controversies (1) to which the United States is a party; (2) between two or more states;[9] (3) between a state and citizens of another state; (4) between citizens of different states; (5) between citizens of the same state claiming lands under grants of different states (a category which quickly became obsolete); (6) between a state, or the citizens thereof, and foreign states, citizens, or subjects; and (7) to all cases affecting ambassadors, other public ministers, and

---

[7] *United States* v. *Bevans* (1818).

[8] Edward S. Corwin (ed.), *The Constitution of the United States of America: Analysis and Interpretation* (Washington: Government Printing Office, 1953), p. 583.

[9] The problem of suits between states has already been discussed in Chap. 6.

consuls. Matters involving these classes of parties can be brought in the federal courts, no matter what the subject matter.

SUITS TO WHICH THE UNITED STATES IS A PARTY    Obviously no constitutional provision would have been necessary to give the United States authority to bring suit as party plaintiff in its own courts. Nor is congressional authorization necessary to enable the United States to sue.[10] Like other parties, however, the United States must have an interest in the subject matter and a legal right to the remedy sought. Thus in 1935 the Supreme Court refused to take jurisdiction of a suit by the United States against West Virginia to determine the navigability of certain rivers in that state, on the ground that there were no legal issues, merely differences of opinion between the two governments.[11]

The principal problems arise, not where the United States is a plaintiff, but where it is a defendant. The principle of sovereign immunity establishes that the government cannot be sued without its consent. Where such consent is given by Congress, the United States can be sued only in accordance with the conditions stated. The government has been suable on contracts in the Court of Claims since 1855, but could not be sued in torts until the passage of the Federal Tort Claims Act in 1946. Even under that statute, there are considerable limits on the government's liability for torts of its employees.

Government corporations are in a special category so far as liability to suit is concerned. They have generally been created in order to operate business enterprises for the government with something like the freedom of private corporations, and this includes freedom to sue and be sued. Congress can of course relieve government corporations from liability to suit, but where it makes no provision one way or the other, the Supreme Court has held the practice of corporate liability to be so well established as to render the corporation subject to suit.[12]

When no consent to sue the government has been given, it may be possible to sue officials acting for the government. In practice it is often very difficult for courts to decide whether a suit which is nominally against a government official is actually a suit against the government. For example, a suit against the Secretary of the Treasury to review a decision about the rate of duty on sugar was held to be suit against the United States because of its effect on the revenue system of the government.[13] One general rule which courts have tended to apply is that a suit in which the judgment

[10] *Dugan* v. *United States* (1818). The Voting Rights Act of 1965 expressed the sense of Congress that the use of poll taxes as a suffrage requirement abridged the right to vote; it directed the Attorney General to institute court action against state enforcement of poll taxes.
[11] *United States* v. *West Virginia* (1935).
[12] *Keifer & Keifer* v. *Reconstruction Finance Corporation* (1939).
[13] *Louisiana* v. *McAdoo* (1914).

would affect the United States or its property is a suit against the United States. On the other hand, cases in which action adverse to the interests of a plaintiff is taken by a government official, who is alleged to be acting beyond his statutory authority or under an unconstitutional statute, are generally held not to be suits against the government.

The leading case on establishing official liability to suit is *United States v. Lee* (1882), which involved the claim of the government to possession of the Robert E. Lee mansion in Arlington, Virginia, through a tax sale. Lee's heirs brought suit for ejectment against the federal officials in charge, and by a five to four vote the Supreme Court held this was not a suit against the United States until it had been determined whether the officers were acting within the scope of their lawful authority. Here the Court found that government possession was based on an unlawful order of the President, and concluded: "No man in this country is so high that he is above the law. No officer of the law may set that law at defiance with impunity."

CONTROVERSIES BETWEEN A STATE AND CITIZENS OF ANOTHER STATE    This provision of the Constitution was generally assumed to extend federal jurisdiction only to suits by a state as plaintiff against citizens of another state as defendants. However, in *Chisholm v. Georgia* (1793), the Supreme Court imprudently interpreted it as permitting a state to be made a defendant in a suit brought by citizens of another state. Georgia then refused to permit the decree to be enforced, and widespread protests against the Court's action resulted in its prompt reversal by adoption of the Eleventh Amendment. Later the Court itself admitted that the *Chisholm* decision had been erroneous.[14]

Since states cannot be sued by citizens of other states in the federal courts, or in their own courts without their consent, no judicial means may be available to compel a state to honor debts owed to private citizens. As already noted, an effort by citizens of New Hampshire to use their state government as a collection agency to recover on defaulted Louisiana bonds failed.[15] When similar bonds were donated outright to South Dakota, however, that state was successful in collecting from North Carolina on them, though four justices thought that even this was a violation of the Eleventh Amendment.[16]

In general, the question as to when a suit is one against a state, and so forbidden by the Eleventh Amendment, is determined on much the same rules as govern federal immunity to suit.[17] Thus, suits against state officers involving state property or suits asking for relief which call for the exercise

---

[14] *Hans v. Louisiana* (1890).
[15] *New Hampshire v. Louisiana* (1883).
[16] *South Dakota v. North Carolina* (1904).
[17] See *Governor of Georgia v. Madrago* (1828); *Kennecott Copper Co. v. State Tax Commission* (1946).

of official authority are considered suits against the state and so prohibited. But suits against state officials alleged to be acting in excess of their statutory authority or under an unconstitutional statute are maintainable.[18]

As a plaintiff, suing citizens of another state, a state may act to protect its own legal rights, or as *parens patriae* to protect the health and welfare of its citizens. The *parens patriae* concept will justify suits brought to protect the welfare of the people as a whole, but not to protect the private interests of individual citizens, though this distinction is often difficult to make. In 1945 the Court permitted Georgia as *parens patriae* to sue twenty railroads for alleged rate-fixing conspiracy. "If the allegations of the bill are taken as true," the Court said, "the economy of Georgia and the welfare of her citizens have seriously suffered as the result of this alleged conspiracy." [19]

Under this clause states are limited to civil proceedings. They cannot seek to enforce their penal laws against citizens of other states in the federal courts.[20] Moreover, states may not seek judicial redress which would be inconsistent with the distribution of powers under the federal Constitution. In *Massachusetts* v. *Mellon* (1923) the state had sought in its *parens patriae* status to enjoin a federal grant-in-aid statute. Justice Sutherland said, in frustrating this effort:

> It cannot be conceded that a State, as *parens patriae*, may institute judicial proceedings to protect citizens of the United States from the operation of the statutes thereof. While the State, under some circumstances, may sue in that capacity for the protection of its citizens . . . it is no part of its duty or power to enforce their rights in respect of their relations with the Federal Government. In that field it is the United States, and not the State, which represents them as *parens patriae*, when such representation becomes appropriate.

CONTROVERSIES BETWEEN CITIZENS OF DIFFERENT STATES    Interesting jurisdictional questions are created by the "diversity of citizenship" clause. For natural persons the tests of state citizenship are domicile in a state, which may be established by residence there, acquisition of property, payment of taxes, or acquisition of the suffrage. If there are multiple parties in a diversity suit, all the persons on one side of the case must be citizens of different states from all persons on the other side.[21] In the case of corporations the Court has adopted the fiction that all the stockholders of a corporation are citizens of the state of incorporation.[22]

[18] See *Osborn* v. *Bank of the United States* (1824).
[19] *Georgia* v. *Pennsylvania R. Co.* (1945). In 1966 the state of Delaware, as *parens patriae* for its citizens, sued the other forty-nine states, seeking to enjoin them from following the unit-vote system in casting their electoral votes for President, a practice which Delaware maintained discriminated against its voters and those of the other smaller states. See Chap. 16.
[20] *Wisconsin* v. *Pelican Insurance Co.* (1888).
[21] *Strawbridge* v. *Curtiss* (1806).
[22] *Muller* v. *Dows* (1877).

The ease of access to the federal courts thus provided for corporations led to substantial abuses. The classic example was the *Kentucky Taxicab Case* (1928). Here a taxicab company, incorporated in Kentucky and doing business in a Kentucky city, wanted to enter into an exclusive contract to provide taxicab service at a railroad station. Knowing that Kentucky courts would invalidate such a contract as contrary to state law, the corporation dissolved itself and reincorporated the identical business in Tennessee. In its new guise it entered into the contract, and then brought suit in federal court to prevent a competing company from interfering with the carrying out of the contract. Since the federal court was not bound by the Kentucky law, this stratagem succeeded.[23]

The *Kentucky Taxicab Case* would be decided differently today, because in 1938 an extremely important reversal of doctrine occurred on the Supreme Court with respect to the law to be applied in diversity cases. This is an interesting story, which goes back to the original Judiciary Act of 1789. Section 34 of that act provided that in diversity cases at common law the laws of the several states should be the rules of decision of the federal courts. In *Swift* v. *Tyson* (1842) Justice Story for the Supreme Court decided that "the laws of the several states" referred only to state statutes, and did not cover the unwritten or common law of the states. Thus in the absence of state statutes controlling a case, federal courts were free to adopt and apply such general principles of law as they thought fitting and applicable.

The principle of the *Tyson* case was subsequently extended from negotiable instruments to other matters, such as wills, torts, real estate titles, and contracts, until by 1888 there were twenty-eight kinds of cases in which federal courts were free to apply different rules of law in diversity cases than those of the state courts. Thus in every state the federal and state courts had their own version of commercial common law, with all the attendant confusion that was bound to result, and plaintiffs were free to shop around for the court in which their case would have the best chance of success.

Profound discontent developed with the *Tyson* rule, which was attacked as a wasteful and confused way to handle a delicate problem of federal-state relations. Justice Holmes, who became the spearhead in the fight on *Swift* v. *Tyson*—Miller and Field had preceded him—was motivated not only by respect for state courts, but also by his pragmatic view of law. Law, he said, "does not exist without some definite authority behind it." He had no patience with the notion of a "transcendental body" of law hanging in the air waiting to be divined by the independent judgment of federal courts. An impressive literature of protest against *Swift* v. *Tyson* appeared in the law reviews. Charles Warren in 1923 published an article with newly discovered evidence which seemed to show that Story's interpretation of section 34 was

[23] *Black & White Taxicab Co.* v. *Brown & Yellow Taxicab Co.* (1928).

incorrect. Liberals in Congress proposed legislation to terminate the *Tyson* rule.

All this had an effect. In 1934 the Court decided that in a case "balanced with doubt," the federal court's independent judgment should be subordinated to the state decisions.[24] This was the only warning given before the roof fell in. *Erie Railroad* v. *Tompkins* was decided in 1938. Counsel in the case had not questioned the *Tyson* precedent. The interpretation of section 34 was not before the Court. Yet Justice Brandeis not only overruled *Swift* v. *Tyson,* he also held that by its previous interpretation of section 34 the Court had committed an unconstitutional action. This is the first and only time in its history that the Supreme Court has accused itself of having made an unconstitutional decision. What it was saying, in effect, was that if Congress should wish to reinstate the *Tyson* rule, it could not do so without amending the Constitution.

The facts of the *Erie* case may help to show the policy considerations which went into this decision. Tompkins, a citizen of Pennsylvania, was seriously injured by a freight train while he was walking along the railroad right of way. He was a trespasser, and by the common law of Pennsylvania railroads were not liable to trespassers except for wanton or willful negligence. So his attorneys filed suit, not in the state courts of Pennsylvania, but in the federal court in New York, the state in which the railroad was incorporated. The lower federal courts awarded Tompkins a judgment of $30,000, holding that it was unnecessary to consider what Pennsylvania law provided, for the question was one of general law to be decided by the federal courts in the exercise of their independent judgment. To this situation Justice Brandeis reacted by stating this new rule of decision:

> Except in matters governed by the Federal Constitution or by Acts of Congress, the law to be applied in any case is the law of the State. And whether the law of the State shall be declared by its Legislature in a statute or by its highest court in a decision is not a matter of federal concern. There is no federal general common law.

The essential intent of the ruling, Justice Frankfurter said in 1945, was to ensure that, in all diversity cases, "the outcome of the litigation in the federal court should be substantially the same, so far as legal rules determine the outcome of a litigation, as it would be if tried in a State court." [25] At first the Supreme Court's tendency was to push its mandate rather far. For example, the Court held that the *Erie* rule required the enforcement of state procedural as well as substantive law.[26] Again, in situations where the highest state court had not passed on a matter of state law, the Supreme Court held that the federal district court must descend the state judicial hierarchy

[24] *Mutual Life Insurance Co.* v. *Johnson* (1934).
[25] *Guaranty Trust Co.* v. *New York* (1945).
[26] *Ibid.*

until it did find a court which had ruled on the matter, and then be guided by that ruling.[27]

However, increasing experience with the *Erie* rule led the Supreme Court to recognize "countervailing factors" which reflect a federal interest in diversity litigation, and where these are deemed to be of overriding importance, to apply federal policy rather than state law. In fact, Judge Henry J. Friendly contends that the *Erie* denial of any federal *general* common law has left the Supreme Court freer to develop a "specialized federal common law" which overrides state law on subjects of national concern and within national legislative power.[28]

CASES INVOLVING FOREIGN STATES AND CITIZENS    The language giving federal jurisdiction over controversies "between a state, or the citizens thereof, and foreign states, citizens or subjects" is not quite as broad as it sounds. Under principles of international law foreign states cannot be sued in American courts without their consent,[29] not even by American states, and conversely foreign powers cannot sue American states in the federal courts.[30] But an American state can sue foreign citizens, foreign states can sue American citizens, American citizens can sue foreigners, and vice versa.

Giving foreign states access to American courts is in accord with the general principle of comity in international law. To be able to sue in American courts, a foreign government must be recognized by the United States, and of course it must submit to the procedures and rules of decisions of American courts.

CASES AFFECTING AMBASSADORS, MINISTERS, AND CONSULS    When Article III gives the federal courts jurisdiction over cases affecting ambassadors, other public ministers, and consuls, naturally it is referring to diplomatic personnel accredited by foreign states to the United States, not to American ambassadors to other countries.[31] Since ambassadors and ministers representing foreign governments in the United States are exempt from jurisdiction of American courts under international law, the effect of this provision is principally to permit foreign diplomats to bring suit in American federal courts against private individuals.

Consuls are not entitled to the same immunity, and federal courts can

---

[27] *West* v. *American Telephone & Telegraph Co.* (1940); *Fidelity Union Trust Co.* v. *Field* (1940); but see *King* v. *Order of United Commercial Travelers* (1948).

[28] "In Praise of Erie—and of the New Federal Common Law," 19 *Record, City of New York Bar* 64–109 (1964). See *Clearfield Trust Co.* v. *United States* (1943); *Textile Workers Union* v. *Lincoln Mills* (1957); Alexander M. Bickel and Harry H. Wellington, "Legislative Purpose and the Judicial Process: The Lincoln Mills Case," 71 *Harvard Law Review* 1–39 (1957).

[29] *The Exchange* v. *McFaddon* (1812).

[30] *Monaco* v. *Mississippi* (1934).

[31] *Ex parte Gruber* (1925).

take jurisdiction of cases concerning them. They may also be dealt with in state courts where appropriate. In *Popovici* v. *Agler* (1930) a Rumanian vice-consul, having married in Ohio, had been sued for divorce and alimony in an Ohio court. He objected to the state court's jurisdiction, claiming that diplomatic officials could be sued only in the federal courts, but Justice Holmes said the constitutional provisions must be interpreted in the light of the fact that domestic relations were reserved to the states at the time the Constitution was adopted.

## FEDERAL–STATE COURT RELATIONS: CONCURRENCY OF JURISDICTION

Though the Judiciary Act of 1789 provided for a complete system of lower federal courts, the statute, as already noted, withheld from the federal courts much of the jurisdiction they were capable of exercising. In fact, from 1789 to the Civil War the lower federal courts were in effect subsidiary courts, principally designed as protection to citizens litigating outside their own states. But after the Civil War the new feelings of nationalism motivated Congress to invest the federal judiciary with enormously increased powers. The Removal Act of March 3, 1875, provided that any suit involving a right given by the Constitution, laws, and treaties of the United States could be begun in the federal courts, or if begun in state courts could be removed to the federal courts for disposition.

Jurisdiction over cases within the judicial power of the United States may thus be exercised either by federal or state courts, except in certain areas where Congress has entrusted jurisdiction *exclusively* to the federal courts. Important areas now exclusively within federal jurisdiction include crimes defined by the United States, federal seizures on land or water, admiralty and maritime jurisdiction, bankruptcy proceedings, actions arising under patent and copyright laws, suits against consuls, suits for penalties and forfeitures incurred under the laws of the United States, and most of the remedies against the United States or federal agencies that have been specially defined by statute.

States have occasionally sought to place restrictions on the right of removal of civil suits from state courts, particularly in dealing with foreign (i.e., out-of-state) corporations. These efforts have usually been held unconstitutional. *Terral* v. *Burke Construction Co.* (1922) concerned a state law providing that when a foreign corporation removed a suit into federal court, its license to do business within the state would be revoked. The Supreme Court held this was an attempt to curtail the free exercise of a constitutional right, and consequently invalid.

When state courts exercise jurisdiction over cases falling within the judicial power of the United States, they operate under the control of the

"supremacy clause" of the Constitution. Article VI, after making the Constitution, laws, and treaties of the United States "the supreme law of the land," continues: "And the judges in every state shall be bound thereby, any thing in the Constitution or laws of any state to the contrary notwithstanding."

Enforcement of this obligation through Supreme Court review of state court decisions, as established in the cases of *Martin* v. *Hunter's Lessee* (1816) and *Cohens* v. *Virginia* (1821), has been discussed in Chapter 5. All things considered, the Supreme Court, like Congress, has been extremely considerate of the position of state courts. This deference is exemplified in its practice of not reviewing a decision of a state court if that decision rests on a nonfederal ground adequate to support it. Section 25 of the Judiciary Act of 1789 limits the Supreme Court to reviewing "final" judgments of the highest state court in which a decision could be had. This ensures that state systems of justice will have full opportunity to settle their own questions before the Supreme Court intervenes.

An interesting aspect of concurrency is the positive obligation which the federal government has sometimes imposed on state courts to enforce federal laws. During the early decades, before the federal courts were so well established, this practice was fairly common. The Fugitive Slave Act of 1793, the Naturalization Act of 1795, and the Alien Enemies Act of 1798, all imposed positive duties on state courts to enforce federal law. In 1799 Congress authorized state trial of criminal offenses under the Post Office Act. Great reliance was placed on state courts for the enforcement of Jefferson's Embargo Acts.

This early effort to relieve the federal courts came to grief. The New England courts were hostile to the Embargo Acts, and the Northern courts generally resisted enforcement of the Fugitive Slave Law. The argument was widely heard that one sovereign cannot enforce the penal laws of another, and the Supreme Court for a time endorsed this position by its holding in *Prigg* v. *Pennsylvania* (1842).

More recently, the Federal Employers' Liability Act of 1908, covering injuries to railroad employees, not only gave concurrent jurisdiction in suits arising under the act to state courts, but even prohibited removal of cases begun in state courts to the federal courts. The purpose was to prevent railroads from fleeing to the federal courts if the injured workman felt he would be better off in the state court. Under this statute a state court can be compelled to enforce federal remedies which are contrary to state policy, the Supreme Court ruled in *Second Employers' Liability Cases* (1912).

The basic constitutional issue was reconsidered in *Testa* v. *Katt* (1947). The Emergency Price Control Act of 1942 provided that persons who had been overcharged in violation of the act could sue for treble damages in any court of competent jurisdiction. When such a suit was brought in Rhode Island, the state supreme court held this to be "a penal statute in the international sense," which state courts could not be required to enforce. The

Supreme Court unanimously reversed this ruling, Justice Black reminding Rhode Island that "state courts do not bear the same relation to the United States that they do to foreign countries." Although Congress could not require Rhode Island to provide courts for the enforcement of these suits, since the state does have courts which enforce similar claims, it may require the state to apply the federal law.

A suitor who seeks to defend rights under the federal Constitution, laws, or treaties by filing his suit in federal court cannot be denied his choice of a federal forum merely because state courts are also available to hear such claims. The Supreme Court did, however, approve "abstention" by federal courts in certain narrowly limited special circumstances in *Railroad Commission of Texas* v. *Pullman Co.* (1941). One of these circumstances is where a state statute, challenged as unconstitutional in federal court, is susceptible to a construction by the state courts that would avoid or modify the constitutional question. Abstention cannot be ordered simply to give the state courts the first opportunity to vindicate the federal claim. In *Zwickler* v. *Koota* (1967) the Supreme Court held that abstention should not have been applied in a case where a state statute was attacked as repugnant to the First Amendment on its face.

### FEDERAL–STATE COURT RELATIONS: CONFLICTS OF JURISDICTION

A dual system of courts faces, in addition to the confusions of concurrency, the frictions of jurisdictional conflicts. Coercive writs may be sought in one jurisdiction against the operation of the other. States may try to impose barriers to removal of cases to federal courts. States may attempt to punish in state courts federal officials who commit some transgressions in the execution of their official duties within the state. State courts have on occasion even refused to comply with Supreme Court orders.

Such frictions may require adoption of appropriate federal legislation, but to a considerable extent the two systems of courts handle their own problems by application of principles of comity. Comity, says Corwin, is "a self-imposed rule of judicial morality whereby independent tribunals of concurrent or coordinate jurisdiction exercise a mutual restraint in order to prevent interference with each other and to avoid collisions of authority." [32] Exercise of the principles of comity is most often required where writs of injunction or habeas corpus are used by one system of courts against the other level of government.

JUDICIAL CONFLICT THROUGH INJUNCTIONS    In general, neither state nor federal courts may enjoin each other's proceedings or judgments. State courts

[32] *Op. cit.,* p. 626.

have been forbidden to take such action by Supreme Court decisions.[33] The reason given has been not the paramount jurisdiction of the federal courts, but rather the complete independence of the two judicial systems in their respective spheres of action.

Federal courts were forbidden to enjoin proceedings in state courts by act of Congress in 1793. But this bar is not applicable where Congress has expressly authorized a stay of proceedings in state courts, or where an injunction is necessary to protect the lawfully acquired jurisdiction of a federal court or to prevent the relitigation of issues previously adjudicated and finally settled by federal court decree.

Congress has also limited the power of federal courts to issue injunctions affecting the states by other statutes. The tax injunction act of 1937 forbids federal district courts to enjoin the collection of state and local taxes where an adequate remedy exists in state courts. Again, the Johnson Act of 1934 forbids the federal courts to enjoin or suspend the operation of public utility rates which have been fixed by state order after reasonable notice and hearing, if there is an adequate remedy in state courts.

Federal courts do, however, exercise the extremely important power of restraining state officials from enforcing unconstitutional state statutes. This power to enjoin state officials from bringing criminal or civil proceedings to enforce an invalid statute was first asserted by the Supreme Court in *Osborn v. Bank of the United States* (1824), but the rule then was that an injunction could issue only after a finding of unconstitutionality had been made in a lawsuit. In 1908 this requirement was abandoned in *Ex parte Young*, which held that the attorney general of a state could be enjoined from proceeding to enforce a state statute in the state courts *pending* a determination of its constitutionality.

The *Young* decision was sharply criticized in Congress, which in 1910 passed a law prohibiting the issuance of injunctions by a single federal judge to restrain the enforcement of state laws; a three-judge court was required to sit in all cases seeking "to interpose the Constitution against enforcement of a state policy." The Supreme Court has also since about 1940 tended to exercise a moderating influence on such invalidation of state legislation through injunctions against state officials.[34]

The civil rights problems of the 1960s imposed new strains on relations between federal and state courts, which may be illustrated by the case of *Dombrowski* v. *Pfister* (1965). Officers of a civil rights organization active in Louisiana filed suit in a federal district court requesting an injunction against imminent prosecutions under two state anti-Communist laws. The complaint alleged that the statutes were unconstitutional and that the defendants, who were various state officials, had threatened prosecution solely

[33] *McKim* v. *Voorhies* (1812); *United States ex rel. Riggs* v. *Johnson County* (1868).
[34] See *Railroad Commission* v. *Rowan & Nichols Oil Co.* (1940, 1941); *Burford* v. *Sun Oil Co.* (1943); *American Federation of Labor* v. *Watson* (1946).

for the purpose of discouraging the organization's civil rights activities. A three-judge court dismissed the complaint, but the Supreme Court reversed by a vote of five to two.

The Supreme Court held in *Dombrowski* that the provisions of these statutes were so vague and so susceptible of unconstitutional application that their very existence tended to have a "chilling effect upon the exercise of First Amendment rights." Therefore, an injunction should issue immediately, restraining state officials from enforcing or threatening to enforce the statutes until they received an adequate "narrowing construction" in a state declaratory judgment proceeding.

JUDICIAL CONFLICT THROUGH HABEAS CORPUS    The first important controversies in this area arose during the Civil War period from the attempted use of habeas corpus by state courts to release prisoners in federal custody. The most famous case was *Ableman* v. *Booth* (1859), already discussed, in which the Supreme Court took a strong and correct line on national supremacy in dealing with the action of a Wisconsin judge who had released a prisoner held by a federal officer on charges of violating the Fugitive Slave Law. As late as 1872, in *Tarble's Case*, Wisconsin again asserted power to release persons in federal custody, and again the Supreme Court denied this power, saying that neither government "can intrude with its judicial process into the domain of the other, except so far as such intrusion may be necessary on the part of the National government to preserve its rightful supremacy in cases of conflict of authority."

The use of habeas corpus by the federal courts to test the constitutionality of state court convictions for violations of state criminal laws is based on a statute of 1867 extending the remedy of the writ to any person in custody "in violation of the Constitution, or of any treaty or law of the United States." This measure was adopted by the Radical Republican Congress in anticipation of Southern resistance to the new constitutional guarantees. As Justice Brennan has commented: "A remedy almost in the nature of removal from the state to the federal courts of state prisoners' constitutional contentions seems to have been envisaged." [35]

The result of the 1867 statute has been to create "an utterly unique relationship between the state and federal sovereigns," under which "state and federal courts jointly and severally administer federal law relevant to state criminal proceedings." [36] The major accommodation between the two systems has been the Supreme Court's requirement that the defendant exhaust his state remedies, before seeking review on habeas corpus in a federal district court.[37] However, where a state prisoner fails to comply with a state procedural requirement and consequently loses the opportunity to present

[35] *Fay* v. *Noia* (1963).

[36] Curtis R. Reitz, "Federal Habeas Corpus: Impact of an Abortive State Proceeding," 74 *Harvard Law Review* 1315, 1324 (1961).

[37] *Ex parte Hawk* (1944); *Darr* v. *Burford* (1950); *Brown* v. *Allen* (1953).

in the state court federal questions relevant to the power of the state to hold him in custody, the Supreme Court ruled in *Fay* v. *Noia* (1963) that he is not barred thereby from subsequent resort to the federal courts for relief through habeas corpus.[38]

Applications by convicted state prisoners for habeas corpus from federal courts have increased rapidly—from 127 in 1941 to 1,232 in 1962.[39] In 1953 Justice Jackson made reference in *Brown* v. *Allen* to this multiplicity of petitions, "so frivolous, so meaningless, and often so unintelligible that this worthlessness of the class discredits each individual application." He proposed to reduce this deluge to "manageable proportions" by certain procedural safeguards in granting habeas corpus.

State resentment over this situation was expressed in 1955 by the introduction of restrictive legislation in Congress. The bill proposed would have permitted federal judges to entertain habeas corpus writs on behalf of persons in custody pursuant to judgment of a state court only on a ground presenting a substantial federal constitutional question (1) which had not theretofore been raised and determined, (2) which there had been no fair and adequate opportunity theretofore to raise and have determined, and (3) which could not thereafter be raised and determined in a state court proceeding subject to Supreme Court review on certiorari.[40] Thus the purpose of this bill was to limit federal judicial review of state criminal convictions in so far as possible to the normal channels of certiorari to the Supreme Court, and to discourage collateral attacks on state convictions through habeas corpus petitions to the federal district courts.

All efforts to adopt such legislation have failed, and in fact the fears that habeas corpus actions would swing open the prison gates appear to have been unfounded. A study by the Administrative Office of the U.S. Courts in 1958 revealed that in the preceding nine years, only twenty-four federal habeas corpus petitioners had won release from state penitentiaries. But Justice Clark, dissenting in *Fay* v. *Noia*, argued that such decisions would increase the flood of petitions, "98% of them . . . frivolous," and make it impossible for the Court to locate the few meritorious applications which might come to it.

The 1867 act may also be utilized by persons held under state authority for criminal acts done under federal authority. The constitutionality of this usage was upheld in *Tennessee* v. *Davis* (1880). A federal revenue officer was arrested in Tennessee on a murder charge. His defense was that he had acted in pursuance of official duties, and he petitioned to have the case removed to the federal court. The Supreme Court admitted that Davis's crime was one against state rather than federal law, but upheld the removal, point-

[38] See also *Irvin* v. *Dowd* (1959). *Fay* v. *Noia* overruled the *Darr* v. *Burford* requirement that exhaustion of remedies must include application for review of the state court decision on certiorari to the United States Supreme Court.
[39] Data given in *Fay* v. *Noia*.
[40] H.R. 5649, 84th Cong.; House Report no. 1200, 84th Cong., 1st sess. (1955).

ing out that the federal government must act through its officers within the states.

> If, when thus acting, and within the scope of their authority, those officers can be arrested and brought to trial in a State court, for an alleged offense against the law of the State, yet warranted by the Federal authority they possess, and if the general government is powerless to interfere at once for their protection, . . . the operations of the general government may at any time be arrested at the will of one of its members.

The complication of a dual system of courts is one which other leading federal governments, such as Australia, Canada, and India, have avoided. In those countries there is only one federal court, superimposed on a complete system of state courts. By contrast, the American system, as Justice Douglas has noted, may seem to be in many respects "cumbersome, expensive, and productive of delays in the administration of justice. . . . It has required judicial statesmanship of a high order to prevent unseemly conflicts between the two judicial systems." But, he concludes, "the days of crisis have passed; regimes and attitudes of harmony and cooperation have developed; and the tradition of deference of one court system to the other has brought dignity and a sense of responsibility to each." [41]

### SELECTED REFERENCES

*The Constitution of the United States of America: Analysis and Interpretation,* Sen. Doc. no. 39, 88th Cong., pp. 597–696, 709–726. Washington: Government Printing Office, 1964.

CROSSKEY, WILLIAM W., *Politics and the Constitution in the History of the United States,* chap. 26. Chicago: The University of Chicago Press, 1953.

DOUGLAS, WILLIAM O., *We the Judges,* chap. 3. Garden City, N.Y.: Doubleday & Company, Inc., 1956.

FRANKFURTER, FELIX, and JAMES M. LANDIS, *The Business of the Supreme Court: A Study in the Federal Judicial System.* New York: The Macmillan Company, 1928.

HARRIS, ROBERT J., *The Judicial Power of the United States.* Baton Rouge, La.: Louisiana State University Press, 1940.

HART, HENRY M., JR., and HERBERT WECHSLER, *The Federal Courts and the Federal System,* chap. 4. Brooklyn, N.Y.: The Foundation Press, Inc., 1953.

[41] William O. Douglas, *We the Judges* (Garden City, N.Y.: Doubleday & Company, Inc., 1956), p. 135. Another potential source of conflict between state and federal courts, the authorization given by an 1866 statute to apply for removal of certain civil rights cases from state to federal courts, will be discussed in Chap. 33.

# 9

## Judicial review

The phrase "judicial review" may be applied to several types of processes. It may describe the control which courts exercise over subordinate corporations or units of government, such as municipalities, or over public officials exercising delegated legislative and administrative powers. Courts will customarily review the actions of such officers or units of government to determine whether they are acting within their powers, and will punish or grant redress for acts found to be *ultra vires* (i.e., outside lawful authority). This is the commonest type of judicial review.

Second, federal systems of government have a characteristic form of judicial review, whereby courts are made responsible for enforcing the agreed-on division of functions between the central government and the component state or provincial governments. Such a division of functions is a necessary feature in any federal system, and by the process of judicial review the courts are made responsible for umpiring and enforcing the rules of the federal system. This power necessarily includes authority to declare invalid any state legislation or other state action which infringes on the constitutional authority of the central government or the other states in the federation. It would be extremely difficult to operate a federal system without such an umpire. As already noted, section 25 of the Judiciary Act of 1789 explicitly provided for Supreme Court review of cases decided in state

courts where the constitutionality of state statutes was at issue. Justice Holmes once said:

> I do not think the United States would come to an end if we lost our power to declare an act of Congress void. I do think the Union would be imperilled if we could not make that declaration as to the laws of the several states. For one in my place sees how often a local policy prevails with those who are not trained to national views.[1]

The third type of judicial review is the power of the Supreme Court to declare acts of Congress unconstitutional. In more general terms, this is the review by courts over the acts of the legislative and executive departments of the same government. There is no superior-subordinate relationship as there is in the first two types of review. Here the courts, though coordinate parts of the government, nevertheless have the authority to declare actions of the other two branches invalid as contrary to the basic law. That explains why this system is often referred to as one of "judicial supremacy." It is judicial review in this third form which Americans customarily think of when the phrase is employed, for such power is enjoyed by American courts at both the federal and state levels.

It used to be customary to attribute the unique status of the Supreme Court, in comparison with the world's other high tribunals, to the Court's power of invalidating acts of Congress. To a certain extent this was true. No such authority resided in the highest courts of Britain or France. Switzerland, a federation which borrowed somewhat from American experience, deliberately rejected in 1848 the American pattern of judicial review and made the legislature the final interpreter of its constitution. The Canadian and Australian federations did give to their high courts authority to pass on the constitutionality of legislation, but their constitutions, lacking such broad protective standards as due process of law or equal protection of the laws, did not provide as much opportunity for judicial assertion of authority over constitutional interpretation as in the United States.

Within the present century, however, the enormous prestige of the Supreme Court has led to adoption of a similar pattern of judicial power in several parts of the democratic world. Leaving aside certain Latin American examples, the period just since World War II has seen systems of judicial review established in Italy, Germany, and India. The Italian Constitution of 1947 made provision for a Constitutional Court with jurisdiction over disputes concerning the constitutionality of laws. Legislative implementation of the court was delayed, and it was not inaugurated until 1956. The Western German basic law of 1949 set up a Federal Constitutional Court with wide jurisdictional powers; since it began operation in 1951 it has handed down several extremely important constitutional decisions. The Indian Con-

---

[1] "Law and the Court," *Speeches* (Boston: Little, Brown and Company, 1934), p. 102.

stitution of 1949 set up a Supreme Court with power to review the constitutionality of actions of the central and state governments, a power which
has been used with force and independence. The world-wide influence of
the American Supreme Court's example is additional reason for inquiry into
the origins of its great powers.

## THE PREHISTORY OF JUDICIAL REVIEW

The theory on which the American practice of judicial review is based may
be summarized as follows: that the written Constitution is a fundamental
law, subject to change only by an extraordinary legislative process, and as
such superior to common and statutory law; that the powers of the various
departments of government are limited by the terms of the Constitution;
and that judges are expected to enforce the provisions of the Constitution as
the superior law and to refuse to enforce any legislative act or executive
order in conflict therewith. What are the foundations of this theory in American thought and experience?

FOUNDATIONS OF JUDICIAL REVIEW    First there is the obvious influence of
natural law, the belief that human conduct is guided by fundamental and
immutable laws which have natural or divine origin and sanction. In English
experience natural law was invoked first as a limitation on the king, and by
Coke in the famous *Dr. Bonham's Case* (1610) against Parliament. "When
an act of parliament is against common right or reason," said Coke, "the
common law will control it and adjudge such act to be void." This view
failed to establish itself in England, but in the American Colonies conditions
were more propitious. With few lawbooks, and with an increasing disrespect
for English legal precedents, the colonists tended to fall back on the Bible
or popular notions of natural law as their guides. Locke supplied the systematic statement of this position, concluding: "the fundamental law of Nature
being the preservation of mankind, no human sanction can be good or valid
against it."

Another factor was the confirmed practice in American experience of
reducing the basic laws to writing. The Mayflower Compact of 1620, the
Fundamental Orders of Connecticut in 1639, the charters granted to the
colonies from 1620 to 1700—always the colonists sought to legitimize and
to limit collective action by fundamental written instruments. But the provision of machinery for enforcing these fundamental laws was not given
much attention. During the Colonial period there was review machinery of
a sort in the powers of disallowance exercised by the Privy Council in England over the acts of colonial legislatures. When the English yoke was thrown
off, the initial Revolutionary enthusiasm saw the free popular legislatures
as a self-sufficient guarantee against oppression of liberties. But it took only
a little experience with all-powerful legislatures to demonstrate the abuses

of unchecked authority, and at least three states experimented with special institutional arrangements to protect the fundamental law from encroachment.

The Pennsylvania constitution of 1776 required a council of censors to be chosen every seven years to inquire whether the constitution had been preserved inviolate. It was authorized to pass public censures, order impeachments, and recommend the repealing of laws which appeared contrary to the principles of the constitution. The first council met in 1783 but was not very successful. Vermont adopted the Pennsylvania plan verbatim, and there it persisted until 1869. New York, by its constitution of 1777, provided for a Council of Revision, consisting of the governor, chancellor, and judges of the state supreme court, which was to review all bills about to become laws and exert a kind of veto power on those it adjudged inconsistent with the spirit of the constitution.

These plans appeared to assume that the courts could not be relied on to enforce the state constitutions, or would not be empowered to declare legislation unconstitutional. In fact, however, there were some nine cases decided in eight states between 1776 and 1789 which purported to declare state legislative acts unconstitutional. Actually the facts in these nine cases are scanty and dubious. The best known is *Trevett* v. *Weeden* (1786), in which a Rhode Island court invalidated an act of the state Assembly requiring the acceptance of paper money as legal tender. The judges appear to have anticipated that the decision would get them in trouble, and consequently, sought to cloak the holding in technical language. When they were called before an angry Legislature to explain the reasons for their decision, they denied the Legislature's right to make such a demand.

JUDICIAL REVIEW IN THE CONVENTION    It is a never-ending puzzle why judicial review, which has become one of the outstanding features of the operation of the American Constitution, was not even mentioned in that document. What actually happened was that a group in the Convention, led by Wilson and Madison, wanted to establish something like the New York Council of Revision, composed of the executive and a "convenient number" of the national judiciary, with a veto power over congressional legislation. This plan was defeated three times in the Convention. Several members objected that under this plan judges who would later have to decide on the validity of the law in a case would have prejudged the matter and that the separation of powers would be thus violated. But Madison on June 6 strongly defended the plan. The executive would need both control and support. Associating judges with him in his revisionary capacity would perform both functions, and would also enable the judicial department "the better to defend itself against Legislative encroachments," Madison thought.

In the debate on the veto power, then, judicial review in this rather peculiar form was considered and rejected in favor of a purely executive

veto. When the original plan failed, its sponsors proposed that the Supreme Court as a whole exercise revisionary powers over legislation. All bills would go both to the President and the Supreme Court, and either could object, whereupon the bill would need to be repassed by a two-thirds vote if either the President or a majority of the Court had objected, and by three-fourths if both had objected. This novel idea was defeated on August 15, three states to eight.

No further effort was made in the Convention to give the Supreme Court explicit revisionary powers over congressional legislation. This does not prove, of course, that the framers were opposed to judicial review as such. But the absence of explicit language did leave room for doubt, and controversy still persists as to their intentions. Charles A. Beard thought that his book, *The Supreme Court and the Constitution,* published in 1912, had settled what Felix Frankfurter in 1924 regarded as an "empty controversy." [2] Beard presented evidence that seventeen of the twenty-five men most influential in the Convention "declared, directly or indirectly, for judicial control." [3] But in 1953 William W. Crosskey concluded after a review of the same evidence that the Constitution had not intended to authorize general judicial review of acts of Congress,[4] and in 1958 Learned Hand took the equivocal position that judicial review was "not a logical deduction from the structure of the Constitution but only a practical condition upon its successful operation." [5]

The debates at the state ratifying conventions have been searched for statements favoring judicial review, particularly by members of the Convention, and some can be found—Marshall in Virginia, Wilson in Pennsylvania, Ellsworth in Connecticut. More attention has been given to Hamilton's clear presentation, in No. 78 of *The Federalist,* of the doctrine of a written constitution as a superior enactment, the preservation of which rests particularly with judges. A "limited constitution," he contended, "can be preserved in practice no other way than through the medium of courts of justice, whose duty it must be to declare all acts contrary to the manifest tenor of the Constitution void." Such authority does not "by any means suppose a superiority of the judicial to the legislative power," Hamilton concluded. "It only supposes that the power of the people is superior to both."

[2] Charles A. Beard, *The Supreme Court and the Constitution,* with an introduction by Alan F. Westin (Englewood Cliffs, N.J.: Prentice-Hall, Inc., 1962), pp. 1, 35.
[3] *Ibid.,* p. 47.
[4] *Politics and the Constitution in the History of the United States* (Chicago: The University of Chicago Press, 1953), chap. 28.
[5] *The Bill of Rights* (Cambridge, Mass.: Harvard University Press, 1958), p. 15.

## THE ESTABLISHMENT OF JUDICIAL REVIEW

With the passage of the Judiciary Act and the inauguration of the federal court system, the fate of judicial review was in the hands of the Supreme Court itself. As we have seen, its initial history did not suggest that it would be able to win a position of respect and power. When John Marshall was named Chief Justice of a Federalist Court in 1801, there were few cases awaiting adjudication, the Jeffersonians were about to assume control of the other two branches of government, and prospects for the Court were dim.

Yet within two years that Court, dominated by Marshall, had successfully asserted its authority to invalidate acts of Congress in one of the cleverest coups of American history. One week before he was to leave office President Adams appointed forty-two new justices of the peace for the District of Columbia. The formal commissions of appointment had not been made out and delivered by Secretary of State John Marshall, who was holding the two positions simultaneously, when Jefferson became President on March 4, 1801, and he ordered his Secretary of State, James Madison, not to deliver them.

Four of the frustrated appointees, headed by William Marbury, petitioned the Supreme Court for a writ of mandamus to compel Madison to deliver the commissions. Madison ignored a preliminary order issued by Marshall, and then Congress shut the Court down for a year to keep it from passing on the validity of the repeal of the Federalist Judiciary Act of 1801. Consequently Marbury's petition could not be acted on until 1803.

Marshall had a difficult problem to solve. He seemed to face two alternatives. He could order Madison to deliver the commissions, but it was certain Jefferson would countermand the order, and the Court would be exposed as powerless to enforce its order. Or he could avoid a test of strength with the executive by refusing to issue the writ, with the same result of advertising the Court's powerlessness. It is a measure of Marshall's genius that he escaped from this apparent dead end by manufacturing a third alternative, which enabled him to claim for the Court an infinitely greater power than Marbury had asked it to exercise, yet in a fashion which Jefferson could not possibly thwart.

This is how it was done. Marbury had applied for mandamus under section 13 of the Judiciary Act of 1789, which provided that "The Supreme Court . . . shall have power to issue . . . writs of mandamus, in cases warranted by the principles and usages of law, to any courts appointed, or persons holding office, under the authority of the United States." Marbury did not go first to a lower court. Under this statute he filed his petition directly with the Supreme Court. But Article III of the Constitution provides that the Supreme Court shall have original jurisdiction only in cases affecting ambassadors, ministers, and consuls and in cases where a state is a party. Marshall professed to believe that the statutory provision conflicted with the

constitutional provision, and that Congress had attempted, contrary to the Constitution, to expand the original jurisdiction of the Supreme Court.

Of course, this was preposterous, and Marshall knew it. Section 13 had been drawn by Oliver Ellsworth, later the third Chief Justice of the United States; it had been passed by the First Congress, which contained many ex-members of the Convention; and it had been actually enforced in 1794 by a Court which contained three ex-members of the Convention. The provision could be, and had been, interpreted in such a way as to raise no questions about adding to the Court's original jurisdiction. It could be taken to mean that the Court had power to issue the writ of mandamus whenever that remedy was appropriate in the disposition of cases properly brought in the Supreme Court, either on appeal or under its original jurisdiction. Thus in a case brought in the Court's original jurisdiction by a state, mandamus would be one of the available remedies. But such an interpretation would not have suited Marshall's purposes.

The proof of Marshall's intent is only too apparent in his opinion. If this was intended as a bona fide holding that the Court lacked jurisdiction to hear the case, he should have made that ruling and then stopped. Jurisdiction is the first thing a court must establish, and if it is found lacking, then the court can do nothing but dismiss the case. Marshall, however, wanted to read Jefferson a lecture. Consequently the first question asked in his decision was whether Marbury had a right to the commission. He concluded that he did, and that Madison had wrongfully withheld it. Then he asked a second question—whether the laws of the country afforded Marbury a remedy for the right that Madison had violated. He said that they did. Only after this detour through some interesting political questions did Marshall come to the jurisdictional question as to whether Marbury was entitled to the remedy for which he had applied. And only then did Marshall announce his newly discovered conflict between section 13 and Article III.

Admiration for Marshall's skill is of course irrelevant to the basic question. Likewise we may pass over the ethical question presented by Marshall's deciding a case which arose out of his own negligence as Secretary of State. The important matter is the logic of Marshall's demonstration that the Court must have the power to invalidate acts of Congress which it holds to be contrary to the Constitution. The case he makes is a strong one, admittedly profiting from Hamilton's argument in No. 78 of *The Federalist*. Marshall started from the proposition that the government of the United States as created by the Constitution is a limited government, and that "a legislative act, contrary to the constitution, is not law." Then what is the obligation of a court when it is asked to enforce such a statute? For Marshall the answer was obvious.

> If a law be in opposition to the constitution; if both the law and the constitution apply to a particular case, so that the court must either decide that case conformable to the law, disregarding the constitution, or

conformable to the constitution, disregarding the law; the court must determine which of these conflicting rules governs the case: this is of the very essence of judicial duty.

After all, Marshall continued, the judicial power extends to cases arising "under the constitution." Is the Court to be forbidden to look into the Constitution when a case arises under it? Must it look only at the statute? Further, he noted that the judges take an oath to support the Constitution. It would be nothing less than immoral to compel them to participate as knowing instruments in the violation of the document they have sworn to support.

This argument has been ratified by time and by practice, and there is little point in quibbling with it. Of course the President also takes an oath to support the Constitution. Does not Marshall's argument then give him the right to refuse to enforce an act of Congress which he regards as unconstitutional? Equally questionable was the bland assumption by both Hamilton and Marshall that a judicial finding of repugnance between a statute and the Constitution was "equivalent to an objective contradiction in the order of nature and not a mere difference of opinion between two different guessers." [6] As Thomas Reed Powell says, "they both covered up this possibly question-begging difficulty by saying in somewhat different form that judges are expert specialists in knowing or finding the law." But we now know beyond the shadow of doubt that constitutional interpretation is a matter of opinion, and that judicial expertise is no guarantee of correctness or wisdom.

Few now find such arguments against judicial review convincing. Yet there is a basic uneasiness which will not die, and which occasionally boils up into bitter conflict, about the supremacy the Supreme Court has assumed in constitutional interpretation. There was, in fact, a less extreme position which the Court could have claimed for itself, which would nonetheless have enabled it to come up with the same disposition of the *Marbury* case. It could have claimed supremacy, not for its interpretations of the Constitution as a whole, but only over those portions of the Constitution pertaining to judicial organization and jurisdiction. Marbury's problem, of course, fell in this area. It could have been argued that the separation of powers principle required each branch to be the interpreter of its own constitutional authority. The judiciary would mark out its own area of constitutional power, but would intervene in the constitutional problems of the other two branches only when disputes arose between them. In *Marbury* v. *Madison,* however, "coequality" was rejected in favor of a policy of judicial supremacy.

This is not the place for a detailed history of the Supreme Court's subsequent use of its power to declare acts of Congress unconstitutional. After *Marbury,* no act of Congress was invalidated until the Missouri Compromise (already repealed) was voided by the disastrous *Dred Scott* decision in 1857.

[6] Thomas Reed Powell, *Vagaries and Varieties in Constitutional Interpretation* (New York: Columbia University Press, 1956), p. 14.

By contrast, from 1865 to 1964, seventy-two acts of Congress were held unconstitutional in whole or in part by the Supreme Court.[7] The climax came in 1935 and 1936 when a Court dominated by four reactionary justices handed down twelve decisions holding acts of Congress unconstitutional.

The "Court-packing" plan which President Roosevelt proposed in 1937 to smash this judicial blockade was by no means the first effort to limit the Supreme Court's powers over congressional legislation. One recurring proposal has been to require an extraordinary majority of the Court to invalidate legislation. In 1868, a bill passed the House which would have required a two-thirds vote of the Court for this purpose. In 1921 a constitutional amendment was proposed in Congress that would have required all but two justices to concur in a declaration of unconstitutionality. Such proposals were motivated by the five to four votes which had been the margin of decision in many important instances.

During the Progressive era in the early part of the twentieth century, the recall of judges was widely advocated, and was actually provided for in some states. In 1912 the Progressive party platform advocated, not the recall of judges, but the recall of judicial decisions. LaFollette, in his bid for the Presidency in 1924, proposed an amendment authorizing Congress to reenact a law declared unconstitutional by the Supreme Court, thereby nullifying the decision. After the child labor law was held unconstitutional in 1918, Senator Owen presented a bill to reenact the law with a clause prohibiting the Supreme Court from invalidating it. No action was ever taken along any of these lines.

After his tremendous victory in the 1936 election, President Roosevelt felt strong enough to challenge the Court. As already noted, he chose the device of increasing the size of the Court, which had been juggled several times previously in American history for political purposes, but he presented his plan in a maladroit fashion. He made no reference to the constitutional crisis which had arisen out of the Supreme Court's dogged refusal to keep abreast of the times. Instead he painted a dubious picture of delay in federal court litigation, of the Supreme Court's heavy burden, and of the need for a "constant infusion of new blood." After one of the bitterest political battles in American history, the original plan was defeated in Congress. Instead, a liberalized retirement bill was passed. Moreover, even before the final defeat of the Court-packing plan, the Supreme Court made a historic change of direction (often referred to as "the switch in time that saved nine"), which was confirmed by President Roosevelt's subsequent appointments to the Court.

The *Brown* decision in 1954 ushered in a period during which the Supreme

---

[7] *The Constitution of the United States of America*, Sen. Doc. no. 39, 88th Cong., 1st sess. (Washington: Government Printing Office, 1964), pp. 1387–1401. The same source lists 656 state constitutional or statutory provisions and 84 municipal ordinances held unconstitutional by the Supreme Court from 1789 to 1963; pp. 1403–1537.

Court was almost constantly in difficulties with some members of Congress and some sections of the populace, but again the institution of judicial review emerged unscathed. It should be obvious that the exercise of such power by the judiciary would not have been tolerated in a democratic government unless it had been wielded with a reasonable measure of judicial restraint and with some attention, as Mr. Dooley said, to the election returns. It therefore becomes appropriate to examine such systematic doctrines or practices as the Court has developed to limit its powers of judicial review.

### JUDICIAL SELF–RESTRAINT: JUSTICIABLE QUESTIONS

There are always procedural techniques available to the Court by which it can avoid having to express an opinion on embarrassing or difficult issues. As already noted, the Court has almost complete control over its business through grant or refusal of writs of certiorari. Certiorari, moreover, is granted on the Court's own terms. In the famous 1951 Smith Act case involving prosecution of the leaders of the American Communist Party, *Dennis* v. *United States,* the Court accepted the evidential findings of the court of appeals as final and limited its review to two relatively narrow constitutional issues. When the Court finally granted a full review of Smith Act convictions in a 1957 case, *Yates* v. *United States,* it came to much different conclusions from those it had reached in the *Dennis* case.

The all too familiar technique of the law's delay may also be utilized to rescue the Court from difficult situations, by postponing decisions until the heat has gone out of an issue. The Court's castigation of Lincoln's trials of civilians before military tribunals during the Civil War was delivered from the safe vantage point of 1866, and martial law in Hawaii during World War II was voided in 1946. But these methods of judicial self-restraint have not been dignified by the kind or caliber of rationalizations to which we now turn.

ADVISORY OPINIONS    The Supreme Court is a court of law, and it has followed a fairly consistent policy of refusing to deal with issues unless they are presented as cases or controversies in the framework of a bona fide lawsuit. In application, this means that the federal courts will not issue advisory opinions, indicating what the law would be on a hypothetical state of facts. One can of course think of many circumstances in which it would be convenient to have an advance opinion from the Supreme Court on the constitutionality of proposed legislation or contemplated executive action. In fact, President Washington in 1793, through his Secretary of State, requested an advisory opinion from the Supreme Court regarding a proposed treaty, but the Court refused the opinion as beyond its competence to give.

If the Supreme Court did give advisory opinions, as supreme courts in several states are obligated to do on request of the governor or legislature,

the Court would presumably not have the advantage of arguments by opposing counsel, nor would the opinions be binding should a genuine case or controversy subsequently come along raising the same issue. The granting of advisory opinions would almost certainly result in constant political embroilment and a substantial dissipation of the Court's influence and prestige.

The ban on advisory opinions is not a barrier to declaratory judgment actions, which are sometimes mistakenly confused with advisory opinions. In 1934 Congress passed the Federal Declaratory Judgment Act authorizing the federal courts to declare rights and other legal relations in cases of "actual controversy," and providing that "such declaration shall have the force and effect of a final judgment or decree and be reviewable as such." [8]

The declaratory judgment is a statutory, nontechnical method of securing a judicial ruling in cases of actual controversy, but without requiring the parties to put themselves in jeopardy by taking action based on their conflicting legal interpretations. No coercive order is normally issued in a declaratory judgment proceeding, for the assumption is that once the law has been declared the parties will act according to it. However, the judgment may be made the basis of further relief, if necessary, or quite commonly a petition for writ of injunction is joined with a declaratory judgment action.

"FRIENDLY" SUITS    From the principle that a lawsuit must pit against each other parties with adverse legal interests grows the practice in the federal courts of refusing to accept so-called "friendly suits." Obviously, if the interests of the opposing parties are actually not adverse, then motivation for bringing out all the relevant facts will be lacking, and the trial court will have no assurance that justice is being done. Particularly is this important when the constitutionality of a federal statute is being attacked, because both parties might actually be antagonistic to the statute.

Such a situation may be closely approached where a stockholder seeks to enjoin the corporation in which he owns stock from complying with an allegedly unconstitutional statute. Several significant pieces of constitutional litigation have occurred under these circumstances. For example, the federal income tax was declared unconstitutional in a suit brought by a common stockholder to enjoin the corporation's breach of trust by paying voluntarily a tax which was claimed to be illegal.[9]

When a stockholder of the Alabama Power Company sued to enjoin that company from carrying out its contract to sell a portion of its properties to the TVA, Justice Brandeis, speaking for four members of the Court, de-

---

[8] The act was upheld in *Aetna Life Ins. Co.* v. *Haworth* (1937). For an interesting case in which the Court regarded the declaratory judgment as inappropriate, see *Public Affairs Associates* v. *Rickover* (1962).

[9] *Pollock* v. *Farmers' Loan & Trust Co.* (1895). See also *Smith* v. *Kansas City Title & Trust Co.* (1921); *Carter* v. *Carter Coal Co.* (1936).

clared that the Court should decline to permit constitutional issues to be raised by the device of stockholders' suits.[10] That the government's case will at least be adequately presented in such controversies is now guaranteed by the provisions of the act of 1937 requiring that the United States be made a party in any case where the constitutionality of an act of Congress is questioned.

TEST CASES    Many suits are carefully planned and brought up to the Supreme Court as "test cases" to secure rulings on disputed constitutional issues. Organizations such as the American Civil Liberties Union and the National Association for the Advancement of Colored People devote much effort to finding good test cases involving constitutional principles on which they hope to draw a favorable ruling from the Supreme Court.

When a new and controversial federal statute is enacted and suits are begun challenging its constitutionality, the Department of Justice customarily selects the case in which it feels the government has the strongest position to carry to the Supreme Court. Sometimes, of course, there is no choice. The case in which the Supreme Court declared the National Industrial Recovery Act unconstitutional, *Schechter Poultry Corp.* v. *United States* (1935), was, as Attorney General Jackson said, "far from ideal as a test case," [11] but circumstances compelled the government to use it.

Test cases must meet all the requirements of a valid case or controversy. If a case is too obviously "staged" simply for the purpose of drawing a court opinion, the Supreme Court may decline to accept it, as is demonstrated by the famous case of *Muskrat* v. *United States* (1911). In 1906 Congress authorized certain named Indians who had been given allotments of land to sue the United States in the Court of Claims in order to determine the validity of acts of Congress restricting alienation of Indian land and increasing the number of persons entitled to share in it. The Attorney General was designated by the act to defend the case. The Supreme Court dismissed the suits when they were brought, on the ground that the United States had "no interest adverse to the claimants." The United States and the Indians were not in dispute as to their respective property rights. Instead, this was a "made-up" case, the object and purpose of which were "wholly comprised in the determination of the constitutional validity of certain acts of Congress." Thus Congress cannot through legislation create a case or controversy merely by stating an issue and by designating parties to present each side.[12]

[10] *Ashwander* v. *Tennessee Valley Authority* (1936).

[11] Robert H. Jackson, *The Struggle for Judicial Supremacy* (New York: Alfred A. Knopf, Inc., 1941), p. 113.

[12] In *United States* v. *C.I.O.* (1948), testing the constitutionality of the Taft-Hartley Act ban on political expenditures by labor unions, Justice Frankfurter charged that "each side was at least unwittingly the ally of the other" in bringing the case before the Court, and for that reason he would have declined review of the case.

STANDING TO SUE    Not every person with the money to bring a lawsuit is entitled to litigate the legality or constitutionality of government action in the federal courts. In order to have standing to maintain such a suit, the individual must establish the sufficiency of his interest in the controversy, and this involves satisfying the courts on two main points: (1) that his interest is one that is peculiarly personal to him, and not one which he shares with all other citizens generally; and (2) that the interest he is defending is a legally protected interest, or right, which is immediately threatened by government action.[13]

On the first point, the necessity for a personal interest can be demonstrated by two cases where the Court came to opposite conclusions as to whether such an interest was present. In 1921 Congress passed a maternity act providing grants-in-aid for states which would cooperate in a federal program to reduce maternal and infant mortality and protect the health of mothers and infants. Suit to enjoin the operation of the statute on grounds of unconstitutionality was brought in the District of Columbia by a Mrs. Frothingham, who sought to sustain her standing in court by alleging that she was a taxpayer of the United States and that the effect of the appropriations authorized by this act would be to increase the burden of future taxation and thereby take her property without due process of law.

The Supreme Court unanimously denied her standing to bring the suit. Although taxpayers' suits are rather common in local and state courts, Justice Sutherland pointed out in *Massachusetts v. Mellon* (1923):

> . . . the relation of a taxpayer of the United States to the Federal Government is very different. His interest in the moneys of the Treasury—partly realized from taxation and partly from other sources—is shared with millions of others; is comparatively minute and indeterminable; and the effect upon future taxation, of any payment out of the funds, so remote, fluctuating and uncertain, that no basis is afforded for an appeal to the preventive powers of a court of equity.

The party who attacks the constitutionality of a federal statute, Sutherland continued, "must be able to show not only that the statute is invalid but that he has sustained . . . some direct injury as the result of its enforcement, and not merely that he suffers in some indefinite way in common with people generally."

The second example grew out of action in 1937 by the Legislature of Kansas in passing on ratification of the child labor amendment proposed to the states by Congress in 1924. The forty members of the Kansas Senate

[13] Individuals who meet these tests and who are also representative of a larger group may bring a "class action" in their own behalf and in behalf of "all others similarly situated." A class action is permitted by the Federal Rules of Civil Procedure where a number of persons have a common legal right and the group is "so numerous as to make it impractical to bring them all before the court." A number of Negro civil rights suits have been brought as class actions.

divided equally on the vote, and the lieutenant governor, presiding officer of the Senate, then cast the deciding vote in favor of ratifying the amendment, which was also ratified by the lower house. Subsequently the senators who had voted against ratification sought mandamus in the Kansas supreme court to compel the secretary of state to certify that the amendment had not been ratified, on the dual ground that the lieutenant governor had no right to vote and that in any case the amendment was not validly before the states because of the length of time that had elapsed since it was first adopted by Congress.

The Supreme Court in *Coleman* v. *Miller* (1939) divided five to four on the issue of standing to sue. The Court majority, through Chief Justice Hughes, said: "The plaintiffs include twenty senators, whose votes against ratification have been overridden and virtually held for naught although if they are right in their contentions their votes would have been sufficient to defeat ratification. We think that these senators have a plain, direct and adequate interest in maintaining the effectiveness of their votes." On the other hand the four dissenters, led by Justice Frankfurter, held that the Kansas legislators had no distinctive claim entitling them to judicial relief. "What is it that they complain of, which could not be complained of here by all their fellow citizens?" Indeed, whether the amendment had died of old age was not even an issue special to Kansas; it was the common concern of every citizen of the United States. Frankfurter concluded: "We can only adjudicate an issue as to which there is a claimant before us who has a special, individualized stake in it. One who is merely the self-constituted spokesman of a constitutional point of view can not ask us to pass on it."

The "directness" of the impact of a challenged action on the person bringing the suit is frequently the determining factor in establishing the existence of a "special, individualized stake" in the controversy. Government action may directly affect the legal interests of one person, while causing only consequential detriment to another. Normally the second party would have no standing to protest in that situation, but conditions may exist where this test does not yield a realistic result. Thus in *Truax* v. *Raich* (1915), an Arizona statute requiring employers of five or more persons to give 80 per cent of their jobs to United States citizens was successfully challenged by an alien employee, even though prosecution under the act was imposed on the employer, not the employee. Obviously, the Supreme Court said, the discharge of the alien complainant by his employer would be solely for the purpose of meeting the requirements of the act and avoiding prosecution. "It is, therefore, idle to call the injury [to the employee] indirect or remote. It is also entirely clear that unless the enforcement of the act is restrained the complainant will have no adequate remedy."

Alleged indirectness of interest was again no bar in *Pierce* v. *Society of Sisters* (1925). Oregon adopted a constitutional amendment in 1922 requiring parents or guardians of children between the ages of eight and sixteen

years to send them to a public school, and the failure to do so was a misdemeanor. A religious order which maintained a school got a court order restraining enforcement of the provision, though the direct effect of the act was on parents, not on schools. The Supreme Court affirmed, not only on the ground that the law would cause irreparable injury to the business and property of the religious group, but more importantly because the law "unreasonably interferes with the liberty of parents and guardians to direct the upbringing and education of children under their control." Thus the religious order was permitted to plead the rights of parents to strengthen its own somewhat less direct interest in the situation.[14]

The second element in standing to sue, and thereby to raise constitutional questions, depends as noted above upon establishing the existence of a right which is immediately threatened by government action. A "right" may be defined as a legally protected interest. A right can be guaranteed by the Constitution, or conferred by statute, or may even have a common-law basis. A right contrasts with a privilege, which the government may grant and withdraw at its discretion.

In *Coleman* v. *Miller* the right asserted by the twenty senators, which the Supreme Court majority accepted as sufficient, was their right "under the Constitution of the United States to have their votes given effect." The right successfully defended by the religious order in the Oregon public school case was the right not to have their property taken without due process of law. The alien in *Truax* v. *Raich* who challenged the Arizona law on employment of aliens asserted his right to equal protection of the laws.

Where a right cannot be demonstrated, however, judicial review is unavailable, no matter how real or obvious the damage done by government action. The Latin phrase is *damnum absque injuria,* that is, damage not recognized as a basis for judicial relief. *Alabama Power Co.* v. *Ickes* (1938) involved an attempt by a power company to enjoin the New Deal Public Works Administration from making grants to Alabama cities which would permit them to build municipal power systems competing with the established private company. The Supreme Court held that the company lacked standing to challenge the government's action, since it had no monopoly rights in the cities it served. "If its business be curtailed or destroyed by the operations of the municipalities, it will be by lawful competition from which no legal wrong results."

Judicial review over entire areas of governmental action may be limited or entirely foreclosed by inability to establish that rights are involved. Government pensions and grants are normally on a privilege basis which does

[14] See also *Barrows* v. *Jackson* (1953), where a California property owner who had breached the obligations of a racial restrictive covenant forbidding sale of property to any but Caucasians was permitted to defend her action by invoking the constitutional rights of non-Caucasians, even though such persons were unidentified and not before the court or directly involved in the case in any way.

not subject them to judicial review. There is normally no protected interest in contracting with the government.[15] The original concept was that access to the mails was a privilege, and there are still doubts as to the extent of judicial review over the Post Office. Whether public employment is a privilege and whether dismissals under the federal loyalty-security programs are subject to procedural protections and judicial review will be discussed later in this volume. Similarly the limitations on the constitutional rights of aliens, and their correspondingly limited access to the courts, will be examined subsequently.

In the past the Court was sometimes charged with delaying decisions on genuine controversies by undue insistence on standards of litigability. In *United Public Workers* v. *Mitchell* (1947) the Hatch Act forbidding federal employees to engage in political activities was challenged by employees who asserted that they wished to engage in political activities and were prevented from doing so by the statute. The Court majority held that this was a hypothetical situation, and only decided the case because one employee had actually violated the act. In *Doremus* v. *Board of Education* (1952), the Court refused review of a taxpayers' suit challenging the constitutionality of Bible reading in the New Jersey schools, on the ground that Bible reading did not increase the cost of education.

However, the more recent Court appears to have substantially relaxed the standing requirement. In the school prayer case, *Engel* v. *Vitale* (1962), there was what Arthur E. Sutherland, Jr., referred to as a "rather curious sparseness of mention of the petitioning plaintiffs or of their children." [16] Since the children were under no coercion to participate in the prayer, and since the prayer did not cause any demonstrable increase in the costs of school operation, the Court could have used the standing issue to avoid deciding the case if it had wished. The following year in the Bible-reading case, *School District of Abington Township* v. *Schempp* (1963), Justice Clark's opinion for the Court took note of the standing problem but only in a footnote which said: "The parties here are school children and their parents, who are directly affected by the laws and practices against which their complaints are directed. These interests surely suffice to give the parties standing to complain."

More recently the standing issue has been raised concerning federal financial aid to education. When the Elementary and Secondary Education Act of 1965 was going through Congress, legislators who objected to the prospect of federal funds being used to aid church-related schools expressed concern that the doctrine of *Massachusetts* v. *Mellon* might prevent the Supreme Court from passing on the establishment of religion issue which

---

[15] *Perkins* v. *Lukens Steel Co.* (1940).
[16] "Establishment according to Engel," 76 *Harvard Law Review* 25, 45 (1962). See also Louis L. Jaffe, "Standing to Secure Judicial Review: Public Actions," 74 *ibid.* 1265 (1961).

they believed was raised by these grants. However, efforts to amend the bill to authorize taxpayers' suits testing the constitutionality of such grants failed.

In spite of this failure, suits were immediately brought against grants to religious schools. In the principal test case, *Flast* v. *Gardner* (1967), complainants sought to enjoin the Secretary of the Department of Health, Education and Welfare from paying out funds to finance guidance services and instruction in reading, arithmetic and other subjects in religiously operated schools and to purchase textbooks for use in such schools. A three-judge federal district court in New York by a two to one vote followed *Massachusetts* v. *Mellon* and held that the plaintiffs as federal taxpayers lacked standing to bring the suit. The Supreme Court granted certiorari to review this decision in October, 1967, thus opening up the distinct possibility that it might be prepared to overrule *Massachusetts* v. *Mellon* and permit taxpayers' suits, at least on First Amendment issues.

This would be a popular move in Congress. In 1966 and again in 1967 the Senate passed bills (S. 2097, 89th Cong.; S. 3, 90th Cong.) granting taxpayers, citizens, and institutions standing to challenge alleged First Amendment infringements under a number of federal spending statutes. The bills endeavored to guard against a flooding of court dockets by requiring all such suits to be brought in the district court for the District of Columbia and within sixty days of the awarding of a federal grant or loan.

### JUDICIAL SELF-RESTRAINT: SEPARATION OF POWERS

The Supreme Court operates constantly under the pressures imposed by the necessity of coexistence with its governmental colleagues in a separation of powers system. As a matter of prestige, it cannot allow itself to be put in a position of subservience to the President or Congress, or to be made to look ridiculous by handing down decrees which will not be enforced. But, by the same token, it seeks to reduce to a minimum the situations in which it seems to assert its superiority over Congress and the President. Because the judicial assumption of power to declare acts of Congress unconstitutional is its most striking claim of judicial superiority, the Supreme Court has sought in numerous ways to restrict its performance in this role.

In 1936, Justice Brandeis, concurring in *Ashwander* v. *Tennessee Valley Authority*, undertook to review the standards the Court had developed to avoid passing on constitutional questions. Among them were the following: (1) The Court will not anticipate a question of constitutional law in advance of the necessity of deciding it, nor is it the habit of the Court to decide questions of a constitutional nature unless absolutely necessary to a decision of the case. (2) The Court will not formulate a rule of constitutional law broader than is required by the precise facts to which it is to be applied. (3) The Court will not pass upon a constitutional question, although properly presented by the record, if there is also present some other ground upon which the case may be disposed of. Thus, if a case can be

decided on either of two grounds, one involving a constitutional question, the other a question of statutory construction or general law, the Court will decide only the latter. (4) When the validity of an act of the Congress is drawn in question, and even if a serious doubt of constitutionality is raised, it is a cardinal principle that the Court will first ascertain whether a construction of the statute is fairly possible by which the question may be avoided. Illustrations of the application of these rules by the Court will be found in later chapters.[17]

Turning to judicial-executive relations, respect for the President and a desire to avoid embarrassing clashes with executive authority have clearly been strong motivating factors in the Court's behavior. As Corwin says: "While the Court has sometimes rebuffed presidential pretensions, it has more often labored to rationalize them; but most of all it has sought on one pretext or other to keep its sickle out of this 'dread field.'" He goes on to point out that the tactical situation is such as to make successful challenge of the President somewhat more difficult than that of Congress, for "the Court can usually assert itself successfully against Congress by merely 'disallowing' its acts, [whereas] presidential exercises of power will generally have produced some change in the external world beyond ordinary judicial competence to efface."

Marshall had been one of the first to recognize the judicial untouchability of the President operating in the executive field. So far as the President's "important political powers" were concerned, he said, the principle is that "in their exercise he is to use his own discretion, and is accountable only to his country in his political character, and to his own conscience."[18] In two important post-Civil War cases the Court ratified this doctrine and extended it to include even the President's duty to enforce the law. *Mississippi* v. *Johnson* (1867) was an action by Mississippi seeking to restrain President Johnson from enforcing certain Reconstruction acts on the ground of their alleged unconstitutionality. The state sought to minimize the seriousness of its request to the Court by contending that President Johnson in enforcing these laws was performing a "mere ministerial duty" requiring no exercise of discretion. The Court rejoined that the President's duty to see that the laws were faithfully executed was "purely executive and political," and went on:

> An attempt on the part of the judicial department of the government to enforce the performance of such duties by the President might be justly characterized, in the language of Chief Justice Marshall, as "an

[17] In *Dennis* v. *United States* (1966) certain union officials who had initially sought to circumvent the non-Communist oath provisions of the Taft-Hartley Act by perjury and deceit were subsequently denied the right to challenge the constitutionality of the act, on the ground that "a claim of unconstitutionality will not be heard to excuse a voluntary, deliberate and calculated course of fraud and deceit."

[18] Edward S. Corwin (ed.), *The President: Office and Powers* (New York: New York University Press, 4th rev. ed., 1957), pp. 16, 25.

absurd and excessive extravagance." It is true that in the instance before us the interposition of the court is not sought to enforce action by the Executive under constitutional legislation, but to restrain such action under legislation alleged to be unconstitutional. But we are unable to perceive that this circumstance takes the case out of the general principles which forbid judicial interference with the exercise of Executive discretion.

A similar effort by Georgia to enjoin the Secretary of War and the generals commanding the Georgia military district from enforcing the Reconstruction acts was likewise frustrated by the Court on the ground that they represented the executive authority of the government.[19]

Judicial interposition in the President's conduct of foreign affairs is also forbidden to the Court by its own self-denying ordinances. This matter will be discussed in detail in a later chapter, but here it is relevant to note an excellent statement by Justice Jackson of the rationale for judicial self-limitation in this field. He said, in a 1948 case:

> The President, both as Commander-in-Chief and as the Nation's organ for foreign affairs, has available intelligence services whose reports are not and ought not to be published to the world. It would be intolerable that courts, without the relevant information, should review and perhaps nullify actions of the Executive taken on information properly held secret. Nor can courts sit *in camera* in order to be taken into executive confidences. But even if courts could require full disclosure, the very nature of executive decisions as to foreign policy is political, not judicial. Such decisions are wholly confided by our Constitution to the political departments of the government, Executive and Legislative. They are delicate, complex, and involve large elements of prophecy. They are and should be undertaken only by those directly responsible to the people whose welfare they advance or imperil. They are decisions of a kind for which the Judiciary has neither aptitude, facilities nor responsibility and have long been held to belong in the domain of political power not subject to judicial intrusion or inquiry.[20]

THE "POLITICAL QUESTION" DOCTRINE    In a substantial number of instances, the Supreme Court has announced its refusal to decide a controversy because it involved a "political question." When this has occurred, considerations of potential conflict with the political branches of the government, such as have just been discussed, have usually been supplemented by professions of doubt as to judicial competence to handle the issues involved or particularly difficult enforcement problems. Significant statements of the political question doctrine as a limitation on judicial action have already been noted in *Luther* v. *Borden* (1849) and *Coleman* v. *Miller* (1939). Chief Justice Hughes said in the latter case that he would not attempt a definition of "the class of

[19] *Georgia* v. *Stanton* (1868).
[20] *Chicago & Southern Air Lines* v. *Waterman S.S. Corp.* (1948).

questions deemed to be political and not justiciable," but he did indicate that the two dominant considerations were "the appropriateness under our system of government of attributing finality to the action of the political departments, and also the lack of satisfactory criteria for a judicial determination."

As already noted, the political question doctrine was relied on by Justice Frankfurter in *Colegrove* v. *Green* (1946) as a rationalization for judicial refusal to correct population inequalities in congressional election districts. But Justice Brennan's opinion for the Court majority in *Baker* v. *Carr* (1962) limited the application of the doctrine to separation of powers situations. At present, then, the doctrine amounts to nothing more than a general self-imposed obligation on the Court to show appropriate deference to the President and Congress.

John P. Roche has attacked the political question doctrine as illogical, and based on circular reasoning: "Political questions are matters not soluble by the judicial process; matters not soluble by the judicial process are political questions. As an early dictionary explained, violins are small cellos, and cellos are large violins." [21] His own analysis is that the Court tends to resort to judicial self-restraint only when the conditions of American political life make that course prudent.

It is now generally assumed that the Supreme Court must be available to answer any constitutional question. Self-restraint counsels the Court to reach constitutional issues reluctantly and to be chary of disagreeing with legislatures or executives, whether national or state. But self-restraint is not the ultimate in judicial wisdom. The Court's primary obligation is not to avoid controversy. Its primary obligation is to bring all the judgment its members possess and the best wisdom that the times afford, to the interpretation of the basic rules propounded by the Constitution for the direction of a free society. The Supreme Court has a duty of self-restraint, but not to the point of denying to the nation the guidance on basic democratic problems which its unique situation equips it to provide.

## SELECTED REFERENCES

BLACK, CHARLE L., JR., *The People and the Court: Judicial Review in a Democracy*. New York: The Macmillan Company, 1960.

CAHN, EDMOND (ed.), *Supreme Court and Supreme Law*, chap. 2. Bloomington, Ind.: Indiana University Press, 1954.

CARR, ROBERT K., *The Supreme Court and Judicial Review*. New York: Holt, Rinehart and Winston, Inc., 1942.

[21] "Judicial Self-restraint," 49 *American Political Science Review* 762–772 (1955).

CORWIN, EDWARD S., *Court over Constitution: A Study of Judicial Review as an Instrument of Popular Government.* Princeton, N.J.: Princeton University Press, 1938.

———, *The Doctrine of Judicial Review.* Princeton, N.J.: Princeton University Press, 1914.

———, *The "Higher Law" Background of American Constitutional Law.* Ithaca, N.Y.: Great Seal Books, Cornell University Press, 1955.

CROSSKEY, WILLIAM W., *Politics and the Constitution in the History of the United States,* chaps. 28, 29. Chicago: The University of Chicago Press, 1953.

DAHL, ROBERT A., "Decision-making in a Democracy: The Role of the Supreme Court as a National Policy-maker," 6 *Journal of Public Law* 279–295 (1958).

DEAN, HOWARD E., *Judicial Review and Democracy.* New York: Random House, Inc., 1966.

DIETZE, GOTTFRIED, "America and Europe—Decline and Emergence of Judicial Review," 44 *Virginia Law Review* 1233–1272 (1958).

HAINES, CHARLES GROVE, *The American Doctrine of Judicial Supremacy.* Berkeley, Calif.: University of California Press, 1932 (second edition).

HART, HENRY M., JR., and HERBERT WECHSLER, *The Federal Courts and the Federal System,* chap. 2. Brooklyn, N.Y.: The Foundation Press, Inc., 1953.

HYNEMAN, CHARLES S., *The Supreme Court on Trial.* New York: The Atherton Press, 1963.

JACKSON, ROBERT H., *The Struggle for Judicial Supremacy.* New York: Alfred A. Knopf, Inc., 1941.

———, *The Supreme Court in the American System of Government.* Cambridge, Mass.: Harvard University Press, 1955.

JAFFE, LOUIS L., "Right to Judicial Review," 71 *Harvard Law Review* 401, 769 (1958).

LEVY, LEONARD W. (ed.), *Judicial Review and the Supreme Court: Selected Essays.* New York: Harper & Row, Publishers, Incorporated, 1967.

MC WHINNEY, EDWARD, *Judicial Review in the English-speaking World.* Toronto, Canada: University of Toronto Press, 1956.

POWELL, THOMAS REED, *Vagaries and Varieties in Constitutional Interpretation,* chaps. 1, 2. New York: Columbia University Press, 1956.

SWISHER, CARL B., *The Supreme Court in Modern Role.* New York: New York University Press, 1958.

WRIGHT, BENJAMIN F., *The Growth of American Constitutional Law.* Boston: Houghton Mifflin Company, 1942.

# Part 4

## The legislature

# 10

## Membership

The institutions and powers of the American Congress are provided for in the first article of the Constitution, which comprises in bulk somewhat over half the original document. The major considerations involved in the creation of a bicameral legislature have already been reviewed, as well as the principles which were to control the composition of the two houses. Our more detailed inquiry into the constitutional experience of Congress may begin with an examination of the provisions and practices relating to membership in the House of Representatives and Senate.

### THE SENATE

The membership of the Senate, though not its size, is fixed by Article I, section 3, which provides for two senators from each state. Thus the size of the Senate is related directly to the number of states, and with the admission of new states it has grown from an original membership of 26 to its present 100. Article V guarantees that "no State, without its consent, shall be deprived of its equal suffrage in the Senate."

The Constitution originally provided that senators would be chosen from each state by its legislature. This arrangement gave effect to the idea that the Senate represented state governments rather than the people of the states. At first the legislatures were left entirely free to decide how they

would select senators. In 1866, however, Congress did intervene to the extent of providing that if the two houses of a state legislature voting separately were unable to agree on a senator, they should meet in joint session and decide the matter by majority vote.

The movement for direct election of senators was motivated partly by the scandals and deadlocks which characterized legislative elections, and partly by the development of a more progressive tone in the country. Some states succeeded in taking the matter largely out of the hands of their legislatures by introducing a form of senatorial primary. Eventually the Seventeenth Amendment was adopted, becoming effective in 1913, and providing for the election of senators by direct popular vote.

## APPORTIONMENT OF REPRESENTATIVES

Representation in the House is based on population. For this purpose Article I provided for an "enumeration," or census, to be made within three years after the first meeting of the Congress and to be repeated every ten years thereafter. In determining the basis for representation, all "free persons" and indentured servants were to be counted, plus "three fifths of all other persons." This latter provision was a delicate method of referring to Negro slaves, whom the slaveholding states wished to include in the electoral base, whereas the other states wanted them excluded, along with "Indians not taxed" (i.e., living in their tribal relationship). Until the first census was taken, Article I, section 2, allotted sixty-five seats to the respective states on the basis of a rough estimate of their populations. The number of representatives was not to exceed 1 for every 30,000 in the electoral base, but each state was to have at least one representative.

The only subsequent constitutional provision affecting representation in the House was made by the Fourteenth Amendment. The abolition of slavery by the Thirteenth Amendment knocked out the three-fifths compromise provision and automatically gave all Negroes full weight for representation purposes. The Fourteenth Amendment recognized this change by language in section 2 apportioning representatives "among the several states according to their respective numbers, counting the whole number of persons in each State, excluding Indians not taxed."

Foreseeing the probable refusal to permit voting by Negroes in the South, the Northern-dominated Congress provided in the same section for reduction in the representation of any state which denied to any of its adult male citizens the right to vote, except for participation in rebellion or other crime. In spite of long-continued and widespread denial of voting rights to Negroes in Southern states, enforcement of this provision was never attempted, and it was regarded as a dead letter in the Constitution. However, with the development of the civil rights movement in the 1960s, renewed attention was given to this sanction, and it was one of the grounds for the unsuccessful effort to block the seating of the Mississippi delegation at the beginning

of the Eighty-ninth Congress. Various futile efforts to enforce the reduction of representation of Southern states by court proceedings were also undertaken.

The actual working out of the apportionment process depends not only upon the decennial census, but also upon subsequent adoption of a new apportionment plan which will give effect to the changes in the state population pattern. The Constitution provides no machinery for this purpose, but it is a task which obviously belongs to Congress. The general procedure was originally that Congress, within a year or two after the census results were available, would pass a reapportionment statute giving effect to the new population figures. Since no state ever liked to have its representation reduced, the total number of seats in the House was increased in every apportionment except one (1842), until it finally reached the figure of 435 under the 1911 statute.

Following the census of 1920 Congress for the first time found itself unable to agree on an apportionment plan, since the alternatives were either to reduce the representation of eleven states or again increase the size of the House. This experience made it clear that there was no means of compelling Congress to perform its constitutional duty on apportionment. Finally in 1929 a permanent reapportionment statute was adopted for the 1930 census and all subsequent ones. This law freezes the size of the House at 435. After each census the Census Bureau prepares for the President a table showing the number of inhabitants of each state and the number of representatives to which each state would be entitled under two alternative methods of handling the population fractions left over after the state populations have been divided by the country-wide ratio. The President then transmits the information to Congress at the beginning of its next regular session. A reapportionment according to the method of computation employed in the previous apportionment then goes into effect unless within sixty days Congress itself enacts a different one.

The admission of Alaska and Hawaii, each with one seat, temporarily raised the number of members in the House to 437. But with the 1960 apportionment, the size of the House automatically reverted to 435. Accommodating the two new states within the 435 total, plus varying rates of population growth since 1950, resulted in an apportionment under which sixteen states lost twenty-one seats while nine states gained nineteen seats. In an effort to ease the resulting political problems in certain states the House seriously considered raising the number of seats to 438, but finally abandoned the idea.

## DISTRICTING FOR THE HOUSE

Fixing the number of representatives from each state is only the first part of the election process. It is still necessary to divide the states into election districts, unless the representatives are to be elected from the state at large,

which was initially a fairly common practice. The districting responsibility is in general left to the states, under the provision of Article I, section 4, that "the times, places and manner of holding elections for Senators and Representatives, shall be prescribed in each state by the legislature thereof."

However, the section goes on to provide that "the Congress may at any time by law make or alter such regulations." Under this authority Congress by the apportionment act of 1842 required every state entitled to more than one representative to be divided by its legislature into districts "composed of contiguous territory," each returning one member. The acts of 1901 and 1911 added a "compact" qualification for districts in an effort to limit the practice of gerrymandering.[1] But the 1929 act omitted any requirement for contiguous, compact, or even equal districts.[2] In *Wood* v. *Broom* (1932) the Supreme Court held that this omission was intentional and had repealed the requirements of the previous laws. Consequently the Court could take no action to correct state redistricting acts setting up gerrymandered districts.

The Court initially held itself powerless also to remedy a state's failure to redistrict at all. The case of *Colegrove* v. *Green* (1946) presented the situation of Illinois, where the rural-dominated Legislature refused after 1901 to revise the state's congressional districts because it would have been compelled to increase the proportion of seats going to Chicago. When subsequent censuses entitled Illinois to additional seats in the House, they had to be filled at large. The differential between the most and least populous congressional districts, which had been only 25,000 in 1897, grew to 400,000 in 1928 and 800,000 in 1946. In many other states there was a similar refusal to give metropolitan areas the seats to which they were entitled by population.

In the *Colegrove* case, the Supreme Court refused to intervene in congressional districting matters on the ground that this was a matter for the "exclusive authority" of Congress. If the Supreme Court got involved it would, according to Justice Frankfurter, be entering a "political thicket." Moreover, the Court feared that any relief it could give would be negative; it could declare the existing system invalid, but could not draw new district lines, with the result that Illinois might be thrown into the forthcoming congressional elections, then only a few months away, with the necessity of electing all its House members at large.

[1] Gerrymandering is the practice whereby the majority party in the state legislature draws district lines which will concentrate the strength of the opposition party into as few districts as possible and spread the strength of its own party over as many districts as possible. The usual result of gerrymandering is a number of odd-shaped districts.

[2] In fact, the statute does not even require election of House members by districts. The 1842 act requiring districting had proved unenforceable; see Roland Young, *The American Congress* (New York: Harper & Row, Publishers, Incorporated, 1958), pp. 29–30. New Mexico and Hawaii each elected their two representatives at large in the 89th Congress, while Maryland, Ohio, and Texas each elected one representative at large. New Mexico and Hawaii continued this practice in the 90th Congress.

This was a four to three decision, and the fourth vote for the majority was cast by Justice Rutledge, who did not agree with Frankfurter's general view that the courts had no responsibility over House districts, but who did favor judicial abstention in this case because he thought intervention just preceding the election would do more harm than good. The three dissenters —Justices Black, Douglas, and Murphy—contended that the failure to redistrict was "willful legislative discrimination" amounting to a denial of equal protection of the laws.

Though judicial power to handle legislative districting issues was thus denied by only three members of the Court, the *Colegrove* decision was generally understood as establishing the principle of judicial nonintervention in legislative apportionments or electoral systems, and was cited as a precedent by the Court in refusing to review several subsequent state election cases.[3] But in 1960 the *Colegrove* rule came up for a new examination in *Gomillion* v. *Lightfoot,* an electoral-district controversy in which the Supreme Court did find that it could act. An Alabama state law had redefined the city boundaries of Tuskegee so as to place all but four or five of the city's Negro voters outside the city limits, without removing a single white voter or resident. The statute was unanimously declared unconstitutional by the Supreme Court.

Justice Frankfurter, author of the *Colegrove* opinion, also spoke for the Court in *Gomillion,* and he denied the Tuskegee ruling in any way weakened or contradicted the *Colegrove* rationale. The two situations were different; in Illinois there had simply been a failure of the Legislature to act, but in Alabama the Legislature had committed a positive discriminatory act. In *Colegrove* there had been "dilution" of the strength of the urban appellants' votes as a result of failure to redistrict, whereas in Tuskegee petitioners had been completely deprived of their votes in the city by affirmative legislative action. "When a legislature thus singles out a readily isolated segment of a racial minority for special discriminatory treatment, it violates the Fifteenth Amendment," concluded Frankfurter.

While the two decisions could be differentiated in this way, the *Gomillion* case did suggest that the *Colegrove* principle of judicial nonintervention might have been weakened. Efforts were under way at this time in various states to test the *Colegrove* rule. Already in 1958 a federal court in Minnesota had ordered the Legislature to redistrict that state's congressional districts. In 1959 a group of voters in Tennessee began a challenge of that state's legislative districts which three years later brought from the Supreme Court the famous decision in *Baker* v. *Carr* (1962) already discussed in Chapter 5.

The Court's ruling in *Baker* was simply that legislative districting controversies of this kind were justiciable, and should be heard by the federal courts. Suits challenging congressional district lines were immediately filed

[3] *South* v. *Peters* (1950); *MacDougall* v. *Green* (1948).

in numerous states, and it was a Georgia case, *Wesberry* v. *Sanders* (1964), which won the race to the Supreme Court. The Georgia district in which the city of Atlanta was located had a 1960 population of 823,000, as compared with the average of 394,000 for all ten Georgia districts. Residents of that district sued to enjoin state officials from conducting a congressional election. The trial court had dismissed the complaint on the basis of the *Colegrove* opinion. The Supreme Court, however, held that the controversy was justiciable and that such disparity in the population of congressional districts was contrary to the constitutional requirement that representatives in Congress be chosen "by the people of the several states."

The Court's vote on the issue of justiciability was eight to one, Justice Harlan being the only dissenter. Justice Black, the Court's spokesman, completed the liquidation of *Colegrove* which *Baker* v. *Carr* had begun. Justice Frankfurter's opinion in *Colegrove* was referred to by Black as a "minority" view. As for Frankfurter's position that Article I, section 4, gave Congress exclusive authority to protect the right of citizens to vote for congressmen, Black rejoined that "the right to vote is too important in our free society to be stripped of judicial protection by such an interpretation."

When Justice Black went on to hold that the Constitution required the Court to enforce equality of congressional districts, Stewart and Clark joined Harlan in dissent. Black derived the principle of equal congressional districts from certain of Madison's statements at the Constitutional Convention and in *The Federalist*, and more specifically from the language in Article I about the choosing of representatives "by the people of the several States." It was the clear intention of the Convention, he asserted, to make "population . . . the basis of the House of Representatives." He continued:

> To say that a vote is worth more in one district than in another would not only run counter to our fundamental ideas of democratic government, it would cast aside the principle of a House of Representatives elected 'by the People,' a principle tenaciously fought for and established at the Constitutional Convention.

Justice Black summed up his position in this concluding paragraph:

> While it may not be possible to draw congressional districts with mathematical precision, that is no excuse for ignoring our Constitution's plain objective of making equal representation for equal numbers of people the fundamental goal for the House of Representatives. That is the high standard of justice and common sense which the Founders set for us.

Justice Harlan's dissent was strongly worded, even alarmist. He thought the Court had declared "constitutionally defective the very composition of a coordinate branch of the Federal Government" and placed "in jeopardy the seats of almost all the members of the present House." His position was that the Constitution did not require equal congressional districts and that

even if it did, Congress had exclusive supervisory power over this matter. Representatives from Georgia *were* elected "by the people," he asserted, and this was all Article I required. As for discussions in the Constitutional Convention on which Black relied, Harlan found "nothing which suggests even remotely that the delegates had in mind the problem of districting within a State." The constitutional right to equal election districts asserted by the Court majority, he charged, had been "manufactured out of whole cloth."

Further judicial action in the Georgia case was made unnecessary when the state Legislature, only four days after *Wesberry* was decided, passed a bill redistricting the state's congressional seats for the first time since 1931, giving Atlanta the representatives to which it was entitled by population and making the population in each district roughly equal.

Harlan's language about declaring the composition of the House "constitutionally defective" was of course not justified. Legislatures in two other states—Michigan and Connecticut—passed redistricting acts in time for the 1964 elections, but in the other states where suits had been begun the courts permitted the 1964 elections to be held on the basis of the existing district lines. Thus the major impact of the ruling was postponed until after the 1964 elections.

Another result of the *Wesberry* decision was to stimulate Congress to work on the problem of equal districts. There had been no new apportionment legislation since 1929, and that act had omitted previous requirements for contiguity, compactness, and equality of population. After *Wesberry* the House Judiciary Committee took up a long-slumbering measure drafted by Representative Celler providing that congressional districts must be composed of compact and contiguous territory, varying not more than 15 per cent from the average population of the state's congressional districts. The bill passed the House in 1965, but failed to get Senate attention. In 1967 the House proposed to approve variations of 30 per cent, while the Senate demanded only 10 per cent. The conferees, unable to compromise, went off on a tangent and produced a bill forbidding further enforcement of congressional redistricting until 1972, after the next census. The Senate rejected this crude attempt to coerce the federal courts. Congress has thus failed to take any position on the districting issue, other than a minor 1967 law forbidding at-large elections for the House except in Hawaii and New Mexico.

It is impractical to follow in detail the congressional redistricting actions in the various states after 1964. Within one year after *Wesberry*, no less than thirteen of the forty-five states with more than one representative had redistricted, and by 1967, 288 districts in thirty states had been redistricted.

In *Wright* v. *Rockefeller* (1964) the Court refused to move into a different congressional districting problem. It declined to hold invalid four Manhattan districts which had allegedly been gerrymandered on racial lines. According to the complaint, white citizens had been concentrated in one of the

districts by "irrational" and discriminatory district lines, while Negroes and Puerto Ricans had been squeezed into the other three districts. Gerrymandering there certainly had been, but the Court majority concluded there was no preponderance of evidence that the motivation was racial.

### TERMS

The two-year term for members of the House now seems fairly short, but it must be remembered that it was adopted at a time when democratic theory stressed the need for annual elections. In the Convention, Madison argued that a one-year term would be "almost consumed in preparing for and traveling to and from the seat of national business," and he favored a three-year term.

Proposals for extending the term to four years have often been made, most recently by President Johnson in 1966. Pointing to the accelerating volume of legislation, the increasingly complex problems, the longer sessions of Congress, and the increasing costs of campaigning, he urged a four-year term to attract better men to the House, give them more time to develop an understanding of national problems, and free them from the pressures and costs of biennial campaigns.

President Johnson's proposal called for representatives to be elected at the same time as the President, thus eliminating the midterm elections to the House which now provide some opportunity for public reaction to the administration in power. This feature was widely condemned even by those who favored the four-year term, and in Congress a bill was presented providing for staggered terms, one half of the House being elected every two years. Even in this modified form there was no substantial support for the change, and no action was taken.

The six-year term for senators [4] is one of the major factors in the peculiar role which the Senate fills in the American system. Legally, the fact that only one-third of the seats fall vacant every two years gives the Senate the status of a "continuing body," compared with the House which must reconstitute itself every two years.

### QUALIFICATIONS

Article I lays down certain qualifications for senators and representatives as to age, citizenship, and residence. A senator must be thirty years of age, nine years a citizen of the United States, and an inhabitant of the state from

[4] In 1967 an effort was made under the recall provisions of Idaho law to start recall proceedings against Senator Frank Church. Such an effort, if successful, would squarely challenge the constitutional provision for a six-year term for senators, as the Senate would undoubtedly hold in determining whether a vacancy existed.

which he is elected.[5] A representative need be only twenty-five years old and a citizen for seven years, but the residence requirement is the same. By custom a representative must reside not only in the state but in the district from which he is elected.

Members of Congress are disqualified for appointment to executive office by Article I, section 6, which provides: "No person holding any office under the United States, shall be a member of either house during his continuance in office." Thus to accept an executive appointment, a member of Congress must resign his seat, and a federal official who is elected to Congress must resign his post before he takes his seat. Members of Congress, however, have been appointed on many occasions to represent the United States on international commissions and at diplomatic conferences. Such diplomatic assignments are not considered "offices" in the constitutional sense, being for specific, temporary purposes and carrying with them no extra compensation.

A second disqualification affecting congressmen is also stated in Article I, section 6: "No Senator or Representative shall, during the time for which he was elected, be appointed to any civil office under the authority of the United States, which shall have been created, or the emoluments whereof shall have been increased during such time." The purpose of this restriction seems to have been to prevent Congress from feathering the nests of its members by creating jobs to which they could be appointed, but it is a rather inept provision which has achieved no useful purpose on the few occasions it has been invoked.[6]

Each house is authorized by Article I, section 5, to "be the judge of the elections, returns and qualifications of its own members." The "qualifications," it seems clear, are those stated in the Constitution. In the Convention, Madison opposed a suggestion that Congress itself should have the power to set qualifications for its members, fearing it might be used by a stronger legislative faction to keep out "partizans of a weaker faction." In *The Federalist*, No. 60, Hamilton wrote that the qualifications of legislators were fixed by the Constitution "and are unalterable by the legislature."

However, on several occasions both houses have in effect enforced additional qualifications by refusing to seat duly elected members who met the constitutional qualifications. The Test Oath Act of 1862 imposed as a qualification on all members of Congress (as well as other federal officials) the taking of an oath that they had not participated in rebellion against the United States.

Individual congressmen have been disqualified on several grounds. The House refused to seat a Utah polygamist in 1900. Victor L. Berger of Wis-

---

[5] Though he lived in Virginia, voted in Massachusetts, and was elected a Massachusetts delegate to the 1964 Democratic national convention, Robert F. Kennedy on August 25, 1964, announced his candidacy for the United States Senate from New York, established residence in that state, and was elected in November, 1964.

[6] See *Ex parte Levitt* (1937).

consin, a Socialist, was refused his seat by the House in 1919 because of his conviction under the Espionage Act for opposing the war. His constituents reelected him, and he was again denied his seat. Before his election for a third time, his conviction was reversed by the Supreme Court, and the House then seated him. In the late 1920s the Senate refused to seat Frank L. Smith of Illinois and William S. Vare of Pennsylvania because of scandals in connection with their campaign funds.

In 1967 Adam Clayton Powell, Negro congressman from New York and the most influential member of his race in a public position, was excluded from his seat in Congress. He had been convicted in 1966 of criminal contempt of court for failing to pay a defamation of character judgment against him in 1963. His autocratic manner of conducting the affairs of the House Education and Labor Committee, of which he was chairman, his highly publicized travels at public expense with feminine members of his staff, and his cashing of the salary checks issued to his estranged wife who performed no functions for the committee, had built up nationwide criticism. As the ninetieth Congress opened, the House voted not to seat him pending the outcome of a special investigation by a select committee into his fitness to serve as a member of the House, and the Democratic caucus removed him as chairman of his committee.

The select committee recommended that Powell be seated but that he be severely censured, lose his seniority, and be assessed $40,000 to reimburse the House for unjustified expenditures. The House, spurred into emotional action by a flood of correspondence from angry constituents, rejected the committee recommendations and the advice of its leadership in both parties, and voted to exclude Powell and to declare his seat vacant.

Powell's response was twofold. He ran in the special election to fill the vacancy and was reelected with 86 per cent of the vote. He also filed suit in federal district court for an injunction ordering the House to seat him, on the ground that it had exceeded its constitutional powers in excluding him when he possessed the constitutional qualifications for membership. In *Powell* v. *McCormack* the district judge dismissed the suit on the ground that it involved a "political question" which the separation of powers principle barred the courts from considering. In February, 1968, the court of appeals likewise ruled against Powell. One judge relied on the political question ground, but the other two rejected Powell's constitutional contentions on the merits, adopting the questionable position that the House is not obligated to seat a duly elected member, but can appraise his activities and fitness at the time he presents his credentials.

## EXPULSION AND CENSURE

Congressmen are not subject to impeachment, not being regarded as "civil officers" of the United States. The Constitution does provide, however, that

each house may expel its members by a two-thirds vote, or punish them for "disorderly behavior." Congress is the sole judge of the reasons for expulsion. The offense need not be indictable. In 1797 the Senate expelled William Blount for conduct which was not performed in his official capacity nor during a session of the Senate nor at the seat of government. The Supreme Court has recorded in a dictum its understanding that the expulsion power "extends to all cases where the offence is such as in the judgment of the Senate is inconsistent with the trust and duty of a member." [7]

When the Southern states seceded in 1861, their senators were not expelled. The Senate simply noted that the seats had "become vacant." However, two Missouri senators were subsequently expelled for acts against the Union. Formal censure proceedings have been brought against only four of its members in Senate history. Senator Joseph McCarthy was censured in 1954 for conduct "contrary to Senatorial traditions." In 1967 Senator Thomas J. Dodd was censured for conduct tending "to bring the Senate into dishonor and disrepute." Specifically he was charged with using for his personal benefit funds obtained from the public through political testimonial dinners intended to finance his election campaigns.

In the case of Adam Clayton Powell the correct constitutional course of action for the House, if it desired to remove him, would have been to seat him and then to censure and expel him. In fact, after the Dodd censure vote, Powell offered to accept censure if readmitted to the House; and he charged that the difference in the action of the two houses was because "Powell is black and Dodd is white."

### THE FILLING OF VACANCIES

Vacancies may occur in either house of Congress by death, resignation, expulsion, or the acceptance of a disqualifying office. So far as the House is concerned, Article I, section 2, makes the following provision for special elections: "When vacancies happen in the representation from any state, the executive authority thereof shall issue writs of election to fill such vacancies." For senators, who were originally chosen by state legislatures, section 3 of Article I authorized temporary state executive appointments to fill vacancies occurring during recesses of the legislature. The Seventeenth Amendment superseded this provision with a general authorization to state governors to call a special election, but the amendment also provided "that the legislature of any state may empower the executive thereof to make temporary appointments until the people fill the vacancies by election as the legislature may direct."

In practice almost all states have authorized their governors to proceed on this basis. The result is that Senate vacancies are usually filled immediately by an appointee who serves until the next general election in his state,

[7] *In re Chapman* (1897).

at which time a senator is elected for the remainder of the original term. On the other hand, the states often leave House vacancies unfilled rather than incur the expense of a special election, particularly if there are only a few months remaining of the term.

## PRIVILEGES AND IMMUNITIES OF MEMBERS

Article I, section 6, provides in part: "The Senators and Representatives . . . shall in all cases, except treason, felony and breach of the peace, be privileged from arrest during their attendance at the session of their respective houses, and in going to and returning from the same; and for any speech or debate in either house, they shall not be questioned in any other place." Immunity from arrest during sessions of the legislature was one of the protections asserted by the English Parliament in its struggle with the Crown, and embodied in the English Bill of Rights. It is of comparatively minor significance in the American Constitution. The phrase, "treason, felony or breach of the peace" has been interpreted by the Court as withdrawing all criminal offenses from the scope of the privilege.[8] Thus the only area left for its operation is arrests in civil suits, which were common when the Constitution was adopted, but are now seldom made. The immunity does not apply to service of process in either civil or criminal cases.

Much more important is the freedom of speech guaranteed to congressmen by the provision that they should not be questioned "in any other place" for any speech or debate. This means that they cannot be sued for libel or slander, or in any other way held legally accountable for statements made in their official capacity except by the House or Senate itself. Not only words spoken on the floor of Congress, but written reports, resolutions offered, the act of voting, and all things done in a session by one of its members relating to the business before it, are covered. This was the ruling in *Kilbourn* v. *Thompson* (1881), where the Court held that members of the House were not liable to suit for false imprisonment because they had instituted legislative proceedings as a result of which the plaintiff was arrested.[9]

The broad protection of the "speech or debate" clause was reaffirmed in *United States* v. *Johnson* (1966). A congressman had made a speech on the

---

[8] *Williamson* v. *United States* (1908).

[9] A more recent illustration is *Dombrowski* v. *Eastland* (1967) where the Court ruled that a senator could not be sued on charges of conspiracy to violate the civil rights of a group of civil rights advocates in Louisiana. Members of Congress, the Court said, "should be protected not only from the consequences of litigation's results but also from the burden of defending themselves." However, the Court held that counsel for Senator Eastland's internal security subcommittee must stand trial on charges of conspiring with the Senator and Louisiana officials to stage an illegal raid in New Orleans. The immunity doctrine "is less absolute, although applicable, when applied to officers or employees of a legislative body, rather than to legislators themselves."

floor of the House in return for payment by private interests, and was convicted of conspiring with these interests to defraud the United States. The government contended that the "speech or debate" clause forbade only prosecutions based on the content of a speech, such as libel actions, but not those founded on the antecedent unlawful conduct of accepting a bribe. However, the Supreme Court held unanimously that the purpose of the clause, growing as it did out of the long struggle of Parliament for independence from the king and his courts, was to protect legislators from "intimidation by the executive and accountability before a possibly hostile judiciary," and that consequently any judicial inquiry into the motivation of a congressman's speech was in violation of the Constitution.

Adam Clayton Powell was convicted of libel in 1963 for comments made on a television program, where he was not protected by his congressional immunity.

*Tenney* v. *Brandhove* (1951) related to the question of legislative immunity in the California Legislature, but in supporting the immunity claimed there the Court had occasion to discuss the issue generally. Brandhove brought suit against members of a California legislative committee, alleging that the committee had summoned him before it not for a legislative purpose but to intimidate him and to prevent him from using his constitutional rights of free speech. Justice Frankfurter reviewed the development in the English Parliament of legislative immunity and its transfer to this country in both federal and state constitutions. Immunity serves a broad purpose. "Legislators are immune from deterrents to the uninhibited discharge of their legislative duty, not for their private indulgence but for the public good. One must not expect uncommon courage even in legislators." Justice Douglas, dissenting, thought that even legislative immunity had its limits. "It is one thing to give great leeway to the legislative right of speech, debate, and investigation. But when a committee perverts its power, brings down on an individual the whole weight of government for an illegal or corrupt purpose, the reason for the immunity ends."

### SELECTED REFERENCES

BAKER, GORDON E., *The Reapportionment Revolution*, chap. 5. New York: Random House, Inc., 1966.

Congressional Quarterly, *Congressional Districting*. Washington: Congressional Quarterly Service, 1962.

———, *Representation and Apportionment*. Washington: Congressional Quarterly Service, 1966.

HACKER, ANDREW, *Congressional Districting: The Issue of Equal Representation*. Washington, D.C.: The Brookings Institution, 1963.

HAYNES, GEORGE H., *The Senate of the United States: Its History and Practice,* vol. I, chaps. 3, 4. Boston: Houghton Mifflin Company, 1938.

JEWELL, MALCOLM E., *The Politics of Reapportionment,* parts 3, 4. New York: The Atherton Press, 1962.

KEY, V. O., JR., *Politics, Parties, and Pressure Groups,* chaps. 20, 22. New York: Thomas Y. Crowell Company, 1958 (fourth edition).

LEWIS, ANTHONY, "Legislative Apportionment and the Federal Courts," 71 *Harvard Law Review* 1057–1098 (1958).

"The Power of a House of Congress to Judge the Qualifications of Its Members," 81 *Harvard Law Review* 673–684 (1968).

"The Reapportionment of Congress," 40 *American Political Science Review* 153–157 (March, 1951).

SCHMECKEBIER, LAURENCE F., *Congressional Apportionment.* Washington, D.C.: The Brookings Institution, 1941.

WILLOUGHBY, WILLIAM F., *Principles of Legislative Organization and Administration.* Washington, D.C.: The Brookings Institution, 1934.

YOUNG, ROLAND, *The American Congress,* chap. 2. New York: Harper & Row, Publishers, Incorporated, 1958.

# 11

## Legislative powers and procedure

The first words in the Constitution, following the Preamble, are: "All legislative powers herein granted shall be vested in a Congress of the United States." These grants cover a remarkable variety of powers. The strictly legislative or "lawmaking" role of Congress is exercised by the passing of statutes, which are of four general types: (1) public laws which formulate authoritative rules of conduct, substantive or procedural, applicable generally or to all classes of persons or events specified in the statute; (2) private acts which apply to named individuals, usually for the purpose of adjusting claims against the government; (3) revenue acts which provide the government's funds; and (4) appropriation acts which make revenues available for expenditure for specified purposes.

This chapter is not concerned with the lawmaking power in specific substantive fields, as granted by the long series of authorizations in Article I, section 8, or elsewhere in the Constitution. Subsequent chapters will be devoted to experience with the most important of these grants—the regulation of commerce, and taxation and fiscal authority. In this chapter the problem is rather to describe the general constitutional principles which have been developed and applied in determining the existence and extent of legislative power.

Neither is it necessary or possible here to account for all the numerous functions which Congress performs in addition to its lawmaking role. Most

of these functions are covered elsewhere in this volume. The role of Congress in proposing amendments to the Constitution—what may be called its *constituent* power—has already been examined. The *electoral* functions which fall to the House and Senate if no candidate for the Presidency or vice presidency secures a majority in the electoral college, and their joint role in canvassing the electoral vote, will be treated in connection with the discussion of the President, as will also the *executive* authority of the Senate in consenting to the ratification of treaties and giving advice and consent to appointments. The *investigative* function of Congress, which is auxiliary to all of its other duties, has raised so many important constitutional questions that Chapter 12 is devoted entirely to that matter.

There remain, then, for brief review in this chapter only the *judicial* role of Congress in performing the function of impeachment, and its *administrative* powers of supervision and control over the federal establishment. Finally, a brief account of constitutional provisions on legislative procedure concludes the chapter.

### PRINCIPLES OF LEGISLATIVE POWER

As the legislative organ of a government of delegated powers, Congress must be able to support any exercise of legislative authority as both authorized and not forbidden by the Constitution. There are two types of authorizations in Article I, section 8. The first seventeen clauses specifically enumerate a series of powers, ranging all the way from punishment of counterfeiting to the declaration of war. Then clause 18 is a general authorization "to make all laws which shall be necessary and proper for carrying into execution the foregoing powers, and all other powers vested by this Constitution in the government of the United States, or in any department or officer thereof."

The relationship of this last clause, referred to in the ratification debates as "the sweeping clause," to the enumerated powers preceding it quickly became the subject of controversy between Federalists and Jeffersonians, between broad and strict constructionists. The issue was joined over Hamilton's plan for a national bank, as presented to the First Congress. There was no authorization in the Constitution for Congress to create a bank; in fact, the Convention had specifically refused to grant to Congress even a restricted power to create corporations. On President Washington's invitation, Hamilton and Jefferson submitted their respective views on whether he should sign the bill; they are classical expositions of divergent theories of constitutional interpretation.

Jefferson emphasized the "necessary" in the necessary and proper clause. Since all the enumerated powers could be carried out without a bank, it was not necessary and consequently not authorized. Hamilton, on the other hand, argued that the powers granted to Congress included the right to employ

"all the *means* requisite and fairly applicable to the attainment of the *ends* of such power," unless they were specifically forbidden or immoral or contrary to the "essential ends of political society."

The Hamiltonian theory of a broad and liberal interpretation of congressional powers was successful in persuading Washington to sign the bank bill, and it has generally predominated in subsequent constitutional development. In 1819 Marshall gave the definitive statement of this view in the great case of *McCulloch* v. *Maryland*. Congressional authority to create a bank (the second Bank of the United States, incorporated by statute in 1816) was again the issue. Marshall found implied congressional power to establish a bank in its expressly granted powers to collect taxes, to borrow money, to regulate commerce, to declare and conduct a war; for "it may with great reason be contended, that a government, entrusted with such ample powers, on the due execution of which the happiness and prosperity of the nation so vitally depends, must also be entrusted with ample means for their execution." A corporation was such a means. "It is never the end for which other powers are exercised."

Marshall analyzed the necessary and proper clause at length. He rejected the strict Jeffersonian interpretation, which "would abridge, and almost annihilate this useful and necessary right of the legislature to select the means." His final, and famous, conclusion was:

> Let the end be legitimate, let it be within the scope of the constitution, and all means which are appropriate, which are plainly adapted to that end, which are not prohibited, but consistent with the letter and spirit of the constitution, are constitutional.

Perhaps the principal doctrinal challenge of a general character which federal legislative power has had to meet since *McCulloch* v. *Maryland* is the contention that the powers reserved to the states under the Tenth Amendment constitute a limitation on expressly granted congressional authority. This position has already been discussed in Chapter 5 under the heading of "dual federalism," and it is consequently unnecessary to deal with it here.

Notice may be taken, however, of a view which is at the opposite extreme from dual federalism. This is the theory put forward by James Wilson of Pennsylvania during the Convention period that "whenever an object occurs, to the direction of which no particular state is competent, the management of it must, of necessity, belong to the United States in Congress assembled." [1] This contention of sovereign and inherent power in Congress was repeated by counsel in the case of *Kansas* v. *Colorado* (1907). The steps in the argument were that complete legislative power must be vested either in the state or national governments; that the states are limited to internal affairs;

---

[1] James De Witt Andrews, *Works of James Wilson* (Chicago: Callaghan and Company, 1896), vol. 1, p. 558.

and that "consequently all powers which are national in their scope must be found vested in Congress." The Court rejected this position as in violation of the Tenth Amendment, and held that powers of a national character not delegated to Congress were "reserved to the people of the United States."

In constitutional theory, then, Congress does not derive its authority from any doctrine of sovereign and inherent power.[2] Delegation by the Constitution is the source of federal legislative authority. However, as the subsequent discussion of the commerce power particularly will indicate, Wilson's assertion that Congress must have the power required to deal with national problems has gradually been accepted, and a broad doctrine of implied power, based on the necessary and proper clause, has been a supplemental source of great significance in equipping Congress with authority commensurate with its responsibilities.

### DELEGATION OF LEGISLATIVE POWER

There is a Latin saw, *delegata potestas non potest delegari,* which may be translated as meaning that delegated power cannot be redelegated. The Supreme Court accepts this prohibition as applied to Congress. And yet delegation of legislative power is an absolute necessity of practical government and has been practiced from almost the beginning of the Republic. The Supreme Court has recognized this necessity. Chief Justice Taft once said that the extent and character of permissible delegation "must be fixed according to common sense and the inherent necessities of the governmental co-ordination."[3] The Court has thus been placed in a dilemma, which it has been able to resolve only by tortuous explanations and legal fictions that what is delegation in fact is not delegation in law.

The reasons why Congress must indulge in extensive delegation of legislative power are well known. The legislative machinery is ponderous. Congressmen may succeed well enough in the task of formulating general policies, but lack the time and expert information needed to prescribe the specific methods for carrying out those policies. Moreover, a piece of legislation once enacted is extremely hard to amend, whereas the problems with which the legislation aims to deal may be constantly changing. These legislative limitations have become increasingly obvious with the expansion of governmental intervention into the management of the economy, and in emergency or wartime periods the pressure on Congress to authorize broad delegations

---

[2] This issue has been reargued by Crosskey, who contends that a construction of the Constitution according to eighteenth-century rules, giving effect to the Preamble, the general welfare clause, and the necessary and proper clause, supports the view that the framers intended Congress to have "a general national legislative authority." W. W. Crosskey, *Politics and the Constitution in the History of the United States* (Chicago: The University of Chicago Press, 1953), pp. 391–393.

[3] *J. W. Hampton, Jr., & Co.* v. *United States* (1928).

of its powers to the executive is especially great. Finally, Congress some-times uses the delegation technique when it realizes that a problem exists, but is uncertain how to handle it. By delegation the "hot potato" can be passed on to other hands.

In consequence of such legislative grants, an enormous quantity of ad-ministrative rules and regulations, filling many volumes of the Federal Code of Regulations, has been issued. Much of this quasi-legislative output simply governs the form and procedure of government action, but a large propor-tion is actually elaboration, definition, or amplification of the substantive provisions of federal statutes. To avoid giving the impression that delegation is always to the executive branch, mention should be made of the act of 1934 delegating to the Supreme Court the power to prescribe rules of civil procedure for the federal courts.

Marshall was the first to rationalize a legislative delegation. In *Wayman* v. *Southard* (1825) he distinguished "important subjects, which must be entirely regulated by the legislature itself, from those of less interest, in which a general provision may be made, and power given to those who are to act under such general provisions to fill up the details." This suggestion that delegation may be employed only in dealing with less important sub-jects has proved completely untenable. On the other hand, the legal fiction that delegation is merely a "filling up the details" of a statute has been a perennially useful one. In *United States* v. *Grimaud* (1911) the Court was confronted with a statute authorizing the Secretary of Agriculture to make rules and regulations with respect to grazing on national forest reservations, which it upheld on the ground that it was "impracticable" for Congress itself to adopt such regulations, covering as they did "local conditions." In em-powering the Secretary of Agriculture to act, "Congress was merely con-ferring administrative functions upon an agent, and not delegating to him legislative power." The fact that the statute provided penalties for violation of the grazing rules did not elevate the regulations "from an administrative to a legislative character."

Marshall's conception of "filling up the details" of course demands that there be an announced general legislative plan into which the details fit. Consequently the Court has consistently demanded that Congress supply standards to guide and control the acts of delegatees. But the Court has normally been willing to accept rather broad and general standards as meeting constitutional requirements—such as the standard that the Inter-state Commerce Commission shall fix rates that are "just and reasonable," [4] or the standard that the Federal Communications Commission shall grant licenses to radio stations when it is in the "public convenience, interest or necessity" to do so.[5]

[4] Upheld in *Interstate Commerce Commission* v. *Illinois Central R.R. Co.* (1910).
[5] Upheld in *Federal Radio Commission* v. *Nelson Brothers* (1933).

CONTINGENT LEGISLATION    Particular attention must be given to a special type of delegation, that made in so-called "contingent legislation." Here the delegation is not of power to make rules or fill in details; it is delegation of authority to determine facts or make predictions which are to have the effect of suspending legislation, or alternatively, of bringing it into effect. Thus in 1809 Congress passed an act which prohibited the importation of goods from certain foreign countries but permitted the prohibition to lapse in case the President ascertained and proclaimed that those countries were no longer molesting the seaborne commerce of the United States. The McKinley tariff of 1890 illustrates the alternative type of contingent legislation. It authorized the admission of certain articles free of duty, but added that if a foreign country producing any of these commodities should impose upon American products duties found by the President to be "reciprocally unequal and unreasonable," then the President would have power to suspend the duty-free status of the foreign commodities, and duties set out in the act would become payable.

The Supreme Court has ruled in a series of cases that this formula for delegation of legislative power, like the delegation of power to fill in details, does not violate constitutional standards. The 1809 Embargo Act was cleared of this charge in the case of *The Brig Aurora* (1813). In upholding the flexible tariff arrangements of the McKinley tariff in *Field* v. *Clark* (1892), the Court denied that the President had been endowed with any real legislative power. The only legislative action taken was "when Congress declared that the suspension should take effect upon a named contingency." The President's role was not that of legislator, but "mere agent of the lawmaking department to ascertain and declare the event upon which its expressed will was to take effect." [6]

DELEGATION AND THE NEW DEAL    After well over a century of judicial rationalization of legislative delegation, there was a widespread assumption that this area was one of the dead letters of American constitutional law. When unconstitutional delegation was charged in the so-called "Hot Oil" case, *Panama Refining Co.* v. *Ryan* (1935), the government did not take it seriously and devoted only 13 pages of its 427-page brief to the point. There was universal amazement when the Court ruled that in giving the President authority to exclude from interstate commerce oil produced in excess of state regulations, Congress had not met constitutional tests by supplying an adequate standard to guide or control the President in the use of this power. Chief Justice Hughes charged that Congress had in effect authorized the President "to pass a prohibitory law," but had declared no policy with respect to exercise of the power, set up no standard for the President's action, and required no finding by the President before he enacted the pro-

[6] See also *J. W. Hampton, Jr., & Co.* v. *United States* (1928).

hibition. In short, "the Congress left the matter to the President without standard or rule, to be dealt with as he pleased."

This was certainly an exaggerated statement, as Justice Cardozo said in dissent. As he saw it, the President was given choice, "though within limits, as to the occasion, but none whatever as to the means." He was not "left to roam at will among all the possible subjects of interstate transportation." His discretion "is not unconfined and vagrant. It is canalized within banks that keep it from overflowing." As for Hughes's objection that the President had made no finding to support the regulations he issued, Cardozo could only conclude that Hughes was confused. Findings may be a necessity under contingent legislation, but this act was not of that character. "If findings are necessary as a preamble to general regulations, the requirement must be looked for elsewhere than in the Constitution of the nation," Cardozo concluded.

It seems clear from this talk about findings and standards that the Court in the *Panama* case failed to accord to the President the normal presumption of validity or breadth of executive action, justifying Cardozo's tart comment that "the Constitution of the United States is not a code of civil practice." But four months later when *Schechter Corp.* v. *United States* (1935) was decided, even Cardozo was convinced that the National Industrial Recovery Act had gone too far in giving the President authority to promulgate industrial codes of fair competition. One year later, in *Carter* v. *Carter Coal Co.* (1936), the Guffey Coal Act was invalidated, partly because it was held to delegate legislative power to set up a code of mandatory regulations for the coal industry. This time the delegation was doubly condemned since it was not even to government officials, but to representatives of the coal industry.

RECENT DELEGATION DECISIONS    These three decisions were handed down in the heat of the Court's battle with the New Deal. After the smoke of that controversy had cleared away, there was no further serious difficulty with delegation charges. In 1939 the Federal Tobacco Inspection Act and the Agricultural Marketing Agreement Act were upheld, though Justice Roberts and a dissenting minority in the latter case charged that the standards set up to govern the Secretary of Agriculture were "so vague as in effect to invest him with uncontrolled power of legislation." [7]

The Fair Labor Standards Act, authorizing the fixing of minimum industry wages by an elaborate hearing procedure, was similarly cleared in *Opp Cotton Mills* v. *Administrator of Wage and Hour Division* (1941). It was charged that such statutory standards for determining wages as "due regard to economic and competitive conditions" and "without substantially curtailing employment," were so vague and indefinite as to provide practically no

[7] *Currin* v. *Wallace* (1939); *United States* v. *Rock Royal Co-operative* (1939); *Hood & Sons* v. *United States* (1939).

congressional guide or control. Justice Stone admitted that the statute left room for the exercise of "judgment."

> But where, as in the present case, the standards set up for the guidance of the administrative agency, the procedure which it is directed to follow and the record of its action which is required by the statute to be kept . . . are such that Congress, the courts and the public can ascertain whether the agency has conformed to the standards which Congress has prescribed, there is no failure of performance of the legislative function.

World War II brought even greater pressure for legislative delegations. In *Yakus* v. *United States* (1944) legislative authority given the Office of Price Administration to fix maximum prices under the Emergency Price Control Act of 1942 was upheld, and *Bowles* v. *Willingham* (1944) performed a similar function for rent controls. The standards fixed in the act were admittedly broad, but were satisfactory to all members of the Court except Roberts. So far as rent controls were concerned, the Administrator was empowered to fix maximum rents in any "defense-rental area" whenever in his judgment that action was necessary or proper in order to effectuate the purposes of the act. In establishing maximum rents he was directed to "give due consideration" to the rent level on April 1, 1941, but he could choose any date up to a year earlier or a later date. The rents fixed were to be such as "in his judgment" would be "generally fair and equitable." The standards for fixing of prices were similarly broad and discretionary.

In both decisions the Court majority took a firmly practical tone, based on their obvious conclusion that controls were a wartime necessity. As Chief Justice Stone said in the *Yakus* case: "The Constitution as a continuously operative charter of government does not demand the impossible or the impracticable." Justice Roberts, on the other hand, thought that the Administrator was left absolutely uncontrolled in arriving at his "judgments," and that the *Schechter* decision had been overruled.

The Renegotiation Act of 1942 authorized defense officials to renegotiate war contracts when it appeared that "excessive profits" were being earned by the contractor. There was no statutory definition of excessive profits, but the responsible administrative officials developed a definition for their guidance, which Congress in 1944 wrote into the act itself by amendment. This circumstance was relied on in *Lichter* v. *United States* (1948) to charge that the original statute was an unconstitutionally vague delegation, but Justice Burton replied for the Court:

> The fact that this term later was further defined both by administrative action and by statutory amendment indicates the probable desirability of such added definition, but it does not demonstrate that such further definition was a constitutional necessity essential to the validity of the original exercise by Congress of its war powers in initiating a new solution of an unprecedented problem.

These wartime delegations may, as Corwin has contended, have exceeded "any previous pattern of delegated legislation touching private rights directly." [8] But the Court's attitude on subsequent peacetime delegations continued to be extremely permissive, as *United States* v. *Sharpnack* (1958) demonstrates. It has been congressional policy to provide that state laws on minor criminal offenses shall apply to federal enclaves within states, such as Army or Air Force bases. This has typically been accomplished by successive federal assimilative crimes acts which adopt the existing state criminal laws on matters not covered by federal law for federal enclaves. But in 1948 Congress, seeking to avoid the necessity of repeated enactments, passed a statute making *future* state laws applicable as well as those on the state statute books at the time the federal act was passed. The Supreme Court upheld this statute against the charge that Congress had abdicated its lawmaking function to the states. Only Justices Douglas and Black, dissenting, would have held the statute invalid on the principle of the *Schechter* decision.

Nevertheless, the decisions do indicate that there are limits which Congress must observe in drafting legislation, and they may be summarized as follows. Congress must define the subject of the delegation, and provide a recognizable standard or criterion to guide the agent to whom legislative powers are delegated.[9] Where contingent legislation is involved, a definite finding with respect to the contingency specified in the statute must be made. Legislative power must be delegated only to public officials, not to private persons or organizations. Finally, Congress must itself provide any penal sanctions for the violation of administrative legislation.

### THE IMPEACHMENT POWER

Congress functions in a quasi-judicial capacity in connection with the process of impeachment, which is established by Article II, section 4, as a means of removing from office "the President, Vice President and all civil officers of the United States." Under Article I, the House of Representatives

[8] Edward S. Corwin, *Total War and the Constitution* (New York: Alfred A. Knopf, Inc., 1947), p. 45.
[9] In *Zemel* v. *Rusk* (1965) the Court held that the Passport Act of 1926, under which the Secretary of State imposed area restrictions on travel by American citizens (Cuba was the forbidden area in this case), did not constitute an invalid delegation because in *Kent* v. *Dulles* (1958) the Court had interpreted the act to authorize only those passport refusals and restrictions "which it could fairly be argued were adopted by Congress in light of prior administrative practice." In *Mora* v. *McNamara* (1967), where the Court denied certiorari in a case brought by three soldiers who contended the war in Vietnam was illegal and that they could be held guilty as war criminals if they participated in it, Justice Stewart dissented. He believed the Court was obliged to consider whether the Gulf of Tonkin Resolution which President Johnson relied on to support the Vietnam campaign was "a constitutionally impermissible delegation of all or part of Congress' power to declare war. . . ."

has "the sole power of impeachment." It exercises this power by passing, by majority vote, "articles of impeachment" which perform the function of an indictment.

The Senate is given "the sole power to try all impeachments." At the trial the House acts as the prosecutor through an appointed committee of managers, and the Senate sits as a court. Its presiding officer is the Vice President, unless the impeachment proceedings involve the President, in which case the Chief Justice of the United States presides. This arrangement is specified by the Constitution in order to remove the Vice President from a situation where his own interests would be so directly involved. Though the Senate is under no obligation to follow all the technical rules of judicial procedure, it accords to the accused the principal rights he would have in a law court, including benefit of counsel and compulsory process for obtaining witnesses. The Constitution requires a two-thirds vote of the senators present for conviction.

Experience with the impeachment process has not been extensive, but it has been sufficient to settle certain problems raised by the constitutional provisions. Impeachment is not applicable to military and naval officers, who are not "civil officers." Members of Congress likewise may not be subjected to impeachment. Though "civil," they are not "officers," for Article I, section 6, provides that "no person holding any office under the United States, shall be a member of either house during his continuance in office." Impeachment charges were brought against Senator William Blount of Tennessee by the House in 1798, but the Senate, after expelling him, declared him exempt from impeachment and dismissed the charges for want of jurisdiction.

Apart from the Blount affair, impeachment actions have been brought against nine federal judges, four of whom were convicted, and two members of the executive branch, President Andrew Johnson in 1868 and Secretary of War Belknap in 1876. Neither was convicted. Belknap sought to evade trial by resigning his office, but the Senate heard the case anyway, thus establishing the proposition that a civil officer can be impeached after he has left office. In such a case the penalty of "removal from office" which the Constitution specifies as a possible judgment would be impossible, but the other stated penalty of "disqualification to hold and enjoy any office of honor, trust or profit under the United States" could of course still be applied. The Constitution forbids any punishment other than these two for an officer convicted on impeachment, but such a conviction is no bar to subsequent prosecution in the regular courts for any wrongful acts. Prosecution under these conditions would not constitute double jeopardy.

Article II, section 4, gives as grounds for impeachment "treason, bribery, or other high crimes and misdemeanors." Treason is defined in Article III, and the meaning of bribery is obvious. "High crimes and misdemeanors" is a less definite category of offenses, however. In practice, it seems to cover any misconduct which affects the public welfare or indicates unfitness on

the part of the official. One of the charges against President Andrew Johnson was that he made public speeches denunciatory of Congress. Judge Archbald was convicted in 1912 on the basis of acts which were not indictable and which were not committed while in the discharge of his official duties. The President's power of granting pardons for offenses against the United States does not apply to cases of impeachment.

Tradition and the cumbersome nature of the impeachment process combine to prevent its present-day use for partisan political purposes. The impeachment of President Andrew Johnson in 1868, which failed of its purpose by only one vote in the Senate, was of course motivated by vindictive partisan passions. That defeat was highly salutary for the future of American politics. Loose talk about impeachment is now sometimes heard in the heat of political controversy, but it is seldom taken seriously. As Jefferson foresaw, the threat of impeachment now "is not even a scarecrow."

## THE POWER OF ADMINISTRATIVE SUPERVISION

The Constitution is not as clear as it might be in allocating responsibility for direction and control of the federal administrative establishment. To be sure, the President has the power to require the opinion in writing of the heads of departments on any subject relating to the duties of their offices, and he has the tremendous leverage which comes with the power to appoint. However, Congress also has a powerful constitutional basis from which to assert supervisory authority. The Senate's advice and consent must be secured for all important appointments. By its legislative authority, Congress can set up, abolish, or modify agencies, offices, and activities. Through its power to appropriate, it controls the nature and extent of administrative programs. Through the power to investigate, it can expose and embarrass officials or operations which are legislatively disapproved.

With these potentialities, it is not surprising that Congress has enjoyed considerable success in asserting legislative powers of supervision over the actions of federal officials. Historically, the basic conflict was over authority to direct the actions of department heads. The federal department head has an interesting duality of obligation which normally causes no trouble, but which on some occasions may expose him to conflicting pressures. As an appointee of the President, he is obligated to carry out administration policies, and he serves at the President's pleasure. On the other hand, Congress, which is authorized by Article I, section 8, clause 18, to make all laws necessary and proper for carrying into execution powers vested by the Constitution "in any department or officer" of the government, may impose statutory responsibilities upon the heads of departments and stipulate what actions are to be taken and how they are to be carried out.

Suppose a congressional statute and a presidential directive conflict, which is a department head to obey? This is a real dilemma. If Congress

can assign executive functions to the departments and direct how they are to be administered, it could strip the President of control over the executive branch. On the other hand, if the President has complete discretion to direct the work of his subordinates, then Congress would find it futile to specify the processes of law enforcement, or to hold any officers accountable for actions taken at the direction of the President.

This duality was recognized in an interesting fashion when the great departments of the government were established. Both the State and War Departments, which handle affairs belonging peculiarly to the President's constitutional area of authority, were by their basic statutes directed to report to the President. But the Secretary of the Treasury, whose functions relating to the raising and spending of money were closer to the sphere of Congress, was directed to "make report and give information to either branch of the legislature . . . respecting all matters referred to him by the Senate or House . . . and generally to perform all such services relative to the finances, as he shall be directed to perform" by Congress. Similarly, the Post Office, on its permanent establishment in 1794, and the Interior Department, created in 1849, were not placed under the control of the President by statute.

Thus there was raised the possibility that the President's executive role might be limited to control over foreign affairs and the armed services, while officers concerned with fiscal policy and internal affairs would look to Congress for direction and control. In these latter areas the responsibility of the President to see that the laws were faithfully executed might have involved, as Attorney General Wirt argued in 1825, nothing more than the obligation to remove or to prosecute criminally negligent officials.

That such a fragmentation of the executive power would actually occur was rendered unlikely by Washington's insistence on the personal loyalty of his department heads. But the later attrition of executive power, particularly under Madison, Monroe, and John Quincy Adams, revived this possibility. It was consequently not until Jackson's vigorous assertion of presidential prerogatives that the theory and practice of unified executive control was established.

It was the controversy over the United States Bank that furnished Jackson with the opportunity to dramatize his position. When Secretary of the Treasury Duane refused to obey Jackson's instructions to withdraw government funds from the Bank, Jackson promptly removed him and appointed a new Secretary who took the desired action. The vigor with which Jackson asserted his constitutional responsibilities and the popular success of his maneuver against the Bank completely overshadow the judicial defeat he suffered on a somewhat similar test of constitutional power, in the case of *Kendall* v. *Stokes* (1838). In a controversy over an alleged indebtedness of the United States for transportation of mail, Postmaster General Kendall, at the behest of the President, refused to make payment. Congress then

passed a special act ordering payment, but Kendall still refused. A mandamus action to force payment was then brought, and the Supreme Court affirmed Kendall's obligation to make the payment, regardless of presidential directives. Every officer in every branch of the government, the Court said, is not "under the exclusive direction of the President." Admittedly the President can direct them in the discharge of "certain political duties." But "it would be an alarming doctrine, that congress cannot impose upon any executive officer any duty they may think proper, which is not repugnant to any rights secured and protected by the constitution; and in such cases, the duty and responsibility grow out of and are subject to the control of the law, and not to the direction of the President." Particularly was this true for actions "of a mere ministerial character," such as were involved here.

The principle of *Kendall* v. *Stokes* is of course still valid. To contend that the President could order a Cabinet member not to obey an act of Congress, unless he challenged its constitutionality, would amount to vesting him with the dispensing power. The Court's decision preserves the right of Congress to entrust statutory duties to various executive officers and agencies, and prevents the President from himself taking over the making of decisions which have been committed by Congress to the discretion of his subordinates. There are in the executive branch scores of "independent" commissions, agencies, or boards, the decisions of which are not even in theory subject to review by the President.

The constitutional limits of the *Kendall* v. *Stokes* principle are that the courts can be relied on to see that congressional directives do not deprive the President of his power to exercise the powers guaranteed him by the Constitution. The political limits are in the ample powers of self-protection available to the President who may, as Jackson did, remove any subordinate who rates a congressional directive higher than one from the President. There can be little doubt that as precedents, the Duane removal outranks *Kendall* v. *Stokes* in constitutional significance.

The *Kendall* decision was cited in 1927 by W. F. Willoughby in support of his argument that Congress had the relationship of a board of directors to the federal administration. To Congress, Willoughby thought, belonged the functions of direction, supervision, and control of the administrative establishment—"reaching decisions regarding the character of work to be undertaken and the means to be employed in performing such work; giving the necessary directions for its performance; and subsequently exercising such supervision and control over the persons to whom the work is entrusted as will ensure that it is being properly and efficiently done." To the executive belonged only the tasks of execution—"carrying out, or putting into execution, the orders so given."

Willoughby went on to warn that Congress must not push its powers of direction, supervision, and control too far, lest it go beyond its competence and set up "a rigidity of organization, procedure, and work that will be

destructive of efficiency in action." [10] Even as thus limited, however, the comparison with a board of directors is inappropriate and confusing. The President does not get his executive authority from Congress. It comes straight from the Constitution through the electoral process. While Congress has an undeniable claim under the necessary and proper clause to enact legislation governing executive operations, it is also undeniably true that the single-headed Presidency is in an incomparably better position to direct, supervise, and control the administrative branch than is the multitudinous Congress. Experience has been so clear on this point as to convince even Congress, which has gone far toward yielding to the executive two important functions which clearly belong to the legislature—control of finances and departmental organization.

The Budget and Accounting Act of 1921 established the principle and practice of the executive budget, under which the President is responsible for formulating and presenting to Congress a complete and detailed expenditure plan for the following fiscal year. To be sure, Congress retains authority to modify these recommendations in any way it sees fit, and the President, lacking any power of item veto, must approve the appropriation acts as adopted by Congress, though he has occasionally asserted the power to "impound" and refused to spend appropriated funds.

As for organization of the federal establishment, Congress has by a series of reorganization acts (in 1933, 1939, 1945, 1949, and 1953) authorized the President to prepare reorganization plans for submission to Congress. These plans go into effect automatically unless vetoed by one or both houses of Congress within a specified time period, the provisions for veto varying somewhat in the different statutes. Numerous reorganization plans have been put into effect in this fashion, perhaps the most important being those establishing the Executive Office of the President under the 1939 act, and creating the Department of Health, Education, and Welfare under the act of 1953.

Although Congress has thus recognized the superior resources of the executive in arriving at budgeting and organizational decisions of a broad legislative character, it has conversely asserted on occasion powers of control over decisions which seem clearly administrative in character. Particularly significant have been statutes requiring the approval of congressional committees for specific administrative actions.[11] Attorneys General since at least the time of President Wilson have advised the executive that such legislation is unconstitutional.

For example, the Defense Department Appropriation Act, 1956, required that decisions of the Armed Forces to dispose of or to transfer to private

[10] W. F. Willoughby, *Principles of Public Administration* (Baltimore: The Johns Hopkins Press, 1927), pp. 9, 33.

[11] See Joseph P. Harris, *Congressional Control of Administration* (Washington, D.C.: The Brookings Institution, 1964); Robert W. Ginnane, "The Control of Federal Administration by Congressional Resolutions and Committees," 66 *Harvard Law Review* 569–611 (1953).

industry nonmilitary functions performed by civilian personnel, such as running laundries, had to be reported to the appropriations committees of the House and Senate, which could disapprove the decisions and forbid such action. President Eisenhower, forced to approve the act because the funds were essential, nevertheless notified Congress that the executive branch would regard this provision as invalid.

In 1965 President Johnson vetoed the military construction bill because it contained a provision preventing the Defense Department from closing defense installations until 120 days after filing a report with the House and Senate armed services committees, and such reports would be accepted only between January 1 and April 30 of each year. The President's veto message contended that it would be a violation of the separation of powers for him to be prevented for eight months of each year from closing military installations. Congress upheld the veto and eliminated the offending provision from the bill in favor of a simple thirty-days'-notice requirement, which the President accepted.

The executive has also taken the position that Congress has no constitutional power to compel it to spend money for projects authorized by Congress. Secretary of Defense McNamara between 1962 and 1966 aroused congressional wrath, first by reluctance to continue the production of manned bombers, and later by declining to build nuclear-powered frigates. In 1962 the House Armed Services Committee proposed legislation "directing" the Secretary to proceed with bomber construction, but a constitutional clash was averted by compromise language.

### LEGISLATIVE PROCEDURE

The constitutional provisions governing legislative procedure require little explication. Article I, section 4, provides that "the Congress shall assemble at least once in every year, and such meeting shall be on the first Monday in December, unless they shall by law appoint a different day." Since by law each Congress terminated on March 4 of the odd years, the "lame duck" session beginning in December of the even years was automatically limited to about three months. This circumstance encouraged legislative filibustering, that is, the deliberate consumption of time in debate in order to prevent the adoption of legislation. Another objection to this time schedule was that congressmen elected in November of the even years did not normally begin service until the next December, thirteen months later. In the meantime, congressmen who had been defeated in November returned to Washington in December and sat in Congress until March 4. The term "lame duck" was applied to these congressmen who, repudiated at the polls, continued to represent their constituents through an entire congressional session. Lame duck Congresses were finally terminated when the Twentieth Amendment, sponsored by Senator Norris, was adopted in 1933. Under its

provisions the terms of senators and representatives end at noon on January 3, and the two regular sessions of each Congress begin on that date.

The President is authorized by Article II, section 3, to call "both houses, or either of them," into special session. He may indicate in his call the reasons for bringing them into special session, but Congress is in no way limited thereby as to the subjects it can take up. The same section authorizes the President to adjourn Congress in case of disagreement between the two houses as to time of adjournment, but Congress has been careful never to offer an occasion for such use of presidential power.

The presiding officer of the House is its Speaker. Although the election of this officer is provided for by Article I, section 2, no constitutional qualifications are laid down. The House presumably could even choose a non-member for Speaker, but this has never been considered. The practice is for the majority party to select its candidate in caucus, and then to support him unanimously when the vote is taken. Unlike the Speaker in the English House of Commons, who must preserve strict impartiality, the American Speaker continues to be a partisan and is in fact the most powerful member of his party in the House. He has a vote and may on rare occasions take the floor to participate in debate.

The Senate has for its presiding officer the Vice President. When serving in this capacity his title is President of the Senate. He has no vote except in case of a tie ( Art. I, sec. 3). Giving the Vice President this function in the Senate is a clear defiance of the principle of separation of powers, but the framers apparently concluded that this was the only way to give the Vice President a useful occupation. The Constitution authorizes the Senate to choose a President pro tempore, to preside in the absence of the Vice President, "or when he shall exercise the office of President of the United States." As in the House, the majority party caucuses to agree on the President pro tempore, who is typically chosen on grounds of seniority.

Article I, section 5, provides that "a majority of each [house] shall constitute a quorum to do business." Both houses have adopted the practice of counting, for quorum purposes, only those members chosen, sworn, and living, whose membership has not been terminated by resignation or expulsion. Thus when there are vacancies in the membership of either house, the majority required for a quorum is proportionately reduced.

Each house "may determine the rules of its proceedings" ( Art. I, sec. 5). An elaborate code of rules, procedures, and precedents has been developed by each house. The House readopts its rules, usually with few or no changes, at the beginning of each session, but the Senate regards itself as a "continuing body," a view which the Supreme Court has ratified,[12] and consequently its rules remain in force from Congress to Congress unless they are specifically amended. Actually the amendment of the Senate rules is an extremely

---

[12] *McGrain* v. *Daugherty* (1927).

difficult operation, if there is any substantial opposition to the change, for the existing rules guarantee unlimited debate and so make it possible to kill proposed motions to change the rules by filibuster. The result is that senators who desire a change in rules of necessity have had to attack the concept of the Senate as a continuing body.

In March, 1917, a filibuster led by Senators LaFollette and Norris, which tied the Senate up until the end of its session on March 4, prevented adoption of a bill, favored by seventy-five senators, to arm merchant ships against submarine attacks. President Wilson issued a bitter denunciation of this "little group of willful men" who, "representing no opinion but their own, have rendered the great government of the United States helpless and contemptible." The public outcry was so great that as the next session opened Senator Walsh of Montana presented a resolution denying that the Senate's rules carried over from one Congress to the next. To head off this resolution the Senate approved a change in Rule 22 providing that debate could be limited by a two-thirds vote of the Senate. Having accomplished his purpose of obtaining a cloture rule, Walsh then dropped the resolution.

The cloture rule, however, was interpreted as not applying to motions proposing a change in the rules, and in 1949 the Senate wrote this provision into Rule 22. In 1953 and again in 1957 a group of Senate liberals, who were particularly concerned about the impossibility of getting any civil rights legislation past a Senate filibuster, sought at the opening of Congress to establish that the rules do not carry over automatically. The 1957 effort drew an advisory ruling from Vice President Nixon to the effect that, while the Senate was a continuing body, its rules were subject to adoption by majority vote at the beginning of each Congress. In spite of this ruling, the motion to take up new rules was defeated.

In practice it has proved very difficult to impose cloture. The procedure adopted in 1917 was that a cloture motion, proposed by sixteen Senators, must be voted on within two days and adopted by a two-thirds vote. Originally, this was two-thirds of the Senators present and voting, but in 1949 the requirement was raised to two-thirds of the entire Senate membership. From 1917 to 1959, out of twenty-two cloture votes only four succeeded.

In 1959, Rule 22 was revised to return to the earlier requirement of two-thirds of Senators present and voting. Changes in rules were also made subject to cloture. If cloture is voted, thereafter debate is limited to one hour for each Senator, and no new amendments can be offered to a bill except by unanimous consent. Motions clearly designed to delay action are out of order.

Cloture under the 1959 rule was not invoked successfully until 1962, when by a vote of sixty-three to twenty-seven the filibuster which ten liberal Senators were waging against a bill to establish a private corporation to run the communications-satellite program was broken. In June, 1964, the Senate for the first time in its history shut off a Southern filibuster by a vote of

seventy-one to twenty-nine and thus made it possible for the Civil Rights Act of 1964 to be passed. Cloture was imposed again in passing the Voting Rights Act of 1965.

Efforts to ease the cloture rule, imposed successfully only seven times in almost half a century, have continued. At the beginning of the 1967 session a resolution authorizing cloture by a three-fifths majority of those present and voting was defeated when a cloture motion to end debate on the resolution secured only a fifty-three to forty-six vote, whereas sixty-six (two-thirds of those present and voting) would have been required for adoption.

A House or Senate rule may become the subject of judicial construction if it is applied in such a way as to affect private rights. In *United States* v. *Smith* (1932) the Court ruled that the Senate was not justified by its rules in seeking to reconsider its confirmation of a presidential appointee to the Federal Power Commission. In *Christoffel* v. *United States* (1949) the Court interpreted the House rule on committee quorums as requiring that a quorum must be established as present at the exact time when testimony was given, if that testimony was to be made the basis for a subsequent perjury prosecution. Four justices, dissenting, argued that a quorum once established should be presumed to continue unless and until a point of no quorum was raised.

Each house is required by Article I, section 5, to "keep a journal of its proceedings, and from time to time publish the same, excepting such parts as may in their judgment require secrecy." In a judicial proceeding, the journal of either house will be accepted as unchallengeable proof of the facts as to existence of a quorum or what the vote was on any particular question.[13] However, a bill which has been duly passed and authenticated by both houses and signed by the President may not be challenged by resort to the journals. In *Field* v. *Clark* (1892) an effort to show from the journals that one section of a bill which had been passed by both houses had been omitted from the act in its authenticated and approved version, was frustrated by this rule.

In addition to its journals Congress publishes the *Congressional Record*, which purports to be a verbatim record of the proceedings in each house. In fact, through revisions and extensions of remarks it includes much additional material.

Finally, the Constitution provides that a yea and nay vote may be demanded on any question at the desire of one-fifth of those present (Art. I, sec. 5). A yea and nay vote is also required on the question of passing a bill over the President's veto (Art. I, sec. 7).

---

[13] *United States* v. *Ballin* (1892).

## SELECTED REFERENCES

BENDINER, ROBERT, *Obstacle Course on Capitol Hill*. New York: McGraw-Hill Book Company, 1964.

BOLLING, RICHARD, *House out of Order*. New York: E. P. Dutton & Co., Inc., 1965.

BURDETTE, FRANKLIN L., *Filibustering in the Senate*. Princeton, N.J.: Princeton University Press, 1940.

CLARK, JOSEPH S., *The Senate Establishment*. New York: Hill and Wang, Inc., 1963.

DOUGLAS, PAUL H., *The Filibuster*. Columbus, Ohio: The Walter J. Shepard Foundation, Ohio State University, 1957.

FENNO, RICHARD, *The Power of the Purse*. Boston: Little, Brown and Company, 1966.

GALLOWAY, GEORGE B., *The Legislative Process in Congress*. New York: Thomas Y. Crowell Company, 1953.

GRIFFITH, ERNEST, *Congress: Its Contemporary Role*. New York: New York University Press, 1961 (third edition).

HARRIS, JOSEPH P., *Congressional Control of Administration*. Washington, D.C.: The Brookings Institution, 1964.

HYNEMAN, CHARLES S., *Bureaucracy in a Democracy*, part 2. New York: Harper & Row, Publishers, Incorporated, 1950.

JAFFE, LOUIS L., "An Essay on Delegation of Legislative Power," 47 *Columbia Law Review* 359–376, 561–593 (April, May, 1947).

MACMAHON, ARTHUR W., "Congressional Oversight of Administration: The Power of the Purse," 58 *Political Science Quarterly* 161–190, 380–414 (June, September, 1943).

MAC NEIL, NEIL, *Forge of Democracy: The House of Representatives*. New York: David McKay Company, Inc., 1963.

MATTHEWS, DONALD R., *U.S. Senators and Their World*. Chapel Hill, N.C.: The University of North Carolina Press, 1960.

MILLETT, JOHN D., and LINDSAY ROGERS, "The Legislative Veto and the Reorganization Act of 1939," 1 *Public Administration Review* 176–189 (Winter, 1941).

TRUMAN, DAVID B. (ed.), *The Congress and America's Future*. Englewood Cliffs, N.J.: Prentice-Hall, Inc., 1965.

WAHLKE, JOHN C., and HEINZ EULAU (eds.), *Legislative Behavior: A Reader in Theory and Research*. New York: The Free Press of Glencoe, 1959.

WHITE, WILLIAM S., *Home Place: The Story of the United States House of Representatives*. Boston: Houghton Mifflin Company, 1965.

WILSON, WOODROW, *Congressional Government*. Boston: Houghton Mifflin Company, 1885.

# 12

## The investigatory power

One of the most important functions which Congress performs is nowhere authorized in the Constitution. The power to investigate is an implied power, supplementary to specifically assigned legislative responsibilities. It is scarcely too much to say that none of the constitutionally recognized functions of Congress could be performed satisfactorily without the authority to secure the facts on which informed legislative decisions can be made. Woodrow Wilson concluded in 1885 that "the informing function of Congress should be preferred even to its legislative function." [1] Yet it is also true that the exercise of investigatory powers has been marked on occasions by such abuses as to bring the entire legislative branch into disrepute. Walter Lippmann once spoke of "that legalized atrocity, the Congressional investigation, in which congressmen, starved of their legitimate food for thought, go on a wild and feverish manhunt, and do not stop at cannibalism." [2]

There are many varieties of congressional investigations, conducted for varying purposes by differing kinds of committees. In addition to the regular standing committees of the two houses, special *ad hoc* investigating committees may be set up by each house or by the two houses jointly for

[1] *Congressional Government* (Boston: Houghton Mifflin Company, 1885), p. 303.
[2] *Public Opinion* (New York: Harcourt, Brace & World, Inc., 1922), p. 289.

conducting specific inquiries. Since the adoption of the Legislative Reorganization Act of 1946, the great bulk of all investigations have been carried on by regular standing committees.

### THE CONSTITUTIONAL BASIS

The first congressional investigation took place in 1792, when the House appointed a committee to inquire into the disaster that had befallen the St. Clair expedition against the Indians. No significant issues pertaining to the constitutionality of the investigatory power, however, reached the Supreme Court until the case of *Kilbourn* v. *Thompson* in 1881. This proceeding grew out of an investigation by the House into the bankrupt firm of Jay Cooke and Company and its interest in a District of Columbia real estate pool. The United States as one of the creditors of the firm was dissatisfied with the settlement in the bankruptcy proceedings, and the House adopted a resolution directing a committee to undertake an investigation, with power to send for persons and papers.

The Court's decision pointed out that the resolution contained no suggestion of contemplated legislation, and that the matter in fact was one on which Congress could not validly legislate; moreover, the settlement was still pending in bankruptcy court, where the United States was free to press its claims. Consequently the Court held that the House had "not only exceeded the limit of its own authority, but assumed a power which could only be properly exercised by another branch of the government." Three limitations on the congressional power to investigate were derivable from the *Kilbourn* decision: (1) the right of inquiry was confined by the principle of the separation of powers; (2) the inquiry must deal with a subject on which Congress could validly legislate; and (3) the resolution setting up the investigation must suggest an interest in legislating on that subject.

Following *Kilbourn* v. *Thompson* the judicial attitude toward congressional investigatory power gradually became more favorable. The case of *In re Chapman* (1897) arose out of a Senate investigation into published charges that senators were yielding to corrupt influences in considering a tariff bill, and Chapman got involved by refusing to answer questions pertinent to the inquiry. The Court, taking note of the constitutional authority of both houses to punish or expel members, held that the inquiry related to the integrity and fidelity of senators in the discharge of their duties, and so was "within the range of the constitutional powers of the Senate." As for the fact that the Senate resolution setting up the inquiry made no reference to any contemplated censure or expulsion, the Court declared that it was not essential for the Senate to declare in advance what it meditated doing, and that the Court would be unjustified in assuming that the Senate was making the investigation without a legitimate object. Thus one of the rules of the *Kilbourn* case was quickly abandoned.

These two nineteenth-century decisions were the principal precedents for the Court when in 1927 it came to decide *McGrain* v. *Daugherty*. This important case arose out of the Senate inquiry into Harry M. Daugherty's conduct of the Department of Justice under President Harding. The Senate resolution specifically directed a select committee to look into Daugherty's failure to prosecute the key figures of the Teapot Dome scandal as well as violators of the antitrust acts and other federal statutes. In the course of its work the committee had occasion to subpoena the brother of the Attorney General, Mally S. Daugherty. When he failed to appear, the Senate directed its sergeant-at-arms to bring him before the bar of the Senate. But Daugherty secured a writ of habeas corpus from a federal district court, and after a hearing the court discharged him on the ground that the Senate was exceeding its proper legislative powers in making this investigation.

The Supreme Court reversed the lower court in an opinion written by Justice Van Devanter. He put forth two general propositions to guide the Court's ruling:

> One, that the two houses of Congress, in their separate relations, possess not only such powers as are expressly granted to them by the Constitution, but such auxiliary powers as are necessary and appropriate to make the express powers effective; and, the other, that neither house is invested with "general" power to inquire into private affairs and compel disclosures, but only with such limited power of inquiry as is shown to exist when the rule of constitutional interpretation just stated is rightly applied. . . . It is a necessary deduction from the decisions in *Kilbourn* v. *Thompson* and *In re Chapman* that a witness rightfully may refuse to answer where the bounds of the power are exceeded or the questions are not pertinent to the matter under inquiry.

Here is a clear statement of two grounds available to witnesses for testing congressional exercise of investigatory power. Did either of them justify Mally Daugherty's refusal to testify? The lower court thought that he had a defense on the claim that the Senate was not seeking information for a legislative purpose, but was conducting a trial of the former Attorney General. The Supreme Court did not see it that way. The subject under investigation was "the administration of the Department of Justice—whether its functions were being properly discharged or were being neglected or misdirected. . . . Plainly the subject was one on which legislation could be had and would be materially aided by the information which the investigation was calculated to elicit." As for the actual intentions of Congress, Van Devanter stated a rule of presumed validity: "The only legitimate object the Senate could have in ordering the investigation was to aid it in legislating; and we think the subject-matter was such that the presumption should be indulged that this was the real object."

## THE LEGISLATIVE CONTEMPT POWER

The instrument through which Congress brings pressure on witnesses before its committees is the power to punish refusal to testify as contempt of Congress. In 1798 Congress adopted a statute empowering committees to take testimony on oath, with the usual "pains, penalties and disabilities" of perjury for false testimony. There were no provisions covering persons who refused to appear as witnesses, or who refused to talk once they had appeared. However, it was assumed that Congress was equipped for these situations by possession of its inherent power to punish for contempt. The existence of this power was judicially confirmed in 1821 when, in the case of *Anderson* v. *Dunn*, the Court upheld the right of the House to attach and punish a person other than a member for contempt of its authority—in fact, an attempt to bribe one of its members. The Court considered that the contempt power was essential to the effective exertion of the expressly granted powers of Congress, and therefore was implied.

Thus it is clear that either house can issue its own process, enforceable by its sergeant-at-arms, to cause the arrest and imprisonment of any person adjudged by the house to be in contempt of its authority. There need be no participation by the courts in this procedure. However, legislative imprisonment, according to *Anderson* v. *Dunn*, may not be extended beyond the session of the body in which the contempt occurred. Experience with legislative judgments of contempt showed that these proceedings tended to be lengthy and irregular, and the absence of the procedural protections of the law courts was generally disapproved.

Consequently Congress passed an act in 1857 providing that any person refusing to appear before a committee or to answer questions pertinent to an inquiry should, in addition to existing pains and penalties, be deemed guilty of a misdemeanor and be subject to indictment and punishment. In operation this statute requires the following steps. First, the committee before which the alleged contempt occurred must recommend a contempt citation to the parent body, which must vote the citation. The congressional action is then transmitted to the federal district attorney, who presents the matter to a federal grand jury. If an indictment is voted, the case is then tried in a federal district court, with appeal to the court of appeals and, if certiorari is granted, to the Supreme Court.

The 1857 act did not preclude the House or Senate from continuing to punish contempts directly, and in fact summary proceedings were common through the nineteenth century. As late as 1934 the Senate convicted a witness of contempt and sentenced him to ten days in jail.[3] Such convictions could be reviewed on habeas corpus, but obviously judicial proceedings under the 1857 act provide much more satisfactory judicial protection of the

---

[3] Carl Beck, *Contempt of Congress* (New Orleans, La.: The Hauser Press, 1959), p. 213.

rights of witnesses. Congress has now completely abandoned any use of its summary procedures.

By turning contempt-of-Congress prosecutions over to the federal courts, Congress has conceded that judges are to fix the constitutional limits of the investigatory power, and that persons charged with contempt are to receive all the protections of judicial trials. Federal judges, however, may feel under some pressure in handling such cases to construe the congressional investigating power very broadly and to defer to the congressional judgment as to what information is needed for the proper performance of legislative tasks.

This attitude appeared to prevail in the cases which reached the courts after World War II, principally involving the House Committee on Un-American Activities and the Subcommittee on Investigations of the Senate Committee on Government Operations, under the chairmanship of Senator Joseph McCarthy. These committees were upheld in a series of lower federal court decisions in the decade after the war, and the Supreme Court refused even to grant certiorari in the more significant of these cases.[4] This was a period when abusive and coercive tactics against witnesses became standard operating procedures of several congressional committees, but the Supreme Court's inaction seemed to indicate that there were no enforceable constitutional limits on investigatory procedures.

### CONSTITUTIONAL DEFENSES FOR WITNESSES

What constitutional grounds are available for witnesses who do not wish to testify before congressional committees? Putting the question another way, what are the constitutional limits on the power of Congress to compel testimony?

First, the witness is protected by the self-incrimination ban in the Fifth Amendment.[5] If he "takes the Fifth," claiming that evidence he is asked to give would tend to incriminate him, he can safely decline to answer further questions and he is protected from possible prosecution for contempt. The role of the Fifth Amendment in forestalling committee investigators first came to general public attention during the televised hearings of the Kefauver crime committee in 1950 and 1951, but the peak of its notoriety was reached during Senator McCarthy's investigations into subversion, when he coined the phrase "Fifth Amendment Communists" to describe all those who invoked its protection.

The Fifth Amendment can be employed only to conceal conduct which might be subject to criminal prosecution if revealed. A witness refusing to testify on grounds of self-incrimination is in a strong position. He is not admitted to have conclusive power to determine that his answer to a question will tend to incriminate him, but on the other hand he cannot be forced

---

[4] *United States* v. *Josephson* (1947); *Barsky* v. *United States* (1948).
[5] For a fuller discussion of the Fifth Amendment, see Chap. 30.

to tell what he is hiding by his silence, for if it were truly incriminating the constitutional protection would have been breached. Thus a committee chairman must necessarily allow great latitude to the witness in permitting him to judge for himself the consequences of answering any particular question.

Witnesses who feel they have something to conceal from a committee face a difficult practical problem in determining the point at which they should claim the privilege of silence. On numerous occasions witnesses have refused on the advice of counsel to answer questions which seemed on the surface completely innocent. One reason for this caution was demonstrated by the Supreme Court's decision in *Rogers* v. *United States* (1951). Jane Rogers, subpoenaed by a federal grand jury, testified that she had been treasurer of the Communist Party in Denver. Having made this admission, she then sought to end her testimony and refused to give the name of the person to whom she had turned over the Party's books. A divided Supreme Court ruled that she had waived the privilege of silence by her initial testimony, and that the further questions she had refused to answer did not involve a "reasonable danger of further crimination."

Although a claim of the Fifth Amendment is a completely effective method of justifying silence before a congressional committee, it almost invariably does great damage to the reputation of the claimant and may also be the basis for punitive actions of various kinds against him. Persons in both public and private employment have lost their jobs as a result of refusing to testify before congressional committees. The widespread unfavorable attitude toward claimants of the Fifth Amendment supplies the background for the Supreme Court's spirited defense of this controversial right in the cases of *Emspak* v. *United States* and *Quinn* v. *United States,* decided on the same day in 1955.

Both Quinn and Emspak had refused to answer questions before the House Committee on Un-American Activities, but their pleas under the Fifth Amendment had been "deliberately phrased in muffled terms." The government charged that they were trying to "obtain the benefit of the privilege without incurring the popular opprobrium which often attaches to its exercise." The Supreme Court majority, however, held that they had given adequate notice of their intention to invoke the privilege. Chief Justice Warren noted in the *Quinn* case that "no ritualistic formula is necessary." If the committee had been in any doubt as to the ground on which refusal to testify was based, it should have asked the witness whether he was in fact relying on the Fifth Amendment. In the *Emspak* opinion the Chief Justice added: "If it is true that in these times a stigma may somehow result from a witness' reliance on the Self-Incrimination Clause, a committee should be all the more ready to recognize a veiled claim of the privilege. Otherwise, the great right which the Clause was intended to secure might be effectively frustrated by private pressures."

As already noted, two other defenses were recognized in *McGrain* v. *Daugherty*—a witness may refuse to answer when the committee is exceeding the bounds of its power,[6] and when the questions are not pertinent to the matter under inquiry. A witness who refuses to answer on these grounds runs a considerable risk, however, for if he is prosecuted for contempt and the court holds he was mistaken in his appraisal of the committee's powers or the pertinency of the questions, then he will go to jail.

Some witnesses before the House Un-American Activities Committee in the 1940s refused to answer questions on the ground that the committee was infringing their rights under the First Amendment. They contended that the committee was attempting by forced exposure of their views and activities to abridge their freedom of speech and association and to punish them for their opinions. This claim met with no success in the courts until 1957, when in *Watkins* v. *United States* the Supreme Court unexpectedly cracked down on the Un-American Activities Committee and for the first time since the *Kilbourn* decision in 1881 endeavored to develop new constitutional doctrine limiting congressional investigatory power.

In the *Watkins* case a labor union official refused to answer questions put by the Un-American Activities Committee as to whether certain persons were members of the Communist Party. He agreed to testify concerning persons whom he believed to be active current Communists, but refused to answer questions about former members who to his best knowledge had long since removed themselves from the movement. He contended that such questions were not authorized by law or relevant to the work of the committee; answers would accomplish no purpose except exposure of past activities. Two lower courts held Watkins guilty of contempt.

By a vote of six to one the Supreme Court reversed the conviction. The basic proposition in the opinion was a reiteration of the well-established doctrine that the power of Congress to investigate, while broad, is not unlimited. As Chief Justice Warren explained, "there is no general authority to expose the private affairs of individuals without justification in terms of the functions of Congress." Moreover, no committee can act as a law-enforcement or trial agency. Under our system of separation of powers those are functions of the executive and judicial departments. The Chief Justice added at this point that "investigations conducted solely for the personal aggrandizement of the investigators or to 'punish' those investigated are indefensible." In short, "no inquiry is an end in itself; it must be related to and in furtherance of a legitimate task of Congress."

Having reasserted this general principle, the Chief Justice nevertheless found it unnecessary to examine the legitimacy of the committee's purposes in questioning Watkins. While he had no doubt "that there is no congres-

[6] In *United States* v. *Rumely* (1953) the Supreme Court held that a House committee had exceeded the authorization it had received from the parent body.

sional power to expose for the sake of exposure," Warren was understandably reluctant to get involved in "testing the motives of committee members." Instead, Watkins was upheld on the more readily demonstrable proposition that the committee's investigatory authorization was unconstitutionally broad.

The Court ruled that in setting up committees or specifying their jurisdiction, the House or Senate must instruct the committee members "on what they are to do with the power delegated to them." The instructions to the committee must "spell out that group's jurisdiction and purpose with sufficient particularity" so that a witness and a reviewing court may have some basis for judging as to whether the questions asked are pertinent to the committee's legislative purpose. In addition to the pertinency test, such instructions are necessary if the House or Senate itself is to have any real responsibility for the committees which are purporting to act for the parent body.

In the *Watkins* case the Court held that the Un-American Activities Committee had failed this test. Its jurisdiction was stated by the House so broadly as to cover any subject it might conceivably wish to examine. Starting from an admittedly justifiable need by Congress to be informed of efforts to overthrow the government by force and violence so that adequate legislative safeguards could be erected, the committee had radiated outward "infinitely to any topic thought to be related in some way to armed insurrection."

There are many objections to running a committee in this free-wheeling fashion, but the Supreme Court was particularly concerned in the *Watkins* case with the resulting threat to the First Amendment rights of witnesses. Chief Justice Warren wrote:

> Clearly, an investigation is subject to the command that the Congress shall make no law abridging freedom of speech or press or assembly. . . . An investigation is part of lawmaking. . . . The First Amendment may be invoked against infringement of the protected freedoms by law or by law-making.

Since the ruling did not rest on First Amendment grounds, Warren's comments about the First Amendment must be regarded as dicta, but he did explain how congressional investigations could infringe the First Amendment:

> Abuses of the investigative process may imperceptibly lead to abridgement of protected freedoms. The mere summoning of a witness and compelling him to testify, against his will, about his beliefs, expressions or associations is a measure of governmental interference. And when those forced revelations concern matters that are unorthodox, unpopular, or even hateful to the general public, the reaction in the life of the witness may be disastrous.

A companion decision to *Watkins* was *Sweezy* v. *New Hampshire* (1957), in which the Court invalidated a state legislative inquiry by a six to two

vote.[7] The New Hampshire Legislature had constituted the attorney general of the state as a one-man legislative committee and directed him to determine whether there were in the state any "subversive persons" as defined in the state subversive activities law. Sweezy was twice subjected to sweeping inquiries into his activities and beliefs by the attorney general. Sweezy answered many questions, specifically denying that he had ever been a member of the Communist Party, but he refused to answer questions which he regarded as not pertinent to the subject under inquiry, as well as any questions about his opinions or beliefs. The contempt charge was based on his refusal to answer questions concerning his activities in the Progressive party, which ran Henry Wallace for President in 1948, and the ideas he expressed in a guest lecture at the University of New Hampshire in 1954.

As in *Watkins*, the Chief Justice used some broad condemnatory language, but ultimately based his decision on the narrower ground of absence of legislative control over the use of the investigatory power. Justice Frankfurter, concurring, dealt with the more basic issue of the Legislature's right to ask such questions, which he found unjustified in the circumstances of this proceeding.

### CONTEMPT AFTER *WATKINS*

The *Watkins* decision brought the Court under violent criticism from some sectors of Congress and many other influential sources of opinion throughout the country. There were various proposals in Congress—to withdraw contempt prosecutions from the appellate jurisdiction of the Supreme Court, to make Congress the final judge of the pertinency of committee questions, to specify the jurisdiction of the Un-American Activities Committee more clearly.[8] However, the case for any such legislation was soon liquidated by the Court's retreat from the *Watkins* holding in *Barenblatt* v. *United States* (1959). The six-judge *Watkins* majority was here reduced to a four-judge minority by the defection of Justices Harlan and Frankfurter. Joining them were Clark, who had been the sole dissenter in *Watkins*, Whittaker, who had not participated in *Watkins*, and Stewart, appointed after the *Watkins* decision.

Justice Harlan, who wrote the *Barenblatt* opinion, did not specifically overrule *Watkins*. In part he accomplished his result by distinguishing *Watkins* from *Barenblatt* on the difference in the facts of the two cases. What were the differences?

> 1.   Watkins was a labor union official questioned on the subject of communism in labor, whereas Barenblatt was a college professor who was questioned in an inquiry into communism in education.

[7] Decisions involving state legislative investigations are included in this chapter, since the principles applied are also relevant to congressional investigations.
[8] See C. Herman Pritchett, *Congress versus the Supreme Court: 1957–1960* (Minneapolis: The University of Minnesota Press, 1961), pp. 45–48.

2.  Watkins had testified to his own relationship with the Communist Party but had refused to answer questions about the past membership of other persons in the Party, whereas the three counts on which the Supreme Court upheld Barenblatt's conviction were refusals to answer questions pertaining to his own present or past membership in the Party.

3.  In *Watkins*, "the petitioner had made specific objection to the Sub-committee's questions on the ground of pertinency; the question under inquiry had not been disclosed in any illuminating manner; and the questions asked the petitioner were not only amorphous on their face, but in some instances clearly foreign to the alleged subject matter of the investigation"; whereas Barenblatt "raised no objections on the ground of pertinency at the time any of the questions were put to him," and in any case pertinency was made to appear "with undisputable clarity."

There were also, of course, important similarities in the two cases, to which Harlan did not call attention. Barenblatt was before the same committee, which was operating under the same vague mandate and using the same tactics of exposure and publicity seeking which the Court had castigated in *Watkins*.

Having established certain factual differences between the two cases, Harlan undertook as the second stage in his reasoning to minimize or render inapplicable the constitutional holding of *Watkins*. Warren had apparently held the mandate of the committee to be unconstitutionally vague, so that it was impossible for a witness before the committee to determine whether questions asked were pertinent to the committee's legitimate legislative purpose. But according to Harlan's version, the Court had reversed Watkins' conviction "solely" on the ground that he had not been adequately apprised of the subject matter of the investigation, and the vagueness of the mandate was only one of the factors in this failure. If the committee informed the witness in some other fashion of the purposes of its inquiry, then the vagueness of the mandate would not be a constitutional defect.

Moreover, the *Barenblatt* decision released the House from any necessity of clarifying the jurisdiction of the committee. The rule under which the committee had been set up, Harlan said, "comes to us with a 'persuasive gloss of legislative history,' . . . which shows beyond doubt that in pursuance of its legislative concerns in the domain of 'national security' the House has clothed the Un-American Activities Committee with pervasive authority to investigate Communist activities in this country."

Since the vagueness and pertinency issues, which had been determinative in *Watkins*, were thus disposed of, the Court proceeded to the ultimate question, which it had managed to talk about but not to decide in *Watkins* —namely, the applicability of the First Amendment. It had taken over twenty years since the Un-American Activities Committee first began to ask individuals about their connection with the Communist Party for the Court

to come to grips with this problem. Now its answer was a strong affirmation of the superiority of congressional power over the protection of the First Amendment.

Congressional power to legislate in the field of Communist activity, Harlan said, was undoubted. "In the last analysis this power rests on the right of self-preservation, 'the ultimate value of any society.'" Congress had proceeded on the assumption that the Communist Party aims at overthrow of the government of the United States by force and violence. The Court itself, Harlan went on, had in numerous decisions refused to consider the Communist Party "as an ordinary political party, and has upheld federal legislation aimed at the Communist problem which in a different context would certainly have raised constitutional issues of the gravest character." In balancing "the competing private and public interests at stake," the public needs here were regarded by Harlan as real and urgent.

Finally, Harlan reached the "exposure" issue. One of Warren's many dicta in *Watkins* was that "there is no congressional power to expose for the sake of exposure," which he had promptly offset by disclaiming any judicial intent to inquire into the "motives" of committee members. Consequently the way had been prepared for Harlan to say: "So long as Congress acts in pursuance of its constitutional power, the judiciary lacks authority to intervene on the basis of the motives which spurred the exercise of that power."

Four members of the Court would not concede that "abuses" by legislative investigating committees touching the First Amendment rights of witnesses were beyond judicial authority to control. Justice Black wrote the principal dissent, in which Chief Justice Warren and Justice Douglas concurred, while Justice Brennan wrote a short dissent confined to the exposure issue.

Black had three main reasons for judging the committee action invalid. First, he stood on the *Watkins* holding about vagueness of the mandate, which Harlan had abandoned. Second, he declared that the committee action infringed the First Amendment. He attacked Harlan's "balancing" principle, saying that in effect it rewrote the First Amendment to read:

> Congress shall pass no law abridging freedom of speech, press, assembly and petition, unless Congress and the Supreme Court reach the joint conclusion that on balance the interest of the Government in stifling these freedoms is greater than the interest of the people in having them exercised.

Even if balancing was a proper method of determining the meaning of the First Amendment, Black thought the majority had done it badly here. Harlan had balanced the right of the government to preserve itself against Barenblatt's right not to talk. What should have been thrown into the scale was the interest of society, of the people as a whole "in being able to join organizations, advocate causes and make political 'mistakes' without later being subjected to governmental penalties for having dared to think for themselves." On the other side of the scale, the congressional interest was

vastly overstated as "self-preservation," with no mention that the legislative power to make laws affecting speech and association is limited, and particularly where education is concerned.

Finally, Black contended that "the chief aim, purpose and practice" of the House committee was the illegal one of trying witnesses and punishing them "by humiliation and public shame." Black cited in proof of this intent the long history of committee practice, and concluded:

> The Court today fails to see what is here for all to see—that exposure and punishment is the aim of this Committee and the reason for its existence. To deny this aim is to ignore the Committee's own claims and the reports it has issued ever since it was established. I cannot believe that the nature of our judicial office requires us to be so blind, and must conclude that the Un-American Activities Committee's "identification" and "exposure" of Communists and suspected Communists, like the activities of the Committee in *Kilbourn* v. *Thompson*, amount to an encroachment on the judiciary which bodes ill for the liberties of the people of this land.

As the *Watkins* decision was distinguished almost to death by *Barenblatt*, so the *Sweezy* case received the same treatment in *Uphaus* v. *Wyman* (1959), decided the same day as *Barenblatt*, with the same five to four division on the Court. Uphaus, a minister and a pacifist, was executive director of an organization called World Fellowship, Inc., which maintained a summer camp in New Hampshire. The attorney general of the state, acting as a one-man legislative investigating committee under the same statutory authorization to determine whether there were "subversive persons" in the state that was involved in the *Sweezy* case, demanded the names of all persons who had attended the camp over a two-year period. Uphaus refused to produce the guest list, and was convicted of civil contempt.

Justice Clark upheld the contempt conviction, noting that evidence offered in court connected Uphaus with many "Communist front" activities and indicated that at least nineteen speakers invited to talk at World Fellowship had either been members of the Communist Party or had connections with organizations on the United States Attorney General's list of subversive organizations. The state legislature had made a legislative finding that "subversive persons" posed a serious threat to the security of the state. Thus the investigation was undertaken to protect a basic governmental interest which outweighed rights in the "associational privacy" of a public camp furnishing board and lodging. The "exposure" to which persons who had been guests at the camp were subjected was simply "an inescapable incident of an investigation into the presence of subversive persons within a State."

Justice Brennan, for the minority, could find no valid legislative purpose in this inquiry. Rather, it was "an investigation in which the processes of law-making and law-evaluating were submerged entirely in exposure of individual behavior—in adjudication, of a sort, however much disclaimed,

through the exposure process." The emphasis of the report to the legislature prepared by the state attorney general was entirely on "individual guilt, individual near-guilt, and individual questionable behavior." The record showed that "the investigatory objective was the impermissible one of exposure for exposure's sake," which had been condemned in *Watkins*. While most legislative investigations unavoidably involve exposure of some sort, here "exposure was the very core, and deliberately and purposefully so, of the legislative investigation." This was, to quote *Kilbourn* v. *Thompson*, a classic example of "a fruitless investigation into the personal affairs of individuals."

The Supreme Court went even beyond *Barenblatt* in two 1961 decisions, *Wilkinson* v. *United States* and *Braden* v. *United States*. Wilkinson had gone to Atlanta to organize opposition sentiment against the Un-American Activities Committee which was holding hearings there, and was subpoenaed to appear before the committee within one hour after he arrived in the city. Braden had circulated a petition, which had been signed by 200 Negroes, asking the House not to permit the committee to conduct hearings in the South. He was required to go from Rhode Island to Atlanta for questioning about the petition.

A five-judge majority supported the inquiry in both cases, Justice Stewart holding that *Barenblatt* had settled the major issues of congressional authorization and First Amendment relevance. The only new factor was the claim that the sole reason for interrogating Wilkinson was to expose him to public censure because of his activities against the committee. Stewart thought that the Court could not "speculate as to the motivations" of the committee. In any case, Wilkinson was not summoned "as the result of an indiscriminate dragnet procedure." He had been identified at a prior hearing as a Communist Party member and the committee had reason to believe at the time he was summoned that he was an active Communist engaged primarily in propaganda activities, which was the subject of the Atlanta investigation.

Braden's claim differed slightly from Wilkinson's in that he had been asked whether he was a member of the Communist Party at the time he affixed his signature to the letter to Congress. Since the right to petition the government for the redress of grievances is guaranteed by the First Amendment, Braden contended that the committee had no proper legislative purpose but was bent on prosecuting him for exercising a constitutional right. But the Court majority could not see that these circumstances distinguished the two cases.

The dissenters in both cases were Black, Douglas, Warren, and Brennan. Justices Black and Douglas contended that the *Barenblatt* decision was not a precedent for these cases, since here the committee was using the contempt power to punish those who dared to criticize it, a purpose not authorized by the resolution establishing the committee. Wilkinson's identification as a Communist was meaningless, Black continued. It rested only on the

testimony of a "paid informant" of the committee, and he observed: "Every member of this Court has, on one occasion or another, been so designated."

### CONTEMPT AFTER *BRADEN*

It thus appeared that the Court had recognized a practically unlimited power of congressional inquiry, and that the intimations of stricter judicial control in *Watkins* and *Sweezy* had been a temporary aberration. But after *Braden* and *Wilkinson* the Court again executed a change of direction, and from 1961 to 1966 it reversed almost every contempt conviction which came before it.[9] These reversals were accomplished for the most part without challenging the scope of investigatory power or querying the motives of the investigators. They were achieved primarily by strict judicial enforcement of the rules on pertinency, authorization, and procedure, plus strict observance of the constitutional standards governing criminal prosecutions. A few illustrations will suffice to show the new trend.

*Deutch* v. *United States* (1961), decided by a five to four vote, involved a graduate student at Cornell who testified before the Un-American Activities Committee about his Communist Party membership but, like Watkins, refused to answer questions involving other persons. Justice Stewart for the majority held that the government had failed to carry its burden of proving the pertinence of the questions. The subcommittee which subpoenaed Deutch was charged with investigating Communist infiltration in the Albany, New York, area, particularly in the field of labor. The questions Deutch was asked had nothing to do with the Albany area or Communist infiltration into labor unions. Indeed, Justice Stewart took "judicial notice of the fact that Ithaca is more than one hundred and sixty-five miles from Albany."

*Yellin* v. *United States* (1963) concerned a steel company employee in Gary, Indiana, who was subpoenaed to testify by the Un-American Activities Committee concerning "colonization" by the Communist Party in basic industry. Four days before the hearing Yellin's attorney sent a wire to the committee's general counsel in Washington requesting that Yellin be heard in executive session rather than in a public hearing. Since the counsel had already left for Gary, the staff director replied and denied the request, though he had no authority from the committee to take such action. In fact, the committee's rules provided that if a majority of the members believed interrogation of a witness in a public hearing might endanger national security or unjustly injure his reputation, the committee must first hear the

[9] The only exception was *Hutcheson* v. *United States* (1962), where the Court upheld the contempt conviction of a labor union official who had refused to answer questions of a Senate committee looking into criminal and improper practices in the labor field, concerning actions for which he was then being prosecuted in state court.

witness in executive session. The Court majority held that this rule and the committee's past practice under it did give witnesses some rights and privileges, and that Yellin was entitled to have the committee follow its rules and give him consideration according to the standards laid down in the rules.

*Russell* v. *United States* (1962) covered six persons, four of whom had refused to testify at a Senate inquiry aimed primarily at employees of *The New York Times*. Justice Stewart for the Court majority held the indictments insufficient because they did not identify the subject under inquiry at the time of the defendants' refusal to answer. The Senate committee counsel in dealing with witnesses had denied that the purpose was "to investigate Communist infiltration of the press," but positive indication of the purpose was limited to such broad statements as that "we are simply investigating communism wherever we find it." The district judge held that the questions were pertinent to the subject under inquiry without indicating what he thought the subject was. Before the Supreme Court the government contended the subject was "Communist activity in news media."

In view of this confused record Justice Stewart held that the indictment had failed to perform its primary office—to inform the defendant of the nature of the accusation against him. The defendants could not be guilty of a criminal offense unless the questions they refused to answer were in fact pertinent to a specific topic under committee inquiry at the time. Justices Clark and Harlan dissented, Clark warning that "this continued frustration of the Congress . . . indicates . . . that the time may have come" for Congress to revert to summary contempt proceedings.[10]

On only two occasions since *Braden* and *Wilkinson* has the Court relied on a broad constitutional ground to limit investigatory powers. In *Gibson* v. *Florida Legislative Investigation Committee* (1963) the president of the Miami branch of the National Association for the Advancement of Colored People had been ordered to appear before a committee of the state Legislature which had been set up to investigate organizations active in the field of race relations, with particular attention to infiltration of Communists into such organizations. He was directed to bring with him membership records of the organization.

Gibson appeared before the committee without the records, and said he would not bring them for the purpose of answering questions concerning membership in the NAACP, because that would interfere with the free exercise of Fourteenth Amendment associational rights of members and prospective members of the organization. He did, however, volunteer to answer questions about membership on the basis of his personal knowledge.

---

[10] Other cases in which the Court reversed contempt convictions on grounds of lack of pertinency of the questions, or failure to follow proper procedures, are *Christoffel* v. *United States* (1949), *Sacher* v. *United States* (1958), *Flaxer* v. *United States* (1958), *Scull* v. *Virginia* (1959), *Slagle* v. *Ohio* (1961), and *Gojack* v. *United States* (1966).

The legitimacy of NAACP concern about the effect publicity concerning its membership lists might have on its ability to maintain the organization had been established by the decisions in *NAACP* v. *Alabama* (1958) and *Bates* v. *City of Little Rock* (1960).[11] To justify a state demand which intrudes into this area of constitutionally protected rights, the Court majority held that the state must "convincingly show a substantial relation between the information sought and a subject of overriding and compelling state interest." Justice Goldberg for the Court majority found nothing in the record to demonstrate the existence of any substantial relationship between the NAACP and subversive activities. An admittedly lawful group, the NAACP did not forfeit its rights to privacy of association simply because the general subject matter of the inquiry was Communist subversion or infiltration. In *Barenblatt* the Court had defended the right of legislative inquirers to proceed "step by step" in making their case, but Goldberg here qualified that statement by saying: "Step by step or in totality, an adequate foundation for inquiry must be laid before proceeding in such a manner as will substantially intrude upon and severely curtail or inhibit constitutionally protected activities or seriously interfere with similarly protected associational rights."

In *DeGregory* v. *Attorney General of New Hampshire* (1966) an inquiry of the same type as those involved in *Sweezy* and *Uphaus* was, like *Gibson*, held to have been justified by no "compelling state interest." The record was found to be "devoid of any evidence that there is any Communist movement in New Hampshire." Moreover, the inquiry had concerned petitioner's activities prior to 1957, and Justice Douglas thought that "the staleness of both the basis for the investigation and its subject matter makes indefensible such exposure of one's associational and political past."

Whether the courts can enjoin the holding of a congressional inquiry has not yet been determined. Such action would require judges to assert in advance of the hearing that the committee contemplated, or that the hearing amounted to, unconstitutional interference with protected rights. In May, 1965, counsel for Dr. Stamler, who had been subpoenaed to appear at an Un-American Activities Committee hearing in Chicago, sought to enjoin the hearing on a variety of constitutional grounds. A federal district judge dismissed the suit as premature; the court felt obliged to assume that the committee would not abuse the constitutional rights of witnesses.

Dr. Stamler attended the hearing but refused to testify, since doing so would have rendered his case moot. In November, 1966, the court of appeals reversed the district court in *Stamler* v. *Willis*, holding that Dr. Stamler's suit raised substantial First Amendment problems not settled by *Barenblatt*, and directed that a three-judge court be convened to hear the case. In spite of the pendency of this suit, the House voted a contempt citation against Stamler in July, 1967.

[11] For a discussion of these cases see Chap. 27.

A similar injunction action was instituted in August, 1966, against a hearing which the Un-American Activities Committee proposed to hold in Washington on the operations of groups opposing the war in Vietnam. A federal judge in the District of Columbia issued a temporary injunction, relying on the Supreme Court's decision in *Dombrowski* v. *Pfister* (1965) which approved enjoining the enforcement of state anti-Communist laws because of the "chilling effect" which the very existence of these laws had on First Amendment rights. However, this injunction was dissolved the next day by a three-judge panel, and the hearing proceeded amid scenes of wild disorder. Two of the witnesses brought suit before a three-judge court in *Krebs* v. *Ashbrook* (1967) to have the committee adjudged unconstitutional, but failed by a vote of two to one. Both the *Stamler* and *Krebs* cases could bring new Supreme Court consideration of the First Amendment issue in congressional investigations.

## THE DILEMMA OF JUDICIAL CONTROL

In 1949 Justice Jackson wrote: "It would be an unwarranted act of judicial usurpation . . . to assume for the courts the function of supervising congressional committees. I should . . . leave the responsibility for the behavior of its committees squarely on the shoulders of Congress." [12] Unfortunately Congress has been too often remiss in assuming this responsibility, and one reason is precisely judicial involvement in enforcing contempt citations. When Congress itself tried contempts, its tendency was to consider the circumstances of the committee action rather carefully, and often the parent body refused to support the committee's contention that a contempt charge was warranted. [13] But now that the courts make the final decision, committee requests for a contempt citation are approved by the full House or Senate almost automatically.

The failure of Congress to insist on appropriately protective committee procedures also increases judicial responsibility. Committee rules of procedure, though generally much improved in recent years, still leave something to be desired. Unfairness may result from limiting the right of representation by counsel, or permitting witnesses to make defamatory charges about persons who have had no advance warning that they are to be named, or holding one-man subcommittee sessions, or denying requests for closed (or sometimes for open) hearings. Rules which exist may not be enforced;

[12] *Eisler* v. *United States* (1949).
[13] In ninety-four cases initiated by committees of Congress prior to 1945, the parent body reversed the committee in thirty-four. Beck, *op. cit.*, p. 188. But from 1950 to 1965 the House automatically approved every one of the 129 contempt citations requested by the Un-American Activities Committee. Incidentally, only nine of these citations resulted in final convictions. *The New York Times*, February 8, 1966.

the Un-American Activities Committee has a rule against releasing in advance the names of persons subpoenaed for its hearings, but somehow the newspapers usually have the names well before the hearings.

The American Civil Liberties Union proposed in 1965 an eleven-point program for fair investigatory procedures. It included a requirement that committees hold executive sessions to screen defamatory, prejudicial, or adverse information in order to determine its reliability before exposing it publicly. The affected individuals would be given adequate notice and the opportunity to appear at the executive session to present their defense. An individual who invoked his privilege against self-incrimination at the closed hearing would not be recalled to answer the same questions in a public hearing. The ACLU also proposed that each house set up a supervisory committee to screen committee recommendations for contempt citations, hoping that this would result in more careful and more objective recommendations to the parent body.

Perhaps the principal objection to Justice Jackson's position is that Congress, which is entitled directly and summarily to punish contempt, has voluntarily chosen to make it a misdemeanor triable in the courts. If contempt is to be criminally punishable, then the courts must apply the same standards of constitutional protection and interpretation that they enforce in other criminal prosecutions. The Supreme Court could not let federal judges become mere rubber stamps for authenticating congressional contempt citations.

The difficulty comes in determining what constitutional standards the courts should require legislative committees to observe. The broad principle which emerged from *Kilbourn* and *McGrain* was that investigations must be for a "proper legislative purpose." They must be an aid to lawmaking; they must not attempt to take over the powers of law enforcement; they must not be used to inquire into private affairs. But these standards are helpful only in the most flagrant cases of legislative abuse of power, and they assert a measure of control over legislative investigations which the Court has been reluctant to translate from theory into practice. As Martin Shapiro has said: "Having asked too much, the Court receives nothing." [14]

Drawing back from the implications of its rule that committees must have a valid legislative purpose, the Court as early as *Kilbourn* announced that it would *presume* the existence of such a purpose. Boldly asserting that there is no right to expose private affairs for the sake of exposure, the Court quickly added in *Watkins* that it would of course not question the motives of legislators. Unable or unwilling to control the subject matter of congressional investigations, the Court has fallen back on policing their procedures. This explains the emphasis in recent decisions on pertinency, authorization, and notice. Unable to enforce the First Amendment against congressional

[14] *Law and Politics in the Supreme Court* (New York: The Free Press of Glencoe, 1964), p. 68.

committees, the Court is the more zealous in applying the Fifth.[15] It is a pragmatic solution for a difficult dilemma.

## SELECTED REFERENCES

BARTH, ALAN, *Government by Investigation*. New York: The Viking Press, Inc., 1955.

BECK, CARL, *Contempt of Congress*. New Orleans, La.: The Hauser Press, 1959.

BUCKLEY, WILLIAM F., JR. (ed.), *The Committee and Its Critics*. Chicago: Henry Regnery Company, 1962.

CARR, ROBERT K., "Constitutional Liberty and Congressional Investigations," in Alfred H. Kelly (ed.), *Foundations of Freedom in the American Constitution*. New York: Harper & Row, Publishers, Incorporated, 1958.

————, *The House Committee on Un-American Activities, 1945–1950*. Ithaca, N.Y.: Cornell University Press, 1952.

"Congressional Investigations: A Symposium," 18 *University of Chicago Law Review* 421–661 (Spring, 1951).

DIMOCK, MARSHALL E., *Congressional Investigating Committees*. Baltimore: The Johns Hopkins Press, 1929.

DOUGLAS, WILLIAM O., *We the Judges*, chap. 4. Garden City, N.Y.: Doubleday & Company, Inc., 1956.

GOODMAN, WALTER, *The Committee: The Extraordinary Career of the House Committee on Un-American Activities*. New York: Farrar, Straus & Giroux, Inc., 1968.

GRISWOLD, ERWIN N., *The Fifth Amendment Today*. Cambridge, Mass.: Harvard University Press, 1955.

HOOK, SIDNEY, *Common Sense and the Fifth Amendment*. New York: Criterion Books, 1957.

KALVEN, HARRY, JR., "Congressional Testing of Linus Pauling," 16 *Bulletin of the Atomic Scientists* 383–390 (1960), 17 *ibid.* 12–19 (1961).

————, "Mr. Alexander Meiklejohn and the Barenblatt Opinion," 27 *University of Chicago Law Review* 315–328 (1960).

MC GEARY, M. NELSON, *The Development of Congressional Investigative Power*. New York: Columbia University Press, 1940.

MEIKLEJOHN, ALEXANDER, "The Barenblatt Opinion," 27 *University of Chicago Law Review* 329–340 (1960).

OGDEN, AUGUST R., *The Dies Committee*. Washington, D.C.: The Catholic University of America Press, 1943.

SHAPIRO, MARTIN, *Law and Politics in the Supreme Court*, chap. 2. New York: The Free Press of Glencoe, 1964.

TAYLOR, TELFORD, *Grand Inquest: The Story of Congressional Investigations*. New York: Simon and Schuster, Inc., 1955.

[15] For example, self-incrimination in the *Emspak* and *Quinn* cases, and grand jury indictment in the *Russell* case. It is noteworthy that of all the decisions reviewed in this chapter, the only two where an investigation was condemned on grounds that a valid legislative purpose was lacking, *Gibson* and *DeGregory*, came from state legislative committees, not congressional.

# 13

## Taxation and fiscal powers

The broadest constitutional grant of fiscal authority to Congress is that in Article I, section 8, clause 1: "The Congress shall have power to lay and collect taxes, duties, imposts and excises, to pay the debts and provide for the common defence and general welfare of the United States."[1] The possession of adequate sources of revenue and broad authority to use public funds for public purposes are essential conditions for carrying on an effective government. Consequently the first rule for judicial review of tax statutes is that a heavy burden of proof lies on anyone who would challenge any congressional exercise of fiscal power. In almost every decision touching the constitutionality of federal taxation, the Supreme Court has stressed the breadth of congressional power and the limits of its own reviewing powers. "The power to tax involves the power to destroy," said Marshall in *McCulloch* v. *Maryland* (1819). The authorization of the Constitution "reaches every subject,"[2] it embraces "every conceivable power of taxation."[3] If the authority to tax is exercised oppressively, "the responsibility of the legislature

---

[1] The four terms used to describe governmental levies are broad enough to cover any known form of taxation. "Duties" and "imposts" are interchangeable terms describing customs dues levied on goods imported from foreign countries; "excises" refer to internal revenue taxes on the manufacture, sale, use, or transfer of property within the United States.

[2] *License Tax Cases* (1867).

[3] *Brushaber* v. *Union Pacific R.R.* (1916).

is not to the courts, but to the people by whom its members are elected." [4] Yet in spite of such statements, the fiscal powers of Congress are not unlimited, and judicial review has a role to play here as elsewhere. The Constitution includes certain specific limitations on the taxing power, and to the interpretations of these restraints we turn first.

## SPECIFIC LIMITATIONS ON THE TAXING POWER

DIRECT TAXATION    Article I, section 9, states the following prohibition: "No capitation, or other direct, tax shall be laid, unless in proportion to the census or enumeration herein before directed to be taken." But what is a "direct" tax? When this provision was under discussion in the Constitutional Convention, King asked precisely this question, and according to Madison's notes, "No one answered." The Supreme Court was first called on to give an answer in *Hylton* v. *United States* (1796), when a tax on carriages was attacked as a direct tax, and consequently as one that had to be apportioned among the states on the basis of population. Alexander Hamilton appeared as special counsel for the government.

The Court unanimously held the tax to be indirect and thus constitutional. Justice Paterson, who had been a member of the Convention, recalled that the provision had been inserted in the Constitution in order to assure the Southern delegates that their slaves and land would not be subjected to special taxes not applicable elsewhere in the country. The Court ruled that the prohibition, as an exception to the general taxing power, should be narrowly interpreted, and suggested that no tax should be regarded as "direct" unless it could be conveniently apportioned. This tax of course could not be fairly apportioned, and so it was classified by the Court as an "excise" on the use of carriages. The only taxes which the judges thought must clearly be regarded as direct were capitation and land taxes.

During the Civil War, Congress for the first time resorted to income taxation as a source of federal revenue, with no provision for apportionment. The Supreme Court upheld the law in *Springer* v. *United States* (1881) on the ground that an income tax was not a direct tax. Congress thus had every reason to be confident of its authority when in 1894 it levied a tax of 2 per cent on incomes in excess of $4,000. This statute was a great victory for the progressive forces of the country, and a sectional triumph for the South and West over the industrial Northeast, where persons with such incomes were mostly located. Before the Supreme Court the tax was depicted as a "Communist march" against the rights of property, and the Court was told that it had never heard nor would ever hear a case more important than this.

The tax was to go into effect on January 1, 1895. The general rule in tax matters is that one pays the tax first and litigates later. However, a device for an immediate test case was found in an equity suit brought against a

[4] *Veazie Bank* v. *Fenno* (1869).

corporation by one of its stockholders to prevent a threatened breach of trust by the allegedly illegal payment of the tax from the corporate treasury. The income of the corporation was derived mainly from real estate and from stocks, bonds, and other personal property.

The Court handed down two decisions in *Pollock* v. *Farmers' Loan & Trust Co.* (1895). In the first it ruled that, since taxes on real estate are direct taxes, taxes on the income or rents from real estate must similarly be considered direct. The decision also invalidated taxation of income from municipal bonds. However, the Court had been evenly divided, with one member absent because of illness, on the main issue as to whether taxes on the income from stocks and bonds were also to be regarded as direct. In the second decision the Court, by a vote of five to four, ruled that such taxation was direct, and went on to hold the entire tax invalid, thus reversing the law of the preceding hundred years. This surrender of the Court to entrenched wealth, in the same year that it refused to apply the Sherman Act against the sugar trust [5] and upheld the conviction of Eugene V. Debs for violating an injunction during the Pullman strike,[6] revealed only too clearly the judiciary's alignment on the side of capital, and earned the Court a popular reputation as a tool of special privilege which was not dispelled for forty years.

A campaign to "repeal" the Court's decision by adoption of a constitutional amendment got under way immediately, and was finally successful in 1913. Meantime, the Court, perhaps not unaffected by the storm it had aroused, refused to use the *Pollock* precedent to invalidate other questioned taxes. An inheritance tax was upheld as an excise in *Knowlton* v. *Moore* (1900), and in *Flint* v. *Stone Tracy Co.* (1911) the Court similarly approved a 1909 statute levying a 1 per cent tax on the net income of corporations.

The Sixteenth Amendment provides: "The Congress shall have power to lay and collect taxes on incomes, from whatever source derived, without apportionment among the several States, and without regard to any census or enumeration." Congress quickly took advantage of the amendment to pass an income tax law, which now provides the principal revenue source for the federal government.

The authorization to tax incomes "from whatever source derived" has been interpreted, in spite of its breadth, as subject to certain limitations. The purpose of the language, the Court initially held in *Brushaber* v. *Union Pacific R.R.* (1916), was merely to correct the error of the *Pollock* decision and to restore income taxation to the category of indirect taxes. The *scope* of the taxing power remained as before. For example, the judicial rule against federal taxation of the salaries of state employees, discussed below, was unaffected by the Sixteenth Amendment.

A second restriction was stated by the Court in *Eisner* v. *Macomber*

[5] *United States* v. *E. C. Knight Co.* (1895).
[6] *In re Debs* (1895).

(1920), where it held that stock dividends could not be treated as taxable income. Stock dividends were not "income" but capital, and consequently still fell under the apportionment rule. In spite of vigorous subsequent attacks on *Eisner* v. *Macomber,* the principle of the decision has been maintained, though sometimes narrowed in application.

THE UNIFORMITY REQUIREMENT    After the affirmative grant of power in the first part of Article I, section 8, clause 1, the clause concludes with this proviso: "But all duties, imposts and excises shall be uniform throughout the United States." Since all direct taxes must be apportioned among the states on the basis of population, it follows that only indirect taxes can be subject to the rule of uniformity. This requirement simply means that the thing or activity taxed must be taxed at the same rate throughout the United States. It is "geographical" uniformity that is demanded.

The Supreme Court gave an authoritative interpretation of this language when it considered the inheritance tax levied by Congress during the Spanish-American War. The law exempted legacies of less than $10,000 from taxation, and taxed legacies over that amount at a variable rate according to the amount and the degree of relationship of the beneficiary to the deceased. The law was attacked on two grounds: if direct, it had to be apportioned; if indirect, it had to be uniform, whereas the rates were variable and progressive.

As already noted, the Court in *Knowlton* v. *Moore* (1900) held the tax not to be a direct tax on the property inherited, but rather a tax on the right of the beneficiary to inherit, and so indirect. On the second charge, the Court denied that "intrinsic" uniformity was intended. Such an interpretation would render "throughout the United States" mere surplusage. Geographical uniformity was what the framers had in mind. A 1926 amendment to the inheritance tax law permitting a deduction from the federal tax for like taxes paid to a state, was held in *Florida* v. *Mellon* (1927) not to be unconstitutional on geographic uniformity grounds because Florida levied no such tax.

TAXES ON EXPORTS    Article I, section 9, clause 5, provides: "No tax or duty shall be laid on articles exported from any state." As already noted, this provision was demanded by the agrarian states to ensure that the national government could not interfere with export of their surplus agricultural products.[7]

Not every tax bearing on exports is forbidden by this clause. A tax levied directly on the articles exported or on the right to export them is, of course, covered. So are stamp taxes on foreign bills of lading which evidence the

[7] Conversely, the states, by Art. I, sec. 10, clause 2, are forbidden, without the consent of Congress, to lay imposts or duties on imports or exports, except what may be absolutely necessary to enforce their inspection laws.

exports, and stamp taxes on marine insurance policies covering the exports. But a tax on the income of a domestic corporation engaged in the export business is not an export tax. Nor is a general tax laid on all property equally, including goods intended for export, unconstitutional if it is not levied on goods in the actual course of exportation or because of their intended exportation. The Court has had to decide in a considerable number of cases at just what point the process of exportation begins. Naturally the prohibition on export taxes does not prevent Congress from regulating exports in other ways.[8]

### TAXATION FOR NONREVENUE PURPOSES

In addition to these specifically stated limits on the federal taxing power, the Supreme Court has found certain implied restrictions which derive from the inherent nature of the federal system. The task of discovering and applying these judicially constructed restrictions is obviously one which, if not performed with discretion, may result in judicial assumption of important policy functions.

One major constitutional issue has grown out of congressional efforts to use the taxing power for purposes which are primarily regulatory, and which result in the raising of comparatively little revenue, or sometimes none at all. Does this mixture of motives invalidate a tax statute? Must the taxing power be limited to revenue purposes only? The Supreme Court has not thought so, except in a very few instances and under quite unusual circumstances.

The protective tariff is a clear case of using taxation for goals other than the raising of revenue. The first tariff law was passed in 1789, but the Supreme Court had no occasion to pass on the constitutionality of this form of taxation until 1928. Then, in *J. W. Hampton, Jr., & Co. v. United States,* the Court was able to cite in its support some 140 years of practice and the fact that it does bring in revenue. "So long as the motive of Congress and the effect of its legislative action are to secure revenue for the benefit of the general government, the existence of other motives in the selection of the subjects of taxes can not invalidate Congressional action," wrote Chief Justice Taft.

Other regulatory or prohibitory taxes have come before the Court with less impressive genealogy, but have been no less firmly upheld. Two types of rationalizations can be distinguished in the Court's approach to these problems. The first sustains the questioned tax on the ground that the taxing power is being employed to help enforce another of the federal government's specifically granted powers. In this posture the constitutional case for the

[8] The provision in Art. I, sec. 9, clause 6, that "no preference shall be given by any regulation of commerce or revenue to the ports of one state over those of another" has yielded judicial interpretations of only minor importance.

tax is strengthened by its auxiliary relationship to an admittedly valid federal purpose.

The potentialities of this argument were first demonstrated in *Veazie Bank* v. *Fenno* (1869). Congress had passed a national banking act authorizing the incorporation of national banks with power to issue currency notes. In 1866 Congress supplemented this act by another imposing a 10 per cent tax on any state bank notes thereafter put in circulation. The purpose of the tax was admittedly to drive out of circulation all state bank notes, but it was upheld by the Supreme Court. The principal constitutional objection made was that Congress had no power to impair a franchise granted by a state. The Court replied that Congress had the unquestioned power to issue notes to circulate as money, which it had undertaken to exercise through the national banking act. To secure the full benefit of this legislation, "Congress may restrain, by suitable enactments, the circulation as money of any notes not issued under its own authority. Without this power, indeed, its attempts to secure a sound and uniform currency for the country must be futile." [9]

Regulatory or prohibitory taxes have also been upheld, however, even when there was no relationship to other powers of Congress, and where they had to stand or fall on their own merits. In this situation the Supreme Court's reasoning has typically stressed the impropriety of any judicial questioning of the motives of Congress. The classic case is *McCray* v. *United States* (1904), which involved an act of Congress levying a tax of 10 cents per pound on oleomargarine artificially colored yellow to look like butter, and only ¼ cent per pound on uncolored margarine. There could be no doubt that the statute was adopted at the behest of the dairy industry to handicap the sale of a competitive product. But the Court denied that "the motives or purposes of Congress are open to judicial inquiry in considering the power of that body" to enact legislation. The statute was on its face an excise tax, and so it followed that it was within the power of Congress.

The principle of the *McCray* case was again endorsed in *United States* v. *Doremus* (1919), where Congress used a small tax requirement to compel the registration of persons engaged in the narcotics trade. "The act may not be declared unconstitutional because its effect may be to accomplish another purpose as well as the raising of revenue," said the Court, but four justices dissented on the ground that the statute was a bold attempt to exercise police power reserved to the states.

The *Doremus* minority position won control of the Court three years later in *Bailey* v. *Drexel Furniture Co.* (1922), also known as the *Child Labor*

[9] Other decisions made on similar reasoning were the *Head Money Cases* (1884) and *Sunshine Anthracite Coal Co.* v. *Adkins* (1940). In the former an act of 1882 had levied on shipowners a tax of 50 cents for each immigrant brought to the United States. The Court said flatly that the power thus exercised "is not the taxing power," considering it rather as a mere incident "of that branch of foreign commerce which is involved in immigration."

*Tax Case*. This decision invalidated the Federal Child Labor Tax Act, passed in 1919 to replace the 1916 Child Labor Act based on the commerce clause, which the Supreme Court had held unconstitutional in *Hammer* v. *Dagenhart* (1918). The clumsily drafted 1919 law levied a tax of 10 per cent on the annual net profits of businesses which at any time during the year employed children in violation of the standards prescribed in the act. The Court, while denying that it had any right or desire to inquire into congressional motives, concluded that this "so-called tax" revealed on its face that it was not a revenue measure, but rather a penalty to regulate child labor. The justices particularly noted the provision that the tax was not to be imposed unless the employer *knowingly* hired children under the age limit, and pointed out: "*Scienter* is associated with penalties, not with taxes." Similarly in *United States* v. *Constantine* (1935), a grossly disproportional federal excise tax, amounting to $1,000, imposed only on retail liquor dealers carrying on business in violation of local law, was declared unconstitutional.

It is not easy for the Court to arrive at such conclusions, for they necessarily involve a finding that Congress has been guilty of improper motives, and has used a constitutional subterfuge to accomplish ends which the Constitution forbids. Moreover, the contention that the taxing power of Congress is limited by the regulatory powers reserved to the states by the Tenth Amendment derives from the same dual federalism reasoning embodied in the discredited case of *Hammer* v. *Dagenhart* (1918).[10] Although the Court abandoned dual federalism in interpreting the federal commerce power and specifically overruled *Hammer* v. *Dagenhart* in *United States* v. *Darby Lumber Co.* (1941), some members of the Court illogically continued to apply the doctrine against the federal taxing power.

The principal case is *United States* v. *Kahriger* (1953), where the Court upheld the challenged tax but both majority and minority used dual federalism reasoning. Following the Kefauver nationwide investigation into gambling and racketeering in 1950, Congress levied a tax on persons engaged in the business of accepting wagers and required that they register with the Collector of Internal Revenue. One of the charges against the tax was that it infringed on the police powers of the states. Justice Reed for the majority thought this was a relevant issue and noted that the legislative history indicated a congressional motive to suppress gambling, but finally upheld the statute on the ground that the Court could intervene only if there were provisions in the act "extraneous to any tax need." Justice Frankfurter's dissent, condemning the tax by rationale straight out of *Hammer* v. *Dagenhart*, argued that "when oblique use is made of the taxing power as to matters which substantively are not within the powers delegated to Congress, the Court cannot shut its eyes to what is obviously, because designedly, an attempt to control conduct which the Constitution left to the responsibility

[10] See the discussion of dual federalism in Chap. 5.

of the States, merely because Congress wrapped the legislation in the verbal cellophane of a revenue measure." [11]

Justices Black and Douglas dissented in *Kahriger* on the ground that requiring a person to register and confess that he was engaged in the illegal business of gambling amounted to self-incrimination contrary to the Fifth Amendment. Justice Reed sought to counter the rather obvious logic of this position by contending that the privilege against self-incrimination "has relation only to past acts," whereas the wagering tax was assessed on "the business of wagering in the future." Fifteen years later, in *Marchetti* v. *United States* (1968) and *Grosso* v. *United States* (1968), the Court with only one dissent overruled *Kahriger* and voided the tax on self-incrimination grounds.

### INTERGOVERNMENTAL TAX IMMUNITY

A second major implied limitation on congressional power to tax is the immunity to federal taxation of state governments, their property, and activities. This immunity rule rests on no specific language of the Constitution. Rather it is a judicially constructed doctrine, based on certain assumptions by the Supreme Court about the conditions for successful operation of a federal system.

INITIAL DEVELOPMENT OF THE DOCTRINE     Actually, the immunity doctrine was first developed by the Supreme Court, in the famous case of *McCulloch* v. *Maryland* (1819), to protect *federal* activities from *state* taxation. The Bank of the United States, incorporated by Congress in 1816, had a branch in Maryland. The bank was politically unpopular, and in 1818 the state legislature imposed a tax on all banks in the state not chartered by the state legislature, which McCulloch, cashier of the branch bank, refused to pay. Marshall upheld the bank's position. After a notable argument demonstrating the power of Congress to incorporate the bank, which is discussed in Chapter 11, he went on to consider the state's claim to taxing power. The ruling principle, he began, is "that the constitution and the laws made in pursuance thereof are supreme; that they control the constitution and laws of the respective States, and cannot be controlled by them." From this axiom Marshall deduced three corollaries: "1. That a power to create implies a power to pre-

---

[11] See also *Sonzinsky* v. *United States* (1937), where the Court upheld a license tax on manufacturers of, or dealers in, firearms likely to be used in criminal activities, such as sawed-off shotguns and machine guns, but only because the tax was not attended by any "offensive regulation." A provision of the same act which made it a crime to obtain a weapon of the lethal type covered by the statute without registering the gun with the government was held unconstitutional in *Haynes* v. *United States* (1968) on the ground that it constituted compulsory self-incrimination.

serve. 2. That a power to destroy, if wielded by a different hand, is hostile to, and incompatible with, these powers to create and to preserve. 3. That where this repugnancy exists, that authority which is supreme must control, not yield, to that over which it is supreme." Since the power to tax is, in Marshall's words, "the power to destroy," it followed that the Maryland tax was unconstitutional.

The *McCulloch* principle was reiterated by Marshall in *Osborn* v. *United States Bank* (1824), and a basis was laid for its expansion by a dictum that all contractors who dealt with the government were entitled to immunity from taxation on such transactions. In *Weston* v. *Charleston* (1829) Marshall barred state taxation of obligations of the United States. Then in 1842 the Court held in *Dobbins* v. *Erie County* that a state had no power to tax the office, or the emoluments of the office, of a federal officer.

State immunity from federal taxation was first asserted by the Court in *Collector* v. *Day* (1871), where the salary of a Massachusetts judge was declared to be immune from the Civil War federal income tax. Justice Nelson grounded the Court's holding directly on the *McCulloch* and *Dobbins* precedents, saying: "If the means and instrumentalities employed by [the federal] government to carry into operation the powers granted to it are, necessarily, and, for the sake of self-preservation, exempt from taxation by the States, why are not those of the States depending upon their reserved powers, for like reasons, equally exempt from Federal taxation?"

Only Justice Bradley pointed to the obvious flaw in this reasoning. State taxation of the instruments of the federal government is a very different thing from federal taxation of the instruments of a state government. State taxation "involves an interference with the powers of a government in which other States and their citizens are equally interested with the State which imposes the taxation." But when Congress levies a tax affecting the states, every state has a voice in the decision through its representatives, and so the states are actually consenting to their own taxation. There is thus a political check on possible abuse of the federal taxing power against the states, whereas a state legislature is subject to no such sense of restraint in levying a tax whose incidence is nationwide.

*Collector* v. *Day* must be considered, however, in the light of the times. The Court was uneasy about the dominance of the Radical Reconstructionists in Congress and the expansion of federal power which their plans contemplated. It was uncertain how much new authority the Civil War amendments to the Constitution had granted to Washington. The Court had just upheld the prohibitive federal tax on the notes of state banks, and the possibility that the taxing power might be used with even more destructive effect against the states was certainly in the minds of the justices.

If Reconstruction was responsible for *Collector* v. *Day* and the birth of the state immunity doctrine, then the Court's economic biases must be

charged with its continuance and enlargement in *Pollock* v. *Farmers' Loan & Trust Co.* (1895), which exempted from federal taxation state and local bonds and the interest therefrom. But in 1905 the immunity principle suffered a significant defeat in *South Carolina* v. *United States*. South Carolina had gone into the business of dispensing alcoholic beverages, the entire profit from the operation going to the state. The state claimed immunity from the regular federal internal revenue taxes levied on liquor dealers, but the Supreme Court denied the claim. The justices thought that the framers of the Constitution had not contemplated state participation in business enterprises, and that consequently tax exemption must be limited to those functions "which are of a strictly governmental character." The Court was also motivated by the fear that if tax exemption was permitted in this area, entrance by the states into other businesses would have the effect of seriously reducing federal revenues, and thus the whole internal revenue structure might be imperiled.

THE IMMUNITY BOOM    The Court of the 1920s reverted to a broader view of tax immunity, though this expansion principally affected state rather than federal taxation. In *Gillespie* v. *Oklahoma* (1922) a state tax applied to income accruing to the lessee of some Indian oil lands was held invalid by a five to four vote, the majority reasoning that the lessee was an instrumentality of the United States used by the government "in carrying out duties to the Indians." Another five to four decision in *Panhandle Oil Co.* v. *Mississippi* (1928) invalidated a state gasoline tax collected on gasoline sold to the federal government. Still another five to four decision, *Long* v. *Rockwood* (1928), held it unconstitutional for a state to tax royalties received from a patent granted by the United States. Justice McReynolds sought to support this fantastic decision by arguing that taxing the royalties from federal patents would interfere with the federal efforts to promote science and invention. In 1929 *Macallen Co.* v. *Massachusetts* held a state corporate franchise tax invalid because interest from national and state bonds was included in measuring the tax.

This immunity boom had considerably less impact on the federal taxing power. To be sure, *Indian Motocycle Co.* v. *United States* (1931) held invalid a federal sales tax on the sale of a motorcycle to a municipal police department, and in *Burnet* v. *Coronado Oil & Gas Co.* (1932) a five to four vote invalidated a federal tax imposed on the income which private persons derived from leasing state-owned oil lands. But a counterweight was supplied by *Metcalf* v. *Mitchell* (1926), which held that consulting engineers had to pay federal income tax on the fees they received for professional services rendered to state and local governments. In the same direction went *University of Illinois* v. *United States* (1933), which required a state university to pay customs duties on the importation of scientific apparatus, and

*Allen* v. *Regents of the University System of Georgia* (1938), applying the federal admissions tax to athletic contests of a state university.

COLLAPSE OF THE IMMUNITY DOCTRINE    The immunity boom finally collapsed in the latter 1930s, after the Court had been reoriented by the first few Roosevelt appointments. The extensions of the immunity principle had rested on the thinnest kind of a Court majority, and represented an extreme view of what constituted a "burden" on government operations. The basis for reversing these decisions had been laid by the dissenting opinions which Justices Holmes and Brandeis, later joined by Stone, had written. It was Holmes who effectively disposed of Marshall's dictum when he rejoined in his *Panhandle* dissent: "The power to tax is not the power to destroy while this Court sits." Holmes left the Court in 1932, and Brandeis early in 1939, so that the major task of translating the minority view of the preceding decade into the majority position of the Roosevelt Court fell to Stone. He had consistently argued that immunity from intergovernmental taxation was not to be supported by merely theoretical conceptions of interference with the functions of government. He demanded that any burdens alleged to result be proved by economic data. This view won a preliminary victory in *Educational Films Corporation* v. *Ward* (1931), which Stone wrote, and which impliedly overruled the *Macallen* decision, and in 1932 *Fox Film Corporation* v. *Doyal* specifically overruled *Long* v. *Rockwood*, decided only four years earlier.

It was not until 1938, however, that the real reversal of doctrine began. The initial blow came in *Helvering* v. *Mountain Producers Corporation* (1938), as the Court by a five to two vote overruled the *Gillespie* and *Burnet* cases. Here Wyoming had leased certain school lands to an oil corporation on terms which gave the state a substantial share of the royalties. Reversing its earlier view, the Court held that where one operating under a government contract is merely being taxed on his profits in the same way that others engaged in the same business are taxed, he cannot show that the effect of the tax on the state "is other than indirect and remote."

Next the long-standing reciprocal exemption of state and federal employees from taxation on their income fell. Such immunity had been reaffirmed as late as 1937 in two decisions, *New York ex rel. Rogers* v. *Graves* and *Brush* v. *Commissioner*. However, when the Court was asked in *Helvering* v. *Gerhardt* (1938) to rule on the liability of Port of New York Authority employees to federal income taxation, it was prepared to reverse the time-honored rule on the ground that immunity from federal taxation should not be allowed beyond that vitally necessary for the continued existence of the states. A nondiscriminatory tax on the net income of state employees, concluded Justice Stone for the Court, could not possibly obstruct the performance of state functions. In cases "where the tax laid upon individuals affects

the state only as the burden is passed on to it by the taxpayer," immunity cannot be allowed "when the burden on the state is so speculative and uncertain that if allowed it would restrict the federal taxing power without affording any corresponding tangible protection to the state government." [12]

As for taxes collected directly from the state, the basic principle is still the *South Carolina* doctrine that immunity does not apply to activities thought not to be essential to the preservation of state government. This position was reiterated by the Court in *New York* v. *United States* (1946), which involved the right of the United States to tax the sale of mineral waters bottled by the State of New York at Saratoga Springs. The Court agreed that the state was liable for the taxes, but it was less sure of its reasons than it had been in 1905. Justice Frankfurter felt that the absence of discrimination against the state was the important factor; New York was required to pay only what private persons would pay on the same subject matter. But Chief Justice Stone thought that a tax might be nondiscriminatory and still interfere unduly with a state's performance of its "sovereign functions." He preferred to uphold the tax on the ground that immunity would withdraw from federal taxing power "a subject of taxation of a nature which has been traditionally within that power from the beginning." Justices Douglas and Black, dissenting, contended that the decision "disregards the Tenth Amendment, places the sovereign States on the same plane as private citizens, and makes the sovereign States pay the federal government for the privilege of exercising the powers of sovereignty guaranteed them by the Constitution." They would have overruled the *South Carolina* decision.

The immunity doctrine is thus no longer a substantial limitation on the congressional taxing power. Of course Congress cannot levy a property tax on a state capitol building, or a stamp tax on writs served by state courts, or any other tax which falls directly on an essential state activity. But of the taxes thus prohibited, the only one of practical importance is the tax on income from state and municipal bonds.[13] Even here, it seems not unlikely that the Court would support Congress if it ever took the initiative in subjecting income from these bonds to the federal income tax.

The same principles now confine federal exemption from state taxation to the "possessions, institutions, and activities of the Federal Government itself." [14] When a state tax falls on a party who is in contractual relationship

---

[12] Immunity of federal employees from state taxation was denied in *Graves* v. *O'Keefe* (1939). The decision specifically overruled *Collector* v. *Day* and *Rogers* v. *Graves,* and impliedly overruled the *Dobbins* and *Brush* cases also. A 1940 federal statute gives nonresident servicemen present in a state in compliance with military orders broad immunity from the state's personal property and income taxation. See *California* v. *Buzard* (1966).

[13] See *Commissioner of Internal Revenue* v. *Shamberg's Estate* (1945).

[14] *United States* v. *Allegheny County* (1944). In *Department of Employment* v. *United States* (1966) the Court held that the American Red Cross is an instrumentality of the United States, for purposes of immunity from state taxation, and that Congress had not waived that immunity.

with the government, the tax is valid, even if it is clear that the tax will be passed on to the government or proportionately increase its costs. Thus in *Alabama* v. *King & Boozer* (1941) the Court upheld a state sales tax imposed on a government contractor relating to materials purchased by him for use in the performance of a government cost-plus contract.[15]

More difficult problems arise when a private party is utilizing government property in manufacture of materials for the government, as often happens on defense contracts. The general distinction here is that the state may not levy a *property* tax on such property, even though it is in private hands and the tax is to be collected from the private taxpayer,[16] but that it may levy a *privilege* tax on the activities of such persons, even though these activities involve the use of government property, and the value or amount of such property is the partial or exclusive basis for measurement of the tax.[17] The Court by a five to four vote in *City of Detroit* v. *Murray Corporation of America* (1958) even upheld a state tax on these latter grounds which was styled by the Michigan statutes as a "personal property tax," though Justice Frankfurter contended that the effect of the decision was to encroach on the basic exemption granted by *McCulloch* v. *Maryland* and to "jettison what has been part of our constitutional system for almost 150 years."

## THE POWER TO SPEND

Revenues are raised by taxation in order to be spent for public purposes. What are the constitutional limitations on the spending power? The basic principle of legislative control over the purse, established by the British Parliament after a long struggle with the Crown, is safeguarded by the provision in Article I, section 9, that "No money shall be drawn from the Treasury, but in consequence of appropriations made by law." But are there any constitutional limits upon the purposes for which Congress may appropriate federal funds? Clearly Congress can spend money to achieve any of the purposes delegated to it by the Constitution, such as regulating commerce among the states or taking the census. But can reliance also be placed upon the rather enigmatic language of the taxing clause which speaks of paying the debts and providing for "the common defence and general welfare"?

SPENDING AND THE GENERAL WELFARE    On occasions it has been urged that the general welfare clause is an independent grant of legislative power to the federal government, quite unrelated to the preceding clause of the same sentence which deals with taxation. In other words, this argument

[15] See also *James* v. *Dravo Contracting Co.* (1937).
[16] *United States* v. *Allegheny County* (1944).
[17] *United States and Borg-Warner Corp.* v. *City of Detroit* (1958); *United States* v. *Township of Muskegon* (1958).

treats the comma after "excises" as though it were a semicolon (as in fact it was up until practically the end of the Constitutional Convention). Crosskey argues vehemently that this interpretation of the general welfare clause as quite independent of the taxing power is what the framers intended, but this position has never been authoritatively accepted. Story contended in his *Commentaries* that adoption of this view would have the tremendous result of transforming the federal government from one of delegated powers into one "of general and unlimited powers."

Rejection of this independent status for the general welfare clause leaves it with what can be called a "purposive" function. However, two purposive theories have been put forward, identified with Madison and Hamilton. Madison asserted that the phrase, "common defence and general welfare," was nothing more than a summary of all the specifically enumerated powers in the subsequent clauses of Article I, section 8. In No. 41 of *The Federalist* he sought by this contention to answer the arguments of those who thought that this language constituted "an unlimited commission" for the federal government. "Nothing is more natural nor common," he wrote, "than first to use a general phrase, and then to explain and qualify it by a recital of particulars." So Congress could spend only for the express functions stated elsewhere in the Constitution. Hamilton, on the other hand, contended that the general welfare clause conferred a power separate and distinct from the enumerated powers, and that Congress consequently had a substantive power to tax and to appropriate, limited only by the requirement of furthering the general welfare of the United States.

Up to 1936 the Supreme Court had never undertaken to settle this argument, principally because a suit attacking federal spending could be prosecuted only by a litigant who had a sufficient legal interest in federal expenditures to give him a standing to sue. As already noted, *Massachusetts v. Mellon* (1923) had ruled that payment of federal income taxes did not entitle a person to challenge congressional appropriations in court. But to the rule that it is normally impossible to secure a court test of federal spending power, the case of *United States* v. *Butler* (1936) stands as an important exception. The Agricultural Adjustment Act of 1933 provided for federal payments to farmers who would cooperate in the government's program of price stabilization through production control. The money paid the farmers was to come from processing taxes on agricultural commodities which were authorized by the same statute. This statutory joinder of a spending program with the tax arrangements for financing it was quite unusual, and gave the Court, at that time in a bitterly anti-New Deal mood, an opening which it quickly exploited.

Butler, as receiver for the Hoosac Mills, resisted the collection of taxes on cotton processed at that plant. He could not expect to win on this issue, for the processing tax was obviously a bona fide exercise of the federal taxing power. But once Butler had gotten his case into court as a tax case, he

transformed it into an attack on the spending power by challenging the tax, not as a tax, but as a means of providing money for a program of agricultural production control which he alleged to be an unconstitutional invasion of the powers of the states—in short, "as a step in an unauthorized plan." The Court ratified this stratagem by ruling that the tax and the spending were in fact "parts of a single scheme."

Thus it was that the *Butler* case gave the Court an opportunity to settle the argument which Madison and Hamilton had begun. The justices settled it in Hamilton's favor, ruling that the general welfare clause meant that congressional power to spend was "not limited by the direct grants of legislative power found in the Constitution." The only limitation was that taxing and spending, in order to meet the general welfare standard, would have to be on "matters of national, as distinguished from local welfare."

This was an important victory for the spending power, but the Court immediately proceeded to make it a hollow one by transferring the argument to an entirely new issue. Whether the spending was for national rather than local welfare was of no importance, Justice Roberts concluded for the *Butler* majority, since, as a statutory plan to regulate and control agricultural production, the act invaded the reserved rights of the states and was consequently invalid under the Tenth Amendment. Congress could not "under the pretext of the exertion of powers which are granted" seek to accomplish "a prohibited end."

The *Butler* decision was little more than a nine-day wonder. As a barrier to federal agricultural regulation it was soon bypassed as the type of program it condemned was reenacted by Congress under the commerce power and upheld by a more cooperative Court in *Mulford* v. *Smith* (1939) and *Wickard* v. *Filburn* (1942). As a general threat to the spending power, it was dispelled in 1937 when the Court upheld the tax provisions of the Social Security Act. *Steward Machine Co.* v. *Davis* involved the unemployment compensation section of the act, which provided for a federal payroll tax on employers of a certain percentage of the wages they paid to employees. The proceeds of the tax went into the general federal treasury. If employers paid state taxes into an unemployment fund set up under a satisfactory state law, they could credit such payments against the federal tax up to 90 per cent.

The Court denied by a five to four vote that these tax provisions were an attempt to coerce the states or to invade their reserved powers. The states were given, true enough, a compelling inducement to provide unemployment compensation, but the Court viewed this not as coercion but as freedom to adopt such social legislation without putting the employers of some states at a disadvantage compared with employers in other states without unemployment compensation. The *Butler* case was specifically distinguished in the *Steward* decision on the grounds that here the proceeds of the tax were not earmarked for a special group; that the state had itself passed,

and could at its pleasure repeal, the unemployment compensation law which was a condition of the credit; and that the relief of unemployment was an end for which nation and state could lawfully cooperate.

A second decision on the same day, *Helvering* v. *Davis,* sustained the Social Security Act system of old-age benefits. The argument on this head had been that the taxing power was being used to benefit a particular class of persons, but the Court believed Congress might reasonably conclude that provision for old-age security would promote the general welfare. The discretion to make such decisions "belongs to Congress, unless the choice is clearly wrong, a display of arbitrary power, not an exercise of judgment."

APPROPRIATIONS AND THE REMOVAL POWER    Because the legislative power to appropriate is so broad and so difficult to question, Congress has sometimes been tempted to use it to achieve purposes which it lacks more direct constitutional power to accomplish. An excellent example concerns removal of officials of the executive branch. The only provision which the Constitution makes for legislative removal is by the complicated process of impeachment, already discussed. But cannot Congress accomplish the same end by providing in appropriation acts that no funds are to be paid to particular individuals, thus driving them out of office?

It was this very interesting question that was raised in the case of *United States* v. *Lovett* (1946). The House, under the prodding of Representative Martin Dies, had adopted a rider to an appropriation act forbidding the use of money appropriated in the statute to pay the salaries of three named federal officials. President Roosevelt, unable to veto the rider without killing the entire act, signed it with a forceful charge that it was unconstitutional. The Court's decision condemned the legislation on the ground that it constituted a bill of attainder, instead of on such possible broader grounds as that it violated the separation of powers by usurping the executive removal power or amounted to an unconstitutional substitute for the impeachment process.

## BORROWING AND MONETARY POWERS

Clauses 2 and 5 of Article I, section 8, give Congress power "to borrow money on the credit of the United States" and "to coin money, regulate the value thereof, and of foreign coin." These authorizations have figured incidentally in several constitutional episodes already discussed. Thus, the holding in *McCulloch* v. *Maryland* (1819) that Congress had the implied power to establish a national bank drew authority in part from clause 5, as did *Veazie Bank* v. *Fenno* (1869) in upholding federal power to tax state bank notes out of existence. However, there are two major crises in American history in which the interpretation of these powers was directly and importantly

at issue. The first led up to and was resolved by the *Legal Tender Cases* (1871), the second by the *Gold Clause Cases* (1935).

In Chapter 2 it was pointed out how important the currency problem was in the minds of the members of the Constitutional Convention. Their dislike for "cheap money" led them to prohibit states from coining money, emitting bills of credit, or making anything but gold and silver coin legal tender in payment of debts. Their distrust of paper money even led them to strike out an authorization to Congress to "emit bills of credit" which was included in the original draft of the borrowing clause. However, they did not go so far as to forbid the federal government to issue paper money, and in fact the existence of this power was assumed to be included within the borrowing power as soon as the government began operations.

In connection with the financing of the Civil War, Congress went further and made "greenbacks" (i.e., bills of credit) legal tender at face value in the payment of debts between private individuals. In *Hepburn* v. *Griswold* (1870) the Court by a vote of four to three held the legal tender acts unconstitutional in so far as they required the acceptance of greenbacks in fulfillment of contracts made before the acts were passed, and ruled that creditors would be deprived of due process if compelled to accept depreciated paper money in payment of such debts. Chief Justice Chase, who as Secretary of the Treasury during the Civil War had supported the legal tender legislation, wrote the majority opinion, which also cast doubt on the constitutionality of the requirement that the notes be accepted in payment of debts incurred *after* the laws were passed. The minority contended that the legal tender measures had been necessary and proper to the exercise of the war power, and had saved the federal government from a collapse of credit.

The *Hepburn* holding, if maintained, would have had a tremendous impact, for the nation's economy had adjusted to the use of greenbacks, and many debtors would have been ruined if required to repay their borrowings in hard money. So the popular pressure for reconsideration was very great. On the day the decision was announced, President Grant sent the nominations of two new justices to the Senate. With their votes, the *Hepburn* decision was overruled five to four in the *Legal Tender Cases* (1871).[18]

The new majority held that a congressional power could be implied from a group of expressly granted powers, and by lumping together the war power, borrowing power, and power to coin money, the Court found adequate support for the legal tender provision. As for taking of property without due process, the revised view was that loss due to the legal tender provision was no more a legal deprivation of property than a loss due to changes in the purchasing power of money. In spite of this emphasis on the war power, *Juilliard* v. *Greenman* (1884) upheld legal tender notes in peacetime. The new amalgam of powers which it cited in support included those

[18] *Knox* v. *Lee* and *Parker* v. *Davis*.

to lay taxes, pay debts, borrow money, coin money, and regulate the value of money.

Though the Supreme Court in the *Legal Tender Cases* held that creditors who had merely specified for payment in "lawful money" had to accept legal tender at face value, in *Trebilcock* v. *Wilson* (1872) it added that Congress had not intended to, and possibly could not constitutionally, require creditors who had specified for payment in gold dollars to accept greenbacks at face value. After this decision many creditors insisted on "gold clauses" (i.e., language requiring payment in gold dollars) in bonds, and by 1933 almost all public and private bonds contained such clauses.

The *Gold Clause Cases* (1935) grew out of legislative and executive action in 1933 reducing the gold content of the dollar, with the intention of cheapening money, raising prices, and rescuing agriculture and industry from depression. As elements in the devaluation program, gold payments by the Treasury were suspended, and persons owning gold or gold certificates were required to turn them in to the Treasury in exchange for other currency. Provisions in both private contracts and government bonds for payment in gold were abrogated.

This program of course led to a flurry of litigation. The leading decision came in *Norman* v. *Baltimore & Ohio Railroad Co.* (1935). The holder of a railroad bond promising payment of interest in gold coin of the United States demanded his interest in gold or in an increased number of devalued dollars equal in gold content to the dollars promised before devaluation. By a five to four vote the Court denied this claim. The contract was interpreted as requiring the payment of money, not the delivery of gold bullion. Congress has broad powers of control over the monetary system, and these powers can not be frustrated by contracts between private parties creating vested rights outside the scope of congressional control. Finally, the Court thought Congress might reasonably conclude that abrogation of the gold clauses in private contracts was an appropriate means of carrying out this revised monetary policy. Justice McReynolds, expressing his dissent, blurted out to the packed courtroom: "As for the Constitution, it does not seem too much to say that it is gone." [19]

Whether Congress could abrogate the gold clause in the government's own contracts was another matter. *Perry* v. *United States* (1935) concerned a government bond issued in 1918 which promised that the principal and interest would be paid in United States gold coin "of the present standard of value." By a vote of eight to one the Court held that the obligation incurred in exercise of the power to borrow money must be given preference over the

[19] For an account of the extraordinary measures which President Roosevelt was prepared to take in case the Court had not upheld the government in the *Gold Clause Cases*, see William E. Leuchtenberg, "The Origins of Franklin D. Roosevelt's 'Court-Packing' Plan," in Philip B. Kurland (ed.), *The Supreme Court Review: 1966* (Chicago: The University of Chicago Press, 1966), pp. 352–354.

government's power to regulate the value of money, and consequently that the promise to pay in gold coin could not be abrogated. However, five justices ruled that the person bringing the suit could recover only for actual losses as a result of the government's action, and since there had been none in this case, he was not entitled to sue. Justice Stone in a separate opinion pointed to the Court's dilemma in undertaking to suggest that

> . . . the exercise of the sovereign power to borrow money on credit . . . may nevertheless preclude or impede the exercise of another sovereign power, to regulate the value of money; or to suggest that although there is and can be no present cause of action upon the repudiated gold clause, its obligation is nevertheless, in some manner and to some extent, not stated, superior to the power to regulate the currency which we now hold to be superior to the obligation of the bonds.

Congress proceeded to ensure that these dilemmas would cause the Court no further trouble by passing a statute denying consent to sue the government on these grounds.

### SELECTED REFERENCES

CORWIN, EDWARD S., *Court over Constitution*, chap. 4. Princeton, N.J.: Princeton University Press, 1938.

———, *The Twilight of the Supreme Court*, chap. 4. New Haven, Conn.: Yale University Press, 1934.

CROSSKEY, WILLIAM W., *Politics and the Constitution in the History of the United States*, pp. 393–408. Chicago: The University of Chicago Press, 1953.

CURTIS, CHARLES P., JR., *Lions under the Throne*, chap. 14. Boston: Houghton Mifflin Company, 1947.

DUNNE, GERALD T., *Monetary Decisions of the Supreme Court*. New Brunswick, N.J.: Rutgers University Press, 1960.

KONEFSKY, SAMUEL J., *Chief Justice Stone and the Supreme Court*, chap. 1. New York: The Macmillan Company, 1945.

POWELL, THOMAS REED, "The Waning of Intergovernmental Tax Immunities," 58 *Harvard Law Review* 633–674 (May, 1945); "The Remnant of Intergovernmental Tax Immunities," 58 *ibid.* 757–805 (July, 1945).

STERN, ROBERT L., "The Problems of Yesteryear—Commerce and Due Process," in Robert G. McCloskey (ed.), *Essays in Constitutional Law*, chap. 5. New York: Alfred A. Knopf, Inc., 1957.

# 14

## The commerce power

The commerce clause has a classic, but deceptive, simplicity. "The Congress shall have power," says Article I, section 8, clause 3, "to regulate commerce with foreign nations, and among the several states, and with the Indian tribes." With this sparse formula the drafters of the Constitution placed in the hands of the federal government a power, the absence of which in the central government under the Articles of Confederation had been largely responsible for the decision to frame a new Constitution.

The language, be it noted, is in terms of a positive grant of power to Congress. The commerce clause does not say what power to "regulate commerce," if any, is left to the states. Nor is any definition attempted of the key words in the clause. As much as any part of the Constitution, this clause has derived its meaning from experience.

Congress undertook the regulation of foreign commerce immediately, but it was quite slow in testing the extent of its constitutional power over commerce among the states. It was not until the adoption of the Interstate Commerce Act in 1887 that the federal government really entered the domestic regulatory field. Consequently, during the first century of the nation's history the commerce clause problems which the Supreme Court was asked to decide grew for the most part out of *state* regulation challenged as infringing the constitutionally protected but largely unexercised power of Congress to regulate commerce among the states.

## GIBBONS v. OGDEN

The first case in which the commerce clause figured before the Supreme Court was *Gibbons* v. *Ogden* (1824), one of the landmarks in American constitutional law. It has been customary to credit Marshall with deciding this case in accordance with his own strongly nationalistic views. Actually, his assertion of federal power was less broad and forthright than it might have been. Marshall could write clearly enough when he wanted to, but as Frankfurter says, this opinion "was either unconsciously or calculatedly confused." [1]

Robert Fulton, the inventor, and Robert R. Livingston had been granted an exclusive right by the State of New York to navigate its waters by steamboat. Ogden had a license from them to engage in navigation. Gibbons, on the other hand, was seeking to operate steamboats between New York and New Jersey under a license granted to him by the federal government. Ogden sought to enjoin Gibbons from using vessels within New York waters, to which Gibbons responded that his boats, being licensed under an act of Congress, could not be excluded by any state law. For our present purposes the important part of the Supreme Court's ruling is Marshall's discussion of the character and extent of the congressional power to regulate commerce.

Daniel Webster, appearing before the Supreme Court as counsel for Gibbons, argued for the broadest possible scope of federal power. The authority of Congress to regulate commerce, he contended, "was complete and entire." It went as far as the concept of commerce went, and "in such an age as this, no words embraced a wider field than commercial regulation. Almost all the business and intercourse of life may be connected, incidentally more or less, with commercial regulations." Naturally, in Webster's view, commerce included navigation. Opposing counsel, on the other hand, would limit commerce "to traffic, to buying and selling, or the interchange of commodities," and would exclude navigation from its scope.

Marshall agreed with Webster about navigation being necessarily a part of commerce:

> Commerce, undoubtedly, is traffic, but it is something more: it is intercourse. It describes the commercial intercourse between nations, and parts of nations, in all its branches. . . . The power over commerce, including navigation, was one of the primary objects for which the people of America adopted their government.

But Marshall failed to claim for Congress the "complete and entire" power over commerce for which Webster had contended. He did seem to start out in that direction. Congressional power over commerce with foreign nations, he said, was admittedly complete. It comprehended "every species of commercial intercourse between the United States and foreign nations." More-

[1] Felix Frankfurter, *The Commerce Clause under Marshall, Taney and Waite* (Chapel Hill, N.C.: The University of North Carolina Press, 1937), p. 17.

over, "commerce, as the word is used in the constitution, is a unit, every part of which is indicated by the term."

Now, since commerce is a unit, and since as applied to foreign nations it covers all commercial intercourse, does it not carry the same meaning when applied to commerce "among the several states?" The word "among," continued Marshall, "means intermingled with. A thing which is among others, is intermingled with them. Commerce among the States, cannot stop at the external boundary line of each State, but may be introduced into the interior." Then, having laid the basis for claiming complete federal power to regulate commerce, Marshall drew back.

> It is not intended to say that these words comprehend that commerce which is completely internal, which is carried on between man and man in a State, or between different parts of the same State, and which does not extend to or affect other States. Such a power would be inconvenient, and is certainly unnecessary.

Note that Marshall does not say that such a power was not intended or made possible by the Constitution. He says only that it would be "inconvenient" and "unnecessary" for Congress to exercise such power. Then he adds, in what is the most important single sentence of the decision: "Comprehensive as the word 'among' is, it may very properly be restricted to that commerce which concerns more States than one." He gives several reasons for this limitation, but the most important is this:

> The genius and character of the whole government seem to be, that its action is to be applied to all the external concerns of the nation, and to those internal concerns which affect the States generally; but not to those which are completely within a particular State, which do not affect other States, and with which it is not necessary to interfere, for the purpose of executing some of the general powers of the government.

Consequently, "the completely internal commerce of a State . . . may be considered as reserved for the State itself."

This whole discussion was largely unnecessary to the actual decision in *Gibbons* v. *Ogden*, which turned on the Court's finding of a conflict between the state and federal statutes. In these circumstances, "the acts of New York must yield to the law of congress," Marshall said. Breaking up the steamboat monopoly was a popular action, but the long-range constitutional importance of the ruling lay in Marshall's rejection of Webster's case for a complete federal power to regulate commerce, and his establishment of a divided authority over commerce, which has been the source of some of the most perplexing problems in American constitutional law.

Subsequently this distinction came to be referred to as that between "interstate" and "intrastate" commerce, and the test for distinguishing between the two categories was whether commerce crossed a state line or not. Marshall, however, did not use these two labels, and his conception of

commerce "which concerns more States than one" was considerably more sophisticated. He felt compelled to concede that the "completely internal commerce of a State" was not within federal power, yet he defined such commerce as that which did not "extend to or affect other States"—certainly not the same thing as saying it is commerce which does not cross a state line.

Marshall's subtle distinctions, however, were soon lost in hard and fast dichotomies. Justice McLean, who thought he was expounding Marshall's views, said in *The Passenger Cases* (1849): "All commercial action within the limits of a State, and which does not extend to any other State or foreign country, is exclusively under state regulation." Chief Justice Taney, whose goals were definitely not those of Marshall, claimed to be stating Marshall doctrine in *The License Cases* (1847) when he spoke of "internal or domestic commerce, which belongs to the States, and over which congress can exercise no control."

### INTERSTATE AND INTRASTATE COMMERCE

So it came about that Marshall, who had a unitary conception of commerce, by his decision in *Gibbons* v. *Ogden* laid the basis for splitting commerce among the states into two parts, designated by two terms which he never used. The power of Congress to regulate commerce among the states was assumed to be correctly stated as the power to regulate interstate commerce.

INTERSTATE COMMERCE     Under this approach, the crossing of a state line is the basic justification for federal regulatory authority. Whatever moves across state lines—goods, commodities, persons, intelligence, or whatever—comes within the ambit of congressional power. The breadth of definition which Marshall claimed for "commerce" has been maintained and even expanded. For he qualified "intercourse" by the preceding word "commercial," whereas subsequent decisions of the Supreme Court have made it clear that there need be no actual commercial character to an interstate movement to bring it under the commerce power. The people who cross an interstate bridge "may be as truly said to be engaged in commerce as if they were shipping cargoes of merchandise from New York to Liverpool." [2] In *Caminetti* v. *United States* (1917), the Mann Act, which is based on the commerce power, was held to apply to the transportation of a woman across state lines for immoral purposes, even though no commercial motive was present.

Of course the major transportation industries offer the classic type of interstate commerce. Congressional power over navigation was settled by the *Gibbons* case, and there was no constitutional doubt as to the power of Congress to pass the Interstate Commerce Act for the regulation of the railroads in 1887. In the *Pipe Line Cases* (1914), the Court upheld federal

[2] *Covington Bridge Co.* v. *Kentucky* (1894).

authority to regulate the transportation of oil and gas in pipelines from state to state, even though the pipelines were not common carriers and transported only the oil and gas of their owners. Regulation of the trucking industry was asserted by the Motor Carrier Act of 1935. Interstate movement of electric power came under federal control in the Federal Power Act of 1935, and the Natural Gas Act of 1938 provided for much the same powers in that field.

What is sent across state lines need not be tangible. Federal control over the interstate transmission of intelligence by telegraph was asserted by the Court in 1878, when it said that the powers of the commerce clause "are not confined to the instrumentalities of commerce, or the postal service known or in use when the Constitution was adopted, but they keep pace with the progress of the country, and adapt themselves to the new developments of time and circumstances."[3] Federal control over radio transmission, provided for in 1927 by the Federal Radio Act, was upheld in 1933, Chief Justice Hughes saying: "No state lines divide the radio waves, and national regulation is not only appropriate but essential to the efficient use of radio facilities."[4]

An activity which does not itself involve movement across state lines may be regarded as interstate commerce because of the use of the instrumentalities of such commerce. The classic case is that of the correspondence schools which are interstate commerce because of their necessitous reliance on the United States mails.[5] Regulation of public utility holding companies under the federal act of 1935 was upheld on the ground that their subsidiaries usually operate on an interstate basis, and that the services which the holding company performs for its subsidiaries involve continuous and extensive use of the mails and other facilities of interstate commerce.[6]

In all these decisions the Court has emphasized the unity of interstate transportation. An interstate journey cannot be broken up into the component parts which occur within each state. As Marshall said, "Commerce among the States cannot stop at the external boundary line of each State." In *Wabash Railway Co.* v. *Illinois* (1886) the Court struck down a state claim to regulate the charges for that portion of an interstate journey which took place within the state. "Whatever may be the instrumentalities by which this transportation [from New York to Illinois] is effected, it is but one voyage."

INTRASTATE COMMERCE    All this emphasis upon the crossing of a state line as the basic test for commerce logically led to the conclusion that what did not cross a state line was not interstate commerce. Marshall himself appeared to lay the foundation for this position by one of the many dicta

---

[3] *Pensacola Telegraph Co.* v. *Western Union Telegraph Co.* (1878).
[4] *Federal Radio Commission* v. *Nelson Bros.* (1933).
[5] *International Text Book Co.* v. *Pigg* (1910).
[6] *Electric Bond & Share Co.* v. *S.E.C.* (1938).

propounded in *Gibbons* v. *Ogden.* Speaking of the right of states to enforce inspection laws for the purpose of improving "the quality of articles produced by the labor of a country," he said that these laws "act upon the subject before it becomes an article . . . of commerce among the States." Thus he appeared to divide into two separate, self-contained processes the production of articles and their transportation in commerce. This artificial distinction, which seems inconsistent with his basic conception of the unity of commerce, was developed by later justices into a limitation of tremendous importance on the completeness of the federal commerce power. In application it worked two ways. First, it helped to *uphold state* regulation or taxation as applied to commercial interests which were claiming immunity from state control on the ground that interstate commerce was involved. Second, it helped to *defeat federal* regulation by limiting congressional power; and this second effect became more significant after 1890 as Congress began to use its regulatory powers for the first time in a significant fashion.

An illustration of the first category is supplied by *Kidd* v. *Pearson* (1888), involving a state prohibition law which forbade the manufacture of alcohol for sale outside the state. This law was upheld on the ground of the clear distinction between manufacturing and commerce. Manufacture is the fashioning of raw materials into a changed form for use. Commerce is buying and selling and the transportation incidental thereto. If the regulation of commerce included regulation of all manufactures that were intended to be the subject of commercial transactions, the Court said, then "Congress would be invested, to the exclusion of the States, with the power to regulate . . . every branch of human industry."

As an example of the second category, consider what the production-distribution distinction did to the enforcement of the Sherman Act. In *United States* v. *E. C. Knight Co.* (1895) this statute was held inapplicable to a sugar monopoly which had acquired nearly complete control of the manufacture of refined sugar within the United States. The reason was simple. "Commerce succeeds to manufacture, and is not a part of it." Commerce among the states does not begin until goods "commence their final movement from the State of their origin to that of their destination." The monopolistic acts here charged "related exclusively to the acquisition of the Philadelphia refineries and the business of sugar refining in Pennsylvania, and bore no direct relation to commerce between the States." In other decisions the Court applied the same principle to mining,[7] lumbering,[8] fishing, farming, oil production,[9] and generation of hydroelectric power.[10]

[7] *United Mine Workers* v. *Coronado Coal Co.* (1922); *Oliver Iron Mining Co.* v. *Lord* (1923).
[8] *Coe* v. *Errol* (1886).
[9] *Champlin Refining Co.* v. *Corporation Commission* (1932).
[10] *Utah Power and Light* v. *Pfost* (1932).

THE BEGINNING OF INTERSTATE COMMERCE     This separation between production and distribution has enormous practical consequences. If the Congress cannot regulate production, and the states cannot burden interstate distribution, it becomes vital to determine just where one process stops and the other begins. Suppose logs are cut and hauled to the banks of an interstate stream, where they are held until high water permits them to be floated downstream. They may be stranded temporarily by low water, and may pass through several states before they reach their destination. Just where did interstate transportation begin, and was this status lost by stops in transit? The same problem is encountered with goods placed on railroads or trucks for interstate transit, which may be temporarily interrupted en route.

Situations of just this character have led to an enormous amount of litigation. In general, the rule is that interstate commerce begins when goods are delivered to a common carrier for transit outside the state, or when they actually start a continuous journey between two states. The local movement of goods preparatory to their delivery to a common carrier is not part of the interstate journey. In 1947 the government argued that Chicago taxicabs were engaged in interstate commerce because of the important role they play in taking rail passengers from one station to another, but the Supreme Court was not convinced. "From the standpoints of time and continuity, the taxicab trip may be quite distinct and separate from the interstate journey. To the taxicab driver, it is just another local fare." [11]

After the continuous interstate journey has begun, temporary interruptions in the course of transportation do not legally break the continuity of the journey. Logs temporarily halted by low water in a stream were held in *Coe* v. *Errol* (1886) to retain their interstate character and so to be immune from local taxation by the state in which they were stranded. An interstate shipment of goods in a freight car may be sidetracked, transferred to another car, or even wrecked without losing its interstate exemption from local regulation or taxation.

THE ENDING OF INTERSTATE COMMERCE     Determination of the point at which an interstate journey ends and state authority resumes is an equally important problem. Marshall dealt with such an issue in the second commerce case which his Court decided, *Brown* v. *Maryland* (1827). In this case the goods involved were imports from abroad into Maryland, and that state sought to levy a license tax on the importer. Article I, section 10, forbids the states to lay duties on imports, and Marshall, searching for a practical rule on the subject, held that imported goods retained their character as imports as long as they remained unsold in the original package. The "original package" doctrine has continued to be used as a judicial rule of thumb. So far as interstate (as opposed to foreign) commerce is concerned, its effect is to forbid states to exert their police power on goods

[11] *United States* v. *Yellow Cab Co.* (1947).

shipped in from other states while remaining in the original packages, unsold, unbroken, and unused. Stated positively, this doctrine protects the first sale of goods within the state while in the original package.

Since the original package has this important protective character, it is not surprising that numerous controversies have arisen as to just what the original package is in different circumstances. A Tennessee statute of 1897 forbade the sale of cigarettes in the state. An effort was made to evade the law by importing cigarettes into the state in the form of small cardboard boxes containing ten cigarettes each, which were transported loose in baskets. The purpose was to establish the small boxes as the original packages and thus to prevent the state from interfering with the first sale. The Supreme Court, however, held that the form, size, and weight of an original package must be adopted in good faith, and not for the purpose of evading state law. If there was an original package here, presumably it was the basket.[12] Later a futile attempt was made to frustrate an Iowa law taxing cigarette dealers by shipping cigarettes into the state without even a basket, the small boxes apparently being "shoveled into and out of a car, and delivered to plaintiffs in that condition." [13]

A different kind of artifice with respect to the terminal point of interstate commerce was attempted in *Walling* v. *Jacksonville Paper Co.* (1943). This company had seven branch houses which received their stock from outside the state, but sold and delivered only within the state. The question was whether employees in these branch houses were covered by the Fair Labor Standards Act. They seemed to be engaged in interstate commerce, for most of the paper products they handled were ordered specifically for local merchants and printed up with their names in out-of-state plants. However, the company sought to break the interstate chain by trucking all incoming orders into the branch warehouse, and then loading them back on trucks for the local delivery. The Supreme Court refused to permit this "ritual of placing goods in a warehouse" to defeat the congressional purpose of controlling the entire interstate movement. "There is a practical continuity of movement of the goods until they reach the customers for whom they are intended. That is sufficient. Any other test would allow formalities to conceal the continuous nature of the interstate transit which constitutes commerce."

### THE POWER TO "REGULATE"

Although the federal power to regulate commerce is thus not a "complete" power, wherever the power does exist it is "plenary." Consequently the breadth of regulatory power which Congress may exercise within its recognized scope of authority has seldom been successfully questioned. Efforts to read restrictive interpretations into the word "regulate" have almost

[12] *Austin* v. *Tennessee* (1900).
[13] *Cook* v. *Marshall County* (1905).

uniformly failed. Regulation, the Court has said, means not only protection and promotion, but also restriction and even prohibition.

The railroad field was the first in which Congress really tested the extent of its regulatory authority. The Interstate Commerce Act of 1887, setting up a regulatory commission with rather limited powers, was upheld by the Court in *Interstate Commerce Commission v. Brimson* (1894) as a necessary and proper means of enforcing congressional authority. In 1916 Congress took what then seemed the rather extreme step of providing in the Adamson Act for the eight-hour day and specifying wage and overtime rates on the railroads. The Court by a bare five to four margin approved the statute in *Wilson v. New* (1917) as necessary to prevent the interruption of commerce by a nationwide strike. The even more drastic plan for recapture of excess rail earnings in the Transportation Act of 1920 was upheld by the Court in 1924.[14]

THE COMMERCE POWER AS A NATIONAL POLICE POWER   A severe test of congressional power over commerce was presented when Congress began, around the turn of the century, to explore the possibilities of using the commerce clause as a kind of national police power. An act of 1895 made it unlawful to transport lottery tickets into a state from another state or a foreign country. An earlier statute excluding lottery tickets from the mails had been upheld by the Court,[15] but the new law raised much more difficult questions, and the Court had the issues argued before it three times. Finally, by a five to four vote the law was upheld in *Champion v. Ames* (1903). Harlan's opinion overruled the objection that regulation did not extend to complete prohibition, and accepted the prevention of harm to the public morals as an appropriate goal of the commerce power, without any showing of effect on the safety or efficiency of commerce. The states were free to take action against intrastate traffic in lottery tickets. Why then could not Congress provide that "commerce shall not be polluted by the carrying of lottery tickets from one State to another?"

The Court was clearly aware that if Congress could not prohibit the interstate traffic in lottery tickets, a no-man's-land would be created where neither federal nor state regulation could enter. It was also cognizant of the argument that if lottery tickets could be excluded from commerce by Congress, then all commerce might be subject to prohibition at the "arbitrary whim" of Congress. Harlan replied that the Court would wait until such cases arose, but he did note that the power of Congress, "although plenary, cannot be deemed arbitrary, since it is subject to such limitations or restrictions as are prescribed by the Constitution."

On the authority of *The Lottery Case*, the Supreme Court upheld the Food and Drug Act of 1906, which prohibited the introduction of impure foods

[14] *Dayton–Goose Creek R. Co. v. United States* (1924).
[15] *In re Rapier* (1892).

and drugs into the states by means of interstate commerce.[16] Since the statute declared adulterated foods "outlaws" of commerce, they could be seized wherever found, so long as they were in the original unbroken packages; for the purpose of the act was not merely to prevent interstate movement of such articles, but the use of them. The Mann Act (1910), forbidding the transportation of women in interstate commerce for the purpose of prostitution and debauchery, was upheld in 1913 on the basis of these precedents.[17] "Of course it will be said that women are not articles of merchandise," the Court wrote, "but this does not affect the analogy of the cases." The applicable principle was the simple one "that Congress has power over transportation 'among the several States'; that the power is complete in itself, and that Congress, as an incident to it, may adopt not only means necessary but convenient to its exercise, and the means may have the quality of police regulations."

THE CHILD LABOR DECISION     This technique of closing the channels of interstate commerce, which had been uniformly successful in meeting constitutional tests, was then applied by Congress in the Federal Child Labor Act of 1916. This statute prohibited transportation in interstate commerce of the products of factories, mines, or quarries where children under the age of fourteen had been permitted to work more than eight hours a day or six days a week or at nights. In the historic case of *Hammer* v. *Dagenhart* (1918) the statute was declared unconstitutional by a five to four vote.

The power to regulate commerce, said Justice Day for the majority, is the power "to control the means by which commerce is carried on," not the right "to forbid commerce from moving." To establish the correctness of this view the Court, of course, had somehow to deal with the contrary precedents just reviewed. Instead of overruling them, Day labored to explain that lottery tickets, impure food, and prostitutes are harmful in and of themselves, whereas goods produced by child labor "are of themselves harmless." In the case of the harmful categories, their regulation in interstate commerce could only be satisfactorily achieved by banning their movement altogether. But with harmless commodities, prohibition of their interstate movement by Congress was unconstitutional. What this argument amounts to is that Congress can prevent harm to consumers after the interstate journey ends, but cannot prevent harm to producers before the journey begins. Of course this is the purest sophistry, and it was fittingly answered by Justice Holmes in his dissent.

> The notion that prohibition is any less prohibition when applied to things now thought evil I do not understand. But if there is any matter upon which civilized countries have agreed . . . it is the evil of premature and excessive child labor. I should have thought that if we were

[16] *Hipolite Egg Co.* v. *United States* (1911).
[17] *Hoke* v. *United States* (1913).

to introduce our own moral conceptions where in my opinion they do not belong, this was preëminently a case for upholding the exercise of all its powers by the United States.

The more reputable part of Day's argument rested on the well-established doctrine that manufacturing, mining, and the like are intrastate commerce, subject to local regulation. In this statute Congress professed to observe the distinction between production and distribution and in form regulated only the latter. But in fact, Day said, the aim was "to standardize the ages at which children may be employed in mining and manufacturing within the States." Congress cannot use *its* admitted powers to oust the states from the exercise of *their* admitted powers. "The grant of authority over a purely federal matter was not intended to destroy the local power always existing and carefully reserved to the States in the Tenth Amendment to the Constitution."

This is a classic statement of the doctrine of dual federalism—that the powers delegated to the national government are nevertheless limited by the reserved powers of the states. When this view had been pressed upon the Court in *The Lottery Case,* Harlan had rejected it in positive fashion: "If it be said that the act of 1895 is inconsistent with the Tenth Amendment, reserving to the States respectively or to the people the powers not delegated to the United States, the answer is that the power to regulate commerce among the States has been expressly delegated to Congress."

Holmes subjected Day's logic to more extensive analysis in his *Hammer* dissent. Certainly what Congress had done—forbidding the transportation of goods in interstate commerce—was within the power expressly given to Congress by the commerce clause, if considered only as to its immediate effects. If it was to be declared unconstitutional, it would have to be because of its possible reaction upon the conduct of the states—in this case, because of its effect upon their freedom to permit child labor. "But if an act is within the powers specifically conferred upon Congress, it seems to me that it is not made any less constitutional because of the indirect effects that it may have, however obvious it may be that it will have those effects, and that we are not at liberty upon such grounds to hold it void."

Holmes went on to point out how often the exercise of a federal power limited state freedom. For example, federal taxation of state bank notes had driven them out of circulation. But his main emphasis was upon the admitted right of Congress to regulate interstate commerce. When states seek to send their products across a state line, "they are no longer within their rights. If there were no Constitution and no Congress their power to cross the line would depend upon their neighbors. Under the Constitution such commerce belongs not to the States but to Congress to regulate."

Obviously Holmes was right, but the majority view in *Hammer* v. *Dagenhart* remained at least in theory the official interpretation until the decision was overruled in 1941. Influential as it may have been, it was never anything

but an exception to the general rule, which as stated by Harlan in *The Lottery Case* is that the power to regulate commerce "is plenary, is complete in itself, and is subject to no limitations except such as may be found in the Constitution." It was the general rule, not the exception, which the Court followed in upholding the power of Congress over interstate commerce in stolen motor vehicles in 1925 [18] and kidnapped persons in 1936.[19]

## THE CONCEPT OF "EFFECT UPON COMMERCE"

In spite of this emphasis on transportation across state lines as the basis for congressional power over commerce, there were other doctrinal developments on the Supreme Court which laid the basis for the twentieth-century growth of the commerce power. This expansion came about primarily by application of the concept of "effect upon commerce." Under this doctrine, Congress could regulate not only commercial activities where state lines were crossed, but also such activities as *affected* interstate commerce.

Like all else in this field, the effect doctrine traces back to Marshall's opinion in the *Gibbons* case. There he said, in spelling out the area of commercial regulation remaining in the hands of the states under the commerce clause, that "it is not intended to say that these words comprehend that commerce . . . which does not extend to or affect other States." When the double negative is eliminated, this is an affirmation that Congress *can* regulate commerce within a state which affects other states.

By 1900 it was clear that congressional power over commerce would have to be freed from its exclusively "interstate" connotations if substantial expansion of congressional power over the industrial and commercial life of the country was to occur. Marshall's effect doctrine was available for this purpose. Of course, "effect" is a vague word; it may be useful if we endeavor to classify various types of situations where activities of a geographically intrastate character have such obvious impact on commerce among the states as to make application of the effect doctrine reasonable.

EFFECT THROUGH INTERMINGLING    First we may note that it is possible for intrastate commerce to be physically so intermingled or intertwined with interstate commerce that the two cannot practically be divided for regulatory purposes; under these circumstances interstate commerce can simply not be regulated without also regulating intrastate commerce. A good example of this situation is supplied by *Southern Railway Co.* v. *United States* (1911). The case arose when the company hauled on its interstate railroad in *intrastate* traffic three cars not equipped with safety couplers as required by the federal Safety Appliance Act. The statute specifically applied, not only to equipment used in interstate commerce, but also to cars "used in

[18] *Brooks* v. *United States* (1925).
[19] *Gooch* v. *United States* (1936).

connection therewith." The Court approved this assertion of federal control over railroad cars which did not themselves cross state lines, saying: "This is so, not because Congress possesses any power to regulate intrastate commerce as such, but because its power to regulate interstate commerce is plenary and consequently may be exerted to secure the safety of the persons and property transported therein and of those who are employed in such transportation, no matter what may be the source of the dangers which threaten it."

"STREAM OF COMMERCE"    A second situation is the so-called "stream of commerce." The case commonly regarded as the fount of this notion was *Swift & Co.* v. *United States* (1905). Chicago stockyards firms had been charged with conspiracy in restraint of trade, and they objected that the purchase and sale of cattle in Chicago was not commerce among the states. Justice Holmes replied for the Court:

> Commerce among the States is not a technical legal conception, but a practical one, drawn from the course of business. When cattle are sent for sale from a place in one State, with the expectation that they will end their transit, after purchase, in another, and when in effect they do so, with only the interruption necessary to find a purchaser at the stock yards, and when this is a typical, constantly recurring course, the current thus existing is a current of commerce among the States, and the purchase of the cattle is a part and incident of such commerce.

A subsequent decision to the same effect in a comparable situation was that of Chief Justice Taft in *Stafford* v. *Wallace* (1922). Here the constitutionality of the Packers and Stockyards Act of 1921 was at issue, as applied to commission men and livestock dealers in the Chicago stockyards. In upholding the act, Taft spoke of "the various stockyards of the country as great national public utilities to promote the flow of commerce from the ranges and farms of the West to the consumers in the East." In *Chicago Board of Trade* v. *Olsen* (1923) the same rationale was employed to uphold the federal Grain Futures Act, regulating boards of trade and members thereof engaged in sale of "futures" in grain. It was argued that futures sales contracts are paper transactions resulting in no actual interstate transfer of grain, but the Court, with Taft again writing the opinion, held that futures sales closely *affected* the price of cash sales and hence were of great significance to the interstate grain trade.

THE SHREVEPORT DOCTRINE    Still a third type of situation in which the effect of local commerce on interstate commerce has achieved constitutional significance is illustrated by the famous *Shreveport Rate Case* (1914). The situation was that Shreveport, Louisiana, competed with Houston and Dallas, Texas, for the trade of the intervening Texas territory. Interstate rates from Shreveport to Texas cities, regulated by the ICC, were higher than the

intrastate rates fixed by the Texas Railroad Commission from Dallas and Houston to the same cities for comparable distances. Thus Shreveport was placed at a competitive disadvantage because of the interstate character of its commerce into Texas. The ICC agreed that it could not permit interstate traffic to be thus burdened, and issued an order requiring Texas *intrastate* rates from Dallas and Houston to be equalized with the interstate rates from Shreveport into Texas.

Justice Hughes wrote a strong opinion for the Court upholding federal power to exercise such control over intrastate commerce. The commerce power of Congress is "complete and paramount. . . . It is of the essence of this power that, where it exists, it dominates. Interstate trade was not left to be destroyed or impeded by the rivalries of local governments." Congress was given power by the commerce clause to see "that the agencies of interstate commerce shall not be used in such manner as to cripple, retard or destroy it." Consequently,

> Wherever the interstate and intrastate transactions of carriers are so related that the government of the one involves the control of the other, it is Congress, and not the State, that is entitled to prescribe the final and dominant rule, for otherwise Congress would be denied the exercise of its constitutional authority and the State, and not the Nation, would be supreme within the national field.

DIRECT VERSUS INDIRECT EFFECT    These various rationalizations of federal control on the basis of intermingling, stream of commerce, or effect on commerce, might appear to open the way for complete exclusion of state regulation, and an achievement of that completeness of the federal commerce power for which Webster had argued in the *Gibbons* case. The Supreme Court, however, did not mean to go so far as that, and consequently there runs through all these cases an insistence by the Court that it is holding back something from the completeness of federal power. It is not *any* effect on commerce, however minimal, which justifies congressional control over intrastate activities. The Court tried a variety of semantic devices in the 1920s and 1930s in an attempt to indicate what kinds of effects justify federal control and what do not—the relation must be "close," the effect must be "substantial"—but the test most often suggested as a standard for judicial review of congressional action was "directness" as opposed to "indirectness" of effect.

The Court first began to talk in terms of direct and indirect effects in the early antitrust cases. Thus in the *Sugar Trust Case* [20] the Court held that the chance "trade or commerce might be indirectly affected" by a sugar company merger was not enough to entitle the government to a Sherman Act decree. At this point the Court's dogma was that sale of a product was incidental to its production, and could never affect commerce other than incidentally

[20] *United States* v. *E. C. Knight Co.* (1895).

or indirectly. But as time went on the Court became less sure on this point. In Holmes's opinion in the *Swift* case, sales became an element in an interstate stream, an integral part of an entire interstate movement. Chief Justice Taft in the *Chicago Board of Trade* case went even further in defining the kind of effect which justified federal control as "whatever amounts to more or less constant practice, and threatens to obstruct or unduly to burden the freedom of interstate commerce."

Clearly the direct-indirect test was a slippery one, with which different courts could get different results. Where Congress or its agent, the ICC, had clearly claimed an area of intrastate commerce under the effect doctrine, the Court tended to acquiesce. As Taft said in the *Chicago Board of Trade* case, "It is primarily for Congress to consider and decide the fact of the danger [to commerce] and meet it. This court will certainly not substitute its judgment for that of Congress in such a matter unless the relation of the subject to interstate commerce and its effect upon it are clearly non-existent."

But where the statute was a general one, like the Sherman Act, then the Court had to satisfy itself, as an original proposition, that the facts of the particular case demonstrated not merely the *existence*, but the *directness* of the effects upon commerce. In the three decades following the *Swift* decision in 1905, a predominantly conservative Court did find such directness in most of the important controversies, thus expanding the federal commerce power. The result of this expansion was not only to justify federal regulation of business, but also to permit the Court to strike at labor unions and their practices under federal law.

Early applications of the Sherman Act against labor organizations, as in the *Danbury Hatters Case*,[21] led Congress to attempt to exempt labor unions from its scope by section 6 of the Clayton Act (1914). However, the Court substantially interpreted this provision out of existence, and found directness of effect on commerce in such intrastate labor actions as a violent strike by the United Mine Workers against a coal company [22] and the *Bedford Cut Stone* case of 1927.[23] In the latter proceeding the Court enjoined a secondary boycott by the national stonecutters' union, whose members had been refusing to handle stone cut by the leading nonunion Indiana limestone quarry. The product against which the strikes were called had come to rest in various states, and had ceased to be a subject of interstate commerce. Interference for a local object would normally not be a burden on commerce, the Court admitted. But here the interference was held to have as a primary aim restraint of the interstate sale and shipment of stone. The conduct of the union directly and substantially curtailed the national flow in commerce of a large proportion of the building limestone production of the entire country, and so was a combination in restraint of trade under the Sherman Act.

[21] *Loewe* v. *Lawlor* (1908).
[22] *Coronado Coal Co.* v. *United Mine Workers* (1925).
[23] *Bedford Cut Stone Co.* v. *Journeymen Stone Cutters' Assn.* (1927).

Again, in 1934 racketeering labor union practices of poultry handlers in the New York area were held to amount to an antitrust conspiracy burdening the free movement of live poultry in commerce. The Court said it was immaterial whether the interstate commerce in question had terminated before the union practices occurred, for "intrastate acts will be enjoined whenever necessary or appropriate for the protection of interstate commerce." [24]

This was the status of the law and the Court's holdings when the National Recovery Administration legislation came up for judicial review in the famous case of *Schechter Poultry Corp.* v. *United States* (1935). The NRA was a major reliance of the New Deal in its attack on the Depression. Under the statute, codes of fair practice had been adopted for most of the industries of the country, large and small, fixing minimum wages and maximum hours, and regulating unfair or destructive competitive practices. President Roosevelt's high hopes for the NRA as a kind of partnership between capital and labor had not been fulfilled, and it was near collapse by the time the Supreme Court mercifully administered the *coup de grâce* in 1935. Our concern, however, is with the constitutional theory of the decision.

The statute's assertion of federal control was over transactions "in or affecting interstate or foreign commerce." The Schechter Corporation was a Brooklyn slaughterhouse operator which purchased live poultry in New York or Philadelphia, trucked it to the Brooklyn plant, slaughtered it, and then sold it to local retail dealers in Brooklyn. The live poultry code did not concern transportation or the practices of commission men. It dealt with hours and wages in the slaughterhouse and the company's local selling practices. Chief Justice Hughes for a unanimous Court held that these activities of the Schechter Corporation were not "transactions in interstate commerce."

Consequently the Schechter Corporation could be brought under the NRA only by one of the several "effect" notions. Would the "stream of commerce" doctrine apply? The Court said no.

> The mere fact that there may be a constant flow of commodities into a State does not mean that the flow continues after the property has arrived and has become commingled with the mass of property within the State and is there held solely for local disposition and use. So far as the poultry here in question is concerned, the flow in interstate commerce had ceased. The poultry had come to a permanent rest within the State.

Was there a direct effect upon interstate commerce which would justify the regulation? Again the answer was negative. Any effects present were indirect. The distinction between direct and indirect effects, Hughes said, "is clear in principle," but he impliedly admitted that he could not state it by falling back on illustration from individual cases the Court had decided

[24] *Local 167 I.B.T.* v. *United States* (1934).

in the past. What he was clear about, however, was that "the distinction between direct and indirect effects of intrastate transactions upon interstate commerce must be recognized as a fundamental one, essential to the maintenance of our constitutional system. Otherwise . . . there would be virtually no limit to the federal power and for all practical purposes we should have a completely centralized government." And he added, after mentioning the government's contention that such centralized powers were necessary to meet the economic emergency in the country: "It is not the province of the Court to consider the economic advantages or disadvantages of such a centralized system. It is sufficient to say that the Federal Constitution does not provide for it."

One year later a sharply divided Court did a reprise on this theme in *Carter* v. *Carter Coal Co.* (1936), which invalidated the coal industry codes set up under the Bituminous Coal Conservation Act of 1935. This time it fell to Justice Sutherland to write the opinion, and he dared to do what Hughes had been unwilling to attempt in the *Schechter* case, namely, to define the difference between a direct and an indirect effect on commerce.

> The word "direct" implies that the activity or condition invoked or blamed shall operate proximately—not mediately, remotely, or collaterally—to produce the effect. It connotes the absence of an efficient intervening agency or condition. And the extent of the effect bears no logical relation to its character. The distinction between a direct and an indirect effect turns, not upon the magnitude of either the cause or the effect, but entirely upon the manner in which the effect has been brought about. If the production by one man of a single ton of coal intended for interstate sale and shipment . . . affects interstate commerce indirectly, the effect does not become direct by multiplying the tonnage, or increasing the number of men employed, or adding to the expense or complexities of the business, or by all combined.

Sutherland then went on to underline the application of these principles to the current problem:

> Much stress is put upon the evils which come from the struggle between employers and employees over the matter of wages, working conditions, the right of collective bargaining, etc., and the resulting strikes, curtailment and irregularity of production and effect on prices; and it is insisted that interstate commerce is *greatly* affected thereby. But . . . the conclusive answer is that the evils are all local evils over which the federal government has no legislative control. The relation of employer and employee is a local relation. . . . And the controversies and evils, which it is the object of the act to regulate and minimize, are local controversies and evils affecting local work undertaken to accomplish that local result. Such effect as they may have upon commerce, however extensive it may be, is secondary and indirect. An increase in the greatness of the effect adds to its importance. It does not alter its character.

This opinion was the dead end of the directness-indirectness dogma. It illuminated as by a flash of lightning a judicial dream world of logical abstractions, where there was no difference between one ton of coal and a million tons of coal, where considerations of degree were not cognizable by the law. Production was local. A production crisis in every part of the country simultaneously could never add up to a national problem with which Congress could deal; it could never have anything other than an indirect effect on commerce.

Sutherland sought to demonstrate that this fantastic result was required by the precedents.[25] But the effect doctrine had been proved to be flexible enough to accommodate earlier legislative efforts to deal with intrastate commercial activities. "A survey of the cases," said Cardozo, dissenting along with Brandeis and Stone, "shows that the words [direct and indirect] have been interpreted with suppleness of adaptation and flexibility of meaning." He was thinking of Holmes in the *Swift* case, Hughes in the *Shreveport* holding, Taft in *Chicago Board of Trade* v. *Olsen.* These were pragmatic and realistic appraisals of the federal commerce power which expose Sutherland's elaborate conceptualism in the *Carter* case as absurdly irrelevant to the issues before the country. The commerce power, Cardozo summed up, should be "as broad as the need that evokes it."

### THE COMMERCE POWER AFTER 1937

Neither the Court nor the country could live with the doctrine of *Carter* v. *Carter Coal Co.* Within a year the standard stated by Justice Cardozo in dissent there became the majority view of the Court. The vehicle for this return to reality was *National Labor Relations Board* v. *Jones & Laughlin Corp.* (1937), involving the constitutionality of the National Labor Relations Act. This case was decided some two months after President Roosevelt had sent his Court-packing plan to Congress, while the Court was still the center of violent political controversy. The decision, which saw Chief Justice Hughes and Justice Roberts joining the liberal trio of Brandeis, Cardozo, and Stone in upholding the statute, was widely regarded as the Court's contribution toward restoration of peaceful relations by acceptance of the New Deal.

THE WAGNER ACT    The National Labor Relations Act, popularly known as the Wagner Act, aimed to protect the right of employees to organize into

[25] Also, as Robert A. Horn has pointed out, Sutherland struck down the miners' wages provision which was not even in effect; he then turned around and, despite the severability provision, held the regulation of prices of coal sold in interstate commerce (admittedly within congressional power) void because the costs of local production of coal had so inevitable an *effect* on the prices in interstate commerce that Congress, despite what it said, could not have meant to deal only with the latter.

labor unions and to bargain collectively with their employers. The statute defined certain types of interference with these rights as unfair labor practices, and set up the NLRB with authority to compel employers to cease and desist from such practices. There was widespread employer resistance to the statute, and obviously it could not be applied to production industries if the *Schechter* and *Carter* view of the commerce clause was correct.

The key jurisdictional provision in the Wagner Act was that empowering the NLRB to forbid any person from engaging in any unfair labor practice "affecting commerce." The Jones & Laughlin Company was one of the nation's major steel producers, with integrated operations in several states. The particular unfair labor acts charged in this case took place in one of the company's Pennsylvania plants, and the constitutional question was whether these practices had a sufficient effect upon commerce to justify congressional control.

Chief Justice Hughes, writing the Court's opinion and holding that they did, needed to construct no new doctrine. Hughes was merely repeating well-established rules when he said:

> Although activities may be intrastate in character when separately considered, if they have such a close and substantial relation to interstate commerce that their control is essential or appropriate to protect that commerce from burdens and obstructions, Congress cannot be denied the power to exercise that control.

So the familiar question returned—did the labor relations of this steel producer have a direct or an indirect effect upon commerce? Hughes gave a practical, not a theoretical, answer.

> In view of respondent's far-flung activities, it is idle to say that the effect would be indirect or remote. It is obvious that it would be immediate and might be catastrophic. We are asked to shut our eyes to the plainest facts of our national life and to deal with the question of direct and indirect effects in an intellectual vacuum.

This, of course, was precisely what Sutherland had done in the *Carter* opinion. Hughes continued:

> When industries organize themselves on a national scale, making their relation to interstate commerce the dominant factor in their activities, how can it be maintained that their industrial labor relations constitute a forbidden field into which Congress may not enter when it is necessary to protect interstate commerce from the paralyzing consequences of industrial war?

In restoring what he called a "practical conception" of interstate commerce, Hughes did not overrule the *Schechter* and *Carter* decisions, but he said as little about them as was feasible. He actually cited the *Schechter* case for some of its positive assertions about congressional power, and then inserted a general saving clause which warned that federal control over

intrastate commerce "must be considered in the light of our dual system of government and may not be extended so as to embrace effects upon interstate commerce so indirect or remote that to embrace them, in view of our complex society, would effectually obliterate the distinction between what is national and what is local, and create a completely centralized government."

The stress which the Hughes opinion placed on the importance and nationally integrated character of the steel industry certainly suggested that these factors were important in justifying the Court's decision. But on the same day the Court also upheld the application of the Wagner Act to a trailer manufacturer [26] and to a small manufacturer of men's clothing [27] on the authority of the *Jones & Laughlin* decision. Apparently a business did not after all need to be one whose interruption by strike would be "catastrophic" in order to justify coverage by the statute.

For a couple of years after the *Jones & Laughlin* decision, there was a flurry of cases searching for loopholes in its doctrine, but none was found.[28] After 1939 cases testing the constitutional coverage of the NLRB virtually disappeared from the Supreme Court's docket. The lines of Wagner Act jurisdiction had been drawn so broadly that there was no further necessity for the Court to take on such problems. The Board did continue to run into an occasional unfavorable decision in the federal courts of appeals, but it appeared to be almost literally true that in no labor relations case over which the NLRB was willing to claim jurisdiction as affecting commerce would the Supreme Court deny the validity of the claim. Indeed, the NLRB eventually undertook voluntarily to limit its own jurisdiction, setting up categories of cases which it could have legitimately handled but which it announced it would not accept.

THE FAIR LABOR STANDARDS ACT    As the Wagner Act furnished the occasion for bringing down the *Schechter* and *Carter* decisions, it fell to another labor statute, the Fair Labor Standards Act, to demolish *Hammer v. Dagenhart*. This 1938 statute, also called the Wages and Hours Act, was the last major piece of New Deal legislation adopted. The formula it employed was similar to that of the 1916 federal child labor law, Congress making it unlawful to ship in interstate commerce goods produced in violation of the wage and hour standards set by the act. The coverage of the act was not as broad as that of the Wagner Act. Where that statute had applied to unfair labor practices "affecting commerce," the Fair Labor Standards Act was made applicable to employees "engaged in commerce or in the production of goods

[26] *NLRB v. Fruehauf Trailer Co.* (1937).
[27] *NLRB v. Friedman–Harry Marks Clothing Co.* (1937).
[28] See *Consolidated Edison Co. v. NLRB* (1938); *Santa Cruz Fruit Packing Co. v. NLRB* (1938); *NLRB v. Fainblatt* (1939). Later cases upholding a broad interpretation of NLRB authority are *Polish Alliance v. Labor Board* (1944), *Guss v. Utah Labor Board* (1957), and *NLRB v. Reliance Fuel Oil Corp.* (1963).

for commerce." The Fair Labor Standards Act also differed from the Wagner Act in that no administrative tribunal like the NLRB was set up to enforce it. Enforcement lay in the regular courts, either through suits brought by individual complainants or by the government administrator of the act.

The basic decision upholding the constitutionality of this act was *United States v. Darby,* announced unanimously by the Court in 1941. As Justice Stone said, there would have been little need for any extended discussion of the constitutional issue, since Congress was asserting its clear power over the movement of goods across state lines, if it had not been for *Hammer v. Dagenhart.* Stone's attention was consequently devoted primarily to disposing of that derelict on the stream of the law.

> In that case it was held by a bare majority of the Court over the powerful and now classic dissent of Mr. Justice Holmes . . . that Congress was without power to exclude the products of child labor from interstate commerce. The reasoning and conclusion of the Court's opinion there cannot be reconciled with the conclusion which we have reached, that the power of Congress under the Commerce Clause is plenary to exclude any article from interstate commerce subject only to the specific prohibitions of the Constitution.
>
> *Hammer v. Dagenhart* has not been followed. The distinction on which the decision was rested that Congressional power to prohibit interstate commerce is limited to articles which in themselves have some harmful or deleterious property—a distinction which was novel when made and unsupported by any provision of the Constitution—has long since been abandoned. . . . The thesis of the opinion that the motive of the prohibition or its effect to control in some measure the use or production within the states of the article thus excluded from the commerce can operate to deprive the regulation of its constitutional authority has long since ceased to have force.
>
> The conclusion is inescapable that *Hammer v. Dagenhart* was a departure from the principles which have prevailed in the interpretation of the Commerce Clause both before and since the decision and that such vitality, as a precedent, as it then had has long since been exhausted. It should be and now is overruled.

The *Darby* decision, clear-cut as it was, did not suffice to settle the jurisdictional questions under the Fair Labor Standards Act in the definitive fashion that the *Jones & Laughlin* decision had achieved for the Wagner Act. "When these provisions first came here," Justice Frankfurter said in 1945, "we made it abundantly clear that their enforcement would involve the courts in the empiric process of drawing lines from case to case, and inevitably nice lines." [29] Two reasons account for the continuing stream of wage and hour cases after 1941. First, the absence of any administrative

[29] *10 East 40th Street v. Callus* (1945).

tribunal like the ICC or the NLRB to perform enforcement functions under the act withheld from the courts, in Frankfurter's words, "the benefit of a prior judgment, on vexing and ambiguous facts, by an expert administrative agency."

Second is the fact that Congress in enacting the statute did not see fit to exhaust its constitutional power over commerce. By failing to make the Wages and Hours Act applicable to all employment "affecting commerce," Congress prevented the Court from using the Wagner or Sherman Act precedents. In FLSA cases it must be established to the satisfaction of the courts in each instance that the employees involved are engaged "in commerce" or "in the production of goods for commerce."

Application of these statutory standards has required the drawing of some rather fine lines. Since type of work done by the employee, and not the nature of the employer's business, determines coverage, it is possible for an employer to have some workers who are covered and others who are not. Thus an examination of the nature of the duties of individual employees and their relation to interstate commerce or the production of goods for commerce is usually required to settle a disputed case. The original act specified that "an employee shall be deemed to have been engaged in the production of goods if such an employee was engaged . . . in any process or occupation necessary to the production thereof, in any State." Because the Court tended to interpret this language as authorizing a fairly broad coverage of fringe workers,[30] Congress in 1949 amended the statute to apply only to workers "directly essential" to production. In 1961 another amendment declared that any company doing an annual business in excess of 1 million dollars was engaged in interstate commerce for the purposes of the act.

AGRICULTURAL REGULATION    The initial New Deal effort to handle the farm problem by invoking the federal taxing power was defeated by the Court in the *Butler* decision. Although the Court was not construing the commerce power there, it almost appeared to be saying that the welfare of agriculture could never be a legitimate concern of the federal government. Of course the Court quickly withdrew from this untenable position. Congress soon found a stopgap after *Butler* in soil conservation, for which farm payments similar to those of the unconstitutional production control program were available. As a more permanent approach Congress turned to marketing controls. The Agricultural Marketing Act of 1937, under which milk marketing agreements were set up to control prices in the major milk-sheds of the country, was held constitutional by the Court in two 1939 decisions involving the New York and Boston areas. The Court said that since most of the milk under agreements moved in interstate commerce and the

[30] See *Kirschbaum* v. *Walling* (1942); *Borden Co.* v. *Borella* (1945); *Martino* v. *Michigan Window Cleaning Co.* (1946).

intrastate milk was inextricably mixed with interstate milk, the regulation of prices of all milk in these markets was a valid exercise of the commerce power.[31]

The Agricultural Adjustment Act of 1938 utilized a new control device, marketing quotas. In 1939 such quotas on tobacco marketing were upheld by the Court in *Mulford* v. *Smith*. The Court emphasized that the statute did not purport to limit production but merely to control the sales of tobacco in interstate commerce so as to prevent the flow of commerce from causing harm. But how tenuous a relationship to interstate commerce the Court was willing to accept was dramatically demonstrated in *Wickard* v. *Filburn* (1942). Here a farmer raising 23 acres of wheat, none of it intended for interstate commerce since all was to be consumed on the farm or fed to stock, was held to have such an effect on interstate commerce as to be liable to the marketing penalties imposed by the act of 1938.

As Justice Jackson recognized, the Court, in spite of the "great latitude" permitted to the commerce power in its post-1937 decisions, had not yet held that production might be regulated "where no part of the product is intended for interstate commerce or intermingled with the subjects thereof." Now in *Wickard* v. *Filburn* it was prepared to do so, and Jackson's justification of this result is the high-water mark of commerce clause expansionism. The guiding principle is that, "even if appellee's activity be local and though it may not be regarded as commerce, it may still, whatever its nature, be reached by Congress if it exerts a substantial economic effect on interstate commerce, and this irrespective of whether such effect is what might at some earlier time have been defined as 'direct' or 'indirect.' "

Examining the economics of the wheat industry, the Court concluded that local consumption of homegrown wheat "constitutes the most variable factor in the disappearance of the wheat crop." It would consequently have "a substantial influence on price and market conditions," and Congress could justifiably have concluded "that wheat consumed on the farm where grown, if wholly outside the scheme of regulation, would have a substantial effect in defeating and obstructing its purpose to stimulate trade therein at increased prices."

Up to 1967 federal meat inspection was limited to products moving in interstate commerce, leaving some 15 per cent of fresh meat and 25 per cent of processed meat to state inspection. After shocking evidence was produced of unsanitary conditions in some of the 15,000 federally uninspected intrastate plants, Congress passed the Wholesome Meat Act of 1967, giving the states two years to revise their systems to federal standards. If a state failed to act, the Department of Agriculture would impose federal inspection. The Department would have access to intrastate plants at all times, and power to act against any plant distributing adulterated products. No

[31] *United States* v. *Rock Royal Cooperative* (1939); *H. P. Hood & Sons* v. *United States* (1939). See also *United States* v. *Wrightwood Dairy Co.* (1942).

question was raised about the constitutional power of Congress to adopt this statute.

NAVIGABLE STREAMS AND FEDERAL POWER PROJECTS     Another important area of congressional interest concerns navigable waters and the hydroelectric power derived from them. Here the basic decision is *United States* v. *Appalachian Electric Power Co.* (1940). The Federal Water Power Act of 1920 made it unlawful to construct a dam for water power development in a navigable water of the United States without first securing a license from the Federal Power Commission. This license controls service, rates, and profits of the licensee, and provides for recapture of the project by the government after fifty years on payment of the net investment therein.

In the *Appalachian* case the contention was that the New River in West Virginia was not navigable, and that even if it were, the government had no right to impose the conditions set forth in the license, since most of them had nothing to do with navigation or its protection. The Court held that the New River was navigable and announced a revised test of navigability which greatly increased federal authority. Previously the rule had been: "Those rivers must be regarded as public navigable rivers in law which are navigable in fact. And they are navigable in fact when they are used, or are susceptible of being used, in their ordinary condition, as highways for commerce." Modifying this test, Justice Reed now said for the Court: "To appraise the evidence of navigability on the natural condition only of the waterway is erroneous. Its availability for navigation must also be considered." The New River, while not then navigable, could be made so by the expenditure of a not unreasonable sum of money, and so it was navigable in law.

In the *Appalachian* case the Court also held that the government's power over navigable waters was not restricted to control relating to navigation. The power being exercised was the commerce power, of which navigation is only a part. "Flood protection, watershed development, recovery of the cost of improvements through utilization of power are likewise parts of commerce control. . . . Navigable waters are subject to national planning and control in the broad regulation of commerce granted the Federal Government."

Of course the federal government may itself build dams in navigable streams under its commerce power, and the same constellation of navigation, irrigation, and flood control purposes, with power as a by-product, may thus be promoted under the commerce power. Attempts to question the legitimacy of and the motives behind the construction of federal multiple-purpose dams where power generation was an important factor have uniformly failed. The Boulder Canyon Project Act of 1928 was upheld in *Arizona* v. *California* (1931). The constitutionality of the TVA power-development program was supported by a federal trial court in 1938 against an

attack by eighteen private power companies, but the Supreme Court found it unnecessary to pass on the constitutional issue, holding that the utilities had suffered no legal injury from TVA activities and consequently had no ground for bringing the suit.[32]

THE SHERMAN ACT    The breadth of the commerce clause has also been demonstrated in recent Sherman Act prosecutions. In 1942 the Department of Justice secured indictments against an underwriters' association which represented a membership of nearly two hundred fire insurance companies, charging conspiracy to fix rates and monopolize trade and commerce. This prosecution challenged a famous Supreme Court decision dating back to 1869, *Paul* v. *Virginia*, which had held that the writing of insurance was a local activity, not interstate commerce. "These contracts are not articles of commerce in any proper meaning of the word," the Court said. They are not "subjects of trade and barter," they are not "commodities" shipped from one state to another and then put up for sale. Though written by an out-of-state company, they do not become effective until delivered by the local agent. "They are, then, local transactions, and are governed by local law." The effect of the decision was to uphold a state law requiring insurance companies not incorporated in the state to secure a license and deposit bonds with the state treasurer before doing business in the state.

On the basis of this decision, the insurance business developed into one of gigantic proportions in the nation while retaining constitutionally its local status. But in *United States* v. *South-Eastern Underwriters Assn.* (1944), the Supreme Court terminated this anomalous situation. Justice Black, speaking for a four-judge majority, started by noting that *Paul* v. *Virginia* and all the other precedents holding the insurance business not to be commerce were cases where the validity of state statutes had been at issue, and the question had been the extent to which the commerce clause might automatically deprive states of the power to regulate insurance. It was in these circumstances that the Court had consistently upheld state regulatory authority. The *South-Eastern* case was the first in which the Court had been asked to pass on the applicability of a federal statute to companies doing an interstate insurance business.

Coming at the problem from this angle, an entirely different line of precedents became applicable. All the cases in which the transportation or movement across state lines of lottery tickets, stolen automobiles, kidnapped persons, and the like, had been held to be interstate commerce and subject to federal regulation were the controlling authorities. If activities of these variegated sorts were interstate commerce, then Black felt that "it would indeed be difficult now to hold that no activities of any insurance company can ever constitute interstate commerce." Although a contract of insurance

---

[32] *Tennessee Electric Power Co.* v. *T.V.A.* (1939). See also *Oklahoma ex rel. Phillips* v. *Guy Atkinson Co.* (1941).

might not in itself be interstate commerce, the entire transaction of which it is a part is a chain of events crossing state boundaries. "No commercial enterprise of any kind which conducts its activities across state lines has been held to be wholly beyond the regulatory power of Congress under the Commerce Clause. We cannot make an exception of the business of insurance." [33]

On only two subsequent occasions has an antitrust suit been defeated on commerce grounds. In 1947 the Court held that taxicab service at Chicago railroad stations was not part of interstate commerce.[34] Then in 1953 the Court turned down an antitrust action brought by professional baseball players who were attacking the "reserve clause" in their contracts which gives the organized baseball club first signing a player the continuing and exclusive right to his services. In a 1922 case the Court had denied that baseball was interstate commerce,[35] and now in *Toolson* v. *New York Yankees* (1953) it refused to reexamine that holding, on the ground that if there were evils in organized baseball to which the antitrust laws should be applied, it was up to Congress to enact new legislation for that purpose. Of course this position was directly contrary to that taken in the *South-Eastern Underwriters* case, and there can be little doubt that the Court's reluctance to upset baseball's established arrangements was due to a belief that the sport could not survive if the reserve clause was invalidated.[36]

THE COMMERCE CLAUSE AND CIVIL RIGHTS    In a 1946 decision sustaining the "death sentence" provision of the Public Utility Holding Company Act, the Supreme Court said: "The federal commerce power is as broad as the economic needs of the nation." [37] Recent experience has shown that it is also as broad as the social needs. In the Civil Rights Act of 1964 Congress undertook to ban racial discrimination in public accommodations throughout the

[33] After this decision Congress passed a statute permitting the states to continue to regulate and tax the insurance business, and exempted it from any federal statutes, with the exception of the Sherman Act and three others. The Supreme Court upheld this statute in *Prudential Insurance Co.* v. *Benjamin* (1946) and *Robertson* v. *California* (1946).

[34] *United States* v. *Yellow Cab Co.* (1947).

[35] *Federal Baseball Club* v. *National League of Professional Baseball Clubs* (1922).

[36] In 1966 a Wisconsin antitrust suit against the former Milwaukee Braves seeking to force them to return from Atlanta was dismissed by the state supreme court, on the ground that the failure of Congress to take any action since the Supreme Court's 1922 decision meant that baseball was immune from antitrust laws and that Congress intended the game to police itself. The Supreme Court denied certiorari in *Wisconsin* v. *Milwaukee Braves, Inc.* (1966). On the constitutional situation of professional athletic competition, see "The Super Bowl and the Sherman Act: Professional Team Sports and the Antitrust Laws," 81 *Harvard Law Review* 418–434 (1967).

[37] *American Power & Light Co.* v *SEC* (1946). The "death sentence" was a statutory requirement that holding companies be simplified and reorganized, and their operations limited to those of an integrated public utility system.

country. The constitutional foundations for the statute were the commerce clause and the equal protection clause. However, in *Heart of Atlanta Motel, Inc.* v. *United States* (1964) and *Katzenbach* v. *McClung* (1964), the Supreme Court found the commerce clause alone fully adequate to support the statute.

The act applied to three classes of business establishments—inns, hotels, and motels; restaurants and cafeterias; and theaters and motion picture houses—if their operations "affect commerce." The act defined what it meant by affecting commerce. Any inn, motel, or other establishment which provides lodging to transient guests affects commerce per se. Restaurants and cafeterias affect commerce if they serve interstate travelers or if a substantial portion of the food they serve or products they sell have "moved in commerce." Motion picture houses and theaters affect commerce if they customarily present films or performances which "move in commerce."

The two 1964 test cases were brought by an Atlanta motel and a Birmingham restaurant. The Court, noting that it was applying principles "first formulated by Chief Justice Marshall in *Gibbons* v. *Ogden*," unanimously upheld the act as applied to both. Only two questions need be asked, said Justice Clark for the Court: did Congress have a rational basis for finding that racial discrimination by places of public accommodation affected commerce; and were the means it selected to eliminate that evil reasonable and appropriate? The answer to both was in the affirmative. The fact that Congress was using the commerce power to legislate against "moral wrongs" was irrelevant, so far as the constitutional foundation for the enactment was concerned.

Justice Black's concurring opinion offered a dramatic commentary on the scope of the commerce power. Searching for an illustration of a business which might be excluded by the Constitution from congressional regulation, he came up with the suggestion that "some isolated and remote lunch room which sells only to local people and buys almost all its supplies in the locality may possibly be beyond the reach of the power of Congress to regulate commerce." He agreed that the Court should not allow "remote, possible, speculative" effects on commerce to be accepted as adequate constitutional grounds "to uproot and throw into the discard all our traditional distinctions between what is purely local . . . and what affects the national interest." But, he added, isolated, individual, local events when added to many others of a similar nature may impose a burden on commerce by reducing its volume or distorting its flow, and Congress was justified in concluding that racial discrimination did impose such a burden.[38]

[38] In 1966 President Johnson proposed that Congress, acting under the commerce power, enact a federal ban on racial discrimination in access to housing. Senator Dirksen protested that such a law was unconstitutional, but it was clearly within the principle of the *Heart of Atlanta* decision. The bill was defeated in 1966, but in 1968 Senator Dirksen found it possible to support a similar federal open housing bill.

In 1967 the House demonstrated that the commerce power could be employed to restrain as well as to protect civil rights. Reacting to Negro riots in the cities and the apparent connection with these disturbances of traveling "black power" agitators such as Stokely Carmichael, the House on July 19 passed by a vote of 347 to 70 a bill making it a federal crime to use the facilities of interstate commerce or to cross state lines to incite a riot or violence. The debate saw Southern representatives who had objected to federal intervention through the Civil Rights Act of 1964 now saying that federal action was needed, while civil rights liberals opposed the bill as federal interference in what was primarily a state and local matter. The bill was brought up again in 1968 with administration support.

The New Deal crisis was largely produced by the Supreme Court's failure to ratify the principles "first formulated by Chief Justice Marshall in *Gibbons v. Ogden*." Those principles have now been so fully accepted that, although there are in theory still limits on the power of Congress to regulate commerce, the Court, as it said in 1946, will not even attempt "to draw the outer limits of this plenary power." [39]

## SELECTED REFERENCES

ALFANGE, DEAN, *The Supreme Court and the National Will,* chap. 7. Garden City, N.Y.: Doubleday & Company, Inc., 1937.

CARR, ROBERT K., *The Supreme Court and Judicial Review,* chap. 6. New York: Holt, Rinehart and Winston, Inc., 1942.

CORWIN, EDWARD S., *The Twilight of the Supreme Court,* chap. 1. New Haven, Conn.: Yale University Press, 1934.

CROSSKEY, WILLIAM W., *Politics and the Constitution in the History of the United States,* part 1. Chicago: The University of Chicago Press, 1953.

DOUGLAS, WILLIAM O., *We the Judges,* chap. 6. Garden City, N.Y.: Doubleday & Company, Inc., 1956.

FRANKFURTER, FELIX, *The Commerce Clause under Marshall, Taney and Waite.* Chapel Hill, N.C.: The University of North Carolina Press, 1937.

HAINES, CHARLES GROVE, and FOSTER H. SHERWOOD, *The Role of the Supreme Court in American Government and Politics, 1835–1864,* chap. 5. Berkeley, Calif.: University of California Press, 1957.

HAMILTON, WALTON H., and DOUGLAS ADAIR, *The Power to Govern: The Constitution—Then and Now.* New York: W. W. Norton & Company, Inc., 1937.

KELLY, ALFRED H., and WINFRED A. HARBISON, *The American Constitution: Its Origins and Development,* chap. 27. New York: W. W. Norton & Company, Inc., 1963 (third edition).

PRITCHETT, C. HERMAN, *The Roosevelt Court: A Study in Judicial Politics and Values, 1937–1947,* chap. 8. New York: The Macmillan Company, 1948.

[39] *North American Co.* v. *SEC* (1946).

STERN, ROBERT L., "The Problems of Yesteryear—Commerce and Due Process," in Robert G. McCloskey (ed.), *Essays in Constitutional Law*, pp. 150–180. New York: Alfred A. Knopf, Inc., 1957.

WOOD, STEPHEN B., *Constitutional Politics in the Progressive Era: Child Labor and the Law*. Chicago: The University of Chicago Press, 1968.

# 15

## The commerce power and the states

In the Republic's early years Congress, which admittedly possessed regulatory power over commerce among the states, generally failed to exercise it or used it very incompletely. The states, on the other hand, were continually adopting legislation which, intentionally or not, touched interstate commerce. It then became the duty of the Supreme Court to decide whether the Constitution left room for the states to exercise those controls, or whether regulatory power belonged exclusively to Congress. The Court is now in the second century of its wrestling with these issues, and no end is in sight.

### THE EXCLUSIVENESS ISSUE

Whether and to what extent the commerce power is an exclusive power of Congress was a major focus of Marshall's three discussions concerning the commerce clause. In *Gibbons* v. *Ogden* (1824) New York State had clearly undertaken to assert authority over interstate navigation using New York waters. In *Brown* v. *Maryland* (1827) the state had levied a rather heavy license tax on importers of foreign articles and had forbidden them to sell the goods they imported until they paid the tax. In *Willson* v. *Black-Bird Creek Marsh Co.* (1829) a dam built across a navigable creek under authority of a Delaware law had been broken by a vessel. When the owners of the

dam brought an action of trespass against the owner of the vessel, he defended on the ground that the creek was a navigable highway which had been unlawfully obstructed by the dam.

After Marshall, problems of similar character came before the Taney Court. In *The License Cases* (1847) liquor purchased in one state was sold in another state without the vendor obtaining the license required by law in the state of sale. *The Passenger Cases* (1849) arose when New York and Massachusetts imposed on masters of ships coming into the state from foreign ports a tax for each passenger aboard, the proceeds of which were used to defray the costs of examining passengers for contagious diseases and to maintain a hospital for those found to be diseased.

THE CONCURRENT POWER THEORY    Judicial discussion in this series of cases developed several theories of exclusiveness in federal-state relations under the commerce clause. The first may be called the theory of "concurrent power." According to this view no field of regulation was exclusively reserved to Congress by the commerce clause. Both Congress and the states had authority to range over the entire field of commerce. The only limitation on state power to regulate commerce was the supremacy clause of Article VI; that is, a federal statute would definitely displace any conflicting state statute. In the absence of such conflicting legislation, the states would be free to go as far as they liked.

This argument was made on behalf of the state in *Gibbons* v. *Ogden*. It was contended that the state had the regulatory power prior to the adoption of the Constitution, and that it was retained by the Tenth Amendment. The affirmative grant of regulatory power to Congress did not oust the states, "unless in its own nature . . . the continued exercise of it by the former possessor is inconsistent with the grant," which was alleged not to be the case here. To support the concurrent theory, the analogy of the taxing power was used. The Constitution gives Congress power to lay and collect taxes, but this grant clearly does not interfere with the exercise of the same power by the states. Why does not the same situation prevail with respect to the commerce power?

Marshall met this argument head on, and refuted it. The commerce and taxing powers are similar neither in their terms nor their nature.

> The power of taxation . . . is a power which, in its own nature, is capable of residing in, and being exercised by, different authorities at the same time. . . . When, then, each government exercises the power of taxation, neither is exercising the power of the other. But, when a State proceeds to regulate commerce with foreign nations, or among the several States, it is exercising the very power that is granted to Congress, and is doing the very thing which Congress is authorized to do.

THE DORMANT POWER THEORY    At the opposite pole from the concurrent power doctrine was the so-called "dormant power" theory. Where the former

gave maximum range to state authority, the latter reduced state power to a minimum. Stated succinctly, the dormant view was that the grant of commerce power to Congress, even though unexercised by Congress, necessarily prevented the states from regulating commerce and invalidated any regulations which impinged on commerce.

Justice Johnson's concurring opinion in *Gibbons* v. *Ogden* forthrightly adopted this view; New York's action in granting a monopoly affecting interstate commerce was invalid whether or not there was conflicting legislation by Congress, he contended. But Marshall avoided taking a position on the issue. In discussing state power, he said, "we may dismiss . . . the inquiry, whether it is surrendered by the mere grant to congress, or is retained until congress shall exercise the power. We may dismiss that inquiry because it has been exercised, and the regulations which congress deemed it proper to make, are now in full operation." In the *Black-Bird* case there was, in Marshall's view, no conflicting federal act (though actually Willson's vessel was licensed under the same federal statute as Gibbons's boat had been), but again Marshall avoided deciding that the state act authorizing damming of a navigable creek was "repugnant to the power to regulate commerce in its dormant state" by holding that the state power being used was the police power rather than the commerce power.

Thus the dormant power theory won no explicit official endorsement from the Court, but at the same time it was not definitively rejected, as the concurrent notion had been. So it continued to figure in Supreme Court discussions. It was avowed by part of the Court in *The License Cases* (1847), where the justices were so badly split that no opinion for the Court was possible. Two years later in *The Passenger Cases* (1849), the dormant power theory finally achieved a victory as the Court held state taxing power to have been abridged "by mere affirmative grants of power to the general government." This was Taney's characterization of the opinion, and naturally he protested it, saying: "I cannot foresee to what it may lead." Actually it led nowhere, for in another three years the dormant doctrine was abandoned by every member of the Court except one in the great case of *Cooley* v. *Port Wardens of Philadelphia* (1852). Before we get to that point, however, we must trace the fortunes of still another unsuccessful doctrine of the period.

THE MUTUAL EXCLUSIVENESS THEORY    This third theory is that of "mutual exclusiveness." The defeat of the concurrent doctrine in the *Gibbons* case had established that there must be some degree of exclusiveness in the congressional commerce power, some areas of regulation from which the states were excluded. The question was, how much exclusiveness, and how was it to be determined? One possible answer was that the field of commercial regulation was divided into two parts by a definite line. On one side of the line the federal government could regulate; the other side belonged to the states; each had to keep out of the other's territory. Their powers, in short, were mutually exclusive.

Marshall seemed in the *Gibbons* case to mark off a sphere of regulation belonging exclusively to the states. He referred there to "that immense mass of legislation, which embraces everything within the territory of a State, not surrendered to a general government." Becoming more specific, he alleged that "inspection laws, quarantine laws, health laws of every description, as well as laws for regulating the internal commerce of a state, and those which respect turnpike roads, ferries, etc., are component parts of this mass. No direct general power over these objects is granted to congress; and, consequently, they remain subject to state legislation."

Similarly, though he did not state it so clearly, Marshall appeared to argue that Congress had exclusive jurisdiction over its sphere, and thus neither the state nor the nation could exercise the powers of the other. But then he very cleverly recaptured for the federal government much of the authority which he had appeared to give away to the states. "It is obvious," he says, "that the government of the Union, in the exercise of its express powers . . . may use means that may also be employed by a State, in the exercise of its acknowledged powers." In other words, to regulate commerce among the states it may be necessary to regulate commerce within a state. Thus he grafted onto his talk about mutually exclusive state and national powers what Crosskey calls the "doctrine of inevitable concurrency as to the means of their execution." [1] But of course this confusion made no difference, because Marshall decided the case on the quite different ground of collision between a state and a federal act.

This strange performance may make some sense if we note that mutual exclusiveness was Jeffersonian doctrine, put forward to protect state claims in opposition to federal power. Marshall may have felt that he could best restrain this view by appearing to accept it while at the same time smothering its impact in a welter of words. In the *Black-Bird* case he continued his apparent tactics of mollification of states' rights sentiment without yielding up the substance of federal power. State authorization of the dams was justified, Marshall said, by "the circumstances of the case." The legislative aims were the draining of swamps, with consequent improvement of health and enhancement of property values. Thus it was action taken under the state's police power, not a regulation of commerce, that was involved, and there was no need to avow or disavow mutual exclusiveness. It was not until the *Cooley* discussion in 1852 that the Court definitely rejected mutual exclusiveness, its suport by that time having dwindled, as in the case of the dormant power theory, to one member of the Court.

THE SELECTIVE EXCLUSIVENESS THEORY    The winner in this doctrinal conflict was the theory of "selective exclusiveness." Interestingly enough, this

---

[1] W. W. Crosskey, *Politics and the Constitution in the History of the United States* (Chicago: The University of Chicago Press, 1953), p. 695.

was precisely the view Webster had urged on the Court in his original *Gibbons* argument. His contention there was "that the power of Congress to regulate commerce was complete and entire, and, to a certain extent, necessarily exclusive." By this he meant that some, but not all, areas of commercial regulation were absolutely foreclosed to the states by the constitutional grant of power to Congress. Who would decide in which areas Congress had exclusive power? Presumably that would fall to the Supreme Court. Marshall knew that if he agreed with Webster, he would have to claim for the Court a breadth of discretionary power which was bound to be unpopular with the Jeffersonians. It was perhaps for this reason that he failed to adopt straightforwardly Webster's doctrine of selective exclusiveness, but sought to achieve much the same result by the devious route of mutual exclusiveness plus inevitable concurrency in means of execution.

In any case Webster was finally vindicated by *Cooley* v. *Port Wardens of Philadelphia* (1852). A state act of 1803 provided that ships in the port of Philadelphia arriving from or bound to any foreign port must engage a local pilot. Failure to do so would result in a fine equal to half the cost of pilotage, payable to the board of wardens of the port to the use of a fund for superannuated pilots and their dependents. By an act of 1789 Congress had in effect adopted all then existing state harbor regulations, and provided that pilots should continue to be regulated in conformity "with such laws as the States may respectively hereafter enact for the purpose, until further legislative provision shall be made by Congress."

Justice Curtis, writing the Court's opinion, was confronted first of all with the necessity of finally deciding one way or the other on the dormant power theory. For if the mere grant of the commercial power to Congress *ipso facto* deprived the states of all power to regulate pilots, then Congress could not confer on the states the power thus to legislate, and the act of 1789 would be void. So the Court had to start from first principles:

> The grant of commercial power to congress does not contain any terms which expressly exclude the States from exercising an authority over its subject-matter. If they are excluded, it must be because the nature of the power, thus granted to congress, requires that a similar authority should not exist in the States. . . . But when the nature of a power like this is spoken of . . . it must be intended to refer to the subjects of that power, and to say they are of such a nature as to require exclusive legislation by congress.

Thus Curtis shifted gears from the theoretical problem of the "nature" of the commerce power to the pragmatic examination of the "subjects" of that power. In this real world Curtis's first observation was that the subjects of regulation are "exceedingly various" and "quite unlike in their nature." Such heterogeneity of subjects quickly led Curtis to conclude that the rules by which they were regulated must be similarly adaptable. Whereas "some imperatively demand . . . a single uniform rule, operating equally on the

commerce of the United States in every port," others "as imperatively demand . . . that diversity, which alone can meet the local necessities."

This analysis clearly doomed the dormant power theory, and Curtis wrote its epitaph in these words: "It is the opinion of a majority of the court that the mere grant to congress of the power to regulate commerce, did not deprive the States of power to regulate pilots." Instead, Curtis accepted the principle of selective exclusiveness as the Court's rule for the future, in these two pregnant sentences:

> Either absolutely to affirm, or deny that the nature of this power requires exclusive legislation by congress, is to lose sight of the nature of the subjects of this power, and to assert concerning all of them, what is really applicable but to a part. Whatever subjects of this power are in their nature national, or admit only of one uniform system, or plan of regulation, may justly be said to be of such a nature as to require exclusive legislation by congress.

Subjects lacking in these characteristics, by the same token, were not within the exclusive power of Congress. Pilotage laws, Curtis concluded, were in this latter category.

> The Act of 1789 contains a clear and authoritative declaration by the first congress, that the nature of this subject is such, that until congress should find it necessary to exert its power, it should be left to the legislation of the States; that it is local and not national; that it is likely to be best provided for, not by one system, or plan of regulations, but by as many as the legislative discretion of the several States should deem applicable to the local peculiarities of the ports within their limits.

SUMMARY    The *Cooley* decision marks the end of the formative period for constitutional theory on federal-state relations under the commerce clause. From this period certain basic principles emerged. First, the commerce clause, by its own force and effect, gave Congress exclusive power to regulate certain kinds of commerce and voided any state infringement on those areas. This principle represented a defeat for Madison's contention that the national commerce power internally was intended only as a negative and preventive provision to keep the states from injuring each other, rather than as a power to be used for the positive purposes of the general government. It likewise represented a defeat for Taney.

Second, the rule developed by the Court conceded that there were areas where commerce among the states or with foreign nations might constitutionally be regulated by the states. Marshall had sought to leave room for such state action by giving it another name—regulation of a "police" character. This was sheer quibbling, which Taney properly exposed in *The License Cases.*

Third, in the determination of this question of constitutional power, the

Supreme Court was to be an active participant. True, the grant of regulatory power is to Congress. But Congress gives its attention to commerce only sporadically, whereas the Court is continuously on tap. For over a century since *Cooley* it has consistently performed the role of umpire, enforcing the laws of Congress against conflicting state laws, invalidating state statutes discriminating against commerce, and determining whether the states are entering fields belonging to the national government under the Constitution.

## STATE REGULATION AND COMMERCE

Thomas Reed Powell used to say that he could easily state the principles of the commerce clause in three sentences: "Congress may regulate interstate commerce. The states may also regulate interstate commerce, but not too much. How much is too much is beyond the scope of this statement." [2] The Supreme Court cannot evade the question of "how much is too much" that easily. In fact, this is precisely the issue it has faced in literally hundreds of cases since *Cooley* was decided.

In these federal-state commercial controversies, the decisions are complicated and often seem contradictory. It is hard to derive understandable principles out of the welter of factual situations with which the Court has dealt. Admittedly the issues are complex, but it must be frankly recognized that part of the confusion results from the fact that the judicial decisions have reflected, in Justice Rutledge's words, "not logic alone, but large choices of policy, affected . . . by evolving experience of federalism." [3]

It is easy to say that the conflict has been between a nationalism as represented by Marshall and the states' rights interests which Taney symbolized. But these are labels which do little toward promoting an understanding of judicial motivation over the years. Nearly all the members of the Court have been nationalists in the sense that they knew the economic history of the Confederation and were resolved to prevent fractionization of American commerce or the setting up of trade barriers around each state.

But a nationalist view on the question of state regulation of commerce may be motivated, not by concern for an unobstructed national market, but by a laissez-faire hostility toward business regulation or taxation in general. If these motives are involved, then there may be a liberal-conservative tinge to the decisions, and the judicial lineups may seem somewhat confused. In the preceding chapter, the liberal position was that of justifying a broad extent of federal power under the commerce clause, as against conservative restrictions on federal regulatory authority. But in these federal-state conflicts, the liberal doctrine has called for limiting the inhibitions which the federal commerce clause imposes on the states, while the conserva-

---

[2] Thomas Reed Powell, *Vagaries and Varieties in Constitutional Interpretation* (New York: Columbia University Press, 1956), p. ix.
[3] *Prudential Insurance Co.* v. *Benjamin* (1946).

tive has emphasized federal power as a limitation on state regulation or taxation.

Take the case of *Di Santo* v. *Pennsylvania* (1927). Pennsylvania required that persons selling steamship tickets to or from foreign countries had to be licensed. Filing of a bond was involved, and a showing that the person was actually an agent for steamship companies. The law was plainly designed to prevent fraud on the public, but the Court majority struck it down as a regulation of foreign commerce, over the dissent of Holmes, Brandeis, and Stone. It is fairly clear that the decision did not register an intent to protect commerce, but simply distaste for all business regulation. In *California* v. *Thompson* (1941) a liberalized Court overruled the *Di Santo* decision, and in numerous other cases made it evident that its dominant motive was to clear the channels for a reasonable amount of state regulation or revenue.

STATE REGULATION IN THE ABSENCE OF FEDERAL LEGISLATION    Turning to the cases, it is helpful to divide them into two categories. First we may consider those in which state legislation impinging on commerce among the states is challenged and there is no conflicting federal legislation. Here the alleged conflict is directly with the commerce clause, and the Court must decide whether state regulation is consistent with the area of free trade carved out by the Constitution itself.

In such situations the Court may conclude that the state regulation is either valid or invalid. A holding of validity will be basically on the grounds developed by Curtis in the *Cooley* decision, namely, that the problem is essentially a local one in which there is no necessity for a uniform national rule. The case of *Bob-Lo Excursion Co.* v. *Michigan* (1948) well illustrates this situation. The Michigan civil rights act had been invoked against a Detroit amusement park company which operated an excursion steamer to an island on the Canadian side of the Detroit River. The company had refused to transport a Negro girl to the island, and in court the defense was that the state law could have no applicability to foreign commerce. The Supreme Court majority, however, held that this commerce was only technically foreign, and was in fact "highly local," the island being "economically and socially, though not politically, an amusement adjunct of the city of Detroit." Moreover, there was nothing in the Michigan law "out of harmony, much less inconsistent, with our federal policy in the regulation of commerce between the two countries." The Court concluded: "It is difficult to imagine what national interest or policy, whether of securing uniformity in regulating commerce, affecting relations with foreign nations or otherwise, could reasonably be found to be adversely affected by applying Michigan's statute to these facts or to outweigh her interest in doing so."

Commonly associated with the assertion that the situation is essentially local is the supporting rationalization that the state law constitutes no burden on commerce. Even where a law does have some clearly burdening

effects, it may still be rescued by showing that the burden falls uniformly on the commerce affected without discrimination in favor of any group or locality. An interesting example of this position is found in *South Carolina Highway Department* v. *Barnwell Brothers* (1938).

South Carolina law prohibited on the highways of that state motor trucks and trailers wider than 90 inches and heavier than 20,000 pounds. These limits were substantially stricter than those in adjacent states, so that trucks meeting legal requirements elsewhere might not be able to operate in South Carolina. A general federal statute regulated interstate trucks, but it did not cover size and weight. In these circumstances the Court permitted the state law to stand. The "essentially local" requirement of the *Cooley* case was met. "Few subjects of state regulation," said Justice Stone, "are so peculiarly of local concern as is the use of state highways." Certainly the statute imposed a burden on commerce, but it fell on all truckers equally. If there had been any evidence that the state was seeking to favor its own citizens, the result would probably have been different.[4]

When the Court majority tips the scale in the other direction, and state legislation is invalidated, the discussion usually still follows the line of the *Cooley* case, but the answers are different. The Court finds that in the particular situation, unless a national, uniform rule is enforced, the burden on commerce will be too serious to be borne. Again, the best way of getting a sense of the argument is to give examples.

In *Southern Pacific Co.* v. *Arizona* (1945), Arizona had passed a train-length law prohibiting operation within the state of trains more than fourteen passenger cars or seventy freight cars in length. The statute was justified as a safety measure, the hazards to trainmen from "slack action" being allegedly greater on longer trains. The railroad brotherhoods who sponsored the legislation were also perhaps not unmindful of the fact that it would create more jobs. The Court majority concluded that the claims for increased safety were slight and dubious, and were outweighed by the "national interest in keeping interstate commerce free from interferences which seriously impede it and subject it to local regulation which does not have a uniform effect on the interstate train journey which it interrupts." If there was to be regulation of train lengths, the Court indicated that it would have to come from Congress, since national uniformity was "practically indispensable to

---

[4] A New Mexico newspaper and radio station were enjoined from accepting or publishing within the state a Texas optometrist's advertising, under a state law forbidding price advertising on eye glasses. The Court in *Head* v. *New Mexico Board of Examiners* (1963) upheld the statute as a valid exercise of the police power and not discriminatory against interstate commerce or operating to disrupt its uniformity.

In *Brotherhood of Locomotive Engineers* v. *Chicago R.I. & P.R. Co.* (1966) a state "full-crew" law which exempted all the state's intrastate railroads from burdens which almost all the interstate railroads had to meet was upheld on the ground that no proof of arbitrary discrimination against interstate commerce had been offered.

the operation of an efficient and economical national railway system." There might seem to be some conflict between this decision and *Barnwell Brothers*, but the Court explained that states have a much more extensive control over their highways than over interstate railroads.

In *Morgan* v. *Virginia* (1946) the Virginia law requiring the separation of white and colored passengers on all motor carriers within the state was invalidated so far as it affected buses in interstate travel. Having just asserted in the *Southern Pacific* case that states had unusual powers of control over motor vehicle traffic, the Court now had to make clear that this point had no particular relevance to the present case. The important thing was whether an undue burden would result from permitting local rules to govern seating in interstate buses. The Court held that there would be real disturbances to the comfort of passengers and their freedom of choice in selecting accommodations. "It seems clear to us that seating arrangements for the different races in interstate motor travel require a single, uniform rule to promote and protect national travel." [5]

*Bibb* v. *Navajo Freight Lines* (1959) saw the Court strike down an Illinois statute requiring plastic contour rear-fender mudguards on trucks operating in the state, and making the conventional mudflap, which is legal in forty-five states, illegal in Illinois. The Court regarded this as a nondiscriminatory but nevertheless unconstitutionally severe burden on commerce. [6]

Where the burden takes the form of a complete obstruction to commerce, then the case against the state regulation involved is very strong indeed. In *Edwards* v. *California* (1941) the Court held unconstitutional a California statute making it a misdemeanor for anyone knowingly to bring or assist in bringing into the state a nonresident "indigent" person. In 1967 several lower federal and state courts held on the basis of the *Edwards* decision that state laws requiring one year of residence in the state before welfare payments could be made were unconstitutional, and in *Shapiro* v. *Thompson* (1968) the Supreme Court agreed to rule on the Connecticut residency statute in this regard.

During the 1960s a number of American cities, under pressure of right-wing organizations, adopted ordinances intended to prevent the local sale of goods produced in Iron Curtain countries, such as Polish hams. These ordinances typically required stores which dealt in such goods to buy a license —in Birmingham the fee was $5,000—and to display signs saying that the

[5] In *Colorado Anti-discrimination Commission* v. *Continental Air Lines* (1963) an airline was charged with violation of the state antidiscrimination act because of refusal to hire a Negro pilot. The airline contended that the *Morgan* case required interstate carriers to be free from diverse state regulations in the field of racial discrimination. But the Supreme Court held that there was no such need for uniform regulation in this situation, and that the act imposed no undue burden on the airline.

[6] Contrariwise, in *Dean Milk Co.* v. *City of Madison* (1951) a milk-inspection ordinance which had the effect of excluding Illinois milk from Madison, Wisconsin, was invalidated, not because it was burdensome but because it discriminated against Illinois milk producers.

store carried "Communist goods." Such ordinances were clearly unconstitutional, but the movement died out without drawing a Supreme Court decision. A federal court ruling that an Oregon law requiring imported meats to be labeled with the name of the country of origin was unconstitutional as a violation of the commerce clause was affirmed by the Supreme Court in *Short* v. *Ness Produce Co.* (1967).

In *Joseph E. Seagram & Sons, Inc.* v. *Hostetter* (1966), the Court ruled that a New York liquor law requiring brand owners to file prices with affirmation that they did not exceed those in any other part of the United States did not on its face place an unconstitutional burden on commerce. Justice Stewart pointed out that the Twenty-first Amendment "demands wide latitude for regulation by the State."

STATE POWER WHERE FEDERAL LEGISLATION EXISTS    Now we turn to situations where Congress has adopted legislation regulating interstate commerce, with which state action is alleged to conflict. The Court's problem in these cases is simpler—to decide whether Congress has completely occupied the field, or whether it has left some room for nonconflicting state legislation. There is likely, nevertheless, to be opportunity for considerable difference of opinion even here, since legislative intent is often difficult to appraise.

Perhaps the most interesting group of recent cases concerns those in which state labor laws have been attacked as in conflict with the national labor relations acts. In this field, "the statutory implications concerning what has been taken from the states and what has been left to them," says Justice Frankfurter, "are of a Delphic nature, to be translated into concreteness by the process of litigating elucidation."[7] As a consequence the decisions, of which there are many, defy easy summary.

Most of the cases have gone against the states, on the ground that Congress had preempted the field by its regulatory legislation. An important decision was *Hill* v. *Florida* (1945), where a state statute providing for compulsory licensing of labor union business agents was held to conflict with the purposes of the Wagner Act. State laws interfering with the right to strike, in public utilities as well as in private businesses, have been invalidated.[8]

Similarly, states have been forbidden to enjoin peaceful picketing[9] or to award damages therefor.[10] Relief, by damages or otherwise, has been denied for unfair labor practices.[11] State antitrust laws cannot be used to prevent the effectuation of collective bargaining agreements,[12] or to enjoin a strike

---

[7] *International Association of Machinists* v. *Gonzales* (1958).

[8] *International Union* v. *O'Brien* (1950); *Amalgamated Association* v. *Wisconsin Employment Relations Board* (1951); *Motor Coach Employees* v. *Missouri* (1963).

[9] *Garner* v. *Teamsters Union* (1953). For a more general treatment of the picketing problem, see Chap. 23.

[10] *San Diego Unions* v. *Garmon* (1957, 1959).

[11] *Guss* v. *Utah Labor Board* (1957).

[12] *Teamsters Union* v. *Oliver* (1959).

as a restraint of trade.[13] Since the Railway Labor Act expressly sanctions union shop agreements, a state right-to-work law cannot be invoked to abrogate such agreements.[14]

In general, states have not been permitted to duplicate remedies provided by federal legislation.[15] But the Court has allowed a damage suit for breach of contract in a state court by a worker who alleged that his union had illegally expelled him.[16] The Court likewise held that an employee kept out of a plant by threats of striking union members might sue the union for damages in the state courts instead of securing relief through the NLRB.[17]

Perhaps the most important decision upholding state power against federal preemption claims in the labor field was *Allen-Bradley Local* v. *Wisconsin Employment Relations Board* (1942), in which the Court held that federal legislation was not intended to impair a state's powers to punish or in some instances to prevent offensive conduct relating to "such traditionally local matters as public safety and order and the use of streets and highways." In this case state action was approved against mass picketing, threats of physical violence against workers, and obstruction of access to a plant by strikers.[18]

Another significant decision favorable to the states was *DeVeau* v. *Braisted* (1960). The New York–New Jersey waterfront compact, dealing with labor racketeering in New York Harbor, and state legislation implementing it, disqualified felons from holding office in waterfront labor organizations. The Supreme Court held that congressional consent to the compact eliminated any ground for the contention that such regulations conflicted with federal labor legislation, though a minority believed the situation to be indistinguishable from *Hill* v. *Florida*.

This issue of federal preemption and federal-state statutory conflict has been faced in many fields other than labor relations.[19] An interesting recent case from another area is *Huron Portland Cement Co.* v. *Detroit* (1960), where the Court upheld a conviction for violation of Detroit's smoke-abatement ordinance by a vessel in the Detroit harbor, even though the ship was

---

[13] *Weber* v. *Anheuser-Busch, Inc.* (1955).

[14] *Railway Employees Department* v. *Hanson* (1956).

[15] *Garner* v. *Teamsters Union* (1953).

[16] *International Association of Machinists* v. *Gonzales* (1958).

[17] *International Union* v. *Russell* (1958).

[18] See also *United Automobile Workers* v. *Wisconsin Employment Relations Board* (1956). In *Brotherhood of Locomotive Engineers* v. *Chicago R.I. & P.R. Co.* (1966) an Arkansas "full-crew" law was upheld against the charge that a 1963 act of Congress had preempted the field.

[19] See the discussion of *Pennsylvania* v. *Nelson* (1956), and the preemption controversy to which it gave rise in Congress, in Chap. 5. In *Railroad Transfer Service* v. *Chicago* (1967) involving a transfer service for passengers and baggage between Chicago railroad stations, the Court held that the Interstate Commerce Act had preempted the field and invalidated attempts by the city to require the service to secure a license which gave the city a veto power over its operations.

operating in interstate commerce and its boiler met the standards of federal legislation.

CONGRESSIONAL LEGITIMIZATION OF STATE REGULATION    There has been a notable line of cases upholding the right of Congress to legitimize state trade barriers where the motivation had general public approval. This technique was first employed to assist states which wished to prohibit the sale of intoxicating liquor. In 1890 the Court ruled in *Leisy* v. *Hardin* that Iowa could not, "in the absence of congressional permission to do so," prevent the first sale in the original package of liquor brought into the state. Within a few months Congress reacted to this decision by passing the Wilson Act rendering intoxicating liquor upon arrival in a state or territory "subject to the operation and effect of the laws of such state or territory enacted in the exercise of its police powers, to the same extent as though such . . . liquors had been produced in such state or territory, and . . . not . . . exempt therefrom by reason of being introduced therein in original packages or otherwise." The Court promptly sustained the validity of this legislation in *In re Rahrer* (1891), saying, "No reason is perceived why, if Congress chooses to provide that certain designated subjects of interstate commerce shall be governed by a rule which divests them of that character at an earlier period of time than would otherwise be the case, it is not within its competency to do so."

Congress then went further, and passed the Webb-Kenyon Act of 1913 over the veto of President Taft, whose Attorney General told him it was unconstitutional. This statute prohibited the shipment of liquor into any state where it was intended to be used in violation of state law. Thus it had the effect of divesting liquor of the protection of its interstate character even before it had begun to move in commerce and before it had come into the state where its illegal use was intended. The Supreme Court upheld the law, saying it was but an extension of the principle of the Wilson Act, for the purpose of "making it impossible for one State to violate the prohibitions of the laws of another through the channels of interstate commerce." [20] The substance and much of the exact language of the Webb-Kenyon Act were subsequently written into the Twenty-first Amendment. "Since that amendment," said Justice Brandeis in 1939, "the right of a State to prohibit or regulate the importation of intoxicating liquor is not limited by the commerce clause." [21]

These legislative techniques for divesting liquor of its character as interstate commerce were almost exactly repeated in dealing with the products of convict labor. Several states had a policy of using prisoners for the production of goods which were then offered for sale in the open market. The

[20] *Clark Distilling Co.* v. *Western Maryland R. Co.* (1917).
[21] *Finch Co.* v. *McKittrick* (1939). See also *Indianapolis Brewing Co.* v. *Liquor Control Commission* (1939).

states which did not exploit their prisoners in this way resented the competition of convict-made goods, but were unable to prevent their importation and sale in the original package. In 1929 Congress passed the Hawes-Cooper Act, which followed the Wilson Act in providing that such products on coming into a state should be immediately subject to the laws of that state, and this statute was upheld by the Court.[22] Then Congress went on to enact in 1935 a statute on the Webb-Kenyon model, called the Ashhurst-Summers Act, which prohibited the transportation of convict-made goods into any state where their sale or use would be contrary to state law. This statute was unanimously approved by the Court, Chief Justice Hughes asserting that Congress was not delegating its powers to the states, but merely exercising them in such a way as to aid the states in carrying out their police powers.[23]

### STATE TAXATION AND THE IMPORTS–EXPORTS CLAUSE

State taxation of commerce presents special problems not met in the preceding discussion of state regulation. For one thing, another provision of the Constitution is here called into play as a supplement to the commerce clause, the imports-exports clause of Article I, section 10. This clause reads, in part: "No state shall, without the consent of Congress, lay any imposts or duties on imports or exports, except what may be absolutely necessary for executing its inspection laws." Another differentiating factor is that, as we saw earlier in this chapter, the taxing power is admittedly a concurrent power, whereas the commerce power is not.

Both the imports-exports clause and the commerce clause were first applied to a state effort to tax foreign commerce in the famous case of *Brown* v. *Maryland* (1827). Here a state act required importers of foreign articles to have a license in order to be able to sell these goods. The state contended that this was an occupational tax, not a tax on imports, but Marshall pierced through this verbiage. "No goods would be imported if none could be sold." Under the Articles of Confederation the states had seen enough of what happened when there was no check on the power to tax imports so that, jealous as they were of their position, they had sanctioned this prohibition on such taxation in the Constitution.

However, Marshall recognized that freedom of imports from taxation could not be a perpetual immunity. At some point imports must become assimilated with the general mass of property in a state and subject to state taxation. Marshall suggested the "original package" doctrine for determining when this point was reached:

> It is sufficient for the present to say, generally, that when the importer has so acted upon the thing imported, that it has become incorporated

---

[22] *Whitfield* v. *Ohio* (1936).
[23] *Kentucky Whip & Collar Co.* v. *Illinois Central R. R. Co.* (1937).

and mixed up with the mass of property in the country, it has, perhaps, lost its distinctive character as an import, and has become subject to the taxing power of the State; but while remaining the property of the importer, in his warehouse, in the original form or package in which it was imported, a tax upon it is too plainly a duty on imports to escape the prohibition in the constitution.

Although Marshall was rather tentative in putting forth the original package doctrine, it proved to have great survival value. For 132 years, as Justice Frankfurter said in 1959, the Court followed the doctrine "without a single deviation." Indeed, in *Hooven & Allison Co.* v. *Evatt* (1945) the Court apparently extended its principle to apply, not only to imports for sale, but also to imports for the importer's own use or consumption. The Court majority here held that bales of hemp and other fibers imported from the Philippines by a rope company and stored in the original packages in its warehouse pending use in manufacturing were not taxable.

However, there were four dissenting justices in the *Hooven* case, indicating substantial concern about this limitation on state taxing powers. By 1959 the dissenting position had won control of the Court, and by a seven to two vote in *Youngstown Sheet & Tube Co.* v. *Bowers* the Court took a much stricter view as to when imports began to be used in manufacturing and lost their tax immunity. The new rule was that inventories of imported materials "essential to current manufacturing requirements" were subject to taxation.

State tax officials immediately began to explore the extent of this new freedom to levy on inventories of imports. Since few manufacturers import materials which they do not intend to process within a reasonable time, it may be that the *Youngstown* rule will completely eliminate tax immunity for the manufacturer-importer.[24] But there is no logical reason why the seller-importer should enjoy any more protection than the manufacturer-importer. In fact, there is no good reason why any imports deserve protection from a general property tax. The original purpose of the imports clause was to prevent discrimination against foreign goods, and to bar taxes which would benefit states through which the imports first pass at the expense of interior states of final destination and use. But a general property tax does not offer a threat on either of these grounds, where the imports have come to rest and are held for sale or use. On policy grounds, then, the Supreme Court is justified in a very restrictive interpretation of the tax immunity provided by the imports clause.

The Twenty-first Amendment, which leaves the states completely unconfined by traditional commerce clause limitations when they restrict the importation of intoxicating liquors for distribution or consumption within their borders, does not repeal the imports-exports clause. Consequently the

---

[24] This seemed the likely result of the Supreme Court's refusal to grant certiorari in *Virtue Bros.* v. *County of Los Angeles* (1966).

states are still forbidden to tax liquor imports while in the original package.[25] Similarly, states may not prohibit the sale of untaxed liquor to airline passengers leaving on overseas flights, for delivery to them on arrival at their foreign destination.[26]

The problem as to when goods being sent out of the country constitutionally become "exports," and thus immune from state taxation, cannot be settled by the original package doctrine, and the Court has been forced to make numerous rather fine distinctions based on the facts of particular cases. In general the tendency, particularly in recent years, has been to protect the state power to tax as long as there is any possible chance that the goods might not actually go into export.

Normally export is considered to have begun when delivery has been made to a common carrier for export.[27] This formula will not fit all situations, however. In a 1949 case a South American corporation had purchased a cement plant in California and employed a common carrier to dismantle it and prepare it for shipment to South America. In the midst of this process the state imposed a personal property tax on so much of the dismantled plant as had not already been shipped out of the country. Justice Douglas said for the Court,

> It is not enough that there is an intent to export, or a plan which contemplates exportation, or an integrated series of events which will end with it. . . . It is the entrance of the articles into the export stream that marks the start of the process of exportation. Then there is certainty that the goods are headed for their foreign destination and will not be diverted to domestic use. Nothing less will suffice.[28]

The imports-exports clause refers to imports from or exports to foreign countries. This might be thought self-evident, but actually Marshall in the *Brown* case assumed that the original package doctrine would "apply equally to importations from a sister State." This dictum was questioned by a minority of the Court in *The License Cases* (1847), and abandoned in *Woodruff* v. *Parham* (1869). This ruling did not leave interstate commerce the prey of unlimited state taxation, of course, as the next section will indicate. As Justice Miller said in *Woodruff*, the commerce clause by its own force would restrain state taxation which discriminated injuriously against the products of other states.

## STATE TAXATION AND COMMERCE

The Supreme Court has examined the impact of state taxes on interstate commerce in a staggering number of cases, but from the decisions two gen-

[25] *Department of Revenue* v. *James B. Beam Distilling Co.* (1964).
[26] *Hostetter* v. *Idlewild Bon Voyage Liquor Corp.* (1964).
[27] *Spalding & Brothers* v. *Edwards* (1923).
[28] *Empresa Siderurgica* v. *Merced County* (1949).

eral principles emerge more or less clearly. First, the Court has generally been resolved that state tax power shall not be used to discriminate against interstate commerce. Second, it has been equally certain that the status of interstate commerce should not be used to permit business operations to escape paying a fair share of local tax burdens. Application of these conflicting principles has been most difficult, partly because of the impossibility of being certain about the final incidence of the disputed taxes.

TAXATION OF PROPERTY IN INTERSTATE TRANSIT    Perhaps the best place to start is with the principle that property cannot be taxed while it is actually in interstate transit. The Court made this clear in the *State Freight Tax Case* (1873), which involved a Pennsylvania statute requiring every company transporting freight within the state to pay a tax at specified rates per ton of freight carried. This tax was held a burdensome regulation of commerce so far as it applied to freight "taken up within the State and carried out, or taken up in other States and brought within her limits." [29]

This rule immediately gives rise to a whole host of practical problems of a type already discussed. When does interstate transit actually begin? What is the tax status of goods whose interstate transit is temporarily interrupted? Light was thrown on both these questions by the famous case of *Coe* v. *Errol* (1886). Logs cut in New Hampshire lay on the shore or in the river, there awaiting spring floods which would carry them downstream and out of the state. The Court held these logs subject to local taxation, Justice Bradley saying: "Goods do not cease to be part of the general mass of property in the State, subject . . . to taxation in the usual way, until they have been shipped, or entered with a common carrier for transportation to another State, or have been started upon such transportation in a continuous route or journey." Other logs, cut in Maine, were stranded in New Hampshire by low water, and efforts were made to tax them there. These logs, the Court ruled, were "already in the course of commercial transportation, and . . . clearly under the protection of the Constitution." But later cases have made clear that where there is a bona fide break in the interstate journey, and the goods have not yet been restored to the current of interstate commerce, a local nondiscriminatory tax can be laid. [30]

When interstate transit has terminated, *Woodruff* v. *Parham* makes the goods immediately taxable, and the original package gives no protection. [31] In this respect there is a difference between the operation of the states' taxing and police powers, for the original package, as we know, does generally protect against police regulations. The reports are full of cases, however,

---

[29] The same principle condemns state taxes on persons coming into or leaving a state. *Crandall* v. *Nevada* (1868), concurring opinion; *Gloucester Ferry Co.* v. *Pennsylvania* (1885).
[30] *General Oil Co.* v. *Crain* (1908).
[31] See *Sonneborn Bros.* v. *Cureton* (1923).

disputing as to whether interstate commerce has actually terminated for tax purposes. One familiar problem concerns the distinction between drummers and peddlers.

Peddlers are persons engaged in the local sale of goods from stocks which they carry with them, and even though their stocks may have been brought in from outside the state, interstate transit is deemed to have ceased, and they are subject to nondiscriminatory license fees.[32] However, a tax which falls with intentional discriminatory incidence on goods originating outside the state is unconstitutional. This was first decided in *Welton* v. *Missouri* (1876), where a peddler's license tax confined to the sale of goods manufactured outside the state was invalidated.

Unlike a peddler, a drummer carries only samples with him and takes orders for subsequent delivery. When this delivery is made from outside the state, in consequence of a contract of sale, the Court held in 1887 that state taxes may not constitutionally be levied. This was the famous case of *Robbins* v. *Shelby County Taxing District*, in which the Court ruled that "the negotiation of sales of goods which are in another state, for the purpose of introducing them into the state in which the negotiation is made, is interstate commerce."

The principle of the *Robbins* case subsequently came under attack. *Best and Co.* v. *Maxwell* (1940) seemed to say that taxes on drummers were bad only if they were discriminatory. North Carolina had levied an annual tax of $250 on persons, not regular retail merchants of the state, who displayed samples in hotel rooms for the purpose of securing retail orders, whereas retail merchants paid only an annual tax of $1 for the privilege of doing business. But in *Nippert* v. *City of Richmond* (1946) the Court returned to full-fledged support of the *Robbins* doctrine, Justice Rutledge saying: "The drummer is a figure representative of a by-gone day. But his modern prototype persists under more euphonious appellations. So endure the basic reasons which brought about his protection from the kind of local favoritism the facts of this case typify."

The principle of the *Robbins* case was broad enough to cover more than drummers. It was soon applied to the taking of orders without samples being shown, and to sales which were not consummated until actual delivery of the goods. With the development of the mail-order business, the possibility of substantial tax losses for the states arose, particularly when the Depression drove nearly all states to a heavy reliance on the sales tax. Two things happened, however. First, the states developed a "use" tax, which was a levy at the same rate as the state sales tax, imposed on the use of goods purchased outside the state. Use within the state is of course a taxable event occurring after interstate commerce has ended. The use tax was upheld by the Court in *Henneford* v. *Silas Mason Co.* (1937), largely on the ground that it involved no discrimination.

[32] *Howe Machine Co.* v. *Gage* (1880).

Obvious administrative difficulties in collecting use taxes from individual purchasers led the states to experiment with requiring collection of the tax by the out-of-state sellers of goods. At first the Court seemed disposed to permit this service to be enforced only when the seller actually had some established business in the state. In two 1941 decisions the state of Iowa was upheld in requiring Chicago mail-order houses to collect the Iowa use tax on shipments from Chicago to Iowa customers. Both companies also operated retail stores in Iowa, and the Court held that they were thereby "receiving benefits from Iowa for which it has the power to exact a price." [33] But in 1944 the Court enforced the same obligation on an out-of-state corporation not licensed to do business in the state and carrying on no operations in Iowa other than the solicitation of orders by traveling salesmen.[34]

Ten years later, however, the Court refused to extend this precedent to cover the case of a Delaware store which had no salesmen in Maryland, but whose advertisements went into Maryland by newspaper, radio, and direct mail, and whose delivery trucks made regular deliveries there. Maryland sought to enforce collection of its use tax by seizing the concern's delivery truck while it was in the state. Five justices declared this violated due process, but four would have upheld the store's obligation to collect the tax.[35] In *National Bellas Hess, Inc.* v. *Illinois* (1967) the Court by a vote of six to three ruled that mail-order houses could not be required to collect state or local use taxes on interstate transactions conducted entirely by mail or common carrier.

A second reaction on the Court was that for a time it permitted a somewhat expanded coverage for state sales taxes, and in the process qualified to a certain extent the impact of the *Robbins* case. *McGoldrick* v. *Berwind-White Coal Mining Co.* (1940) held that, in the absence of congressional action, a New York City general sales tax could be collected on coal shipped from Pennsylvania to a New York purchaser to fulfill a contract entered into in New York City. The Court considered the tax as similar to a use tax in its effect, and ruled that delivery of the coal within the state was local activity sufficient to sustain the tax.

Three justices dissented from this decision, and the view they represented regained control of the Court in 1944 with *McLeod* v. *Dilworth Co.* Here a divided Court ruled that a sales tax could not be validly imposed by a state on sales to its residents where the orders were accepted in, and the goods shipped from, another state, with title passing on delivery to the carrier. A sales tax could not be made to do the work of a use tax, said Justice Frank-

---

[33] *Nelson* v. *Sears, Roebuck & Co.* (1941); *Nelson* v. *Montgomery Ward & Co.* (1941). See also *Felt & Tarrant Mfg. Co.* v. *Gallagher* (1939).
[34] *General Trading Co.* v. *State Tax Cmsn.* (1944).
[35] *Miller Bros Co.* v. *Maryland* (1954). In *American Oil Co.* v. *P. G. Neill* (1965) the Court followed this precedent in striking down an excise tax where a corporation could show there were no in-state activities connected with out-of-state sales.

furter. Similarly in *Freeman* v. *Hewit* (1946) Frankfurter invalidated Indiana's tax on the proceeds of securities sold by a local resident on the New York exchange, though the minority contended that the receipt of the proceeds from the sale was a purely local incident not protected by the commerce clause.

TAXATION OF THE INTERSTATE COMMERCE PRIVILEGE    The inherent dilemma in the Court's approach to the problem of state power to tax the privilege of engaging in interstate commerce is obvious when the principles of two of the earlier cases are placed side by side. In *Paul* v. *Virginia* (1869) the Court held that a corporation chartered by one state could do business in other states only with their consent, which might be granted "upon such terms and conditions as those States may think proper to impose." One such condition, it might seem, would be the taking out of a license and the paying of a license fee. But when the Court was confronted in 1888 with a state license tax on a telegraph company doing both a domestic and an interstate business, it said: "Can a State prohibit such a company from doing such a business within its jurisdiction, unless it will pay a tax and procure a license for the privilege? If it can, it can exclude such companies, and prohibit the transaction of such business altogether. We are not prepared to say that this can be done." [36] After further reflection, the Court in 1891 was prepared to say that it could not be done. "To carry on interstate commerce is not a franchise or a privilege granted by the State; it is a right which every citizen of the United States is entitled to exercise under the Constitution and laws of the United States." [37] On many subsequent occasions the Court has reaffirmed that a state has no power to refuse or tax the privilege of doing interstate business.[38]

Where a corporation is doing both an intrastate and interstate business, the state can, it is true, levy a privilege tax on the doing of the intrastate business. The fact that the intrastate and interstate business of a corporation may be quite closely related has caused some practical difficulties in determining the validity of intrastate license taxes, but in 1936 Justice Brandeis said: "No decision of this Court lends support to the proposition that an occupation tax upon local business, otherwise valid, must be held void merely because the local and interstate branches are for some reason inseparable." [39]

The states may of course attempt to do by indirection what they cannot do directly. Many state tax statutes have been ruled invalid on the ground that, no matter what they might be called, they were in reality levies on the privilege of doing an interstate business. One of the best-known cases is

[36] *Leloup* v. *Port of Mobile* (1888).
[37] *Crutcher* v. *Kentucky* (1891). But compare *Maine* v. *Grand Trunk Railway Co.* (1891).
[38] See *International Textbook Co.* v. *Pigg* (1910); *Spector Motor Service* v. *O'Connor* (1951).
[39] *Pacific Telephone & Telegraph Co.* v. *Tax Cmsn.* (1936).

*Western Union Telegraph* v. *Kansas ex rel. Coleman* (1910), where a percentage tax on the total capitalization of all foreign corporations doing or seeking to do a local business in the state was declared to be a burden on the company's interstate business and on its property located and used outside the state.

On the other hand, "franchise taxes" are not condemned by their name.[40] If the franchise tax is merely a "just equivalent" of other taxes, it is valid however calculated.[41] When it is in addition to other taxes, its validity will be determined on the basis of the facts of the case, including the apportionment doctrine to be discussed shortly.[42]

TAXATION OF THE AGENCIES OF INTERSTATE COMMERCE    The states may not tax interstate commerce, yet they admittedly may tax domestic business and all property within their borders. This is another dilemma. With the same concerns often doing both local and interstate business, and with their property being employed in both types of commerce, how are the above principles to be applied?

Naturally a state can tax the fixed property of a foreign corporation which is located within the state. But what about the movable property? Can it tax, for example, only the railroad cars that happen to be within its boundaries on tax assessment day? Even with respect to the fixed property, there are problems in determining the value of property for tax purposes. The property of an interstate railroad, or a telegraph company, or a pipeline, has value as a unit. One state may contain the expensive terminal properties of a railroad, while in another state there may be little more than track. Yet the track mileage in Iowa has greater value than its mere worth as ties and rails, because it is a necessary link in traffic with Chicago. Thus Iowa may justifiably seek to measure taxes on railroad property in the state by some apportionment device which takes into account the contribution made by Iowa to the total operation of the road.

The first recognition by the Supreme Court of the validity of the apportionment principle came in 1888, when Massachusetts was sustained in taxing Western Union on account of the property owned and used by it in the state, taking as the basis for the assessment such proportion of the value of its capital stock as the length of its lines within the state bore to the company's total mileage throughout the country.[43] Similar capital stock apportionment formulas were subsequently approved for the Pullman Company in Pennsylvania and a railroad express company in Ohio.[44] Thus it was

---

[40] *Maine* v. *Grand Trunk Railway Co.* (1891); *Memphis Natural Gas Co.* v. *Stone* (1948).
[41] *Railway Express Agency, Inc.* v. *Virginia* (1959).
[42] See, for example, *Ford Motor Co.* v. *Beauchamp* (1939), and *International Harvester Co.* v. *Evatt* (1947).
[43] *Western Union Telegraph Co.* v. *Massachusetts* (1888).
[44] *Pullman's Palace Car Co.* v. *Pennsylvania* (1891); *Adams Express Co.* v. *Ohio* (1897).

firmly established that values created by interstate commerce could be taxed, provided the state used a formula which the Court considered a fair measure for the protection provided by the state.

Mathematical exactitude in fixing the apportionment would not be demanded. "The difficulty of making an exact apportionment is apparent," the Court said in 1931, "and hence, when the State has adopted a method not intrinsically arbitrary, it will be sustained until proof is offered of an unreasonable and arbitrary application in particular cases." [45] Nor would the fact that the apportionment of "going concern" value resulted in a figure far above the actual value of corporate property in the state be taken as a necessary objection to its validity. In the express company case, property worth about $70,000 was taxed at a valuation of more than $500,000.

Once the apportionment principle was accepted, the states used their ingenuity in finding various indexes of corporate prosperity against which to apply it. Sometimes corporate net income was taxed on an apportionment basis. In general, a state tax on net income of a concern engaged in both intrastate and interstate commerce does not raise serious questions about burdening the interstate commerce.[46] Even in *Northwestern States Portland Cement Co.* v. *Minnesota* (1959), where an Iowa cement company carried on no business in Minnesota of a local character severable from interstate commerce, the Supreme Court upheld an apportioned tax on net income.

Far more important, however, are state taxes based on corporate gross receipts. Maine made the initial effort in this direction, and in 1891, the Court upheld its tax levied on such proportion of the revenues of railroads operating in the state as their mileage within the state bore to their total mileage.[47] The Court's general principle is that taxation measured by gross receipts is constitutional if fairly apportioned; "the simple but controlling question is whether the state has given anything for which it can ask return." [48] This is the positive justification for the right to tax. But there is also the countervailing principle that interstate commerce cannot be subjected to the burden of "multiple taxation." [49] The Court has recognized that it might approve a basis for corporate taxation which, if applied by every state within which the corporation does business, would have confiscatory effects. The requirement for apportionment is relied on to prevent this result. But of course an apportioned tax may still carry the risks of multiple or burdensome taxation.[50]

In *General Motors Corporation* v. *Washington* (1964), the recent Court indicated that it is more concerned with justifying than with limiting gross

[45] *Hans Rees' Sons* v. *North Carolina* (1931).
[46] *United States Glue Co.* v. *Oak Creek* (1918).
[47] *Maine* v. *Grand Trunk Railway Co.* (1891).
[48] *Wisconsin* v. *J. C. Penney Co.* (1940).
[49] *Michigan-Wisconsin Pipe Line Co.* v. *Calvert* (1954); see also *Gwin, White & Prince* v. *Henneford* (1939).
[50] See *Joseph* v. *Carter & Weekes Stevedoring Co.* (1947).

receipts taxes. Here the tax was measured by gross wholesale sales of motor vehicles and parts in the state. Though the tax was unapportioned, the Court upheld it on the ground that taxable local business was so mingled with interstate business that the state was justified in attributing all sales in Washington to its local activity. The company claimed that multiple taxation might result, since interstate sales might also be taxable in other states. But the Court held no actual showing of such a burden had been made.

The apportionment principle, originating largely in connection with railroad transportation, has not been so directly applicable to navigation and air transport. For vessels the general rule is that they are taxable only at their home port, unless they have acquired actual situs in another state by continuous employment there, and this rule prevents multiple taxation.[51] However, in 1949 the apportionment principle was successfully applied by Louisiana to a barge line operating on the Mississippi.[52] Minnesota was able to utilize a version of the home port theory in winning the Court's approval for a personal property tax on the entire air fleet of Northwest Airlines, a Minnesota corporation, even though only a fraction of the fleet was in the state on tax day.[53]

Taxation of motor vehicles has largely avoided apportionment problems. Every truck entering a state can be charged a toll for its use of state highways, and the only question is whether the tax is within reasonable bounds. Since the basic decision in *Hendrick* v. *Maryland* (1915) comparatively few taxes on motor vehicles have been declared invalid on commerce grounds.[54] The tax may be based on truck capacity or mileage, or it may be a flat fee.[55] It may even be based on fair market value of the motor vehicles used.[56] A carrier has no right to question a tax levy on the ground that the money is not actually being used by the state for road upkeep.[57]

COURT OR CONGRESS AS TAX UMPIRE    Since the 1930s the Supreme Court has manifested an increased unwillingness to strike down state tax measures on constitutional grounds. Perhaps the initial cause was the desperate financial situation of the states during the Depression, when the Court clearly felt under some compulsion to approve the new taxes developed to save the states from bankruptcy. Another factor was the uncertainty of some justices as to the validity of their credentials as tax umpires. Around 1940 Justices Black and Douglas, joined for a time by Frankfurter, revived the Taney doctrine that the responsibility of enforcing the commerce clause involves

---

[51] *Gloucester Ferry Co.* v. *Pennsylvania* (1885); *Old Dominion S.S. Co.* v. *Virginia* (1905).
[52] *Ott* v. *Mississippi Barge Line Co.* (1949).
[53] *Northwest Airlines* v. *Minnesota* (1944).
[54] Examples are *Interstate Transit* v. *Lindsey* (1931); *Ingels* v. *Morf* (1937).
[55] *Aero Mayflower Transit Co.* v. *Georgia Public Service Cmsn.* (1935).
[56] *Capitol Greyhound Lines* v. *Brice* (1950).
[57] *Dixie Ohio Express* v. *State Revenue Cmsn.* (1939).

so much discretion that it belongs more appropriately to Congress.[58] Although this "leave-it-to-Congress" attitude enjoyed some minor successes, the Court soon returned to its role as umpire of the federal system. As Frankfurter said in *Freeman* v. *Hewit* (1946), "The Commerce Clause was not merely an authorization to Congress to enact laws for the protection and encouragement of commerce among the States, but by its own force created an area of trade free from interference by the States."

The Court's continued leniency toward state taxation impinging on interstate commerce eventually did lead Congress to enter this field for the first time. After the decision in *Northwestern States Portland Cement Co.* v. *Minnesota* (1959), upholding the right of a state to impose a net income tax on the purely interstate business of a foreign corporation, Congress enacted a statute limiting the power of states to tax the net income of interstate corporations, which either overruled the *Northwestern* decision or assured there would be no further extension of state taxing power in this area.[59] A House committee then undertook a study of state taxation of interstate commerce, and in 1965 made recommendations for legislation on state sales taxes and gross receipts taxes as well as uniform apportionment formulas.[60] It appears that Congress may at long last undertake part of the burden which the Supreme Court has been carrying in this difficult field of federalism.

## SELECTED REFERENCES

*The Constitution of the United States of America: Analysis and Interpretation,* Sen. Doc. no. 39, 88th Cong., pp. 205–282. Washington: Government Printing Office, 1964.

CORWIN, EDWARD S., *The Commerce Power versus States Rights.* Princeton, N.J.: Princeton University Press, 1936.

DOUGLAS, WILLIAM O., *We the Judges,* chap. 7. Garden City, N.Y.: Doubleday & Company, Inc., 1956.

KALLENBACH, JOSEPH E., *Federal Cooperation with the States under the Commerce Clause.* Ann Arbor, Mich.: The University of Michigan Press, 1942.

KONEFSKY, SAMUEL J., *Chief Justice Stone and the Supreme Court,* chap. 2. New York: The Macmillan Company, 1945.

PRITCHETT, C. HERMAN, *The Roosevelt Court: A Study in Judicial Politics and Values, 1937–1947,* chap. 4. New York: The Macmillan Company, 1948.

[58] See Taney's dissent in *Pennsylvania* v. *Wheeling Bridge Co.* (1852); the dissent of Black, Douglas, and Frankfurter in *McCarroll* v. *Dixie Greyhound Lines* (1940); and Black's concurring opinion in *Northwest Airlines* v. *Minnesota* (1944).

[59] Pub. L. no. 86–272 (1959). In *Mouton* v. *International Shoe Co.* (1964) the Supreme Court declined to review a state court decision upholding the constitutionality of this statute.

[60] See House Reports nos. 565, 952, 89th Cong., 1st sess. (1965).

# Part 5

The executive

# 16

## Qualifications and election

The creation of the Presidency of the United States by the Constitutional Convention was political invention of a very high order. While there can have been in 1787 no conception of the powerful and multifaceted office which history and practice were to make of the Presidency, the basis was laid for this development by the bold decisions of the Founders.

Their duality of views on the presidential office has already been noted. On one side was the preference for an executive which would be nothing more than an institution for carrying the will of the legislature into effect, with an incumbent appointed by and accountable to the legislature. On the other side was the strong-executive faction, which wanted a single-headed office independent of the legislature. As the Convention deliberated, the key decisions increasingly favored the latter view.

In the controversy over ratification of the Constitution, fear of these strong executive powers was one of the motives most widely exploited by opponents of the new charter. Hamilton in No. 67 of *The Federalist* ridiculed the efforts that had been made to present the office as possessed of practically royal prerogatives. As for the unity of the executive, he contended that far from being a danger, it made the institution more susceptible of popular surveillance and control, while at the same time guaranteeing energy in the office, "a leading character in the definition of good government."

What the "energy" of George Washington and his successors has made

of the office cannot be recounted here. Our concern is the much narrower one of examining the basis which the specific provisions of Article II, as judicially interpreted, have provided for the presidential office, and the authority which these provisions have conferred, or the limits they have imposed, upon presidential power. Thus confined, much of the flesh and blood of the Presidency is outside the scope of our consideration. For the Supreme Court has only infrequently been called on to resolve the constitutional issues of the Presidency. Where executive action has impinged on private rights, or occasionally in cases of conflict between the President and Congress, judicial intervention to define the constitutional situation has been successfully invoked. But over the broad political reaches of presidential power the judicial influence has been minor. In the area of the present chapter, which deals with the qualifications and electoral arrangements for the Presidency, judicial interpretation has seldom been important.

### QUALIFICATIONS

The Constitution provides that "No person except a natural born citizen, or a citizen of the United States, at the time of the adoption of this Constitution, shall be eligible to the office of President." The clause making eligible persons who were citizens of the United States at the time of the adoption of the Constitution was of only temporary significance, but it was necessary since every adult in the United States in 1787, who had been born in this country, had been born a British subject.

Every person born in the United States and subject to its jurisdiction is a citizen and, of course, a natural-born citizen. Persons born abroad and acquiring citizenship by the process of naturalization are thus excluded from eligibility to the Presidency. But persons born abroad to American citizen parents are considered natural-born American citizens.[1]

The other qualifications of the President as stated in Article II are that he shall have attained the age of thirty-five years, and have been for fourteen years a resident within the United States. The assumption that this fourteen-year period need not be continuous preceding accession to the office is borne out by the fact that Herbert Hoover had not been a continuous resident of the United States for fourteen years when he was elected President in 1928. Although these are the only constitutional qualifications which must be met for eligibility to the Presidency, in effect Congress has added to them by

[1] Congress so provided by Act of March 26, 1790, 1 Stat. 415. In spite of this statute some effort was made in 1967 to prove that George Romney, Governor of Michigan, who was born of American parents in Mexico, was not eligible for the Presidency. As Corwin says, "Should . . . the American people ever choose for President a person born abroad of American parents, it is highly improbable that any other constitutional agency would venture to challenge their decision. . . ." *The President: Office and Powers* (New York: New York University Press, 1957), p. 33.

providing that persons convicted of various federal crimes shall, in addition to other penalties, be incapable of holding office under the United States.

## PRESIDENTIAL ELECTION AND THE CONSTITUTION

THE ORIGINAL PLAN    The constitutional solution of the problem of presidential selection was to provide that each state should "appoint, in such manner as the legislature thereof may direct, a number of electors, equal to the whole number of Senators and Representatives to which the State may be entitled in the Congress." That the electors should not be holders of federal office was guaranteed by the further provision that "no Senator or Representative, or person holding an office of trust or profit under the United States, shall be appointed an elector."

The choosing of the President was thus to be in the hands of a selected group of citizens in each state, equal in number to that state's congressional delegation. But the resemblance to Congress went no further. Instead of assembling in the capital, the electors were to "meet in their respective States, and vote by ballot for two persons, of whom one at least shall not be an inhabitant of the same State with themselves." The results of the vote were to be transmitted to the president of the Senate, who would open the sealed certificates in the presence of both houses, and the votes would then be counted. The person with the greatest number of votes was to be the President, provided he had a majority of the whole number of electors. If two candidates were tied, and both had more than a majority, the House was immediately to choose between them. If no candidate had a majority, then the House would choose from the five highest on the list. In either event the House was to vote by states, "the representation from each State having one vote," with a majority required to elect. After the choice of the President, the person having the next greatest number of votes was to be Vice President, and in the event of a tie, the Senate was to choose between the contenders.

The intention of the framers as to the role of the electors was not entirely clear. Hamilton thought the electors could freely choose candidates for President on the basis of their own judgment and experience, but others have argued that the electoral plan was a step toward, not away from, popular election and that the electors were to be bound by pledges they had given in securing appointment.[2] In any case, the unanimity of agreement on Washington prevented any difficulties arising in the first two elections.

With the development of political parties, the electoral plan was immediately in trouble. The result of the 1796 balloting was to give the Presidency and vice presidency to different parties, with John Adams and Thomas Jefferson ranking first and second in the electoral voting.

[2] Lucius Wilmerding, Jr., *The Electoral College* (New Brunswick, N.J.: Rutgers University Press, 1958), pp. 19–22.

This was a minor defect, however, compared with the result in 1800. Jefferson and Aaron Burr, as the Republican candidates for President and Vice President, were both named by each Republican elector, so that a tie resulted. Everyone understood that Jefferson was the Presidential choice, but the tie threw the election into the House, voting by states. There the Federalists were tempted to thwart their great opponent by casting their votes for Burr, and it took prolonged balloting and the influence of Hamilton before the House finally elected Jefferson in February, 1801.

PROBLEMS UNDER THE TWELFTH AMENDMENT   This experience exposed a constitutional defect so serious that immediate repair was needed. Consequently the Twelfth Amendment was adopted in 1804, and it still controls the electoral process. It made the following changes: (1) the electors were to ballot separately for President and Vice President; (2) if no candidate for President received a majority, the House, voting as before by states, was to choose "from the persons having the highest numbers not exceeding three on the list"; (3) the Vice President also had to receive a majority of the electoral votes, and if no one achieved a majority, the Senate was to choose between the two highest candidates; (4) if the choice of President fell to the House, and it had not made a choice by March 4, the Vice President was to act as President; and (5) it was specifically provided that no person constitutionally ineligible to the office of President should be eligible to that of Vice President.

This was an improvement, but the election of 1824 showed how unsatisfactory was the alternative of selection by the House. The breakdown of the congressional caucus in that election caused votes to be cast for a number of candidates, the three highest being Andrew Jackson with ninety-nine, John Quincy Adams, eighty-four, and William H. Crawford, forty-one. Henry Clay, Speaker of the House and one of the defeated candidates, swung the vote to Adams, to the vast outrage of the Jackson forces, who claimed that the House was morally bound to select the candidate with the highest electoral vote. Adams offered the consolation of Cabinet posts to all the defeated candidates, but only Clay accepted, and his appointment as Secretary of State was popularly taken as proof that Adams had secured the Presidency by a bargain with Clay. The uproar of 1824 led to no constitutional revision, however, and the subsequent development of a mature two-party system kept further electoral difficulties from arising until 1876.

The Hayes-Tilden election controversy was an incredibly tangled affair. The truth seems to be that the Democrats stole the election in the first place, and the Republicans then stole it back. There was no doubt that Tilden, the Democratic candidate, had a popular majority. He was conceded 184 electoral votes, one less than a majority, and Hayes had 165, while 20 were in dispute. Disagreement centered on Louisiana, South Carolina, and Florida, from which rival sets of returns had been sent in amid charges of fraud and

violence, and Oregon, where one elector was in dispute. A majority of the Senate was Republican and a majority of the House was Democratic. If the president of the Senate decided which votes to count, Hayes would win, whereas if the election was thrown into the House, Tilden would be elected.

The Twelfth Amendment provides that the president of the Senate should open the certificates, but does not say who should do the counting or decide what votes to count. With the two houses hopelessly deadlocked, a completely extraconstitutional compromise was eventually enacted at the end of January, 1877. A fifteen-man Electoral Commission was created, composed of five members of the House (three Democrats and two Republicans), five Senators (three Republicans and two Democrats), and five members of the Supreme Court. Four of the justices were designated in the act by reference to their judicial circuits, and they were evenly divided as to parties. The fifth justice, chosen by these four, was Joseph P. Bradley of New Jersey, a Republican, whose vote gave the Republicans an eight to seven margin on each of the issues before the Commission.

Bradley's position was that the Constitution required Congress to accept the returns as authenticated by the state election officials, and gave no power to conduct an inquiry into the conduct of the elections. Consequently the Commission majority counted for Hayes the nineteen votes from the three Southern states as reported by state officials. But the lone Oregon vote, on which the election now depended, had been certified by the state officials for Tilden on the ground that the Republican elector, who had a higher vote, had been ineligible because at the time of his election he held "an office of trust and profit under the United States." The Republican majority of the Commission conveniently discovered that this was an issue on which it could challenge the certification of the state officials, and accepted the vote of the Republican elector, thus electing Hayes by a vote of 185 to 184.

There was momentary talk of violence by the defeated Democrats, but cooler heads prevailed. The act setting up the Commission had reserved any right existing under the Constitution to question in the courts the titles of the victorious candidates, but no case was ever brought. Thus was the country rescued from the consequences of a faulty electoral system by a device entirely unknown to the Constitution. In 1887 Congress by statute provided that any dispute over appointment of electors was to be conclusively settled by the state itself, provided it did so at least six days before the time for the meeting of the electors. If a state failed to perform this function and its electoral vote remained in dispute, it would not be counted unless both houses of Congress agreed. So the 1876 dilemma need not be reenacted, and no subsequent presidential election has posed the threat of comparable breakdown in electoral machinery. But certain basic characteristics of the electoral college system remain as perennial subjects of controversy.

## ELECTORAL COLLEGE PROBLEMS

DISTORTION OF THE POPULAR VOTE    The first objection to the electoral college system is the disproportion it usually yields between the electoral vote and the popular vote. The electoral college margin of the winning candidate is typically much greater than his majority in the popular vote. This does no real harm, of course, and may even have some psychological value when it results in giving a clear electoral college majority to a candidate who secured only a plurality in the popular vote.

But electoral college distortion can also have the opposite consequence of deflating a popular vote majority or plurality into an electoral vote minority. In three presidential elections—1824, 1876, and 1888—the winning candidate did not lead in the popular vote. However, in two of these three cases, it is hardly fair to blame the electoral system for the perversion of the popular mandate. In 1824 this responsibility rests on the House for failing to select the popular favorite, Jackson, and similarly in 1876 it was the Electoral Commission which made the decisions that kept Tilden out of office. Thus the 1888 experience, when Harrison was elected with 100,000 fewer votes than Cleveland, is the only bona fide case of the electoral college yielding a minority President. Nevertheless, it may well be argued that even one case is one too many, and that the mere existence of such a possibility is a grave defect in an electoral system.[3]

THE UNIT VOTE    Actually, the major reason for this potentiality of electoral miscarriage is not a constitutionally required feature of the electoral system. The primary cause of distortion is the practice (which, with minor exceptions, all states have followed for well over a century) of each state casting its electoral votes as a unit for the candidate securing a majority or plurality of the popular votes in that state, rather than using some plan of proportional division of the electors.

The Constitution does not control the manner in which the states shall "appoint" their electors, and a great variety of means have been employed. In the first three presidential elections, choice of electors by the state legislatures was the usual method. Thereafter popular election became the rule, and at first several states used the district plan, which meant that a state's electoral vote could be divided among the candidates. By 1832, however, all states had abandoned the district plan, and it has since been employed only rarely. With the statewide general ticket system of choosing electors, it is virtually impossible for a split result to occur. No state is likely to abandon the present plan on its own initiative, for a proportional division of its vote while other states retained the block principle would minimize its electoral college importance.

[3] In 1948 a shift of 29,294 votes in California, Illinois, and Ohio would have elected Dewey over Truman, even though Truman would still have had a national plurality of more than 2,077,000 popular votes.

The unit-vote system makes each of the big states, where the parties are usually rather evenly balanced, a glittering jackpot. The parties must give major attention to capturing votes in the large states, where the potential payoff is so great, while largely disregarding the smaller states. The candidates are usually selected from the large states, and the parties must direct their appeals to the interests of their urban and industrial residents. Senator Goldwater's strategy in 1964 of deliberately abandoning the large states of the industrial East and seeking to build an electoral majority out of the West and South was a formula for disaster. Moreover, with the entire electoral vote of each large state subject to determination by the margin of a few thousand votes, bad weather, fraud, appeals to minority groups, and other fortuitous circumstances may determine the choice of President.

Another effect of the unit-vote system is that it prevents voters who supported the losing candidate in each state from having any impact on the electoral result. Though a candidate may secure only 51 per cent of the popular votes, he is awarded the entire electoral vote of the state, and those who opposed him are in effect coerced by the system into supporting him. In 1966 the state of Delaware filed an unusual suit with the Supreme Court in its original jurisdiction, contending that the unit-voting system abridged the political rights of individuals by canceling each state's minority votes, gave the large states a favored position, created the possibility of minority Presidents, and in general guaranteed distortion and debasement in the electoral process. The Supreme Court dismissed the suit.[4]

OTHER DISTORTING FACTORS     The unit system of casting electoral votes is not the only cause of the typical lack of correspondence between the electoral and popular results. There is in addition the overweighting of the electoral vote of the less populous states, which results from giving each state, large or small, two electoral votes on the basis of its two Senators.

A further factor in causing skewed electoral results is the varying rate of voter turnout in the states. In the South, where the real contests until recently were decided in the Democratic primaries, the final elections have tended to be routine, attracting relatively few voters. The past disfranchisement of Negro voters in the area also contributed to low turnout, so that in general each electoral vote cast by a Southern state represented only a fraction of the voters per electoral vote elsewhere.

Finally, shifts in population and varying rates of population growth among the states between census periods cause additional disproportion between popular and electoral votes. In the election of 1960 each state still cast the number of electoral votes it had been awarded under the census of 1950. Thus California had only thirty-two electoral votes in the 1960 election, whereas her population as shown by the 1960 census would have entitled the state to forty votes.

[4] *Delaware v. New York* (1966).

THE STATUS OF ELECTORS    A second disturbing feature of the present system is the status of the electors. Successful operation of the electoral college system requires that the electors regard themselves as automatons, whose sole function is to cast an electoral vote for the candidates of their party. Actually the system worked this way until 1948, with only a few exceptions. In 1821 an elector who should have voted for Monroe cast his vote for John Quincy Adams, reportedly to prevent a unanimous result and thus to preserve for Washington the honor of being the only President ever selected unanimously. In the disputed election of 1876, James Russell Lowell, a Hayes elector from Massachusetts, was urged to cast his vote for Tilden and thus end the controversy which seemed to be threatening the stability of the nation, but he refused to do so on the ground that it would be "treacherous, dishonorable, and immoral" to fail to comply with his election mandate.

General acceptance of the automatic character of the electors' function is reflected in the fact that their names do not even appear on the ballot in almost three-fourths of the states. However, in recent elections there have been organized efforts in certain Southern states to claim for electors the freedom of choice which presumably was theirs in the original constitutional theory. In part this freedom has been asserted by individual electors. But it has also been claimed by state legislatures who have provided for unpledged slates of electors, under no instructions from the electorate and completely free to vote their own choices in the electoral college.

In 1948 a Democratic elector from Tennessee, who was also on the slate of electors for the States' Rights Dixiecrats, cast his electoral vote for Thurmond instead of Truman. In 1956 one of Alabama's Democratic electors refused to support Stevenson and cast his vote for an Alabama circuit judge.

In 1960 several slates of electors unpledged to any candidate were on state ballots. Georgia's twelve Democratic electors were not pledged to support Kennedy, and only five of Alabama's eleven Democratic electors were so pledged. In Mississippi there were two sets of Democratic electors, one unpledged, while in Louisiana the States' Rights party's electors were unpledged. In the actual balloting the six unpledged Alabama electors and all eight Mississippi electors voted for Senator Harry F. Byrd of Virginia. So did one of the Republican electors from Oklahoma, Henry D. Irwin. After Kennedy's narrow victory at the polls, Irwin and an Alabama attorney made contact with all the victorious electors of both parties urging them to withhold their electoral votes or to vote for a third candidate, in the hope that Kennedy would be deprived of his electoral vote majority and the election be thrown into the House. But the plan failed, and no elector except Irwin violated his pledge. In the 1964 electoral vote there were no defections.

Various efforts have been made to ensure that electors will actually vote for the nominees of their party. In most states electors are now required to give signed or oral pledges to this effect. However, in 1964 only California and Oregon had state laws requiring electors to honor their pledges. An

Alabama statute of this kind, subsequently repealed, was upheld by the Supreme Court in *Ray* v. *Blair* (1952).

Since voters can support a presidential candidate only by voting for a pledged set of electors, the possibility arises that a state can completely deny to its citizens the opportunity to vote for a major party candidate. This happened in 1948 when the Alabama States' Rights Democrats took over the party organization and chose a list of electors pledged to vote against the party's nominees. No list of electors pledged to Truman and Barkley was on the Alabama ballot. Again in 1964 the Democratic nominees received no votes in Alabama because the only Democratic slate of electors was unpledged. In fact, three states in 1964—Alabama, Mississippi, and Georgia—had laws providing that electors could not be pledged to a candidate. However, the Republican electors received a majority in all three states and did cast their votes for the Republican candidates.

ELECTION BY THE HOUSE     A third feature of the present system which is almost universally condemned is the choice of a President by the House, voting by states, in the event that no candidate receives a majority of the electoral vote. Since the Twelfth Amendment has been in effect, this has happened only once, in 1824, and it yielded a result in conflict with the voters' choice. Much more serious results are possible if the experience is ever repeated, as it very nearly was in 1948. Had Truman lost Ohio and California—and his combined majority in these two states was 25,472 out of 6,700,000 votes cast—the election would have been thrown into the House, because of the success of the third-party candidate in four states.

In the House as constituted on January 3, 1949, twenty-one state delegations had a Democratic majority, twenty had a Republican majority, three were evenly divided, and four represented states carried by the States' Rights ticket. It is hard to overestimate the turmoil which would have been involved in getting twenty-five of these delegations to agree on Truman, Dewey, or Thurmond in the short period from January 3 to noon of January 20, the hour when the new President's term was to begin. If no President had been selected by that time, then the Vice President, chosen from between Alben Barkley and Earl Warren by the Senate, which had fifty-four Democrats, would have begun to act as President.

Again, in 1960 a shift of only a few thousand votes in key states carried by Kennedy with narrow margins would have left him, as well as Nixon, without an electoral college majority and enabled the Byrd electors to throw the choice of President into the House.

### PROPOSALS FOR ELECTORAL REFORM

Reform of the electoral college system has been perennially discussed, but the difficulty of taking action has always been that there was no consensus on an alternative. Many proposals have been considered by congressional

committees, particularly the Senate Judiciary Subcommittee on Constitutional Amendments under the chairmanship first of Senator Kefauver and later Senator Bayh.[5] However, the closest Congress came to action was in 1950, when the so-called Lodge-Gossett proportional-vote amendment passed the Senate by the necessary majority but failed in the House.

A principal reason for this inability to agree on any change in the electoral arrangements is that, in spite of the defects pointed out above, many persons feel, with considerable justification, that the present system has worked reasonably well. It has produced Chief Executives comparable in quality, if not generally superior, to those of other democratic nations. It has met crises successfully. No President has had to be chosen by the House since 1824. No President has been elected with fewer popular votes than his opponent since 1888. The method has been a strong source of support for the two-party system by handicapping the development of third parties. Although eleven men who received less than 50 per cent of the popular vote have been elected President,[6] only two were supported by less than 45 per cent of the electorate—Lincoln with 39.79 per cent in 1860 and Wilson with 41.85 per cent in 1912.

Defenders of the present system admit, of course, that the casting of electoral votes by state units gives predominant campaign importance to the large states, the large cities, and key minority groups in the large cities. But their response is that it is appropriate for urban influences to control in electing the President because the state legislatures and both houses of Congress are overweighted in representation of rural areas and the small states. Thus one imbalance tends to correct the other.[7] In 1956 the then-Senator John F. Kennedy, speaking in opposition to changes in the electoral system, said: "It is not only the unit vote for the Presidency we are talking about, but a whole solar system of government. If it is proposed to change the balance of power of one of the elements of the solar system, it is necessary to consider the others."

As already pointed out, the unit system is not required by the Constitution, and any state could abandon it if it chose. In 1966 President Johnson proposed to Congress the adoption of an amendment which, among other changes, would have made the unit vote mandatory for the states. This feature of his proposal drew little support, but the presidential initiative did result in renewed interest in the whole subject of electoral college revision.

[5] See the references to hearings of the subcommittee, at the conclusion of this chapter.
[6] This figure would be increased to fourteen by adding the three Presidents—Adams (1824), Hayes (1876), and Harrison (1888)—who were elected although they had fewer popular votes than their opponents.
[7] This situation is less true since the Supreme Court required state legislatures and the House of Representatives to follow the rule of one man, one vote.

THE PROPORTIONAL-VOTE PLAN    The proportional-vote plan is usually referred to as the Lodge-Gossett amendment after its two initial sponsors. This plan would give candidates for the Presidency such proportion of the electoral vote in each state as the candidate received of the total vote cast for the Presidency in that state, percentages being figured to three places beyond the decimal point. This plan would make the relation between the electoral and popular vote exactly proportional, but would not correct the distortions arising from the small state advantage in electoral votes, differences in the rate of turnout, or census lag in dividing electoral votes among the states.

Fears have been expressed that the proportional electoral count might encourage the formation of third parties or a whole group of splinter parties. The present block system has been a barrier to the success of third parties, for unless they can get the top vote in one or more states, they get no credit at all for their popular votes in the electoral college. But under a proportional system of recording the vote, all votes cast are given effect and the chances of a party with a mere plurality vote winning the Presidency are increased. For this reason the Lodge-Gossett plan, when before the Senate in 1950, was revised by addition of the Lucas amendment, requiring a 40 per cent plurality in the electoral vote to elect a President. If no candidate had such a proportion, the election would be thrown into Congress, the House and Senate, sitting jointly, to elect the President from the top two candidates.

In addition to reflecting more accurately the popular strength of the candidates, the proportional plan would retain the importance of the states in the electoral process, and would encourage turnout and the growth of the second party in previously one-party states, since every vote cast would be given effect in the count. Objections to the plan, in addition to its possible encouragement of splinter parties, are that the large states would lose their present commanding position, while the small states woud not give up their advantage of two electoral votes regardless of size, and that it would still be possible for a candidate to be elected President with fewer popular votes than his opponent. Indeed, if the votes in the 1960 election had been counted by the proportional system, Nixon, with 113,000 fewer votes than Kennedy, would have been elected with 266.075 electoral votes to 265.623 for Kennedy.

THE DISTRICT-VOTE PLAN    The district plan, originally sponsored by Senator Mundt, would require electors to be chosen by districts, using either the existing congressional districts or the same number of districts drawn specifically for presidential elections. The two electoral votes awarded to each state by reason of its Senate seats would of course continue to be subject to statewide election. Unlike the proportional plan, which dispenses with electors, the district plan would retain the position of elector, and the candidate for elector receiving a plurality of the votes in his district would

be elected. If no candidate achieved a majority in the electoral vote, the President would be chosen from among the highest three candidates by the senators and representatives sitting jointly and voting as individuals.

The arguments for the district plan are that it would eliminate the electoral distortions and emphasis on the large states that result from the unit-vote plan; that by using congressional districts it would give exactly the same kind of representative quality to the electoral vote as is found in Congress; and that, unlike the proportional plan, it would discourage third parties because they would have to carry individual congressional districts in order to have any electoral impact.

Against the district plan the arguments are that it is preferable to have different bases for the election of President and members of Congress; that the temptation to gerrymander congressional districts would be too great to control, since gerrymandering would now pay off twice, both in congressional and presidential elections; that many states would continue to vote as a unit, since the winning party is often dominant in the entire state; and that rural and one-party states would be advantaged at the expense of urban areas.

THE DIRECT NATIONWIDE VOTE    The simplest and most direct plan for electing the President would be to abandon the electoral college system entirely, ignore state lines, and throw all the voters of the nation into a single electorate for choice of the President. The case for this method is overwhelming. The votes of all individuals would be equal. Since all votes count in the national total, political activity would be encouraged in all areas, including previously one-party states.

The direct nationwide vote is the most democratic system. The President, as the only elected national official (along with the Vice President), should be chosen by the nation and responsible to it. Only direct election can guarantee that the man elected President will be the one with more popular votes than any other candidate. Under the unit, proportional, or district plan it is possible for a candidate to lose in the popular vote and win in the electoral vote; all three systems are lotteries where the relation between the popular and electoral votes is subject to chance.

Direct election would of course eliminate the electoral vote advantage now enjoyed by the small states, and for this reason it was long assumed that a constitutional amendment abolishing the electoral vote system could never secure ratification by three-fourths of the states. But in fact the small-state advantage has been more than offset by the advantage the unit system gives to the large states. Increasingly it has become evident that the only practicable way to remedy these inequities is to abandon the states as electoral areas. In 1966 the United States Chamber of Commerce and an American Bar Association Commission on Electoral College Reform both supported direct election, and a poll of 2,700 state legislators conducted by

Senator Burdick showed 59 per cent favoring direct election, 17 per cent for the proportional plan, 13 per cent for districts, and 10 per cent for retaining the present electoral college setup.

Direct election would create some problems calling for decision. An absolute majority of the popular votes could hardly be required for election; as already noted, fourteen past Presidents polled less than 50 per cent of the vote. On the other hand, if a plurality is sufficient to elect, this might encourage splinter parties to enter candidates and fragment the national vote. A President who took office on the basis of a 30 per cent plurality would be in a very weak position to exercise national leadership.

The direct election bill introduced by Senator Bayh in the Eighty-ninth Congress, S.J. Res. 163, provided that a candidate to be elected must receive a plurality of at least 40 per cent of the popular vote. Only one American President has ever been elected with less than this percentage, and that was Lincoln in 1860 when there were four major candidates. The figure of 40 per cent represents a respectable consensus, and should be relatively easy for one candidate to achieve in case of a three-way race.

But if 40 per cent or some other minimum plurality is adopted, provision must be made for the eventuality that no candidate may achieve that minimum. There are two possibilities. One is a runoff election limited to the top two candidates. The other is election by Congress, with members of both houses sitting jointly and voting as individuals. The first is democratic but expensive and a complete novelty at the national level. The second is less democratic but simpler and sanctioned by past practice.

Direct national election of the President would call for consideration of voter qualifications, which are now fixed by the states, subject to federal constitutional provisions. The states would of course continue to provide the election machinery, and they could be left with major responsibility over voter qualifications. The Bayh bill provides that all persons eligible under state law to vote for members of Congress would also be eligible to vote for President, except that the states could adopt less restrictive residence requirements for voting in the presidential election.[8] It is possible that direct election of the President might cause states to reduce their age limits for voting, in order to increase the relative weight of their state in the national poll. Four states already have lowered the voting age below twenty-one, and it is likely that other states would join the parade under this stimulus. The Bayh bill would take care of any possible excesses in competitive reduction of the age limit by empowering Congress to fix a uniform minimum age for presidential elections. Chances for adoption of the direct vote plan were improved when Senate minority leader Everett Dirksen joined with Bayh during the 1967 session in sponsoring the amendment.

---

[8] More than twenty states already have adopted more lenient residence requirements for voting in presidential elections than for electing other officials.

### TERM AND TENURE

The decision of the Convention for a four-year term was based in large part on the delegates' preference for presidential re-eligibility. When Washington declined a third term, he did so for reasons of personal convenience. But when Jefferson announced in 1807 that he would withdraw after two terms, he stressed Washington's example and raised the issue to one of principle, arguing that indefinite re-eligibility would undermine the elective system and turn the Presidency into a life tenure post. The subsequent examples of Madison, Monroe, and Jackson gave the two-term tradition almost unassailable validity. In fact Jackson while President repeatedly urged a constitutional amendment making the President directly elective for a single term only, of from four to six years.

The first concerted attack on the two-term tradition came in 1876 from a group of Republican politicians who wanted Grant to run for a third term, but the resistance was overwhelming. In 1908 Theodore Roosevelt, having served three and a half years of McKinley's term and one term in his own right, stated that "the wise custom which limits the President to two terms regards the substance and not the form," and stated flatly that "under no circumstances will I be a candidate for or accept another nomination." However, by 1912 he had changed his mind, and unsuccessfully sought a third term. Calvin Coolidge found himself in somewhat the same position in 1928, but he never definitely stated his view on the application of the two-term tradition in his case, merely announcing that he did not "choose to run for President in 1928."

Thus it was left for Franklin Roosevelt definitely to breach the tradition in 1940, when the electorate concluded that maintenance of the two-term limit was less important than retaining his experienced leadership in a world at war. Election for a precedent-shattering fourth term was quickly followed by Roosevelt's death on April 12, 1945.

The tragic denouement of this experiment with unlimited re-eligibility, combined with pent-up Republican frustration over four successive defeats by the same candidate, quickly produced a move for writing the two-term rule into the Constitution. When the Republicans won control of the Eightieth Congress they immediately pushed through such an amendment, which was ratified in 1951. The Twenty-second Amendment provides that no person shall be elected to the office of President more than twice, and that no person who has held the office of President, or acted as President, for more than two years of a term to which some other person was elected President, shall be elected more than once. This provision would have made Theodore Roosevelt ineligible in 1912 and Coolidge in 1928.

In support of the two-term limit, it can be argued that the physical toll of eight years in the Presidency under present conditions is all that any man can safely endure and that it is desirable to have an automatic limit on presi-

dential ambitions. On the other hand, this provision forecloses the possibility of retaining an experienced President for a third term in times of emergency, and it may substantially weaken the authority of the President in the closing years of his second term.

## SUCCESSION

Apart from the expiration of his term, the President's tenure in office may be terminated by resignation, impeachment, inability to perform his duties, or death. No man has yet resigned the Presidency, and impeachment has been attempted only once, against Andrew Johnson. On the other hand, eight Presidents have died in office, and there have been three instances when substantial doubt existed about the ability of the President to perform his duties.

THE STATUS OF THE VICE PRESIDENT    The constitutional provision for these contingencies is found in Article II, section 1, as follows: "In case of the removal of the President from office, or of his death, resignation, or inability to discharge the powers and duties of the said office, the same shall devolve on the Vice President." Another relevant provision is found in the Twelfth Amendment, which requires that the Vice President have the same qualifications as the President.

The vagueness of the constitutional language on succession has been the cause of much controversy. What is it that devolves upon the Vice President when the President dies, resigns, or is impeached? Is it the "office" of President, or only the "powers and duties" of the office? Does the Vice President become President, or does he simply "act" as President until a new President is elected?

An excellent case can be made for the latter alternative, both on the basis of the language of the Constitution and on what is known about the intention of the framers from other evidence. Certainly the drafters intended that only an acting President be installed under the circumstances described in the latter part of the same paragraph, which provides: "And the Congress may by law provide for the case of removal, death, resignation or inability, both of the President and Vice President, declaring what officer shall then act as President." The point is then driven home by the rest of the paragraph: "And such officer shall act accordingly, until the disability be removed, or a President shall be elected." There is also the language of the Twelfth Amendment, which prescribes what shall be done if no candidate secures the requisite majority of votes in the electoral college or the House: "Then the Vice President shall act as President, as in the case of the death or other constitutional disability of the President."

There was no need to construe the constitutional language on succession until 1841, when President Harrison died after only one month in office. It

therefore fell to Vice President John Tyler to establish the practice in this all-important respect. Tyler was on his Virginia farm when Harrison died on April 4, and the Cabinet sent him a notice of the fact, addressing him as Vice President. Tyler took the oath prescribed by the Constitution on April 6, but the certificate of the judge who administered the oath noted that Tyler deemed himself "qualified to perform the duties and exercise the powers and offices of President . . . without any other oath" than the one he had taken as Vice President. He nevertheless took the presidential oath, since "doubts may arise, and for greater caution."

This statement of Tyler's would indicate that he initially thought of himself as an acting President, and his Cabinet appears to have taken the same position. However, on April 9 Tyler issued an "inaugural address" in which he spoke of himself as having been called "to the high office of President of this Confederacy." The claim was not accepted without controversy. John Quincy Adams recorded in his diary on April 16 his view that Tyler's position was "in direct violation both of the grammar and context of the Constitution." When Congress met on May 31, the customary resolutions were proposed informing the President that Congress was ready to proceed to business. Amendments were offered in both houses to strike out the word "President" and insert instead "Vice President, now exercising the office of President," but they were defeated. Thus the institution of acting President was strangled at birth.

The ghost of the issue which Tyler decided has walked only once. The original resolution offered in 1867 looking toward the impeachment of Andrew Johnson referred to him as "Vice-President of the United States, discharging the powers and duties of the office of President." However, in the House Judiciary Committee this terminology was dropped, and it was against "the President of the United States" that the impeachment proceedings were directed. The Twentieth Amendment terminated any possible doubt on this matter by providing, in section 3: "If, at the time fixed for the beginning of the term of the President, the President elect shall have died, the Vice President elect shall become President." The Twenty-fifth Amendment added: "In case of the removal of the President from office or of his death or resignation, the Vice President shall become President."

SUCCESSION BEYOND THE VICE PRESIDENT   The Constitution authorizes Congress to declare what "officer shall . . . act as President" in case neither the President nor Vice President is living or able to serve. Congress acted on this authorization in 1792, by passing a statute which provided for the succession first of the President pro tempore of the Senate and then of the Speaker of the House. It was not contemplated that these officials would have much time in office, however, for the statute required immediate steps to be taken for choosing a successor through the electoral college, who would be elected for a full four-year term. If any President had ever been elected

under this statute, the synchronization of presidential elections with congressional would of course have been destroyed. But the act of 1792 never had to be utilized.

In 1886 Congress adopted a different theory of presidential succession, providing that the heads of the seven Cabinet departments then existing, beginning with the Secretary of State, should constitute the line of succession after the Vice President. This act repealed the 1792 provision requiring immediate election of a new President, but it substituted therefor a direction to the acting President to assemble Congress within twenty days if it was not in session, thus apparently intending to give Congress a chance to arrange for election of a President if it should see fit to do so.

Thus the law stood when Harry Truman became President to serve out the last three years and nine months of Franklin Roosevelt's fourth term. Truman was disturbed by the fact that during this long period when there would be no Vice President, succession would go to the man whom he named as Secretary of State. He felt that it was undemocratic for him to be in a position to name his successor, and in a special message to Congress on June 19, 1945, he urged revision of the 1886 law to place the Speaker of the House and the President pro tempore of the Senate ahead of the Cabinet in the line of succession. The Republican Eightieth Congress adopted these proposals in the Presidential Succession Act of 1947.

Under this statute the Speaker of the House, upon resigning as Speaker and as a member of the House, is to act as President when a successor to the Presidency is needed and there is no Vice President. If there is no Speaker, or if he fails to qualify, the President pro tempore of the Senate, upon resigning his post and his Senate seat, is to act as President. In either event the acting President is to serve for the remainder of the current presidential term, unless he is filling in because the President-elect or Vice President-elect had failed to qualify or the President was temporarily disabled; in such a situation his status would terminate if and when the President did qualify or the disability was removed. Cabinet officers follow in the line of succession according to the seniority of their departments.[9] A Cabinet officer must resign his departmental headship on taking the presidential oath of office, but his occupancy of the office would last only until there was a Speaker or President pro tempore available to succeed him. The statute clearly states that the title of all successors taking presidential office under the act will be "Acting President."

The act of 1947 was a bad piece of legislation. Placing the Speaker and President pro tempore ahead of the Secretary of State and other Cabinet members was ill-advised, considering that Secretaries of State have tended

[9] The order of departments is as follows: State, Treasury, Defense, Attorney General, Post Office, Interior, Agriculture, Commerce, and Labor. The newest Cabinet departments, all created since 1947—Health, Education, and Welfare; Housing and Urban Development; and Transportation—are of course not included in the line of succession.

to be men of greater stature, ability, and prominence than the heads of the two houses of Congress. Moreover, having the succession pass to congressional officers opens the way for transfer of party control over the Presidency, if Congress is controlled by the party which lost the last presidential election. Finally, since the Speaker or President pro tempore serves out the remainder of the four-year term after taking office, even though the congressional term to which he was elected may have expired in the meantime, there is the possibility of a new kind of "lame duck" President.

The constitutional flaws in the statute are equally serious, running counter as it does to the theory of separation of powers. The Constitution requires that the person named by Congress as a successor must be an "officer" of the United States. It also declares that no person holding "any office under the United States" is eligible to a seat in Congress. Consequently a member of Congress cannot be an "officer of the United States," and so is ineligible to act as President. Thus the act of 1792 was clearly unconstitutional, because it provided that the acting President was to retain his seat in Congress and his post as President pro tempore or Speaker. The 1947 act chose the other horn of the dilemma, requiring the Speaker or President pro tempore to resign his legislative post and seat *before* becoming Acting President. But it is only as they hold these posts that they are entitled to act as President. Thus the 1947 act seems also to be clearly contrary to the Constitution.

In 1965 Congress found a solution to this problem without repealing the 1947 statute. It adopted and sent to the states for ratification the Twenty-fifth Amendment, which provides in section 2 that "whenever there is a vacancy in the office of the Vice President, the President shall nominate a Vice President who shall take office upon confirmation by a majority vote of both houses of Congress."

This provision solves the problem of succession beyond the Vice President by eliminating the possibility that this eventuality will ever occur (except in some catastrophe where both the President and Vice President met death simultaneously). There will always be a Vice President in office, ready to take over the Presidency if need arises. Appointment of a new Vice President by the President ensures that there will be no change in party control of the Presidency, which might occur if the Speaker of the House succeeded to the post. Confirmation by both houses of Congress ensures that the new Vice President will have the confidence of the legislature and presumably of the country. The Twenty-fifth Amendment constitutes an admirable solution of a problem as old as the Constitution.

### PRESIDENTIAL INABILITY

The Constitution takes account of the President's possible "inability to discharge the powers and duties of the said office," and as in the case of death

or removal, the Vice President is directed to take over. However, unlike death or removal, inability may be only a temporary condition which can pass away and leave the President as fit as ever to continue his duties. If the original constitutional intention that the Vice President would be only an Acting President under all contingencies had come to fruition, there would be little difficulty in the Vice President's filling in temporarily for a disabled President. But the fact that the office of Acting President is unknown to our history in other eventualities has resulted in some doubt as to its applicability in cases of inability.

Three American Presidents have suffered serious disability during their terms of office. President Garfield was shot on July 2, 1881, and lingered on until his death on September 19. During this period he was able to perform only one official act, the signing of an extradition paper. A majority of Garfield's Cabinet believed that any performance of presidential functions by Vice President Arthur would automatically oust Garfield from the Presidency, on the theory that there could not be two Presidents at the same time. Consequently Arthur took no action.

On September 26, 1919, President Wilson suffered a collapse and was disabled for many weeks. For over three months he saw no one except his wife and the doctors. Mrs. Wilson gave him such state papers as she thought he could handle; others were referred by her to Cabinet members. Secretary of State Lansing at the onset of the President's illness tried to secure support for having Vice President Marshall take over Wilson's powers and duties, but was unsuccessful. Then Lansing took the initiative in calling several Cabinet meetings. When Wilson heard of this, he regarded it as an assumption of Presidential authority, and requested Lansing's resignation.

President Eisenhower had three serious illnesses in a little over two years. First was his heart attack in September, 1955, followed by an operation for ileitis in June, 1956, and then by a slight stroke in November, 1957. He had organized the Presidency for the first time on the staff principle with which he was familiar from his military experience, with substantial delegations of authority which kept many of the normal concerns of his predecessors from coming to his attention. He had moreover made greater use of his Vice President than had been customary in the past. During Eisenhower's convalescences the role of the Vice President was somewhat expanded, including the chairing of Cabinet meetings and sessions of the National Security Council, but the primary responsibility for keeping the wheels turning was assumed by the White House staff, headed by Sherman Adams.[10]

Each of these emergencies created a temporary power vacuum and

---

[10] President Kennedy's almost instantaneous death by assassination prevented any inability problem arising on November 22, 1963. President Johnson underwent operations in 1965 and 1966, but he was unconscious or incapacitated for only a brief period on each occasion.

aroused concern about our constitutional unpreparedness for handling situations of such great potential danger. Each emergency could have been eased by having the Vice President become Acting President for a temporary period. This did not occur, a principal reason being uncertainty as to the effect this assumption of responsibility would have on the status of the disabled President.

In the absence of any legislation or constitutional consensus on this problem, President Eisenhower wisely took the initiative and in March, 1958, made public an agreement he had reached with Vice President Nixon concerning a possible future inability. This agreement called for the Vice President to serve as "acting President, exercising the powers and duties of the office until the inability had ended." Then the President "would resume the full exercise of the powers and duties of the office." President Kennedy entered into a similar agreement with Vice President Johnson in 1961, as did President Johnson with Vice President Humphrey in 1965.

The assassination of President Kennedy in 1963 was a grim reminder that the various succession problems had not been solved, and led Congress to adopt the Twenty-fifth Amendment in 1965. Section 3 of the amendment gave constitutional recognition to the Eisenhower-Nixon type of arrangement by providing that the President, if unable to discharge the powers and duties of his office, could transfer them to "the Vice President as Acting President" by filing a written declaration of inability with the President of the Senate and the Speaker of the House. The President could resume his powers and duties by a written declaration to the same two officers.

The most difficult problem that the drafters of the Twenty-fifth Amendment foresaw was the possibility that the President might suffer a mental illness and not recognize his inability. Stripping a President of his office against his will is a grave prospect, yet the need for such action could arise. Section 4 consequently provided a formula which it was hoped would protect all interests in such a crisis. The Vice President and a majority of the Cabinet "or such other body as Congress may by law provide" were authorized to declare the President unable to serve by written notice to the heads of the two houses of Congress, and on the filing of such a declaration the Vice President would become Acting President.

The President could resume his powers by written notice to the two houses that the inability had ceased to exist. However, if the Vice President and a majority of the Cabinet (or other designated body) within four days thereafter notified Congress that in their opinion the President had not recovered from his disability, then Congress would have to decide the issue. It would assemble within forty-eight hours and reach a decision within twenty-one days. If two-thirds of both houses voted that the President was unable to discharge his duties, the Vice President would continue as Acting President. Otherwise the President would resume his office. Hopefully, no

occasion will ever arise calling for the use of this machinery, but it is valuable insurance against emergency.

## SELECTED REFERENCES

CORWIN, EDWARD S. (ed.), *The President: Office and Powers, 1787–1957*, chap. 2. New York: New York University Press, 1957 (fourth revised edition).

————, and LOUIS W. KOENIG, *The Presidency Today*, chap. 4. New York: New York University Press, 1956.

DAVID, PAUL, "The Vice-Presidency: Its Institutional Evolution and Contemporary Status," 29 *Journal of Politics* 721–748 (1967).

*Electing the President*, A Report of the Commission on Electoral College Reform, American Bar Association. Chicago: American Bar Association, 1967.

"The Electoral College," Subcommittee on Constitutional Amendments of the Judiciary Committee, U.S. Sen., 87th Cong., 1st sess., 1961. Washington: Government Printing Office, 1961.

FEERICK, JOHN D., *From Failing Hands: The Story of Presidential Succession*. New York: Fordham University Press, 1965.

HANSEN, RICHARD, *The Year We Had No President*. Lincoln, Nebr.: University of Nebraska Press, 1962.

KALLENBACH, JOSEPH E., *The American Chief Executive*. New York: Harper & Row, Publishers, Incorporated, 1966.

————, "The New Presidential Succession Act," 41 *American Political Science Review* 931–941 (1947).

————, "Our Electoral College Gerrymander," 4 *Midwest Journal of Political Science* 162–191 (1960).

KEFAUVER, ESTES, "The Electoral College: Old Reforms Take On a New Look," 27 *Law and Contemporary Problems* 188–212 (1962).

"Method of Nomination and Election of the President and Vice President," Hearings before the Subcommittee on Constitutional Amendments of the Judiciary Committee, U.S. Sen., 88th Cong., 1st sess., 1963. Washington: Government Printing Office, 1963.

"Nomination and Election of President and Vice President," Hearings before the Subcommittee on Constitutional Amendments of the Judiciary Committee, U.S. Sen., 87th Cong., 1st sess., 1961. Washington: Government Printing Office, 1961.

PIERCE, NEAL, *The People's President*. New York: Simon and Schuster, Inc., 1968.

"Presidential Inability," Hearings before the Subcommittee on Constitutional Amendments of the Judiciary Committee, U.S. Senate, 88th Cong., 1st sess., 1963. Washington: Government Printing Office, 1963.

"Presidential Inability and Vacancies in the Office of Vice President," Hearings before the Subcommittee on Constitutional Amendments of the Judiciary Committee, U.S. Senate, 88th Cong., 2d sess., 1964. Washington: Government Printing Office, 1964.

SILVA, RUTH C., "The Lodge-Gossett Resolution: A Critical Analysis," 44 *American Political Science Review* 86–99 (1950).

———, *Presidential Succession.* Ann Arbor, Mich.: The University of Michigan Press, 1951.

———, "Presidential Succession and Disability," 21 *Law and Contemporary Problems* 646–662 (1956).

SMITH, GENE, *When the Cheering Stopped.* New York: William Morrow and Company, Inc., 1964.

WILMERDING, LUCIUS, JR., *The Electoral College.* New Brunswick, N.J.: Rutgers University Press, 1958.

# 17

## Executive powers in general

In turning to a general discussion of presidential authority, it is particularly important to recall the limitations of this volume. It is not a constitutional history. It is not a compendium of governmental practice under the Constitution. Thus, in discussing the subject of executive powers under the Constitution there can be no thought of undertaking any detailed account, either chronological or analytical, of the development of the theory or practice of executive power. Our concern is the more limited one of focusing attention on the problems of interpretation and controversy to which the constitutional language pertaining to executive power has given rise. For reasons having to do with the separation of powers, already noted, the courts have usually been reluctant to intervene in controversies over executive power. Nevertheless, there have been opportunities for some strikingly important expressions of judicial opinion on these problems.

### THE PRESIDENT AND LAWMAKING

We begin with the paradox that some of the President's most important executive powers are legislative. They are legislative in the sense that the Constitution gives him a role to play in relation to Congress as an institution and in relation to its adoption of legislation.

First, the President has certain functions in connection with the convening

and adjourning of Congress. The regular annual sessions of Congress are stipulated by the Constitution, but the President is authorized by Article II, section 3, "on extraordinary occasions, [to] convene both houses, or either of them," in special session, a power which has often been exercised. He has the power to adjourn Congress, but only in case the two houses disagree with respect to the time of adjournment, an eventuality which has never occurred.

Again, the President has an important role as the initiator of legislative programs, based on the following language from Article II, section 3: "He shall from time to time give to the Congress information of the state of the Union, and recommend to their consideration such measures as he shall judge necessary and expedient." Accordingly, a "State of the Union" message is submitted to Congress by the President at or near the beginning of each regular session. Executive influence on formulation of the legislative program, of course, does not stop here. The policy leadership of the administration is continuously manifested by the preparation of draft bills, testimony before congressional committees by department heads and other officials of the executive branch, and use of the President's vast powers as party leader and manipulator of public opinion.

APPROVAL OF LEGISLATION    The role of the President in the final approval of legislation is carefully safeguarded by the Constitution. Under Article I, section 7, "every bill" and "every order, resolution, or vote to which the concurrence of the Senate and House of Representatives may be necessary" must be presented to the President for approval or disapproval. There are only three exceptions to this general rule of presidential participation. First, the requirement is by its terms not applicable to actions affecting only a single house, such as adopting rules of procedure, appointing officers and employees, establishing special committees, or passing resolutions not purporting to have any legislative effect. Second, as already noted in Chapter 3, the President does not participate formally in the process of proposing amendments to the Constitution.

Third, joint actions of the two houses in the form of *concurrent resolutions* are customarily not submitted to the President. Concurrent resolutions are adopted by both houses of Congress, but normally not for strictly lawmaking purposes. They are used, for example, in correcting errors in bills after they have been adopted, setting up joint committees of the two houses, or fixing the time for adjournment. Technically it would seem that the concurrent resolution is an evasion of the constitutional requirements. The evasion, however, is unimportant so long as concurrent resolutions are not used for lawmaking purposes. But there have been instances where this limitation was not observed, and under these conditions the concurrent resolution is a potential threat to the constitutional right of the President to participate in the lawmaking process.

For example, the Lend-Lease Act of 1941 delegated certain temporary powers to the President, the expiration date being June 30, 1943. However, Congress, not satisfied with fixing this date, provided that the powers should lapse earlier if Congress should pass a concurrent resolution declaring that the powers conferred "are no longer necessary to promote the defense of the United States." Similar provisions were included in other legislation granting wartime powers. The purpose of such language was to make possible the termination of these programs by legislative action which would not be subject to the presidential veto power.

Corwin supports the constitutionality of such use of the concurrent resolution, on both legal and policy grounds. Since Congress is free not to delegate its powers, he contends that it is free to do so on certain stipulated conditions. "Why, then, should not one condition be that the delegation shall continue only as long as the two houses are of opinion that it is working beneficially?" The answer is that the "opinion" of the two houses can only be expressed by adopting a law, and the Constitution explicitly guarantees the President's right to participate in lawmaking.

On policy grounds, Corwin suggests that, since legislative delegations are often necessarily broad, the only way to keep delegation from becoming abdication is "by rendering the delegated powers recoverable without the consent of the delegate." [1] This may be a "common-sense" method of securing an equilibrium between President and Congress, and a President may acquiesce for policy reasons in a practice which invades his constitutional prerogative of participating in lawmaking. But if he chooses to protest, as President Roosevelt did concerning the Lend-Lease Act,[2] his constitutional position is clearly sound.

It does not appear that Congress has ever actually made use of these powers it has claimed to terminate legislation by concurrent resolution. The one area where the device has been employed for at least quasi-legislative purposes is in connection with reorganization acts passed by Congress in 1939 and 1945. The Reorganization Act of 1939 authorized the President to prepare reorganization plans affecting the government departments, which would become automatically effective after a certain period unless during that period both houses had passed a concurrent resolution stating that Congress was opposed to the reorganization plan. The 1945 act had the same provisions, but the Reorganization Acts of 1949 and 1953 dropped the concurrent resolution and permitted either house to veto reorganization plans.

If the concurrent resolution as employed for this purpose is constitutionally questionable, then of course, the later arrangements for veto by a single house are even more so. There may be a constitutional question here, but

---

[1] Edward S. Corwin (ed.), *The President: Office and Powers, 1787–1957* (New York: New York University Press, 4th rev. ed., 1957), p. 130.
[2] Robert H. Jackson, "A Presidential Legal Opinion," 66 *Harvard Law Review* 1353–1361 (1953).

it is obviously not one arising out of an attempt to exclude the President from participating in the legislative process. In fact, the President and Congress reverse their usual roles under the reorganization acts, with the President drafting legislation and Congress exercising the approval or veto power.[3]

EXECUTIVE VETO POWER    The President's power to veto legislation is referred to as a "qualified" or "suspensive" veto, since it can be overridden by a two-thirds vote of both houses. Nevertheless, it is scarcely possible to overestimate the contribution which the veto power makes to executive authority. The number of times the President exercises the veto is of course no index to its importance. The mere existence of the power is a constant factor in congressional thinking, and legislative planning is generally circumscribed by realization of the necessity of producing measures which the President will be willing to sign.

Thinking and practice with respect to use of the veto power have varied greatly during our history. The first six Presidents usually vetoed bills only on the ground that they were unconstitutional or technically defective. Jackson was the first President to adopt a policy of vetoing bills simply because he considered them objectionable in aim and content, but even so he vetoed only twelve bills in eight years. Only fifty-one vetoes were recorded up to the Civil War.

Eight Presidents—the most recent being Garfield—never vetoed a single measure. Grover Cleveland and Franklin Roosevelt, on the other hand, used the veto 414 and 631 times respectively. No presidential veto was overridden until Tyler's administration, and it still occurs very infrequently. Even Franklin Roosevelt, who originated more than one-third of all the vetoes in American history up to that time, was reversed only nine times. Among recent Presidents, Truman had 250 vetoes, Eisenhower 181, and Kennedy 25. Truman's vetoes were overridden twelve times, Eisenhower's twice, and Kennedy's never.

If the President decides to veto a bill, he returns it unsigned within ten days to the house in which it originated, accompanying it with a statement of his objections. The veto stands unless, with a quorum present, it is overridden by a two-thirds vote in each house. On the question of repassage of the bill, the way each member votes must be recorded, which imparts a greater sense of responsibility to the action.

The President can permit a bill to become law without his signature by failing to return it with his signature within ten days after he has received it. This procedure is used when the President does not approve of a bill, but

---

[3] On the general subject of the "legislative veto," see Joseph P. Harris, *Congressional Control of Administration* (Washington, D.C.: The Brookings Institution, 1964), Chap. 8; Joseph Cooper and Ann Cooper, "The Legislative Veto and the Constitution," 30 *George Washington Law Review* 467–516 (1962).

feels it impossible or impolitic to veto it. However, in these circumstances the bill will become law only if Congress is still in session after the ten days have expired. If Congress adjourns within the ten-day period, the bill does not become law, and is said to have been given a "pocket veto."

A pocket veto is an absolute veto, since the adjournment of Congress prevents any attempt at repassage of the bill. The Supreme Court has taken the position that any adjournment of Congress, and not merely the final adjournment at the end of a Congress, is sufficient to permit use of the pocket veto. In the so-called *Pocket Veto Case* (1929), it was the adjournment of the first session of the Sixty-ninth Congress which was involved, but the Court ruled that the President had been effectively prevented from observing the constitutional requirement of returning the bill to the house in which it originated.

The President must by practice accept or reject a bill *in toto;* he has no "item veto." Thus there is a temptation for Congress to attach legislation which the President is known to oppose, as a "rider" to some vitally important bill. Numerous proposals to give the President an item veto, primarily with respect to appropriations measures, have uniformly failed.

PROBLEMS RE SIGNING BILLS    There are certain circumstances in which the power of the President to approve bills has been questioned. For almost 150 years it was assumed that the President could not sign bills after the adjournment of the Congress which passed them. The reasoning apparently was that the President in signing bills was participating in the legislative power, and that the legislative power of a Congress expired when the session terminated. Consequently it was presidential practice to go to the Capitol on the last day of each session in order to sign the final bills. It was President Wilson who challenged this notion by signing several bills after the final adjournment of the Sixty-ninth Congress. In *Edwards* v. *United States* (1932) the Supreme Court sustained the President's right so to sign bills in a case based on action by President Hoover.

A problem on which no ruling has yet been given is whether bills passed less than ten days before the end of a President's term, on which he takes no action, may be approved or vetoed by the incoming President. A dictum of the Court in the *Edwards* case says that the incoming President may not approve such a bill, since it was not presented to him. However, President Truman after taking office in 1945 signed several bills which had been presented to the White House prior to President Roosevelt's death, and his power to do so was not challenged.

## THEORIES OF EXECUTIVE POWER

When we turn from the President as participant in lawmaking to the President as operating head of the executive branch, the first relevant constitu-

tional provision is the initial sentence of Article II: "The executive power shall be vested in a President of the United States of America." There has been considerable disagreement as to whether these words comprise a grant of power or are a mere designation of office. If the latter view is taken, then the executive power must be defined by the more or less specific authorizations to the President found elsewhere in Article II, such as the power to grant pardons, to receive ambassadors, to make appointments, or to take care that the laws be faithfully executed.

But is there any reason for concluding that this more restrictive view of executive powers is the correct or preferable one? The main argument against the broader concept is based on a supposed logical difficulty. Why, it is said, should Article II start out with a general grant of executive power, and then be followed by more specific grants? Chief Justice Taft sought to dispose of this query by explaining that the specific grants lend emphasis "where emphasis was regarded as appropriate."[4] On the basis of extensive research into eighteenth-century practices and terminology, Crosskey concludes that draftsmanship of that period typically made use of "a general proposition followed by an incomplete enumeration of particulars, or things which, arguably, are particulars, included within the antecedent general expression."[5]

But perhaps the best reason for regarding the initial sentence of Article II as a grant of power is that only by this method is the President equipped with the broad authority which the chief executive of a state must have. The prime characteristic of executive power is that it is "residual." The executive is always in session, always available to fill in gaps and meet emergencies. In contrast, as Locke says, "the law making power is not always in being, and is usually too numerous and so too slow for the dispatch requisite to execution."[6]

If further support is needed for the position that the "executive power" phrase is a broad grant of power, it can be found in an action of the First Congress, commonly referred to as the "decision of 1789." In setting up the new department of foreign affairs, the House fell into a debate as to how the secretary of the department would be removed. Some members thought the Senate's consent would be necessary, just as in appointment, and others said Congress could provide any arrangement for removal it saw fit under the "necessary and proper" clause. The language actually put into the statute, "whenever the said principal officer shall be removed from office by the President," reflected the majority conclusion that the President already had the right of removal on the basis of his "executive power" under the Constitution.

[4] *Myers* v. *United States* (1926).
[5] W. W. Crosskey, *Politics and the Constitution in the History of the United States* (Chicago: The University of Chicago Press, 1953), p. 379.
[6] John Locke, *Of Civil Government*, book 2, chap. 14.

The only other language approaching the executive power provision in breadth of authorization is the sentence in Article II, section 3: "He shall take care that the laws be faithfully executed." Although this is a notably broad grant of power, it also served the limiting function of emphasizing the American notion of the executive as subordinate to the law, in contrast with the wide prerogative powers of the English executive.

For a satisfactory indication of how these two general grants of executive power have been interpreted and what they have meant in practice, nothing less than a history of the Presidency would be adequate. But fortunately for our purposes, an understanding of the two principal contrasting interpretations of executive power can be supplied by two Presidents, Theodore Roosevelt and William H. Taft. Roosevelt wrote his activist personality and expansive attitude into constitutional law with his "stewardship" conception of the presidential office. His theory was

> . . . that the executive power was limited only by specific restrictions and prohibitions appearing in the Constitution or imposed by the Congress under its Constitutional powers. . . . I declined to adopt the view that what was imperatively necessary for the Nation could not be done by the President unless he could find some specific authorization to do it. My belief was that it was not only his right but his duty to do anything that the needs of the Nation demanded unless such action was forbidden by the Constitution or by the laws.[7]

In conformity with this theory, Roosevelt indicated that he would not have hesitated to take over the anthracite mines in 1902 and to work them in the name of the government, rather than permit them to be closed by a threatened strike, though there was no law authorizing him to do so. A better illustration, since it actually happened, was Roosevelt's action in promotion of his conservation policy. The statutes then in force authorized the President to withdraw from private entry all public lands on which "mineral deposits" had been found. Roosevelt went further, and withdrew land for forest and bird reserves, as well as land on which the existence of minerals was only suspected. He felt justified in taking such action as a steward for the public interest, pending legislation which he hoped Congress would adopt. In any case there was no law against what he had done.

Taft found this position incompatible with his more sedentary view of the Presidency. In lectures which he gave in 1916 after his Presidential term, he said:

> The true view of the Executive functions is, as I conceive it, that the President can exercise no power which cannot be fairly and reasonably traced to some specific grant of power or justly implied and included within such express grant as proper and necessary to its exercise. Such specific grant must be either in the Federal Constitution or in an act of

---

[7] Theodore Roosevelt, *Autobiography* (New York: The Macmillan Company, 1913), pp. 388-389.

Congress passed in pursuance thereof. There is no undefined residuum of power which he can exercise because it seems to him to be in the public interest.[8]

This rebuke to Roosevelt's stewardship notions would have been somewhat more impressive if Taft had acted on it consistently during his Presidency. As a matter of fact, however, he had done almost exactly the same thing as Roosevelt on the public land question. He did cancel many of the Roosevelt orders as invalid, but then he himself withdrew a large tract in California on which oil had been discovered, an act for which there was no congressional authorization. He asked Congress to ratify his action, which it failed to do. In *United States* v. *Midwest Oil Co.* (1915), however, the Supreme Court upheld the Taft order on the ground that it was supported by long-continued usage which Congress had not challenged, in spite of opportunities to do so.

The issue that emerges here, then, is whether the President must always be able to cite a law of the United States or a specific constitutional authorization in support of his actions, or whether the broad "executive power" with which he is vested justifies any actions he conceives as being in the public interest, so long as there is no conflict with existing legislation or constitutional provisions. Locke put this issue in its classical form. Pointing to the relative characteristics of executive and legislature already quoted, he concluded that the executive must always be equipped with discretionary and prerogative powers.

> For the legislators not being able to foresee and provide by laws for all that may be useful to the community, the executor of the laws, having the power in his hands, has by the common law of Nature a right to make use of it for the good of the society, in many cases where the municipal law has given no direction, till the legislative can conveniently be assembled to provide for it. Many things there are which the law can by no means provide for, and those must necessarily be left to the discretion of him that has the executive power in his hands, to be ordered by him as the public good and advantage shall require; nay, it is fit that the laws themselves should in some cases give way to the executive power, or rather to this fundamental law of Nature and government— viz., that, as much as may be, all the members of the society are to be preserved.

The Supreme Court found it necessary to take a position on this issue in *In re Neagle* (1890), and it lined up with Locke. The *Neagle* case grew out of a highly bizarre set of facts. Supreme Court Justice Field, whose judicial circuit included California, had had his life threatened by a disappointed litigant named Terry, and the Attorney General assigned a United States marshal to protect Field while riding the circuit in that state. When Terry

---

[8] William Howard Taft, *Our Chief Magistrate and His Powers* (New York: Columbia University Press, 1916), pp. 139–140.

appeared about to make a physical attack on Field, the marshal, Neagle, killed him. There was some local feeling favorable to Terry, and Neagle was arrested and held by state authorities on a charge of murder. The United States sought Neagle's release on habeas corpus under a provision of the federal statutes making the writ available to one "in custody for an act done or omitted in pursuance of a law of the United States."

The problem was that Congress had enacted no *law* authorizing the President or the Attorney General to assign marshals as bodyguards to federal justices. But the Supreme Court did not propose to interpret "law" so narrowly. "In the view we take of the Constitution . . . any obligation fairly and properly inferrible from that instrument, or any duty of the marshal to be derived from the general scope of his duties under the laws of the United States, is a 'law,' within the meaning of this phrase."

It would be unthinkable, said the Court, which admittedly had a more than academic interest in the matter, for a sovereign government to have "within the domain of its powers no means of protecting . . . judges" in the discharge of their duties. The power must exist somewhere, and the only question was where. The legislature could pass a law, but it had not done so. Then, in language practically paraphrasing Locke, the Court turned to the President, whom it found admirably equipped for performing such a function, through his Cabinet, his appointees, his executive departments, his control over the Armed Forces, through all those who "aid him in the performance of the great duties of his office, and represent him in a thousand acts."

There is "a peace of the United States," the Court went on, and by necessity and design the President is the principal conservator of that peace. The President's duty to see that the laws are faithfully executed is consequently not "limited to the enforcement of acts of Congress . . . according to their *express terms*" but includes also "the rights, duties and obligations growing out of the Constitution itself, our international relations, and all the protection implied by the nature of the government under the Constitution." Thus the duty assigned to the marshal in this affair was properly considered to arise "under the authority of the law of the United States."

This broad interpretation of the laws which the President was obliged faithfully to execute was underlined five years later in the case of *In re Debs.* As already noted, President Cleveland sent troops to Chicago to deal with a railway strike, and had his Attorney General secure a federal court injunction against the strikers. There was no explicit statutory basis for the injunction, but the Supreme Court sustained it on the broad ground that: "Every government, entrusted, by the very terms of its being, with powers and duties to be exercised and discharged for the general welfare, has a right to apply to its own courts for any proper assistance in the exercise of the one and the discharge of the other." Here again the theme was that the right of self-preservation must belong to a government, whether claimed by statute

or not, and that the executive was constitutionally entitled to act in such cases.

In contrast to these strong supports for the doctrine of inherent or implied presidential powers, stands the 1952 decision in the famous *Steel Seizure Case*. Briefly, the facts in *Youngstown Sheet and Tube Co.* v. *Sawyer* were as follows. In the latter part of 1951, a dispute arose between the steel companies and their employees over terms and conditions of employment. On December 18, the steel workers' union gave notice of intention to strike when existing agreements expired on December 31. On December 22, President Truman referred the dispute to the Federal Wage Stabilization Board, and the strike was called off, but the board's subsequent report produced no settlement. On April 4, 1952, notice of a strike on April 9 was issued. A few hours before the strike was to begin, the President issued an executive order directing the Secretary of Commerce to take possession of and operate the steel mills of the country. The President based his action on a contention that the work stoppage would jeopardize national defense, particularly in Korea. The next morning he sent a message to Congress reporting his action, and a second message on April 21. The steel companies obeyed the Secretary's orders under protest, and brought suit for injunction against him in the District of Columbia district court. On April 30, Judge Pine granted a preliminary injunction restraining the Secretary from continuing the seizure. The case went to the Supreme Court with almost unprecedented speed, and on June 2, the Court held by a six to three vote that the President had exceeded his constitutional powers.

Chief Justice Vinson's opinion for the three dissenters was in the spirit of the *Neagle, Debs,* and *Midwest* cases. His theory of the President's seizure was that its purpose was "to faithfully execute the laws by acting in an emergency to maintain the status quo, thereby preventing collapse of the legislative programs [military procurement and anti-inflation] until Congress could act." In the message which he immediately sent to Congress, the President explained this reason for his action "and expressed his desire to cooperate with any legislative proposals approving, regulating or rejecting the seizure of the steel mills."

Vinson argued that action for this purpose was constitutional, for two reasons. First, the relevant statutes in effect at the time gave the President free choice as to what remedy, if any, he should attempt to apply in averting a steel strike. There were on the statute books three laws which might be considered available for use by the President. The first was the Selective Service Act of 1948, which specifically gave the President authority to seize plants failing to produce goods ordered by the Armed Forces for national defense purposes.

The second was the Taft-Hartley Act, which included provisions adopted for the purpose of dealing with nationwide strikes. Under this act the President was authorized to appoint a board of inquiry and thereafter, in proper

cases, seek injunctive relief for an eighty-day period against a threatened work stoppage. The President could invoke that procedure whenever, in his opinion, "a threatened or actual strike . . . affecting an entire industry . . . will, if permitted to occur or to continue, imperil the national health or safety." The act contained no seizure provisions. Consideration was given to the seizure device when Congress was debating the bill, but it was voted down.

The third was the Defense Production Act of 1950, Title II of which delegated to the President power to acquire by condemnation property needed for national defense, when the need was immediate and all other means of securing the property on a fair basis had been exhausted. This provision was obviously not thought of as a way of dealing with strikes, for Title V covered the mediation of labor disputes affecting national defense, though it created no sanctions for the settlement of such disputes. Under this latter authority the President had created the Wage Stabilization Board, and he later added mediation of wage disputes to its duties.

Among the four alternatives available under these three acts, President Truman chose the last by referring the dispute to the Wage Stabilization Board to investigate and make recommendations for fair and equitable terms of settlement. By using this method, he actually secured a ninety-nine-day delay of the strike call, compared with the eighty-day cooling-off period under Taft-Hartley. But the objection was made that the Taft-Hartley Act procedure, which had no provision for seizure, was the one Congress had developed specifically to deal with nationwide strikes. It may well have been a vindictive hostility toward that act, which was passed over his veto, which led President Truman to ignore it, but the fact is that the provisions of the statute leave its invocation within the discretion of the President. He used his discretion, and chose the alternative remedy of the Wage Stabilization Board.

Vinson's second point was that the President, having exhausted the statutory remedy he chose to use, was justified in seizing the mills as a temporary means of averting a strike pending congressional action. Admittedly there was no statutory authorization for the seizure, but Vinson regarded the constitutional grant of "executive power" to the President, and his constitutional responsibility to execute the laws, as providing inherent power for such presidential action. His reading of the Constitution and his interpretation of the purpose of the Founders was that "the Presidency was deliberately fashioned as an office of power and independence." His illustrations ran all the way from Washington's vigorous suppression of the Whiskey Rebellion, Jefferson's initiative in the Louisiana Purchase, and Lincoln's wholly unauthorized Emancipation Proclamation, down to President Roosevelt's World War II nonstatutory seizures of aircraft and industrial plants.

Judge Pine's decision in the district court had challenged such an interpretation of executive powers under the Constitution. He denied that the

President had any "inherent" powers not traceable to an express grant in the Constitution. As his sole authority for this position, he cited the passage from Taft's book already quoted. Judge Pine dismissed Roosevelt's stewardship theory as one which does not "comport with our recognized theory of government." The numerous instances in American history where Presidents have acted on a theory of inherent powers he dismissed as "repetitive, unchallenged, illegal acts."

Judge Pine's action in enjoining the steel seizure was upheld by the Supreme Court, but his denial of inherent powers to the President was not ratified by the Court. Only Black and Douglas approved the Pine position that the President was limited to expressly granted powers, and even they made no specific reference to the Taft statement. Frankfurter and Burton found a consideration of inherent powers unnecessary to decision of the case. Clark fully accepted the doctrine of inherent powers, and Jackson substantially did so. Thus there were at least five votes against Pine's constitutional interpretation.

How then does it happen that the government lost the case? The answer requires an analysis of the position taken by the six majority justices, each of whom wrote an opinion. Black wrote the opinion of the Court, in which Douglas concurred. Like Judge Pine, they took up dogmatic positions based on a hard and fast interpretation of the separation of powers. Black disposed of the entire controversy in thirteen paragraphs, and his argument was on such a plane of lofty moral and constitutional generalities that he did not bother to cite a single Supreme Court decision bearing on the substantive issue. But the other majority justices did not accept this separation of powers dogma. Frankfurter specifically attached a paragraph to Black's opinion for the Court in order to warn that "the considerations relevant to the legal enforcement of the principle of separation of powers seem to me more complicated and flexible than may appear from what Mr. Justice Black has written."

Consequently we must turn away from Black and Douglas to the other four majority justices in search for the real doctrine of the steel decision. All four of their opinions recognize that American constitutional law is a pragmatic affair. Jackson, for example, stressed the folly of any rigorous notions about strict separation of the branches of government. Successful operation of our system requires a combination of "separateness" with "interdependence," "autonomy" with "reciprocity." He thought that "presidential powers are not fixed but fluctuate, depending upon their disjunction or conjunction with those of Congress." He believed that when the President "takes measures incompatible with the expressed or implied will of Congress, his power is at its lowest ebb," and because he was convinced that the President had done that here, he found the action unconstitutional.

Frankfurter likewise approached the problem, not as a matter of laying down the law to the President, but as a matter of balancing the equities in

this particular instance between the two democratic branches of the government, to both of which the Supreme Court owed deference. Examination of congressional actions pertaining to use of presidential seizure powers from 1916 to the passage of the Taft-Hartley Act convinced Frankfurter that Congress had "deemed seizure so drastic a power as to require it to be carefully circumscribed whenever the President was vested with this extraordinary authority." When considering the Taft-Hartley bill, Frankfurter went on, Congress gave considered attention to the seizure device and on "a balance of considerations . . . chose not to lodge this power in the President." It is true that Congress did not write into the act a statutory prohibition on presidential seizure, but it "expressed its will to withhold this power from the President as though it had said so in so many words."

The Court in the *Steel Seizure Case*, then, did not deny the constitutionality of the President's general power to meet emergencies by the exercise of inherent or residual powers. It did not decide that Theodore Roosevelt was wrong and Taft was right. What the decision did hold was that the inherent power of seizure which the President might otherwise have possessed had been eliminated in this situation when Congress decided not to include seizure authority in the Taft-Hartley Act.

### THE POWER OF APPOINTMENT

Basic to executive authority is the President's power to appoint the officials of the administration. Article II, section 2, provides:

> [The President] shall nominate, and by and with the advice and consent of the Senate, shall appoint ambassadors, other public ministers and consuls, judges of the Supreme Court, and all other officers of the United States, whose appointments are not herein otherwise provided for, and which shall be established by law; but the Congress may by law vest the appointment of such inferior officers, as they think proper, in the President alone, in the courts of law, or in the heads of departments.

This language establishes four different methods of appointment—by the President with Senate confirmation, by the President alone, by the courts of law, and by the heads of departments. Congress has no appointment power, except, under Article I, to choose its own officers. Nevertheless, Congress is involved very deeply in the process of appointment, as the following discussion will indicate.

QUALIFICATIONS AND DISQUALIFICATIONS    In creating offices, Congress can specify the qualifications to be possessed by appointees to those offices. Familiar statutory requirements relate to citizenship, residence, age, political affiliation, professional attainments, and so on. Congress has even provided on occasion that presidential appointments shall be made from among a small number of persons named by others. Thus an act of 1920 required that

the Railroad Labor Board consist of three men to be appointed from six nominees by employees, and three to be chosen from six nominees by carriers. The civil service system is, of course, a general limitation on the executive appointment power.

On rare occasions Congress has written qualifications so restrictive as actually to confine appointment to one individual. A classic instance of this sort occurred in 1916, when in conference committee the following language was slipped into an Army reorganization bill which among other things provided for appointment of judge advocates:

> Provided further, That of the vacancies created in the Judge Advocate's Department by this act, one such vacancy, not below the rank of Major, shall be filled by the appointment of a person from civil life, not less than forty-five nor more than fifty years of age, who shall have been for ten years a Judge of the Supreme Court of the Philippine Islands, shall have served for two years as a Captain in the regular or volunteer army, and shall be proficient in the Spanish language and laws.

There was of course only one American with these qualifications, and he was a friend of the chairman of the House conferees. Even worse was a 1941 act setting up a bridge commission to take over and operate an Illinois-Indiana toll bridge, which specifically named the three commissioners, who were to have life terms. This example of congressional appointment was clearly unconstitutional.

SENATORIAL CONFIRMATION AND SENATORIAL COURTESY    The requirement that appointments by the executive shall be subject to approval by the upper house of the legislature is peculiar to the United States, and to the several countries of Central and South America that have used the American Constitution as a model. The Senate's advice and consent is given by a majority of a quorum. The distinction between "officers" who need Senate confirmation and "inferior officers" who do not is entirely in the discretion of Congress. The Constitution apparently assumes that these two categories will cover the field, but in extraconstitutional practice a third and very numerous category, "employees," is recognized, who may be appointed by officers whose status is lower than that of department head.

When the framers of the Constitution spoke of the Senate's "advice" on nominations, they apparently were thinking of collective advice by the Senate acting as a kind of council for the President. But the Senate has never functioned as such a council, and it is obviously impractical for it to offer advice on appointments in any collective fashion. However, advice is given by individual senators, which is made very effective by the practice of "senatorial courtesy." A nomination to a federal office within a state, on which the senator or senators of that state from the President's party have not been consulted, will almost invariably be refused confirmation if the aggrieved senator chooses to make an appeal to his colleagues. Where the

appointment is to an office in Washington, it is normal procedure to consult with the senator of the state from which the appointee comes, but if this is not done the rule of senatorial courtesy is less likely to be applied when confirmation is requested. If the Senate does refuse confirmation for a high-level appointment, it is usually for broad policy reasons, not because the rule of senatorial courtesy has been ignored.

That the Senate, having once consented to a nomination, cannot change its mind is established both by practice and judicial decision. In 1930 President Hoover nominated George Otis Smith as first chairman of the reorganized Federal Power Commission. The Senate confirmed the nomination, and Smith was commissioned. Some of his first acts angered the liberal forces in the Senate. Senate rules permit a motion to reconsider a resolution of confirmation and to recall the notification thereof within the next two days of actual executive session. The Senate had not been in session, so that technically the two days had not expired. Consequently the Senate voted to reconsider the nomination, and rejected it.

President Hoover refused to recognize the Senate reversal, saying it was an attempt to exercise the removal power under the guise of reconsidering a nomination. The Senate ordered the institution of quo warranto proceedings, and the Supreme Court, in *United States* v. *Smith* (1932), upheld Smith's title to the office on the ground that the Senate had never interpreted its rule to cover the case of an appointee already installed in office on the faith of the Senate's original consent. Since the Senate is free to change its rules without notice, the basis of the Court's decision was rather weak, even though the result was obviously correct. It might have been better for the Court to say flatly that any attempt to recall a confirmation resolution after it had been transmitted to the President and the commission had been signed was unconstitutional.

RECESS APPOINTMENTS    Article II, section 2, clause 3, provides: "The President shall have power to fill up all vacancies that may happen during the recess of the Senate, by granting commissions which shall expire at the end of their next session." The word "happen" does not mean that the vacancy must have actually developed while the Senate was in recess. A vacancy occurring during a Senate session, which for any reason remains unfilled by the end of the session, can be filled by a recess appointment. This, plus the fact that a recess appointee can serve throughout the next session of the Senate, opens up the possibility of the President's using recess appointments to keep in office men whom the Senate would refuse to confirm, and this has occasionally happened. In fact, President Jefferson appears to have kept Robert Smith as his Secretary of the Navy for four years without Senate confirmation by this device. Congress has moved against such practices by legislation providing that if the vacancy exists while the Senate is in session, the recess appointee may receive no salary until he has been confirmed by the Senate.

### THE POWER OF REMOVAL

Surprisingly, the Constitution makes no express provision for the removal of federal officials except through the process of impeachment, which is an unwieldy and quite impractical device, useful only on extraordinary occasions. This gap has been filled by executive practice, legislative provisions, and judicial interpretation.

Two principal constitutional issues have arisen in connection with removals. First, is removal solely an executive function, or can the Senate claim a share in removing officials who were appointed subject to Senate confirmation? Hamilton in No. 77 of *The Federalist* expressed the opinion that the consent of the Senate "would be necessary to displace as well as to appoint." But the First Congress, faced with this issue in setting up the Department of State, acted on the theory, as we have already seen, that the President alone possessed the removal power.

In fact Congress tacitly recognized the existence of an unrestrained presidential removal power from 1789 to 1867, and it developed into one of his most effective instruments for control of the executive branch. In 1867, however, Congress passed the Tenure of Office Act, which forbade the removal by the President of department heads without consent of the Senate. President Johnson's attempt to remove his Secretary of War in violation of this act was one of the charges in his impeachment. Following Johnson's term the act was modified, and it was completely repealed in 1887, without ever having been the subject of constitutional test.

Meanwhile, however, Congress had passed in 1876 a law providing that postmasters of the first, second, and third class, appointed for four-year terms, should be subject to removal by the President "by and with the advice and consent of the Senate." The Supreme Court finally had occasion to rule on this law in 1926, in the famous case of *Myers* v. *United States*. President Wilson removed Myers, a first-class postmaster in Portland, Oregon, in 1920 before his four-year term was up, without seeking Senate consent. Myers brought suit in the Court of Claims for his salary for the balance of his four-year term, and the Supreme Court held by a vote of six to three that the law of 1876 was unconstitutional.

Chief Justice Taft's opinion for the Court was one of the longest and most elaborate in its history. First, he relied upon the "decision of 1789," and the subsequent practice of untrammeled removal power. The Tenure of Office Act of 1867 he dismissed as a temporary divergence from legislative policy resulting from partisan controversy. Second, and more importantly, he derived the principle of the removal power directly from the Constitution, specifically from the grant of "executive power" and the "faithful execution of the laws" clause. Obviously, said the Chief Justice, the President "alone and unaided could not execute the laws. He must execute them by the assistance of subordinates." It follows that "in the absence of any express

limitation respecting removals, that as his selection of administrative officers is essential to the execution of the laws by him, so must be his power of removing those for whom he cannot continue to be responsible."

Chief Justice Taft went on to develop this argument in language which seemed to be illumined by his own experience in the presidential office. He said:

> When a nomination is made, it may be presumed that the Senate is, or may become, as well advised as to the fitness of the nominee as the President, but in the nature of things the defects in ability or intelligence or loyalty in the administration of the laws of one who has served as an officer under the President, are facts as to which the President, or his trusted subordinates, must be better informed than the Senate, and the power to remove him may, therefore, be regarded as confined, for very sound and practical reasons, to the governmental authority which has administrative control.

Indeed, there is an imperative need for the President to be able to remove his immediate subordinates, to whom the President delegates exercise of his discretion and discharge of his political duties. Since there is nothing in the Constitution that would permit a distinction between these officials and those engaged in more normal duties, Taft concluded that an unrestricted power to remove attaches to all positions filled by the President.

The Taft opinion failed to convince three members of the Court, including Holmes and Brandeis. Holmes thought the arguments based on constitutional grants of executive power were "spider's webs inadequate to control the dominant facts." However, the Taft decision was sound law because it was sound politics and sound administration in equating the powers of the President with his responsibilities. Where the opinion was unsound was in its attempt to decide more than the case called for. Taft veered off from considerations applicable to a postmastership into dicta about executive officials not in a position of direct responsibility to the President, saying:

> There may be duties of a quasi-judicial character imposed on executive officers and members of executive tribunals whose decisions after hearing affect interests of individuals, the discharge of which the President can not in a particular case properly influence or control. But even in such a case he may consider the decision after its rendition as a reason for removing the officer, on the ground that the discretion regularly entrusted to that officer by statute has not been on the whole intelligently or wisely exercised. Otherwise he does not discharge his own constitutional duty of seeing that the laws be faithfully executed.

This dictum challenged the statutory basis on which Congress had established the Interstate Commerce Commission in 1887, the Federal Trade Commission in 1914, and the Federal Tariff Commission in 1916. To be sure, the statutes setting up these agencies did not require Senate concurrence in removals, but the commissioners were in each case made removable by the

President "for inefficiency, neglect of duty, or malfeasance in office," and the clear implication of this statutory language was that the President was forbidden to remove on any other ground. A restriction of a different sort was placed in the Budget and Accounting Act of 1921, making the Comptroller General subject to removal (aside from impeachment) only by joint resolution of Congress and then only after a hearing which established incapacity, inefficiency, neglect of duty or malfeasance, or conduct involving moral turpitude.

Such legislation raised the second major issue concerning the removal power. Granting that removal is solely an executive function, can the exercise of this executive power be regulated by law? The *Myers* decision was correctly interpreted by Congress as challenging the validity of any restrictions on the President's removal power. Consequently as new quasi-judicial commissions or regulatory agencies were set up, no such restrictive language was inserted in their statutes.[9]

A test of Taft's dictum was inevitable, and it took the form of *Humphrey's Executor* v. *United States* (1935). Humphrey, first appointed to the Federal Trade Commission by President Coolidge, was reappointed by President Hoover in 1931 for a seven-year term. His views were not in accord with the philosophy of the New Deal, and President Roosevelt in 1933 requested Humphrey's resignation, saying: "I do not feel that your mind and my mind go along together on either the policies or the administering of the Federal Trade Commission, and, frankly, I think it is best for the people of this country that I should have a full confidence." When the resignation was not forthcoming, the President removed him. Humphrey died shortly afterwards, but his executor brought suit in the Court of Claims for his salary from the time of removal until his death.

The Supreme Court ruled unanimously that this action had exceeded the President's authority. In view of the fact that the removal was based squarely on Chief Justice Taft's dictum in the *Myers* case, it was, of course, necessary for Justice Sutherland, who wrote the *Humphrey* decision, to disavow the Taft theory. This he did by pointing out that the officer involved in the *Myers* case, a postmaster, was "restricted to the performance of executive functions," and rather lowly ones at that. In contrast, Humphrey was a member of "an administrative body created by Congress to carry into effect legislative policies embodied in the statute," performing its duties "without executive leave." In fact, Sutherland continued, a Federal Trade Commissioner "occupies no place in the executive department and . . . exercises no part of the executive power vested by the Constitution in the President." The Federal Trade Commission is a "quasi-legislative or quasi-judicial" agency,

[9] The statutes setting up the Federal Power Commission, reorganized in 1930, and the Federal Communications Commission and the Securities and Exchange Commission, both created in 1934, lack any limitation on the President's removal power.

which Congress intended to discharge its duties "independently of executive control." Forbidding the President to remove its commissioners except for cause is a legitimate way of implementing that policy, "for it is quite evident that one who holds his office only during the pleasure of another, cannot be depended upon to maintain an attitude of independence against the latter's will."

Sutherland challenged not only the dicta of Taft's opinion, but also its basic constitutional theory. He ignored Taft's interpretation of the executive power clause as a grant of authority. He appeared to whittle down presidential power to two categories. First, there were the prerogatives explicitly granted to the President in the Constitution. The impact of the "decision of 1789," Sutherland said, was limited to this category, since it concerned the Secretary of State, an officer who was "purely executive . . . responsible to the President, and to him alone, in a very definite sense." The second category of presidential responsibility was for those officials who exercised only nondiscretionary or ministerial powers, such as a postmaster. Apart from these two classes of officials, it appeared that Congress was free to impose such limitations as it chose upon the removal power. Congress reacted immediately to the *Humphrey* decision by writing into the National Labor Relations Act, then in the process of enactment, the most stringent provision it had yet applied to a regulatory commission: "Any member of the Board may be removed by the President, upon notice and hearing, for neglect of duty or malfeasance in office, but for no other cause."

Arthur E. Morgan attempted unsuccessfully to use the *Humphrey* decision to invalidate his removal as chairman of the TVA by President Roosevelt in 1938. A federal court of appeals found that the TVA Act did not attempt to eliminate the President's discretionary power to remove board members, nor could the TVA be regarded as a quasi-judicial agency.[10]

In 1958, however, the Supreme Court applied and extended the *Humphrey* doctrine in *Wiener* v. *United States*. Wiener was appointed by President Truman in 1950 to the War Claims Commission, an agency created by the War Claims Act of 1948 to settle certain types of claims growing out of World War II. The statute provided that the terms of office of the three commissioners would expire at the time fixed for winding up the affairs of the agency, which according to a 1952 amendment was March, 1955. There was no other provision in the act bearing on tenure of the commissioners—no provision either granting, limiting, or denying the President's power to remove.

The Eisenhower administration, coming into office in 1953, found Democrats in these three posts paying $14,000 yearly, and desired to have the

---

[10] The Supreme Court refused to review this decision. *Morgan* v. *TVA* (1941). See C. Herman Pritchett, *The Tennessee Valley Authority: A Study in Public Administration* (Chapel Hill, N.C.: The University of North Carolina Press, 1943), pp. 203–216.

positions for deserving Republicans. After one member had died, the resignations of the other two were requested, President Eisenhower writing to them that he regarded it in the national interest that he should have personnel of his own choosing to administer the act. When they refused to resign, they were removed in December, 1953, and three Republicans were appointed. No charges of malfeasance or other misdeeds were made against the original incumbents.

Wiener sued unsuccessfully for his salary in the Court of Claims, which agreed that his agency was quasi-judicial, but pointed out that Congress had placed no limitations on the President's power to remove its members, and consequently the *Humphrey* decision did not apply. However, the Supreme Court unanimously reversed the Court of Claims. Justice Frankfurter noted the parallel between presidential actions in the two cases, both men having been removed from quasi-judicial agencies without effort to show cause, and the purpose in each case having been to permit the President to appoint men of his own selection. The fact that there were specific statutory limits on the removal of Federal Trade Commissioners, whereas there were none in the War Claims Act was regarded as unimportant. Frankfurter reasoned that from the quasi-judicial nature of the agency it could be assumed that "Congress did not wish to have hang over the Commission the Damocles' sword of removal by the President for no reason other than that he preferred to have on that Commission men of his own choosing." Under the *Wiener* decision, then, the President's power of removal, which normally can be exercised at his discretion, may be exercised on quasi-judicial agencies only for cause, regardless of whether Congress has so provided.

The legislation establishing the federal civil service system and providing certain protections for the tenure of government employees is, of course, a valid limitation on the executive power of removal. Similarly, a legislative requirement for the removal of civil servants engaging in political activities has been held constitutional by the Supreme Court.[11] The removal of federal employees on loyalty-security grounds, carried out after 1947 under executive orders issued by Presidents Truman and Eisenhower, is discussed in Chapter 27.

## THE POWER TO PARDON

Article II, section 2, provides that the President "shall have power to grant reprieves and pardons for offenses against the United States, except in cases of impeachment." A pardon is usually thought of as an act of grace to correct a conviction or sentence which seems mistaken, harsh, or disproportionate to the crime. However, American Presidents have on numerous occasions

---

[11] *United Public Workers* v. *Mitchell* (1947).

used the pardoning power to grant amnesty to an entire group.[12] Congress also has the power to grant amnesties, and has done so in remitting penalties incurred under national statutes,[13] and by providing immunity from prosecution for persons testifying before courts or congressional investigating committees.[14] However, Congress cannot interfere with the President's right to issue amnesties. An act of 1870, making proof of loyalty necessary to recover on abandoned property sold by the government during the Civil War, notwithstanding any executive amnesty, was declared unconstitutional by the Supreme Court, which said: "The legislature cannot change the effect of such a pardon any more than the executive can change a law." [15]

The effect of a pardon is to grant exemption from the punishment the law inflicts for a crime. Since imprisonment and fine are the normal punishments, a pardon frees a convicted criminal from serving any uncompleted term of imprisonment and from paying any unpaid fine. Loss of certain civil and political rights is often an additional penalty for conviction of crime. Since a pardon will restore these rights, one may still be sought on behalf of persons who have completed their sentences and paid their fines.

In *Ex parte Garland* (1867) the Supreme Court ruled that the effect of a pardon is to wipe out completely all effects of the conviction for crime, Justice Field stating: "When the pardon is full, it releases the punishment and blots out of existence the guilt, so that in the eye of the law the offender is as innocent as if he had never committed the offence." The case arose out of an 1865 statute providing that any person seeking to practice law in a federal court must take oath that he had never voluntarily borne arms against the United States, nor given aid and comfort to its enemies. Garland had received a full pardon for his Confederate activities, and the Court held that the pardon restored all his civil rights and made him, "as it were, a new man, and gives him a new credit and capacity."

But more recent decisions have made it clear that a conviction for crime may have legal effects that a subsequent pardon cannot blot out. A 1914 case involved prosecution of a man in New York who had previously been convicted of a federal offense and then pardoned. His New York conviction as a second offender was upheld by the Supreme Court, on the ground that a past offense, even though pardoned, could be taken into consideration when punishing a new offense as "a circumstance of aggravation." [16]

Marshall early stated the rule that a pardon must be accepted to be valid,[17] which was followed in *Burdick* v. *United States* (1915). President Wilson had offered a full and unconditional pardon for all offenses against the United States to one Burdick, whose testimony was wanted by a federal

---

[12] Upheld in *Armstrong* v. *United States* (1872).
[13] *The Laura* (1885).
[14] *Brown* v. *Walker* (1896).
[15] *United States* v. *Klein* (1872).
[16] *Carlesi* v. *New York* (1914).
[17] *United States* v. *Wilson* (1833).

grand jury. Burdick, however, refused to accept the pardon, and the Supreme Court unanimously backed him. "The grace of a pardon," said Justice McKenna, "may be only in pretense . . . involving consequences of even greater disgrace than those from which it purports to relieve."

Although the *Burdick* principle has not been abandoned, a way to avoid some of its effect was discovered by President Coolidge, who "remitted" the sentence of a convicted criminal who had announced that he would refuse a pardon. Similarly he commuted the sentence of a federal prisoner so that he could be turned over to Connecticut authorities on a murder charge. A federal judge upheld this action, saying that there was no "right to incarceration" guaranteed by the Constitution.[18] Still a different set of circumstances was presented by a convict whose death sentence had been commuted to life imprisonment in 1909 by President Taft. After nearly two decades of prison life, the prisoner concluded he would be better off dead, and attacked Taft's action as a pardon he had not accepted. Justice Holmes rejoined:

> A pardon in our days is not a private act of grace from an individual happening to possess power. It is a part of the Constitutional scheme. When granted it is the determination of the ultimate authority that the public welfare will be better served by inflicting less than what the judgment fixed.

Thus the only question was whether life imprisonment was a lesser punishment than death, and Holmes thought the "common understanding" was to this effect.[19]

The only directly stated limitation on the President's pardoning power is that it does not apply to cases of impeachment, thus preventing the President from undoing the effect of such legislative punishment. It has been argued that the courts similarly need to be able to safeguard their power to punish for contempt against interference by presidential pardons. This issue was presented in *Ex parte Grossman* (1925). Grossman, having violated an injunction issued under the National Prohibition Act, had been sentenced to a year's imprisonment and fined for contempt of court. President Coolidge commuted the sentence to payment of the fine, but the federal district court refused to recognize the pardon. The Supreme Court reversed, Chief Justice Taft pointing out that in England the king had exercised the power to pardon for contempts, and in the United States the President had done so many times previously. Taft even suggested that, since punishment for contempt is meted out without the protection of trial by jury, there is a special reason why the chance of pardon for contempt should be present "to avoid possible mistake, undue prejudice or needless severity." Taft did agree, however, that the pardoning power should be limited to criminal contempts. Civil

[18] *Chapman* v. *Scott* (1925).
[19] *Biddle* v. *Perovich* (1927).

contempt actions, whose purpose is to enforce the rights of litigants, cannot be frustrated by a pardon.

## SELECTED REFERENCES

BINKLEY, WILFRED E., *President and Congress*. New York: Alfred A. Knopf, Inc., 1962 (third revised edition).

BLACKMAN, JOHN L., JR., *Presidential Seizure in Labor Disputes*. Cambridge, Mass.: Harvard University Press, 1967.

CORWIN, EDWARD S. (ed.), *The President: Office and Powers, 1787–1957*, chaps. 1, 3, 4. New York: New York University Press, 1957 (fourth revised edition).

———, "The Steel Seizure Case: A Judicial Brick without Straw," in Robert G. McCloskey (ed.), *Essays in Constitutional Law*, chap. 8. New York: Alfred A. Knopf, Inc., 1957.

———, and LOUIS W. KOENIG, *The Presidency Today*. New York: New York University Press, 1956.

CUSHMAN, ROBERT E., *The Independent Regulatory Commissions*, chap. 6. Fair Lawn, N.J.: Oxford University Press, 1941.

FENNO, RICHARD F., JR., *The President's Cabinet*. Cambridge, Mass.: Harvard University Press, 1954.

HARRIS, JOSEPH P., *The Advice and Consent of the Senate: A Study of the Confirmation of Appointments by the United States Senate*. Berkeley, Calif.: University of California Press, 1953.

HYMAN, SIDNEY, *The American President*. New York: Harper & Row, Publishers, Incorporated, 1954.

——— (ed.), "The Office of the American Presidency," 307 *The Annals of the American Academy of Political and Social Science* 1–155 (September, 1956).

KALLENBACH, JOSEPH E., *The American Chief Executive*. New York: Harper and Row, Publishers, Incorporated, 1966.

KOENIG, LOUIS W., *The Chief Executive*. New York: Harcourt, Brace & World, Inc., 1964.

MC CONNELL, GRANT, *Steel and the Presidency—1962*. New York: W. W. Norton & Co., Inc., 1963.

———, *The Steel Seizure of 1952*. University, Ala.: University of Alabama Press, 1960.

NEUSTADT, RICHARD E., *Presidential Power: The Politics of Leadership*. New York: John Wiley & Sons, Inc., 1960.

"The Presidential Office," 21 *Law and Contemporary Problems* 607–752 (Autumn, 1956).

REDFORD, EMMETTE S., "The President and the Regulatory Commissions," 44 *Texas Law Review* 288–321 (1965).

ROSSITER, CLINTON, *The American Presidency*. New York: Harcourt, Brace & World, Inc., 1960.

SCHUBERT, GLENDON A., JR., *The Presidency in the Courts,* chaps, 2, 8, 9. Minneapolis: The University of Minnesota Press, 1957.

———, "The Steel Case: Presidential Responsibility and Judicial Irresponsibility," 6 *Western Political Quarterly* 61–77 (1953).

SMITH, J. MALCOLM, and CORNELIUS P. COTTER, *Powers of the President during Crises.* Washington, D.C.: Public Affairs Press, 1960.

WESTIN, ALAN F., *The Anatomy of a Constitutional Law Case: Youngstown Sheet and Tube Co. v. Sawyer.* New York: The Macmillan Company, 1958.

ZINN, CHARLES J., *The Veto Power of the President.* Washington: Government Printing Office, 1951.

# 18

## *Control of foreign relations*

The doctrine of "political questions," we noted in Chapter 9, is available for the Supreme Court's use when an issue of private right which it is asked to decide turns on considerations largely outside judicial competence or authority. It is significant that the political questions doctrine has been perhaps most often invoked by the Court to avoid decisions relating to the conduct of American foreign relations. An early instance was *Foster* v. *Neilson* (1829), where the Court refused to rule on the location of the boundary between Spain and the United States in 1804 because this was "more a political than a legal question," and one on which the courts must accept the decisions of "the political departments."

The development of constitutional principles in the foreign relations field is thus more properly traced through the medium of diplomatic history than constitutional law, and the present chapter will be accordingly of limited scope. The Supreme Court has nevertheless on several occasions stated principles of primary importance in the guidance and rationalization of American practice in the field of foreign relations. Of course the federal courts administer general international law in so far as it is applicable in cases coming before them, but that is a different problem and one outside the confines of the present study.

## THE NATURE OF FEDERAL POWER

The provisions of the Constitution pertaining to foreign relations all take the form of assignments of particular functions to the various branches of the government. These specifically mentioned powers by no means cover the whole range of foreign affairs, and there is no grant of authority over foreign relations in broad terms comparable, say, with the authorization to regulate commerce among the states. On the other hand there are no provisions expressly denying or limiting the federal government's full authority to conduct external relations as a sovereign nation in a world of sovereign nations.

The framers were in fact well aware that there was no choice in this matter. The central government they were instituting would be fatally disabled if it lacked authority to deal with its peers or to meet the ever-recurring crises arising out of its relations abroad. As Hamilton said in No. 23 of *The Federalist:* "The circumstances that endanger the safety of nations are infinite, and for this reason no constitutional shackles can wisely be imposed on the power to which the care of it is committed." Thus the first principle in this area is that governmental power over foreign relations is plenary. The manner of its exercise is in certain respects specified by the Constitution, and the location of responsibility is defined. But the federal government's basic authority to conduct foreign relations is constitutionally unlimited.

What is the constitutional source of this authority, which goes far beyond the sum of the particular functions mentioned in the document? The answer is that authority over foreign affairs is an inherent power, which attaches automatically to the federal government as a sovereign entity, and derives from the Constitution only as the Constitution is the creator of that sovereign entity. As Justice Sutherland said in *United States* v. *Curtiss-Wright Export Corporation* (1936): "The investment of the federal government with the powers of external sovereignty did not depend upon the affirmative grants of the Constitution. The powers to declare and wage war, to conclude peace, to make treaties, to maintain diplomatic relations with other sovereignties, if they had never been mentioned in the Constitution, would have vested in the federal government as necessary concomitants of nationality."

For this reason, Sutherland continued, the source of foreign relations authority contrasted sharply with federal power over internal affairs. "In that field, the primary purpose of the Constitution was to carve from the general mass of legislative powers *then possessed by the states* such portions as it was thought desirable to vest in the federal government, leaving those not included in the enumeration still in the states." But the Constitution could not transfer power over external affairs in this way from the states to the nation because "the states severally never possessed international powers." Rather, on the separation of the colonies "acting as a unit" from Great Britain, "the powers of external sovereignty passed from the Crown not to the colonies severally, but to the colonies in their collective and cor-

porate capacity as the United States of America." Even before the Declaration of Independence, the Colonies were acting through a common agency, the Continental Congress, and when "the external sovereignty of Great Britain in respect of the colonies ceased, it immediately passed to the Union." Thus the Union, existing before the Constitution, "was the sole possessor of external sovereignty and in the Union it remained without change save in so far as the Constitution in express terms qualified its exercise."

Presumably the purpose of Sutherland's conceptualistic analysis, which seems strikingly at variance with the actual historical facts of the Revolutionary period, was to establish that the federal government's power over foreign affairs was inherent, plenary, and exclusive, but it seems an unnecessarily involved way of achieving those ends. Surely the inherent nature of the power to conduct foreign affairs can be deduced from the right of a nation to self-preservation in a world of nations, without elaborate hypotheses about the location and transfer of sovereignty in a revolutionary period. That the power is plenary is established by the absence of any expressed constitutional limitations on its exercise. That the power is exclusive as against the states is sufficiently established by Article I, section 10, which flatly forbids states to enter into "any treaty, alliance, or confederation," or to grant "letters of marque and reprisal." The third clause of section 10 carries further prohibitions, though these may be waived with the consent of Congress. The clause reads:

> No state shall, without the consent of Congress, . . . keep troops, or ships of war in time of peace, enter into any agreement or compact . . . with a foreign power, or engage in war, unless actually invaded, or in such imminent danger as will not admit of delay.

In fact, the consent of Congress has never been asked for any of these purposes, and the clause must now be read as an unqualified bar to the acts specified. Thus the complete incapacity of the states for foreign relationships is fully established by the letter of the Constitution and by practice.

Neither is Sutherland's theory necessary to prevent any possible encroachment on federal authority by the states through their "reserved powers" under the Tenth Amendment. In discussing the commerce clause, we saw how the doctrine of dual federalism for a time made reserved state powers an instrument for denying full exercise by the federal government of its directly granted powers to regulate commerce among the states. But dual federalism never got a foothold in the field of foreign relations, as *Ware* v. *Hylton* (1796) demonstrates. During the Revolutionary War Virginia passed a law sequestering British property and providing that debts owed by citizens of the state to British subjects could be discharged by payment to a designated state officer. This statute was clearly a valid exercise of state powers under international law. However, the treaty of peace between the United States and Great Britain controverted this arrangement and pre-

served the right of British creditors to collect such debts. The Supreme Court held that this exercise by the United States of its treaty power had the effect of nullifying the conflicting Virginia law.

## THE ROLE OF THE PRESIDENT

The principal theoretical writers on government whose works were known and read by the framers—Blackstone, Locke, Montesquieu—were unanimous in contending that the power to conduct foreign relations must rest with the executive. In spite of this fact, the Constitution allocated the power to declare war to Congress, where the authority had vested under the Articles of Confederation. It made the Senate's consent necessary to the ratification of treaties, and by a two-thirds vote. It made the Senate's advice and consent a condition to the appointment of ambassadors. When account is taken of the general lawmaking and appropriating powers of Congress, the exercise of which may be essential to the formulation and execution of foreign policy decisions, it is clear that, as Corwin says, "The Constitution, considered only for its affirmative grants of powers capable of affecting the issue, is an invitation to struggle for the privilege of directing American foreign policy." [1]

For this struggle the President is powerfully equipped by the general characteristics of executive power already noted, by his constitutional authority as Commander in Chief, and by his recognized position as "the Nation's organ for foreign affairs." [2] The Supreme Court has repeatedly recognized the President's primacy and special position in this area, as a further look at the *Curtiss-Wright* decision will demonstrate. The controversy in that case involved a joint resolution adopted by Congress in 1934 authorizing the President by proclamation to prohibit the sale within the United States of arms to certain South American belligerent states. The President promptly issued such a declaration. A conviction for violation of the proclamation and joint resolution was attacked on the ground that the statute constituted an unlawful delegation of legislative power to the President, because action was left to the "unfettered discretion" of the executive with no statutory standards to guide his decision.

As noted in Chapter 11, the Court had just used such grounds to invalidate federal statutes in the *Panama Refining, Schechter,* and *Carter Coal Co.* cases. But in *Curtiss-Wright* Justice Sutherland pointed out that the delegations in those three cases had "related solely to internal affairs," whereas the "whole aim" of the resolution challenged here was "to affect a situation entirely external to the United States." In this latter area the President possessed not only the powers given him by statute, but also "the very delicate,

[1] Edward S. Corwin (ed.), *The President: Office and Powers, 1787–1957* (New York: New York University Press, 4th rev. ed., 1957), p. 171.
[2] This phrase goes back to a statement made by John Marshall in the House of Representatives in 1799. See *ibid.*, pp. 177–178.

plenary and exclusive power of the President as the sole organ of the federal government in the field of international relations." Sutherland went on:

> It is quite apparent that if, in the maintenance of our international relations, embarrassment . . . is to be avoided and success for our aims achieved, congressional legislation which is to be made effective through negotiation and inquiry within the international field must often accord to the President a degree of discretion and freedom from statutory restriction which would not be admissible were domestic affairs alone involved. Moreover, he, not Congress, has the better opportunity of knowing the conditions which prevail in foreign countries. . . . He has his confidential sources of information. He has his agents in the form of diplomatic, consular and other officials.

In the light of these circumstances, the Court concluded that delegations of legislative power to the President in matters involving foreign relations could not be judged by the same standards that would be applied in internal affairs.

More specifically, what powers does the President exercise in his role as "sole organ" of foreign relations for the nation? First of all, he is the channel for communications to and from other nations. He appoints the members of the diplomatic corps through whom official contacts are maintained abroad and receives their reports through the Department of State. Negotiations with foreign countries are conducted under his direction. In collaboration with the Secretary of State he determines the policies to be followed in dealing with foreign nations.

Second, the power of recognizing foreign governments follows from the presidential role in sending and receiving diplomatic representatives. President Washington established the controlling precedent in this area when he received Citizen Genêt and then some months later demanded his recall by France, without consulting Congress on either occasion. Decisions on the establishment of diplomatic relations, as in the recognition of Russia in 1933, or the refusal to recognize Communist China, may have tremendous consequences, but the constitutional responsibility for the decisions rests with the President alone.

Third, the President can use his control of the Armed Forces to implement his foreign policy, and to enforce American rights or interests abroad. In 1844 Tyler disposed the naval and military forces so as to protect Texas against Mexican reprisals because of the pending treaty for annexation of Texas to the United States. Theodore Roosevelt in 1903 "took Panama," as he put it, and later sent the fleet around the world to demonstrate American power and interest in world affairs. President Wilson ordered the arming of American merchant vessels as a countermove to German unrestricted submarine warfare in March, 1917. Troops have been repeatedly employed to protect American lives and property in foreign countries.

These are powers of tremendous impact—so great, in fact, that to a con-

siderable degree they cancel out the most important grant of external authority to Congress, the power to declare war. The President can, by his management of foreign affairs and his use of the Armed Forces, so shape the nation's policy and the development of events as to leave Congress no choice but to declare war. Of all the wars in which the United States has engaged, only two—the War of 1812 and the Spanish-American War—were clearly the product of congressional policy. In the remainder, although legislative sentiment generally supported the policies which led up to the hostilities, the formulation of those policies was predominantly the work of the executive.

TREATIES    On the other hand, the necessity of securing Senate consent by a two-thirds vote for the ratification of treaties has proved in practice to be a real limitation on executive policy making. The framers thought of the Senate as a kind of council with which the President would sit while treaties were under negotiation and from which he would get advice. In fact President Washington tried to use the Senate in this way in August, 1789, going to the Senate chamber in person and presenting seven issues pertaining to a proposed treaty with the Southern Indians on which he wished "advice and consent." The senators preferred not to discuss the matter in the presence of the President, and voted to refer it to a committee of five. Washington, quite indignant, exclaimed: "This defeats every purpose of my coming here," and subsequently withdrew with what William Maclay called "a discontented air." Washington did go back two days later for the Senate's answers to his questions, but the whole experience was so unfortunate that the effort has never been repeated.

Treaties are consequently negotiated by the executive, though congressional leaders are normally appointed to the American delegation to important international conferences as well as to the United Nations. When treaties are sent to the Senate in completed form, their fate is unpredictable. John Hay once wrote: "A treaty entering the Senate is like a bull going into the arena; no one can say just how or when the final blow will fall—but one thing is certain, it will never leave the arena alive." [3] This is highly exaggerated, but the shambles which Senate intervention has sometimes made of United States foreign policy has led many students to conclude that consent to treaty ratification by a majority vote of the two houses of Congress would be preferable to the present arrangement. [4]

The Senate can defeat a treaty entirely, or consent to ratification with amendments. This latter action requires the President, if he still favors the

[3] William R. Thayer, *The Life and Letters of John Hay* (Boston: Houghton Mifflin Company, 1915), vol. 2, p. 393.

[4] A consular treaty was signed with Russia in 1964, but the President did not submit it to the Senate until 1967, for fear it would be defeated. It was approved sixty-six to twenty-eight, with only three more votes than the two-thirds required.

treaty, to secure the acceptance of these amendments by the foreign power involved before the treaty can be ratified. The Senate may also attach reservations, which do not alter the content of the treaty itself, but do qualify the obligations assumed under the treaty by the United States.

EXECUTIVE AGREEMENTS    Partly because of the hazards of Senate treaty approval, the President has made extensive use of "executive agreements" with foreign countries. Since these agreements are not treaties in name, they are not subject to the constitutional requirement of Senate consent. They may be employed for minor matters which it would be inappropriate to embody in a treaty, but in the twentieth century many executive agreements have dealt with matters of major importance. Thus Japanese immigration into the United States was governed for seventeen years by the "Gentlemen's Agreement" of 1907, and the controversial Potsdam and Yalta Pacts were executive agreements.

Executive agreements are often based on acts of Congress authorizing them. If not, they are usually said to find their constitutional authority in the President's power as Commander in Chief or in his position as the sole organ of international relations. Efforts to distinguish the legal effects of executive agreements from treaties have generally been unsuccessful. One contention has been that the force of an executive agreement terminates with the end of the administration which entered into it, but this is not true. For example, the 1940 destroyer deal with Britain provided for United States leases extending ninety-nine years on the British bases involved.

A further contention is that agreements, unlike treaties, are not "law of the land" unless authorized or approved by Congress, and so not noticeable by the courts. But in *United States* v. *Belmont* (1937) the Supreme Court specifically denied this view, holding that the recognition of Soviet Russia in 1933 and the accompanying executive agreements constituted an international compact which the President was authorized to enter into without consulting the Senate. Moreover, such agreements had the same effect as treaties in superseding conflicting state laws. To similar effect was the decision in *United States* v. *Pink* (1942).

The Supreme Court has not determined whether an executive agreement will supersede an earlier act of Congress with which it is in disagreement. In *United States* v. *Guy W. Capps, Inc.* (1955) it was charged that an executive agreement between the United States and Canada was unconstitutional because the President had not utilized a relevant statutory procedure, relying instead on his independent constitutional authority. The court of appeals, citing the *Steel Seizure Case*, held the executive agreement unconstitutional "because it was not authorized by Congress and contravened provisions of a statute dealing with the very matter to which it related." The Supreme Court, however, avoided the constitutional issue and decided the case on other grounds.

### CONGRESS AND FOREIGN RELATIONS

In addition to the power of Congress to declare war and the special role of the Senate in ratifying treaties and confirming ambassadorial appointments, Congress can exercise great influence over foreign policy through its general powers of legislation, appropriation, and investigation. Congress early seized power from the President on the matter of neutrality. In 1793 President Washington, on the outbreak of war between Britain and France, issued a proclamation asserting the intention of the United States to be "friendly and impartial" toward both belligerents. Hamilton wrote a defense of the constitutional right of the President to issue such a proclamation, but the action was offensive to Jeffersonian views of executive power. In 1794 Congress superseded the executive proclamation by passing the first neutrality act, and this precedent has been subsequently accepted as establishing legislative authority over the neutrality issue.

Congress possesses specific constitutional authority to define and punish offenses against the law of nations as well as to regulate foreign commerce. Congress may use its general lawmaking power to frustrate or limit executive foreign policy. In 1924 Congress adopted the Japanese Exclusion Act over the protests of President Coolidge and Secretary of State Hughes, with damaging effects on American foreign relations. The authority to negotiate reciprocal trade agreements, a basic instrument of foreign policy after 1934, had to be won anew from Congress every two or three years. More recently a favorite legislative device has been to impose statutory bans on trade with, or aid to, countries in congressional disfavor.

Congressional legislative power may also step into the breach caused by failure of the treaty process to function successfully. After the defeat of the Treaty of Versailles, it was a joint resolution of Congress which finally brought American participation in the war against the Central Powers to a legal conclusion in 1921. Moreover, it should be noted that American adherence to the United Nations was accomplished by congressional statute, the United Nations Participation Act of 1945.

The appropriations power gives legislative control over any executive policy which requires funds for its implementation, and the fact that appropriations measures must originate with the House serves somewhat to balance the Senate's special role in the foreign relations field. Since the inauguration of the Marshall Plan in 1947, the appropriation for foreign aid has annually precipitated lengthy and often acrimonious debates over foreign policy, and the executive recommendations are almost invariably substantially reduced. In 1966 the President's request for a supplemental appropriation, mostly for the war in Vietnam, was made the occasion for a full-dress televised review of Vietnam policy by the Senate Foreign Relations Committee.

The House and Senate can also use their general investigatory powers to influence foreign policy. During the 1930s Senator Nye's investigations of the armament industry did much to encourage an isolationist attitude toward foreign involvements. In 1966 Senator Fulbright, who was at odds with President Johnson on Vietnam, used his powerful position as chairman of the Senate Foreign Relations Committee to conduct "educational" hearings on China policy and the North Atlantic Treaty Organization as well as Vietnam.

Conscious of the desirability of congressional support for the use of troops outside the country, President Eisenhower in 1955 requested Congress to adopt a joint resolution authorizing his employment of the armed forces to protect Formosa from Chinese attack. Again in 1957 Congress voted support for the President if he should determine there was necessity for use of force against Communist aggression in the Middle East.

These precedents were utilized by President Johnson in 1964. At a time when there were only 20,000 American troops in Vietnam, and after alleged North Vietnamese torpedo boat attacks on two United States destroyers in the Gulf of Tonkin, the President asked Congress for a joint resolution of support to strengthen his hand in dealing with the Vietnam situation. Almost unanimously Congress adopted the so-called Tonkin Gulf Resolution approving and supporting "the determination of the President, as Commander in Chief, to take all necessary measures to repel any armed attack against the forces of the United States and to prevent further aggression."

President Johnson subsequently relied on this resolution as authorizing and justifying the tremendous escalation of military operations in Vietnam and the bombing of North Vietnam, whereas many congressmen felt there had been no such intention and that they had been manipulated into a position where they had to approve the resolution or give an impression of national disunity. Particularly in the Senate various efforts were made to recapture some congressional control over the situation.

Thus, on November 16, 1967, the Foreign Relations Committee adopted unanimously a Fulbright resolution asserting that "the executive and legislative branches of the United States Government have joint responsibility and authority to formulate the foreign policy of the United States," and stating that in the future American armed forces should not be committed to hostilities on foreign territory without "affirmative action by Congress specifically intended to give rise to such commitment."

Again, on November 30 the Senate unanimously adopted the Mansfield Resolution calling on the President to seek United Nations help in ending the war in Vietnam. Shortly thereafter the Senate Foreign Relations Committee began a study of the Tonkin Gulf incident, which some senators suspected had been misrepresented by the administration in order to ensure

congressional support for escalation of the war. Although these efforts had not by early 1968 had any effect on administration policy, they did provide a focus for the widespread opposition to the war.

## CONSTITUTIONAL ASPECTS OF THE TREATY POWER

Article VI provides: "This Constitution, and the laws of the United States which shall be made in pursuance thereof; and all treaties made, or which shall be made, under the authority of the United States, shall be the supreme law of the land." Two problems growing out of this language need consideration here: first, the relationship between treaties and acts of Congress; and second, the relationship of treaties and the treaty-making power to the Constitution itself.

TREATIES AND ACTS OF CONGRESS    Article VI sets treaties and acts of Congress on a par—both are "the supreme law of the land." How then are conflicts between treaties and statutes adjusted? First it is necessary to distinguish between "self-executing" and "non-self-executing" treaties. A treaty is self-executing when it requires no congressional legislation to put it into effect. Thus the provisions of a treaty defining the rights of aliens in the United States would automatically become the "supreme law of the land," and the courts would be obliged to enforce them. A non-self-executing treaty is one in which obligations of future action are undertaken by the political departments of the government. A treaty of alliance with a foreign power, or a treaty which required the appropriation of money by Congress would be illustrations. The courts have no power to enforce such treaties should the government fail to honor the obligation it has undertaken.

In general, where a treaty and a statute conflict, the latter in point of time supersedes the earlier. There are exceptions, however. All acts of Congress prevail over earlier conflicting treaties, but a non-self-executing treaty does not supersede an earlier conflicting act of Congress. The Supreme Court had occasion to state the general rule in the *Head Money Cases* (1884), where Congress had levied a head tax on immigrants coming to the United States despite earlier treaties guaranteeing their free admission. The Court upheld the statute, saying: "So far as a treaty made by the United States with any foreign nation can become the subject of judicial cognizance in the courts of this country, it is subject to such acts as Congress may pass for its enforcement, modification, or repeal."

CONSTITUTIONAL SCOPE OF TREATIES    According to Article VI, laws must be made "in pursuance" of the Constitution in order to have status as supreme law of the land, but treaties need be made only "under the authority of the United States." Considerable effort has been made to conjure up from this difference in wording the bogey of a treaty power which is unlimited by

the Constitution. Some substance seems to be given these fears by the fact that the Supreme Court has never held a treaty unconstitutional, and by the circumstances of the Court's decision in *Missouri* v. *Holland* (1920).

This case arose out of the efforts of the United States to impose limits on the shooting of migratory birds. The first congressional statute passed for this purpose was declared an unconstitutional exercise of federal commerce power in two federal district court decisions, on the ground that the birds were owned by the states in their sovereign capacity for the benefit of their people. The United States then entered into a treaty with Great Britain, reciting the dangers of extermination of birds in their annual migrations between the United States and Canada, providing for closed seasons and other forms of protection, and agreeing that the two powers would take or propose to their legislatures necessary measures for making the treaty provisions effective. In pursuance of this treaty, Congress passed a statute in 1918 prohibiting the killing of migratory birds except in accordance with federal regulations.

The Supreme Court, through Justice Holmes, upheld enforcement of this statute against the charge that the treaty and legislation were an unconstitutional interference with the rights of the states. In part his conclusion rested upon the evanescent nature of the state claim to ownership of the birds. "The whole foundation of the State's rights is the presence within their jurisdiction of birds that yesterday had not arrived, tomorrow may be in another State and in a week a thousand miles away." But more positively his case was based on recognition of the fact that here was "a national interest of very nearly the first magnitude" which could be protected "only by national action in concert with that of another power. . . . But for the treaty and the statute there soon might be no birds for any powers to deal with."

Holmes did not intend to see the only effective means of protecting this national interest frustrated by "some invisible radiation from the general terms of the Tenth Amendment." For "it is not lightly to be assumed that, in matters requiring national action, 'a power which must belong to and somewhere reside in every civilized government' is not to be found." In this instance the authority was to be found in the treaty power. Holmes hastened to add that he did not "mean to imply that there are no qualifications to the treaty-making power"; one such limitation, he suggested, would be any explicit "prohibitory words . . . found in the Constitution." But there were none applicable to this situation. The general deduction which he drew was that "there may be matters of the sharpest exigency for the national well being that an act of Congress could not deal with but that a treaty followed by such an act could."

There is at first glance something startling about a situation whereby ratification of a treaty gives Congress constitutional powers it did not possess in the absence of the treaty. But this result is an inevitable consequence of

the plenary nature of federal power over foreign affairs. The division of functions between federal and state governments made by the Constitution relates only to internal affairs. The complete incapacity of the states for foreign relationships requires that the federal government have authority to deal with all matters which are of legitimate concern to American foreign relations. This does not mean, however, that the treaty power can be used to amend the Constitution, nor does it open up all constitutional rights to revision by treaties. Perhaps the best way to make this clear is to examine the provisions and purposes of the Bricker Amendment which attracted such great public interest in the early 1950s.

## THE BRICKER AMENDMENT

The Bricker Amendment's support was generated by postwar isolationism and resentment against a decade of strong executive leadership and American involvement in foreign affairs. In particular, advocates of the amendment were exercised about proposed United Nations covenants on human rights and genocide, and wanted to establish that no treaty could affect rights guaranteed by the Constitution. They were also hostile to the idea that a treaty can affect the constitutional division of internal functions between federal and state governments. Finally, they wanted to restrict the use of executive agreements, on the ground that they had been used excessively and unwisely. The specific provisions of the Bricker Amendment were revised from time to time, but these three general purposes were consistently maintained.

TREATIES AND CONSTITUTIONAL RIGHTS     The first section of the amendment, in its 1953 version, was as follows: "A provision of a treaty which conflicts with this Constitution shall not be of any force or effect." In so far as the proponents of the amendment were motivated by a genuine fear that the treaty power was not limited by the Constitution, their concern was baseless. First, the peculiar language of Article VI, referring to treaties "made under the authority of the United States," was not intended to indicate that treaties, unlike statutes, did not have to be made "in pursuance" of the Constitution. Its purpose was simply to validate treaties made by the United States *before* the Constitution was adopted, particularly the important peace treaties which concluded the Revolutionary War.

Second, although it is true that the Supreme Court has never held a treaty unconstitutional, it has on several occasions clearly announced that the treaty power is subject to the Constitution. Perhaps the most explicit earlier holding to this effect came in *Geofroy* v. *Riggs* (1890). Justice Field there began by admitting that "the treaty power, as expressed in the Constitution, is in terms unlimited," but he went on to note that it was subject to those implied "restraints which are found in that instrument against the action of

the government or of its departments, and those arising from the nature of the government itself and of that of the States." Since this language was a little vague, Field added: "It would not be contended that [the treaty power] extends so far as to authorize what the Constitution forbids, or a change in the character of the government or in that of one of the States, or a cession of any portion of the territory of the latter, without its consent."

Any doubt which could have remained on the subjection of the treaty power to the Constitution after this decision was completely extinguished by *Reid* v. *Covert* (1957). Justice Black, after quoting Article VI, said:

> There is nothing in this language which intimates that treaties and laws enacted pursuant to them do not have to comply with the provisions of the Constitution. . . . It would be manifestly contrary to the objectives of those who created the Constitution, as well as those who were responsible for the Bill of Rights—let alone alien to our entire constitutional history and tradition—to construe Article VI as permitting the United States to exercise power under an international agreement without observing constitutional prohibitions. In effect, such construction would permit amendment of that document in a manner not sanctioned by Article V.

Thus adoption of the original Bricker Amendment language about the supremacy of the Constitution over the treaty power would have been surplusage, merely confirming the present understanding.

TREATIES AND FEDERALISM    A second purpose of the Bricker Amendment was to reverse the holding in *Missouri* v. *Holland* and to render the national government incapable of assuming the regulation of subjects reserved to the states by entering into a treaty. In its most celebrated form, the so-called "which" clause, the Bricker proposal ran as follows: "A treaty shall become effective as internal law in the United States only through legislation which would be valid in the absence of a treaty."

This language, if added to the Constitution, would have done two things. First, it would require that a treaty, after ratification, be reenacted by Congress if it was to be enforceable in the courts. No treaty could be self-executing within the United States. Following the two present steps of negotiation and Senate consent to ratification, there would have to follow three additional steps—approval by the House, the Senate, and the President, who might by then be a different President from the one who had negotiated the treaty. Under these conditions foreign countries might well have hesitated to enter into treaties with the United States, knowing the perils involved in making the agreements binding.

More important, this language would require that the legislation reenacting the treaty be within the existing powers of Congress. It would prevent the federal government from dealing with any internal problem on the basis of a treaty, on which it lacked authority to legislate under its other constitu-

tional powers. Yet the majority of American treaties, including some of the most important ones, have dealt with matters internally under the jurisdiction of the states. These include such matters as the right to own property, to inherit, to collect debts, to organize a corporation, to escape discriminatory taxes, to have access to courts, to enter a profession, or to enjoy religious freedom. The United States enters into treaties guaranteeing such rights for aliens in the United States so that American citizens can have the benefit of reciprocal protection abroad. If the federal government were prevented by the Bricker Amendment from negotiation on these internal matters, foreign countries would have no incentive to guarantee similar protection of American personal or property rights abroad.

This part of the Bricker Amendment, then, represented an attack on constitutional principles and practices which have been essential features of the conduct of foreign relations since the Revolution. Because of concern about hypothetical dangers to states' rights, backers of the amendment proposed to render the federal government powerless to negotiate for the protection of important American rights and interests.

EXECUTIVE AGREEMENTS    Finally, the Bricker Amendment sought in various ways to limit the President's power to enter into executive agreements. In its early stages it provided that "executive agreements shall not be made in lieu of treaties." If this hopelessly vague language meant anything, it was a complete ban on executive agreements. It was quickly dropped, and the 1953 draft made executive agreements subject to the same limitations imposed on treaties. This provision would have had the fantastic result of requiring all executive agreements, which outnumber treaties ten to one, to be reenacted by Congress, and would subject them to the crippling subject-matter limitations just analyzed.

It is not surprising that, as the purpose and effect of the Bricker Amendment came to be understood, its original support dwindled. Stimulated by imaginary dangers and partisan passions, the Brickerites undertook to deny the plenary power of the federal government to conduct the foreign relations of the nation and, as President Eisenhower said, to deprive the President "of the capacity necessary to carry on negotiations with foreign governments."

## CONTROL OVER PASSPORTS

Throughout most of American history, a passport has not been a legal requirement for entering or leaving the United States. Prior to 1856 various federal, state, and local officials had issued passports or certificates of citizenship which served as letters of introduction to foreign officials requesting treatment according to the usages of international law. In 1856 Congress put an end to these unsystematic practices by passage of the Passport Act, which still remains the basic statute covering the field. That law provides: "The

Secretary of State shall be authorized to grant and issue passports . . . under such rules as the President shall designate and prescribe for and on behalf of the United States, and no other person shall grant, issue, or verify any such passport."

Travel restrictions were imposed during the War of 1812, the Civil War, and World War I. The act of 1918 made it unlawful, in time of war, while a presidential proclamation was in force, for a citizen to leave or enter the United States unless he bore a valid passport. This act was amended in 1941 so that it could be operative in times of "emergency" short of war. Its restrictions were invoked by presidential proclamation in November, 1941, and were maintained in continuous effect thereafter. In the Immigration and Nationality Act of 1952 the same powers were reenacted. Thus from 1941 on the power of the Secretary of State to issue passports gave him the authority to control travel by American citizens abroad. The present general practice of other countries to refuse admission to travelers who do not bear valid passports re-enforces this control.

It has been customary to refer to the Secretary's powers under the 1856 act as "discretionary." In practice, however, this discretion was long exercised within very narrow limits, and principally in the decision of two issues. One was whether the applicant was in fact a citizen or a person "owing allegiance" to the United States, for the act forbade granting passports to any other persons. The other was whether the applicant was trying to escape from legal prosecution, promoting passport fraud, or otherwise engaged in illegal conduct. It is true that other issues were raised from time to time. For example, in 1869 Attorney General Hoar referred to the possibility that the public interest might require denial of a passport to an avowed anarchist, and two decades later Secretary of State Bayard opposed the issuance of passports to Mormons intending to propagate polygamy abroad.

There was no consistent practice of denying passports on grounds of harm to the public interest, however, until the Russian Revolution. Thereafter passports were generally refused to American Communists until 1931. Concern again developed on this matter after World War II, and in 1947 the State Department adopted a policy of refusing passports to Communists or persons engaged in activities which would advance the movement, or whose travel would "prejudice the orderly conduct of foreign relations" or "otherwise be prejudicial to the interests of the United States." During the following decade a substantial number of persons, most of whom denied being Communists, were refused passports on "political" grounds. In the Internal Security Act of 1950 Congress added statutory support by forbidding passports to members of Communist organizations ordered to register as such with the Attorney General.

A number of the applicants who were denied passports brought suit against the State Department to compel their issuance, but none of these

controversies reached the Supreme Court until 1958. Even then the decision in *Kent* v. *Dulles* did not reach the basic constitutional question involved. However, several decisions of the federal courts in the District of Columbia had previously explored the issues, and their rulings are of considerable assistance in this analysis.

First of all, "freedom to travel" has been definitely established by these decisions as a right of American citizens. This ruling was first made by the court of appeals in *Shachtman* v. *Dulles* (1955):

> The denial of a passport . . . causes a deprivation of liberty that a citizen otherwise would have. The right to travel, to go from place to place as the means of transportation permit, is a natural right subject to the rights of others and to reasonable regulation under law. A restraint imposed by the Government of the United States upon this liberty, therefore, must conform with the provision of the Fifth Amendment that "No person shall be . . . deprived of . . . liberty . . . without due process of law."

In basing the right to travel on the Fifth Amendment, the court apparently decided against the relevance of the First Amendment to this problem. However, denial of a passport in order to prevent criticism of American policies abroad might be regarded as interference with the freedom of speech, and denial because of past statements might seem to be punishment for the exercise of First Amendment freedoms. The Supreme Court in *Kent* v. *Dulles* likewise avoided any attempt to invoke the First Amendment, and firmly ratified the Fifth Amendment holding. As Justice Douglas put it:

> The right to travel is a part of the "liberty" of which the citizen cannot be deprived without the due process of law of the Fifth Amendment. . . . Freedom of movement across frontiers in either direction . . . was a part of our heritage. Travel abroad . . . may be necessary for a livelihood. It may be as close to the heart of the individual as the choice of what he eats, or wears, or reads.

Having decided this much, the Supreme Court found it unnecessary to take up the more difficult question of how far this liberty might be curtailed without infringing on due process, because five justices concluded that Congress had not authorized the kinds of curtailment which the State Department had been practicing. Congress had not passed a general passport act since it codified and reenacted the original 1856 statute in 1926, and at that time, Douglas held, State Department practice had "jelled" only around denial because of unlawful conduct or lack of citizenship. There was, to be sure, the 1950 statute denying passports to members of organizations required to register with the Attorney General, but it was not in effect because by 1958 no registration proceedings had been completed and the constitutionality of the act was still undecided. As for the grant of discretion to the Secretary of State in issuing passports, most recently made in the Immigration and Nationality Act of 1952, the Court hesitated "to impute to Congress

. . . a purpose to give him unbridled discretion to grant or withhold a passport from a citizen for any substantive reason he may choose." The four-judge minority, on the other hand, thought that the 1952 act had ratified all prior use by the Secretary of his discretionary powers.

As a result of this decision, the State Department announced that passport applicants would no longer be required to answer questions about Communist Party membership, and passports were immediately granted to Paul Robeson, Corliss Lamont, and others who had been contesting the State Department's denial of passports for years. However, the Department also immediately requested Congress to adopt legislation confirming the powers it had been exercising. The bill proposed would bar the issuance of passports to persons who had been members of the Communist Party or who had engaged in "pro-Communist activity" within the preceding ten years. Representative Walter introduced legislation giving the Secretary broad discretion to deny passports to persons whose travel he thought would be "prejudicial to the interests of the United States." However, Congress failed to enact any new passport legislation.

This left, as the only expressly applicable statute limiting passports, the 1950 Internal Security Act, the registration provisions of which the Court held constitutional in 1961.[5] Thus the passport provisions of the act were brought into effect, and the State Department promptly used them to deny passports to two leading American Communists. The Supreme Court held the legislation unconstitutional in *Aptheker* v. *Secretary of State* (1964).

Justice Goldberg ruled for the Court that the language was unconstitutional on its face because it prohibited the granting of passports to any member of a registered Communist organization, regardless of whether his membership was knowing or unknowing, regardless of his degree of activity in the organization and his commitment to its purpose, or regardless of the purposes for which he wished to travel. After all, he might simply want "to visit a relative in Ireland, or . . . read rare manuscripts in the Bodleian Library of Oxford University." Justice Clark for a three-judge minority thought these were "irrational imaginings" and argued that, at least as applied to admitted Communist leaders, the statute should be upheld.

The Court did not say in *Aptheker* that the right to travel was absolute. It merely held that this particular limitation was too broad and indiscriminate in its scope. In *Zemel* v. *Rusk* (1965) the Court upheld the State Department's refusal to validate passports for travel to Communist Cuba. The broad language of the Passport Act of 1926, which the Court had held in the *Kent* case did not authorize State Department denial of passports to Communists, was here thought to justify the practice of geographical area limitations on travel. The Court majority found that there had been a frequent practice of area restrictions on passports in the decade prior to 1926; thus it could be inferred that Congress intended by the broad language of

[5] *Communist Party* v. *Subversive Activities Control Board* (1961).

the act to maintain such authority in the executive—authority that could be supported by "the weightiest considerations of national security."

Another, and more persuasive, difference from the *Kent* situation was that there the action was taken against an individual because of his views or affiliations, whereas area limitations are imposed "because of foreign policy considerations affecting all citizens." Thus the Court felt there was no possible First Amendment claim that the individual was being restrained from travel because of his views. This was an inhibition on action, not on speech; "the right to speak and publish does not carry with it the unrestrained right to gather information." Justice Douglas, dissenting with Black and Goldberg, admitted that the right to travel was "at the periphery of the First Amendment, rather than at its core," and so could be regulated, but he thought it was done in too broad a fashion here.

Enforcement of these area restrictions has proved frustrating for the State Department, however. William Worthy, a newspaperman, had visited Communist China in 1956 in defiance of the ban on such travel, and in 1957 the State Department refused to renew his passport on the ground that he might not abide by area restrictions in the future. He went to Cuba in 1961 without a passport, and was indicted on his return for entering the country without a passport. The Court of Appeals for the Fifth Circuit ruled that the provision of the Immigration and Nationality Act of 1952 forbidding reentry of an American citizen into the United States without a valid passport was an unconstitutional denial of the fundamental right of free ingress.[6]

The Department of Justice did not take the case to the Supreme Court, deciding to rely instead on the statutory provision forbidding citizens to *depart from* the country without a valid passport. For a test on this issue, criminal charges were brought against American citizens who had traveled to Cuba with passports, otherwise valid, which had not been validated for travel to Cuba. There was no specific language in the statute punishing the violation of State Department area restrictions, and the Department in issuing the Cuba restrictions had made no reference to their enforcement by criminal sanctions. The action had been explained as intended to make clear to travelers in Cuba that because of the absence of normal diplomatic relations the government would not be able to extend normal protective services to Americans visiting there. Consequently the Court unanimously held in *United States* v. *Laub* (1967) and *Travis* v. *United States* (1967) that the criminal indictment must be dismissed. "Crimes are not to be created by inference," said Justice Fortas.

This ruling left open to the State Department the sanction of canceling the passports of persons who visited off-limit countries. In 1959 the Court of Appeals for the District of Columbia upheld such action, and the Supreme Court declined to review the case.[7] Cancellation of the passport of Yale Professor Staughton Lynd in 1966 after his peace mission to North Vietnam

[6] *Worthy* v. *United States* (1964).
[7] *Worthy* v. *Herter* (1959).

led to another test of this power.[8] When Lynd applied for a new passport to go to England, the State Department refused because he would not promise not to go on to North Vietnam. In 1967 the court of appeals for the District of Columbia held that the Passport Act of 1926 does not give the State Department the right to control a person's travel, but only to say where the individual can take his passport. The State Department may make a traveler promise that he will leave his passport with the United States consulate in an approved country before venturing into a prohibited country, but it cannot refuse to issue the passport even if the traveler admits he intends to visit the off-limits country without his passport. The court explained that the passport statute must be read narrowly out of deference to the constitutionally protected right to travel.[9]

This decision eliminated the last effective means available to the government to keep Americans from going to prohibited countries, and led the administration in December, 1967, to request legislation from Congress imposing criminal penalties for unauthorized travel.

## SELECTED REFERENCES

CHAFEE, ZECHARIAH, JR., *Three Human Rights in the Constitution of 1787,* pp. 162–213. Lawrence, Kans.: University of Kansas Press, 1956.

*The Constitution of the United States of America: Analysis and Interpretation,* Sen. Doc. no. 39, 88th Cong., pp. 462–497. Washington: Government Printing Office, 1964.

CORWIN, EDWARD S. (ed.), *The President: Office and Powers 1787–1957,* chap. 5. New York: New York University Press, 1957 (fourth revised edition).

EHRLICH, THOMAS, "Passports," 19 *Stanford Law Review* 129–149 (1966).

*Freedom to Travel: Report of the Special Committee to Study Passport Procedures of the Association of the Bar of the City of New York.* New York: Dodd, Mead, & Company, Inc., 1958.

SCHUBERT, GLENDON A., JR., "Politics and the Constitution: The Bricker Amendment during 1953," 16 *Journal of Politics* 257–298 (1954).

———, *The Presidency in the Courts,* chap. 4. Minneapolis: The University of Minnesota Press, 1957.

SUTHERLAND, ARTHUR E., JR., "Restricting the Treaty Power," in Robert G. McCloskey (ed.), *Essays in Constitutional Law,* chap. 7. New York: Alfred A. Knopf, Inc., 1957.

[8] In 1967 the State Department lifted the ban on travel to Albania, but retained it for Communist China, Cuba, North Korea, and North Vietnam. It also issued regulations limiting the authority of the Secretary of State to impose travel bans. He may do so only when a country is at war with the United States, when armed hostilities are in progress in a country, or when travel "would seriously impair the conduct of United States foreign affairs." *The New York Times,* March 15, 1967.

[9] *The New York Times,* December 21, 1967.

# 19

## The President as Commander in Chief

In No. 74 of *The Federalist* Alexander Hamilton wrote: "Of all the cares or concerns of government, the direction of war most peculiarly demands those qualities which distinguish the exercise of power by a single hand." He was defending the "propriety" of the Commander in Chief clause (Art. II, sec. 2) which reads: "The President shall be Commander in Chief of the army and navy of the United States, and of the militia of the several states, when called into the actual service of the United States." This provision, he added, was "so consonant to the precedents of the State constitutions in general, that little need be said to explain or enforce it."

Hamilton could not foresee the tremendous reservoir of power which this language was to provide for the President. It would amount, he said in No. 69, "to nothing more than the supreme command and direction of the military and naval forces, as first general and admiral of the Confederacy," while the more significant powers of declaring war and of raising and regulating fleets and armies were exercised by Congress. Actually this was an accurate enough forecast of the limited role of the President as Commander in Chief from 1789 to 1861. It was President Lincoln who, in his resolve to maintain the Union, linked together the Presidential power to take care that the laws be faithfully executed with that of Commander in Chief to yield a result approaching constitutional dictatorship.

For ten weeks after the fall of Fort Sumter until he called Congress into

special session, Lincoln met the emergency by a series of actions which were for the most part completely without statutory authorization, though they were subsequently ratified by Congress. He added 40,000 men to the Army and Navy, closed the Post Office to "treasonable correspondence," paid out 2 million dollars from unappropriated funds in the Treasury, proclaimed a blockade of Southern ports, suspended the writ of habeas corpus in several areas, and caused the arrest and military detention of persons suspected of treasonable practices. World Wars I and II, with their progressively greater impact on the civilian economy of the country, saw a proportionate increase in the President's wartime powers, though the expansion was achieved in nearly all cases with greater regard for the constitutional proprieties than was characteristic of the Civil War.

This chapter is concerned with judicial reaction to presidential and congressional exercise of the war power. The number of Supreme Court decisions dealing with these problems is quite large, as might be anticipated in view of the severity of war's impacts on private rights. However, this does not mean that the judiciary has played an extensive role in determining the constitutional limits of the war power. As Clinton Rossiter points out, the Supreme Court has been asked to examine only "a tiny fraction of [the President's] significant deeds and decisions as commander in chief, for most of these were by nature challengeable in no court but that of impeachment— which was entirely as it should have been. The contours of the presidential war powers have therefore been presidentially, not judicially, shaped; their exercise is for Congress and the people, not the Court, to oversee." [1]

## THE STATE OF WAR

THE WAR POWER OF CONGRESS    There have been several alternative theories about the source of the war power of Congress. In No. 23 of *The Federalist* Hamilton seemed to assume that the war power derived from the specific provisions of Article I, section 8, which in clauses 11 to 14 authorizes Congress:

> To declare war, grant letters of marque and reprisal, and make rules concerning captures on land and water;
> To raise and support armies, but no appropriation of money to that use shall be for a longer term than two years;
> To provide and maintain a navy;
> To make rules for the government and regulation of the land and naval forces.

But in *Penhallow* v. *Doane* (1795) the Supreme Court suggested that the war power was an attribute of sovereignty and so not dependent upon these

---

[1] Clinton Rossiter, *The Supreme Court and the Commander in Chief* (Ithaca, N.Y.: Cornell University Press, 1951), p. 126.

specific grants. Marshall in *McCulloch* v. *Maryland* (1819) derived the power to "conduct" a war from the authorization to "declare" it.

The Supreme Court has not subsequently found it essential to come to any firm conclusion on this issue. Among the more recent discussions, *United States* v. *Curtiss-Wright Export Corp.* (1936) supported the status of the war power as inherent in national sovereignty, but in *Lichter* v. *United States* (1948) the Court chose to use the Hamiltonian method of totting up the separate constitutional clauses to produce an aggregate of "war powers."

No matter what the constitutional theory, the judicial result has almost invariably been to support a war power coextensive with war's "felt necessities." Conscription was attacked in the *Selective Draft Law Cases* (1918) on the grounds that the Constitution gave Congress no such power, that conscription amounted to involuntary servitude, and that it encroached on the constitutional power of the states over the militia, but the Court rejected all these contentions.

A number of challenges to selective service were filed during the war in Vietnam, all to no avail. In *Katz* v. *Tyler* (1967) the Supreme Court denied certiorari in a case which charged that the draft law was a violation of the Ninth Amendment and that the American operation in Vietnam was a war of aggression which is outlawed by the Treaty of London of 1945.[2] The trial judge had thrown the suit out on the ground that the objectors lacked standing. In *Mitchell* v. *United States* (1967) the Court likewise denied certiorari in another case based on the Treaty of London, where the trial judge had barred from evidence any testimony as to the legality of the war or about alleged atrocities by American forces in Vietnam as not germane to the charge of failing to report for induction. Justice Douglas dissented, on the ground that these claims presented "sensitive and delicate questions" which should be answered, adding that there is "a considerable body of opinion that our actions in Vietnam constitute the waging of an aggressive 'war.'"

The Court likewise denied certiorari in *Mora* v. *McNamara* (1967) where three soldiers had refused to go to Vietnam on the ground that it was an illegal war, but this time Justice Stewart joined Douglas in thinking the case should be heard. The appeal, he said, raised questions of great magnitude as to whether the Vietnam action was war in the constitutional sense, and if so, whether the President could send men to fight there when no war had been declared by Congress.

Wartime legislation controlling economic freedom and the use of private property has with rare exceptions received the constitutional blessing of the Court. The unsuccessful allegations of unconstitutional delegation against World War II legislation have already been discussed in Chapter

---

[2] The Treaty of London, often called the Nuremberg Charter, was signed by United States representatives but not submitted to the Senate for ratification. It makes soldiers in an aggressive war individually responsible as war criminals, even if they acted under orders.

11. The statement of Justice Douglas in *Bowles* v. *Willingham* (1944), though wholly illogical, is an accurate reflection of the normal judicial attitude when war regulations are challenged: "A nation which can demand the lives of its men and women in the waging of . . . war is under no constitutional necessity of providing a system of price control on the domestic front which will assure each landlord a 'fair return' on his property."

The war power of course does not require the existence of a state of war for its exercise. Even in the more sheltered times of the nineteenth century, it was necessary to prepare for war in time of peace. The Supreme Court found occasion to defend this obvious principle in *Ashwander* v. *Tennessee Valley Authority* (1936), where it supported the peacetime maintenance and operation of the Wilson Dam nitrate and power plants, built under the National Defense Act of 1916, on the ground that they were "national defense assets."

After hostilities end, there is necessarily a period before the state of war is legally terminated and the country readjusts to a peacetime economy. Congressional reliance on its war powers to deal with the problems of the postwar period has seldom been questioned. During World War I the so-called Wartime Prohibition Act was passed on November 22, 1918, eleven days after the armistice. In *Hamilton* v. *Kentucky Distilleries* (1919) the Court unanimously refused to "enquire into the motives of Congress," but noted in support of the legislation "that the treaty of peace has not yet been concluded, that the railways are still under national control by virtue of the war powers, that other war activities have not been brought to a close, and that it cannot even be said that the man power of the nation has been restored to a peace footing." The Court upheld postwar rent control for the District of Columbia in 1921 in *Block* v. *Hirsh,* though by 1924 it did conclude that the emergency had come to an end, and with it the case for rent control.[3]

Similar questions were raised at the close of World War II. The rent control statute passed in 1947 was upheld in *Woods* v. *Miller Co.* (1948), the Court pointing out "that there has not yet been eliminated the deficit in housing which in considerable measure was caused by the heavy demobilization of veterans and by the cessation or reduction in residential construction during the period of hostilities." Justice Douglas warned, however, that the Court did not intend to permit the war power to "be used in days of peace to treat all the wounds which war inflicts on our society," to the point where it would "swallow up all other powers of Congress" and the Ninth and Tenth Amendments as well.

Another important ruling in this period was *Ludecke* v. *Watkins* (1948), involving deportation of a German national in 1946 under the Alien Enemy Act of 1798, which was operative only during periods of a "declared war." Five justices held that the Court could not question the President's power

[3] *Chastleton Corp.* v. *Sinclair* (1924).

to take such action, but Justice Black thought "the idea that we are still at war with Germany in the sense contemplated by the statute . . . is a pure fiction."

THE BEGINNING OF WAR     The legislature's constitutionally protected power to declare war may be rendered meaningless by events which take the decision entirely out of congressional hands. We noted in Chapter 18 that the President through his control over foreign policy and his power to deploy the Armed Forces plays a dominant part in the shaping of events. In recognition of the realities, the framers of the Constitution, who had originally provided that Congress should have the power "to make war," changed the language to "declare" war so that the President would have clear authority to repel attacks.

The legitimacy of President Lincoln's actions in inaugurating the military operations of the Civil War was upheld in the *Prize Cases* (1863). The President had declared a blockade of Confederate ports in April, 1861, and this case concerned four vessels which had been captured and taken as prizes by Union naval vessels. To decide this issue of private rights, the Court had to consider questions of the highest political significance. If it held that the conflict was not a war because it had not been declared so by Congress, then the laws of war would not apply and the prizes would have been illegally taken. If it held that the blockade was legal, but in the process recognized the Confederacy as an independent sovereign, recognition of the Confederate States by foreign governments would be encouraged, with vastly damaging effects for the Union cause.

By a narrow margin the Court avoided both of these positions. Five justices held that the insurrection was a state of war under domestic and international law, so that the President's blockade and the capture of prizes was legitimate. This "greatest of civil wars," Justice Grier said, "sprung forth suddenly from the parent brain, a Minerva in the full panoply of *war*. The President was bound to meet it in the shape it presented itself, without waiting for Congress to baptize it with a name; and no name given to it by him or them could change the fact." Moreover, it was the President who had to determine "what degree of force the crisis demands." The President's blockade proclamation was conclusive evidence for the Court that a state of war existed which demanded recourse to such a measure. At the same time the Court majority accorded no rights of sovereignty to the South.

The Court thus took the view urged by Richard Henry Dana, one of the counsel in the case, that "War is *a state of things,* and not an act of legislative will." In contrast, the minority contended that the conflict was a "personal war" of the President "until Congress assembled and acted upon this state of things." The minority was mindful of the literal language of the Constitution. The majority was mindful of the realities a reviewing court must recognize where it is dealing with the ultimate in political decisions.

The last time that Congress declared war in advance of hostilities was in the Mexican War of 1845. In World Wars I and II the President asked Congress to recognize the existence of a state of war. In the war in Vietnam the Tonkin Gulf Resolution, as previously noted, was regarded by President Johnson as a sufficient congressional authorization for escalated hostilities. Assistant Secretary of State Katzenbach, testifying before the Senate Foreign Relations Committee on August 17, 1967, argued that the Tonkin Gulf Resolution gave the President as much authority as a declaration of war would have. In fact, he alarmed the senators by referring to declarations of war as "outmoded," and contended that a declaration of war would not "correctly reflect the very limited objectives of the United States with respect to Vietnam."

THE ENDING OF WAR    In the absence of any constitutional language indicating how wars are to be ended, judicial responsibility has again been to recognize the political decisions. As for the actual cessation of hostilities by armistice or otherwise, that is, of course, a decision for the President to make. Termination of the legal state of war is effected normally by negotiation of a treaty, but there is American experience with other methods. The Civil War was ended by presidential proclamation, World War I by joint resolution of Congress. "Whatever the mode," said the Supreme Court in *Ludecke* v. *Watkins* (1948), termination of a state of war "is a political act."

OCCUPATION OF TERRITORY    Territory conquered by the United States comes under the control of the President. In a whole series of controversies arising out of incidents following the Mexican War, the Civil War, and the Spanish-American War, the Supreme Court repeatedly denied any right to review presidential actions in these circumstances. The President's authority to establish a government for conquered territory comes neither from the Constitution nor the laws of the United States, but only from the law of war.

The sole instance where the Supreme Court failed to take this position was the first case in which the problem was raised, *Jecker* v. *Montgomery* (1851). During the war with Mexico, a prize court was established by the President at Monterey in conquered Mexican territory, because the Navy could not spare prize crews to take captured ships around Cape Horn to a port of the United States. Chief Justice Taney held this court unconstitutional, since it had not been established by Congress, and explicitly denied the President's power to "establish a court in a conquered country." But the Court never repeated this ruling.[4] For example, in several cases the Court upheld as constitutional the Provisional Court for Louisiana set up by the President after the capture of New Orleans in 1862 as a combined federal-

[4] However, Justice Black repeated the Taney arguments in a dissent in *Madsen* v. *Kinsella* (1952).

state court, for which he defined both jurisdiction and procedure, and fixed salaries to be paid out of the War Department contingent fund.[5]

Following a period of military occupation the President has full authority to establish a system of civil government for conquered territory, which may, however, be superseded by congressional legislation. If the territory is to be retained permanently by the United States, Congress must adopt legislation creating a civil government. But until this is done, the President is the sole source of governmental authority in the area. As the Court said in *Santiago* v. *Nogueras* (1909): "The authority to govern such . . . territory is found in the laws applicable to conquest and cession. That authority is the military power, under the control of the President as Commander-in-Chief."

### THE PRESIDENT AND THE ARMED FORCES

As Commander in Chief the President is the ceremonial, legal, and administrative head of the Armed Forces.[6] He appoints the officers of the services, though Congress determines the grades to which appointments may be made and may specify the qualifications of the appointees, who must also be confirmed by the Senate. The President has an unlimited power to dismiss officers from the service in time of war, but in time of peace Congress has provided that dismissal shall be only in pursuance of the sentence of a general court-martial. He may adopt rules and regulations for the government, safety, and welfare of the Armed Forces, in subordination to Congress's constitutional power "to make rules for the government and regulation of the land and naval forces."

The President may involve himself in such direction of military movements and strategy and the actual conduct of military operations as he sees fit. President Washington accompanied his troops into the field at the time of the Whiskey Rebellion in 1792. One need think only of President Lincoln's telegraphic orders and personal visits to his generals in the field, or President Roosevelt in the chart room of the White House mapping the grand strategy of World War II, or President Johnson personally approving the targets to be bombed in North Vietnam, to appreciate the tremendous potential of the President's role.

As commander of the Armed Forces the President is in control of the most

[5] See *The Grapeshot* v. *Wallerstein* (1870).

[6] The President's position as Commander in Chief gives him the status of a member of the Armed Forces. President Lincoln's assassination was treated as a military crime for this reason—the killing of the Commander in Chief while he was actually in command of the national forces in his headquarters city. A military tribunal of nine officers tried the assassins, and no civil court ever looked into the commission's jurisdiction or proceedings. When the President or his wife is in a government hospital, he is charged the Armed Forces rate of $1.09 per day, and his wife $1.75, which is the rate for members of the family of men on active military duty. *The New York Times*, August 17, 1962.

incomparably powerful machinery of coercion in the country. He may use this power to enforce national laws and treaties within the United States, and he is the agent for enforcing the guarantee which Article IV, section 4, gives to the states against invasion and domestic violence. Presidential practice in this respect, as regulated by congressional acts of 1792, 1795, and 1807, has already been examined in Chapter 5.

Two early Supreme Court decisions emphasize that the President is not judicially accountable for his emergency use of the Armed Forces. One was *Martin* v. *Mott* (1827) involving a presidential order calling out the militia under the act of 1795. Justice Story agreed that the President's power was limited to situations of actual invasion or imminent danger of invasion, but added that "the authority to decide whether the exigency has arisen, belongs exclusively to the President, and . . . his decision is conclusive upon all other persons." Similarly Chief Justice Taney in *Luther* v. *Borden* (1849) denied that any court could question a presidential decision calling out the militia.

Obviously the courts have no power to examine decisions of the President to use the Armed Forces outside the country, and even Congress has hesitated to cramp the President's discretion by legislative limitations. President Wilson's dispatch of troops to Siberia in the summer of 1918, the landing of marines in various Caribbean countries in the 1920s, President Truman's dispatch of troops to Korea in 1950, President Eisenhower's sending of marines to Lebanon in 1958, President Kennedy's Bay of Pigs invasion in 1961, and President Johnson's occupation of the Dominican Republic in 1965, are examples of the use of the Armed Forces to implement presidential policies. In fact, a 1966 study listed 162 instances where the President instructed the military forces to act against enemies without congressional authorization.

### THE PRESIDENT AND MARTIAL LAW

SUSPENSION OF THE WRIT OF HABEAS CORPUS     "Martial law" is a general term covering military rule in domestic areas. In varying degrees it involves military assumption of normal civil lawmaking and enforcement functions. A necessary instrument of a system of martial law is suspension of the writ of habeas corpus, which permits civil or military authorities to hold persons in jail indefinitely without placing charges against them or bringing them to trial.

The Constitution provides in Article I, section 9: "The privilege of the writ of habeas corpus shall not be suspended, unless when in cases of rebellion or invasion the public safety may require it." Suspension of the "privilege" of the writ means that, though courts may continue to issue the writ, the jailer to whom the writ is directed is relieved of the responsibility of obeying the order to produce the prisoner in court. The Constitution

undoubtedly contemplates that Congress should have power to suspend the writ when required by public safety, since the clause is located in the legislative article of the Constitution. However, President Lincoln, acting on his own authority, suspended it several times during the Civil War. In the Habeas Corpus Act of March 3, 1863, Congress, in carefully chosen language, said that the President was authorized to suspend the writ "during the present rebellion," but without indicating where the authorization came from. Before this act was passed, however, there had been a notable clash between Lincoln and Chief Justice Taney over the issue.

In May, 1861, Taney, sitting in the circuit court in Baltimore, under statutory authority from the Judiciary Act of 1789 granted the writ requested by John Merryman, who had been arrested and confined in Fort McHenry because of his secessionist activities. The military authorities refused to honor the writ, and Taney's effort to arrest the commanding general for contempt was likewise frustrated. Taney wrote an opinion holding unconstitutional Lincoln's suspension of the privilege, and directed the clerk of the court to send a copy to the President. "It will then," he added, "remain for that high officer, in fulfillment of his constitutional obligation to take care that the laws be faithfully executed, to determine what measures he will take to cause the civil processes of the United States to be respected and enforced." Lincoln continued to exercise the power which Taney had held unconstitutional, though Merryman was shortly turned over to civil authorities and indicted for treason. Is the law of the Constitution what Taney said, or what Lincoln did? Rossiter's conclusion from the episode is "that in a condition of martial necessity the President has the power to suspend the privilege of the writ of habeas corpus. The most a court or judge can do is read the President a lecture based on *Ex parte Merryman*." [7]

MILITARY TRIALS OF CIVILIANS    In a proclamation of September 24, 1862, President Lincoln coupled suspension of habeas corpus with an order that all persons "guilty of any disloyal practice affording aid and comfort to rebels" should be liable to trial and punishment by "courts-martial or military commissions." This order was effective throughout the United States, and was a direct challenge to the authority of the regular civil courts. Although Congress subsequently ratified the habeas corpus suspension by its act of 1863, it never gave statutory support to trial of civilians by military commissions, which had to rest solely on the President's power as Commander in Chief.

The Court eventually ruled trial by military commissions unconstitutional, but not until the Civil War had been over for a year, in the case of *Ex parte Milligan* (1866). Milligan was arrested at his home in Indiana late in 1864, tried by a military commission, and sentenced to be hanged. In May, 1865, Milligan got a writ of habeas corpus from the federal court in Indianapolis,

[7] *Op. cit.*, p. 25.

and the Supreme Court unanimously ruled that the President had no power to order trial of civilians by military courts in areas where the regular courts were open and operating.

The obvious propriety of this ruling was somewhat clouded by the fact that five members of the Court went further to hold that Congress would not have this authority either. Since Congress had not sought to authorize such trials, the issue was not properly before the Court. Moreover, Justice Davis's opinion for the Court has been criticized for its self-righteous tone and for its sweeping denials that the claim of "necessity" can ever suspend constitutional protections. The Court would have been entitled to more credit for its protestations if the decision had come while hostilities were still in progress —for example, in *Ex parte Vallandigham* (1864), where it deliberately avoided a similar problem on technical grounds. Nevertheless the basic holding of the *Milligan* case was of great value, and has often been cited in subsequent decisions.

There was a considerable similarity between Lincoln's military commissions and the situation which prevailed in Hawaii during the greater part of World War II. Martial law was declared by the Governor of Hawaii immediately after the Japanese attack on December 7, 1941, and the President approved his action two days later. Civil and criminal courts were forbidden to try cases, military tribunals being set up to replace them. In August, 1942, a Honolulu stockbroker was arrested on a charge of embezzling stock. He was brought before a military court, his request for trial by jury was refused, and he was convicted and sentenced to four years' imprisonment. In February, 1944, well over two years after Pearl Harbor, a civilian shipfitter employed in the Honolulu Navy Yard engaged in a brawl with two armed Marine sentries in the yard. By this date, military control of Hawaii had been relaxed, and the courts had been authorized to conduct criminal as well as civil trials. However, prosecutions for violations of military orders, which covered a wide range of day-to-day civilian activities, were still required to be conducted before military tribunals. The shipfitter was convicted before such a court.

These cases came to the Supreme Court in *Duncan* v. *Kahanamoku* (1946) on the contentions that the Hawaii Organic Act had not authorized the trial and punishment of civilians by military courts, and that if it did confer such authority, the act was unconstitutional. The Court majority found it unnecessary to reach the second question, for they held that when Congress had granted the Governor of Hawaii power to declare martial law, it had not meant to supersede constitutional guarantees of a fair trial which apply elsewhere in the United States. The division between civil and military power

> . . . had become part of our political philosophy and institutions prior to the time Congress passed the Organic Act. The phrase "martial law" as employed in that Act, therefore, while intended to authorize the military to act vigorously for the maintenance of an orderly civil govern-

ment and for the defense of the Islands against actual or threatened rebellion or invasion, was not intended to authorize the supplanting of courts by military tribunals.

Justices Burton and Frankfurter dissented. Their position was that "the conduct of war under the Constitution is largely an executive function," in which "executive discretion to determine policy is . . . intended by the Constitution to be supreme," at least on the battlefield. The original declaration of martial law after Pearl Harbor was clearly justified, and the executive authorities should be allowed a reasonable period in which "to decide when and how to restore the battle field to its peace time controls." The dissenting justices felt that the Court in condemning, from the safe vantage point of 1946, the military decisions made in 1941 and 1942 might be establishing a precedent "which in other emergencies may handicap the executive branch of the Government in the performance of duties allotted to it by the Constitution and by the exercise of which it successfully defended the nation against the greatest attack ever made upon it."

There is something to be said for the dissenting position, but the two justices were certainly unduly alarmed about the possibility that a Supreme Court decision might hamper executive power to meet future emergencies. In 1955 a large-scale civil defense test was held, involving the assumption of widespread destruction by atomic bombs. President Eisenhower had purposely not been briefed in advance on actions which might be taken, so that emergency conditions could be simulated as realistically as possible. When the test began the President immediately issued a proclamation of nationwide martial law. There was widespread criticism of this action, and the experience was a valuable one in prompting consideration of alternative methods of meeting emergency situations.

### THE PRESIDENT AND MILITARY JUSTICE

MILITARY TRIALS FOR MILITARY PERSONNEL   The Armed Forces maintain a system of courts-martial for punishment of offenses by their members, under regulations prescribed by Congress. Articles of War were adopted for the Army by Congress in 1789, and for the Navy in 1800. The procedures embodied in the Articles were those of the Revolutionary War, aimed at enforcing discipline rather than administering justice, and they became increasingly unacceptable to the citizen soldiers of World Wars I and II. These protests were recognized by the adoption in 1950 of the Uniform Code of Military Justice, a sweeping overhaul of military law which gave a man in uniform more procedural rights than he would have had as a suspect in civilian courts at that time. In fact, the Code anticipated the major Supreme Court decisions of the next decade by providing free legal counsel in general courts-martial, requiring warning of rights before a suspect could be questioned, and providing free transcripts and counsel for appeals.

In general, courts-martial are totally distinct from the civilian courts, constituting completely separate systems of justice. Courts-martial exercise no part of the judicial power of the United States. The decision of a court-martial must be affirmed by the appropriate command officers and in certain cases by a board of review appointed by a judge advocate general, and a final appeal may be taken on matters of law to the Court of Military Appeals. This is a bench of three civilian judges set up by the Uniform Code of Military Justice, appointed for fifteen-year terms by the President with the advice and consent of the Senate.

The relationship of the guarantees of the Bill of Rights to military trials is somewhat complex. The right to indictment by grand jury is specifically made inapplicable to "cases arising in the land and naval forces," and there is of course no right to trial by jury. Initially it was assumed that only those constitutional rights specifically authorized by Congress applied in courts-martial, and in fact legislation did guarantee the privilege against self-incrimination and the rights to confrontation, counsel, and compulsory process. But in *Wade* v. *Hunter* (1949) the Supreme Court held that the Fifth Amendment's ban on double jeopardy also applied to courts-martial, and in *United States* v. *Tempia* (1967) the Court of Military Appeals applied all the standards of the Supreme Court's decision in *Miranda* v. *Arizona* (1966) for the regular courts to the military legal system. The theory of the *Tempia* decision is that the entire framework of constitutional rights applies in the armed services "except insofar as they are made inapplicable either expressly or by necessary implication." [8]

The Uniform Code of Military Justice specifically prohibits appeal from the Court of Military Appeals to the Supreme Court. However, the writ of habeas corpus furnishes a method whereby detention as a result of a court-martial decision can be reviewed by the civil courts. Such review is strictly limited to the issue of jurisdiction of the court-martial, which may be challenged on the ground that the offense charged was not within its cognizance, that the court was not constituted according to law, or that the punishment

[8] This doctrine raises interesting questions with respect to First Amendment rights in the armed services, first explored in the 1967 court-martial of an army captain who talked against the Vietnam war and refused to teach his medical skills to Green Berets, an elite combat force, on the ground that they were guilty of calculated atrocities in Vietnam. The senior trial judge permitted the war crimes doctrine of Nuremberg to be offered as a defense, but the defense failed to produce a witness with first-hand knowledge of atrocities chargeable to Green Berets. The American Civil Liberties Union, which defended the captain, charged that two articles of the Uniform Code were unconstitutional as infringing on rights of free speech, and also vague and unduly broad in violation of the Fifth Amendment. Article 133 proscribes "conduct unbecoming an officer and a gentleman," and Article 134 proscribes "all disorders and neglects to the prejudice of good order and discipline." The Supreme Court denied certiorari to review the court-martial verdict of guilt in *Levy* v. *Corcoran* (1967). See Ira Glasser, "Judgment at Fort Jackson: the Court-Martial of Captain Howard B. Levy," 4 *Law in Transition Quarterly* 123–156 (1967).

exceeded the limits imposed by the Code. Conformity of court-martial procedures to applicable constitutional standards may also be examined.

With this limited scope of review, it is natural that the Supreme Court has seldom invalidated the decisions of military tribunals. Its reluctance to get involved in the review of court-martial proceedings may be illustrated by one or two examples. In *Humphrey* v. *Smith* (1949) a court-martial conviction for rape was attacked on the ground that the "thorough and impartial investigation" of charges required by the Articles of War before a general court-martial is convened had not been given. The Supreme Court held that it was up to the Army, not the courts, to enforce this requirement. *Wade* v. *Hunter* (1949) involved a trial begun under the jurisdiction of the Third Army in Germany, which was forced to recess for a week because some of the witnesses were ill. When the trial was able to resume, the Third Army was no longer quartered in the vicinity of the crime, so the case was transferred to the Fifteenth Army, which was in the area. A new court-martial was convened, and the soldier was convicted. The Supreme Court held that this procedure did not constitute double jeopardy.

There is one jurisdictional problem concerning courts-martial, however, where the Court's intervention has been quite significant. In *United States ex rel. Hirshberg* v. *Cooke* (1949) the Court held that an enlisted member of the Navy who had been granted honorable discharge in 1946 with the expiration of his enlistment and who had then reenlisted the next day, could not subsequently be tried by court-martial for an offense occurring during his prior enlistment. When Congress adopted the Uniform Code in 1950, it was aware of this decision and wrote in a provision allowing courts-martial to try former members of the Armed Forces after their discharge for offenses committed while in the service. The language was drawn to cover only offenses punishable under military regulations by as much as five years' imprisonment and restricted to those instances in which the accused would otherwise escape trial in any American court.

The Supreme Court by a six to three vote held this provision of the Code unconstitutional in *United States ex rel. Toth* v. *Quarles* (1955). After service in Korea, Toth had been honorably discharged. He returned to his home in Pittsburgh and went to work in a steel plant. Five months later he was arrested by military authorities, charged with having committed murder while in Korea, and flown to Korea to stand trial before a court-martial. His sister instituted habeas corpus proceedings against the Secretary of the Air Force in a District of Columbia court, which ordered his return to the United States.

For the Supreme Court, Justice Black noted that no claim of presidential power as Commander in Chief was involved. The statute had to be justified solely by the power of Congress to "make rules for the government and regulation of the land and naval forces," as supplemented by the "necessary and proper" clause. The provision applied to over three million Americans

who had become veterans since the act was passed (and the number would grow each year), threatening them with military trial, the characteristics of which Black compared quite unfavorably with trial in the civil courts. The Court found there was no sufficient justification for thus depriving so many Americans of their constitutional right to trial by jury and indictment by grand jury, particularly since there was an alternative and perfectly constitutional method which Congress could have used to deal with the problem of crimes committed by servicemen while in service but not discovered until later—namely, to confer on the regular federal courts jurisdiction to try such crimes.

*Wilson* v. *Girard* (1957) involved a serviceman who, unlike Toth, preferred military to civilian trial, but the civil courts in this case were those of Japan. Girard, a member of the Army on duty in Japan, was accused of killing a Japanese woman by firing an empty cartridge case from a rifle grenade launcher on an Army firing range. The United States had a "status of forces" treaty agreement with Japan covering offenses committed in Japan by members of the United States Armed Forces, which provided for American jurisdiction over such offenses, which might, however, be waived in any case by the United States. Waiver was authorized in Girard's case, on the recommendation of the State Department and with the President's approval, and the Japanese authorities were notified that Girard would be turned over for trial. A political storm quickly blew up in Congress over this action, and Girard's relatives sought habeas corpus against Secretary of Defense Wilson. A federal court in the District of Columbia denied the writ but granted an injunction against delivery of Girard to the Japanese.

The Supreme Court reversed this ruling. Its brief opinion pointed out that a sovereign nation has exclusive jurisdiction to punish offenses against its laws committed within its borders, unless it consents to limit or surrender its jurisdiction. Japan had ceded this right in its agreement with the United States, subject to the qualification that the United States would give "sympathetic consideration" to a Japanese request for waiver of its rights in cases where Japan considered the waiver of particular importance. The Supreme Court found nothing in the Constitution, or in any legislation subsequent to the treaty, which prohibited the carrying out of this waiver by the Armed Forces. "In the absence of such encroachments" the Supreme Court bowed out of the picture, leaving "the wisdom of the arrangement . . . exclusively for the determination of the Executive and Legislative Branches." Girard was then tried by a Japanese court, convicted, and given a sentence much lighter than he could have expected from an American court-martial.

MILITARY TRIALS FOR MILITARY DEPENDENTS      Whether military courts may assert jurisdiction over dependents accompanying American service men stationed abroad in occupied territory or at American military bases has given the Supreme Court some trouble. The question was considered in two

1956 cases, *Reid* v. *Covert* and *Kinsella* v. *Krueger*. With three justices dissenting and one reserving his opinion, the Court upheld the jurisdiction of courts-martial in these circumstances. However, a petition for rehearing was subsequently granted, and one year later the Court by a vote of six to two reversed its previous holding.

In both instances wives of military personnel, living on American bases in England and Japan, had killed their husbands. The Uniform Code of Military Justice makes subject to its provisions "all persons serving with, employed by, or accompanying the armed forces without the continental limits of the United States." In an opinion by Justice Black, the Court concluded that this attempt to subject civilians "accompanying" the Armed Forces to courts-martial was unconstitutional.

The reasoning in the *Toth* case, that civilians are entitled to trial by civil courts, would settle the issue here, except for the fact that Toth was arrested in the United States and the two women were arrested abroad. This difference in circumstances was relevant, however, only if constitutional safeguards do not apply to United States government action against a citizen abroad. The Court majority rejected this contention, though there were precedents to the contrary. *In re Ross* (1891) had approved a statutory provision under which American consuls could try American citizens charged with committing crimes in Japan and certain other "non-Christian" countries. In the *Ross* case the Court had flatly held that "the Constitution can have no operation in another country." (It did not explain how the American government, which has no power except that granted by the Constitution, could try citizens abroad if the Constitution had no operation there.) In the *Reid* v. *Covert* rehearing the Court set aside the *Ross* decision as a "relic from a different era" where consular courts, with their long history antedating the Constitution, might have performed some useful function, but which had now been abandoned and should not be "disinterred."

The minority position in the *Reid* v. *Covert* rehearing stressed the practical problems encountered in maintaining American Armed Forces in sixty-three foreign countries and contended that, in effect, wives of servicemen were as much a part of military installations as their husbands.

There was some disagreement on the Court as to whether the reasoning in this case was applicable only when capital crimes were involved. However, in *Kinsella* v. *United States ex rel. Singleton* (1960), the Court majority ruled that military trial of service dependents for noncapital offenses was also unconstitutional. Moreover, American civilian employees of the Armed Forces abroad cannot be tried by military courts for either capital or noncapital offenses, according to *McElroy* v. *United States ex rel. Guagliardo* (1960) and *Grisham* v. *Hagan* (1960).[9]

[9] In 1967 the Armed Forces in Vietnam claimed jurisdiction over American civilians working in Vietnam under military auspices. Chap. 10, sec. 802, of the Uniform Code of Military Justice provides that "in time of war persons serving with or accompanying the armed forces in the field" are subject to the Code. *The New York Times*, February 16, March 3, 1967.

MILITARY TRIALS OF ENEMIES    Courts-martial or military commissions have occasionally been set up by the President, under statutory authorization or his inherent powers as Commander in Chief, to deal with military crimes committed by others than the Armed Forces of the United States. As already noted, a military commission was created to try the assassins of President Lincoln. In 1942 President Roosevelt established a military commission to try eight German saboteurs who had been landed in this country by submarine with the assignment of blowing up factories and bridges. When the case before the tribunal was nearly completed, counsel for the saboteurs, despite an executive order denying them all access to civil courts, got a writ of habeas corpus contending for their right to trial in a civil court.

The Supreme Court unanimously upheld the military trial in *Ex parte Quirin* (1942). It was unnecessary to determine the extent of presidential authority as Commander in Chief, since Congress had provided for the trial of offenses against the law of war by such commissions, and the acts charged against the saboteurs were offenses against the law of war. The constitutional requirements of grand jury indictment and jury trial were held inapplicable to the trial of such offenses by military commissions. As for the *Milligan* decision, which was particularly relied on by counsel for the saboteurs, the Court pointed to the obvious factual differences in that case and held it inapplicable. The significance of the *Quirin* decision is its firm establishment of the authority of the civil courts to examine the jurisdiction of presidentially appointed military commissions.

Following World War II certain Japanese generals who had commanded troops in the Pacific theater were placed on trial before an American military commission in the Philippines. The Supreme Court in *In re Yamashita* (1946) again took jurisdiction, and again upheld the authority of the commission. Its procedures had been particularly under attack, for under the regulations prescribed by General MacArthur the commission had admitted hearsay and opinion evidence, and had allowed defense counsel inadequate time to prepare their defense. But the Court majority held that the commission's procedures and its rulings on evidence were reviewable only by the superior military authorities, not by the courts. Justices Murphy and Rutledge, however, filed eloquent dissents objecting to "departures from constitutional norms inherent in the idea of a fair trial."

*Hirota* v. *MacArthur* (1948) differed from the *Yamashita* case in that the Japanese defendants involved had been tried for war crimes before a military tribunal set up by General MacArthur as the agent for the Allied Powers which had defeated Japan. The defendants sought to file habeas corpus petitions directly with the Supreme Court, but their motions were denied on the ground that courts of the United States could have no jurisdiction over this tribunal because of its international character. It was not "a tribunal of the United States."

Between 1948 and 1950 the Supreme Court was flooded with habeas corpus petitions from Germans confined by order of military courts of the

American occupation forces. The Court uniformly denied these petitions for want of jurisdiction. But eventually one of the cases reached the Supreme Court by way of the District of Columbia courts in 1950. *Johnson* v. *Eisentrager* was originated by twenty-one German nationals in the service of the German government who were located in China during World War II. After the unconditional surrender of Germany, which obligated all forces under German control to cease active hostilities at once, they were alleged to have continued hostile operations by furnishing intelligence concerning American forces to the Japanese. After the Japanese surrender they were taken into custody and convicted by a wholly American military court sitting in China. The prisoners were repatriated to Germany to serve their sentences, under custody of the United States Army.

Habeas corpus was granted by the Court of Appeals in the District of Columbia, on the ground that "any person, including an enemy alien, deprived of his liberty anywhere under any purported authority of the United States is entitled to the writ if he can show that extension to his case of any constitutional rights or limitations would show his imprisonment illegal." The Supreme Court, however, said it had never heard of the writ of habeas corpus being issued by a court "on behalf of an alien enemy who, at no relevant time and in no stage of his captivity, has been within its territorial jurisdiction." Residence within the country was essential to qualify an alien for judicial protection by American courts. Justices Black, Douglas, and Burton, dissenting, pointed out that in both *Quirin* and *Yamashita*, aliens had been permitted to contest convictions for war crimes; the only difference here was that the capture, trial, and imprisonment had taken place outside American territory. They felt it was wholly indefensible to make a prisoner's right to test legality of a sentence depend upon where the government chose to imprison him.

## THE PRESIDENT AND THE HOME FRONT

CONTROL OF THE ECONOMY    In so far as the economic controls increasingly demanded by twentieth-century warfare have been based on congressional enactments, their general judicial ratification has already been noted. There have been some instances, however, where a President has acted without specific statutory support under his general powers as Commander in Chief. Two matters may be singled out for particular attention here.

One was the remarkable message sent to Congress by President Roosevelt on September 7, 1942, requesting the repeal of a certain provision of the Emergency Price Control Act which he considered to be threatening "economic chaos." If Congress failed to take this action by the first of October, he said that he himself would act, under his powers "to take measures necessary to avert a disaster which would interfere with the winning of the war." By this he apparently meant that he intended to disregard the statutory

provision if Congress did not repeal it. He could not, of course, contend that the statute was unconstitutional, only that it was unwise. This assertion of presidential wartime power goes beyond anything that can be supported on constitutional grounds, but the action of Congress in providing a satisfactory change in the statute prevented the issue from becoming a reality.

Both in World War I and II, however, presidential action was taken to seize industrial plants, an interference with the use of private property which admittedly could be justified only on grounds of wartime necessity. President Wilson's seizures were based on statutory authorization, but from 1941 to 1943 President Roosevelt made numerous seizures without any supporting legislation, simply referring to his general authority as President and Commander in Chief. The plants seized were ones important to war production in which labor-management disagreements were threatening, or had already resulted in, stoppage of production. Ultimately Congress authorized presidential seizures of manufacturing and production facilities by the Smith-Connally Act of 1943.

Only one court test of these wartime seizures eventuated, and it led to no definitive ruling by the Supreme Court. After a three-year struggle between Montgomery Ward and the War Labor Board, the President in 1944 ordered the Secretary of War to take possession of the company's properties. The government itself then went to court, seeking an injunction forbidding the company officers from interfering with the seizure. A federal district judge held that Montgomery Ward was engaged in "distribution," not "production," and consequently the statute did not authorize seizure of its facilities, nor did he think the President could take such action under his general war powers. The court of appeals, however, interpreted production more broadly and thereby found statutory support for the seizure. The Supreme Court accepted the case, but then dismissed it as moot because the Army had turned the properties back to the company.[10]

President Truman's seizure of the nation's steel mills in 1952 did not come in a period of declared war, and Justice Black's opinion for the Court in *Youngstown Sheet & Tube Co.* v. *Sawyer* refused to give any consideration to claims that the action could be justified by his status as Commander in Chief. Justice Jackson undertook a more thoughtful statement of reasons for this holding.

> We should not use this occasion to circumscribe, much less to contract, the lawful role of the President as Commander-in-Chief. I should indulge the widest latitude of interpretation to sustain his exclusive function to command the instruments of national force, at least when turned against the outside world for the security of our society. But, when it is turned inward, not because of rebellion but because of a lawful economic struggle between industry and labor, it should have no such in-

[10] *Montgomery Ward and Co.* v. *United States* (1945).

dulgence. . . . The purpose of lodging dual titles in one man was to insure that the civilian would control the military, not to enable the military to subordinate the presidential office. No penance would ever expiate the sin against free government of holding that a President can escape control of executive powers by law through assuming his military role.

THE JAPANESE EVACUATION    The enforced evacuation of Japanese and Japanese-Americans from the West Coast early in World War II by combined executive-legislative action must be regarded, in spite of its subsequent ratification by the Supreme Court, as one of the most unfortunate episodes in the long history of the war power under the Constitution. The deeply rooted opposition to Orientals on the West Coast, combined with the hysteria of the early war period, built up a tremendous pressure to take action against the over 100,000 persons of Japanese ancestry in the area. On February 19, 1942, President Roosevelt issued an executive order empowering the Secretary of War to designate military areas from which any or all persons might be excluded in order to prevent espionage and sabotage. Under this authorization the three West Coast states and part of Arizona were proclaimed military areas and all persons of Japanese ancestry, 70,000 of whom were American citizens, were cleared from these areas. Congress on March 21, 1942, passed a law ratifying and confirming the executive order.

The inevitable constitutional tests of this harsh and unprecedented treatment of American citizens and aliens lawfully resident in the United States, with its untold suffering and loss of property, presented the Supreme Court with a difficult problem. Was it to hold these procedures contrary to due process, or to justify them on the ground that the responsible civil and military leaders claimed they were a military necessity? As usual, the law's delays gave the Court a period of grace before it had to answer. The decision in *Hirabayashi* v. *United States* did not come until June, 1943. Moreover, the circumstances of the case provided an opportunity for the Court to avoid the more difficult constitutional questions. Shortly before the evacuation program had been undertaken, the Army had adopted a curfew regulation requiring all aliens and persons of Japanese ancestry to be in their residences between 8 P.M. and 6 A.M. Hirabayashi, an American-born citizen of alien Japanese parents, was convicted of failure both to obey the curfew and to report for registration for evacuation. Sentence for the two offenses was made to run concurrently.

The Supreme Court took advantage of this fact to limit its review to the curfew, clearly a less drastic interference with liberty than the enforced evacuation, and unanimously upheld it as a temporary emergency war measure. Under the circumstances that existed at the time, the Court concluded that it was not unreasonable for those charged with the national

defense to feel that the Japanese constituted a peculiar danger to national security. Racial discriminations are odious and usually unconstitutional, because justified by no proper legislative purpose. But "in time of war residents having ethnic affiliations with an invading enemy may be a greater source of danger than those of a different ancestry."

In *Korematsu* v. *United States*, decided in December, 1944, the constitutionality of the evacuation program, then in effect for over two and a half years, could no longer be avoided, and the Court upheld it by a divided vote. The majority opinion followed the lines of the earlier decision, holding that the military authorities were not unjustified in concluding that the Japanese residents of the Coast area constituted a potentially grave danger to the public safety, a danger so great and pressing that there was no time to set up procedures for determining the loyalty or disloyalty of individual Japanese. Actually the Court made no effort to use that valuable prerogative of judicial review, the "wisdom of hindsight," to challenge the military conclusions, though it certainly was apparent by the end of 1944 that the fears of sabotage and treachery by West Coast residents of Japanese descent were entirely groundless. Only Justice Murphy charged that the case made by the military had not been based on any demonstrated public necessity, but upon "an accumulation of much of the misinformation, half-truths and insinuations that for years have been directed against Japanese Americans by people with racial and economic prejudices." Justices Roberts and Jackson also dissented, the latter suggesting that even if the military decision was justified, the Court should refuse to enforce it, because Court approval would give constitutional sanction to "a military expedient that has no place in law under the Constitution."

The Court partially recouped its reputation as the defender of individual liberties by *Ex parte Endo* (1944), decided the same day as *Korematsu*. Here the Court upheld the right of a Japanese-American girl, whose loyalty to the United States had been established, to a writ of habeas corpus freeing her from a relocation camp. Justice Douglas's opinion avoided any ruling on the constitutionality of the detention program as a whole by pointing out that neither statute nor executive order anywhere specifically authorized detention. Justice Roberts, concurring in the result, thought the Court had ignored its responsibility to meet squarely the constitutional issue created by the government's action in depriving an admittedly loyal citizen of her liberty for a period of years. The weekend before the *Endo* ruling, and apparently in anticipation of it, the Army ordered the release of all loyal Japanese-Americans from the relocation camps.

In 1947 President Truman's Commission on Civil Rights described the evacuation as "the most striking mass interference since slavery with the right to physical freedom," and recommended that the evacuees be at least partly compensated for their property losses. Congress responded by passing

the Evacuation Claims Act of 1948, under which some thirty-seven million dollars was paid to 26,500 claimants.[11]

## SELECTED REFERENCES

ANTHONY, J. GARNER, *Hawaii under Army Rule*. Stanford, Calif.: Stanford University Press, 1955.

CORWIN, EDWARD S. (ed.), *The President: Office and Powers, 1787–1957*, chap. 6. New York: New York University Press, 1957 (fourth revised edition).

———, *Total War and the Constitution*. New York: Alfred A. Knopf, Inc., 1947.

GRODZINS, MORTON, *Americans Betrayed: Politics and the Japanese Evacuation*. Chicago: The University of Chicago Press, 1949.

HAINES, CHARLES GROVE, and FOSTER H. SHERWOOD, *The Role of the Supreme Court in American Government and Politics, 1835–1864*, chaps. 11, 12. Berkeley, Calif.: University of California Press, 1957.

HUNTINGTON, SAMUEL P., "Civilian Control and the Constitution," 50 *American Political Science Review* 676–699 (September, 1956).

———, *The Soldier and the State: The Theory and Politics of Civil-Military Relations*. Cambridge, Mass.: Harvard University Press, 1957.

MAY, ERNEST R. (ed.), *The Ultimate Decision: The President as Commander in Chief*. New York: George Braziller, Inc., 1960.

MAYERS, LEWIS, *The American Legal System*, chaps. 18–21. New York: Harper & Row, Publishers, Incorporated, 1955.

RANDALL, JAMES G., *Constitutional Problems under Lincoln*. Urbana, Ill.: The University of Illinois Press, 1951 (revised edition).

RANKIN, ROBERT S., *When Civil Law Fails: Martial Law and Its Legal Basis in the United States*. Durham, N.C.: The Duke University Press, 1939.

ROSSITER, CLINTON, *The Supreme Court and the Commander in Chief*. Ithaca, N.Y.: Cornell University Press, 1951.

SCHUBERT, GLENDON A., JR., *The Presidency in the Courts*, chaps. 6–8. Minneapolis: The University of Minnesota Press, 1957.

SWISHER, CARL B., *The Supreme Court in Modern Role*, chap. 4. New York: New York University Press, 1958.

TEN BROEK, JACOBUS, EDWARD N. BARNHART, and FLOYD W. MATSON, *Prejudice, War and the Constitution*, chaps. 5–8. Berkeley, Calif.: University of California Press, 1954.

[11] In *Honda* v. *Clark* (1967) the Supreme Court ordered restored to Japanese-American claimants some ten million dollars in savings deposits seized as "enemy property" in 1942.

# Part 6

## First Amendment freedoms

# 20

## Constitutional basis for protection of individual rights

The one essential quality of constitutionalism, says McIlwain, is as a legal limitation on government. Tom Paine wrote that a constitution is "to liberty, what a grammar is to language." Of course, a written constitution is not necessary to the protection of civil liberties, as English experience so well demonstrates. And the most elaborate safeguards in a written constitution will be meaningless unless the country to which they apply has a tradition which makes freedom a value of the highest order, and unless there are the resources, the opportunities, and the will to protect the principles of an open society from attack or frustration.

The American tradition of civil liberty is composed of many strands. Basic is the Christian-Hebraic belief in the worth of the individual, and acceptance of a moral obligation to shape the institutions of society so that they will promote the unfolding and the enrichment of human character. Centuries of struggle in England to achieve political institutions which would aim toward equality before the law and equalization of political power, resulting in such documents as Magna Carta (1215), the Petition of Right (1628), and the Bill of Rights (1689), were a living part of the early American tradition. The writings of the seventeenth- and eighteenth-century political philosophers, particularly Locke, with their notions about natural law and the origins of government in a compact freely entered into by its citizens, were an essential element in American Revolutionary thought. The Declaration

of Independence put these ideas about liberty and equality into classic phraseology.

All this was the heritage of the new nation, the "common law" of American liberties. If it had never been spelled out in a written constitution, it would nonetheless have continued to be effective in guiding the political decisions of the developing commonwealth. The discussion of the following pages may seem to neglect these traditional factors in favor of a concern with detailed provisions of the written Constitution. The defense can only be that the ideas and the resources supplied by the American heritage are the foundations on which the edifice of constitutional liberty is erected.

## THE BILL OF RIGHTS

As a matter of fact, the theory of the Constitutional Convention was that the traditional liberties did not need much in the way of specific constitutional protection. The basic concept of limited national government was to be achieved by division of functions, separation of powers, checks and balances, calculated to frustrate any drive toward dictatorial power. The drafters of the Constitution relied on the open spaces of the American continent to guarantee escape from confining situations. They saw the boundless resources of the country as insurance of economic opportunity. They conceived that the broad expanse of the Republic would encompass such a variety of interests as to make combination into a domineering majority difficult. Said Madison in No. 10 of *The Federalist:*

> The smaller the society, the fewer probably will be the distinct parties and interests composing it . . . and . . . the more easily will they concert and execute their plans of oppression. Extend the sphere, and you take in a greater variety of parties and interests; you make it less probable that a majority of the whole will have a common motive to invade the rights of other citizens.

Thus individual liberty did not need to be planned for. It would come automatically as the by-product of a system of economic opportunity, social mobility, and political responsibility.

Although this seems to have been the dominant theory of the Convention, it was departed from in a few instances. There are in fact several provisions which bear more or less closely on issues of civil liberty: protection against suspension of the writ of habeas corpus; prohibition of the passage of bills of attainder or ex post facto laws by either Congress or the state legislatures; the ban on religious tests as a qualification for public office; the requirement of trial by jury; the restrictions on conviction for treason; and the guarantee to citizens of each state of all privileges and immunities of citizens in the several states.

When the proposed Constitution went to the states for ratification, it quickly became apparent that the framers' view of civil liberties as needing no special protection in the new charter was not widely shared. In several

of the important states ratification was secured only on the understanding that amendments protecting individual rights would be immediately added to the Constitution. In his first inaugural address, Washington urged Congress to give careful attention to the demand for these amendments.

Madison took the lead in bringing together the various suggestions for amendments, which he presented to the House on June 8, 1789. His original idea was that they should be incorporated into the body of the Constitution at the places where they would appropriately belong. Most of the proposals had to do with limiting the power of Congress over citizens, and these were to follow the clause in Article I, section 9, prohibiting congressional adoption of bills of attainder and ex post facto laws. The new language to be inserted at this point would have prohibited Congress from abridging the freedom of religion, of speech, press, or assembly, and of bearing arms. There were also restrictions on quartering troops, prosecuting citizens for crime, and inflicting punishment. Changes aiming at a fuller guarantee to the citizen of a fair trial by a jury in his own district and the benefits of the common law were to be worked into the jury trial provision of Article III.

When the House took up consideration of the amendments, Roger Sherman of Connecticut objected to the insertion of new material into, and the deletion of superseded material from, the original Constitution, and he was eventually able to convince the House that the amendments should be appended to the Constitution, each complete, independent, and understandable in itself. The House proposals went to the Senate on August 24. There additional changes were made, and some proposed amendments were eliminated entirely, such as a clause exempting conscientious objectors from compulsory military service, and an article specifically prohibiting any of the three departments of government from exercising powers vested in the other two. Twelve amendments were approved by the Senate, and after concurrence by the House, they went to the states on September 25, 1789.

Two of these proposed amendments ultimately failed of ratification. The first had to do with the ratio between population and the number of representatives in the House, and the second would have postponed the effect of any alteration in the compensation of congressmen until an election had intervened. The remaining ten amendments were ratified by the necessary eleven states (there being fourteen states in the Union by that time) on December 15, 1791.

The ten amendments can be thought of as falling into four categories. The First, and justly the most famous of the amendments, covers freedom of speech, press, assembly, and religion. The Second and Third, which are of little contemporary significance, deal with the right of the people to keep and bear arms,[1] and the quartering of soldiers in private homes. The Fourth

---

[1] The Second Amendment protects only the right of the states to maintain and equip a militia and does not guarantee individuals the right to bear arms; *United States* v. *Cruikshank* (1875). See "Firearms: Problems of Control," 80 *Harvard Law Review* 1328–1346 (1967).

through the Eighth are concerned primarily with procedural protections in criminal trials, but other matters are also covered, such as the prohibition on taking of private property for public use without just compensation. Finally, the Ninth and Tenth Amendments are simply declaratory of the existing constitutional situation. The Ninth Amendment provides that the enumeration of certain rights in the Constitution shall not be construed to deny or disparage others retained by the people. The Tenth concerns primarily state powers rather than individual rights, and thus has little bearing on the discussion of the present section of this volume.

Only gradually did the conception grow that these ten amendments constituted a great Bill of Rights. About half the state constitutions at the time did not include a bill of rights in their provisions, and it could easily be argued that these ten amendments accomplished no substantial changes in the constitutional pattern. They took away from Congress few powers which it could reasonably have been thought to have had before the amendments were ratified, and the procedural limitations on criminal trials would no doubt have been carried over from the common law in any event. Crosskey contends that the addition of a bill of rights to the Constitution was unnecessary, and was demanded only because the "ignorant and credulous" had been made suspicious by interests opposed to the ratification of the Constitution.

Unquestionably, however, these "unnecessary" provisions have had a tremendous use and value in the development of American constitutional thinking and practice. No doubt it can be argued that the effects of the Bill of Rights have not been uniformly favorable to the libertarian cause. The mention of these specific guarantees in the Constitution may have led to the assumption, in spite of the Ninth Amendment, that no other rights exist which are deserving of protection. Libertarian thought may sometimes have been diverted from concern with general principles to legal quarrels over the textual meaning of amendments. Still, these certainly must be regarded as minor consequences, far outranked by the positive contributions of these written guarantees.

### CIVIL RIGHTS PROBLEMS TO THE CIVIL WAR

Three-quarters of a century elapsed after the Bill of Rights was added to the Constitution before any more amendments dealing with civil liberties were adopted. No detailed account of the application of constitutional guarantees during that period can or need be attempted. The ex post facto clause was early given a definitive and restricted interpretation in *Calder* v. *Bull* (1798). The Alien and Sedition Acts of 1798 raised some constitutional questions, but they never got to the Supreme Court. As the nineteenth century wore on, all other issues paled into obscurity in the fierce light of the slavery controversy, until that issue was excised by the brutal surgery of the Civil

War. The Court's involvement in civil liberties issues during the first half of the nineteenth century was infrequent, but the little that did happen was inextricably involved in subsequent constitutional thought, and it is impossible to understand the post-Civil War amendments without some grasp of the Court's prior actions in four major respects.

THE BILL OF RIGHTS AND THE STATES    First we may look at the differences of opinion which arose as to whether the provisions of the Bill of Rights, and more particularly the first eight amendments, were applicable to the federal government alone, or whether they also affected the states. It may seem surprising that doubt on such a fundamental point could have been left in the drafting of the amendments, but the fact is that only two of the amendments are specifically stated as restraints upon the United States. They are the First Amendment, which is by its terms made applicable only to Congress, and one clause of the Seventh which provides that "no fact tried by jury, shall be otherwise reexamined in any court of the United States, than according to the rules of the common law." All the other amendments, from the Second through the Eighth, state general libertarian principles, with no indication that their protective effect is only against federal action.

Nevertheless, the Supreme Court as early as 1833, in a unanimous opinion written by Chief Justice Marshall, ruled that these amendments were inapplicable to the states. This was the famous case of *Barron* v. *Baltimore,* and the specific issue was whether the city of Baltimore, by street grading which had diverted streams from their natural courses and rendered Barron's wharf unusable, had deprived him of property without due process of law, contrary to the Fifth Amendment. Obviously his claim could not stand unless the Fifth Amendment applied to state and local governments.

The issue, said Marshall, was of great importance but not of much difficulty.

> The constitution was ordained and established by the people of the United States for themselves, for their own government, and not for the government of the individual states. . . . The powers they conferred on this government were to be exercised by itself; and the limitations on power, if expressed in general terms, are naturally, and, we think, necessarily applicable to the government created by the instrument.

Following this appeal to logic, Marshall turned to history. It was well known that the ratification of the Constitution was not secured without immense opposition. "In almost every convention by which the constitution was adopted, amendments to guard against the abuse of power were recommended. These amendments demanded security against the apprehended encroachments of the general government—not against those of the local governments."

Finally, Marshall's appeal was to the textual provisions of the original Constitution. He called attention to sections 9 and 10 of Article I, both

containing a series of prohibitions on legislative action. But in section 9 the language is general, whereas in section 10 all the prohibitions are imposed specifically on the states. Thus section 9 forbids ex post facto laws and bills of attainder generally, while in section 10 the ban is repeated for the states. Whenever a constitutional provision was meant to affect the states, Marshall concluded, "words are employed which directly express that intent. . . . These amendments contain no expression indicating an intention to apply them to the state governments. This court cannot so apply them."

These are powerful arguments, and they have been fully incorporated into American constitutional development. Nevertheless, *Barron* v. *Baltimore* did not represent a universally accepted view.[2] When it came time to draft the post-Civil War amendments, one of the leading motives of some members of Congress was precisely to liquidate the effects of this decision.

THE MEANING OF PRIVILEGES AND IMMUNITIES    The second dilemma of the pre-Civil War period concerned the meaning of Article IV, section 2—the privileges and immunities clause. The provision that "the citizens of each state shall be entitled to all privileges and immunities of citizens in the several states" was perhaps the vaguest of all the civil rights language in either the original Constitution or the amendments, and a difficult problem was thereby created for reviewing courts. By all odds the best known of the early judicial efforts along this line was that of Justice Bushrod Washington, sitting in federal circuit court in *Corfield* v. *Coryell* (1825). This case, already noted in Chapter 5, involved a New Jersey statute which prohibited any person not a resident of New Jersey from gathering oysters in the state. Washington held that this act was not a violation of Article IV, section 2, because the privileges and immunities which the Constitution protects are those "which are, in their nature, fundamental; which belong, of right, to the citizens of all free governments." He went on to suggest quite a list of rights which met this test: protection by the government; enjoyment of life and liberty; the right to acquire and possess property; the right of a citizen of one state to pass through, or reside in, other states for purposes of trade or profession; protection by the writ of habeas corpus; the right to institute and maintain court actions; exemption from higher taxes than are paid by other citizens of the state; and the elective franchise, as regulated by the laws of the particular state in which it is exercised. "These, and many others which might be mentioned, are, strictly speaking, privileges and immunities."

This language of Washington's, which was well known and widely quoted, sounds, as Fairman says, like "pure natural law." It does not seek to discover the nature of these privileges and immunities by reference to the Bill of

[2] See William W. Crosskey, *Politics and the Constitution in the History of the United States* (Chicago: The University of Chicago Press, 1953), pp. 1056–1082.

Rights or any other part of the Constitution. Rather Washington speaks simply of "fundamental" rights, belonging to "the citizens of all free governments," and then throws in a hodgepodge of activities, some of which, such as the practice of a profession or exercise of the elective franchise, obviously are subject to a wide variety of state regulations. According to Washington, the provision established a uniform, nationwide set of standards, applicable to all states. In effect he revised the sentence to read: "The citizens of each state shall be entitled to all privileges and immunities of citizens of the United States in the several states." This position, as developed and applied into the Civil War period and beyond, Crosskey calls the "old Republican view" of the privileges and immunities clause, a part of the "common faith" of that party. As such it had a great importance in the drafting and adoption of the Fourteenth Amendment.

Opposed to the "Washington–old Republican" interpretation of the privileges and immunities clause was another, which was in fact probably the one intended by the framers. The language can be read as meaning simply that a citizen of one state going into another state is not to be discriminated against because of his out-of-state origin. As a matter of fact, Washington's opinion in *Corfield* v. *Coryell* was so broad that it may seem to support this interpretation also. On this basis there is no need to search for any natural law or fundamental standards; the privileges and immunities to which an individual is entitled are those which are standard in that state, applied without discrimination. Under this view the clause is read as though it said: "The citizens of each state shall be entitled in each of the other states to all privileges and immunities of the citizens of the state in which they shall happen to be."

Under this second interpretation the clause does not bulk so large in its import for civil liberties. It is more of an instrument for interstate adjustment and comity. As the preamble of the corresponding provision in the Articles of Confederation put it, the intent was "the better to secure and perpetuate mutual friendship and intercourse among the people of the different states in this Union." But it seems clear that Representative Bingham, the "old Republican" who subsequently carried the privileges and immunities clause over from Article IV into the Fourteenth Amendment, saw in it a much more potent instrument, a guarantee of certain basic rights, variously defined as those specified elsewhere in the Constitution or, more broadly, as those belonging of right to the citizens of all free governments.

CONSTITUTIONAL ISSUES OF SLAVERY    The slavery problem, which was present in many constitutional guises during the pre-Civil War period, particularly in the form of federal-state controversies touched on in Chapter 5, as a civil liberties issue is long dead and largely outside our present frame of reference. However, the most important and notorious of all the Supreme

Court's decisions on the slavery issue, the case of *Dred Scott* v. *Sandford* (1857), has a bearing on the matter just dealt with, and on the drafting of the Fourteenth Amendment.

A Negro named Dred Scott, a slave in Missouri, had been taken by his owner into the state of Illinois, where slavery had been forbidden by the Northwest Ordinance of 1787, and also into the territory of Upper Louisiana (Minnesota), where slavery was forbidden by the Missouri Compromise. Having then been returned to Missouri, Scott brought suit for his freedom in a Missouri court, on the ground of his periods of residence in free territory. His claim was denied by the state supreme court, which held that Scott's legal status was determined by the law of the state in which he resided.

Taking advantage of the fact that a citizen of New York had become Scott's owner, Scott's friends then brought a similar suit in the federal courts based on diversity of citizenship. The issue of Scott's citizenship, which could have been crucial to the case, was minimized by the judge. He held that citizenship, for purposes of federal court jurisdiction, meant only residence and the power to own property. Consequently he permitted the case to be tried, and ruled against Scott on the merits of his claim to freedom.

The Supreme Court's decision was delayed until just after Buchanan's inauguration in 1857. Ignoring the complex whirl of events in which the case had its setting, we need note only two of the Court's main holdings, as announced by Chief Justice Taney. First, no Negro slave could be a citizen with power to sue in the federal courts. Scott had not become a free man by reason of the Missouri Compromise, because it was unconstitutional. Unless he had some other claim to freed status, he was still a slave and so without right to bring suit in the federal courts.

Second, and more fundamental, Taney contended that Negroes had been regarded as persons of an inferior order when the Constitution was adopted, and that it had not considered them as "citizens." Consequently, all persons of African descent, whether slaves or not, were barred from access to the federal courts under the diversity of citizenship clause and indeed, from the enjoyment of any rights or protections under the Constitution. Specifically, Taney wrote that "persons" of Dred Scott's "class" were not "a portion of this people" or "constituent members of this sovereignty." They were "not included, and were not intended to be included, under the word 'citizens' in the Constitution, and can therefore claim none of the rights and privileges which that instrument provides for and secures to citizens of the United States."

What were the rights and privileges of citizens of the United States which Taney thus foreclosed to all persons of African descent? In addition to the right to sue in the federal courts, there was eligibility to the Congress or the Presidency, which is limited to citizens of the United States. But what about rights guaranteed by the Constitution to "the people" or to "persons"

generally? Taney's use throughout his opinion of "the people" of the American Union as synonymous with "citizens of the United States" certainly suggests that these broader guarantees were no more effective than the narrower ones.

But what about Article IV, section 2? If a state gives its free Negro residents the status of state citizens, would they not be able to claim protection in other states for the privileges and immunities of state citizenship? Taney said no. In his view Article IV, section 2, protected only the rights of citizens of the United States. Each state, he said, might confer "the character of citizen" upon anyone it thought proper, but such a citizen would not be entitled to "the privileges and immunities of a citizen in the other states." To put a "citizen" of any given state on a plane of "perfect equality" with the citizens of every other state as to rights of person and property would be, in effect, to make him a citizen of the United States. And since the Court had started out by saying that persons of Dred Scott's class could not be citizens of the United States, obviously the privileges and immunities clause had to be interpreted so as not to open a loophole in that doctrine.

So the privileges and immunities clause, under the pressure of the slavery issue, was given a very restricted interpretation indeed. Its protections were available only to those citizens of the states who were also citizens of the United States. This prevented the clause from protecting Negroes. But Taney then went on to remove its protection further by holding that it covered only citizens of the United States who were temporarily in other states. There they were entitled to the minimum privileges and immunities generally prevailing in that state. But a state was left perfectly free to create inequalities in rights among its *own* citizens. Thus the privileges and immunities clause was reduced very nearly to a cipher.

THE MEANING OF DUE PROCESS      The due process clause of the Fifth Amendment closely approaches the privileges and immunities clause in vagueness. The Supreme Court has confessed that "few phrases of the law are so elusive of exact apprehension as this." [3] But "due process" did have something in the way of an ascertainable history. It was generally thought to be descended from the Latin phrase "per legem terrae" in the Magna Carta of 1215. In chapter 39 of that document the King promised: "No freeman shall be arrested, or imprisoned, or disseized, or outlawed, or exiled, or in any way molested; nor will we proceed against him, unless by the lawful judgment of his peers or by the law of the land."

The Petition of Right of 1628 prayed that "freemen be imprisoned or detained only by the law of the land, or by due process of law, and not by the King's special command without any charge." In 1819 Daniel Webster tried his hand at defining due process in his argument in the *Dartmouth*

---

[3] *Twining* v. *New Jersey* (1908).

*College* case, describing it as "the general law; a law, which hears before it condemns; which proceeds upon inquiry, and renders judgment only after trial," so that "every citizen shall hold his life, liberty, property, and immunities, under the protection of the general rules which govern society."

The *Dartmouth College* decision did not turn on the due process clause, however, and actually it was not until 1856 that the Supreme Court first interpreted it, in the case of *Murray's Lessee* v. *Hoboken Land & Improvement Company*. An act of Congress had authorized the Treasury Department, without recourse to judicial process, to issue warrants against and make a levy on the property of federal revenue collectors found to be indebted to the United States. The complaint was made that this was a taking of property without due process of law. The Supreme Court upheld the statute, on the ground that the procedure prescribed was not in conflict with any specific provisions of the Constitution, nor with the settled usages under English common and statute law which had been carried over into the practice of this country.

These, then, are the most important pre-Civil War contributions (both positive and negative) made by the Supreme Court to the understanding of civil liberties under the Constitution. The lines of judicial interpretation thus opened up were of great significance when Congress undertook those postwar modifications in the Constitution which John Frank has referred to as constituting "the second American Revolution."

### DRAFTING OF THE FOURTEENTH AMENDMENT

Of the three post-Civil War amendments, only the Fourteenth need concern us here. The Thirteenth Amendment, abolishing slavery and involuntary servitude, which became effective in December, 1865, has been narrowly construed, and so has required subsequent judicial application only in certain minor respects.[4] The Fifteenth Amendment took effect in March, 1870, and

---

[4] The principal application of the Thirteenth Amendment has been to invalidate "peonage" legislation or practices in the states. Peonage is usually achieved by an employer giving an employee an advance of wages and then compelling the worker to stay on the job until the debt is worked off. A number of state statutes have allowed or fostered such a system of indentured labor. The law invalidated in *Bailey* v. *Alabama* (1911) provided that any person who, with intent to injure or defraud, entered into a written contract and obtained money or property, and failed to perform the services contracted for, should be punished as if he had been guilty of theft. What made such laws unconstitutional was their requirement that one man work for another or go to jail. As the Court said in *Pollock* v. *Williams* (1944), a state may not "directly or indirectly command involuntary servitude, even if it was voluntarily contracted for."

There are exceptional circumstances in which compulsory labor is permissible. A state may require able-bodied persons to devote a reasonable amount of their time to such public duties as jury service or repair of the roads [*Butler* v. *Perry* (1916)]. Forced service for military purposes is not interpreted as

guaranteed that the right of citizens of the United States to vote should not be abridged because of race, color, or previous condition of servitude. It is discussed elsewhere.

The Fourteenth Amendment, dating from July, 1868, was infinitely more complex and has resulted in more litigation than any other provision of the Constitution, with the possible exception of the commerce clause. Intense dispute over the intended effect and meaning of the amendment persists to the present day. The purpose of this discussion is to present as fully as space permits the circumstances of the adoption of the amendment, so that a basis will be laid for understanding its subsequent tangled history.

First of all, it should be clear that our concern is almost entirely with the first section of the amendment, which reads:

> All persons born or naturalized in the United States, and subject to the jurisdiction thereof, are citizens of the United States and of the state wherein they reside. No state shall make or enforce any law which shall abridge the privileges or immunities of citizens of the United States; nor shall any state deprive any person of life, liberty, or property without due process of law; nor deny to any person within its jurisdiction the equal protection of the laws.

There are four additional sections, three of them dealing with important political problems resulting from the Civil War, and the last giving Congress power to enforce by appropriate legislation the preceding four sections.[5]

Actually the major attention of Congress and the state legislatures in drafting and ratifying the amendment was concentrated upon the issues of sec-

---

involuntary servitude [*Selective Draft Law Cases* (1918)]. Nor does the Thirteenth Amendment cover special professions which operate under conditions requiring continued service for a specified time, such as seamanship [*Robertson v. Baldwin* (1897)]. In *Heart of Atlanta Motel* v. *United States* (1964) the Court found "no merit" in the contention that, by requiring appellant to rent rooms to Negroes against its will, Congress was subjecting the motel to involuntary servitude.

[5] Section 2 repealed the provisions of Article I, section 2, which counted three-fifths of the slaves in apportionment for representation in Congress. Since it was anticipated that the Southern states would be reluctant to permit the freed Negroes to vote, this section went on to say that if any state denied its citizens the right to vote except for participation in rebellion or other crime, "the basis of representation therein shall be reduced in the proportion which the number of such male citizens shall bear to the whole number of male citizens twenty-one years of age in that state."

Section 3 excluded from federal or state office anyone who had taken an oath as a federal or state official to support the Constitution, and who had subsequently engaged in insurrection or rebellion against the United States or given aid and comfort to its enemies. However, Congress could by a two-thirds vote of each house remove such disability.

Section 4 provided that the validity of the public debt of the United States should not be questioned, and forbade the United States or any state to assume or pay any obligation incurred in aid of insurrection or rebellion against the United States.

tions 2, 3, and 4 rather than upon the first section. But the relative importance of the different sections in practice is strikingly demonstrated by the fact that in the 1964 official annotated edition of the Constitution, out of 263 pages on the Fourteenth Amendment, 255 pages are devoted to the first section and 8 pages to the remaining four.

The formative period of the Fourteenth Amendment was between January 12, 1866, when the first drafts were considered by the Joint Committee on Reconstruction, and June 13 of the same year, when the House concurred in the Senate version. What was it that the Congress, under control of Republican Reconstructionists, was trying to do? Its basic motivation was undoubtedly to protect the rights of the newly freed Negroes, to establish constitutional guarantees which would be effective when, as ultimately would happen, military control was withdrawn from the Southern states. The "Black Codes" of those states had been grossly discriminatory, forbidding Negroes to own property, to have access to the courts, and so on. Since *Barron* v. *Baltimore* had limited the effect of the Bill of Rights to the federal government, the only provision in the Constitution as it then existed which might cover the Negro was the privileges and immunities clause. However, the *Dred Scott* decision, as just noted, eliminated this possibility. Thus new guarantees were needed.

The first move of the Thirty-ninth Congress was toward statutory protection. A civil rights bill was introduced by Senator Trumbull of Illinois on January 5, 1866, and became law on April 9 by passage over President Johnson's veto, two months before the Fourteenth Amendment was adopted by Congress. The Civil Rights Act provided that persons born in the United States were citizens of the United States, and that such citizens, without regard to color, were entitled in every state and territory to the same rights to contract, sue, give evidence, and hold property as were enjoyed by white citizens, and to the equal benefit of all laws for the security of person and property. Any person who under color of law caused any such civil right to be denied would be guilty of a federal offense.

By the Civil Rights Act the federal government asserted its power to control civil rights *within* the several states for the purpose of preventing discrimination against the newly freed Negroes. Where did it get this power? Senator Trumbull cited three sources—the Thirteenth Amendment, the privileges and immunities clause, and the Declaration of Independence. "Liberty and slavery," he said, "are opposite terms." Consequently an unjust encroachment upon liberty was "a badge of servitude which, by the Constitution, is prohibited." As for privileges and immunities, he was relying upon the *Corfield* v. *Coryell* interpretation which saw them as "such fundamental rights as belong to every free person . . . the great fundamental rights of life, liberty, and the pursuit of happiness, and the right to travel, to go where he pleases. This is the right which belongs to the citizen of each State." The Declaration of Independence he threw in for good measure.

However, Trumbull's arguments failed to convince some in Congress who were wholly in favor of the bill. Particularly Representative John A. Bingham of Ohio, an important member of the Joint Committee on Reconstruction, challenged reliance on the privileges and immunities clause because it gave no enforcement authority to Congress. The Thirteenth Amendment argument was not accepted.[6] Consequently there was a strong feeling among the Republican Reconstructionists that the civil rights of the freedmen must be put on a firmer constitutional footing, and one that would not be subject to repeal by a later Congress. Thus discussion of the Fourteenth Amendment proceeded concurrently with the action on the Civil Rights Act.

It is not possible to examine in detail the evolution of the amendment from the first drafts submitted in the Joint Committee on January 12 to its final passage. But we can get a sense of the developmental process by noting the successive versions of the first section proposed by Bingham, whose role entitled him to rate as "father" of the amendment. His first draft said simply: "The Congress shall have power to make all laws necessary and proper to secure to all persons in every State within this Union equal protection in their rights of life, liberty and property."

We note two things about this language. First, it would supply the constitutional authority for legislation which Bingham felt to be lacking for the Civil Rights Act. Second, it was concerned with giving Congress power to protect civil rights, rather than with stating standards of protection which would be enforceable directly by the courts. This latter point deserves underlining, for it is essential to understanding the spirit of the times. The Presidency under Johnson was in eclipse. The Supreme Court, in the aftermath of the *Dred Scott* decision, was at very nearly the lowest point in its history. Congress was in the saddle, and the first thing that occurred to its members was that Congress should undertake the protection of civil liberties by legislation and by securing whatever authority was necessary for such legislation.

[6] However, Mark DeWolfe Howe has recently argued that the Thirteenth Amendment did actually supply constitutional authority for the Civil Rights Act of 1866. He interprets the Amendment's intention to be "that the institution [of slavery] and the badges of inferiority with which it had degraded the Negro should be wholly eradicated." He suggests that the Fourteenth Amendment, as subsequently interpreted by the Supreme Court, had the anomalous result of actually weakening the authority Congress could have exercised under the Thirteenth Amendment, saying: "I have not seen any evidence that when the Fourteenth Amendment was adopted its framers intended to take back any of the congressional authority which the Thirteenth Amendment had created—the authority, that is, to deal with private efforts to perpetuate the inequalities born of slavery." *Civil Rights, the Constitution, and the Courts* (Cambridge, Mass.: Harvard University Press, 1967), pp. 47, 50–51.

An effort was made to revive the "badge of servitude" theory of the Thirteenth Amendment in *Jones* v. *Alfred H. Mayer Co.* (1968), where it was contended by plaintiffs who had been denied opportunity to buy a house for racial reasons that the act of 1866 was an implementation of the Thirteenth Amendment, and that housing discrimination was forbidden by the act as a vestige of slavery.

On January 27 a revised Bingham draft proposed to give Congress legislative power "to secure all persons in every State full protection in the enjoyment of life, liberty and property; and to all citizens of the United States in every State the same immunities and equal political rights and privileges." This was poor drafting. How much protection is "full" protection? Did the "same immunities" mean the same throughout the nation, or merely the same for white and Negro in each state? Bringing "political" rights into the amendment added a whole new field of concern.

The Joint Committee rejected this draft by a tie vote, so Bingham tried again. This time his proposal ran: "Congress shall have power to make all laws which shall be necessary and proper to secure to citizens of each State all privileges and immunities of citizens in the several States; and to all persons in the several States equal protection in the rights of life, liberty and property."

This text was reported to the two houses on February 13. In the House Bingham explained that both parts of his proposal were already in the Constitution and binding on the states, and that he was merely adding the power of Congress to enforce them. Professors Fairman and Crosskey, who have done so much to sharpen our understanding of the issues involved in the drafting of the Fourteenth Amendment, disagree as to what this statement of Bingham's proves. Fairman concludes that Bingham was confused, for the privileges and immunities clause had been given no authoritative interpretation, and could at best have only a limited import, while the Fifth Amendment had been held in *Barron* v. *Baltimore* to be applicable to the federal government only.

Crosskey thinks Bingham knew exactly what he was doing. Bingham believed that the privileges and immunities clause covered those rights conferred in specific terms by other provisions of the Constitution and its amendments, which he referred to as "this immortal bill of rights embodied in the Constitution." As to the effectiveness of these guarantees against the states, Bingham had declared as early as 1859: "Whenever the Constitution guarantees to its citizens a right, either natural or conventional, such guarantee is in itself a limitation upon the States." Since these views were contrary to the position taken by the Supreme Court in the *Barron* and *Dred Scott* cases, the Fourteenth Amendment was intended to repeal those decisions. As Crosskey says, Bingham drew up this draft "upon the assumption that his own constitutional ideas and those of his Republican brethren, and *not* the Supreme Court's constitutional decisions, were the standing law."

If this was Bingham's view and purpose, then one essential element was missing from his formulation. He had failed to do anything about repealing another of the doctrines of the *Dred Scott* case, namely, that persons of African descent, whether slaves or not, could not be citizens of the United States under the Constitution. The Civil Rights Act did have a provision guaranteeing the status of Negroes as citizens of the United States, but the

draft of the Fourteenth Amendment did not, and during the House discussion no one suggested that it was needed.

After a three-day House debate at the end of February, further consideration of Bingham's draft was postponed. In April the Joint Committee undertook further revisions, and on April 28 the first section of the Fourteenth Amendment, in what was to be its final form save only for the first sentence defining citizenship, was adopted. It was again the work of Bingham. In contrast to the draft which the House had debated, this version was not merely a grant of power to Congress. It was a direct obligation on the states. Moreover, the long debate as to whether the amendment should leave the states free to set their own standards on civil rights and merely seek to prevent unequal application of those standards, or whether it should set up general standards of treatment to which the practices in each state must conform, was finally settled. It would do both. So there was an equal protection clause which guaranteed no discrimination, though without the "life, liberty and property" language of the earlier draft. But there was also the privileges and immunities clause carried over from Article IV, section 2, and made applicable to "citizens of the United States." And to this was now added the due process clause from the Fifth Amendment.

The House passed this version on May 10. The Senate took it up on May 23, and there it was handled by Jacob M. Howard of Michigan. It was in fact Howard who, seeing the need for a definition of citizenship, subsequently added the first sentence of the present amendment to fill that gap. Howard devoted more attention to explaining the privileges and immunities clause to the Senate than to the other parts of the first section. He agreed that the privileges and immunities guaranteed by Article IV were somewhat vague, and thought it would be "a somewhat barren discussion" to determine what they were. "But it is certain," he added, "the clause was inserted in the Constitution for some good purpose."

Whatever these privileges and immunities were—and Howard quoted from Justice Washington in *Corfield* v. *Coryell*—they "are secured to the citizen solely as a citizen of the United States and as a party in their courts. They do not operate in the slightest degree as a restraint or prohibition upon State legislation." The Supreme Court, as we have just seen, had ruled to this effect in the *Dred Scott* case. Moreover, the first eight amendments were in the same situation, because of *Barron* v. *Baltimore*. Howard specifically recited the provisions of these amendments and said that the privileges and immunities clause of the Fourteenth Amendment would make this "mass of privileges, immunities, and rights, some of them secured by the second section of the fourth article . . . some by the first eight amendments of the Constitution," effective on the states. "The great object of the first section of this amendment is . . . to restrain the power of the States and compel them at all times to respect these great fundamental guarantees."

With regard to the equal protection and due process clauses, he pointed

out that they would "disable a State from depriving not merely a citizen of the United States, but any person, whoever he may be, of life, liberty, or property without due process of law, or from denying to him the equal protection of the laws of the State." Similarly in the House Bingham had stressed the difference between the protection of "citizens" in the first clause and "persons" in the second and third clauses, and had said that the amendment would protect the "inborn rights of every person," both "citizen and stranger."

It is not feasible to report the additional debate in detail. The Senate approved the resolution, as amended, on June 8, and the House accepted the revised version on June 13. Thus, with the concurrence of the necessary states, were added to the Constitution three important new standards for the protection of civil liberties against state action. Equal protection, a general guarantee against discrimination, was the most specific of the new provisions. The other two—due process, and privileges and immunities— were concepts without precise contours which would have such meaning as they might be given by Congress and, more importantly, by the Supreme Court. To this process of spelling out the implications for individual liberties of the Bill of Rights and the Fourteenth Amendment, we now turn, giving attention first to freedom of speech and press.

## SELECTED REFERENCES

AVINS, ALFRED (ed.), *The Reconstruction Amendments' Debates*. Richmond, Va.: Virginia Commission on Constitutional Government, 1967.

BRANT, IRVING, *The Bill of Rights: Its Origin and Meaning*. Indianapolis: The Bobbs-Merrill Company, Inc., 1965.

CHAFEE, ZECHARIAH, JR., *How Human Rights Got into the Constitution*. Boston: Boston University Press, 1952.

CROSSKEY, WILLIAM W., "Charles Fairman, 'Legislative History,' and the Constitutional Limitations on State Authority," 22 *University of Chicago Law Review* 1–143 (1954).

———, *Politics and the Constitution in the History of the United States*, chaps. 31, 32. Chicago: The University of Chicago Press, 1953.

FAIRMAN, CHARLES, "Does the Fourteenth Amendment Incorporate the Bill of Rights? The Original Understanding," 2 *Stanford Law Review* 5–139 (1949).

———, "A Reply to Professor Crosskey," 22 *University of Chicago Law Review* 144–156 (1954).

———, "The Supreme Court and the Constitutional Limitations on State Governmental Authority," 21 *University of Chicago Law Review* 40–78 (1953).

FLACK, HORACE E., *The Adoption of the Fourteenth Amendment*. Baltimore: The Johns Hopkins Press, 1908.

GRAHAM, HOWARD J., "The Early Anti-slavery Backgrounds of the Fourteenth Amendment," 1950 *Wisconsin Law Review* 479, 610.

HAINES, CHARLES GROVE, and FOSTER H. SHERWOOD, *The Role of the Supreme Court in American Government and Politics, 1835–1864,* chap. 10. Berkeley, Calif.: University of California Press, 1957.

HARRIS, ROBERT J., *The Quest for Equality.* Baton Rouge, La.: Louisiana State University Press, 1960.

JAMES, JOSEPH B., *The Framing of the Fourteenth Amendment.* Urbana, Ill.: The University of Illinois Press, 1956.

KELLY, ALFRED H., "Clio and the Court: An Illicit Love Affair," in Kurland, Philip B. (ed.), *The Supreme Court Review: 1965,* pp. 119–158. Chicago: The University of Chicago Press, 1965.

KENDRICK, BENJAMIN B. (ed.), *The Journal of the Joint Committee of Fifteen on Reconstruction.* New York: Columbia University Press, 1914.

MC LAUGHLIN, ANDREW C., *A Constitutional History of the United States,* chaps. 40, 49. New York: Appleton-Century-Crofts, Inc., 1935.

POUND, ROSCOE, *The Development of Constitutional Guarantees of Liberty.* New Haven, Conn.: Yale University Press, 1957.

RUTLAND, ROBERT A., *The Birth of the Bill of Rights, 1776–1791.* Chapel Hill, N.C.: The University of North Carolina Press, 1955.

TEN BROEK, JACOBUS, *Equal under Law* (originally published as *The Antislavery Origins of the Fourteenth Amendment*). New York: Collier Books, a division of Crowell-Collier Publishing Co., 1965.

# 21

## The judicial approach to civil liberties

"Congress shall make no law . . . abridging the freedom of speech, or of the press." This great principle of an open society was incorporated into the Constitution when the First Amendment was ratified on December 15, 1791. No one who has even the faintest understanding of how democratic self-government functions can harbor any doubt as to the fundamental importance of freedom of ideas. The case against suppression of opinion was put in perhaps its most perfect literary form for modern times by Justice Holmes's dissent in the case of *Abrams* v. *United States* (1919):

> Persecution for the expression of opinions seems to me perfectly logical. If you have no doubt of your premises or your power and want a certain result with all your heart you naturally express your wishes in law and sweep away all opposition. To allow opposition by speech seems to indicate that you think the speech impotent, as when a man says that he has squared the circle, or that you do not care whole-heartedly for the result, or that you doubt either your power or your premises. But when men have realized that time has upset many fighting faiths, they may come to believe even more than they believe the very foundations of their own conduct that the ultimate good desired is better reached by free trade in ideas—that the best test of truth is the power of the thought to get itself accepted in the competition of the market, and that truth is the only ground upon which their wishes safely can be carried out. That at any rate is the theory of our Constitution.

Holmes is here making a "utilitarian" defense of free speech, basing its justification on its value to society. But freedom to speak may also be defended as a natural right which individuals must enjoy if they are to achieve the full potentialities of their intellectual and moral endowments. Interference with such rights would on this basis be objectionable, not because society was deprived of truths it might otherwise have discovered, but because individuals were thwarted in the development and expression of their rational faculties.

Our task, however, is not to discuss generally the philosophical or moral or social case for freedom of expression but rather to examine more specifically the meaning and effect which the libertarian principles of the First Amendment have achieved in American experience through judicial interpretation and enforcement. Judges, of course, are not the only, or even necessarily the most effective, guardians of civil liberties. Learned Hand has warned:

> I often wonder whether we do not rest our hopes too much upon constitutions, upon laws and upon courts. These are false hopes; believe me, these are false hopes. Liberty lies in the hearts of men and women; when it dies there, no constitution, no law, no court can save it; no constitution, no law, no court can even do much to help it. While it lies there it needs no constitution, no law, no court to save it.[1]

But this goes too far. As Paul Freund has pointed out, the argument is based on a false dichotomy between a people either lost beyond saving or secure beyond the need of help.[2] The question is not whether the courts should do everything but whether they can do something. American experience has shown that the judiciary can be a substantial support when constitutional freedoms are threatened, and the Supreme Court by its repeated consideration of these issues has earned a position as the nation's most thoughtful expositor of the principles of a free society.

### HISTORY AND THE FIRST AMENDMENT

The Supreme Court had no occasion to make any significant exploration of the scope and meaning of the First Amendment for more than 100 years after its adoption. But in 1897 the Court did announce a principle which, if consistently followed, would have greatly affected its twentieth-century interpretations of that amendment. In *Robertson* v. *Baldwin* the Court said: "The law is perfectly well settled that the first ten amendments to the Constitution, commonly known as the Bill of Rights, were not intended to lay down any novel principles of government, but simply to embody certain guaranties and immunities which we had inherited from our English ancestors."

[1] Irving Dilliard (ed.), *The Spirit of Liberty* (New York: Alfred A. Knopf, Inc., 1952), pp. 189–190.
[2] "The Supreme Court and Civil Liberties," 4 *Vanderbilt Law Review* 552 (1951).

If the First Amendment was in fact intended to be limited to principles inherited from our English ancestors, then Blackstone's famous definition of the liberty of the press would be a principal guide to its meaning:

> The liberty of the press is indeed essential to the nature of a free state; but this consists in laying no previous restraints upon publications, and not in freedom from censure for criminal matter when published. Every freeman has an undoubted right to lay what sentiments he pleases before the public; to forbid this, is to destroy the freedom of the press; but if he publishes what is improper, mischievous or illegal, he must take the consequence of his own temerity.[3]

If the First Amendment ratifies Blackstone's understanding of freedom of the press, then it is a protection only against previous restraint, or censorship. This is of course an important guarantee and one which has been fully incorporated into American reasoning. Banning of books, preventing newspapers from being published, forbidding or breaking up peaceful assemblies —such actions are associated with dictatorships; they are not permissible under the First Amendment.

But Blackstone offered no principle which would protect speakers or publishers from punishment for what they had said or written. He would permit punishment, not only for speech or publication which is illegal or criminal, but also for matter which is "improper" or "mischievous." His rules would allow broad scope for governmental prosecutions against those who had exercised the right of free speech or free press. English practice, in fact, permitted wide latitude for severe action against the crime of "seditious libel"—that is, defaming or criticizing the government or its officers. If the First Amendment carried over the English law of seditious libel, then freedom of speech and press in America were subject to serious limits.

That this English legacy had in fact persisted was evident when Congress adopted the Sedition Act of 1798. This statute provided punishment for making false, scandalous, and malicious statements against the government of the United States, either house of Congress, or the President, with intent to defame them or bring them into contempt or disrepute, or to stir up the hatred of the people against them, or bring about sedition in any of its various forms. The act was broad enough to make criminal virtually any criticism of the government.

The Federalist members of Congress who passed this legislation as a device for punishing their Jeffersonian critics obviously did not regard it as barred by the First Amendment. However, the violent public reaction against the numerous prosecutions instituted under the act indicated that the Federalists were in error, and subsequent developments, capped by the Supreme Court's decision in *New York Times* v. *Sullivan* (1964), established that there is no law of seditious libel under the American Constitution.[4]

---

[3] Blackstone, *Commentaries*, IV, 151, 152.
[4] See the discussion of seditious libel in Chap. 26.

So it is clear that *Robertson* v. *Baldwin* does not supply the rule for interpreting the First Amendment, in spite of Justice Frankfurter's assertion in *Dennis* v. *United States* (1951) that it represented "the authentic view of the Bill of Rights." As in interpreting the rest of the Constitution, the Supreme Court must find the meaning of the First Amendment within the context of American understandings and the "felt necessities of the times." The Court has in fact been quite fertile in developing insights and standards to guide its interpretation of the First Amendment.

### THE CLEAR AND PRESENT DANGER TEST

The usual reason for seeking to control or punish speech is that the speech threatens to result in dangerous or illegal acts. Ideas do have consequences. "Words," as Judge Learned Hand said in the *Masses* case, "are not only the keys of persuasion, but the triggers of action." [5] The shout of "Fire" in a crowded theater can directly cause the most deadly panic. A person may be persuaded by speech or writing to commit murder. Words may lead to the development of a plan for overthrowing the government.

It is clear that words which directly incite to illegal acts are themselves tainted with illegality. The common law recognized the crime of incitement to violence, and the First Amendment has never been understood as extending its sanctuary to speech criminal in purpose and intent. But it immediately becomes apparent there are questions of degree involved here. How closely related must the speech be to the crime in order to taint the speech with illegality? How clear must the purpose be to incite to crime? What degree of immediacy must there be in the situation? And, since these questions are going to be determined in legal prosecutions, who will be responsible for doing so—the trial judge, or the jurors?

At one extreme, the theory can be adopted that words do not become criminal until they have a tendency to produce immediate breach of the peace. But if this is the rule to be applied, then no new legislation or judicial standards are needed, for the common-law rules on criminal solicitation or incitement cover the case.

But the lawmakers and the public are often unwilling to confine restrictive powers over speech within such narrow limits, particularly in crisis situations. They may begin to move against speech merely because it is unpopular. They may say, as Justice Sanford did in *Gitlow* v. *New York* (1925): "The State cannot reasonably be required to measure the danger from every . . . utterance in the nice balance of a jeweler's scale. A single revolutionary spark *may* kindle a fire that, smouldering for a time, *may* burst into a sweeping and destructive conflagration."

This "remote and indirect tendency" test was in fact operative prior to the adoption of the First Amendment. The English common law of sedition

[5] *Masses Publishing Co.* v. *Patten* (1917).

made words criminal if they cast blame on the government or its officials, on the ground that bringing them into disrepute would *tend* to overthrow the state. The American Sedition Act of 1798 adopted this same standard, but in other respects the act was an advance on the common law of criminal sedition in that it entrusted criminality to the jury rather than the judge, and admitted truth as a defense. This act was rejected by the political process, and the authority of the "remote and indirect tendency" test which it embodied was at least somewhat impaired. But no other standard was stated, nor was there judicial need for one in the federal courts until World War I when enforcement of the Espionage Act of 1917 and the Sedition Act of 1918 forced the issue onto the Supreme Court's calendar.

Justice Holmes was the Court's spokesman in its initial encounters with the free speech problem. The Espionage Act, which prohibited the making of false statements intended to interfere with the successful prosecution of the war, as well as acts obstructing recruiting or causing insubordination in the Armed Forces, was at issue in *Schenck* v. *United States* (1919). The defendants had mailed circulars to men eligible for the draft, declaring conscription to be unconstitutional despotism and urging them to assert their rights. Holmes spoke for a unanimous Court in finding that such speech was not protected by the First Amendment because of the "clear and present danger" that it would result in illegal action:

> The character of every act depends upon the circumstances in which it is done. . . . The most stringent protection of free speech would not protect a man in falsely shouting fire in a theatre and causing a panic. . . . The question in every case is whether the words used are used in circumstances and are of such a nature as to create a clear and present danger that they will bring about the substantive evils that Congress has a right to prevent. It is a question of proximity and degree.

Then he added, with particular reference to the problems of the *Schenck* case: "When a nation is at war many things that might be said in time of peace are such a hindrance to its effort that their utterance will not be endured so long as men fight and that no Court could regard them as protected by any constitutional right."

In the same month, March, 1919, Holmes wrote two more unanimous opinions for the Court, upholding convictions in Espionage Act cases. In *Frohwerk* v. *United States* the culprit had inserted several articles in a Missouri German-language newspaper on the constitutionality and merits of the draft and the purposes of the war. Holmes was obviously in some doubt as to whether the clear and present danger test had been met here, but, because of the inadequacy of the record, he concluded: "It is impossible to say that it might not have been found that the circulation of the paper was in quarters where a little breath would be enough to kindle a flame and that the fact was known and relied upon by those who sent the paper out."

The third case was the conviction of Eugene V. Debs, one of whose

speeches at a Socialist convention was charged with being an attempt to cause insubordination in the Army and obstruct recruiting. The speech was not designed for soldiers, nor did Debs urge his hearers to resist the draft. Nonetheless, Holmes felt unable to go behind the jury's verdict and accepted it as proof that actual interference with the war was intended and was the proximate effect of the words used.[6]

Thus in its first three applications the clear and present danger test proved a rather illusory protection to freedom of speech in wartime. It was, in effect, a rationalization for sending men to jail because of their speech, though it did insist that the relationship between speech and illegal acts must be proximate, not remote and indirect. Professor Zechariah Chafee, Jr., praised the *Schenck* ruling as supplying "for the first time an authoritative judicial interpretation in accord with the purpose of the framers of the Constitution."[7]

In the fall of 1919 Holmes, along with his colleague, Louis D. Brandeis, sought to show that the test did have protective value, but the two justices were unable to carry the Court majority with them. The crime in *Abrams* v. *United States* was printing and circulating pamphlets attacking the government's action in sending American troops to Vladivostok and Murmansk in the summer of 1918 and calling for a general strike of munitions workers. Holmes's dissent is probably his most famous piece of rhetoric; but here we need note only the effort he made to sharpen up and strengthen the clear and present danger test by these words:

> We should be eternally vigilant against attempts to check the expression of opinions that we loathe and believe to be fraught with death, unless they so imminently threaten immediate interference with the lawful and pressing purposes of the law that an immediate check is required to save the country. . . . Only the emergency that makes it immediately dangerous to leave the correction of evil counsels to time warrants making any exception to the sweeping command, "Congress shall make no law . . . abridging the freedom of speech."

In two additional cases during the same term, the same two justices, with Brandeis writing the dissents, protested the Court's failure to apply the "rule of reason" which the clear and present danger test supplied.[8]

Two later foundation stones of the theory remain to be inspected. The first is *Gitlow* v. *New York* (1925), upholding a conviction under the New York criminal anarchy statute for publication of a radical manifesto. Justice Sanford for the Court majority argued that the clear and present danger test had been relevant in Espionage Act cases, for that act made certain actions unlawful and the purpose of the test was to determine at what point words

---

[6] *Debs* v. *United States* (1919).

[7] Zechariah Chafee, Jr., *Free Speech in the United States* (Cambridge, Mass.: Harvard University Press, 1941), p. 82.

[8] *Schaefer* v. *United States* (1920); *Pierce* v. *United States* (1920).

became the equivalent of unlawful acts. But in the New York statute, the legislature had itself determined that certain words of incitement were dangerous. In reviewing such a legislative finding, the sole responsibility of the Supreme Court was to decide whether there was a reasonable basis for the legislative conclusion.

Holmes came up again with some fine prose to the effect that "every idea is an incitement"; but the enduring positive contribution of *Gitlow* was the majority's casual, almost incidental, assumption that the free speech protections of the First Amendment, applicable by their terms only against congressional action, are also effective in the states by reason of the "liberty" provision of the Fourteenth Amendment.

This was a startling constitutional development. Ever since 1884 the Supreme Court had denied that the Fourteenth Amendment imported into the states any of the criminal prosecution provisions of the Fourth through the Eighth Amendments, and as late as 1922 the Court had said that "the Constitution of the United States imposes upon the States no obligation to confer upon those within their jurisdiction . . . the right of free speech." [9] But in 1923 the Court ruled that "liberty" to teach a foreign language in private schools was protected by the Fourteenth Amendment from state infringement.[10] And one week before the *Gitlow* decision the Court invalidated an Oregon law interfering with the "liberty" of parents to send their children to private schools.[11] Although in each case there was a deprivation of property element for schools and teachers, the decisions did clear the way for a holding that liberty of thought, without any property nexus, was protected under the Fourteenth Amendment. And so we find Sanford saying in *Gitlow:* "We may and do assume that freedom of speech and of the press . . . are among the fundamental personal rights and 'liberties' protected . . . from impairment by the States."

Finally, we must note Brandeis's statement in *Whitney* v. *California* (1927), where, speaking for Holmes as well, he wrung out of the clear and present danger test the maximum protection of which it seems capable. A legislative declaration that a danger exists which justifies restrictions on speech and assembly creates, he said, merely a "rebuttable presumption." If the conditions alleged by the legislature do not, in fact, exist, then the courts, guided by the clear and present danger test, must refuse to enforce the statute. Brandeis admitted that the standards for the test had not yet been clearly fixed, and he undertook once more the task of formulation:

> To courageous, self-reliant men, with confidence in the power of free and fearless reasoning applied through the processes of popular government, no danger flowing from speech can be deemed clear and present, unless the incidence of the evil apprehended is so imminent that it may

[9] *Prudential Insurance Co.* v. *Cheek* (1922).
[10] *Meyer* v. *Nebraska* (1923).
[11] *Pierce* v. *Society of Sisters* (1925).

befall before there is opportunity for full discussion. If there be time to expose through discussion the falsehood and fallacies, to avert the evil by the processes of education, the remedy to be applied is more speech, not enforced silence. Only an emergency can justify repression. . . . Moreover, even imminent danger cannot justify resort to prohibition of these functions essential to effective democracy, unless the evil apprehended is relatively serious. Prohibition of free speech and assembly is a measure so stringent that it would be inappropriate as the means for averting a relatively trivial harm to society. . . . The fact that speech is likely to result in some violence or in destruction of property is not enough to justify its suppression. . . . Among free men, the deterrents ordinarily to be applied to prevent crime are education and punishment for violations of the law, not abridgment of the rights of free speech and assembly.

The subsequent history of the clear and present danger test—its development in the 1930s and 1940s and its decline in the 1950s and 1960s—will be found in later chapters. But at this point it may be noted that from 1919 to 1927 its successive statements were eloquent but it kept no one out of jail.

### LEGISLATIVE REASONABLENESS

Looking back, we see that the clear and present danger test was, at first, not a test for the validity of legislation—the Espionage Act was admittedly constitutional—but only a test for determining how closely words had to be related to illegal acts in order to be infected with their illegality. Even in *Gitlow,* Holmes did not appear to challenge the New York statute. He merely doubted whether Gitlow's "redundant discourse" was included in the statutory prohibition. It was not until *Whitney* that clear and present danger was definitely set forth as a basis on which courts, and indeed, all Americans, could "challenge a law abridging free speech and assembly by showing that there was no emergency justifying it."

This development brought the clear and present danger test into direct conflict with an earlier standard of judicial review; namely, that legislative conclusions embodied in statutes must be upheld by courts if there is any basis on which a "reasonable man" could have reached the same conclusion as the legislature. The reasonable man theory was embraced by the majority in *Gitlow* and *Whitney.* Those decisions held that the function of the Court, when confronted with a statute alleged to infringe basic civil liberties, was limited to judging whether a reasonable man could have reached the legislature's conclusion as to the existence of a danger demanding that protective action be taken. As Sanford said in *Gitlow:* "Every presumption is to be indulged in favor of the validity of the statute." Legislatures should be rebuked only if they act "arbitrarily or unreasonably."

Now there is sound authority for the reasonable man theory of judicial review. Holmes himself was ordinarily one of the most ardent exponents of

this test. As he said in his famous dissent to *Lochner* v. *New York* (1905), he would not invalidate any statute "unless it can be said that a rational and fair man necessarily would admit that the statute proposed would infringe fundamental principles as they have been understood by the traditions of our people and our law." Of course, *Lochner* was not a civil liberties case; the issue was whether New York could limit the hours of employment in bakeries. But in 1923 Holmes did apply the reasonable man test in what came very close to being a civil liberty case, *Meyer* v. *Nebraska*. The Court majority here, as previously noted, held invalid a state law which was aimed to prevent the teaching of the German language in the primary schools Holmes refused to go along with this judgment, because he believed that whether children in their early years should hear and speak only English at school was "a question upon which men reasonably might differ and therefore I am unable to say that the Constitution of the United States prevents the experiment being tried."

This quotation epitomizes the doctrine upon which Holmes's reputation for liberalism was based. The reasonable man theory was a method of letting the legislatures have their own way. A conservative Supreme Court, from 1880 on, had insisted on the right to substitute its judgment for that of Congress or the state legislatures as to the constitutionality of laws which changed the rules respecting rights and uses of property. Holmes thought that the Court had no such license from the Constitution to override the views of popularly elected legislatures, except to veto statutes for which no case could possibly be made that would satisfy a reasonable man. This was the core of his liberalism.

Why, then, did Holmes appear to abandon the reasonable man test in the civil liberties field? And could it be liberalism to advocate a doctrine of narrow judicial review in dealing with economic regulation and broad judicial review over regulations limiting freedom of speech and press? This apparent paradox was explained in two different ways on the Roosevelt Court, and the divergence was the basis for some of its classic arguments.

### PREFERRED POSITION

One explanation, adopted on numerous occasions and associated with the judicial quartet of Black, Douglas, Murphy, and Rutledge, was that the reasonable man test, although appropriate in all other fields, did not apply where the basic freedoms of the First Amendment were at issue. There, it was contended, the judiciary had to hold itself and legislatures to higher standards because of the "preferred position" which the Constitution gives to First Amendment freedoms. Stated in an extreme form, the argument is that any law touching communication is infected with presumptive invalidity. A more moderate statement is that, because First Amendment values are so essential to a free society, legislative action infringing those values must

be shown to be not only "reasonably" adapted to the attaining of valid social goals but justified by overwhelmingly conclusive considerations.

The development of the preferred position view must be indicated rather summarily. Holmes himself never made this argument. Its origin might be found in Justice Cardozo's statement in a 1937 decision that First Amendment liberties were on "a different plane of social and moral values." Freedom of thought and speech, he said, is "the matrix, the indispensable condition, of nearly every other form of freedom. . . . Neither liberty nor justice would exist if they were sacrificed." [12] A somewhat similar position was taken a little earlier in the same year, in the case of *Herndon* v. *Lowry*. But the credit for the invention is usually given to Justice Stone, in a footnote which he appended to a 1938 decision.[13]

The case in question concerned application of a congressional act prohibiting transportation of certain types of compounded milk products in interstate commerce, and Stone was rehearsing the familiar arguments for the reasonable man theory of judicial review:

> The existence of facts supporting the legislative judgment is to be presumed, for regulatory legislation affecting ordinary commercial transactions is not to be pronounced unconstitutional unless in the light of the facts made known or generally assumed it is of such a character as to preclude the assumption that it rests upon some rational basis within the knowledge and experience of the legislators.

At this point occurred the footnote:

> There may be narrower scope for operation of the presumption of constitutionality when legislation appears on its face to be within a specific prohibition of the Constitution, such as those of the first ten amendments, which are deemed equally specific when held to be embraced within the Fourteenth. . . . It is unnecessary to consider now whether legislation which restricts those political processes which can ordinarily be expected to bring about repeal of undesirable legislation, is to be subjected to more exacting judicial scrutiny under the general prohibitions of the Fourteenth Amendment than are most other types of legislation. . . . Nor need we enquire . . . whether prejudice against discrete and insular minorities may be a special condition, which tends seriously to curtail the operation of those political processes ordinarily to be relied upon to protect minorities, and which may call for a correspondingly more searching judicial inquiry.

This is admittedly a tentative and qualified pronouncement; Frankfurter, who vigorously challenged the whole preferred position argument as "mischievous," was justified in concluding that it "did not purport to announce any new doctrine" and that, if it had, a footnote would hardly have been an

[12] *Palko* v. *Connecticut* (1937).
[13] *United States* v. *Carolene Products Co.* (1938). For the interesting history of this footnote, see Alpheus T. Mason, *Harlan Fiske Stone: Pillar of the Law* (New York: The Viking Press, Inc., 1956), pp. 512–516.

"appropriate way" of doing so.[14] But within a year and a half the idea which Stone had at least suggested leaped from the footnotes to become the doctrine of an almost unanimous Court, Justice Frankfurter included, in the 1939 handbill cases.[15] Speaking through none other than Justice Roberts, the Court said:

> In every case, therefore, where legislative abridgement of the rights [to freedom of speech and press] is asserted, the courts should be astute to examine the effect of the challenged legislation. Mere legislative preferences or beliefs respecting matters of public convenience may well support regulation directed at other personal activities, but be insufficient to justify such as diminishes the exercise of rights so vital to the maintenance of democratic institutions. And so, as cases arise, the delicate and difficult task falls upon the courts to weigh the circumstances and to appraise the substantiality of the reasons advanced in support of the regulation of the free enjoyment of the rights.

McReynolds was the only dissenter.

The "preferred position" phrase was apparently not actually employed until Stone, by then Chief Justice, used it in 1942 in his dissent from *Jones* v. *Opelika,* where the Court majority upheld municipal license taxes on booksellers as applied to Jehovah's Witnesses and cited the fact that these were general tax ordinances, not levies aimed at this particular group. In reply Stone observed:

> The First Amendment is not confined to safeguarding freedom of speech and freedom of religion against discriminatory attempts to wipe them out. On the contrary, the Constitution, by virtue of the First and Fourteenth Amendments, has put those freedoms in a preferred position. Their commands are not restricted to cases where the protected privilege is sought out for attack. They extend at least to every form of taxation which, because it is a condition of the exercise of the privilege, is capable of being used to control or suppress it.

One year later Justice Douglas restated this thought, but now for the Court majority, in *Murdock* v. *Pennsylvania* (1943), which overruled *Jones* v. *Opelika:* "Freedom of press, freedom of speech, freedom of religion are in a preferred position." The phrase reappeared in several subsequent decisions. Even Justice Jackson, whose subsequent thoughts were most antagonistic to the preferred position argument, lent it support in his 1943 holding in the second flag-salute case.[16] Perhaps the strongest of all the statements along this line was that by Justice Rutledge in *Thomas* v. *Collins* (1945):

> Any attempt to restrict those liberties must be justified by clear public interest, threatened not doubtfully or remotely, but by clear and present danger. The rational connection between the remedy provided

---

[14] *Kovacs* v. *Cooper* (1949).
[15] *Schneider* v. *Irvington* (1939).
[16] *West Virginia State Board of Education* v. *Barnette* (1943).

and the evil to be curbed, which in other contexts might support legislation against attack on due process grounds, will not suffice. These rights rest on firmer foundation. Accordingly, whatever occasion would restrain orderly discussion and persuasion, at appropriate time and place, must have clear support in public danger, actual or impending. Only the gravest abuses, endangering paramount interests, give occasion for permissible limitation.

The task of rebutting the preferred position doctrine was principally assumed by Justice Frankfurter. It was his contention that Holmes by the clear and present danger test had not really challenged the reasonable man theory or intended to develop an alternative to it as a test for the validity of legislation. He was dismayed by the uses to which the Roosevelt Court began to put the clear and present danger test. He contended that it was being used for a purpose other than Holmes had intended—namely, to determine the constitutionality of legislation; that it was being applied in much different areas than Holmes had contemplated, including contempt of court proceedings and violation of petty police regulations; and that the spirit of its use was much different than Holmes would have approved. In dissenting from the Court's decision in *Bridges* v. *California* (1941), he charged that Justice Black's employment of the clear and present danger test with preferred position embellishment was an unthinking "recitation of phrases that are the short-hand of a complicated historic process." In *Pennekamp* v. *Florida* (1946) he came close to denying any meaning at all to the doctrine, saying: " 'Clear and present danger' was never used by Mr. Justice Holmes to express a technical legal doctrine or to convey a formula for adjudicating cases. It was a literary phrase not to be distorted by being taken from its context."

In *Kovacs* v. *Cooper* (1949) Justice Frankfurter, reacting against Justice Reed's acceptance of the "preferred position" phrase in the Court's opinion, made the clearly mistaken claim that this doctrine had "never commended itself to a majority of this Court." But in the same opinion he gave evidence of the persuasiveness of the preferred position idea when he agreed that "those liberties of the individual which history has attested as the indispensable conditions of an open as against a closed society come to this Court with a momentum of respect lacking when appeal is made to liberties which derive from shifting economic arrangements."

### THE ABSOLUTIST–LITERALIST POSITION

Beyond the preferred position argument stands the contention that the First Amendment gives *absolute* protection to the freedoms it names. This approach asserts that the First Amendment means literally what it says—that Congress shall *make no law* which has the effect of limiting, or reducing in compass, freedom of speech and press. On this reasoning any law passed by Congress which abridges the freedom of speech or press is unconstitutional

on its face, and the circumstances alleged to justify it need not even be considered.

The principal proponent of the absolutist position on the Supreme Court has been Justice Black, who summarized his argument in *Smith* v. *California* (1959) as follows:

> I read "no law abridging" to mean *no law abridging*. The First Amendment, which is the supreme law of the land, has thus fixed its own value on freedom of speech and press by putting these freedoms wholly "beyond the reach" of *federal* power to abridge. No other provision of the Constitution purports to dilute the scope of these unequivocal commands of the First Amendment. Consequently, I do not believe that any federal agencies, including Congress and this Court, have power or authority to subordinate speech and press to what they think are "more important interests."

The tenets of the absolutist doctrine, however, have been developed most completely by Alexander Meiklejohn. He writes:

> No one who reads with care the text of the First Amendment can fail to be startled by its absoluteness. The phrase, "Congress shall make no law . . . abridging the freedom of speech," is unqualified. It admits of no exceptions. To say that no laws of a given type shall be made means that no laws of that type shall, under any circumstances, be made. That prohibition holds good in war as in peace, in danger as in security.[17]

Meiklejohn distinguishes between public and private speech. It is public speech, concerned with public issues, for which absolute protection is essential, because in a self-governing system the citizens are the rulers and must be free to examine and discuss all ideas relating to the public issues they must decide:

> Just so far as, at any point, the citizens who are to decide an issue are denied acquaintance with information or opinion or doubt or disbelief or criticism which is relevant to that issue, just so far the result must be ill-considered, ill-balanced planning for the general good. . . . When a question of policy is "before the house," free men choose to meet it not with their eyes shut, but with their eyes open. To be afraid of ideas, any idea, is to be unfit for self-government. Any such suppression of ideas about the common good, the First Amendment condemns with its absolute disapproval. The freedom of ideas shall not be abridged.

Meiklejohn is aware that "twentieth-century America does not accept 'absolutes' so readily as did the eighteenth century." In this pragmatic era

---

[17] Alexander Meiklejohn, *Free Speech and Its Relation to Self-government* (New York: Harper & Row, Publishers, Incorporated, 1948), pp. 17, 26–27. A more recent and expanded version of his views is contained in *Political Freedom: The Constitutional Powers of the People* (New York: Harper & Row, Publishers, Incorporated, 1960).

we think it well to be "reasonable," to "take all factors into consideration," to "avoid extremes." It is just not "practical" to assert an absolute right to freedom of speech, we tend to believe. In reply Meiklejohn seeks support for his view from another protection of speech found in the Constitution which has unquestioningly been treated as an absolute right. That is the provision in Article I, section 6, to the effect that members of Congress "shall not be questioned in any other place" for "any speech or debate in either house."

The parallel is an interesting one: Congress "shall make no law," and congressmen "shall not be questioned." We have already seen in Chapter 11 that the congressional right of free speech is taken at its face value. Congressmen are absolutely protected from prosecution because of what they have said in Congress or its committees or its official publications. Members of Congress may abuse this freedom; they may make false or libelous statements. They may ruin a man's reputation or cause him to lose his employment. But except for possible discipline by the legislature itself, they will go scatheless, simply because the theory of representative government under the Constitution is that absolute freedom of legislative discussion is a greater good and must be protected at all costs.

The Constitution makes a similar judgment, say the absolutists, concerning freedom of speech, because of the importance of freedom of discussion to democratic self-government. The Constitution knows how to grant qualified rights, if that is its purpose and intent. Take the due process clause of the Fifth Amendment. It does not state an absolute prohibition. It does not say that persons shall not be deprived of life, liberty, or property. It says that persons *may* be so deprived, provided due process of law is followed. Life, liberty, and property are qualified rights under the Fifth Amendment. But freedom of speech under the First Amendment is limited by no such qualifications.

The absolutist-literalist position has often been misunderstood or misrepresented. In *Konigsberg* v. *State Bar* (1961), Justice Harlan asserted that the absolutists believed the First Amendment granted "an unlimited license to talk." Meiklejohn indignantly repudiated this "caricature" as unworthy of serious consideration. "Speech, as a form of human action, is subject to regulation in exactly the same sense as is walking, or lighting a fire, or shooting a gun." For Meiklejohn, absolutism means simply that the First Amendment "forbids Congress to abridge the freedom of a citizen's speech, press, peaceable assembly, or petition, whenever those activities are utilized for the governing of the nation." [18]

But literalism-absolutism does create problems for its advocates. A purely literal reading of the First Amendment, which applies by its terms only to

[18] "The First Amendment Is an Absolute," in Philip B. Kurland (ed.), *The Supreme Court Review: 1961* (Chicago: The University of Chicago Press, 1961), pp. 252, 256.

Congress, would have prevented the Court from extending the amendment's coverage to the states as was done in the *Gitlow* case. Chafee denies that Meiklejohn's supposed boundary between public and private speech actually exists: "There are public aspects to practically every subject." [19] To Meiklejohn's charge that Holmes subverted the First Amendment by permitting it to be breached whenever there was a clear and present danger, Chafee responds that the only practicable alternative to Holmes's limited immunity for speech was not absolute immunity but no immunity at all. Black's absolutism led him into a quixotic attack on the validity of the entire law of libel.[20] It is significant that Justice Murphy, as devoted a civil libertarian as ever sat on the Court, admitted in *Chaplinsky* v. *New Hampshire* (1942): "It is well understood that the right of free speech is not absolute at all times and under all circumstances."

### BALANCING

The converse of the absolutist position that the government has *no* power to limit expression in constitutionally protected areas is that the government has *some* power to limit expression in all areas. The extent of this power must be determined in every case by balancing the case for freedom against the case for order or security.

The clear and present danger test was, of course, a form of balancing, but the scales were definitely tipped in favor of freedom; as Justice Brandeis said, the apprehended evil must be not only clear and present but also "relatively serious" and so "imminent" that it could not be averted by the processes of education. Advocates of the preferred position for civil liberties also allowed for balancing, but freedom's thumb on the scales was even heavier here.

The more recent proponents of balancing on the Supreme Court, principally Justice Harlan, weigh freedom against order with no preferences. The basic notion of the balancers, as Emerson has expressed it, is "that the court must, in each case, balance the individual and social interest in freedom of expression against the social interest sought by the regulation which restricts expression." [21]

The balancing formula had its principal application in the 1950s in cases where the Court was passing on the validity of congressional action against Communists. Initially utilized by Chief Justice Vinson in *American Com-*

---

[19] Book review, 62 *Harvard Law Review* 891 (1949).

[20] See Chap. 26; also Edmond Cahn, "Mr. Justice Black and First Amendment 'Absolutes': A Public Interview," 37 *New York University Law Review* 37 (1962).

[21] Thomas I. Emerson, "Toward a General Theory of the First Amendment," 72 *Yale Law Journal* 877 (1963); *Toward a General Theory of the First Amendment* (New York: Random House, Inc., 1966), pp. 53–54.

*munications Association* v. *Douds* (1950), it was most clearly stated by Justice Harlan in *Barenblatt* v. *United States* (1959) for the Court majority in upholding the power of congressional investigation. In some circumstances, Harlan said, the First Amendment would protect an individual from disclosing his associational relationships to a congressional committee. But a witness does not have the right to resist inquiry in all circumstances. Consequently there must be "a balancing by the courts of the competing private and public interests at stake in the particular circumstances shown." Harlan then proceeded to review the individual and the governmental interests at stake, and concluded that "the balance . . . must be struck in favor of the latter."

Justice Black, dissenting in *Barenblatt*, agreed that balancing might be employed by courts to test the validity of a law which "primarily regulates conduct" but which has a minor effect on speech or "indirectly" affects ideas. But he vigorously denied that laws directly abridging First Amendment freedoms could be justified by a balancing process. Such action was a direct challenge to his absolutist interpretation of First Amendment protections. He also protested that Harlan had misused the balancing test because he had balanced "the right of the Government to preserve itself, against Barenblatt's right to refrain from revealing Communist affiliations." The real interest in Barenblatt's silence, Black felt, was not a mere personal one. It was "the interest of the people as a whole in being able to join organizations, advocate causes and make political 'mistakes' without later being subjected to governmental penalties for having dared to think for themselves. . . . It is these interests of society, rather than Barenblatt's own right to silence, which I think the Court should put on the balance against the demands of the Government, if any balancing process is to be tolerated." [22]

Emerson criticizes balancing because it "frames the issues in such a broad and undefined way, is in effect so unstructured, that it can hardly be described as a rule of law at all." It provides "no hard core of doctrine to guide a court," but rather casts it loose "in a vast space . . . to strike a general balance in the light of its own best judgment. . . . If a court takes the test seriously, the factual determinations involved are enormously difficult and time-consuming, and quite unsuitable for the judicial process." But in fact the test does not allow courts to exercise any real degree of independent

[22] Dean Alfange, Jr., agrees with Black, saying that without considering the "paltry purpose" that would be achieved by forcing Barenblatt to testify, Harlan had simply asserted that any investigation into Communist activity is valid, and all witnesses must answer any and all questions pertaining in any way to Communism, no matter how absurd or inconsequential, so that the government's "right of self-preservation" may be vindicated. Alfange continues, "that is hardly balancing; it is total abdication of judicial responsibility." "The Balancing of Interests in Free Speech Cases: In Defense of an Abused Doctrine," 2 *Law in Transition Quarterly* 1, 22 (1965).

judgment, because it gives "almost conclusive weight to the legislative judgment." [23]

On the other hand, Dean Alfange, Jr., feels that the balancing doctrine has been unfairly abused by liberals because it has been unfairly used by its proponents. He defends balancing of interests as a central feature of sociological jurisprudence; it is an activist technique, well adapted to the settlement of First Amendment cases; it is essential to "an accurate appraisal of reality." He concludes: "The alternative to balancing is to prepackage decisions by setting up objective standards in advance, which, because of their unavoidable abstractness, cannot be made adequate to deal with the constantly varying factual situations which each case presents." [24]

### THE TWO-LEVEL THEORY

Finally, the Supreme Court has on occasion sought to solve some of its First Amendment problems by dividing expression into two levels—one level to which the First Amendment applies and a second level of expression which does not deserve constitutional protection. The Court first spelled out this theory in the case of *Chaplinsky* v. *New Hampshire* (1942). Chaplinsky, threatened with arrest after creating a public disturbance by his open denunciations of all religion as a "racket," had told a city marshal of Rochester, New Hampshire, that "you are a God damned racketeer" and "a damned Fascist and the whole government of Rochester are Fascists or agents of Fascists." The Court upheld Chaplinsky's conviction for violating a state statute against calling anyone "offensive or derisive" names in public. Justice Murphy, writing for a unanimous Court, said:

> There are certain well-defined and narrowly limited classes of speech, the prevention and punishment of which has never been thought to raise any Constitutional problem. These include the lewd and the obscene, the profane, the libelous, and the insulting or 'fighting' words—those which by their very utterance inflict injury or tend to incite an immediate breach of the peace. It has been well observed that such utterances are no essential part of any exposition of ideas, and are of such slight social value as a step to truth that any benefit that may be derived from them is clearly outweighed by the social interest in order and morality.

This conception that only speech which has "social value" is protected by the First Amendment solved the Court's immediate problem in the *Chap-*

---

[23] See also criticisms of balancing in Laurent B. Frantz, "The First Amendment in the Balance," 71 *Yale Law Journal* 1424–1450 (1962); Martin Shapiro, *Freedom of Speech: The Supreme Court and Judicial Review* (Englewood Cliffs, N.J.: Prentice-Hall, Inc., 1966), chap. 3; Donald Meiklejohn, "Labels and Libertarians," in Walter F. Murphy and C. Herman Pritchett (eds.), *Courts, Judges and Politics* (New York: Random House, Inc., 1961), pp. 465–469.

[24] *Op. cit.*, p. 28.

*linsky* case, but it has difficult and serious implications which have made the two-level theory of dubious value.[25]

## APPRAISAL

The various doctrines just reviewed are obviously related to the results which their judicial practitioners wished to achieve and the conceptions they had of their judicial responsibilities. In fact, Martin Shapiro, referring to the "polemical origins" of these doctrines, goes so far as to say that it is a "grave error to take them seriously instead of viewing them in their true light as the superficial ploys of the deeper struggle between activist and modest [self-restraint] tendencies on the Court." [26] Without going this far, one can point up the relations between these doctrines and their consequences for judicial review.

The absolutist position involves a maximum of judicial challenge to legislatures with a minimum exercise of judicial judgment, because the absolutist automatically strikes down any legislation which abridges protected liberties. The two-level theory is another manifestation of absolutism, but at the other end of the scale; expressions on the lower level are absolutely *un*-protected, so the judge need neither challenge legislative infringements on expression at that level nor exercise judicial judgment.

The reasonable man test and the balancing technique as employed on the Court may be paired. Both are doctrines of judicial self-restraint and rationalizations for letting legislatures have their own way. The test of reasonableness, as Felix S. Cohen wrote, "makes of our courts lunacy commissions sitting in judgment upon the mental capacity of legislators." [27] Since legislators are seldom lunatics, their actions are seldom without some justification in reason.

The clear and present danger test and the preferred position doctrine are also closely related. Both require judges to take at least a moderately activist stance and to exercise responsible judgment in determining whether the First Amendment has been breached. These tests do not give the automatic answers of the absolutists, but, in contrast to the pseudo-standards of the reasonableness and balancing doctrines, they do supply positive and workable standards to guide judicial judgment.[28]

With this introduction to the principal standards developed by or available to the Supreme Court for interpreting First Amendment freedoms, we now turn to an examination of their application in specific fields of protected expression.

[25] See Chap. 25 on obscenity.
[26] *Op. cit.,* p. 87.
[27] L. K. Cohen (ed.), *The Legal Conscience: Selected Papers of Felix S. Cohen* (New Haven: Yale University Press, 1960), p. 44.
[28] See Shapiro, *op. cit.,* Chap. 4, for a strong defense of the clear and present danger and preferred position tests.

## SELECTED REFERENCES

BERNS, WALTER, *Freedom, Virtue and the First Amendment*, chaps. 4–6. Baton Rouge, La.: Louisiana State University Press, 1957.

BICKEL, ALEXANDER M., *The Least Dangerous Branch*. Indianapolis: The Bobbs-Merrill Company, Inc., 1962.

BLACK, CHARLES L., JR., *The People and the Court: Judicial Review in a Democracy*. New York: The Macmillan Company, 1960.

CAHN, EDMOND, "The Firstness of the First Amendment," 65 *Yale Law Journal* 464–481 (1956).

———, "Justice Black and First Amendment 'Absolutes': A Public Interview," 37 *New York University Law Review* 549–563 (1962).

CHAFEE, ZECHARIAH, JR., *Free Speech in the United States*, chaps. 2, 3. Cambridge, Mass.: Harvard University Press, 1941.

FRANTZ, LAURENT B., "Is the First Amendment Law?" 51 *California Law Review* 729–754 (1963).

KONEFSKY, SAMUEL J., *The Legacy of Holmes and Brandeis: A Study in the Influence of Ideas*. New York: The Macmillan Company, 1956.

LEVY, LEONARD W., *Legacy of Suppression: Freedom of Speech and Press in Early American History*. Cambridge, Mass.: The Belknap Press, Harvard University Press, 1960.

MC KAY, ROBERT B., "The Preference for Freedom," 34 *New York University Law Review* 1182–1227 (1959).

MEIKLEJOHN, ALEXANDER, "The First Amendment Is an Absolute," in Philip B. Kurland (ed.), *The Supreme Court Review, 1961*, pp. 245–266. Chicago: The University of Chicago Press, 1961.

———, *Political Freedom: The Constitutional Powers of the People*. New York: Harper & Row, Publishers, Incorporated, 1960.

MENDELSON, WALLACE, "On the Meaning of the First Amendment: Absolutes in the Balance," 50 *California Law Review* 821–828 (1962).

MILLER, JOHN C., *Crisis in Freedom*. Boston: Little, Brown and Company, 1951.

PRITCHETT, C. HERMAN, *The Roosevelt Court: A Study in Judicial Politics and Values, 1937–1947*, chap. 10. New York: The Macmillan Company, 1948.

SHAPIRO, MARTIN, *Freedom of Speech: The Supreme Court and Judicial Review*. Englewood Cliffs, N.J.: Prentice-Hall, Inc., 1966.

SMITH, JAMES MORTON, *Freedom's Fetters: The Alien and Sedition Laws and American Civil Liberties*. Ithaca, N.Y.: Cornell University Press, 1956.

WECHSLER, HERBERT, "Toward Neutral Principles of Constitutional Law," 73 *Harvard Law Review* 1–35 (1959).

# 22

## Freedom of the press

When Blackstone wrote that "the liberty of the press consists in laying no *previous* restraints upon publications," he was stating a principle which had become established in England by 1695 and in the colonies by 1725. The issue had thus been closed for decades by the time the First Amendment was adopted. Whatever other doubts there might have been about its intent, there could be no question that it was meant to restate the ban on previous restraints of speech and press.

The tradition of press freedom is firmly established in the United States. There has of course been censorship in wartime, though to an increasing degree efforts have been made to develop these controls on a voluntary basis. In the heat of political controversy, as for example over the abolition of slavery in the pre-Civil War period, editors have been beaten or worse, presses have been destroyed, newspapers have been burned or refused delivery through the mails. The lot of the publisher or distributor of unpopular doctrine can be made difficult in various ways. But the fact remains that *legal* efforts to restrain the freedom of the press have been comparatively few.

### THE RIGHT TO PUBLISH

The basic right of the publisher is that he shall not be required to have government permission to publish or be subjected to a governmental ban

on publication. When Blackstone was defining freedom of the press, licensing of publishers was the typical means of government control, and that is obviously unconstitutional under the First Amendment.[1] But in the Supreme Court's first great anticensorship decision, *Near* v. *Minnesota* (1931), control took the form of a statute providing for the abating, as a public nuisance, of "malicious, scandalous and defamatory" newspapers or periodicals and the enjoining of anyone maintaining such a nuisance. The paper involved was a Minneapolis weekly devoted to attacks on the law enforcement officers of the city, who were charged with permitting "Jewish gangsters" to control illegal operations in the area and with deriving graft from those activities.

The statute as applied against this paper was declared unconstitutional by a five to four vote. The minority of Butler, Van Devanter, McReynolds, and Sutherland defended the statute on the ground that it did not constitute prior restraint as that idea had been historically understood. "It does not authorize administrative control in advance such as was formerly exercised by the licensers and censors but prescribes a remedy to be enforced by a suit in equity." Instead of arbitrary administrative action this statute guaranteed the due process of the law courts. Moreover, since the injunction could be issued only *after* a malicious or defamatory publication had appeared and been adjudged a nuisance, it was not a *previous* restraint but the abating of a nuisance already committed. But Chief Justice Hughes replied for the majority that the object of the statute was not punishment but suppression, and concluded: "This is of the essence of censorship."

The second major point of the dissenters was that the reasonable man rule should be applied here. "The Act was passed in the exertion of the State's power of police, and this court is by well established rule required to assume, until the contrary is clearly made to appear, that there exists in Minnesota a state of affairs that justifies this measure for the preservation of the peace and good order of the State." Butler went on: "It is of the greatest importance that the States shall be untrammeled and free to employ all just and appropriate measures to prevent abuses of the liberty of the press."

Hughes in reply did not assert that the protection against previous restraint was "absolutely unlimited." He did, however, deny that it was normally within the legislative range of choice to pass previous restraint legislation, or that there was any obligation on courts to presume the validity of such legislation. The legitimacy of prior restraints could be recognized only in "exceptional cases." He specified four such exceptional situations. One was where the success of the nation's Armed Forces was at stake in time of war, and here he quoted from Holmes in the *Schenck* case, though he did not

---

[1] Licensing of radio and television stations by the government under the commerce power is in a different category, the justification being that only a limited number of channels is available and consequently regulation is necessary if any use at all is to be made of such facilities.

directly invoke the clear and present danger test. Another was when the "primary requirements of decency" were enforced against obscene publications. The third arose where the security of community life had to be protected "against incitements to acts of violence and the overthrow by force of orderly government." Fourth, it might be necessary for equity courts "to prevent publications in order to protect private rights." Only the last two could conceivably be relevant in the *Near* case, but Hughes held them inapplicable. The purpose of the statute was not to redress individual or private wrongs. As for the chance that the circulation of scandal might tend to disturb the public peace, "the theory of the constitutional guaranty is that even a more serious public evil would be caused by authority to prevent publication."

*Near* v. *Minnesota* was followed in 1936 by a decision invalidating an effort to discourage publications by discriminatory taxation. This type of restraint had been common in English and early American history. In 1712 Parliament had imposed a tax on newspapers and advertisements, the main purpose of which was to suppress publication of comments and criticisms objectionable to the Crown. The taxes were particularly effective in limiting circulation of the cheaper popular papers, and their publishers were at the mercy of the Commissioners of Stamps. The duties were vigorously attacked as "taxes on knowledge," and the sending of newspaper stamps to the American Colonies in 1765 was one of the factors leading to the Revolution. Massachusetts imposed a newspaper tax in 1785 which was so violently opposed that it was repealed in a year and replaced by an advertisement tax, which lasted only two years. This Massachusetts experience appears to have been in part responsible for adoption of the First Amendment, and no state law of this sort was adopted from 1788 to 1934.

In the latter year the Louisiana Legislature, under the control of Huey Long, enacted a 2 per cent tax on gross receipts from advertising on all firms publishing newspapers or periodicals having a circulation of more than 20,000 copies per week. It was denominated as a license tax on the privilege of engaging in the business of selling advertising. The statute affected 13 of the 17 daily newspapers published in the state, but did not touch any of the 120 weekly newspapers. The measure was clearly aimed at the city papers, which on the whole were opposing the Long regime, whereas the country press was favorable to Long.

In *Grosjean* v. *American Press Co.* (1936), the Supreme Court unanimously held the tax unconstitutional. It ruled that the First Amendment, applicable here by way of the Fourteenth, outlawed newspaper or advertising taxes, which had a history as "well-known and odious" as newspaper licensing. Judge Cooley was held to have stated the applicable rule when he wrote:

> The evils to be prevented [by the First Amendment] were not the censorship of the press merely, but any action of the government by

means of which it might prevent such free and general discussion of public matters as seems absolutely essential to prepare the people for an intelligent exercise of their rights as citizens.

Newspapers were of course not immune from any of the ordinary forms of taxation:

> But this is not an ordinary form of tax, but one single in kind, with a long history of hostile misuse against the freedom of the press. . . . The tax here involved is bad not because it takes money from the pockets of the appellees. . . . It is bad because, in the light of its history and of its present setting, it is seen to be a deliberate and calculated device in the guise of a tax to limit the circulation of information to which the public is entitled in virtue of the constitutional guaranties.

The First Amendment does not, however,. entitle publishers to any special exemption from governmental regulation of business practices which may be constitutionally applied to businesses generally. The Wagner Act regulating labor relations was held applicable to the press by a five to four vote in *Associated Press* v. *National Labor Relations Board* (1937). The NLRB had ordered the Associated Press to reinstate one of its news editors allegedly discharged because of his activity in organizing and furthering the American Newspaper Guild. The AP contended that, although the statute could be applied to its mechanical employees, its responsibility of furnishing unbiased and impartial news reports required that it have complete freedom in determining for itself the qualifications of its news employees. Justice Roberts responded that the AP retained complete freedom to discharge any employee "save only as a punishment for, or discouragement of," union activities. The Board's regulation was confined to this one matter, and had "no relation whatever to the impartial distribution of news." Similarly the antitrust provisions of the Sherman Act and the wage and hour requirements of the Fair Labor Standards Act [2] have been held applicable to the press.

In *Mills* v. *Alabama* (1966) the Supreme Court held unconstitutional, as applied to the editor of a Birmingham newspaper, a state law making it a crime to electioneer or solicit votes on election day in support of, or in opposition to, any proposition being voted on. The editor had published on election day an editorial urging voters to approve a change to the mayor-council form of city government for Birmingham, a change that was generally understood to be aimed at establishing a more moderate racial policy in the city by eliminating its two most prominent segregationist officials. The state supreme court sustained the criminal conviction of the editor, on the ground that the law was a reasonable election regulation and served the salutary purpose of protecting the public from confusing last-minute charges when, because of lack of time, they could not be answered or their truth determined.

[2] *Associated Press* v. *United States* (1945); *Lorain Journal Co.* v. *United States* (1957); *Oklahoma Press Publishing Co.* v. *Walling* (1946).

In a brief opinion for the Court, Justice Black said it was "difficult to conceive of a more obvious and flagrant abridgement of the constitutionally guaranteed freedom of the press." There was a "fatal flaw" in the reasoning of the lower court. The "last-minute charges" about which it was concerned could still be made on the day preceding the election, and the law would then make it a crime to answer them on election day. This would "silence the press at a time when it can be most effective."

A conflict between freedom of the press and the right of individuals to reasonable protection of their privacy was presented in *Time, Inc.* v. *Hill* (1967). In 1952 a Pennsylvania family named Hill had been held hostage in their home for nineteen hours by three escaped convicts. A novel portraying a similar incident was published in 1953, and was made into a play which appeared on Broadway in 1955. *Life* magazine made a feature story of the play, which it linked directly to the experience of the Hills, even taking pictures of the actors in the house where the Hills lived when the incident occurred. In fact, both the book and play were highly fictionalized accounts, differing in many respects from the family's experience.

The Hills sued for damages under a state law protecting privacy and were awarded $30,000. The Supreme Court by a vote of five to four set the judgment aside. Justice Brennan stressed that the risk of exposure to publicity is "an essential incident of life in a society which places a primary value on freedom of speech and of press." The press cannot be saddled with "the impossible burden of verifying to a certainty the facts associated in news articles with a person's name, picture or portrait, particularly as related to non-defamatory matter." However, Brennan thought the press could be held to the same standard he had previously developed for libel suits in *New York Times* v. *Sullivan* (1964), namely, that "knowing or reckless falsehood" could not be protected. Since it was not clear that the trial judge had charged the jury in these terms, the Court reversed the judgment, though leaving the way open for a new trial. Justice Fortas for the minority regarded the article as a "reckless and irresponsible assault" upon the Hill family, and did not believe that the Court was adequately protecting the constitutional right of privacy.[3]

[3] In *Spahn* v. *Julian Messner* (1966) the New York Court of Appeals enjoined and awarded damages for publication of an unauthorized biography of Warren Spahn, the baseball pitcher, which was an inaccurate and distorted account of his personal and private life with a preponderant percentage of factual errors and fanciful passages. As a "newsworthy" person, factual reporting about him would be protected as being in the public interest, but the court said that did not mean his personality could be fictionalized and exploited for commercial benefit through the medium of an unauthorized biography. However, the Supreme Court vacated the judgment in *Julian Messner* v. *Spahn* (1967) and remanded the case to the lower court for reconsideration in the light of the ruling in *Time, Inc.* v. *Hill*.

In 1965 the daughter of Henry Clay Frick, one of Pittsburgh's industrial tycoons who died in 1919, asked a Pennsylvania court to enjoin publication of a book about her father, on the ground that it unfairly presented him as an

### FREEDOM OF CIRCULATION: HANDBILLS

In an 1878 decision Justice Field stated a truism when he observed: "Liberty of circulating is as essential to that freedom [of the press] as liberty of publishing; indeed, without the circulation, the publication would be of little value." [4] Of course not all publishers are proprietors of newspapers or periodicals, with established channels of distribution. Anyone with a hand printing press is a publisher for purposes of the First Amendment, with full rights not to be hampered by government restrictions in the publishing and circulation of his printed product. This has been established by a series of Supreme Court decisions involving handbills.

The first was *Lovell* v. *Griffin* (1938), in which the Supreme Court unanimously condemned as unconstitutional a municipal ordinance requiring official permission to distribute publications. The ordinance covered distribution "by hand or otherwise" of "literature of any kind," which was made a nuisance unless written permission in advance was obtained from the city manager. Counsel for the city argued that the ordinance was justified because of the "sanitary problem in removing from . . . streets papers, circulars and other like materials." Moreover, it was contended that the petitioner in this case, who was a member of Jehovah's Witnesses selling their literature from door to door, was not a member of the press, and so not "in the class of persons who are entitled to invoke the constitutional provisions touching the freedom of the press."

The Supreme Court held the ordinance "invalid on its face." It was an absolute prohibition of distribution without permit, "not limited to ways which might be regarded as inconsistent with the maintenance of public order or as involving disorderly conduct, the molestation of the inhabitants, or the misuse or littering of the streets." The First Amendment was appropriately invoked, because liberty of the press necessarily embraced the distribution of pamphlets and leaflets. "These indeed have been historic weapons in the defense of liberty, as the pamphlets of Thomas Paine and others in our own history abundantly attest. The press in its historic connotation comprehends every sort of publication which affords a vehicle of information and opinion."

Subsequent decisions have, if anything, widened the protection afforded distribution of handbills. Four cases were grouped in a 1939 decision, *Schneider* v. *State* (*Town of Irvington*), and in all four the state courts had attempted to distinguish the regulations from the circumstances of the

---

exploiter of workingmen. She sued under an untested state law permitting recovery of damages for statements "tending to blacken the memory" of the dead. In 1967 the judge dismissed the suit and in his opinion, upholding the author's right to make an unflattering historical assessment of Frick, came close to calling the suit frivolous. He did not explain why it took two years to arrive at such an obvious conclusion. *The New York Times,* May 26, 1967.

[4] *Ex parte Jackson* (1878).

*Lovell* case. The Supreme Court, with only McReynolds dissenting, struck down all these efforts. Prevention of litter was a major defense in three of the four cases, but Justice Roberts said that the purpose of keeping the streets clean was not sufficient to justify an ordinance prohibiting a person rightfully on a public street from handing out literature to one willing to receive it. Streets are natural and proper places for dissemination of information and opinion. There are other methods of preventing littering without interfering with constitutional rights; one way is to punish those who actually throw the handbills on the street.

The *Schneider* decision recognized that *commercial* soliciting and canvassing could be subjected to regulation, and some subsequent cases have arisen under this heading.[5] In *Jamison* v. *Texas* (1943) a member of Jehovah's Witnesses was distributing handbills, on one side of which was an invitation to a meeting sponsored by the sect; on the other side was a description of two books setting out their religious views which would be mailed or delivered to anyone making a 25-cent contribution. The state contended that this made the handbill a commercial proposition and consequently subject to regulation, but the Supreme Court unanimously rejected this view.

In *Talley* v. *California* (1960) the Court gave further protection to handbill distribution by declaring unconstitutional a state law which required all handbills to have printed on them the names and addresses of the persons who prepared, distributed, or sponsored them. The purpose was to provide a method of identifying those who might be responsible for fraud, false advertising, or libel, but the Court majority thought the identification requirement would tend to restrict freedom of expression. Three dissenting justices were not convinced that the Constitution protects the "freedom of anonymous speech."[6]

## FREEDOM OF CIRCULATION: THE POST OFFICE

Distribution, we have just seen, is accepted by the Court as a part of the right to print. Effective distribution of much printed material is almost impossible without using the U.S. Post Office. Therefore, access to the distribution facilities of the mails should be as broad as the right to print. But this has not been the case. In the Supreme Court's first important treatment of the problem, *Ex parte Jackson* (1878), Justice Field stated the restrictive principle that "the right to designate what shall be carried necessarily involves the right to determine what shall be excluded." To similar effect was the statement of Justice Brown in *Public Clearing House* v. *Coyne* (1904):

[5] See *Valentine* v. *Chrestensen* (1942).

[6] In *Zwickler* v. *Koota* (1967) the Supreme Court considered the constitutionality of a New York law barring the distribution of unsigned campaign literature, and directed a federal district court to hear the case.

"The legislative body in thus establishing a postal service may annex such conditions to it as it chooses."

Congress in 1872 had enacted a statute making unmailable lottery tickets, obscene or indecent publications and devices, and instructions for preventing conception and procuring abortions. *Ex parte Jackson* and a later decision, *In re Rapier* (1892), both upheld the lottery ban, Justice Field saying in the *Jackson* case: "In excluding various articles from the mail, the object of Congress has not been to interfere with the freedom of the press, or with any other rights of the people; but to refuse its facilities for the distribution of matter deemed injurious to the public morals."

These two lottery decisions constituted, until 1957, the principal Supreme Court support for congressional regulation of the mails on the grounds of protecting the public morals. But the banning of literature from the mails because of alleged obscenity certainly presents entirely different problems than does a lottery. Lottery tickets are rather easily identified, but judgments as to what is obscene vary tremendously, and many literary classics have been treated as nonmailable by the Post Office. In addition to obscenity, which it has statutory authority to intercept, the Post Office has also undertaken on occasion to bar certain types of political opinions from the mails.

CONFISCATION OF MAIL    Three instrumentalities have been employed by the Post Office for prior restraint purposes. The first is impounding and confiscation, which has been used primarily against alleged obscene matter and foreign political propaganda. Up until 1957 the Post Office procedures for handling obscene matter deposited in the mails were very arbitrary. Administrative hearings as to the fact of obscenity seemed to be offered only if the interested party threatened legal action to recover his property. Justice Douglas, sitting as a circuit judge, questioned the exercise of the impounding power in a 1954 case, *Stanard* v. *Oleson*. Congress in 1956 passed an act giving the Post Office authority to impound mail suspected of promoting obscenity, as well as fraud and gambling. However, considerable protection, both substantive and procedural, was written into the act.[7] An impounding order expired after twenty days unless the Postmaster General sought a federal court order continuing it. In 1960 Congress stripped the Postmaster General of his power to issue these interim orders and limited him to the seeking of temporary restraining orders in the federal courts.[8]

In 1957 the Post Office adopted regulations covering the procedural rights of persons whose material was alleged to be unmailable. Written notice of the reasons for barring the mail was required, and hearing within ten days before a Post Office examiner was guaranteed, with decision two days after the hearing in the case of a periodical.[9] These procedures were used in the

[7] 70 Stat. 699 (1956).
[8] 74 Stat. 553 (1960).
[9] 39 Code of Federal Regulations 203 (November 9, 1957).

case of *Manual Enterprises, Inc.* v. *Day* (1962) to bar certain magazines from the mails on the ground of obscenity. The Court majority held that the magazines were not obscene, but three members of the Court went further and ruled that Congress had never authorized the Postmaster General to use any administrative processes to close the mails to matters he regarded as obscene. If Congress did grant such authority to the Post Office, they went on, this would raise two further questions: whether Congress can provide that obscenity be determined in any forum except a court, and whether Congress can close the mails to obscenity by any means other than prosecution of the sender.

The same techniques originally developed for handling alleged obscenity were also used by the Post Office on "foreign political propaganda." About 1940 the Post Office, with the cooperation of the Bureau of Customs, began confiscating periodicals and books mailed to residents of the United States from foreign countries which seemed politically questionable. The Russian newspapers *Pravda* and *Izvestia* were typical of the materials intercepted. Statutory authority for such Post Office action was dubious or nonexistent, but whenever suits were filed against the Post Office, it always released the confiscated material to avoid a judicial test of its powers.

In 1961 President Kennedy issued an executive order directing that the practice of intercepting Communist propaganda be stopped. The next year Congress retaliated by passing a statute specifically authorizing the Postmaster General to detain "communist political propaganda" and to deliver it only upon the addressee's request. In *Lamont* v. *Postmaster General* (1965) the Supreme Court unanimously declared this statute unconstitutional, holding that to force an addressee to request in writing that his mail be delivered was an abridgement of First Amendment rights.

THE STOP ORDER    A second Post Office instrument of prior restraint is the "stop order." Issuance of such orders was first authorized by Congress against persons or firms found by the Post Office to be using the mails to defraud. The effect of the order was that all mail addressed to the person or company was intercepted, stamped "fraudulent," and returned to the sender. Postal money orders drawn to the firm would not be paid.

For a number of years the Court either avoided considering or assumed the constitutionality of this procedure.[10] But in the 1922 case of *Leach* v. *Carlile* Justices Holmes and Brandeis filed a vigorous objection to it in a dissenting opinion, Holmes writing: "If the execution of this law does not abridge freedom of speech I do not quite see what could be said to do so." But the dissent proved ineffective. It is true that in *Donaldson* v. *Read Magazine* (1948) a fraud order of very broad effect was considerably limited in

---

[10] See *School of Magnetic Healing* v. *McAnnulty* (1902); *Public Clearing House* v. *Coyne* (1904).

its scope after the Court had indicated doubt as to its constitutionality, but the revised order was then upheld.

In 1950 the Post Office secured from Congress the power to employ this same procedure against firms using the mails to deal in obscenity.[11] One of the initial actions under the new statute was against a company issuing nudist magazines. All mail to the company was stopped, designated unlawful, and returned to senders. The Court of Appeals for the District of Columbia ruled that the Post Office could lawfully issue a stop order only against mail addressed to the company which was directly connected with the specific issues found obscene. The court admitted that such a limitation might not be "practically possible," but the important point was that "there is and can be no finding now that any particular future issue of the . . . magazines will be obscene. . . . To let the present orders stand would permit the Postmaster General to prevent—in practical effect—the continued publication of a magazine without any advance knowledge that its future issues will be in violation of law, and thus to suppress putatively lawful activities." The Supreme Court refused to review this decision on certiorari.[12]

SECOND-CLASS PRIVILEGES   The third type of Post Office prior restraint relates to the granting of second-class mailing privileges. The circulation of publications carried at second-class rates is in effect subsidized by the government, for the rates are much less than the third-class rates which would otherwise have to be paid. Thus second-class mailing privileges are absolutely essential if a periodical publication is to compete successfully in its field.

Originally a publication which sought to secure second-class rates had to meet two tests—that it be regularly issued at stated intervals, and that it be published for dissemination of information of a public character. In 1912 Congress required all periodical publications to file with the Post Office a statement showing their officers and ownership and, for daily newspapers, the average number of copies sold. Moreover, all reading matter for the publication of which money was accepted was required to be plainly marked "advertisement." In 1913 this statute was attacked as a restriction of the freedom of the press "thinly disguised as a regulation of the mails." The Supreme Court, however, ruled that the requirement was a justifiable incident of the valuable second-class privilege given to publishers.[13]

During the first World War the power over second-class privileges was one of two weapons used to effect, with Supreme Court approval, a blatant censorship of the press. The second weapon was the Espionage Act of 1917, one entire title of which was devoted to use of the mails. It provided that any newspaper published in violation of any of the provisions of the act would

[11] 64 Stat. 451 (1950).
[12] *Summerfield* v. *Sunshine Book Co.* (1955).
[13] *Lewis Publishing Co.* v. *Morgan* (1913).

be nonmailable. The law was promptly applied to *The Masses*, a revolutionary antiwar monthly journal, its August, 1917, issue being excluded from the mails.[14] Postmaster General Burleson then refused to grant the September or any future issues second-class privileges, on the ground that since the magazine had skipped the August number, it was no longer a periodical, since it was not regularly issued!

This same one-two punch, as administered to a Socialist paper published by Victor Berger, the *Milwaukee Leader*, was upheld by the Supreme Court in *Milwaukee Publishing Co.* v. *Burleson* (1921). Justice Clarke for the majority took the position that second-class rates were a privilege withdrawable by the Postmaster General when a publication failed to conform to the law. Justice Brandeis thought this power would make the Postmaster General "the universal censor of publications," and Justice Holmes added: "The United States may give up the Post Office when it sees fit, but while it carries it on the use of the mails is almost as much a part of free speech as the right to use our tongues, and it would take very strong language to convince me that Congress ever intended to give such a practically despotic power to any one man."

These protests proved ineffective, and again in World War II precisely the same technique was employed. During the first year of the war, seventy newspapers and other publications were barred from the mails in this way under authority of the revived Espionage Act. In fields unrelated to national security, however, some support for the Holmes-Brandeis position on the powers of the Postmaster General with respect to second-class mail was given by the Supreme Court's 1946 decision in *Hannegan* v. *Esquire*. Postmaster General Walker sought to withdraw second-class privileges from *Esquire*, on the ground that the magazine did not meet the statutory test of being "published for the dissemination of information of a public character, or devoted to literature, the sciences, arts, or some special industry." He argued that the material in *Esquire*, although not obscene in a technical sense, was so close to it that it was "morally improper and not for the public welfare and the public good."

A unanimous Supreme Court held that Congress had not meant to grant the Postmaster General rights of censorship when it attached these conditions to the second-class privilege. Under the statute he was limited to determining whether a publication "contains information of a public character, literature or art"; he was not granted "the further power to determine whether the contents meet some standard of the public good or welfare." The Holmes-Brandeis dissent in *Milwaukee Publishing Co.* was noted, with the comment: "Grave constitutional questions are immediately raised once it is said that the use of the mails is a privilege which may be extended or withheld on any grounds whatsoever."

[14] *Masses Publishing Co.* v. *Patten* (1917).

The same Holmes-Brandeis dissent was quoted with approval by the Court in the 1965 *Lamont* case. It may be, then, that the Court has finally come around to the view that "the use of the mails is almost as much a part of free speech as the right to use our tongues." But it is doubtful whether this position is yet shared by Congress or the Post Office.[15]

### FREE PRESS AND FAIR TRIAL

A free press problem of increasing importance and difficulty relates to the right of newspapers to publish information and comment about current criminal proceedings. The right to a fair trial, as will be discussed in more detail in Chapter 30, includes among other features the right to trial by an unbiased jury. A fair trial requires that the judge and jury make their judgments solely on the basis of the evidence introduced in the courtroom, and of course they must be subjected to no outside pressures in reaching their decisions.

The American tradition of press freedom has given newspapers complete freedom to report the facts of criminal investigations and prosecutions. From the time a crime is committed, newspapers undertake to publish every bit of information they can secure concerning the crime and the criminal, usually with the cooperation of the police and prosecutors. They recount the evidence and the previous criminal record, if any, of the suspect. In particularly gruesome crimes, the press may whip up feeling against the person charged. "Trial by newspaper" may be so complete and effective that the task of securing a jury which has not prejudged the case becomes very difficult. Occasionally a newspaper will go so far as to attempt to exert editorial pressure on the judge or jury while the case is still being tried.

In such a situation there is a fundamental conflict between two constitutional rights—a fair trial and a free press. The basic justification for freedom of the press is that untrammeled public discussion and expression of all conceivable views offers the best chance of achieving truth and wisdom. Public policy making must be subjected to the influence of popular pressures. But in a trial at law the purpose is to safeguard the proceedings as fully as possible *from* popular pressures. The whole judicial apparatus is aimed at limiting a jury or judge to consideration of relevant and probative facts bearing on the controversy. Admittedly there is and must be popular interest in and discussion of the way the judicial function is performed. But while a case is pending in court the public interest in the evenhanded administration of

---

[15] In 1965 a Senate committee became considerably perturbed when it discovered that the Post Office had "mail covers" on some twenty-four thousand persons at the request of various investigative agencies. Their mail was not opened, but the return addresses and any other information on the outside of the mail was recorded. The committee took no action, but the Postmaster General agreed to tighten up and centralize controls over the use of mail covers.

justice requires that the judge and jury be subject to no dictates or pressures but those of their own judgment and consciences.

THE CONTEMPT POWER    The power of judges to punish for contempt, which was examined in Chapter 7, is the principal instrument by which a judge can protect proceedings in his court from newspaper pressure. However, American judges are seriously limited in their use of the contempt power to restrain out-of-court comments about current court proceedings. The English practice is much more restrictive in this connection than the American. Only the barest facts may be published in England concerning a pending prosecution, and anything remotely smacking of comment on the case would lay the offender open to contempt charges. The American tradition, with its great reliance upon elected judges at the state and local level, its rough and ready standards of justice on the frontier, and its general hostility toward restraints, has been much less willing to concede the immunity of judicial proceedings from outside comment. In addition, summary punishment procedures tend to arouse greater resentment when applied to contempts occurring out of court than when committed in the presence of the court.

These attitudes were reflected in a federal statute adopted in 1831 which forbade summary punishments except in the case of misbehavior in the presence of the court, "or so near thereto as to obstruct the administration of justice." This act effected a substantial limitation on the contempt power, but near the turn of the century some federal district courts again undertook summary punishment for publications. The Supreme Court gave approval to this trend in *Toledo Newspaper Co.* v. *United States* (1918), holding that a newspaper publishing objectionable comments about a judge and his conduct of pending litigation was "so near thereto" as to justify summary punishment.[16] Justice Holmes, dissenting with Brandeis, denied that there had been any obstruction of justice, saying: "I think that 'so near as to obstruct' means so near as actually to obstruct—and not merely near enough to threaten a possible obstruction." He added that "a judge of the United States is expected to be a man of ordinary firmness of character."

The *Toledo* decision was overruled in 1941 by *Nye* v. *United States* as the Court adopted the Holmes position that "so near thereto" means physical proximity. Consequently newspapers are protected by statute from summary punishment for comments on federal judicial decisions.

So far as state courts are concerned, the freedom of newspapers from contempt prosecutions derives from the Fourteenth Amendment and the Supreme Court's decision in *Bridges* v. *California* (1941). A radical labor leader, Harry Bridges, and a conservative, labor-baiting newspaper, the *Los Angeles Times,* had with unique impartiality been brought to book for

---

[16] See also *Craig* v. *Hecht* (1923).

contempt. The newspaper was cited by a California judge who was trying a case involving assault by labor union members on nonunion truck drivers. At a time when the defendants had been found guilty, but not yet sentenced, the *Times* said editorially: "Judge A. A. Scott will make a serious mistake if he grants probation to Matthew Shannon and Kennan Holmes. This community needs the example of their assignment to the jute-mill." As for Harry Bridges, while a motion for a new trial was pending in a case involving a dispute between an AFL and a CIO union, he sent a telegram to the United States Secretary of Labor calling the judge's decision "outrageous," threatened that an attempt to enforce it would tie up the entire Pacific Coast, and warned that his union did "not intend to allow state courts to override the majority vote" in NLRB elections.

The Supreme Court reversed both contempt citations by a narrow five to four margin. Justice Black for the majority held there would have to be "a clear and present danger" that such comments would obstruct justice in order for the contempt citations to be justified. The majority saw no such threat. The antilabor position of the paper was well known in the community. The Bridges telegram was simply a statement that if the court's decree was enforced there would be a strike. Such a strike would not have been unlawful, and presumably the judge was not "unaware of the possibility of a strike as a consequence of his decision." Moreover, the telegram was to the Secretary of Labor, who has official responsibility for prevention of strikes and is entitled to all available information about their occurrence. To accept the possibility that such publications would in themselves have a "substantial influence upon the course of justice would be to impute to judges a lack of firmness, wisdom, or honor,—which we cannot accept as a major premise."

As already noted, Justice Frankfurter made a strong attack on the application of the clear and present danger test in these circumstances. Holmes had no thought of using it for such a purpose, he contended.

> A trial is not a "free trade in ideas," nor is the best test of truth in a courtroom "the power of the thought to get itself accepted in the competition of the market." A court is a forum with strictly defined limits for discussion. . . . We cannot read into the Fourteenth Amendment the freedom of speech and of the press protected by the First Amendment and at the same time read out age-old means employed by states for securing the calm course of justice. . . . To assure the impartial accomplishment of justice is not an abridgment of freedom of speech or freedom of the press. . . . In fact, these liberties themselves depend upon an untrammeled judiciary whose passions are not even unconsciously aroused and whose minds are not distorted by extrajudicial considerations.

This argument was continued in two subsequent cases, *Pennekamp* v. *Florida* (1946) and *Craig* v. *Harney* (1947), both of which freed newspapers

from contempt charges.[17] By this line of decisions, Justices Jackson and Frankfurter charged in *Shepherd* v. *Florida* (1951), the Supreme Court had "gone a long way to disable a trial judge from dealing with press interference with the trial process." Louis L. Jaffe, making the same point, said that this series of decisions "has licensed the press to criticize and abuse judges engaged in the decision of lawsuits." [18]

PRETRIAL PUBLICITY    While the Supreme Court has maintained these limitations on the judicial contempt power vis-à-vis the press, it has subsequently come to share the Frankfurter-Jackson concern about "trial by newspaper," particularly the publication of information during the pretrial period. The Court was first confronted with this situation in *Maryland* v. *Baltimore Radio Show* (1950). A state judge had held a radio station in contempt for broadcasting news of the arrest, confession, and past criminal record of a man accused of the brutal murder of an eleven-year-old girl. Because of these public revelations, counsel for the accused felt compelled to waive a jury trial. When the state appellate court reversed the contempt citation, the Supreme Court declined to grant certiorari, an action which so shocked Justice Frankfurter that he wrote a long opinion pointing out that refusal to grant certiorari was not the equivalent of an affirmance.

The Court continued for another decade its disinclination to apply constitutional controls to pretrial publicity. In *Stroble* v. *California* (1952) a confession by the killer of a six-year-old girl was made public with the participation of the prosecutor, and the press branded the man as a "werewolf," but the Court affirmed the conviction.

Not until 1961, in *Irvin* v. *Dowd*, did the Court reverse a state conviction because of pretrial publicity. Here the defendant was a man accused of six murders, whose confession had been issued by the police in press releases which were intensively publicized. Because of the popular indignation generated by the publicity, one change of venue to an adjoining county was granted, but feeling was high there also, and a second change was refused. Convincing evidence of prejudice against the defendant was demonstrated when it took four weeks to select the jury from a panel of 430, of whom 268 had to be excused because of fixed opinions of guilt. Eight of the twelve jurors selected, though claiming not to have fixed opinions, thought the defendant was guilty. The Supreme Court unanimously concluded: "With his life at stake, it is not requiring too much that petitioner be tried in an

---

[17] The more recent Court has followed the same policy of protecting out-of-court comments. In *Wood* v. *Georgia* (1962) a sheriff who had issued to the press very critical statements concerning certain actions by the judges of the county court was freed from a contempt citation on the ground that his comments had not presented any clear and present danger to the administration of justice.

[18] Louis L. Jaffe, "Trial by Newspapers," 40 *New York University Law Review* 504 (1965).

atmosphere undisturbed by so huge a wave of public passion and by a jury other than one in which two thirds of the members admit, before hearing any testimony, to possessing a belief in his guilt."

In *Rideau* v. *Louisiana* (1963) the pretrial publicity was compounded by television. A man accused of murder made a confession, which he subsequently repeated in a filmed television "interview" with the sheriff. The film was shown three times on the local television station; three of the members of the jury which tried him two months later had seen the film. The Supreme Court reversed the conviction on the ground that a change of venue should have been granted so that the jury could have been drawn "from a community of people who had not seen and heard Rideau's televised 'interview.'"

PROBLEMS IN THE CONDUCT OF THE TRIAL    The Court's most recent consideration of the fair-trial problem has involved press activity or other publicity during the trial itself as well as in the pretrial period. *Estes* v. *Texas* (1965) brought before the Court the nationally publicized prosecution for swindling of Billie Sol Estes. The principal issue was the televising of the actual courtroom proceedings. At a two-day pretrial hearing in the case there was live television, radio coverage, and news photography throughout the hearings. At least twelve cameramen operated in the courtroom, cables and wires were snaked across the floor, three microphones were on the judge's bench, and others were beamed at the jury box and counsel table. Admittedly all this activity led to considerable disruption of the hearings.

As a result, changes were made in the arrangements when the case was called for trial. A booth had been constructed at the rear of the courtroom from which the television cameras and newsreel photographers operated. Live telecasting was prohibited during a great portion of the actual trial. Excerpts from the proceedings were shown on regular television news broadcasts.

The Supreme Court reversed the conviction because of this television coverage. Noting that forty-eight states and the federal government forbid television of court proceedings, Justice Clark ruled that the practice was inherently prejudicial to a fair trial. First, there was the impact on the jury, which would be distracted, self-conscious, and uneasy under the increased pressure of public attention. Second, witnesses would be equally subject to the strain of knowing they were performing for a vast audience. Moreover, prospective witnesses could watch the proceedings on television and shape their own subsequent testimony in the light of what had gone before.

Third, television places added responsibilities on the trial judge simply in terms of supervising the physical arrangements, while the temptations such coverage offers to ambitious judges who are elected to their posts are obvious. Fourth, the effect on the defendant "is a form of mental—if not

physical—harassment, resembling a police line-up or the third degree." Justice Clark concluded: "A defendant on trial for a specific crime is entitled to his day in court, not in a stadium, or a city or nationwide arena. The heightened public clamor resulting from radio and television coverage will inevitably result in prejudice. Trial by television is, therefore, foreign to our system."

A minor point in the opinion concerned the charge that television was being discriminated against in favor of newspapers if it was excluded from the courtroom. Justice Clark responded that the reporters for all the communications media were being treated alike. All had access to the courtroom, but none could bring their equipment. The newspaperman could not bring his typewriter or printing press; the television reporter could not bring his camera.

Chief Justice Warren wrote a concurring opinion, in which he forecast the disintegration of the trial process "if the television industry and trial judges were allowed to become partners in the staging of criminal proceedings." Trials would be scheduled for a time to catch the biggest television audience. Recesses would be called to permit station breaks and commercials. Judges might compete in developing interesting mannerisms that would heighten the appeal of their trials and get better ratings. The Chief Justice summed up: "The sense of fairness, dignity and integrity that all associate with the courtroom would become lost with its commercialization. . . . The television camera, like other technological innovations, is not entitled to pervade the lives of everyone in disregard of constitutionally protected rights."

The case of *Sheppard* v. *Maxwell* (1966) grew out of the scandalous press involvement in the nationally famous trial of Dr. Sam Sheppard for the murder of his wife. One Cleveland newspaper in particular conducted a campaign to cast suspicion on Sheppard, to get him indicted, and to convict him in the eyes of the public. Every action in the case took place in a carnival of publicity. The coroner's inquest was held in a school gymnasium with live broadcasting. When Sheppard was brought in to the city hall under arrest, scores of newscasters, photographers, and reporters were awaiting his arrival. In the courtroom three of the four rows of benches were assigned to the communications media, and a press table was even erected inside the bar of the court, so close to Sheppard that he could not consult with his lawyers without being overheard.

A radio station set up broadcasting facilities next door to the jury room, and a debate about the trial was aired on the radio while the jury was being selected. There was a staged television interview with the judge as he entered the courthouse on one occasion. On the first day of the trial, the jury viewed the scene of the murder in company with hundreds of reporters and onlookers, and one newspaper rented a helicopter and flew over the

house while the jurors were there. The jurors were subjected to constant publicity; their pictures appeared in Cleveland newspapers more than forty times.

The Supreme Court was appalled by this travesty. Justice Clark said: "The fact is that bedlam reigned at the courthouse during the trial and newsmen took over practically the entire courtroom, hounding most of the participants in the trial, especially Sheppard." The news media "inflamed and prejudiced the public." Much of the responsibility for this sorry state of affairs rested on the trial judge, Clark charged, noting that both the judge and prosecutor were candidates for judgeships in an election held two weeks after the trial started.

What could the judge have done to prevent this trial from turning into a carnival, without challenging the freedom of the press? First, Clark thought, he should have adopted stricter rules governing the use of the courtroom by newsmen. Their number should have been limited, and their conduct more closely regulated. (They even handled exhibits lying on the counsel table during recesses.) Second, the judge should have "insulated" the witnesses; instead they were interviewed at will by newsmen. Third, "the court should have made some effort to control the release of leads, information and gossip to the press by police officers, witnesses, and the counsel for both sides." The prosecution repeatedly made alleged "evidence" available to the news media which was never offered in the trial. As for the highly distorted reports of the trial in the papers, Clark thought the judge "should have at least warned the newspapers to check the accuracy of their accounts." Because the trial judge "did not fulfill his duty to protect Sheppard from the inherently prejudicial publicity which saturated the community and to control disruptive influences in the courtroom," the Supreme Court ordered Sheppard to be tried again or released.

The deplorable conduct of the press tolerated by the judge during the Sheppard trial, and by the Dallas police after the assassination of President Kennedy, is fortunately exceptional. But there is increasing concern that even the ordinary routines of American newsgathering and publishing may be inconsistent with the right to a fair trial.

Two notable reports have been made on the problem by the organized bar. In 1966 the American Bar Association published the Reardon report proposing rules which would limit statements for dissemination to the public on pending criminal cases by lawyers, court attachés, and law-enforcement officers. From the time of arrest or filing of a charge until the end of the trial, information could not be released outside of court on such matters as prior criminal record, existence or contents of any confession, performance of examinations, identity of prospective witnesses, or possible guilt or innocence. These rules would be made effective as to lawyers through the ABA Canons of Professional Ethics, enforceable by disciplinary proceedings, and as to law-enforcement agencies by internal regulations. On

the touchy question of enforcement against the press, the ABA committee recommended use of the contempt power in limited instances while cases were actually on trial.

In 1967 a committee of the Association of the Bar of the City of New York, under Judge Harold R. Medina, issued a report which likewise proposed a drastic tightening of the Canons of Professional Ethics to halt the flow of prejudicial publicity by lawyers in criminal cases, but took the position that the courts were powerless to impose direct controls on the news media or the police. Instead, the Medina committee urged that strict voluntary codes be adopted by the police and the press in reporting crime news.

The American Newspaper Publishers Association responded with a sharp attack on these proposals. They contended that any interference with news sources concerning criminal investigations and prosecutions would be censorship and that a free press requires not only freedom to print without prior restraint but also free and uninhibited access to information. They denied that pretrial and intrial reporting had any real bearing on the outcome of criminal cases, and contended that the press was actually a positive influence in assuring a fair trial.

Though a consensus of those most immediately concerned thus seems unlikely, the Supreme Court decisions just reviewed have had a rather immediate impact, as many police departments and prosecutors throughout the country have begun to adopt self-limitations on the information released about pending cases. Moreover, the warning of the *Sheppard* case led many judges to take steps toward stricter control of trials. When Sheppard himself was retried in 1966, only fourteen newsmen were admitted to the courtroom and all interviews with participants were banned. In the notorious 1967 Speck murder trial in Illinois, the state supreme court upheld the trial judge's order that prospective jurors could not be named in the press until they were excused or sworn and sequestered, and a reporter who violated this rule was barred from the courtroom.[19]

[19] *The New York Times*, March 2, 1967. On February 19, 1968, the American Bar Association adopted the Reardon report, which has the following results: (1) makes it unethical for any prosecutor or defense lawyer to tell the press anything about a pending case except basic identifying facts; (2) urges police departments to impose similar restrictions on their members, and calls on judges to use their contempt powers to enforce the restrictions on both lawyers and police; (3) calls on courts to adopt judicial standards aimed at securing fairer trials; and (4) proposes that judges use their contempt power to punish newsmen if they publish articles during the course of a trial that are willfully designed to affect the outcome. This action was taken against the protest of the news organizations. *The New York Times*, February 20, 1968.

### SELECTED REFERENCES

AMERICAN BAR ASSOCIATION, *Fair Trial and Free Press.* Chicago: American Bar Association, 1966 (mimeographed).

AMERICAN NEWSPAPER PUBLISHERS ASSOCIATION, *Free Press and Fair Trial.* New York: American Newspaper Publishers Association, 1967.

BERNS, WALTER, *Freedom, Virtue and the First Amendment,* chaps. 1–3. Baton Rouge, La.: Louisiana State University Press, 1957.

COMMISSION ON FREEDOM OF THE PRESS, *A Free and Responsible Press.* Chicago: The University of Chicago Press, 1947.

COWEN, ZELMAN, and others, *Fair Trial vs. a Free Press.* Santa Barbara, Calif.: Center for the Study of Democratic Institutions, 1965.

FELSHER, HOWARD, and MICHAEL ROSEN, *The Press in the Jury Box.* New York: The Macmillan Company, 1966.

"Free Speech vs. Fair Trial in the English and American Law of Contempt by Publication," 17 *University of Chicago Law Review* 540–553 (1950).

FRIENDLY, ALFRED, and RONALD L. GOLDFARB, *Crime and Publicity.* New York: The Twentieth Century Fund, 1967.

GERALD, J. EDWARD, *The Press and the Constitution, 1931–1947.* Minneapolis: The University of Minnesota Press, 1948.

GILLMOR, DONALD M., *Free Press and Fair Trial.* Washington, D.C.: Public Affairs Press, 1966.

GOLDFARB, RONALD L., *The Contempt Power.* New York: Columbia University Press, 1963.

———, "Public Information, Criminal Trials and the Cause Celebre," 36 *New York University Law Review* 810–838 (1961).

JAFFE, LOUIS L., "Trial by Newspapers," 40 *New York University Law Review* 504–524 (1965).

MEDINA, HAROLD R., *Freedom of the Press and Fair Trial.* New York: Columbia University Press, 1967.

MUELLER, GERHARD O. W., "Problems Posed by Publicity to Crime and Criminal Proceedings," 110 *University of Pennsylvania Law Review* 1 (1961).

SPECIAL COMMITTEE ON RADIO AND TELEVISION OF THE ASSOCIATION OF THE BAR OF THE CITY OF NEW YORK, *Radio, Television, and the Administration of Justice: A Documented Survey of Materials.* New York: Columbia University Press, 1965.

THAYER, FRANK, *Legal Control of the Press.* Brooklyn, N.Y.: The Foundation Press, Inc., 1962.

# 23

## Restraint of speech and assembly

In turning from censorship of the press to consider prior restraints on speech, we should bear in mind the different social settings within which these two communications processes operate. Communication via the printed page is essentially a private affair. Even on a crowded subway car, the newspaper readers—as readers—are isolated from each other; they are engaged in no collective experience. The reader makes no noise; he creates no disturbance; he causes no problems.

Communication by speech, on the other hand, is by definition a social experience, which must involve the interaction of at least two persons. Here is the beginning of a community interest in the speech process. Suppose two persons are discussing politics in a private home. Certainly there is no case for governmental restraint here. But wait! What if the discussion becomes an argument and voices are raised, to the annoyance of neighbors? Or suppose one of the discussants applies offensive language to the other, who resents it and starts a brawl? Suppose a weapon is drawn? At some point along the way a speech situation in which the government could have no interest has turned into a matter justifying public intervention, and all this with only two participants.

As we increase the number of discussants and move them from a private to a public location, the opportunities for public intervention are multiplied. Suppose an unpopular group wants to meet in a public school auditorium.

Suppose demonstrators convene in a public park or parade on a public street, thereby creating traffic problems and making it likely that persons unsympathetic to the demonstrators will happen by and be tempted to display their opposition. Suppose that loudspeakers being used at an outdoor meeting annoy by their noise, regardless of the words used, other members of the public rightfully in the area.

Obviously there is no end to the complications that can arise in a speech situation as we move out from a constitutionally protected core into areas where preservation of speech rights must compete with other allowable public interests. Justice Jackson has well contrasted the social settings of printing and speaking:

> Written words are less apt to incite or provoke to mass action than spoken words, speech being the primitive and direct communication with the emotions. Few are the riots caused by publication alone, few are the mobs that have not had their immediate origin in harangue. The vulnerability of various forms of communication to community control must be proportioned to their impact upon other community interests.[1]

These are considerations to be kept in mind as we turn to consider various judicial analyses of the application of previous restraints to speech and assembly situations.


### SPEECH IN THE PUBLIC FORUM

Clearly, private meetings are entitled to the utmost protection under principles of freedom of speech and assembly. The forum is private, listeners are in voluntary attendance, and those who disapprove of what is being said can leave. But what is the situation when *public* facilities—the streets, the parks, or a publicly owned meeting hall—are used for meetings or demonstrations?

The point of departure for judicial consideration of this problem is an opinion written by Justice Holmes in 1895 when he was on the Massachusetts supreme court, *Commonwealth* v. *Davis*, the principles of which were subsequently adopted by the United States Supreme Court.[2] A Boston ordinance required a permit from the mayor for any persons to "make any public address, discharge any cannon or firearm, expose for sale any goods" on Boston Common. Holmes approved the ordinance in a most positive fashion. It was not "directed against free speech generally," he said, but only "toward the modes in which Boston Common may be used." A legislature

> . . . as representative of the public . . . may and does exercise control over the use the public may make of such places. . . . For the Legislature absolutely or conditionally to forbid public speaking in a highway or public park is no more an infringement of the rights of a member of the public than for the owner of a private house to forbid it

[1] *Kunz* v. *New York* (1951).
[2] *Davis* v. *Massachusetts* (1897).

in his house. . . . The Legislature may end the right of the public to enter upon the public place by putting an end to the dedication to public uses. So it may take the lesser step of limiting the public use to certain purposes.

It is instructive to compare this view with that which Holmes later took concerning the Post Office in the *Milwaukee Publishing Co.* case. It will be recalled that there he said the government could give up the Post Office at any time, but so long as it was operated, free speech applied to it. In 1895, however, he was contending that, since Boston Common could be closed to the public entirely, any lesser restriction on public use was necessarily valid. The obviously dubious analogy between a private house and a public park was even more remarkable.

This early Holmes ruling had to be distinguished or disregarded as dictum when the Supreme Court in the 1930s and 1940s began seriously to consider the constitutional status of meetings in public places. *Hague* v. *C.I.O.* (1939), the first such encounter, grew out of a Jersey City ordinance which prohibited assemblies "in or upon the public streets, highways, public parks or public buildings" without a permit from the director of public safety. Under Mayor Hague, who became famous for his boast, "I am the law," the CIO was denied use of public halls in Jersey City on the ground that it was a Communist organization. Members of the CIO were searched when coming into the city, were threatened with arrest if they discussed the Wagner Act, were arrested for distributing printed matter, and were forcibly ejected from the city and put on the boat for New York.

The Supreme Court by a five to two vote held that these invasions of liberty could not be defended as valid police regulations. "Wherever the title of street and parks may rest," wrote Justice Roberts, "they have immemorially been held in trust for the use of the public and time out of mind have been used for the purpose of assembly, communicating thoughts between citizens and discussing public questions." Their use for communication of views on national questions may be regulated in the interests of all, but may not, in the guise of regulations, be abridged or denied.

So it was established that individuals and groups have a right of access to the public forum for discussion of public issues. As Justice Black put it, "One who is rightfully on a street . . . carries with him there as elsewhere the constitutional right to express his views in an orderly fashion." [3] This means that speakers can mount soapboxes on street corners, or address groups in public parks. But it does not follow that their access to the public forum is an absolute right beyond restraint or regulation in the public interest. After all, sidewalks, streets, and parks serve other purposes in addition to communication. In an effort to accommodate and reconcile these conflicting interests, legislatures and city councils have rather generally provided

[3] *Jamison* v. *Texas* (1943).

for some form of restraint on access to the public forum, thereby creating potential First Amendment problems.

## "PURE SPEECH" VERSUS "SPEECH PLUS"

Since, as Justice Jackson says, "the vulnerability of various forms of communication to community control must be proportioned to their impact upon other community interests," some classification of forms of communication with reference to their impact on other legitimate interests should be helpful in determining what controls are constitutionally "proportioned" to this impact.

In fact, the Supreme Court has attempted a classification of this kind in the distinction it has made between "pure speech" and "speech plus." In *Cox* v. *Louisiana* (1965) Justice Goldberg speaks of those "who communicate ideas by pure speech," as contrasted with those "who would communicate ideas by conduct such as patrolling, marching, and picketing on streets and highways." Again in the same opinion he refers to "speech in its pristine form." Pure speech would include, we can assume, communication taking place by the spoken word in face-to-face contacts, addresses or remarks at meetings, speech amplified by mechanical means or on the channels of the various communications media. Pure speech can range from dull expositions to the most emotional harangues. The distinctive qualities of pure speech are that it relies for its effect only on the power of the ideas or emotions that are communicated by speech and that usually the audience is a voluntary one which chooses to listen to the speaker's message.

The idea of "speech plus" was first developed by the Supreme Court in its labor picketing decisions, to take account of the fact that picketing is more than speech. In the 1940 case of *Thornhill* v. *Alabama* the Court broadly assimilated peaceful picketing to freedom of speech, and so protected it by the First Amendment against abridgement. But very soon the Court concluded that this was a partially incorrect conception of picketing, and began to qualify this position. As Justice Douglas said in a 1942 decision: "Picketing by an organized group is more than free speech, since it involves patrol of a particular locality and since the very presence of a picket line may induce action of one kind or another, quite irrespective of the nature of the ideas which are being disseminated." [4]

Justice Harlan used the phrase "speech plus" in *NAACP* v. *Button* (1963). The Court in that case recognized the type of litigation in which the NAACP has engaged to promote Negro rights as "a form of political expression," and so entitled to constitutional protection. Harlan, not satisfied with this analysis, thought that NAACP litigation, "whether or not associated with the attempt to vindicate constitutional rights, is *conduct;* it is speech *plus.*" Jus-

---

[4] *Bakery and Pastry Drivers Local* v. *Wohl* (1942).

tice Goldberg did not use the phrase in *Cox* v. *Louisiana,* but this is what he meant by the words already quoted, the communication of ideas "by conduct such as patrolling, marching, and picketing on streets and highways."

It would of course be a mistake to regard these two phrases, "pure speech" and "speech plus," as designating well-defined and distinct categories. In fact, Kalven is prepared to challenge the distinction as nonexistent or worthless. He suggests that "all speech is necessarily 'speech plus' [since] it is noise and may interrupt some one else." [5] But there is some value in the two concepts if only because they draw attention to the wide range of speech situations. Perhaps that range and its constitutional consequences might better be suggested by a somewhat different threefold distinction: (1) face-to-face communication; (2) meetings in the public forum; and (3) demonstrations and picketing.

### FACE–TO–FACE COMMUNICATION

Face-to-face discussions by two or more persons in the public forum represent the communications process in its most pristine form and involve almost no threat to any countervailing public values. Persons engaged in such dialogues create no problem because of the noise they make, the bulk of their numbers, interference with the use of streets or sidewalks, or danger to public order. For that reason it is generally inconceivable that any restraints can legitimately be imposed on such small groups. Even in countries threatened with serious civil disorder, where public meetings are banned completely as an emergency measure, gatherings of less than a prescribed number are usually permitted.

Since there can be no basis for prior restraint of these face-to-face sessions, any legislation purporting to limit them would be unconstitutional on its face. There is in fact a Supreme Court holding precisely to this effect. In *Thornhill* v. *Alabama* (1940) a picket at a struck plant approached a nonunion worker who was reporting for work at the plant. The picket and the nonstriker had a brief discussion, which convinced the latter to turn around and go back home. The picket was convicted under a state law which forbade picketing or loitering near a place of business for the purpose of influencing other persons not to work there.

The Supreme Court held this statute unconstitutional on its face. The defense of the act was that it was intended to protect the community from the violence and breaches of the peace which might result from picketing. But the act was not narrowly drawn to cover such evils. It would prohibit a single individual from walking along a public sidewalk in front of a plant carrying a placard giving the facts of a labor dispute there. Such a sweeping

---

[5] Harry Kalven, Jr., "The Concept of the Public Forum," in Philip B. Kurland (ed.), *The Supreme Court Review: 1965* (Chicago: The University of Chicago Press, 1965), p. 23.

proscription of freedom was not justified by the asserted evils, the Court concluded.

## MEETINGS IN THE PUBLIC FORUM

A meeting in the public forum differs from a small face-to-face group in that it is typically planned, involves a larger number of people, and distinguishes between speakers and listeners. Such gatherings inevitably create public problems, which lay the basis for public regulation. If the meeting is in a public hall, permission must be secured to use the hall. If it is held in a public park or on a street corner, the meeting may create policing or traffic problems.

Consequently there is a case for some measure of prior restraint on, or control over, meetings in the public forum, which case could not be made in the case of print or face-to-face communication. Experience has shown that the Supreme Court will accept the constitutionality of permit or licensing systems for speech or assembly in the public forum, provided (1) the licensing is used only for the purpose of giving advance notice of traffic or policing problems, (2) the officials who grant the licenses are controlled by strict standards which will prevent the free play of administrative discretion, and (3) no discrimination is practiced.

A good illustrative decision is *Poulos* v. *New Hampshire* (1953). Under authorization by a state statute the city of Portsmouth set aside one of its small parks for open-air public meetings under a permit system. A group of Jehovah's Witnesses was denied a permit to hold a religious service in the park, and they attacked the licensing requirement as unconstitutional restraint. The state supreme court ruled that the statute required "uniform, nondiscriminatory and consistent administration of the granting of licenses for public meetings" and that the denial of a permit to this group had been arbitrary and unreasonable. The Supreme Court through Justice Reed agreed that as thus interpreted the state permit law was constitutional. He considered it "a nonsequitur to say that First Amendment rights may not be regulated because they hold a preferred position in the hierarchy of the constitutional guarantees of the incidents of freedom. . . . Regulation and suppression are not the same, either in purpose or result, and courts of justice can tell the difference."

But not all licensing regulations have met the Court's tests. In *Niemotko* v. *Maryland* (1951) a group of Jehovah's Witnesses requesting use of a city park for religious services was denied a permit by the city council, after a hearing where the Witnesses were queried about their alleged refusal to salute the flag and their interpretation of the Bible. The Supreme Court concluded that the permit was denied because of dislike for the group's views, and unanimously held such action not only an infringement on freedom of speech but also a denial of equal protection of the laws.

The case of *Kunz* v. *New York* (1951), decided the same day, was more difficult. It grew out of a New York City ordinance making it unlawful to hold public worship meetings on the street without first obtaining a permit from the police commissioner. Kunz, whose custom it was to engage in outdoor preaching, in 1946 applied for and received a permit good for the calendar year. In November, 1946, the permit was revoked after a hearing, on evidence that Kunz had ridiculed and denounced other religious beliefs in his meetings. His applications for 1947 and 1948 were disapproved, no reason being given. When he spoke without a permit in Columbus Circle, he was arrested and fined $10.

For the Court majority, this was unjustifiable prior restraint. The ordinance gave to "an administrative official discretionary power to control in advance the right of citizens to speak on religious matters on the streets of New York," with "no appropriate standards to guide his action." To the argument that Kunz's religious meetings had in the past caused some disorder, the Court replied that "there are appropriate public remedies to protect the peace and order of the community if appellant's speeches should result in disorder or violence."

But Justice Jackson, dissenting, felt it was "quixotic" to give "hateful and hate-stirring attacks on races and faiths" the classic protections of free speech. New York City is a "frightening aggregation" of people all legally free to live, labor, and travel where they please.

> Is it not reasonable that the City protect the dignity of these persons against fanatics who take possession of its streets to hurl into its crowds defamatory epithets that hurt like rocks? . . . If any two subjects are intrinsically incendiary and divisive, they are race and religion. . . . These are the explosives which the Court says Kunz may play with in the public streets, and the community must not only tolerate but aid him. I find no such doctrine in the Constitution.

The principle that a permit may not be denied because of fears that the speaking may lead to violence is now rather well established. In 1960 George Lincoln Rockwell, leader of the American Nazi Party, was refused a permit to speak on July 4 in Union Square, New York City, and a state judge upheld the action, saying that the Bill of Rights did not require "loosing self-confessed advocates of violence upon a community at a time and place where it is inevitable that public disorder and riot will result." [6] However, the state supreme court reversed this decision unanimously, and the United States Supreme Court refused to review the ruling.[7]

Again, a New York City Board of Education refusal to permit a neo-Nazi, anti-Semitic group to use a public school auditorium, on grounds that its proposed meeting "might tend to cause dissension or provoke disorder," was reversed by the city's corporation counsel, who said: "Advanced censorship

[6] *The New York Times,* August 31, 1960.
[7] *Morris* v. *Rockwell* (1961).

of speech content, or previous restraint of the free exercise of speech, based merely on prior occurrences, violates the constitutional guarantees of freedom of speech." [8] A group of "beat" poets who applied for a permit to read poetry in Washington Square Park in New York City were told they would have to submit the manuscripts for approval by the Park Department, which anticipated obscenity in the poems, but this ruling was later reversed by the courts, and the meeting was held.[9]

Sound amplification of speech creates special problems which may be thought to justify regulation. The case of *Saia* v. *New York* (1948) concerned a Jehovah's Witnesses minister who gave lectures at a fixed place in a public park on designated Sundays, using sound equipment mounted on top of his car to reach a wider audience. This city had an ordinance forbidding the use of sound-amplification devices except with the permission of the chief of police. Saia had such a permit, but when it expired, renewal was refused on the ground that there had been complaints. The minister proceeded to use his equipment without a permit, and was convicted for the violation.

Justice Douglas, in a short opinion classically illustrating the absolutist position, held the ordinance unconstitutional on its face as a previous restraint on the right of free speech, with no standards prescribed for the exercise of discretion by the chief of police in using his licensing powers. There might be abuses in the use of loudspeakers but, if so, they would have to be controlled by "narrowly drawn statutes" aimed at those abuses, not by giving a police officer power to deny the use of loudspeakers entirely. People might allege that they were annoyed by noise when they were really objecting to the ideas noisily expressed.

In this conflict between the individual's right to speak and the public's right not to be made miserable, four dissenting justices took the side of the public. Justice Frankfurter pointed out that the park in question was a small one; the loudspeaker was powerful enough to cover a large part of the park and might seriously interfere with the recreational uses to which people wished to put the park. Uncontrolled noise disturbs "the refreshment of mere silence, or meditation, or quiet conversation." Justice Jackson's dissent expressed astonishment that the Constitution could be supposed to prevent municipalities from regulating or prohibiting "the irresponsible introduction of contrivances of this sort into public places."

As it turned out, the Court quickly withdrew from the position taken in the *Saia* decision. *Kovacs* v. *Cooper* (1949) arose out of the operation of a sound truck for the purpose of commenting on a local labor dispute. A city ordinance made it unlawful for sound trucks or similar amplifying devices emitting "loud and raucous" noises to be operated on the public streets. On its face this ordinance was more stringent than the one in *Saia*, for it appeared to be a complete prohibition of sound apparatus.

[8] *The New York Times*, February 16, 1966.
[9] *Ibid.*, August 29, 1966.

In a rather cloudy opinion for a five-judge majority of the Court, however, Justice Reed interpreted the ordinance as prohibiting only "loud and raucous" sound trucks. He stated specifically that "absolute prohibition within municipal limits of all sound amplification, even though reasonably regulated in place, time and volume, is undesirable and probably unconstitutional as an unreasonable interference with normal activities." But, on the other hand, "unrestrained use throughout a municipality of all sound amplifying devices would be intolerable," and the loud and raucous test he accepted as a satisfactory one. Though he saved the ordinance in this fashion, he never did make clear whether a sound truck could be operated in other than a loud and raucous manner. The law on sound trucks has consequently been left in a rather unsatisfactory state by the Supreme Court. However, the Court's recognition of the case against amplified sound suggests that fairly stringent regulations may well be constitutional.[10]

### PICKETING IN LABOR DISPUTES

Picketing and demonstrating differ from public meetings in that they typically involve physical movement of the participants. They rely less upon the persuasive influence of speech and more upon the impact of assembling, marching, and patrolling. Their purpose is to bring a point of view—by signs, slogans, singing, or their mere presence—to the attention of the widest possible public, including those uninterested or even hostile. Demonstrators are likely to seek maximum exposure by going where they will be seen and heard by the most people, which increases the possibility of traffic problems, inconvenience to the public, and breach of the peace.

The extent of the constitutional protection that can be claimed for demonstrations and picketing became a matter of great importance with the civil rights movement of the 1960s, which relied so heavily on these methods of commandeering the public forum. The Supreme Court found itself largely lacking in useful precedents to guide its way through these new dilemmas. There was, however, one substantial body of prior decisions which might have some relevance—those dealing with the right of labor organizations to picket. It should be helpful to look at these opinions, both for comparative purposes and because labor picketing is a substantial First Amendment problem in its own right.

It is not so long since picketing of all kinds was held by the courts to be tortious conduct, and peaceful picketing was regarded as a contradiction in terms. Gradually the view developed that peaceful picketing by strikers who had a direct economic interest to serve might be permitted by the state, but "stranger picketing" remained outside the law. In 1921 the Supreme Court cautiously admitted that "strikers and their sympathizers" might main-

---

[10] For an instance of the use of an antinoise statute to jail a civil rights leader, see *Cox* v. *Louisiana* (1965).

tain one picket "for each point of ingress and egress" at a plant or place of business. Unless severely limited in this way, the Court concluded, picketing "indicated a militant purpose, inconsistent with peaceable persuasion." [11]

It is a long jump from 1921 to 1940, when in the case of *Thornhill* v. *Alabama* Justice Murphy, speaking for a majority of the Court, put peaceful picketing of all kinds under the protection of the free speech clause. Foundations for this development had been laid by Justice Brandeis in the 1937 case of *Senn* v. *Tile Layers' Protective Union,* which arose under a Wisconsin statute authorizing the giving of publicity to labor disputes and making peaceful picketing lawful and nonenjoinable. Justice Brandeis's opinion held that a statute thus protecting stranger picketing was not unconstitutional, and noted:

> Clearly the means which the statute authorizes—picketing and publicity—are not prohibited by the Fourteenth Amendment. Members of a union might, without special statutory authorization by a State, make known the facts of a labor dispute, for freedom of speech is guaranteed by the Federal Constitution. The State may, in the exercise of its police power, regulate the methods and means of publicity as well as the use of public streets. If the end sought by the unions is not forbidden by the Federal Constitution the State may authorize working men to seek to attain it by combining as pickets, just as it permits capitalists and employers to combine in other ways to attain their desired economic ends.

The *Thornhill* case, decided three years later, involved the reverse situation of a state law making peaceful picketing a misdemeanor, which as applied in this instance rendered punishable a mere conversation between a picket on company property and a nonunion worker. The Supreme Court, with only McReynolds dissenting, took the position that the coverage of this statute was so broad as on its face to preclude all practicable and effective methods of enlightening the public as to the facts of a labor dispute. Since "in the circumstances of our times the dissemination of information concerning the facts of a labor dispute must be regarded as within that area of free discussion that is guaranteed by the Constitution," the Court concluded that a statute blocking such dissemination so completely must be adjudged unconstitutional.

That picketing was a form of communication and a method of circulating information Justice Murphy regarded as requiring no proof. But there are other ways of looking at picketing than as a type of speech. It is likely that many people respect picket lines simply to avoid trouble or charges of being antiunion rather than because they are intellectually persuaded by the signs the pickets carry. On many picket lines the purpose is not so much publicity as it is economic coercion. The International Brotherhood of Teamsters can shut off the flow of supplies into an establishment by posting a single picket at each of its truck entrances. Of course, this kind of "signal picketing" is a

[11] *American Steel Foundries* v. *Tri-City Central Trades Council* (1921).

far cry from the circulation of ideas which the First Amendment is intended to protect.

The Murphy opinion did not supply any guidance for taking account of these complexities. It merely held that a state could not flatly prohibit all picketing, because of the communication element therein. It did not consider whether the state would be justified in regulating picketing where the communications process results in, or even seeks, damage to other social values protected by law or the Constitution. The case of *Milk Wagon Drivers Union* v. *Meadowmoor Dairies* (1941) promptly presented such a situation. Here the Court held that the Illinois courts were justified in enjoining all picketing in a labor dispute which had been so marred by past violence that it was believed impossible for future picketing to be maintained on a peaceful basis. But the likelihood of violence was not the only ground on which the Court proved willing to support restrictions on picketing. In *Carpenters and Joiners Union* v. *Ritter's Cafe* (1942), Ritter was having a residence built by nonunion labor, but the pickets were operating around his cafe, a mile away, where the pressure would hurt him more. By a five to four vote the Court ruled that Texas had the right to restrict picketing to the area within which a labor dispute arises.

More important as illustrating the conflict between rights of communication and other lawful social interests were a series of cases beginning in 1949. In each case two elements were essential to the Court's justification of the injunction: (1) that these competing values represented public policy as laid down by competent authorities acting within their legal and constitutional powers; and (2) that these interests were, in fact, of greater social value than the rights of communication which were being restrained. It is instructive to see how these findings were reached in the specific cases.

In the first case, *Giboney* v. *Empire Storage & Ice Co.* (1949), the conflict was with Missouri's law on restraint of trade. A union of retail ice peddlers in Kansas City sought agreements with wholesale ice distributors not to sell to nonunion peddlers. Under state law such agreements were punishable by $5,000 fine and five-year prison terms, plus liability to suit for treble damages by the injured parties. Empire, which refused to sign the agreement or discontinue such sales, was picketed and secured an injunction against the picketing. The union's justification was that a labor dispute existed with the company and that the picketers were publicizing only truthful information in exercise of their rights to free speech.

Speaking through Justice Black, the Court unanimously ruled against the union. As for the first test mentioned above, the constitutionality of antitrust legislation was, of course, well established. On the second point, Black agreed that a state could not abridge fundamental freedoms "to obviate slight inconveniences or annoyances," but he said that Missouri's interest in enforcement of its policy against restraints of trade could not be so classified. The union was attempting to enforce its own policy in violation of that offi-

cially declared by the state; the speech restrained was "an essential and inseparable part of a grave offense against an important public law." Consequently, the First Amendment did not immunize that unlawful conduct from state control.

In the *Giboney* case and several others [12] where the conflict was likewise with a policy laid down by state legislation, the Court's task was comparatively easy. But in *Hughes* v. *Superior Court of California* (1950), the determination of illegal purpose rested on judge-made rather than upon statute law. Here a grocery store, about half of whose customers were Negroes, was picketed by a citizens' group with the demand that the store's employees be in proportion to the racial origin of the customers. An injunction against the picketing was upheld by the California supreme court on the ground that the picketing, though peaceful, was for an unlawful purpose—"to demand discriminatory hiring on a racial basis." The court assumed, without deciding the question, that if discrimination in employment did exist, "picketing to protest it would not be for an unlawful objective"; but here the picketers were demanding that employment be based on race and color rather than on individual qualifications, and this was contrary to California's public policy.

Justice Frankfurter, approving this position for a unanimous Court, said it was immaterial that the state policy on this point was expressed by the judicial organ rather than by the legislature. California was free to strike at the evils inherent in a "quota system" of employment by means of a limited injunction rather than by statute law. Justices Black, Minton, and Reed concurred on the basis of the *Giboney* case rather than on the basis of Frankfurter's reasoning.

This indication of differing views grew into full-fledged dissent in the next and most difficult picketing case which the Vinson Court had to decide, *International Brotherhood of Teamsters* v. *Hanke* (1950). The facts were that two used-car businesses in Seattle, operated by their owners without employees, were picketed to enforce a demand that they become union shops. The union was seeking to set up a schedule whereby used-car dealers would be closed evenings and on weekends, and these two self-employers contended they could not afford to operate on this basis. The state courts, in enjoining the picketing, were apparently impressed by the fact that all but 10 of the 115 used-car dealers in Seattle were self-employers, and concluded: "The union's interest in the welfare of a mere handful of members . . . is far outweighed by the interests of individual proprietors and the people of the community as a whole, to the end that little businessmen and property owners shall be free from dictation as to business policy by an outside group having but a relatively small and indirect interest in such policy."

What distinguishes this case from the preceding ones is that the union in

[12] *Building Service Employees Union* v. *Gazzam* (1950); *Local Union No. 10* v. *Graham* (1953).

its picketing was not making an unlawful demand. If Hanke had entered into the contract which the union was demanding, it would presumably have been enforced by the state courts. Thus the injunction was based simply on court disapproval of the union's objectives. Nevertheless, Justice Frankfurter in a four to three decision upheld the injunction on the ground that Washington was free to strike a balance between competing economic interests and that the balance here achieved was not "so inconsistent with rooted traditions of a free people that it must be found an unconstitutional choice."

The *Hanke* principle was reiterated by a five to three vote in *International Brotherhood of Teamsters, Local 695* v. *Vogt* (1957), where pickets had sought to coerce an employer to coerce his employees into joining the union. The principle, as Frankfurter restated it, is that there is "a broad field in which a State, in enforcing some public policy, whether of its criminal or its civil law, and whether announced by its legislature or its courts, [can] constitutionally enjoin peaceful picketing aimed at preventing effectuation of that policy." The only limitation Frankfurter indicated on this broad field was that "blanket prohibitions against picketing" could not be enacted. Douglas, dissenting along with Warren and Black, contended that the proper test of state power was the much more stringent one announced in *Giboney*—"that this form of expression can be regulated or prohibited only to the extent that it forms an essential part of a course of conduct which the State can regulate or prohibit."

These later decisions justify the conclusion that the *Thornhill* principle has now been confined to its narrowest limits, namely, invalidation only of flat restraints against all picketing, leaving legislatures and judges largely free to define public purposes which may override picketing rights. As Justice Frankfurter has summarized the situation: "Picketing, not being the equivalent of speech as a matter of fact, is not its inevitable legal equivalent. Picketing is not beyond the control of a State if the manner in which picketing is conducted or the purpose which it seeks to effectuate gives ground for its disallowance." [13] Kalven has commented that "the state is about as free to regulate [picketing] today as it would have been had the free-speech metaphor never been employed in *Thornhill*." [14]

## PUBLIC DEMONSTRATIONS

Insofar as the constitutional law of labor picketing is relevant for political demonstrations, it suggests that very substantial restraints can be imposed on demonstrations. Actually, there are important differences between the two forms of persuasion. The economic coercion and the moral persuasion

[13] *Hughes* v. *Superior Court of California* (1950).
[14] Harry Kalven, Jr., *The Negro and the First Amendment* (Columbus, Ohio: Ohio State University Press, 1965), p. 134.

(the taboo on crossing a picket line) of labor picketing generally have no parallel in political demonstrations. On the other hand, demonstrations often strive for mass impact, with all the public order problems thus created, whereas in efficiently organized industries there is no need to rely on mass picketing for impact.

For the constitutional law of demonstrations we return again to the foundation supplied by *Hague* v. *C.I.O.* (1939) in the statement that the use of the streets and public places "for purposes of assembly, communicating thoughts between citizens, and discussing public questions [is] a part of the privileges, immunities, rights, and liberties of citizens." This language seems clearly to provide a constitutional justification for demonstrations, a conclusion supported by more recent Supreme Court decisions. Thus in *Edwards* v. *South Carolina* (1963) the Court through Justice Stewart characterized a civil rights rally by some two hundred Negro students on the grounds of the South Carolina state capitol as the exercise of "basic constitutional rights in their most pristine and classic form." Again, in *Cox* v. *Louisiana* (1965), where the leader of some two thousand Negro students lining the sidewalk across from the Baton Rouge courthouse was alleged to have made "inflammatory" remarks urging the students to attempt to enter nearby segregated restaurants, Justice Goldberg, speaking for the Court, said that this part of the speech "obviously did not deprive the demonstration of its protected character under the Constitution as free speech and assembly." [15]

An opposing position has been stated by Justice Black, who denies that "speech plus" is speech at all. In the *Cox* case he wrote: "Picketing, though it may be utilized to communicate ideas, is not speech, and therefore is not of itself protected by the First Amendment. . . . Standing, patrolling, or marching back and forth on streets is conduct, not speech, and as conduct can be regulated or prohibited." Consequently Black concluded that a state would have "the general power . . . to bar all picketing on its streets and highways."

---

[15] Draft-card burning is a novel form of political demonstration which began during the Vietnam war. Congress responded by adopting an amendment to the Selective Service Act making it a crime to burn a draft card. The provision was upheld by two courts of appeals, and the Supreme Court denied certiorari in *Miller* v. *United States* (1967). However, in *O'Brien* v. *United States* (1967) the Court of Appeals for the First Circuit held the law unconstitutional, saying: "We would be closing our eyes . . . if we did not see on the face of the amendment that it was precisely directed at public as distinguished from private destruction. In other words, a special offense was committed by persons . . . who made a spectacle of their disobedience. In singling out persons engaged in protest for special treatment, the amendment strikes at the very core of what the First Amendment protects. It has long been beyond doubt that symbolic action may be protected speech." However, the court ruled that persons who burned their draft cards no longer possessed them, as required by law, and could be convicted on that charge. The Supreme Court granted certiorari to review this decision in *United States* v. *O'Brien* (1967).

This is an extreme view which is impossible to reconcile with the Court's previous decisions. As we saw, the *Thornhill* decision linked the right to publicize the facts of labor disputes with the First Amendment, and forbade blanket prohibition of all picketing. Justice Goldberg, author of the opinion for the Court in *Cox* v. *Louisiana,* did not feel it necessary to reply to Black except in a footnote. There he recognized that Justice Jackson had also argued that "a State or municipality could reserve the streets completely for traffic and other facilities for rest and relaxation of the citizenry," but he cited expressions in *Hague, Kunz, Niemotko,* and *Poulos* in support of the contrary position that at least "some open area must be preserved for outdoor assemblies."

The correct constitutional principle, then, is that political demonstrations and picketing are constitutional rights but may be subjected to regulation which fairly endeavors to accommodate both the rights of the demonstrators and the rights of the public. In *Niemotko,* Justice Frankfurter stated the issue as "how to reconcile the interest in allowing free expression in public places with the protection of . . . the primary uses of streets and parks." This is questionable phrasing if it implies that the rights of expression must always be subsidiary to the other uses of the public forum. Justice Goldberg made the fullest statement of the adjustments that constitutional practice will require in *Cox* v. *Louisiana:*

> The rights of free speech and assembly, while fundamental in our democratic society, still do not mean that everyone with opinions or beliefs to express may address a group at any public place and at any time. The constitutional guarantee of liberty implies the existence of an organized society maintaining public order, without which liberty itself would be lost in the excesses of anarchy. The control of travel on the streets is a clear example of governmental responsibility to insure this necessary order. A restriction in that relation, designed to promote the public convenience in the interest of all, and not susceptible to abuses of discriminatory application, cannot be disregarded by the attempted exercise of some civil right which, in other circumstances, would be entitled to protection. One would not be justified in ignoring the familiar red light because this was thought to be a means of social protest. Nor could one, contrary to traffic regulations, insist upon a street meeting in the middle of Times Square at the rush hour as a form of freedom of speech or assembly. Governmental authorities have the duty and responsibility to keep their streets open and available for movement.

PERMIT SYSTEMS     The duty and responsibility of governmental authorities to keep the streets open obviously justifies them in requiring that persons desiring to parade on the streets secure permits. The Court so held in *Cox* v. *New Hampshire* ( 1941 ), where it unanimously approved the conviction of a group of Jehovah's Witnesses who had marched single file along a downtown city street, carrying placards to advertise a meeting, without securing

the special license required by state statute for "parades or processions" on a public street. The statute, which was the same one that the Court later applied in the *Poulos* case, was held to be a reasonable police regulation, administered under proper safeguards. The Court made clear that it was treating the license requirement as merely a traffic regulation and that the conviction was not for conveying information or holding a meeting.

The constitutionality of a permit system can be challenged in two ways. First, the ordinance or statute may be so restrictive, or give such discretionary power to public officials to deny permits, as to be unconstitutional on its face. For example, a city ordinance of Birmingham, Alabama, authorized a city commission to refuse a parade permit if "in its judgment the public welfare, peace, safety, health, decency, good order, morals or convenience require that it be refused." In *Walker* v. *Birmingham* (1967) the Supreme Court was clear that this ordinance was unconstitutional on its face.

Second, the permit regulations, though phrased with due regard for constitutional requirements, may be administered in a discriminatory or repressive fashion. The authorities may deny permits to some groups, or seek to confine parades to remote areas of the city, or find that demonstrations are never compatible with traffic requirements.

INJUNCTIONS   In addition, or as an alternative, to control by permits, demonstrations may be limited by court injunctions. After the open housing marches led by Martin Luther King in Chicago during the summer of 1966 had resulted in widespread violence, the city obtained an injunction preventing King and his associates from marching in more than one area of the city in any one day, having more than 500 persons in a march, marching at night or during traffic rush hours, or holding a march without giving twenty-four hours' notice to the police. Shortly thereafter a federal judge in Chicago enjoined George Lincoln Rockwell and his American Nazi Party from demonstrating in Jewish neighborhoods during the Jewish high holidays. Picketing at a Baltimore high-rise apartment house led a state judge to limit CORE and the Klan to ten pickets each and assign specific sidewalk space for each group. After a state judge in Natchez, Mississippi, had enjoined all civil rights demonstrations, a federal judge modified the order to permit the demonstrators to walk peacefully two abreast on the public sidewalks, observing all traffic signals, and keeping close to the building line or curb.

These are random examples of judicial involvement in control of demonstrations, and they illustrate how a judge can fashion an order to the particular problem before him. In enjoining Governor Wallace from interfering with Martin Luther King's Selma march, Judge Frank Johnson said in *Williams* v. *Wallace* (1965): "[The] extent of the right to assemble, demonstrate and march peaceably along the highways and streets in an orderly manner should be commensurate with the enormity of the wrongs that are being pro-

tested and petitioned against." Judge Johnson regarded the wrongs here as "enormous."

When a permit for a demonstration has been refused or an injunction issued, the demonstrators have two choices. They can go ahead with their demonstration and risk arrest, or they can bring court action to secure review of the ban. In the *Poulos* case, where a permit was denied Jehovah's Witnesses for a religious service in a public park, the meeting was held anyway, and the speaker was arrested. The Supreme Court, though agreeing that the license was wrongfully refused, ruled in a divided opinion that the applicant was obliged to take advantage of the judicial review provided by the licensing statute; having failed to pursue this remedy, he was properly convicted of speaking without a license. The Court admitted that judicial correction of arbitrary administrative action is "exulcerating and costly," but thought that to allow applicants to hold public meetings without prior safety arrangements was apt to cause breaches of the peace or create public dangers.

The Court took the same position by a five to four vote in *Walker* v. *Birmingham* (1967), where Martin Luther King and some of his followers had defied a state court injunction against racial demonstrations while racial tensions were high in Birmingham in 1963. King contended that the injunction denied his constitutional rights, and he feared that his protest movement would lose its momentum if he paused to litigate the injunction. For the majority Justice Stewart admitted that the injunction raised substantial constitutional issues, but held that it should have been challenged in court, not disobeyed. He sympathized with the "impatient commitment" of the civil rights leaders to their cause, but said, "Respect for judicial process is a small price to pay for the civilizing hand of law, which alone can give abiding meaning to constitutional freedom." Justice Brennan for the minority charged that the Court was ignoring the doctrine of constitutional supremacy and raising Alabama's judicial ruling "above the right of free expression guaranteed by the Federal Constitution."

OBSTRUCTION OF PUBLIC PASSAGES    The public interest in keeping streets and sidewalks open for movement can also be protected by legislation addressing itself directly to this problem. A law forbidding the obstruction of public passages was involved in *Cox* v. *Louisiana* (1965). There 2,000 Negro students had assembled in Baton Rouge on the old state capitol grounds a few blocks from the courthouse. Apparently no parade permit had been requested or secured. Police asked the group to disband. Instead, they began an orderly march toward the courthouse, stopping for a traffic light on the way. As they approached the courthouse, the police chief told Cox the demonstration must be confined to the side of the street across from the courthouse.

The demonstrators lined up on this sidewalk about five deep almost the

entire length of the block. They raised picket signs, prayed, and sang patriotic and religious songs. Cox then directed the students to go to the segregated lunch counters of the adjacent stores and have lunch. At this point the sheriff ordered the demonstrators to disperse. When they did not move, tear gas shells were fired at the crowd by the police, and the demonstration quickly broke up. The next day Cox was arrested, one of the charges being violation of a state statute punishing willful obstruction of "the free, convenient, and normal use of any public sidewalk."

The Supreme Court, through Justice Goldberg, agreed that a state or city had the right to assure the safety and convenience of the people in the use of the public sidewalks and also that in this case the demonstrators had obstructed the sidewalk. However, the statute made a specific exception for the picketing and lawful assembly of labor unions. Moreover, it appeared that city officials had in the past permitted other groups to block the streets by their meetings. Consequently the Court majority held the statute invalid because it denied equal protection of the laws and had not been applied in a "uniform, consistent, and nondiscriminatory" manner.

The inference is clear from Justice Goldberg's language that a nondiscriminatory public passages act would be constitutional. In applying such a statute the Court's problem would be to decide whether in fact the particular demonstration had obstructed the sidewalk. While the Court majority did not reach that issue in *Cox*, Justices White and Harlan, dissenting, thought obstruction had been clearly established. "Two thousand people took possession of the sidewalk in an entire city block. Building entrances were blocked and normal use of the sidewalk was impossible . . . [A]t some point the authorities were entitled to apply the statute and to clear the streets. That point was reached here."

The Court's failure to deal with the issue of obstruction of public passages was repeated five months later in *Cameron* v. *Johnson* (1965). Here a Mississippi statute made unlawful picketing or mass demonstrations which obstruct free access to state or local government buildings. Some civil rights groups sought an injunction against enforcement of the statute from a federal district court, alleging that the language was so vague, ambiguous, and sweeping that it could be used, and in fact had been used, to harass and persecute persons for simple picketing and demonstrating. The federal court found that the act had not been used in this way, and declined to grant the injunction. The Supreme Court in a brief *per curiam* opinion remanded the case for consideration of other issues. Justice Black, joined by Harlan and Stewart, castigated the Court's unenlightening action:

> There are many earnest, honest, good people in this Nation who are entitled to know exactly how far they have a constitutional right to go in using the public streets to advocate causes they consider just. . . . The Court has already waited entirely too long, in my judgment, to perform its duty of clarifying these constitutional issues. . . . Before this

Court relegates the States to the position of mere onlookers in struggles over their streets and the accesses to their public buildings, this Court should at least write an opinion making clear to the States and interested people the boundaries between what they can do in this field and what they cannot.[16]

COURTHOUSE PICKETING    In 1949 Congress passed a statute making it illegal to picket or parade in or near a building housing a federal court, with the intention of interfering with the administration of justice or influencing judges or jurors in the discharge of their duties.[17] This statute resulted from the picketing of federal courthouses by partisans of the defendants during trials involving leaders of the Communist Party, and was adopted by Congress at the urging of the organized bar and the federal judiciary. Several states, including Louisiana, enacted statutes on the same model. In the case of *Cox* v. *Louisiana,* this statute was invoked against Cox, whose demonstrators had taken up positions 125 feet from the courthouse.

Justice Goldberg for the Court found this law to be "a statute narrowly drawn to punish specific conduct that infringes a substantial state interest in protecting the judicial process." It was "on its face a valid law dealing with conduct subject to regulation so as to vindicate important interests of society . . . the fact that free speech is intermingled with such conduct does not bring with it constitutional protection." Justice Black was even stronger in his support for the statute, saying: "The streets are not now and never have been the proper place to administer justice." He warned that minority groups would suffer the most if "street multitudes are allowed to substitute their pressures for the less glamorous but more dependable and temperate processes of law."

Although the Court was thus unanimous in upholding the statute, a majority reversed Cox's conviction on the ground that the sheriff had given the demonstrators permission to stand across the street from the courthouse, and that therefore they could not be regarded as having been so "near" the building as to be in violation of the statute. Four justices dissented vigorously from this rationalization for what Justice Clark called Cox's "brazen

[16] In *Cameron* v. *Johnson* (1968) the Court held that the Mississippi law was not unconstitutional on its face and that the lower federal court was justified in refusing to enjoin its enforcement. The New York police department has a regulation banning demonstrations entirely in the busy Times Square area, but in *Turner* v. *New York* (1967) the Court declined to rule on the case of anti-Vietnam war demonstrators who had been convicted of disorderly conduct in connection with police dispersal of a demonstration in the prohibited area.

In 1967 the New York court of appeals held unconstitutional a New York City law which had been used to prevent persons from setting up tables for the distribution of literature on public sidewalks. The statute, which made it unlawful "to encumber or obstruct any street . . . with any article or thing whatsoever" was held to be so broad as to be subject to discriminatory application. *The New York Times,* December 29, 1967.

[17] 18 U.S.C. 1507.

defiance of the statute." He added: "I never knew until today that a law enforcement official . . . could forgive a breach of the criminal law. I missed that in my law school, in my practice and for two years while I was head of the Criminal Division of the Department of Justice."

RESIDENTIAL PICKETING    A different kind of issue was raised in the summer of 1965 when over one hundred pickets demanding the resignation of Chicago's school superintendent marched around Mayor Daley's home in a residential neighborhood. Residents of the area, resenting the intrusion, threatened the marchers with violence and the police, fearing a riot, arrested some sixty-five of the demonstrators, five of whom were later found guilty of disorderly conduct.

The case for the pickets is that they were peaceful, they were using the public sidewalks, and they were seeking to bring their views to the attention of the mayor. On the other hand, their sheer numbers created a disturbance and constituted an invasion of privacy. It may be contended that a public official can have no private life, but this method of making contact with the mayor has less the character of a petition and more that of harassment, intimidation, and coercion.[18]

## NON–PUBLIC FORUM PROBLEMS

Not all the problems in restraint of speech are generated by conflicts of interest in the public forum. Life's complexities assure speech issues in other spheres. There is, for example, the problem of protecting individuals in their homes from unwanted communications. The householder who does not wish to suffer the annoyance of having solicitors knock on his door can post a "no trespassing" sign, and most of the states have statutes which will permit prosecution for trespass after warning. But can the community on its own account decide that house-to-house visitation is a nuisance and adopt restrictive regulations?

So far as purely commercial visitors are concerned, the community can adopt any kind of regulation without raising First Amendment problems. The town of Green River, Wyoming, was apparently the first to experiment, in 1931, with an ordinance banning house-to-house commercial canvassers. The regulation was upheld by the state supreme court in 1936 against charges that it interfered with interstate commerce, took property without due process, and denied equal protection of the laws. The Supreme Court dismissed the appeal for want of a substantial federal question.[19]

[18] See Alfred Kamin, "Residential Picketing and the First Amendment," 61 *Northwestern University Law Review* 177–236 (1966). In January, 1968, the Illinois supreme court upheld convictions of the picketers on the ground that the police had a right to request the demonstration to be stopped to prevent imminent violence. The court did not rule on the issue whether an official's residence may be picketed. *Chicago Sun-Times*, January 27, 1968.

[19] *Bunger* v. *Green River* (1937).

For noncommercial door-to-door canvassing, the situation is not so simple. *Martin* v. *City of Struthers* (1943) tested an ordinance which made it unlawful for a person distributing "handbills, circulars or other advertisements" to ring the doorbell or otherwise summon the occupant of a residence to the door for the purpose of receiving such material. The ordinance was applied against a member of Jehovah's Witnesses who was distributing a dodger announcing a meeting and lecture. The motivation for the ordinance was to protect the daytime sleep of residents of this industrial town, since many of them were employed on night shifts in factories.

By a six to three vote, the Supreme Court invalidated the ordinance. Justice Black noted that "for centuries it has been a common practice in this and other countries for persons not specifically invited to go from home to home and knock on doors or ring doorbells to communicate ideas to the occupants or to invite them to political, religious, or other kinds of public meetings." To be sure, door-to-door visitation might be a nuisance or a blind for criminal activities. But it was also a customary part of the techniques of many political, religious, and labor groups, and "is essential to the poorly financed causes of little people." An ordinance which substituted community judgment for the desires of individuals, many of whom might be glad to receive the literature, was invalid because in conflict with the freedom of speech and press.

In two 1946 decisions the Court again protected the right of Jehovah's Witnesses to go onto private property—a "company town" and a federal housing development—regardless of the wishes of the proprietors.[20] But *Breard* v. *Alexandria* (1951) gave a different answer. At issue was a Green River ordinance, here applied against salesmen of magazine subscriptions, which gave rise to a free press problem not present in the earlier litigation. Justice Reed for the Court held that the case turned on "a balancing of the conveniences between some householders' desire for privacy and the publishers's right to distribute publications in the precise way that those soliciting for him think brings the best results." Communities which had found house-to-house canvassing obnoxious had a right to control it by ordinance. Magazines could be sold some other way.

Turning to another area, the decision in *Thomas* v. *Collins* (1945) illustrates the Supreme Court's suspicion of license systems for speech where there is no public forum justification. A 1943 Texas statute required all labor union organizers to secure organizers' cards from the secretary of state before soliciting members for their unions. Registration involved supplying the name, union affiliation, and credentials of the organizer, and the secretary of state had no discretion to refuse registration if the application was properly made.

By a five to four vote the Supreme Court invalidated the statute as an interference with freedom of speech and assembly. Two main arguments

[20] *Marsh* v. *Alabama* (1946); *Tucker* v. *Texas* (1946).

had been relied on by the state. The first was that the registration requirement resembled the vocational or business-practice regulations which states
commonly adopt; according to this view, it was to be construed as affecting
only the right to engage in the business of a paid organizer, and not limiting the expression of views on union membership. Justice Rutledge, for the
majority, ruled that it was impossible to make this distinction; it would be
an "incredible feat" for a union leader to make a speech praising unionism
without impliedly suggesting membership to his audience. In the absence of
some grave and imminent threat to the public interest, "restriction so destructive of the right of public discussion" could not be upheld.

The second argument for the statute was that, since the secretary of state
had no discretion to refuse the license, registration was only a "previous
identification" requirement. But the Court argued that if previous identification could be required for speeches on labor unionism, it could be required
for any social, business, religious, or political cause, and speech or assembly
which could not be punished directly could be made a crime by establishment of a previous identification requirement and penalizing failure to
conform with it.

Finally, we may note the limitation on speech which is found in the
Hatch Act of 1939, dealing with political activity of government employees.
The spoils system had been a long-standing abuse in American politics, and
the civil service movement, which gained its greatest initial success with
the Pendleton Act of 1883, aimed at a system of merit appointments. The
Civil Service Commission set up by this act took the position that any political activity by civil servants, even though unrelated to the securing or
retention of government employment, would lessen popular confidence in
the civil service, and so adopted a rule forbidding all civil service employees to take an active part in political management or campaigns. In 1939
Congress put this rule in statutory form by adopting the first Hatch Act.

The effect of this legislation is obviously to restrict the speech rights of
civil servants, but in *United Public Workers* v. *Mitchell* (1947), the Supreme
Court by the narrow margin of four to three upheld the statute. Justice
Reed for the Court majority denied that the act was an unconstitutional
invasion of the rights of free speech or of the Fifth, Ninth, or Tenth Amendments. "To declare that the present supposed evils of political activity are
beyond the power of Congress to redress would leave the nation impotent
to deal with what many sincere men believe is a material threat to the
democratic system." As for the argument that such restrictions, if needed,
should be imposed only on the few upper-level employees who influence
policy determinations, Reed's reply was that it was not unreasonable for
Congress to fear that political influence would be used to build the great
mass of lower-level employees into a political machine.

Justices Black, Douglas, and Rutledge would have held the statute unconstitutional. Douglas contended that if political influences needed to be

limited, the legislation should be more narrowly drawn to get at the specific conduct constituting a clear and present danger. He suggested drawing the line between the administrative class of government employees, who prepare the basic data on which policy decisions are made, and the clerical and industrial employees. Black's argument was in more general terms and more ringing language. He unsparingly castigated a policy which muzzled several million citizens and deprived the body politic of their political participation and interest.

The Hatch Act ban on political activity creates a particular problem in Washington, D.C., and its suburbs, where much of the population is on the federal payroll. Civil Service Commission regulations under the act permit federal officials to run for local office and participate in local campaigns as independents, but not to run on or work for the Democratic or Republican tickets. Federal employee organizations have been increasingly unhappy with these restrictions, and there have been continuing efforts to secure a reexamination of the *United Public Workers* decision in the courts.[21]

### SELECTED REFERENCES

CHAFEE, ZECHARIAH, JR., *Free Speech in the United States.* Cambridge, Mass.: Harvard University Press, 1941.

———, "The Great Liberty: Freedom of Speech and Press," in Alfred H. Kelly (ed.), *Foundations of Freedom in the American Constitution,* chap. 3. New York: Harper & Row, Publishers, Incorporated, 1958.

FREEMAN, HARROP A., and OTHERS, *Civil Disobedience.* Santa Barbara, Calif.: Center for the Study of Democratic Institutions, 1966.

GREGORY, CHARLES O., *Labor and the Law.* New York: W. W. Norton & Company, Inc., 1961 (second revised edition).

HORN, ROBERT A., *Groups and the Constitution,* chap. 4. Stanford, Calif.: Stanford University Press, 1956.

KALVEN, HARRY, JR., "The Concept of the Public Forum: Cox v. Louisiana," in Philip B. Kurland (ed.), *The Supreme Court Review: 1965,* pp. 1–32. Chicago: The University of Chicago Press, 1965.

———, *The Negro and the First Amendment.* Columbus, Ohio: Ohio State University Press, 1965.

KAMIN, ALFRED, "Residential Picketing and the First Amendment," 61 *Northwestern University Law Review* 177–236 (1966).

LANE, EDGAR, *Lobbying and the Law.* Berkeley, Calif.: University of California Press, 1964.

[21] Academic freedom, though not discussed separately in this volume, has constitutional aspects, particularly as concerns freedom of speech and freedom of association (Chap. 27). See generally the important discussion, "Academic Freedom," 81 *Harvard Law Review* 1045–1159 (1968). In *Epperson* v. *Arkansas* (1968) the Court agreed to review a statute forbidding the teaching of evolution in the public schools.

# 24

## Punishment of speech and assembly

The theoretical objection to prior restraint, as seen in the preceding chapters, is that opinion must not be throttled in advance. Abuses of speech or press are not to be anticipated. Expression must be left free, but if in the process abuses occur, they may then be proceeded against, if they rise to the required level of seriousness, and are established by proof in proper judicial proceedings. Censorship is aimed at what *may* be said; its justification can be based only on probabilities and hypotheses. Subsequent punishment for a speech offense must be based on definite acts and real happenings. "A sanction applied after the event," notes Justice Frankfurter, "assures consideration of the particular circumstances of a situation." [1]

All this helps to justify the constitutional preference for subsequent punishment over previous restraint. But obviously it does not mean that subsequent punishment is no danger to constitutional liberties. Severe and certain sanctions against exercise of speech rights can be just as effective in discouraging their assertion as censorship. Moreover, by definition, prior restraint gives advance warning of peril to a person who challenges the restraint, whereas subsequent punishment often turns on questions of degree, and a penalty may be imposed for acts which were thought to be entirely permissible when they were performed. Finally, the mere fact that censor-

[1] *Niemotko* v. *Maryland* ( 1951 ).

ship is generally regarded as an odious practice and flatly unconstitutional means that its successful espousal is less likely, and its judicial rejection relatively certain. On the other hand, there is no comparable stigma attached to subsequent punishment, and legislation effecting it is seldom unconstitutional on its face.

### BREACH OF THE PEACE: THE THREE-STAGE ANALYSIS

Preservation of the peace is a prime responsibility of a community's officials, In all states there are statutes defining such misdemeanors or crimes as breach of the peace, disorderly conduct, inciting to riot, and the like. The South Carolina supreme court defined the common-law crime of breach of the peace in *Edwards* v. *South Carolina* (1963) as follows:

> By "peace" . . . is meant the tranquility enjoyed by citizens of a municipality or community where good order reigns among its members, which is the natural right of all persons in political society. . . .
>
> In general terms, a breach of the peace is a violation of public order, a disturbance of the public tranquility, by any act or conduct inciting to violence. . . . It is not necessary that the peace be actually broken to lay the foundation for a prosecution for this offense. If what is done is unjustifiable and unlawful, tending with sufficient directness to break the peace, no more is required. Nor is actual personal violence an essential element in the offense.

Speech can be, and often is, the direct cause of incitement to breach of the peace. A group assembled to hear speakers or to communicate ideas by demonstrating or picketing can easily develop into a disturbance of the public tranquillity. Law-enforcement officers and courts are continually required to balance the claims of free speech against the claims of law and order.

Reviewing the Supreme Court's experience with these difficult problems, we find that three stages in the judicial analysis can be distinguished. First, the Court must determine whether the speech involved in the prosecution for breach of the peace is of a type which enjoys constitutional protection. Normally there is no difficulty in deciding this issue favorably. But in the case of *Chaplinsky* v. *New Hampshire* (1942), as already noted, the Supreme Court asserted that certain types of speech are so lacking in social utility that they forfeit any claim to standing under the First Amendment. In that opinion it was "insulting or 'fighting' words" which were specifically at issue, but Justice Murphy indicated that "lewd and obscene," "profane," and "libelous" language fell in the same category of unprotected speech. Since 1942 the Court has done a great deal more thinking about the problems of obscenity and libel, which will be discussed in the chapters following. But the two-level principle of the *Chaplinsky* case is presumably still valid for

profane and insulting speech.[2] In the overwhelming majority of speech prosecutions, however, there will be no doubt that the First Amendment is applicable, and the Court can proceed with its analysis.

The second question to be asked is whether the ordinance or statute under which the speaker is being prosecuted, both on its face and as judicially applied in the instant case, validly states or recognizes the constitutional status which protected speech enjoys under the First Amendment. The best case to illustrate this requirement is *Terminiello* v. *Chicago* (1949). The controversy there arose out of a speech on the fascist model made under riotous conditions in a Chicago auditorium in 1946. Terminiello specialized in attacks upon Jews and the Roosevelt administration. On this occasion 800 sympathizers were present in a packed hall, while outside a larger crowd picketed the building in protest, threw rocks through the windows, and sought to force the doors. Police had all they could do to keep the doors shut, and only by their aid was the speaker's party able to enter and leave the building. Following the affair Terminiello was found guilty of disorderly conduct under an ordinance covering "all persons who shall make, aid, countenance, or assist in making any improper noise, riot, disturbance, breach of the peace, or diversion tending to a breach of the peace."

This case seemed to offer the Supreme Court an opportunity and an obligation to consider the facts of this disturbance against a background of free speech theory which would give due weight to the right of a speaker to address willing listeners in a private hall, and the nature of the community's obligation to defend that right against violent interruptions from outsiders. But a five-judge majority, speaking through Justice Douglas, never reached this issue. It appeared from an examination of the record that the trial judge had charged the jury that "breach of the peace" consists of any "misbehavior which violates the public peace and decorum" and that the "misbehavior may constitute a breach of the peace if it stirs the public to anger, invites dispute, brings about a condition of unrest, or creates a disturbance, or if it molests the inhabitants in the enjoyment of peace and quiet by arousing alarm."

The Court majority held that this construction of the ordinance was as relevant and as binding as though the "precise words had been written into the ordinance." Consequently, the issue was whether an ordinance which penalized speech that might "invite dispute" or "bring about a condition of unrest" was constitutional. Justice Douglas's brief opinion, almost without argument and completely without reference to the facts of the riotous meeting, concluded that speech could not be censored or punished on such

[2] It appears that more than half of the 15,000 to 20,000 disorderly conduct arrests in the District of Columbia each year involve cursing, and that in most of these cases the arrest is made on the police officer's initiative without the support of a citizen's complaint. The American Civil Liberties Union in 1967 undertook test cases to establish the right of a person to swear, so long as no violence was threatened.

grounds but only where it was shown likely "to produce a clear and present danger of a serious substantive evil that rises far above public inconvenience, annoyance, or unrest." Consequently, the conviction was reversed.

If the Court had not invalidated the ordinance by this construction, it would have had to proceed to the third stage of the analysis and determine whether the danger of breach of the peace resulting from the speech was so real that it overrode the claims of constitutional protection. This is precisely what the dissenters in *Terminiello,* who found no fault with the ordinance, did. Justice Jackson supplied a detailed summary of the factual situation on which the prosecution was based and which was in the trial judge's mind as he charged the jury. He conveyed some sense of the inflammatory situation at the meeting by quoting at length from the stenographic record of Terminiello's speech and his testimony at the trial. For Jackson, who had been Allied prosecutor in the Nazi war crimes trials at Nuremberg, this exhibition of political, racial, and ideological conflict was not an isolated or unintended collision of forces. "It was a local manifestation of a world-wide and standing conflict between two groups of revolutionary fanatics, each of which had imported to this country the strong-arm technique developed in the struggle by which their kind has devastated Europe." American cities have to cope with this problem. They should not be paralyzed by sweeping decisions which would encourage hostile ideological forces to use city streets as battlegrounds, with resulting destruction of public order.

Terminiello could not have spoken at all, Jackson continued, had it not been for the police protection provided his meeting. "Can society be expected to keep these men at Terminiello's service if it has nothing to say of his behavior which may force them into dangerous action?" The authorities are entitled to place some checks upon those whose behavior or speech calls mobs into being, and the courts should support these checks, so long as the claim of "danger to public order is not invoked in bad faith, as a cover for censorship or suppression. The Preamble declares domestic tranquility as well as liberty to be an object in founding a Federal Government." And, finally: "The choice is not between order and liberty. It is between liberty with order and anarchy without either. There is danger that, if the Court does not temper its doctrinaire logic with a little practical wisdom, it will convert the constitutional Bill of Rights into a suicide pact."

Another case which illustrates the full three-stage analysis, in which the Court was unanimous, is *Cantwell* v. *Connecticut* (1940). Here a member of Jehovah's Witnesses was on a public street seeking converts. In accordance with the practice of his sect, he carried a phonograph and records, which he sought to play for anyone who would listen. He stopped two pedestrians and requested that they listen to a record. They agreed. The record was a violent attack on all organized religious systems and particularly the Catholic Church, which was characterized in offensive terms. The listeners, both Catholics, were angered. They felt like hitting him, but when they made

known their displeasure, Cantwell packed up his phonograph and left. The incident did not draw a crowd or impede traffic, and no blows were struck. Nevertheless, Cantwell was charged with the common-law offense of inciting a breach of the peace, and convicted.

The Supreme Court reversed the conviction. First, the speech was protected; it was "an effort to persuade a willing listener to buy a book or to contribute money in the interest of what Cantwell, however misguided others may think him, conceived to be true religion." Second, the law was valid. Third, there had been no danger of breach of the peace. There had been "no assault or threatening of bodily harm, no truculent bearing, no intentional discourtesy, no personal abuse." Justice Roberts summed up the constitutional principles that should govern such a case:

> In the realm of religious faith, and in that of political belief, sharp differences arise. In both fields the tenets of one man may seem the rankest error to his neighbor. To persuade others to his own point of view, the pleader, as we know, at times, resorts to exaggeration, to vilification of men who have been, or are, prominent in church or state, and even to false statement. But the people of this nation have ordained in the light of history, that, in spite of the probability of excesses and abuses, these liberties are, in the long view, essential to enlightened opinion and right conduct on the part of the citizens of a democracy.

### THE EXPECTATION OF VIOLENCE

To secure a conviction for breach of the peace involving speech, we have seen that the peace need not be actually broken. It may be enough that the speech tended with sufficient directness toward a breach of the peace. But who is to make this determination, and on what grounds?

Initially, of course, the chances of violence must be appraised by the police or other law-enforcement officers present at the scene of the potential disturbance, in deciding whether to arrest the speaker. Then the prosecuting attorney must prove to a trial judge and jury, using primarily evidence supplied by the police, that a breach of the peace had been committed or incited. Finally, the record of the trial-court proceedings will be reviewed by one or more appellate courts to determine whether the conviction can be supported on the facts and the law. Each stage of judicial review moves further away from the immediacy of the events, and relies more and more on a cold written record. On what basis can judges thus remote from the controversy challenge the judgment of the police who were on the scene?

A policeman's lot in a trouble spot is not a happy one. He must appraise the chances of violence, and determine how long he can let the speech or demonstration go on without interfering, in the hope that violence will not actually break out. If he determines that he must intervene, he must decide which of the participating parties offers the greater threat to the peace.

Should he arrest the speaker or those who are threatening the speaker? And how will he later prove in court that his judgment was the one called for by his obligation to preserve the peace?

In the civil rights controversies of the 1960s these problems were faced hundreds of times by law-enforcement officers. And yet there had accumulated by that time only a very few relevant Supreme Court decisions, which in any event could not possibly provide precise guides for handling disturbances, each of which has its own unique set of conditions. Nonetheless, these decisions must be reviewed for such guidance as they can give.

*Feiner* v. *New York* (1951) involved a university student who made a soapbox speech on a Syracuse street corner to publicize a meeting of the Young Progressives of America, his voice being carried over loudspeakers mounted on a car. The seventy-five or so people who gathered, mixed white and Negro, blocked the sidewalk, so that pedestrians had to go out into the street to get around. Feiner spoke in a "loud high-pitched voice," and in the course of his remarks reportedly said that the mayor of Syracuse, President Truman, and Mayor O'Dwyer of New York were all "bums"; that the "American Legion is a Nazi Gestapo"; and that "the Negroes don't have equal rights; they should rise up in arms and fight for their rights." Two police officers, originally attracted by the traffic problem caused by the crowd, mixed in the gathering and became aware of "angry mutterings," "shoving and milling around," and "restlessness." One man in the audience told the officers that if they didn't take that "son of a bitch" off the box, he would. The officers then approached Feiner, and one of them "asked" him to get off the box. When Feiner continued his speech, the officer "told" him to get down. When this failed, the officer "demanded" that he get down, telling him he was under arrest. Feiner asked why he was arrested, and the officer said the charge was "unlawful assembly." The ground was later changed to disorderly conduct.

Speaking for a six-judge majority, Chief Justice Vinson upheld the conviction. The evidence as to whether "a clear danger of disorder" threatened as a result of the speaker's remarks had been weighed by the trial court, and its conclusion had been affirmed by two higher state courts. Feiner had a right to speak, but he had no right to "incite to riot." He was "neither arrested nor convicted for the making or the content of his speech. Rather, it was the reaction which it actually engendered." Besides, he was guilty of "deliberate defiance" of the police officers. But Douglas, dissenting, felt that the record indicated no likelihood of riot. "It shows an unsympathetic audience and the threat of one man to haul the speaker from the stage. It is against that kind of threat that speakers need police protection. If they do not receive it and instead the police throw their weight on the side of those who would break up the meetings, the police become the new censors of speech."

The *Feiner* case did, indeed, approve a formula which could make police suppression of speech quite simple. Any group which wished to silence a

speaker could create a disturbance in the audience, and that would justify police in requesting the speaker to stop. If the speaker refused, he would be guilty of disorderly conduct.

By 1963, when *Edwards* v. *South Carolina* was decided, the civil rights revolution was in full swing and the Court had had more time to think about police obligations in handling speakers and demonstrators. In the *Edwards* situation a group of almost two hundred Negro students had marched onto the grounds of the South Carolina state capitol during the noon hour to submit a protest concerning discrimination against Negroes in the state. They walked in an orderly way through the grounds carrying placards. A crowd of several hundred onlookers gathered in the area, and the city manager recognized some "possible trouble makers" in the crowd. After thirty to forty-five minutes of this demonstration, police officers notified the participants that they would be arrested if they did not disperse in fifteen minutes. Instead of dispersing, the students began to sing patriotic songs loudly, to stamp their feet, clap their hands, and engage in other behavior described as "boisterous" by the city manager. After fifteen minutes, the students were arrested, and were subsequently convicted of the common-law crime of breach of the peace.

With only one dissent, the Supreme Court reversed the convictions. The reasoning followed the three stages already described. First, the students were exercising "basic constitutional rights in their most pristine and classic form." Second, the offense had not been defined in "a precise and narrowly drawn regulatory statute" aimed at "certain specific conduct." Rather, they were convicted of an offense "so generalized" that it was admittedly "not susceptible of exact definition." As in the *Terminiello* case, South Carolina law as interpreted and applied here had sought "to make criminal the peaceful expression of unpopular views," which the Fourteenth Amendment does not permit.

Although this holding would have been sufficient to decide the case, the Court, perhaps mindful of the criticism it had received in *Terminiello* for ignoring the factual situation, went on to the third stage. On the basis of its own "independent examination of the whole record," the Court denied that there had been sufficient danger of breach of the peace to justify the police demand to disperse. The students had "peaceably assembled" and "peaceably expressed their grievances." Not until they were warned to "disperse on pain of arrest did they do more." Even then, there was only a "religious harangue" and the singing of songs. "There was no violence or threat of violence on their part, or on the part of any member of the crowd watching them. Police protection was 'ample.'"

The *Feiner* case, where the Court upheld police action, created some problem in *Edwards*, for the *Feiner* crowd was considerably smaller and the atmosphere almost certainly less tense. Justice Clark, the sole dissenter in *Edwards*, believed that this racial confrontation in a South Carolina setting

had the makings of a "major catastrophe" which the police action may have averted. But Justice Stewart for the *Edwards* majority insisted that the *Feiner* situation had been more threatening, and thus avoided any necessity to overrule the *Feiner* decision.

In *Cox* v. *Louisiana* (1965) there was, in addition to the charges noted in the preceding chapter, also a breach of the peace conviction. The Court found *Cox* strikingly similar to *Edwards,* and reversed the conviction, again with Clark as the sole dissenter. The Court found the speech and assembly involved here constitutionally protected and the law applied "unconstitutionally broad." The Court's independent examination of the record, supported by a television news film of the events which the Court viewed, indicated that the meeting was "orderly and not riotous." The fear of violence was based on the presence of a group of 100 to 300 tense and agitated white citizens who were looking on from across the street. But they were separated from the students by seventy-five armed policemen, a fire truck, and the fire department, and the evidence indicated that they could have handled the crowd. Only after this finding of an absence of danger did Justice Goldberg note, as an additional reason for reversing the conviction, that the breach of the peace statute involved here was "unconstitutionally vague in its overly broad scope."

### TRESPASS AND SIT-INS

Beginning in 1960 the "sit-in" became a favorite and effective device employed in the Negro civil rights movement. The principal targets of sit-ins were variety and drug stores maintaining segregated lunch counters. Negroes were welcome as customers in these stores in all departments except for food service. As a protest against such discrimination, Negroes would take seats at lunch counters and, if refused service, continue to sit there until arrested or ousted by force. They were customarily charged either with breach of the peace resulting from trespass, or criminal trespass (that is, remaining on private property after being requested to leave).

Ordinarily, trespass on private property is clearly illegal and subject to punishment. Does it gain a protected status when it is employed as a form of expression, as a social protest? A sit-in, Justice Harlan readily conceded in *Garner* v. *Louisiana* (1961), "was a form of expression within the range of protections afforded by the Fourteenth Amendment." It was

> . . . as much a part of the 'free trade in ideas' . . . as is verbal expression, more commonly thought of as 'speech.' It, like speech, appeals to good sense and to 'the power of reason as applied through public discussion' . . . just as much as, if not more than, a public oration delivered from a soapbox at a street corner. This Court has never limited the right to speak, a protected 'liberty' under the Fourteenth Amendment . . . to mere verbal expression.

However, Harlan went on to deny that the Fourteenth Amendment would protect "demonstrations conducted on private property over the objection of the owner," which of course was the issue in the sit-in cases. Black put the same view even more forcibly in *Bell* v. *Maryland* (1964): "Unquestionably petitioners had a constitutional right to express these views [against refusal of service] wherever they had an unquestioned legal right to be." But they had no legal right to be on the premises of the restaurant against the owner's will. "The right to freedom of expression is a right to express views—not a right to force other people to supply a platform or a pulpit."

The Court as a whole, however, never endorsed the view that sit-ins involving trespass were illegal. Though it decided a dozen sit-in cases between 1960 and 1964, it never found one that would require it to pass squarely on the constitutional situation of sit-in trespassers. In *Boynton* v. *Virginia* (1960), the defendant remained in a terminal restaurant after service was refused on the basis of race and he was asked to leave. The Court held that under the Interstate Commerce Act the terminal was required to serve all customers without discrimination, and so it had violated its statutory duty and could not validly ask the defendant to leave. Thus there had been no criminal trespass.

In the 1961 group of cases from Louisiana, headed by *Garner*, the convictions had been for the crime of disturbing the peace. The state's claim was that the Negroes had disturbed the peace just "by sitting there." The Supreme Court, after examining Louisiana precedents, concluded that the state breach of the peace statute did not reach peaceful and orderly conduct. Since there was no evidence of any disorderly conduct by the sitters, the Court held their convictions lacked any evidentiary support and denied them due process of law under the Fourteenth Amendment.

In the 1963 cases the convictions were reversed because the policy of segregation which the sit-ins were protesting was governmentally inspired, and so amounted to "state action" in violation of the equal protection clause. For example, in *Peterson* v. *Greenville* a city ordinance required separation of the races in restaurants, and in *Lombard* v. *Louisiana* separation was enforced at the direction of city officials. Thus it was not the "private choice" of the restaurant owners to exclude Negroes, and so there was no trespass issue.

Finally, in *Bell* v. *Maryland* (1964) the Court got a clear case of conviction for criminal trespass in a restaurant where the decision not to serve Negroes was entirely the private choice of the owner, and where the police took no action until the owner swore out warrants of arrest for the sitters who had refused his demand that they leave his restaurant. At last it seemed that the Court would have to uphold a sit-in conviction. But no. In June, 1962, five months *after* these convictions were affirmed by the Maryland supreme court, Baltimore adopted an ordinance prohibiting restaurants and other places of public accommodation from denying service because of race.

The state of Maryland followed soon after with a similar law. Thus by 1964, when these appeals got to the Supreme Court, Maryland law had made conduct such as that of the restaurant owner illegal and had destroyed the basis for a trespass charge. Under these circumstances the Court majority vacated the judgment and remanded the case to the state court so that it might be reconsidered in the light of the supervening change in state law.

Actually, six justices did use this case to express their opinions on the constitutionality of sit-ins, but they were split three to three. Justice Douglas, supported by Goldberg, repeated and elaborated the argument he had first made in *Garner* that restaurants are not really private property, but are devoted to a public use and so are forbidden to deny equal protection directly by the terms of the Fourteenth Amendment. Justice Goldberg, supported by Douglas and the Chief Justice, in a long opinion reached the same conclusion by reopening the argument about the intention of the framers of the Fourteenth Amendment and the authors of the decision in the *Civil Rights Cases* (1883).

On the other side, Justice Black, supported by Harlan and White, insisted that the Court should declare the right of private property owners to protect their control over their property by invoking the trespass laws, and announce that the Fourteenth Amendment, "standing alone, does not prohibit privately owned restaurants from choosing their own customers."

A few weeks after the *Bell* decision, Congress passed the Civil Rights Act of 1964, which made unlawful racial discrimination in access to public accommodations such as restaurants, hotels, and motels. Under the 1964 act it is the owner of the restaurant who refuses service for racial reasons who is guilty of unlawful conduct, not the person who enters the restaurant demanding service. This statute presumably terminates the need for sit-in tactics against private owners providing public accommodations as defined in the act, and liquidates this constitutional issue. In *Hamm* v. *City of Rock Hill* (1964), decided six months after the 1964 statute had been adopted, the Supreme Court by a five to four vote held that the federal act had abated state convictions for trespass occurring before the act was passed.[3]

Demonstrations involving occupation of or sit-ins on public property present a separate problem. In the preceding chapter we saw that the Court had upheld statutes forbidding the blocking of public passages or picketing around courthouses. Can general breach of the peace or criminal trespass charges be used to punish occupation of public buildings or areas adjacent thereto?

In *Edwards* the Court specifically upheld the right of demonstrators to occupy the state capitol grounds in South Carolina for purposes of their demonstration. In *Brown* v. *Louisiana* (1966) a demonstration against segre-

---

[3] In *Burbridge* v. *California* (1967) the Court left standing convictions for trespass and unlawful assembly against demonstrators who had staged sit-ins in San Francisco auto agencies to protest alleged racial job discrimination.

gated library service which took the form of a sit-in (or stand-in) in a small public library building was held by a vote of five to four not to amount to a violation of the breach of the peace law. Five Negroes walked into the library and asked for a certain book. The librarian told them the book was not in the library, but offered to get it from the state library and send it to them through the bookmobile service (there was a separate bookmobile for Negroes). When they made no move to depart, the librarian asked them to leave. No one else was in the library, and they stood quietly until the sheriff arrived and arrested them for breach of the peace.

Justice Fortas for the Court noted that the defendants were lawfully in the library, their deportment was "unexceptionable," and they were "neither loud, boisterous, obstreperous, indecorous nor impolite." The only basis for the charge, then, was the continuation of their presence after an order to leave. The Court assumed that they were making a protest against the library's unlawful policy of segregation; by their "silent and reproachful presence" in a place where they had a right to be they were exercising their constitutional right to petition the government for a redress of grievances.

Justice Black was eloquent in dissent. He felt there was a great difference between a demonstration in the public streets and in public buildings such as libraries, where "order and tranquility of a sort entirely unknown to the public streets are essential to their normal operation." By remaining in this small library when they had no further library business to transact, they brought its operations to a halt. They were not denied service because of their race; they were in fact given all the service that could be given under the circumstances. Black found it highly disturbing if a public library which, as Fortas had said, was a "hallowed place," could be taken over by protesters. If one group could do it for one cause, other groups could do it for other causes. The next step, Black feared, would be to paralyze the schools.

Nine months later, in *Adderly* v. *Florida* (1966), a shift by Justice White made it possible for Black to state this position as the majority view of the Court. A group of Negro students sought to demonstrate at a segregated jail where other students protesting segregation had been lodged the day before. They crowded around the jail door entrance, but at the request of a deputy sheriff fell back a short distance onto the jail driveway where the demonstration continued. The sheriff, on his arrival, told them they were trespassing on jail property and he would give them ten minutes to leave or he would arrest them. Over one hundred did not leave, and were arrested.

Black distinguished this situation from the *Edwards* case. State capitol grounds are open to the public, but jails, built for security purposes, are not. In *Edwards* the demonstrators used a public driveway to enter, here they used a drive intended only for jail purposes. In *Edwards* the charge was the very broad and loose common-law crime of breach of the peace, here there was a statute aimed at conduct of one limited kind, trespassing on the prop-

erty of another with malicious and mischievous intent. Black believed that the state, "no less than a private owner of property, has power to preserve the property under its control for the use to which it is lawfully dedicated." As in the *Brown* case, he denied that "people who want to propagandize protests or views have a constitutional right to do so whenever and however and wherever they please."

Justice Douglas vigorously denied that this could be treated as an ordinary trespass case, or that the sheriff could be analogized to a private owner ordering trespassers off his property. Here was an exercise of the right to petition the government for the redress of grievances, using the only type of access to public officials that was open to the petitioners. The assembly and petition were peaceable. There was no threat to the safety of the jail or interference with its functioning. Douglas agreed that some public places might be inappropriate for protests, but he would not leave the determination of that fact to the particular custodian of the public property or allow him in his discretion to decide what areas could be used for the communication of ideas. This is contrary to the principle of *Kunz* v. *New York* (1951) and many other cases, that infringement of rights of free expression must be made only by narrowly drawn statutes which provide adequate standards to control administrative discretion.

In the disorders attending the "Free Speech Movement" on the Berkeley campus of the University of California in 1964, there was a mass occupation of one of the university buildings, from which the students and nonstudents had to be removed by force. Some 565 persons were convicted for refusal to leave a public building after closing hours, and in *Savio* v. *California* (1967) the Supreme Court dismissed their appeals for want of jurisdiction.

### THE CONSTITUTIONAL CHALLENGE
### OF DIRECT ACTION

The civil rights movement of the 1960s presented to the Supreme Court and to American society in general the dilemma of adjusting to the techniques of direct action and civil disobedience when employed for the morally justifiable goals of racial equality. The terms "direct action" and "civil disobedience" are often equated, but a careful analysis will distinguish between them.

Direct action is a very broad term covering a wide range of challenges to established laws or practices. Direct action may be nonviolent or violent. It may operate within legal limits, or it may deliberately and intentionally violate the law. The purpose of direct action is to dramatize issues, to force grievances on the attention of the community, to create trouble and expense for the community involved, and to compel the "establishment" or the "power structure" to enter into negotiations for correcting the conditions protested. As Martin Luther King, the acknowledged philosopher of the

direct action movement, put it: "Nonviolent direct action seeks to create such a crisis and establish such creative tension that a community that has constantly refused to negotiate is forced to confront the issue." [4]

The direct action program which King led was nonviolent and operated in large part through legal methods such as parades and demonstrations. King's program, however, did include the violation of laws he regarded as unjust. His rationalization was: "There are just laws and there are unjust laws. . . . I would agree with Saint Augustine that 'an unjust law is no law at all.' "

Civil disobedience is an extreme form of direct action. It involves deliberate violation of law, but the violation is not necessarily limited to laws the protestors regard as unjust. Rather, practitioners of civil disobedience will violate admittedly valid laws, such as traffic regulations, in order to dramatize their grievances by creating a maximum of confusion, trouble, and danger for the community. Actual or threatened tactics of civil disobedience have included sitting down in busy street intersections or on major bridges, concerted turning on of water faucets to reduce water pressure, stalling automobiles on expressways, occupying offices of government officials, blocking entrances to construction sites, and the like.

The American Civil Liberties Union issued a statement on civil disobedience in 1968 specifying two categories which the ACLU would not undertake to defend. One was deliberate violation of a law based on the individual's belief that the law was unjust even though it was constitutional. The other was violation of a valid law with which the individual has no quarrel in order to call attention to some other evil. As examples of conduct beyond ACLU concern, the statement mentioned open rebellion or riots, refusal to take part in civil defense drills, refusal to pay federal taxes as a protest against military expenditures, or refusing to register for military service. The ACLU, however, did agree to defend Dr. Benjamin Spock who with four others was indicted in 1968 for an antidraft conspiracy.

The decisions of the Supreme Court examined in this chapter indicate a general predisposition to support nonviolent forms of direct action for civil rights. In the sit-in cases of 1961 and 1963, the Court found various reasons for holding that trespassers could not be punished for resorting to self-help in challenging illegal state-enforced discriminatory treatment. In the 1964 cases the Court majority construed federal and state statutes guaranteeing against discrimination in public accommodations as having abated convictions for trespass which occurred before the statutes were passed.[5]

Several justices warned in the 1964 sit-in cases against carrying protection of civil rights activists too far. In *Hamm* v. *Rock Hill* Justice Black denied

---

[4] "A Letter from Birmingham Jail," July, 1963.
[5] As Justice Stewart put it in *City of Greenwood* v. *Peacock* (1966): "The Civil Rights Act of 1964 as construed in *Hamm* thus specifically and uniquely conferred upon the defendants an absolute right to 'violate' the explicit terms of the state criminal trespass law."

that the Civil Rights Act of 1964 authorized "persons who are unlawfully refused service a 'right' to take the law into their own hands by sitting down and occupying the premises for as long as they choose to stay." In the same case Justice White expressed his doubts that Congress had intended by the 1964 statute "to ratify massive disobedience to the law, so often attended by violence," and added: "Whether persons or groups should engage in non-violent disobedience to laws with which they disagree perhaps defies any categorical answer for the guidance of every individual in every circumstance. But whether a court should give it wholesale sanction is a wholly different question which calls for only one answer."

Justice Black also dissented in *Bell* v. *Maryland* (1964), expressing concern if a private property owner, no matter how prejudiced, could not call on the state to enforce the trespass laws against people he did not want in his restaurant.

> Such a doctrine would . . . severely handicap a State's efforts to maintain a peaceful and orderly society. Our society has put its trust in a system of criminal laws to punish lawless conduct. To avert personal feuds and violent brawls it has led its people to believe and expect that wrongs against them will be vindicated in the courts. Instead of attempting to take the law into their own hands, people have been taught to call for police protection to protect their rights wherever possible. It would betray our whole plan for a tranquil and orderly society to say that a citizen, because of his personal prejudices, habits, attitudes, or beliefs, is cast outside the law's protection and cannot call for the aid of officers sworn to uphold the law and preserve the peace. The worst citizen no less than the best is entitled to equal protection of the laws of his State and of his Nation.

Justice Goldberg undertook to answer these comments for the Court majority: "This statement, to which all will readily agree, slides over the critical question: Whose conduct is entitled to the 'law's protection'?" The question was whether the weight and protective strength of the law would be cast in favor of the claim of the restaurant owner to discriminate or the claim of the demonstrators to service in a public accommodation. Goldberg concluded: "In my view the Fourteenth Amendment resolved this issue in favor of the right of petitioners to public accommodations and it follows that in the exercise of that constitutionally granted right they are entitled to the 'law's protection.'"

So far as massive demonstrations of the type involved in *Edwards* and *Cox* are concerned, we saw that the Court does not claim for "speech plus" the full First Amendment protection enjoyed by "pure speech." Justice Goldberg was very clear in *Cox* that the right of free speech and assembly in the streets is limited by the need to keep the streets orderly and open.

Still, the Court majority upheld the rights of the demonstrators in these two cases, as well as in the *Brown* library stand-in, as against breach of the

peace charges. It was well aware how easily generalized breach of the peace statutes could be manipulated to punish essays in direct action in current civil rights controversies. As Heyman has pointed out:

> First, such [statutory] norms are easily susceptible to discriminatory application against Negroes in communities enormously hostile to nationally ratified Negro aspirations. They give local officials a discretionary whip hand to suppress any form of protest with which they disagree. Second, such rules fail to provide protestants with warning that specific behavior is prohibited. Third, such statutes are particularly useful means to stifle unpopular protest on the grounds that it will stimulate active opposition and thus to avoid the First Amendment duty to protect within reason, not to suppress, the expression of unpopular views.[6]

But again there were warnings from the dissenters. White was willing to grant that the *Cox* demonstration had a right to monopolize the streets for a reasonable time, but "at some point the authorities were entitled to apply the statute and to clear the streets." Justice Black was more forceful: "Those who encourage minority groups to believe that the United States Constitution and federal laws give them a right to patrol and picket in the streets whenever they choose, in order to advance what they think to be a just and noble end, do no service to those minority groups, their cause, or their country."

And in *Brown* v. *Louisiana* he warned: "It is high time to challenge the assumption in which too many people have too long acquiesced, that groups that think they have been mistreated or that have actually been mistreated have a constitutional right to use the public's streets, buildings, and property to protest whatever, wherever, whenever they want, without regard to whom it may disturb."

Obviously the Court has only begun to face the constitutional challenges presented by the various forms of direct action utilized in the civil rights movement. All members of the Court and the country generally can agree with Justice Goldberg's stirring peroration in the *Cox* case:

> Nothing we have said here . . . is to be interpreted as sanctioning riotous conduct in any form or demonstrations, however peaceful their conduct or commendable their motives, which conflict with properly drawn statutes and ordinances designed to promote law and order, protect the community against disorder, regulate traffic, safeguard legitimate interests in private and public property, or protect the administration of justice and other essential governmental functions.
>
> Liberty can only be exercised in a system of law which safeguards order. We reaffirm the repeated holdings of this Court that our constitutional command of free speech and assembly is basic and fundamental

[6] Ira Michael Heyman, "Civil Rights 1964 Term: Responses to Direct Action," in Philip B. Kurland (ed.), *The Supreme Court Review: 1965* (Chicago: The University of Chicago Press, 1965), pp. 159, 184–5.

and encompasses peaceful social protest, so important to the preservation of the freedoms treasured in a democratic society. We also reaffirm the repeated decisions of this Court that there is no place for violence in a democratic society dedicated to liberty under law, and that the right of peaceful protest does not mean that everyone with opinions or beliefs to express may do so at any time and at any place. There is a proper time and place for even the most peaceful protest and a plain duty and responsibility on the part of all citizens to obey all valid laws and regulations.

But the translation of these principles into decisions in individual controversies will certainly continue to arouse vigorous controversy. As Heyman has said: "Simplistic analyses supporting either the protestants or law and order are insufficient. Hard questions in a variety of factual situations must be answered. Sweeping statements avoid the hard questions and only exacerbate already emotion-laden issues." [7]

## SELECTED REFERENCES

BLACK, CHARLES L., JR., "Problems of the Compatibility of Civil Disobedience with American Institutions of Government," 43 *Texas Law Review* 492 (1965).

HEYMAN, IRA MICHAEL, "Civil Rights 1964 Term: Responses to Direct Action," in Philip B. Kurland (ed.), *The Supreme Court Review: 1965,* pp. 159–186. Chicago: The University of Chicago Press, 1965.

KALVEN, HARRY, JR., *The Negro and the First Amendment,* chaps. 3, 4. Columbus, Ohio: Ohio State University Press, 1965.

KEETON, MORRIS, "The Morality of Civil Disobedience," 43 *Texas Law Review* 507 (1965).

KING, DONALD B., and CHARLES W. QUICK (eds.), *Legal Aspects of the Civil Rights Movement.* Detroit: Wayne State University Press, 1965.

LEWIS, THOMAS P., "The Sit-in Cases: Great Expectations," in Philip B. Kurland (ed.), *The Supreme Court Review: 1963,* pp. 101–151. Chicago: The University of Chicago Press, 1963.

PAULSEN, MONRAD G., "The Sit-in Cases of 1964: 'But Answer Came There None,'" in Philip B. Kurland (ed.), *The Supreme Court Review: 1964,* pp. 137–170. Chicago: The University of Chicago Press, 1964.

SCHWELB, FRANK E., "The Sit-in Demonstration: Criminal Trespass or Constitutional Right," 36 *New York University Law Review* 779–809 (1961).

[7] *Ibid.,* p. 186.

# 25

## Obscenity

Like the civil rights revolution, the sexual revolution of the 1950s and 1960s created difficult problems of applying old constitutional standards to new claims for freedom. Legal restraints on obscenity and legal standards governing the degree of frankness in discussions of sexual matters date in England from the passage of Lord Campbell's Act in 1857. A few years later in the United States the crusading zeal of Anthony Comstock led to the passage of regulatory legislation in many states.

American courts, including the United States Supreme Court, assumed the constitutionality of antiobscenity laws almost without discussion. As we have seen, the Supreme Court made no attempt to develop free speech doctrine until 1919, and then it was concerned only with political speech. The failure even to recognize that obscenity laws might raise constitutional questions is evident in Chief Justice Hughes's opinion in *Near* v. *Minnesota,* where he simply assumed that one of the exceptions to the rule of no prior restraints on publications was enforcement of "the primary requirements of decency . . . against obscene publications." The same view was reflected in Justice Murphy's acceptance in *Chaplinsky* of "the lewd and obscene" as classes of speech "the prevention and punishment of which has never been thought to raise any Constitutional problem."

During this period, however, proceedings against well-known literary works under state obscenity laws or federal postal and customs regulations

required the courts to undertake a more careful consideration of the problem. Judge Woolsey's 1934 decision that James Joyce's *Ulysses* was not obscene was a striking portent of change.[1] Other well-known prosecutions of the period involved Lillian Smith's *Strange Fruit*, Kathleen Winsor's *Forever Amber*, and Erskine Caldwell's *God's Little Acre*.

In 1948 the first such case reached the Supreme Court, a prosecution of *Memoirs of Hecate County* by the distinguished critic Edmund Wilson. However, the Court was divided four to four, and so unable to hand down a decision.[2] In 1956 Federal Court of Appeals Judge Jerome Frank wrote a remarkable opinion delineating the conflict between obscenity laws and free speech theory, and appealing to the Supreme Court to deal with the constitutional issues.[3] It did so the following year in the landmark case of *Roth* v. *United States*.

## LEGAL TESTS FOR OBSCENITY

The first step in understanding the constitutional law of obscenity is to ask why obscenity has been made criminally punishable. What is the evil against which legislatures have been endeavoring to protect society? In general, there would seem to be two classes of concerns. First, obscenity has been regarded as bad in and of itself. It is indecent. It is a violation of good moral standards. It appeals to "prurient interest" and "stimulates impure sexual thoughts." It arouses feelings of disgust and revulsion or, alternatively, it induces unhealthy psychological excitement. In the words of the federal postal law, the obscene is the "lewd," the "lascivious," the "filthy."

Second, obscenity may be regarded as criminally punishable because of its evil effects on individuals and society. Obscene materials, it is alleged, will have a tendency to deprave the minds or characters of persons exposed to it. It will corrupt the public morals. It will lead to immoral or antisocial sexual conduct. It will result in the advocacy of improper sexual values.

It was this second approach which was embodied in the first widely accepted legal definition of obscenity, that framed in 1868 by Justice Cockburn in the English case of *Queen* v. *Hicklin*. He said: "I think the test of obscenity is this, whether the tendency of the matter charged as obscenity is to deprave and corrupt those whose minds are open to such immoral influences, and into whose hands a publication of this sort may fall."

Under the pressure of this "effects" test, Justice Cockburn had to specify *who* was being depraved and corrupted, and his answer was, "those whose minds are open to such immoral influences." It was this feature of the *Hicklin* test which rendered it ultimately unacceptable, for, as Judge Learned Hand said in *United States* v. *Kennerly* (1913), it "would forbid

---

[1] *United States* v. *One Book Entitled "Ulysses"* (1934).
[2] *Doubleday & Co.* v. *New York* (1948).
[3] *United States* v. *Roth* (1956).

all which might corrupt the most corruptible." Hand did not think that "society is prepared to accept for its own limitations those which may perhaps be necessary to the weakest of its members. . . . To put thought in leash to the average conscience of the time is perhaps tolerable, but to filter it by the necessities of the lowest and least capable seems a fatal policy."

Hand's protest was echoed by Justice Frankfurter in *Butler* v. *Michigan* (1957), where a state statute had made it an offense to sell to the general public books that might have a deleterious effect upon the young:

> The State insists that by thus quarantining the general reading public against books not too rugged for grown men and women in order to shield juvenile innocence, it is exercising its power to promote the general welfare. Surely, this is to burn the house to roast the pig. . . . The incidence of this enactment is to reduce the adult population of Michigan to reading only what is fit for children.

The *Hicklin* test ignored literary and other social values, judged a whole book by passages taken out of context, and tested for obscenity by the tendency of the passages alone to deprave the minds of those open to such influence and into whose hands the book might come. Nevertheless, this test became so thoroughly established in the United States that in 1913 Judge Learned Hand felt compelled to give it effect in the *Kennerly* decision, even though he personally rejected it in the following memorable language:

> I hope it is not improper for me to say that the rule as laid down, however consonant it may be with mid-Victorian morals, does not seem to me to answer to the understanding and morality of the present time. . . . I question whether in the end men will regard that as obscene which is honestly relevant to the adequate expression of innocent ideas, and whether they will not believe that truth and beauty are too precious to society at large to be mutilated in the interests of those most likely to pervert them to base uses.

It was not until the 1930s that this remarkably sage counsel began to be effective in judicial decisions.[4] In the celebrated *Ulysses* case of 1934, Judge Augustus N. Hand in the court of appeals explicitly repudiated the *Hicklin* rule and replaced it with this new standard:

> While any construction of the statute that will fit all cases is difficult, we believe that the proper test of whether a given book is obscene is its dominant effect. In applying this test, relevancy of the objectionable parts to the theme, the established reputation of the work in the estimation of approved critics, if the book is modern, and the verdict of the

---

[4] See *United States* v. *Dennett* (1930); *United States* v. *One Obscene Book Entitled "Married Love"* (1931); *United States* v. *One Book Entitled "Contraception"* (1931).

past, if it is ancient, are persuasive pieces of evidence; for works of art are not likely to sustain a high position with no better warrant for their existence than their obscene content.[5]

The abandonment of the *Hicklin* test permitted more civilized judgments on literary works, but it left the legal tests for obscenity vague, and it did nothing toward reconciling obscenity prosecutions with free speech theory. It was this task which the Supreme Court finally undertook in the *Roth* case.

## THE TWO-LEVEL THEORY

*Roth* v. *United States* and its companion case, *Alberts* v. *California,* required the Court to rule on the constitutionality of both federal and state obscenity laws. The task, so long avoided, turned out to be surprisingly easy. Justice Brennan, writing for the majority, held there was no First Amendment problem because obscenity was "not within the area of constitutionally protected speech." The First Amendment extends to "all ideas having even the slightest redeeming social importance—unorthodox ideas, controversial ideas, even ideas hateful to the prevailing climate of opinion. . . . But implicit in the history of the First Amendment is the rejection of obscenity as utterly without redeeming social importance." Since obscenity is not "protected speech," there is no necessity to show any connection with unlawful action in order to justify criminal punishment. Rather, "convictions may be had without proof either that obscene material will perceptibly create a clear present danger of antisocial conduct, or will probably induce its recipients to such conduct." It is sufficient to allege, as had been done in these cases, that the materials circulated had incited "impure sexual thoughts."

So the obscene is not constitutionally protected. But what is obscene? That was the question which the Court now had to answer, and it was not so easy. Brennan made clear that he did not mean to say all discussions of sex were obscene; indeed, sex is "a great and mysterious motive force in human life . . . one of the vital problems of human interest and public concern." Consequently it was necessary to find a legal test for obscenity to supplant the *Hicklin* test which would fully protect the right to deal with sexual subjects. This is the test he proposed: "whether to the average person, applying contemporary community standards, the dominant theme of the material taken as a whole appeals to prurient interest."

The improvements in this standard over *Hicklin* are obvious. It is the average person, not the most susceptible person, whose morals are to be protected. The dominant theme of the material taken as a whole is the basis for judgment, not isolated passages from a book. Applying contemporary community standards recognizes that obscenity is a relative concept. Since

[5] *United States* v. *One Book Entitled "Ulysses"* (1934).

the trial courts in both *Roth* and *Alberts* had defined obscenity consistently with this standard, Justice Brennan concluded that the convictions should be upheld.

Justices Douglas and Black, dissenting, denied Brennan's basic constitutional premise that obscenity can be punished because of the thoughts it provokes, with no proof that it has incited overt acts or antisocial conduct. "The test of obscenity the Court endorses today gives the censor free range over a vast domain. To allow the State to step in and punish mere speech or publication that the judge or the jury thinks has an *undesirable* impact on thoughts but that is not shown to be a part of unlawful action is drastically to curtail the First Amendment."

Justice Harlan also dissented so far as enforcing the federal statute was concerned. The charge against Roth was selling a book which tended to "stir sexual impulses and lead to sexually impure thoughts." He suggested that much of the great literature of the world could be stigmatized under such a view of the statute, and he believed that the federal government had no power "to bar the sale of books because they might lead to any kind of 'thoughts.'" But so far as the constitutionality of the state law was concerned, he felt obliged to accept as not irrational the legislature's conclusion that distribution of certain types of literature might induce criminal or immoral sexual conduct. He approved application of the state law in the *Alberts* case because his own "independent perusal" of the material convinced him that its suppression would not unconstitutionally "interfere with the communication of 'ideas' in any proper sense of that term."

Because the *Roth* decision upheld the constitutionality of obscenity laws, and because it flatly denied that obscenity was entitled to any constitutional protection under the First Amendment, the opinion when it was first handed down was widely considered to be a forecast of strong judicial support for further obscenity prosecutions. Certainly the four dissenters regarded the *Roth* reasoning as dangerously broad. Harlan, for example, found "lurking beneath its disarming generalizations" a number of problems which left him with "serious misgivings" as to the future effect of the decision.

However, it soon appeared that the Court recognized the dangers of the two-level theory, and intended to define the concept of obscenity very strictly. *Kingsley International Pictures Corp.* v. *Regents* (1959) required the Court to review the banning of the film version of "Lady Chatterley's Lover." The state statute involved forbade the showing of motion pictures which portray "acts of sexual immorality . . . as desirable, acceptable or proper patterns of behavior." This film was held by the state courts to have portrayed approvingly an adulterous relationship, and so the denial of a license to exhibit it was upheld.

Justice Stewart for a unanimous Court reversed this decision. What New York had done was to censor a motion picture "because that picture advo-

cates an idea"—the idea "that adultery under certain circumstances may be proper behavior." This idea might well be contrary to moral standards, religious precepts, and legal codes. But, said Stewart, the Constitution does not protect only those ideas "that are conventional or shared by a majority. It protects advocacy of the opinion that adultery may sometimes be proper, no less than advocacy of socialism or the single tax." By endeavoring to prevent the expression of certain ideas, the state had "struck at the very heart of constitutionally protected liberty." There can be no prosecution, then, for "thematic obscenity." Ideas cannot be obscene.

The next important step in limiting the obscenity concept was taken in *Manual Enterprises, Inc.* v. *Day* (1962), where Justice Harlan wrote the opinion. As already noted, he had been concerned over the breadth of the "prurient interest" test announced in *Roth,* and in *Manual* he was able to narrow it by adding a second test. In his view, "prurient interest" was only another way of stating the *Hicklin* "effect" test of depraving and corrupting. He believed that conviction for obscenity should require proof of *both* the elements analyzed earlier in this chapter; there must be prurient interest effect *and* "patent offensiveness." He pointed out that some acknowledged masterpieces of art or literature might have a dominant theme appealing to prurient interest, and he would rank such works as obscene only if their "indecency" was self-demonstrating. On the basis of the patent offensiveness test, Harlan absolved of obscenity the material involved in *Manual*—magazines with photographs intended to appeal to male homosexuals. He found the magazines to be "dismally unpleasant, uncouth, and tawdry," but not "beyond the pale of contemporary notions of rudimentary decency."

A third test, likewise restrictive of the scope of the obscenity concept, was put forward by Justice Brennan in *Jacobellis* v. *Ohio* (1964). Its foundation was his statement in the *Roth* case that obscenity is "utterly without redeeming social importance." At that time he had simply been defending the two-level theory and justifying the constitutionality of laws against obscenity. But his statement was also relevant as a test *for* obscenity. If it is true that obscenity is "utterly without redeeming social importance," then it must be equally true that anything *with* redeeming social importance cannot be obscene. This was what Brennan spelled out in the *Jacobellis* case, which dealt with censorship of the film "The Lovers." He wrote that

> . . . material dealing with sex in a manner . . . that has literary or scientific or artistic value or any other form of social importance, may not be branded as obscenity and denied the constitutional protection. Nor may the constitutional status of the material be made to turn on a 'weighing' of its social importance against its prurient appeal, for a work cannot be proscribed unless it is 'utterly' without social importance.

Thus the Court had by 1964 set up three tests for obscenity—prurient interest appeal, patent offensiveness, and utterly without redeeming social value.

In the famous *Fanny Hill* case of 1966 (*A Book Named "John Cleland's Memoirs of a Woman of Pleasure"* v. *Attorney General of Massachusetts*) the Court made it clear that the three tests were separate and that a book had to fail all three before it could be adjudged obscene. The supreme court of Massachusetts had granted that the book might have "some minimal literary value," but did not think that gave it any social importance. Since it appealed to prurient interest and was patently offensive, the state court held it obscene. Justice Brennan for the Supreme Court ruled that this was a misinterpretation of the social value criterion. "Each of the three federal constitutional criteria is to be applied independently; the social value of the book can neither be weighed against nor canceled by its prurient appeal or patent offensiveness." Since the state court admitted the book had a "modicum of social value," that was enough to rescue it from the charge of obscenity.

Both Justices White and Clark attacked this use of the "social importance" test to rescue *Fanny Hill*. White said: "In my view, 'social importance' is not an independent test of obscenity but is relevant only to determining the predominant prurient interest of the material." The test would protect "well written" obscenity, leaving only "the poorly written" vulnerable.

## HARD–CORE PORNOGRAPHY

Though the justices encountered some difficulties in applying these standards, there did emerge a clear majority view that there was a class of materials, called "hard-core pornography," which was not protected by the First Amendment. Some members of the Court believed that nothing else would meet the Court's three tests for obscenity. Justice Harlan said in *Manual Enterprises:* "At least one important state court and some authoritative commentators have considered *Roth* and subsequent cases to indicate that only 'hard-core' pornography can constitutionally be reached under this or similar state obscenity statutes." In *Jacobellis* Justice Stewart wrote: "I have reached the conclusion . . . that under the First and Fourteenth Amendments criminal laws in this area are constitutionally limited to hard-core pornography."

Presumably the materials in *Roth* and *Alberts* must have been hard-core pornography, since the convictions were upheld, though they were not so described at the time. The Solicitor General in arguing the *Roth* case contended that the federal statute was essential to prevent the country from being flooded with hard-core pornography, which constituted 90 per cent of the material proceeded against under the statute. He defined hard-core pornography as erotic objects, books, photographs, and movies depicting "every conceivable kind of normal and abnormal sexual relations."

Margaret Mead explains pornography as "calculated to stimulate sex feelings independent of the presence of another loved and chosen human being."

Pornography is "daydream material calculated to feed the auto-erotic desires of the immature and perverted and senile," sums up William Lockhart.[6]

The Supreme Court, however, has not yet attempted to define or explain hard-core pornography. Chief Justice Warren in *Jacobellis* asked: "Who can define 'hard-core pornography' with any greater clarity than 'obscenity'?" Justice Stewart in the same case confessed: "I shall not attempt . . . to define the kinds of material I understand to be embraced within [hard-core pornography]; and perhaps I could never succeed in intelligibly doing so. But I know it when I see it, and the motion picture involved in this case is not that." Although admirable for its candor, this statement was not very helpful to others in identifying what Stewart insisted was "a distinct and easily identifiable class of material," and so in *Ginzburg* v. *United States* (1966) he added: "In order to prevent any possible misunderstanding, I have set out in the margin a description, borrowed from the Solicitor General's brief, of the kind of thing to which I have reference."

### THE FOURTH TEST: PANDERING

If the obscenity laws applied only to hard-core pornography, then distributors of salacious literary materials had little reason to fear prosecution. The result undoubtedly was an increase in the openness with which sexually stimulating materials were published and advertised. When the magazine *Eros,* announced as a quarterly "devoted to the subjects of Love and Sex," was founded in 1962 by Ralph Ginzburg, he said in an advertisement that it was "the result of recent court decisions that have realistically interpreted America's obscenity laws and that have given to this country a new breath of freedom of expression. . . . *Eros* takes full advantage of this new freedom of expression. It is *the* magazine of sexual candor."

Ginzburg had misinterpreted the extent of the new freedom. He was prosecuted and convicted under the federal obscenity statute for the publication of *Eros* and certain other materials, and sentenced to five years in prison. The Supreme Court, some members of which had apparently become concerned over the commercial exploitation of sex resulting from its earlier decisions, unexpectedly affirmed the conviction by a vote of five to four in *Ginzburg* v. *United States* (1966).

In justification for this ruling, Justice Brennan for the majority announced a new, fourth test for obscenity—the setting or context in which the publications claimed to be obscene were presented to the public. The Court conceded that Ginzburg's publications "standing alone . . . might not be obscene." But when viewed "against a background of commercial exploitation

---

[6] William Lockhart and Robert McClure, "Obscenity Censorship: The Core Constitutional Issue—What Is Obscene?" 7 *Utah Law Review* 289 (1961); also *Selected Essays on Constitutional Law* 670 (1963).

of erotica solely for the sake of their prurient appeal," a different conclusion was justified.

Each of the accused publications, the Court found, had been "originated or sold as stock in trade of the sordid business of pandering." The "leer of the sensualist" permeated the advertising. The publisher "deliberately emphasized the sexually provocative aspects of the work, in order to catch the salaciously disposed." He engaged in the "exploitation of interests in titillation by pornography." The magazine was even mailed from Middlesex, New Jersey, after arrangements to mail it from Intercourse, Pennsylvania, had proved unsuccessful.

Justice Brennan did not state the new "context" test very precisely. He simply affirmed for the Court that "the question of obscenity may include consideration of the setting in which the publications were presented as an aid to determining the question of obscenity." He did not discuss the relationship of the context test to the other three tests, except to say that "in close cases evidence of pandering may be probative with respect to the nature of the material in question and thus satisfy the *Roth* test." But surely the holding is that the setting test can override the other three, since materials otherwise not clearly obscene can become "illicit merchandise" because of the way in which they are presented.

In *Mishkin* v. *New York* (1966), decided the same day as *Ginzburg*, the Court by a vote of six to three upheld the criminal conviction of a man who published and arranged for the writing of books concerned largely with deviant sexual practices. The New York courts applied hard-core pornography as their obscenity standard, which of course met the Supreme Court's constitutional requirements. The principal feature of interest in *Mishkin* was its treatment of the "average person" aspect of the *Roth* test. Counsel for Mishkin argued that books emphasizing flagellation, fetishism, lesbianism, and masochism such as were here at issue were so deviant that they would not appeal to the prurient interest of an "average" person, but instead would "disgust and sicken" him. Justice Brennan countered this legalism by the following adjustment of "the prurient-appeal requirement to social realities": "Where the material is designed for and primarily disseminated to a clearly defined deviant sexual group, rather than the public at large, the prurient-appeal requirement of the *Roth* test is satisfied if the dominant theme of the material taken as a whole appeals to the prurient interest in sex of the members of that group."

The obscenity field, which had been complicated enough prior to *Ginzburg*, was reduced to what C. Peter Magrath calls a "disaster area"[7] by *Ginzburg* and its two companion cases, *Fanny Hill* and *Mishkin*. One problem with *Ginzburg* is the obvious lack of due process. The Court, as Black

---

[7] C. Peter Magrath, "The Obscenity Cases: Grapes of Roth," in Philip B. Kurland (ed.), *The Supreme Court Review: 1966* (Chicago: The University of Chicago Press, 1966), p. 56.

and Harlan charged, had rewritten the federal obscenity statute into an antipandering law, on the basis of which, Stewart agreed, Ginzburg had been found guilty of offenses—pandering, titillation, commercial exploitation —with which he had not been charged. Although Brennan cited one federal court decision, *United States* v. *Rebhuhn* (1940), to establish that the relationship of pandering to obscenity had been previously accepted, pandering had not been seriously discussed in the *Ginzburg* case in the lower court opinions, in the briefs, or in the oral arguments.

Of broader significance, the pandering test was likely to prove unusable or at least completely unpredictable in application. In the *Fanny Hill* case there was no evidence of pandering in the record, but if there had been, Brennan said it could have been used to help resolve the obscenity issue. Clark, on the other hand, would have applied the pandering test because he thought the publisher was fully aware of the "prurient appeal" of the book. Surely the character of the advertising or the motives of a book's publishers are irrelevant to a decision on the obscenity of the book.

The *Ginzburg* decision is perhaps best understood as one of Mr. Dooley's "illiction returns" decisions, a reassurance by the Court to the country that the permissiveness of its standards on obscenity did have limits. In fact, the decision was widely interpreted in this manner, and it stimulated many proposals for the drafting of new obscenity legislation. However, in *Redrup* v. *New York* (1967) the Court, throwing out obscenity convictions based on two "pulp" books and ten "girlie" magazines, made it clear that its standards for the suppression of obscenity were still strict. Further evidence of this fact was given when on the last day of the term in 1967 the Court reversed no less than thirteen state and federal obscenity convictions, usually citing *Redrup*. One of these cases, *Aday* v. *United States,* had involved an incredible ten-year sentence for sending an allegedly obscene book through the mails. Significantly, on the same day the Court did affirm in *Landau* v. *Fording* a conviction in a case where the California courts had found a film to constitute hard-core pornography.

The 1967 opinions recapitulated the differences among the Court's members on the obscenity issue. Black and Douglas believe the federal and state governments are utterly without power to suppress or punish obscenity. Stewart would permit action only against hard-core pornography. Brennan and Fortas stand by the "prurient interest," "patent offensiveness," and "utter lack of social value" tests. Clark, Warren, and White would use prurient interest alone and undiluted. Harlan would limit the federal government to action against hard-core pornography, but would permit the states greater leeway.

The *Redrup* case suggested that the Court, though thus fractured, might coalesce on two policy positions. First, *Redrup* indicated that the Court would regard favorably statutes reflecting "a specific and limited state concern for juveniles." Second, the Court would react unfavorably to "any sug-

gestion of an assault upon individual privacy by publication in a manner so obtrusive as to make it impossible for an unwilling individual to avoid exposure to it." The *Redrup* opinion also reiterated the pandering test, but because of its inherent problems it seems unlikely to be employed except in cases of unusual provocation.[8]

## OBJECTIVITY AND STANDARDS

Review of obscenity convictions offers the Supreme Court an unusual problem. Normally the Court is limited to examining the record of the proceedings in the courts below and the legal arguments in the briefs. The Court must take the word of witnesses who testified about the facts at issue. But in an obscenity case the material adjudged obscene is available for direct first-hand examination by the justices if they wish, and in fact this is the general practice on the Supreme Court. The justices read the books or magazines and have a showing of the movies that have been found obscene in lower courts. In *Jacobellis* Justice Brennan wrote: "We have viewed the film." In *Kingsley International Pictures Corp.*, Justice Frankfurter expressed the opinion he formed "after viewing the picture." [9]

Under these circumstances, can the Supreme Court's rulings have any other basis than the personal tastes of the justices? The subjectivity of their obscenity decisions has been frankly admitted by several justices. In *Roth* Justice Harlan recognized that since the constitutional standards on obscenity "do not readily lend themselves to generalized definitions, the constitutional problem in the last analysis becomes one of particularized judgments which appellate courts must make for themselves." Justice Stewart's test for hard-core pornography was knowing it when he saw it. Justice Brennan in *Bantam Books Inc.* v. *Sullivan* (1963) agreed that it was "a dim and uncertain line" which separated constitutionally protected expression from obscenity.

The judicial reactions to the film "Lady Chatterley's Lover" were frankly personal. Justice Frankfurter said: "As one whose taste in art and literature

---

[8] On the first of the above points, see *Ginsberg* v. *New York* (1968), where the Court approved the constitutionality of a statute making it a crime to sell any material to children under seventeen years of age that presents a salacious view of nudity, sexual conduct, or sado-masochistic abuse. On the second issue, see *Fort v. Miami* (1967), where the Court, with three justices dissenting, let stand an obscenity conviction of a sculptor who displayed in his yard life-sized statues of males and females in erotic embrace.

[9] Justice Black is the only recorded exception to this practice. After noting that several of his colleagues had relied on their personal appraisal of "Lady Chatterley's Lover" for their conclusion that New York could not bar its showing, he said: "Unlike them, I have not see the picture." In *Mishkin* he noted: "Neither in this case nor in *Ginzburg* have I read the alleged obscene matter." His position is that "this Court is without constitutional power to censor speech or press regardless of the particular subject discussed," and so there is no need for him to judge the particular works in controversy.

hardly qualifies him for the *avant-garde,* I am more than surprised that the New York authorities should have banned 'Lady Chatterley's Lover.' " Justice Harlan's comment was: "I cannot regard this film as depicting anything more than a somewhat unusual, and rather pathetic, 'love triangle,' lacking in anything that could properly be termed obscene or corruptive of the public morals by inciting the commission of adultery." Justice Black recorded his disapproval of a practice under which "every member of the Court must exercise his own judgment as to how bad a picture is, a judgment which is ultimately based at least in large part on his own standard of what is immoral."

Are there any methods by which obscenity judgments can be made less subjective? We have just seen how Justice Black avoids these "policy controversies, which have so little in common with lawsuits." Chief Justice Warren in *Jacobellis* protested against the Court establishing itself "as an ultimate censor, in each case reading the entire record, viewing the accused material, and making an independent *de novo* judgment on the question of obscenity." Instead, he would apply a "sufficient evidence" standard to the record. "This is the only reasonable way I can see to obviate the necessity of this Court's sitting as the Super Censor of all the obscenity purveyed throughout the Nation." Applying this standard, he would have allowed the Ohio courts' judgment that "The Lovers" was obscene to stand.

Justice Harlan had still another solution. He would apply the sufficient evidence rule to the states, but continue strict Supreme Court supervision over federal obscenity prosecutions, because he believed that Congress had "no substantive power over sexual morality." Moreover, he said in *Roth,* he found it tolerable, if not necessarily wise or desirable, that the people of one state might be prevented from reading D. H. Lawrence. "But that no person in the United States should be allowed to do so seems to me to be intolerable." Harlan reiterated this "split-level First Amendment theory" in the *Fanny Hill* case, but secured no support for it elsewhere on the Court.

During the oral argument in the 1966 obscenity cases, various members of the Court questioned counsel about how they should discharge their responsibilities. Chief Justice Warren, referring to the twenty-three books involved, said: "Do we have to read all of them to determine if they have social importance? I'm sure this Court does not want to be the final censor to read all the prurient material in the country to determine if it has social value. If the final burden depends on this Court, it looks to me as though we're in trouble." [10]

So far, however, the Court majority has insisted there is no alternative to this case-by-case review. Obscenity is a "constitutional fact." Only if material is in fact obscene is it constitutional to punish its purveyors, and unless the Court makes an independent review of the facts in each case, it is abdi-

---

[10] *The New York Times,* December 8, 1965.

cating its responsibility to enforce constitutional standards. Justice Brennan in *Jacobellis* protested that the Court acts no differently in obscenity cases than in other areas where it passes on the constitutionality of "criticism of judges and public officials, advocacy of governmental overthrow, or speech alleged to constitute a breach of the peace." He could not see why the Court is called a "super-censor" when it makes an "independent constitutional judgment" on the facts of each obscenity proceeding to determine whether the material was constitutionally protected. Both Justices Harlan and Frankfurter in *Kingsley International Pictures Corp.* made the same point; censorship statutes could never be "self-executing" and consequently the Court could not hope to avoid the necessity for "individualized adjudication."

One final problem with the Court's standards in obscenity cases should be noted. The *Roth* principle relates obscenity to "contemporary community standards." What does this mean? Under the federal obscenity law, obviously there must be "a national standard of decency," as Justice Harlan said in *Manual Enterprises*. But in a state prosecution, does community refer to the locality, and can obscenity standards vary from place to place?

Chief Justice Warren argued in *Jacobellis* that there was in fact "no provable 'national standard'" and that it would be "unreasonable to expect local courts to divine one." But the Court majority disagreed, holding that "community" as used in *Roth* meant "society at large." It is true, Justice Brennan said, "that local communities throughout the land are in fact diverse. . . . Communities vary, however, in many respects other than their toleration of alleged obscenity, and such variances have never been considered to require or justify a varying standard for application of the Federal Constitution." Brennan concluded: "It is, after all, a national Constitution we are expounding."

It is customary in obscenity trials for literary experts to be offered as witnesses, testifying as to the social importance of the challenged works and their relation to community standards. How much weight is given to this "expert" testimony is uncertain. In the oral argument in the *Fanny Hill* case, testimony of scholars asserting the literary and historical value of the book was questioned by counsel for the state, who said that if such evidence was credited, it would be virtually impossible ever to brand a book as obscene, because some evidence could always be found of a book's supposed value.

Justice Frankfurter spoke up in behalf of the expert witnesses in *Smith v. California* (1959). He argued that anyone charged with obscenity had the implicit right "to enlighten the judgment of the tribunal, be it the jury or . . . the judge, regarding the prevailing literary and moral community standards and to do so through qualified experts . . . for community standards or the psychological or physiological consequences of questioned literature can as a matter of fact hardly be established except through experts." The refusal of the trial judge in the *Smith* case to allow experts to testify led Frankfurter to conclude that due process had been denied.

## THE TECHNIQUES OF MORALS CENSORSHIP: BOOKS

Legislative limitations on the circulation of allegedly obscene literature usually employ the technique of subsequent punishment. In *Smith* v. *California* (1959) the Supreme Court imposed a limitation on prosecution techniques, by declaring unconstitutional a Los Angeles ordinance which made it a crime for anyone to have in his possession for sale obscene books. The fault in the ordinance was that it did not require the bookseller to be aware of the obscene contents of a book to justify a conviction. If a seller were absolutely liable for having obscene books in his possession, the Court felt that he would tend to restrict the books he sold to those he had personally inspected, and this would be a serious bar to the free flow of communications.

Public alarm over the growing rate of juvenile delinquency and crime and the possible contribution of comic and pocket books to these evils has recently led to new forms of restraint on the distribution of print. Many volunteer citizen groups have been active in this field. They typically operate by developing lists of publications they consider objectionable, and their members then urge distributors and dealers not to handle these items. So long as this remains an activity of private citizens, no constitutional questions are raised. However, in a number of instances public officials have taken these lists, or developed lists of their own, and have threatened distributors with prosecution if they stocked books on the list.

In *Bantam Books, Inc.* v. *Sullivan* (1963) the Supreme Court declared a practice similar to this unconstitutional.[11] The Rhode Island Legislature had created a Commission to Encourage Morality in Youth with the duty to "educate" the public concerning obscene publications and to recommend prosecution of violations of the laws on obscenity. The commission undertook the practice of notifying book distributors on official stationery that certain publications handled by them had been found objectionable for sale to youths under eighteen. These letters customarily thanked the distributors in advance for their cooperation, and reminded them that it was the commission's duty to recommend prosecution for purveyors of obscenity. Copies of the lists of objectionable publications were also circulated to local police departments. Usually distributors stopped further circulation of listed publications.

The defense of the commission program was that it was merely "exhorting" and "advising," not "regulating." But the Supreme Court regarded the commission as engaged in the deliberate suppression of publications, acting "under color of state law." Through a system of "informal sanctions," the commission had largely obviated the need to employ criminal sanctions, and thus had eliminated the safeguards of the criminal process. This was prior restraint and, said Justice Brennan, citing *Near* v. *Minnesota,* "any system

[11] See also *Holding* v. *Blankenship* (1967).

of prior restraints of expression comes to this Court bearing a heavy presumption against its constitutional validity." Justice Harlan, dissenting, agreed that the commission had made some ill-advised and overbearing utterances, but believed the majority was not giving due regard to the state's concern with the problem of juvenile delinquency.

The Court reconciled its *Bantam Books* decision with the earlier judgment in *Kingsley Books* v. *Brown* (1957), which went in the opposite direction. A New York statute authorized the chief executive or legal officer of any city or town in the state to bring an injunction against the sale of any indecent books or other materials. The person whom it was sought to enjoin was entitled to a trial of the issues within one day and the court was to give its decision two days after the trial ended. If the injunction was granted, the material was to be surrendered to the sheriff or seized by him, and destroyed.

This statute had also been attacked as violating the principle of *Near* v. *Minnesota*, but the Court had upheld it by a five to four vote. Justice Frankfurter for the majority thought there was little resemblance between the two cases. In *Near* a court was enjoining future issues of a publication because its past issues had been found to be offensive and derogatory to a public official. Here a court was enjoining circulation of material already published, which had been found in a judicial proceeding to be obscene. Both statutes are prior restraint, but Frankfurter thought this phrase was not a "self-wielding sword," nor could it serve as a "talismanic test." The kind of prior restraint applied in this case seemed to him no more restrictive an interference with freedom of publication than criminal punishment after the event would be.

Chief Justice Warren, dissenting, charged that book seizure "savors too much of book burning." The New York statute, totally ignoring the "manner of use" of the book, or the "setting in which it is placed," put the book itself on trial, not its seller. "It is the conduct of the individual that should be judged, not the quality of art or literature. To do otherwise is to impose a prior restraint and hence to violate the Constitution. Certainly in the absence of a prior judicial determination of illegal use, books, pictures and other objects of expression should not be destroyed."

This decision seemed to open up very dangerous prospects. A noisy pressure group makes up its list, a politically ambitious mayor or district attorney files suit for injunction, a complaisant judge grants it—and a book is enjoined over an entire state, as bad in and of itself, under all circumstances. Copies are seized and destroyed, "like diseased cattle and impure butter."

The Supreme Court's subsequent decisions indicated its awareness of these possibilities. In *Bantam Books* the Court explained that it had "tolerated" the New York law only because "it operated under judicial superintendence and assured an almost immediate judicial determination of the validity of the restraint." It has declined to approve several similar statutes which lacked the protections of the New York law. In *Marcus* v. *Search Warrant* (1961)

warrants issued under a Missouri search and seizure statute gave the police virtually unlimited authority to seize any publications which they considered to be obscene; the warrants were issued on complaints lacking any specific description of the publications to be seized, and without prior submission of any publications to the judge issuing the warrant. The Court held these procedures to be deficient for lack of safeguards to prevent suppression of nonobscene books protected by the Constitution.

A *Quantity of Copies of Books* v. *Kansas* (1964) took a similar position on a similar Kansas law. However, because of the *Marcus* decision, the attorney general of Kansas had involved a county judge in the seizure proceedings. A warrant had been secured from the judge directing seizure of certain paperback novels, and after seizure the judge held a hearing and found the books obscene. The Supreme Court held that the failure to afford a hearing on the question of obscenity before the warrant was issued made this procedure constitutionally deficient.

Justice Brennan did not say the Kansas procedure was "prior restraint," but Justice Harlan, dissenting, thought this was an "unarticulated premise" lurking in the opinion. In contrast, Harlan regarded this as a penal law taking effect after the event of publication, and he also believed the Kansas procedure fully met the procedural requirements of the *Kingsley Books* decision. It seems clear that the more recent Court majority proposes to confine the *Kingsley Books* rule to as narrow a scope as possible.

### THE TECHNIQUES OF MORALS CENSORSHIP: MOVIES

State censorship of motion pictures was approved by the Court in the 1915 case of *Mutual Film Corp.* v. *Industrial Commission of Ohio*. The motion picture of that era was of course only an entertaining novelty rather completely devoid of any ideational content, and it was readily assimilated to burlesque or other theatrical spectacles which were customarily subjected to control on moral grounds. Moreover, the 1915 decision antedated the Court's concern with civil liberties problems.

Over the years both motion pictures and the Court changed. The movies came somewhat closer to being commentaries on the social scene, and in documentary films and newsreels they rivaled the newspapers in reporting current events. Yet censorship continued to be practiced, and there were even some noteworthy instances of its application to newsreels. These developments were not lost on the Supreme Court, and during the 1940s several justices intimated that moving pictures were entitled to the protection of the First and Fourteenth Amendments.[12]

It was not until 1952, however, that the 1915 censorship decision was overruled. *Burstyn* v. *Wilson* concerned Rossellini's film *The Miracle*, which had been licensed for exhibition in New York and shown for about two months.

[12] See *United States* v. *Paramount Pictures* (1948).

After a Catholic campaign against the film, appropriate administrative review was undertaken, and the license was withdrawn on the ground that the picture was "sacrilegious." A state statute authorized denial of a license to a movie found to be "obscene, indecent, immoral, inhuman, sacrilegious, or . . . of such a character that its exhibition would tend to corrupt morals or incite to crime."

Justice Clark wrote the Court's opinion holding that states could not constitutionally censor motion pictures on the ground that they are sacrilegious. First, Clark definitely brought movies within the protection of the First Amendment, by way of the Fourteenth. Contrary to the view in the *Mutual Film* case that they were merely spectacles, Clark said: "It cannot be doubted that motion pictures are a significant medium for the communication of ideas."

The rest of Clark's opinion was a little puzzling. He seemed to base his rejection of censorship on the rather narrow ground that "sacrilege," the standard applied in the case, was too loose and meaningless and set the censor "adrift upon a boundless sea amid a myriad of conflicting currents of religious views, with no charts but those provided by the most vocal and powerful orthodoxies." He warned that the Court was expressing no opinion on "whether a state may censor motion pictures under a clearly drawn statute designed and applied to prevent the showing of obscene films." But nevertheless his opinion did contain one rather strong sentence related less to the vagueness issue and more to the general invalidity of prior restraints: "From the standpoint of freedom of speech and the press, it is enough to point out that the state has no legitimate interest in protecting any or all religions from views distasteful to them which is sufficient to justify prior restraints upon the expression of those views."

This ambiguity in the Court's position continued to be characteristic of subsequent decisions.[13] In *Kingsley International Pictures Corp.* v. *New York* (1959) the Court reviewed the application of the New York law, as it had been revised in 1954 to meet the *Burstyn* criticisms, against "Lady Chatterley's Lover." As already noted, the Court decided that the law was being applied to censor ideas. Since it was unconstitutional for that reason, the Court had no occasion to decide whether it was also unconstitutional on general prior restraint grounds.

The next case, *Times Film Corp.* v. *Chicago* (1961), was a test case seeking to force the Court to rule directly on the constitutionality of motion-picture censorship. An exhibitor applied for a permit to exhibit "Don Juan" in Chicago and paid the license fee, but refused to submit the film for examination by the board of censors. He then sought an injunction to pre-

[13] In the next four decisions after *Burstyn*, the Court invalidated the censorship of five different films, but without writing an opinion in any of the cases. *Gelling* v. *Texas* (1952); *Superior Films* v. *Ohio Department of Education* (1954); *Holmby Productions* v. *Vaughn* (1955); *Times Film Corp.* v. *Chicago* (1957).

vent the city from interfering with the showing of the film, on the ground that the ordinance amounted to unconstitutional prior restraint. But the Supreme Court refused to be pushed into a ruling on the broad issue of the censor's basic authority, or to admit that there might be a right to show every motion picture at least once without restraint. The Court implied that there was a public interest in preventing the showing of obscene motion pictures, and it would, as in the earlier cases, talk only about standards and procedures for the exercise of this power.

Then, in *Freedman* v. *Maryland* (1965) an exhibitor used the one remaining tactic to force a ruling on movie censorship from the Court. He showed a film in public without submitting it to the state board of censors. But once more the Court refused to oblige with a ruling on censorship per se. This time, however, it frankly admitted its concern about the "peculiar dangers to constitutionally protected speech" inherent in motion-picture censorship, and took the important step of laying down strict new procedural requirements for such systems.

First, the burden of proving that the film is unprotected expression must rest on the censor. Second, the censor must, within a specified brief period after a movie is presented to him, either issue a license or go to court to restrain the showing of the film. Third, the procedure must assure a prompt final judicial decision. Since the Maryland law did not provide these protections, it was unconstitutional.

At the time of this ruling, only four states and a few municipalities had active censorship programs. Following the decision, the New York supreme court held that state's law unconstitutional, and the Legislature did not pass a new one. The Chicago city council, however, amended its ordinance to give effect to the Supreme Court's requirements. But in *Teitel Film Corp.* v. *Cusack* (1968) the Court held the revised ordinance unconstitutional as failing to meet the *Freedman* promptness test, since it would take an exhibitor at least fifty days to get into court for a review of a Chicago censor board ban.

State laws punishing the showing of obscene films are not affected of course, by the censorship decisions.[14] Nor has the Supreme Court expressed any opinion concerning plans, now widely discussed, for ordinances requiring the classification of motion pictures and the exclusion of children from those given an "adult only" rating. A Dallas ordinance of this sort was upheld by a federal district court in 1966.[15] Finally, the Supreme Court has never explained what are the peculiar characteristics of films which permit them to be subjected to a system of prior restraint which would be clearly unconstitutional if applied to books.

[14] *Jacobellis* v. *Ohio* (1964) involved a conviction for possessing and exhibiting an allegedly obscene film.
[15] The Supreme Court held the ordinance unconstitutional because its standards were too vague in *Interstate Circuit, Inc.* v. *Dallas* (1968).

## SELECTED REFERENCES

CAIRNS, ROBERT B., JAMES C. N. PAUL, and JULIUS WISHNER, "Sex Censorship: The Assumptions of Anti-obscenity Laws and the Empirical Evidence," 46 *Minnesota Law Review* 1009 (1962).

CARMEN, IRA H., *Movies, Censorship and the Law.* Ann Arbor, Mich.: The University of Michigan Press, 1966.

ERNST, MORRIS L., and ALAN U. SCHWARTZ, *Censorship: The Search for the Obscene.* New York: The Macmillan Company, 1964.

HENKIN, LOUIS, "Morals and the Constitution: The Sin of Obscenity," 63 *Columbia Law Review* 391 (1963).

KALVEN, HARRY, JR., "The Metaphysics of the Law of Obscenity," in Philip B. Kurland (ed.), *The Supreme Court Review: 1960*, pp. 1–45. Chicago: The University of Chicago Press, 1960.

KUH, RICHARD H., *Foolish Figleaves? Pornography in—and out of—Court.* New York: The Macmillan Company, 1967.

LOCKHART, WILLIAM, and ROBERT MC CLURE, "Censorship of Obscenity: The Developing Constitutional Standards," 45 *Minnesota Law Review* 5 (1960).

———, and ———, "Literature, the Law of Obscenity, and the Constitution," 38 *Minnesota Law Review* 295 (1954).

MAGRATH, C. PETER, "The Obscenity Cases: Grapes of Roth," in Philip B. Kurland (ed.), *The Supreme Court Review: 1966*, pp. 7–77. Chicago: The University of Chicago Press, 1966.

"Obscene Literature," 18 *Vanderbilt Law Review* 2084 (1965).

"Obscenity and the Arts" (a symposium), 20 *Law and Contemporary Problems* 532–688 (1955).

"Obscenity in the Mails: Post Office Department Procedures and the First Amendment," 58 *Northwestern University Law Review* 664 (1963).

PAUL, JAMES C. N. and MURRAY L. SCHWARTZ, *Federal Censorship: Obscenity in the Mail.* New York: The Free Press of Glencoe, 1961.

SCHWARTZ, LOUIS B., "Moral Offenses and the Model Penal Code," 63 *Columbia Law Review* 669 (1963).

# 26

## Libel

When Chief Justice Hughes declared prior restraint of the press unconstitutional in *Near* v. *Minnesota*, he emphasized that both public and private redress against abuses of the liberty accorded the press were available through the libel laws. When Justice Murphy developed in *Chaplinsky* v. *New Hampshire* his theory that certain limited classes of speech had such slight social value that they were not protected by the First Amendment, he included the "libelous" along with the lewd, the profane, and the insulting. When Congress passed the Sedition Act in 1798, punishing libel of the government, the assumption was that the First Amendment did not forbid such legislation. It is only very recently that the Supreme Court has seriously begun to examine the constitutional status of laws punishing libel.

First some definitions and distinctions are in order. *Libel* is the defamation of character by print or other visual presentation such as television. *Slander* is defamation by oral presentation. Defamation itself needs definition. The act of 1798 spelled out the concept as "false, scandalous and malicious writing . . . with the intent . . . to bring into contempt or disrepute; or to excite . . . the hatred of the good people of the United States."

Prosecutions for libel can be *civil* or *criminal*. The theory of a criminal prosecution is that libel is an offense against the peace and good order of the community, likely to incite acts of physical retaliation. In earlier times when there were no laws punishing defamation, dueling developed as a

method by which wounded feelings of honor could be avenged. Criminal punishment for libel provides a lawful means of redress and is designed to avert the possibility that libelous utterances will provoke an enraged victim to breach of the peace. Libels of the government or public officials may be made criminally punishable, as by the Sedition Act of 1798. Criminal libel statutes provide for fines and sentences of imprisonment within defined limits. The act of 1798 specified maximum sentences of $5,000 fine and five years in prison.

A civil prosecution for libel is a suit for monetary damages brought by the victim against the publisher of the libel. The civil suit has generally tended to supplant criminal prosecutions for libel in the area of private defamation. As Justice Brennan said in *Garrison* v. *Louisiana* (1964), the civil remedy "enabled the frustrated victim to trade chivalrous satisfaction for damages [and] substantially eroded the breach of the peace justification for criminal libel laws."

Damages in a civil suit may be of two types—*compensatory* and *punitive*. Compensatory damages are intended to reimburse the individual for actual financial loss resulting, for example, from loss of employment or earning power or reputation occasioned by the libel. The amount of such losses can be reasonably well established by evidence. Punitive damages are exemplary in character, intended to compensate the victim for his suffering and to punish the libeler for malicious intent. There is no objective standard for determining the amount of punitive damages, and they have tended to escalate in recent years. When Theodore Roosevelt won a libel suit after he had left the Presidency against a newspaper which had charged he cursed and was intoxicated while campaigning, he was awarded damages of 6 cents. But more recently a college football coach who had been accused in a *Saturday Evening Post* story of giving his team's signals to an opponent was awarded $60,000 in compensatory damages and 3 million dollars in punitive damages, which was cut to $400,000 on appeal. A television actor who lost his job because he was blacklisted by a right-wing organization was awarded damages totalling 2.25 million dollars, which was cut to $550,000 on appeal.

### SEDITIOUS LIBEL

Seditious libel is defamation of the government and its officials and is punished criminally. American experience with seditious libel was strongly influenced by English practice. The English law of seditious libel permitted punishment for publications tending to bring into hatred or contempt, or to excite disaffection against, the king, the government, Parliament, or the administration of justice. The English law of libel was initially developed by the Star Chamber, which made no use of a jury. After the Star Chamber was abolished in 1641, the King's Bench was influenced by its tradition and permitted juries only a limited role, such as finding facts as to authorship

or publication, reserving for the bench the question of whether these facts constituted a libel. A long line of oppressive libel prosecutions finally led to Fox's Libel Act in 1792, which allowed the jury to find a general verdict in cases of criminal libel. The American Sedition Act of 1798 also entrusted the determination of criminality to the jury, and in addition admitted truth as a defense.

It was the contention of Zechariah Chafee in his influential book, *Free Speech in the United States,* that the First Amendment was intended to abolish the law of seditious libel, a position also accepted by Justice Holmes. This view has been questioned by Leonard Levy, who argues that it was not until after adoption of the act of 1798 that opinion crystallized against seditious libel.[1] He points out that Jefferson, although he attacked the act of 1798 and its use against his partisans, was willing to see his Federalist opponents prosecuted for seditious libel in the states after he became President.

The Sedition Act expired by its terms in 1801, and it never reached the Supreme Court for a constitutional test. Fines levied against those convicted were subsequently repaid by act of Congress on the ground that the act had been unconstitutional, and President Jefferson pardoned all those found guilty under the act. Calhoun in a report to the Senate in 1836 assumed the act had been invalid, as did Justice Holmes in *Abrams* v. *United States* (1919) and Justice Jackson in *Beauharnais* v. *Illinois* (1942).

Finally, in *New York Times Co.* v. *Sullivan* (1964) the Court flatly ruled the act had been inconsistent with the First Amendment "because of the restraint it imposed upon criticism of government and public officials." In fact, Justice Brennan, who wrote the opinion for the Court, suggested that the right to criticize official conduct was "the central meaning of the First Amendment." Harry Kalven has translated this holding into the proposition that "defamation of the government is an impossible notion for a democracy." He goes on: "In brief, I suggest, that the presence or absence in the law of the concept of seditious libel defines the society. . . . If . . . it makes seditious libel an offense, it is not a free society no matter what its other characteristics." [2]

---

[1] Leonard W. Levy, *Legacy of Suppression* (Cambridge, Mass.: The Belknap Press, Harvard University Press, 1960). For comments on Levy's position, see Martin Shapiro, *Freedom of Speech: The Supreme Court and Judicial Review* (Englewood Cliffs, N.J.: Prentice-Hall, Inc., 1966), p. 93; Alexander Meiklejohn, "The First Amendment Is an Absolute," in Philip B. Kurland (ed.), *The Supreme Court Review: 1961* (Chicago: The University of Chicago Press, 1961), pp. 263–264.

[2] "The New York Times Case: A Note on 'The Central Meaning of the First Amendment,'" in Philip B. Kurland (ed.), *The Supreme Court Review: 1964* (Chicago: The University of Chicago Press, 1964), p. 205. See Justice Brennan's comment on Kalven's interpretation, in "The Supreme Court and the Meiklejohn Interpretation of the First Amendment," 79 *Harvard Law Review* 1, 10 (1965).

So far as prosecutions for libel on government are concerned, then, the Supreme Court has held, as reiterated by Justice Brennan in *Rosenblatt* v. *Baer* (1966), that "the Constitution does not tolerate [them] in any form." There is complete freedom to criticize government and public policies. But the government acts through individual public officials. Does that mean there is also complete freedom to criticize or defame public officials? That is a different problem, to which we now turn.

## LIBEL OF PUBLIC OFFICIALS

Prosecutions for alleged libel of public officials may be either civil or criminal. The case of *New York Times Co.* v. *Sullivan* (1964) was a civil suit. *The New York Times* had printed as a paid advertisement a criticism of the treatment of Negroes in Montgomery, Alabama. The ad was submitted by reputable persons, but it was later discovered that it contained some factual errors. The police commissioner of Montgomery, though not mentioned in the ad either by name or specific reference to his office, contended that criticism of the Montgomery "police" constituted a libel of him. The case was tried in Alabama.

The trial judge ruled that the statements in the ad were "libelous per se." He instructed the jury that legal injury was implied from the bare fact of publication, that compensatory (or general) damages did not need to be alleged or proved but were presumed, and also that "falsity and malice" were presumed, thus justifying punitive damages as well. The judge refused to require that the verdict differentiate between compensatory and punitive damages.

The Alabama jury awarded damages of $500,000, an amount one thousand times greater than the maximum fine provided by the Alabama criminal defamation statute. Another commissioner who sued on the basis of the same ad also got a $500,000 judgment, eleven additional libel suits were filed against *The Times* seeking a total of 5.6 million dollars, while five suits asking 1.7 million dollars were brought at the same time against the Columbia Broadcasting System based on its coverage of Alabama civil rights controversies. This indicates the magnitude of the threat to the solvency of major communications media which these libel proceedings had raised.

The Supreme Court unanimously reversed the *Sullivan* libel judgment on the ground that the Alabama libel law, as applied against *The New York Times*, failed to provide safeguards for freedom of speech and press required by the Constitution. The earlier statements in such cases as *Near* and *Chaplinsky* that the Constitution does not protect libelous publications were now qualified. A libel law, like any other, must meet constitutional standards; "libel can claim no talismanic immunity from constitutional limitations."

The *New York Times* case, Justice Brennan said for the Court, had to be

considered "against the background of a profound national commitment to the principle that debate on public issues should be uninhibited, robust, and wide-open, and that it may well include vehement, caustic, and sometimes unpleasantly sharp attacks on government and public officials." This advertisement, as an expression of grievance and protest on a major public issue, clearly qualified for constitutional protection.

Had it forfeited that standing by the falsity of some of the statements and the alleged defamation of the police commissioner? The Court did not think so. Erroneous statement is inevitable in free debate. "A rule compelling the critic of official conduct to guarantee the truth of all his factual assertions—and to do so on pain of libel judgments virtually unlimited in amount" would be fatal to robust debate on public issues. It would impose a "pall of fear and timidity . . . upon those who would give voice to public criticism." A defense for "erroneous statements honestly made" is essential to the survival of First Amendment freedoms.

Injury to official reputation, Justice Brennan went on, likewise "affords no warrant for repressing speech that would otherwise be free." Criticism of the official conduct of government officers "does not lose its constitutional protection merely because it is effective criticism and hence diminishes their official reputations."

The Court did, however, attach one important reservation to this broad constitutional protection for freedom of comment. Defamatory falsehood relating to official conduct would be actionable if made with "actual malice," that is, "with knowledge that it was false or with reckless disregard of whether it was false or not." But actual malice would have to be proved. Recognizing that this particular case might be tried again, the Court thought it wise to warn that the facts presented in the Alabama trial would not sustain a finding of actual malice on the part of *The New York Times*. Nor did the Court find any sufficient evidence in the record to transmute the general, "impersonal" criticisms of Alabama government into personal criticism, and hence potential libel, of the officials of that government.

Justices Black, Douglas, and Goldberg would have gone further than the Court. They argued for "absolute, unconditional" freedom of publications from libel suits. Black contended that the press must have "an absolute immunity for criticism of the way public officials do their public duty." He charged that "state libel laws threaten the very existence of an American press virile enough to publish unpopular views on public affairs and bold enough to criticize the conduct of public officials." The "actual malice" test, he thought, was "an elusive, abstract concept, hard to prove and hard to disprove." It would be an uncertain, "evanescent protection for the right critically to discuss public officers."

Justice Goldberg, responding to the contention that "deliberately and maliciously false statements have no conceivable value as free speech,"

argued that the real issue was whether constitutional freedoms are effectively safeguarded "by a rule allowing the imposition of liability upon a jury's evaluation of the speaker's state of mind."

Later in the same year the Supreme Court applied the principles of the *New York Times* case in a prosecution for criminal defamation, *Garrison* v. *Louisiana* (1964). A district attorney had issued a public statement disparaging the judicial conduct of eight criminal court judges, and had been found guilty of libel. The Supreme Court, again through Justice Brennan, held that where criticism of public officials is concerned, criminal libel statutes serve no interests distinct from those served by civil libel laws, and therefore are subject to the same limitations.

Again, however, the Court made an exception for "the knowing or reckless falsehood." A lie "knowingly and deliberately published about a public official" should enjoy no immunity. "For the use of the known lie as a tool is at once at odds with the premises of democratic government and with the orderly manner in which economic, social, or political change is to be effected." Calculated falsehoods do not enjoy constitutional protection because they are in the *Chaplinsky* category of utterances which are "no essential part of any exposition of ideas." Justices Black, Douglas, and Goldberg again would have given complete protection against criminal libel prosecutions. Douglas charged that the Court's "actual malice" rule allowed the unconstitutional law of seditious libel to remain partially effective.[3]

Another conviction of criminal libel for criticism of public officials was reversed in *Ashton* v. *Kentucky* (1966). A college student endeavoring to aid unemployed miners in a Kentucky coal-mining community published a pamphlet of limited circulation making serious charges against the local police and the owner of the town newspaper, in connection with a labor dispute. The trial court defined the common-law crime of criminal libel in Kentucky as "any writing calculated to create disturbances of the peace." The Supreme Court, citing *Terminiello* v. *Chicago*, held that, as so defined, the elements of the crime were so indefinite and uncertain that it could not be enforced as a penal offense.

Since public officials are protected against libel only by the rule of "actual malice," it becomes important to define "public official." In the *New York Times* case the Court remarked that it would not there undertake "to determine how far down into the lower ranks of government employees the 'public official' designation would extend for purposes of this rule." But it did get into this issue in *Rosenblatt* v. *Baer* (1966). In that case a newspaper columnist had been found guilty of libeling a man employed by the commissioners of a New Hampshire county to operate a county ski recreation area. Justice Brennan, following the principle that criticism of those responsible for government operations must be free, held that the "public

---

[3] The rule of the *New York Times* and *Garrison* cases was applied in *Henry* v. *Collins* (1965) and *Beckley Newspapers Corp.* v. *Hanks* (1967).

official" designation "applies at the very least to those among the hierarchy of government employees who have, or appear to the public to have, substantial responsibility for or control over the conduct of governmental affairs."

Justice Douglas wanted to go further. He believed that not only public officials at all levels but any persons whose activities had an impact on public affairs—government contractors, "industrialists who raise the price of a basic commodity," labor leaders who combine "trade unionism with bribery and racketeering"—should be open to criticism without raising fear of libel suits. The important question for him was "whether a public *issue,* not a public official, is involved."

Justice Stewart, on the other hand, was afraid the Court, in protecting the right of free discussion under the First Amendment, was neglecting "the right of a man to the protection of his own reputation from unjustified invasion and wrongful hurt. . . . The protection of private personality . . . is left primarily to the individual States under the Ninth and Tenth Amendments." He would not permit the First Amendment to undermine the right of the states to safeguard the "rights and values of private personality [which] far transcend mere personal interests. Surely if the 1950s taught us anything, they taught us that the poisonous atmosphere of the easy lie can infect and degrade a whole society." He would prevent a state from converting its law of defamation into a law of seditious libel, but that was as far as he would go.

A word should be said about libelous utterances *by* public officials. As we have already seen, members of Congress enjoy an absolute immunity from legal liability for any statements they may make in their official capacity. The President is recognized by the courts to be free from judicial process. The Supreme Court's decision in *Barr* v. *Matteo* (1959) extended immunity from libel prosecution to all federal administrative officials for statements made within the "outer perimeter" of their official duty. Thus government officials have absolute protection against prosecution for libel, whereas persons who allegedly libel government officials have the qualified protection provided by the actual malice rule.

### PRIVATE DEFAMATION

Prosecution for private defamation—that is, libel of one private individual or corporation by another private person—may be either civil or criminal. However, we have seen that criminal redress for private defamation has now practically disappeared.

We have also noted the disagreement on the Supreme Court as to what consequences, if any, attach to the distinction between defamation of public officials and private defamation. Justice Black has concluded that all libel suits are constitutionally forbidden by the First Amendment, no matter who

is involved. This position derives from his absolutist view of constitutional standards. He believes that the First Amendment "intended that there should be no libel or defamation law in the United States under the United States Government, just absolutely none so far as I am concerned." [4] Thus he would leave individuals, public or private, with no legal redress against the most malicious or scandalous assaults on their reputations.

On the other hand, Justice Goldberg said in his *New York Times* concurring opinion: "Purely private defamation has little to do with the political ends of a self-governing society." Presumably he meant to suggest that punishment of private defamation did not raise substantial First Amendment problems.

This is no doubt true in many situations, but certainly prosecutions for private defamation can create serious public issues. Newspapers, magazines, and other media of mass communication are often the targets of libel suits. If the libel laws permit heavy damages to be assessed for private defamation, willingness of the communications media to carry stories on controversial issues may be seriously diminished. A 1964 survey showed that libel suits seeking damages of 288 million dollars were pending in three Southern states alone, almost all against newspapers and television companies based on their reporting of civil rights controversies. [5]

Recognizing this threat to free communication, the courts have responded by extending the *New York Times* rule protecting comment about public officials to private individuals who engage in public controversy. Immediately after the *New York Times* decision had been handed down, it was applied by the Federal Court of Appeals for the Second Circuit in a libel suit brought by Linus Pauling, the famous physicist, against *The New York Daily News,* which had referred to him as a "loudmouth" and "pro-Communist." The court ruled that newspapers should be protected when presenting fair comment, without malice, on the activities of non-office holders engaged in debate on public issues. [6] Similarly, a subsequent suit by Pauling against *The National Review* was dismissed by a New York State judge who held that Pauling had limited his legal remedies to sue over being called a Communist collaborator because he had "made himself a public figure engaged voluntarily in public discussion of matters of grave public concern and controversy." [7]

The Supreme Court took up this issue in two 1967 decisions, and unanimously agreed that constitutional safeguards against libel suits should extend beyond public officials to "public figures," either those who thrust themselves into the vortex of public disputes or who have a status in life that commands

[4] Edmond Cahn, "Justice Black and First Amendment Absolutes: A Public Interview," 37 *New York University Law Review* 549 (1962).
[5] *The New York Times,* April 4, 1964.
[6] *Pauling* v. *News Syndicate Co.* (1964).
[7] *The New York Times,* April 20, 1966.

the White Circle League and asked for financial contributions. Beauharnais was convicted of violating the statute and was fined $200.

The Supreme Court upheld the conviction and statute by a five to four vote, Justice Frankfurter writing the opinion. Every state, he noted, provides for the punishment of libels directed at individuals. Clearly, it is libelous falsely to charge a person "with being a rapist, robber, carrier of knives and guns, and user of marijuana." The question, then, is whether the Fourteenth Amendment prevents states from punishing libels "directed at designated collectivities and flagrantly disseminated." His answer was that the Illinois Legislature might reasonably have decided to seek ways "to curb false or malicious defamation of racial and religious groups, made in public places and by means calculated to have a powerful emotional impact on those to whom it was presented." Where the individual is "inextricably involved" in the group, speech which could be libelous if directed to the individual may also be treated as libelous when directed at the group.

Justices Black, Douglas, Reed, and Jackson dissented, though Jackson's position differed from that of the other three. To Black, this decision manifested the shocking results of the reasonable man test in the civil liberties field. By treating the Illinois statute as a libel law, Frankfurter had taken the case out of the context of all the Court's free speech decisions on "the bland assumption that the First Amendment is wholly irrelevant. It is not even accorded the respect of a passing mention." Such a law, Black was sure, would present "a constant overhanging threat to freedom of speech, press and religion."

Justice Jackson agreed with the majority on the constitutionality of the group libel law, but thought that convictions would have to meet the clear and present danger test by taking into account the "actual or probable consequences" of the libel. In this case there should have been an appraisal of the particular form, time, place, and manner of the communication. Is a leaflet inherently less dangerous than the spoken word, because less "emotionally exciting?" Is the publication "so foul and extreme" as to defeat its own ends? Perhaps its appeal for money, "which has a cooling effect on many persons," would negate its inflammatory tendencies. Perhaps it would impress the passer-by "as the work of an irresponsible who needed mental examination." By failing to insist on such an inquiry into the circumstances, Jackson thought the majority had failed to achieve a constitutional balance between state power and individual rights.

Subsequent developments have demonstrated the error of the *Beauharnais* decision and undermined its authority. It failed to consider the close relationship between group libel and seditious libel.[8] It sought to remove important areas of public discussion from the protection of the First Amendment. It failed to understand, as the Court later put it in the *New York*

[8] Harry Kalven, Jr., *The Negro and the First Amendment* (Columbus, Ohio: Ohio State University Press, 1965), chap. 1.

*Times* case, the constitutional flaw in a law which "dampens the vigor and limits the variety of public debate." Even hatemongers have rights in a free society.

Group libel laws punish the act of discussion itself. If the debate becomes too vigorous, the breach of the peace laws are available. It is significant that when Illinois revised its criminal code in 1961, the three criminal libel laws on the books were merged into a single brief statute keyed to breach of the peace.[9] On the other hand, it should be noted that England, faced for the first time with racial problems, has adopted the group libel formula. The Race Relations Act of 1965 makes it unlawful to stir up in a public place "hatred against any section of the public in Great Britain distinguished by color, race or ethnic or national origins."

## SELECTED REFERENCES

BETH, LOREN P., "Group Libel and Free Speech," 39 *Minnesota Law Review* 167–184 (1955).

BRANT, IRVING, "Seditious Libel: Myth and Reality," 39 *New York University Law Review* 1–19 (1964).

CHAFEE, ZECHARIAH, JR., *Free Speech in the United States.* Cambridge, Mass.: Harvard University Press, 1941.

KALVEN, HARRY, JR., *The Negro and the First Amendment.* Columbus, Ohio: Ohio State University Press, 1965.

———, "The New York Times Case: A Note on 'The Central Meaning of the First Amendment,'" in Philip B. Kurland (ed.), *The Supreme Court Review: 1964,* pp. 191–221. Chicago: The University of Chicago Press, 1964.

———, "The Reasonable Man and the First Amendment: Hill, Butts, and Walker," in Philip B. Kurland (ed.), *The Supreme Court Review: 1967,* pp. 267–309. Chicago: The University of Chicago Press, 1967.

LEVY, LEONARD W., *Jefferson and Civil Liberties: The Darker Side.* Cambridge, Mass.: The Belknap Press, Harvard University Press, 1963.

———, *Legacy of Suppression: Freedom of Speech and Press in Early American History.* Cambridge, Mass.: The Belknap Press, Harvard University Press, 1960.

PHELPS, ROBERT H., and E. DOUGLAS HAMILTON, *Libel.* New York: The Macmillan Company, 1967.

RIESMAN, DAVID, "Democracy and Defamation: Control of Group Libel," 42 *Columbia Law Review* 727–780 (1942).

SHAPIRO, MARTIN, *Freedom of Speech: The Supreme Court and Judicial Review.* Englewood Cliffs, N.J.: Prentice-Hall, Inc., 1966.

TANENHAUS, JOSEPH, "Group Libel," 35 *Cornell Law Quarterly* 261–302 (1950).

[9] *Ibid.,* pp. 7, 174.

# 27

## Freedom of association

There is no provision in the Constitution specifically protecting freedom of association, yet the right of individuals to organize into groups for political, economic, religious, and social purposes is universally recognized. The constitutional basis for this freedom must be derived from the right of assembly and the freedoms of speech, press, and religion. The Supreme Court has often remarked upon "the close nexus between the freedoms of speech and assembly," and noted how "effective advocacy of both public and private points of view, particularly controversial ones, is undeniably enhanced by group association." [1]

Because it is so closely linked with these First Amendment freedoms, discussion of associational freedom in this volume is partly subsumed under other headings—for example, in dealing with political parties, labor unions, and religious groups. In this chapter our concern is primarily with unpopular organizations whose rights of association have been under the most pressure.

Associative freedom, of course, is not absolute for any group, any more than are the freedoms of speech, press, and assembly. The freedom of group life is always subject to some degree of regulation in the public interest. Totalitarians carry this regulation to the point of completely subjecting all groups to the purposes of the state. Anarchists go to the other extreme in

[1] *National Association for the Advancement of Colored People* v. *Alabama* (1958).

proposing that the state abdicate its functions to groups. The liberal state seeks to encourage the maximum of group freedom compatible with the general public welfare.

Robert Horn in his penetrating study of groups and the Constitution has classified the variety of relationships which can exist between government and groups.[2] For our present purposes three categories may be sufficient.

First, there is the policy of freedom from governmental interference or influence; the government simply keeps hands off. This policy of *laissez faire* is one that dictatorships or closed societies cannot risk. They must maintain control over all groups, even the most innocuous, to insure that they will not be used to challenge the regime.

Second, the government may assist groups, as by encouraging their formation, giving them appropriate privileges and powers, or even subsidizing them. So far as religious groups are concerned, there are constitutional limits on such assistance growing out of the establishment of religion clause in the Constitution, which will be discussed in the next chapter. When the public interest would be furthered thereby, the government may forbid private individuals to interfere with the rights of persons who are members of groups or wish to form groups, and may even require individuals to enter into legal relations with groups. Here we need think only of the many laws forbidding discrimination against racial groups or interference with the formation of labor unions or those requiring employers to bargain collectively with unions.

Third, the government may impose limitations on groups to prevent them from performing acts injurious to their own members, to persons outside the group, or even to the welfare of the state itself. It is in this third area, of course, where constitutional issues of freedom of association can arise. The variety of restrictions on the freedom of group activity is limited only by legislative imagination. They range all the way from mere discouragement of groups or membership by official policy to the actual outlawry of particular groups, making membership in them subject to criminal punishment. Although such extreme measures are now uncommon in democratic countries, in the past almost all groups—churches, labor unions, political parties, secret societies—have been illegal at one time or another.

In recent American experience, the organization whose associational rights have been under greatest pressure is the Communist Party. To meet the threat which communism appeared to present to American security, after the Russian Revolution established a basis for the Party's world-wide operations, much restrictive and punitive legislation was passed both by Congress and the state legislatures, and reviewing courts have had to struggle with very difficult problems in reconciling traditional and basic associative free-

[2] Robert A. Horn, *Groups and the Constitution* (Stanford, Calif.: Stanford University Press, 1956).

doms with society's right to counter organized efforts conceived to threaten its way of life and undermine national security.

In addition, the civil rights movement of the 1950s and 1960s brought into prominence two groups on the opposite sides of that struggle, the National Association for the Advancement of Colored People (hereafter NAACP) and the Ku Klux Klan, which have to a lesser degree encountered challenges to their continued operation. More recently difficulties have also been experienced by organizations of the New Left such as Students for a Democratic Society and the Student Nonviolent Coordinating Committee, as well as organizations on the far right such as the John Birch Society, the Minutemen, and the American Nazi Party.

## THE COMMUNIST PARTY AND GUILT BY ASSOCIATION

The Supreme Court's introduction to the interpretation of statutory restrictions on radicals came during and immediately after World War I, involving the Espionage Act of 1917 and the Sedition Act of 1918. Both enactments had to be construed in a wartime setting, which hardly encouraged the Court to be venturesome in protecting the speech rights of the assorted Socialists, pacifists, pro-Germans, Communists, and anarchists who were prosecuted under those statutes. The more significant of the decisions— particularly the *Abrams, Schenck,* and *Debs* cases—have already been commented on, and the ineffectiveness of the clear and present danger test, first developed in these cases, has been noted.

The "Red scare" stirred up by the Bolshevik revolution persisted for some time after the war, particularly in the form of the raids conducted by Attorney General A. Mitchell Palmer and his efforts toward the deportation of alien radicals. But the national return to normalcy largely took the federal government out of the anti-Communist field, and the Sedition Act was repealed in 1921. There remained the states, many of which had legislation on the books aimed at radicals of various sorts. Some of these laws had been passed after the assassination of President McKinley in 1901 by an anarchist, and were directed at "criminal anarchy" or "criminal syndicalism." It was a New York statute of this sort which was involved in *Gitlow* v. *New York* (1925).

Gitlow was a member of the Left Wing Section of the Socialist party, a group which opposed moderate socialism and soon became the United States Communist Party. He was business manager of the party paper in which a "Left Wing Manifesto" was published, containing typical Communist language about the necessity of accomplishing the Communist revolution through class struggle, general strikes, and the power of the proletariat. Gitlow was convicted of criminal anarchy on the basis of this publication, and the Supreme Court upheld the conviction, though in the process it made

the startling and unexpected concession that the First Amendment was effective against the states.

Thus the *Gitlow* case opened the way for Supreme Court review of all state laws under which political radicals were convicted, and in *Whitney* v. *California* (1927) the Court appeared to adopt the rule of guilt by association. Miss Whitney's crime, under the California Syndicalism Act, was that she participated, without protest, in the convention which set up the Communist Labor party of California, and was elected an alternate member of its state executive committee. She testified that it was not her purpose that this party should be an instrument of terrorism or violence, or violate any law, but the party was found to have been formed to teach criminal syndicalism, and as a member of the party she participated in the crime.

The Supreme Court upheld this conviction on the ground that "united and joint action involves . . . greater danger to the public peace and security than the isolated utterances and acts of individuals," but Justices Brandeis and Holmes did not agree. Brandeis said:

> The felony which the statute created is a crime very unlike the old felony of conspiracy or the old misdemeanor of unlawful assembly. The mere act of assisting in forming a society for teaching syndicalism, of becoming a member of it, or of assembling with others for that purpose is given the dynamic quality of crime. There is guilt although the society may not contemplate immediate promulgation of the doctrine. Thus the accused is to be punished, not for contempt, incitement or conspiracy, but for a step in preparation, which, if it threatens the public order at all, does so only remotely. The novelty in the prohibition introduced is that the statute aims, not at the practice of criminal syndicalism, nor even directly at the preaching of it, but at association with those who propose to preach it.

On the other hand, Brandeis could not accept the claim of Miss Whitney that the statute was unconstitutional on its face. He did contend that it could be applied only after satisfying the clear and present danger test which, as already noted, he here elaborated and made more stringent. But because Miss Whitney had not raised the clear and present danger question or requested that the judge or jury determine the existence of such conditions, and because there was evidence in the record showing a conspiracy on the part of the IWW to commit present serious crimes, which would be aided by the activity of the Communist Labor party, he and Justice Holmes felt they could not object to the judgment of the state court.

The Hughes Court of the 1930s, however, took a considerably different line on such state convictions. In three important decisions—*Stromberg* v. *California* (1931), *DeJonge* v. *Oregon* (1937), and *Herndon* v. *Lowry* (1937) —the convictions of admitted Communists were reversed. Miss Stromberg had raised a red flag every morning at a children's summer camp. DeJonge had addressed a public meeting called by the Communist Party to protest

police violence against strikers. Herndon was a Communist organizer in Georgia who possessed inflammatory literature addressed to Negroes. In each case the Court voided the conviction on the basis of well-established rules of criminal law.

One such rule employed was that a crime cannot be defined in vague and indefinite terms. In the *Stromberg* case, the law made it a felony to display a red flag as an "emblem of opposition to organized government." Chief Justice Hughes held that this language was so loose as to permit the punishment of the fair use of the opportunity for free political discussion. Herndon had been convicted under a pre-Civil War statute aimed to prevent slave insurrections, never before used, and providing penalties up to death for attempting to persuade persons "to join in any combined resistance to the lawful authority of the State." Justice Roberts said that to convict under this language, a jury would have to engage in "pure speculation as to future trends of thought and action." If a jury thought that action now might result in violence in twenty or even fifty years, who could say they were wrong? The law thus amounted to "a dragnet which may enmesh anyone who agitates for a change of government if a jury can be persuaded that he sought to have some effect in the future conduct of others."

A second point made in these rulings was the elementary one that a person cannot be convicted on the basis of a charge not contained in the indictment. DeJonge had been indicted for conducting a meeting, but he had been convicted because he was a member of the Communist Party. Admittedly nothing illegal was done at the meeting, but the state court's theory was that the Communist Party had no right of peaceable assembly, because the Legislature had determined that the organization aimed at force and violence. "Consistently with the Federal Constitution," said Chief Justice Hughes, "peaceable assembly for lawful discussion cannot be made a crime," and he added: "Conviction upon a charge not made would be sheer denial of due process."

But perhaps the most significant feature of these decisions was the insistence of the Court that conviction must be for personal guilt and not on the basis of guilt by association. Miss Stromberg's Communist affiliations were ignored. In the DeJonge affair, the objectives of the Communist Party, to which the state courts had devoted a great deal of attention, were set aside as irrelevant, the Chief Justice saying: "Notwithstanding those objectives, the defendant still enjoyed his personal right of free speech and to take part in a peaceable assembly having a lawful purpose, although called by that Party." As for Herndon, convicted for holding recruiting meetings for the Communist Party and possessing Communist Party literature, Justice Roberts ruled there was no evidence that he used inciting language in his meetings. As for the incendiary literature, the proof wholly failed to show that he had read these documents, approved of them, or distributed them.

Thus this series of cases gave considerable support for associative freedom

as applied to members of the Communist Party. Gitlow was held guilty of issuing a publication with a forbidden and illegal purpose, but Stromberg, DeJonge, and Herndon, judged on their own actions, and not on the basis of motives which might be imputed to them because of their membership in the Communist Party, were within the protection of the Constitution.

The Court of the 1940s continued this refusal to accept the rule of guilt by association. *Schneiderman* v. *United States* (1943) concerned an admitted member and official of the Communist Party who had become a naturalized citizen in 1927. In 1939 the government brought proceedings to cancel his citizenship, an action authorized by law where citizenship had been fraudulently or illegally procured. The government charged that Schneiderman, as a Communist during the five years preceding his naturalization, could not have met the statutory requirement of being "attached to the principles of the Constitution of the United States, and well disposed to the good order and happiness of the same." Conflicting testimony was given in court as to whether Marxian theory advocated the use of force and violence as a method of attaining its objective, and the Supreme Court majority, speaking through Justice Murphy, concluded that the case had not been proved.

Again in 1945 the Court had another opportunity to consider, this time somewhat less directly, the status of the Communist Party in the case of *Bridges* v. *Wixon.* Harry Bridges, an alien West Coast labor leader, was subjected to deportation proceedings as a member of or affiliated with the Communist Party, which was alleged to advocate the overthrow of the government by force or violence. The court majority concluded that Bridges's membership in the Party had not been proved, and that his "affiliation" had simply taken the form of cooperating with it in the attainment of legitimate trade union goals. The relevance of this holding to our present problem is the Court's admission that the Communist Party *could* engage in "wholly lawful activities." It followed that membership in the Party or affiliation with it did not necessarily attaint a person.

### THE SMITH ACT

Apart from the Espionage and Sedition Acts of World War I, numerous other statutes have aimed at radicals or revolutionaries. A general law makes unlawful seditious conspiracy "to overthrow, put down, or to destroy by force the Government of the United States, or to levy war against them, or to oppose by force the authority thereof." The Immigration Act of 1917 requires the exclusion and deportation of aliens who advocate the overthrow of the government by force and violence, and declares ineligible for naturalization aliens who are members of organizations so advocating. The Hatch Act of 1939 prohibits employment by the government of members of organizations advocating overthrow of "our constitutional forms of government."

What was destined to become the most famous of the anti-Communist

measures was the Alien Registration Act of 1940, better known as the Smith Act. Actually alien registration was only one of the five purposes of the act. Its major importance was as a peacetime sedition act, the first federal peacetime restrictions on speaking and writing by American citizens since the ill-fated Sedition Act of 1798. Section 2 of the statute makes it unlawful knowingly to advocate or teach the overthrow of any government in the United States by force or violence, to print or distribute written matter so advocating, or to organize or knowingly become a member of any group which so advocates. Section 3 makes punishable conspiracy to accomplish any of these ends.

The language of the Smith Act is less drastic than the Sedition Act of 1798 in that it forbids only the advocacy of force, and not mere political criticism of government officials. But it is more restrictive in at least one respect. The law makes it a crime to belong to an organization that is subsequently found to advocate the overthrow of the government by force, regardless of what the individual says or does. The act does not mention the Communist Party by name, but there can be no doubt that the framers of the statute believed the Party advocated force and violence and intended the act to apply to it and its members.

The first use of the Smith Act came in 1943, when the leaders of the Socialist Workers party, a small Trotskyite group with headquarters in Minneapolis, were convicted under the act. These people were admitted Marxists but bitter enemies of the Communist Party. The lower court followed the *Gitlow* decision in declaring that clear and present danger from the party's revolutionary doctrines need not be proved, since Congress had made a finding as to the existence of the danger.[3] The Supreme Court, in spite of the obvious importance of this ruling, declined to grant certiorari.

Then in 1948 the Truman administration, apparently goaded by the Republican charges of being "soft on communism," began a dramatic prosecution in New York of eleven leaders of the American Communist Party under the Smith Act. The indictment made two charges against them: (1) willfully and knowingly conspiring to organize as the United States Communist Party a society, group, and assembly of persons who teach and advocate the overthrow and destruction of the government of the United States by force and violence, and (2) knowingly and willfully advocating and teaching the duty and necessity of overthrowing and destroying the government by force and violence. No overt revolutionary acts other than teaching, advocating and conspiring were alleged.

The trial before Judge Medina was full of sensations and lasted for nine months. The ultimate conviction was upheld by the court of appeals, Chief Judge Learned Hand writing the opinion. The Supreme Court then granted certiorari limited to questions of the constitutionality of the Smith Act, "inherently or as construed and applied in the instant case." By a vote of six to

[3] *Dunne* v. *United States* (1943).

two, with Chief Justice Vinson writing the opinion, the Court confirmed the convictions in *Dennis* v. *United States* (1951).

The major issue confronting the Court was how to reconcile with the free speech guarantee of the Constitution convictions which treated speaking and teaching as criminal offenses. For, admittedly, the eleven had taken no action with the immediate intention of initiating a revolution. Vinson sought to validate the statute by construing it as being "directed at advocacy, not discussion." But that did not solve the problem completely. For advocacy has two aspects. It is action against which, when aimed toward unlawful ends, the government had the undoubted power to protect itself. But it also "contains an element of speech," as Vinson agreed; and consequently his opinion for the Court majority had inevitably to return to the clear and present danger test.

Vinson's argument amounted to a substantial reinterpretation of the Holmes-Brandeis doctrine, which he purported to follow. His principal affirmative contribution was his definite rejection of the Court's restrictive holding in the *Gitlow* case that any statute punishing advocacy of overthrow of the government is valid and that the courts are limited to determining whether in a particular case the evidence supported the conviction. He thereby preserved the right of full judicial review, but at the same time he rejected the Holmes-Brandeis position that courts must invalidate convictions under such statutes unless the likelihood of success for the subversive activity was immediate and pressing. Vinson thought that the conviction must be upheld whenever the facts as determined by the Court indicated some appreciable probability at some point in time of successful overthrow of the government. The actual formula he adopted was that used by Learned Hand in the court of appeals: "whether the gravity of the 'evil,' discounted by its improbability, justifies such invasion of free speech as is necessary to avoid the danger." Obviously, said Vinson, the clear and present danger test "cannot mean that before the Government may act, it must wait until the *putsch* is about to be executed, the plans have been laid and the signal is awaited. . . . We must therefore reject the contention that success or probability of success is the criterion."

Jackson and Frankfurter each added their own interpretations of clear and present danger. For Jackson, the problem was easy. Holmes and Brandeis had developed this test in cases which presented only "technical or trivial violations . . . arising before the era of World War II revealed the subtlety and efficacy of modernized revolutionary techniques used by totalitarian parties." Jackson would save the test, "unmodified, for application as a 'rule of reason' in the kind of case for which it was devised," namely, hot-headed speeches on street corners or circulation of a few incendiary pamphlets. But when the issue is the probable success of a world-wide revolutionary conspiracy, it is futile for the courts to attempt prophecy in the guise of a legal

decision. "The judicial process simply is not adequate to a trial of such far-flung issues."

Frankfurter took the occasion to state again his rejection of the clear and present danger test, which had, he contended, by reason of the Court's recent decisions become nothing but a formula, an inflexible dogma supporting "uncritical libertarian generalities." What was called for was not the application of a formula but a "candid and informed weighing of the competing interests." Moreover, this weighing is, in the first instance, for legislatures to undertake, "and the balance they strike is a judgment not to be displaced by ours, but to be respected unless outside the pale of fair judgment."

Justice Black, dissenting, charged that the Court's decision repudiated "directly or indirectly" the clear and present danger rule: "I cannot agree that the First Amendment permits us to sustain laws suppressing freedom of speech and press on the basis of Congress' or our own notions of mere 'reasonableness.' Such a doctrine waters down the First Amendment so that it amounts to little more than an admonition to Congress." He would hold Section 3 of the Smith Act "a virulent form of prior censorship of speech and press," and "unconstitutional on its face."

Douglas took up a subsidiary clear and present danger issue; namely, whether the trial judge had been correct in limiting the jury to determining the fact of guilt under the statute, while reserving to himself as a matter of law the finding as to whether a danger existed sufficient to justify the application of the statute. Vinson held that this question was properly one for the judge to decide; but Douglas regarded it as "so critical an issue in the case" that it should have gone to the jury. However, he could not see how either judge or jury could have decided the question of danger on the basis of a record which contained no evidence on the "strength and tactical position" of the Communist Party in the United States. In the absence of such evidence, he himself could see no danger from these "miserable merchants of unwanted ideas." "Free speech—the glory of our system of government—should not be sacrificed on anything less than plain and objective proof of danger that the evil advocated is imminent."

The Court, however, had cut itself off from consideration of the evidence relied on to prove the alleged conspiracy by its questionable action in granting certiorari limited only to the constitutionality of the statute. Actually the government's case was a most peculiar one. The evidence presented at the trial was primarily concerned with what was in the basic texts of Marxism-Leninism extending all the way back to 1848, as distributed by the Communist Party and discussed at their meetings. The guilt of the Communist leaders was established by connecting them with the organization of the Party and the teaching of these texts. By allowing the validity of convictions based on such textual analyses to be established by default, the Supreme Court permitted the assumption that it had accepted the principle of guilt

by association; illegal conspiracy could be established by demonstrating activities—any kind of activities—in furtherance of the organizational work of the Communist Party.

The *Dennis* decision encouraged the government to bring similar prosecutions, based on similar evidence, against the lesser Party leaders throughout the country. The government was almost uniformly successful in these subsidiary suits, in none of which did the Supreme Court grant certiorari until October, 1955, when it agreed to review the conviction of fourteen California Communists. This time no limitation was imposed on the grant of certiorari, and the result was the shattering decision in *Yates* v. *United States* (1957). By a vote of six to one the Court, while not challenging the constitutionality of the Smith Act as established by the *Dennis* decision, reversed the convictions of five of the fourteen defendants and laid down conditions for Smith Act trials which made it much more difficult to secure any future convictions.

Justice Harlan, writing the majority decision, concerned himself with three main issues. The first was a problem of statutory interpretation. The Smith Act makes it unlawful to "organize" a group which advocates the overthrow of the government by force and violence, and the indictment here charged the defendants with both "organization" and "advocacy." Harlan held that the term "organize" in the act referred only to the formation of the Communist Party in the United States in its present form, an event which took place in 1945, and that since the date of the indictment was 1951, the three-year statute of limitations had run on that part of the indictment. Because the Court was unable to tell whether the jury would have rendered a verdict of guilty if only the advocacy charge had been before them, the elimination of the organizing charge required the entire verdict to be set aside.

Harlan's second point was that the trial judge's instructions to the jury did not adequately distinguish between "advocacy of abstract doctrine and advocacy directed at promoting unlawful action." The trial judge had apparently been misled by the looseness of some of Vinson's language in *Dennis,* but Harlan now reinterpreted *Dennis* to make it clear that that decision had actually been based on this distinction. In his restatement of Vinson's holding, Harlan completely abandoned any reliance on the clear and present danger test. The problem of the prosecution in both cases was to prove advocacy directed at promoting unlawful action. The *Dennis* ruling, said Harlan, was not based on any contention that "the defendant's advocacy was directed at, or created any danger of, immediate overthrow." Rather, "it did establish that the advocacy was aimed at building up a seditious group and maintaining it in readiness for action at a propitious time." Harlan continued:

> The essence of the *Dennis* holding was that indoctrination of a group in preparation for future violent action, as well as exhortation to imme-

diate action, by advocacy found to be directed to "action for the accomplishment" of forcible overthrow, to violence "as a rule or principle of action," and employing "language of incitement" . . . is not constitutionally protected when the group is of sufficient size and cohesiveness, is sufficiently oriented towards action, and other circumstances are such as reasonably to justify apprehension that action will occur.

This concise, one-sentence summary of the *Dennis* decision is worth several paragraphs of Vinson's wrestlings with the clear and present danger test. As so interpreted, *Dennis* provided a clear contrast to the view of the *Yates* trial judge that "mere doctrinal justification of forcible overthrow, if engaged in with the intent to accomplish overthrow, is punishable *per se* under the Smith Act." That sort of advocacy, Harlan concluded, "even though uttered with the hope that it may ultimately lead to violent revolution, is too remote from concrete action to be regarded as the kind of indoctrination preparatory to action which was condemned in *Dennis*." Consequently, the trial judge's charge to the jury furnished it "wholly inadequate guidance" on the central point in the case and supplied a second reason why the convictions could not be allowed to stand.

Third, Harlan looked at the evidence on which the convictions had been secured. True, the Court had already reversed the convictions on the two preceding grounds, but it also had a duty to determine whether evidence in the record was "palpably insufficient" to justify a new trial. Of course all the evidence relating to the "organizing" aspect of the conspiracy had to be thrown out, which "diluted" the case very substantially. But even the evidence on the advocacy point was valueless to the extent that it was intended only to prove advocacy of the abstract doctrine of forcible overthrow. There had to be evidence of "Party advocacy or teaching in the sense of a call to forcible action at some future time."

In such evidence the Court found the record "strikingly deficient." The government's theory was that the Marxist-Leninist texts which it offered in evidence demonstrated the conspiratorial character of the Communist Party, and that conspiracy on the part of the defendants was proved by then connecting them with the Party. This was easy, because they were all admittedly active in the Party. But Harlan insisted that the Party's advocacy of forcible action had to be shown by acts, not by texts.

> At best this voluminous record shows but a half dozen or so scattered incidents which, even under the loosest standards, could be deemed to show such advocacy. Most of these were not connected with any of the petitioners, or occurred many years before the period covered by the indictment. We are unable to regard this sporadic showing as sufficient to justify viewing the Communist Party as the nexus between these petitioners and the conspiracy charged.

What the Court was saying was that evidence of activity in the Communist Party would not meet the requirements in this case. Some of the

Party's activities might be wholly lawful. The defendants could be convicted only on the basis of their individual acts other than their mere relations with the Party. On this basis five of the defendants were completely cleared. There was no evidence in the record to connect them with the conspiracy charged except that they had long been members and officers of the Communist Party of California.

As for the other nine defendants, the Court was not prepared to go so far. There was evidence involving them—Party classes, an "underground apparatus," board meetings held in a devious and conspiratorial manner—which might meet the Court's tests. "We are not prepared to say, at this stage of the case, that it would be impossible for a jury, resolving all conflicts in favor of the Government and giving the evidence . . . its utmost sweep, to find that advocacy of action was also engaged in when the group involved was thought particularly trustworthy, dedicated, and suited for violent tasks."

The Black-Douglas dissents in the *Dennis* case were partially vindicated by the *Yates* decision, though again in *Yates* Black and Douglas found themselves in disagreement with the majority opinion. While concurring in the result, they would have held the Smith Act completely unconstitutional and directed the acquittal of all defendants. In fact, this latter result was achieved six months later when the Department of Justice "reluctantly" requested the trial court to dismiss the indictments against the remaining nine defendants on the ground that "the evidentiary requirements laid down by the Supreme Court" could not be satisfied. Also on the basis of the *Yates* ruling, indictments were dismissed against  six Communists in Pittsburgh and eleven in Puerto Rico; courts of appeals reversed convictions of seven who had been tried in Hawaii, four in Seattle, five in New Haven, and four in Philadelphia. It appeared that the Smith Act had been rendered virtually useless as an instrument for jailing Communists and that the more than one hundred convictions under the act had been largely illegal.[4]

Thus the Court, which had appeared to accept guilt by association in *Dennis*, in *Yates* moved back toward its traditional insistence on proof of individual wrongdoing. But section 2 of the Smith Act, which makes unlawful mere membership in a group advocating forcible overthrow of the government, remained to be construed by the Court. When it came up for review in the case of *Scales* v. *United States* (1961), the Court was asked to hold it unconstitutional because it imputed guilt on the basis of associations and sympathies rather than because of concrete personal involvement in criminal conduct.

The Court, however, upheld the constitutionality of section 2 by employing the strict standards of evidence of the *Yates* decision and by interpreting section 2 as applying only to "knowing," "active," members who had a

---

[4] The *Yates* decision also impeded government efforts to denaturalize naturalized citizens on the basis of Communist Party membership. See *Nowak* v. *United States* (1958) and *Maisenberg* v. *United States* (1958).

"specific intent to bring about violent overthrow." The Court repeated that it would not permit convictions supported only by such evidence as

> . . . the teaching of Marxism-Leninism and the connected use of Marxist 'classics' as textbooks; the official general resolutions and pronouncements of the Party at past conventions; dissemination of the Party's general literature . . . ; the secrecy of meetings and the clandestine nature of the Party generally; [or] statements by officials evidencing sympathy for and alliance with the U.S.S.R.

On the contrary, the Court would insist on at least two "patterns of evidence" to support a finding of illegal advocacy:

> (a)   the teaching of forceful overthrow, accompanied by directions as to the type of illegal action which must be taken when the time for the revolution is reached; and
> (b)   the teaching of forceful overthrow, accompanied by a contemporary, though legal, course of conduct clearly undertaken for the specific purpose of rendering effective the later illegal activity which is advocated.

The Court majority found that Scales was linked to illegal advocacy by this latter kind of evidence. He had been the director of a secret school for the advanced education of selected young Party members. He once remarked that the Party was setting up underground means of communication, and in 1951 he himself went "underground." In his presence, students at the school were once shown how to kill a man with a pencil, a technique which, it was said, might come in handy on a picket line. He had often said that the goals of communism could only be achieved by violent revolution that would have to start internally with the working classes. Such evidence met the *Dennis* and *Yates* tests for *present* advocacy of *future* action toward violent overthrow.

Justice Douglas, dissenting along with Warren, Black, and Brennan, contended that Scales was charged with no unlawful acts and therefore that the Court had legalized guilt by association. The majority sought to refute this charge by reversing another section 2 conviction on the same day in *Noto* v. *United States* (1961). In Noto's trial, Justice Harlan ruled, the kind of evidence that had convicted Scales was lacking. Justice Black interpreted the *Noto* decision as telling the government that it had not had sufficient up-to-date information on the present policies of the Communist Party, and he added: "I cannot join an opinion which implies that the existence of liberty is dependent upon the efficiency of the Government's informers."

## THE INTERNAL SECURITY ACT OF 1950

The Internal Security Act of 1950, also known as the McCarran Act, got its start as the Mundt-Nixon bill in 1948, and was passed over President Tru-

man's veto. The immigration and naturalization provisions of the statute are discussed in Chapter 35. Here we are concerned with two aspects of the act.

First, section 4 provides: "It shall be unlawful for any person knowingly to combine, conspire, or agree with any other person to perform any act which would substantially contribute to the establishment within the United States of a totalitarian dictatorship." There is a proviso that this language does not apply "to the proposal of a Constitutional amendment." This language avoids the "force or violence" test of the Smith Act, and according to Representative Nixon was needed because Communists had developed techniques for taking over governments without using force or violence. But such a loose definition of sedition is rather clearly unconstitutional, and the Department of Justice has brought no prosecutions under section 4.

Much more important are the requirements of registration imposed in sections 1 and 2 on Communist organizations, and the disabilities that flow from such registration. Communist organizations are ordered to register with the Attorney General, and a Subversive Activities Control Board is established to determine which organizations should be required to register. Upon issuance of such an order by the board, the organization must register, disclose names and addresses of its officers, and give an accounting of sources of money and expenditures. Among the sanctions incurred by a registered organization are the following: its mail and radio broadcasts must be identified as Communist propaganda; members may not hold nonelective federal positions; they commit a crime if they apply for or use a United States passport; and their right to work in defense plants is limited.

The Subversive Activities Control Board was organized in November, 1950. The Attorney General almost immediately filed a petition to compel the Communist Party of the United States to register as a Communist-action organization. After many misadventures,[5] the board finally got a favorable ruling from the Supreme Court eleven years later in *Communist Party* v. *Subversive Activities Control Board* (1961). The Party had contended that the registration provisions were fraudulent and that the real purpose of the statute was to impose impossible requirements in order to lay a foundation for criminal prosecution of the Party and its officers and members—in effect "outlawing" the Party. There is much evidence that this was in fact the intention of Congress, but the Court accepted the statute as a bona fide registration law and upheld it on that basis. The Court majority declined to consider the constitutionality of any of the sanctions which the act applied to registered organizations on the ground that, since the Party had not yet registered, they had not come into effect. Justice Frankfurter wrote:

> Although they become operative as soon as a registration order is made final, their application remains in a very real sense problematical.

[5] See *Communist Party* v. *Subversive Activities Control Board* (1956).

We cannot now foresee what effect, if any, upon the Party the denial of tax exemption will have. . . . We do not know that, after such an order is in effect, the Party will wish to utilize the mails. . . . It is wholly speculative now to foreshadow whether, or under what conditions, a member of the Party may in the future apply for a passport, or seek government or defense-facility or labor-union employment, or, being an alien, become a party to a naturalization or a denaturalization proceeding. None of these things may happen.

Naturally, these things did happen. The registration order having been upheld by the Supreme Court, prosecutions were brought against two leaders of the Communist Party to revoke their passports. In *Aptheker* v. *Secretary of State* (1964), the Court declared the passport provisions of the 1950 statute unconstitutional because they too broadly and indiscriminately restricted the right to travel.

The government had no more success in compelling enforcement of the registration requirement. The Party's officials refused to register after the 1961 decision, and the government then brought action against them for failure to register. A federal district court conviction was reversed by the court of appeals in 1963, because the government had not proved that some person was available who would run the risk of incriminating himself by registering on behalf of the Party. The court held that no one could be forced by a registration proceeding to declare his association with a Party that has been labeled criminal.[6] The Supreme Court denied certiorari.

In 1965 the government brought another prosecution in which it hoped to supply the missing proof. It presented in court two FBI informants within the Party who testified that they would have volunteered to register for the Party if asked. A federal district court jury convicted the Party on this evidence and levied the maximum fine of $230,000. This conviction was reversed in 1967, the court of appeals holding the McCarran Act "hopelessly at odds" with the Fifth Amendment's guarantee against self-incrimination. The Department of Justice decided not to appeal this decision to the Supreme Court.[7]

The 1950 statute provides that if a Communist-action organization does not register as ordered, the individual members of the organization must register. Since no individual members took this step, the SACB brought action to require two Party members to register. In *Albertson* v. *SACB* (1965) the Supreme Court unanimously held that this would constitute compulsory self-incrimination. Justice Clark noted that as Attorney General in 1948 he had advised the Senate Judiciary Committee that such a registration requirement would be unconstitutional.

[6] *Communist Party* v. *United States* (1963).
[7] *The New York Times,* March 4, April 5, 1967.

Following the failure of two more SACB efforts to compel alleged "Communist-front" organizations to register,[8] this record of futility was completed in *United States* v. *Robel* (1967), where the Court declared unconstitutional by a vote of 6 to 2 the provision of the McCarran Act making it a crime for any member of a Communist-action organization "to engage in any employment in any defense facility." The Court was not prepared to rescue this provision, as it had done with section 2 of the Smith Act in *Scales* v. *United States* (1961), by interpreting it as applying only to active members with the specific intent to overthrow the government. Rather the precedent applied was *Aptheker*, and the statute was invalid because its language swept "indiscriminately across all types of associations with Communist-action groups, without regard to the quality or degree of membership. . . . The statute quite literally establishes guilt by association alone, without any need to establish that an individual's association poses the threat feared by the Government in proscribing it." [9]

With the Internal Security Act rendered useless by Supreme Court decisions, Congress came to the rescue of the moribund SACB in December, 1967, by amending the statute to eliminate the requirement for Communist organizations and members to register themselves. Instead, the new act established a procedure under which the SACB would hold hearings on cases referred to it by the Attorney General and would itself determine whether individuals and organizations were Communist. The names of those found to be Communist would be placed on a public register.

### THE PUBLIC SERVICE AND SUBVERSION

An important motive of legislation or administrative action aimed at the Communist Party has been to keep its members out of public employment or other posts where they would be in a position to undertake subversive activities.

---

[8] *American Committee for Protection of Foreign Born* v. *SACB* (1965) and *Veterans of the Abraham Lincoln Brigade* v. *SACB* (1965). In 1966 the Attorney General initiated action against the W. E. B. DuBois Clubs of America seeking to compel them to register as a Communist-front organization. See *DuBois Clubs of America* v. *Clark* (1967), in which the Court declined to enjoin the SACB from proceeding with the hearing. Justices Douglas and Black, dissenting, would have granted the injunction on the ground that the registration provisions of the McCarran Act were unconstitutional on their face, that the decision in *Dennis* v. *United States* (1951) had no longer any validity, and that the "harassment" of minority groups by public hearings and probing into their views had the same "chilling" effect on associational freedoms the Court had condemned in *Dombrowski* v. *Pfister* (1965).

[9] In *Schneider* v. *Smith* (1968) the Court unanimously held that the Coast Guard had exceeded the authority given by the Magnuson Act of 1950 by inquiring into seamen's beliefs and associations before granting them seamen's licenses. Three justices added that the Coast Guard's procedure would have been unconstitutional, even if clearly specified by law.

LOYALTY OATHS    Both federal and state laws customarily require public employees to take some kind of oath of loyalty to the government. An oath denying membership in the Communist Party was first upheld by the Supreme Court in *Garner* v. *Board of Public Works* (1951), Justice Frankfurter saying: "In the context of our time, such membership is sufficiently relevant to effective and dependable government, and to the confidence of the electorate in its government."

However, the Court quickly imposed some limits on such oaths. In *Wieman* v. *Updegraff* (1952) the Court unanimously insisted that the mere fact of membership was not sufficient grounds for exclusion from the public service; it must be a "knowing" association. In this case an Oklahoma law excluded from the state service persons who had been members of proscribed organizations, regardless of whether they had knowledge of the character of the organizations. The Court ruled that such an "indiscriminate classification of innocent with knowing activity . . . offends due process."

By 1966 a majority of the Court was ready to go further, and *Elfbrandt* v. *Russell* apparently reversed the *Garner* decision, by striking down an Arizona loyalty-oath law which provided punishment for anyone taking the oath who was or later became a knowing member of an organization having for one of its purposes the overthrow of the government. Justice Douglas for a five-judge majority relied on the principle of the *Aptheker* case. To punish mere knowing membership was to adopt the rule of guilt by association; beyond knowing membership there also had to be a "specific intent" to further the illegal aims of the organization before punishment was justified. Four dissenting justices charged that this was a departure from earlier decisions holding that a state was "entitled to condition public employment upon its employees abstaining from knowing membership in the Communist Party."

Loyalty-oath statutes have also been invalidated on other grounds. In *Cramp* v. *Board of Public Instruction* (1961), a Florida act requiring state employees to swear that they had never lent their "aid, support, advice, counsel, or influence to the Communist Party" was held lacking in "terms susceptible to objective measurement" and so failed to inform what the state commanded or forbade. *Baggett* v. *Bullitt* (1964) involved two Washington provisions which required teachers to swear that they were not "subversive persons" and that they would "by precept and example promote respect for the flag . . . reverence for law and order and undivided allegiance to the government of the United States." The Court held these provisions "invalid on their face because their language is unduly vague, uncertain and broad."

In *Whitehill* v. *Elkins* (1967) the Court declared unconstitutional the Maryland law requiring state employees to swear they were not subversive persons which it had earlier upheld per curiam in *Gerende* v. *Board of Supervisors* (1951). The *Gerende* decision was now distinguished on the

ground that at that time the attorney general of the state had interpreted the law to apply only to persons attemping to alter the form of government by force or violence. A Texas loyalty oath for state employees was invalidated in *James* v. *Gilmore* (1968). But a New York law requiring merely an oath to uphold the federal and state constitutions was approved by the Court in *Knight* v. *Board of Regents* (1968).

A very famous non-Communist oath, applying not to public officials but to labor union officers, was that required by the Labor Management Relations Act of 1947, better known as the Taft-Hartley Act. Section 9(h) of this act denied the protections and services of the act to any labor organization unless each of its officers filed an affidavit with the National Labor Relations Board "that he is not a member of the Communist Party or affiliated with such party, and that he does not believe in, and is not a member of or supports any organization that believes in or teaches, the overthrow of the United States Government by force or by any illegal or unconstitutional methods." Here for the first time in this series of measures the Communist Party was definitely named.

In *American Communications Association* v. *Douds* (1950), the Supreme Court upheld the validity of the oath. The congressional purpose, according to Chief Justice Vinson, was to remove political strikes as an obstruction to interstate commerce. Congress had such power under the commerce clause unless results were achieved which were forbidden by other provisions of the Constitution. He agreed that political freedoms were limited by the statute because its effect was to exert "pressures upon labor unions to deny positions of leadership to certain persons who are identified by particular beliefs and political affiliations." Normally, beliefs and affiliations are "irrelevant to permissible subjects of government action," but that does not mean they are "never relevant." Here the Court conceived that beliefs and affiliations bore a reasonable relation to the apprehended evil. The persons identified by the statute did not cause damage by speech, and it was not their speech that the statute sought to restrain, but rather their use of force through the political strike. "Speech may be fought with speech. . . . But force may and must be met with force."

Justice Black, dissenting, could not believe that "the Commerce Clause restricts the right to think." He stood on "the basic constitutional precept that penalties should be imposed only for a person's own conduct, not for his beliefs or for the conduct of others with whom he may associate. Guilt should not be imputed solely from association or affiliation with political parties or any other organization, however much we abhor the ideas which they advocate." The test oath was in itself a suspect weapon, Black felt, for "history attests the efficacy of that instrument for inflicting penalties and disabilities on obnoxious minorities." His final word was: "Never before has this Court held that the Government could for any reason attaint persons for their political beliefs or affiliations. It does so today."

The Taft-Hartley oath was repealed in 1959. It had proved ineffective, since Communists were willing to take the oath, which meant that the only sanction was a perjury prosecution presenting serious difficulties of proof. Congress substituted a provision making it a crime for a member of the Communist Party to serve as an officer or employee of a labor union (73 Stat. 519, 536). In *United States* v. *Brown* (1965) the Court by a five to four vote held this provision unconstitutional as a bill of attainder. The minority contended that this was simply conflict-of-interest legislation of a type previously upheld, and that the *Brown* decision had overruled *Douds*.

Another type of loyalty oath was involved in *Speiser* v. *Randall* (1958), which held unconstitutional the statutory procedure for enforcing a California constitutional provision requiring all individuals and organizations claiming any exemption from state property taxes to file loyalty oaths. The effect of the enforcement procedure was to place on taxpayers the burden of showing that they did not advocate overthrow of the government. In ordinary tax cases, it is permissible to require taxpayers, on challenge, to prove the accuracy of their own declarations. But in this situation, Justice Brennan noted, "the transcendent value of speech is involved." He continued:

> The man who knows that he must bring forth proof and persuade another of the lawfulness of his conduct necessarily must steer far wider of the unlawful zone, than if the State must bear these burdens. . . . In practical operation, therefore, this procedural device must necessarily produce a result which the State could not command directly. It can only result in a deterrence of speech which the Constitution makes free.

If the state wished to deny tax exemption to persons or organizations on grounds of disloyalty, it would have to "bear the burden of persuasion to show that the appellants engaged in criminal speech."

The loyalty-oath requirement has been carried to ridiculous extremes. It has been required of college students receiving loans under the National Defense Education Act, of certain classes of applicants under the Medicare Act, and even of members of private organizations such as the motion pictures directors' union.[10] At one time Indiana required a loyalty oath from

---

[10] The Medicare Act of 1965 required persons over sixty-five who were not covered by Social Security to sign an oath that they were not members of a Communist-action group, in order to be eligible for benefits. The provision was upheld by a federal judge in New York but declared unconstitutional as a violation of the First Amendment by a California federal court. The Solicitor General announced that the government would accept the California ruling and cease enforcing the statute. He suggested that the Supreme Court nullify the New York ruling by regarding that case as moot, which the Court did in *Weiss* v. *Gardner* (1967). The California case was *Reed* v. *Gardner* (1966).

The loyalty-oath requirement for membership in the screen directors' union was invalidated by a federal court of appeals in 1966, and the Supreme Court refused to review the decision; *Directors' Guild of America, Inc.* v. *Hurwitz* (1966).

professional wrestlers. It has never been shown that loyalty oaths are of the slightest effect in dealing with subversion. Communists have no hesitation in signing such oaths, as the Taft-Hartley experience showed. Those who object are usually persons of principle who feel it is demeaning to be coerced into professing one's loyalty, which in a free society should be taken for granted until proof to the contrary is submitted.

REMOVAL OF PUBLIC EMPLOYEES    The loyalty oath was supplemented in many jurisdictions by statutory programs for the removal of public employees on loyalty grounds. The New York law was upheld by the Court in *Adler* v. *Board of Education* (1952). This law required the Board of Regents to make, after notice and hearing, a listing of organizations which it found to advocate, advise, teach, or embrace the doctrine that the government should be overthrown by force or violence or any unlawful means. Membership of a schoolteacher in any such listed organization was "prima facie evidence for disqualification for appointment to or retention in" any school position, but before an individual was severed from or denied employment, he was to be given a full hearing and the right of judicial review.

The Court upheld the law by a six to two vote. For the majority, Minton contended that the "guilt by association" point had been disposed of by the *Garner* opinion, and he added:

> We adhere to that case. A teacher works in a sensitive area in a schoolroom. There he shapes the attitude of young minds towards the society in which they live. In this, the state has a vital concern. . . . That the school authorities have the right and the duty to screen the officials, teachers, and employees as to their fitness to maintain the integrity of the schools as a part of ordered society, cannot be doubted. One's associates, past and present, as well as one's conduct, may properly be considered in determining fitness and loyalty. From time immemorial, one's reputation has been determined in part by the company he keeps.

Justices Black and Douglas, dissenting, argued the social unwisdom of censorship, particularly as applied to teachers. Said Douglas:

> The present law proceeds on a principle repugnant to our society—guilt by association. A teacher is disqualified because of her membership in an organization found to be "subversive." . . . The mere fact of membership in the organization raises a prima facie case of her own guilt. She may, it is said, show her innocence. But innocence in this case turns on knowledge; and when the witch hunt is on, one who must rely on ignorance leans on a feeble reed. . . .
>
> The very threat of such a procedure is certain to raise havoc with academic freedom. Youthful indiscretions, mistaken causes, misguided enthusiasms—all long forgotten—become the ghosts of a harrowing present. Any organization committed to a liberal cause, any group organized to revolt against an hysterical trend, any committee launched to sponsor an unpopular program becomes suspect. These are the organizations into

which Communists often infiltrate. Their presence infects the whole, even though the project was not conceived in sin. A teacher caught in that mesh is almost certain to stand condemned. Fearing condemnation, she will tend to shrink from any association that stirs controversy. In that manner freedom of expression will be stifled.

The *Adler* decision was eventually overruled by a five to four vote in *Keyishian* v. *Board of Regents* (1967), a case brought by professors in the New York State university system. Brennan for the majority disposed of *Adler* on the ground that the Court there had not considered charges that the statutory standards were too vague and uncertain in their application, and also because of intervening decisions holding that "mere membership" in the Communist Party could not be constitutionally penalized.

Brennan reached out to bring under review the entire mass of provisions included in the Feinberg law and its amendments, which he characterized as "a highly efficient *in terrorem* mechanism," a "regulatory maze," and a "complicated and intricate scheme." Academic freedom, he said, is "a special concern of the First Amendment, which does not tolerate laws that cast a pall of orthodoxy over the classroom." While New York could protect its educational system from subversion, it could not do so by vague and uncertain standards, but only by "sensitive tools" which clearly inform teachers of the sanctions being established. In one area the law was admittedly specific, namely, making Communist Party membership as such prima facie evidence of disqualification for teaching. But the Court found this provision invalid because, as in *Elfbrandt*, it imposed sanctions on "mere knowing membership without any showing of specific intent to further the unlawful aims of the Communist Party."

The dissenters (Clark, Harlan, Stewart, and White) contended that the majority, in moving against the "overbroad sweep" of the Feinberg law, had by "its broadside swept away one of our most precious rights, namely, the right of self-preservation." The issue, Clark said, was simply this:

> May the State provide that one who, after a hearing with full judicial review, is found to wilfully and deliberately advocate, advise, or teach that our Government should be overthrown by force or violence or other unlawful means; or who wilfully and deliberately prints, publishes, etc., any book or paper that so advocates *and who personally* advocates such doctrine himself; or who wilfully and deliberately becomes a member of an organization that advocates such doctrine, is prima facie disqualified from teaching in its university? My answer, in keeping with all of our cases up until today, is "Yes"!

Another rather common state action has been the removal of public employees who refuse to give information about alleged subversive connections, whether by taking the Fifth Amendment before a legislative committee or by some other method. In three important cases the Court divided five to four on the constitutional aspects of such action. In the first, *Slochower* v.

*Board of Higher Education of New York City* (1956), a Brooklyn College professor had taken the Fifth Amendment before a Senate committee on all questions covering his political associations before 1941. He was discharged under a provision of the New York charter that whenever an employee utilized the privilege against self-incrimination to avoid answering a question relating to his official conduct, his employment tenure "shall terminate" and the office "shall be vacant." The Court majority, speaking through Justice Clark, held that the charter provision as interpreted here had converted the employee's claim of privilege "into a conclusive presumption of guilt. Since no inference of guilt was possible from the claim before the federal committee, the discharge falls of its own weight as wholly without support."

Justice Clark went on to express the view that Slochower had no "constitutional right" to his job, and that it would be perfectly proper for "the city authorities themselves to inquire into Slochower's fitness." This was precisely what happened in *Lerner* v. *Casey* (1958) and *Beilan* v. *Board of Public Education, School District of Philadelphia* (1958). Lerner was a New York subway conductor, Beilan a public school teacher. Lerner refused to tell New York City authorities whether he was a member of the Communist Party, and was dismissed as a person of "doubtful trust and reliability" because of his "lack of candor." Beilan refused to tell his superintendent whether he had held a certain position in the Communist Party in 1944, and later took the Fifth Amendment before a House committee; he was dismissed for "incompetency."

The Court majority (Harlan, Burton, Frankfurter, Clark, and Whittaker) upheld the official action in both cases, contending that the employees were not removed because of a Fifth Amendment plea (as in Slochower's case), or because of their beliefs or associations, or because they were "security risks," but only because their refusal to answer questions put by their employers constituted evidence of their unreliability and incompetency. The four dissenters could not accept such "transparent denials" of the real reasons for the removals. Again, in *Nelson* v. *County of Los Angeles* (1960) the majority upheld a discharge for insubordination based on refusal to answer questions before the House Un-American Activities Committee, a decision which came very close to overruling *Slochower*.

A different type of removal action was held unconstitutional by the Court in *Shelton* v. *Tucker* (1960). An Arkansas statute required every teacher in the public schools and state colleges, as a condition of employment, to file annually a list of every organization to which he had belonged or contributed in the preceding five years. The act was upheld in the federal district court on the basis of *Garner* and *Adler*, but the Supreme Court by a five to four vote ruled the requirement invalid. Justice Stewart for the majority agreed that the state had a right to investigate the competence and fitness of persons hired as teachers, but considered such an "unlimited and indiscriminate" inquiry a threat to associational freedom going "far beyond what might be

justified in the exercise of the State's legitimate inquiry into the fitness and competency of its teachers."

THE FEDERAL LOYALTY-SECURITY PROGRAM    President Truman set up a loyalty program for federal employees in 1947, and President Eisenhower continued it in somewhat revised form in 1953. All employees and applicants for employment were required to undergo a loyalty check, in which the FBI assisted in an investigative role. The Department of Justice prepared a list of subversive organizations to help guide the decisions of agency loyalty boards. Hearings were held by these boards when damaging information was received concerning an employee or applicant, but some of the customary protections of the hearing procedure—particularly the right to be informed of the source of the charges and the right to confront the persons making the accusations—were not guaranteed in these proceedings.

The loyalty-security program was widely attacked as denying procedural due process. In *Joint Anti-Fascist Refugee Committee* v. *McGrath* (1951), the Court majority held that the Attorney General had not accorded necessary procedural protections to the organizations he labeled as subversive, the listing being made, as Justice Frankfurter said, "without notice, without disclosure of any reasons justifying it, without opportunity to meet the undisclosed evidence or suspicion on which designation may have been based, and without opportunity to establish affirmatively that the aims and acts of the organization are innocent."

On the more serious question whether the hearings accorded individual civil servants met due process standards, the Court divided four to four in *Bailey* v. *Richardson* (1951). Consequently no opinion could be written, but most of the justices used the *Joint Anti-Fascist* case, decided the same day, to express their views. The general rule on public employment has been that it is not a right, and consequently that it is not the business of the courts to question the decisions of administrative superiors about the fitness of their employees to perform their assigned tasks. The relevant federal statutes require only notice of removal and an opportunity to reply to charges, except for veterans, who have by statute the right of appeal to the Civil Service Commission.

There can be little doubt that this is the proper policy under all ordinary circumstances. No one would contend that, in order to discharge a federal employee for inefficiency, his superiors should hold a quasi-judicial hearing and provide for judicial review of the decision. But removals under the loyalty-security program are not ordinary removals. A loyalty charge puts an employee on trial not only for his job but for his reputation and his professional standing. Removal on loyalty grounds may make it impossible for him to secure any other employment for which he is fitted. He is condemned as a person unworthy of trust and confidence. These considerations convinced four members of the Court that loyalty hearings must meet full due process

standards. But since the Court was evenly divided, the decision of the lower court remained in effect, and it had rejected the due process claims.

In several subsequent cases the Supreme Court considered aspects of the loyalty-security system, but largely avoided the constitutional issues.[11] However, in *Greene* v. *McElroy* (1959), which dealt with the industrial security program in effect for private plants doing work for the government that involved access to secret information, the Court did object strongly to loyalty hearings which "failed to comport with our traditional ideas of fair procedure." Chief Justice Warren thought it was a principle of our jurisprudence that "where governmental action seriously injures an individual, and the reasonableness of the action depends on fact findings, the evidence used to prove the Government's case must be disclosed to the individual so that he has an opportunity to show that it is untrue."

As a consequence of the *Greene* decision President Eisenhower issued an executive order which significantly enlarged the right of accused security risks in industrial establishments to confront and cross-examine their accusers. Procedural protections in the loyalty hearings of government employees were also generally improved by the agencies involved. However, when the commanding officer of the Naval Gun Factory in Washington revoked the security clearance of a cafeteria worker without any procedure whatever, the Court upheld the action by a five to four vote in *Cafeteria & Restaurant Workers Union* v. *McElroy* (1961) on the ground that as proprietor of a military establishment the government had "unfettered control" of its operations.[12]

ADMISSION TO THE BAR    In several states constitutional issues have been raised by denial of admission to the bar to applicants because of some question about possible present or past membership in the Communist Party. In two 1957 cases, *Schware* v. *New Mexico Board of Bar Examiners* and *Konigsberg* v. *State Bar of California*, the Supreme Court reversed such action. Schware had been denied admission on the ground that he did not meet the requirement of "good moral character," primarily because of his admitted membership in the Party from 1932 to 1940. The Court held this was no basis for an inference of bad moral character two decades later. Justice Black pointed out that at that time the Communist Party was a "lawful political party with candidates on the ballot in most States." Presumably some members of the Party during that period had illegal aims and engaged in illegal activities, but "it cannot automatically be inferred that all members shared their evil purposes or participated in their illegal conduct."

[11] *Peters* v. *Hobby* (1955); *Cole* v. *Young* (1956); *Service* v. *Dulles* (1957); *Taylor* v. *McElroy* (1959); *Vitarelli* v. *Seaton* (1959). See also *Harmon* v. *Brucker* (1958).
[12] See also *Williams* v. *Zuckert* (1963).

Konigsberg had declined on constitutional grounds to answer questions concerning his political beliefs. There was some disagreement on the Supreme Court as to whether the examiners had barred him because of his non-co-operation or because of negative findings as to character and loyalty. A five-judge majority adopted the latter explanation, and reversed the board's conclusion as contrary to the evidence.

Following this decision, the state bar committee again held hearings at which Konigsberg again refused to answer any questions relating to his alleged membership in the Communist Party. The committee refused to certify him, this time clearly on the ground that his refusal to answer had obstructed a full investigation into his qualifications. In the second *Konigsberg* case (1961) the Supreme Court upheld the state action by a vote of five to four, on the ground that a state can require a bar applicant "to provide unprivileged answers to questions having a substantial relevance to his qualifications." In another case decided the same day, *In re Anastaplo,* the Court by the same division upheld the action of an Illinois bar committee in denying an applicant admission to the bar. In Anastaplo's case there was never any suggestion from any source of Communist Party membership. He had simply taken a stand on principle against discussing his political beliefs with the examiners, who had no derogatory information whatever about the applicant but decided to punish him for his stubbornness.

### THE STATUS OF THE COMMUNIST PARTY
### AND ITS MEMBERS

As a result of congressional legislation and judicial decisions, the Communist Party appears to exist in a curious half-world—neither wholly legal nor wholly illegal. It would be a comparatively easy step to "outlaw" the Party and drive it completely underground in the United States. In fact, that appeared to be the intent of the Communist Control Act of 1954, which deprived the Communist Party of all "rights, privileges, and immunities attendant upon legal bodies created under the jurisdiction of the laws of the United States or any political subdivision thereof." The justification for this outlawry of the Party, the act declared, was "its role as the agency of a hostile foreign power [which] renders its existence a clear present and continuing danger to the security of the United States."

However, Congress faced the dilemma that if the Party was outlawed by the act of 1954, it could scarcely be required to register under the act of 1950. Consequently the 1954 statute provided that the Party was to retain legal status sufficient to enable it to register under the Internal Security Act. No effort was ever made to enforce the 1954 statute, but its curious provisions well summarize official policy toward the Communist Party, which has been to keep it legal enough so that it can be successfully prosecuted for its illegalities, a strategy which has been only partly successful.

The Supreme Court has accepted the congressional position that the Communist Party is not a bona fide political party and so it and its members are not entitled to the usual constitutional protections of speech and association. Congress first stigmatized the Communist Party by name in the Taft-Hartley Act of 1947 with the non-Communist oath provisions. In *American Communications Association* v. *Douds* (1950) the Supreme Court agreed that "Congress could rationally find that the Communist Party is not like other political parties in its utilization of positions of union leadership as means by which to bring about strikes and other obstructions of commerce for purposes of political advantage." Justice Jackson affirmed that "the Communist Party is something different in fact from any other substantial party we have known, and hence may constitutionally be treated as something different in law."

In the *Dennis* case the Court found a basis for conviction of leaders of the Communist Party in the fact that it was "a highly organized conspiracy, with rigidly disciplined members subject to call when the leaders . . . felt that the time had come for action, coupled with the inflammable nature of world conditions, similar uprisings in other countries, and the touch-and-go nature of our relations with countries with whom petitioners were in the very least ideologically attuned."

As Justice Goldberg summarized the situation in *Gibson* v. *Florida Legislative Investigation Committee* (1963), because "the Communist Party is not an ordinary or legitimate political party . . . membership therein is *itself* a permissible subject of regulation and legislative scrutiny." Consequently, witnesses before congressional committees are not protected by the First Amendment from being compelled to answer questions as to their membership in the Communist Party.[13] Applicants for admission to the bar can be compelled to reveal whether they are members of the Party.[14] Decisions which may now be questionable because of *Keyishian* hold that government employees, applicants for public employment, and officers of labor unions may be required to take an oath that they are not members of the Party.[15] Members of the Party can be convicted of the crime of being knowing, active leaders in its operation.[16] Naturalized citizens can lose their citizenship because of present or past membership in the Party.[17] Aliens deported from the United States because of past Communist Party membership can be denied their social security benefits.[18] In 1966 a veteran of the United States Armed Forces who was decorated for heroism in World War

[13] *Barenblatt* v. *United States* (1959).
[14] *Konigsberg* v. *State Bar of California* (1961).
[15] *Garner* v. *Board of Public Works* (1951); *American Communications Association* v. *Douds* (1950).
[16] *Scales* v. *United States* (1961).
[17] See Chap. 35.
[18] *Flemming* v. *Nestor* (1960).

II but was convicted of violation of the Smith Act in 1949 was denied burial in Arlington Cemetery.

On the other hand, the Communist Party has not been formally or effectively outlawed. It remains, at least in part, above ground. It is listed in telephone directories. It publishes a newspaper. The Supreme Court on several occasions has recognized that it engages in some "wholly lawful activities." [19] Consequently both the Party and its members enjoy some constitutional protection. The officers and members are covered by the self-incrimination clause of the Fifth Amendment.[20] It is a bill of attainder to make it a crime for a Communist to be an officer of a labor union.[21] It is a denial of the constitutional right to travel to bar all members of the Party from applying for or using passports.[22] In 1966 the Communist-disclaimer oath required of applicants under the Medicare Act was ruled unconstitutional by a three-judge district court as a violation of First Amendment rights.[23] Finally, the *Keyishian* decision appears to cast some doubt on Goldberg's statement in *Gibson* that membership in the Party "is *itself* a permissible subject of regulation."

### THE NAACP AND THE KU KLUX KLAN

If one were to appraise freedom of association in the United States solely on the basis of the preceding Communist Party experience, it would seem clear that associational freedom has been seriously circumscribed. Justices Black and Douglas in particular have argued that the rights of the Communist Party cannot be attacked without opening up all organizations to similar government control, but the Court majority has denied that this need be true, and has endeavored rather successfully to prevent these limitations from being applied to other groups.

There is, to be sure, an embarrassing Supreme Court opinion dating back to 1928, *Bryant* v. *Zimmerman.* A 1923 New York statute required any unincorporated association which demanded an oath as a condition of membership to file with state officials copies of its constitution, bylaws, and oath, together with a list of its officers and members. This law was drafted with the Ku Klux Klan in mind, and the Supreme Court upheld it as applied to the Klan, which refused any compliance with the statute. The Court's decision was based on the particular character of the Klan's activities, involving acts of unlawful intimidation and violence.

This reasoning is of course similar to that which the Court has used more recently to uphold anti-Communist legislation. But the statute is clearly a

---

[19] *Bridges* v. *Wixon* (1945); *Yates* v. *United States* (1957).
[20] *Communist Party* v. *United States* (1963); *Albertson* v. *SACB* (1965).
[21] *United States* v. *Brown* (1965).
[22] *Aptheker* v. *Secretary of State* (1964).
[23] *Reed* v. *Gardner* (1966).

serious restraint on associational freedom, and it seems unlikely that the Court would uphold the statute today as applied to any organization except the Communist Party. As Justice Douglas pointed out in *Gibson* v. *Florida Legislative Investigation Committee*, in 1928 "the incorporation of the First Amendment into the Fourteenth had only recently been adumbrated . . . and the full exposition of the right of association that is part of the periphery of the First Amendment had not yet been made."

That "full exposition" of which Douglas spoke has occurred primarily in the Court's recent decisions involving the NAACP. After the *Brown* decision in 1954, the activities of the NAACP in seeking to promote school desegregation aroused great hostility in most of the Southern states. Its members were subjected to economic coercion and often to physical violence. There were also many efforts through legislation and court action to hamper or terminate the work of the organization.

Alabama, like other states, has a statute requiring out-of-state corporations to register and meet certain requirements before doing business in the state. The NAACP, organized under the laws of New York, had a regional office in Alabama, but did not comply with the statute, from which it considered itself exempt. After 1954 the organization was particularly active in the state seeking enforcement of the Supreme Court's ruling against racial segregation in the public schools. In retaliation Alabama officials brought court action in 1956 to enjoin the association from conducting business in the state, in the course of which the organization was ordered to produce its records, including names and addresses of all members in Alabama. The association filed the qualifying forms required by statute and produced all records requested except the membership lists, the disclosure of which it contended the state could not constitutionally compel. For this failure the organization was held in contempt and fined $100,000.

The Supreme Court ruled in *NAACP* v. *Alabama* (1958) that compelled disclosure of the membership lists would abridge the rights of members to engage in lawful association in support of their common beliefs. For the association was able to make

> . . . an uncontroverted showing that on past occasions revelation of the identity of its rank-and-file members has exposed these members to economic reprisal, loss of employment, threat of physical coercion, and other manifestations of public hostility. . . . [Justice Harlan continued:] Under these circumstances, we think it apparent that compelled disclosure of . . . membership is likely to affect adversely the ability of petitioner and its members to pursue their collective effort to foster beliefs which they admittedly have the right to advocate, in that it may induce members to withdraw from the Association and dissuade others from joining it because of fear of exposure of their beliefs shown through their associations and of the consequences of this exposure.

The fact that it was "private community pressures" rather than state action which would penalize disclosure of membership was irrelevant. "The crucial factor is the interplay of governmental and private action, for it is only after the initial exertion of state power represented by the production order that private action takes hold." Moreover, the exclusive announced purpose of the court action was to determine whether the association was doing business in Alabama in violation of the state foreign corporation registration act. This was not, concluded Justice Harlan, "a controlling justification for the deterrent effect on the free enjoyment of the right to associate which disclosure of membership lists is likely to have." [24]

Although the Court did not stress this fact, it obviously assumed that the NAACP was a "lawful" organization—it spoke of the members as associating "to pursue their lawful private interest"—and on this basis distinguished the 1928 Klan decision which had upheld a state demand for names of members. Again in *Bates* v. *City of Little Rock* (1960) the Court unanimously invalidated a demand that city officials be furnished with a list of the members of a local branch of the NAACP. This information was called for on the ground that it was necessary to determine whether the organization was subject to a local occupation license tax, but the Court ruled that there was no showing that production of the membership list bore any "reasonable relationship" to achievement of the governmental purpose of taxation.

In *Shelton* v. *Tucker* (1960), already discussed, the interest of the legislature in requiring all schoolteachers to list their organizations was admittedly to flush out NAACP members, and Shelton was such a member, but the Court decided the case on general principles without reference to the character of the organization.

The NAACP has concentrated much of its effort on court suits to compel desegregation, and here also it has been subjected to pressure. A Virginia law, typical of those in many other states, forbids the stirring up of litigation or the improper solicitation of legal business. This legislation was aimed at "ambulance chasing" and other unethical legal practices, but because the NAACP admittedly seeks out test cases on which it can go to court, it was accused of violating the statute in Virginia.

In *NAACP* v. *Button* (1963) the Supreme Court upheld the association's litigation procedures, and in the decision recognized litigation as "a form of political expression." The Court said that "in the context of NAACP objectives, litigation is not a technique of resolving private differences; it is a means of achieving the lawful objectives of equality of treatment by all government, federal, state, and local, for the members of the Negro com-

[24] For subsequent developments in this case, see *NAACP* v. *Alabama* (1964); George R. Osborne. "The NAACP in Alabama," in C. Herman Pritchett and Alan F. Westin (eds.), *The Third Branch of Government* (New York: Harcourt, Brace & World, Inc., 1963), pp. 149–203.

munity in this country." Indeed, "for such a group, association for litigation may be the most effective form of political association." [25]

So far as the Ku Klux Klan is concerned, the only Supreme Court decision is the now rather dubious one in *Bryant* v. *Zimmerman* (1928). Violence by Klan members led President Johnson in 1965 to urge that Congress pass legislation restricting the Klan's activities, and the House Committee on Un-American Activities undertook an investigation of the Klan for the purpose of drafting such legislation. The bill presented in 1966 would have made it a felony for members of a "clandestine organization" to commit or conspire to commit acts in a broad area of violence, kidnapping, or intimidation against other persons' rights. Both the Attorney General and the American Civil Liberties Union pointed out various constitutional problems in the bill. Individual acts of violence or lawlessness can and should be punished, but legislation assessing criminality on the basis of group membership and activities moves into the area of guilt by association.

The Communist Party, then, remains the only organization which has suffered legal punishment with Court approval, and even here the judicial tendency has been to withdraw from earlier acceptance of legislative restrictions on the Party. Recent Court decisions have made both the Smith Act and the Internal Security Act virtually unenforceable. "Outlawry" of the Party is almost unanimously opposed. Any new legislation aimed at subversion will have to accept the very firm status which associational freedom has now achieved.

## SELECTED REFERENCES

ABERNATHY, GLENN, *The Right of Assembly and Association*. Columbia, S.C.: The University of South Carolina Press, 1961.

BONSAL, DUDLEY B., *The Federal Loyalty-Security Program: Report of the Special Committee of the Association of the Bar of the City of New York*. New York: Dodd, Mead & Company, Inc., 1956.

BONTECOU, ELEANOR, *The Federal Loyalty-Security Program*. Ithaca, N.Y.: Cornell University Press, 1953.

BROWN, RALPH S., JR., *Loyalty and Security: Employment Tests in the United States*. New Haven, Conn.: Yale University Press, 1958.

CHAFEE, ZECHARIAH, JR., *Free Speech in the United States*. Cambridge, Mass.: Harvard University Press, 1941.

CHASE, HAROLD W., *Security and Liberty: The Problem of Native Communists, 1947–1955*. Garden City, N.Y.: Doubleday & Company, Inc., 1955.

[25] In *Brotherhood of Railroad Trainmen* v. *Virginia ex rel. Virginia State Bar* (1964) and *United Mine Workers* v. *Illinois State Bar Assn.* (1967), the Court followed the *Button* case in upholding forms of group legal service to organization members.

COOK, THOMAS I., *Democratic Rights versus Communist Activity*. Garden City, N.Y.: Doubleday & Company, Inc., 1954.

CUSHMAN, ROBERT E., *Civil Liberties in the United States: A Guide to Current Problems and Experience*, chap. 7. Ithaca, N.Y.: Cornell University Press, 1956.

DOWELL, ELDRIDGE F., *A History of Criminal Syndicalism Legislation in the United States*. Baltimore: The Johns Hopkins Press, 1939.

FELLMAN, DAVID, *The Constitutional Right of Association*. Chicago: The University of Chicago Press, 1963.

———, *The Defendant's Rights*, pp. 213–235. New York: Holt, Rinehart and Winston, Inc., 1958.

GARDNER, DAVID P., *The California Oath Controversy*. Berkeley, Calif.: University of California Press, 1967.

GELLHORN, WALTER (ed.), *The States and Subversion*. Ithaca, N.Y.: Cornell University Press, 1952.

HOOK, SIDNEY, *Heresy, Yes—Conspiracy, No*. New York: The John Day Company, Inc., 1953.

HORN, ROBERT A., *Groups and the Constitution*, chaps. 6, 7. Stanford, Calif.: Stanford University Press, 1956.

HYMAN, HAROLD M., *To Try Men's Souls: Loyalty Tests in American History*. Berkeley, Calif.: University of California Press, 1959.

ISRAEL, JEROLD H., "Elfbrandt v. Russell: The Demise of the Oath?" in Philip B. Kurland (ed.), *The Supreme Court Review: 1966*, pp. 193–252. Chicago: The University of Chicago Press, 1966.

LATHAM, EARL, *The Communist Controversy in Washington: From the New Deal to McCarthy*. Cambridge, Mass.: Harvard University Press, 1966.

MURRAY, ROBERT K., *Red Scare: A Study in National Hysteria, 1919–1920*. Minneapolis: The University of Minnesota Press, 1955.

PACKER, HERBERT L., *Ex-Communist Witnesses*. Stanford, Calif.: Stanford University Press, 1962.

PELTASON, JACK W., "Constitutional Liberty and the Communist Problem," in Alfred H. Kelly (ed.), *Foundations of Freedom in the American Constitution*, chap. 4. New York: Harper & Row, Publishers, Incorporated, 1958.

PRITCHETT, C. HERMAN, *The Political Offender and the Warren Court*. Boston: Boston University Press, 1958.

RICE, CHARLES E., *Freedom of Association*. New York: New York University Press, 1962.

ST. JAMES, WARREN, *The NAACP: A Case Study in Pressure Groups*. New York: Exposition Press, 1958.

SWISHER, CARL B., *The Supreme Court in Modern Role*, chap. 3. New York: New York University Press, 1958.

VOSE, CLEMENT E., *Caucasians Only: The Supreme Court, the NAACP, and the Restrictive Covenant Cases*. Berkeley, Calif.: University of California Press, 1959.

# 28

## Religious freedom and establishment

Freedom to worship God according to the dictates of individual conscience was one of the dominant motives in the founding of the American Colonies, and it might have been expected that provisions guaranteeing that right would have an important place in the Constitution. In fact, the Founders left the original Constitution almost devoid of language on the relationships of government and religion, thus conforming with their general practice in the civil liberties field. The sole exception was the provision of Article VI that "no religious test shall ever be required as a qualification to any office or public trust under the United States." Even this language was protested by Roger Sherman of Connecticut, who thought prohibition of religious tests for office was unnecessary, "the prevailing liberality being a sufficient security against such tests."

Actually, the "prevailing liberality" had not kept religious tests from being rather common in the Colonies and states. The early constitutions of several states disfranchised or excluded from office Catholics, Jews, and nonbelievers. In Massachusetts and Maryland, the office of governor was closed to all except Christians. In four more states, the governor had to be a Protestant. New York and Virginia were exceptional in taking no account of religious opinion for officeholding.

The adoption of the First Amendment repaired the omissions of the original Constitution on religious freedom by the addition of the following

language: "Congress shall make no law respecting an establishment of religion, or prohibiting the free exercise thereof." The states were thus specifically excluded from the ambit of the First Amendment, though many states had similar provisions in their own constitutions. In 1940, however, the Supreme Court held that the free exercise clause in the First Amendment had been made applicable to the states by the Fourteenth Amendment's guarantee of "liberty." This step was a logical sequence to the Court's ruling in the 1925 *Gitlow* decision applying the free speech and press provisions of the First Amendment to the states. Clearly, freedom to propagate religious convictions is hardly distinguishable from free speech generally, and the Supreme Court so held in *Cantwell* v. *Connecticut*.[1]

It was not until 1947, in *Everson* v. *Board of Education of Ewing Township,* that the Supreme Court had occasion to deal with state-religion relationships in an establishment context. But when it did so, it assumed without discussion that the establishment provision of the First Amendment was just as binding on the states as the freedom of religion language. To some the applicability of the establishment clause to the states has not seemed as obvious as it did to the Court. Corwin has argued that the "liberty" protected by the Fourteenth Amendment logically includes freedom of religion, but that establishment of religion is quite unrelated to the concept of liberty. Consequently, he contends state establishment of religion is perfectly constitutional unless it is of such a nature as to deprive persons of their freedom of religion. However, in practice this position would mean that a local religious majority could use its position to obtain local preferential treatment. By holding that the states are bound by both of the religious sections of the First Amendment, the Supreme Court moved to eliminate such divisive and dangerous possibilities. As Justice Brennan said in *School District of Abington Township* v. *Schempp* (1963), "the religious liberty embodied in the Fourteenth Amendment would not be viable if the Constitution were interpreted to forbid only establishments ordained by Congress."

Judicial interpretation of the free exercise and establishment principles has been affected by the differences in their developmental history. The principle of religious freedom or toleration was the older and the more firmly grounded in 1791. The tragic results of religious persecution and discrimination, of punishment for matters of conscience and belief, had long been demonstrated in England and on the continent by the time of the founding of the American nation, and the theoretical and practical case for toleration was well developed in English writing.

The establishment provision, on the other hand, was in flat contradiction

---

[1] Six years earlier, in *Hamilton* v. *Board of Regents* (1934), Justice Cardozo had anticipated this ruling by writing in a concurring opinion: "I assume for present purposes that the religious liberty protected by the First Amendment against invasion by the nation is protected by the Fourteenth Amendment against invasion by the states."

to the English practice then current, and some variety of establishment was found in several of the American states at the time the Constitution was adopted. Thus the principle of separation of church and state was an American invention whose application remained to be worked out in practice.

## FREE EXERCISE OF RELIGION

Free exercise of religion is closely related to freedom of expression generally, and it is natural that principles from the broader field can be used, sometimes without further refinement, to dispose of free exercise issues. In fact, one of the most important actions ever taken by the Supreme Court to guarantee free exercise of religion did not even rely on First Amendment principles. This was the case of *Pierce* v. *Society of Sisters* (1925), in which a Catholic religious order sued to test the constitutionality of an Oregon law requiring all children to attend only public schools for the first eight grades. In upholding the constitutional right of children to attend nonpublic schools where religious education could be provided, the Court struck down the law simply as an interference with the "business and property" of private and parochial schools.

It is possible for other constitutional provisions to be invoked to protect free exercise. For example, in *Niemotko* v. *Maryland* (1951) some Jehovah's Witnesses were arrested for making proselyting speeches in a public park without having secured a permit to do so. The Court held that permission had been denied because the city officials disliked the Witnesses and their views, and consequently the convictions violated the equal protection clause. Again, *Lovell* v. *Griffin* (1938) protected the right of Jehovah's Witnesses to sell the sect's literature from door to door without a permit, on free press grounds. *Saia* v. *New York* (1948) upheld the right of a Jehovah's Witnesses preacher to use a sound truck in a public park for his sermons, on free speech reasoning.

By reliance on general free expression principles to handle religious freedom claims, the Court has to that extent avoided the necessity of developing any special doctrinal content or tests for enforcement of the free exercise clause. It has assumed that the right to distribute religious pamphlets is no different from the right to distribute pamphlets dealing with other kinds of ideas. It has assumed that religious meetings in public parks deserve the same claim to protection as political rallies.

There are some obvious reasons for equating political and religious freedoms. If religious freedom is not the same as political freedom, then it must enjoy either less or more protection. The first alternative would result in discrimination against religious groups, which is not compatible with the free exercise clause. The second would amount to preference for religious freedom over general speech and press claims, and would raise possible establishment problems. This is the dilemma the Court must face when and if it

undertakes to discuss religious freedom as a value separate from the general context of other civil liberties.

FREE EXERCISE AND PRIOR RESTRAINT    One important principle which carries over from the free speech field to free exercise of religion is the ban on prior restraints, as the Court made clear in *Cantwell* v. *Connecticut* (1940). Here a state statute had made it a crime for any person to solicit or canvass from house to house for any religious or philanthropic cause without securing the prior approval of the secretary of the county welfare council, who was authorized to determine whether the cause was a bona fide religious one, conforming to reasonable standards of efficiency and integrity. The Court unanimously held this statute to abridge freedom of religion; a requirement of prior approval by a public official, which may be refused in his discretion, constitutes "a censorship of religion as the means of determining its right to survive," said Justice Roberts.

In *Jones* v. *Opelika* (1942) the prior restraint alleged took the form of municipal license fees on transient merchants or book agents as applied in three different cities to Jehovah's Witnesses engaged in door-to-door peddling of religious tracts. None of these ordinances discriminated against the sale of religious literature, nor were they drafted with the Witnesses in mind. They were ordinary taxes on the privilege of peddling. When religious advocates resort to commercial methods to raise funds for religious propaganda, the Court held, it is natural and proper to subject them to the payment of a fee. "The First Amendment does not require a subsidy in the form of fiscal exemption."

Four dissenting justices, however, thought these taxes were "in reality taxes upon the dissemination of religious ideas, a dissemination carried on by the distribution of religious literature for religious reasons alone and not for personal profit." After the appointment of Justice Rutledge to the Court a few months later, the issue was reconsidered and in *Murdock* v. *Pennsylvania* (1943) the decision of the previous year was overruled. The incidental collection of small sums for books or tracts to help finance the spread of religion was not regarded by the new Court majority as making this evangelism commercial, any more than passing the collection plate makes a church service commercial.

Another instance of a prior restraint invalidated on religious grounds was *Kunz* v. *New York* (1951). Here an ordinance making it unlawful to hold public worship meetings on the streets without first obtaining a permit from the city police commissioner was declared unconstitutional because it gave "an administrative official discretionary power to control in advance the right of citizens to speak on religious matters on the streets of New York."

ANTISOCIAL CONDUCT    Another free speech principle which the Court has applied in the religion field is the distinction between speech and action. In

*Cantwell* Justice Roberts said that free exercise of religion embraces "two concepts,—freedom to believe and freedom to act. The first is absolute but, in the nature of things, the second cannot be. Conduct remains subject to regulation for the protection of society."

Experience has shown only too clearly that religious beliefs often require, or are used to justify, unorthodox, bizarre, or even dangerous kinds of practices ranging all the way from polygamy to use of drugs and snake handling. De Tocqueville referred to the large number of "strange sects" in the United States, and observed that "religious insanity is very common." [2]

The Supreme Court has ruled that actions or practices which are made criminal by law or which are outrageously offensive to public morality are not rendered immune from punishment because of alleged religious motivation. To deal with such problems the Court developed the "secular regulation rule," which is stated by David Manwaring as follows: "There is no constitutional right to exemption on religious grounds from the compulsion of a general regulation dealing with nonreligious matters." [3]

The Court first developed this rule in dealing with the Mormon practice of polygamy. A congressional statute had made polygamy illegal in the territories of the United States, and in *Reynolds* v. *United States* (1878) the Court upheld the constitutionality of the statute against the Mormon contention that polygamy was required by their religion and that consequently punishing polygamy would deny them the free exercise of their religion. The Court thought the situation was exactly the reverse. Since a law against polygamy in the territories was clearly within the constitutional powers of Congress as a general secular regulation, the Mormons were actually asking for favored treatment from the law, namely, exemption from a statute which would be enforced on all others whose religious principles did not include polygamy.

*Prince* v. *Massachusetts* (1944) saw the Court preferring a secular regulation for the welfare of children over a claim for religious freedom, but by only a five to four margin. A nine-year-old girl, accompanied by her aunt, who was a Jehovah's Witness, sold literature of the Witnesses on downtown street corners at night. A Massachusetts statute forbade boys under twelve and girls under eighteen to sell newspapers or other merchandise on the streets, and provided punishment for parents and guardians who permitted children to do so.

The Court majority was not willing to grant that the religious motivation present in the case limited the state's normal range of protective authority over children. Propagandizing activities on the public streets were likely to result in the same kinds of problems "whether in religious, political or other

---

[2] Alexis de Tocqueville, *Democracy in America* (New York: Alfred A. Knopf, Inc., 1948), vol. 2, p. 134, note 19.

[3] David R. Manwaring, *Render unto Caesar: The Flag-salute Controversy* (Chicago: The University of Chicago Press, 1962), p. 51.

matters," and Massachusetts was justified in concluding that an "absolute prohibition" of involvement of children was necessary to accomplish the state's purpose.

Justice Murphy, one of the dissenters, did not doubt the right of the state to have general child welfare regulations, but he insisted that when they infringed on a religious exercise, then there had to be a grave, immediate, and substantial danger as justification. He could see no such dangers in this situation. He thought that the evils a legislature might normally envisage with children on the streets would not be present when there was a religious motivation involved.

Secular regulations aimed at protecting public health and safety usually prevail over religious objections or scruples.[4] In *Jacobson* v. *Massachusetts* (1905) the Supreme Court upheld a state compulsory vaccination law over religious and other objections. Refusal to accept medical aid or blood transfusion on religious grounds has led to numerous court decisions. When official action is taken to provide medical care for children against the wishes of their parents, the courts have uniformly upheld the intervention. But in a 1965 Illinois case where an adult woman without minor children was dying because of her religious objection to transfusion and the hospital obtained a court order appointing a conservator who approved the transfusion, the state supreme court, hearing the case after her death, ordered the appointment expunged, on the ground that the refusal had created no clear and present danger and that the order had interfered with her basic constitutional rights.[5]

Various state decisions have upheld laws forbidding commercial fortune telling when applied to palm reading as a religious practice, or laws prohibiting the handling of snakes in religious services. Faith healers cannot use religious liberty as a defense in prosecutions for the unlicensed practice of medicine. In *Ballard* v. *United States* (1944) the Court held that a cult leader could be prosecuted for mail fraud, provided the jury was not allowed to pass on the truth of the religious claims he made but only his good faith in professing to believe them.

THE FLAG-SALUTE CASES    The resistance of Jehovah's Witnesses to the compulsory flag salute in the public schools presented the Supreme Court with a particularly perplexing secular regulation issue. The Witnesses instruct their children that saluting the flag constitutes worship of a "graven image," and is contrary to Bible teaching. The conflict in conscience thus set up in schools requiring the salute was brought to the Supreme Court in

---

[4] David Fellman, *Religion in American Public Law* (Boston: Boston University Press, 1965), pp. 21–29.

[5] *In re Brooks' Estate* (1965). In *George* v. *United States* (1966) the Supreme Court refused to review the appeal of a Jehovah's Witness who had been forced to accept a blood transfusion by a federal court order after he entered a Veterans Administration hospital with a bleeding ulcer.

*Minersville School District* v. *Gobitis* (1940), where the Court decided, with only Justice Stone dissenting, that the compulsory flag salute did not infringe the constitutional rights of the protesting children. Justice Frankfurter, who wrote the majority opinion, stressed that "national unity is the basis of national security," and such unity

> . . . is fostered by all those agencies of the mind and spirit which may serve to gather up the traditions of a people, transmit them from generation to generation, and thereby create that continuity of a treasured common life which constitutes a civilization. "We live by symbols." The flag is the symbol of our national unity, transcending all internal differences, however large, within the framework of the Constitution.

Justice Frankfurter argued that this was "legislation of general scope not directed against doctrinal loyalties of particular sects." The free exercise clause did not, he said, relieve the individual from obedience to a general law not aimed at the promotion or restriction of religious beliefs. The mere possession of religious convictions which contradict the relevant concerns of a political society does not relieve the citizen from the discharge of political responsibilities. The only question was whether a school board was justified in thinking that requiring the flag salute would help to further legitimate educational ends, and Frankfurter did not see how the Supreme Court could deny that the school board might legitimately hold such a view.

Justice Frankfurter's position was thus that the state had a constitutional right to compel all school children to salute the flag. There was no discrimination against those who had religious scruples against this ceremony. In fact, as in the *Reynolds* case, if their religious scruples were regarded as exempting them from the exercise, they would be receiving preference because of their religion over all other students who had no such scruples.

The *Gobitis* decision unleashed a wave of persecution against the Witnesses, and the ruling was rather generally condemned in the press.[6] Justice Stone, the sole dissenter, accepted religious objections as a valid ground for refusing to salute the flag. He thought that, while voluntary expressions of loyalty might promote national unity, compulsory exercises by children in violation of their own and their parents' religious convictions were not so important a method of promoting national unity as to override the constitutional guarantee of free exercise.

Three years later, *West Virginia State Board of Education* v. *Barnette* (1943) accomplished the important result of reversing the *Gobitis* holding while at the same time avoiding Stone's solution of religious preference. Justice Jackson for the new majority stated the issue as whether any child, regardless of religious belief, could be compelled to engage in a compulsory flag-salute exercise. He answered: "We think the action of the local authori-

---

[6] See Manwaring, *op. cit.*

ties in compelling the flag salute and pledge transcends constitutional limitations on their power and invades the sphere of intellect and spirit which it is the purpose of the First Amendment . . . to reserve from all official control." Since the state could not compel *any* student to engage in the flag salute, there was no need to develop a justification for giving preferential treatment to particular religious groups.

THE LICENSE TAX CASES     It was in the municipal license tax cases that the Supreme Court finally recognized a claim for religious exemption from secular regulations. As already noted, *Jones* v. *Opelika* (1942) tested the constitutionality of municipal license taxes on Jehovah's Witnesses who were selling religious literature from door to door. In this initial consideration of the problem, the Court majority upheld the taxes. Justice Reed's opinion for the Court thought that "ordinary commercial methods of sales of articles to raise propaganda funds" were subject to state taxation, no matter if it was a religious organization that was involved. He regarded as proper "nondiscriminatory regulation of operations which are incidental to the exercise of religion or the freedom of speech or the press"; this was quite different from any interference with "the religious rite itself or the unmixed dissemination of information."

Four justices dissented from this position. Justice Murphy, one of the dissenters, condemned the tax as an interference with the free exercise of religion. He espoused for the first time on the Court a preferred position for religious freedoms over other First Amendment values: "Important as free speech and a free press are to a free government and a free citizenry, there is a right even more dear to many individuals—the right to worship their Maker according to their needs and the dictates of their souls and to carry their message or their gospel to every living creature." This desire, he suggested, might constitute a "more precious" reason for action in a free exercise of religion case than in a free speech or press situation.

Within a year the dissenters won control of the Court on this issue. *Murdock* v. *Pennsylvania* (1943), with Justice Douglas speaking for the Court, defined the actions of the Witnesses in distributing their literature as a religious rite. "The hand distribution of religious tracts is an age-old form of missionary evangelism," and "selling" the literature to defray expenses does not make it a commercial operation, any more than the passing of a collection plate in church makes the church service a commercial project. The impact of this tax on Jehovah's Witnesses was the equivalent of imposing a tax for the privilege of delivering a sermon, and the state "may not impose a charge for the enjoyment of a right granted by the federal constitution."

Justice Frankfurter, dissenting, pointed out the problem involved in any grant of a special position to religious commercial operations. Street hawkers create conditions which require municipalities to spend money.

To say that the Constitution forbids the states to obtain the necessary revenue from the whole of a class that enjoys these benefits and facilities, when . . . no discrimination is suggested . . . and the exaction is not claimed to be actually burdensome, is to say that the Constitution requires not that the dissemination of ideas in the interest of religion shall be free but that it shall be subsidized by the state. Such a claim offends the most important of all aspects of religious freedom in this country, namely, that of the separation of church and state.

SECULAR REGULATION AND THE ALTERNATIVE MEANS TEST    The secular regulation rule was applied to uphold Sunday closing laws in 1961, but with a qualification which was to result in a substantial modification in the Court's subsequent attitude on free exercise problems. Two of the *Sunday Closing Cases, Gallagher* v. *Crown Kosher Super Market* and *Braunfeld* v. *Brown,* involved challenges to Sunday closing laws in two states by Orthodox Jewish merchants who contended that, since their religion required that they close their shops on Saturday, a Sunday closing law limited them to a five-day week and was a restraint of the free exercise of their religion.

Two justices agreed with this position. Justice Stewart thought that the state could not constitutionally compel "an Orthodox Jew to choose between his religious faith and his economic survival." Justice Douglas felt that when a state uses its coercive powers "to compel minorities to observe a second Sabbath, not their own," the state was aiding and preferring one religion over another, contrary to the Constitution.

The Court majority, however, speaking through Chief Justice Warren, upheld the Sunday closing laws as secular regulations. While they had admittedly been religious in their origin, the Court regarded them now as purely an effective device for providing a uniform day of rest. Moreover, the laws were secular regulations which did not make any religious activity unlawful, merely more expensive.

However, Warren's opinion made an important addition to the secular regulation rule. This is the key sentence: "If the State regulates conduct by enacting a general law within its power, the purpose and effect of which is to advance the State's secular goals, the statute is valid despite its indirect burden on religious observances *unless the State may accomplish its purpose by means which do not impose such a burden.*" (Italics added.) This is substantially a new test for secular regulations, which now will be upheld against claims of interference with free exercise only if there appear to be no practicable alternative means whereby the legislative purpose can be accomplished. Applying the test in *Braunfeld,* the Chief Justice evaluated the availability of alternative means for achieving the secular goal of a common day of rest, and found none that seemed practicable.

The potentialties of this new test became apparent when in *Sherbert* v. *Verner* (1963) its effect was to invalidate a state law. A Seventh Day Adventist textile worker was discharged for refusal to work on Saturday, and

no other work was available in the area for one who would not work on Saturday. She filed a claim for unemployment compensation, which was denied on the ground that her refusal to accept suitable work meant that she was not "available for work" as required by statute.

Justice Brennan for the Court ruled that this denial of benefits was a burden on the free exercise of the woman's religion. Admittedly the law had a valid secular purpose. But the pressure on her to violate her Sabbath was as much an infringement on the free exercise of her religion as a fine imposed for Saturday worship. Sunday observers are protected from having to make such a choice. The opinion does not rely on this claim of discrimination, however. It rests rather on the ground that there is an available alternative here which will preserve the free exercise of religion—namely, to grant exemption from the statute for refusal to work for religious reasons. This requirement that a state must grant preference to religious reasons for refusing to work over nonreligious reasons disturbed Justices Harlan and White, dissenting, who would have applied the traditional secular regulation rule.

The *Sherbert* holding was subsequently applied in state courts to overturn the conviction of Navajo members of the Native American Church for using peyote in their religious ceremonies; [7] to free a woman from a contempt sentence for refusal on religious grounds to serve on a jury; [8] and to hold that children could not be compelled to stand while the national anthem was being played in school.[9]

PREFERRED STATUS FOR RELIGIOUS FREEDOM    A review of these secular regulation cases shows that the Court has at least on occasions recognized free exercise of religion as superior to other freedom of expression claims, and has granted exemption from secular rules to religious devotees that would not have been available to others. This preference for religion is the position which Justice Murphy first put forward in *Jones* v. *Opelika* (1942), and the ground on which Justices Black and Douglas relied in the 1943 flag-salute case.

The opposition to this view was led by Justice Frankfurter, who contended that the state must neither hurt nor help religion. In *Murdock* v. *Pennsylvania* (1943) he responded to Justice Murphy: "The essence of the religious freedom guaranteed by our Constitution is therefore this: no religion shall either receive the state's support or incur its hostility." In the second flag-salute

---

[7] *People* v. *Woody* (1964). In 1966 Dr. Timothy Leary announced that he had founded a new religion, the League of Spiritual Discovery, based on the sacramental use of the drug LSD, as well as peyote and marijuana.

[8] *In re Jenison* (1963).

[9] *Sheldon* v. *Fannin* (1963). But in *Garber* v. *Kansas* (1967) the Court, with three justices dissenting, let stand a Kansas conviction of a member of the Amish religion who refused, on religious grounds, to send his daughter to a public school.

case he answered Black and Douglas: "The validity of secular laws cannot be measured by their conformity to religious doctrines. It is only in a theocratic state that ecclesiastical doctrines measure legal right or wrong."

The Frankfurter position is powerfully supported by Philip B. Kurland in his *Religion and the Law,* the theme of which is that "the freedom and separation clauses should be read as a single precept that government cannot utilize religion as a standard for action or inaction because these clauses prohibit classification in terms of religion either to confer a benefit or to impose a burden." [10]

But perhaps the most effective statement of the position that religion should not be singled out for special freedoms is that of Justice Jackson in *Douglas* v. *City of Jeanette* (1943), a companion case to *Murdock:*

> In my view, the First Amendment assures the broadest tolerable exercise of free speech, free press, and free assembly, not merely for religious purposes, but for political, economic, scientific, news, or informational ends as well. When limits are reached which such communications must observe, can one go farther under the cloak of religious evangelism? Does what is obscene, or commercial, or abusive, or inciting become less so if employed to promote a religious ideology? I had not supposed that the rights of secular and non-religious communications were more narrow or in any way inferior to those of avowed religious groups.

But, it may be asked, if the free exercise clause carries protections in no way different from those attaching to the speech and press provisions, why does the First Amendment make special mention of religious freedom? Jackson replies: "The history of religious persecution gives the answer. Religion needed specific protection because it was subject to attack from a separate quarter. . . . It was to assure religious teaching as much freedom as secular discussion, rather than to assure a greater license, that led to its separate statement."

The Frankfurter-Jackson-Kurland position, while appealing in its simplicity and evenhandedness, would impose too rigid a control on courts, legislatures, and administrators in making the adjustments demanded in the real world. It would certainly require the abolition of tax exemption for churches. It would forbid Congress to grant exemption from military service to conscientious objectors to war on religious grounds. It would prevent such a minor gesture of understanding and goodwill as Congress made in 1965 to the Old Order Amish, a nonconformist religious group of some nineteen thousand persons who believe that any form of insurance shows a lack of faith in God. In passing the Medicare-Social Security Act of 1965, Congress took account of their position and permitted self-employed persons to withdraw from the Social Security system if they were members of a recognized religious sect conscientiously opposed to public and private insurance.

[10] *Religion and the Law* (Chicago: Aldine Publishing Co., 1962), p. 18.

DEFINING RELIGION    Recognition of the right of religious claimants to override secular regulations inescapably involves determining what religion is. To carry out a policy of preference for religious freedom, the Supreme Court must either define religion itself, or allow groups and individuals to make their own definitions of religion.

The Court's initial tendency was to undertake its own definition of religion, as was demonstrated in the Mormon cases. In *Davis* v. *Beason* (1890) the territory of Idaho had made it a prerequisite to exercise of the franchise that the voter take an oath he was not a member of any organization which advised or practiced the "crime of bigamy or polygamy." Davis, a Mormon, was denied the right to vote. Since he was not himself a polygamist, he had lost the franchise because of his belief in polygamy as expressed in his church membership. To uphold the statute the Court had to deny that polygamy could be a religious belief, and to do this it sought to develop an objective test or definition of religion: "The term 'religion' has reference to one's views of his relations to his Creator, and to the obligations they impose of reverence for his being and character, and of obedience to his will." Religious liberty permits each individual "to entertain such notions respecting his relations to his Maker and the duties they impose as may be approved by his judgment and conscience, and to exhibit his sentiments in such form of worship as he may think proper, not injurious to the equal rights of others."

On the basis of this definition, the Court somehow concluded that polygamy could not be "a tenet of religion." Rather it was, by "the general consent of the Christian world in modern times," a crime, and "crime is not the less odious because sanctioned by what any particular sect may designate as religion." Similarly in *Church of Jesus Christ of Latter-day Saints* v. *United States* (1890) the Court found that the Mormon Church could not be considered a religious corporation, because one of its principal tenets, polygamy, was merely supposed or imagined to be religious. As a parallel, the Court pointed to the Thugs of India, who "imagined that their belief in the right of assassination was a religious belief; but their thinking so did not make it so."

Judges have also been involved in defining religion in connection with tax exemption for religious organizations [11] and conscientious objectors to war (to be considered shortly), but the recent tendency of the Supreme Court has been to allow groups and individuals to define religion for themselves, and to recognize opinion and action religiously motivated in good faith as constitutionally protected, even though this means accepting views which seem, as Justice Douglas said in the *Ballard* case, "incredible, if not preposterous, to most people." In *Murdock* v. *Pennsylvania,* as we have seen, the Court allowed Jehovah's Witnesses to decide for themselves that selling their literature from door to door was a part of their religion. In *Fowler* v.

[11] See Fellman, *op. cit.*, pp. 43–51.

*Rhode Island* (1953) the Court said: "It is no business of courts to say that what is a religious practice or activity for one group is not religion under the protection of the First Amendment."

This likewise seems to be the position toward which the courts are moving on the Black Muslim issue. This Negro group, which preaches black supremacy and complete separation of the races, has all the normal features of a religion, but its members when in prison have often been denied access to the literature of their religion or the opportunity to hold services. The reasons given have been that the sect is not a religion but rather a political and racist movement, and that their preachings of hatred for white people would be dangerous in prisons. In *Cooper* v. *Pate* (1963) the Supreme Court reversed the action of a lower court which had refused to hear the complaint of a Black Muslim in an Illinois penitentiary that he was denied permission to purchase religious publications and certain other privileges solely because of his religious beliefs. The federal district court then ruled that Muslims must be allowed to have the Koran, to be visited by Islamic ministers, and to hold religious services. There had been no showing of "clear and present danger to prison security" from such visits or services, Judge Austin said. As for the prison official's charge that Black Muslims do not teach the true religion of Islam, the judge replied: "As religion is not a subject of knowledge but only a matter of opinion, it is not the function of this court to determine the merits of an alleged religion, however excellent or fanatical or preposterous said religion may seem." [12]

There is no reason to doubt, however, that the courts will still disallow claims for religious status which go beyond all bounds of belief. Even in the *Murdock* case Justice Douglas said: "We do not intimate or suggest . . . that any conduct can be made a religious rite and by the zeal of the practitioners swept into the First Amendment." In 1966 a federal court in Phoenix convicted for mail fraud a cult leader who claimed that betting on dog races was part of his religious belief.

Theism, moreover, is coming to be regarded as no longer a necessary element in religion. In *Torcaso* v. *Watkins* (1961) a Maryland requirement of a "declaration of belief in the existence of God" as a qualification for public office in the state was declared unconstitutional by a unanimous Court, as an invasion of "freedom of belief and religion." Government may not "aid those religions based on a belief in the existence of God as against those religions founded on different beliefs." [13]

While no case has yet been decided by the Supreme Court, several lower courts have held that tax exemptions for places of religious worship must be

[12] *Chicago Sun-Times,* June 8, 1965.

[13] On October 11, 1965, the Maryland supreme court in *Schowgurow* v. *State* ruled that requiring jurors to swear to a belief in God was unconstitutional, and reversed the conviction of a Buddhist who had objected that nonbelievers in God were excluded from the grand jury which indicted him and the trial jury which convicted him.

interpreted to include nontheistic groups.[14] Constitutional questions were avoided in these cases by looking at the social function of these groups rather than at the content of their beliefs.

CONSCIENTIOUS OBJECTORS TO WAR    Every American conscription law has granted exemption from military service to conscientious objectors who met the statutory definition. The Draft Act of 1917 gave exemption to objectors affiliated with a "well-recognized religious sect or organization . . . whose existing creed or principles [forbid] its members to participate in war in any form." This limitation of exemption to members of particular sects seems clearly invalid as a discrimination against other religions, but in fact the Secretary of War ruled that "personal scruples against war" would be considered as constituting conscientious objection.[15]

In adopting the 1940 Selective Training and Service Act Congress made it unnecessary to belong to a pacifist religious sect if the claimant's own opposition to war was based on "religious training and belief." This phrase was defined in the 1948 act as follows: ". . . an individual's belief in a relation to a Supreme Being involving duties superior to those arising from any human relation, but [not including] essentially political, sociological, or philosophical views or a merely personal moral code."

The Supreme Court construed this language in *United States* v. *Seeger* (1965). The case involved three young men, none of whom was a member of an orthodox religious group or willing to declare a belief in a Supreme Being. However, none was "an avowedly irreligious person or . . . an atheist." All were found by the Court to have a sincere and meaningful belief which occupied a place in their lives "parallel to that filled by the orthodox belief in God." The Court interpreted the statutory phrase "Supreme Being" as meaning not the orthodox God but a "broader concept of a power or being, or a faith, 'to which all else is subordinate or upon which all else is ultimately dependent.' " The language denying the rights of conscientious objection based upon a "merely personal moral code" meant "a moral code which is not only personal but which is the sole basis for the registrant's belief and is in no way related to a Supreme Being."

The Court thought that this interpretation of the statute did not place an impossible burden on the Selective Service officials. The test was "simple of application" and "essentially . . . objective"—whether the claimed belief occupies "the same place in the life of the objector as an orthodox belief in God holds in the life of one clearly qualified for exemption." The Court went on to say that, while of course the "truth" of an objector's belief could not be questioned, whether the belief was "truly held" could be examined.

---

[14] See *Washington Ethical Society* v. *District of Columbia* (1957); *Fellowship of Humanity* v. *County of Alameda* (1957).
[15] The general constitutionality of the draft act was upheld in *Arver* v. *United States* (*Selective Draft Law Cases*) (1918).

The *Seeger* ruling, it will be noted, was simply an exercise in statutory construction; no constitutional position was taken. Justice Douglas, concurring, pointed out that if the Court had held that the right of conscientious objection was limited to those "who embraced one religious faith rather than another," that would be discrimination in violation of the free exercise clause and also a denial of equal protection.

The widespread opposition to the war in Vietnam, often expressed on moral grounds, led some to assert that the right to object to particular wars on grounds of conscience should be recognized. The American Civil Liberties Union supported this position in a 1966 statement which said that "no person [should] be compelled to participate in armed conflict when he believes it to be in violation of his conscience to do so, and equally wrong to yield his conscience to his government, whether on moral, social, philosophical or religious grounds." The statement continued:

> The individuals who should qualify as conscientious objectors to a particular war are . . . those who find such participation in such a war to be so great a wrong that even government's command will not relieve them of responsibility for committing that wrong. For civil libertarians conscience so central to a man's belief becomes an aspect of religious liberty protected by the First Amendment—whether or not the objector calls his conscience "religious." [16]

THE LIBERTY OF CHURCHES    While courts will become involved in the internal affairs of churches only with the greatest reluctance, there are disputes, particularly those involving property rights, which they cannot avoid. State courts have accepted suits brought by individuals for reinstatement of membership, suits filed for reinstatement of a pastor or to prevent a discharged pastor from conducting services, cases involving the right of a church to buy and sell property, and cases concerning burial rights.[17] In suits between competing factions of a local congregation, the general rule is that the will of the majority prevails, and courts will limit their inquiry to determining which is the majority. But where hierarchical or centrally organized churches are involved, the courts will follow the decision of the proper institutional authority, as the Supreme Court has done in two noteworthy cases.

In the first, *Watson* v. *Jones* (1872), a Presbyterian church in Louisville, Kentucky, had split over the slavery issue, and the two groups took their respective claims to the church property to the courts. In *Kedroff* v. *St. Nich-*

---

[16] Decisions denying naturalization to alien conscientious objectors unwilling to swear that they would defend the United States by force of arms—*United States* v. *Schwimmer* (1929), *United States* v. *Macintosh* (1931), *United States* v. *Bland* (1931)—were reversed in *Girouard* v. *United States* (1946). An unsuccessful claim of conscientious objection to an "unjust war" was denied review by the Supreme Court in *Spiro* v. *United States* (1968).

[17] Fellman, *op. cit.*, pp. 59–63.

*olas Cathedral of Russian Orthodox Church* (1952) the New York Legislature had sought to free the Russian Orthodox churches in America from control by the Moscow church authorities by making them subject to an autonomous Russian Church in America. The statute provided that in all other respects the churches should conform to the doctrine and discipline of the Eastern Orthodox Church.

In both these cases the Supreme Court held that principles of religious liberty precluded state intervention. The dispute over the Louisville church property would have to be decided by the church hierarchy, and its decision would be binding on the courts. The New York law transferring control over churches from one group of persons to another was an inadmissible use of state power. Justice Jackson, dissenting in the latter case, thought that New York had a right to make its own property laws, and apply them to churches. But Justice Frankfurter replied: "St. Nicholas Cathedral is not just a piece of real estate. . . . What is at stake here is the power to exercise religious authority." The church, not the state, must make the decisions on location of such power.[18]

In *First Unitarian Church of Los Angeles* v. *County of Los Angeles* (1958) an effort to deny tax exemption to a church unless its officers signed a loyalty oath was struck down for due process reasons without reaching freedom of religion issues.

### ESTABLISHMENT OF RELIGION

There have been two general views as to the intention of the establishment clause. One position holds that it was meant to outlaw only the kind of establishment that existed in Europe in 1791, namely, an official, publicly supported church. This view contends that the evil in establishment is the preferential treatment of one religion over others. It argues that the establishment clause does not forbid state contacts with religion or state support of religious activities so long as all religions are treated equally and no discrimination is involved.

The other view contends that establishment refers to any government support of or connection with religion. This position holds that the no-establishment principle requires the complete separation of church and state, and forbids any public financial support to religious institutions, even if made available on a nonpreferential basis. The Supreme Court has consistently espoused this second position, and the supporting arguments for this interpretation can be summarized briefly.

[18] On remand, the New York Court of Appeals reached on common-law grounds the same conclusion as in the first decision. The Supreme Court, in *Kreshik* v. *St. Nicholas Cathedral* (1960), again reversed, holding that it was no more proper for a court to intervene in this religious dispute than for the Legislature to do so.

First there is the evidence supplied by the framing of the First Amendment. Congress considered and rejected language that would clearly have adopted the first position stated above. In the Senate three motions, all aimed directly and narrowly against laws preferring one "sect" or "denomination" over others were defeated. However, the Senate then adopted another comparatively narrow ban: "Congress shall make no law establishing articles of faith or a mode of worship." The House, which had previously adopted broad prohibitory language against laws "establishing religion," rejected the Senate's version. A conference committee of the two houses, including James Madison as chairman of the House conferees, abandoned the Senate proposal and drafted the present language which forbids "an establishment of religion" rather than merely an established church.

Second, the phrase "establishment of religion" must be given the meaning that it had in the United States in 1791, rather than its European connotation. In America there was no establishment of a single church, as in England. Four states had never adopted any establishment practices. Three had abolished their establishments during the Revolution. The remaining six states—Massachusetts, New Hampshire, Connecticut, Maryland, South Carolina, and Georgia—changed to comprehensive or "multiple" establishments. That is, aid was provided to all churches in each state on a non-preferential basis, except that the establishment was limited to churches of the Protestant religion in three states and to those of the Christian religion in the other three states. Since there were almost no Catholics in the first group of states, and very few Jews in any state, this meant that the multiple establishment practices included every religious group with enough members to form a church. It was this nonpreferential assistance to organized churches that constituted "establishment of religion" in 1791, and it was this practice that the amendment forbade Congress to adopt.

Third, Jefferson and Madison were the dominant figures in developing the constitutional policy on establishment, and they both espoused strict separation of church and state. A bill providing for tax support of religion had been presented to the Virginia Legislature in 1784. Those who professed no religion were permitted by the bill to direct that their tax be used for general educational purposes. Madison attacked this bill in his famous "Memorial and Remonstrance against Religious Assessments," which was so persuasive that the bill was not even presented in the 1785 session. Instead, Jefferson's Act for Establishing Religious Freedom was passed by the Virginia Legislature.

During their terms as President, moreover, both Jefferson and Madison took very strict positions on establishment. Both believed that presidential proclamations of Thanksgiving Day were contrary to the Constitution. They also regarded as unconstitutional tax exemption for churches, payment from government funds to chaplains in Congress and the armed services, and

nonpreferential land grants for the support of churches. It is significant that a 1796 treaty with Tripoli, a Moslem country, negotiated under President Washington and ratified by the Senate, stated that there was no ground for religious differences between the two nations because "the government of the United States of America is not, in any sense, founded on the Christian religion."

NATIONAL ESTABLISHMENT PROBLEMS    The Supreme Court has had little occasion to consider the limits which the establishment clause imposes on Congress. For the most part the issues that have arisen have been settled by practice. Thanksgiving Day proclamations and chaplains in Congress have long been accepted. Chaplains in the armed services seem clearly justified on the ground that it would be a violation of religious freedom to take men away from their homes and churches and make no provision for their continued worship and spiritual guidance. Compulsory chapel attendance at the four armed services academies seems a more questionable policy; it was attacked in 1966 by the Lutheran Church as an infringement of the constitutional rights of the cadets and midshipmen. The use of the phrase "In God We Trust" on United States coins and the phrase "under God" which Congress added to the Pledge of Allegiance in 1954 have aroused only minor concern.

The Supreme Court has never yet held any congressional action unconstitutional as an establishment of religion. In 1899 a case came up involving an appropriation for hospitals in the District of Columbia. Part of this money was allocated by the District government for construction of an isolation wing for a Catholic hospital. The Court refused to enjoin this expenditure, distinguishing between the hospital corporation and the order of nuns which controlled it, and noting that the hospital was open to everyone.[19] In 1908 another injunction suit against the Commissioner of Indian Affairs sought to prevent payments of money to the Bureau of Catholic Indian Missions for Catholic schools among the Sioux Indians. The Court held there was no case because the payments were from funds held in trust by the government for the benefit of Indian tribes, and consequently the commissioner was acting in a quasi-private capacity as a trustee. The Court admitted that the decision might have been otherwise if regular public funds were involved.[20]

Perhaps the most authoritative indication of what cannot be done by Congress under the establishment clause was given by a Senate committee which in 1853 investigated the constitutionality of chaplains. Its conclusion was that laws "in favor of any church, or ecclesiastical association, or system of religious faith" would be invalid if they provided "endowment at the public expense, peculiar privileges to its members, or disadvantages or pen-

[19] *Bradfield* v. *Roberts* ( 1899 ).
[20] *Quick Bear* v. *Leupp* ( 1908 ).

alties upon those who should reject its doctrines or belong to other communions." [21]

ESTABLISHMENT AND THE STATES    Establishment problems have arisen in the states principally in the field of public education. Even though the First Amendment had not then been applied to the states, a strong national interest developed on the issue as early as the 1870s. President Grant in his annual message to Congress in 1875 proposed a constitutional amendment prohibiting the teaching of religion in the public schools and forbidding school funds from being used directly or indirectly in aid of any religious sect. The Republican party had such a plank in its platform in 1876 and 1880. An amendment making the provisions of the First Amendment on religion applicable to the states, and specifically banning use of public school funds by religious sects, passed the House overwhelmingly in 1876, but failed to receive a two-thirds majority in the Senate. But what Congress failed to do in 1876, the Supreme Court substantially did in 1925 when it made the First Amendment applicable to the states by way of the "liberty" language in the Fourteenth.

There was no immediate application of this principle in the establishment field, however. The issue was ignored in a 1930 case, *Cochran v. Louisiana State Board of Education,* where it might have been exploited. The state of Louisiana under a free textbook program was supplying books to students in parochial as well as public schools. The constitutional objection raised was that this involved a taking of property for private use contrary to the due process clause. The Court ruled, however, that the appropriation of tax funds was for a public purpose, and thus upheld the program.

THE NEW JERSEY BUS CASE AND THE PUPIL BENEFIT THEORY    *Everson v. Board of Education of Ewing Township* (1947) involved a New Jersey statute which authorized local boards of education to make rules and contracts for transportation of children to and from schools, whether public or private. Under this statute the Ewing township board arranged to reimburse parents of public and Catholic school pupils for money expended by them for transportation of their children on the regular public transportation system.

A taxpayer brought suit challenging on constitutional grounds the right of the board to reimburse parents of parochial school students, but lost in the Supreme Court by a five to four vote. Justice Black's opinion for the majority (including Douglas, Murphy, Vinson, and Reed) dealt principally with the objection that the statute amounted to an establishment of religion. To assist in applying the establishment clause to the New Jersey bus problem, Black reviewed European and American colonial history of government-

[21] Senate Report no. 376, 32d Cong., 2d sess. (1853).

supported churches, concluding that the First Amendment means at least this much:

> Neither a state nor the Federal Government can set up a church. Neither can pass laws which aid one religion, aid all religions, or prefer one religion over another. Neither can force nor influence a person to go to or to remain away from church against his will or force him to profess a belief or disbelief in any religion. No person can be punished for entertaining or professing religious beliefs or disbeliefs, for church attendance or non-attendance. No tax in any amount, large or small, can be levied to support any religious activities or institutions, whatever they may be called, or whatever form they may adopt to teach or practice religion.

On the basis of these principles Black acknowledged that the New Jersey statute approached the "verge" of constitutional power. Indeed, looking at the establishment of religion clause as forbidding the contribution of "tax-raised funds to the support of an institution which teaches the tenets and faith of any church"—and Black admitted this is what the provision means—it would be hard to support the statute. But he escaped from the necessity of reaching this conclusion by moving over to the free exercise of religion clause, which he interpreted as commanding New Jersey not to "hamper its citizens in the free exercise of their own religion." The state must not exclude any individuals, *"because of their faith, or lack of it,* from receiving the benefits of public welfare legislation."

Fearful that this argument might prove too much, Black hurried on to say that of course a state could limit its provision of transportation assistance to public school children only. But in fact, he added, the states have generally not taken this line. They already furnish many services to church schools with general approval, such as fire and police protection, sidewalks, and public highways. The First Amendment "requires the state to be a neutral in its relations with groups of religious believers and non-believers; it does not require the state to be their adversary. State power is no more to be used so as to handicap religions than it is to favor them." His argument closed with the contention that this New Jersey action did not constitute "the slightest breach" in the wall between church and state, which "must be kept high and impregnable."

Four justices (Frankfurter, Jackson, Rutledge, and Burton) could not accept this view of state financial aid as public welfare legislation beneficial to children and their parents rather than as assistance in the providing of religious education. Justice Rutledge thought the issue was simple: "Does New Jersey's action furnish support for religion by use of the taxing power?" No one denies that the Catholic schools give religious instruction; and transportation, Rutledge argued, "is as essential to education as any other element." If providing transportation is merely "public welfare legislation," then there can be "no possible objection to more extensive support of religious education by New Jersey." Moreover, if the public can aid religions,

it can also regulate them. This is the first step in the direction of an establishment of religion, Rutledge concluded.

The *Everson* decision, of course, merely held that providing tax-supported bus transportation to religious schools was not contrary to the federal Constitution. It did not say that such transportation had to be provided. In fact, David Fellman reports that "the great weight of authority among the state courts is against bus transportation" as forbidden by state constitutional provisions limiting or prohibiting the expenditure of public moneys for sectarian education.[22] This issue remains a constant source of controversy in state legislatures and state courts.

Partly because of these state constitutional provisions, which are often quite specific in banning state expenditures for religious purposes,[23] the "pupil benefit" theory endorsed by the Supreme Court in *Everson* has been utilized less than might have been expected to justify additional forms of public aid to religious schools. Almost invariably state courts have struck down the granting of public money to parochial schools for general expenses of operation or to cover tuition costs.[24] On the question of supplying textbooks to parochial school children, the state courts have been divided. A 1965 New York statute requiring public schools to "lend" textbooks to students in private and parochial schools was reviewed by the Supreme Court in *Board of Education* v. *Allen* (1968).

The pupil benefit theory was of course the justification for the provisions in the "GI Bill" passed by Congress in 1944, under which returning veterans could attend denominational schools to which federal payments were made directly.[25] Similarly, all children who attend tax-exempt schools were made eligible for the benefits of the National School Lunch Act.[26]

THE "RELEASED TIME" CASES    Although the Supreme Court upheld the bus-transportation practices of the *Everson* case, the narrow margin by which it did so, and the fact that the entire Court agreed that the establishment provision had a much wider scope than merely to prohibit an established church, obviously opened the way to more litigation. The next case was *McCollum* v. *Board of Education* (1948), in which the Court decided that a "released time" program of religious education in the public schools

[22] Fellman, *op. cit.*, p. 83.
[23] The New York State constitution provides in Article XI, section 3: "Neither the state nor any subdivision thereof shall use its property or credit or any public money . . . directly or indirectly, in aid or maintenance . . . of any school or institution of learning wholly or in part under the control or direction of any religious denomination."
[24] Fellman, *op. cit.*, p. 72. In 1961 the Vermont supreme court held that tuition payments by a local school district for students at parochial schools were in violation of the federal Constitution, and the Supreme Court denied certiorari; *Swart* v. *School District* (1961).
[25] 58 Stat. 287, 290 (1944).
[26] 60 Stat. 230 (1946).

of Champaign, Illinois, violated the establishment clause. Under this program public school children, on consent of their parents, attended classes in Protestant, Catholic, or Jewish religious instruction during school hours and in the school building. The religious teachers were not paid by the schools, but were under the supervision of the school superintendents, and attendance was compulsory for participants in the program.

Justice Black, speaking for six justices, held that under this plan tax-supported school buildings were being used in disseminating religious doctrines, and the state's public school machinery was being employed to provide pupils for religious classes—a clear violation of the *Everson* principle that the wall between church and state "must be kept high and impregnable." Justice Jackson, concurring, agreed that the Champaign religious classes went beyond permissible limits, but he was worried over the prospect of the Supreme Court becoming a "super board of education for every school district in the nation." Without a clearer statement of legal principles to provide guidance to both educators and judges than Black's opinion provided, he feared that the wall of separation between church and state was likely to become "as winding as the famous serpentine wall designed by Mr. Jefferson for the University he founded." Only Justice Reed would have held the Champaign plan constitutional.

The *McCollum* decision created a furore in church circles, for similar released time programs were widely in effect throughout the country. It was against this background that the Court was offered a second opportunity to consider the issue, in ruling on the New York program of released time religious education in *Zorach* v. *Clauson* (1952). The New York plan called for religious instruction outside the schools, thus differing sufficiently from the Champaign arrangement to win the approval of six justices, including three who had voted against the Champaign plan (Douglas, Vinson, and Burton) and two who had not been on the Court at the time of the earlier decision (Clark and Minton).

Under the New York City program, students were released from classes during the school day, on written request of their parents, in order to attend religious exercises or classes in religious centers off the school grounds. Those not released stayed in the school classrooms. The churches made weekly reports to the schools of children who had not reported for religious instruction. Because the program involved "neither religious instruction in public school classrooms nor the expenditure of public funds," Douglas ruled for the majority that the *McCollum* case was not controlling.

There were two elements in Douglas's argument, the first of which was more persuasive than the second. He began by demonstrating that any rigid system of separation between church and state would be absurd and impossible. It would make church and state aliens to each other—

> . . . hostile, suspicious, and even unfriendly. Churches could not be required to pay even property taxes. Municipalities would not be per-

mitted to render police or fire protection to religious groups. Policemen who helped parishioners into their places of worship would violate the Constitution. Prayers in our legislative halls; the appeals to the Almighty in the messages of the Chief Executive; the proclamations making Thanksgiving Day a holiday; "so help me God" in our courtroom oaths—these and all other references to the Almighty that run through our laws, our public rituals, our ceremonies would be flouting the First Amendment. . . . We cannot read into the Bill of Rights such a philosophy of hostility to religion.

Nevertheless, Douglas agreed that there are certain things the government cannot do under the religious clauses of the First Amendment, and he undertook to draw up a list just as Black had done in the *Everson* case:

Government may not finance religious groups nor undertake religious instruction nor blend secular and sectarian education nor use secular institutions to force one or some religion on any person. . . . The government must be neutral when it comes to competition between sects. It may not thrust any sect on any person. It may not make a religious observance compulsory. It may not coerce anyone to attend church, to observe a religious holiday, or to take religious instruction.

But did not the New York plan here under attack actually coerce students to "take religious instruction"? Douglas thought not. The situation was merely that of schools closing their doors or suspending their operations "as to those who want to repair to their religious sanctuary for worship or instruction. . . . The public schools do no more than accommodate their schedules to a program of outside religious instruction." But this latter statement cannot possibly be squared with the facts, as the dissenters (Black, Jackson, and Frankfurter) promptly pointed out. The schools do not close their doors or suspend their operations. Students who do not participate in the religious program are compelled to attend other school activities. Thus the state in the New York program was clearly making "religious sects beneficiaries of its power to compel children to attend secular schools." As Jackson put it, the school "serves as a temporary jail for a pupil who will not go to Church."

Neither of the released time decisions had quite the effects that were anticipated. *McCollum* did not stop all the on-premises programs of religious education, and *Zorach* did not encourage many new ones to start. *McCollum* was simply ignored in many communities which continued to use the public schools for religious training, though in some cases token rental payments were made.[27] *Zorach*, in turn, did not stir up the additional litiga-

---

[27] See Gordon Patric, "The Impact of a Court Decision: Aftermath of the McCollum Case," 6 *Journal of Public Law* 455 (1957), reprinted in Walter F. Murphy and C. Herman Pritchett (eds.), *Courts, Judges, and Politics* (New York: Random House, Inc., 1961), pp. 577–583.

tion that had been predicted, and was followed by only a modest increase in the number of pupils attending released time programs.[28]

RELIGIOUS EXERCISES IN THE PUBLIC SCHOOLS     By important decisions in 1962 and 1963 the Supreme Court flatly and almost unanimously rejected religious exercises in public school programs of education as unconstitutional. Bible reading in the public schools had been declared contrary to the constitutions of several states as early as the 1870s. A test under the federal Constitution finally reached the Supreme Court in *Doremus* v. *Board of Education* (1952), where a New Jersey court had upheld as not "sectarian" the reading, without comment, of five verses from the Old Testament, together with the Lord's Prayer, at the opening of each public school day. However the Supreme Court declined to pass on the issue, on the technical ground that the plaintiffs lacked standing to maintain the suit.

*Engel* v. *Vitale* (1962) arose out of the action of the New York State Board of Regents, which has general supervisory authority over the state public schools, in composing a twenty-two-word prayer so bland that it was thought to be nonsectarian, and recommending its daily recital in the public schools as part of a general program of moral and spiritual training. By a vote of six to one the Supreme Court held the prayer unconstitutional as an establishment of religion.

Justice Black's opinion for the Court was not very long or very complex, for he did not regard the problem as a difficult one. Obviously the saying of "the Regents' prayer is a religious activity." Moreover, the prayer "was composed by governmental officials as a part of a governmental program to further religious beliefs." The establishment clause must at least mean that "in this country it is no part of the business of government to compose official prayers for any group of the American people to recite as a part of a religious program carried on by government."

Justice Black had arrived at this holding by the end of his fourth paragraph. The remaining seven paragraphs of his opinion were devoted in considerable part to a rehearsal of the evils resulting from establishment, both in England and the American Colonies, and a statement of the purposes of the establishment provision:

> Its first and most immediate purpose rested on the belief that a union of government and religion tends to destroy government and to degrade religion. . . . The Establishment Clause . . . stands as an expression of principle on the part of the Founders of our Constitution that religion is too personal, too sacred, too holy, to permit its "unhallowed perver-

[28] See Frank J. Sorauf, "*Zorach* v. *Clauson*: The Impact of a Supreme Court Decision," 53 *American Political Science Review* 777 (1959); "The Released Time Case," in C. Herman Pritchett and Alan F. Westin (eds.), *The Third Branch of Government* (New York: Harcourt, Brace & World, Inc., 1963), pp. 118–148.

sion" by a civil magistrate. Another purpose of the Establishment Clause rested upon an awareness of the historical fact that governmentally established religions and religious persecutions go hand in hand.

On this latter point Justice Black admitted that this officially approved prayer did not "amount to a total establishment of one particular religious sect to the exclusion of all others." In fact this was a relatively insignificant matter compared with governmental encroachments on religion which were common two centuries earlier. But he cited the advice of James Madison that "it is proper to take alarm at the first experiment on our liberties," for the principle that can support a first experiment can later be used to support a broad establishment of religion.

Justice Black was also careful to deny that the Court's decision indicated "a hostility toward religion or toward prayer." All that the Court was saying was that "government in this country should stay out of the business of writing and sanctioning official prayers and leave that purely religious function to the people themselves and to those the people choose to look to for religious guidance."

Justice Black did not invoke the free exercise clause in the *Engel* case, for two reasons. First, the prayer was considered "denominationally neutral" or nonsectarian. Second, participation in the prayer on the part of pupils was voluntary, which might be regarded as taking care of those who objected to the prayer. Justice Black apparently thought that under these conditions it would be difficult to demonstrate an interference with any pupil's free exercise of religion, although he admitted that "indirect coercive pressure upon religious minorities" could exist under the plan.

Justice Stewart, the sole dissenter, could not see how an "official religion" was established "by letting those who want to say a prayer say it." He seemed to interpret the establishment clause in accordance with the first of the two positions stated at the beginning of this section, a view never before asserted by any member of the Court in any of its establishment decisions. He also attacked the use of the phrase "wall of separation between church and state" as an accurate or useful guide to the decision of establishment problems. It is a phrase, he said, "nowhere to be found in the Constitution." It is a phrase, however, that the Court has used in every establishment decision since 1878.

The reaction to the *Engel* decision, particularly since it came only three months after the controversial ruling in *Baker* v. *Carr*, was explosive in the extreme. Only a minority of those expressing their opinions—and this minority notably included President Kennedy—appeared to have made an effort to understand the Court's position. For most, their conclusion was simply that the Supreme Court was against prayer. The Court was variously charged with "tampering with America's soul," with having stated its "disbelief in God Almighty." A representative in Congress from Alabama cried out: "They put the Negroes in the schools and now they've driven God out."

A number of constitutional amendments were immediately introduced in Congress to authorize prayers in the public schools.

Time was to show that sober second thought would yield more understanding of and support for the Court's position than the initial reactions indicated. The Court itself, unmoved by the outcry against *Engel*, in the next term reiterated its position in *School District of Abington Township* v. *Schempp* (1963). At issue here were the practices in two Pennsylvania and Maryland schools of beginning the school day with reading of the Bible or recitation of the Lord's Prayer. The Court held these to be unquestionably "religious exercises" and so, again with only Justice Stewart dissenting, unconstitutional. The *Schempp* opinions added to or elaborated on the *Engel* reasoning in several ways.

First, where Justice Black in *Engel* had relied on history, Justice Clark in *Schempp* relied on the Court's precedents. From eight opinions "in the past score of years" Clark drew this rule: "To withstand the strictures of the Establishment Clause there must be a secular legislative purpose and a primary effect that neither advances nor inhibits religion." The constitutional command is for a " 'wholesome' neutrality."

Second, Justice Clark noted that this wholesome neutrality would not prevent the study of the Bible or of religion in public schools, "when presented objectively as part of a secular program of education." Justices Goldberg and Harlan, concurring, underlined this point. They warned against any "untutored devotion to the concept of neutrality" or "pervasive devotion to the secular" which would lead to "hostility to the religious."

Third, Clark denied that "the concept of neutrality, which does not permit a State to require a religious exercise even with the consent of the majority of those affected, collides with the majority's right to free exercise of religion." The free exercise clause prohibits the use of state action to deny the rights of free exercise to anyone, but "it has never meant that a majority could use the machinery of the State to practice its beliefs." Clark also denied that forbidding religious exercises in schools establishes a "religion of secularism."

Justice Stewart disagreed on this point, asserting that "a compulsory state educational system so structures a child's life that if religious exercises are held to be an impermissible activity in schools, religion is placed at an artificial and state-created disadvantage." Consequently, he thought that "permission of such exercises for those who want them is necessary if the schools are truly to be neutral in the matter of religion." But the implications of this argument are clearly unacceptable. As Louis H. Pollak has pointed out, it would impose on the state "an affirmative duty to provide religious education to those children whose parents could not afford to send them to private schools." [29]

[29] Louis H. Pollak, "Public Prayers in Public Schools," 77 *Harvard Law Review* 62, 75 (1963).

Fourth, the *Schempp* opinions more satisfactorily than *Engel* explain why religious exercises in public schools are forbidden when some other public religious manifestations are not.[30] As Justice Brennan said in his concurrence, the Court had no intention of declaring unconstitutional "every vestige, however slight, of cooperation or accommodation between religion and government." He proceeded at some length to suggest why prayer at the beginning of a legislative session or "In God We Trust" on coins did not involve the "particular dangers to church and state which religious exercises in the public schools present." He even reduced the distinction to a set of categories; what the establishment clause forbids are "those involvements of religious with secular institutions which (a) serve the essentially religious activities of religious institutions; (b) employ the organs of government for essentially religious purposes; or (c) use essentially religious means to serve governmental ends, where secular means would suffice."

Finally, the *Schempp* decision spelled out why the Court was invoking the establishment rather than the free exercise clause. As Justice Clark said, "It is necessary in a free exercise case for one to show the coercive effect of the enactment as it operates against him in the practice of his religion," whereas no coercion need be shown to support an establishment violation. Consequently it is much easier to satisfy the "standing" requirement in an establishment suit than in a free exercise case. In fact, the issue of standing, which in *Doremus* v. *Board of Education* (1952) the Court used to avoid deciding a Bible-reading case, was practically ignored by the Court in the *Engel* and *Schempp* cases. It is also significant to note, as Pollak does,[31] that if the Court had relied only on the free exercise clause in *Engel* and *Schempp*, this would have meant that "prayer programs were constitutionally unobjectionable unless and until challenged, and, therefore, that school boards would have been under no discernible legal obligation, as assuredly they now are, to suspend ongoing prayer programs on their own initiative." [32]

[30] In *Engel*, Justice Stewart had suggested that the Court would logically have to declare unconstitutional the practice of opening each session of the Supreme Court with the invocation "God save the United States and this Honorable Court." But Justice Black replied that there was a clear difference between religious exercises organized and sponsored by the public schools, and patriotic or ceremonial "manifestations in our public life of belief in God."

[31] *Loc. cit.*, p. 70.

[32] In *Chamberlain* v. *Dade County Board of Public Instruction* (1964) the Court reversed a Florida supreme court ruling upholding public school prayers and "devotional" Bible reading. The state court had, however, enjoined the showing of religious films and the holding of Christmas and Channukah programs. The state court had declined to consider issues raised by baccalaureate services in schools, a religious census among pupils, and a religious test for teachers. The Supreme Court in *Chamberlain* dismissed these issues for want of properly presented federal questions.

In *DeKalb County Community School District* v. *Despain* (1968) the Court let stand a lower court ruling that a prayer in verse form recited by kindergarten children was still a prayer after the word "God" and "Amen" were eliminated from it, and so was unconstitutional.

The opposition originally aroused by *Engel* was revived by *Schempp,* though it did not reach the same intensity. There was much resistance to the rulings; for example, in Alabama the state board of education made Bible reading part of the required curriculum. But when Representative Becker of New York in 1964 proposed a constitutional amendment which would permit voluntary prayers and Bible reading in the schools, testimony at the hearings revealed that the Court's decisions were supported by the great majority of the religious leaders of the country, and the amendment was not even reported out of committee.

In 1966 Senator Dirksen sought to revive the issue with an amendment providing that nothing in the Constitution should prohibit public school authorities "from providing for or permitting the voluntary participation by students or others in prayer," but no authority was given "to prescribe the form or content of any prayer." Again the testimony of religious leaders and constitutional experts was overwhelmingly against the proposal, and it was defeated on September 21, 1966, by a vote of forty-nine to thirty-seven, nine less than the required two-thirds majority. Although many violations of the rulings continued to occur, considerable attention was given to developing school opening exercises which would have an inspirational character without being religious.

FEDERAL AID TO EDUCATION    Under various federal statutes, such as the National Defense Education Act, Congress has provided for loans or grants to colleges and universities for buildings or educational programs. Religious institutions of higher learning have generally been eligible for such aid, with the limitation that no funds can go for buildings used for religious instruction or for chapels or for schools of divinity or theology. Since taxpayers' suits testing the constitutionality of federal spending are forbidden by the principle of *Massachusetts* v. *Mellon* (1923), the Supreme Court has never passed on these grants.

There is no such problem with respect to taxpayers' suits in the state courts, and in 1966 the supreme court of Maryland invalidated grants of 2 million dollars in state tax funds for the construction of buildings at one Methodist and two Catholic colleges, even though the buildings were not to be used for religious purposes. The state court analyzed in detail the religious aspects of the institutions and concluded that each projected a religious "image." Grants to a fourth college, also religious-connected, were upheld on the ground that it was essentially secular in character. The Supreme Court declined to review the Maryland court's decision.[33]

Prior to 1965 no substantial federal financial aid in the elementary and secondary education field had ever been provided. The principal reason why all the proposals for federal aid to education had failed of enactment in Congress was Catholic refusal to support legislation which did not include

[33] *Board of Public Works of Maryland* v. *Horace Mann League* (1966).

aid for religious schools. President Johnson successfully bypassed this barrier and secured passage of the Elementary and Secondary Education Act of 1965 by proposing assistance primarily to schools serving children from low-income families. The act as passed made funds available in various ways for improving the education of students in both religious and public schools.

Most of the funds go to public school districts in "poverty-impacted" areas, to be used to meet the special educational needs of educationally deprived children, but through "shared time" or "dual enrollment" programs, eligible children attending nonpublic schools may also participate in these benefits. Second, the act provides funds for the purchase of textbooks and library materials. The title to these books remains in the public school district, but in fact they are used by the pupils of both public and nonpublic schools. Finally, the act provides for supplemental education centers where remedial instruction, laboratories, specialized teachers, and counselors are to be available for both public and nonpublic students.

The legislation was carefully designed so that all the funds are channeled to public sources, and no financial aid goes for the teaching of religious subjects. On the other hand, federal funds are used to bear part of the cost of educating pupils in religious schools, and decisions of public school boards may be affected by the necessity of accommodating their programs to those of religious schools. Because the costs of education for nonpublic schools will be reduced by public assumption of such expensive items as science laboratories and gymnasia, more religious groups may find it feasible to set up their own schools, and the present dominant position of the public schools could conceivably be undermined.

The case for the act is that the aid is for the benefit of the pupil rather than the school, and thus supported by the *Everson* decision. It can also be argued that the act meets the test of the *Schempp* case, namely, that there must be a "secular legislative purpose and a primary effect that neither advances nor inhibits religion," and that, under the *Pierce* ruling, churches have been accepted as performing a public function in providing education. Against the act it can be argued that there is no real distinction between direct and indirect aid to religious schools, since both strengthen the sectarian institutions by freeing their own funds for religious use and enabling them to give religious training to more students.

TAX EXEMPTION    State law uniformly grants property tax exemption to churches, and the federal tax statutes also extend exemption on income taxes for gifts to religious institutions as well as in connection with taxes on estates, gifts, and admissions. The administration of such exemptions requires official determination of what are bona fide religious organizations, which sometimes involves difficult decisions.[34] While tax exemption clearly

[34] See Fellman, *op. cit.*, pp. 46–51.

constitutes an aid to religion, it has been uniformly upheld. Usually the grounds stressed are that religious organizations promote social and moral welfare, and to some extent relieve the state of responsibilities in protecting and advancing the interests of its citizens.

More recently, the heightened concern over separation of church and state, stimulated in part by Supreme Court decisions, has led to some reconsideration of the case for tax exemption, but thus far without any impact on the practice. The Maryland supreme court in 1966 unanimously rejected a suit brought to abolish the state's tax exemption for church buildings as an indirect aid to religion. The court stressed that all charities are exempt, and that a major part of church work is charitable in nature. The Supreme Court refused to review this ruling.[35]

### SELECTED REFERENCES

BETH, LOREN P., *The American Theory of Church and State*. Gainesville, Fla.: University of Florida Press, 1958.

BLANSHARD, PAUL, *Religion and the Schools*. Boston: Beacon Press, 1963.

BLUM, VIRGIL C., *Freedom in Education: Federal Aid for All Children*. Garden City, N.Y.: Doubleday & Company, Inc., 1965.

BOLES, DONALD E., *The Bible, Religion, and the Public Schools*. Ames, Iowa: The Iowa State University Press, 1965 (third edition).

BROWN, ERNEST J., "Quis Custodiet Ipsos Custodes?—The School Prayer Cases," in Philip B. Kurland (ed.), *The Supreme Court Review: 1963*, pp. 1–33. Chicago: The University of Chicago Press, 1963.

CORWIN, EDWARD S., "The Supreme Court as National School Board," 23 *Thought* 665–683 (1948).

DIERENFIELD, RICHARD, *Religion in American Public Schools*. Washington, D.C.: Public Affairs Press, 1962.

DRINAN, ROBERT F., *Religion, the Courts, and Public Policy*. New York: McGraw-Hill Book Company, 1963.

FELLMAN, DAVID, *Religion in American Public Law*. Boston: Boston University Press, 1965.

GALANTER, MARC, "Religious Freedoms in the United States: A Turning Point?" 1966 *Wisconsin Law Review* 217–296 (1966).

GIANNELLA, DONALD A. (ed.), *Religion and the Public Order: An Annual Review of Church and State and of Religion, Law, and Society*. Chicago: The Unversity of Chicago Press, 1966.

———, "Religious Liberty, Nonestablishment, and Doctrinal Development," 80 *Harvard Law Review* 1381–1431 (1967), 81 *ibid.* 513–590 (1968).

[35] *Cree* v. *Goldstein* (1966); *Murray* v. *Goldstein* (1966). A somewhat related issue was presented in *Harris* v. *City of New York* (1958), where the Court declined to pass on a claim that the sale of land, cleared for a redevelopment project with public funds, at a reduced price to a Catholic university constituted a subsidy to religion. See also *Gart* v. *Cole* (1959).

HORN, ROBERT A., *Groups and the Constitution,* chaps. 2, 3. Stanford, Calif.: Stanford University Press, 1956.

HOWE, MARK DEWOLFE, *The Garden and the Wilderness.* Chicago: The University of Chicago Press, 1965.

KATZ, WILBER G., *Religion and American Constitutions.* Evanston, Ill.: Northwestern University Press, 1964.

KAUPER, PAUL G., *Religion and the Constitution.* Baton Rouge, La.: Louisiana State University Press, 1964.

KERWIN, JEROME G., *Catholic Viewpoint on Church and State.* Garden City, N.Y.: Hanover House, Doubleday & Company, Inc., 1960.

KURLAND, PHILIP B., "Of Church and State and the Supreme Court," 29 *University of Chicago Law Review* 1–96 (1961).

———, "The Regents' Prayer Case," in Philip B. Kurland (ed.), *The Supreme Court Review: 1962,* pp. 1–33. Chicago: The University of Chicago Press, 1962.

———, *Religion and the Law.* Chicago: Aldine Publishing Co., 1962.

LINCOLN, CHARLES E., *The Black Muslims in America.* Boston: Beacon Press, 1961.

LUND, SISTER CANDIDA, "The Sunday Closing Cases," in C. Herman Pritchett and Alan F. Westin (eds.), *The Third Branch of Government,* pp. 276–308. New York: Harcourt, Brace & World, Inc., 1963.

MANWARING, DAVID R., *Render unto Caesar: The Flag-salute Controversy.* Chicago: The University of Chicago Press, 1962.

MARNELL, WILLIAM H., *The First Amendment: The History of Religious Freedom in America.* Garden City, N.Y.: Doubleday & Company, Inc., 1964.

MURRAY, JOHN COURTNEY, "Law or Prepossessions?" in Robert G. McCloskey (ed.), *Essays in Constitutional Law,* chap. 10. New York: Alfred A. Knopf, Inc., 1957.

———, *We Hold These Truths.* Garden City, N.Y.: Doubleday & Company, Inc., 1960.

OAKS, DALLIN H. (ed.), *The Wall between Church and State.* Chicago: The University of Chicago Press, 1963.

PFEFFER, LEO, *Church, State, and Freedom.* Boston: Beacon Press, 1966.

SIBLEY, MULFORD Q., and PHILIP E. JACOB, *Conscription of Conscience: The American State and the Conscientious Objector, 1940–1947.* Ithaca, N.Y.: Cornell University Press, 1952.

SORAUF, FRANK J., "The Released Time Case," in C. Herman Pritchett and Alan F. Westin (eds.), *The Third Branch of Government,* pp. 118–148. New York: Harcourt, Brace & World, Inc., 1963.

"State Sunday Laws and the Religious Guarantees of the Federal Constitution," 73 *Harvard Law Review* 729–746 (1960).

STEDMAN, MURRAY S., *Religion and Politics in America.* New York: Harcourt, Brace & World, Inc., 1964.

STOKES, ANSON PHELPS, and LEO PFEFFER, *Church and State in the United States.* New York: Harper & Row, Publishers, Incorporated, 1964 (revised edition).

TUSSMAN, JOSEPH (ed.), *The Supreme Court on Church and State.* Fair Lawn, N.J.: Oxford University Press, 1962.

WHALEN, WILLIAM J., *Armageddon around the Corner: A Report on Jehovah's Witnesses*. New York: The John Day Company, Inc., 1962.

WILSON, JOHN F. (ed.), *Church and State in American History*. Boston: D. C. Heath and Company, 1965.

# Part 7

## Due process and equal protection

# 29

## Due process standards

The concept of due process, introduced into the Constitution in the Fifth Amendment as a limitation on Congress, and repeated in the Fourteenth Amendment as a limitation on the states, is perhaps the most expansive and adaptable of the Constitution's many broad phrases. As Justice Frankfurter has eloquently said:

> "Due process," unlike some legal rules, is not a technical conception with a fixed content unrelated to time, place and circumstances. Expressing as it does in its ultimate analysis respect enforced by law for that feeling of just treatment which has been evolved through centuries of Anglo-American constitutional history and civilization, "due process" cannot be imprisoned within the treacherous limits of any formula. Representing a profound attitude of fairness between man and man, and more particularly between the individual and government, "due process" is compounded of history, reason, the past course of decisions, and stout confidence in the strength of the democratic faith which we profess. Due process is not a mechanical instrument. It is not a yardstick. It is a process.[1]

The due process concept does not depend for its constitutional foundation solely on the two clauses of the Fifth and Fourteenth Amendments. All of the amendments from the Fourth through the Eighth embody important due process rights, mostly concerned with protection against abuses in the process

[1] *Joint Anti-Fascist Refugee Committee* v. *McGrath* (1951).

of criminal prosecutions. Moreover, the Fourteenth Amendment contains the related, and somewhat more specific, guarantee of equal protection of the laws, as well as the looser and less significant standard of privileges and immunities of citizens of the United States. All these provisions add up to a set of vital guarantees of the status of free individuals in an open society.

### DUE PROCESS AND LEGISLATION

The due process clause of the Fifth Amendment, as pointed out in Chapter 21, is generally traced to the Magna Carta of 1215, in one chapter of which the king promised: "No freeman shall be arrested, or imprisoned, or disseized, or outlawed, or exiled, or in any way molested; nor will we proceed against him, unless by the lawful judgment of his peers or by the law of the land." In England it was thus the king who was limited by due process. By contrast, anything Parliament enacted was "the law of the land," and not subject to judicial check. But in one of its first opinions interpreting the due process clause, *Murray's Lessee* v. *Hoboken Land & Improvement Co.* (1856), the Supreme Court held that in America due process was a limitation on the legislature as well as on the executive and the judiciary.

The problem in the *Murray* case was whether legislation providing for distress warrant levies on the property of federal tax collectors found to be indebted to the United States amounted to constitutional procedure. The Court said:

> That the warrant now in question is legal process, is not denied. It was issued in conformity with an act of Congress. But is it "due process of law"? The Constitution contains no description of those processes which it was intended to allow or forbid. It does not even declare what principles are to be applied to ascertain whether it be due process. It is manifest that it was not left to the legislative power to enact any process which might be devised. The article is a restraint on the legislative as well as on the executive and judicial powers of the government, and cannot be so construed as to leave Congress free to make any process "due process of law" by its mere will.

A second contribution of the *Murray* decision, written by Justice Curtis, was its effort to ascertain and state the principles upon which the Court would rely in deciding whether a particular process was "due" process. Curtis thought there were two tests that should be used. First, "we must examine the constitution itself, to see whether this process be in conflict with any of its provisions." He did not say where he would look in the Constitution, but obviously he must have been thinking of the specific "process" guarantees found primarily in the Bill of Rights. If this search turned up a conflict, then of course the process was not "due process," and that would be the end of it.

In the *Murray* situation, however, no such conflict was found, and so

Curtis went on to announce a second test—"those settled usages and modes of proceeding existing in the common and statute law of England, before the emigration of our ancestors, and which are shown not to have been unsuited to their civil and political condition by having been acted on by them after the settlement of this country." This was a test based on English and early American practice. A process otherwise unforbidden by the Constitution might still turn out to be contrary to Anglo-Saxon traditions, and if so it would not be due process of law. For the purposes of the *Murray* case Curtis conducted a search which showed that a summary method for the recovery of debts due the government had been provided for "by the common and statute law of England prior to the emigration of our ancestors, and by the laws of many of the States at the time of the adoption of this amendment," and consequently the statute "cannot be denied to be due process of law."

By the *Murray* decision, then, Congress was brought under the purview of the due process clause, and a standard for determining whether legislative action constituted due process was stated. The adoption of the Fourteenth Amendment meant that state legislatures were placed in a similar position. Thus the Supreme Court became responsible for testing the procedures stipulated by both federal and state statutes, so far as they affected life, liberty, or property, on due process grounds. As the Court summed up in *Hurtado* v. *California* (1884):

> It is not every act, legislative in form, that is law. Law is something more than mere will exerted as an act of power. It must be not a special rule for a particular person or a particular case, . . . thus excluding, as not due process of law, acts of attainder, bills of pains and penalties, acts of confiscation, acts reversing judgments, and acts directly transferring one man's estate to another, legislative judgments and decrees, and other similar, special, partial and arbitrary exertions of power under the forms of legislation. Arbitrary power, enforcing its edicts to the injury of the persons and property of its subjects, is not law, whether manifested as the decree of a personal monarch or of an impersonal multitude.

With this broad conception of the judicial responsibility for enforcing due process, it is perhaps not surprising that the Supreme Court soon moved from a review of the *procedures* which legislatures established in statutes affecting property or personal rights, to a concern with the *substance* of the legislation itself. The transformation of due process, which is by definition a procedural concept, into a set of substantive property rights enforceable by the courts, is one of the most interesting episodes in American constitutional law, to which Chapter 31 is devoted in its entirety.

## DUE PROCESS IN JUDICIAL PROCEEDINGS

As already noted, there are two sources of due process concepts in the Constitution. First, there are the two due process clauses of the Fifth and

Fourteenth Amendments. Second, there are the more specific procedural protections in criminal trials included in the Fourth through the Eighth Amendments, plus the bill of attainder, ex post facto, and jury trial provisions in the original Constitution. So far as the federal courts are concerned, obviously their procedures must conform with all applicable provisions of the Bill of Rights.

The obligations of the state courts, however, are not so clear. In fact, the adoption of the Fourteenth Amendment plunged the Supreme Court into a major constitutional controversy on this issue which has not yet been entirely settled. The issue is whether the state courts are bound simply by the general obligation of the Fourteenth Amendment to render due process, or whether the due process clause "incorporated" all the specific due process guarantees of the Bill of Rights and obligated the Supreme Court to enforce them upon the states.

DUE PROCESS AS A GENERAL CONCEPT    The Court's initial position, and one it maintained steadfastly into the 1950s, was that state courts were controlled only by the general concept of due process. In *Pennoyer* v. *Neff* (1877) due process was spoken of rather vaguely as requiring "a course of legal proceedings according to those rules and principles which have been established in our systems of jurisprudence for the protection and enforcement of private rights." Due process in judicial proceedings, the Court thought, required principally that litigants have the benefit of a full and fair trial in the courts, and that their rights be measured, not by laws made to affect them individually, but by general provisions of law applicable to all those in like condition. Judicial procedures might vary according to circumstances, but they would be *due* procedures if they followed the established forms of law or if, adapting old forms to new problems, they preserved the principles of liberty and justice. There is a noteworthy paragraph in Justice Matthews's decision in *Hurtado* v. *California* (1884) which stressed the creative character of the due process concept:

> The Constitution of the United States was ordained, it is true, by descendants of Englishmen, who inherited the traditions of English law and history; but it was made for an undefined and expanding future, and for a people gathered and to be gathered from many nations and of many tongues. And while we take just pride in the principles and institutions of the common law, we are not to forget that in lands where other systems of jurisprudence prevail, the ideas and processes of civil justice are also not unknown. . . . There is nothing in Magna Charta, rightly construed as a broad charter of public right or law, which ought to exclude the best ideas of all systems and of every age; and as it was the characteristic principle of the common law to draw its inspiration from every fountain of justice, we are not to assume that the sources of its supply have been exhausted. On the contrary, we should expect that

the new and various experiences of our own situation and system will mould and shape it into new and not less useful forms.

A later Court in *Snyder* v. *Massachusetts* (1934) summed up that a state was "free to regulate the procedure of its courts in accordance with its own conception of policy and fairness unless in so doing it offends some principle of justice so rooted in the traditions and conscience of our people as to be ranked as fundamental."

JURISDICTION    Of the basic components in judicial due process, perhaps the most fundamental is jurisdiction. Jurisdiction has been defined as the power to create legal interests. But legal interests cannot be created if they cannot be enforced. The state must have actual physical power over persons or things if it is to render effective decrees which concern them. A state has jurisdiction over a person (such proceedings are called *in personam* actions) if he is physically present within the state, or if he is domiciled in the state but is temporarily absent, or if he has consented to the exercise of jurisdiction over him.

Corporations, being fictitious persons, can manifest their presence in states outside their state of origin only by activities carried on in their behalf. In general, such activities must be "continuous and systematic" in order to meet the "presence" test. As the Court said in *International Shoe Co.* v. *Washington* (1945), the due process clause "does not contemplate that a state may make binding a judgment *in personam* against an individual or corporate defendant with which the state has no contacts, ties, or relations." Furthermore, "the casual presence of the corporate agent or even his conduct of single or isolated items of activities in a state in the corporation's behalf are not enough to subject it to suit on causes of action unconnected with the activities there." On the other hand, "some single or occasional acts of the corporate agent . . . because of their nature and quality and the circumstances of their commission, may be deemed sufficient to render the corporation liable to suit." [2]

Jurisdiction over things, usually exerted by actions *in rem*, may be exercised over property within the state, even though the owner is not within the state and control over him is never obtained. Thus a state can permit attachment of property within its borders owned by a nonresident, for the purpose of satisfying a debt owed by him to a citizen of the state, or in settlement of a claim for damages by the citizen against the nonresident.

[2] See *Travelers Health Assn.* v. *Virginia* (1950). In the case of *New York Times Co.* v. *Sullivan* (1964), the Alabama courts asserted jurisdiction over a libel suit against the newspaper because 394 copies containing the alleged libel out of an edition of 650,000 had been circulated in Alabama, 35 of them in Montgomery County where the suit arose. *The New York Times* contended that this was an inadequate basis for jurisdiction, but entered a general appearance in the action; the Supreme Court ruled that under Alabama law this amounted to waiving the jurisdictional objection.

NOTICE AND HEARING   Jurisdiction, though potentially possessed, may not be exercised in a judicial proceeding until it has been perfected by appropriate notice which acquaints all parties of the institution of proceedings calculated to affect their rights. It is contrary to due process for a person to be deprived of property rights by a decree in a proceeding in which he does not appear, or is not served with process or effectively made a party to the case. The standard method of giving notice is by personal service, i.e., summons delivered to the defendant personally. However, various forms of substituted service, as by mail or newspaper publication, may meet the legal requirements. In general due process requires the best notice that is possible under the circumstances.[3] In *Walker* v. *City of Hutchinson* (1956) the Court held that newspaper notice of condemnation of property for street-widening purposes was not sufficient, where the city had the property owner's name and could have notified him by mail. Where a mother, after divorce and remarriage, got an adoption decree for her daughter by her first marriage without notice to the father, the decree was held void in *Armstrong* v. *Manzo* (1965).

Due process requires that a party to judicial proceedings be afforded an opportunity to be heard at some stage before final judgment is entered. This includes the right to present such arguments, testimony, or evidence as may be pertinent to the case. The hearing must be before a fair and impartial tribunal.

In general, the Supreme Court for some seven decades was inclined to leave state courts alone provided they observed these general due process requirements of jurisdiction, notice, and fair hearing. Due process did not require the states to adopt specific measures of procedure or doctrines of law. Its effect was negative—to keep the state courts within broad bounds—rather than positively to enforce certain mandatory procedures.

THE INCORPORATION ARGUMENT   Throughout this entire period, however, there was a minority view on the Court which insisted that the Fourteenth Amendment had incorporated the due process standards of the Bill of Rights and obligated the Court to enforce them on the states. The Court did not encounter this problem immediately on adoption of the Fourteenth Amendment, for at first litigation centered on the privileges and immunities clause, which was thought to be more promising in its protective potentialities than the due process clause. But in the *Slaughter-House Cases* (1873) the Court confined the privileges and immunities clause to the narrow protection of those rights peculiar to national citizenship, making it inapplicable to property rights and trials in state courts.

Attention then turned to the due process clause of the Fourteenth Amendment, which got its first significant examination in *Hurtado* v. *California* (1884). Instead of being indicted by a grand jury, Hurtado had been

[3] *Mullane* v. *Central Hanover Bank & Trust Co.* (1950). See the discussion of personal service in divorce cases in Chap. 6.

brought to trial for murder on information after examination and commitment by a magistrate, as permitted by the California constitution. Thus the question before the Supreme Court was whether such departure from grand jury indictment violated due process of law.

On the basis of Justice Curtis's first test in the *Murray* case, due process had clearly been violated, for the Fifth Amendment makes indictment by grand jury mandatory for all capital or otherwise infamous crimes. However, Justice Matthews made the *Murray* rule seem to approve the *Hurtado* result. The "real syllabus" of the Curtis holding, Matthews said, is "that a process of law, which is not otherwise forbidden, must be taken to be due process of law, if it can show the sanction of settled usage both in England and in this country; but it by no means follows that nothing else can be due process of law." Then, having recognized Curtis's first test by the clause, "which is not otherwise forbidden," he proceeded to ignore it and to work from the last thought in the sentence, which is substantially Curtis's second test—the test of historical practice.

Matthews was able to show that grand jury indictment was not even known at the time of Magna Carta, or for centuries thereafter. In fact, some of the early practices had been so barbarous that he suggested "it is better not to go too far back into antiquity for the best securities for our 'ancient liberties.'" In any case, it would not be wise for the states to be bound to any fixed set of procedures in criminal cases.

> It is more consonant to the true philosophy of our historical legal institutions to say that the spirit of personal liberty and individual right, which they embodied, was preserved and developed by a progressive growth and wise adaptation to new circumstances and situations of the forms and processes found fit to give, from time to time, new expression and greater effect to modern ideas of self-government.

For those who might find this liberal philosophy unconvincing, Matthews had a more pedantic argument. Since the Fifth Amendment contains both the guarantee of due process and of indictment by grand jury, and since it must be assumed that no part of the Constitution is superfluous, it follows that due process as used in the Fifth Amendment does not include indictment by grand jury. When the same phrase is repeated in the Fourteenth Amendment, it must be given the same meaning. Thus Matthews emerged with the remarkable conclusion, directly opposed to that of Curtis, that the due process clauses in both the Fifth and Fourteenth Amendments must be interpreted to *exclude* any rights specified elsewhere in the Constitution.

Justice Harlan was the only dissenter in the *Hurtado* case; he was an incorporationist. To him the Fourteenth Amendment evinced "a purpose to impose upon the States the same restrictions, in respect of proceedings involving life, liberty and property, which had been imposed upon the general government." Again in *Maxwell* v. *Dow* (1900) he dissented in the most extensive examination the Fourteenth Amendment had received up to that

time. He was thoroughly aroused by the fact that the development of substantive due process had made it possible for the Court to protect property
rights against state legislative action, while procedural rights in state courts
remained unprotected, and he commented bitterly:

> If then the "due process of law" required by the Fourteenth Amend-
> ment does not allow a State to take private property without just com-
> pensation, but does allow the life or liberty of the citizen to be taken in
> a mode that is repugnant to the settled usages and the modes of pro-
> ceeding authorized at the time the Constitution was adopted and which
> was expressly forbidden in the National Bill of Rights, it would seem
> that the protection of private property is of more consequence than the
> protection of the life and liberty of the citizen.

This entire argument was resumed in *Twining* v. *New Jersey* (1908). The
state practice under fire in *Twining* was self-incrimination; the jury, under
state law, had been instructed that they might draw an unfavorable inference
from the defendant's failure to testify in denial of evidence offered against
him. Justice Moody for the Court upheld the law, but recognizing the weakness of the *Hurtado* decision, announced that the Court preferred to rest its
decision "on broader grounds" than were there stated. The important thing
was whether exemption from self-incrimination was "a fundamental principle
of liberty and justice which inheres in the very idea of free government and
is the inalienable right of a citizen of such a government."

How can judges proceed to answer such a question? One way, Moody
asserted, was "to inquire how the right was rated during the time when the
meaning of due process was in a formative state and before it was incorporated in American constitutional law." He found that it was omitted from
the great declarations of English liberty, and that in fact English courts and
Parliaments dealt with the exemption "as they would have dealt with any
other rule of evidence." Moreover, only four of the thirteen original states
insisted that this rule should be included in the Constitution, and two of
these states did not have it in their own constitutions at the time. Thus the
historical evidence demonstrated that "the privilege was not conceived to be
inherent in due proces of law, but on the other hand a right separate, independent, and outside of due process." Moody went on to note that the
exemption was unknown outside the common-law countries, and was not
observed "among our own people in the search for truth outside the administration of the law." So, "salutary as the principle may seem to the great
majority, it cannot be ranked with the right to hearing before condemnation,
the immunity from arbitrary power not acting by general laws, and the
inviolability of private property."

After the *Twining* decision the incorporation controversy was relatively
quiescent at the Supreme Court level for three decades. Then in 1937 *Palko*
v. *Connecticut* offered an opportunity for reexamining the issue. In the interim
the incorporation theory had achieved a very great success in another area.

As already noted, *Gitlow* v. *New York* (1925) had admitted that the "liberty" protected by the Fourteenth Amendment against deprivation without due process included the freedoms of speech and press guaranteed by the First Amendment. If the First Amendment was incorporated into the Fourteenth, why were not the other guarantees in the Bill of Rights similarly situated?

It fell to Justice Cardozo to answer this question in the *Palko* case. The defendant had been convicted of second-degree murder and given a life sentence, but the state appealed the conviction, as was authorized by state law, and the state supreme court, finding there had been error in the trial to the prejudice of the state, ordered a new trial. The second time the defendant was convicted of murder in the first degree and sentenced to death. The question was whether the effect of the second trial was to place the defendant twice in jeopardy for the same offense.

Cardozo began by once more flatly rejecting the incorporation thesis. To the extent that some of the first eight amendments had been made effective against the states, that was not because they were incorporated in the Fourteenth Amendment when it was adopted, but because they had been found by the Supreme Court "to be implicit in the concept of ordered liberty." Cardozo admitted that when one looked at the line drawn by the Court between rights which meet this test and those which do not, it might seem "wavering and broken." But "reflection and analysis" would disclose a "rationalizing principle."

> The right to trial by jury and the immunity from prosecution except as the result of an indictment may have value and importance. Even so, they are not of the very essence of a scheme of ordered liberty. To abolish them is not to violate a "principle of justice so rooted in the traditions and conscience of our people as to be ranked as fundamental." . . . Few would be so narrow or provincial as to maintain that a fair and enlightened system of justice would be impossible without them. What is true of jury trials and indictments is true also . . . of the immunity from compulsory self-incrimination. . . . This too might be lost, and justice still be done.

On the other hand, fredom of thought and speech, as guaranteed by the First Amendment, is on "a different plane of social and moral values. . . . Of that freedom one may say that it is the matrix, the indispensable condition, of nearly every other form of freedom." So these freedoms have been "absorbed" into the Fourteenth Amendment, for "neither liberty nor justice would exist if they were sacrificed."

With this groundwork, it remained only for Cardozo to conclude that double jeopardy of the type presented in this case was not a value on the high plane represented by the First Amendment. All the state was asking was that the case against the defendant go on "until there shall be a trial free from the corrosion of substantial legal error." If there had been an error adverse to the accused, admittedly he could get another trial. To give the

state a reciprocal privilege was "no seismic innovation. The edifice of justice stands, its symmetry, to many, greater than before."

Justice Black was in his first term on the Court when the *Palko* decision was made, and he did not dissent, though Butler did. This is interesting, for ten years later Black, in *Adamson* v. *California* (1947), led an assault on this entire line of cases which lacked only one vote of achieving success. The issue was again self-incrimination, this time as presented by a state statute permitting the failure of a defendant to explain or to deny evidence against him to be commented on by the court and by counsel and to be considered by the judge and the jury. For the defendant with a previous criminal record, the problem posed by this rule is that if he chooses to go on the witness stand to explain or deny evidence, he is then subject to cross-examination which can bring out his prior convictions. If he fails to take the stand, the assumption is that he cannot refute the evidence or has something to hide.

By a five to four vote, the Court held this statutory provision not contrary to due process. Justice Reed for the majority stood by the *Palko* rejection of the incorporation argument. The only question was whether a state statute permitting comment on the refusal of a defendant to take the stand met the Supreme Court's notions as to allowable procedure. Reed made practically no effort to answer by reference to standards outside the value systems of the individual justices, such as historical practice. Instead, he said very frankly, "We see no reason why comment should not be made upon his silence. . . . When evidence is before a jury that threatens conviction, it does not seem unfair to require him to choose between leaving the adverse evidence unexplained and subjecting himself to impeachment through disclosure of former crimes."

Black's dissent, which spoke for Douglas, Murphy, and Rutledge as well, was a powerful defense of the incorporation theory. In a lengthy appendix to his opinion, he marshaled the historical data favorable to the incorporation view, such as the speeches of Bingham and Howard already referred to, and concluded: "My study of the historical events that culminated in the Fourteenth Amendment . . . persuades me that one of the chief objects that the provisions of the Amendment's first section, separately, and as a whole, were intended to accomplish was to make the Bill of Rights, applicable to the states." The Court, he went on, had repeatedly declined to appraise this historical evidence. Instead, it had reiterated a "natural law" formula under which it had substituted "its own concepts of decency and fundamental justice for the language of the Bill of Rights. . . . I would follow what I believe was the original purpose of the Fourteenth Amendment—to extend to all the people of the nation the complete protection of the Bill of Rights."

Justice Frankfurter, concurring in the Court's majority opinion, devoted himself to answering Black and to ridiculing the "notion that the Fourteenth Amendment was a covert way of imposing upon the States all the rules which it seemed important to Eighteenth Century statesmen to write into the

Federal Amendments." Actually, substantial victory for the incorporation position was only a decade away. The story of those developments, however, must await the more detailed examination of due process requirements for criminal prosecutions which is the subject of the following chapter.[4]

## SELECTED REFERENCES

CROSSKEY, WILLIAM W., "Charles Fairman, 'Legislative History,' and the Constitutional Limitations on State Authority," 22 *University of Chicago Law Review* 1–143 (1954).

———, *Politics and the Constitution in the History of the United States*, pp. 1102–1116. Chicago: The University of Chicago Press, 1953.

FAIRMAN, CHARLES, "Does the Fourteenth Amendment Incorporate the Bill of Rights? The Original Understanding," 2 *Stanford Law Review* 5–139 (1949).

———, "A Reply to Professor Crosskey," 22 *University of Chicago Law Review* 144–156 (1954).

———, "The Supreme Court and the Constitutional Limitations on State Governmental Authority," 21 *University of Chicago Law Review* 40–78 (1953).

FLACK, HORACE E., *The Adoption of the Fourteenth Amendment*. Baltimore: The Johns Hopkins Press, 1908.

FRANKFURTER, FELIX, "Memorandum on 'Incorporation' of the Bill of Rights into the Due Process Clause of the Fourteenth Amendment," 78 *Harvard Law Review* 746–783 (1965).

[4] Due process is not necessarily judicial process. Administrative agencies and officers often have considerable authority to take action affecting the rights of property and of person. Where they are given such power, however, the obligations of due process become applicable to them. This means that the requirements of jurisdiction, notice, hearing, and general fairness of procedure must be observed in administrative actions. An enormous body of what is called "administrative law" has grown up as a consequence, which cannot be covered in this volume. See Kenneth C. Davis, *Administrative Law and Government* (St. Paul, Minn.: West Publishing Company, 1960); Louis L. Jaffe, *Judicial Control of Administrative Action* (Boston: Little, Brown and Company, 1965).

# 30

## Criminal prosecutions

One of the Supreme Court's most important functions is to maintain constitutional standards for the criminal prosecutions conducted in both federal and state courts. The significance which the Constitution attaches to such protection is indicated by the fact that five of the ten amendments comprising the Bill of Rights are largely devoted to specifying the standards and procedures to be observed in criminal prosecutions. These amendments contain not only the broad guarantee of due process of law, but numerous specific procedural protections such as indictment by grand jury and speedy and public trial, as well as safeguards against self-incrimination, unreasonable searches and seizures, double jeopardy, and cruel and unusual punishments. In addition to enforcing these constitutional provisions, the Supreme Court has the general responsibility over administration of justice in the federal courts which comes from its position at the apex of the judicial hierarchy. This supervisory authority, the Court has said, "implies the duty of establishing and maintaining civilized standards of procedure and evidence." [1]

[1] *McNabb* v. *United States* (1943). In *Yates* v. *United States* (1958) the Court made a highly unusual use of its supervisory power by itself reducing a sentence for contempt of court after the district judge who imposed the original sentence had failed to respond to the Supreme Court's "gentle intimations" that the sentence should be reduced.

## CRIMES AGAINST THE UNITED STATES

There are four principal references to federal crimes in the Constitution: "counterfeiting the securities and current coin of the United States," "piracies and felonies committed on the high seas," and "offences against the law of nations," all found in Article I, section 8; and "treason against the United States," which is defined in Article III, section 3. Obviously these four crimes do not account for the content of the United States Criminal Code, and there is no federal common law of crimes.[2] All the other multitudinous crimes on the federal statute books have been defined and made punishable by congressional exercise of implied power. Any law which Congress has the power to adopt, it also has the power to enforce by making violation a crime. Thus the power "to establish post offices and post roads" clearly implies the power to punish theft from the mails. Of the crimes which achieve the distinction of constitutional mention, only one, treason, has a history and a constitutional significance justifying consideration here.

The constitutional provision on treason is short. "Treason against the United States shall consist only in levying war against them, or in adhering to their enemies, giving them aid and comfort. No person shall be convicted of treason unless on the testimony of two witnesses to the same overt act, or on confession in open court." The intent of the framers in these words is well known; they were seeking to make convictions for treason very difficult to obtain. The members of the Convention "almost to a man had themselves been guilty of treason under any interpretation of British law."[3] They had been "taught by experience and by history to fear abuse of the treason charge almost as much as they feared treason itself." They believed that a government had to deserve the loyalty of its citizens, and that opposition to the abuses of a tyrannical government was justified and should not be punished as treason.

Consequently the Convention wrote into the Constitution every limitation on treason convictions "that the practice of governments had evolved or that politico-legal philosophy to that time had advanced." The result of this restrictive approach has been to render treason litigation comparatively unimportant in American constitutional development. The Supreme Court never had occasion to review a treason conviction until the case of *Cramer* v. *United States* in 1945. In the brief for that case, all previous proceedings in which construction of the treason clause had been involved were collected, and they totaled nineteen. As Justice Jackson said in his *Cramer* decision: "We have managed to do without treason prosecutions to a degree that probably would be impossible except while a people was singularly confident of external security and internal stability."

[2] *United States* v. *Hudson and Goodwin* (1812).
[3] This quotation and those immediately following are from *Cramer* v. *United States* (1945).

The treason provision has, however, been invoked often enough to demonstrate its problems of interpretation. The Aaron Burr conspiracy led to two treason rulings by Chief Justice Marshall. In *Ex parte Bollman* (1807) he warned that "the crime of treason should not be extended by construction to doubtful cases." He confined the meaning of levying war to the actual waging of war or the actual assembling of men for that purpose. In presiding over the trial of Burr,[4] Marshall ruled that Burr, not having been present at the actual assemblage of men, could be convicted of procuring or levying of war only upon the testimony of two witnesses to his having procured the assemblage. The result was practically to limit convictions for "levying war" to actual participants in armed hostilities.

In more recent times treason charges have usually been based not on the "levying war" clause, but on the offense of "adhering" to the nation's enemies, "giving them aid and comfort." In *Cramer* v. *United States* (1945) the Supreme Court divided five to four in applying this constitutional provision. Cramer had befriended two of the German saboteurs who were landed in the United States by submarine in 1942 for the purpose of sabotaging the American war effort. He met and lunched with them in public places, and took a large sum of money from one for safekeeping. The only overt acts established by two witnesses were the public meetings. The Court majority concluded that Cramer's eating and drinking in a public place "was no part of the saboteurs' mission and did not advance it."

Two years later the Supreme Court for the first time in its history sustained a treason conviction. *Haupt* v. *United States* (1947) grew out of the same incident of the German saboteurs, the defendant being the father of one of them. When the son turned up in Chicago on his mission, the father took him into his house, accompanied him when he sought employment in a plant manufacturing bomb sights, and purchased an automobile for him. This time the Court held the constitutional standard of treason had been met. The "harboring and sheltering" which Haupt had provided his son, an overt act established by two witnesses, was of direct value to his traitorous enterprise, in a way that Cramer's public meetings with the saboteurs had not been.

Since 1947 only one additional treason case has reached the Supreme Court, and it added little to the law.[5] Following the Korean War the Defense Department referred over two hundred cases of possible treason arising out of that conflict to the Department of Justice, but actual prosecutions were few. They seem likely to continue to be few. The strictness of the constitutional standard of proof was commended by Chief Justice Marshall in the first of the *Burr* cases, and Justice Jackson in *Cramer* took a similar view of the inherent dangers in a treason charge because of the "passion-rousing potentialities" of accusations of "treachery and of general intent to betray."

[4] *United States* v. *Burr* (1807).
[5] *Kawakita* v. *United States* (1952).

The treason offense, he concluded, "is not the only nor can it well serve as the principal legal weapon to vindicate our national cohesion and security."

In fact, to a considerable degree prosecutions under various antisubversive and espionage laws, which do not present such difficult problems of proof, have substituted for treason prosecutions. In the famous case of the Rosenbergs, who were executed in 1952 after conviction under the Espionage Act for giving aid to a country, not an enemy, the offense was held to be distinct from treason, so that neither the two-witness rule nor the overt act requirement was applicable.[6]

## CRIMINAL PROCEDURE IN THE ORIGINAL CONSTITUTION

For the most part the original Constitution did not concern itself with spelling out the procedural protections in federal prosecutions, but there were four exceptions. One, the prohibition on suspension of the writ of habeas corpus, has been discussed in Chapter 19. A second, the jury trial provisions of Article III, was quickly superseded by the Sixth Amendment. Only the prohibitions on bills of attainder and ex post facto laws need be examined here.

BILLS OF ATTAINDER    Both Congress and the states were forbidden by Article I, sections 9 and 10, to pass any "bill of attainder." These provisions were adopted to outlaw the practice of legislative punishment common in England, where individuals could be condemned to death by special act of Parliament called a bill of attainder. Legislative acts inflicting lesser punishments were designated "bills of pains and penalties." As interpreted by the Supreme Court, the bill of attainder provisions forbid all legislative acts, "no matter what their form, that apply either to named individuals or to easily ascertainable members of a group in such a way as to inflict punishment on them without a judicial trial."[7]

The bill of attainder provisions were first applied after the Civil War. A congressional act requiring attorneys practicing in the federal courts to take an oath that they had never given aid to persons engaged in hostility to the United States was held unconstitutional in *Ex parte Garland* (1867). In *Cummings* v. *Missouri* (1867) a state constitutional provision seeking to exclude persons who had aided the Confederacy from following certain professions—a minister was involved in this case—was invalidated on similar grounds.

No other legislation was held to constitute a bill of attainder until 1946, when in *United States* v. *Lovett* the Court voided an act of Congress which had prohibited the payment of compensation to three named government

[6] *United States* v. *Rosenberg* (1952).
[7] *United States* v. *Lovett* (1946).

employees who had been charged with subversive activities by the House Un-American Activities Committee. In *Communist Party* v. *SACB* (1961) Justice Black, dissenting, contended that the Internal Security Act of 1950 was a "classical bill of attainder" because it constituted a legislative finding of guilt against members of the Communist Party. The majority said, in rebuttal: "The Act is not a bill of attainder. It attaches not to specified organizations but to described activities in which an organization may or may not engage."

However, Black's view became that of the Court majority in *United States* v. *Brown* (1965) where, as already reported, a 1959 statute making it a crime for a member of the Communist Party to serve as an officer or employee of a labor union was held unconstitutional. It would be legitimate, said Chief Justice Warren, for Congress to adopt a generally applicable rule decreeing that any person who commits certain acts or possesses certain characteristics should not hold union office, leaving to courts and juries the task of deciding what persons fell in those categories. But this act designated the persons who possessed the feared characteristics—members of the Communist Party—and this made the act a bill of attainder.

EX POST FACTO LAWS    The passage of ex post facto laws is also forbidden to both Congress and the states. An ex post facto law is "a law made after the doing of the thing to which it relates, and retroacting upon it." The reason for inserting such sweeping prohibitions in the Constitution was apparently to be found in the freedom with which state legislatures in that era had passed paper money or legal tender laws setting aside existing contracts, so that what had been lent in gold and silver could be repaid in paper. However, in *Calder* v. *Bull* (1798) the Supreme Court construed the ex post facto clauses as covering only penal and criminal laws.

Every law that makes criminal an act done before the passage of such law that was innocent when done, or that aggravates a crime or makes it greater than when it was committed, or that changes the punishment and inflicts a greater penalty than the law annexed to the crime when committed, or that alters the rules of evidence, permitting less or different evidence to convict a person of an offense committed prior to its passage, or that operates in any way to the disadvantage of one accused of a crime committed prior to the enactment of the law is an ex post facto law. The clause is directed against legislative action only. It does not reach erroneous or inconsistent decisions of the courts.

A law cannot be held to be ex post facto unless it imposes punishment in the legal sense for past acts. A deportation law authorizing the Secretary of Labor to expel aliens for criminal acts committed before its passage was held not ex post facto, since deportation is not classified as punishment, but as a discretionary exercise of sovereign power.[8] Similarly, a statute terminat-

---

[8] *Mahler* v. *Eby* (1924).

ing payment of Social Security benefits to an alien following deportation for Communist affiliation was declared not ex post facto on the ground that it was not a penalty.[9]

The right to practice a business or profession may be denied to one who was convicted of an offense before the statute was enacted, if the offense can reasonably be regarded as a continuing disqualification. Thus *DeVeau* v. *Braisted* (1960) upheld a statute excluding convicted felons from offices in New York waterfront unions, unless pardoned or holding a parole board's good conduct certificate. But the Civil War test oaths invalidated as bills of attainder in *Garland* and *Cummings* were also held to be ex post facto, on the assumption that they bore no reasonable relation to fitness to perform professional duties.

### UNREASONABLE SEARCHES AND SEIZURES

Because of the close connection between searches and arrests, a few preliminary words are in order concerning the power to arrest. English law recognized broad powers of arrest; even private citizens could arrest, and all felony arrests could be made without warrant. In fact, arrest warrants were accepted only reluctantly, and primarily for the purpose of protecting those making arrests from tort liability. But the common law, with its strong bias toward property rights, did not grant any power to search the premises of suspected offenders on the basis of "reasonable suspicion."

The Fourth Amendment recognizes warrants of arrest, which can be issued only on "probable cause." However, the amendment does not say that warrants are required for an arrest. This would be completely impractical, since it would preclude officers from making arrests for offenses committed in their presence or where immediate action was necessary to apprehend a law violator. Provided there is probable cause for the arrest, no arrest warrant is needed even if it is possible to get one. Probable cause for arrest exists where facts and circumstances within the officer's knowledge and of which he has "reasonably trustworthy information [are] sufficient in themselves to warrant a man of reasonable caution in the belief that an offense has been or is being committed."[10] In *McCray* v. *Illinois* (1967) the Court held by a vote of five to four that the police are not required to disclose in court the names of informants who supplied the information on the basis of which an arrest was made.

SEARCHES AND WARRANTS    The Fourth Amendment safeguards "the people" in their "persons, houses, papers, and effects" from "unreasonable" searches and seizures. What is the test of reasonableness in searches? The

[9] *Flemming* v. *Nestor* (1960).
[10] *Brinegar* v. *United States* (1949). See also *Rugendorf* v. *United States* (1964).

amendment relies primarily upon requirement of a search warrant, issued "upon probable cause, supported by oath or affirmation, and particularly describing the place to be searched, and the persons or things to be seized." Warrants are issued by judicial officers, who are brought into the procedure in order to exert a neutral or at least modifying influence upon the police. As Justice Murphy has said: "In their understandable zeal to ferret out crime and in the excitement of the capture of a suspected person, officers are less likely [than judges] to possess the detachment and neutrality with which the constitutional rights of the suspect must be viewed." [11]

The requirement of particularity in the amendment reflects the purpose of definitely forbidding such general warrants as the hated "writs of assistance" under which British officers searched houses for smuggled goods during the Colonial period. The impact of the particularity requirement is illustrated by *Federal Trade Commission* v. *American Tobacco Co.* (1924), where the federal agency had sought to compel the company to turn over all the letters and telegrams received by it from its jobber customers for an entire year. Justice Holmes for the Court condemned this venture as a "fishing expedition" into private papers "on the possibility that they may disclose evidence of crime," and said this was contrary to the spirit of the Fourth Amendment.[12]

A judicial officer has "probable cause" for issuance of a warrant if he is presented with an affidavit setting forth apparent facts which would lead a reasonably discreet and prudent man to believe that the offense charged had been committed.[13] An affidavit resting on hearsay, that is, one which relies on the observations of an informer rather than an officer, meets the probable cause test if the informer had previously given correct information and if there is corroboration from other sources.[14]

SEARCH WITHOUT A WARRANT    Most constitutional issues as to search and seizure arise, however, not out of failure to observe the requirements in securing warrants, but out of failure to secure any search warrant at all.

---

[11] *Trupiano* v. *United States* (1948).

[12] In *Stanford* v. *Texas* (1965) a magistrate acting under a state statute outlawing the Communist Party issued a warrant authorizing search of a home for all books and records concerning the state Party and its operations. Officers made a five-hour search and found no Communist records, but carried away some 2,000 items, including books, insurance policies, marriage certificate, and household bills. The Supreme Court held the warrant invalid, saying that "the constitutional requirement that warrants must particularly describe the 'things to be seized' is to be accorded the most scrupulous exactitude when the 'things' are books, and the basis for their seizure is the ideas which they contain."

[13] There was probable cause for issuance of a search warrant when officers had seen large amounts of sugar and five-gallon cans being taken into a house and had smelled fermenting mash when walking past the house; *United States* v. *Ventresca* (1965).

[14] *Jones* v. *United States* (1960).

Such failure does not automatically void a search or seizure. It depends upon the circumstances.

First, search without a warrant may be made in connection with a valid arrest. For example, an officer making an arrest, with a warrant of arrest, or on the basis of trustworthy information, or for a crime committed in the officer's presence, may search the person of the suspect and seize any instruments of the crime which are in plain sight. However, the officer must have a justification for the arrest if any accompanying search is to be upheld. In *Henry* v. *United States* (1959) two FBI agents investigating interstate whiskey thefts had received a tip that a certain person might be implicated. After observing the loading of cartons into his auto on two occasions, they stopped the car, took the cartons to their office, and discovered that they were stolen radios. The Supreme Court held that the arrest had occurred when the car was stopped, and that the agents had inadequate grounds for an arrest at that time. Consequently the seizure was illegal. However, in *Draper* v. *United States* (1959) an arrest and seizure by federal narcotics agents was ruled valid where the agents had only a tip that a man arriving on a certain train, dressed in a certain way, walking fast, and carrying a tan bag, would be carrying narcotics.

The "plain sight" rule has been the subject of some rather confused interpretations. In *Harris* v. *United States* (1947) the Court by a five to four vote upheld a search of a four-room apartment with only an arrest warrant. But the following year, in *Trupiano* v. *United States* the Court, again divided five to four, invalidated a seizure without a warrant of a still on a New Jersey farm where the illegal equipment was in plain sight, the reason being that the agents had had plenty of time to secure a warrant and seemed to have willfully disregarded the warrant requirement.

To complete the confusion, the Court then swung back toward the *Harris* position in *United States* v. *Rabinowitz* (1950). A stamp dealer had been arrested on a warrant in his one-room office for selling stamps fraudulently overprinted to give them a higher value for philatelists. A search was then made of the office for additional fraudulent stamps, over five hundred of which were found. Although the officers had thought to bring experts along to identify the stamps, they had not thought to secure a search warrant. The Court, by a five to three vote, held that the search was nevertheless reasonable, since the office was open to the public, small, and under the immediate control of the occupant. *Trupiano* was overruled, to the extent that it required "a search warrant solely upon the basis of the practicability of procuring it rather than upon the reasonableness of the search after a lawful arrest."

The FBI went too far in *Kremen* v. *United States* (1957). Armed with arrest warrants for two fugitives from justice who had been convicted under the Smith Act, the FBI also arrested two other occupants of a mountain cabin, seized documents found on their persons, and removed the entire

contents of the cabin to FBI headquarters. The Court held that this went "beyond the sanction of any of our cases."

The famous Russian spy case, *Abel* v. *United States* (1960), upheld a search where an administrative warrant of arrest rather than one issued by a judicial officer had been used. Abel, an alien, was arrested in his hotel room by agents of the Immigration and Naturalization Service as a preliminary to deportation proceedings. They acted under authority of a warrant issued by their own agency, since deportation is a civil proceeding, not punishment for crime. FBI agents were present at the time of the arrest but did not participate in it or in the search of Abel's person and his room. After the prisoner had been taken away by the INS men, the FBI agents did search the room, with the consent of the hotel management, and found evidence used in Abel's subsequent conviction of espionage.

The Supreme Court by a five to four vote upheld the validity of this arrest on an administrative warrant. The dissenters charged that the FBI, suspecting espionage but unable to prove it, wanted to avoid having to secure a regular judicial warrant which would have required a description of the things to be seized. So the FBI called in the immigration people to make the arrest, under cover of which they could pursue their own investigation. But the Court majority concluded that the decision to proceed administratively was made in good faith. Since the arrest was valid, the search was valid as incident to a lawful arrest.

Whether armed with a warrant or not, officers cannot break down a door to effect a lawful arrest and the seizure of incriminating evidence unless they are refused admission after giving clear notice of their authority and purpose.[15] In *Wong Sun* v. *United States* (1963) an agent, on the basis of information too vague to sustain a request for an arrest warrant, sought entry to a Chinese laundry at 6:00 A.M. by pretending he had some laundry there; after being refused admission he identified himself, broke open the door, and seized the fleeing suspect. The Court by a five to four vote held this to be an unlawful entry and an unauthorized arrest.

In *Chapman* v. *United States* (1961) the Court held unconstitutional seizure of a still in a rented house by officers acting without a warrant but with the permission of the landlord, who in fact had discovered the still when he entered the house in the absence of the tenant. Since the tenant was not there when the officers arrived either, the search could not be justified as incident to an arrest.

Generally, the fact that evidence is available to officers which would justify issuance of a search warrant does not relieve them of the necessity to secure such a warrant. In *Jones* v. *United States* (1958) the Court held that protracted observation by federal agents of mash flowing from a house

---

[15] *Miller* v. *United States* (1958). But police can enter a house in "hot pursuit" of a suspect, and search the house for the felon, his weapons, and the fruits of the crime; *Warden* v. *Hayden* (1967).

did not justify search and seizure of contraband distilling equipment without a warrant. Similarly, in *Johnson* v. *United States* (1948) the odor of burning opium coming from a hotel room was held insufficient to justify entry without a warrant.

The Fourth Amendment can be violated by guileful as well as forcible or stealthy intrusions into a constitutionally protected area. In *Gouled* v. *United States* (1921) a business acquaintance, acting under orders of federal officers, obtained entry into Gouled's office by falsely purporting only to pay a social visit. In Gouled's absence, the intruder ransacked the office and seized certain private papers of an incriminating nature. The Court held this an unconstitutional search and seizure.[16]

This precedent did not help James Hoffa, who was convicted in 1964 of jury tampering on the basis of evidence provided by one of his associates, Partin, who had been a frequent visitor to Hoffa's hotel room but who was secretly an informer for the government. Hoffa contended that Partin's role vitiated the consent Hoffa had given for Partin's repeated entries into the suite, and that by listening to Hoffa's statements Partin had conducted an illegal search for verbal evidence.

The Supreme Court, however, in *Hoffa* v. *United States* (1966), held that the security of his hotel room on which Hoffa was entitled to rely had not been breached. Partin was present by invitation, and Hoffa's revelations were voluntary. What Hoffa had relied on was "his misplaced confidence that Partin would not reveal his wrongdoing." Similarly, the Court held in *Lewis* v. *United States* (1966) that a drug pusher who had invited an undercover agent into his home and sold him narcotics there could not contend that there had been an unconstituitonal invasion of the "sanctity" of his home.

The right to search an automobile on probable cause without a warrant was first recognized during the prohibition era in *Carroll* v. *United States* (1925), the justification being that an auto can be quickly moved out of the jurisdiction where the warrant must be sought. The Court did not, however, hold that the Fourth Amendment is simply inapplicable to moving vehicles, as it might have done by relying on their obvious differences from dwelling places. Instead, the *Carroll* ruling was that where the securing of a warrant was reasonably practical it must be used.

The doctrine of the *Carroll* case has been maintained and even extended. In *Brinegar* v. *United States* (1949), where there was no congressional authorization for warrantless searches as there had been in *Carroll*, the Court, over a brilliant dissent by Jackson, extended the principle of war-

---

[16] The Court also ruled in *Gouled* that even in a lawful search the police could seize only illegal articles, such as narcotics, weapons, or fruits of a crime, and not "mere evidence" of crime such as articles of clothing. In 1967 the Court overruled the "mere evidence" rule in *Warden* v. *Hayden*, holding that the principal object of the Fourth Amendment is the protection of privacy rather than the protection of property.

rantless search of automobiles to all federal offenses and gave a very loose interpretation to probable cause, which in this case was based on past illegal conduct of the driver. There is some indication, however, that the more recent Court is enforcing stricter standards of probable cause.[17]

Search of an automobile may also be tested on grounds of reasonableness. In *Preston* v. *United States* (1964) a man was arrested in his automobile for vagrancy. The police took custody of the car because they did not want to leave it in the street, but the Court held this gave them no right to search the car. However, in *Cooper* v. *California* (1967) the car of a man arrested on narcotics charges was held as evidence pending forfeiture proceedings as required by statute. By a five to four vote the Court held a search under these circumstances was justified.

THE EXCLUSIONARY RULE IN FEDERAL TRIALS    The principal sanction against search and seizure by federal officials is that any evidence secured by such methods is barred from use in federal trials. This rule excluding illegally procured evidence was established by the Supreme Court in *Weeks* v. *United States* (1914), and it was initially thought to be only a rule of evidence promulgated by the Court under its authority to control the rules of evidence in federal courts, not a requirement derived from the Fourth Amendment. But since the holding in *Mapp* v. *Ohio* (1961), to be considered shortly, the Court appears to regard it as a constitutional mandate.

Originally this exclusionary rule applied only if federal agents were the guilty parties in procuring the evidence. If the evidence was illegally secured by state police or stolen by private parties and then turned over to federal officers on a "silver platter," it could be employed in a federal trial. But in *Elkins* v. *United States* (1960) the Supreme Court by a vote of five to four abandoned the "silver platter" doctrine.[18]

STATE SEARCHES AND SEIZURES    The Supreme Court had no occasion to make a definitive ruling on the application of the unreasonable search and seizure requirements of the Fourth Amendment to the states until *Wolf* v. *Colorado* (1949). This case involved an abortionist who had been convicted on the basis of records seized in an unauthorized search of his office. Justice Frankfurter, writing the Court's opinion, concluded that freedom from unreasonable search and seizure was an essential element in the concept of "ordered liberty," and so entitled to Fourteenth Amendment protection against state action.

> The security of one's privacy against arbitrary intrusion by the police
> —which is at the core of the Fourth Amendment—is basic to a free

[17] See *One 1958 Plymouth Sedan* v. *Pennsylvania* (1965).
[18] The "silver platter" rule never did apply to evidence secured by wire tapping, because of the statutory ban on use of wire-tap evidence in federal courts. See *Benanti* v. *United States* (1957).

society. . . . The knock at the door, whether by day or by night, as a prelude to a search, without authority of law but solely on the authority of the police, did not need the commentary of recent history to be condemned as inconsistent with the conception of human rights enshrined in the history and the basic constitutional documents of English-speaking peoples.

The next question was whether the state was forbidden to use the illegally secured evidence in the trial. It would not be admissible in a federal court, but six justices in *Wolf* v. *Colorado* voted not to embody the exclusionary rule in the Fourteenth Amendment. Justice Frankfurter, after a survey of practice on this point, concluded that "most of the English-speaking world does not regard as vital . . . the exclusion of evidence thus [illegally] obtained." Accordingly the Court "must hesitate to treat this remedy as an essential ingredient of the right." The sanctions suggested by Frankfurter, if evidence secured by illegal invasion of privacy was nonetheless used in court, were "the remedies of private action and such protection as the internal discipline of the police, under the eyes of an alert public opinion, may afford."

A strong dissent came from Justices Murphy, Rutledge, and Douglas. Justice Holmes had once said that without the exclusion of evidence as a sanction, the Fourth Amendment "might as well be stricken from the Constitution." Now the Court was reversing that view with a "bland citation of 'other remedies'." Murphy proceeded to demonstrate that these other remedies were either unavailable or unrealistic, and he summed up: "The conclusion is inescapable that but one remedy exists to deter violations of the search and seizure clause. That is the rule which excludes illegally obtained evidence."

The Court's subsequent dilemmas in applying the *Wolf* rule may be illustrated by three decisions. The first, *Rochin* v. *California* (1952), was a prosecution for illegal possession of narcotics. Having information that Rochin was selling dope, three deputy sheriffs entered his house and forced open his bedroom door. Rochin was sitting on the bed partly dressed, and his common-law wife was in bed. There were two capsules on the night stand, which Rochin seized and put in his mouth. The deputies jumped on him and tried to extricate the capsules. This failing, they handcuffed him and took him to a hospital, where at the direction of the officers a doctor pumped his stomach and produced the capsules, which contained morphine. The capsules were the chief evidence on which he was convicted.

Justice Frankfurter for a unanimous Court invalidated the conviction. The *Wolf* rule would have admitted evidence secured illegally, but the conduct here went beyond any acceptable bounds.

> It is conduct that shocks the conscience. Illegally breaking into the privacy of the petitioner, the struggle to open his mouth and remove what was there, the forcible extraction of his stomach's contents—this

course of proceeding by agents of government to obtain evidence is bound to offend even hardened sensibilities. They are methods too close to the rack and the screw to permit of constitutional differentiation.

Next came *Irvine* v. *California* (1954), where official conduct was also shocking, but not too shocking to permit application of the *Wolf* rule. The police suspected Irvine of illegal bookmaking. In his absence from home, they had a locksmith go there and make a door key. Two days later they entered the house with his key and installed a concealed microphone, boring a hole in the roof through which wires were strung to a neighboring garage, where officers were posted with listening devices. Subsequently they twice reentered the house to move the microphone into better positions. At the trial, the officers were allowed to testify to conversations heard by this method.

The Court majority, Justice Jackson writing the opinion, said that this was "trespass, and probably a burglary," but according to *Wolf* there was no basis for denying the state's right to get a conviction by use of such methods. "We adhere to *Wolf* as stating the law of search-and-seizure cases."

Four justices thought the *Irvine* procedure was unconstitutional regardless of the *Wolf* rule, and Frankfurter, author of *Wolf*, was included in the four. He contended that the *Wolf* ruling did not affect the decision on exclusion of the evidence in this case, because here there was "additional aggravating conduct which the Court finds repulsive," as there had also been in the *Rochin* case. There had been no direct physical violence in *Irvine*, as there had been in *Rochin*, but there had been "a more powerful and offensive control over the Irvines' life," a control which enabled police to hear every word said in a private home for an entire month.

The third case was *Breithaupt* v. *Abram* (1957). A truck driven by Breithaupt in New Mexico collided with another car and three persons were killed. An almost empty whisky bottle was found in the truck. Breithaupt, seriously injured, was taken to a hospital unconscious. When liquor was detected on his breath, the police directed a doctor to secure a sample of his blood by use of a hypodermic needle. Testimony regarding the blood test was admitted in evidence at the trial, and an expert gave his opinion that the amount of alcohol found in the blood was sufficient to induce intoxication.

By a six to three vote the Court distinguished these circumstances from those in the *Rochin* case and upheld the conviction. Justice Clark pointed out that blood tests are "routine"; they do not shock the conscience or offend the sense of justice; there is nothing brutal or offensive about them. Intoxication is one of the reasons for the "increasing slaughter on our highways," and the interests of society in reducing these hazards outweigh "so slight an intrusion" on the person.

The Court's effort to distinguish the *Rochin* case was unconvincing, as

the three dissenters (Warren, Black, and Douglas) pointed out. In each case the operation was performed by a doctor in a hospital. In each case body fluids were extracted. Both operations are common, "scientific," and cause no lasting ill effects. In both cases evidence which had been obtained from a man on an involuntary basis was used to convict him.[19]

The *Wolf* rule on evidence had apparently emerged unscathed from this series of encounters, but actually its days were numbered. In the 1960 *Elkins* decision, where the Court abandoned the "silver platter" rule for federal prosecutions, the Court majority through Justice Stewart took note of the fact that the states were definitely moving away from the freedom the *Wolf* decision gave them and toward adoption of the federal exclusionary rule.

Then in *Mapp* v. *Ohio* (1961), the Court by a five to three vote overruled *Wolf*. Cleveland police officers, suspecting that a law violator was hiding in a certain house, broke in the door, manhandled a woman resident, searched the entire premises, and discovered some obscene materials in a trunk. The woman was convicted of possession of these materials. The state court, pointing out that the objects had not been taken from the defendant's person by brutal or offensive physical force (as in *Rochin*), permitted their use in evidence on the basis of *Wolf*. But the Supreme Court disposed of *Wolf*, Justice Clark saying:

> The ignoble shortcut to conviction left open to the State [by *Wolf*] tends to destroy the entire system of constitutional restraints on which the liberties of the people rest. Having once recognized that the right to privacy embodied in the Fourth Amendment is enforceable against the States, and that the right to be secure against rude invasions of privacy by state officers is, therefore, constitutional in origin, we can no longer permit that right to remain an empty promise.

Following the rationale of the *Mapp* decision, the Court asserted in *Ker* v. *California* (1963) that "the standard of reasonableness is the same under the Fourth and Fourteenth Amendments." This means, said the Court in *Aguilar* v. *Texas* (1964) that the requirements for obtaining a search warrant are the same in both federal and state jurisdictions; the *Aguilar* case held that a search warrant issued on the basis of an affidavit which recited "mere conclusions" was not valid.[20] But in the *Ker* case itself the Court suggested that "a healthy federalism depends upon the avoidance of needless conflict between state and federal courts," and approved a search which would have been unlawful if carried out by federal officials because of the supervisory powers the Supreme Court has over federal courts which it does not exercise over state courts.

[19] In *Schmerber* v. *California* (1966) the Court again upheld compulsory blood tests for drivers, this time against the contention that the tests amounted to compulsory self-incrimination.

[20] Other searches were held invalid in *Beck* v. *Ohio* (1964) and *Stoner* v. *California* (1964).

When a new constitutional standard is laid down by the Court, it is generally given retroactive effect. But in *Linkletter* v. *Walker* (1965) the Court ruled that the *Mapp* doctrine would not be applied to invalidate state criminal convictions which had become final before the decision was rendered. The existence of the *Wolf* rule prior to *Mapp* had had consequences which could not be ignored. "The past cannot always be erased by a new judicial declaration."

*Monroe* v. *Pape* (1961) held that police officers could be sued under federal civil rights laws for damages resulting from an unconstitutional search and seizure. Here Chicago police had broken into a home in the early hours of the morning, ransacked and destroyed most of the furniture, taken the occupant to the police station, interrogated him for ten hours on a murder charge, and then released him.

Search warrants must be secured by city officials seeking to inspect private premises for possible violations of fire, health, and building regulations, but the warrants do not need to meet the same "probable cause" tests required in a criminal investigation. The Court so held in two 1967 cases, *Camara* v. *Municipal Court*, where a city public health inspector without a warrant had been refused entrance to an apartment, and *See* v. *Seattle*, involving an effort to inspect a commercial warehouse under the fire code. In these opinions, decided by a vote of six to three, the Court overruled the earlier five to four holding in *Frank* v. *Maryland* (1959).

Police on occasions set up roadblocks and stop all motorists for questioning. Such procedures are valid for enforcing traffic laws, for example, checking drivers' licenses. But if the object is to arrest or search, probable cause must be first established.

In 1968 the Supreme Court reviewed the constitutionality of state "stop and frisk" laws which authorize police to search individuals if they suspect that a crime is being planned or committed or that the policeman is in danger of attack.[21] Problems have also been raised by a California law which requires persons on the street to identify themselves and account for their presence on demand of the police.

WIRE TAPPING AND ELECTRONIC EAVESDROPPING   Normally the search and seizure clause protects against the seizure of physical objects useful in effecting criminal convictions, but it may also be invoked against alleged unreasonable "search" of a person's spoken words. This possibility was illustrated by the famous wire-tapping case, *Olmstead* v. *United States* (1928). Federal prohibition agents had secured evidence against a gang of rumrunners by tapping their telephones and recording the conversations, and convictions were secured on the basis of this evidence. The Court majority determined that there had been no actual search and seizure in this case. The agents

---

[21] *Sibron* v. *New York* (1968); *Peters* v. *New York* (1968); *Terry* v. *Ohio* (1968).

had never entered the quarters of the suspects, but had done the tapping in the basements of apartment buildings. "The evidence was secured by the use of the sense of hearing and that only."

Justice Holmes, dissenting, noted that wire tapping was a crime in the state of Washington, where these acts occurred, and said that the United States should have no part in such a "dirty business." Justice Brandeis, also dissenting, felt that the conception of a "search" should not be confined to actual physical entry.

> The progress of science in furnishing the Government with means of espionage is not likely to stop with wire-tapping. Ways may some day be developed by which the Government, without removing papers from secret drawers, can reproduce them in court. . . . Advances in the psychic and related sciences may bring means of exploring unexpressed beliefs, thoughts and emotions. . . . Can it be that the Constitution affords no protection against such invasions of individual security?

The Court did, however, point out in *Olmstead* that Congress had power to adopt "controlling legislation" in this field, and in the 1934 Communications Act Congress followed this suggestion by providing that "no person not being authorized by the sender shall intercept any communication and divulge or publish the . . . contents . . . of such intercepted communication to any person." Subsequently the Court in *Nardone* v. *United States* (1937) held that this law rendered inadmissible in federal trials evidence as to an interstate communication secured by wire tapping. Later the Court extended this interpretation to apply also to intrastate communications [22] and to indirect or derivative use of evidence secured in this fashion.[23]

The effort in *Olmstead* to invoke the Fourth Amendment against wire tapping failed because the Court majority was unable to reconcile a new technique for searching and seizing with its traditional conception that there is no search without a trespass and no seizure without a physical object. It might have been expected that the Roosevelt Court, which was so largely guided by the views of Holmes and Brandeis, would have taken the first opportunity to adopt their dissenting position in *Olmstead*. But when the occasion presented itself in *Goldman* v. *United States* (1942), only Frankfurter, Stone, and Murphy were prepared to do so. Douglas confessed ten

---

[22] *Weiss* v. *United States* (1939).

[23] *Nardone* v. *United States* (1939). See also *Rathbun* v. *United States* (1957); *Benanti* v. *United States* (1957). The Department of Justice, relying on an interpretation of the Communications Act by Attorney General Jackson, contended that it was not a criminal violation to intercept conversations by wire tapping so long as the results were not divulged in court. Consequently federal agencies admittedly carried on wire tapping on a large scale, though supposedly only with the express consent of the Attorney General and only in cases of national security or where human life was in danger. All efforts in Congress to amend the 1934 act and to authorize wire tapping by federal agents had failed up to 1968, though they were actively continuing.

years later, in *On Lee* v. *United States,* that his failure to join them had been an error. Black supported *Olmstead* because of his literalist interpretation of the Fourth Amendment as applying only to tangible objects.

In the *Goldman* case the Court for the first time encountered the practice of electronic eavesdropping or "bugging." No use is made of telephone lines; instead, bugs are planted in locations permitting conversations to be overheard at a distance. In *Goldman* government agents had used a detectaphone sensitive enough to pick up conversations in an adjoining office, the words being heard through the wall with no physical intrusion into the adjacent office. Since *Olmstead* had ruled that words are not protected against seizure, and since there had been no search involving physical trespass, the Court majority held that the Fourth Amendment had not been violated.

If trespass does occur during a bugging operation, then of course it becomes an unconstitutional search and seizure under the *Olmstead-Goldman* doctrine. In *Silverman* v. *United States* (1961) police officers in the District of Columbia had occupied a vacant house and driven a "spike mike" through the party wall of an adjoining row house. The spike made contact with the heating duct of the house and all conversations in the house were audible to the officers next door. The Supreme Court held that the projection of the spike into the adjoining house, "by even a fraction of an inch," amounted to an unauthorized physical penetration of a constitutionally protected area.

A more complicated bugging problem was presented by *On Lee* v. *United States* (1952). There the Court held admissible statements made by the accused to a supposed friend on his own premises which, through a transmitter concealed on the person of the "friend," were broadcast to a federal agent outside. The *On Lee* ruling, to which four justices dissented, was reaffirmed in *Lopez* v. *United States* (1963). Here a federal agent investigating possible evasion of excise taxes by a restaurant owner was offered a bribe to call off the investigation. The agent returned with a pocket wire recorder on his person and secured a recording which was used at the trial. The Court majority denied this was eavesdropping. The agent was lawfully on the premises, and the recording was simply corroborating evidence of what he had heard with his own ears.

A controversy between former Attorney General Robert F. Kennedy and J. Edgar Hoover in 1966 led to the disclosure that federal agents had systematically engaged in unconstitutional bugging operations. The Supreme Court reacted by ordering a new trial in the case of *Black* v. *United States* (1966) after the Justice Department admitted entering his Washington hotel suite to place a bug. The Department filed with the Court a memorandum recognizing its obligation not to use evidence obtained in violation of a defendant's protected rights, and launched a review of past prosecutions in which bugging had occurred. By mid-1967 the Department had reported fifteen cases of this sort, in most of which the Court then reversed the

convictions. In July 1967 Attorney General Clark issued sweeping new regulations forbidding all wire tapping and virtually all eavesdropping by federal agents except in national security cases.

These actions ran counter to the opinion of many legislators and law enforcement officers, both state and national, that wire tapping and eavesdropping are necessary to meet the threat of organized crime. Several states had passed laws permitting eavesdropping if authorized in advance by a judge. The New York law of this type provided that a judge could authorize up to two months of eavesdropping if a district attorney, attorney general, or police officer above the rank of sergeant swore there was "reasonable ground" to believe it might reveal evidence of crime.

The Supreme Court declared this statute unconstitutional in *Berger* v. *New York* (1967) by a vote of five to four. Instead of yielding to pressure, the Court actually strengthened its stand against eavesdropping by abandoning the *Olmstead-Goldman* rule that the Fourth Amendment did not protect against the search and seizure of words. Justice Clark for the *Berger* majority held the state law in direct violation of the Fourth Amendment. He regarded this two-month period of eavesdropping as the equivalent of a series of intrusions pursuant to a single showing of probable cause. He also objected that the particularization required for a search warrant and the notice of search given by a warrant were not provided by the New York law. The broad sweep of the Court's language, particularly Clark's suggestion that "notice" of eavesdropping would have to be given, left it uncertain as to whether any practical eavesdrop law could be drafted which would meet the Court's objection.

A few months later *Katz* v. *United States* (1967) gave the Court a chance to take a more tenable position. Here federal agents had secured evidence against a gambler by bugging a public telephone booth which he used to place bets. By an eight to one vote the Court reversed the conviction, but in so doing it outlined a procedure by which bugging could be constitutionally employed.

First, however, the Court completed the dismantling of *Olmstead* and its progeny, particularly the conception that the Fourth Amendment forbids only physical invasion of a constitutionally protected area. What the Fourth Amendment actually protects, said Justice Stewart, is "people, not places. What a person knowingly exposes to the public, even in his own home or office, is not a subject of Fourth Amendment protection. But what he seeks to preserve as private, even in an area accessible to the public, may be constitutionally protected."

The fact that Katz was in a public glass-enclosed telephone booth where he could be readily seen was irrelevant. He was constitutionally entitled to make a private telephone call which would not be broadcast to government agents by a bug on top of the phone booth. The fact that there was no

physical penetration of the agents into the phone booth was also irrelevant. The Court, Stewart said, has departed from the "narrow view" of the *Olmstead* case that property interests or technical notions of trespass control the right of the government to search and seize. Specifically overruling *Olmstead* and *Goldman,* Stewart concluded: "The Government's activities in electronically listening to and recording the petitioner's words violated the privacy upon which he justifiably relied while using the telephone booth and thus constituted a 'search and seizure' within the meaning of the Fourth Amendment."

However, Stewart then went on to explain how the requirements of the the Fourth Amendment could be met in this kind of situation. The government had in fact proceeded quite cautiously in this case. The agents did not begin their electronic surveillance until their investigation had established a strong probability that Katz was using the telephone to transmit gambling information to persons in other states in violation of federal law. Moreover, the agents confined their listening to the brief periods he was in the booth, and did not listen to any other persons.

Consequently the Court regarded this as a "very limited search and seizure" which would have met the standards of the Fourth Amendment if government agents had followed "the procedure of antecedent justification that is central to the Fourth Amendment," and had secured prior judicial approval for the eavesdropping. The Court referred for support to its favorable decision in *Osborn* v. *United States* (1966), where on the basis of a sworn statement that one of James Hoffa's attorneys had endeavored to bribe a prospective juror, the two federal judges in the district where the trial was being conducted had authorized the use of a tape recorder for the specific and limited purpose of ascertaining the truth of the allegation. Thus the Court in *Osborn* and *Katz* has offered Congress and the states a formula for constitutional bugging—namely, antecedent judicial authorization justified by investigation and a showing of probable cause and for a strictly limited law enforcement purpose.

### SELF-INCRIMINATION

The Fifth Amendment provides that no one "shall be compelled in any criminal case to be a witness against himself." The privilege against self-incrimination was well established in England by the last half of the seventeenth century, its adoption marking a great advance over earlier practices when suspects were not only required to give such testimony but were tortured to force them to do so. The privilege came to this country as part of the English common law, and was included in the Virginia Bill of Rights of 1776, drafted by George Mason.

There has been considerable diversity of opinion concerning the privilege. On the one hand, it has been regarded as "one of the great landmarks in

man's struggle to make himself civilized," [24] and as the epitome of the Anglo-Saxon assumption that a man is presumed innocent until proved guilty. Justice Stephen J. Field said: "The essential and inherent cruelty of compelling a man to expose his own guilt is obvious to every one." [25] On the other hand, it has been subjected to a classic attack by Jeremy Bentham, and in 1925 Charles Evans Hughes recommended serious consideration of its abolition.

The first, and most obvious, effect of the Fifth Amendment is that the defendant in a criminal trial cannot be required to take the witness stand. It is improper for opposing counsel to call attention to failure of a defendant to take the stand in his own defense, and by federal statute a jury must be instructed that the defendant's failure to testify creates no presumption against him.[26] If he does take the stand, then he lays himself open to cross-examination which may bring out evidence damaging to his cause.

Before a grand jury, congressional committee, or administrative tribunal, the situation is different. Since there has been no indictment for crime, a person from whom evidence is sought cannot refuse to be a witness, but once he has gone on the witness stand, he can decline to answer particular questions on the ground of self-incrimination. It is normally very difficult to challenge a witness who refuses to testify on Fifth Amendment grounds without forcing him to reveal the conduct which the Constitution entitles him to conceal. It is agreed that a witness may refuse to give not only answers which constitute an admission of guilt but also those which merely furnish evidence of guilt or supply leads to obtaining such evidence. However, he may not refuse to talk when the danger of incrimination is "of an imaginary and unsubstantial character, having reference to some extraordinary and barely possible contingency, so improbable that no reasonable man would suffer it to influence his conduct." [27]

This is the "real danger versus imaginary possibility" test, but in 1955 Justice Harlan in *Emspak* v. *United States* charged that the Court had practically given up this standard, and was approving the refusal of witnesses to answer questions which could not conceivably be incriminatory. In the *Emspak* case the questions the witness had refused to answer all had to do with persons under suspicion of communism. The Court majority held that this circumstance justified Emspak in refusing to answer, but Harlan thought this was "painting with too broad a brush." The inference he drew from the record was that Emspak's real motive was to avoid being a "stool pigeon" against his associates, and this was not a "legal excuse for refusing to answer nonincriminating questions."

[24] Erwin N. Griswold, *The Fifth Amendment Today* (Cambridge, Mass.: Harvard University Press, 1955), p. 7.

[25] *Brown* v. *Walker* (1896).

[26] See *Bruno* v. *United States* (1939); *Grunewald* v. *United States* (1957).

[27] Quoted in *Emspak* v. *United States* (1955) from an 1861 decision by the Court of Queen's Bench, *The Queen* v. *Boyes*, 1 B. & S. 311.

The Fifth Amendment does not justify a person in refusing to testify about matters which would merely impair his reputation or tend to disgrace him.[28] A divided Court has held that where a witness or defendant has voluntarily answered some questions, he may not refuse to answer related questions on the ground of self-incrimination.[29] As already noted in *Albertson* v. *SACB* (1965), it would constitute self-incrimination to require persons to register as members of the Communist Party.

An individual who has acquired income in an illegal manner cannot refuse on self-incrimination grounds to make out an income tax return, but he could refuse to answer incriminating questions concerning it.[30] Even though criminal conduct would be disclosed by the answers, a person may not refuse to testify if the conduct is no longer punishable because the statute of limitations has run or because he has been granted immunity from prosecution by statute.

The granting of immunity to witnesses whose testimony is particularly wanted has been authorized by Congress in several statutes. The constitutionality of its use by the Interstate Commerce Commission under an act of 1893 was upheld by a five to four vote in *Brown* v. *Walker* (1896). The majority admitted that, interpreted literally, the self-incrimination clause authorizes a witness "to refuse to disclose any fact which might tend to incriminate, disgrace or expose him to unfavorable comments," and as so interpreted would render the immunity act unconstitutional. But the Fifth Amendment could also be read as having for its object only "to secure the witness against a criminal prosecution, which might be aided directly or indirectly by his disclosure." The Court regarded this second interpretation as yielding a better balance between private right and public welfare. "If [a witness] secure legal immunity from prosecution, the possible impairment of his good name is a penalty which it is reasonable he should be compelled to pay for the common good."

The four dissenters in *Brown* v. *Walker* thought it was obvious that the immunity act reduced the scope of the constitutional protection. Justice Field was particularly indignant at this breaching of "the shield of absolute silence." The Fifth Amendment, he said, "gives absolute protection to a person called as a witness in a criminal case against the compulsory enforcement of any criminating testimony against himself. . . . No substitute for the protection contemplated by the amendment would be sufficient were its operation less extensive and efficient."

The frequent blockage of government inquiries into subversion by claims of the privilege against self-incrimination led the Eisenhower administration to propose, and Congress to adopt, the Immunity Act of 1954, under which witnesses can be compelled to testify before courts, grand juries, or congres-

---

[28] *Hale* v. *Henkel* (1906).
[29] *Rogers* v. *United States* (1951); *Brown* v. *United States* (1958).
[30] *United States* v. *Sullivan* (1927).

sional committees in national security cases by granting them immunity from prosecution for any criminal activities they may confess. The act was upheld in *Ullmann* v. *United States* (1956), Justice Frankfurter writing the majority opinion. Ullmann, who had earlier pleaded the Fifth Amendment before a congressional committee and a grand jury when questioned about a wartime espionage ring in Washington, was granted immunity under the 1954 act so that a grand jury could secure his testimony. In his opinion Frankfurter, mindful of attacks of the McCarthy variety upon the Fifth Amendment, warned that its protection must not be downgraded or its effectiveness diminished. However, he did not believe it was interpreting the amendment in a "hostile or niggardly spirit" to uphold the immunity act. *Brown* v. *Walker* had settled that the protection of the amendment relates only to the infliction of penalties affixed to criminal acts. Immunity from criminal penalties removes that danger. "Once the reason for the privilege ceases, the privilege ceases."

Attorneys for Ullmann had sought to distinguish *Brown* v. *Walker* on the ground that Ullmann, by being forced to testify concerning possible espionage, would be subjected to disabilities that had not been present in the earlier case. If any participation in subversive activities were brought out in the coerced testimony, Ullmann might face loss of his job, expulsion from a labor union, ineligibility for a passport, and in general be subjected to public opprobrium. But the Court's reply was that these were not criminal penalties.

Justice Douglas, dissenting with Black, thought that *Brown* v. *Walker* should be overruled. Under its doctrine the constitutionally guaranteed privilege of silence was being traded away "for a partial, undefined, vague immunity." The 1954 statute protected individuals from criminal punishment but exposed them to the punishment of infamy and disgrace. Today, said Douglas, "the disclosure that a person is a Communist practically excommunicates him from society." But fundamentally the question for Douglas was not one of measuring the equivalence of protections or the severity of penalties. "My view is that the Framers put it beyond the power of Congress to *compel* anyone to confess his crimes. The evil to be guarded against was partly self-accusation under legal compulsion. But that was only a part of the evil. The conscience and dignity of man were also involved."

Finally, the protection against self-incrimination puts limits not only on the use of a defendant's words, but also on the use of his books or papers. Forcing a person to turn over incriminating written materials is in effect requiring him to testify against himself, in violation of the Fifth Amendment. It also amounts to an unreasonable seizure under the Fourth Amendment. As the Supreme Court said in *Boyd* v. *United States* (1886), with respect to the production of records the two provisions "run almost into each other."

However, records of corporations constitute an important exception to the immunity principle. *Hale* v. *Henkel* (1906) held that a corporation is not protected by the self-incrimination clause, and so cannot contest a subpoena on those grounds, though it may do so on the basis of the Fourth Amendment. Similarly, corporate officials may not withhold testimony or documents on the ground that their corporation would be incriminated, nor may the custodian of corporate books or records withhold them on the ground that he personally might be incriminated by their production.[31] The same principles were applied to labor unions in *United States* v. *White* (1944). But in *Curcio* v. *United States* (1957) the Court held that when a custodian of union records failed to produce them before a grand jury, he could not be required to explain or account under oath for their nonproduction if he claimed that doing so would tend to incriminate him.

The same reasoning that applies to corporate records even more clearly covers public documents, which must be produced by the official in possession even though they serve to incriminate him. In several regulatory statutes where Congress has required records to be kept to furnish information on transactions subject to government regulation, the courts have ruled that these records take on the status of "quasi-public" documents and no immunity applies in connection with them.[32]

SELF-INCRIMINATION IN STATE COURTS    As noted in the preceding chapter, the Fifth Amendment ban on self-incrimination was long regarded as inapplicable to state prosecutions. In two major decisions, *Twining* v. *New Jersey* (1908) and *Adamson* v. *California* (1947), the Court upheld state statutes permitting the drawing of unfavorable inferences from the defendant's failure to take the witness stand. The privilege against self-incrimination was not regarded as necessary to a system of "ordered liberty."

To similar effect was *Feldman* v. *United States* (1944), where by a four to three margin the Court held that the Fifth Amendment did not protect a person in refusing to give testimony before a state body which might lead to a federal prosecution. Justice Frankfurter upheld this result as required by our system of dual sovereignties, and the only limitation he admitted on the practice was that there must be no "complicity" of federal officers in the state proceeding. Justice Black, dissenting, bitterly attacked this ruling as cutting into the "very substance" of the Fifth Amendment on the basis of "dialectics" and "syllogistic reasoning" about the necessities of the federal system. The argument was repeated in *Knapp* v. *Schweitzer* (1958), with the same result, but with four justices favoring reversal of the *Feldman* rule.

*Cohen* v. *Hurley* (1961), another five to four ruling, held that New York could disbar an attorney who invoked the privilege and refused to testify before a judicially established committee of inquiry looking into "ambu-

[31] *Wilson* v. *United States* (1911); *Essgee Co.* v. *United States* (1923).
[32] *Shapiro* v. *United States* (1948). But see *Marchetti* v. *United States* (1968).

lance chasing." The majority held that disbarment was based, not on his exercise of the self-incrimination privilege, but on his refusal to discharge obligations which as a lawyer he owed the court.

But only two months after *Cohen,* the *Mapp* decision began a constitutional revolution which eventually dethroned the "ordered liberty" test and incorporated all the major protections of the Bill of Rights into the Fourteenth Amendment. *Malloy* v. *Hogan* (1964) by another vote of five to four overruled the long-established doctrine of *Twining* and *Adamson* and bestowed the Fifth Amendment's protection against self-incrimination on defendants in state courts. In *Malloy* a man had refused to answer questions in a state gambling inquiry and had been committed to jail for contempt. Justice Brennan for the majority wrote: "The Twining view of the privilege has been eroded. . . . It would be incongruous to have different standards determine the validity of a claim of privilege . . . depending on whether the claim was asserted in a state or federal court. Therefore, the same standards must determine whether an accused's silence in either a federal or state proceeding is justified."

Justice Harlan, one of the dissenters, agreed that principles of justice inherent in due process should forbid a state to imprison a person solely because he refused to give evidence which might incriminate him. But he objected to the majority's "wholesale incorporation" of federal requirements into the Fourteenth Amendment, for this would make applicable to the states the entire body of federal law that had grown up in this field, in inevitable "disregard of all relevant differences which may exist between state and federal criminal law and its enforcement." Justice Harlan admitted that the *Mapp* and *Ker* decisions had incorporated the Fourth Amendment into the Fourteenth Amendment, but he thought that there was nothing in those decisions "to suggest that the Fifth Amendment went along as baggage."

The *Malloy* ruling was applied in *Griffin* v. *California* (1965) to invalidate the practice, permitted by California law, of permitting both prosecutor and judge to comment on failure of an accused to take the witness stand. Harlan concurred with reluctance, saying the decision exemplified "the creeping paralysis with which this Court's recent adoption of the 'incorporation' doctrine is infecting the operation of the federal system." For substantially the same reasons as given in the *Linkletter* case, the Court decided in *Tehan* v. *Shott* (1966) that the *Griffin* rule would not be given retroactive application.[33]

Reverberations from *Malloy* were also felt in *Spevack* v. *Klein* (1967), which overruled *Cohen* v. *Hurley.* Like *Cohen,* the *Spevack* case involved disbarment of an attorney for refusal to answer questions in a disciplinary proceeding. The Court held that, since the self-incrimination clause had been absorbed into the Fourteenth Amendment, its protection extended to

---

[33] In *Chapman* v. *California* (1967) the Court held that failure to follow the *Griffin* rule was not "harmless error."

lawyers as well as other persons, and that it should not be "watered down by imposing the dishonor of disbarment and the deprivation of a livelihood as a price for asserting it." [34]

On the same day that *Malloy* was decided, the Court overruled *Feldman* and held in *Murphy* v. *Waterfront Commission of New York Harbor* (1964) that evidence which a person was compelled to give before a state tribunal under guarantee of immunity from state prosecution could not be used against him in a federal prosecution. The basis for the *Feldman* decision, questionable enough when it was handed down in 1944, had been completely undercut by the *Elkins* ruling that evidence illegally seized by state officials could not be used in federal courts. Even Justice Harlan concurred in *Murphy*. Though insisting that the *Feldman* result was still justified by the Constitution, he agreed that the Supreme Court under its general supervisory powers over the federal courts must prevent their use of this kind of coerced evidence.[35]

*Schmerber v. California* (1966) subjected the 1957 *Breithaupt* ruling on compelled blood tests for drunken drivers to review under the new judicial doctrines of the 1960s, and, rather surprisingly, *Breithaupt* survived by a five to four vote. Following an auto accident and removal of the driver to the hospital, a police officer noted indications of intoxication, placed the man under arrest, and directed a physician to take a blood sample, despite the man's refusal, on advice of counsel, to consent thereto. A report of the chemical analysis, showing intoxication, was admitted in evidence at the trial.

Justice Brennan for the majority upheld this action against both self-incrimination and search and seizure claims, though the dissenters argued principally the self-incrimination issue. To accomplish what Justice Black, dissenting, regarded as the "extraordinary feat" of holding that a person who is compelled to give his blood to help the state convict him is not being required to be a witness against himself, Brennan had to narrowly interpret the privilege as protecting an accused "only from being compelled to testify against himself, or otherwise provide the State with evidence of a testimonial or communicative nature." Here extraction of the blood and its chemical analysis involved "not even a shadow of testimonial compulsion upon or enforced communication by the accused." His "testimonial capacities were in no way implicated; indeed, his participation, except as a donor, was irrelevant to the results of the test."

---

[34] In *Garrity* v. *New Jersey* (1967), a companion case to *Spevack* v. *Klein*, the Court ruled that where police officers were given the choice of incriminating themselves or forfeiting their jobs and pension rights, and they chose to make confessions, the confessions were not voluntary and could not be used in subsequent criminal prosecutions in state courts.

[35] The important self-incrimination decision, *Miranda* v. *Arizona* (1966), will be discussed in connection with right to counsel.

## COERCED CONFESSIONS

The Fifth Amendment forbids the use in federal courts of confessions secured under conditions of physical or mental coercion, for in such cases the defendant would obviously have been under compulsion to testify against himself. In recent years additional limitations have been placed by the Supreme Court upon the use of confessions in federal prosecutions.

Federal statutes require suspects on apprehension to be taken before the nearest judicial officer "without unnecessary delay" for hearing, commitment, or release on bail. When suspects are taken before a committing magistrate, the law officers must show probable cause for the arrests, and the suspects must be informed of their right to remain silent and to have counsel. The motive of the police in delaying this process is usually to attempt to secure a confession before the suspect learns of his rights.[36]

In *McNabb* v. *United States* (1943) two men suspected of shooting a revenue officer were taken into custody by federal officials and questioned over a period of two days, without the presence of friends or counsel, until a confession was secured. The Supreme Court voided the conviction, not on the ground that the confession was coerced, but because of violation of the "without unnecessary delay" provision.

There was considerable criticism of the *McNabb* rule as placing a substantial impediment in the path of law enforcement, but the Court reaffirmed it in *Mallory* v. *United States* (1957). This decision, which voided a death sentence for rape in the District of Columbia, set off a concerted effort in Congress to revise the *McNabb* rule by new legislation providing that a confession or other evidence otherwise admissible should not be excluded solely because of delay in the arraignment. These initial efforts failed, but in 1967 Congress passed an act revising the *McNabb-Mallory* rule by permitting police in the District of Columbia to detain suspects for up to three hours of interrogation before having them arraigned.

COERCED CONFESSIONS IN STATE COURTS    Confessions extorted by force and violence are contrary to the most elemental notions of due process and any convictions based on them are void. The Supreme Court was first confronted with such a situation in *Brown* v. *Mississippi* (1936). The facts of brutality and torture by state officers were uncontroverted, and no evidence other than the coerced confessions of murder was presented at the trial. The state's defense was the *Twining* argument that immunity from self-incrimination was not an essential element in due process of law. Chief Justice Hughes replied for a unanimous Court that *Twining* simply gave

---

[36] Since the *Escobedo* and *Miranda* decisions, of course, suspects must be informed of these rights as soon as they are arrested or subjected to interrogation.

a state some freedom to experiment with the procedures of criminal prosecution. But that freedom is "the freedom of constitutional government and
is limited by the requirement of due process of law. Because a State may
dispense with a jury trial, it does not follow that it may substitute trial by
ordeal. The rack and torture chamber may not be substituted for the witness stand."

More difficult questions arise where confessions are secured by coercion
which is mental rather than physical. At first the Court was reluctant to
move against psychological coercion.[37] But in *Ashcraft* v. *Tennessee* (1944)
a Court majority adopted the rule of "inherent coerciveness." Ashcraft had
been convicted of murder on a confession elicited by thirty-six hours of continuous questioning under electric lights by relays of officers, investigators,
and lawyers. Such a situation was held to be "so inherently coercive that
its very existence is irreconcilable with the possession of mental freedom
by a lone suspect against whom the full coercive force is brought to bear."
Justice Jackson disagreed on the ground that a confession obtained by
questioning, "even if persistent and prolonged," is different from one obtained by the use of violence. "Interrogation *per se* is not, while violence
*per se* is, an outlaw."

This stand against psychological coercion was generally maintained in
subsequent decisions, though usually by a divided Court.[38] To give only
one example, *Fikes* v. *Alabama* (1957) involved a Negro of low mentality
who had been kept incommunicado for a week, had not been arraigned,
and had been questioned intermittently. Justice Frankfurter's conclusion
for the Court was that none of these circumstances standing alone would
justify a reversal, but that "in combination they bring the result below the
Plimsoll line of 'due process.'"

Whether a confession was voluntary or coerced must be decided without
reference to its probable truth. The Court briefly departed from this rule
in *Stein* v. *New York* (1953), which assumed that involuntary confessions
are excluded solely because they are untrustworthy and that if there is
independent evidence of the reliability of a confession it need not be rejected because it was involuntary. However, the Court rejected this view
in *Rogers* v. *Richmond* (1961), and overruled *Stein* in *Jackson* v. *Denno*
(1964). The latter decision held that the voluntariness of a decision must
be determined prior to its admission into evidence before the jury.[39]

As the *Fikes* case indicated, the Court at that time, contrary to the
*McNabb-Mallory* rule in the federal courts, did not regard confessions
secured while a suspect was illegally detained by the police as unconstitu-

---

[37] *Lisenba* v. *California* (1941).
[38] *Malinski* v. *New York* (1945), *Haley* v. *Ohio* (1948), *Watts* v. *Indiana*
(1949), *Turner* v. *Pennsylvania* (1949), *Harris* v. *South Carolina* (1949), and
*Leyra* v. *Denno* (1953) were all decided by five to four votes.
[39] See also *Sims* v. *Georgia* (1967).

tional for that reason alone. A divided Court upheld confessions secured between arrest and arraignment in *Gallegos* v. *Nebraska* (1951), *Stroble* v. *California* (1952), and *Brown* v. *Allen* (1953). In the latter case a preliminary hearing was not given until eighteen days after the arrest.

In 1958 the question was first raised as to whether a confession would be regarded as coerced which was secured after a suspect had been denied the opportunity to consult a lawyer during his questioning by the police. In *Crooker* v. *California* (1958) and *Cicenia* v. *La Gay* (1958) the Court treated this as a denial of counsel rather than as a coercion issue, and by votes of five to four and five to three in the two cases held that denial of access to counsel did not automatically invalidate the confessions. These decisions were reversed in *Escobedo* v. *Illinois* (1964), but consideration of that decision and the related case of *Miranda* v. *Arizona* (1966) falls in the following section.

### THE RIGHT TO COUNSEL

In establishing an accused person's right to have "the assistance of counsel for his defense," the Sixth Amendment represented an important advance over common-law practices. The actual wording of the amendment implies that the assistance of counsel is a privilege of which the accused has a right to avail himself, but not a mandatory feature of all criminal trials. In the Federal Crimes Act of 1790, Congress imposed a statutory duty on the courts to assign counsel to represent the defendant in capital cases, from which it could be logically implied that there was no such obligation in other types of cases. Up until 1938 it was the general understanding that where a person desired counsel, but for lack of funds or any other reason was not able to obtain counsel, the court was under no obligation in a noncapital case to secure counsel for him.

The Supreme Court abruptly and decisively changed this rule in *Johnson* v. *Zerbst* (1938), a counterfeiting prosecution in which it held that "the Sixth Amendment withholds from federal courts, in all criminal proceedings, the power and authority to deprive an accused of his life or liberty unless he has or waives the assistance of counsel." The Court justified this new interpretation of the amendment by adding that the "right to be heard would be, in many cases, of little avail if it did not comprehend the right to be heard by counsel." The right to counsel can be waived, but the waiver must be intelligent and understanding, and judicial determination on this point depends "upon the particular facts and circumstances . . . including the background, experience, and conduct of the accused." [40]

It is conceivable that the requirement of representation by counsel may

---

[40] See *Von Moltke* v. *Gillies* (1948).

be met in form but not in substance. A conviction may be attacked on the ground that counsel assigned by the court was incompetent, but in any such claim a heavy burden of proof rests on the defendant. Of course, counsel to be effective should have adequate opportunity to prepare and present his case, and should be present at all stages of the trial.

RIGHT TO COUNSEL IN STATE TRIALS   The Supreme Court first considered the issue of right to counsel in state court trials in the famous First Scottsboro case, *Powell* v. *Alabama* (1932). The case involved seven Negro boys, ignorant and illiterate, who were charged with the rape of two white girls in an open gondola car of a freight train passing through Alabama. They were taken from the train near Scottsboro and jailed there. Public excitement was high, and they were guarded by state militia at all stages of the proceedings. At the arraignment they pleaded not guilty. They were not asked whether they had, or were able to employ, counsel, or wished to have counsel appointed. The presiding judge did appoint "all the members of the bar" as counsel for the purpose of arraigning the defendants, but this "expansive gesture" produced no results.

The first case came to trial with no counsel for the defense. As the trial began an out-of-state lawyer said some people had asked him to come down, and that he would be willing to appear along with local counsel that the court might appoint. A member of the local bar then agreed that he would help the out-of-state lawyer. As the Supreme Court subsequently noted:

> With this dubious understanding, the trials immediately proceeded. The defendants, young, ignorant, illiterate, surrounded by hostile sentiment, haled back and forth under guard of soldiers, charged with an atrocious crime regarded with especial horror in the community where they were to be tried, were thus put in peril of their lives within a few moments after counsel for the first time charged with any degree of responsibility began to represent them.

The state supreme court ruled that this arrangement met the requirements of the state constitution. The Supreme Court, however, said that did not decide the matter under the Fourteenth Amendment. "The right to the aid of counsel," wrote Justice Sutherland, is of a "fundamental character." In this country, "historically and in practice," a hearing has always included "the right to the aid of counsel when desired and provided by the party asserting the right." The Court went on to indicate why this should be so:

> The right to be heard would be, in many cases, of little avail if it did not comprehend the right to be heard by counsel. Even the intelligent and educated layman has small and sometimes no skill in the science of law. If charged with crime, he is incapable, generally, of determining for himself whether the indictment is good or bad. He is unfamiliar with the rules of evidence. Left without the aid of counsel he may be put on

trial without a proper charge, and convicted upon incompetent evidence, or evidence irrelevant to the issue or otherwise inadmissible. He lacks both the skill and knowledge adequately to prepare his defense, even though he have a perfect one. He requires the guiding hand of counsel at every step in the proceedings against him. Without it, though he be not guilty, he faces the danger of conviction because he does not know how to establish his innocence.

All these factors would operate even with intelligent defendants. Considering all the additional prejudicial circumstances in this case, the Court was clear that "the failure of the trial court to give . . . reasonable time and opportunity to secure counsel was a clear denial of due process."

But the Court did not stop there. If these defendants were unable to get counsel, even though opportunity were offered, then the due process clause required the trial court "to make an effective appointment of counsel." This was new law, and so it was natural that the Court should state careful limits for the new principle:

> Whether this would be so in other criminal prosecutions, or under other circumstances, we need not determine. All that it is necessary now to decide, as we do decide, is that in a capital case, where the defendant is unable to employ counsel, and is incapable adequately of making his own defense because of ignorance, feeble-mindedness, illiteracy, or the like, it is the duty of the court, whether requested or not, to assign counsel for him as a necessary requisite of due process of law; and that duty is not discharged by an assignment at such a time or under such circumstances as to preclude the giving of effective aid in the preparation and trial of the case.

To an unusual degree the principle of the *Powell* case was tied to the individual circumstances of that case. In *Betts* v. *Brady* (1942) the circumstances were different and the Court's holding was different. Betts, under indictment for robbery in Maryland, requested the court to appoint counsel for him, since he was financially unable to secure legal aid. The judge refused, on the ground that it was not the practice in that county to appoint counsel for indigent defendants except in murder and rape prosecutions. The trial proceeded before the judge, acting without a jury.

Betts's contention was that the *Powell* case required appointment of counsel in all state criminal cases. Justice Roberts, who spoke for the Supreme Court, admitted there was some ground for such a conclusion in the *Powell* opinion, but pointed out that the actual holding in the case had been limited to its specific facts. The question whether the *Powell* rule applied to all criminal cases was therefore a new one. "Is the furnishing of counsel in all cases whatever dictated by natural, inherent, and fundamental principles of fairness?"

The Court then proceeded to make the same kind of examination of the constitutions and statutes of the original states which, as applied in

*Powell*, had resulted in the conclusion that aid of counsel "when desired and provided by the party asserting the right" was a fundamental requirement of a fair hearing. However, the Court's conclusion as to the mandatory *furnishing* of counsel was that "in the great majority of the States, it has been the considered judgment of the people, their representatives and their courts that appointment of counsel is not a fundamental right, essential to a fair trial. On the contrary, the matter has generally been deemed one of legislative policy." Whereas in *Powell* the Court had pointed out the great disadvantages any layman would encounter without legal guidance in a court of law, here Roberts said the defendant was "of ordinary intelligence and ability to take care of his own interests on the trial of [a] narrow issue." Therefore no constitutional error had been made.

Justice Black was joined by Douglas and Murphy in a vigorous dissent against this holding. Black of course believed that the Sixth Amendment was incorporated in the Fourteenth, but he was willing to argue the matter on the ground of fundamental fairness chosen by the majority, saying: "A practice cannot be reconciled with 'common and fundamental ideas of fairness and right,' which subjects innocent men to increased dangers of conviction merely because of their poverty." The majority opinion had admitted that in eighteen states the statutes required the courts to appoint in all cases where defendants were unable to procure counsel, and "any other practice seems to me to defeat the promise of our democratic society to provide equal justice under the law."

State counsel cases continued to come to the Court in unusual numbers, well over twenty in the decade following *Betts* v. *Brady*. The Court under the *Betts* rule had to consider the "special circumstances" in each case to determine whether the denial of counsel had amounted to a constitutional defect in the trial. In several instances absence of counsel was held unobjectionable even though the possibility of serious unfairness seemed to exist.[41] But in most cases the Court did find that the circumstances required the furnishing of counsel. This was generally true, for example, where the offense was a capital one; [42] where the conduct of the trial judge appeared to be questionable; [43] where the defendant was young or ignorant or otherwise handicapped; [44] or where the points of law involved were too technical for a layman to grasp.[45] In fact, after 1950 the Supreme Court never affirmed a state criminal conviction where denial of counsel was claimed.

Clearly the Court was moving toward a firmer position on the necessity for counsel in state trials. Finally, in the celebrated case of *Gideon* v. *Wainwright* (1963), the Court overruled *Betts* v. *Brady* and held that rep-

[41] See *Canizio* v. *New York* (1946); *Bute* v. *Illinois* (1948).
[42] See *Tomkins* v. *Missouri* (1945).
[43] See *Townsend* v. *Burke* (1948) and *White* v. *Ragen* (1945).
[44] See *De Meerleer* v. *Michigan* (1947); *Marino* v. *Ragen* (1947); *Moore* v. *Michigan* (1957).
[45] See *Rice* v. *Olson* (1945).

resentation by counsel is a constitutional necessity in all state criminal trials.[46] Justice Black wrote the opinion in *Gideon*, and thus had the opportunity to turn his *Betts* dissent into the law of the Constitution. Gideon was an uneducated ne'er-do-well who, convicted of a minor crime in Florida without the assistance of counsel, stubbornly and unaided from his prison cell drafted a petition printed painfully with pencil on lined paper to the Supreme Court. The Court agreed to hear his claim and appointed a member of a leading Washington law firm, Abe Fortas, who in 1965 was himself to be appointed to the Court, to represent Gideon.

The Court was unanimous in concluding that the right to counsel was fundamental and essential to a fair trial. In fact, twenty-two states had filed briefs as friends of the Court arguing for this position, while only two states had come forward to support Florida's position. Even Justice Harlan agreed that the "special circumstances" rule had been "substantially and steadily eroded" and that *Betts* should be overruled; he only objected that it was entitled to "a more respectful burial" than Justice Black had given it.[47] The decision was generally well received in the legal profession, and programs for supplying counsel to indigent defendants were promptly inaugurated or existing programs improved throughout most of the states.

THE RIGHT TO COUNSEL IN THE PRETRIAL PERIOD    As already noted, the problem of the right to counsel during the pretrial period was first raised by *Crooker* v. *California* (1958). The Court agreed there that a due process problem could be presented by deprivation of counsel during any part of the pretrial proceedings, provided the suspect "is so prejudiced thereby as to infect his subsequent trial with an absence of 'that fundamental fairness essential to the very concept of justice.'" However, the Court refused to regard every denial of a pretrial request to contact counsel as infringement of a constitutional right. In the *Crooker* case, though a capital offense was involved, the Court ruled that denial of counsel during interrogation had not invaded the defendant's constitutional rights because he was a college graduate with a year of law school, and was aware of his right to remain silent.

The Court arrived at a similar conclusion in *Cicenia* v. *La Gay* (1958). A flat holding that any state denial of a defendant's request to confer with counsel during police questioning, "irrespective of the particular circumstances involved . . . would mean that state police could not interrogate

---

[46] This decision is the subject of a fascinating book by Anthony Lewis, *Gideon's Trumpet* (New York: Random House, Inc., 1964).

[47] See Jerold H. Israel, "Gideon v. Wainwright: The 'Art' of Overruling," in Philip B. Kurland (ed.), *The Supreme Court Review: 1963* (Chicago: The University of Chicago Press, 1963), pp. 211–272. The decision was given retroactive effect because, as later explained in *Linkletter* v. *Walker* (1965), the principle applied in *Gideon* "went to the fairness of the trial—the very integrity of the fact-finding process," and there could be no assurance that a defendant convicted without the aid of counsel had received a fair trial.

a suspect before giving him an opportunity to secure counsel," and the Court majority thought such an "inflexible rule" would be inconsistent with the latitude the states needed in administration of their systems of criminal justice.

The "special circumstances" rule, however, was to suffer the same fate of erosion here as in *Gideon*. The process began the following year in *Spano* v. *New York* (1959), where a defendant already indicted for first-degree murder was questioned by police officers who ignored his requests to contact an attorney and got a confession from him after an eight-hour session. The Court unanimously reversed the conviction, four justices relying directly on the denial of counsel. As Justice Douglas said, the period after indictment and before trial might have been "the only stage when legal aid and advice would help him." [48]

The major decision was *Escobedo* v. *Illinois* (1964). Escobedo, under suspicion of murder, was questioned intensively by police officers who repeatedly denied his request to see his attorney and likewise rebuffed the persistent attempts of the attorney to see his client. Escobedo was not informed of his right to refuse to answer police questions, and eventually he made a confession.

The Supreme Court, having already agreed in *Spano* that counsel could not be denied after indictment, now concluded by a vote of five to four that no "meaningful distinction" could be drawn between interrogation before and after formal indictment. Justice Goldberg spoke for the Court majority:

> We hold, therefore, that where, as here, the investigation is no longer a general inquiry into an unsolved crime but has begun to focus on a particular suspect, the suspect has been taken into police custody, the police carry out a process of interrogations that lends itself to eliciting incriminating statements, the suspect has requested and been denied an opportunity to consult with his lawyer, and the police have not effectively warned him of his absolute constitutional right to remain silent, the accused has been denied 'the assistance of counsel' in violation of the Sixth Amendment to the Constitution as 'made obligatory upon the States by the Fourteenth Amendment,' *Gideon* v. *Wainwright* . . . and that no statement elicited by the police during the interrogation may be used against him at a criminal trial.

Justice Goldberg took account of objections that this rule would greatly reduce the number of confessions secured because, as Justice Jackson had once said, "any lawyer worth his salt will tell the suspect in no uncertain terms to make no statement to police under any circumstances." Goldberg replied that "no system worth preserving" should have to fear that an

[48] *Massiah* v. *United States* (1964), a federal narcotics case, followed *Spano* in holding that the securing of incriminating statements from a defendant under indictment, by a ruse of government agents which involved electronic eavesdropping, was a denial of the right to counsel under the Sixth Amendment.

accused would be made aware of his constitutional rights. Moreover, officers could still gather evidence from witnesses and undertake other "proper investigative efforts." The Court's holding was only that "when the process shifts from investigatory to accusatory—when its focus is on the accused and its purpose is to elicit a confession—our adversary system begins to operate, and, under the circumstances here, the accused must be permitted to consult with his lawyer."

The *Escobedo* ruling was clear evidence of the Supreme Court's great concern about police abuses in interrogating suspects and its belief in the virtues of the adversary process, the protections of which it was extending from the trial to the pretrial period. *Escobedo* also represented an effort to substitute an objective test for the constitutionality of interrogation in place of the subjective, balancing, case-by-case examination of circumstances which the Court had been forced into in its previous decisions.

But *Escobedo* left many questions unanswered. When did warning of their rights have to be given to suspects? Did *Escobedo* preclude any questioning at all in the absence of counsel? Must counsel be supplied for indigents or others unable to secure counsel? And did *Escobedo* operate retroactively to invalidate every prior prosecution where conviction had been secured in violation of its standards? *Escobedo* quickly became the focus of a nationwide debate on law enforcement and the whipping boy of all who blamed the increase in crime on the "coddling of criminals" by such Court decisions.

The Supreme Court took an important step toward clarifying its standards and stepping up its war on police abuses in *Miranda* v. *Arizona* (1966) and three companion cases, all involving the use of confessions obtained by police interrogation without informing the suspects of their right to remain silent and to see counsel. The Court reversed the convictions in all these cases by a vote of five to four, on the ground that incommunicado police detention is inherently coercive. In the process it laid down a stiff code of conduct for police interrogation, including the following requirements:

> 1. A person held in custody for interrogation must first be informed in clear and unequivocal terms that he has the right to remain silent.
> 2. He must be warned that anything he says can and will be used against him in court.
> 3. He must be given the right to consult with counsel prior to questioning and to have counsel present during questioning if he desires.
> 4. Failure to request counsel does not constitute a waiver of the right to have counsel.
> 5. If the accused is unable to secure a lawyer, one must be appointed for him.

The *Miranda* decision added new fuel to the flames started by *Escobedo*. Many law-enforcement officers contended that the new rules would make

it impossible any longer to solve crimes by securing confessions. On the other hand, it was argued that police now concentrate on confessions because that is easier than going out to look for evidence, and that *Miranda* would force them to do a more creative job. Also, several studies purported to show that confessions are not presently involved in the great majority of convictions.

Some commentators who shared the Court's goals were nonetheless critical of the *Miranda* decision, on the ground that the Court had undertaken the essentially legislative task of adopting a complete code of law-enforcement procedures, a responsibility which belongs to legislatures, and on which substantial progress was being made in some areas. But the Supreme Court obviously felt that police malpractices were so widespread that the normal procedure of criticizing past abuses in individual cases was inadequate to correct them, and that consequently it must spell out in detail a code of constitutional conduct for the police. Chief Justice Warren gave assurance that the decision was not intended to hamper the traditional function of police officers in investigating crime; persons not under restraint could be questioned; any statements freely and voluntarily given would be admissible in evidence. He also suggested that the role of confessions in securing convictions had been overplayed; in all four of these cases there was very good evidence against the suspects besides the confessions. Finally, he encouraged "Congress and the States to continue their laudable search for increasingly effective ways of protecting the rights of the individual while promoting efficient enforcement of our criminal laws."

One week after *Miranda*, the Court held in *Johnson* v. *New Jersey* (1966) that neither the *Escobedo* nor the *Miranda* decision was to be applied retroactively. Law-enforcement agencies had fairly relied on prior cases in obtaining incriminating statements during the years preceding these two cases, and retroactivity in their application would seriously disrupt administration of the criminal laws, the Court held; but they would apply to prosecutions begun after the cases were announced. For persons whose trials were already completed, the case law on coerced confessions would still be available as a basis for appeals.[49]

[49] In *Davis* v. *North Carolina* (1966) the *Miranda* standards were used as a factor in judging voluntariness of a confession, even though the trial took place prior to *Miranda*. The Court declined to accept a case, *DeJoseph* v. *Connecticut* (1966), raising the issue whether the right to counsel applies in misdemeanor cases. In *United States* v. *Wade* (1967) and *Gilbert* v. *California* (1967) the Court held that a defendant has a constitutional right to have counsel present if he is required to take part in a police lineup for identification before trial, but did not question the constitutionality of the lineup technique itself. "We have no doubt that compelling the accused merely to exhibit his person for observation by a prosecution witness prior to trial involves no compulsion on the accused to give evidence having testimonial significance." The *Gilbert* case also ruled that the taking of handwriting samples before the defendant saw his lawyer was not a violation of any constitutional right. In

## INDICTMENT BY GRAND JURY

English practices with respect to indictment by grand jury and trial by jury, which were still in process of transition in the period of colonization, were not transferred bodily to the New World. There was initially a period of pronounced hostility toward the legal profession and its methods, and the law was applied in a rude and nontechnical fashion. There thus arose "the great difference between the limits of the jury trial in different States" that Alexander Hamilton commented on in *The Federalist*, No. 83, with the result that "no general rule could have been fixed upon by the Convention which would have corresponded with the circumstances of all the States." Consequently in its provisions for federal criminal prosecutions the Constitution made no mention of the grand jury whatever. The Fifth Amendment filled in this gap by the provision that "no person shall be held to answer for a capital or otherwise infamous crime, unless on a presentment or indictment of a grand jury."

The purpose of the grand jury provision is to require prosecuting officers to prove to a body of laymen that there is a prima facie case of criminal violation so that citizens will not be subjected to the expense and indignity of a criminal trial without reasonable cause. If the grand jury finds the evidence sufficiently strong, it votes an indictment or a "true bill."

This is one area where the states are not required to follow federal standards. In some twenty-eight states the grand jury has been abolished,[50] and a prosecuting officer may bring a person to trial by filing an "information" against him. The Supreme Court upheld this practice in *Hurtado* v. *California* (1884), and has never reversed this decision.


## TRIAL BY JURY

The Constitution provides for jury trials in criminal cases by the Sixth Amendment (and also by Article III, section 2, of the original Constitution), and in civil cases "where the value in controversy shall exceed twenty dollars" by the Seventh Amendment. Since the Sixth Amendment merely says that the accused "shall enjoy the right" to a trial by jury, jury trial in federal courts is not an institutional requirement, but only a "valuable privilege" which a person accused of crime may forego at his election. However, "before any waiver can become effective, the consent of government counsel and the sanction of the court must be had, in addition to

---

*Mempa* v. *Rhay* (1967) the Court extended the requirement of counsel to post-trial hearings where revocation of probation would result in substantial confinement.

[50] England, the land of its birth, has also abolished the grand jury. The Fifth Amendment of the United States Constitution specifically waives the grand jury requirement for "cases arising in the land or naval forces, or in the militia, when in actual service in time of war or public danger."

the express and intelligent consent of the defendant." [51] Waiver may be made by the accused in an informal manner, without the use of a written instrument, and without the advice of counsel.

The right to trial by jury in federal criminal cases has been held to be limited to those who, under the Fifth Amendment, are subject to indictment or presentment by grand jury. This means that there is a class of petty crimes for which jury trial cannot be claimed, but exactly where the line is to be drawn has caused the courts some trouble. Other situations in which jury trial may not be claimed include charges of criminal contempt of court [52] and petitions for the writ of habeas corpus; deportation proceedings for aliens and disbarment proceedings for attorneys, which are civil, not criminal; and extradition proceedings, which are administrative, not judicial. Moreover, trials by courts-martial are not affected by the Sixth Amendment, the provision of the Fifth Amendment waiving the grand jury requirement "in the land or naval forces" having been also read into the Sixth. [53]

In *Patton* v. *United States* (1930) the Supreme Court stated the three essential elements in trial by jury as trial by a panel of twelve, supervision by a judge, and unanimity of verdict. Elimination of any of these elements, the Court said, would constitute a denial of the constitutional right to jury trial. In the *Patton* case, one of the jurors had become incapacitated during the trial and both sides stipulated that it should proceed with eleven jurors, with court approval. The Supreme Court ruled that waiving one member was the same as waiving the entire jury, however. It is similarly clear that any effort to tamper with the unanimous verdict requirement would be unconstitutional, and the presence of the same judge throughout the trial is also a mandatory requirement.

The jury, according to the amendment, must be "impartial." This raises the whole question of jury composition and method of selection. Bias, although difficult to guard against, may be thought of (1) as being simply a matter of opinion, or (2) as growing out of or being associated with social or economic status of jurors. Bias in the first sense is protected against by the right to challenge prospective jurors for cause. At the Aaron Burr trial for treason, his attorney argued that a juror to be selected must have a mind

---

[51] *Patton* v. *United States* (1930). The requirement that the government consent to a defendant's waiver of a jury trial was upheld in *Singer* v. *United States* (1965). In 1967 a federal district judge held the federal kidnapping law unconstitutional because it would discourage a defendant from asserting his right to trial by jury; the law specified the death penalty for a kidnapper who harmed his victim, provided "the verdict of the jury shall so recommend." The possibility of a death penalty could be avoided by waiving a jury trial. The Supreme Court agreed with this position in *United States* v. *Jackson* (1968).

[52] But see the conditions under which jury trials may be required in criminal contempt cases, in *United States* v. *Barnett* (1964) and *Cheff* v. *Schnackenberg* (1966).

[53] *Ex parte Milligan* (1866).

"perfectly indifferent and free from prejudice," but Chief Justice Marshall said this was too stringent a standard. A closed mind would be objectionable, but casual opinions on the subject should not disqualify a venireman. Obviously the challenged bias must have some direct relation to the issues of the case; thus a person who has conscientious scruples against the death penalty is generally excluded from the jury in a capital case.

The main protection against bias resulting from a juror's race or employment or class status is the principle that no intentional discrimination against any group or sector of the population is to be permitted in jury selection. The Supreme Court has struck down restrictive practices in federal jury selection, even when their purpose was benign.[54] Exclusion of women from federal juries was condemned in *Ballard* v. *United States* (1946). The 1949 Smith Act prosecution of Communist Party leaders in New York was bogged down for seven weeks by defense efforts to establish that poor people, manual workers, Negroes, Jews, women, and members of the Communist and American Labor parties were deliberately excluded from federal jury panels in New York, in favor of "rich, propertied and well-to-do." Judge Medina found there had been no such deliberate or planned discrimination, and the trial then proceeded.

Practices in federal jury selection are not uniform. A 1961 Justice Department survey showed the ninety-two federal district courts had ninety-two systems of selecting juries. Two of the commonly used methods violate the cross-section principle. One is the "key man" system, under which outstanding citizens recommend the veniremen; this method was held unconstitutional by a federal court of appeals in *Rabinowitz* v. *United States* (1966). The second is to draw the venire from available lists—of telephone subscribers, voters, property owners, even church members. The Johnson administration proposed a federal jury reform bill in 1967 which would require random selection of jurors from voter registration lists.[55] The American Civil Liberties Union contends that the best procedure is the survey system, the method used by public opinion pollsters in surveying the population.

A special problem in impartiality concerns the service of government employees on federal juries, a matter of great importance in the District of Columbia. In criminal and other cases to which the government is a party, the question has been raised as to whether government employees can be

---

[54] In *Thiel* v. *Southern Pacific Co.* (1946) the practice invalidated was that of automatically excusing from jury service all persons working for a daily wage, since the fee for jurors was inadequate to compensate them for loss of wages. In *Glasser* v. *United States* (1942) the Court indicated that intentional selection of jurors from among women who had taken League of Women Voters "jury classes" would not be approved.

[55] The bill was enacted into law in March, 1968. It requires random selection from "a fair cross section of the community," and bars discrimination on account of race, color, religion, sex, national origin, or economic status.

free from bias in favor of the government.[56] In *Dennis* v. *United States* (1950) the Supreme Court upheld the conviction of a well-known Communist by a jury which included seven government employees. Justice Frankfurter, dissenting, felt that it was simply recognizing "the facts of life" to see that government employees would be "peculiarly susceptible" to the pressures generated by antagonism toward a politically unpopular group.

JURY TRIAL IN STATE COURTS     As in the case of grand juries, the Supreme Court has permitted the states to follow trial jury practices different from those in the federal courts. *Maxwell* v. *Dow* (1900) held that state trial juries can be composed of fewer than twelve. But both the due process clause and the equal protection clause require the Supreme Court to review state jury selection practices where charges of discrimination are made.

The chief problems, both in the selection of grand and trial juries, have resulted from discrimination against Negroes. As early as 1880, a Virginia judge charged with excluding Negroes from jury lists because of their race and color was found guilty of denying equal protection.[57] In the same year, a West Virginia statute requiring juries to be composed exclusively of white male citizens was likewise held unconstitutional.[58] However, where a state statute made no discrimination against Negroes, the fact that no Negroes had sat on the grand and trial juries in a murder case was not a constitutional objection to conviction. Petitioners had no right to have Negroes on the jury, the Court said.[59] Thus, so long as open discrimination against Negroes was avoided, it was possible for the Southern states to follow a successful exclusion policy based on practice and custom.

This system operated undisturbed by the Supreme Court until 1935, when it was challenged in *Norris* v. *Alabama*, known as the *Second Scottsboro* case. Following the Supreme Court's reversal in the first case on grounds of denial of counsel, a second trial had been held in another county and the defendants again convicted. This second conviction was attacked on the ground that Negroes were systematically excluded from the grand jury in the county where the indictment was found, and from the trial jury in the county where the trial was held. The Supreme Court unanimously sustained this contention, finding that in each of the two counties no Negroes had ever been called for jury service within the memory of the oldest inhabitants or any officer of the courts. This was in spite of the fact that there were Negro citizens in each county well able to render jury service, and that Negro citizens had been called on to serve

---

[56] See *Crawford* v. *United States* (1909); *United States* v. *Wood* (1936); *Frazier* v. *United States* (1948).
[57] *Ex parte Virginia* (1880).
[58] *Strauder* v. *West Virginia* (1880).
[59] *Virginia* v. *Rives* (1880).

on federal juries in that district. "For this long-continued, unvarying, and wholesale exclusion of Negroes from jury service," Chief Justice Hughes concluded, "we find no justification consistent with the constitutional mandate." The great advance of the *Norris* decision was that it permitted discriminatory practices to be inferred from the facts showing the actuality of unequal treatment.

The *Norris* rule was a fairly clear one, and for a time it took care of the situation.[60] Soon, however, things got more complicated as techniques were developed for evading the spirit of the Court's rulings. In the case of *Akins* v. *Texas* (1945) the jury commissioners had carefully placed one Negro on the grand jury. The commissioners freely admitted that the limitation of Negro representation to one juror was intentional, but the Supreme Court was unable to find any loophole in this technical compliance with constitutional requirements. Mathematical exactitude or proportional representation of races or groups, the Court said, was not required to meet the equal protection guarantee.

The authority of the *Akins* ruling was subsequently impaired by the somewhat confused decision in *Cassell* v. *Texas* (1950). Four justices held the proceedings illegal because the commissioners admitted that they chose jurymen only from among those with whom they were personally acquainted, and that they knew no available Negroes who were qualified. Three other justices, including Frankfurter, who had supported the *Akins* ruling, reached the same result, but on the ground that in twenty-one consecutive grand jury panels there had never been more than one Negro. To them this fact demonstrated that the commissioners believed the presence of one Negro on the panel satisfied the Supreme Court's standards. What the Court actually required, Frankfurter said, was a basis of selection that did not "consciously take color into account." Arbitrary limitation is "purposeful discrimination." [61]

The Court found discrimination to exist in *Avery* v. *Georgia* (1952), where the names of prospective Negro jurors were placed in the jury box on yellow tickets, and in *Whitus* v. *Georgia* (1967), where the names of prospective jurors were selected from the books of the county tax receiver, which were maintained on a racially segregated basis. But it seems evident that Supreme Court decisions alone will not end racial discrimination in jury selection in numerous Southern counties. The administration's civil rights bill in 1966 contained provisions prohibiting racial discrimination in the selection of state jurors, but it was defeated in Congress.

[60] See *Smith* v. *Texas* (1940); *Hill* v. *Texas* (1942); *Eubanks* v. *Louisiana* (1958).

[61] In *Brown* v. *Allen* (1953) the Court approved selection of jurors from taxpayers' lists. Negroes amounted to 33 per cent of the county's population, but only 16 per cent of the taxpayers. The Court majority thought this was a "good faith effort to secure competent juries" which should not be condemned "merely because of varying racial proportions."

In 1954 the Supreme Court for the first time extended the rule against racial discrimination in jury composition to a group other than Negroes. *Hernandez* v. *Texas* presented the allegation that persons of Mexican descent were systematically excluded from jury service in Jackson County, Texas, and the Supreme Court unanimously agreed. The state contended that only two classes—white and Negro—existed within the contemplation of the Fourteenth Amendment. Chief Justice Warren gave a sociological reply:

> Throughout our history differences in race and color have defined easily identifiable groups which have at times required the aid of the courts in securing equal treatment under the laws. But community prejudices are not static, and from time to time other differences from the community norm may define other groups which need the same protection. Whether such a group exists within a community is a question of fact. When the existence of a distinct class is demonstrated, and it is further shown that the laws, as written or as applied, single out that class for different treatment not based on some reasonable classification, the guarantees of the Constitution have been violated.

*Fay* v. *New York* (1947) tested the constitutionality of New York's so-called "blue-ribbon" juries.[62] A conviction was attacked on the ground that laborers, operatives, craftsmen, foremen, and service employees were "intentionally and deliberately excluded" from the jury. It was contended that the panel was chosen "with a purpose to obtain persons of conservative views, persons of the upper economic and social stratum in New York County, persons having a tendency to convict defendants accused of crime, and to exclude those who might understand the point of view of the laboring man." Statistical tables were submitted comparing the occupational distribution in New York County with that of the special jury panel, and the underrepresentation of manual workers on the panel was quite apparent. However, Justice Jackson for the Court majority held that there was no proof of a deliberate purpose to discriminate against this group, and went on:

> Even in the Negro cases, this Court has never undertaken to say that a want of proportionate representation of groups, which is not proved to be deliberate and intentional, is sufficient to violate the Constitution. . . . If the Court has hesitated to require proportional representation where but two groups need be considered and identification of each group is fairly clear, how much more imprudent would it be to require proportional representation of economic classes.

### THE SIXTH AMENDMENT

The Sixth Amendment spells out certain other protections of the trial procedure. An accused is entitled to a "speedy and public trial." Trials have been challenged for lack of speed rather infrequently. Of necessity speed

---

[62] Blue-ribbon juries were abolished in New York in 1965.

is a relative concept, subordinate to the broader protections of the amendment. But it was this provision which terminated the trial of John David Provoo in 1955 for alleged treasonous activities in aid of the Japanese during World War II. The presiding judge held that a fair trial could not be had in 1955 on charges brought in 1949 for acts alleged to have been committed in 1942–1945, where the defendant had already been held in jail for five years and afforded no opportunities to locate or interview witnesses, many of whom had died in the meantime.[63]

In *Klopfer* v. *North Carolina* (1967) the Court held that the speedy trial provision of the Sixth Amendment is also applicable to the states. A university professor's 1964 trial for a sit-in trespass had resulted in a hung jury. Over a year later the prosecutor secured a *nolle prosequi* order (meaning that he did not at that time intend to prosecute the case further), but with leave to reinstate the indictment. Thus the threat that he might be tried at a later time was left hanging over Klopfer. The Court held that such unjustified postponement of trial was a denial of the right to a speedy trial, "which is as fundamental as any of the rights secured by the Sixth Amendment."

The requirement of the Sixth Amendment that "the accused shall enjoy the right . . . to be informed of the nature and cause of the accusation" is intended to make it possible for the defendant to prepare his defense adequately. Failure to meet this standard may be the result of either the statute defining the crime or the indictment charging it. However, vagueness in the statute is more properly attacked on the basis of the due process clause of the Fifth Amendment, thus limiting the purview of the Sixth Amendment to the indictment process.

A case illustrating this feature of the Sixth Amendment was the government's prosecution of Owen Lattimore on charges growing out of his testimony before a Senate subcommittee under Senator McCarthy's chairmanship. Lattimore was indicted on seven counts of perjury, the key count being that he had lied when he testified that he had never been "a sympathizer, or any other kind of promoter of Communism or Communist interests." In 1953 District Judge Youngdahl dismissed this count as vague and indefinite, a ruling which was upheld by the court of appeals. The government then secured a new two-count indictment, charging that Lattimore had lied when he denied that he was a follower of the Communist line or a promoter of Communist interests. In 1955 Judge Youngdahl dismissed both counts, saying: "To require defendant to go to trial for perjury under charges so formless and obscure as those before the Court would be unprecedented and would make a sham of the Sixth Amendment and the Federal rule requiring specificity of charges."[64]

[63] *United States* v. *Provoo* (1955). But see *Pollard* v. *United States* (1957) and *United States* v. *Ewell* (1966).
[64] *United States* v. *Lattimore* (1954, 1955).

The right to be informed of the nature and cause of the accusation also has some relevance to the Supreme Court's insistence that criminal statutes must be sufficiently specific in their terms to define and give adequate notice of the kind of conduct which they forbid. This is the familiar rule that criminal statutes may be held "void for vagueness." The applicable principle has been stated by the Supreme Court:

> That the terms of a penal statute creating a new offense must be sufficiently explicit to inform those who are subject to it what conduct on their part will render them liable to its penalties, is a well-recognized requirement, consonant alike with ordinary notions of fair play and the settled rules of law. And a statute which either forbids or requires the doing of an act in terms so vague that men of common intelligence must necessarily guess at its meaning and differ as to its application, violates the first essential of due process of law.[65]

The Sixth Amendment right of a defendant "to be confronted with the witnesses against him" was held in *Pointer* v. *Texas* (1965) to be a "fundamental right" obligatory on the states. Here the transcript of testimony given by a witness at the preliminary hearing was introduced at the trial because the witness had left the state and was unavailable to testify. The Supreme Court ruled that this denied the defendant's right to confront the witness and cross-examine him by counsel.[66]

In *Turner* v. *Louisiana* (1965) the jury during a three-day period of sequestration in a murder trial was in the charge of two deputy sheriffs who were also witnesses for the state. The Court held that this close association undermined the basic guarantees of trial by jury, including confrontation and cross-examination.[67]

The Immigration and Nationality Act of 1952 automatically, without prior judicial or administrative proceedings, imposed the penalty of forfeiture of citizenship on persons who, in time of war or emergency, leave or remain outside the United States to evade military service. In *Kennedy* v. *Mendoza-Martinez* (1963) the Court held this provision void as withholding a cluster of rights guaranteed by the Fifth and Sixth Amendments, namely, notice, confrontation, trial by jury, compulsory process for obtaining witnesses, and aid of counsel.

The unique "one-man grand jury" system of Michigan was held by the Court in *In re Oliver* (1948) to deny several Sixth Amendment trial rights.

[65] *Connally* v. *General Construction Co.* (1926). For illustrative decisions see *Lanzetta* v. *New Jersey* (1939) and *Winters* v. *New York* (1948). In *Bouie* v. *Columbia* (1964) sit-in convictions were reversed not because of vague statutory language but because of "unforeseeable and retroactive judicial expansion of narrow and precise statutory language."

[66] See also *Douglas* v. *Alabama* (1965); *Brookhart* v. *Janis* (1966); *Smith* v. *Illinois* (1968).

[67] Similarly in *Parker* v. *Gladden* (1966) the Court voided a conviction where a court bailiff assigned to shepherd the sequestered jury had made prejudicial comments about the defendant to the jury members.

The case arose when a Michigan judge, sitting as a grand jury, concluded that a witness testifying before him in a secret session was not telling the truth. He thereupon assumed his role as judge, and with no break in the proceedings, charged the witness with contempt, immediately convicted him, and sentenced him to sixty days in jail. The only other persons present during this weird procedure were two other judges who sat as advisers, plus the court staff. The trial had, of course, proceeded without counsel, but there had also been a failure to give the accused anything definite as to the nature and cause of the accusation against him—the charge was that his story did not "jell." Moreover, although this charge was based in part on testimony of another witness before the judge–grand jury the same day, the accused was denied any opportunity to be confronted with the witnesses against him. On all these points the Supreme Court held the proceeding unconstitutional.

Finally, the Sixth Amendment right of a defendant to have compulsory process for obtaining witnesses in his favor was held in *Washington* v. *Texas* (1967) to be incorporated into the due process clause and made binding on the states.

## DUE PROCESS, FAIR TRIAL, AND EQUAL PROTECTION

Both federal and state trials are subject to requirements of fairness which may be grounded in general conceptions of due process or equal protection rather than in the more specific procedural language of the Bill of Rights. It is a denial of due process if a prosecutor knowingly offers false evidence or suppresses evidence favorable to a defendant.[68] In *Miller* v. *Pate* (1967) a sex-murder conviction was reversed because the prosecutor had deliberately misrepresented paint on a pair of men's shorts as blood.[69]

A conviction based on insufficient evidence, or totally devoid of evidentiary support, is a denial of due process. In *Thompson* v. *Louisville* (1960) a conviction for loitering and disorderly conduct and in *Garner* v. *Louisiana* (1961) a conviction for disturbing the peace by a civil rights sit-in were held completely devoid of support in the evidence. Moreover, due process limits the power of Congress or state legislatures to make the proof of one fact or group of facts evidence of the ultimate fact on which guilt is predicated.[70]

The Supreme Court's concern for equal protection has been manifested

---

[68] *Mooney* v. *Holohan* (1935).

[69] See also *Giles* v. *Maryland* (1967) involving suppression of evidence in a rape case.

[70] *Tot* v. *United States* (1943). *United States* v. *Romano* (1965) held unconstitutional a federal statute providing that the mere presence of a person at an illegal still should be deemed sufficient evidence to authorize conviction for possession and custody of the still, unless the defendant explained such presence to the satisfaction of the jury.

in a series of decisions aiming to ensure that indigence will not be a bar to taking appeals from criminal convictions. The leading case is *Griffin* v. *Illinois* (1956), which held it unconstitutional discrimination for a state to furnish free stenographic transcripts of trials only for review of constitutional questions and to indigent defendants under death sentence. This restriction prevented other defendants, unable to purchase a transcript, from exercising their right to appellate review.[71]

In *Douglas* v. *California* (1963) the Court for similar reasons struck down a state criminal procedure under which appellate courts could deny an indigent's request for appointment of counsel if they believed the appointment would be valueless.[72] *Swenson* v. *Bosler* (1967) held that poor defendants must be provided with lawyers when they appeal to higher state courts, even if they do not specifically request such aid.

*Tumey* v. *Ohio* (1927) held that a fair trial was denied because the judge had a pecuniary interest in finding the defendant guilty. By a state statute the mayor of every city in Ohio had jurisdiction to try bootlegging offenses committed anywhere in his county, and half the fines collected went to the municipal treasury. In this case the city had an ordinance providing that the mayor should receive, in addition to his salary, the amount of his costs in such cases. Costs were payable by the defendant only in case of conviction, and it was contended that this monetary interest in a conviction disqualified the mayor from sitting. The Supreme Court upheld this claim, Chief Justice Taft saying: "It certainly violates the Fourteenth Amendment, and deprives a defendant in a criminal case of due process of law, to subject his liberty or property to the judgment of a court the judge of which has a direct, personal, substantial, pecuniary interest in reaching a conclusion against him in his case." [73]

A more complex problem of Supreme Court supervision over state criminal justice arises when the charge of unfairness in the trial is based on allegations that the verdict was affected by outside pressures not apparent on the record. There was a slogan on the frontier, "Give him a fair trial and then hang him." Is a lynching transformed into a fair trial when the requisite forms of legal action are gone through?

This was a question the Supreme Court first encountered in *Frank* v.

[71] See also *Burns* v. *Ohio* (1959) and *Douglas* v. *Green* (1960). *Rinaldi* v. *Yeager* (1966) held that the cost of transcripts cannot be taken from the prison wages of indigents subsequent to failure of an appeal. See generally the note, "Discrimination Against the Poor and the Fourteenth Amendment," 81 *Harvard Law Review* 435–453 (1967).

[72] See also *Draper* v. *Washington* (1963); *Lane* v. *Brown* (1963); *Anders* v. *California* (1967); *Entsminger* v. *Iowa* (1967).

[73] See also *In re Murchison* (1955). In *Giaccio* v. *Pennsylvania* (1966) the Court declared invalid a state law allowing juries to assess court costs against persons charged with misdemeanors and found not guilty. Justice Stewart said that allowing a jury to punish a defendant after finding him not guilty "violates the most rudimentary concept of due process of law."

*Mangum* (1915). Frank, a native New Yorker, had gone to Georgia to manage a factory owned by his uncle. In 1913 he was convicted of the murder of a girl who worked in the plant. The trial was conducted in an atmosphere poisonous with anti-Semitism and hatred of "foreigners" from New York. After appeals to the state courts had failed, a writ of habeas corpus was sought from the federal district court, on grounds of mob domination of the trial. The Supreme Court upheld the lower court's refusal to intervene, saying that the findings of the state supreme court, far removed from the atmosphere of the trial, must be accepted.

Justices Holmes and Hughes did not think so. This was a habeas corpus action which "cuts through all forms and goes to the very tissue of the structure. It comes in from the outside, not in subordination to the proceedings, and although every form may have been preserved opens the inquiry whether they have been more than an empty shell." Holmes went on to say that "mob law does not become due process of law by securing the assent of a terrorized jury." The proof of mob law here was that the trial judge had requested the defendant and his lawyers not to be in the courtroom when the verdict was brought in, because of the "probable danger of violence" if there was an acquittal or disagreement, and Holmes continued: "It is our duty . . . to declare lynch law as little valid when practiced by a regularly drawn jury as when administered by one elected by a mob intent on death." That Holmes was right about the temper of the proceedings was tragically proved a little later when Frank, under sentence of death, was taken from the state prison farm and lynched.

Eight years later, in *Moore* v. *Dempsey* (1923), Holmes had a chance to repeat these views in a majority opinion which, in effect, though not in terms, overruled the *Frank* decision. There had been race riots and a reign of terror in Arkansas. The Holmes opinion, as Max Lerner says, gives rapid glimpses of the entire pattern of power and opinion in the sharecropping South: "the attempts to organize in the face of landowner terrorism, the meeting in the Negro church, the armed attack, the manhunt by vigilantes, the lynching mob, the Committee of Seven, the torturing of witnesses, the intimidation of counsel, the skeleton trial, the resolutions by the American Legion and Rotary and Lions Clubs, the attempts to appease the mob spirit by hastening execution." [74]

These were the facts. Now what was the law? Was habeas corpus available? Certainly it should not be used to correct "mere mistakes of law" in the course of the trial.

> But if the case is that the whole proceeding is a mask—that counsel, jury and judge were swept to the fatal end by an irresistible wave of public passion, and that the State Courts failed to correct the wrong, neither perfection in the machinery for correction nor the possibility that

[74] Max Lerner, *The Mind and Faith of Justice Holmes* (Boston: Little, Brown and Company, 1946), p. 347.

the trial court and counsel saw no other way of avoiding an immediate outbreak of the mob can prevent this Court from securing to the petitioners their constitutional rights.

*Kent* v. *United States* (1966) and *Application of Gault* (1967) dealt with the issue of procedural protections in juvenile courts. The general conception of such courts has been that the state is acting through them as *parens patriae* and not as adversary, and that the proceedings against juveniles are civil and not criminal. Consequently it has been the usual practice that the child is not entitled to the constitutional rights of adult offenders, such as bail, indictment, public or jury trial, immunity against self-incrimination, or counsel. He can claim only the fundamental due process right to fair treatment.

In the *Kent* case the juvenile court of the District of Columbia had waived without a hearing its jurisdiction over a sixteen-year-old boy accused of housebreaking, robbery, and rape, thus permitting him to be indicted and tried in the regular courts where the maximum sentence for these crimes was much greater, including the possibility of execution. The Supreme Court ruled that a valid waiver order under these circumstances required at least a hearing, access by counsel to the reports considered by the juvenile court judge, and a statement of reasons for the decision to waive jurisdiction. Justice Fortas in the course of his opinion expressed concern that a child in juvenile courts might be receiving "the worst of both worlds: that he gets neither the protections accorded to adults nor the solicitous care and regenerative treatment postulated for children."

The Court went farther in the *Gault* case, where a fifteen-year-old boy who had made a lewd telephone call was committed to the state industrial school as a delinquent, with the possibility of remaining there until the age of twenty-one. For an adult, the maximum punishment for such an offense would have been a fine of $50 or imprisonment for not more than two months. The boy's parents brought a habeas corpus action, alleging that they had been given inadequate notice of the charges, that the complainant had not testified, that they had not been offered the assistance of counsel, that the boy had not been warned his testimony could be used against him, that no transcript had been made of the trial, and that Arizona law did not permit appeal of a juvenile court decision.

Justice Fortas, though recognizing the benign purposes which the informal procedures of juvenile courts had been intended to achieve, felt that the intelligent enforcement of due process standards would not compel the states to displace the substantive benefits of the juvenile process and would correct such grievous disregard of procedural protections as was demonstrated by this case. "Under our Constitution," said Fortas, "the condition of being a boy does not justify a kangaroo court." Specifically, he held that in a juvenile proceeding there must be notice of charges; notice of right to be represented by counsel and appointment of counsel if the parents are

unable to afford counsel; the right to confront and cross-examine complainants and other witnesses; and adequate warning of the privilege against self-incrimination and the right to remain silent. Justice Stewart, the only outright dissenter, charged that the decision converted juvenile proceedings into criminal prosecutions and was inviting "a long step backwards into the nineteenth century."

The conviction of an accused person while he is legally incompetent violates due process,[75] and state procedures must be adequate to protect this right.[76] The first formulation of an insanity test for judging criminal responsibility was the "right-wrong" criterion promulgated in *M'Naghten's Case* (1843), namely, that "at the time of the committing of the act, the party accused was labouring under such a defect of reason, from disease of the mind, as not to know the nature and quality of the act he was doing; or, if he did know it, that he did not know he was doing what was wrong." The federal courts adopted the *M'Naghten* rule, and then supplemented it with the "irresistible impulse" test after this modification had been approved by the Supreme Court in *Davis* v. *United States* (1895).

This remained the basis for judging criminal responsibility in all the federal courts until 1954, when the District of Columbia Court of Appeals adopted a new test for insanity in *Durham* v. *United States*. This rule was "simply that an accused is not criminally responsible if the unlawful act was the product of mental disease or mental defect." The *Durham* rule set off a vigorous debate, but was not adopted by other courts and was expressly repudiated by three federal circuits. *Durham* was criticized because of the inherent vagueness in its terms, its overemphasis on the causal relationship between "disease" and "product," and its lack of utility for juries, which must make a social judgment, not a medical analysis.

In 1961 the Court of Appeals for the Third Circuit in *United States* v. *Currens* proposed another test, somewhere between *M'Naghten* and *Durham*, which was intended to utilize the newer psychological knowledge and still be meaningful to a jury of laymen. The *Currens* test is this: "The jury must be satisfied that at the time of committing the prohibited act the defendant, as a result of mental disease or defect, lacked substantial capacity to conform his conduct to the requirements of the law which he is alleged to have violated." The Supreme Court had not by 1968 expressed its opinion in this very difficult field.

### DOUBLE JEOPARDY

The Fifth Amendment in archaic language forbids the government to put any person twice "in jeopardy of life or limb" for the same offense. The underlying idea, as Justice Black has said, "is that the State with all its

[75] *Bishop* v. *United States* (1956).
[76] *Pate* v. *Robinson* (1966).

resources and power should not be allowed to make repeated attempts to convict an individual for an alleged offense, thereby subjecting him to embarrassment, expense and ordeal and compelling him to live in a continuing state of anxiety and insecurity, as well as enhancing the possibility that even though innocent he may be found guilty." [77] Enforcement of this provision depends upon the views taken as to what constitutes "jeopardy" in a legal proceeding, and what constitutes "sameness" in an offense.

On the first question, an accused person has of course been placed in jeopardy when he has been tried by a court of competent jurisdiction and either acquitted or convicted. The government may not appeal such a verdict or institute a second prosecution for the same offense.[78] It is not even necessary for a trial to have reached the stage of a verdict to bring the jeopardy rule into operation; otherwise a prosecutor or judge would be able to stop a trial when it began to appear that the jury might not convict, in order to leave the way open for a second trial. On the other hand, when a jury fails to agree on a verdict and is discharged by the judge, a second trial is permissible, the theory being that it is merely a continuation of the first.[79] And trial by a court which is subsequently found to lack jurisdiction cannot place the defendant in jeopardy, no matter how far the proceedings are carried.

The accused may waive his constitutional immunity against double jeopardy. He does this when he requests a new trial, or appeals from a verdict of guilty. If a conviction is set aside on appeal, the defendant may be tried a second time for the same offense,[80] and the accused assumes the risk of receiving a heavier penalty than in the first trial. But according to *Green* v. *United States* (1957), he cannot be subjected to the risk of being convicted on a more serious charge than in the first trial. However, he may be tried on a different theory in the second trial; in *Forman* v. *United States* (1960) a defendant was convicted of a subsidiary conspiracy after the statute of limitations had run on the main conspiracy involved in the first trial.

The "same offense" provision means the same identical offense as defined by the same governmental jurisdiction. The test of identity of offenses is whether the same evidence is required to prove them. If not, the fact that two charges grow out of one transaction does not make a single offense where two or more are defined by the statutes.[81] Thus Congress may provide for both civil and criminal prosecution for the same act or failure to act,

[77] *Green* v. *United States* (1957). Courts-martial are governed by the double jeopardy provision; see *Wade* v. *Hunter* (1949).
[78] When a federal trial judge directs acquittal of a defendant, even though he acts on erroneous grounds, the double jeopardy clause precludes a second trial. *Fong Foo* v. *United States* (1962).
[79] *United States* v. *Perez* (1824).
[80] *United States* v. *Ball* (1896).
[81] *Morgan* v. *Devine* (1915); *United States* v. *Ewell* (1966).

or it may separate a conspiracy to commit a substantive offense from the actual commission of the offense, and attach a different penalty to each. A person who refused to testify before a Senate committee was not subjected to double jeopardy by being punished for contempt of the Senate and also indicted for a misdemeanor for such refusal.[82]

The Narcotic Drugs Act, as amended, provides for three separate offenses in connection with the vending of illicit drugs. In *Gore* v. *United States* (1958) a defendant was convicted of a single sale on each of two separate days under all three provisions, a total of six counts, and was given a separate sentence on each count. The Court held this was not double jeopardy. Decisions like this and *Abbate* v. *United States* (1959), to be considered shortly, led the Attorney General of the United States to announce, as reported in *Petite* v. *United States* (1960), that it would be the general policy of the government not to make several offenses arising from a single transaction the basis of multiple prosecutions.

DOUBLE JEOPARDY IN STATE COURTS     As already noted, *Palko* v. *Connecticut* (1937) held that the federal double jeopardy rule was not binding on the states and that a statute permitting the state to appeal a criminal conviction was not inconsistent with the standard of "ordered liberty."

A bizarre form of double jeopardy problem came to the Court's attention in *Louisiana ex rel. Francis* v. *Resweber* (1947). Francis had been duly convicted of murder and sentenced to death. He was placed in the electric chair, but because of some mechanical difficulty, it did not operate, and the prisoner was returned to his cell. Redress was then sought in the courts on the ground that a second trip to the electric chair would constitute double jeopardy contrary to the Fifth Amendment and cruel and unusual punishment in violation of the Eighth Amendment. The Supreme Court said: "We shall examine the circumstances under the assumption, but without so deciding, that violation of the principles of the Fifth and Eighth Amendments, as to double jeopardy and cruel and unusual punishment, would be violative of the due process clause of the Fourteenth Amendment." The Court was able to leave the constitutional problem in this equivocal state, since it found that, even if the two standards were applicable, they had not been violated.

In two 1958 decisions a double jeopardy problem was raised by the prosecution of different offenses at consecutive trials, even though the crimes arose out of the same occurrence. In *Hoag* v. *New Jersey*, a man who was alleged to have robbed five tavern patrons was tried for the robbery of three of them, and was acquitted because of the unexpected failure of four of the state's witnesses to identify the defendant. The state then tried Hoag for robbery of a fourth patron, who was the only witness at the first trial to

[82] *In re Chapman* (1897).

identify the defendant, and this time the jury convicted. By a five to three vote the Supreme Court upheld the state's action on the ground that, while a single trial would have been "preferable practice," the Fourteenth Amendment did not lay down an inflexible rule making multiple trials unconstitutional, and the circumstances of this case did not result in "fundamental unfairness." Chief Justice Warren, dissenting, thought that the state had relitigated "the same issue on the same evidence before two different juries."

*Ciucci* v. *Illinois* involved a man accused of killing his wife and three children. The initial prosecution for one of the murders brought conviction and a twenty-year sentence. Dissatisfied with this outcome, the prosecutor instituted a second trial for another of the murders, which yielded a forty-five-year sentence. The state then made a third effort, and was finally rewarded by a death sentence. The Court upheld these tactics by a five to four vote.[83]

DOUBLE JEOPARDY IN A FEDERAL SYSTEM    Where both federal and state governments make the same act an offense, the Supreme Court has held that it is not double jeopardy for each government to prosecute and punish. This rule provoked considerable dissatisfaction during the era of national prohibition, but the Court justified dual prosecution in *United States* v. *Lanza* (1922) as resulting from our system of "two sovereignties, deriving power from different sources, capable of dealing with the same subject-matter within the same territory. . . . It follows that an act denounced as a crime by both national and state sovereignties is an offense against the peace and dignity of both."

This principle was developed further in two 1959 decisions. In *Abbate* v. *United States* several individuals who conspired in Illinois to blow up telephone properties in Mississippi were convicted on a conspiracy charge in Illinois, and were subsequently found guilty of the same acts by a federal court in Mississippi. In *Bartkus* v. *Illinois* a man was tried by a federal court for robbery of an Illinois bank and acquitted. He was then indicted for the same crime by an Illinois grand jury, convicted, and sentenced to life imprisonment.

The Supreme Court, by a divided vote, denied that the double jeopardy standard had been violated in either case. The dissenters in *Bartkus* contended that the state prosecution was really a second federal prosecution originated by the federal officers who, defeated in their effort to convict Bartkus in federal court, had induced state authorities to institute the second prosecution and turned over their evidence and their witnesses to the state.

[83] In *Cichos* v. *Indiana* (1966) the Court declined for technical reasons to rule on the claim that the double jeopardy provision was binding on the states.

## EXCESSIVE BAIL

"Excessive bail shall not be required," the Eighth Amendment says, copying a similar provision in the English Bill of Rights of 1689. Bail is the pledge of money or property by an accused person or his sureties in order to guarantee his appearance for trial. Admission to bail provides a means whereby an individual may obtain his freedom while awaiting trial. Apart from humanitarian considerations and the presumption that a person is innocent until proved guilty, it provides the accused with a better opportunity to prepare his defense. The constitutional provision has been construed as a limitation both on Congress, in adopting statutes governing admission to bail, and on federal courts, in fixing bail in individual cases.

The Eighth Amendment does not make admission to bail an absolute right in all circumstances. In the Judiciary Act of 1789, Congress provided that a person arrested for a noncapital offense *shall* be admitted to bail, thereby conceding that bail can be refused in capital cases in the discretion of the judge.

Bail is excessive, the Supreme Court has said, when it is set "at a figure higher than an amount reasonably calculated" to fulfill the purpose of assuring the presence of the accused at the trial.[84] The Federal Rules of Criminal Procedure itemize the factors to be considered by the court in fixing bail as follows: "The nature and circumstances of the offense charged, the weight of the evidence against him, the financial ability of the defendant to give bail and the character of the defendant."

The Supreme Court applied the excessive bail provision in *Stack* v. *Boyle* (1951). Twelve "second-string" Communist leaders had been taken into custody in Los Angeles on Smith Act indictments, and bail of $50,000 fixed for each defendant. The government's reason for asking such high bail was that four Communist leaders convicted a few months earlier in New York had vanished and forfeited their bail. The Supreme Court unanimously held that in the circumstances bail in such amount was excessive, Chief Justice Vinson saying:

> It is not denied that bail for each petitioner has been fixed in a sum much higher than that usually imposed for offenses with like penalties and yet there has been no factual showing to justify such action in this case. The Government asks the courts to depart from the norm by assuming, without the introduction of evidence, that each petitioner is a pawn in a conspiracy and will, in obedience to a superior, flee the jurisdiction. To infer from the fact of indictment alone a need for bail in an unusually high amount is an arbitrary act. Such conduct would inject into our system of government the very principles of totalitarianism which Congress was seeking to guard against in passing the statute under which petitioners have been indicted.

[84] *Stack* v. *Boyle* (1951).

In *Carlson* v. *Landon* (1951) the Court refused to interfere with the Attorney General's denial of bail for active alien Communists held pending determination of their deportability, even though there was no contention that they would attempt to disappear or evade deportation orders. The bail provision of the Eighth Amendment was held inapplicable since deportation is not a criminal proceeding.

Widespread concern about abuses of the bail system led Congress in 1966 to pass the administration-sponsored Bail Reform Act, which requires the release on personal recognizance or on unsecured bond of persons charged with noncapital federal offenses unless a judicial officer finds that release would "not reasonably assure" appearance as required. Bail reform in the states is also underway.

### CRUEL AND UNUSUAL PUNISHMENTS

The Eighth Amendment's ban on "cruel and unusual punishments" outlaws such penalties as torture or lingering death, but under current moral standards does not interfere with summary execution by hanging, shooting, electrocution, or lethal gas. It is conceivable, however, that sentiment might some day develop to the point where capital punishment would be generally regarded as "cruel." Since "cruel" is not a technical term, with a definite meaning at common law at the time of adoption of the Eighth Amendment, it would seem that its interpretation can be modified in the light of changes in public opinion. The constitutional standard, in addition to barring punishments cruel in themselves, also relates to punishments which are out of all proportion to the offense.[85]

In *Trop* v. *Dulles* (1958) Chief Justice Warren held for the Court that imposing loss of citizenship on a member of the Armed Forces convicted by court-martial of wartime desertion was a cruel and unusual punishment. Warren took account of the fact that desertion may be punished by death, but denied that the existence of the death penalty was "a license to the Government to devise any punishment short of death within the limit of its imagination." Conceiving that the basic concept underlying the Eighth Amendment "is nothing less than the dignity of man," the Chief Justice went on to say:

> We believe . . . that use of denationalization as a punishment is barred by the Eighth Amendment. There may be involved no physical mistreatment, no primitive torture. There is instead the total destruction of the individual's status in organized society. It is a form of punishment more primitive than torture, for it destroys for the individual the political existence that was centuries in the development.

A California law making it a crime to be a drug addict was held to be cruel and unusual punishment in *Robinson* v. *California* (1962). The statute

[85] See *Weems* v. *United States* (1910); *Badders* v. *United States* (1916).

did not require any proof that the defendant bought or used drugs or had any in his possession. The mere status of being an addict, which could be established by needle marks in the arm, was sufficient. The Court regarded addiction as an illness rather than a crime, and thought that ninety days in jail for being ill was cruel and unusual punishment.[86]

Capital punishment, abolished by thirteen states, has come under increasing pressure, counsel for condemned defendants in a number of cases arguing that it is cruel and unusual punishment. In *Rudolph v. Alabama* (1963) the Court, with three justices dissenting, denied certiorari in a case where it was contended that the death penalty for a convicted rapist who had not taken or endangered life was cruel and unusual.

Other constitutional objections to the death penalty have been based on due process and equal protection grounds. It is argued that state statutes commonly prescribe no standards for imposition of the death penalty, giving unconstitutionally broad discretion to juries and judges; that persons who object to the death penalty are excluded from juries in capital cases; and that in the South the death sentence for rape is imposed almost exclusively upon Negroes. The Supreme Court in *Witherspoon v. Illinois* (1968) and *Bumper v. North Carolina* (1968) agreed to rule on the second of these contentions, and in *Maxwell v. Bishop* (1967) it ordered a federal court to hear a case presenting the third claim. While it seems unlikely that the Supreme Court will hold capital punishment flatly unconstitutional, some tightening of standards in capital cases seems probable.

### CONCLUSION

Two main themes have emerged from this discussion of the Supreme Court's recent experience with the standards of criminal prosecution. First is the Court's insistence on requiring state standards to be substantially identical with those applicable in federal courts. The Court, which from 1884 to 1961 sought to hold the states only to general standards of due process, fairness, and ordered liberty, has now imposed on the states the more specific requirements of the Fourth Amendment as to unreasonable searches and seizures; the Fifth Amendment privilege against self-incrimination; the Sixth Amendment guarantee of counsel, speedy and public trial, confrontation of witnesses, and compulsory process; and the Eighth Amendment prohibition against cruel and unusual punishments. Double jeopardy seems a likely candidate for addition to this list. Some of these steps were taken by

---

[86] After having refused in *Budd v. California* (1966) to hear an appeal making the contention that criminal conviction of chronic alcoholics constituted cruel and unusual punishment, the Court reversed itself and in *Powell v. Texas* (1967) agreed to hear such a claim. In *In re Andrada* (1965) the Court declined to accept a case claiming that state-ordered sexual sterilization was cruel and unusual punishment.

an unanimous Court; the "right to counsel" decision in *Gideon* is an example. Others were disputed and achieved by five to four decisions.

The constitutional theory by which these new standards for state courts were supported is a matter of importance. The initial effort to make the Bill of Rights effective against the states, we have seen, was based on the assertion that the Fourteenth Amendment had "incorporated" its provisions. But the first success achieved in this direction, the decision in *Gitlow* v. *New York* (1925) making the principles of the First Amendment binding on the states, did not use "incorporation" language. It simply said that the freedoms of the First Amendment were protected against state impairment because they are "fundamental." Later decisions held that the First Amendment was "made applicable" to the states by the Fourteenth or that the Fourteenth had "absorbed" the First.

The objection to the incorporation theory, as Justice Frankfurter, its most vehement latter-day opponent, saw it, was that it was a "mechanical device" by which the provisions of the Bill of Rights were supposed to have been "automatically infused into the Fourteenth Amendment before the ink had dried." [87] Incorporation was incompatible with his conception of the federal system; he believed the states were left free to experiment with criminal procedures except for those that were fundamental to a free society. He did not regard all the provisions of the Fourth through the Eighth Amendments, which he referred to in *Adamson* as rules which "seemed important to Eighteenth Century statesmen," as of equal importance. The Seventh Amendment requirement of jury trial in suits at common law involving more than twenty dollars is a glaring example.

When Justice Cardozo in *Palko* v. *Connecticut* (1937) summed up fifty years of judicial refusal to accept the incorporation position, he explained that the First Amendment values had been "absorbed" into the Fourteenth because they were essential to a system of ordered liberty, whereas those of the Fourth through the Eighth were not then thought to be. Of course this left the way open for a similar "absorption" of these values in case the Court concluded at some later time that they were also essential or fundamental.

This is, in fact, the way the recent revolution in state criminal procedures occurred. In 1949, when *Wolf* v. *Colorado* held that the states may not conduct unreasonable searches and seizures, Justice Frankfurter explained this was because such practices are inconsistent with ordered liberty in a free society. On the other hand, the exclusionary rule applied in the federal courts was held not to be binding on the states in the same decision; it was not basic, and other sanctions were available to the states.

This latter aspect of the *Wolf* decision was reconsidered and reversed in

[87] Felix Frankfurter, "Memorandum on 'Incorporation' of the Bill of Rights into the Due Process Clause of the Fourteenth Amendment," 78 *Harvard Law Review* 746–783 (1965).

*Mapp* v. *Ohio* (1961), which made the exclusionary rule mandatory on the states. Justice Clark's opinion in *Mapp* seemed to rest on an incorporation argument, and it was so interpreted by Justice Harlan, dissenting, who spoke also for Justice Frankfurter. Whereas *Wolf*, he said, had been based on the "principle of privacy" which is at the core of the Fourth Amendment, *Mapp* appeared to make "the Fourth Amendment *as such*" the rule for the states, thus establishing a "precise equivalence . . . between the requirements of the Fourth and Fourteenth Amendments."

If Justice Harlan was correct, this was a foundation on which Justice Black, when he wrote the *Gideon* opinion, could have based a solid incorporationist victory. Black had been the most vehement of the Court's critics of "ordered liberty" and partial absorption. He had repeatedly objected to this "natural law" formula under which judges could substitute their "own concepts of decency and fundamental justice for the language of the Bill of Rights."

But Black did not choose to press his victory, now that the substance of his position had been won. Instead, he "accepted" the assumption of *Betts* v. *Brady* against which he had so long campaigned. The right to counsel was to be effective in the states, not because it was incorporated in the Fourteenth Amendment, but because it was "fundamental and essential to a fair trial." On this reasoning he was able to get a unanimous Court, including Justice Harlan.

However, Harlan's acquiescence was short-lived, for he found the "creeping incorporationism" of *Mapp* at work again in *Ker* v. *California* (1963) and *Malloy* v. *Hogan* (1964). Now he was certain that the Court had abandoned "fundamental fairness" in favor of identical standards for federal and state prosecutions. It is true that Justice Brennan for the Court majority in *Malloy* specifically refused to base his opinion on the incorporation argument (noting that only ten justices in the Court's history had accepted it). But Justice Harlan thought that if this was not incorporationism, it was something just as bad—a holding that "the Due Process Clause of the Fourteenth Amendment is a shorthand directive to this Court to pick and choose among the provisions of the first eight Amendments and apply those chosen, freighted with their entire accompanying body of federal doctrine, to law enforcement in the States."

The second theme, which is obvious from the discussion of the chapter, is the recent Court's strong insistence on the establishment of strict procedural protections in criminal prosecutions. This issue has involved the justices in a fundamental value conflict between the claims of the individual to be put in peril of his life or liberty only in a fashion compatible with fundamental concepts of fairness and the claims of society for the maintenance of order and security. Justices, like other men, attach varying weights to these values, and the contrasting positions are well summed up in the 1953 decision of *Stein* v. *New York*. The Court there held that, even though

a defendant had been deprived in his trial of constitutional rights, he was not entitled to a new trial if the state could show that there was sufficient evidence, apart from that unconstitutionally admitted, to justify the jury in finding guilt. Justice Jackson said: "We are not willing to discredit constitutional doctrines for protection of the innocent by making of them mere technical loopholes for the escape of the guilty. . . . The people of the State are also entitled to due process of law." But for Justices Douglas, Black, and Frankfurter, dissenting, this was a degradation of constitutional protections provided, as Frankfurter said, "not out of tenderness for the accused but because we have reached a certain stage of civilization"—a civilization which, Douglas added, "by respecting the dignity even of the least worthy citizen, raises the stature of all of us."

## SELECTED REFERENCES

ALLEN, FRANCIS A., "Federalism and the Fourth Amendment: A Requiem for Wolf," in Philip B. Kurland (ed.), *The Supreme Court Review: 1961*, pp. 1–48. Chicago: The University of Chicago Press, 1961.

*The Constitution of the United States of America: Analysis and Interpretation*, Sen. Doc. no. 39, 88th Cong., pp. 925–1030, 1214–1278. Washington: Government Printing Office, 1964.

CROSSKEY, WILLIAM W., *Politics and the Constitution in the History of the United States*, chaps. 11, 32. Chicago: The University of Chicago Press, 1953.

DASH, SAMUEL, *The Eavesdroppers*. New Brunswick, N.J.: Rutgers University Press, 1959.

DIAMOND, BERNARD L., "From *M'Naghten* to *Currens* and Beyond," 50 *California Law Review* 189–205 (1962).

DOUGLAS, WILLIAM O., *The Right of the People*. Garden City, N.Y.: Doubleday & Company, Inc., 1958.

FELLMAN, DAVID, *The Defendant's Rights*. New York: Holt, Rinehart and Winston, Inc., 1958.

————, *The Defendant's Rights under English Law*. Madison, Wis.: The University of Wisconsin Press, 1966.

GRISWOLD, ERWIN N., *The Fifth Amendment Today*. Cambridge, Mass.: Harvard University Press, 1955.

HELLER, FRANCIS H., *The Sixth Amendment to the Constitution of the United States*. Lawrence, Kans.: University of Kansas Press, 1951.

HOOK, SIDNEY, *Common Sense and the Fifth Amendment*. New York: Criterion Books, 1957.

HURST, WILLARD, "Treason in the United States," 58, *Harvard Law Review* 226–272, 395–444, 806–857 (1944–1945).

INBAU, FRED E., and JOHN E. REID, *Criminal Interrogation and Confessions*. Baltimore: The Williams and Wilkins Company, 1962.

LANDYNSKI, JACOB W., *Search and Seizure and the Supreme Court.* Baltimore: The Johns Hopkins Press, 1966.

LONG, EDWARD V., *The Intruders: The Invasion of Privacy by Government and Industry.* New York: Frederick A. Praeger, Inc., 1967.

MANSFIELD, JOHN H., "The Albertson Case: Conflict between the Privilege against Self-incrimination and the Government's Need for Information," in Philip B. Kurland (ed.), *The Supreme Court Review: 1966*, pp. 103–166. Chicago: The University of Chicago Press, 1966.

MAYERS, LEWIS, *Shall We Amend the Fifth Amendment?* New York: Harper & Row, Publishers, Incorporated, 1959.

MORRISON, STANLEY, "Does the Fourteenth Amendment Incorporate the Bill of Rights? The Judicial Interpretation," 2 *Stanford Law Review* 140–173 (1949).

MURPHY, WALTER F., *Wiretapping on Trial: A Case Study in the Judicial Process.* New York: Random House, Inc., 1965.

National Legal Aid and Defender Association, *Defender Newsletter.* Chicago: American Bar Center (monthly).

PAULSEN, MONRAD G., "Kent v. United States: The Constitutional Context of Juvenile Cases," in Philip B. Kurland (ed.), *The Supreme Court Review: 1966*, pp. 167–192. Chicago: The University of Chicago Press, 1966.

TREBACH, ARNOLD S., *The Rationing of Justice: Constitutional Rights and the Criminal Process.* New Brunswick, N.J.: Rutgers University Press, 1964.

# 31

## Substantive due process

Due process was, as the term implies, originally a procedural concept. In the preceding chapter its application to control the procedures of criminal prosecutions in federal and state courts was examined. But due process has also developed, in the hands of the Supreme Court, a substantive guise under which it serves as a constitutional limitation, not merely on legislative or executive *procedure,* but on legislative or executive power *to act at all.* How was a procedural concept transformed into a limitation on the substance of governmental power? How did we develop what Crosskey calls this "constitutional heresy"?

### PROCEDURE INTO SUBSTANCE

In *Murray's Lessee* v. *Hoboken Land & Improvement Co.* (1856) Congress was warned that it could not simply adopt any process it chose as due process of law. At almost this same time the first hints of the extension of due process to cover questions of substantive power were given. An 1855 act of the New York Legislature forbade all owners of intoxicating liquors to sell them under any conditions except for medicinal purposes. Storing of such liquors when not designed for sale was forbidden except in dwelling houses. Violation of these provisions was made a misdemeanor, and the liquors involved were declared nuisances to be destroyed by summary

process. This drastic statute left many owners of liquor no alternative but to destroy their own property, for if they waited for the state to destroy it, they would incur penalties for their inaction. The highest New York court, in the 1856 case of *Wynehamer* v. *New York*, held this statute unconstitutional under the state due process clause. The court concluded that the harsh operation of this statute on liquors lawfully owned at the time the act went into effect amounted to an act of destruction not within the power of government to perform, "even by the forms which belong to 'due process of law.'"

This was novel doctrine, which had the potentiality of undermining all legislative power. A dissenting judge in the *Wynehamer* case pointed out that if "property" was so protected by the due process clause, then "liberty" must be equally protected. "It might be urged, with precisely the same pertinency and force, that a statute which prohibits certain vicious actions, and declares them criminal, deprives persons of their liberty, and is therefore in derogation of the constitution." Courts of other states were reluctant to follow the *Wynehamer* lead. The Supreme Court of Rhode Island was fearful of the sterilizing effect of this doctrine of vested rights on social change. "Pushed to its necessary conclusions the argument goes to the extent, that once make out that anything real or personal is property, as everything in a general sense is, and legislation as to its uses and vendability . . . must stop at the precise point at which it stood when the thing first came within the protection of this clause." [1]

Nevertheless the position stated by the *Wynehamer* majority soon began to appear in other influential quarters. In 1857 Chief Justice Taney in the *Dred Scott* case held the Missouri Compromise void because, among other reasons, it violated the due process clause of the Fifth Amendment, saying: "An act of Congress which deprives a citizen of the United States of his liberty or property, merely because he came himself or brought his property into a particular Territory of the United States, and who had committed no offense against the laws, could hardly be dignified with the name of due process of law." This argument had not been made by counsel in the case, and Taney spoke for only two of his colleagues in voicing it. Three other majority justices reached their finding of unconstitutionality on different grounds, while Justice Curtis in his dissent refuted the Taney position, pointing to earlier state and federal laws against the slave trade.

Taney's view as to the power of the due process clause as a defense both of liberty and property against substantive legislative power was to be confirmed by events. The Supreme Court in *Hepburn* v. *Griswold* (1870) set aside the Legal Tender Act of 1862 on the ground, among others, that retroactive application of the law deprived creditors of property without due

---

[1] *State* v. *Paul* (1858); *State* v. *Keeran* (1858); quoted in Edward S. Corwin, *Liberty against Government* (Baton Rouge, La.: Louisiana State University Press, 1948), p. 110.

process of law. However, the authority of the *Hepburn* case was nullified when its holding was reversed two years later, so we must press on a little further to witness the legitimizing of substantive due process at the highest judicial level. In this process our attention turns from the due process clause of the Fifth Amendment to that of the Fourteenth, for it was state legislative action rather than federal which was by all odds the more important in impinging on vested property rights during the latter part of the nineteenth century.

The initial effort to protect property rights under the Fourteenth Amendment was made in the *Slaughter-House Cases* (1873). Counsel for the New Orleans butchers who were attacking the slaughterhouse monopoly granted by state statute was John A. Campbell, former justice of the Supreme Court. He argued that the Fourteenth Amendment had not been intended merely to guarantee the rights of the newly freed Negroes. This purpose was only incidental to the Amendment's broader goal of protecting "laissez-faire individualism." The colonists who settled this continent were seeking "freedom, free action, free enterprise." A monopolistic charter such as was here involved abridged "privileges and immunities," denied "equal protection of the laws," and was a deprivation of "liberty."

Justice Miller's majority opinion was largely confined to the privileges and immunities point. As for due process and equal protection, Miller observed that they had "not been much pressed" by counsel, and he felt that it was "sufficient to say that under no construction" of the due process clause "that we have ever seen, or any that we deem admissible" could the Louisiana law be held "a deprivation of property." There were four dissenters. Justice Field took his stand primarily on the privileges and immunities clause, but Justice Bradley dissented squarely on due process grounds:

> [The] right to choose one's calling is an essential part of that liberty which it is the object of government to protect; and a calling, when chosen, is a man's property and right. Liberty and property are not protected where these rights are arbitrarily assailed. . . . In my view, a law which prohibits a large class of citizens from adopting a lawful employment, or from following a lawful employment previously adopted, does deprive them of liberty as well as property, without due process of law.

Justice Swayne developed the same theme. "Liberty is freedom from all restraints but such as are justly imposed by law. Beyond that line lies the domain of usurpation and tyranny." But who was to determine what restraints might "justly" be imposed by law? This was the question the Court faced four years later in the famous case of *Munn* v. *Illinois* (1877), the first Fourteenth Amendment decision in which both majority and minority concentrated on the due process clause.

An Illinois law fixing the maximum charges for storage of grain in warehouses and elevators had been attacked as taking property without due

process of law. Chief Justice Waite for the majority upheld the statute. The police power of a state legislature, he said, was like the power of the British Parliament, subject only to explicit prohibitions in state or national constitutions. The common law had recognized a category of businesses "affected with a public interest," such as inns, gristmills, and ferries, which "must submit to be controlled by the public for the common good." Whether a business fell within this category was primarily for the legislature to determine. Judicial intervention would be permissible only in cases where the Court was able to say of its own knowledge that no "state of facts could exist" which would justify the legislative conclusion. As for the rates and charges fixed by a legislature for businesses affected with a public interest, they were not subject to judicial review. "For protection against abuses by legislatures the people must resort to the polls, not to the courts."

This decision has generally been regarded as a great victory for liberalism and a judicial refusal to recognize due process as a limit on the substance of legislative regulatory power. Of course that was the immediate result achieved, and Justices Field and Strong protested this statement of legislative supremacy, which they regarded as "subversive" of the rights of property and liberty. But in fact Waite had not denied the claims of substantive due process. That could have been accomplished by a flat rejection of the due process argument, as was done in the *Slaughter-House Cases*. Instead, Waite gave careful consideration to the due process point, and only upheld the legislation after recognizing that a judicial case needed to be made for it on due process grounds, which he did by carving out "businesses affected with a public interest" as an exception to ordinary private property, which could not be so treated.

It must be admitted that this judicial acceptance of substantive due process was not readily apparent, even to the members of the Court, and one year later, in *Davidson* v. *New Orleans* (1878), Justice Miller took the occasion to criticize the efforts of counsel to press this misguided notion of due process on the Supreme Court. He said:

> It is not a little remarkable, that while this provision [due process] has been in the Constitution . . . as a restraint upon the authority of the Federal government, for nearly a century . . . this special limitation upon its powers has rarely been invoked in the judicial forum or the more enlarged theatre of public discussion. But while it has been a part of the Constitution, as a restraint upon the power of the States, only a very few years, the docket of this court is crowded with cases in which we are asked to hold that State courts and State legislatures have deprived their own citizens of life, liberty, or property without due process of law. There is here abundant evidence that there exists some strange misconception of the scope of this provision as found in the Fourteenth Amendment. In fact, it would seem, from the character of many of the cases before us, and the arguments made in them, that the clause under consideration is looked upon as a means of bringing to the test of the

decision of this court the abstract opinions of every unsuccessful litigant in a State court of the justice of the decision against him, and of the merits of the legislation on which such a decision may be founded.

But Miller and Waite were no match for the true believers in substantive due process like Field and Bradley, who knew what they wanted, and soon the Court began to consider openly the "merits" of state legislation.

## THE POLICE POWER: HEALTH, MORALS, AND SAFETY

The police power is simply the power of government to take appropriate action to protect and foster the public welfare. It is one of the residual powers retained by the states in the American constitutional system. The federal government possesses no police power under that name, but as already noted, the commerce, taxing, and other specifically granted powers can be used by the federal government to achieve much the same purposes.

A power so broad, so all-encompassing, was bound to generate countervailing pressures. Traditionally the police power has been employed to deal with nuisances, to combat the spread of disease, to secure public safety, to safeguard public morals. Illness or death, demoralization, destruction of property—these are such obvious social ills that legislation aimed clearly at their prevention need have little fear of meeting judicial tests of constitutionality. Nevertheless, substantive due process demands that judges assess the case for the legislation on the basis of their own independent judgment and not simply accept the legislative certification that the use of the police power was justified.

An early statement of the Court's new position was given by Justice Harlan in *Mugler* v. *Kansas* (1887), where the constitutionality of a state prohibition act was being challenged. The Court had to review the law, Harlan said, because

> . . . not . . . every statute enacted ostensibly for the promotion of [the public welfare] is to be accepted as a legitimate exertion of the police powers of the State. There are, of necessity, limits beyond which legislation cannot rightfully go. . . . The courts are not bound by mere forms, nor are they to be misled by mere pretences. They are at liberty—indeed, are under a solemn duty—to look at the substance of things, whenever they enter upon the inquiry whether the legislature has transcended the limits of its authority. If, therefore, a statute purporting to have been enacted to protect the public health, the public morals, or the public safety, has no real or substantial relation to those objects, or is a palpable invasion of rights secured by the fundamental law, it is the duty of the courts to so adjudge, and thereby give effect to the Constitution.

HEALTH AND WELFARE LEGISLATION   Public health and welfare measures often impose serious limitations on individual liberty, but judicial permis-

siveness has been the rule in their interpretation. No citations need be given to establish the justification of quarantines for contagious diseases, regulations on the sale of dangerous drugs, inspection requirements for restaurants and food processors or handlers, prohibition of the sale of unwholesome or adulterated foods. The Pennsylvania antioleomargarine statute approved in *Powell* v. *Pennsylvania* (1888) was accepted as a health measure, though one might have justifiable doubts that this was the major purpose of the enactment. Justice Harlan, in an orgy of double negatives, ruled that the Court

> . . . cannot adjudge that the defendants' rights of liberty and property . . . have been infringed by the statute of Pennsylvania, without holding that, although it may have been enacted in good faith for the objects expressed in its title, namely, to protect the public health and to prevent the adulteration of dairy products and fraud in the sale thereof, it has, in fact, no real or substantial relation to those objects. . . . The court is unable to affirm that this legislation has no real or substantial relation to such objects.[2]

Reasonable regulation of professions or occupations which have a close relationship to public health, such as doctors, dentists, druggists, nurses, beauticians, barbers, plumbers, and the like, is readily supportable as a protection of the public welfare, for obvious reasons which need not be elaborated. Such regulation, moreover, may extend beyond the basic considerations of health to cover activities only tangentially related.[3] Thus in a well-known decision the Supreme Court upheld an Oregon statute which forbade dentists to advertise in any competitive or spectacular manner. The Court's view was that, under the police power, a state might properly provide safeguards not only against deception, but also against practices tending to demoralize the profession by forcing its members into an unseemly rivalry which would enlarge the opportunities of the least scrupulous.[4]

But there are two Supreme Court decisions which, better than any others, illustrate the presumption of validity which almost automatically attaches to legislation for health purposes. The first is *Jacobson* v. *Massachusetts* (1905), upholding a state requirement of vaccination against smallpox. The

[2] One of the few instances where deference was not given to legislation asserted to have a health purpose was attributable to the ultra-laissez-faire Court of the 1920s. *Weaver* v. *Palmer Brothers* (1926) invalidated a Pennsylvania statute forbidding the use of shoddy in the manufacture of bedding materials, over the protest of Holmes, Brandeis, and Stone.

[3] An exception was the case of *Liggett Co.* v. *Baldridge* (1928), involving a Pennsylvania law requiring all stockholders of a corporation owning drugstores to be licensed pharmacists. The Court said: "The claim, that mere ownership of a drug store by one not a pharmacist bears a reasonable relation to the public health, finally rests upon conjecture, unsupported by anything of substance." Actually the purpose of the statute was to prevent further expansion of chain drugstores, and Holmes and Brandeis voted to uphold it.

[4] *Semler* v. *Oregon State Board of Dental Examiners* (1935).

statute applied to adults in any area where the board of health certified that vaccination was necessary for the public health or safety. Jacobson refused to be vaccinated, contending it was injurious or dangerous. He offered to prove his contentions in court, but his evidence was excluded as incompetent and immaterial.

The Supreme Court, with Brewer and Peckham dissenting, upheld the state court. Justice Harlan for the majority made a most illuminating statement in justification of refusal to listen to Jacobson's evidence. He was quite willing to believe that there were those, some of them perhaps even doctors, who attached little or no value to vaccination. But

> . . . what everybody knows the court must know, and therefore the state court judicially knew, as this court knows, that an opposite theory accords with the common belief and is maintained by high medical authority. We must assume that when the statute in question was passed, the legislature of Massachusetts was not unaware of these opposing theories, and was compelled, of necessity, to choose between them. It was not compelled to commit a matter involving the public health and safety to the final decision of a court or jury. It is no part of the function of a court or a jury to determine which one of two modes was likely to be the most effective for the protection of the public against disease. That was for the legislative department to determine in the light of all the information it had or could obtain.

This did not mean, Harlan continued, that the courts could never question the constitutionality of a legislative decision. "If a statute purporting to have been enacted to protect the public health, the public morals or the public safety, has no real or substantial relation to those objects, or is, beyond all question, a plain, palpable invasion of rights secured by the fundamental law, it is the duty of the courts to so adjudge, and thereby give effect to the Constitution." But here vaccination is not in "palpable conflict" with the Constitution, nor can it be contended that it has no "real or substantial relation" to the public health. "Since then vaccination, as a means of protecting a community against smallpox, finds strong support in the experience of this and other countries, no court, much less a jury, is justified in disregarding the action of the legislature simply because in its or their opinion that particular method was—perhaps or possibly—not the best either for children or adults."

"Presumed validity" clearly gave the right result here, in supporting a legislative measure backed by the great weight of scientific evidence against resistance by the ignorant or the misguided. But suppose that a legislature, enticed by the allurements of allegedly scientific findings, winds up on the side of the crackpots. In that situation we might be less happy with the result achieved by presuming a justification for the legislative action.

Consider the case of *Buck* v. *Bell*, decided in 1927 with only one dissent, and with Justice Holmes writing the Court's opinion. Virginia had a statute

under which persons affected with hereditary insanity, idiocy, imbecility, feeblemindedness, or epilepsy could be subjected to compulsory sexual sterilization. This operation could be performed only on inmates of state institutions, and adequate provisions were made by the statute for notice, hearing, and judicial review before such operations were performed. In this particular case the law was applied to Carrie Buck, a seventeen-year-old "feeble-minded" female inmate of a state institution whose mother was also a "feeble-minded" inmate of the same institution, and who had given birth to an allegedly mentally defective child just before admission to the institution. The contention was that if she were rendered incapable of childbearing, she could be released from the institution and become self-supporting. In the judicial proceedings held to authorize the operation there was presented, in addition to evidence concerning the mental and social status of Carrie Buck, testimony in support of the statute by eugenicists to the effect that feeblemindedness was hereditary and incurable.

Justice Holmes's opinion supporting the sterilization order, and accepting without question the scientific justification for the statute, was very brief. This is the heart of it.

> We have seen more than once that the public welfare may call upon the best citizens for their lives. It would be strange if it could not call upon those who already sap the strength of the State for these lesser sacrifices, often not felt to be such by those concerned, in order to prevent our being swamped with incompetence. It is better for all the world, if instead of waiting to execute degenerate offspring for crime, or to let them starve for their imbecility, society can prevent those who are manifestly unfit from continuing their kind. The principle that sustains compulsory vaccination is broad enough to cover cutting the Fallopian tubes. . . . Three generations of imbeciles are enough.

Seldom has so much questionable doctrine been compressed into five sentences of a Supreme Court opinion. The first two sentences state a completely unacceptable standard for measuring legislative action. If it were true that, because the state can demand the supreme sacrifice of life itself, it is thereby justified in demanding any lesser sacrifice, then every constitutional protection could be disregarded at will. Because the government can require a man to lay down his life in battle, it does not follow that he can be deprived of freedom of speech or the right to trial by jury. Moreover, it is a rather perverse view which sees the *Jacobson* decision as a precedent broad enough to cover Carrie Buck. As Walter Berns has said: "It is a broad principle indeed that sustains a needle's prick in the arm and an abdominal incision, if only in terms of the equipment used. It becomes something else again in terms of the results obtained: no smallpox in the one case and no children in the other." [5]

[5] "Buck v. Bell: Due Process of Law?" 6 *Western Political Quarterly* 764 (1953).

Most significant of all, however, was Holmes's apparent failure to realize that there could be any question as to the scientific theories on which this legislation was based. In the *Jacobson* case the Court had at least recognized that vaccination was not universally accepted. Perhaps Holmes's action was the fault of the way the case was presented in the lower courts, where the eugenic evidence offered to support the policy had been countered only by legal arguments that "legislation of this kind carried with it the danger of giving the state the power to rid itself of citizens it deemed undesirable according to its own standards, and that this might even be applied to races." Actually it could have been shown that the Virginia Legislature and the other states with similar sterilization laws had been responding to the propaganda of a small but active organization expounding racist or elitist doctrines founded on allegedly scientific eugenic principles, the validity of which reputable scientists deny.

If the Supreme Court had known these facts, perhaps it still should have refused to question the statute, simply saying, as Waite did in the *Munn* case, that the resort in case of legislative error is to the polls, not to the courts. This would be a proper response, except for the fact that since the *Munn* decision the Court had assumed the responsibility of testing the substance of legislation on due process grounds—of determining whether a challenged statute has any "real or substantial relation" to the public health, or whether it effects "a plain, palpable invasion of rights secured by the fundamental law." If these are really the goals of the Court's inquiry, then it signally failed to make the kind of investigation in *Buck* v. *Bell* which would have resulted in a genuine review of legislative action on substantive due process grounds.

PROTECTION OF PUBLIC MORALS    The commonest offenses against public morality are gambling, drunkenness, blasphemy, obscenity, and irregular sexual conduct. Most legislation aimed at the prevention and punishment of activities generally regarded in the society as offensive to moral standards is unlikely to generate constitutional objections. But it is only too well known that fanatics and bigots often seek on allegedly moral grounds the passage of legislation which amounts to serious invasions of privacy and coercion of individuals with different standards of morality.

The most striking example was the adoption of prohibition of intoxicating liquor in the United States and in many of the states. Substantive due process was never invoked against prohibition legislation. In *Mugler* v. *Kansas*, Justice Harlan wrote:

> There is no justification for holding that the State, under the guise merely of police regulation, is here aiming to deprive the citizen of his constitutional rights; for we cannot shut out of view the fact, within the knowledge of all, that the public health, the public morals, and the public safety, may be endangered by the general use of intoxicating

drinks; nor the fact, established by statistics accessible to every one, that the idleness, disorder, pauperism, and crime existing in the country are, in some degree at least, traceable to this evil.

The Supreme Court recognized in the *Mugler* case that the effect of the statute would be to render practically worthless property invested in the liquor business at a time when it was a perfectly legal occupation, but this was not contrary to due process.[6] Moreover, the *Mugler* decision even held it was permissible for the legislature to prohibit individuals from manufacturing intoxicating liquors for their own use, on the ground that such a loophole might cause the prohibitory plan to fail. Along the same line, a subsequent decision held that the mere possession of intoxicating liquor might be prohibited.[7] Indeed, a state might prohibit the sale of *nonintoxicating* malt liquors in order to make effective its prohibition against the sale of intoxicants.[8] The general attitude of the Supreme Court toward prohibition of liquor was well summed up in a 1900 decision:

> Intoxicating liquors belong to a class of commodities which, in the opinion of a great many estimable people, are deleterious in their effects, demoralizing in their tendencies, and often fatal in their excessive indulgence. . . . It may be that their evil effects have been exaggerated. . . . It is, however, within the power of each State to investigate the subject and to determine its policy in that particular. If the legislative body come deliberately to the conclusion that a due regard for the public safety and morals requires a suppression of the liquor traffic, there is nothing in the commercial clause of the Constitution, or in the Fourteenth Amendment to that instrument, to forbid its doing so.[9]

As for federal action, the so-called Wartime Prohibition Act, passed ten days after the Armistice in 1918, was upheld on the basis of the government's war powers in 1919.[10] The adoption of the Eighteenth Amendment of course wrote prohibition into the Constitution.

Long before scientific proof of the dangers of cigarette smoking became available, some states sought to prohibit cigarettes on both health and morals grounds. A Tennessee statute of this sort was sustained by the Supreme Court in *Austin* v. *Tennessee* (1900) with the following justification:

> Cigarettes do not seem until recently to have attracted the attention of the public as more injurious than other forms of tobacco; nor are we now prepared to take judicial notice of any special injury resulting from their use or to indorse the opinion of the Supreme Court of Tennessee that "they are inherently bad and bad only." At the same time we should be shutting our eyes to what is constantly passing before them were we to affect an ignorance of the fact that a belief in their deleterious effects,

[6] See also *Boston Beer Co.* v. *Massachusetts* (1878).
[7] *Crane* v. *Campbell* (1917).
[8] *Purity Extract & Tonic Co.* v. *Lynch* (1912).
[9] *Austin* v. *Tennessee* (1900).
[10] *Hamilton* v. *Kentucky Distilleries and Warehouse Co.* (1919).

particularly upon young people, has become very general, and that communications are constantly finding their way into the public press denouncing their use as fraught with great danger to the youth of both sexes. Without undertaking to affirm or deny their evil effects, we think it within the province of the legislature to say how far they may be sold, or to prohibit their sale entirely, . . . provided . . . there be no reason to doubt that the act in question is designed for the protection of the public health.

In 1932 a Utah statute which forbade billboard or streetcar advertising of tobacco was upheld by the Supreme Court, Justice Brandeis saying: "The law deals confessedly with a subject within the scope of the police power. No facts are brought to our attention which establish either that the evil aimed at does not exist or that the statutory remedy is inappropriate." [11]

SAFETY     Legislative regulations adopted to protect public safety and order likewise seldom present problems to reviewing courts. One need mention only such familiar types of restrictions as those affecting the muzzling of dogs, the carrying of concealed weapons, the transportation or storing of explosives or inflammables, the control of fire hazards in buildings, or the promotion of safety in highway, rail, and air traffic.

To give only one example of the expected judicial reaction to safety legislation, state regulation of the size and weight of motor trucks was upheld in *Sproles* v. *Binford* (1932), Chief Justice Hughes saying:

Limitations of size and weight are manifestly subjects within the broad range of legislative discretion. . . . When the subject lies within the police power of the State, debatable questions as to reasonableness are not for the courts but for the legislature, which is entitled to form its own judgment, and its action within its range of discretion cannot be set aside because compliance is burdensome.

BEYOND HEALTH, MORALS, AND SAFETY     The public welfare which states can promote by use of the police power has on occasion been defined in terms broader than the traditional categories of health, morals, and safety. Increasingly the Supreme Court has accepted promotion of public convenience or prosperity, or even aesthetic purposes, as justifying legislative interference with liberty or property.

*Euclid* v. *Ambler Realty Co.* (1926), upholding the constitutionality of zoning, was a landmark case in the development of a broader judicial attitude toward police power regulation. Zoning ordinances typically divide a city into various classes of residential, commercial, and manufacturing districts, and buildings and land use within each area must conform to the regulations for this district. Such restrictions of course constitute a serious limitation on freedom of the owner to employ his property as he sees fit,

[11] *Packer Corp.* v. *Utah* (1932).

and the Supreme Court held two hearings in the *Euclid* case before it approved the zoning regulations by a five to four vote.

Many of the purposes which zoning seeks to achieve—limits on heights of buildings and billboards, exclusion of offensive trades from residential districts, and so on—had, it is true, already been judicially approved.[12] But a zoning ordinance wrapped up all these restrictions in a general plan and imposed them in a blanket fashion. Thus the Court noted in the *Euclid* case that all industrial establishments, the inoffensive as well as the offensive, would be excluded from the areas designated as residential. However, Justice Sutherland, who spoke for the majority, did not find this a problem. These questions of degree are often encountered. "The bad fades into the good by such insensible degrees that the two are not capable of being readily distinguished and separated in terms of legislation."

More serious was the exclusion of all businesses and trades, including hotels and apartment houses, from residential districts. This was a more extreme control than any the Court had ever approved in the past. To support such restrictions Sutherland rehearsed the findings and the philosophy of the zoning experts as set forth in numerous reports.

> These reports, which bear every evidence of painstaking consideration, concur in the view that the segregation of residential, business, and industrial buildings will make it easier to provide fire apparatus suitable for the character and intensity of the development in each section; that it will increase the safety and security of home life; greatly tend to prevent street accidents, especially to children, by reducing the traffic and resulting confusion in residential sections; decrease noise and other conditions which produce or intensify nervous disorders; preserve a more favorable environment in which to rear children, etc. With particular reference to apartment houses, it is pointed out that the development of detached house sections is greatly retarded by the coming of apartment houses, . . . interfering by their height and bulk with the free circulation of air and monopolizing the rays of the sun which otherwise would fall upon the smaller homes, and bringing, as their necessary accompaniments, the disturbing noises incident to increased traffic and business, and the occupation, by means of moving and parked automobiles, of larger portions of the streets, thus detracting from their safety and depriving children of the privilege of quiet and open spaces for play, enjoyed by those in more favored localities. . . . Under these circumstances, apartment houses, which in a different environment would be not only entirely unobjectionable but highly desirable, come very near to being nuisances.

Reasoning of this sort, Sutherland concluded, was "sufficiently cogent to preclude us from saying, as it must be said before the ordinance can be declared unconstitutional, that such provisions are clearly arbitrary and

[12] See *Welch* v. *Swasey* ( 1909); *Cusack* v. *Chicago* (1917).

unreasonable, having no substantial relation to the public health, safety, morals, or general welfare."

The *Euclid* decision established the constitutionality of new and far-reaching controls on use of property, but it is significant that Sutherland's defense was based primarily on the old concept of nuisances. It was not until the decision in *Berman* v. *Parker* (1954), involving the constitutionality under the Fifth Amendment of a slum-clearance and redevelopment program in the District of Columbia, that Justice Douglas for a unanimous Court accepted aesthetics as a proper public purpose in its own right.

> Public safety, public health, morality, peace and quiet, law and order —these are some of the more conspicuous examples of the traditional application of the police power to municipal affairs. Yet they merely illustrate the scope of the power and do not delimit it. . . . Miserable and disreputable housing conditions may do more than spread disease and crime and immorality. They may also suffocate the spirit by reducing the people who live there to the status of cattle. They may indeed make living an almost unsufferable burden. They may also be an ugly sore, a blight on the community which robs it of charm, which makes it a place from which men turn. The misery of housing may despoil a community as an open sewer may ruin a river. . . .
>
> The concept of the public welfare is broad and inclusive. . . . The values it represents are spiritual as well as physical, aesthetic as well as monetary. It is within the power of the legislature to determine that the community should be beautiful as well as healthy, spacious as well as clean, well-balanced as well as carefully patrolled.

### ECONOMIC REGULATION

It is only when we come to consider legislation regulating economic activities that we see the full potentialities of the doctrine of substantive due process. Judges who were willing to accept state intervention to protect the public health and developed reasons for justifying it, tended to be much less ready to accept state intervention in the economy and much more likely to produce rationalizations for striking down state action. As early as 1897, in *Allgeyer* v. *Louisiana*, the Supreme Court announced the principle that the right to make contracts was a part of the liberty guaranteed by the due process clause, and stated the doctrine of freedom of contract in a most forthright fashion:

> The "liberty" mentioned in [the Fourteenth] Amendment means not only the right of the citizen to be free from the mere physical restraint of his person, as by incarceration, but the term is deemed to embrace the right of the citizen to be free in the enjoyment of all his faculties; to be free to use them in all lawful ways; to live and work where he will; to earn his livelihood by any lawful calling; to pursue any livelihood or avocation, and for that purpose to enter into all contracts which may be

proper, necessary and essential to his carrying out to a successful conclusion the purposes above mentioned.

The immediate beneficiaries of this judicial antagonism toward economic regulation were customarily business corporations. A word should be said about how corporations came within the protection accorded to "persons" under the due process clause. It is rather anomalous that the Fourteenth Amendment for a half century after its adoption should have been of very little value to the Negroes in whose behalf it was primarily adopted, while it should so quickly have been accepted by the Court as a protector of corporate rights. Some have argued that this was not an accident. The "conspiracy theory" of the Fourteenth Amendment presents it as a deliberate Trojan horse which, purporting merely to protect Negro rights, smuggled into the Constitution the principle of judicial review over state legislation affecting corporate property interests. Supporting this contention is the argument made before the Supreme Court in 1885 by Roscoe Conkling, a member of the joint congressional committee which drafted the amendment, that the committee had purposely inserted the term "person" rather than "citizen" in the due process and equal protection clauses in order to cover corporations.[13]

Actually it requires no such theory, which in any event is now rather thoroughly discredited, to explain the development of judicial concern for corporate rights. A knowledge of the temper of the times is sufficient. In *Santa Clara County* v. *Southern Pacific Rr. Co.* (1886) the Court was unanimous in asserting that the Fourteenth Amendment covered corporations, Chief Justice Waite saying: "The Court does not wish to hear argument on the question." No dissent was expressed until 1938, when Justice Black sought to repeal a half century of holdings by denying that the amendment had been intended to apply to corporations.[14] Again in 1949 Douglas joined Black in reasserting this view, but at the same time they admitted that "history has gone the other way." [15]

JUDICIAL ACCEPTANCE OF ECONOMIC REGULATION    Many types of economic regulation encountered little opposition from the courts. Economic legislation was often presented as based on health considerations, and where courts were convinced that the health rationale was valid they would usually concede constitutionality. This was generally true, for example, of laws

[13] *San Mateo County* v. *Southern Pacific Rr. Co.* (1885). See Howard Jay Graham, "The 'Conspiracy Theory' of the Fourteenth Amendment," 47 *Yale Law Journal* 371–403 (1938), 48 *ibid.* 171–194 (1938).

[14] *Connecticut General Life Inc. Co.* v. *Johnson* (1938).

[15] *Wheeling Steel Corp.* v. *Glander* (1949). Considering the importance of groups in a liberal democratic society, it would be a dubious and even illiberal policy to guarantee rights to individuals while denying them to organized groups. See the defense of group rights in *Joint Anti-Fascist Refugee Committee* v. *McGrath* (1951).

regulating hours of work in industrial employment. In *Holden* v. *Hardy* (1898) the Supreme Court, with only two dissents (Brewer and Peckham), upheld a Utah statute providing for an eight-hour day in mines and smelters. This law was clearly tied in with the protection of life and health. It only affected workers in two occupations which the legislature had judged to be dangerous when too long pursued. Since there were reasonable grounds for holding this conclusion to be true, the Court would not review the legislative decision.

More importantly, the Court went on to challenge the whole freedom of contract idea by pointing out that the workers and owners were not on an equal bargaining basis. Consequently the self-interest of the workers was not a safe guide, and in the interests of the public health the legislature could impose its authority to protect one party to the contract against himself. This case was brought by the employer, who argued solicitously that the law interfered with the right of his employees to contract freely. "The argument," the Court rejoined, "would certainly come with better grace and greater cogency from the latter class."

*Muller* v. *Oregon* (1908) unanimously upheld a ten-hour law applying to women in industry. Taking "judicial cognizance" of factors which make women the weaker sex, the Court held that "she is properly placed in a class by herself, and legislation designed for her protection could be sustained, even when like legislation is not necessary for men and could not be sustained." The Court acknowledged its debt to "the brief filed by Mr. Louis D. Brandeis," which gathered an enormous amount of information on foreign and state laws limiting hours for women, and official reports stressing the dangers to women from long hours of labor. Such laws and opinions "may not be, technically speaking, authorities," the Court said, but "they are significant of a widespread belief that woman's physical structure, and the functions she performs in consequence thereof, justify special legislation restricting or qualifying the conditions under which she should be permitted to toil."

So health considerations provided the Court with police power justification for some hours legislation. For a time it also appeared that health arguments would legitimize regulation of wages, even though the connection with health was more indirect here and the assault on freedom of contract was more painful to employers. An Oregon minimum wage law came up to the Supreme Court in 1917. The Oregon supreme court had upheld the law on the strength of the *Muller* principle, finding it a protection for women's health and also for their morals. In *Stettler* v. *O'Hara*, the Supreme Court split four to four, with Brandeis abstaining, and thus the state court decision was left in effect. Within the next six years three more state supreme courts upheld minimum wages for women, relying upon the *Stettler* case.

Even the regulation of prices, a still more direct incursion on the principles of *laissez faire*, was initially approved in the case of *Munn* v. *Illinois*

(1877) where, as already noted, the Court upheld the fixing of rates for Chicago grain elevators on the ground that they fell within a category of businesses recognized by the common law as "affected with a public interest." Chief Justice Waite said:

> Property does become clothed with a public interest when used in a manner to make it of public consequence, and affect the community at large. When, therefore, one devotes his property to a use in which the public has an interest, he, in effect, grants to the public an interest in that use, and must submit to be controlled by the public for the common good, to the extent of the interest he has thus created.

In later decisions the Court added such business operations as insurance companies,[16] stockyards,[17] and tobacco warehouses [18] to the category of businesses affected with a public interest and so subject to regulation of rates and charges. The *Munn* principle was also applied in *Davidson* v. *New Orleans* (1878) to hold that businesses subject to control of rates were not entitled under the due process clause to judicial review of the question of just compensation.

Workmen's compensation acts presented no due process difficulties for the Supreme Court. Under the common law, courts had developed certain defenses to which employers were entitled when sued for damages by injured workmen. One was the doctrine of contributory negligence, which prevented the employee from receiving damages if the injury had been in any way due to his own negligence. Another was the fellow-servant rule, which blocked recovery if the injury was due to negligence of a fellow employee. There was also the assumption of risk doctrine, which held that an employee entering an employment assumed all the ordinary risks that went with that employment and left him free to recover only for extraordinary or unanticipated risks. Such rules as these made it very difficult for employees to secure redress for industrial injuries.

In the early part of the twentieth century state legislatures began to feel that industrial accidents should be recognized as a cost of production, and compensated for by the employer. Laws of various types aiming at this goal were passed. In 1917 the Supreme Court upheld the New York law, saying that although it no doubt limited freedom of contract to some extent, this was a legitimate exercise of the police power for protection of the health, safety, and welfare of an important group of individuals.[19] In 1919 the Supreme Court summed up its experience with state compensation acts as follows:

> These decisions have established the propositions that the rules of law concerning the employer's responsibility for personal injury or death of

[16] *German Alliance Insurance Co.* v. *Lewis* (1914).
[17] *Cotting* v. *Godard* (1901).
[18] *Townsend* v. *Yeomans* (1937).
[19] *New York Central Ry. Co.* v. *White* (1917).

an employee arising in the course of the employment are not beyond alteration by legislation in the public interest; that no person has a vested right entitling him to have these any more than other rules of law remain unchanged for his benefit; and that, if we exclude arbitrary and unreasonable changes, liability may be imposed upon the employer without fault, and the rules respecting his responsibility to one employee for the negligence of another and respecting contributory negligence and assumption of risk are subject to legislative change.[20]

JUDICIAL REJECTION OF ECONOMIC REGULATION   Although these illustrations of judicial acceptance of economic regulation are significant, they are not fully representative of the Supreme Court's position for the first third of the twentieth century. During this period the Court grew steadily more critical of legislative efforts to deal with what were widely regarded as economic abuses or evils and more inflexible in its interpretation of the due process clause.

*Lochner* v. *New York* (1905) sounded the Court's call to battle against welfare economics. This case involved a state law which forbade bakery employees to work for more than ten hours a day or sixty hours a week. In spite of the fact that the Court had upheld a ten-hour law for miners in *Holden* v. *Hardy* (1898), it now declared the New York statute unconstitutional, by a five to four vote.

The law, said Justice Peckham for the majority, could be upheld only as a measure "pertaining to the health of the individual engaged in the occupation of a baker." Did the health of bakers need protection? Peckham did not think so, and he gave two reasons. First, "to the common understanding the trade of a baker has never been regarded as an unhealthy one." Second, statistics regarding trades and occupations show that although "the trade of a baker does not appear to be as healthy as some other trades, [it] is also vastly more healthy than still others." Since there were no special health hazards about baking, then, to permit bakers' hours to be regulated would be to permit general legislative control of hours in industry. This was so unthinkable to Peckham that it clinched his argument.

The majority opinion did not bother to hide its distaste for such legislative interference. "Statutes of the nature of that under review, limiting the hours in which grown and intelligent men may labor to earn their living, are mere meddlesome interferences with the rights of the individual." Unless the Court called a halt, we would all be "at the mercy of legislative majorities." The Court must pierce through legislative pretenses when laws purporting to protect the public health or welfare were "in reality, passed from other motives."

There was nothing in Peckham's opinion to suggest that it would come with better grace if employee freedom of contract were defended by employees rather than employers. There was nothing about any inequality of

[20] *Arizona Employers' Liability Cases* (1919).

bargaining power on the part of employees. In fact, Peckham inferred that such notions were an insult to red-blooded American workingmen. "There is no contention that bakers as a class are not equal in intelligence and capacity to men in other trades or manual occupations, or that they are not able to assert their rights and care for themselves without the protecting arm of the State, interfering with their independence of judgment and of action. They are in no sense wards of the State."

The Peckham opinion, which has long been a museum piece, called forth some of Justice Holmes's best-known phrases.

> This case is decided upon an economic theory which a large part of the country does not entertain. . . . The Fourteenth Amendment does not enact Mr. Herbert Spencer's Social Statics. . . . I think that the word liberty in the Fourteenth Amendment is perverted when it is held to prevent the natural outcome of a dominant opinion, unless it can be said that a rational and fair man necessarily would admit that the statute proposed would infringe fundamental principles as they have been understood by the traditions of our people and our law.

In this instance, Holmes thought that it did not need "research to show that no such sweeping condemnation can be passed upon the statute before us."

Of course Holmes was right in saying that *Lochner* was decided "upon an economic theory." But it is also true that it was decided on a legal theory— that use of the police power was limited to grounds of health, morals, and safety. Holmes concluded that a "reasonable man" might think the New York law "a proper measure on the score of health." But actually it was not a health law. It was, as Peckham charged, a labor law. Holmes knew this, too, and was ready to approve it as a labor law, because "men whom I certainly could not pronounce unreasonable would uphold it is a first instalment of a general regulation of the hours of work." But the Court majority was not willing to follow Holmes's "reasonable man" so far or so fast.

Eighteen years later the *Lochner* ruling was invoked in *Adkins* v. *Children's Hospital* (1923) to strike down a District of Columbia minimum wage law for women. It had been widely thought that *Lochner* had lost much of its authority, for in the interim the Court had upheld the Oregon ten-hour law for women, and in *Bunting* v. *Oregon* (1917) it had approved a ten-hour law for both men and women in industry without ever mentioning the *Lochner* decision. Consequently, as Chief Justice Taft said in his *Adkins* dissent, there was reason to assume that the *Lochner* case had been "overruled *sub silentio*." But for the five-judge majority in *Adkins*, *Lochner* was still the law.

The *Adkins* opinion, written by Justice Sutherland, was a paean to freedom of contract in its purest form, with no nonsense about the special needs of women or inequality of bargaining position. The Court saw the statute as

> . . . simply and exclusively a price-fixing law, confined to adult women . . . who are legally as capable of contracting for themselves as men. It

> forbids two parties having lawful capacity . . . to freely contract with
> one another in respect of the price for which one shall render service
> to the other in a purely private employment where both are willing, per-
> haps anxious, to agree, even though the consequence may be to oblige
> one to surrender a desirable engagement and the other to dispense with
> the services of a desirable employee.

Sutherland had two main reasons why this was unconstitutional. First,
the standards set up by statute to guide the administering board in fixing
minimum wages were too vague and fatally uncertain. The sum necessary
to maintain a woman worker in good health and protect her morals is not
precise or unvarying. It will depend on her temperament, her habits, her
moral standards, her independent resources, and so on. It cannot be determined "by a general formula prescribed by a statutory bureau."

Second, the law was invalid because it took account "of the necessities of
only one party to the contract," compelling the employer to pay the minimum wage whether or not the employee was worth that much to him. There
are two elements in every contract of employment—"the amount to be paid
and the service to be rendered"—and they are balanced against each other
by the contracting parties. But this law upset the balancing process by
fixing the amount to be paid arbitrarily with no relation to the work the
employee was engaged to do or the efficiency with which she performed it.
Such an arrangement was, to Sutherland, quite literally "immoral," and he
concluded: "A statute which prescribes payment . . . solely with relation
to circumstances apart from the contract of employment, the business affected by it and the work done under it, is so clearly the product of a naked,
arbitrary exercise of power that it cannot be allowed to stand under the
Constitution."

Chief Justice Taft, dissenting, thought that the *Adkins* case was controlled
by the *Muller* decision, and he could see no difference in principle between
regulating maximum hours and minimum wages. Holmes agreed.

> The bargain is equally affected whichever half you regulate. *Muller* v.
> *Oregon*, I take it, is as good law today as it was in 1908. It will need
> more than the Nineteenth Amendment to convince me that there are no
> differences between men and women, or that legislation cannot take
> those differences into account. I should not hesitate to take them into
> account if I thought it necessary to sustain this act. . . . But after
> *Bunting* v. *Oregon* . . . I had supposed that it was not necessary, and
> that *Lochner* v. *New York* . . . would be allowed a deserved repose.

Holmes went on to admit that he personally had doubts about this statute,
but they were irrelevant according to his standard of judicial review. "When
so many intelligent persons, who have studied the matter more than any of
us can, have thought that the means are effective and are worth the price,
it seems to me impossible to deny that the belief reasonably may be held
by reasonable men."

Following the *Adkins* decision, many states assumed that a minimum wage law which *did* take into account the value-of-service-rendered principle would be constitutional, and passed statutes including such provisions. A New York law of this type came before the Supreme Court in *Morehead* v. *Tipaldo* (1936), in the midst of the Court's furious battle against the New Deal. The four surviving members of the *Adkins* majority—Sutherland, Butler, Van Devanter, and McReynolds—joined with Justice Roberts to invalidate the New York law. The value-of-service feature in the New York law was held insufficient to meet the *Adkins* objection, which was dogmatically restated in these words: "The State is without power by any form of legislation to prohibit, change or nullify contracts between employers and adult women workers as to the amount of wages to be paid."

This bland reiteration in 1936 of a conclusion which had had little enough support in the palmy days of 1923 was one of the great mistakes of Supreme Court history, and did more to destroy the country's confidence in the Court as then constituted than some of its more publicized anti-New Deal decisions. The ruling earned the dissent of as distinguished a foursome as ever sat on the high court—Chief Justice Hughes and Justices Brandeis, Cardozo, and Stone. The Chief Justice wrote a long dissent which was a devastating refutation of Butler's majority view, but for present purposes it may be preferable to note Stone's effort to point out to the majority some of the facts of life in 1936.

> In the years which have intervened since the *Adkins* case we have had opportunity to learn that a wage is not always the resultant of free bargaining between employers and employees; that it may be one forced upon employees by their economic necessities and upon employers by the most ruthless of their competitors. We have had opportunity to perceive more clearly that a wage insufficient to support the worker does not visit its consequences upon him alone; that it may affect profoundly the entire economic structure of society and, in any case, that it casts on every taxpayer, and on government itself, the burden of solving the problems of poverty, subsistence, health and morals of large numbers in the community. Because of their nature and extent these are public problems. A generation ago they were for the individual to solve; today they are the burden of the nation.

Here for the first time in an economic regulation case a Supreme Court justice burst out of the traditional health and morals boundaries on state police power and asserted—what was shortly to become axiomatic for the Court—that public power is as broad as is necessary to meet urgent public problems.

During this period the Court also struck out at legislative efforts to protect the organization of labor unions. Congress in 1898 adopted legislation outlawing the so-called "yellow-dog" contract, an agreement not to join a labor union which many employers forced workers to sign as a condition of

employment. Discharging an employee of an interstate railroad on grounds of his membership in a labor organization was made a criminal offense against the United States. This statute was declared unconstitutional by the Supreme Court in the 1908 case of *Adair* v. *United States,* on familiar freedom of contract grounds.

Justice Harlan agreed that legislatures could limit this freedom where its exercise was "inconsistent with the public interests or . . . hurtful to the public order or . . . detrimental to the common good," but the yellow-dog contract did not fall in any of these categories.

> It is not within the functions of government . . . to compel any person in the course of his business and against his will to accept or retain the personal services of another, or to compel any person, against his will, to perform personal services for another. . . . The right of the employé to quit the service of the employer, for whatever reason, is the same as the right of the employer, for whatever reason, to dispense with the services of such employé.

Thus the Court, with evenhanded justice, was protecting the right of the employee not to work, as well as the right of the employer to fire, though the former situation was not before the Court. Reminiscent of Anatole France, who spoke of the majestic equality of the law which forbids both rich and poor to steal bread, beg in the streets, or sleep under bridges, Harlan concluded: "In all such particulars the employer and the employé have equality of right, and any legislation that disturbs that equality is an arbitrary interference with the liberty of contract which no government can legally justify in a free land."

Holmes dissented in the *Adair* case and also in *Coppage* v. *Kansas* (1915), where the Court struck down a comparable state statute. He said in the latter case: "In present conditions a workman not unnaturally may believe that only by belonging to a union can he secure a contract that shall be fair to him. . . . If that belief, whether right or wrong, may be held by a reasonable man, it seems to me that it may be enforced by law in order to establish the equality of position between the parties in which liberty of contract begins." He would therefore have overruled the *Adair* decision.

In the area of legislative rate and price fixing, the Court's initial favorable attitude as manifested in *Munn* v. *Illinois* was reversed by significant decisions in the 1920s. In *Tyson & Brother* v. *Banton* (1927) a New York law forbidding the resale of theater tickets at more than a 50-cent markup was declared unconstitutional by a five to four vote. Theaters, said Justice Sutherland, are not public utilities or affected with a public interest. They enjoy no government grant or privilege. Justice Holmes, dissenting, thought that "theaters are as much devoted to public use as anything well can be. We have not that respect for art that is one of the glories of France. But to many people the superfluous is the necessary, and it seems to me that Gov-

ernment does not go beyond its sphere in attempting to make life livable for them."

The following year the Court by a six to three vote in *Ribnik* v. *McBride* (1928) held unconstitutional New Jersey's effort to regulate the fees charged by employment agencies. Such businesses are "essentially private," and there is no more justification for fixing their rates than for setting the prices for food or housing or fuel.[21]

Legislative efforts at business regulation were not confined to price fixing, of course.[22] In 1920 a Kansas statute declared that food, clothing, fuel, and transportation industries were affected with a public interest, and endeavored to subject them to compulsory arbitration and fixing of wages and working conditions by an industrial relations court. The Supreme Court ruled that a packing company was a "private" concern which could not be constitutionally subjected to such controls.[23] Nebraska in 1921 established maximum weight for loaves of bread, and provided penalties for selling or making bread in other weights. The Court invalidated this measure, which was presented as one to protect consumers from fraud, calling it arbitrary interference with a private business.[24] However, the Court later upheld a statute of the same sort with somewhat modified enforcement standards.[25]

Oklahoma had varying experiences in undertaking to regulate by the licensing power businesses which it conceived to fall within the public interest. In 1929 the Court upheld a state law declaring the business of operating a cotton gin to be one having a public interest, and requiring a showing of public necessity before it could be undertaken.[26] But in the famous case of *New State Ice Co.* v. *Liebmann* (1932), the Court refused to grant such status to the ice business, holding that it was "as essentially

[21] In *Williams* v. *Standard Oil Co.* (1929) the Court with only one dissent declared unconstitutional a Tennessee statute authorizing a state official to fix the prices at which gasoline should be sold within the state. Enterprises in this field were private businesses, the Court said, and did not belong in the public interest category.

[22] In 1914 the people of Washington state had adopted by the initiative process a law prohibiting the taking of fees from persons seeking employment. By a five to four vote in *Adams* v. *Tanner* (1917) the Court declared this measure unconstitutional. Justice McReynolds said there was "nothing inherently immoral or dangerous to public welfare in acting as paid representative of another to find a position." It was in fact a useful business which could be regulated but not destroyed. Justice Brandeis, dissenting along with Holmes, Clarke, and McKenna, pointed out that the law did not forbid employment agencies from charging *employers* for their services, but that even if the agencies were put out of business by the law, the Court must give some heed to abuses and inadequacies the state was trying to correct.

[23] *Wolff Packing Co.* v. *Court of Industrial Relations* (1923); see also *Dorchy* v. *Kansas* (1924).

[24] *Burns Baking Co.* v. *Bryan* (1924).

[25] *Petersen Baking Co.* v. *Bryan* (1934).

[26] *Frost* v. *Corporation Commission* (1929).

private in its nature as the business of the grocer, the dairyman, the butcher.
. . . [It] bears no such relation to the public as to warrant its inclusion in
the category of businesses charged with a public use."

Finally, the Court's earlier reluctance to undertake judicial review of
public utility rate fixing disappeared. *Smyth* v. *Ames* (1898) held that due
process required the courts not merely to review the reasonableness of rates
but also to determine whether the rates permitted a fair return on a fair
valuation of property devoted to public use. *Smyth* v. *Ames* opened up over
forty years of confusion, as regulatory commissions tried to guess what
standards reviewing courts would employ and the methods they would require to be used in determining fair value of utility property.

THE ABANDONMENT OF ECONOMIC DUE PROCESS    The structure of substantive due process which the Supreme Court built in these economic cases
was probably its most original intellectual achievement during the first third
of the twentieth century.[27] Edward S. Corwin referred to substantive due
process as "the most important field of American constitutional law." [28]
These were the cases for which the Court was best known up to 1933; these
were the decisions which primarily gave the Court its reputation as the
bastion of conservatism, the protector of property rights, "the sheet anchor
of the Republic."

Then, within a few years, it was all over, and the Court had completely
rejected substantive due process as a guide. This striking reversal began
with *Nebbia* v. *New York* (1934), as the Court by a five to four vote accepted the validity of a depression-born law regulating milk prices. A New
York State statute had established a milk control board with power to fix
minimum and maximum retail prices, and in this case the objective had been
to prevent ruinous price cutting by fixing minimum prices. Justice Roberts
spoke for the majority, which included also Hughes, Brandeis, Stone, and
Cardozo.

Roberts began by admitting that the milk industry had never been regarded as affected with a public interest and had none of the characteristics
relied on in the past in attributing such status—no public grant or franchise,
no monopoly, no obligation to serve all comers, no devotion of property to
a use which the public might itself appropriately undertake. But that made
no difference. It was a misconception to think that the power to regulate
depended upon holding a franchise or enjoying a monopoly. Munn had no
franchise nor anything that could "fairly be called a monopoly." Nor was
there any mystical power in the standard, "affected with a public interest."
This phrase, rightly understood, "is the equivalent of 'subject to the exercise

---

[27] The only competitor would be the clear and present danger test, but it was
the product of only two members of the Court, Justices Holmes and Brandeis,
and their interpretation of the test was not accepted by the Court majority.
[28] *Op. cit.*, p. 64.

of the police power'; . . . nothing more was intended by the expression."
Then came the heart of the *Nebbia* decision.

> It is clear that there is no closed class or category of businesses af-
> fected with a public interest, and the function of courts in the application
> of the Fifth and Fourteenth Amendments is to determine in each case
> whether circumstances vindicate the challenged regulation as a reason-
> able exertion of governmental authority or condemn it as arbitrary or
> discriminatory. . . . The phrase "affected with a public interest" can,
> in the nature of things, mean no more than that an industry, for ade-
> quate reason, is subject to control for the public good.

The *Nebbia* decision was followed by others supporting state and federal
price fixing in a variety of fields.[29] However, the contrary decisions of the
1920s had not been specifically overruled, and when a Nebraska statute
fixing rates which private employment agencies might charge an applicant
for employment came before that state's supreme court in 1940, the court
rather unimaginatively declared the law unconstitutional on the authority of
*Ribnik* v. *McBride*. The Supreme Court unanimously reversed the state
court in *Olsen* v. *Nebraska* (1941). "The drift away from *Ribnik* v. *McBride*,"
said Justice Douglas, "has been so great that it can no longer be deemed a
controlling authority." In *Gold* v. *DiCarlo* (1965) the Court without opinion
upheld a New York law limiting theater-ticket-broker surcharges, in effect
overruling the 1927 *Tyson* decision.

In 1937 the Court upheld minimum wage laws for women in *West Coast
Hotel Co.* v. *Parrish*. This case arose under the Washington state minimum
wage law which, be it noted, had been passed in 1913 and enforced continuously thereafter, quite irrespective of the *Adkins* ruling. The act, like
that of the District of Columbia, contained no value-of-service standard, and
so seemed more in defiance of the *Adkins* decision than the New York law
had been. But Chief Justice Hughes upheld the Washington law, construct-
ing his majority opinion out of quotations from Taft and Holmes, and asking
such questions as "What can be closer to the public interest than the health
of women and their protection from unscrupulous and overreaching employers?" More important, he wrote the principles of Stone's *Morehead* dissent into the law of the land, thereby finally releasing the police power from
dependence on health and morals considerations. The opinion concluded
with a direct overruling of the *Adkins* decision. Nothing was said about
*Lochner,* but this time we can be sure, with Taft, that it had been overruled
*sub silentio.*

In 1941 the Court upheld the minimum wage and maximum hours regu-

---

[29] *Townsend* v. *Yeomans* (1937), upholding a Georgia statute fixing maximum
warehouse charges for the handling and selling of leaf tobacco; *United States*
v. *Rock Royal Co-Operative, Inc.* (1939), upholding the power of Congress
to fix minimum prices for milk under the commerce clause; *Sunshine Anthracite Coal Co.* v. *Adkins* (1940), upholding the price-fixing provisions of the
federal Bituminous Coal Act of 1937.

lations of the Fair Labor Standards Act, passed in 1938. The validity of this statute under the commerce clause, as determined in *United States* v. *Darby Lumber Co.* (1941), has already been discussed. Due process objections to the statute were disposed of in one short paragraph which cited *Holden*, *Muller*, and *Bunting* on hours, and *West Coast Hotel* on wages. The federal act covered men as well as women, so that *West Coast Hotel* was no precedent at all on minimum wages for men. But the sexual distinction, which as late as 1937 had been absolutely vital in establishing constitutional power, was by 1941 completely unimportant to the Court. The world had moved fast, and the Court along with it.

In *Federal Power Commission* v. *Hope Natural Gas Co.* (1944) the Court definitely repudiated the judicial control over rate making which it had assumed in *Smyth* v. *Ames.* The *Adair* and *Coppage* doctrine on labor organization was gradually outflanked, but the two decisions were not specifically repudiated until 1949 in *Lincoln Federal Labor Union* v. *Northwestern Iron & Metal Co.* Involved were a North Carolina statute and a Nebraska constitutional amendment outlawing the closed shop. No person was to be denied an opportunity to work in the two states either because he was or because he was not a member of a labor organization. The Supreme Court unanimously upheld these laws against free speech, equal protection, and due process charges.

It is not the mere reversal of position in these economic due process cases which is surprising. That was bound to happen. The Court could not continue to live in the nineteenth century. It had to abandon the exaggerated pretensions toward judicial control over economic policy which substantive due process had been used to justify. It had to assume that Congress and the state legislatures were as likely to act as reasonable men when they passed economic regulations as when they legislated for the public health, safety, and welfare.

But the Court did not merely retreat to the test of reasonableness which it employed in *Jacobson* v. *Massachusetts* and *Buck* v. *Bell.* As Robert McCloskey has so well pointed out, the Court appeared to say that it would no longer subject economic legislation to *any* constitutional test.[30] It would abandon any responsibility for reviewing legislative decisions on economic problems and, returning to the spirit of *Munn*, tell plaintiffs to carry their objections to the legislature, not the courts.

Thus in *Olsen* v. *Nebraska* Justice Douglas for a unanimous Court stated that differences of opinion on the needfulness or appropriateness of a law "suggest a choice which 'should be left where . . . it was left by the Constitution—to the states and to Congress.'" Again, *Day-Brite Lighting* v.

[30] "Economic Due Process and the Supreme Court," in Philip B. Kurland (ed.), *The Supreme Court Review: 1962* (Chicago: The University of Chicago Press, 1962), pp. 34–62.

*Missouri* (1952) involved a state law which provided that employees could absent themselves from their jobs for four hours on election days, and forbade employers to deduct wages for their absence. The Court majority admitted that the social policy embodied in the law was debatable, but said: "Our recent decisions make plain that we do not sit as a super-legislature to weigh the wisdom of legislation nor to decide whether the policy it expresses offends the public welfare."

*Williamson* v. *Lee Optical of Oklahoma* (1955) asked the Court to review a statute which was the product of an interest group struggle in the Oklahoma legislature, and represented a victory for the ophthalmologists and optometrists of the state over the opticians. It forbade any person not in the first two categories from fitting lenses to the face or duplicating or replacing lenses into frames, except on the prescription of an ophthalmologist or optometrist.

The trial court held that there was no sound health or welfare reason why opticians should not be able to fit old glasses into new frames or to duplicate lenses without a prescription. The Supreme Court agreed that this might be "a needless, wasteful requirement in many cases," but said:

> It is for the legislature, not the courts, to balance the advantages and disadvantages of the new requirement. . . . The day is gone when this Court uses the Due Process Clause of the Fourteenth Amendment to strike down state laws, regulatory of business and industrial conditions, because they may be unwise, improvident, or out of harmony with a particular school of thought.

Finally, in *Ferguson* v. *Skrupa* (1963) the Court upheld a Kansas statute prohibiting anyone except lawyers from engaging in the business of "debt adjustment," overruling *Adams* v. *Tanner* (1917) in the process. Black, condemning again the *Lochner-Coppage-Adkins-Burns* line of cases, repeated that "it is up to legislatures, not courts, to decide on the wisdom and utility of legislation." Justice Harlan registered the sole protest against judicial abdication; insisting that the Court could not shirk the responsibility to judge even in this field, he assumed that task and concurred in upholding the statute as bearing "a rational relation to a constitutionally permissible objective."

EQUAL PROTECTION AND ECONOMIC REGULATION    It may be appropriate at this time to consider the relationship of the equal protection clause of the Fourteenth Amendment to economic regulation, although the principal discussion of equal protection is reserved to a later chapter. The principal impact of the equal protection standard has been against racial discrimination. In fact, during the Supreme Court's first discussion of the Fourteenth Amendment in the *Slaughter-House Cases* (1873), Justice Miller, taking note of the obvious origin of the amendment in concern for Negro rights,

doubted very much "whether any action of a State not directed by way of discrimination against the negroes as a class, or on account of their race, will ever be held to come within the purview" of the equal protection clause.

As it turned out, this prediction was doubly confounded. The Court proved very reluctant to use the equal protection clause as an instrument for protection of the civil rights of Negroes and, at the same time, eager to invent uses for it as a bar to business regulation. Robert J. Harris reports that, out of 554 decisions of the Supreme Court up to 1960 in which the equal protection provision was involved, 426 (77 per cent) dealt with legislation affecting economic interests, while only 78 (14 per cent) concerned state laws allegedly imposing racial discrimination or acts of Congress designed to eliminate it.[31]

Judicial review under the equal protection clause, however, was never carried to the extremes which characterized the application of substantive due process. The Court generally understood that legislatures in dealing with the regulation of economic life must classify and make distinctions based on differences in degree. In *Barbier* v. *Connolly* (1885) the Court upheld a San Francisco ordinance which prohibited the night operation of laundries within a certain section of the city, on the ground that it was a reasonable precaution against fire. "It is not legislation discriminating against any one. All persons engaged in the same business . . . are treated alike." Justice Field, who wrote the opinion, went on to talk about the impact of the equal protection clause in words which have been often quoted. The clause, he said, was not designed

> . . . to interfere with the power of the State, sometimes termed its police power, to prescribe regulations to promote the health, peace, morals, education, and good order of the people, and to legislate so as to increase the industries of the State, develop its resources, and add to its wealth and prosperity. From the very necessities of society, legislation of a special character, having these objects in view, must often be had in certain districts, such as for draining marshes and irrigating arid plains. Special burdens are often necessary for general benefits—for supplying water, preventing fires, lighting districts, cleaning streets, opening parks, and many other subjects. Regulations for these purposes may press with more or less weight upon one than upon another, but they are designed, not to impose unequal or unnecessary restrictions upon any one, but to promote, with as little individual inconvenience as possible, the general good. Though . . . necessarily special in their character, they do not furnish just ground of complaint if they operate alike upon all persons and property under the same circumstances and conditions. Class legislation, discriminating against some and favoring others, is prohibited, but legislation which, in carrying out a public purpose, is

[31] *The Quest for Equality* (Baton Rouge, La.: Louisiana State University Press, 1960), p. 59.

limited in its application, if within the sphere of its operation it affects alike all persons similarly situated, is not within the amendment.

The decided cases are full of warnings against judicial interference with legislative classifications. The differences between persons or things on which the classification is based need not be scientific or marked, so long as there are some practical distinctions.[32] A classification must be clearly and actually arbitrary to be held invalid, and not merely possibly so.[33] Every presumption as to facts which could conceivably justify the legislative classification will be assumed.[34] The state may do what it can to prevent what it deems an evil, and stop short of those cases in which the harm to the few concerned is thought less important than the harm to the public that would result if the rules laid down were made mathematically exact.[35] Legislative reform may take one step at a time, addressing itself to the phase of the problem which seems most acute to the legislative mind.[36] The legislature may select one phase of one field and apply a remedy there, neglecting the others.[37]

In spite of such judicial permissiveness, a few regulatory statutes now and again have been snagged by the Supreme Court on the equal protection hook.[38] In several fields, classifications originally declared invalid have later been approved. As we already know, this happened in the field of minimum wage laws for women. Another example is found in state antimonopoly laws, several of which have exempted agricultural products and livestock in the hands of the producer from their scope. An Illinois law of this type was held unconstitutional by the Supreme Court in 1902,[39] but in 1940 the Court upheld a similar provision in a Texas statute, saying that the earlier precedent had been "eroded" by the passage of time.[40]

The traditional "liberal" position, with its emphasis on judicial self-restraint, has generally disapproved of striking down state economic legislation on equal protection grounds, which Justice Holmes once referred to as the "usual last refuge of constitutional arguments." [41] However, equal protection was still able to stir up some good arguments on the liberal Court of the 1940s. For example, *Kotch* v. *Board of River Port Pilot Commissioners* (1947) involved a Louisiana statutory plan of licensing pilots for the port of New Orleans. Members of the licensing board were themselves pilots,

[32] *Orient Ins. Co.* v. *Daggs* (1899).
[33] *Bachtel* v. *Wilson* (1907).
[34] *Crescent Cotton Oil Co.* v. *Mississippi* (1921).
[35] *Dominion Hotel* v. *Arizona* (1919).
[36] *Semler* v. *Oregon State Board of Dental Examiners* (1935).
[37] *A.F. of L.* v. *American Sash Co.* (1949).
[38] *Smith* v. *Cahoon* (1931); *Mayflower Farms* v. *Ten Eyck* (1936); *Hartford Steam Boiler Inspection and Ins. Co.* v. *Harrison* (1937).
[39] *Connolly* v. *Union Sewer Pipe Co.* (1902).
[40] *Tigner* v. *Texas* (1940).
[41] *Buck* v. *Bell* (1927).

and they operated the certification process in such a way that only selected relatives and friends of present pilots could secure licenses. Four members of the Court thought this was a "wholly arbitrary exercise of power," condemned by the principle of the *Yick Wo* case even though the basis for discrimination was consanguinity rather than race. But the majority, through Justice Black, ruled that the Court should not interfere with "the right and power of a state to select its own agents and officers." [42]

More recently, the Court took the same position in *Williamson* v. *Lee Optical of Oklahoma* (1955), the due process aspects of which have already been covered. An equal protection issue was raised by the fact that this strict legislative regulation of opticians in fitting and replacing lenses completely exempted sellers of "ready-to-wear" glasses from control. The Court unanimously upheld the legislature, saying: "For all this record shows, the ready-to-wear branch of this business may not loom large in Oklahoma or may present problems of regulation distinct from the other branches."

The Court was not so permissive, however, in *Morey* v. *Doud* (1957). An Illinois statute exempted money orders of the American Express Company from the requirement that any firm issuing money orders in the state must secure a license and submit to state regulation. The state argued that the world-wide operations and unquestioned solvency of this company made the exemption reasonable, but for the first time in several decades the Court refused to defer to the legislative judgment on an economic classification issue. Justices Frankfurter, Harlan, and Black, dissenting, charged the majority was viewing significant distinctions with a glass eye, and returning to the long-discredited role of "Superlegislature."

### SUBSTANTIVE DUE PROCESS AND THE RIGHT TO PRIVACY

The paradox of substantive due process is that its rise and decline were simultaneous. For we know that due process, during the same period when it was being abandoned as a source of judicial control over state regulation of business and industrial conditions, was being developed by the Court into an unprecedentedly strong check on the substance of legislation infringing civil liberties.

We are already familiar with the rationale for this development. Standing alone and uninterpreted, due process is a vague standard which courts should not attempt to apply to limit legislative discretion. But where due process is a carrier for the meanings stated in the First Amendment, then a court can legitimately veto legislation without laying itself open to the charge of thwarting the democratic process. Stanley Morrison has pointed out how this doctrine solves the problem of a judicial liberal such as Justice

[42] See also *Goesart* v. *Cleary* (1948); *Railway Express Agency* v. *New York* (1949).

Black, making it possible for him "to abolish substantive due process in the economic field and to preserve it in the field of civil liberties." [43]

But does this reasoning adequately safeguard the essential values of a democratic society? It protects the libertarian goals stated in the Bill of Rights, but it does not state a basis for judicial protection of newer values not adequately perceived when the Bill of Rights was drawn up. The best illustration is sterilization legislation such as was involved in *Buck* v. *Bell*. There is nothing specific in the Bill of Rights to justify Supreme Court invalidation of such a law, yet it is highly unlikely that the Court of the 1960s would accept the Holmes opinion.

Actually, a later Court came very close to overruling *Buck* v. *Bell*. *Skinner* v. *Oklahoma* (1942) involved a state habitual-criminal sterilization act, under which persons convicted two or more times of felonies involving moral turpitude could be rendered sexually sterile. Douglas wrote the majority opinion striking down the law on equal protection grounds, which made it unnecessary for him to reconsider *Buck* v. *Bell*. But both Stone and Jackson wrote concurring opinions cutting much of the ground out from under the *Buck* decision and its presumption of legislative validity. Stone said, satirically:

> If we must presume that the legislature knows—what science has been unable to ascertain—that the criminal tendencies of any class of habitual offenders are transmissible regardless of the varying characteristics of its individuals, I should suppose that we must likewise presume that the legislature, in its wisdom, knows that the criminal tendencies of some classes of offenders are more likely to be transmitted than those of others.

Jackson went further in suggesting his doubts as to the constitutionality of sterilization on eugenic grounds: "I . . . think the present plan to sterilize the individual in pursuit of a eugenic plan to eliminate from the race characteristics that are only vaguely identified and which in our present state of knowledge are uncertain as to transmissibility presents . . . constitutional questions of gravity." While he admitted that these constitutional questions had been decided in favor of the legislation in *Buck* v. *Bell*, he implied that, so far as he was concerned, the failure to overrule the *Buck* decision here was simply because the Oklahoma law was unconstitutional on other grounds, for he warned: "There are limits to the extent to which a legislatively represented majority may conduct biological experiments at the expense of the dignity and personality and natural powers of a minority."

Substantive due process is a necessary doctrine for any judge who wants to be in a position occasionally to argue with "legislatively represented majorities." Justice Jackson needed substantive due process in order to

---

[43] Stanley Morrison, "Does the Fourteenth Amendment Incorporate the Bill of Rights: The Judicial Interpretation," 2 *Stanford Law Review* 140–173 (1949).

question the decision of the Missouri Legislature in the *Day-Brite Lighting* case. Dissenting there, he said:

> There must be some limit to the power to shift the whole voting burden from the voter to someone else who happens to stand in some economic relationship to him. Getting out the vote is not the business of employers. . . . It is either the voter's own business or the State's business. I do not question that the incentive which this statute offers will help swell the vote; to require that employees be paid time-and-a-half would swell it still more, and double-time would do even better. But does the success of an enticement to vote justify putting its cost on some other citizen?

In fact, subsequent experience suggests the Court cannot live with the Black doctrine that it should enforce due process only when it is spelled out in the Constitution. *Griswold* v. *Connecticut* (1965) saw the Court in a most creative mood. It wanted to argue with a legislature, but it had no specific constitutional provisions on which to base its argument. And so it created a constitutional foundation for its position, just as it had done with substantive due process three-quarters of a century earlier.

At issue in *Griswold* was a Connecticut law forbidding the use of contraceptives or advice as to their use, for violation of which the medical and executive directors of a New Haven planned-parenthood center were convicted. Justice Douglas, speaking for the Court, held that this law interfered with "a right of privacy older than the Bill of Rights." Admittedly this zone of privacy is not specified in the Constitution, but he found it within the "penumbra" of several fundamental constitutional guarantees. There is the right of association in the penumbra of the First Amendment. There is the recognition of the privacy of the home in the Third and Fourth Amendments, as well as the zone of personal privacy derived from the self-incrimination clause of the Fifth Amendment. Finally, there is the Ninth Amendment's warning that the enumeration of certain rights in the Constitution does not mean that there are not others "retained by the people." Justices Harlan and White relied on the due process clause to come to the same conclusion that the law was invalid.[44]

[44] The right to privacy thus placed on a broad constitutional foundation by the Court has been at least inferentially recognized and applied by the Court in a number of other contexts discussed elsewhere in this volume. The common law protected privacy by actions against trespass, assault, deceit, and libel and slander. The rise of the sensational mass-circulation press with its commercial invasions of privacy led to some successful common-law actions, and a statutory effort to protect privacy from commercial exploitation was examined by the Court in *Time, Inc.* v. *Hill* (1967). Privacy of association was recognized by the Court in *NAACP* v. *Alabama* (1958) and *Gibson* v. *Florida Legislative Investigation Committee* (1963). In *Sweezy* v. *New Hampshire* (1957) Justice Frankfurter referred to "political privacy." The right to anonymity in public expression was recognized by the Court in *Talley* v. *California* (1960). Privacy of the body, related to the Fifth Amendment's protec-

For Justice Black, this creation of a right of privacy out of general constitutional language was an exact parallel to the Court's earlier creation of property rights out of the due process clause. The Court's reasoning in *Griswold*, for him, came straight out of *Lochner, Coppage*, and *Adkins*. This was the same "natural law due process philosophy" which he thought the Court had abandoned and which he charged was "no less dangerous when used to enforce this Court's views about personal rights than those about economic rights." He reiterated his willingness "to hold laws unconstitutional where they are forbidden by the Federal Constitution." But where the Court had no guide as specific as the First Amendment, then he denied that the Court had power "to sit as a supervisory agency over acts of duly constituted legislative bodies and set aside their laws because of the Court's belief that the legislative policies adopted are unreasonable, unwise, arbitrary, capricious or irrational."

But why should the due process clause have substantive impact only through the First Amendment? Why, as McCloskey asks, is "liberty of economic choice . . . less indispensable to the 'openness' of a society than freedom of expression?" Justice Douglas made the same point in *Barsky* v. *Board of Regents* (1954), where he said in dissent: "The right to work, I had assumed, was the most precious liberty that man possesses. Man has indeed as much right to work as he has to live, to be free, to own property."

Are rights of such importance to be left without judicial protection? It does not seem likely. It is true that in the *Barsky* case the Court majority followed the rule of judicial noninterference in the economic field and sustained administrative suspension of a physician's license against a charge of unreasonableness. But in 1957 on a bar-admission case Justice Black himself declared for the Court that state-imposed qualifications "must have a rational connection with the applicant's fitness or capacity" to practice the profession.[45]

It is significant that Justice Douglas, having read the Court out of the picture in *Olsen* v. *Nebraska, Day-Brite Lighting* v. *Missouri,* and *Williamson* v. *Lee Optical,* found it necessary to read it at least partially back in again in *Poe* v. *Ullman* (1961):

> The error of the old Court, as I see it, was not in entertaining inquiries concerning the constitutionality of social legislation but in applying the

tion against self-incrimination, was an element in the decisions in *Rochin* v. *California* (1952), *Breithaupt* v. *Abram* (1957), and *Schmerber* v. *California* (1966). The marital privacy issue in *Griswold* had earlier been examined by some members of the Court in dissenting opinions in *Poe* v. *Ullman* (1961). The best general discussion of the privacy issue is Alan F. Westin, *Privacy and Freedom* (New York: Atheneum, 1967).

[45] *Schware* v. *Board of Bar Examiners* (1957). The Court maintained its insistence on the judicially enforced "rational connection rule" in three 1961 decisions—*Cohen* v. *Hurley, In re Anastaplo,* and *Konigsberg* v. *State Bar*—even though the majority found in each case that the restriction was rationally justified.

standards that it did. . . . Social legislation dealing with business and economic matters touches no particularized prohibition of the Constitution, unless it be the provision of the Fifth Amendment that private property should not be taken for public use without just compensation. If it is free of the latter guarantee, it has a wide scope for application. Some go so far as to suggest that whatever the majority in the legislature says goes . . . that there is no other standard of constitutionality. That reduces the legislative power to sheer voting strength and the judicial function to a matter of statistics. . . . While the legislative judgment on economic and business matters is "well-nigh conclusive," . . . it is not beyond judicial inquiry.

The American system of "judicial inquiry," it seems safe to conclude, cannot operate without the concept of substantive due process. Nor can the Supreme Court evade its obligation to judge whether legislation bears "a rational relation to a constitutionally permissible objective."

## SELECTED REFERENCES

BERNS, WALTER, "Buck v. Bell: Due Process of Law?" 6 *Western Political Quarterly* 762–775 (1953).

*The Constitution of the United States of America: Analysis and Interpretation,* Sen. Doc. no. 39, 88th Cong., pp. 1082–1146. Washington: Government Printing Office, 1964.

CORWIN, EDWARD S., *Liberty against Government: The Rise, Flowering and Decline of a Famous Juridical Concept,* chaps. 3, 4. Baton Rouge, La.: Louisiana State University Press, 1951.

DOUGLAS, WILLIAM O., *We the Judges,* chap. 8. Garden City, N.Y.: Doubleday & Company, Inc., 1956.

HAMILTON, WALTON H., "Affectation with Public Interest," 39 *Yale Law Journal* 1089–1112 (1930).

HOLT, J. C., *Magna Carta.* New York: Cambridge University Press, 1966.

KELLY, ALFRED H., and WINFRED A. HARBISON, *The American Constitution: Its Origins and Development,* chaps. 19, 20. New York: W. W. Norton & Company, Inc., 1963 (third edition).

LERNER, MAX, "The Supreme Court and American Capitalism," in Robert G. McCloskey (ed.), *Essays in Constitutional Law,* chap. 4. New York: Alfred A. Knopf, Inc., 1957.

MC CLOSKEY, ROBERT G., "Economic Due Process and the Supreme Court," in Philip B. Kurland (ed.), *The Supreme Court Review: 1962,* pp. 34–62. Chicago: The University of Chicago Press, 1962.

ROCHE, JOHN P., "Entrepreneurial Liberty and the Fourteenth Amendment," 4 *Labor History* 3–31 (1963).

# 32

## Contracts, eminent domain, and taxation

The Constitution does not leave the safeguarding of property solely to a judicially developed doctrine of substantive due process. In this chapter the impact of the Constitution on the protection of property rights will be examined in three different contexts—contracts, eminent domain, and taxation. In two of these areas specific protective language occurs in the Constitution. The states are forbidden to impair the obligation of contracts, and the federal government is forbidden to take private property without just compensation. However, the due process clause backstops and intertwines with these more detailed provisions, and the judicial problem is basically similar in all three areas.

### THE PROTECTION OF CONTRACTS

Article I, section 10, forbids any state to "pass any . . . law impairing the obligation of contracts." This language, commonly referred to as the contract clause, qualifies as one of the Constitution's enigmas. The fact that the clause has comparatively little present-day significance should not be permitted to minimize the outstanding role which it played in an earlier period. In the absence of a due process requirement applicable to the states, the contract clause was invoked against state legislation early and often. Even after the Fourteenth Amendment was adopted, it took some time, as we

know, for substantive due process to develop and to supply judicial rationalization for protection of the freedom of contract. As Benjamin F. Wright has noted in his definitive study, up to 1889 the contract clause had been considered by the Court in almost 40 per cent of all cases involving the validity of state legislation. During that period it was the constitutional justification for seventy-five decisions in which state laws were held unconstitutional, almost half of all those in which legislation was declared invalid by the Supreme Court.[1] But with the development of substantive due process, there was less and less occasion to invoke the contract clause.

Another reason why the contract clause has seemed to be primarily of historical interest is that the significant development of the doctrine in this field took place prior to 1865. In this process Marshall's contribution was preeminent. His four great contract decisions, written between 1810 and 1819—*Fletcher* v. *Peck* (1810), *New Jersey* v. *Wilson* (1812), *Sturges* v. *Crowninshield* (1819), and *Dartmouth College* v. *Woodward* (1819)—are among the most significant decisions that the Supreme Court has ever handed down. By employing a far broader conception of contract than had prevailed in 1787, and by combining this conception with the principles of eighteenth-century natural law, Marshall was able to make of the contract clause a powerful instrument for the protection of the vested rights of private property.

Before going further, some explanation of terms is in order. A contract is a mutual and legally enforceable agreement between at least two parties under which each or both undertake to do or to refrain from doing certain things. A contract is analyzable into two elements: the agreement, which comes from the parties, and the obligation, which comes from the law and makes the agreement binding on the parties. If a party to a valid contract fails to perform the obligation he has assumed, the other party has two kinds of remedies available. He may sue in a law court for damages, or if damages would not be an adequate remedy or would be difficult to assess, he may sue in a court of equity for a writ of specific performance. Contracts may be written or unwritten, express or implied,[2] executory or executed.[3]

THE ORIGINAL UNDERSTANDING    The "intention of the framers" concerning the contract clause is almost impossible to determine. The most general assumption has been that the clause was desired by propertied interests who

---

[1] Benjamin F. Wright, *The Contract Clause of the Constitution* (Cambridge, Mass.: Harvard University Press, 1938), p. 95.

[2] An implied contract is one not created or evidenced by express agreement of the parties, but inferred by the law, as a matter of reason and justice, from their acts or conduct.

[3] An executory contract is one which requires some future act to be done. An executed contract is one where nothing remains to be done by either party, and where the transaction is completed at the moment the arrangement is made. An executed contract is not properly a contract at all, except reminiscently, since the parties are no longer bound by a contractual tie.

wanted to protect themselves against the kind of state legislation favoring debtors that had been passed during the hard times of the 1780s—issuance of paper money which was given legal tender status in payment of private debts, granting debtors postponements beyond the contract date for payment of debts, or permitting them to pay debts in installments or in commodities. But this problem was thought to have been met by the provisions forbidding the states to emit bills of credit, coin money, or give anything but specie the quality of legal tender (Art. I, sec. 10), and also by bestowing on the federal government the power to coin money and regulate its value (Art. I, sec. 8). In the debates on ratification, when the contract clause was mentioned at all, which appears to have been very seldom, it was generally assumed to be a part of the monetary restrictions imposed on the states by the Constitution.

MARSHALL AND PUBLIC CONTRACTS    The common understanding of the time, moreover, was that the clause affected only private contracts, that is, contracts between individuals. Yet in the series of important contract cases decided by the Marshall Court, practically all dealt with public contracts. The Supreme Court's first case interpreting the contract clause, *Fletcher* v. *Peck* (1810), was one of the most controversial and unpopular that body has ever handed down, because it had the effect of protecting the perpetrators of the outrageous Yazoo land frauds. The case had its origin in the action of the Georgia legislature which in 1795 was induced by bribery to direct the sale of public lands, comprising most of what is now the states of Alabama and Mississippi, to four land companies. Public anger quickly removed these legislators, and the new legislature in 1796 revoked the sale of the previous year, but the land companies had already disposed of some of the land to speculators and prospective settlers, who sought redress in various ways.

In the suit which was cooked up to test the legislative action, Marshall ruled that whether the original sale had been procured by fraud was not a proper subject of judicial inquiry, and concentrated on the contract issue and the injustice of the repeal act to the innocent purchasers from the land companies. How did he turn this land grant into a contract? Marshall argued that a grant is a contract executed, and that the grant contains an implied contract that the grantor will not reassert his right over the thing granted. This interpretation has little relation to the ordinary understanding of the "obligation" of contract, which is to perform or fulfill the terms of an executory contract. But even conceding that a grant is a contract, how is it established that the contract clause, contrary to the original understanding, applies to public contracts? Marshall cited no authorities. He merely asserted that the words of the clause "are general, and are applicable to contracts of every description."

Perhaps because of these weaknesses, Marshall seemed hesitant about

resting his argument entirely on the contract clause. He also invoked in a rather vague way the ex post facto and bill of attainder provisions, though *Calder* v. *Bull* (1798) had already held the ex post facto clause to be confined to criminal cases. In addition, and almost in the same breath, he suggested that the limits on the Georgia legislature came not from the Constitution, but from "the nature of society and of government." In his concluding paragraph, he could do no better than say that the rescinding act was invalidated "either by general principles, which are common to our free institutions, or by the particular provisions of the constitution of the United States."

This sorry performance inflamed public opinion, which was already antagonistic to the nationalistic trends of the Marshall Court on states' rights grounds. Nevertheless, the doctrine that the contract clause covered public contracts remained firmly established. Marshall himself quickly conquered the doubts he had exhibited in *Fletcher* v. *Peck*, and in *New Jersey* v. *Wilson* (1812) applied the contract clause to prevent a state from exercising one of its most fundamental powers, taxation. The New Jersey colonial legislature had in 1758 entered into an agreement with an Indian tribe which gave them perpetual tax exemption on the land where they resided. In 1801 the Indians, wishing to move to New York, secured the consent of the New Jersey legislature to sell the land. The new owners claimed the tax exemption ran with the land, but the state argued that a perpetual exemption had been given only because the Indians were forbidden to alienate the land, and that if this provision could be repealed, so could the tax exemption. Marshall invalidated the legislative attempt to tax the land, without ever mentioning the basic issue of the right of a state to bargain away its indispensable taxing power.

Next came *Dartmouth College* v. *Woodward* (1819), which held that a corporate charter was a contract. Though this case concerned a college, it was largely business corporations which were to benefit from the decision. Dartmouth College was chartered by the Crown in 1769 as a seminary for the education of young Indians. Subsequently the clientele of the college changed and it became involved in New Hampshire politics. In 1816 a Republican majority in the legislature passed an act changing the name to Dartmouth University, increasing the board of trustees from twelve to twenty-one, vesting appointment of the new members in the governor and council, and providing for a board of overseers, appointed by the governor, with veto power over the actions of the trustees. The new authorities proceeded to oust the old trustees, who brought suit against the college secretary to recover the college charter, seal, and records.

For the Supreme Court, Marshall invalidated the state legislation on the ground that a charter of incorporation is a contract protected against legislative infringement. This doctrine was sheer creation on Marshall's part. In both *Fletcher* v. *Peck* and *New Jersey* v. *Wilson* there had been dis-

cernible contracts entered into by two parties for a consideration. But it could not possibly have occurred to the Founding Fathers that a charter granted by the Crown was a contract.

Forced to admit that this kind of grant was not within the original intention of the contract clause, Marshall came up with the following celebrated rule of constitutional construction:

> It is not enough to say, that this particular case was not in the mind of the Convention, when the article was framed, nor of the American people, when it was adopted. It is necessary to go farther, and to say that, had this particular case been suggested, the language would have been so varied, as to exclude it, or it would have been made a special exception. The case being within the words of the rule, must be within its operation likewise, unless there be something in the literal construction so obviously absurd, or mischievous, or repugnant to the general spirit of the instrument, as to justify those who expound the constitution in making it an exception.

In this instance, Marshall felt, there was no such reason. Would the Founders have excluded "contracts made for the advancement of literature" from the protection accorded ordinary contracts? Certainly not. It was a small college, but there were those who loved it.

LIMITATIONS ON THE PROTECTION OF PUBLIC CONTRACTS    These three decisions raised a truly alarming specter of a venal or unwise legislature giving away the public birthright or even divesting the government of its essential taxing power—actions which would be irremediable under the contract clause. It is hardly surprising that a doctrine so potentially dangerous tended to generate its own correctives, which can be summarized under three headings.

First, the Darthmouth College decision itself recognized that the state may insert as a condition in the corporate charter the right to "amend, alter, and repeal" the same. This reservation is then part of the contract, and exercise of the power does not impair the contractual obligation. Again, the reservation may be, not in the contract itself, but in general legislation which has the effect of incorporating the reservation in all charters of subsequent date. Especially after the Dartmouth ruling, such reservations were commonly provided, both by statutory and constitutional provisions.

Second, there is the rule of strict construction of public contracts or grants, which stems from Chief Justice Taney's famous decision in *Charles River Bridge* v. *Warren Bridge* (1837). The Charles River Bridge, a privately owned toll structure, was incorporated in 1785, and its franchise was extended in 1792. In 1828 Massachusetts incorporated the Warren Bridge and authorized it to build and operate a toll bridge near the other bridge. After a short period the Warren Bridge was to become free and part of the public highway; this would of course be fatal to the toll bridge. Taney,

speaking for the Court, ruled that the state had not given the Charles River Bridge an exclusive charter. There was no express language in the contract that another bridge would not be established nearby. Public grants or franchises are to be strictly construed, and nothing passes to the grantee by implication. Taney added: "While the rights of private property are sacredly guarded, we must not forget that the community also have rights, and that the happiness and well being of every citizen depends on their faithful preservation."

The rule of strict construction has been applied to public utility franchises generally [4] and to grants of tax exemption. Marshall himself stated that tax exemption grants are never to be presumed, but must be specifically set forth.[5] But efforts to attack the holding in *New Jersey* v. *Wilson*, and to establish the principle that taxation is an inalienable power which no legislature can barter away, have never succeeded.[6]

While taxation has thus not been given the status of an inalienable governmental power, the police power and eminent domain have been so recognized, constituting the third of the general limitations on the constitutional protection accorded to public grants. The subordination of all charter rights and privileges to the power of eminent domain was first stated by the Supreme Court in 1848.[7] Vermont, which had granted an exclusive right to construct a bridge, subsequently made a new grant to a competing company, at the same time providing compensation for the old bridge. The Court held that state sovereignty rendered all the principal powers of a state inalienable, and that corporate franchises were always subject to being taken by eminent domain.

In 1869 the Illinois legislature granted the Illinois Central Railroad title to nearly a thousand acres of submerged land on the Chicago lakefront, and then took it back four years later. The Supreme Court approved by a four to three vote, Justice Field saying: "Such abdication is not consistent with the exercise of that trust which requires the government of the State to preserve such waters for the use of the public." [8] Even an explicit agreement by a state not to exercise the power of eminent domain has been held to have no binding effect.[9]

The leading cases on inalienability of the police power were decided in 1878 and 1880. In *Fertilizing Co.* v. *Hyde Park* (1878), a franchise to operate a fertilizer factory was rendered valueless by a municipal ordinance prohibiting the transportation of offal through the streets, and forbidding the operation of such a factory within the town limits. The Court ruled,

[4] *Skaneateles Water Works Co.* v. *Skaneateles* (1902); *Knoxville Water Co.* v. *Knoxville* (1906).
[5] *Providence Bank* v. *Billings* (1830).
[6] *Piqua Branch of the State Bank* v. *Knoop* (1853) is the leading case.
[7] *West River Bridge Co.* v. *Dix* (1848).
[8] *Illinois Central Railroad* v. *Illinois* (1892).
[9] *Pennsylvania Hospital* v. *Philadelphia* (1917).

though not without dissent, that since the franchise contained no express exemption from the power to abate a nuisance, the contract was made subject to the police power of the state. In *Stone* v. *Mississippi* (1880) a lottery franchise had been granted for a definite term of years, but two years later a new constitution was adopted which forbade lotteries. The unanimous Court ruled that "the power of governing is a trust committed by the people to the government, no part of which can be granted away."

CONTRACTS BETWEEN PRIVATE PERSONS    Only about 10 per cent of the Supreme Court's contract cases have involved private contracts, but in that number are cases of considerable interest and importance. Again we go back to the Marshall Court for the beginning of the story. *Sturges* v. *Crowninshield* (1819) involved the validity of a New York bankruptcy act as applied to a contract of debt made *before* the law was passed. Of course the Constitution gives Congress power to enact "uniform laws on the subject of bankruptcies throughout the United States," but Congress had not at this time exercised its power so as to cover the field fully. Consequently Marshall took the position that until Congress did so act, the states were free to regulate "such cases as the laws of the Union may not reach." But Marshall then went on to declare the state law in violation of the contract clause. His objection, moreover, was not to the particular provisions of this law. He contended that the contract clause meant that contracts were free from all legislative regulation. The sole exception he was willing to allow was for laws abolishing imprisonment for debt.

Although Marshall carried the Court for this extreme view in *Sturges,* he was unable to do so in *Ogden* v. *Saunders* (1827), where the bankruptcy law being questioned was in force *before* the contract was made. Marshall would have declared this law unconstitutional also, but for the only time in his thirty-four years as Chief Justice he was in the minority on a constitutional issue. Dissenting with Duval and Story, he argued that the framers had intended to prevent all legislative interference with contracts, not merely "retrospective laws." Realizing that his reliance on intent of the Constitution was shaky, he also invoked natural law. "Individuals do not derive from government their right to contract, but bring that right with them into society." No just government may interfere with this right, except to substitute legal remedies for personal force or to regulate or prohibit mischievous agreements.

If the Marshall view had prevailed, *Ogden* v. *Saunders* would have been the foundation for judicial supervision over state legislation under the contract clause comparable with that which developed under the due process clause sixty years later. But the majority held that the *Sturges* decision had to be limited to contracts already made. A statute in effect at the time a contract is entered into is a part of the contract, and therefore cannot be held to impair its obligation. The true meaning of the contract clause, said Justice

Johnson, was to protect against "arbitrary and tyrannical legislation over existing rights." Bankruptcy legislation was no more in this category than laws regulating usurious contracts or the collection of gaming debts. This view of insolvency laws has been consistently maintained since.

State authority to modify contractual remedies is derived from the police power, and we have already seen that the police power cannot be frustrated by public contracts. Even less should private contracts be permitted to override public policy. Thus a state prohibition act is not invalid because it nullifies contracts for the sale of beer,[10] and contracts of employment may legitimately be modified by later workmen's compensation laws.[11] As the Supreme Court said in 1905, "Parties by entering into contracts may not estop the legislature from enacting laws intended for the public good." [12]

There may be real difficulty in determining how far a legislature may reasonably go when the "public good" sought under the police power is such a controversial problem as the relief of debtors. The most famous debtor relief case of recent times is *Home Building and Loan Assn. v. Blaisdell* (1934), where the Court by a five to four vote upheld depression legislation passed by Minnesota to prevent the wholesale loss of mortgaged properties by debtors unable to meet their obligations. On application from the mortgagor, state courts could extend the existing one-year period of redemption from foreclosure sales for an additional limited time. During this period in which the mortgagor was allowed to retain possession, he was obliged to apply the income or reasonable rental value to the payment of taxes, interest, insurance, and the mortgage indebtedness.

In upholding the law Chief Justice Hughes stressed the government's emergency powers. "While emergency does not create power," he said, "emergency may furnish the occasion for the exercise of power." The states have a reserved power to protect the interests of their citizens in time of emergency. They also have an obligation not to impair contracts. These two powers "must be construed in harmony with each other." One must not be used to destroy the other. Certainly "state power exists to give temporary relief from the enforcement of contracts in the presence of disasters due to physical causes such as fire, flood or earthquake." The same power must exist "when the urgent public need demanding such relief is produced by other and economic causes." Hughes concluded: "The question is no longer merely that of one party to a contract as against another, but of the use of reasonable means to safeguard the economic structure upon which the good of all depends. . . . The principle of this development is . . . that the reservation of the reasonable exercise of the protective power of the State is read into all contracts."

Shortly thereafter, less carefully drawn moratorium legislation in two

[10] *Boston Beer Co.* v. *Massachusetts* ( 1878 ).
[11] *New York Central R. Co.* v. *White* ( 1917 ).
[12] *Manigault* v. *Springs* ( 1905 ).

other states was invalidated by the Court,[13] but these decisions do not detract from the authority of the *Blaisdell* opinion. In 1945 Justice Frankfurter for a unanimous Court said that the Hughes opinion had left "hardly any open spaces of controversy concerning the constitutional restrictions of the Contract Clause upon moratory legislation." The *Blaisdell* principle was restated by Frankfurter to say that

> When a widely diffused public interest has become enmeshed in a network of multitudinous private arrangements, the authority of the State "to safeguard the vital interests of its people" . . . is not to be gainsaid by abstracting one such arrangement from its public context and treating it as though it were an isolated private contract constitutionally immune from impairment.[14]

The recent experience with the contract clause in the protection of private contracts against legislation growing out of the Depression demonstrates the present-day superfluity of the clause. The federal government is confined by no contract clause, but the Supreme Court had no difficulty in using the due process clause of the Fifth Amendment to declare the Frazier-Lemke moratorium legislation unconstitutional in 1935.[15] The due process clause of the Fourteenth Amendment is similarly available to challenge any state law which is questionable on contract grounds. The obligation of contracts clause has become, in the words of Corwin, "a tail to the due process of law kite . . . a fifth wheel to the Constitutional Law coach." [16]

### EMINENT DOMAIN

Eminent domain is the power of government to take private property when it is needed for a public purpose. Since such authority is an incident of sovereignty, it requires no explicit constitutional recognition. The Fifth Amendment assumes the existence of this power in the national government when it imposes the requirement of "just compensation" on its use. The same amendment, of course, contains broader language prohibiting the federal government from taking property without due process of law. At the state level there is the due process clause in the Fourteenth Amendment but no "just compensation" language. Despite these differences in constitutional phraseology, certain significant constitutional questions apply to exercise of the eminent domain power by both the states and the federal government: what is a public purpose? what is a taking of property? and what is just compensation?

[13] *Worthen Co.* v. *Thomas* (1934); *Worthen Co.* v. *Kavanaugh* (1935).

[14] *East New York Savings Bank* v. *Hahn* (1945).

[15] *Louisville Joint Stock Land Bank Co.* v. *Radford* (1935).

[16] Edward S. Corwin, *The Constitution of the United States of America: Analysis and Interpretation* (Washington: Government Printing Office, 1953), p. 362. A recent example is *City of El Paso* v. *Simmons* (1965).

PUBLIC PURPOSE    Where a public agency itself proposes to use land for a public building, highway, park, or other facility for general public use, the public character of the taking is obvious. But the taking need not be for a use to which all the public will have access. Condemnation of property for public housing projects, in which only a small percentage of the population can live, is now thoroughly established. The "access" test is not relevant here; rather public purpose results from the contribution of public housing to slum clearance, reduction of crime and disease, lowering of police and fire costs, and general community improvement.[17]

Eminent domain power is customarily granted to public utility corporations, which have no difficulty in meeting the public use test. Even private corporations or individuals may be considered to qualify under sufficiently pressing circumstances. For example, in the arid West, a taking for a right of way across a neighbor's land for the enlargement of an irrigation ditch thereon to enable the taker to obtain water for irrigation on land that would otherwise be valueless was upheld.[18] Similar justification was found for a right of way across a placer mining claim for the aerial bucket line of a mining corporation.[19] "Mill acts" in various states have authorized riparian owners to dam streams for the operation of mills, and the resultant flooding of land of other private owners has generally been upheld, if compensation was paid.[20]

The tendency of the Supreme Court to give great weight to legislative determinations of what is a public use has been reinforced by recent developments. In *United States ex rel. TVA* v. *Welch* (1946) Justice Black said in the opinion for the Court: "We think that it is the function of Congress to decide what type of taking is for a public use." Justice Douglas added, in *Berman* v. *Parker* (1954): "Subject to specific constitutional limitations, when the legislature has spoken, the public interest has been declared in terms well-nigh conclusive." So far as state cases are concerned, the Supreme Court has tended to follow the decisions of the state courts. In a 1908 case the Court could recall no instance "where this Court has condemned as a violation of the Fourteenth Amendment a taking upheld by the State court as a taking for public uses." [21]

THE TAKING OF PROPERTY    There is sometimes a dispute in eminent domain cases over what is to be considered a "property right" for which compensation must be paid. When a lock and dam belonging to a navigation company was condemned, the government had to pay for the franchise to charge tolls as well as for the tangible property which was taken.[22] On the

---

[17] *City of Cleveland* v. *United States* (1945).
[18] *Clark* v. *Nash* (1905).
[19] *Strickley* v. *Highland Boy Gold Mining Co.* (1906).
[20] *Otis Co.* v. *Ludlow Mfg. Co.* (1906).
[21] *Hairston* v. *Danville & W. R. Co.* (1908).
[22] *Monongahela Nav. Co.* v. *United States* (1893).

other hand, where the government orders the removal or alteration of a bridge across a navigable river, on the ground that it is an obstruction to navigation, that is not a taking of property within the meaning of the Constitution.[23]

There is no private property in the running water of a navigable stream. Consequently, if the government has occasion to condemn land on a navigable stream for a power project, it need not pay the "power value" of the land, for it already owns the flowing water which creates the power potential.[24] Likewise, if downstream river improvement activities raise the water level of a navigable stream and deprive an upstream power producer of some of its fall of water, the government is under no constitutional obligation to pay for the loss.[25] On non-navigable streams, however, *United States v. Cress* (1917) recognized private ownership of the running water, and thus opened the way for private capitalization of power potential. The government has made a determined but thus far unsuccessful attempt to induce the Court to reverse the rule of the *Cress* case.[26]

Property need not be literally or fully "taken" in order to establish a basis for claiming compensation. An individual may remain in possession of his property, and still find that by reason of governmental action his use or enjoyment of the property has been seriously impaired. Property is taken within the meaning of the Constitution "when inroads are made upon an owner's use of it to an extent that, as between private parties, a servitude has been acquired either by agreement or in course of time." [27]

For example, *United States v. Causby* (1946) concerned a chicken farm which adjoined an airport leased by the United States. Bombing planes roared over the farm day and night on a glide path carrying them only 83 feet above the farm. The chicken business had to be abandoned because as many as ten chickens a day were killed by flying into walls in their fright. The Supreme Court ruled that the government action constituted a taking of the property, saying: "The flight of airplanes, which skim the surface but do not touch it, is as much an appropriation of the use of the land as a more conventional entry upon it." [28]

Such liability on the part of the government, however, is limited by the doctrine of "consequential damages." Acts done in the proper exercise of governmental power, and not encroaching on private property, though their

[23] *Hannibal Bridge Co.* v. *United States* (1911).
[24] *United States* v. *Chandler-Dunbar Water Co.* (1913); *United States* v. *Twin City Power Co.* (1956). But see *United States* v. *Virginia Electric Co.* (1961).
[25] *United States* v. *Willow River Power Co.* (1945).
[26] *United States ex rel. TVA* v. *Powelson* (1943); *United States* v. *Willow River Power Co.* (1945); *Grand River Dam Authority* v. *Grand-Hydro* (1948).
[27] *United States* v. *Dickinson* (1947).
[28] Similarly *Griggs* v. *Allegheny County* (1962) held that the noise, vibration, and danger resulting from airplane use of a new county airport constituted a taking of an air easement over the plaintiff's property.

consequences may impair its use, are not generally regarded as a taking of property. Changes in grade level of a street do not require compensation to owners whose access to their property is impaired. The government does not have to compensate a riparian owner for cutting off his access to navigable waters by changing the course of the stream in order to improve navigation.[29] A whole series of railroad cases has held that abutting property owners have no claim for compensation because of smoke, noise, danger of fires, or other normal results of railroad operation.

Restrictions on use of property in wartime have been held not to constitute a taking of property, even when they extend to a complete ban on its use, as in the *Wartime Prohibition Cases* (1919) of World War I. The most recent holding to this effect came in *United States* v. *Central Eureka Mining Company* (1958). During World War II there was a critical need for nonferrous metals, whereas gold mining was classified as nonessential. At first gold mines were simply prevented from buying any new machinery or supplies. Later, the War Production Board ordered the closing of all gold mines, apparently in the hope that the laborers thus displaced would move into nonferrous-metal mining where there were critical shortages. The ban was lifted in 1945. The Supreme Court held that these "temporary restrictions" did not constitute a taking of private property. Justice Harlan, dissenting, thought that if the government had seized the gold mines to accomplish its purpose of diverting the miners into other employment, it would certainly have owed compensation, and added: "When the Government proceeds by indirection, and accomplishes by regulation what is the equivalent of outright physical seizure of private property, courts should guard themselves against permitting formalities to obscure actualities."

JUST COMPENSATION    So far as state takings are concerned, the Supreme Court has pretty well kept out of disputes over the adequacy of compensation. Unless a state court has, by its rulings of law, prevented an owner from receiving substantially any compensation at all, the Court will not intervene. "All that is essential is that in some appropriate way, before some properly constituted tribunal, inquiry shall be made as to the amount of compensation, and when this has been provided there is that due process of law which is required by the Federal Constitution."[30]

In federal takings, however, the Supreme Court has been more concerned with the standards applied. An owner of land to be condemned is entitled to "market value fairly determined." That value may reflect not only the use to which the property is presently devoted but also that to which it may be readily converted. But a reasonable probability of the land's being devoted to a more profitable purpose must be shown if it is to affect the compensation awarded.

[29] *United States* v. *Commodore Park, Inc.* (1945).
[30] *Backus (A.) Jr. & Sons* v. *Fort Street Union Depot Co.* (1898).

In *United States ex rel. TVA* v. *Powelson* (1943) the value of the site for the TVA's Hiwassee Dam was set by the courts at about 1 million dollars plus some severance damages. The owner contended that the land had a fair market value of 7.5 million dollars. He arrived at this claim by figuring that the property, plus other land he owned, plus adjoining tracts owned by other people which he could acquire by use of the eminent domain power which North Carolina had granted him, could be the basis for a four-dam hydroelectric project. The Supreme Court denied the claim. The United States was not required to pay the owner for the loss of a business prospect based on an unexercised power of eminent domain. "The sovereign must pay only for what it takes, not for opportunities which the owner may lose," at least where the project is "only a speculative venture—a promotional scheme wholly *in futuro.*"

The conventional criterion for determining just compensation is what the property would bring in the free and open market. But what if there is no free market? During World War II several interesting cases arose where price ceilings had replaced the free market. Because foreign sources of pepper were cut off, by 1944 one company owned practically all the pepper that was left in the United States. It refused to sell to the Army at the low ceiling price which had been set in 1941, and so the Army seized what it needed. The Supreme Court in *United States* v. *Commodities Trading Corp.* (1950) held that the ceiling price was the just price.[31] In certain wartime purchases of commodities not covered by ceiling prices, the Court declined to accept market price as the just price because it was unduly affected by wartime emergency.[32]

## DUE PROCESS IN TAXATION

The power of Congress to tax has already been discussed in Chapter 13. Here we are concerned only with limitations which the due process and equal protection clauses of the Fourteenth Amendment may impose upon the states. Because the taxing power is essential to the existence of the states, constitutional restrictions tend to be interpreted as favorably to the state as possible.

PUBLIC PURPOSE    One general limitation is that taxes must be levied for a public purpose. A tax levy may be challenged on this ground because its proceeds go to private individuals for private benefit, or because the expenditure, though by a public agency, is for a purpose not regarded as appropriate for the state to undertake. It was the first of these contentions which was invoked in the leading case of *Citizens' Savings and Loan Assn.*

---

[31] See also *United States* v. *Felin & Co.* (1948).
[32] *United States* v. *Cors* (1949); *United States* v. *Westinghouse Electric & Mfg. Co.* (1950).

v. *Topeka* (1875). The city had issued bonds and given the proceeds to a bridge company to induce it to locate its plant in that city. When suit was brought because the city defaulted on the bonds, the Supreme Court ruled the bonds illegal because issued for a private purpose.

Obviously the *Topeka* principle is strictly limited in its impact. Most public programs aim to provide assistance of one form or another to individuals; this is the public purpose they perform, and the legitimacy of such purposes is questioned so seldom as to provide few court decisions. In 1930 a Louisiana statute providing for free school books to the school children of the state was attacked in so far as it was applied to aid students in private or parochial schools. The Supreme Court, however, held that it was the school children who were the beneficiaries of these expenditures, not the private schools. The interest of the state was its broad concern for education. "Individual interests are aided only as the common interest is safeguarded," said Chief Justice Hughes.[33]

Again, the unemployment compensation act of Alabama was upheld by the Supreme Court in 1937 as fulfilling a public purpose. Support of the poor had long been accepted, the Court noted. Unemployment compensation supported by tax funds was a new method of attacking an old public problem. "When public evils ensue from individual misfortunes or needs, the legislature may strike at the evil at its source. If the purpose is legitimate because public, it will not be defeated because the execution of it involves payments to individuals."[34]

The second type of public purpose controversy has occurred when states or municipalities have undertaken busines operations characteristically carried on in the United States by private enterprise. Because there is no fixed line between the public and private sphere of operations, the Supreme Court has never invalidated state activities on this ground. The principal test was supplied by the North Dakota Nonpartisan League's extensive program of state ownership inaugurated in 1919, including a state bank, a state mill and grain elevator, a state housing commission, and a state industrial commission to manage these businesses and utilities. The state supreme court upheld the program, and the United States Supreme Court, refusing to be drawn into a discussion as to what was a "proper" public function, said that the localities were the best judges as to what governmental services they required.[35]

JURISDICTION  A state must have jurisdiction of property in order to tax it; otherwise there is a taking of property without due process of law. No problem is involved in applying this rule to real property, such as land. It has a fixed situs, and can be taxed only by the state in which it is physically

---

[33] *Cochran v. Louisiana State Board of Education* (1930).
[34] *Carmichael v. Southern Coal & Coke Co.* (1937).
[35] *Green v. Frazier* (1920); see also *Jones v. City of Portland* (1917).

located. For personal property of a tangible character, such as automobiles, household possessions, or domestic animals, the rule of taxation by the state in which the property is actually located likewise prevails, even though it may not be the state in which the owner is domiciled.[36] The theory is that the state of situs is providing protection and benefits to the property, and so is entitled to levy taxes on it.

The really difficult problems are encountered in the taxation of intangibles, such as stocks, bonds, or certificates of indebtedness. The general rule here is that the situs of intangibles for taxing purposes is in the state where the owner or creditor has his domicile. In Latin this rule reads "mobilia sequuntur personam." However, there are other competing principles of taxation. Mortgages on real estate may be taxed by the state in which the mortgaged property is located as well as by the state in which the mortgagee is domiciled. Corporate stock may be taxed at the domicile of the owner, at the commercial situs of the issuing corporation, and at the domicile of the issuing corporation. As for state or municipal bonds, there have been four different views concerning situs for taxation—the domicile of the owner, the domicile of the debtor, the place where the bonds are actually physically located, and within the jurisdiction where the owner has caused them to become integral parts of a localized business.[37]

The Supreme Court has said that the Fourteenth Amendment does not require the fixing of a single exclusive place for the taxation of intangibles, nor does it invalidate multiple taxation. Justice Holmes, speaking for the Court in *Blackstone* v. *Miller* (1903), ruled that debts were taxable both at the domicile of the debtor and that of the creditor. "There are many circumstances," wrote Justice Stone in *Curry* v. *McCanless* (1939), "in which more than one state may have jurisdiction to impose a tax and measure it by some or all of the taxpayer's intangibles." Legal interests growing out of the complex relationships between persons may be too diverse in respect to different taxing jurisdictions to permit unitary treatment.

The issue of multiple taxation of intangibles has been particularly pressing in the field of inheritance taxation. Inheritance taxes are levied, not on the property inherited, but on the transmission of the property or the enjoyment of the legal privilege of taking property by will or descent. Thus the state of the deceased person's domicile may levy inheritance taxes in an amount determined by the value of the property transmitted. Other states may, however, be the situs of some of the property involved and may also seek to levy taxes measured by the value of such portion of the estate.

The Supreme Court has not been too consistent in its treatment of the multiple taxation problem. At first inheritance taxation by both the domiciliary and the situs state was generally permitted. But to the property-

---

[36] *Union Refrigerator Transit Co.* v. *Kentucky* (1905); *Frick* v. *Pennsylvania* (1925).
[37] *Farmers' Loan & Trust Co.* v. *Minnesota* (1930).

minded Court of the late 1920s double taxation seemed sacrilegious, and in *Farmers' Loan & Trust Co.* v. *Minnesota* (1930) the Court took a firm stand against it, overruling *Blackstone* v. *Miller* (1903) in the process. The 1930 case involved a resident of New York who died leaving a considerable sum in Minnesota state bonds. When both New York and Minnesota sought to levy an inheritance tax on the same transfer, the Minnesota tax was voided on the ground that that state had no jurisdiction over the bonds.

Justice Holmes, along with Brandeis, dissented, but not so strongly as he did in *Baldwin* v. *Missouri* (1930), which involved the same question. This was the last dissent Holmes wrote on the Court, and one of his most famous:

> I have not yet adequately expressed the more than anxiety that I feel at the ever increasing scope given to the Fourteenth Amendment in cutting down what I believe to be the constitutional rights of the States. As the decisions now stand, I see hardly any limit but the sky to the invalidating of those rights if they happen to strike a majority of this Court as for any reason undesirable. I cannot believe that the Amendment was intended to give us *carte blanche* to embody our economic or moral beliefs in its prohibitions.

Brandeis and Stone joined in this dissent. The same trio, speaking through Stone, also protested in *First National Bank of Boston* v. *Maine* (1932), when the Court majority held that Maine had no power to tax the transfer of shares of stock in a Maine corporation owned by a citizen of Massachusetts and located in Massachusetts.

The dissenting view soon became the majority position of the Roosevelt Court. *Curry* v. *McCanless* (1939), as decided by a five to four vote, drastically limited the no-double-taxation rule, though the facts of the case were not such as to require an overruling of the earlier decisions. But in 1942, *State Tax Commission of Utah* v. *Aldrich* presented a factual situation identical with that in the *Maine* case, and by a seven to two vote the 1932 decision was overruled, presumably taking down with it the others in that same line. The reasoning of the new line of cases was that stated by Stone in *Curry* v. *McCanless:*

> From the beginning of our constitutional system control over the person at the place of his domicile and his duty there, common to all citizens, to contribute to the support of government have been deemed to afford an adequate constitutional basis for imposing on him a tax on the use and enjoyment of rights in intangibles measured by their value. . . . But when the taxpayer extends his activities with respect to his intangibles, so as to avail himself of the protection and benefit of the laws of another state, in such a way as to bring his person or . . . [his intangibles] within the reach of the tax gatherer there, the reason for a single place of taxation no longer obtains.

Under this doctrine it is still possible for a tax on intangibles to be invalidated, but it cannot be done solely on the ground of multiple taxation.

States may levy income taxes on two bases, consistent with due process of law. They may tax the entire net income of individuals resident in the state whether received from inside or outside the state. The jurisdiction here is founded on the protection which the state furnishes its residents as to their persons, their right to receive income, and to the enjoyment of it. Second, states may tax that portion of a nonresident's net income derived from property owned or from any business, trade, or profession carried on by him within its borders. Jurisdiction here is based on the state's dominion over and protection of the property or the activity from which income is derived. Thus double state taxation of income is also possible.

EQUAL PROTECTION    The equal protection clause has been of comparatively minor significance as a restriction on tax legislation. In an 1890 decision the Court outlined the breadth of permissible legislative power to classify for tax purposes, noting that the equal protection clause does not prevent a state

> . . . from adjusting its system of taxation in all proper and reasonable ways. It may, if it chooses, exempt certain classes of property from any taxation at all, such as churches, libraries and the property of charitable institutions. It may impose different specific taxes upon different trades and professions, and may vary the rates of excise upon various products; it may tax real estate and personal property in a different manner; it may tax visible property only, and not tax securities for payment of money; it may allow deductions for indebtedness, or not allow them. All such regulations, and those of like character, so long as they proceed within reasonable limits and general usage, are within the discretion of the state legislature.[38]

Application of these principles has meant that the Court is even less likely to challenge legislative classifications under the taxing power than under the police power. Inheritance tax laws typically involve numerous discriminatory features—exemption of small estates, graduated tax rates, variation of tax rates according to whether the estate goes to lineal descendants, collateral heirs, or persons unrelated by blood—but they have uniformly been upheld against claims of denial of equal protection.[39] The same is true of the exemption and progressive rate features of income taxes.

The Court has announced that it will invoke the equal protection clause in instances of "clear and hostile discriminations against particular persons and classes, especially such as are of an unusual character, unknown to the

[38] *Bell's Gap R. Co.* v. *Pennsylvania* (1890).
[39] *Magoun* v. *Illinois Trust & Savings Bank* (1898).

practice of our governments."[40] But instances of judicially condemned intentional discrimination are few. In 1912 the Court even went so far as to uphold a Montana law which taxed hand laundries operated by men in which over two women were employed.[41] But a gross sales tax graduated at increasing rates with the volume of sales was declared unconstitutional,[42] as was a gross receipts tax on corporations operating taxicabs, but not applied to individual operators.[43]

During the 1929 depression, sentiment against the newly developing chain stores led many states to adopt busines taxes bearing more heavily on chains than on single establishments. An Indiana law imposed an occupation tax on the operation of retail stores, graduated according to the number of stores owned. By a five to four vote the Court held that such a tax was justified by advantages in organization, management, and type of business transacted which chains enjoyed over other types of stores. "The fact that a statute discriminates in favor of a certain class does not make it arbitrary, if the discrimination is founded upon a reasonable distinction, . . . or if any state of facts reasonably can be conceived to sustain it."[44]

The Court also upheld a Louisiana law which counted all the stores in the chain, even those outside the state, in applying the graduated tax principle, on the ground that the tax was actually levied on the number of stores in the state.[45] However, a Florida law which increased the tax on chain stores when they were located in more than one county was held to be arbitrary and so unconstitutional.[46]

Foreign corporations offer a tempting target for state legislatures, and it is in this area that the equal protection clause has probably been most often successfully invoked. Even so, equal protection does not require identical taxes on all foreign and domestic corporations in every case. A state is not required to admit foreign corporations to carry on interstate business within its borders, and so it may arbitrarily exclude them or license them upon any terms it sees fit, apart from exacting surrender of rights derived from the Constitution.[47] Even after they are admitted, annual license fees may be increased and may be charged at a higher rate than is imposed on domestic corporations.[48] But after foreign corporations have paid what the state requires in the way of franchise or privilege tax, "the adopted corporations are entitled to equal protection with the state's own corporate progeny,

[40] *Bell's Gap R. Co.* v. *Pennsylvania* (1890).
[41] *Quong Wing* v. *Kirkendall* (1912).
[42] *Stewart Dry Goods Co.* v. *Lewis* (1935).
[43] *Quaker City Cab Co.* v. *Pennsylvania* (1928).
[44] *State Board of Tax Commissioners* v. *Jackson* (1931).
[45] *Great A. & P. Tea Co.* v. *Grosjean* (1937).
[46] *Liggett Co.* v. *Lee* (1933).
[47] *Hanover Fire Insurance Co.* v. *Harding* (1926).
[48] *Philadelphia Fire Assn.* v. *New York* (1886); *Lincoln Nat. Life Insurance Co.* v. *Read* (1945).

at least to the extent that their property is entitled to an equally favorable *ad valorem* tax basis." [49]

## SELECTED REFERENCES

*The Constitution of the United States of America: Analysis and Interpretation,* Sen. Doc. no. 39, 88th Cong., pp. 378–410, 986–996, 1149–1185. Washington: Government Printing Office, 1964.

CROSSKEY, WILLIAM W., *Politics and the Constitution in the History of the United States,* chap. 12. Chicago: The University of Chicago Press, 1953.

DUNHAM, ALLISON, "Griggs v. Allegheny County in Perspective: Thirty Years of Supreme Court Expropriation Law," in Philip B. Kurland (ed.), *The Supreme Court Review: 1962,* pp. 63–106. Chicago: The University of Chicago Press, 1962.

MAGRATH, C. PETER, *Yazoo: Law and Politics in the New Republic: The Case of Fletcher v. Peck.* Providence, R.I.: Brown University Press, 1966.

WRIGHT, BENJAMIN F., JR., *The Contract Clause of the Constitution.* Cambridge, Mass.: Harvard University Press, 1938.

[49] *Wheeling Steel Corp. v. Glander* (1949).

# 33

## Equal protection of the laws

"Equal protection of the laws" is a phrase born with the Fourteenth Amendment, the first specific recognition of the doctrine of equality in the Constitution. The dictum of the Declaration of Independence that "all men are created equal," which was effectively used in the antislavery campaign, had a somewhat different import. Charles Sumner came closer to the equal protection notion with his phrase, "equality before the law," which he developed in 1849 in contending before the Massachusetts supreme court that separate public schools for Negro children would be unconstitutional. Later he sought to get the principle of equal rights into the Constitution by way of the Thirteenth Amendment, his suggestion being: "All persons are equal before the law, so that no person can hold another as a slave."

But it was Representative Bingham who gave final form to the idea. In December, 1865, he proposed a constitutional amendment authorizing Congress "to secure to all persons in every State of the Union equal protection in their rights, life, liberty, and property." Within the same month Senators Wilson and Trumbull introduced the bill which became the Civil Rights Act of 1866, in which all inhabitants were guaranteed "full and equal benefit of all laws and proceedings for the security of person and estate." When Bingham came to prepare his draft of the Fourteenth Amendment, "equal protection in their rights" and "equal benefit of all laws" were merged to produce "equal protection of the laws."

The fact that the states are bound by an equal protection clause, whereas the federal government is not, raises a question whether Congress is free to enact class legislation or discriminatory measures that would be forbidden in the states. The answer is that it has not worked out this way in practice. As will be demonstrated in the present chapter, either by means of the due process clause in the Fifth Amendment, or by statutory construction, the Supreme Court has generally prevented any diversity of standards on class legislation between federal and state levels.

But if due process incorporates the concept of equal protection, what is the value of the equal protection clause? Crosskey argues, in fact, that the modern theories of the Supreme Court on due process have made the equal protection language "a quite unnecessary and superfluous part of the Constitution." [1] Chief Justice Taft's contention that equal protection provided relief from types of discrimination to which due process did not extend was a dictum [2] which subsequent decisions have found it difficult to support. Nevertheless, equal protection, even though really a part of due process, admittedly sharpens up the rather vague contours of that concept and provides a criterion by which class legislation or legal discrimination can be tested and invalidated.

## THE ORIGINAL UNDERSTANDING

There are two methods by which one can undertake to decipher the original intention of the equal protection clause. One is the method used by Crosskey, which infers intent from analysis of the language used, as logically construed and with the meaning which would normally be derived from those words by a person of that period who knew the relevant judicial history. Applying this method, Crosskey is convinced that the equal protection clause was intended primarily to remedy the weaknesses and uncertainties of the privileges and immunities clause of the original Constitution, which were summarized in Chapter 20. The equal protection clause would have this effect by giving "to each individual within each state—whether there permanently or not—a right that the sanctions of the state's tort law and criminal law, in particular, should be as freely and completely available, both legislatively and administratively, in defense of his interests, as in defense of those of any other individual within the state."

The protection, be it noted, is extended to "persons." This means that neither citizen nor alien may be subjected to discrimination which rests on a purely personal basis. "Inequalities in rights established by the states, which depend upon skin color or any other purely personal characteristic; which depend upon the fact, that a man is the particular 'person' he happens

---

[1] W. W. Crosskey, *Politics and the Constitution in the History of the United States* (Chicago: The University of Chicago Press, 1953), p. 1158.
[2] *Truax* v. *Corrigan* (1921).

to be; or which depend upon the fact that others are favorites of those in authority are examples of the kind of thing which the Equal Protection Clause forbids," concludes Crosskey.[3]

A second method of interpreting the intention of the equal protection clause is to examine congressional legislation adopted or proposed during the period in which the Fourteenth Amendment was added to the Constitution. The evidence of contemporary interpretation of congressional powers is certainly significant for such a purpose, in spite of the obvious difficulties in determining or appraising congressional intent in the chaotic conditions of the post-Civil War era.

Obviously Congress was thinking primarily of the newly freed Negroes when it drafted the Fourteenth Amendment. Their problems were of two sorts. The first was political. How could they be guaranteed the right to vote and to full political participation in the Southern states? Congress sought to include some formula for this purpose in the Fourteenth Amendment, but ultimately all it was able to produce was the provision in section 2 of the amendment reducing representation in the House for any state which denied the vote to qualified citizens.

The second problem was guaranteeing the civil, as distinct from the political, rights of the freedmen. This was the area that equal protection was meant to cover—but what fields, and how fully? There can be no doubt that the equal protection clause was meant to end discrimination enforced upon Negroes by the "Black Codes" of certain states which limited their right to hold property, specified criminal offenses for Negroes only, and hampered their access to the courts in a variety of ways. In 1862 Congress had repealed the Black Codes in the District of Columbia and prohibited exclusion of witnesses on account of color in court cases there. The Civil Rights Act of 1866, passed just prior to congressional adoption of the Fourteenth Amendment, spelled out clearly the purpose to guarantee Negroes equality in courts and commerce, by giving

> . . . citizens, of every race and color . . . the same right, in every State and Territory . . . to make and enforce contracts, to sue, be parties, and give evidence, to inherit, purchase, lease, sell, hold, and convey real and personal property, and to full and equal benefit of all laws and proceedings for the security of person and property, as is enjoyed by white citizens, and shall be subject to like punishment, pains, and penalties, and to none other.

Congressional intent in other areas of discrimination is less clear. The impact which equal protection was intended to have on segregation is certainly open to doubt. The problem of segregation was never squarely faced during the incubation period of the amendment. There was a widespread assumption of a dichotomy between "civil" equality and "social" equality. The former was a matter which the law must control, but the latter was a

[3] Crosskey, *op. cit.*, pp. 1098–1101.

matter of taste, with which the law had nothing to do. Just where the dividing line was between the two areas was not too clear, however.

Geographical segregation—that is, governmental restriction of Negroes to certain sections of a city or their exclusion from areas by limiting their right to buy or live on particular pieces of property—was clearly forbidden under congressional interpretations of that period. Segregation in transportation, it would seem, was almost equally condemned by congressional attitudes of the time, which held that transportation companies had a common-law duty to take all comers, and that making any distinctions in the operation of this duty because of color denied an equal right to contract for transportation.

Concerning hotels and theaters, there was substantially more disagreement. Hotels were generally thought, like railroads, to have a common-law obligation to serve all comers, but there were problems of location as to rooms and at dining tables where preferences in tastes could legitimately be indulged. Theaters were scarcely in the same public utility category as railroads and hotels, but they were nevertheless subject to extensive regulation of various sorts.

On segregation in education, the situation was the most confused of all. At the close of the Civil War, Negroes were generally excluded from education altogether in both North and South. The primary problem was to get any kind of education at all for Negroes, not whether the schools were to be separate or mixed. In the District of Columbia, separate schools for Negroes were established as they were freed during the war, so that a pattern of segregation was established before Congress could take a position on the subject. Several abortive efforts were made subsequently to legislate against school segregation, but the main battle was in connection with the Civil Rights Act of 1875. On May 22, 1874, an amendment permitting separate but equal schools was defeated in the Senate, twenty-six to twenty-one, and the next day the Senate passed the bill forbidding school segregation by a vote of twenty-nine to sixteen. However, when the House considered the measure a year later, it deleted the school clause, and it remained out of the final statute.

The Civil Rights Act of 1875, then, forbade racial separation or discrimination in public conveyances, hotels, and theaters,[4] and also required equality in jury service. The constitutional basis for the statute cited in the congressional debates was primarily the equal protection clause, with privileges and immunities as a subordinate support. There are two matters of

---

[4] The actual language of sec. 1 was "that all persons within the jurisdiction of the United States shall be entitled to the full and equal enjoyment of the accommodations, advantages, facilities, and privileges of inns, public conveyances on land or water, theaters, and other places of public amusement; subject only to the conditions and limitations established by law, and applicable alike to citizens of every race and color, regardless of any previous condition of servitude."

major significance to note about this act. The first is that, apart from the jury provisions, it was directed at discriminatory actions not primarily of public officials, but of private individuals operating services traditionally subject to public regulation.

Second, the Civil Rights Act was based on an unquestioned assumption that Congress had plenary legislative power to enforce the protections of the Fourteenth Amendment, that its authority was as broad as was necessary to correct abuses which might be found, and that it could be invoked to punish acts of omission, or failure to enforce the law, as well as affirmative discriminatory acts. There was this significant difference in the two situations. When a state discriminated by affirmative state action, redress simply required the negating of that action. But where the discrimination arose out of actions by private individuals which the state failed to prevent or punish, then redress necessarily required the assertion of power to coerce state officials into a positive program of law enforcement. Thus the latter situation involved substantially greater congressional control over state and local government than the former.

Nevertheless, both in the act of 1875 and in the earlier Ku Klux (Second Enforcement) Act of 1871, Congress asserted its power to legislate affirmatively in behalf of a racial group which states might neglect to protect from the actions of private persons. There can be no doubt that a large majority in Congress at this time shared the view that Congress could enforce the Fourteenth Amendment on the states by affirmative legislation, and that a state denied equal protection when it tolerated widespread abuses against a class of citizens because of their color without seriously attempting to protect them by enforcing the law.

Within a decade the Supreme Court decided that Congress had been completely wrong on both these points. There is scarcely a more striking instance in American constitutional history of outright judicial disregard of congressional intent. In the *Civil Rights Cases* of 1883, the Supreme Court concluded that the Congress which had drafted the Fourteenth Amendment and which had provided for its enforcement by major enactments in 1871 and 1875 had not understood the amendment or congressional powers under it. By means of what Justice Harlan in his dissenting opinion called "a subtle and ingenious verbal criticism," the Court proceeded to sacrifice "the substance and spirit" of the amendment.

Justice Bradley's opinion is indeed a masterpiece of ingenuity. He started by giving literal effect to the language that "no state" shall deny equal protection, saying: "It is State action of a particular character that is prohibited. Individual invasion of individual rights is not the subject-matter of the amendment." The congressmen who had drafted and interpreted this language apparently had no such understanding of its meaning, but only one Supreme Court justice, Harlan, agreed with them. Railroads, he said, might

be owned by private companies, but they were "none the less public high-ways," and the state may regulate their entire management. With railroads, and also with inns, "no matter who is the agent, or what is the agency, the function performed is *that of the State.*" As to places of public amusement, "the authority to establish and maintain them comes from the public," and "a license from the public . . . imports, in law, equality of right, at such places, among all the members of that public."

The defeat of the Harlan position meant that Congress was stripped of any power to correct or to punish individual discriminatory action. Only *state* action was subject to the amendment. Bradley then undertook a second exercise in strict construction, this time operating on section 5 of the amendment. What did that section give Congress power to do? Why, "to enforce the prohibition" on state legislation or "State action of every kind" denying equal protection of the laws; further,

> . . . to adopt appropriate legislation for correcting the effects of such prohibited State laws and State acts, and thus to render them effectually null, void, and innocuous. This is the legislative power conferred upon Congress, and this is the whole of it. It does not invest Congress with power to legislate upon subjects which are within the domain of State legislation; but to provide modes of relief against State legislation, or State action, of the kind referred to. It does not authorize Congress to create a code of municipal law for the regulation of private rights; but to provide modes of redress against the operation of State laws, and the action of State officers . . . when these are subversive of the fundamental rights specified in the amendment.

In other words, Congress was limited to the *correcting* of *affirmative* state action. "Until some State law has been passed, or some State action through its officers or agents has been taken, adverse to the rights of citizens sought to be protected by the Fourteenth Amendment, no legislation of the United States under said amendment, nor any proceeding under such legislation, can be called into activity." The Civil Rights Act was not corrective legislation. It was "primary and direct." It was a code of conduct which ignored state legislation, and assumed "that the matter is one that belongs to the domain of national regulation." Since the law was thus based on a misconstruction of the Fourteenth Amendment, and since it was not regarded by the Court as having any demonstrable relationship with the Thirteenth Amendment, it was unconstitutional.

Perhaps one other thing needs to be said in concluding this examination of congressional and judicial views in the formative period of the equal protection clause. When the Court first discussed the equal protection clause in the *Slaughter-House Cases* (1873), Justice Miller, taking note of the obvious origin of the amendment in concern for Negro rights, doubted "very much whether any action of a State not directed by way of discrimination against the negroes as a class, or on account of their race, will ever be held

to come within the purview" of the clause. This was, of course, a very bad piece of prophecy, which Miller himself soon recanted.

### RACIAL EQUALITY IN COMMERCE

The clearest agreement on the meaning of equal protection, we have seen, concerned equality of races in courts and commerce. In Chapter 30 the application of equal protection in guaranteeing the representativeness of state juries has already been covered. So far as equality in commerce is concerned, the first important application of the clause against racial discrimination occurred in *Yick Wo* v. *Hopkins* (1886). A San Francisco ordinance made it unlawful to operate a laundry, except in a brick or stone building, without securing the consent of the board of supervisors. Masquerading as a safety measure, this ordinance in actual use discriminated against Chinese laundry operators. The fact of discrimination was demonstrated to the satisfaction of the Supreme Court, which determined that there had been a "practical denial" of equal protection of the laws.

> Though the law itself be fair on its face and impartial in appearance, yet, if it is applied and administered by public authority with an evil eye and an unequal hand, so as practically to make unjust and illegal discrimination between persons in similar circumstances, material to their rights, the denial of equal justice is . . . within the prohibition of the Constitution.

In *Truax* v. *Raich* (1915), the discrimination resulting from operation of an Arizona law was against aliens, rather than on a strictly racial basis. The statute required that if a company or person employed more than five workers, 80 per cent of them must be native-born citizens of the United States or qualified electors. A native of Austria employed as a cook in a restaurant was fired because of the provisions of this law. The Supreme Court held that the police power of the states, while broad, did not

> . . . go so far as to make it possible for the State to deny to lawful inhabitants, because of their race or nationality, the ordinary means of earning a livelihood. It requires no argument to show that the right to work for a living in the common occupations of the community is of the very essence of the personal freedom and opportunity that it was the purpose of the [Fourteenth] Amendment to secure.

Using alien status as the basis for limitation of economic opportunities is not necessarily contrary to the equal protection clause.[5] It all depends upon the case that can be made for the legislative classification. Thus California had an Alien Land Law forbidding aliens ineligible for American citizenship to acquire agricultural land, which was initially accepted by the Supreme Court.[6] However, this was a fundamental limitation on the right

[5] See *Clarke* v. *Deckebach* (1927); *Heim* v. *McCall* (1915).
[6] *Terrace* v. *Thompson* (1923); *Cockrill* v. *California* (1925).

to earn a livelihood of the same order as that involved in *Truax* v. *Raich,* and eventually the Court had to reconsider the issue in *Oyama* v. *California* (1948).

Under the act, property acquired or transferred in violation of the act escheats (i.e., reverts) to the state as of the date of acquisition. Oyama, an ineligible alien, had purchased in 1934 several acres of agricultural land in the name of his six-year-old son Fred, an American citizen. In 1944 the state filed a petition to declare an escheat of the land on the ground that the conveyance had been made in violation of the law. Chief Justice Vinson for a six-judge majority concluded that the state law discriminated against Fred Oyama and that the discrimination was based solely on his parent's country of origin. The Chief Justice assumed, "for purposes of argument only," that the law was constitutional, but invalidated it on the ground that the means chosen to enforce it exceeded constitutional limits.

*Takahashi* v. *Fish and Game Commission* (1948) involved California's wartime attempt to ban Japanese from commercial fishing. A 1943 amendment to the state fish and game code prohibited the issuance of fishing licenses to "alien Japanese." In 1945 the language was changed to "a person ineligible to citizenship," in an effort to put the ban on a less vulnerable basis. A seven-judge majority, speaking through Justice Black, flatly declared the prohibition unconstitutional. Black did not deny that a state might apply some laws "exclusively to its alien inhabitants as a class" but held that such power "is confined within narrow limits."

### GEOGRAPHICAL SEGREGATION

By geographical segregation is primarily meant racial limitations with respect to housing. The equal protection clause, we have seen, was clearly intended to protect equal rights in buying or disposing of property. After the *Civil Rights Cases* (1883), this protection would still be effective against state action which violated equal rights in property ownership, and the Supreme Court so held when cases came up for review. Baltimore, in 1910, was apparently the first city to adopt a municipal segregation ordinance. Shortly afterward, the same procedure was followed by other Southern cities. The Louisville ordinance came before the Supreme Court in *Buchanan* v. *Warley* (1917) and was invalidated on the ground that it was an unconstitutional interference with the right of a property owner to dispose of his real estate. Attempts to circumvent the *Buchanan* decision were defeated in both state and federal courts, and by 1930 the unconstitutionality of municipal segregation ordinances was firmly established.[7]

The field was thus left to a second protective device—restrictive covenants entered into by property owners binding themselves not to sell or

[7] See *Harmon* v. *Tyler* (1927); *City of Richmond* v. *Deans* (1930); *City of Birmingham* v. *Monk* (1951).

lease their property to Negroes or certain other social, national, or religious groups. Because this type of agreement results from action by private persons, not by the state, it was at first generally successful in meeting constitutional tests.

The first restrictive covenant case to reach the Supreme Court, *Corrigan* v. *Buckley* (1926), was dismissed on grounds of lack of jurisdiction, but Justice Sanford for the Court did hold that such private covenants were not contrary to the Constitution or to public policy. Not until 1948 did the Supreme Court reconsider this position. Then it handed down two unanimous decisions upholding the validity of restrictive covenants but denying them judicial enforcement. The first decision, *Shelley* v. *Kraemer*, concerned actions brought to enforce restrictive covenants in the states of Missouri and Michigan. Chief Justice Vinson found it relatively easy to reconcile the Court's new view with its previous decisions. *Corrigan* v. *Buckley*, he pointed out, had concerned only the right of private individuals to enter into such covenants, and he here reiterated the conclusion of the *Corrigan* case that "restrictive agreements standing alone cannot be regarded as violative of any rights guaranteed . . . by the Fourteenth Amendment."

But in *Shelley* v. *Kraemer* the Court was willing to push beyond this point and to consider the status of action by state courts to enforce these covenants. "It cannot be doubted," said the Chief Justice, "that among the civil rights intended to be protected from discriminatory state action by the Fourteenth Amendment are the rights to acquire, enjoy, own and dispose of property." The question, then, was whether judicial enforcement of restrictive covenants amounted to "state action." The Court answered:

> We have no doubt that there has been state action in these cases in the full and complete sense of the phrase. The undisputed facts disclose that petitioners were willing purchasers of properties upon which they desired to establish homes. The owners of the properties were willing sellers; and contracts of sale were accordingly consummated. It is clear that but for the active intervention of the state courts, supported by the full panoply of state power, petitioners would have been free to occupy the properties in question without restraint.

The fact that "the particular pattern of discrimination, which the State has enforced, was defined initially by the terms of a private agreement" made no difference. "State action, as that phrase is understood for the purposes of the Fourteenth Amendment, refers to exertions of state power in all forms."

The second decision, *Hurd* v. *Hodge* (1948), involved two cases arising in the District of Columbia, where the equal protection clause could not be invoked. Consequently, it was contended that judicial enforcement was forbidden by the due process clause of the Fifth Amendment. The Court, speaking again through the Chief Justice, found it unnecessary to base its

decision upon constitutional grounds at all. Primary reliance was placed upon section 1 of the Civil Rights Act of 1866, which guarantees to "all citizens" the same rights as white citizens "to inherit, purchase, lease, sell, hold, and convey real and personal property." The Court held that judicial enforcement of restrictive covenants would be a violation of this section. Even in the absence of the statute, however, the Court indicated that judicial enforcement would be contrary to the public policy of the United States, which the Supreme Court would have power to enforce in the exercise of its supervisory powers over the courts of the District of Columbia.

Since these two decisions left restrictive covenants legal, even though unenforceable, the question soon arose as to whether a signer of a covenant who breached its provisions could be sued for damages by other participants in the covenant. In *Barrows* v. *Jackson* (1953) a California property owner who had failed to live up to the conditions of a covenant was sued by three neighbors on the ground that the value of their property had dropped sharply since Negroes moved in. But six justices thought that the Supreme Court should not permit or require California to coerce a property owner to pay damages for failure to observe a covenant that California had no right to incorporate in a statute or enforce in equity and which federal courts could not enforce because contrary to public policy.[8]

### SEGREGATION IN PUBLIC TRANSPORTATION

Separate accommodations for Negroes on public transportation were the rule in the Southern States at the time the Fourteenth Amendment was adopted. After the Civil War, Congress took several steps against this practice, culminating in the Civil Rights Act of 1875. One of the *Civil Rights Cases* (1883) arose out of the exclusion of a Negro woman from the ladies' car of an interstate train. But, as we have already seen, the Supreme Court held the Fourteenth Amendment applicable only against state action, and ruled that the actions of a railroad or its employees did not fall into this category.

This decision at least left open the possibility that *state* action *enforcing* segregation would be contrary to the equal protection clause. But this defense fell in the famous case of *Plessy* v. *Ferguson* (1896). Here a Louisiana statute *requiring* segregation of the two races on public carriers was held by the Supreme Court not to violate the Fourteenth Amendment. Said Justice Brown: "The object of the amendment was undoubtedly to enforce the absolute equality of the two races before the law, but in the nature of things it could not have been intended to abolish distinctions based upon color, or to enforce social, as distinguished from political equality, or a commingling of the two races upon terms unsatisfactory to either."

The Court denied that the enforced separation of the two races stamped

[8] But see *Leeper* v. *Charlotte Park Commission* (1956).

the colored race with a "badge of inferiority." "If this be so, it is not by reason of anything found in the act, but solely because the colored race chooses to put that construction upon it." Thus *Plessy* v. *Ferguson* gave the Supreme Court's blessing to the view that segregation was compatible with equality. "Separate but equal" was the formula for reconciling the protection of the Fourteenth Amendment with a system of state-enforced segregation. Justice Harlan dissented, protesting that "our Constitution is color-blind, and neither knows nor tolerates classes among citizens."

Elimination of the equal protection clause still left the federal commerce power as a possible barrier to segregated transportation facilities. The Civil Rights Act of 1875 did not attempt to rely on the commerce power, but the Interstate Commerce Act of 1887 did contain in section 3(1) a ban on "undue or unreasonable prejudice or disadvantage" in service rendered in interstate commerce. This provision was almost immediately invoked to test segregated facilities, but the Interstate Commerce Commission ruled against the claim, saying:

> The disposition of a delicate and important question of this character, weighted with embarrassments arising from antecedent legal and social conditions, should aim at a result most likely to conduce to peace and order, and to preserve the self-respect and dignity of citizenship of a common country. And, while the mandate of the statute must be our paramount guide, we may be assisted by the knowledge familiar to all of past and present circumstances relating to our diverse population, and such lights of reason and experience as surround the question, in giving effect with the least amount of friction to the purposes of the law.

A second alternative under the commerce clause was to attack state laws pertaining to segregated transportation in the courts as an unconstitutional burden on commerce. This was done successfully in *Hall* v. *DeCuir* (1878), but the catch was that the state law voided there was an 1869 Louisiana Reconstruction statute *prohibiting* discrimination on account of race or color. The Court regarded this matter as one on which uniformity of practice was required, and consequently only Congress could adopt regulations on the subject.

It was not until 1890 that the Supreme Court encountered the opposite kind of statutory situation. An 1888 Mississippi statute required all railways carrying passengers in the state to provide "equal but separate" accommodations for white and Negro passengers. It seemed obvious that the Supreme Court, which in *DeCuir* had declared a state statute *prohibiting* segregation an unconstitutional burden on interstate commerce, would have to make a similar holding against a state statute *requiring* discrimination. By a seven to two vote, however, the Court avoided the simple but honest logic of this position by acceptance of Mississippi's contention that the act applied solely to commerce within the state, and so raised no interstate commerce question.[9]

[9] *Louisville, New Orleans & Texas R. Co.* v. *Mississippi* (1890).

*Hall* v. *DeCuir* had not been overruled, however; it had merely been distinguished. So efforts to challenge segregation on commerce grounds continued to be made. The Court avoided the issue in a variety of ways. For example, in *McCabe* v. *Atchison, Topeka & Santa Fe* (1914), where an injunction was sought against the Oklahoma "separate coach" law of 1907, the Court denied that a case for relief in equity had been made out. However, the decision insisted that the separate but equal standard in the Interstate Commerce Act demanded "substantial equality of treatment of persons traveling under like conditions," and the failure to supply first-class accommodations for Negroes because there was less demand for them was rebuked by Justice Hughes.

Finally, in *Mitchell* v. *United States* (1941) the Court squarely upheld a charge of denial of equal treatment brought by a Negro congressman from Illinois who had been refused Pullman accommodations in Arkansas. The ruling, however, did not challenge the constitutionality of segregation in interstate commerce. It merely insisted that accommodations must be "substantially equal" to meet the constitutional test, and from this point of view went no further than the *McCabe* decision.

There was evident, however, a changed temper on the Court, which needed merely the appropriate occasion to become manifest. The opportunity came in 1946, when *Morgan* v. *Virginia* was decided. This case arose out of the prosecution of a Negro woman who was making an interstate bus trip from Virginia to Baltimore and who refused to move to the back of the bus on the request of the driver so that her seat would be available for white passengers. The Supreme Court found the state law to be a burden on commerce in a matter where uniformity was necessary.

The Court, having thus willingly rediscovered the relationship of the commerce clause to segregation, in its very next case was embarrassed to find that the commerce clause could be relied on to protect as well as to condemn discrimination. In *Bob-Lo Excursion Co.* v. *Michigan* (1948), as already noted, the Court upheld a conviction under the Michigan Civil Rights Act of a Detroit amusement park company which refused to transport a Negro girl on its boat to an island on the Canadian side of the Detroit River. Although this was technically foreign commerce, to which the state law could not apply, the Court majority held that it was actually "highly local." The *DeCuir* and *Morgan* cases were distinguished on the ground that they did not involve such "locally insulated" situations. Moreover, in neither of those cases had complete exclusion from transportation facilities been attempted. Justice Jackson, dissenting, rejoined: "The Court admits that the commerce involved in this case is foreign commerce, but subjects it to the state police power on the ground that it is not very foreign."

*Bob-Lo* highlighted the Court's problem in attempting to achieve equalitarian goals through the cold-blooded and clumsy constitutional concept of

commerce.[10] Justice Douglas gave expression to this feeling in his concurring opinion; he would have preferred to base the decision upon the more appealing foundation of the equal protection clause. Ultimately, in 1956, the Court did just that. But first the ICC demonstrated that the same goal could be reached by a reinterpretation of the Interstate Commerce Act.

In November, 1955, the ICC issued an order that racial segregation on trains and buses crossing state lines would have to be terminated by January 10, 1956. The decision applied also to public waiting rooms in railway and bus terminals. The order was based on a finding that these segregated practices subjected Negro passengers to undue and unreasonable prejudice and disadvantage, in violation of the 1887 statute. The ICC courageously quoted from its own decision to the contrary effect in 1887, and indicated why it had now changed its mind:

> "Present circumstances relating to our diverse population" are different from those in 1887 . . . and "lights of reason and experience" are clearer. It is hardly open to question that much progress in improved race relations has been made since then and that more can be expected. . . . We are therefore now free to place greater emphasis on steps "to preserve the self-respect and dignity of citizenship of a common country" which this commission in 1887 balanced against "peace and order."

This ICC ruling of course affected only interstate commerce. Intrastate practices could be brought into line only through the equal protection clause. In 1956, the Supreme Court took this step by affirming a lower court ruling that an Alabama statute and a Montgomery ordinance requiring segregation of races on intrastate buses violated the equal protection and due process clauses.[11] This decision was a result of, and an anticlimax to, the historic Court decisions of May, 1954, invalidating segregation in public education, and it is to that area that we now turn.

### SEGREGATION IN EDUCATION

The fraudulent character of the protection afforded by the "separate but equal" rule was perhaps most obvious in the field of education. By any test which might be applied, Negro schools in states where segregation was the rule were markedly inferior to white schools. For many years, however, the Supreme Court persistently avoided getting itself into situations where it would have to recognize this fact.

The story starts in 1899, with *Cumming* v. *Richmond County Board of Education*. This case arose out of the decision of a Georgia school board to discontinue the existing Negro high school in order to use the building and facilities for Negro elementary education. No new high school for Negroes was established, though the existing white high schools were continued.

[10] See also *Henderson* v. *United States* (1950).
[11] *Gayle* v. *Browder* (1956).

Negro taxpayers sought to restrain the school board from using money to support white high schools until equal facilities for Negro students were provided. The unanimous Supreme Court decision avoided discussion of the segregation issue. It denied that discontinuance of the Negro high school was a violation of equal protection of the laws, but laid more stress on the conclusion that an injunction which would close the white high schools was not the proper legal remedy and would not help the colored children. Justice Harlan concluded with a reminder that the management of schools was a state matter in which the federal government could intervene only in the case of a "clear and unmistakable disregard" of constitutional rights.

A Kentucky law requiring segregation of white and Negro students in all educational institutions, private and public, was upheld as applied to a private institution in *Berea College* v. *Kentucky* (1908). Again the Court found a way to avoid passing on the segregation issue. It argued that this was merely a matter between Kentucky and a corporation which it had created. The statute could be regarded as an amendment to the college's corporate charter, and the state could withhold privileges from one of its corporations which it could not constitutionally withhold from an individual. Justices Harlan and Day, dissenting, contended that the Court should meet the issue head on and not hide behind the law of corporations. They were convinced that, at least as applied to private institutions where there was "voluntary meeting" of the two races "for innocent purposes," this statute was definitely unconstitutional.

Having successfully avoided the issue twice, the Court then felt able to act as though established practice had foreclosed discussion of the question. *Gong Lum* v. *Rice* (1927) concerned a child of Chinese descent who was required to attend a Negro school in Mississippi under the state constitutional obligation that separate schools be maintained for children of "the white and colored races." As to the equal protection problem posed by this arrangement, Chief Justice Taft said for the Court: "Were this a new question, it would call for very full argument and consideration, but we think that it is the same question which has been many times decided to be within the constitutional power of the state legislature to settle without intervention of the federal courts under the Federal Constitution." The fifteen state and lower federal court decisions cited by the Chief Justice to support this conclusion, however, could not hide the fact that there had been no Supreme Court ruling directly on the issue of segregation in educational institutions and that there had never been "full argument and consideration" by that body.

As in the transportation field, the pattern of segregation in education thus achieved a solid constitutional foundation. The more liberally oriented Court of the later 1930s was able, however, again as in the transportation area, to effect a substantial change of direction within the confines of the doctrine by stressing the need for *equality* in segregation. Missouri refused

to admit Negroes to its state law school, providing instead that the state would pay tuition fees for any of its Negro citizens who could obtain admission to law schools in neighboring states where segregation was not enforced. Lloyd Gaines refused this arrangement and brought suit to compel the registrar of the University of Missouri to admit him as a law student. The Supreme Court through Chief Justice Hughes upheld Gaines's position.[12] The limited demand for legal education within the state could not justify Missouri in shifting its responsibility to provide equal educational opportunities to some other state. By operating a white law school, the state was providing privileges to white students which it denied to Negroes because of their race. Equality of treatment was the only basis on which segregation was constitutionally justifiable.

Missouri met this ruling by setting up a separate, and inferior, law school for Negroes, and other Southern states adopted the same device. How far was the Supreme Court prepared to go in insisting upon equality of facilities? The test came in 1950. *McLaurin* v. *Oklahoma State Regents* involved a Negro who sought admission to the state university as a Ph.D. candidate in education. The Legislature, under pressure of the *Gaines* ruling, had amended the state law to permit the admission of Negroes to institutions of higher learning in cases where such institutions offered courses not available in the Negro schools. However, the program of instruction for such Negro students was to be given "upon a segregated basis." Accordingly, McLaurin was admitted to the University of Oklahoma graduate school but was subjected to certain segregation practices in classrooms, library, and cafeteria. These separations, which the state defended as "merely nominal," were declared unconstitutional by a unanimous Court. Such restrictions on McLaurin, Chief Justice Vinson wrote, "impair and inhibit his ability to study, to engage in discussions and exchange views with other students, and, in general, to learn his profession."

*Sweatt* v. *Painter*, decided the same day, involved the petition of a Negro student for admission to the University of Texas Law School. The facts were that Sweatt had applied for admission to the law school in 1946 and had been rejected solely because he was a Negro. When the university set up a separate law school for Negroes in 1947, Sweatt refused to attend and secured a hearing on the issue of the equality of facilities at the newly established school. The Texas courts ruled that the "privileges, advantages, and opportunities for the study of law" at the Negro law school were "substantially equivalent" to those available at the university law school.

The Supreme Court disagreed. Chief Justice Vinson's opinion contrasted the faculty, the student body, the library, the alumni, and the other facilities of the two institutions. In comparison with the University of Texas Law School, judged by the Court to be "one of the nation's ranking law schools,"

[12] *Missouri ex rel. Gaines* v. *Canada* (1938). See also *Sipuel* v. *Board of Regents of the University of Oklahoma* (1948).

was the Negro law school with five full-time professors, a student body of twenty-three, a library of 16,500 volumes, and one alumnus who had become a member of the Texas bar. "It is difficult to believe that one who had a free choice between these law schools would consider the question close." Above all, the Court considered that a law school limited to Negroes, a minority of the Texas population, could not be an effective "proving ground for legal learning and practice":

> The law school to which Texas is willing to admit petitioner excludes from its student body members of the racial groups which number 85% of the population of the State and include most of the lawyers, witnesses, jurors, judges and other officials with whom petitioner will inevitably be dealing when he becomes a member of the Texas Bar. With such a substantial and significant segment of society excluded, we cannot conclude that the education offered petitioner is substantially equal to that which he would receive if admitted to the University of Texas Law School.

This language made it clear that the Supreme Court had concluded that no law school limited to Negroes could meet the requirement of the equal protection clause. But the Court based its conclusion on the necessary and inescapable "inequality" of the education offered by such school, not upon a condemnation of the principle of segregation. Considering the temper of the times and the significance of the world-wide battle against racial discrimination, it was obvious that pressure would continue on the Court to terminate the doctrine of separate but equal which gave constitutional respectability to racial segregation.

And so the issue continued to knock on the Court's portals. The pressure, moreover, shifted from graduate professional and university education, where the breaking-down of segregation barriers presented a lesser problem because of the comparatively few Negro students involved, to public education at the primary and secondary levels. In December, 1952, the Court held hearings on five appeals in such cases, in all of which the lower courts had upheld segregation laws but demanded that educational facilities be made equal. On June 8, 1953, the Court announced the cases would be reargued on October 12 and set out a series of five questions to which counsel were requested to address themselves. Two of the five questions related to the intent of the Congress and the state legislatures which drafted and ratified the Fourteenth Amendment and whether they understood that it would abolish segregation in public schools.

*Brown* v. *Board of Education of Topeka* and the other school segregation cases [13] were finally decided on May 17, 1954. The vote was unanimous, an unexpected development which was immediately hailed as a diplomatic triumph for Chief Justice Warren, who wrote the opinion. It was a surprisingly brief statement of thirteen paragraphs. First, Warren noted that the

[13] *Briggs* v. *Elliott; Davis* v. *County School Board of Prince Edward County; Gebhart* v. *Belton; Bolling* v. *Sharpe.*

historical background and the circumstances surrounding the adoption of the Fourteenth Amendment were at best "inconclusive" as to the intention of the drafters. But in any case the Court could not "turn the clock back to 1868 when the Amendment was adopted, or even to 1896 when *Plessy* v. *Ferguson* was written." The decision had to consider public education "in the light of its full development and its present place in American life throughout the Nation." Warren continued:

> Today, education is perhaps the most important function of state and local governments. Compulsory school attendance laws and the great expenditures for education both demonstrate our recognition of the importance of education to our democratic society. It is required in the performance of our most basic public responsibilities, even service in the armed forces. It is the very foundation of good citizenship. Today it is a principal instrument in awakening the child to cultural values, in preparing him for later professional training, and in helping him to adjust normally to his environment. In these days, it is doubtful that any child may reasonably be expected to succeed in life if he is denied the opportunity of an education. Such an opportunity, where the state has undertaken to provide it, is a right which must be made available to all on equal terms.

Thus the Court finally came to grips with the constitutionality of the "separate but equal" doctrine, which it had avoided in six preceding public education cases. "Does segregation of children in public schools solely on the basis of race, even though the physical facilities and other 'tangible' factors may be equal, deprive the children of the minority group of equal educational opportunities? We believe that it does." For this precedent-shattering conclusion, the Court's justification was surprisingly brief and simple. "To separate [children in grade and high schools] from others of similar age and qualifications solely because of their race generates a feeling of inferiority as to their status in the community that may affect their hearts and minds in a way unlikely ever to be undone." Consequently, "separate educational facilities are inherently unequal."

*Bolling* v. *Sharpe* was handled in a separate decision from the other four cases, since it arose in the District of Columbia where the equal protection clause was not applicable. In a brief opinion, Warren held that the due process clause of the Fifth Amendment required the same result. It would be "unthinkable" that the Constitution imposed a lesser duty on the federal government than on the states. Equal protection is a more specific safeguard than due process, to be sure, and the concepts are not "interchangeable." But the liberty protected by the due process clause includes "the full range of conduct which the individual is free to pursue, and it cannot be restricted except for a proper governmental objective. Segregation in public education is not reasonably related to any proper governmental objective, and thus it imposes on Negro children of the District of Columbia a burden that consti-

tutes an arbitrary deprivation of their liberty in violation of the Due Process Clause."

These holdings still left the problem of putting this potentially explosive doctrine into effect. Further hearings were held in April, 1955, and on May 31 the Supreme Court announced its plan of action. The cases would be remanded to the courts where they had originated, which would fashion decrees of enforcement on equitable principles and with regard for "varied local school problems." The local courts would consider whether the actions or proposals of the various school authorities constituted "good faith implementation of the governing constitutional principles." They would require "a prompt and reasonable start toward full compliance" with the 1954 ruling, but once such a start had been made, the courts might find that additional time was necessary to carry out the ruling in an effective manner. Such delays, however, would have to be proved "necessary in the public interest and . . . consistent with good faith compliance at the earliest practicable date." During this period of transition to full compliance, the courts where the cases originated would retain jurisdiction of them. Thus the Supreme Court committed its prestige in an experiment in judicially enforced revision of human behavior patterns without precedent in American experience.

### ENFORCEMENT OF THE *BROWN* DECISION

At first it seemed that the prestige of the Court might substantially temper the expected resistance to the *Brown* decree. The Court may have expected that it would receive some support from Congress and the President in winning acceptance for the ruling, but no such aid was forthcoming. On the contrary, ninety-six Southern congressmen signed a manifesto in 1956 challenging the legality of the Court's decision, and President Eisenhower, while declaring that he would enforce the law, persistently declined to attempt any organization of support for the ruling. Under the circumstances it is not surprising that progress toward the goal of desegregating education was slow and uneven.

STATE PROGRAMS OF RESISTANCE    In the states of the "Old South" the legislatures, led by Virginia, promptly adopted complete batteries of new laws aimed to frustrate efforts to achieve integration. In many instances these laws were recognized even by their sponsors to be unconstitutional, but they were gestures of defiance and testing them in court would take time. The principal legislative devices were the following:

*1. Interposition*    Interposition has already been discussed in Chapter 5. This doctrine is incompatible with the plain terms of Article VI of the Constitution and conflicts with an unbroken line of precedents dating back to 1803. Virginia and Louisiana reinforced their interposition resolutions

with legislation withdrawing consent to be sued on matters relating to public school operations. This withdrawal of consent may affect state courts, but not federal. An action against an officer or agency attempting to enforce an unconstitutional statute is not a suit against the state.[14]

2. *State police power*   A 1954 Louisiana statute and constitutional amendment invoked the state's police power as a means of preserving racial separation. These acts ordered segregation maintained solely because of the possible threats to the public peace which integration might bring. The lower federal courts made short shrift of this plan.[15] The court of appeals wrote: "The use of the term police power works no magic in itself. Undeniably the States retain an extremely broad police power. This power, however, as everyone knows, is itself limited by the protective shield of the Federal Constitution." Equally invalid was the effort of Mississippi to prevent desegregation by making it a crime to attend a mixed school. A state cannot impose criminal penalties on a citizen because he obeys a federal court order.

3. *Pupil placement*   Nine Southern states quickly adopted pupil-placement laws. In general these statutes laid down broad principles, such as nearness to schools, scholastic aptitude of the pupil, and wishes of the parents, as guides for school boards in assigning students to various institutions. In fact, the pattern of segregation was preserved under these statutes by reassigning pupils to their present schools and by assigning new pupils on the basis of race. Requests to transfer from one school to another had to go through an elaborate set of administrative hearings before there could be appeal to the courts. The few Negro students who attempted to thread this maze were invariably frustrated. Nevertheless, the Supreme Court in its only test of a pupil-placement law, *Shuttlesworth* v. *Birmingham Board of Education* (1958), affirmed a lower court holding which upheld the law on the "presumption" that it was not being used to discriminate against Negro pupils.[16]

4. *Private schools*   The core of the resistance plans was the "private school" concept. State laws authorized the closing of public schools where necessary to avoid desegregation. In some instances the buildings were leased to private groups which operated them on a segregated basis, and public funds were used to pay the tuition of students at these schools. Such

[14] See *Osborn* v. *Bank of the United States* (1824); *Ex parte Young* (1908).
[15] *Bush* v. *Orleans Parish* (1956); *Orleans Parish* v. *Bush* (1957).
[16] For a graphic account of how pupil-placement plans worked, see J. W. Peltason, *Fifty-eight Lonely Men* (New York: Harcourt, Brace & World, Inc., 1961), pp. 79–92.

plans immediately encountered unfavorable court decisions,[17] but Prince Edward County, Virginia, which was involved in one of the original 1954 cases, kept its public schools closed and paid tuition for white children in private schools until 1964. Then the Supreme Court in *Griffin* v. *County School Board of Prince Edward County* held it unconstitutional for one county to close its public schools under state law while they remained open in all other counties.

In addition to legal barriers to desegregation, delay was occasioned by threatened or actual violence. Major incidents occurred at Clinton, Tennessee, in 1956; at Little Rock, Arkansas, in 1957; at New Orleans in 1960; and at the University of Mississippi in 1962. President Eisenhower's intervention at Little Rock and President Kennedy's action in the University of Mississippi case have already been mentioned in Chapter 5. In *Cooper* v. *Aaron* (1958) the Supreme Court held that the violent resistance to the Little Rock school board's desegregation plan was "directly traceable" to the Governor and state Legislature and warned that the constitutional rights of children not to be discriminated against in school admission because of race "can neither be nullified openly and directly by state legislators or state executive or judicial officers, nor nullified indirectly by them through evasive schemes for segregation."

THE ENFORCEMENT PROBLEM    Achieving desegregation of the public schools by lawsuits was inevitably a slow and difficult process. In the first place, the issue of segregation had to be raised in each individual school district by persons or groups who would take the responsibility, run the risks, and incur the costs of filing a suit. Usually this task had to be assumed by organized Negro groups, typically the NAACP. In some sections of the South reprisals against those active in the NAACP were so severe and effective that no one would initiate action against school segregation.

Second, the local school boards, acting either on their own initiative or under the compulsion of a federal district court order, had to prepare a desegregation plan. School boards, even when they were willing to act, usually preferred to wait for a court mandate in order to justify themselves to the segregationists in the community.

Third, the federal district judges had to order the desegregation plans into effect. At the time enforcement of the *Brown* decision got under way there were forty-eight federal district judges in the eleven Southern states. They were nearly all native Southerners, sharing the views of the white Southern establishment, subject to the social pressures of their communities, per-

---

[17] See *Aaron* v. *Cooper* (1958); *Harrison* v. *Day* (1959); *Hall* v. *St. Helena Parish School Board* (1961). In *Louisiana Financial Assistance Commission* v. *Poindexter* (1968) the Supreme Court affirmed the unconstitutionality of a 1962 state law which gave state tuition grants to students who attended private, segregated schools.

sonally unsympathetic to the *Brown* ruling. It is not surprising that they tended to move very slowly, and in some cases not at all, in implementing school desegregation plans.

Fourth, the Federal Courts of Appeals for the Fourth and Fifth Circuits, located in Richmond and New Orleans, composed of ten judges, had the responsibility of reviewing the decisions of the district judges. Generally the appellate court judges, somewhat further removed from the pressures of local situations than the district judges, took a conscientious view of their obligations to enforce the Supreme Court's ruling, and they overturned many of the district court decisions.

Fifth, there was the Supreme Court itself, which maintained its strong and unanimous stand against segregation. After the 1955 mandate, however, the Court endeavored to give the lower courts the maximum opportunity and the maximum responsibility for pressing toward the constitutional goal of integration, not only for the schools but for other public facilities. The desegregation requirement was extended to bus transportation, public parks and golf courses, swimming pools, public auditoriums, courtroom seating, and airport restaurants by Supreme Court rulings which merely reversed or affirmed lower court decisions by *per curiam* opinions or without any opinion.[18] Since the *Brown* opinion had been limited to demonstrating why segregation in education was unconstitutional, there were some who felt that the Court was neglecting its responsibility to spell out constitutional principles by failing to provide a reasoned argument against segregation in other areas of public activity.[19]

CONGRESSIONAL AND PRESIDENTIAL ACTION    The Supreme Court received no substantial support on the segregation issue from the other two branches of the federal government for almost a decade, apart from the military actions in Little Rock and in Oxford, Mississippi. It is true that in 1957 Congress passed the first civil rights act since the post-Civil War period, but the statute was principally concerned with voting rights, and efforts to include a provision authorizing the Attorney General to bring school desegregation suits were defeated.

President Kennedy was initially inclined to think that new civil rights legislation was not needed, but after police dogs, cattle prods, and fire hoses had been used against demonstrating Negroes in Birmingham in the spring of 1963, he changed his mind and submitted an omnibus civil rights bill to

[18] *Mayor of Baltimore* v. *Dawson* (1955), public recreation; *Holmes* v. *City of Atlanta* (1955), municipal golf courses; *Gayle* v. *Browder* (1956), buses; *New Orleans City Park Improvement Assn.* v. *Detiege* (1958), public parks; *State Athletic Cmsn.* v. *Dorsey* (1959), athletic contests; *Turner* v. *Memphis* (1962), airport restaurants; *Johnson* v. *Virginia* (1963), courtroom seating; *Schiro* v. *Bynum* (1964), auditoriums; *Lee* v. *Washington* (1968), jails.

[19] See Herbert Wechsler, "Toward Neutral Principles of Constitutional Law," 73 *Harvard Law Review* 1, 22 (1959).

Congress. Following the assassination, President Johnson made adoption of the program one of his primary purposes, and with his persuasive leadership a bipartisan majority in Congress passed the Civil Rights Act of 1964. Title IV of that act authorized the Attorney General to bring school desegregation suits in the name of the United States.

The 1964 act also included in Title VI a general provision prohibiting racial discrimination in any local or state program receiving federal financial assistance. This sanction became of very great importance when, in the Education Act of 1965, as already noted, Congress adopted President Johnson's plan for federal financial assistance to elementary and secondary schools. To become eligible for these grants in the fall of 1965, all public schools had to certify that they were integrated or file acceptable plans for achieving complete integration by the fall of 1967.

This financial prod had a powerful impact, but even so progress was quite slow in some areas. In 1966 the Office of Education issued "guidelines" requiring "significant progress" from year to year toward desegregation in school systems receiving federal aid. For example, school systems operating under so-called "free choice" plans—where students are presumably free to attend schools of their own choosing—should show 15 to 18 per cent of their pupils in desegregated schools by the second year of the program.

The "white backlash" of 1966 created difficult enforcement problems for the Office of Education, and the guidelines were bitterly attacked by Southern representatives in Congress. The resistance centered in Alabama, where the Legislature in 1966 passed a law declaring the guidelines null and void and prohibiting Alabama schools from signing any statements of compliance with them. The federal district court in Montgomery declared this law unconstitutional.[20] Moreover, a three-judge federal panel in March, 1967, ordered the state board of education to begin desegregation of all public schools by the fall of 1967.[21] An attack on the quota and percentage requirements of the guidelines was rebuffed by the Court of Appeals for the Fifth Circuit in the same month; it ordered integration in all six Southern states by the fall of 1967, an order the Supreme Court declined to stay in *Caddo Parish School Board* v. *United States* (1967).

APPRAISAL     By 1967, twelve years after the *Brown* mandate, progress toward desegregation in the schools was either encouraging or discouraging, depending on one's interpretation. By the fall of 1966, in the eleven states

[20] *The New York Times,* May 4, 1967.
[21] *Ibid.,* March 23, 1967. The Supreme Court affirmed this order in *Wallace* v. *United States* (1967). The district court's order was unusual in that it directed the state board to monitor the progress of local school officials. Previous orders were directed to the local boards themselves. In *Green* v. *New Kent County School Board* (1967) the Court agreed to decide whether freedom of choice plans satisfy desegregation requirements when they fail to break down the pattern of racial segregation in Southern schools.

of the Old South, over 360,000 Negro children—12.5 per cent of the total Negro school population—were in desegregated schools. This was double the amount of desegregation that had been achieved by the previous year, yet civil rights groups considered this record little more than tokenism. Moreover, the national mood was less favorable to the civil rights cause after the riots of 1966 and 1967 and the rise of the "Black Power" movement.

In the North there had been almost no progress in dealing with "*de facto* segregation"—that is, schools which are segregated because the neighborhood-school principle in all-Negro neighborhoods produces all-Negro schools. The primary fault here is with the housing barriers that force Negroes to live in restricted localities, and the long-range solution is to break up the ghettoes. But the more active civil rights groups contend that a segregated school is contrary to the *Brown* doctrine whether produced by state law or by the housing pattern, and have proposed that *de facto* segregation be terminated by bussing white pupils into Negro neighborhoods and Negro pupils into white areas. This drastic step has not achieved very wide acceptance, and the reaction of courts which have been asked to order such corrective action has been mixed.[22]

Another tactic was represented by suits begun in Detroit and Chicago in 1968, alleging that variations in educational opportunity violate the equal protection clause, and seeking to compel the states to make more money available for slum area schools. Tax resources vary widely in different school districts because of disparities in local tax bases and rates, and state aid tends to reward the richer schools. The result in both states is that there are wealthy districts which spend six or seven times as much per pupil as the poor districts. The suits contend that the constitutional goal of equal educational opportunities requires the states not merely to equalize spending in all districts but to provide more funds for education in disadvantaged districts where needs are greater because children lack the preschool background and extracurricular educational experience enjoyed by children in better areas.

### STATE MISCEGENATION LAWS

In many states marriage between Negroes and whites has been a criminal act, carrying penalties up to ten years' imprisonment. The Supreme Court

[22] Federal courts of appeals ruled that *de facto* segregation was not unconstitutional in *Bell* v. *School Board of Gary* (1963), *Downs* v. *Board of Education of Kansas City, Kansas* (1964), and *Deal* v. *Cincinnati Board of Education* (1966). In *Springfield School Committee* v. *Barksdale* (1965) a federal district court order requiring steps to remedy *de facto* segregation was vacated by the court of appeals because the school authorities were voluntarily undertaking such a program. In *Hobson* v. *Hansen* (1967) Judge J. Skelly Wright made a scathing attack on *de facto* segregation and the entire school system of the District of Columbia, and ordered a variety of remedial actions to be taken.

had never passed directly on the constitutionality of such laws, but in *Pace* v. *Alabama* (1882) it upheld an Alabama statute whose penalties for fornication between a white person and a Negro were more severe than those provided in the general fornication statute.

Miscegenation laws were uniformly upheld in state courts until 1948, when the California supreme court in *Perez* v. *Lippold* ruled that state's law unconstitutional by a vote of four to three. The law provided that no license could be issued for the marriage of a white person with a Negro, mulatto, Mongolian, or Malay, and declared all such marriages illegal and void. The court majority held that the legislation violated equal protection by impairing, solely on the basis of race, the right of individuals to marry, and amounted to an arbitrary and unreasonable discrimination against certain racial groups. The *Pace* decision was distinguished on the ground that it had dealt only with adultery and nonmarital intercourse which are not, like marriage, basic rights.

The Supreme Court managed for a long time to avoid this socially sensitive issue, even though the state laws involved seemed questionable under the *Brown* decision. In 1955 the Virginia supreme court in *Naim* v. *Naim* upheld that state's miscegenation law. Distinguishing the *Brown* ruling, the state court reasoned that intermarriage of the races, unlike education, was not a foundation of good citizenship or a right which must be available to all on equal terms. The Fourteenth Amendment, the court said, did not prevent the states from preserving the "racial integrity" of their citizens or preventing a "mongrel breed."

The Supreme Court took this case for consideration but then, in a transparently evasive maneuver, remanded it on the ground that the inadequacy of the record prevented the constitutionality of the miscegenation issue from being considered in a clear-cut fashion. The Virginia court, however, declined to reopen the case, and the Supreme Court then dismissed the second appeal on the ground that the state court's action had left the case "devoid of a properly presented federal question."

Presumably the Supreme Court felt that the *Brown* decision had created enough problems for one decade without adding the issue of mixed marriages. But by 1964 it was ready to move cautiously. In *McLaughlin* v. *Florida* the Court unanimously declared unconstitutional a statute which made it a crime for a white person and a Negro, not married to each other, to habitually live in and occupy the same room at night. The state court had upheld the law on authority of the *Pace* decision, but the Supreme Court now ruled that *Pace* had embodied too narrow a view of the equal protection clause. Any classification based solely on race, said Justice White for the Court, must bear a heavy burden of justification. He found no such justification here, but his opinion seemed to assume that a justification might conceivably be possible. Justice Stewart thought this was too cautious; he would not admit that under any circumstances a state law could make "the color

of a person's skin the test of whether his conduct is a criminal offense."

Florida also had a law against mixed marriages, but the Court in *McLaughlin* was careful to avoid expressing any opinion on its validity. However, this issue was squarely raised by a 1966 Virginia supreme court decision, and in *Loving* v. *Virginia* (1967) the Supreme Court unanimously declared the Virginia antimiscegenation law unconstitutional. Holding that marriage is one of the "basic civil rights of man," Chief Justice Warren said: "To deny this fundamental freedom on so unsupportable a basis as . . . racial classifications . . . so directly subversive of the principle of equality at the heart of the Fourteenth Amendment, is surely to deprive all the state's citizens of liberty without due process of law." The opinion obviously also invalidated similar laws in fifteen other states.

### STATE ACTION

An important factor in the expanding effectiveness of the equal protection clause against racial discrimination has been the Supreme Court's recent interpretation of the "state action" requirement of the Fourteenth Amendment. The Court's initial statement on state action in the *Civil Rights Cases* (1883) was that the Fourteenth Amendment forbade only those denials of due process or equal protection "sanctioned in some way by the state" or "done under state authority." But whether an act falls within these categories is not always easy to determine.

ACTIONS OF STATE OFFICIALS    Normally there is no doubt that actions by state or local officials in their official capacity constitute state action. This is obvious when they act under authorization of a specific state law, but it is also generally true when they take discriminatory action without authorization of law or even contrary to law. An early holding of the Supreme Court was in *Ex parte Virginia* (1880), where a county judge had been indicted for excluding Negroes from jury service. The Court said: "Whoever . . . acts in the name and for the State, and is clothed with the State's power, his act is that of the State."

The Civil Rights Act of 1866, passed before adoption of the Fourteenth Amendment, made punishable racial discrimination by persons acting "under color of any law." This phrase has since been rather generally employed in civil rights statutes, and it has come to be accepted as one of the tests of state action. The Supreme Court in *United States* v. *Classic* (1941) applied the statute to officials guilty of election fraud, saying: "Misuse of power, possessed by virtue of state law and made possible only because the wrongdoer is clothed with the authority of state law, is action taken 'under color of' state law."

In the gruesome case of *Screws* v. *United States* (1945), where a sheriff

had beaten a Negro prisoner to death in his jail, the defense against a federal civil rights prosecution was that the sheriff, having acted in abuse of his official capacity, could not be regarded as having acted under color of law. The Court majority rejected this view, Justice Rutledge contending that the sheriff had acted with the "power of official place," but Justice Roberts, dissenting, could not see how conduct "in flagrant defiance of State law, may be attributed to the State."

More recently the Girard College case involved the Court in some difficult distinctions as to state action. Girard College in Philadelphia was created under terms of a will probated in 1831, which provided for the establishment and operation of a school for "white male orphans." The college was administered by the board of directors of city trusts, admittedly a state agency. In *Pennsylvania* v. *Board of City Trusts* (1957) the Supreme Court held that refusal to admit Negroes to the school was discrimination by state action. The state courts then substituted private individuals as trustees, who continued the exclusionary policy. The Supreme Court denied certiorari to review this action in *In re Girard College Trusteeship* (1958), thus apparently accepting the contention that state action was no longer involved. However, the school was subsequently opened to Negroes by a 1968 court of appeals ruling reinterpreting the will "in this changed world." [23]

*Evans* v. *Newton* (1966) was somewhat similar to the Girard College case. Under the terms of a will funds were given to the city of Macon, Georgia, for creation of a park for white persons only. When it appeared that as a public park Negroes would have to be admitted, the city resigned as trustee and a court appointed three private individuals as the new trustees. The Supreme Court, admitting that "what is 'private' action and what is 'state' action is not always easy to determine," held the park was still public because "the momentum it acquired as a public facility is . . . not dissipated *ipso facto* by the appointment of 'private' trustees." Justice Douglas also suggested that "the service rendered even by a private park of this character is municipal in character." Justice Harlan, dissenting, was alarmed by this latter proposition. If there can be no such thing as a private park, he wondered how there could be such a thing as a private school, for the service rendered by schools is even more important to the public than parks.

INACTION OF STATE OFFICIALS     A somewhat different question arises when injury is done to a person's civil rights as a result of official failure to act. Can official inaction be treated as "state action"? *Lynch* v. *United States* (1951) involved review of the conviction of a Georgia sheriff who had

---

[23] In 1967 the Court vacated a ruling by a federal district judge in Virginia who had refused to bar state officials from enforcing the clause in the will establishing Sweet Briar Institute that limited its student body to "white girls and young women"; *Sweet Briar Institute* v. *Button.*

allowed Negro prisoners in his custody to be kidnapped and beaten by a Ku Klux mob. The sheriff claimed that he had been overpowered, but the evidence indicated that if he had not actively cooperated with the mob, at least he had offered no resistance and had made no effort to arrest its members. A Georgia federal court jury found him guilty of having acted under color of law to deprive a citizen of his protected rights, and the court of appeals agreed that official inaction, where designed to injure, may be punished. "There was a time when the denial of equal protection of the laws was confined to affirmative acts, but the law now is that culpable official inaction may also constitute a denial of equal protection."

In *Terry* v. *Adams* (1953) a group of private citizens regularly conducted an unofficial primary prior to the regular Democratic primary to select candidates for office in a Texas county who would then be entered in the regular primary. The theory of this pre-primary was that it was private action from which Negroes could be constitutionally excluded, but the Supreme Court ruled that the pre-primary had become "an integral part" of the election process. Both Justices Black and Frankfurter emphasized that state inaction was the root of the offense. According to Black, the state had permitted "circumvention" to produce the equivalent of a discriminatory election, and Frankfurter referred to the state's "abdication."

DISCRIMINATION IN PUBLIC ACCOMMODATIONS    The *Civil Rights Cases* (1883), as we have seen, held that the Fourteenth Amendment did not prevent discrimination in such privately owned public accommodations as hotels and theaters. Although that decision has never been overruled, the situation of public accommodations has been drastically changed by judicial interpretation and by state and federal statutes.

In the first place, any significant relationship between the state and the enterprise may be interpreted as transferring to the latter the constitutional obligations of the state. The leading case is *Burton* v. *Wilmington Parking Authority* (1961), involving a parking facility owned and operated by an agency of the state of Delaware. To help finance the building some of the space was leased to commercial operations. This case arose when a restaurant located on the premises refused service to a Negro. The Supreme Court majority held that its location in, and relationship to, the parking facility had cost the restaurant its "purely private" character. The revenue from this and other commercial leases was an indispensable part of the state's plan to operate the project on a self-sustaining basis. The relationship between the restaurant and the parking enterprise was mutually beneficial. By its inaction in failing to require the restaurant to serve all comers, the state was held to have made itself a party to the refusal of service.

The sit-in cases already discussed in Chapter 24 furnish additional illustrations of how public accommodations may come under the state action rule. In *Peterson* v. *Greenville* (1963) restaurant discrimination was state

action because a city ordinance required separation of the races. In *Lombard* v. *Louisiana* (1963) there was no ordinance, but the Court held that city officials had coerced the restaurant manager to operate a segregated facility, which made it state action. *Griffin* v. *Maryland* (1964) held that an amusement park's exclusion of Negroes was state action because, to enforce this policy, the park employed a deputy sheriff who, though working on his off-duty hours, wore his badge and purported to exercise the powers of a deputy sheriff at the park.

However, there must be some link of this kind between the state and the enterprise, however tenuous or indirect, to justify treating the discriminatory action of public accommodations as state action under the Fourteenth Amendment. The Supreme Court has stopped short of a holding that public accommodations are by the very nature of their service public agencies governed by the equal protection clause. This was the position taken by the first Justice Harlan in his dissent to the *Civil Rights Cases*, and it has been revived on the recent Court by Justices Douglas and Goldberg.

In *Garner* v. *Louisiana* (1961) Justice Douglas, speaking only for himself, argued that restaurants could not be considered ordinary private property but were of necessity in the public domain because they have to have permits to operate and are subject to broad public powers of inspection. In *Bell* v. *Maryland* (1964) he amplified this position, now supported by Goldberg. Douglas denied that any constitutional rights of privacy are involved in a business that has voluntarily chosen to serve the public. Most such public accommodations are of a corporate character, owned by stockholders who never see the customers in their establishments and have no personal rights that are being protected by refusal of service to certain classes. The reasons for discrimination in these situations are purely business reasons. Justice Goldberg, starting from the principle that "the Declaration of Independence states the American creed," built his opinion on the "fundamental purpose" of the Fourteenth Amendment, though he almost certainly greatly overstated the historical arguments concerning the intention of the amendment.

Three other justices in the *Bell* case—Black, Harlan, and White—controverted this position, contending that restaurants were no different from other private property and that a restaurant owner must be protected in his constitutional rights to occupy, enjoy, and use his property. The Fourteenth Amendment standing alone, without any statutory implementation, does not allow people "to force their way into his restaurant and remain there over his protest," Black concluded.

Actually, the Court found it unnecessary to choose between these two positions in *Bell* v. *Maryland,* for it was able to dispose of the case without reaching the constitutional issue. After the sit-in convictions which the Court was reviewing in *Bell,* the Maryland Legislature passed a law guaranteeing free access to public accommodations in the state. Because of this change in the legal situation, six justices, including Douglas and Goldberg, voted to

remand the case to the state court on the assumption that it would now want to reverse the convictions.

The Supreme Court's wisdom in delaying its consideration of the constitutional situation of public accommodations was demonstrated when, only twelve days after the *Bell* decision, the Civil Rights Act of 1964 was signed. In this statute, also called the Public Accommodations Act, Congress took over from the Supreme Court the responsibility of determining what rights of access there should be to the most important types of public accommodations. Under the statute full and equal access without discrimination or segregation is guaranteed with respect to hotels and motels, restaurants, and catering establishments of all kinds, places of entertainment and sports exhibitions, gasoline stations, and such bars and barber shops as are physically within the premises of a covered establishment. Boarding houses with not more than five rooms for rent are not covered, nor are private clubs or other establishments not in fact open to the public.

This statute, as already noted in Chapter 14, invoked the commerce clause as authority for its enactment, and it was on this basis that the Supreme Court promptly upheld the act in *Heart of Atlanta Motel* v. *United States* (1964). But Congress also relied on the Fourteenth Amendment by defining the applicability of the act to cover discrimination and segregation required by action of the state or carried on "under color of any law" or "any custom or usage required or enforced by officials of the State." In the *Heart of Atlanta* case the Supreme Court found it unnecessary to consider this second basis for congressional action, since the commerce power alone was sufficient for the decision. This ruling relieved the Court from the necessity of reconsidering the *Civil Rights Cases* of 1883, the decision in which was held here to be "inapposite, and without precedential value."

PRIVATE DISCRIMINATION AND STATE ACTION    The state action rule of the Fourteenth Amendment leaves individuals free to discriminate for any reason in their personal relationships, in granting access to their homes, or in the operation of private associations. As Justice Goldberg said in his *Bell* opinion, "Rights pertaining to privacy and private association are themselves constitutionally protected liberties," and courts will safeguard the privilege of every person "to close his home or club to any person . . . on the basis of personal prejudices including race."

But how far beyond the home or the club does this guarantee of the right to discriminate extend? The principal problems have concerned the buying, selling, and renting of property. We have already noted that in *Shelley* v. *Kraemer* (1948) the Court regarded restrictive covenants, which are voluntary contractual agreements among property owners not to sell their property to persons of particular race or color, as legal so far as the contracting parties were concerned; but their judicial enforcement was barred because that would constitute discriminatory state action by the

courts. The implications of this ruling seemed rather sweeping. It was argued that, if obtaining court aid in carrying out a private activity converts such private action into state action, then very few of life's activities would be left in the private sector, and almost all private activity could be required to conform to state standards.

Clearly the opinion did not mean to go this far. The Court itself said that it was erecting "no shield against merely private conduct, however discriminatory or wrongful." Louis Pollak suggested that the *Shelley* doctrine must be interpreted only to prevent the state from enforcing a discrimination by one who did not wish to discriminate.[24] After all, judicial enforcement of the restrictive covenant in *Shelley* would have permitted remote owners to prevent the acquisition of property by a willing Negro buyer who had found a willing white seller. If a person is unwilling to sell or to admit others onto his property, no matter how blatantly discriminatory his reasons, the *Shelley* rule does not prevent the courts from enforcing his full freedom of choice, said Justice Black in *Bell* v. *Maryland.*

Some states have adopted "open occupancy" laws which make illegal refusal to sell or to rent to persons because of their race or color, and these statutes have generally met state constitutional tests. The experience of California has received the most attention. The Unruh Civil Rights Act of 1959 and the Rumford Act of 1963 barred racial discrimination in the sale or rental of any private dwelling of more than four units, and the State Fair Employment Practice Commission was empowered to prevent violations. In 1964 California voters, by a margin of almost two to one, approved an amendment to the state constitution which nullified the effect of these acts and provided that property owners had "absolute discretion" to sell or rent to persons of their choice.

In 1966 the California supreme court by a vote of five to two in *Mulkey* v. *Reitman* declared the amendment unconstitutional as state action in violation of the equal protection clause. By adopting the amendment, the court said, the state had become "at least a partner in the . . . act of discrimination," adding that when "the electorate assumes to exercise the law-making function," it is "as much a state agency as any of its elected officials." In *Reitman* v. *Mulkey* (1967) the Supreme Court upheld this position by a vote of five to four, Justice White for the majority ruling that the amendment made the right to discriminate "one of the basic policies of the state." After the amendment was passed, "the right to discriminate, including the right to discriminate on racial grounds, was embodied in the state's basic charter, immune from legislative, executive or judicial regulation at any level of the state government. Those practicing racial discriminations need no longer rely on their personal choice. They could now evoke express constitutional authority." Under this ruling racial discrimination by private persons vio-

---

[24] "Racial Discrimination and Judicial Integrity," 108 *University of Pennsylvania Law Review* 1, 13 (1959).

lates the Fourteenth Amendment if the state takes any action encouraging such discrimination.[25]

## FEDERAL PROTECTION OF CIVIL RIGHTS

The federal character of the American constitutional system has resulted in some peculiarly difficult problems in enforcing the equal protection standard of the Fourteenth Amendment. Judicial redress against discriminatory state action must usually be sought in state courts in cases brought on the initiative of the injured individual. Where state courts and state opinion are hostile to the efforts of a minority group to assert its claims to constitutional protections, or where individuals lack the resources to bring court actions, the standards of the federal Constitution may very well go unenforced. This was the historical situation of the Negro in the South following adoption of the Fourteenth and Fifteenth Amendments, though it has also been faced in a less intense fashion by groups in other parts of the country.

Under these circumstances the question arises of direct federal action—legislative, executive, or judicial—to secure the more effective enforcement of federal constitutional standards. As we have seen, the original expectation was that the protections of the Fourteenth Amendment would be made effective by congressional legislation, which would furnish the foundation for a positive federal program of protection for civil rights. Of course it did not work out that way. The early civil rights acts of 1866, 1870, 1871, and 1875 proved largely valueless. With a hostile Supreme Court and an uninterested public, much of the legislative product of Radical Reconstruction was declared unconstitutional, or repealed by later Congresses. What was left was largely ignored and unused by enforcement authorities. There were perennial proposals for new legislation, particularly antilynching and antipoll tax measures, but they could never get through Congress over Southern opposition.

During the New Deal period, interest was heightened in these problems. In 1939 Attorney General Frank Murphy established a Civil Rights Section in the Criminal Division of the Department of Justice, which undertook to enforce such of the civil rights laws as remained on the statute books. President Truman appointed a Committee on Civil Rights, which issued a distinguished report, *To Secure These Rights*, in 1947. But efforts to adopt a federal fair employment practices act failed, though substantial progress was made toward eliminating discrimination in employment by voluntary programs and by the banning of discrimination on government contracts.

[25] See the extensive discussion by Charles L. Black, Jr., " 'State Action,' Equal Protection, and California's Proposition 14," 81 *Harvard Law Review* 69–109 (1967). As already noted, an effort in Congress to adopt a national open housing requirement as part of the 1966 civil rights bill failed. But in *Jones* v. *Alfred H. Mayer Co.* (1968) the plaintiffs contended that housing discrimination was already illegal under the Civil Rights Act of 1866.

After the *Brown* decision in 1954, there was renewed attention to the possibility of federal enforcement of civil rights, which led to adoption of the Civil Rights Act of 1957. This statute dealt largely with protection of voting rights, which is the subject of the next chapter. But it also set up a Civil Rights Commission to take testimony, gather information, and make recommendations to Congress on needed civil rights legislation. In addition a new Civil Rights Division in the Department of Justice was given statutory status.

The 1957 statute was followed by the Civil Rights Act of 1960, also concerned primarily with voting rights, and then the Civil Rights Act of 1964, dealing principally with equal access to public accommodations. In 1966 a Senate filibuster defeated a House-passed bill forbidding discrimination in the sale or rental of housing. But in 1968 Congress passed a civil rights act with strong open housing provisions, the final House action coming shortly after the assassination of Martin Luther King, Jr.

Of the four civil rights acts passed since 1957, none deals with the problem of "Southern justice," that is, the century-old system in some Southern states where all too often crimes against Negroes go unpunished and efforts by Negroes to secure redress in the courts against wrongs go unheard. The opportunity for federal officials and courts to step into such situations has depended very largely on two inadequate statutes dating from the Reconstruction period. Section 241 of Title 18 of the United States Code provides a fine of up to $5,000 and imprisonment of up to ten years for a conspiracy by two or more persons to "injure, oppress, threaten, or intimidate any citizen" from exercising, or because he has exercised, any right or privilege "secured" to him by the Constitution or laws of the United States.

The other relevant criminal statute is section 242. It provides a fine of $1,000 or one year in prison, or both, for any person who, acting "under color of any law, statute, ordinance, regulation, or custom," willfully deprives any inhabitant of the United States of any of the rights, privileges, or immunities "secured or protected" by the Constitution or laws of the United States. This second section is broader than the conspiracy statute in that its shield covers all "inhabitants," not merely "citizens." Moreover, section 242 refers to substantive acts and not just to conspiracies, and therefore can be used against a single individual who commits unlawful acts providing he is acting "under color of" law.

A technical difference between the two statutes, but one with important consequences, is that section 241 covers rights "secured" by the Constitution or federal laws, which was originally given a limited interpretation as the equivalent of rights of national citizenship, such as the right to vote in national elections, to petition Congress for redress of grievances, and to use the federal courts.

Section 242, on the other hand, covers not only "secured" rights but also rights "protected" against state infringement, including the guarantees of

due process and equal protection. Consequently the federal government could safeguard the more limited class of "secured" rights against deprivation both by private individuals under 241 and by state officials under 242, but was limited by the state-action requirement of the Fourteenth Amendment in prosecuting violations of the more significant "protected" rights under section 242.

These two statutes had not been much used up until the 1960s, and had not been very effective. In *Screws* v. *United States* (1945), where a sheriff beat his prisoner to death, a conviction under section 242 was reversed and a new trial ordered because the judge had not charged the jury that the deprivation of constitutional rights must be "willful." A minority of three justices in *Screws* thought that section 242 was flatly unconstitutional. In two 1951 decisions growing out of an instance of police brutality in Florida, the Court upheld a conviction under section 242 in *Williams* v. *United States* but reversed on the same facts under section 241 in *United States* v. *Williams* because of their limited interpretation of "secured" rights.

Violence against civil rights workers and Negroes in the South in the 1960s led to widespread demands for more effective intervention by the federal government, and the Department of Justice made renewed efforts to use sections 241 and 242, which were successful in the cases of *United States* v. *Price* (1966) and *United States* v. *Guest* (1966). The *Price* case was an aftermath of the murder of three young civil rights workers near Philadelphia, Mississippi, in 1964. The Department of Justice, reluctant to turn over evidence gathered by the FBI to a local grand jury, secured a federal indictment against eighteen suspects under sections 241 and 242. The federal district judge, relying on *United States* v. *Williams*, dismissed the conspiracy indictment under 241.

The Supreme Court in *Price* unanimously overruled the district judge, and in the process broadened the interpretation of this section to cover not only rights of national citizenship but also Fourteenth Amendment rights. Justice Fortas pointed out that the Court had actually been divided four to four in *United States* v. *Williams*, and that Justice Frankfurter's more restrictive view had prevailed only because the ninth justice, Black, had gone along for an entirely different reason. As interpreted in *Price*, section 241 embraces "*all* of the rights and privileges secured to citizens by *all* of the Constitution and *all* of the laws of the United States." The Court felt that the history of this Reconstruction legislation made clear its broad sweep—"the violent denial of legal process was one of the reasons motivating enactment of the section"—and declared: "We are not at liberty to seek ingenious analytical instruments for excluding from its general language the Due Process Clause of the Fourteenth Amendment." In the 1967 trial which this holding made possible, Price and six associates were found guilty, the first convictions for a civil rights slaying in Mississippi.

*United States* v. *Guest* (1966) grew out of the murder of Lemuel A. Penn,

a resident of Washington, D.C., which occurred when he was driving through Georgia. Two men were tried for the murder in a Georgia court and acquitted. Conspiracy indictments under section 241 against six men were dismissed by a federal judge, who was then reversed by the Supreme Court on grounds similar to those in *Price*. There was one important difference in the two cases, however, which led to an interesting division on the Court. In *Price* several local law-enforcement officers had been involved, so that state action in the denial of due process was clearly present. But in *Guest* all the six men indicted for having conspired to injure Penn in the free exercise and enjoyment of his rights were private individuals. The Court majority through Justice Stewart concluded that since the equal protection clause is a guarantee only against state action, section 241 can "secure" rights only against state action. However, the Court held that here the indictment had satisfied this requirement because it charged cooperative state action in the conspiracy, namely, that one of the means used to deny the right to equal utilization of public facilities was causing the arrest of Negroes on false reports that such Negroes had committed criminal acts.

Three justices, speaking through Justice Brennan, challenged this holding that there had to be state action to support a denial of equal protection charge under section 241. They construed the section as reaching wholly private action which interferes with Fourteenth Amendment rights and upheld it as a constitutional exercise of congressional enforcement power under section 5 of the amendment. Three additional justices from the *Guest* majority—Clark, Black, and Fortas—agreed that section 5 empowers Congress to enact laws punishing all conspiracies, with or without state action, that interfere with Fourteenth Amendment rights.

In this rather indirect fashion the Supreme Court finally effectively overruled the *Civil Rights Cases* of 1883 insofar as that decision limited the power of Congress under section 5 of the Fourteenth Amendment to the adoption of "appropriate legislation for correcting the effects of . . . prohibited state law and state acts" only. Taken along with the broad decision in *South Carolina* v. *Katzenbach* that under section 2 of the Fifteenth Amendment (which is almost identical with section 5 of the Fourteenth) Congress can use "any rational means" to effectuate the purpose of the amendment, it is clear that the way is open for Congress to adopt much more effective standards for the protection of civil rights than sections 241 and 242 have provided.

CIVIL SUIT    Two statutes generally paralleling the criminal sanctions just discussed allow damage suits against state officers and private persons who violate constitutional rights. Section 1983 of Title 42 of the United States Code (formerly Title 8, sec. 43) provides for civil suit against any person acting under "color of any statute, ordinance, regulation, custom, or usage" who deprives a citizen of his constitutional rights. This corresponds closely

to section 242 of the criminal code. It can be used to deter "unlawful law enforcement" by making the official who exceeds legal bounds liable for monetary damages.[26] But its most important use has been in combination with other provisions of the United States Code to obtain an injunction or declaratory judgment against the enforcement of unconstitutional laws or policies. In this manner the white primary was invalidated, as was segregation in public schools, buses, and parks.

The second statute under which civil suits may be brought is now codified as section 1985 of Title 42 (formerly Title 8, sec. 47), which allows a damage suit against two or more persons who conspire to deprive or do deprive "any person or class of persons of the equal protection of the laws, or of equal privileges and immunities under the laws." This section presented constitutional difficulties, brought out in *Collins* v. *Hardyman* (1951), so long as the Court insisted that equal protection could be defended only against state action or against persons acting under color of law. But the *Guest* decision, as we have just seen, suggests that this limitation may no longer exist.

OTHER CIVIL RIGHTS MEASURES    A statute of 1866, codified as section 1443, Title 28, authorized the removal of civil rights cases under certain circumstances from state to federal courts. Denial of removal petitions was not subject to appeal to the Supreme Court until so provided by the Civil Rights Act of 1964. In *Georgia* v. *Rachel* (1966) the Court held that the federal district court involved must grant a hearing to determine whether defendants under prosecution in state courts for a restaurant sit-in had been ordered to leave the restaurant solely for racial reasons. If so, their rights of free access to public accommodations under the 1964 Civil Rights Act would have been challenged, and they would be entitled to removal of the case to federal court.

However, in another case decided the same day, *City of Greenwood* v. *Peacock* (1966), the Court by a five to four vote held that removal would not be ordered on allegations that the defendants had been arrested and charged solely because they were Negroes or were engaged in helping Negroes to assert their civil rights. The majority asserted that the removal statute was not intended "to work a wholesale dislocation of the historic relationship between the state and the federal courts in the administration

[26] The Supreme Court applied this statute in *Monroe* v. *Pape* (1961) in a suit brought against lawless actions of the Chicago police in breaking into a home at night, humiliating the occupants, ransacking the house, and arresting the husband, all without search or arrest warrants. Justice Frankfurter, the sole dissenter, protested the "unwisdom of extending federal criminal jurisdiction into areas of conduct conventionally punished by state penal law." In *Pierson* v. *Ray* (1967) the Court found the *Monroe* decision inapplicable, and held that the defense of good faith and probable cause was available to police officers in a suit under section 1983 for false arrest and imprisonment.

of the criminal law." If the defendants really were being prosecuted because they were Negroes, Justice Stewart said, there were other possible remedies in the federal courts by way of injunction, habeas corpus, and appeal.

Justice Douglas for the dissenters in *Peacock* contended that "the federal regime was designed from the beginning to afford some protection against local passions and prejudices by the important pretrial federal remedy of removal." He added:

> These defendants' federal civil rights may, of course, ultimately be vindicated if they persevere, live long enough, and have the patience and the funds to carry their cases for some years through the state courts to this Court. But it was precisely that burden that Congress undertook to take off the backs of this persecuted minority and all who espouse the cause of their equality.

A major problem in "Southern justice" has been the refusal of white jurors to convict white persons charged with the violation of civil rights of Negroes. The civil rights bill of 1966, as passed by the House, prohibited discrimination in the selection of federal and state jurors, and authorized federal district courts to suspend state jury qualifications, to require use of objective criteria in selection of jurors, to appoint a master to act as jury official, and to require preservation of jury records. By 1968 white juries had convicted white defendants in several civil rights cases.

Finally, it should be noted that federal courts can act directly against persons who interfere with the enforcement of federal court orders. When city officials of Grenada, Mississippi, in 1966 made no effort to protect Negro children, attending a school desegregated by court order, from being beaten by white adults, the Department of Justice requested an injunction from the federal district court ordering Grenada officials to protect the children in the future and to arrest and prosecute those who assaulted them.

### SELECTED REFERENCES

BERMAN, DANIEL M., *A Bill Becomes a Law: The Civil Rights Act of 1960*. New York: The Macmillan Company, 1962.

BICKEL, ALEXANDER M., "The Original Understanding and the Segregation Decision," 69 *Harvard Law Review* 1–65 (1955).

———, *Politics and the Warren Court*. New York: Harper & Row, Publishers, Incorporated, 1965.

BLAUSTEIN, ALBERT P., and CLARENCE C. FERGUSON, JR., *Desegregation and the Law*. New York: Random House, Inc., 1962 (second revised edition).

CAHN, EDMOND, "Jurisprudence," 30 *New York University Law Review* 150–169 (1955).

Congressional Quarterly, *Revolution in Civil Rights*. Washington, D.C.: Congressional Quarterly Service, 1965.

*The Constitution of the United States of America: Analysis and Interpretation,* Sen. Doc. no. 39, 88th Cong., pp. 1279–1321. Washington: Government Printing Office, 1964.

FRANK, JOHN P., and ROBERT F. MUNRO, "The Original Understanding of 'Equal Protection of the Laws,'" 50 *Columbia Law Review* 131–169 (1950).

GARFINKEL, HERBERT, "Social Science Evidence and the School Segregation Cases," 21 *Journal of Politics* 37–59 (1959).

GOLDWIN, ROBERT A. (ed.), *One Hundred Years of Emancipation.* Chicago: Rand McNally & Company, 1964.

GRIMES, ALAN P., *Equality in America.* Fair Lawn, N.J.: Oxford University Press, 1964.

HARRIS, ROBERT J., *The Quest for Equality.* Baton Rouge, La.: Louisiana State University Press, 1960.

LEWIS, ANTHONY, *Portrait of a Decade: The Second American Revolution.* New York: Random House, Inc., 1964.

PELTASON, JACK W., *Fifty-eight Lonely Men: Southern Federal Judges and School Desegregation.* New York: Harcourt, Brace & World, Inc., 1961.

*Race Relations Law Reporter.* Nashville, Tenn.: Vanderbilt University School of Law, 1956–

TEN BROEK, JACOBUS, *Equal under Law.* New York: Collier Books, a division of Crowell-Collier Publishing Co., 1965.

TUSSMAN, JOSEPH (ed.), *The Supreme Court on Racial Discrimination.* Fair Lawn, N.J.: Oxford University Press, 1963.

United States Commission on Civil Rights, *1961 Commission on Civil Rights Report: Part IV, Education; Part VII, Equal Justice under Law.* Washington: Government Printing Office, 1961.

———, *Racial Isolation in the Public Schools.* Washington: Government Printing Office, 1967.

# 34

## The franchise

The framers of the Constitution had to deal with the problem of the franchise only in connection with the selection of members of the House of Representatives, since senators were elected by the state legislatures and presidential electors were appointed in such manner as the state legislatures might direct. Eventually the responsibility for electing the President and members of both houses of Congress devolved upon this same national electorate. Although the states have the major responsibility under the Constitution of determining the standards for voting eligibility, in recent years Congress has come increasingly to concern itself, through constitutional amendment and through legislation, with the problem of discriminatory denial of the right to vote in certain states.

### CONSTITUTIONAL FOUNDATION OF THE RIGHT TO VOTE

The basic provision in the Constitution governing the right to vote in federal elections is Article I, section 2, which provides that electors for members of the House in the several states "shall have the qualifications requisite for electors of the most numerous branch of the state legislature." By this device the Constitution assured election of the House on a popular base but avoided creation of a national electorate separate from the state electorates, which were defined by legal provisions varying widely from state to state.

Second, there is the "times, places and manner" clause of Article I, section 4. As already noted, Congress first took action under this authority in 1842, when it required that members of the House should be elected by districts rather than on a general state ticket. An act of 1866 regulated the procedure of state legislatures in choosing senators. The first comprehensive federal statute on elections came in 1870, motivated by the political problems of the Reconstruction period. The Enforcement Act of 1870 and subsequent measures made federal offenses of false registration, bribery, voting without legal right, making false returns of votes cast, interference in any manner with officers of elections, or the neglect by any such officer of any duty required of him by state or federal law.

In addition to these two provisions of Article I, four of the amendments to the Constitution have a bearing on elections and the electorate. The equal protection clause of the Fourteenth Amendment has been applied, as we shall see, to forbid discriminatory practices by state election officials. The Fourteenth Amendment also contains the threat of reduction of representation for denial of the right to vote. When it appeared that this provision would not achieve its purpose of securing the suffrage for Negroes, the Fifteenth Amendment was adopted in 1870, specifically guaranteeing that "the right of citizens of the United States to vote shall not be denied or abridged by the United States or by any state on account of race, color, or previous condition of servitude." The Nineteenth Amendment, adopted in 1920, uses the same formula to guarantee women the right to vote. The Fourteenth, Fifteenth, and Nineteenth Amendments all authorize Congress to enforce their provisions by appropriate legislation. The Twenty-fourth Amendment, adopted in 1964, provides that the right to vote in a federal election shall not be denied for failure to pay a poll tax or any other tax.

In spite of the Fifteenth Amendment's use of the phrase "the right to vote," the Supreme Court was at first reluctant to give effect to such a right. Under Article I, section 2, participation in federal elections depends upon state laws prescribing the electorate, and so it is strictly true, as the Supreme Court held in the early case of *Minor* v. *Happersett* (1875), that "the Constitution of the United States does not confer the right of suffrage upon anyone." Mrs. Minor had sought to compel election officials in Missouri, where suffrage was limited to male citizens, to accept her vote on the ground that she had a right to vote as a citizen of the United States under the Fourteenth Amendment, but the Court decisively rejected this contention. The following year the Court took a similarly negative attitude toward the Fifteenth Amendment, contending that it did not confer the right to vote on anyone, bu merely "invested the citizens of the United States with a new constitutional right which is . . . exemption from discrimination in the exercise of the elective franchise." [1]

Within a decade, however, the Court had reconsidered this doctrine. *Ex*

[1] *United States* v. *Reese* (1876); *United States* v. *Cruikshank* (1876).

*parte Yarbrough* (1884) affirmed the conviction of several Klansmen for conspiring to prevent a Negro by intimidation from voting for a member of Congress. They were held to have violated the Enforcement Act of 1870, which provided punishment in cases of conspiracy to injure or intimidate a citizen in the exercise of any federal right. In spite of *Minor* v. *Happersett*, there was a *right* involved in this case. The earlier decision, explained the Court, merely meant that state law, not the federal Constitution, determined what classes of citizens could exercise the franchise. But once state law had determined who was eligible to vote by statutory provisions covering state elections, then the federal Constitution through Article I, section 2, stepped in to guarantee their *right* to vote for members of Congress.

Similarly the Court took a new view of the Fifteenth Amendment. In the same case Justice Miller held that, contrary to the Court's original position, the amendment might "under some circumstances . . . operate as the immediate source of a right to vote." Where state constitutions or laws made being white a qualification for voting, the amendment would annul the word "white" and leave a Negro "in the enjoyment of the same right as white persons."

### STATE LIMITATIONS ON THE FRANCHISE

The states are left free, then, to fix conditions on exercise of the franchise, so long as they do not infringe any constitutional limitations or valid congressional statutes interpreting and enforcing those limitations. The principal types of restrictions imposed by the states which have raised no constitutional issues are the following.

*1. Citizenship*    All states require that voters be citizens of the United States, although in the past aliens were permitted to vote in some states. Not until 1928 was there a presidential election in which no alien was eligible to vote.

*2. Residence*    All states require a certain period of residence in the state and locality as a qualification for the franchise. This is a reasonable requirement for participation in state and local elections,[2] but it is an irrelevant qualification in voting for President, and about half of the states have now adopted special residence requirements for presidential elections. These laws extend the right to vote either to new residents, even though they do not meet the residence requirements for voting in other elections, or to former residents until they are eligible to vote in their new states.

In *Carrington* v. *Rash* (1965) the Supreme Court ruled that Texas had carried its residence restrictions too far when it provided that any member of the Armed Forces who moved to Texas during the course of his military

[2] See *Pope* v. *Williams* (1904).

duty was prohibited from voting in the state so long as he remained in the Armed Forces. The Court agreed that Texas had a right to require that voters be bona fide residents, but anyone who met that test could not be denied opportunity for equal political representation. "'Fencing out' from the franchise a sector of the population because of the way they may vote is constitutionally impermissible."

3. *Age*    The general voting age set by the states has been twenty-one, but Georgia reduced it to eighteen in 1943. In Kentucky it is also eighteen, in Alabama nineteen, and in Hawaii twenty.[3]

4. *Conviction of crime*    The states generally make conviction and confinement for felony or infamous crime a disqualification for voting until civil rights are restored. A statute of this kind was upheld by the Supreme Court in *Green* v. *New York City Board of Elections* (1968).

5. *Insanity*    Persons who are idiots, insane, or under guardianship are specifically disqualified from voting in almost all states.

On the other hand, some states have adopted limitations on the franchise which are obviously discriminatory on their face, and which the Supreme Court has had no hesitation in declaring unconstitutional. Perhaps the best known is the "grandfather clause" involved in *Guinn* v. *United States* (1915). An Oklahoma law imposed a literacy test for voting, but gave exemption for persons whose ancestors had been entitled to vote in 1866. The Court held this provision to be a clear attempt to evade the Fifteenth Amendment. Oklahoma rejoined with a new election registration law which permitted a twelve-day registration period but exempted from the registration requirement those who had voted in the 1914 election under the unconstitutional grandfather clause. The Court held this law also invalid in *Lane* v. *Wilson* (1939).

More difficult are statutory conditions on exercise of the franchise which are not discriminatory on their face, but which can be administered in a discriminatory manner. The principal instruments in this category are poll taxes, literacy tests, and requirements to understand or interpret the Constitution.

POLL TAXES    Poll (or head) taxes were once a familiar source of revenue, but gradually fell into disuse. They were revived around 1900 by a number of states and made a condition of the franchise as a deliberate device to reduce the possibility of Negro voting. At the Virginia constitutional convention in 1902 which adopted a poll-tax requirement for that state, its

---

[3] Reduction of the voting age in other states seems likely. In 1967 the Gallup Poll reported that 64 per cent of adults favored lowering the voting age to eighteen.

principal sponsor frankly stated that the purpose was "to discriminate to the very extremity of permissible action under the limitations of the Federal Constitution, with a view to the elimination of every negro voter who can be gotten rid of, legally." [4]

In practice the poll tax was a very substantial bar to the voting of Negroes and poor whites. While the amount of the tax was usually around $2, that was a large sum for many, and there was usually a provision that unpaid back taxes had to be paid if a person wanted to start voting. Moreover, the tax requirement was a source of corruption in elections, taxes often being paid by candidates in return for voting support.

On its face, however, the poll tax was not discriminatory, and in *Breedlove* v. *Suttles* (1937) the Supreme Court refused to hold that its use constituted a denial of equal protection or a violation of the Fifteenth Amendment. However, it was gradually abandoned, and by 1960 was maintained by only five states—Alabama, Arkansas, Mississippi, Texas, and Virginia.

LITERACY TESTS    In 1960 over twenty states had a literacy requirement for voting. Such a test had been upheld by the Supreme Court in *Guinn* v. *United States* (1915) as so clearly within state power as to require no discussion. The Court unanimously adhered to this view in the North Carolina case of *Lassiter* v. *Northampton County Board of Elections* (1959), Justice Douglas saying: "Illiterate people may be intelligent voters. Yet in our society where newspapers, periodicals, books, and other printed matter canvass and debate campaign issues, a State might conclude that only those who are literate should exercise the franchise."

Though not charged in this case, the Court in *Lassiter* did recognize that a literacy test, fair on its face, might be used for discriminatory purposes. Since there was overwhelming evidence that the test was in fact used for this purpose in some Southern states, the Civil Rights Commission in its 1961 report on voting recommended that literacy be established by a method which would be objective and not subject to manipulation, namely, by accepting attainment of the sixth grade in school as fulfilling the literacy requirement. The New York literacy law had this provision.

A special problem was presented in New York, where the requirement of literacy in English excluded from the franchise those members of the large Puerto Rican community who were literate only in Spanish. This issue was raised in *Cardona* v. *Power* (1966) but was avoided by the Court majority; four justices who did express an opinion on the question were evenly divided as to whether the English requirement was a denial of equal protection to Spanish-speaking citizens.

INTERPRETATION OF THE CONSTITUTION    Particularly in Southern states, literacy tests have been combined with a requirement to understand or

[4] Quoted in *Harman* v. *Forssenius* (1965).

interpret provisions of the state or federal constitutions. In *Williams* v. *Mississippi* (1898) the Supreme Court upheld such a law because on its face it did not discriminate against Negroes. But a half century later, in *Davis* v. *Schnell* (1949), the Court affirmed a lower court ruling that an Alabama "understand and explain" law was invalid on its face because of its legislative setting and the great discretion it vested in the registrar.

This decision had little impact on the continued widespread use of such requirements for achieving disfranchisement on racial grounds. As concern about the denial of Negro voting rights escalated in the 1950s, it became increasingly clear that the "understanding" test was one of the principal techniques by which Southern registrars excluded Negroes from the franchise. In their completely uncontrolled discretion they gave impossibly hard questions to Negro registrants and refused them registration because of technical or inconsequential errors.

When Negroes did nevertheless begin to qualify in some numbers, state statutes were revised to raise the barriers even higher. In 1954 Mississippi added to the reading and interpreting requirement the additional obligation to demonstrate to the registrar "a reasonable understanding of the duties and obligations of citizenship under a constitutional form of government." In 1960 a new voting qualification, "good moral character," was adopted, and in 1962 the state Legislature provided that application forms must be filled out "properly and responsively" by the applicant without any assistance, and that a registrar could not tell an applicant why he failed the test because to do so might constitute assistance.

This account of legal barriers to voting does not suggest adequately the fertility of Southern legislatures in devising additional hurdles for would-be Negro voters, nor of course does it take into account the use of intimidation and violence to prevent Negro registration or to punish those who voted or participated in voter-registration campaigns. The Civil Rights Commission summarized the situation in its 1961 voting report by pointing out that in at least one hundred twenty-nine counties in ten Southern states less than 10 per cent of eligible Negroes were registered. In seventeen representative "black belt" counties where Negroes constituted a majority of the population, only about 3 per cent were found to be registered.

## THE CONSTITUTIONAL STATUS OF PRIMARY ELECTIONS

Another device, which was successful for a time in achieving racial discrimination, was to bar Negroes from primary elections. The authority of the Constitution and Congress over primaries was thrown into serious doubt by the decision in *Newberry* v. *United States* (1921). In the Corrupt Practices Act of 1910 Congress had restricted campaign expenditures in securing nomination as well as in the election, and Truman H. Newberry was convicted of violating this statute in his successful campaign for a Michigan

Senate seat in 1918. The Supreme Court set aside his conviction, five justices holding that when the Constitution referred to election it meant the "final choice of an officer by the duly qualified electors," and that the primary was "in no real sense part of the manner of holding the election."

This ruling was weakened because one of the majority, Justice McKenna, thought that the constitutional situation would be different if Congress had passed the statute in question *after* the adoption of the Seventeenth Amendmen providing for the direct election of senators. The four-judge minority was clear that the primary was part of the election process, and also argued that Congress had the inherent power, entirely apart from Article I, section 4, to safeguard the purity of the process by which its members were elected.

In spite of the dubious majority in this case, Congress seemingly accepted this check on its powers and expressly excluded primary elections from the purview of the new Corrupt Practices Act passed in 1925. The Southern states also took the *Newberry* ruling as indicating that no constitutional protections covered primary elections, and so they set about discriminating against Negro voters in primaries in a perfectly open fashion. In 1923 the Texas Legislature flatly prohibited Negroes from voting in that state's Democratic primaries. When this statute was tested in *Nixon* v. *Herndon* (1927), the Supreme Court avoided a reconsideration of the constitutional status of primaries and their relationship to the Fifteenth Amendment. Instead it invalidated the statute on the ground that it was a "direct and obvious infringement" of the equal protection clause in the Fourteenth Amendment.

The Texas Legislature then came back with another law authorizing political parties in the state, through their state executive committees, to prescribe the qualifications for voting in their primaries. The theory of this statute was that what the state could not do directly because of the Fourteenth Amendment, it could authorize political parties to do. The Democratic state executive committee then excluded Negroes from primary elections, but in *Nixon* v. *Condon* (1932) the Court held that the party committee had acted as the agent of the state, which made the action equivalent to that by the state itself, and so unconstitutional as an official denial of equal protection.

In neither of these decisions did the Court question the *Newberry* assertion that party primaries were outside the protection of the Constitution; it was only the fact that state legislation was the basis for party action in these cases which made the Fourteenth Amendment applicable. Taking advantage of this situation, the Texas Democratic party convention, immediately after the *Condon* decision, on its own authority and without any state legislation on the subject, adopted a resolution confining party membership to white citizens. By unanimous vote the Court concluded in *Grovey* v. *Townsend* (1935) that this action did not infringe the Fourteenth Amendment because it was taken by the party and not by the state.

The Supreme Court thus endorsed the view that political parties are private clubs uncontrolled by constitutional limitations on official action, and that the primaries they hold are constitutionally no part of the election process. Both of these propositions are so directly contrary to the obvious facts of party operation that they were bound to fall sooner or later of their own weight. The occasion for disposing of the *Newberry* doctrine came in 1941. *United States* v. *Classic* involved a prosecution brought by the Civil Rights Section of the U.S. Department of Justice against election officials in Louisiana who had tampered with the ballots in a primary where candidates for representative in Congress were chosen. The Court pointed out that Louisiana election laws made the primary "an integral part" of the process of electing congressmen, and that in fact the Democratic primary in Louisiana was "the only stage of the election procedure" where the voter's choice was of significance. The Court was thus taking a highly realistic view in its conclusion that the authority given Congress by Article I, section 4, "includes the authority to regulate primary elections when, as in this case, they are a step in the exercise by the people of their choice of representatives in Congress."

The *Classic* opinion did not even mention *Grovey* v. *Townsend*, but it clearly left the private club theory on very shaky legal ground. Consequently a new test case from Texas was begun, which resulted in a direct reversal of the *Grovey* decision by the Court in *Smith* v. *Allwright* (1944). The Court held that after the *Classic* ruling, party primaries could no longer be regarded as private affairs nor the parties conducting them as unaffected with public responsibilities. Noting that parties and party primaries in Texas were in fact regulated at many points by state statutes, the Court reasoned that a party required to follow these directions was "an agency of the State," and if it practiced discrimination against Negroes, that was "state action within the meaning of the Fifteenth Amendment."

Inasmuch as the *Smith* decision stressed the extensive statutory regulation of parties and party primaries in Texas as proof that a party so regulated was "an agency of the State," South Carolina immediately resorted to the stratagem of repealing all its statutes pertaining to party primaries, hoping thus to pass off the Democratic party in that state as a "private voluntary association of individuals," which could then exclude Negroes constitutionally by "club rules." The lower federal courts, however, refuted this contention, and the Supreme Court refused even to grant certiorari in the case of *Rice* v. *Elmore* (1948).

In *Terry* v. *Adams* (1953) the Court, with only one justice dissenting, applied the principle of *Smith* v. *Allwright* to invalidate the unofficial primaries conducted in a Texas county by the Jaybird party, a Democratic political organization which excluded Negroes. The winners in the Jaybird primaries then entered the regular Democratic party primaries, where over a sixty-year period they were never defeated for county office. In fact, other

candidates seldom filed. The Court ruled that the "Jaybird primary has become an integral part, indeed the only effective part, of the elective process that determines who shall rule and govern in the county," and consequently that the Fifteenth Amendment was applicable and must be observed.

## FEDERAL PROTECTION OF VOTING RIGHTS

Although the Supreme Court had thus made commendable efforts to enforce the Fourteenth and Fifteenth Amendments in voting cases, discrimination against Negroes in some states was so firmly established that lawsuits alone were quite incapable of dealing with the problem. As in the area of school segregation, help from Congress and the President was essential.

EXIT THE POLL TAX    Efforts in Congress to abolish the poll tax as a voting requirement date back to the early 1940s. In the military voting law of 1942, Congress did in fact provide that in time of war no soldier could be denied the right to vote because of failure to comply with a state law imposing a poll tax. Five times between 1942 and 1949 bills to ban the poll tax by statute passed the House but died in the Senate, three times as a result of Southern filibuster.

There was some uncertainty in Congress as to whether it would require a constitutional amendment rather than a statute to outlaw the poll tax. Finally in 1962 the Senate acquiesced in an amendment banning the poll tax in federal elections, which was ratified in 1964 as the Twenty-fourth Amendment.

Recognizing that a broadened electorate would threaten its long-established power, the Byrd political organization in Virginia immediately put through the state legislature a law requiring voters in federal elections either to pay a poll tax or to file a certificate of residence at least six months prior to each election. The Supreme Court in *Harman* v. *Forssenius* (1965) held this law unconstitutional as an abridgement of the right to vote, because it imposed a material and burdensome requirement on persons who wished to exercise their constitutional right to vote in federal elections without paying a poll tax.

The poll tax after the Twenty-fourth Amendment remained as a restriction on the franchise in *state* elections in four states, Arkansas having abolished the requirement in 1964. The House proceeded to adopt a poll-tax ban in state elections in the 1965 voting rights bill, but the Senate demurred and the act as passed simply contained in section 10 a finding that poll taxes were used to discriminate in some areas and that the constitutional right to vote was "denied or abridged" by payment of taxes as a precondition for voting. The act authorized the Attorney General to seek court action against enforcement of poll taxes in state and local elections. He brought such suits in the four states, and three-judge federal courts in Alabama and Texas

early in 1966 held the tax invalid in those states. There was an immediate increase of 25 per cent in the number of registered voters in Texas.[5]

A few weeks later the Supreme Court in *Harper* v. *Virginia State Board of Elections* (1966), a case which had been started by Virginia Negroes, declared the Virginia poll tax unconstitutional as an "invidious discrimination" and a denial of equal protection. "Voter qualifications have no relation to wealth nor to paying or not paying this or any other tax." The right to vote, the Court added, "is too precious, too fundamental to be so burdened or conditioned." The contrary decision in *Breedlove* v. *Suttles* was overruled. Justice Black, dissenting, had no doubt that Congress could have abolished the poll tax in state elections by legislation, but he thought that for the Court to take this step itself on the authority of the Fourteenth Amendment was to resort to natural-law reasoning and to usurp the power of amending the Constitution.

THE CIVIL RIGHTS ACTS OF 1957, 1960, AND 1964    The Civil Rights Act of 1957 gave to the Attorney General the power to initiate injunction proceedings to protect the right to vote. The significance of this statutory power in more effective protection of the franchise is obvious. A criminal proceeding for denial of the right to vote is harsh, it comes after the election is over, and conviction by a local jury is likely to be difficult. A civil proceeding for an injunction, initiated by an individual to protect his right to vote, can be brought only when he knows in advance that a state officer intends to deny this right, and when he has the courage and the money to start such an action. The Attorney General with his resources for investigation and litigation is in an infinitely stronger position to act for protection of indivdual rights.

Since the injunction was the enforcement device provided by the bill, congressional attention centered on possible abuses of the judicial contempt power. Opponents of the legislation sought to limit its effectiveness by providing for trial by jury in the case of individuals held in contempt of court for failing to abide by injunctions. Normally, a defendant does not have the right to jury trial in contempt cases, either in federal or state courts, and any general provision of such a right would make chaos of the judicial enforcement of court orders. As finally adopted, the 1957 act did grant a right to jury trial, but within very narrow limits—only in civil rights cases where the individual was found guilty of criminal contempt and where the judge imposed a fine in excess of $300 or a jail sentence in excess of forty-five days. In such cases, a second trial with a jury had to be provided if the defendant insisted.

The results under the 1957 act were quite disappointing. By 1965, seventy suits had been filed, thirty had been concluded, and none had been lost,

---

[5] *The New York Times*, March 23, 1966.

but resulting increases in Negro registration were minimal. Court action had to be taken to secure registration records, which often were found to have been destroyed. Even when a suit proving discrimination was won, many Negroes were reluctant to register.[6]

The Civil Rights Act of 1960 endeavored to make the 1957 act more effective by authorizing the Department of Justice to secure registration records without bringing lawsuits. The 1960 act also empowered federal judges to appoint referees to register for voting in federal and state elections qualified Negroes who had been refused registration, in areas where a pattern of discrimination had been established by suits brought under the 1957 statute. However, it appears that no referees were actually appointed.

Both the 1957 and 1960 statutes placed the burden for correcting voting discrimination upon federal district judges, who were usually unsympathetic with this goal. It soon became clear that case-by-case litigation could hardly make a significant dent in the hardened areas of resistance to Negro voting. By 1964 only 6.7 per cent of voting-age Negroes in Mississippi were registered, in Alabama 21.6 per cent, in Virginia 27.7 per cent, and in Louisiana 31.6 per cent. Intimidation and new state legislative barriers largely frustrated federal efforts to increase Negro registration. In Dallas County, Alabama, four years of litigation by the Justice Department and two federal court findings of discrimination resulted in increasing Negro registration from 156 to 383, out of 15,000 Negroes of voting age.

The Civil Rights Act of 1964 dealt primarily with access to public accommodations, but it did impose new federal controls on the registration process by requiring state registrars to apply voting-qualification standards equally, to disregard minor errors in registration forms, and to administer literacy tests in writing.

THE VOTING RIGHTS ACT OF 1965      By 1965 it was clear that drastic federal action was required if the blockade to Negro voting was to be broken. The constitutional basis for the Voting Rights Act of 1965, which was passed after cloture had been imposed in the Senate, was section 2 of the Fifteenth Amendment, which authorizes Congress to enforce, by "appropriate" measures, the ban on racial discrimination in voting.

This historic act flatly declared that "no voting qualification or prerequisite to voting" was to be imposed to deny or abridge the right of any citizen to vote on account of race or color. The act concentrated on four types of "tests or devices": (1) literacy and understanding tests; (2) educational achievement or knowledge of any particular subject; (3) good moral character; and (4) proof of qualifications by voucher of registered voters. The use of such tests or devices, which had accounted for the great bulk of "legal" discrimination, was prohibited in any state or political sub-

[6] *The New York Times,* March 16, 1965.

division where less than 50 per cent of the persons of voting age were registered on November 1, 1964, or had voted in the presidential election of November, 1964.

The 50 per cent test was of course a very rough index of voting discrimination. Its use made the statute applicable to six Southern states—Alabama, Georgia, Louisiana, Mississippi, South Carolina, and Virginia—but also to Alaska, twenty-six counties in North Carolina, and a few other scattered counties. It did not apply to Arkansas, Texas, and Florida, where in some sections there were large Negro populations but few Negro voters, because those states did not use literacy tests.

In states and counties covered by the act, voting qualifications of the above four types were suspended, and they could be restored only by a suit brought in the district court of the District of Columbia proving that such tests or devices had not been used for purposes of racial discrimination in the preceding five years.[7] Moreover, such states had to obtain the approval of the Attorney General before enacting any new voting-qualification laws.

The 1965 statute also provided for appointment by the United States Civil Service Commission of voting examiners in any political subdivision where the Attorney General certified that they were needed to enforce the Fifteenth Amendment. These examiners were to register all applicants meeting the voting requirements of state law, insofar as these requirements had not been suspended by the statute. The Attorney General acted promptly to place federal examiners in counties with the worst records of discrimination, and within six months the number of Negroes registered in Alabama had doubled.

The Supreme Court upheld the constitutionality of the Voting Rights Act in *South Carolina* v. *Katzenbach* (1966). Admittedly the statute amounted to an unprecedented abridgement of the power to set voting qualifications for the states caught by the 50 per cent test. They lost the right to enforce registration laws which could still be enforced in all other states. They had to get the consent of the District of Columbia federal court to resume enforcement of suspended statutes, and permission from the Attorney General to adopt new voting-qualification laws.

This was, as the Supreme Court recognized, an "inventive" use of congressional power to enforce the Fifteenth Amendment. But the Court also recognized that the provocation had been great. Congress had tried milder measures, and they had not worked. Now, in the 1965 act, Congress was manifesting a "firm intention" to rid the country of racial discrimination in voting, and the states had only themselves to blame for the drastic remedies adopted.

The Court stated the basic constitutional principle involved in these

---

[7] Alaska won exemption from the 1965 act by this procedure in 1966.

words: "As against the reserved powers of the States, Congress may use any rational means to effectuate the constitutional prohibition of racial discrimination in voting." The means here employed were rational, the Court held. South Carolina contended that the coverage formula was "awkwardly designed in a number of respects and that it disregards various local conditions which have nothing to do with racial discrimination," but the Court found the formula "rational in both practice and theory." Congress had learned that widespread and persistent discrimination in voting had typically entailed the misuse of tests and devices, and this was the evil for which the new remedies were specifically designed. The Court was unanimous, except that Justice Black regarded the provisions requiring review of state laws by the District of Columbia court and the Attorney General as unconstitutional.

New York was exempt from the effect of the 1965 statute, and consequently its requirement of literacy in English for voting would not have been affected. But at the urging of the state's two senators, Congress inserted a provision prohibiting the states from imposing an English-language literacy test, for the purpose of securing "the rights under the fourteenth amendment of persons educated in American-flag schools in which the predominant classroom language was other than English." Completion of the sixth grade in such a school was to be accepted as meeting the literacy requirement.

While this provision was regarded by many as of dubious constitutionality, the Supreme Court upheld it in *Katzenbach* v. *Morgan* (1966) as appropriate legislation under section 5 of the Fourteenth Amendment to enforce the equal protection clause. By prohibiting New York from denying the franchise to large segments of its Puerto Rican community, Congress was helping that community gain nondiscriminatory treatment in public services through enhancement of its political power.

> It was well within congressional authority to say that this need of the Puerto Rican minority for the vote warranted federal intrusion upon any state interests served by the English literacy requirement. . . . Congress might have also questioned whether denial of a right deemed so precious and fundamental in our society was a necessary or appropriate means of encouraging persons to learn English.

The change accomplished by federal pressure and the impact of the civil rights movement in increasing Negro voting was dramatic. According to the Southern Regional Council, the 1,092,992 Negro voters registered in 1960 in the Old Confederacy had increased to 2,503,140 in 1966, and over the same period the percentage of Negroes of voting age registered had risen from 28.2 to 50.1.[8] In 1961 the United States Civil Rights Commission was so disheartened by the record of state discrimination that it recommended

[8] *The New York Times,* July 26, 1966.

the federal government take over the fixing of qualifications for voting. It proposed that Congress, acting under section 2 of the Fifteenth Amendment and sections 2 and 5 of the Fourteenth Amendment, enact legislation providing that all citizens of the United States shall have the right to vote in federal and state elections, which may not be abridged by any state for any cause except for failure to meet reasonable age or length-of-residence requirements, legal confinement, or conviction of a felony.[9] The Voting Rights Act of 1965 plus the Twenty-fourth Amendment and the *Harper* decision have achieved much the same result.

## SELECTED REFERENCES

BERMAN, DANIEL M., *A Bill Becomes a Law*. New York: The Macmillan Company, 1966 (second edition).

BICKEL, ALEXANDER M., "The Voting Rights Cases," in Philip B. Kurland (ed.), *The Supreme Court Review: 1966*, pp. 79–102. Chicago: The University of Chicago Press, 1966.

CARR, ROBERT K., *Federal Protection of Civil Rights: Quest for a Sword*. Ithaca, N.Y.: Cornell University Press, 1947.

KOMMERS, DONALD P., "The Right to Vote and Its Implementation," 39 *Notre Dame Lawyer* 365–410 (1964).

MARSHALL, BURKE, *Federalism and Civil Rights*. New York: Columbia University Press, 1964.

OGDEN, FREDERIC D., *The Poll Tax in the South*. University, Ala.: University of Alabama Press, 1958.

President's Commission on Registration and Voting Participation, *Report*. Washington: Government Printing Office, 1963.

President's Committee on Civil Rights, *To Secure These Rights*. Washington: Government Printing Office, 1947.

United States Commission on Civil Rights, *Voting*. Washington: Government Printing Office, 1961.

[9] United States Commission on Civil Rights, *Voting* (Washington: Government Printing Office, 1961), p. 139.

# Citizenship, naturalization, and immigration

The original Constitution said very little on the important subject of citizenship. There was one clear grant of power to Congress—"to establish an uniform rule of naturalization"—in Article I, section 8. In addition, the Constitution mentioned both state and national citizens several times, but did not define either type of citizenship or indicate the relationship between them. Neither did the Constitution express a preference between the two principal rules which modern civilized nations have employed for determining citizenship—the *jus sanguinis,* under which one acquires the citizenship of one's parents, or the *jus soli,* under which one becomes a citizen of the country of birth. These gaps were subsequently filled by the Fourteenth Amendment, but the extent of congressional power over such matters as expatriation and the control of aliens has been left to be defined by executive practice, congressional legislation, and judicial interpretation.

## CITIZENSHIP

The Constitution did not make it clear whether national citizenship was anterior to state citizenship, or vice versa. The states' rights position was that a person derived national citizenship from his status as a state citizen. This issue was finally dealt with by the Supreme Court in the *Dred Scott* case (1857), where the majority accepted the priority of state over national

citizenship. Individuals born in the United States derived their citizenship from their status as descendants of persons "who were at the time of the adoption of the Constitution recognized as citizens in the several States [and] became also citizens of this new political body."

For persons born outside the United States, however, there was no such relationship between national and state citizenship. A state could grant state citizenship to anyone living in the state, but that would not make the recipient a citizen of the United States. National citizenship could be conferred only under the authority of Congress to establish "an uniform rule of naturalization." There was one grand exception to these principles, however. According to Chief Justice Taney in the *Dred Scott* case, a Negro was unable to attain United States citizenship either from a state or by virtue of birth in the United States, even if he were a free man descended from a Negro residing as a free man in a state at the date of ratification of the Constitution.

The Fourteenth Amendment reversed the *Dred Scott* decision and cleared up the uncertainties of the original Constitution. A definition of citizenship was provided for the first time: "All persons born or naturalized in the United States and subject to the jurisdiction thereof, are citizens of the United States and of the state wherein they reside." This language recognized the citizenship of Negroes, and made it clear that state citizenship now signifies little more than residence within the state. As the Supreme Court pointed out in the *Slaughter-House Cases:* "Not only may a man be a citizen of the United States without being a citizen of a State, but an important element is necessary to convert the former into the latter. He must reside within the State to make him a citizen of it, but it is only necessary that he should be born or naturalized in the United States to be a citizen of the Union."

The Fourteenth Amendment adopts *jus soli* as its principal rule of citizenship. Birth in the United States confers citizenship on the children of alien parents, even if the parents are themselves ineligible to citizenship. This was decided in *United States* v. *Wong Kim Ark* (1898). The only qualification to this rule is that stated by the amendment—the person must not only be born in the United States but also be "subject to the jurisdiction thereof." In the *Wong Kim Ark* case the Court visualized four categories of persons who would fall under this exception—children of foreign sovereigns or their ambassadors and ministers (but not consuls); children born on foreign public ships while in American territorial waters; children of enemies born within and during a hostile occupation of American territory; and children of members of Indian tribes owing direct allegiance to their several tribes. This latter holding was based on an 1884 decision of the Court which denied citizenship to Indians living in the tribal relationship,[1]

[1] *Elk* v. *Wilkins* (1884).

but in 1924 Congress authorized the issuance of certificates of citizenship to Indians living in tribes, so that this fourth exception has ceased to be effective.

Children born to United States citizens abroad are by act of Congress also United States citizens, provided the citizen parent had had a period of residence in the United States prior to the birth of the child. To this extent the United States follows the rule of *jus sanguinis* as well as *jus soli*. The various classes of persons who are citizens at birth on either of these two bases are defined in Title III of the Immigration and Nationality Act of 1952, which codifies much previous legislation.

### NATURALIZATION

At first it was thought that the power of Congress "to establish an uniform rule of naturalization" might be shared with the states, but in *Chirac* v. *Chirac* (1817) Marshall ruled that it belonged exclusively to Congress. State courts of record may be used to administer the naturalization oath, but this is merely an arrangement of convenience.

There is no constitutional "right" to be naturalized. Congress has complete discretion to determine what classes of aliens are eligible to naturalization. As the Supreme Court has said, the power of Congress "is not trammeled, and it may grant or withold the privilege of naturalization upon any grounds or without any reason, as it sees fit." [2] But, once Congress has enacted a statute defining eligibility for naturalization, then "there is a statutory right in the alien to submit his petition and evidence to a court, to have that tribunal pass upon them, and, if the requisite facts are established, to receive the certificate." [3]

Post-Civil War statutes confined eligibility to white persons and those of African descent. By the Nationality Act of 1940 Congress, in furtherance of our "good neighbor" policy toward Latin America, extended the privilege to descendants of races indigenous to the Western Hemisphere. In 1943 Chinese persons or persons of Chinese descent were made eligible, Filipinos and people indigenous to India were accorded the same privilege in 1946. In 1952 the Immigration and Nationality Act provided in sweeping language that "the rights of a person to become a naturalized citizen of the United States shall not be denied or abridged because of race."

The act of 1952 also terminated the policy of denying the privilege of naturalization to conscientious objectors. In Chapter 28 we saw how the Supreme Court had at first upheld this policy, which was based on administrative rulings and not on any statutory commands. But in *Girouard* v. *United States* (1946) these earlier decisions were reversed and overruled.

[2] *Terrace* v. *Thompson* (1923).
[3] *Tutun* v. *United States* (1926).

This was a matter for congressional decision, the Court said, and the will of Congress would not be inferred from its acquiescence in an administrative practice.

In 1952 Congress supplied positive legislation on this question. It provided that a person, to be admitted to citizenship, must take an oath to support and defend the Constitution, to bear true faith and allegiance to the United States, and when required by law, to bear arms. But persons who are conscientious objectors to war "by reason of religious training and belief" are given the alternative of performing work of national importance under civilian direction or noncombatant service in the armed forces.

Political opinion still remains as a restriction on naturalization, however. In fact, while limitations on other grounds have been disappearing, concern with political beliefs has been increasing. This trend began in 1906, when Congress sought to keep anarchists from becoming citizens by requiring a petitioner for naturalization to state that "he is not a disbeliever in or opposed to organized government, or a member of or affiliated with any organization or body of persons teaching disbelief in or opposed to organized government." This statute made beliefs and associations, not actions, the basis for refusal of naturalization, and established a standard for naturalized citizens which natural-born citizens did not have to meet.

In the Nationality Act of 1940, this language was considerably expanded, the new provisions being aimed at Communists, though the act was careful not to designate them or their party by name. Within the next few years the Supreme Court exhibited a reluctance to apply general language of this sort to the Communist Party of the United States. As we have already seen, both *Schneiderman* v. *United States* (1943) and *Bridges* v. *Wixon* (1945) held that the Communist Party was not necessarily, in all its operations, illegal. Consequently Congress became more specific in the Internal Security Act of 1950, which denied naturalization to any person belonging to or affiliated with any "Communist action organization" which is required to register under the terms of the Subversive Activities Control Act of 1950. Advocacy of "the economic, international, and governmental doctrines of any other form of totalitarianism" was also proscribed.

Even the 1950 language still made it necessary for the government to establish by complicated administrative and judicial proceedings that the Communist Party was a "Communist-action" organization, and this was too slow for Congress. In the Immigration and Nationality Act of 1952 there was finally adopted a flat prohibition on naturalization of any person "who is a member of or affiliated with . . . the Communist Party of the United States," or its "direct predecessors or successors." Thus all responsibility was taken away from the courts to determine the character of the Communist Party in relation to naturalization matters.

Naturalization is of course typically granted to individuals who meet the

statutory requirements and complete the stipulated procedures.[4] However, naturalization may also be extended to all the members of a group, without consideration of their individual fitness. Such collective naturalization has typically been extended to inhabitants of territories and dependencies acquired by the United States. Such status can be conferred either by treaty or by act of Congress. In the case of the Louisiana Territory, Florida, and Alaska, the treaty of annexation promised that the inhabitants would be admitted as soon as possible to all the rights and immunities of United States citizenship. But the treaty of peace with Spain in 1898 provided that cession of Spanish colonies to the United States was not to operate as a naturalization of their inhabitants; rather their civil rights and political status would be determined by Congress. By statute Congress then declared Puerto Ricans and Filipinos to be citizens of their respective islands. This status was retained by inhabitants of the Philippines until independence of the country was achieved in 1946, but Puerto Ricans were made citizens of the United States in 1917. Congress granted citizenship to the residents of Texas on its annexation in 1845, to the inhabitants of the Hawaiian Islands in 1900, and to those of the Virgin Islands in 1927.

### DENATURALIZATION

There are two ways by which American citizenship may be lost: denaturalization and expatriation. Denaturalization is the process of canceling a certificate of naturalization by official action for cause, and by definition can only be employed against persons who have secured their citizenship by naturalization.

The original purpose of denaturalization procedures, as authorized by act of 1906, was to provide a method of canceling citizenship secured by the use of fraudulent documents or where entry into the United States was illegal. But the denaturalization procedure thus made available can also be employed against naturalized citizens who hold unpopular political views. During World War I a considerable number of naturalized citizens who expressed sympathy for Germany were denaturalized, and World War II saw a similar drive on both Nazis and Communists. The theory in these cases was that naturalization had been illegally procured because no Nazi or Communist could meet the required statutory test—namely, that during the five years immediately preceding his application he must have "behaved as a man of good moral character, attached to the principles of the Constitution of the United States, and well disposed to the good order and happiness of the same."

[4] When an alien father becomes naturalized, the effect is also to naturalize his minor children living in the United States. An alien wife must secure naturalization independently of her husband's action.

The Supreme Court in *Schneiderman* v. *United States* (1943) refused to uphold the denaturalization of an admitted Communist Party official under the Nationality Act of 1940. Justice Murphy for the majority reasoned that since this was a proceeding to revoke the privilege of citizenship after it had been enjoyed for twelve years, the burden of proof was on the government to show by "clear, unequivocal and convincing" evidence that citizenship had been illegally acquired.[5]

The following year the Court, applying the same rule on burden of proof, unanimously protected an alleged Nazi from denaturalization in *Baumgartner* v. *United States* (1944). However, in 1946 the Court found in *Knauer* v. *United States* a case which met the statutory standard. The evidence showed that before and after his naturalization in 1937 Knauer had followed "a clear course of conduct . . . designed to promote the Nazi cause in this country." He was not, the Court concluded, "an underling caught up in the enthusiasm of a movement, driven by ties of blood and old associations to extreme attitudes, and perhaps unaware of the conflict of allegiance implicit in his actions. Knauer is an astute person. He is a leader. . . . His activities portray a shrewd, calculating, and vigilant promotion of an alien cause."

The 1952 statute now controls the denaturalization process. It provides that any naturalized person who takes the oath with mental reservations or conceals beliefs and affiliations which by law disqualify one for naturalization, is subject to having his certificate canceled after an appropriate judicial proceeding. Furthermore, the 1952 act adds a new hazard. If a naturalized citizen within five years after his naturalization becomes a member of an organization which would have precluded him from being eligible for naturalization, "it shall be considered prima facie evidence that such person was not attached to the principles of the Constitution of the United States and was not well disposed to the good order and happiness of the United States at the time of naturalization." In the absence of countervailing evidence this will be sufficient ground for canceling the certificate as having been obtained by "willful misrepresentation."

Denaturalization has been employed also against criminals and racketeers. The Department of Justice has on several occasions announced special drives aimed at naturalized citizens in these categories, with denaturalization being used to make them subject to deportation.

The constitutionality of the denaturalization power, long taken for granted, was attacked by Justices Murphy and Rutledge in the two cases of *Knauer* v. *United States* (1946) and *Klapprott* v. *United States* (1949). Their position was that the Constitution makes only one distinction between natural-born and naturalized citizens; the latter are ineligible for the Presidency. They contended that in no other way can the status of naturalized

---

[5] The *Schneiderman* principle was applied to void denaturalization proceedings in *Nowak* v. *United States* (1958) and *Maisenberg* v. *United States* (1958), with some reliance also on *Yates* v. *United States* (1957).

citizens be made inferior. But if they can be stripped of citizenship on grounds and by procedures which could not be applied to natural-born citizens, then there are in effect "two classes of citizens, one free and secure except for acts amounting to forfeiture within our tradition; the other, conditional, timorous and insecure because blanketed with the threat that some act or conduct, not amounting to forfeiture for others, will be taken retroactively to show that some prescribed condition had not been fulfilled and be so adjudged." They denied that any such difference was contemplated when Congress was given power to provide for naturalization. "The power to naturalize is not the power to denaturalize," concluded Rutledge in the *Knauer* case. But this position has failed to win any other converts on the Court.[6]

The result is that there truly are two classes of citizens, as Murphy and Rutledge charged. This will continue to be true, so long as conduct *subsequent* to naturalization can open the door to loss of citizenship. For naturalized citizens the exercise of First Amendment freedoms is attended by risks not incurred by natural-born citizens. Correction of this condition does not require that the power of denaturalization be denied, but only that its use be limited to cases of willful and material fraud in procuring naturalization papers.

### EXPATRIATION

Expatriation refers to the loss of citizenship as the result, intended or unintended, of voluntary action taken by a citizen, either natural-born or naturalized. The original English view was that a person owed perpetual allegiance to the country of his birth, and that he could not expatriate himself without the consent of that country. There was initially some inclination in the United States to follow the English rule. In 1868, however, Congress adopted a statute declaring explicitly that the "right of expatriation is a natural and inherent right of all people, indispensable to the enjoyment of the rights of life, liberty, and the pursuit of happiness."

The motivation for this declaration was primarily to establish that persons naturalized by the United States did not continue to owe allegiance to any foreign government. In making expatriation depend upon the voluntary action and intent of the individual, Congress raised no question about its constitutional power over expatriation. But in 1907 Congress passed a law stating various circumstances which would result in expatriation, and thus created for the first time the possibility that the action of a citizen might be

---

[6] However, the Douglas opinion in *Schneider* v. *Rusk* (1964), *infra*, rejects "second-class citizenship" for naturalized citizens and adopts the Murphy-Rutledge premise that "the rights of citizenship of the native born and of the naturalized person are of the same dignity and are coextensive." The *Schneider* rule has not yet been applied in a denaturalization proceeding.

regarded by law as resulting in loss of citizenship, contrary to any intention the individual might have had.

The Citizenship Act of 1907 declared that expatriation occurred when an American citizen became naturalized in a foreign state or took an oath of allegiance to a foreign state. The statute also provided that a naturalized citizen who resided for three years in the foreign state from which he came, or for five years in any other foreign state, would be presumed to have ceased to be an American citizen. The presumption did not by itself effect expatriation, however, and might be overcome by the presentation of countervailing evidence.[7]

Another provision of the 1907 act specified that an American woman citizen expatriated herself on marrying an alien. The Supreme Court upheld the constitutionality of this questionable piece of legislation in *MacKenzie* v. *Hare* (1915). The Court conceded that a change of citizenship cannot be arbitrarily imposed, but contended that the power of the United States as a sovereign nation rendered it competent to provide that an individual voluntarily entering into certain specified relationships should suffer loss of citizenship as a consequence. However, this particular provision was repealed by the Cable Act of 1922, except as to American women who married aliens ineligible to American citizenship. Even this restriction was eliminated in 1931, thus removing marriage as an automatic instrument of expatriation.[8]

The Nationality Act of 1940 added new grounds for expatriation. As codified in the Immigration and Nationality Act of 1952, the law states twelve conditions under which individual action results in expatriation. At least six of these conditions could cause loss of citizenship contrary to the intention of the individual. Three involve relationships with a foreign state—serving in the armed forces of a foreign power without authorization and with consequent acquisition of foreign nationality; assuming public office under the government of a foreign state, for which only nationals of that state are

---

[7] The effect of such a presumptive loss of citizenship on a child of expatriated parents was litigated in the well-known case of *Perkins* v. *Elg* (1939). An American-born child of naturalized American parents was taken by them to their former country, where they resumed their former allegiance. The Court held that the residence of the child in that country during minority did not result in loss of citizenship, provided that on attaining majority he elected to retain it and returned to the United States. The holding of the *Elg* case is now substantially enacted into law by the Immigration and Nationality Act of 1952.

[8] In *Savorgnan* v. *United States* (1950) a native-born American woman applied for and obtained Italian citizenship in the United States before marrying an Italian consular officer in 1940 and going to Italy with him during the war years 1941 to 1945. She then returned to the United States and sought to establish her American citizenship, which she contended she had never intended to renounce. The Supreme Court avoided deciding whether her Italian naturalization had automatically expatriated her, but did determine that she had lost her citizenship by taking up residence in Italy.

eligible; and voting in an election or participating in a plebiscite in a foreign state.

The constitutionality of this latter provision was upheld by a five to four vote of the Supreme Court in *Perez* v. *Brownell* (1958). The majority, through Justice Frankfurter, held that Congress was entitled under its implied powers to enact legislation for the regulation of foreign affairs, and that this authority might "reasonably be deemed to include a power to deal generally with the active participation, by way of voting, of American citizens in foreign political elections." Congress could reasonably believe that such activities "might well become acute, to the point of jeopardizing the successful conduct of international relations." Finally, Frankfurter concluded that loss of nationality was one of the consequences which Congress could attach to such voting as a means of avoiding this potential embarrassment in the conduct of foreign relations. The four dissenters were Warren, Black, Douglas, and Whittaker.

In *Marks* v. *Esperdy* (1964) the Court considered the provision making service in the armed forces of another power grounds for expatriation, and divided four to four, which had the effect of affirming the lower court decision upholding the law. Marks was a native-born American citizen who fought in the Cuban army under Castro, and he became a stateless person by this decision. The government relied on the *Perez* case in taking action against Marks.

On the same day, however, the Court by a vote of five to three in *Schneider* v. *Rusk* (1964) declared unconstitutional the statutory provision authorizing expatriation of naturalized citizens who have lived for three years continuously in the territory of the foreign state of which they were formerly nationals. The Court here did not regard *Perez* as controlling. Rather Justice Douglas for the majority saw the issue as one of due process. Native-born citizens can reside abroad indefinitely without suffering loss of citizenship, but naturalized citizens cannot. This creates "a second-class citizenship," said Douglas, and proceeds on the "impermissible presumption that naturalized citizens as a class are less reliable and bear less allegiance to this country than do the native born." [9]

Other grounds for loss of citizenship under the 1952 law are essentially of a penal character—conviction and discharge from the armed services for desertion in time of war; conviction of treason or an attempt at forceful overthrow of the United States; and fleeing or remaining outside the United States in time of war or proclaimed emergency in order to evade military training. Since these conditions would normally not result in an expatriated person's simultaneously gaining citizenship in another country, the usual consequence would be that the individual would become stateless.

[9] It was estimated that some fifty thousand American expatriates living abroad had their citizenship rights restored by the *Schneider* decision. *The New York Times*, September 23, 1964.

The first of these grounds for expatriation was considered by the Court in *Trop* v. *Dulles* (1958). Deciding on the same day as *Perez* v. *Brownell*, the Court nonetheless came to an opposite conclusion, because of a switch in sides by Justice Brennan. Chief Justice Warren, speaking also for Black, Douglas, and Whittaker, repeated, but now on the winning side, the doctrine of constitutional protection for citizenship which he had urged unsuccessfully in *Perez*. There he had contended that citizenship is not subject to the general powers of the government.

> What is this government, whose power is here being asserted? And what is the source of that power? The answers are the foundation of our republic. To secure the inalienable rights of the individual, "Governments are instituted among Men, deriving their just powers from the consent of the governed." I do not believe the passage of time has lessened the truth of this proposition. It is basic to our form of government. This government was born of its citizens, it maintains itself in a continuing relationship with them, and, in my judgment, it is without power to sever the relationship that gives rise to its existence. I cannot believe that a government conceived in the spirit of ours was established with power to take from the people their most basic right.
>
> Citizenship *is* man's basic right for it is nothing less than the right to have rights. Remove this priceless possession and there remains a stateless person, disgraced and degraded in the eyes of his countrymen.

In the *Trop* case the Chief Justice carried the argument forward with these telling words:

> Citizenship is not a license that expires upon misbehavior. . . . And the deprivation of citizenship is not a weapon that the Government may use to express its displeasure at a citizen's conduct, however reprehensible that conduct may be. As long as a person does not voluntarily renounce or abandon his citizenship, . . . his fundamental right of citizenship is secure.

In addition, as already noted in Chapter 30, the Chief Justice expressed the view that this legislation amounted to cruel and unusual punishment.

The authority of Warren's position was diminished because Justice Brennan, who supplied the necessary fifth vote for the majority, voted as he did only because he thought that expatriation as a punishment for desertion did not have the "requisite rational relation" to the war power that voting in a foreign election had to the power to regulate the conduct of foreign relations.

This dialogue was continued in the 1963 cases of *Kennedy* v. *Mendoza-Martinez* and *Rusk* v. *Cort*. Both dealt with the provision depriving Americans of their citizenship for leaving, or remaining outside of, the United States to evade military service, and both ruled by votes of five to four that the statute was unconstitutional. Justice Goldberg for the majority was silent about Warren's cruel and unusual punishment idea. Instead, he based his

holding on the contention that denationalization for draft evasion was penal in its character, and consequently that expatriation procedures must provide the protections of the Fifth and Sixth Amendments. The other four members of the majority—Warren, Black, Douglas, and Brennan—would have gone further and denied the right of the government to expatriate, regardless of what procedures were used.

The replacement of Goldberg by Fortas gave this absolutist position the fifth vote it needed to become the Court's rule in *Afroyim* v. *Rusk* (1967). Afroyim, a naturalized citizen, lost his citizenship for voting in a 1951 election for Israel's parliament. For the five-judge majority Black held that the citizenship clause of the Fourteenth Amendment protects every citizen against "forcible destruction" of his citizenship. "Our holding does no more than to give to this citizen that which is his own, a constitutional right to remain a citizen in a free country unless he voluntarily relinquishes that citizenship." Black concluded: "In our country the people are sovereign and the government cannot sever its relationship to the people by taking away their citizenship." [10]

The Court has a strong case for forbidding the use of expatriation as a form of punishment for conduct of which Congress disapproves, since the result is normally to leave the ex-citizen stateless, and since there is always the alternative of the criminal law as a sanction. But Black's absolutism also forbids Congress to establish any criteria for determining whether a citizen has shifted his allegiance to a foreign country with resultant loss of citizenship, and seems to override the concession Warren had made in his *Perez* dissent that expatriation would follow from action by which a citizen "manifests allegiance to a foreign state . . . so inconsistent with the retention of citizenship" that renunciation can properly be implied.

### EXCLUSION OF ALIENS

The absolute power of Congress to exclude aliens from the United States is firmly established. An alien who seeks admission to this country may not do so under any claim of right. Admission is a privilege granted only on such terms as the Congress may prescribe.

RACIAL EXCLUSION    In 1882, Congress passed a law suspending Chinese immigration for ten years, the first restriction on what had previously been complete freedom to enter the United States. In 1887, a Chinese laborer who had lived in this country for twelve years returned to China bearing a certificate authorizing him to reenter the United States. Seven days before

---

[10] The *Afroyim* decision clearly invalidated all statutes providing for expatriation of citizens because of involvement in the affairs of a foreign state, but presumably did not affect the government's power to denaturalize where naturalization was obtained by fraud.

his return in 1888, Congress passed a law annulling all outstanding certificates and abrogating the right of reentry. The statute contravened treaties between the United States and China, but the Supreme Court in the *Chinese Exclusion Case* (1889) upheld the congressional action. The power to exclude aliens, the Court said, is an incident of sovereignty. Without that authority, the United States "would be to that extent subject to the control of another power."

The policy of Chinese exclusion, extended in 1892 for another ten years, was made permanent by statute in 1902. Japanese exclusion was substantially achieved by President Roosevelt's Gentlemen's Agreement with Japan in 1907, a device which avoided direct affront to Japanese national pride. Congress was not satisfied, however, until it wrote Japanese exclusion into the law in 1924. Actually the Japanese exclusion act did not mention Japan. It merely denied admission to all aliens "ineligible to citizenship." This formula excluded also the natives of other Far Eastern countries and the Pacific islands. The "barred zone" provisions of a 1917 law excluded natives of India, parts of Russia, and several other countries.

The abandonment of the principle of racial exclusion came in three stages. In 1943, while China was an ally in World War II, Congress repealed Chinese exclusion on the request of the President. In 1946, as the Philippines became independent and India neared that status, admission of races indigenous to those two countries was permitted. Finally, in the Immigration and Nationality Act of 1952, all explicit racial restrictions on admission were repealed. However, the quota law of 1924, which was substantially continued by the 1952 act, heavily favored immigrants from Northern and Western Europe and effectively restricted immigration from other parts of the world.

The quota system was finally repealed in 1965. The new immigration act retained an annual ceiling—120,000 a year from the Western Hemisphere and 170,000 from the rest of the world. First preference under the act was to unite families separated by the operation of the old quota system; close relatives of United States citizens receive 74 per cent of the openings. Preference was also given to members of professions or persons of exceptional ability in the sciences and arts (to a total of 17,000 per year), and to workers with skills needed in the American labor force. Anyone without close relatives or labor skill can be admitted only if the Secretary of Labor certifies that the immigrant will not replace an American worker or lower his pay.

EXCLUSION ON GROUNDS OF OPINION    In the wake of McKinley's assassination by an anarchist, Congress in 1903 passed a law providing for the exclusion of anarchists, or persons believing in assassination or the overthrow of government by force and violence, or belonging to organizations teaching such doctrines.[11] These provisions were extended in subsequent acts to

[11] Upheld by the Supreme Court in *Turner* v. *Williams* (1904).

include persons and organizations who advocate the unlawful destruction of property. In 1939 the Supreme Court ruled that these barriers applied only to persons who at the time of entry into the United States were members of the proscribed types of organizations.[12] Congress immediately amended the law to make it applicable to previous membership as well.

The Subversive Activities Control Act of 1950 banned the admission of aliens who were members of or affiliated with the Communist Party in any country, or who sought to enter the United States to engage in activities which would endanger the welfare or safety of this country. The act also excluded aliens if "there is reason to believe" that after entry they would be likely to engage in activity "subversive to the national security." The Immigration and Nationality Act of 1952 took over these categories, and even added a few more. But it also effected certain alleviations by providing that persons who had joined proscribed organizations involuntarily, or while less than sixteen years of age, or for the purpose of obtaining employment or the essentials of living, or who had for at least five years prior to application for entry actively opposed the doctrines of these organizations, could be granted visas if the consular officer found it was in the public interest to do so, and admitted if the Attorney General approved.

ADMINISTRATIVE FINALITY    The administrative machinery required to administer the exclusion policy is of concern here only so far as it raises constitutional issues. The thousands of alien inspections which must be conducted by immigration officers in carrying out the exclusion process make obvious the case for speedy summary action. Recognizing the breadth of congressional power and the need for administrative discretion, the courts have placed exclusion procedures largely outside the scope of constitutional protection.

The first important ruling on procedural issues was in *Nishimura Ekiu* v. *United States* (1892). The statute provided that the immigration inspector's decision on the right of any alien to land, when adverse to that right, should be final unless appealed to the superintendent of immigration, whose action was subject to review by the Secretary of the Treasury. The statute said nothing about the finality of the Secretary's decision, but the Court held that where "a statute gives a discretionary power to an officer, to be exercised by him upon his own opinion of certain facts, he is made the sole and exclusive judge of the existence of those facts, and no other tribunal, unless expressly authorized by law to do so, is at liberty to re-examine or controvert the sufficiency of the evidence on which he acted." [13]

The well-known case of *United States* v. *Ju Toy* (1905) presented a different situation, in that the person denied permission to reenter the country claimed to be a native-born citizen of the United States. The Supreme Court

---

[12] *Kessler* v. *Strecker* (1939).
[13] See also *Lem Moon Sing* v. *United States* (1895).

by a six to three vote held that here also the Secretary's decision must be treated as final. Justice Holmes wrote for the Court majority:

> The petitioner, although physically within our boundaries, is to be regarded as if he had been stopped at the limit of our jurisdiction and kept there while his right to enter was under debate. If, for the purpose of argument, we assume that the Fifth Amendment applies to him and that to deny entrance to a citizen is to deprive him of liberty, we nevertheless are of opinion that with regard to him due process of law does not require a judicial trial. That is . . . the almost necessary result of the power of Congress to pass exclusion laws.

But Justice Brewer, dissenting, thought this was "a star chamber proceeding." "Banishment is a punishment and of the severest sort. There can be no punishment except for crime. The petitioner has been guilty of no crime. . . . Yet . . . with only an examination before a ministerial officer, he is compelled to suffer punishment as a criminal, and is denied the protection of either a grand or petit jury."

The Court did shortly make it clear that the administrative process of exclusion was not entirely immune from judicial control. In *Chin Yow* v. *United States* (1908) the Court held violative of due process the refusal of an inspector to permit certain witnesses offered by the alien to testify. Justice Holmes noted that under *Ju Toy* the decision of the Secretary is final, "but that is on the presupposition that the decision was after a hearing in good faith, however summary in form." Judicial review of administrative procedure, moreover, is not limited to cases where citizenship is claimed.[14]

Thus the technical argument that a person who has been refused admission on arrival in the United States may be considered as stopped at the border and not entitled to the constitutional rights of a resident has not been allowed to interfere with judicial enforcement of due process standards in exclusion proceedings.[15] In such cases the person held for return abroad is in fact imprisoned, and if he is a citizen, wrongly. As Justice Holmes said in the *Chin Yow* case: "*De facto* he is locked up until carried out of the country against his will." The method of testing the legality of this restraint of liberty is by petition for writ of habeas corpus. On habeas corpus the federal district court does not give a *de novo* trial, but confines itself to an examination of the record of the administrative proceedings, to see whether the actions of the immigration officers meet the test of due process of law.

[14] See *Tod* v. *Waldman* (1924).

[15] But by a five to four vote the Court used this technical argument in *Leng May Ma* v. *Barber* (1958) to hold that such an alien, admitted on parole while admissibility was being determined, was not "within the United States" for purposes of the statute authorizing the Attorney General to withhold deportation of an alien to a country where he was likely to be subjected to "physical persecution." Douglas, Warren, Black, and Brennan, in dissent, protested this "hostile reading" of a "humane provision of our law." See also *Rogers* v. *Quan* (1958).

If the alien has had the benefit of the good faith application of the procedures Congress has specified, that is all to which due process entitles him.

That a hearing in exclusion cases rests upon congressional beneficence and not constitutional right was dramatically demonstrated by *United States ex rel. Knauff* v. *Shaughnessy* (1950). Kurt Knauff, a naturalized United States citizen and army veteran who was a civilian employee of the Army at Frankfurt, sought to bring his German-born wife to the United States in 1948, but she was excluded without a hearing by order of the Attorney General on the ground that her admission would be prejudicial to the interests of the United States. This procedure was duly authorized by regulations adopted under authority of a 1941 statute which provided that the President may issue "reasonable rules, regulations and orders" to govern the entrance of aliens during a period of national emergency. Mrs. Knauff brought habeas corpus proceedings, contending that exclusion without a hearing was in violation of the Fifth Amendment and congressional statutes. By a four to three vote the Court rejected her claims. The Fifth Amendment did not apply. "Whatever the procedure authorized by Congress is, it is due process as far as an alien denied entry is concerned."

In *Shaughnessy* v. *United States ex rel. Mezei* (1953) the Court again approved exclusion without a hearing, this time by a five to four vote. Mezei came to the United States in 1923 and lived in New York for twenty-five years. He married and had a home there but did not become a citizen. In 1948 he sailed for Europe. Returning to the United States in 1950, he was excluded on security grounds without a hearing, the action purportedly being based on confidential information which it would be prejudicial to the public interest to disclose. After Mezei had spent almost two years on Ellis Island, a federal district court agreed that he was unlawfully confined and ordered his release on a writ of habeas corpus. The court of appeals affirmed his freedom. But in 1953, the Supreme Court by a bare majority held that the courts could not interfere in an exclusion proceeding grounded on danger to national security, and Mezei was returned to Ellis Island.

Justice Jackson, one of the dissenters, charged that this action amounted to executive imprisonment, "considered oppressive and lawless since John, at Runnymede, pledged that no free man should be imprisoned, dispossessed, outlawed, or exiled save by the judgment of his peers or by the law of the land." He granted the right of administrative detention of aliens, but he insisted that aliens also had rights, derived from the Constitution, which Congress must respect. This was particularly the case where the excluded alien had a long period of residence in this country, and was really seeking to "return home." Congress may not authorize "United States officers to take without due process of law the life, the liberty or the property of an alien who has come within our jurisdiction; and that means he must meet a fair hearing with fair notice of the charges."

The present situation, then, is one of administrative finality, with judicial

intervention limited to determining whether there has been a fair hearing when Congress provides for a hearing. The Immigration and Nationality Act of 1952 authorizes the Attorney General to exclude aliens "on the basis of information of a confidential character." Where this happens, even though a hearing is held, a reviewing court in a habeas corpus proceeding would not even have before it the facts on the basis of which the exclusion order was made. As Justice Murphy said in *Bridges* v. *Wixon:* "The Bill of Rights is a futile authority for the alien seeking admission . . . to these shores."

### CONTROL OF ALIENS AND DEPORTATION

Aliens admitted to the United States remain under a system of surveillance which does not apply to citizens. The Alien Registration Act of 1940 provides that all aliens over the age of fourteen must register annually and be fingerprinted. Failure to do so is a criminal offense. This act, taken in conjunction with other laws regulating immigration and naturalization, was held by the Supreme Court in *Hines* v. *Davidowitz* (1941) to constitute a comprehensive and uniform system for the regulation of all aliens, and to preclude enforcement of a Pennsylvania alien-registration law. Aliens are also subject to deportation on a variety of statutory grounds.

THE POWER TO BANISH    The first American experience with deportation statutes came with the notorious Alien and Sedition Acts of 1798. One of that group of statutes, the Naturalization Act, raised the residence requirement for naturalization from five to fourteen years in the hope of cutting off the Republican party's supply of foreign-born voters. Another, the Alien Enemies Act, authorized the President in time of war or threatened invasion to seize, secure, or remove from the country all resident aliens who were citizens of the enemy nation. A third, the Alien Act, authorized the President for a two-year period to expel from the country any alien whom he considered dangerous to the public peace or safety, or whom he believed to be plotting against the country. This latter statute was attacked by Jefferson in the famed Kentucky Resolution of 1798 as giving the President unconstitutional power to expel aliens without the protections of a criminal trial.

Nearly a century passed with no new deportation laws on the statute books. Then, as the policy of Chinese exclusion was adopted, it seemed necessary as an enforcement measure to provide for the expulsion of illegal entrants. The act of 1892 required all Chinese laborers in the United States who were entitled to remain here to secure a certificate of residence. A person without such a certificate was to be deemed unlawfully within the country, and subject to arrest and deportation.

The Supreme Court upheld this statute by a six to three vote in the famous case of *Fong Yue Ting* v. *United States* (1893). Justice Gray for the majority asserted that the right of the government "to expel or deport foreigners,

who have not been naturalized . . . rests upon the same grounds, and is as absolute and unqualified as the right to prohibit and prevent their entrance into the country." Admittedly the limited judicial hearing provided by the statute did not meet the constitutional requirements for criminal trials, but the Court held that "the order of deportation is not a punishment for crime." Gray was even of the opinion that Congress could have ordered deportation of aliens lacking certificates of residence by direct executive action, without any judicial trial or examination at all.

Chief Justice Fuller and Justices Brewer and Field dissented from this reasoning in as strong language as judicial propriety would permit. Field, who had written the *Chinese Exclusion* decision upholding the absolute and inherent right of Congress to exclude aliens, said there was a tremendous difference between exclusion and deportation; the precedents applicable to the former gave no legitimacy to the latter. Brewer thought that the barbarity of the ruling would lead followers of Confucius to wonder on what ground Americans were sending missionaries to China, and added a powerful protest against the view that the power to deport was inherent in sovereignty. Chief Justice Fuller summed up the statute as "a legislative sentence of banishment, and, as such, absolutely void."

The dissenters also attacked the holding that deportation was not punishment. Deportation, said Field, was a penalty imposed on an alien for failure to get a certificate. "That is the punishment for his neglect, and that being of an infamous character can only be imposed after indictment, trial, and conviction." Moreover, the punishment "is beyond all reason in its severity. It is out of all proportion to the alleged offence. It is cruel and unusual." Brewer added: "Every one knows that to be forcibly taken away from home, and family, and friends, and business, and property, and sent across the ocean to a distant land, is punishment; and that oftentimes most severe and cruel."

The eloquent arguments of the minority were fruitless in 1893, and have remained so. The two basic propositions of *Fong Yue Ting*—that Congress has the inherent power to order deportation, and that deportation is not criminal punishment—are firmly established in the subsequent decisions. Indeed, deportation, which was at first conceived of only as a method for expelling aliens who had entered the country illegally, was soon employed by Congress to remove aliens who had entered legally but had subsequently violated a condition attached to continued residence. Thus the Immigration Act of 1917 provided for the deportation of aliens convicted of a crime involving moral turpitude committed within five years after entry, where a sentence of one year or more was levied, and also of aliens convicted and sentenced more than once for crimes involving moral turpitude, with no time limit.

Other statutory grounds for deportation, now codified in the Immigration and Nationality Act of 1952, are violation of alien-registration requirements,

peddling of narcotic drugs, addiction to narcotics, becoming a public charge within five years after entry, or membership in a subversive organization. Deportation for past membership in the Communist Party was upheld by the Supreme Court in *Harisiades* v. *Shaughnessy* (1952). Justice Jackson, speaking for the majority, recognized that "as world convulsions have driven us toward a closed society the expulsion power has been exercised with increasing severity, manifest in multiplication of grounds for deportation, in expanding the subject classes from illegal entrants to legal residents, and in greatly lengthening the period of residence after which one may be expelled." But had this process reached a point "where it is the duty of this Court to call a halt upon the political branches of the Government"? Jackson did not think so. The policy toward aliens is "vitally and intricately interwoven with contemporaneous policies in regard to the conduct of foreign relations, the war power, and the maintenance of a republican form of government," which are "so exclusively entrusted to the political branches of government as to be largely immune from judicial inquiry or interference."

But Justices Black and Douglas disagreed. They insisted that *Fong Yue Ting* had been wrongly decided, and was inconsistent with the philosophy of constitutional law developed in other decisions for the protection of resident aliens. Douglas said:

> An alien, who is assimilated in our society, is treated as a citizen so far as his property and his liberty are concerned. He can live and work here and raise a family, secure in the personal guarantees every resident has and safe from discriminations that might be leveled against him because he was born abroad. Those guarantees of liberty and livelihood are the essence of the freedom which this country from the beginning has offered the people of all lands. If those rights, great as they are, have constitutional protection, I think the more important one—the right to remain here—has a like dignity.

A provision of the 1952 statute authorizing deportation of aliens affected with a "psychopathic personality" has been interpreted by immigration authorities to justify the deportation of homosexuals.[16] Another provision of the act allows the Attorney General to deport a denaturalized person to any country which will accept him if his native country refuses to do so. This means that an alien may be deported to a country in which he has never lived.

The administrative procedures used in deportation have often seemed unnecessarily harsh. For example, in 1961 an alien known as a racketeer

---

[16] The Supreme Court upheld this interpretation in *Boutilier* v. *Immigration and Naturalization Service* (1967). Justice Douglas, dissenting, thought that the term "psychopathic personality" was "a treacherous one like 'Communist' or in an earlier day 'Bolshevik,'" and was "much too vague for constitutional standards." In 1965, after Boutilier had been ordered deported, Congress added "sexual deviation" to the statute as grounds for exclusion or deportation. See also *Rosenberg* v. *Fleuti* (1963).

was arrested when he walked into the immigration office in New Orleans for the regular alien registration. Without being allowed to phone his family or obtain clothes or money, he was handcuffed, driven to the airport, and flown in a government plane to Guatemala. Though he had been given no notice, the local newspapers and television stations had been notified to be on hand.[17]

To minimize somewhat the present rigors of the deportation law, the American Civil Liberties Union has proposed a ten-year statute of limitations for deportable conduct, thus protecting aliens from the threat of deportation for acts in the distant past. The ACLU also suggests that any child admitted to this country for permanent residence before his fourteenth birthday should be immunized from deportation.[18]

PROCEDURAL PROTECTIONS    The Supreme Court has continued to maintain, as in *Fong Yue Ting*, that deportation is not criminal punishment, but the corollary of this doctrine, that procedural protections can consequently be waived, has been somewhat undermined by subsequent decisions. In 1922 the Court decided that the *Ju Toy* rule of administrative finality as to a claim of citizenship in an exclusion case did not apply to deportation proceedings. When a person within the country against whom a warrant of arrest in expulsion proceedings had been issued presented substantial evidence tending to establish a claim to citizenship, he was held in *Ng Fung Ho* v. *White* (1922) to be entitled to a judicial trial of the issue. The question, Justice Brandeis said, was whether "a resident of the United States who claims to be a citizen [can] be arrested and deported on executive order." The Court was unwilling to see the fact of citizenship determined in this way.

Where no claim of citizenship is made in a deportation proceeding, the alien is not entitled to a judicial trial, but he is entitled to a fair hearing. This was first determined in the *Japanese Immigrant Case* (1903),[19] where the Court interpreted the legislation as requiring a hearing, at least for aliens who had not entered clandestinely and who had been here some time even if illegally. This interpretation, which challenged the *Fong Yue Ting* dictum approving summary executive action, was regarded as necessary to bring the statute "into harmony with the Constitution." The same holding was repeated in *Wong Yang Sung* v. *McGrath* (1950), where Justice Jackson said

[17] *The New York Times,* April 6, 1961.
[18] By way of illustration, the Court approved in 1960 deportation to Finland of a fifty-two-year-old alien who had lived in this country since he was a baby, on grounds of Communist Party membership between 1937 and 1939. *Niukkanen* v. *McAlexander* (1960). See also *Galvan* v. *Press* (1954); *Rowoldt* v. *Perfetto* (1957); *Gastelum-Quinones* v. *Kennedy* (1963). The latter two cases apply the rule that to deport for membership in the Communist Party the government must prove that the membership was a "meaningful association" and that the alien understood the "political implications" of membership.
[19] *Yamataya* v. *Fisher* (1903).

that without a hearing "there would be no constitutional authority for deportation."

In some recent decisions the Court has even tended to judge fairness of a deportation hearing by the standards of criminal proceedings. Thus in *Bridges* v. *Wixon* (1945) Justice Douglas concluded for the Court that the deportation order was based largely on "hearsay" statements, which "certainly would not be admissible in any criminal case as substantive evidence." The same attitude was apparent in *Jordan* v. *DeGeorge* (1951), where the Court was considering whether conviction of crimes involving "moral turpitude" was an unconstitutionally vague ground for deportation. Chief Justice Vinson, noting that the purpose of the "void for vagueness" rule is to warn individuals of the criminal consequences of their conduct, said: "Despite the fact that this is not a criminal statute, we shall nevertheless examine the application of the vagueness doctrine to this case. We do this in view of the grave nature of deportation."

Such procedural protections do not apply to the deportation of alien enemies in time of war. The Alien Enemy Act of 1798 is still in force, and its use was upheld in *Ludecke* v. *Watkins* (1948). A German enemy alien, who had been interned in the United States during World War II, was ordered deported to Germany in January, 1946, when the shooting war was over, but before the legal state of war had been terminated. Justice Frankfurter for the Court ruled that the President was acting under his war powers and that the order of deportation was not judicially reviewable. Four justices dissented, Justice Douglas contending that it was "foreign to our system" for any officer of the government to be given discretion to "override due process."

Aliens whose deportation is sought are customarily released on bail while the proceedings are pending. However, under the Internal Security Act of 1950 and the Immigration and Nationality Act of 1952 the Attorney General is authorized to hold aliens against whom charges have been brought, in custody without bail at his discretion. This power was upheld by a sharply divided Court in *Carlson* v. *Landon* (1952).

The 1952 statute authorizes the Attorney General to retain an alien in custody for an additional period of six months *after* the final order of deportation is issued in order to "effect the alien's departure." During this six months' period the alien is subject to the "supervision" of the Attorney General, and may be required "to give information under oath as to his nationality, circumstances, habits, associations, and activities, and such other information, whether or not related to the foregoing, as the Attorney General may deem fit and proper."

*United States* v. *Witkovich* (1957) involved the attempt of the Attorney General to compel an alien under "supervision" to answer questions as to whether he subscribed to the *Daily Worker* or was a member of the Communist Party, and numerous other demands aimed at establishing possible

Communist connections. The Supreme Court held these questions invalid. The statute should be interpreted to authorize only questions "reasonably calculated to keep the Attorney General advised regarding the continued availability for departure of aliens whose deportation is overdue." Any broader interpretation of the statute would raise constitutional questions, the Court implied.

This review makes clear the extremely broad power of Congress over deportation. The effort to reverse the principles of the *Fong Yue Ting* decision has failed. Nevertheless, by statutory interpretation, and by assimilating deportation procedures in certain instances to those of criminal prosecutions, the Supreme Court has softened somewhat the absolutism of the congressional power over aliens.[20]

### SELECTED REFERENCES

APPLEMAN, IRVING, "Supreme Court on Expatriation: An Historical Review," 23 *Federal Bar Journal* 351 (1963).

———, "That New Immigration Act," 52 *American Bar Association Journal* 717 (1966).

ARMSTRONG, MICHAEL F., "Banishment: Cruel and Unusual Punishment," 111 *University of Pennsylvania Law Review* 758 (1963).

"Deportation and Exclusion," 71 *Yale Law Journal* 760–792 (1962).

GORDON, CHARLES, "Due Process of Law in Immigration Proceedings," 50 *American Bar Association Journal* 34 (1964).

———, "Finality of Immigration and Nationality Determinations," 31 *University of Chicago Law Review* 433–466 (1964).

"Involuntary Loss of Citizenship by Naturalized Citizens Residing Abroad," 49 *Cornell Law Quarterly* 52–80 (1963).

KONVITZ, MILTON R., *The Alien and the Asiatic in American Law,* Ithaca, N.Y.: Cornell University Press, 1946.

———, *Civil Rights in Immigration.* Ithaca, N.Y.: Cornell University Press, 1953.

PRITCHETT, C. HERMAN, *Civil Liberties and the Vinson Court,* chap. 6. Chicago: The University of Chicago Press, 1954.

Report of the President's Commission on Immigration and Naturalization, *Whom We Shall Welcome.* Washington: Government Printing Office, 1952.

[20] See *Immigration and Naturalization Service* v. *Errico* (1966). In *Woodby* v. *Immigration and Naturalization Service* (1966) the Court held that no order for deportation may be entered unless it is found by clear, unequivocal, and convincing evidence that facts alleged as grounds for deportation are true. But compare this with a naturalization proceeding, *Berenyi* v. *District Director* (1967), where the Court held that it could not review concurrent findings of fact by two courts below; they had upheld a finding that applicant was not a person of good moral character because he had lied in denying having once been a member of the Communist Party in Hungary, though the evidence that he was not a Communist was overwhelming.

ROCHE, JOHN P., "The Expatriation Cases," in Philip B. Kurland (ed.), *The Supreme Court Review: 1963*, pp. 325–356. Chicago: The University of Chicago Press, 1963.

VAN VLECK, WILLIAM C., *The Administrative Control of Aliens: A Study in Administrative Law and Procedure*. New York: The Commonwealth Fund, 1932.

# Appendixes

## Constitution of the United States of America

WE THE PEOPLE of the United States, in Order to form a more perfect Union, establish Justice, insure domestic Tranquility, provide for the common defence, promote the general Welfare, and secure the Blessings of Liberty to ourselves and our Posterity, do ordain and establish this CONSTITUTION for the United States of America.

### ARTICLE I

*Section 1*    All legislative Powers herein granted shall be vested in a Congress of the United States, which shall consist of a Senate and House of Representatives.

*Section 2*    [1.] The House of Representatives shall be composed of Members chosen every second Year by the People of the several States, and the Electors in each State shall have the Qualifications requisite for Electors of the most numerous Branch of the State Legislature.

[2.] No Person shall be a Representative who shall not have attained to the Age of twenty five Years, and been seven Years a Citizen of the United States, and who shall not, when elected, be an Inhabitant of that State in which he shall be chosen.

[3.] Representatives and direct Taxes [1] shall be apportioned among the several States which may be included within this Union, according to their respective Numbers, which shall be determined by adding to the whole Number of free Persons, including those bound to Service for a Term of Years, and excluding

---

[1] Modified as to direct taxes by the Sixteenth Amendment.

Indians not taxed, three fifths of all other Persons.[2] The actual Enumeration shall be made within three Years after the first Meeting of the Congress of the United States, and within every subsequent Term of ten Years, in such Manner as they shall by Law direct. The Number of Representatives shall not exceed one for every thirty Thousand, but each State shall have at Least one Representative; and until such enumeration shall be made, the State of New Hampshire shall be entitled to chuse three, Massachusetts eight, Rhode-Island and Providence Plantations one, Connecticut five, New-York six, New Jersey four, Pennsylvania eight, Delaware one, Maryland six, Virginia ten, North Carolina five, South Carolina five, and Georgia three.

[4.] When vacancies happen in the Representation from any State, the Executive Authority thereof shall issue Writs of Election to fill such Vacancies.

[5.] The House of Representatives shall chuse their Speaker and other Officers; and shall have the sole Power of Impeachment.

*Section 3*    [1.] The Senate of the United States shall be composed of two Senators from each State, chosen by the Legislature thereof,[3] for six Years; and each Senator shall have one Vote.

[2.] Immediately after they shall be assembled in Consequence of the first Election, they shall be divided as equally as may be into three Classes. The Seats of the Senators of the first Class shall be vacated at the Expiration of the second Year, of the second Class at the Expiration of the fourth Year, and of the third Class at the Expiration of the sixth Year, so that one third may be chosen every second Year; and if Vacancies happen by Resignation, or otherwise, during the Recess of the Legislature of any State, the Executive thereof may make temporary Appointments until the next Meeting of the Legislature, which shall then fill such Vacancies.

[3.] No Person shall be a Senator who shall not have attained to the Age of thirty Years, and been nine Years a Citizen of the United States, and who shall not, when elected, be an Inhabitant of that State for which he shall be chosen.

[4.] The Vice President of the United States shall be President of the Senate, but shall have no Vote, unless they be equally divided.

[5.] The Senate shall chuse their other Officers, and also a President pro tempore, in the Absence of the Vice President, or when he shall exercise the Office of President of the United States.

[6.] The Senate shall have the sole Power to try all Impeachments. When sitting for that Purpose, they shall be on Oath or Affirmation. When the President of the United States is tried, the Chief Justice shall preside: And no Person shall be convicted without the Concurrence of two thirds of the Members present.

[7.] Judgment in Cases of Impeachment shall not extend further than to removal from Office, and disqualification to hold and enjoy any Office of honor, Trust or Profit under the United States: but the Party convicted shall nevertheless be liable and subject to Indictment, Trial, Judgment and Punishment, according to Law.

*Section 4*    [1.] The Times, Places and Manner of holding Elections for Senators and Representatives, shall be prescribed in each State by the Legislature

---

[2] Replaced by the Fourteenth Amendment.
[3] Modified by the Seventeenth Amendment.

thereof; but the Congress may at any time by Law make or alter such Regulations, except as to the Places of chusing Senators.

[2.] The Congress shall assemble at least once in every Year, and such Meeting shall be on the first Monday in December, unless they shall by Law appoint a different Day.[4]

Section 5     [1.] Each House shall be the Judge of the Elections, Returns and Qualifications of its own Members, and a Majority of each shall constitute a Quorum to do Business; but a smaller Number may adjourn from day to day, and may be authorized to compel the attendance of absent Members, in such Manner, and under such Penalties as each House may provide.

[2.] Each House may determine the Rules of its Proceedings, punish its Members for Disorderly Behaviour, and, with the Concurrence of two thirds, expel a Member.

[3.] Each House shall keep a Journal of its Proceedings, and from time to time publish the same, excepting such Parts as may in their Judgment require Secrecy; and the Yeas and Nays of the Members of either House on any question shall, at the Desire of one fifth of those Present, be entered on the Journal.

[4.] Neither House, during the Session of Congress, shall, without the Consent of the other, adjourn for more than three days, nor to any other Place than that in which the two Houses shall be sitting.

Section 6     [1.] The Senators and Representatives shall receive a Compensation for their Services, to be ascertained by Law, and paid out of the Treasury of the United States. They shall in all Cases, except Treason, Felony and Breach of the Peace, be privileged from Arrest during their Attendance at the Session of their respective Houses, and in going to and returning from the same; and for any Speech or Debate in either House, they shall not be questioned in any other Place.

[2.] No Senator or Representative shall, during the Time for which he was elected, be appointed to any civil Office under the Authority of the United States, which shall have been created, or the Emoluments whereof shall have been encreased during such time; and no Person holding any Office under the United States, shall be a member of either House during his Continuance in Office.

Section 7     [1.] All Bills for raising Revenue shall originate in the House of Representatives; but the Senate may propose or concur with Amendments as on other Bills.

[2.] Every Bill which shall have passed the House of Representatives and the Senate, shall, before it become a Law, be presented to the President of the United States; If he approve he shall sign it, but if not he shall return it, with his Objections to that House in which it shall have originated, who shall enter the Objections at large on their Journal, and proceed to reconsider it. If after such Reconsideration two thirds of that House shall agree to pass the Bill, it shall be sent, together with the Objections, to the other House, by which it shall likewise be reconsidered, and if approved by two thirds of that House, it shall become a Law. But in all such Cases the Votes of both Houses shall be determined by yeas and Nays, and the Names of the Persons voting for and against the Bill shall be entered on the Journal of each House respectively. If any Bill shall not be returned by the President

---

[4] Modified by the Twentieth Amendment.

within ten Days (Sundays excepted) after it shall have been presented to him, the same shall be a Law, in like Manner as if he had signed it, unless the Congress by their Adjournment prevent its Return, in which Case it shall not be a Law.

[3.] Every Order, Resolution, or Vote to which the Concurrence of the Senate and House of Representatives may be necessary (except on a question of Adjournment) shall be presented to the President of the United States; and before the same shall take Effect, shall be approved by him, or being disapproved by him, shall be repassed by two thirds of the Senate and House of Representatives, according to the Rules and Limitations prescribed in the Case of a Bill.

*Section 8*    The Congress shall have Power [1.] To lay and collect Taxes, Duties, Imposts and Excises, to pay the Debts and provide for the common Defence and general Welfare of the United States; but all Duties, Imposts and Excises shall be uniform throughout the United States;

[2.] To borrow Money on the credit of the United States;

[3.] To regulate Commerce with foreign Nations, and among the several States, and with the Indian Tribes;

[4.] To establish an uniform Rule of Naturalization, and uniform Laws on the subject of Bankruptcies throughout the United States;

[5.] To coin Money, regulate the Value thereof, and of foreign Coin, and fix the Standard of Weights and Measures;

[6.] To provide for the Punishment of counterfeiting the Securities and current Coin of the United States;

[7.] To establish Post Offices and post Roads;

[8.] To promote the Progress of Science and useful Arts, by securing for limited Times to Authors and Inventors the exclusive Right to their respective Writings and Discoveries;

[9.] To constitute Tribunals inferior to the supreme Court;

[10.] To define and punish Piracies and Felonies committed on the high Seas, and Offences against the Law of Nations;

[11.] To declare War, grant Letters of Marque and Reprisal, and make Rules concerning Captures on Land and Water;

[12.] To raise and support Armies, but no Appropriation of Money to that Use shall be for a longer Term than two Years;

[13.] To provide and maintain a Navy;

[14.] To make Rules for the Government and Regulation of the land and naval Forces;

[15.] To provide for calling forth the Militia to execute the Laws of the Union, suppress Insurrections and repel Invasions;

[16.] To provide for organizing, arming, and disciplining, the Militia, and for governing such Part of them as may be employed in the Service of the United States, reserving to the States respectively, the Appointment of the Officers, and the Authority of training the Militia according to the discipline prescribed by Congress;

[17.] To exercise exclusive Legislation in all Cases whatsoever, over such District (not exceeding ten Miles square) as may, by Cession of particular States, and the Acceptance of Congress, become the Seat of the Government of the United States, and to exercise like Authority over all Places purchased by the Consent of

the Legislature of the State in which the same shall be, for the Erection of Forts, Magazines, Arsenals, dock-Yards, and other needful Buildings;—And

[18.] To make all Laws which shall be necessary and proper for carrying into Execution the foregoing Powers, and all other Powers vested by this Constitution in the Government of the United States, or in any Department or Officer thereof.

*Section 9*  [1.] The Migration or Importation of such Persons as any of the States now existing shall think proper to admit, shall not be prohibited by the Congress prior to the Year one thousand eight hundred and eight, but a Tax or duty may be imposed on such Importation, not exceeding ten dollars for each Person.

[2.] The Privilege of the Writ of Habeas Corpus shall not be suspended, unless when in Cases of Rebellion or Invasion the public Safety may require it.

[3.] No Bill of Attainder or ex post facto Law shall be passed.

[4.] No Capitation, or other direct, Tax shall be laid, unless in Proportion to the Census or Enumeration herein before directed to be taken.[5]

[5.] No Tax or Duty shall be laid on Articles exported from any State.

[6.] No Preference shall be given by any Regulation of Commerce or Revenue to the Ports of one State over those of another: nor shall Vessels bound to, or from, one State, be obliged to enter, clear, or pay Duties in another.

[7.] No Money shall be drawn from the Treasury, but in Consequence of Appropriations made by Law; and a regular Statement and Account of the Receipts and Expenditures of all public Money shall be published from time to time.

[8.] No Title of Nobility shall be granted by the United States: And no Person holding any Office of Profit or Trust under them, shall, without the Consent of the Congress, accept of any present, Emolument, Office, or Title, of any kind whatever, from any King, Prince, or foreign State.

*Section 10*  [1.] No State shall enter into any Treaty, Alliance, or Confederation; grant Letters of Marque and Reprisal; coin Money; emit Bills of Credit; make any Thing but gold and silver Coin a Tender in Payment of Debts; pass any Bill of Attainder, ex post facto Law, or Law impairing the Obligation of Contracts, or grant any Title of Nobility.

[2.] No State shall, without the Consent of the Congress, lay any Imposts or Duties on Imports or Exports, except what may be absolutely necessary for executing its inspection Laws: and the net Produce of all Duties and Imposts, laid by any State on Imports or Exports, shall be for the Use of the Treasury of the United States; and all such Laws shall be subject to the Revision and Controul of the Congress.

[3.] No State shall, without the Consent of Congress, lay any Duty of Tonnage, keep Troops, or Ships of War in time of Peace, enter into any Agreement or Compact with another State, or with a foreign Power, or engage in War, unless actually invaded, or in such imminent Danger as will not admit of delay.

ARTICLE II

*Section 1*  [1.] The executive Power shall be vested in a President of the United States of America. He shall hold his Office during the Term of four Years,

---

[5] Modified by the Sixteenth Amendment.

and, together with the Vice President, chosen for the same Term, be elected, as follows

[2.] Each State shall appoint, in such Manner as the Legislature thereof may direct, a Number of Electors, equal to the whole Number of Senators and Representatives to which the State may be entitled in the Congress: but no Senator or Representative, or Person holding an Office of Trust or Profit under the United States, shall be appointed an Elector.

[3.] The Electors shall meet in their respective States, and vote by Ballot for two Persons, of whom one at least shall not be an Inhabitant of the same State with themselves. And they shall make a List of all the Persons voted for, and of the Number of Votes for each; which List they shall sign and certify, and transmit sealed to the Seat of the Government of the United States, directed to the President of the Senate. The President of the Senate shall, in the Presence of the Senate and House of Representatives, open all the Certificates, and the Votes shall then be counted. The Person having the greatest Number of Votes shall be the President, if such Number be a Majority of the whole Number of Electors appointed; and if there be more than one who have such Majority, and have an equal Number of Votes, then the House of Representatives shall immediately chuse by Ballot one of them for President; and if no Person have a Majority, then from the five highest on the List the said House shall in like Manner chuse the President. But in chusing the President, the Votes shall be taken by States, the Representation from each State having one Vote; A quorum for this Purpose shall consist of a Member or Members from two thirds of the States, and a Majority of all the States shall be necessary to a Choice. In every Case, after the Choice of the President, the Person having the greatest Number of Votes of the Electors shall be the Vice President. But if there should remain two or more who have equal Votes, the Senate shall chuse from them by Ballot the Vice President.[6]

[4.] The Congress may determine the Time of chusing the Electors, and the Day on which they shall give their Votes; which Day shall be the same throughout the United States.

[5.] No Person except a natural born Citizen, or a Citizen of the United States, at the time of the Adoption of this Constitution, shall be eligible to the Office of President; neither shall any Person be eligible to that Office who shall not have attained to the Age of thirty five Years, and been fourteen Years a Resident within the United States.

[6.] In Case of the Removal of the President from Office, or of his Death, Resignation, or Inability to discharge the Powers and Duties of the said Office, the Same shall devolve on the Vice President, and the Congress may by Law provide for the Case of Removal, Death, Resignation, or Inability, both of the President and Vice President, declaring what Officer shall then act as President, and such Officer shall act accordingly, until the Disability be removed, or a President shall be elected.

[7.] The President shall, at stated Times, receive for his Services, a Compensation, which shall neither be encreased nor diminished during the Period for which he shall have been elected, and he shall not receive within that Period any other Emolument from the United States, or any of them.

[6] This paragraph was replaced in 1804 by the Twelfth Amendment.

[8.] Before he enter on the Execution of his Office, he shall take the following Oath or Affirmation:—"I do solemnly swear (or affirm) that I will faithfully execute the Office of President of the United States, and will to the best of my Ability, preserve, protect and defend the Constitution of the United States."

*Section 2*    [1.] The President shall be Commander in Chief of the Army and Navy of the United States, and of the Militia of the several States, when called into the actual Service of the United States; he may require the Opinion, in writing, of the principal Officer in each of the executive Departments, upon any Subject relating to the Duties of their respective Offices, and he shall have Power to grant Reprieves and Pardons for Offences against the United States, except in Cases of Impeachment.

[2.] He shall have Power, by and with the Advice and Consent of the Senate, to make Treaties, provided two thirds of the Senators present concur; and he shall nominate, and by and with the Advice and Consent of the Senate, shall appoint Ambassadors, other public Ministers and Consuls, Judges of the supreme Court, and all other Officers of the United States, whose Appointments are not herein otherwise provided for, and which shall be established by Law: but the Congress may by Law vest the Appointment of such inferior Officers, as they think proper, in the President alone, in the Courts of Law, or in the Heads of Departments.

[3.] The President shall have Power to fill up all Vacancies that may happen during the Recess of the Senate, by granting Commissions which shall expire at the End of their next Session.

*Section 3*    He shall from time to time give to the Congress Information of the State of the Union, and recommend to their Consideration such Measures as he shall judge necessary and expedient; he may, on extraordinary Occasions, convene both Houses, or either of them, and in Case of Disagreement between them, with Respect to the Time of Adjournment, he may adjourn them to such Time as he shall think proper; he shall receive Ambassadors and other public Ministers; he shall take Care that the Laws be faithfully executed, and shall Commission all the Officers of the United States.

*Section 4*    The President, Vice President and all civil Officers of the United States, shall be removed from Office on Impeachment for, and Conviction of, Treason, Bribery, or other high Crimes and Misdemeanors.

ARTICLE III

*Section 1*    The judicial Power of the United States, shall be vested in one supreme Court, and in such inferior Courts as the Congress may from time to time ordain and establish. The Judges, both of the supreme and inferior Courts, shall hold their Offices during good Behaviour, and shall, at stated Times, receive for their Services, a Compensation, which shall not be diminished during their Continuance in Office.

*Section 2*    [1.] The judicial Power shall extend to all Cases, in Law and Equity, arising under this Constitution, the Laws of the United States, and Treaties made, or which shall be made, under their Authority;—to all Cases affecting Ambassadors, other public Ministers and Consuls;—to all Cases of admiralty and maritime Jurisdiction;—to Controversies to which the United States shall be a Party; —to Controversies between two or more States;—between a State and Citizens of

another State; [7]—between Citizens of different States;—between Citizens of the same State claiming Lands under Grants of different States, and between a State, or the Citizens thereof, and foreign States, Citizens or Subjects.

[2.] In all Cases affecting Ambassadors, other public Ministers and Consuls, and those in which a State shall be Party, the supreme Court shall have original Jurisdiction. In all the other Cases before mentioned, the supreme Court shall have appellate Jurisdiction, both as to Law and Fact, with such Exceptions, and under such Regulations as the Congress shall make.

[3.] The Trial of all Crimes, except in Cases of Impeachment, shall be by Jury; and such Trial shall be held in the State where the said Crimes shall have been committed; but when not committed within any State, the Trial shall be at such Place or Places as the Congress may by Law have directed.

*Section 3*    [1.] Treason against the United States, shall consist only in levying War against them, or in adhering to their Enemies, giving them Aid and Comfort. No Person shall be convicted of Treason unless on the Testimony of two Witnesses to the same overt Act, or on Confession in open Court.

[2.] The Congress shall have Power to declare the Punishment of Treason, but no Attainder of Treason shall work Corruption of Blood, or Forfeiture except during the Life of the Person attainted.

ARTICLE IV

*Section 1*    Full Faith and Credit shall be given in each State to the public Acts, Records, and judicial Proceedings of every other State. And the Congress may by general Laws prescribe the Manner in which such Acts, Records and Proceedings shall be proved, and the Effect thereof.

*Section 2*    [1.] The Citizens of each State shall be entitled to all Privileges and Immunities of Citizens in the several States.

[2.] A Person charged in any State with Treason, Felony, or other Crime, who shall flee from Justice, and be found in another State, shall on Demand of the executive Authority of the State from which he fled, be delivered up, to be removed to the State having Jurisdiction of the Crime.

[3.] No Person held to Service or Labour in one State, under the Laws thereof, escaping into another, shall, in Consequence of any Law or Regulation therein, be discharged from such Service or Labour, but shall be delivered up on Claim of the Party to whom such Service or Labour may be due.

*Section 3*    [1.] New States may be admitted by the Congress into this Union; but no new State shall be formed or erected within the Jurisdiction of any other State; nor any State be formed by the Junction of two or more States, or Parts of States, without the Consent of the Legislatures of the States concerned as well as of the Congress.

[2.] The Congress shall have Power to dispose of and make all needful Rules and Regulations respecting the Territory or other Property belonging to the United States; and nothing in this Constitution shall be so construed as to Prejudice any Claims of the United States, or of any particular State.

*Section 4*    The United States shall guarantee to every State in this Union a Republican Form of Government, and shall protect each of them against Invasion;

[7] Restricted by the Eleventh Amendment.

and on Application of the Legislature, or of the Executive (when the Legislature cannot be convened) against domestic Violence.

### ARTICLE V

The Congress, whenever two thirds of both Houses shall deem it necessary, shall propose Amendments to this Constitution, or, on the Application of the Legislatures of two thirds of the several States, shall call a Convention for proposing Amendments, which, in either Case, shall be valid to all Intents and Purposes, as Part of this Constitution, when ratified by the Legislatures of three fourths of the several States, or by Conventions in three fourths thereof, as the one or the other Mode of Ratification may be proposed by the Congress; Provided that no Amendment which may be made prior to the Year One thousand eight hundred and eight shall in any Manner affect the first and fourth Clauses in the Ninth Section of the first Article; and that no State, without its Consent, shall be deprived of its equal Suffrage in the Senate.

### ARTICLE VI

[1.] All Debts contracted and Engagements entered into, before the Adoption of this Constitution, shall be as valid against the United States under this Constitution, as under the Confederation.

[2.] This Constitution, and the Laws of the United States which shall be made in Pursuance thereof; and all Treaties made, or which shall be made, under the Authority of the United States, shall be the supreme Law of the Land; and the Judges in every State shall be bound thereby, any Thing in the Constitution or Laws of any State to the Contrary notwithstanding.

[3.] The Senators and Representatives before mentioned, and the Members of the several State Legislatures, and all executive and judicial Officers, both of the United States and of the several States, shall be bound by Oath or Affirmation, to support this Constitution; but no religious Test shall ever be required as a Qualification to any Office or public Trust under the United States.

### ARTICLE VII

The Ratification of the Conventions of nine States, shall be sufficient for the Establishment of this Constitution between the States so ratifying the Same.

## AMENDMENTS

### AMENDMENT I

Congress shall make no law respecting an establishment of religion, or prohibiting the free exercise thereof; or abridging the freedom of speech, or of the press; or the right of the people peaceably to assemble, and to petition the Government for a redress of grievances.

### AMENDMENT II

A well regulated Militia, being necessary to the security of a free State, the right of the people to keep and bear Arms, shall not be infringed.

AMENDMENT III

No Soldier shall, in time of peace be quartered in any house, without the consent of the Owner, nor in time of war, but in a manner to be prescribed by law.

AMENDMENT IV

The right of the people to be secure in their persons, houses, papers, and effects, against unreasonable searches and seizures, shall not be violated, and no Warrants shall issue, but upon probable cause, supported by Oath or affirmation, and particularly describing the place to be searched, and the persons or things to be seized.

AMENDMENT V

No person shall be held to answer for a capital, or otherwise infamous crime, unless on a presentment or indictment of a Grand Jury, except in cases arising in the land or naval forces, or in the Militia, when in actual service in time of War or public danger; nor shall any person be subject for the same offence to be twice put in jeopardy of life or limb; nor shall be compelled in any criminal case to be a witness against himself, nor be deprived of life, liberty, or property, without due process of law; nor shall private property be taken for public use, without just compensation.

AMENDMENT VI

In all criminal prosecutions the accused shall enjoy the right to a speedy and public trial, by an impartial jury of the State and district wherein the crime shall have been committed, which district shall have been previously ascertained by law, and to be informed of the nature and cause of the accusation; to be confronted with the witnesses against him; to have compulsory process for obtaining witnesses in his favor, and to have the Assistance of Counsel for his defence.

AMENDMENT VII

In suits at common law, where the value in controversy shall exceed twenty dollars, the right of trial by jury shall be preserved, and no fact tried by a jury shall be otherwise re-examined in any Court of the United States, than according to the rules of the common law.

AMENDMENT VIII

Excessive bail shall not be required, nor excessive fines imposed, nor cruel and unusual punishments inflicted.

AMENDMENT IX

The enumeration in the Constitution, of certain rights, shall not be construed to to deny or disparage others retained by the people.

AMENDMENT X

The powers not delegated to the United States by the Constitution, nor prohibited by it to the States, are reserved to the States respectively, or to the people.
[The first ten Amendments were adopted in 1791.]

AMENDMENT XI

The Judicial power of the United States shall not be construed to extend to any suit in law or equity, commenced or prosecuted against one of the United States by Citizens of another State, or by Citizens or Subjects of any Foreign State. [Adopted in 1798.]

AMENDMENT XII

The Electors shall meet in their respective states, and vote by ballot for President and Vice-President, one of whom, at least, shall not be an inhabitant of the same state with themselves; they shall name in their ballots the person voted for as President, and in distinct ballots the person voted for as Vice-President, and they shall make distinct lists of all persons voted for as President, and of all persons voted for as Vice-President, and of the number of votes for each, which lists they shall sign and certify, and transmit sealed to the seat of the government of the United States, directed to the President of the Senate;—The President of the Senate shall, in the presence of the Senate and House of Representatives, open all the certificates and the votes shall then be counted;—The person having the greatest number of votes for President, shall be the President, if such number be a majority of the whole number of Electors appointed; and if no person have such majority, then from the persons having the highest numbers not exceeding three on the list of those voted for as President, the House of Representatives shall choose immediately, by ballot, the President. But in choosing the President, the votes shall be taken by states, the representation from each state having one vote; a quorum for this purpose shall consist of a member or members from two-thirds of the states, and a majority of all the states shall be necessary to a choice. And if the House of Representatives shall not choose a President whenever the right of choice shall devolve upon them, before the fourth day of March next following, then the Vice-President shall act as President, as in the case of the death or other constitutional disability of the President.—The person having the greatest number of votes as Vice-President, shall be the Vice-President, if such number be a majority of the whole number of Electors appointed, and if no person have a majority, then from the two highest numbers on the list, the Senate shall choose the Vice-President; a quorum for the purpose shall consist of two-thirds of the whole number of Senators, and a majority of the whole number shall be necessary to a choice. But no person constitutionally ineligible to the office of President shall be eligible to that of Vice-President of the United States. [Adopted in 1804.]

AMENDMENT XIII

*Section 1*     Neither slavery nor involuntary servitude, except as a punishment for crime whereof the party shall have been duly convicted, shall exist within the United States, or any place subject to their jurisdiction.

*Section 2*     Congress shall have power to enforce this article by appropriate legislation. [Adopted in 1865.]

AMENDMENT XIV

*Section 1*     All persons born or naturalized in the United States, and subject to the jurisdiction thereof, are citizens of the United States and of the State

wherein they reside. No State shall make or enforce any law which shall abridge the privileges or immunities of citizens of the United States; nor shall any State deprive any person of life, liberty, or property, without due process of law; nor deny to any person within its jurisdiction the equal protection of the laws.

*Section 2*    Representatives shall be apportioned among the several States according to their respective numbers, counting the whole number of persons in each State, excluding Indians not taxed. But when the right to vote at any election for the choice of electors for President and Vice President of the United States, Representatives in Congress, the Executive and Judicial officers of a State, or the members of the Legislature thereof, is denied to any of the male inhabitants of such State, being twenty-one years of age, and citizens of the United States, or in any way abridged, except for participation in rebellion, or other crime, the basis of representation therein shall be reduced in the proportion which the number of such male citizens shall bear to the whole number of male citizens twenty-one years of age in such State.

*Section 3*    No person shall be a Senator or Representative in Congress, or elector of President and Vice President, or hold any office, civil or military, under the United States, or under any State, who, having previously taken an oath, as a member of Congress, or as an officer of the United States, or as a member of any State legislature, or as an executive or judicial officer of any State, to support the Constitution of the United States, shall have engaged in insurrection or rebellion against the same, or given aid or comfort to the enemies thereof. But Congress may by a vote of two-thirds of each House, remove such disability.

*Section 4*    The validity of the public debt of the United States, authorized by law, including debts incurred for payment of pensions and bounties for services in suppressing insurrection or rebellion, shall not be questioned. But neither the United States nor any State shall assume or pay any debt or obligation incurred in aid of insurrection or rebellion against the United States, or any claim for the loss or emancipation of any slave; but all such debts, obligations and claims shall be held illegal and void.

*Section 5*    The Congress shall have power to enforce, by appropriate legislation, the provisions of this article. [Adopted in 1868.]

### AMENDMENT XV

*Section 1*    The right of citizens of the United States to vote shall not be denied or abridged by the United States or by any State on account of race, color, or previous condition of servitude.

*Section 2*    The Congress shall have power to enforce this article by appropriate legislation. [Adopted in 1870.]

### AMENDMENT XVI

The Congress shall have power to lay and collect taxes on incomes, from whatever source derived, without apportionment among the several States, and without regard to any census or enumeration. [Adopted in 1913.]

### AMENDMENT XVII

The Senate of the United States shall be composed of two Senators from each State, elected by the people thereof, for six years; and each Senator shall have

one vote. The electors in each State shall have the qualifications requisite for electors of the most numerous branch of the State legislatures.

When vacancies happen in the representation of any State in the Senate, the executive authority of such State shall issue writs of election to fill such vacancies: *Provided,* That the legislature of any State may empower the executive thereof to make temporary appointments until the people fill the vacancies by election as the legislature may direct.

This amendment shall not be so construed as to affect the election or term of any Senator chosen before it becomes valid as part of the Constitution. [Adopted in 1913.]

## AMENDMENT XVIII

*Section 1*    After one year from the ratification of this article the manufacture, sale, or transportation of intoxicating liquors within, the importation thereof into, or the exportation thereof from the United States and all territory subject to the jurisdiction thereof for beverage purposes is hereby prohibited.

*Section 2*    The Congress and the several States shall have concurrent power to enforce this article by appropriate legislation.

*Section 3*    This article shall be inoperative unless it shall have been ratified as an amendment to the Constitution by the legislatures of the several States, as provided in the Constitution, within seven years from the date of the submission hereof to the States by the Congress. [Adopted in 1919.]

## AMENDMENT XIX

The right of citizens of the United States to vote shall not be denied or abridged by the United States or by any State on account of sex.

Congress shall have power to enforce this article by appropriate legislation. [Adopted in 1920.]

## AMENDMENT XX

*Section 1*    The terms of the President and Vice President shall end at noon on the 20th day of January, and the terms of Senators and Representatives at noon on the 3d day of January, of the years in which such terms would have ended if this article had not been ratified; and the terms of their successors shall then begin.

*Section 2*    The Congress shall assemble at least once in every year, and such meeting shall begin at noon on the 3d day of January, unless they shall by law appoint a different day.

*Section 3*    If, at the time fixed for the beginning of the term of the President, the President elect shall have died, the Vice President elect shall become President. If a President shall not have been chosen before the time fixed for the beginning of his term, or if the President elect shall have failed to qualify, then the Vice President elect shall act as President until a President shall have qualified; and the Congress may by law provide for the case wherein neither a President elect nor a Vice President elect shall have qualified, declaring who shall then act as President, or the manner in which one who is to act shall be selected, and such person shall act accordingly until a President or Vice President shall have qualified.

*Section 4*    The Congress may by law provide for the case of the death of any of the persons from whom the House of Representatives may choose a President whenever the right of choice shall have devolved upon them, and for the case of the death of any of the persons from whom the Senate may choose a Vice President whenever the right of choice shall have devolved upon them.

*Section 5*    Sections 1 and 2 shall take effect on the 15th day of October following the ratification of this article.

*Section 6*    This article shall be inoperative unless it shall have been ratified as an amendment to the Constitution by the legislatures of three-fourths of the several States within seven years from the date of its submission. [Adopted in 1933.]

### AMENDMENT XXI

*Section 1*    The eighteenth article of amendment to the Constitution of the United States is hereby repealed.

*Section 2*    The transportation or importation into any State, Territory, or possession of the United States for delivery or use therein of intoxicating liquors, in violation of the laws thereof, is hereby prohibited.

*Section 3*    This article shall be inoperative unless it shall have been ratified as an amendment to the Constitution by conventions in the several States, as provided in the Constitution, within seven years from the date of the submission hereof to the States by the Congress. [Adopted in 1933.]

### AMENDMENT XXII

*Section 1*    No person shall be elected to the office of the President more than twice, and no person who has held the office of President, or acted as President, for more than two years of a term to which some other person was elected President shall be elected to the office of the President more than once. But this Article shall not apply to any person holding the office of President when this Article was proposed by the Congress, and shall not prevent any person who may be holding the office of President, or acting as President, during the term within which this Article becomes operative from holding the office of President or acting as President during the remainder of such term.

*Section 2*    This Article shall be inoperative unless it shall have been ratified as an amendment to the Constitution by the legislatures of three-fourths of the several States within seven years from the date of its submission to the states by the Congress. [Adopted in 1951.]

### AMENDMENT XXIII

*Section 1*    The District constituting the seat of Government of the United States shall appoint in such manner as the Congress may direct:

A number of electors of President and Vice President equal to the whole number of Senators and Representatives in Congress to which the District would be entitled if it were a State, but in no event more than the least populous State; they shall be in addition to those appointed by the States, but they shall be considered, for the purposes of the election of President and Vice President, to be electors appointed by a State; and they shall meet in the District and perform such duties as provided by the twelfth article of amendment.

*Section 2*    The Congress shall have power to enforce this article by appropriate legislation. [Adopted in 1961.]

AMENDMENT XXIV

*Section 1*    The right of citizens of the United States to vote in any primary or other election for President or Vice President, for electors for President or Vice President, or for Senator or Representative in Congress, shall not be denied or abridged by the United States or any State by reason of failure to pay any poll tax or other tax.

*Section 2*    The Congress shall have power to enforce this article by appropriate legislation. [Adopted in 1964.]

AMENDMENT XXV

*Section 1*    In case of the removal of the President from office or of his death or resignation, the Vice President shall become President.

*Section 2*    Whenever there is a vacancy in the office of the Vice President, the President shall nominate a Vice President who shall take office upon confirmation by a majority vote of both Houses of Congress.

*Section 3*    Whenever the President transmits to the President pro tempore of the Senate and the Speaker of the House of Representatives his written declaration that he is unable to discharge the powers and duties of his office, and until he transmits to them a written declaration to the contrary, such powers and duties shall be discharged by the Vice President as Acting President.

*Section 4*    Whenever the Vice President and a majority of either the principal officers of the executive departments or of such other body as Congress may by law provide, transmit to the President pro tempore of the Senate and the Speaker of the House of Representatives their written declaration that the President is unable to discharge the powers and duties of his office, the Vice President shall immediately assume the powers and duties of the office as Acting President.

Thereafter, when the President transmits to the President pro tempore of the Senate and the Speaker of the House of Representatives his written declaration that no inability exists, he shall resume the powers and duties of his office unless the Vice President and a majority of either the principal officers of the executive departments or of such other body as Congress may by law provide, transmit within four days to the President pro tempore of the Senate and the Speaker of the House of Representatives their written declaration that the President is unable to discharge the powers and duties of his office. Thereupon Congress shall decide the issue, assembling within forty-eight hours for that purpose if not in session. If the Congress, within twenty-one days after receipt of the latter written declaration, or if Congress is not in session, within twenty-one days after Congress is required to assemble, determines by two-thirds vote of both Houses that the President is unable to discharge the powers and duties of his office, the Vice President shall continue to discharge the same as Acting President; otherwise, the President shall resume the powers and duties of his office. [Adopted in 1967.]

## MEMBERS OF THE UNITED STATES SUPREME COURT 1789-1968

| *Chief Justices* | *State* | *Term* | *Appointed by* | *Life Span* |
|---|---|---|---|---|
| John Jay | N.Y. | 1789–1795 | Washington | 1745–1829 |
| John Rutledge | S.C. | 1795* | " | 1739–1800 |
| Oliver Ellsworth | Conn. | 1796–1800 | " | 1745–1807 |
| John Marshall | Va. | 1801–1835 | J. Adams | 1755–1835 |
| Roger B. Taney | Md. | 1836–1864 | Jackson | 1777–1864 |
| Salmon P. Chase | Ohio | 1864–1873 | Lincoln | 1808–1873 |
| Morrison R. Waite | Ohio | 1874–1888 | Grant | 1816–1888 |
| Melville W. Fuller | Ill. | 1888–1910 | Cleveland | 1833–1910 |
| Edward D. White | La. | 1910–1921 | Taft | 1845–1921 |
| William H. Taft | Conn. | 1921–1930 | Harding | 1857–1930 |
| Charles E. Hughes | N.Y. | 1930–1941 | Hoover | 1862–1948 |
| Harlan F. Stone | N.Y. | 1941–1946 | F. D. Roosevelt | 1872–1946 |
| Fred M. Vinson | Ky. | 1946–1953 | Truman | 1890–1953 |
| Earl Warren | Calif. | 1953– | Eisenhower | 1891– |

| *Associate Justices* | | | | |
|---|---|---|---|---|
| John Rutledge | S.C. | 1789–1791 | Washington | 1739–1800 |
| William Cushing | Mass. | 1789–1810 | " | 1732–1810 |
| James Wilson | Pa. | 1789–1798 | " | 1742–1798 |
| John Blair | Va. | 1789–1796 | " | 1732–1800 |
| James Iredell | N.C. | 1790–1799 | " | 1751–1799 |
| Thomas Johnson | Md. | 1791–1793 | " | 1732–1819 |
| William Paterson | N.J. | 1793–1806 | " | 1745–1806 |
| Samuel Chase | Md. | 1796–1811 | " | 1741–1811 |
| Bushrod Washington | Va. | 1798–1829 | J. Adams | 1762–1829 |
| Alfred Moore | N.C. | 1799–1804 | " | 1755–1810 |
| William Johnson | S.C. | 1804–1834 | Jefferson | 1771–1834 |
| Henry B. Livingston | N.Y. | 1806–1823 | " | 1757–1823 |
| Thomas Todd | Ky. | 1807–1826 | " | 1765–1826 |
| Joseph Story | Mass. | 1811–1845 | Madison | 1779–1845 |
| Gabriel Duval | Md. | 1811–1835 | " | 1752–1844 |
| Smith Thompson | N.Y. | 1823–1843 | Monroe | 1768–1843 |
| Robert Trimble | Ky. | 1826–1828 | J. Q. Adams | 1777–1828 |
| John McLean | Ohio | 1829–1861 | Jackson | 1785–1861 |
| Henry Baldwin | Pa. | 1830–1844 | " | 1780–1844 |
| James M. Wayne | Ga. | 1835–1867 | " | 1790–1867 |
| Philip P. Barbour | Va. | 1836–1841 | " | 1783–1841 |

* Unconfirmed recess appointment.

| Associate Justices | State | Term | Appointed by | Life Span |
|---|---|---|---|---|
| John Catron | Tenn. | 1837–1865 | Jackson | 1786–1865 |
| John McKinley | Ala. | 1837–1852 | Van Buren | 1780–1852 |
| Peter V. Daniel | Va. | 1841–1860 | " | 1784–1860 |
| Samuel Nelson | N.Y. | 1845–1872 | Tyler | 1792–1873 |
| Levi Woodbury | N.H. | 1846–1851 | Polk | 1789–1851 |
| Robert C. Grier | Pa. | 1846–1870 | " | 1794–1870 |
| Benjamin R. Curtis | Mass. | 1851–1857 | Fillmore | 1809–1874 |
| John A. Campbell | Ala. | 1853–1861 | Pierce | 1811–1889 |
| Nathan Clifford | Maine | 1858–1881 | Buchanan | 1803–1881 |
| Noah H. Swayne | Ohio | 1862–1881 | Lincoln | 1804–1884 |
| Samuel F. Miller | Iowa | 1862–1890 | " | 1816–1890 |
| David Davis | Ill. | 1862–1877 | " | 1815–1886 |
| Stephen J. Field | Calif. | 1863–1897 | " | 1816–1899 |
| William Strong | Pa. | 1870–1880 | Grant | 1808–1895 |
| Joseph P. Bradley | N.J. | 1870–1892 | " | 1813–1892 |
| Ward Hunt | N.Y. | 1872–1882 | " | 1810–1886 |
| John M. Harlan | Ky. | 1877–1911 | Hayes | 1833–1911 |
| William B. Woods | Ga. | 1880–1887 | " | 1824–1887 |
| Stanley Matthews | Ohio | 1881–1889 | Garfield | 1824–1889 |
| Horace Gray | Mass. | 1881–1902 | Arthur | 1828–1902 |
| Samuel Blatchford | N.Y. | 1882–1893 | " | 1820–1893 |
| Lucius Q. C. Lamar | Miss. | 1888–1893 | Cleveland | 1825–1893 |
| David J. Brewer | Kans. | 1889–1910 | B. Harrison | 1837–1910 |
| Henry B. Brown | Mich. | 1890–1906 | " | 1836–1913 |
| George Shiras, Jr. | Pa. | 1892–1903 | " | 1832–1924 |
| Howell E. Jackson | Tenn. | 1893–1895 | " | 1832–1895 |
| Edward D. White | La. | 1894–1910 | Cleveland | 1845–1921 |
| Rufus W. Peckham | N.Y. | 1895–1909 | " | 1838–1909 |
| Joseph McKenna | Calif. | 1898–1925 | McKinley | 1843–1926 |
| Oliver W. Holmes | Mass. | 1902–1932 | T. Roosevelt | 1841–1935 |
| William R. Day | Ohio | 1903–1922 | " | 1849–1923 |
| William H. Moody | Mass. | 1906–1910 | " | 1853–1917 |
| Horace H. Lurton | Tenn. | 1909–1914 | Taft | 1844–1914 |
| Charles E. Hughes | N.Y. | 1910–1916 | " | 1862–1948 |
| Willis Van Devanter | Wyo. | 1910–1937 | " | 1859–1941 |
| Joseph R. Lamar | Ga. | 1910–1916 | " | 1857–1916 |
| Mahlon Pitney | N.J. | 1912–1922 | " | 1858–1924 |
| James C. McReynolds | Tenn. | 1914–1941 | Wilson | 1862–1946 |
| Louis D. Brandeis | Mass. | 1916–1939 | " | 1856–1941 |
| John H. Clarke | Ohio | 1916–1922 | " | 1857–1945 |
| George Sutherland | Utah | 1922–1938 | Harding | 1862–1942 |
| Pierce Butler | Minn. | 1922–1939 | " | 1866–1939 |
| Edward T. Sanford | Tenn. | 1923–1930 | " | 1865–1930 |
| Harlan F. Stone | N.Y. | 1925–1941 | Coolidge | 1872–1946 |
| Owen J. Roberts | Pa. | 1930–1945 | Hoover | 1875–1955 |
| Benjamin N. Cardozo | N.Y. | 1932–1938 | " | 1870–1938 |

| *Associate Justices* | *State* | *Term* | *Appointed by* | *Life Span* |
|---|---|---|---|---|
| Hugo L. Black | Ala. | 1937– | F. D. Roosevelt | 1886– |
| Stanley F. Reed | Ky. | 1938–1957 | " | 1884– |
| Felix Frankfurter | Mass. | 1939–1962 | " | 1882–1965 |
| William O. Douglas | Conn. | 1939– | " | 1898– |
| Frank Murphy | Mich. | 1940–1949 | " | 1890–1949 |
| James F. Byrnes | S.C. | 1941–1942 | " | 1879– |
| Robert H. Jackson | N.Y. | 1941–1954 | " | 1892–1954 |
| Wiley B. Rutledge | Iowa | 1943–1949 | " | 1894–1949 |
| Harold H. Burton | Ohio | 1945–1958 | Truman | 1888–1964 |
| Tom C. Clark | Tex. | 1949–1967 | " | 1899– |
| Sherman Minton | Ind. | 1949–1956 | " | 1890–1965 |
| John M. Harlan | N.Y. | 1955– | Eisenhower | 1899– |
| William J. Brennan, Jr. | N.J. | 1956– | " | 1906– |
| Charles E. Whittaker | Mo. | 1957–1962 | " | 1901– |
| Potter Stewart | Ohio | 1958– | " | 1915– |
| Byron R. White | Colo. | 1962– | Kennedy | 1917– |
| Arthur J. Goldberg | Ill. | 1962–1965 | " | 1908– |
| Abe Fortas | Tenn. | 1965– | Johnson | 1910– |
| Thurgood Marshall | Md. | 1967– | " | 1908– |

# Index of cases

*Aaron* v. *Cooper,* 357 U.S. 566 (1958), 131, 727

*Abbate* v. *United States,* 359 U.S. 187 (1959), 647–648

*Abel* v. *United States,* 362 U.S. 217 (1960), 606

*Abington Township School District* v. *Schempp,* 374 U.S. 203 (1963), 553, 577–580

*Ableman* v. *Booth,* 21 How. (1859), 76, 155

*Abrams* v. *United States,* 250 U.S. 616 (1919), 412, 417, 511

*Adair* v. *United States,* 208 U.S. 161 (1908), 676, 680

*Adams* v. *Tanner,* 244 U.S. 590 (1917), 677, 681

*Adams Express Co.* v. *Ohio,* 165 U.S. 194 (1897), 301

*Adamson* v. *California,* 332 U.S. 46 (1947), 596–597, 620, 652

*Aday* v. *United States,* 388 U.S. 447 (1967), 499

*Adderly* v. *Florida,* 385 U.S. 39 (1967), 484–485

*Adkins* v. *Children's Hospital,* 261 U.S. 525 (1923), 673–675, 679

*Adler* v. *Board of Education of New York City,* 342 U.S. 485 (1952), 540–541

*Aero Mayflower Transit Co.* v. *Georgia Public Service Cmsn.,* 295 U.S. 285 (1935), 303

*Aetna Life Insurance Co.* v. *Haworth,* 300 U.S. 227 (1937), 116, 168

*Afroyim* v. *Rusk,* 387 U.S. 253 (1967), 769

*Aguilar* v. *Texas,* 378 U.S. 108 (1964), 611

*Akins* v. *Texas,* 325 U.S. 398 (1945), 637

*Alabama* v. *Arizona,* 291 U.S. 286 (1934), 110

——— v. *King & Boozer,* 314 U.S. 1 (1941), 245

*Alabama Power Co.* v. *Ickes,* 302 U.S. 464 (1938), 172

*Alaska Packers Assn.* v. *Industrial Accident Cmsn.,* 294 U.S. 532 (1935), 105

*Alberts* v. *California,* 354 U.S. 476 (1957), 493, 496

*Albertson* v. *Subversive Activities Control Board,* 382 U.S. 70 (1965), 535, 547, 618

*Allen* v. *Regents of the University System of Georgia,* 304 U.S. 439 (1938), 243

*Allen-Bradley Local* v. *Wisconsin Employment Relations Board,* 315 U.S. 740 (1942), 292

*Allgeyer* v. *Louisiana,* 165 U.S. 578 (1897), 668

*Amalgamated Assn.* v. *Wisconsin Employment Relations Board,* 340 U.S. 383 (1951), 291

*American Committee for Protection of Foreign Born* v. *Subversive Activities Control Board,* 380 U.S. 503 (1965), 536

*American Communications Assn.* v. *Douds,* 339 U.S. 382 (1950), 426–427, 538, 546

*American Federation of Labor* v. *American Sash Co.,* 335 U.S. 538 (1949), 683

v. *Watson,* 312 U.S. 246 (1941), 154

*American Insurance Co.* v. *Canter,* 1 Pet. 511 (1828), 93, 133

*American Oil Co.* v. *P. G. Neill,* 380 U.S. 451 (1965), 299

*American Power and Light Co.* v. *SEC,* 329 U.S. 90 (1946), 277

*American Steel Foundries* v. *Tri-City Central Trades Council,* 257 U.S. 184 (1921), 460

*Anastaplo, In re,* 366 U.S. 82 (1961), 122, 545, 687

*Anders* v. *California,* 386 U.S. 738 (1967), 642

*Anderson* v. *Dunn,* 6 Wheat. 204 (1821), 217

*Andrada, In re,* 380 U.S. 953 (1965), 651

*Aptheker* v. *Secretary of State,* 378 U.S. 500 (1964), 369, 535, 537, 547

*Arizona* v. *California,* 283 U.S. 423 (1931), 275

*Arizona Employers' Liability Cases,* 250 U.S. 400 (1919), 672

*Armstrong* v. *Manzo,* 380 U.S. 545 (1965), 592

*Armstrong* v. *United States,* 13 Wall. 154 (1872), 349

*Arver* v. *United States (Selective Draft Law Cases),* 245 U.S. 366 (1918), 374, 565

*Ashcraft* v. *Tennessee,* 322 U.S. 143 (1944), 624

*Ashton* v. *Kentucky,* 384 U.S. 195 (1966), 514

*Ashwander* v. *Tennessee Valley Authority,* 297 U.S. 288 (1936), 168–169, 174–175, 375

*Associated Press* v. *National Labor Relations Board,* 301 U.S. 103 (1937), 434

v. *United States,* 326 U.S. 1 (1945), 434

v. *Walker,* 388 U.S. 130 (1967), 517

*Atherton* v. *Atherton,* 181 U.S. 155 (1901), 102

*Austin* v. *Tennessee,* 179 U.S. 343 (1900), 259, 665

*Avery* v. *Georgia,* 345 U.S. 559 (1952), 637

*Bachtel* v. *Wilson,* 204 U.S. 36 (1907), 683

*Backus (A.) Jr. & Sons* v. *Fort Street Union Depot Co.,* 169 U.S. 557 (1898), 700

*Badders* v. *United States,* 240 U.S. 391 (1916), 650

*Baggett* v. *Bullitt,* 377 U.S. 360 (1964), 537

*Bailey* v. *Alabama,* 219 U.S. 219 (1911), 404

*Bailey* v. *Drexel Furniture Company,* 259 U.S. 20 (1922), 35, 238–239

*Bailey* v. *Richardson,* 341 U.S. 918 (1951), 543

*Bakelite Corp., Ex parte,* 279 U.S. 438 (1929), 133, 135

*Baker* v. *Carr,* 369 U.S. 186 (1962), 57, 84–86, 90, 177, 185

*Bakery and Pastry Drivers Local* v. *Wohl,* 315 U.S. 769 (1942), 454

*Baldwin* v. *Missouri,* 281 U.S. 586 (1930), 704

*Ballard* v. *United States,* 329 U.S. 187 (1946), 557, 563, 635

Bantam Books Inc. v. Sullivan, 372 U.S. 58 (1963), 500, 503–504

Barbier v. Connolly, 113 U.S. 27 (1885), 682

Barenblatt v. United States, 360 U.S. 109 (1959), 222–226, 229, 427, 546

Barr v. Matteo, 360 U.S. 564 (1959), 515

Barron v. Baltimore, 7 Pet. 243 (1833), 399–400, 406, 408–409

Barrows v. Jackson, 346 U.S. 249 (1953), 172, 717

Barsky v. Board of Regents, 347 U.S. 442 (1954), 687

Barsky v. United States, 167 F. 2d 241 (1948), 218

Bartkus v. Illinois, 359 U.S. 121 (1959), 648

Bates v. City of Little Rock, 361 U.S. 516 (1960), 229, 549

Baumgartner v. United States, 322 U.S. 665 (1944), 511, 764

Beauharnais v. Illinois, 343 U.S. 250 (1952), 518–519

Beck v. Ohio, 379 U.S. 89 (1964), 611

Becker v. Philco Corp., 389 U.S. 979 (1967), 518

Beckley Newspapers Corp. v. Hanks, 389 U.S. 81 (1967), 514

Bedford Cut Stone Co. v. Journeymen Stone Cutters' Assn., 274 U.S. 37 (1927), 266

Beilan v. Board of Public Education, School District of Philadelphia, 357 U.S. 399 (1958), 542

Bell v. Maryland, 378 U.S. 226 (1964), 482–483, 487, 735–737

Bell v. School Board of Gary, 324 F. 2d 209 (1963), cert. den. 377 U.S. 924 (1964), 730

Bell's Gap R. Co. v. Pennsylvania, 134 U.S. 232 (1890), 705–706

Benanti v. United States, 355 U.S. 96 (1957), 608, 613

Berea College v. Kentucky, 211 U.S. 45 (1908), 721

Berenyi v. District Director, 385 U.S. 630 (1967), 779

Berger v. New York, 388 U.S. 41 (1967), 615

Berman v. Parker, 348 U.S. 26 (1954), 668, 698

Best and Co. v. Maxwell, 311 U.S. 454 (1940), 298

Betts v. Brady, 316 U.S. 455 (1942), 627–629, 653

Bibb v. Navajo Freight Lines, 359 U.S. 520 (1959), 290

Biddle v. Perovich, 274 U.S. 480 (1927), 350

Bishop v. United States, 350 U.S. 961 (1956), 645

Black v. United States, 385 U.S. 26 (1966), 614

Black & White Taxicab Co. v. Brown & Yellow Taxicab Co., 276 U.S. 518 (1928), 148

Blackstone v. Miller, 188 U.S. 189 (1903), 703–704

Block v. Hirsh, 256 U.S. 135 (1921), 375

Bloom v. Illinois, 386 U.S. 1003 (1967), 120

Board of Education v. Allen, 228 N.E. 2d 791, 309 U.S. 1031 (1968), 572

Board of Public Works of Maryland v. Horace Mann League, 385 U.S. 97 (1966), 579

Bob-Lo Excursion Co. v. Michigan, 333 U.S. 28 (1948), 288, 719

Bolling v. Sharpe, 347 U.S. 497 (1954), 723–724

Bollman, Ex parte, 4 Cr. 75 (1807), 143, 600

Bond v. Floyd, 385 U.S. 116 (1966), 92–93

A Book Named "John Cleland's Memoirs of a Woman of Pleasure" v. Attorney General of Massachusetts, 383 U.S. 413 (1966), 496, 499, 501–502

Borden Co. v. Borella, 325 U.S. 679 (1945), 273

Boston Beer Co. v. Massachusetts, 97 U.S. 25 (1878), 665, 696

Bouie v. Columbia, 378 U.S. 347 (1964), 640

Boutilier v. Immigration and Naturalization Service, 387 U.S. 118 (1967), 776

Bowles v. Willingham, 321 U.S. 503 (1944), 202, 375

Boyd v. United States, 116 U.S. 616 (1886), 619

Boynton v. Virginia, 364 U.S. 454 (1960), 482

Braden v. United States, 365 U.S. 431 (1961), 226

*Bradfield* v. *Roberts,* 175 U.S. 291 (1899), 569

*Bradford Electric Light Co.* v. *Clapper,* 286 U.S. 145 (1932), 105

*Bradley* v. *Fisher,* 13 Wall. 335 (1871), 139

*Braunfeld* v. *Brown,* 366 U.S. 599 (1961), 560

*Breard* v. *Alexandria,* 341 U.S. 622 (1951), 471

*Breedlove* v. *Suttles,* 302 U.S. 277 (1937), 749, 754

*Breithaupt* v. *Abram,* 352 U.S. 432 (1957), 610, 622, 687

*Bridges* v. *California,* 314 U.S. 252 (1941), 423, 443–444

*Bridges* v. *Wixon,* 326 U.S. 135 (1945), 526, 547, 762, 774, 778

*Brig Aurora, The,* 7 Cr. 382 (1813), 200

*Briggs* v. *Elliott,* 347 U.S. 483 (1954), 723

*Brinegar* v. *United States,* 338 U.S. 160 (1949), 603, 607

*Brookhart* v. *Janis,* 384 U.S. 1 (1966), 640

*Brooks* v. *United States,* 267 U.S. 432 (1925), 263

*Brooks' Estate, In re,* 205 N.E. 2d 435 (1965), 557

*Brotherhood of Locomotive Engineers* v. *Chicago, R. I. & P. R. Co.,* 382 U.S. 423 (1966), 289, 292

*Brotherhood of Railroad Trainmen* v. *Virginia ex rel. Virginia State Bar,* 377 U.S. 1 (1964), 550

*Brown* v. *Allen,* 344 U.S. 443 (1953), 155–156, 625, 637

*Brown* v. *Board of Education,* 347 U.S. 483 (1954), 349 U.S. 294 (1955), 57, 76, 117, 723–730

*Brown* v. *Louisiana,* 383 U.S. 131 (1966), 483–485, 487–488

*Brown* v. *Maryland,* 12 Wheat. 419 (1827), 258, 281, 294

*Brown* v. *Mississippi,* 297 U.S. 278 (1936), 623

*Brown* v. *United States,* 356 U.S. 148 (1958), 618

*Brown* v. *United States,* 359 U.S. 41 (1959), 118

*Brown* v. *Walker,* 161 U.S. 591 (1896), 349, 617–619

*Bruno* v. *United States,* 308 U.S. 287 (1939), 617

*Brush* v. *Commissioner,* 300 U.S. 352 (1937), 243–244

*Brushaber* v. *Union Pacific R. R.,* 240 U.S. 1 (1916), 233, 235

*Bryant* v. *Zimmerman,* 278 U.S. 63 (1928), 547, 550

*Buchanan* v. *Warley,* 245 U.S. 60 (1917), 715

*Buck* v. *Bell,* 274 U.S. 200 (1927), 662–664, 680, 683, 685

*Budd* v. *California,* 385 U.S. 909 (1966), 651

*Building Service Employees Union* v. *Gazzam,* 339 U.S. 532 (1950), 462

*Bumper* v. *North Carolina,* 389 U.S. 1034 (1968), 651

*Bunger* v. *Green River,* 300 U.S. 638 (1937), 470

*Bunting* v. *Oregon,* 243 U.S. 426 (1917), 673

*Burbridge* v. *California,* 386 U.S. 1030 (1967), 483

*Burdick* v. *United States,* 236 U.S. 79 (1915), 349–350

*Burford* v. *Sun Oil Co.,* 319 U.S. 315 (1943), 154

*Burnet* v. *Coronado Oil and Gas Co.,* 285 U.S. 393 (1932), 242–243

*Burns* v. *Ohio,* 360 U.S. 252 (1959), 642

*Burns* v. *Richardson,* 384 U.S. 73 (1966), 91

*Burns Baking Co.* v. *Bryan,* 264 U.S. 504 (1924), 677

*Burstyn* v. *Wilson,* 343 U.S. 495 (1952), 505–506

*Burton* v. *Wilmington Parking Authority,* 365 U.S. 715 (1961), 734

*Burton's Lessee* v. *Williams,* 3 Wheat. 529 (1818), 108

*Bush* v. *Orleans Parish,* 138 F. Supp. 336 (1956), 726

*Bush* v. *Orleans School Board,* 364 U.S. 500 (1960), 77

*Bute* v. *Illinois,* 333 U.S. 640 (1948), 628

*Butler* v. *Michigan,* 352 U.S. 380 (1957), 492

*Butler* v. *Perry,* 240 U.S. 328 (1916), 404


*Caddo Parish School Board* v. *United States,* 386 U.S. 1001 (1967), 729

*Cafeteria & Restaurant Workers Union* v. *McElroy,* 367 U.S. 886 (1961), 544

*Calder* v. *Bull,* 3 Dall. 386 (1798), 602, 692

*California* v. *Buzard,* 382 U.S. 386 (1966), 244

    v. *Southern Pacific Co.,* 157 U.S. 229 (1895), 130

    v. *Thompson,* 313 U.S. 109 (1941), 288

*Camara* v. *Municipal Court,* 387 U.S. 523 (1967), 612

*Cameron* v. *Johnson,* 381 U.S. 741 (1965), 468–469

*Caminetti* v. *United States,* 242 U.S. 470 (1917), 255

*Canizio* v. *New York,* 327 U.S. 82 (1946), 628

*Cantwell* v. *Connecticut,* 310 U.S. 296 (1940), 477–478, 553, 555–556

*Capitol Greyhound Lines* v. *Brice,* 339 U.S. 542 (1950), 303

*Cardona* v. *Power,* 384 U.S. 672 (1966), 749

*Carlesi* v. *New York,* 233 U.S. 51 (1914), 349

*Carlson* v. *Landon,* 342 U.S. 524 (1952), 650, 778

*Carmichael* v. *Southern Coal & Coke Co.,* 301 U.S. 495 (1937), 702

*Carpenters and Joiners Union* v. *Ritter's Cafe,* 315 U.S. 722 (1942), 461

*Carrington* v. *Rash,* 380 U.S. 89 (1965), 747

*Carroll* v. *Lanza,* 349 U.S. 408 (1955), 105

*Carroll* v. *United States,* 267 U.S. 132 (1925), 607

*Carter* v. *Carter Coal Co.,* 298 U.S. 238 (1936), 168, 201, 268–269

*Cary* v. *Curtis,* 3 How. 236 (1845), 142

*Cassell* v. *Texas,* 339 U.S. 282 (1950), 637

*Chamberlain* v. *Dade County Board of Public Instruction,* 377 U.S. 402 (1964), 578

*Champion* v. *Ames,* 188 U.S. 321 (1903), 260, 262–263

*Champlin Refining Co.* v. *Corporation Commission,* 286 U.S. 210 (1932), 257

*Chaplinsky* v. *New Hampshire,* 315 U.S. 568 (1942), 426, 428, 475, 490, 509

*Chapman, In re,* 166 U.S. 661 (1897), 191, 215, 647

*Chapman* v. *California,* 386 U.S. 18 (1967), 621

*Chapman* v. *Scott,* 10 F. 2d 156 (1925), 350

*Chapman* v. *United States,* 365 U.S. 610 (1961), 606

*Charles River Bridge* v. *Warren Bridge,* 11 Pet. 420 (1837), 693–694

*Chastleton Corp.* v. *Sinclair,* 264 U.S. 543 (1924), 375

*Cheff* v. *Schnackenberg,* 384 U.S. 373 (1966), 120, 634

*Chicago & Southern Air Lines* v. *Waterman S.S. Co.,* 333 U.S. 103 (1948), 176

*Chicago Board of Trade* v. *Olsen,* 262 U.S. 1 (1923), 264, 266

*Child Labor Tax Case* (see *Bailey* v. *Drexel Furniture Company*)

*Chin Yow* v. *United States,* 208 U.S. 8 (1908), 772

*Chinese Exclusion Case* (*Chae Chan Ping* v. *United States*), 130 U.S. 581 (1889), 770, 775

*Chirac* v. *Chirac,* 2 Wheat. 259 (1817), 761

*Chisholm* v. *Georgia,* 2 Dall. 419 (1793), 34, 52, 146

*Christoffel* v. *United States,* 338 U.S. 84 (1949), 212, 228

*Church of Jesus Christ of Latter-Day Saints* v. *United States* (*Mormon Church* v. *United States*), 136 U.S. 1 (1890), 563

*Cicenia* v. *LaGay,* 357 U.S. 504 (1958), 625, 629

*Cichos* v. *Indiana,* 385 U.S. 76 (1966), 648

*Citizen's Saving and Loan Assn.* v. *Topeka,* 87 U.S. 655 (1875), 701–702

*City of Birmingham* v. *Monk,* 341 U.S. 940 (1951), 715

*City of Cleveland* v. *United States,* 323 U.S. 329 (1945), 698

*City of Detroit* v. *Murray Corp. of America,* 355 U.S. 489 (1958), 245

*City of El Paso* v. *Simmons,* 379 U.S. 497 (1965), 697

*City of Greenwood* v. *Peacock,* 384 U.S. 808 (1966), 486, 742–743

*City of Richmond* v. *Deans,* 281 U.S. 704 (1930), 715

*Ciucci* v. *Illinois,* 356 U.S. 571 (1958), 648

*Civil Rights Cases,* 109 U.S. 3 (1883), 483, 712–713, 715, 717, 732, 734–736, 741

*Clark* v. *Nash,* 198 U.S. 361 (1905), 698

*Clark Distilling Co.* v. *Western Maryland R. Co.,* 242 U.S. 311 (1917), 293

*Clarke* v. *Deckebach,* 274 U.S. 392 (1927), 714

*Clearfield Trust Co.* v. *United States,* 318 U.S. 363 (1943), 150

*Cochran* v. *Louisiana State Board of Education,* 281 U.S. 370 (1930), 570, 702

*Cockrill* v. *California,* 268 U.S. 258 (1925), 714

*Coe* v. *Coe,* 334 U.S. 378 (1948), 103

*Coe* v. *Errol,* 116 U.S. 517 (1886), 257–258, 297

*Cohen* v. *Hurley,* 366 U.S. 117 (1961), 620–621, 687

*Cohens* v. *Virginia,* 6 Wheat. 264 (1821), 74, 152

*Cole* v. *Young,* 351 U.S. 536 (1956), 544

*Colegrove* v. *Green,* 328 U.S. 549 (1946), 85, 177, 184–185

*Coleman* v. *Miller,* 307 U.S. 433 (1939), 36, 40, 171–172, 176

*Collector* v. *Day,* 11 Wall. 113 (1871), 241, 244

*Collins* v. *Hardyman,* 341 U.S. 651 (1951), 742

*Colorado Anti-Discrimination Commission* v. *Continental Air Lines,* 372 U.S. 714 (1963), 290

*Commissioner of Internal Revenue* v. *Shamberg's Estate,* 323 U.S. 792 (1945), 244

*Commonwealth* v. *Davis,* 162 Mass. 510 (1895), 452

*Communist Party* v. *Subversive Activities Control Board,* 351 U.S. 115 (1956), 534; 367 U.S. 1 (1961), 369, 534–535, 602

— v. *United States,* 331 F. 2d 807, cert. den. 377 U.S. 968 (1963), 535, 547

*Connally* v. *General Construction Co.,* 269 U.S. 385 (1926), 640

*Connecticut General Life Ins. Co.* v. *Johnson,* 303 U.S. 77 (1938), 669

*Connolly* v. *Union Sewer Pipe Co.,* 184 U.S. 540 (1902), 683

*Consolidated Edison Co.* v. *National Labor Relations Board,* 305 U.S. 197 (1938), 271

*Cook* v. *Marshall County,* 196 U.S. 261 (1905), 259

*Cooley* v. *Board of Wardens of the Port of Philadelphia,* 12 How. 299 (1852), 283, 285–286

*Cooper* v. *Aaron,* 358 U.S. 1 (1958), 58, 77, 127, 727

*Cooper* v. *California,* 386 U.S. 58 (1967), 608

*Cooper* v. *Pate,* 378 U.S. 546 (1963), 564

*Coppage* v. *Kansas,* 236 U.S. 1 (1915), 676, 680

*Corfield* v. *Coryell,* 6 Fed. Cases 3230 (1823), 99, 400–401, 406, 409

*Coronado Coal Co.* v. *United Mine Workers,* 268 U.S. 295 (1925), 266

*Corrigan* v. *Buckley,* 271 U.S. 323 (1926), 716

*Cotting* v. *Godard,* 183 U.S. 79 (1901), 671

*Covington Bridge Co.* v. *Kentucky,* 154 U.S. 204 (1894), 255

*Cox* v. *Louisiana,* 379 U.S. 536 (1965), 454–455, 459, 464–465, 467–470, 481, 487–488

*Cox* v. *New Hampshire,* 312 U.S. 569 (1941), 465–466

*Coyle* v. *Smith,* 221 U.S. 559 (1911), 78

*Craig* v. *Harney,* 331 U.S. 367 (1947), 444

*Craig* v. *Hecht,* 263 U.S. 255 (1923), 443

*Cramer* v. *United States,* 325 U.S. 1 (1945), 599–600

*Cramp* v. *Board of Public Instruction,* 368 U.S. 278 (1961), 537

*Crandall* v. *Nevada,* 6 Wall. 35 (1868), 297

*Crane* v. *Campbell,* 245 U.S. 304 (1917), 665

*Crawford* v. *United States,* 212 U.S. 183 (1909), 636

*Cree* v. *Goldstein,* 385 U.S. 816 (1966), 581

*Crescent Cotton Oil Co.* v. *Mississippi,* 257 U.S. 129 (1921), 683

*Crider* v. *Zurich Ins. Co.,* 380 U.S. 39 (1965), 105

*Crooker* v. *California,* 357 U.S. 433 (1958), 625, 629

*Crutcher* v. *Kentucky,* 141 U.S. 47 (1891), 300

*Cumming* v. *Richmond County Board of Education,* 175 U.S. 528 (1899), 720

*Cummings* v. *Missouri,* 4 Wall. 277 (1867), 601, 603

*Curcio* v. *United States,* 354 U.S. 118 (1957), 620

*Currin* v. *Wallace,* 306 U.S. 1 (1939), 201

*Curry* v. *McCanless,* 307 U.S. 357 (1939), 703–704

*Curtis Publishing Co.* v. *Butts,* 388 U.S. 130 (1967), 517

*Cusack* v. *Chicago,* 242 U.S. 526 (1917), 667


*Danbury Hatters Case* (1908) (see *Loewe* v. *Lawlor*)

*Darr* v. *Burford,* 339 U.S. 200 (1950), 155–156

*Dartmouth College* v. *Woodward,* 4 Wheat. 518 (1819), 52, 403–404, 690, 692–693

*Davidson* v. *New Orleans,* 96 U.S. 97 (1878), 659, 671

*Davis* v. *Beason,* 133 U.S. 333 (1890), 563

*Davis* v. *County School Board of Prince Edward County,* 347 U.S. 483 (1954), 723

*Davis* v. *Massachusetts,* 167 U.S. 43 (1897), 452

*Davis* v. *North Carolina,* 384 U.S. 737 (1966), 632

*Davis* v. *Schnell,* 336 U.S. 933 (1949), 750

*Davis V. United States,* 160 U.S. 469 (1895), 645

*Day-Brite Lighting* v. *Missouri,* 342 U.S. 421 (1952), 680–681, 686–687

*Dayton-Goose Creek R. R. Co.* v. *United States,* 263 U.S. 456 (1924), 260

*Deal* v. *Cincinnati Board of Education,* 369 F. 2d 55 (1966), 730

*Dean Milk Co.* v. *City of Madison,* 340 U.S. 349 (1951), 290

*Debs, In re,* 158 U.S. 564 (1895), 81, 235, 337

*Debs* v. *United States,* 249 U.S. 211 (1919), 416–417

*DeGregory* v. *Attorney General of New Hampshire,* 383 U.S. 825 (1966), 229

*DeGroot* v. *United States,* 5 Wall. 419 (1867), 134

*DeJonge* v. *Oregon,* 299 U.S. 353 (1937), 524–526

*DeJoseph* v. *Connecticut,* 220 A. 2d 752, cert. den. 385 U.S. 982 (1966), 632

*DeKalb County Community School District* v. *Despain,* 390 U.S. 906 (1968), 578

*Delaware* v. *New York,* 385 U.S. 895 (1966), 147, 313

*DeLima* v. *Bidwell,* 182 U.S. 1 (1901), 93

*DeMeerleer* v. *Michigan,* 329 U.S. 663 (1947), 628

*Dennis* v. *United States,* 339 U.S. 162 (1950), 636

*Dennis* v. *United States,* 341 U.S. 494 (1951), 56, 118, 167, 415, 528–531, 536, 546

*Dennis* v. *United States,* 384 U.S. 855 (1966), 175

*Department of Employment* v. *United States,* 385 U.S. 355 (1966), 244

*Department of Revenue* v. *James B. Beam Distilling Co.,* 377 U.S. 341 (1964), 296

*Deutch* v. *United States,* 367 U.S. 456 (1961), 227

*DeVeau* v. *Braisted,* 363 U.S. 144 (1960), 292, 603

*Dillon* v. *Gloss,* 256 U.S. 368 (1921), 36

*Dinis* v. *Volpe,* 389 U.S. 570 (1968), 91

*Directors' Guild of America* v. *Hurwitz,* 385 U.S. 971 (1966), 539

*DiSanto* v. *Pennsylvania,* 273 U.S. 34 (1927), 288

*Dixie Ohio Express* v. *State Revenue Cmsn.,* 306 U.S. 72 (1939), 303

*Dobbins* v. *Erie County,* 16 Pet. 435 (1842), 241, 244

*Dombrowski* v. *Eastland,* 387 U.S. 82 (1967), 192

*Dombrowski* v. *Pfister,* 380 U.S. 479 (1965), 154–155, 230, 536

*Dominion Hotel* v. *Arizona,* 249 U.S. 265 (1919), 683

*Donaldson* v. *Read Magazine,* 333 U.S. 178 (1948), 439

*Dorchy* v. *Kansas,* 264 U.S. 286 (1924), 677

*Doremus* v. *Board of Education*, 342 U.S. 429 (1952), 173, 575, 578

*Doubleday* v. *New York*, 335 U.S. 848 (1948), 491

*Douglas* v. *Alabama*, 380 U.S. 415 (1965), 640

*Douglas* v. *California*, 372 U.S. 353 (1963), 642

*Douglas* v. *City of Jeanette*, 319 U.S. 157 (1943), 562

*Douglas* v. *Green*, 363 U.S. 192 (1960), 642

*Downes* v. *Bidwell*, 182 U.S. 244 (1901), 93

*Downs* v. *Board of Education of Kansas City, Kansas*, 336 F. 2d 988, cert. den. 380 U.S. 914 (1965), 730

*Draper* v. *United States*, 358 U.S. 307 (1959), 605

*Draper* v. *Washington*, 372 U.S. 487 (1963), 642

*Dred Scott* v. *Sandford*, 19 How. 393 (1857), 53, 105, 165, 402–403, 406, 408–409, 657, 759–760

*DuBois Clubs of America* v. *Clark*, 389 U.S. 309 (1967), 536

*Dugan* v. *United States*, 3 Wheat. 172 (1818), 145

*Duncan* v. *Kahanamoku*, 327 U.S. 304 (1946), 381–382

*Dunne* v. *United States*, 138 F. 2d 862 (1943), 527

*Durham* v. *United States*, 214 F. 2d 862 (1954), 645

*Durousseau* v. *United States*, 6 Cr. 307 (1810), 130

*Dusch* v. *Davis*, 387 U.S. 112 (1967), 91

*East New York Savings Bank* v. *Hahn*, 326 U.S. 230 (1945), 697

*Educational Films Corp.* v. *Ward*, 282 U.S. 379 (1931), 243

*Edwards* v. *California*, 314 U.S. 160 (1941), 290

*Edwards* v. *South Carolina*, 372 U.S. 229 (1963), 464, 475, 480–481, 483–484, 487

*Edwards* v. *United States*, 286 U.S. 482 (1932), 333

*Eisler* v. *United States*, 338 U.S. 189 (1949), 230

*Eisner* v. *Macomber*, 252 U.S. 189 (1920), 235–236

*Electric Bond and Share Co.* v. *S.E.C.*, 303 U.S. 419 (1938), 256

*Elfbrandt* v. *Russell*, 384 U.S. 11 (1966), 537, 541

*Elk* v. *Wilkins*, 112 U.S. 94 (1884), 760

*Elkins* v. *United States*, 364 U.S. 206 (1960), 608, 611, 622

*Empresa Siderurgica* v. *Merced County*, 337 U.S. 154 (1949), 296

*Emspak* v. *United States*, 349 U.S. 190 (1955), 219, 617

*Endo, Ex parte*, 323 U.S. 283 (1944), 391

*Engel* v. *Vitale*, 370 U.S. 421 (1962), 57, 173, 575–579

*Entsminger* v. *Iowa*, 386 U.S. 748 (1967), 642

*Epperson* v. *Arkansas*, 88 S. Ct. 1024 (1968), 473

*Erie Railroad* v. *Tompkins*, 304 U.S. 64 (1938), 149–150

*Escobedo* v. *Illinois*, 378 U.S. 478 (1964), 625, 630–632

*Essgee Co.* v. *United States*, 262 U.S. 151 (1923), 620

*Estes* v. *Texas*, 381 U.S. 532 (1965), 446–447

*Estin* v. *Estin*, 334 U.S. 541 (1948), 102, 104

*Eubanks* v. *Louisiana*, 356 U.S. 584 (1958), 637

*Euclid* v. *Ambler Realty Co.*, 272 U.S. 365 (1926), 666–668

*Evans* v. *Gore*, 253 U.S. 245 (1920), 139

*Evans* v. *Newton*, 382 U.S. 296 (1966), 733

*Everson* v. *Board of Education of Ewing Township*, 330 U.S. 1 (1947), 553, 570–572, 580

*Exchange, The* v. *McFaddon*, 7 Cr. 116 (1812), 150

*Fairfax's Devisee* v. *Hunter's Lessee*, 7 Cr. 603 (1813), 73

*"Fanny Hill" Case, The* (see *A Book Named "John Cleland's Memoirs of a Woman of Pleasure"* v. *Attorney General of Massachusetts*)

*Farmers' Loan and Trust Co.* v. *Minnesota*, 280 U.S. 204 (1930), 703–704

*Fay* v. *New York*, 332 U.S. 261 (1947), 638

*Fay* v. *Noia*, 372 U.S. 391 (1963), 155–156

*Federal Baseball Club* v. *National League of Professional Baseball Clubs*, 259 U.S. 200 (1922), 277

*Federal Power Commission* v. *Hope Natural Gas Co.*, 320 U.S. 591 (1944), 680

*Federal Radio Commission* v. *General Electric Co.*, 281 U.S. 464 (1930), 134
v. *Nelson Bros.*, 289 U.S. 266 (1933), 199, 256

*Federal Trade Commission* v. *American Tobacco Co.*, 264 U.S. 298 (1924), 604

*Feiner* v. *New York*, 340 U.S. 315 (1951), 479–480

*Feldman* v. *United States*, 322 U.S. 487 (1944), 620, 622

*Fellowship of Humanity* v. *Alameda County*, 315 P. 2d 395 (1957), 565

*Felt & Tarrant Mfg. Co.* v. *Gallagher*, 306 U.S. 62 (1939), 299

*Ferguson* v. *Skrupa*, 372 U.S. 726 (1963), 681

*Fertilizing Co.* v. *Hyde Park*, 97 U.S. 659 (1878), 694

*Fidelity Union Trust Co.* v. *Field*, 311 U.S. 169 (1940), 150

*Field* v. *Clark*, 143 U.S. 649 (1892), 200, 212

*Fikes* v. *Alabama*, 352 U.S. 191 (1957), 624

*Finch Co.* v. *McKittrick*, 305 U.S. 395 (1939), 293

*First National Bank* v. *Yankton County*, 101 U.S. 129 (1880), 93

*First National Bank of Boston* v. *Maine*, 284 U.S. 312 (1932), 704

*First Unitarian Church of Los Angeles* v. *County of Los Angeles*, 357 U.S. 545 (1958), 567

*Flast* v. *Gardner*, 389 U.S. 895 (1967), 174

*Flaxer* v. *United States*, 358 U.S. 147 (1958), 228

*Flemming* v. *Nestor*, 363 U.S. 603 (1960), 546, 603

*Fletcher* v. *Peck*, 6 Cr. 87 (1810), 690–692

*Flint* v. *Stone Tracy Co.*, 220 U.S. 107 (1911), 235

*Florida* v. *Mellon*, 273 U.S. 12 (1927), 236

*Fong Foo* v. *United States*, 369 U.S. 141 (1962), 646

*Fong Yue Ting* v. *United States*, 149 U.S. 698 (1893), 774–776

*Ford Motor Co.* v. *Beauchamp*, 308 U.S. 331 (1939), 301

*Forman* v. *United States*, 361 U.S. 416 (1960), 646

*Fort* v. *Miami*, 389 U.S. 918 (1967), 500

*Fortson* v. *Dorsey*, 379 U.S. 433 (1965), 91

*Fortson* v. *Morris*, 385 U.S. 231 (1966), 92

*Foster* v. *Neilson*, 2 Pet. 253 (1829), 353

*Fowler* v. *Rhode Island*, 345 U.S. 67 (1953), 563–564

*Fox Film Corp.* v. *Doyal*, 286 U.S. 123 (1932), 243

*Frank* v. *Mangum*, 237 U.S. 309 (1915), 642–643

*Frank* v. *Maryland*, 359 U.S. 360 (1959), 612

*Frazier* v. *United States*, 335 U.S. 497 (1948), 636

*Freedman* v. *Maryland*, 380 U.S. 51 (1965), 507

*Freeman* v. *Hewit*, 329 U.S. 249 (1946), 300, 304

*Frick* v. *Pennsylvania*, 268 U.S. 473 (1925), 703

*Frohwerk* v. *United States*, 249 U.S. 204 (1919), 416

*Frost* v. *Corporation Cmsn.*, 278 U.S. 515 (1929), 677

*Gallagher* v. *Crown Kosher Super Market*, 366 U.S. 617 (1961), 560

*Gallegos* v. *Nebraska*, 342 U.S. 55 (1951), 625

*Galvan* v. *Press*, 347 U.S. 522 (1954), 777

*Garber* v. *Kansas*, 389 U.S. 51 (1967), 561

*Garland, Ex parte*, 4 Wall. 333 (1867), 122, 349, 601, 603

*Garner* v. *Board of Public Works*, 341 U.S. 716 (1951), 537, 546

Garner v. Louisiana, 368 U.S. 157 (1961), 481–483, 641, 735

Garner v. Teamsters Union, 346 U.S. 485 (1953), 291–292

Garrison v. Louisiana, 379 U.S. 64 (1964), 510, 514

Garrity v. New Jersey, 385 U.S. 493 (1967), 622

Gart v. Cole, 263 F. 2d 244; cert. den. 359 U.S. 978 (1959), 581

Gastelum-Quinones v. Kennedy, 374 U.S. 469 (1963), 777

Gault, In re, 387 U.S. 1 (1967), 644

Gayle v. Browder, 352 U.S. 903 (1956), 720, 728

Gebhart v. Belton, 347 U.S. 483 (1954), 723

Geer v. Connecticut, 161 U.S. 519 (1896), 99

Gelling v. Texas, 343 U.S. 960 (1952), 506

General Motors Corp. v. Washington, 377 U.S. 436 (1964), 302

General Oil Co. v. Crain, 209 U.S. 211 (1908), 297

General Trading Co. v. State Tax Cmsn., 322 U.S. 335 (1944), 299

Genesee Chief, The v. Fitzhugh, 12 How. 443 (1852), 144

Geofroy v. Riggs, 133 U.S. 258 (1890), 364

George v. United States, 382 U.S. 1010 (1966), 557

Georgia v. Pennsylvania R. Co., 324 U.S. 439 (1945), 147

v. Rachel, 384 U.S. 780 (1966), 742

v. Stanton, 6 Wall. 50 (1868), 176

Gerende v. Board of Supervisors of Elections, 341 U.S. 56 (1951), 537–538

German Alliance Insurance Co. v. Lewis, 233 U.S. 389 (1914), 671

Giaccio v. Pennsylvania, 382 U.S. 399 (1966), 642

Gibbons v. Ogden, 9 Wheat. 1 (1824), 52, 253–255, 257, 263, 279, 281–285

Giboney v. Empire Storage and Ice Co., 336 U.S. 490 (1949), 461–463

Gibson v. Florida Legislative Investigation Committee, 372 U.S. 539 (1963), 228, 546–548, 686

Gideon v. Wainwright, 372 U.S. 335 (1963), 56, 628–629, 653

Gilbert v. California, 388 U.S. 263 (1967), 632

Giles v. Maryland, 386 U.S. 66 (1967), 641

Gillespie v. Oklahoma, 257 U.S. 501 (1922), 242–243

Ginsberg v. New York, 389 U.S. 965 (1968), 500

Ginzburg v. United States, 383 U.S. 463 (1966), 497–499

Girard College Trusteeship, In re, 138 A. 2d 844; cert. den. 357 U.S. 570 (1958), 733

Girouard v. United States, 328 U.S. 61 (1946), 761

Gitlow v. New York, 268 U.S. 652 (1925), 415, 417–419, 426, 523–524, 553, 595, 652

Glasser v. United States, 315 U.S. 60 (1942), 635

Glidden Co. v. Zdanok, 370 U.S. 530 (1962), 131, 134

Gloucester Ferry Co. v. Pennsylvania, 114 U.S. 196 (1885), 297, 303

Goesart v. Cleary, 335 U.S. 464 (1948), 684

Gojack v. United States, 384 U.S. 702 (1966), 228

Gold v. DiCarlo, 380 U.S. 520 (1965), 679

Gold Clause Cases, 294 U.S. 240, 330 (1935), 249–251

Goldman v. United States, 316 U.S. 129 (1942), 613–616

Gomillion v. Lightfoot, 364 U.S. 339 (1960), 185

Gong Lum v. Rice, 275 U.S. 78 (1927), 721

Gooch v. United States, 297 U.S. 124 (1936), 263

Gordon v. United States, 117 U.S. 697 (decided 1864, reported 1886), 134

Gore v. United States, 357 U.S. 386 (1958), 647

Gouled v. United States, 255 U.S. 298 (1921), 607

Governor of Georgia v. Madrazo, 1 Pet. 110 (1828), 146

Grand River Dam Authority v. Grand-Hydro, 335 U.S. 359 (1948), 699

Grapeshot, The v. Wallerstein, 9 Wall. 129 (1870), 378

Graves v. O'Keefe, 306 U.S. 466 (1939), 244

*Gray* v. *Sanders,* 372 U.S. 368 (1963), 86–87, 92

*Great A. & P. Tea Co.* v. *Grosjean,* 301 U.S. 412 (1937), 706

*Green* v. *Frazier,* 253 U.S. 233 (1920), 702

*Green* v. *New Kent County School Board,* 389 U.S. 1003 (1967), 729

*Green* v. *New York City Board of Elections,* 389 U.S. 1048 (1968), 748

*Green* v. *United States,* 355 U.S. 184 (1957), 646; 356 U.S. 165 (1958), 119

*Greene* v. *McElroy,* 360 U.S. 474 (1959), 544

*Griffin* v. *California,* 380 U.S. 609 (1965), 621

*Griffin* v. *County Board of Prince Edward County,* 337 U.S. 218 (1964), 727

*Griffin* v. *Illinois,* 351 U.S. 12 (1956), 642

*Griffin* v. *Maryland,* 378 U.S. 130 (1964), 735

*Griggs* v. *Allegheny County,* 369 U.S. 84 (1962), 699

*Grisham* v. *Hagan,* 361 U.S. 278 (1960), 386

*Griswold* v. *Connecticut,* 381 U.S. 479 (1965), 686–687

*Grosjean* v. *American Press Company,* 297 U.S. 233 (1936), 433–434

*Grossman, Ex parte,* 267 U.S. 87 (1925), 350

*Grosso* v. *United States,* 390 U.S. 62 (1968), 240

*Grovey* v. *Townsend,* 295 U.S. 45 (1935), 751–752

*Gruber, Ex parte,* 269 U.S. 302 (1925), 150

*Grunewald* v. *United States,* 353 U.S. 391 (1957), 617

*Guaranty Trust Co.* v. *New York,* 326 U.S. 99 (1945), 149

*Guinn* v. *United States,* 238 U.S. 347 (1915), 748–749

*Guss* v. *Utah Labor Board,* 353 U.S. 1 (1957), 271, 291

*Gwin, White & Prince* v. *Henneford,* 305 U.S. 434 (1939), 302

*Haddock* v. *Haddock,* 201 U.S. 562 (1906), 102–103

*Hague* v. *C.I.O.,* 307 U.S. 496 (1939), 453, 464–465

*Hairston* v. *Danville & W. R. Co.,* 208 U.S. 598 (1908), 698

*Hale* v. *Henkel,* 201 U.S. 43 (1906), 618, 620

*Haley* v. *Ohio,* 332 U.S. 596 (1948), 624

*Hall* v. *DeCuir,* 95 U.S. 485 (1878), 718–719

*Hall* v. *St. Helena Parish School Board,* 197 F. Supp. 649, 287 F. 2d 376, cert. den. 368 U.S. 830 (1961), 727

*Hamilton* v. *Board of Regents,* 293 U.S. 245 (1934), 553, 665

*Hamilton* v. *Kentucky Distilleries and Warehouse Co.,* 251 U.S. 146 (1919), 375

*Hamm* v. *City of Rock Hill,* 379 U.S. 306 (1964), 483, 486–487

*Hammer* v. *Dagenhart,* 247 U.S. 251 (1918), 35, 72, 73, 239, 261–262, 272

*J. W. Hampton, Jr. & Co.* v. *United States,* 276 U.S. 394 (1928), 198, 200, 237

*Hannegan* v. *Esquire,* 327 U.S. 146 (1946), 441

*Hannibal Bridge Co.* v. *United States,* 221 U.S. 194 (1911), 699

*Hanover Fire Insurance Co.* v. *Harding,* 272 U.S. 494 (1926), 706

*Hans* v. *Louisiana,* 134 U.S. 1 (1890), 146

*Hans Rees' Sons* v. *North Carolina,* 283 U.S. 123 (1931), 302

*Harisiades* v. *Shaughnessy,* 342 U.S. 580 (1952), 776

*Harman* v. *Forssenius,* 380 U.S. 528 (1965), 749, 753

*Harmon* v. *Brucker,* 355 U.S. 579 (1958), 544

*Harmon* v. *Tyler,* 273 U.S. 668 (1927), 715

*Harper* v. *Virginia State Board of Elections,* 383 U.S. 663 (1966), 754

*Harris* v. *City of New York,* 357 U.S. 907 (1958), 581

*Harris* v. *South Carolina,* 338 U.S. 68 (1949), 624

*Harris* v. *United States,* 331 U.S. 145 (1947), 605

*Harris* v. *United States,* 382 U.S. 162 (1965), 118

*Harrison* v. *Day,* 106 S. E. 2d 636 (1959), 727

*Hartford Steam Boiler Inspection and Ins. Co.* v. *Harrison,* 301 U.S. 459 (1937), 683

*Haupt* v. *United States,* 330 U.S. 631 (1947), 600

*Hawk, Ex parte,* 321 U.S. 114 (1944), 155

*Hawke* v. *Smith,* 253 U.S. 221 (1920), 38, 40

*Haynes* v. *United States,* 390 U.S. 85 (1968), 240

*Head* v. *New Mexico Board of Examiners,* 374 U.S. 424 (1963), 289

*Head Money Cases,* 112 U.S. 580 (1884), 143, 238, 362

*Heart of Atlanta Motel* v. *United States,* 379 U.S. 241 (1964), 278, 405, 736

*Heim* v. *McCall,* 239 U.S. 175 (1915), 714

*Helvering* v. *Davis,* 301 U.S. 619 (1937), 248

*Helvering* v. *Gerhardt,* 304 U.S. 405 (1938), 243

*Helvering* v. *Mountain Producers Corp.,* 303 U.S. 376 (1938), 243

*Henderson* v. *United States,* 339 U.S. 816 (1950), 720

*Hendrick* v. *Maryland,* 235 U.S. 610 (1915), 303

*Henneford* v. *Silas Mason Co.,* 300 U.S. 577 (1937), 298

*Henry* v. *Collins,* 380 U.S. 356 (1965), 514

*Henry* v. *United States,* 361 U.S. 98 (1959), 605

*Hepburn* v. *Griswold,* 8 Wall. 603 (1870), 249, 657–658

*Hernandez* v. *Texas,* 347 U.S. 475 (1954), 638

*Herndon* v. *Lowry,* 301 U.S. 242 (1937), 421, 524–526

*Hill* v. *Florida,* 325 U.S. 538 (1945), 291

*Hill* v. *Texas,* 316 U.S. 400 (1942), 637

*Hines* v. *Davidowitz,* 312 U.S. 52 (1941), 774

*Hipolite Egg Co.* v. *United States,* 220 U.S. 45 (1911), 261

*Hirabayashi* v. *United States,* 320 U.S. 81 (1943), 390

*Hirota* v. *MacArthur,* 338 U.S. 197 (1948), 387

*Hoag* v. *New Jersey,* 356 U.S. 464 (1958), 647

*Hobson* v. *Hansen,* 269 F. Supp. 401 (1967), 730

*Hoffa* v. *United States,* 385 U.S. 293 (1966), 607

*Hoke* v. *United States,* 227 U.S. 308 (1913), 261

*Holden* v. *Hardy,* 169 U.S. 366 (1898), 670, 672

*Holding* v. *Blankenship,* 387 U.S. 94 (1967), 503

*Hollingsworth* v. *Virginia,* 3 Dall. 378 (1798), 38

*Holmby Productions* v. *Vaughn,* 350 U.S. 870 (1955), 506

*Holmes* v. *City of Atlanta,* 350 U.S. 879 (1955), 728

*Home Building and Loan Assn.* v. *Blaisdell,* 290 U.S. 398 (1934), 696–697

*Honda* v. *Clark,* 386 U.S. 484 (1967), 392

*H. P. Hood & Sons* v. *United States,* 307 U.S. 588 (1939), 201, 274

*Hooven & Allison Co.* v. *Evatt,* 324 U.S. 652 (1945), 295

*Hostetter* v. *Idlewild Bon Voyage Liquor Corp.,* 377 U.S. 324 (1964), 296

*Howe Machine Co.* v. *Gage,* 100 U.S. 676 (1880), 298

*Hughes* v. *Superior Court of California,* 339 U.S. 460 (1950), 462–463

*Humphrey* v. *Smith,* 336 U.S. 695 (1949), 384

*Humphrey's Executor* v. *United States,* 295 U.S. 602 (1935), 346–347

*Huntington* v. *Attrill,* 146 U.S. 657 (1892), 105

*Hurd* v. *Hodge,* 334 U.S. 24 (1948), 716

*Huron Portland Cement Co.* v. *Detroit,* 362 U.S. 440 (1960), 292

*Hurtado* v. *California,* 110 U.S. 516 (1884), 569–590, 592–594, 633

*Hutcheson* v. *United States,* 369 U.S. 599 (1962), 227

*Hylton* v. *United States,* 3 Dall. 171 (1796), 234

*Illinois Central Railroad* v. *Illinois,* 146 U.S. 387 (1892), 694

*Immigration and Naturalization Service* v. *Errico,* 385 U.S. 214 (1966), 779

*Indian Motorcycle Co.* v. *United States,* 283 U.S. 570 (1931), 242

*Indianapolis Brewing Co.* v. *Liquor Control Cmsn.*, 305 U.S. 391 (1939), 293

*Ingels* v. *Morf*, 300 U.S. 290 (1937), 303

*Insular Cases, The*, 182 U.S. 1, 222, 244 (1901), 93–94

*International Assn. of Machinists* v. *Gonzales*, 356 U.S. 617 (1958), 291–292

*International Brotherhood of Teamsters* v. *Hanke*, 339 U.S. 470 (1950), 462–463

*International Brotherhood of Teamsters, Local 695* v. *Vogt*, 354 U.S. 284 (1957), 463

*International Harvester Co.* v. *Evatt*, 329 U.S. 416 (1947), 301

*International Shoe Co.* v. *Washington*, 326 U.S. 310 (1945), 591

*International Textbook Co.* v. *Pigg*, 217 U.S. 91 (1910), 256, 300

*International Union* v. *O'Brien*, 339 U.S. 454 (1950), 291

*International Union* v. *Russell*, 356 U.S. 634 (1958), 292

*Interstate Circuit, Inc.* v. *Dallas*, 387 U.S. 903 (1967), 507

*Interestate Commerce Cmsn.* v. *Brimson*, 154 U.S. 447 (1894), 260

*Interstate Commerce Cmsn.* v. *Illinois Central R. R.*, 215 U.S. 452 (1910), 199

*Interstate Transit* v. *Lindsey*, 283 U.S. 183 (1931), 303

*Irvin* v. *Dowd*, 359 U.S. 394 (1959), 156

*Irvin* v. *Dowd*, 366 U.S. 717 (1961), 445

*Irvine* v. *California*, 347 U.S. 128 (1954), 610

*Jackson, Ex parte*, 96 U.S. 727 (1878), 436–438

*Jackson* v. *Denno*, 378 U.S. 368 (1964), 624

*Jacobellis* v. *Ohio*, 378 U.S. 184 (1964), 495–497, 500–502, 507

*Jacobson* v. *Massachusetts*, 197 U.S. 11 (1905), 557, 661–664, 680

*James* v. *Dravo Construction Co.*, 302 U.S. 134 (1937), 245

*James* v. *Gilmore*, 389 U.S. 572 (1968), 538

*Jamison* v. *Texas*, 318 U.S. 413 (1943), 437, 453

*Japanese Immigrant Case* (*Yamataya* v. *Fisher*), 189 U.S. 86 (1903), 777

*Jecker* v. *Montgomery*, 13 How. 498 (1851), 377

*Jenison, In re*, 125 N.W. 2d 588 (1963), 561

*Johnson* v. *Eisentrager*, 339 U.S. 763 (1950), 388

*Johnson* v. *New Jersey*, 384 U.S. 719 (1966), 632

*Johnson* v. *United States*, 333 U.S. 10 (1948), 607

*Johnson* v. *Virginia*, 373 U.S. 61 (1963), 728

*Johnson* v. *Zerbst*, 304 U.S. 458 (1938), 625

*Joint Anti-Fascist Refugee Committee* v. *McGrath*, 341 U.S. 123 (1951), 543, 587, 669

*Jones* v. *Alfred H. Mayer Co.*, 389 U.S. 968 (1968), 407, 738

*Jones* v. *City of Portland*, 245 U.S. 217 (1917), 702

*Jones* v. *Opelika*, 316 U.S. 584 (1942), 422, 555, 559, 561

*Jones* v. *United States*, 137 U.S. 202 (1890), 93

*Jones* v. *United States*, 357 U.S. 493 (1958), 606

*Jones* v. *United States*, 362 U.S. 257 (1960), 604

*Jordan* v. *DeGeorge*, 341 U.S. 223 (1951), 778

*Joseph* v. *Carter & Weekes Steveforing Co.*, 330 U.S. 422 (1947), 302

*Joseph E. Seagram & Sons, Inc.* v. *Hostetter*, 384 U.S. 35 (1966), 291

*Juilliard* v. *Greenman*, 110 U.S. 421 (1884), 249

*Julian Messner* v. *Spahn*, 387 U.S. 239 (1967), 435

*Kansas* v. *Colorado*, 206 U.S. 46 (1907), 110, 197

*Katz* v. *Tyler*, 386 U.S. 942 (1967), 374

*Katz* v. *United States*, 389 U.S. 347 (1967), 615–616

*Katzenbach* v. *McClung*, 379 U.S. 294 (1964), 278

*Katzenbach* v. *Morgan*, 384 U.S. 641 (1966), 757

*Kawakita* v. *United States*, 343 U.S. 717 (1952), 600

*Kedroff* v. *St. Nicholas Cathedral or Russian Orthodox Church*, 344 U.S. 94 (1952), 566–567

*Keifer & Keifer* v. *Reconstruction Finance Corp.*, 306 U.S. 375 (1939), 145

*Kendall* v. *Stokes*, 12 Pet. 524 (1838), 206–207

*Kennecott Copper Corp.* v. *State Tax Cmsn.*, 327 U.S. 573 (1946), 146

*Kennedy* v. *Mendoza-Martinez*, 372 U.S. 144 (1963), 640, 768

*Kent* v. *Dulles*, 357 U.S. 116 (1958), 203, 368

*Kent* v. *United States*, 383 U.S. 541 (1966), 644

*Kentucky* v. *Dennison*, 24 How. 66 (1861), 106–107

*Kentucky Taxicab Case* (see *Black & White Taxicab Co.* v. *Brown & Yellow Taxicab Co.*)

*Kentucky Whip and Collar Co.* v. *Illinois Central R. Co.*, 299 U.S. 334 (1937), 294

*Ker* v. *California*, 374 U.S. 23 (1963), 611, 621, 653

*Kessler* v. *Strecker*, 307 U.S. 22 (1939), 771

*Keyishian* v. *Board of Regents*, 385 U.S. 589 (1967), 541, 546–547

*Kidd* v. *Pearson*, 128 U.S. 1 (1888), 257

*Kilbourn* v. *Thompson*, 103 U.S. 168 (1881), 192, 215, 220, 226, 231

*Kilgarlin* v. *Hill*, 386 U.S. 120 (1967), 91

*King* v. *Order of United Commercial Travelers*, 333 U.S. 153 (1948), 150

*Kingsley Books, Inc.* v. *Brown*, 354 U.S. 436 (1957), 504–505

*Kingsley International Pictures* v. *Regents*, 360 U.S. 684 (1959), 494–495, 500, 502, 506

*Kinsella* v. *Krueger*, 351 U.S. 470 (1956), 386

*Kinsella* v. *Singleton*, 361 U.S. 234 (1960), 386

*Kirk* v. *Gong*, 389 U.S. 574 (1968), 91

*Kirschbaum* v. *Walling*, 316 U.S. 517 (1942), 273

*Klapprott* v. *United States*, 335 U.S. 601 (1949), 764

*Klopfer* v. *North Carolina*, 386 U.S. 213 (1967), 639

*Knapp* v. *Schweitzer*, 357 U.S. 371 (1958), 620

*Knauer* v. *United States*, 328 U.S. 654 (1946), 764–765

*Knight* v. *Board of Regents*, 390 U.S. 36 (1968), 538

*Knowlton* v. *Moore*, 178 U.S. 41 (1900), 235–236

*Knox* v. *Lee* (*Legal Tender Cases*), 12 Wall. 457 (1871), 249

*Knoxville Water Co.* v. *Knoxville*, 200 U.S. 22 (1906), 694

*Konigsberg* v. *State Bar of California*, 353 U.S. 252 (1957), 122, 544

*Konigsberg* v. *State Bar of California*, 366 U.S. 36 (1961), 122, 425, 545–546, 687

*Korematsu* v. *United States*, 323 U.S. 214 (1944), 391

*Kotch* v. *Board of River Port Pilot Commissioners*, 330 U.S. 552 (1947), 683

*Kovacs* v. *Cooper*, 336 U.S. 77 (1949), 422–423, 458–459

*Krebs* v. *Ashbrook*, 275 F. Supp. 111 (1967), 230

*Kremen* v. *United States*, 353 U.S. 346 (1957), 605

*Kreshik* v. *St. Nicholas Cathedral*, 363 U.S. 190 (1960), 567

*Kunz* v. *New York*, 340 U.S. 290 (1951), 452, 457, 465, 485, 555

*Lamont* v. *Postmaster General*, 381 U.S. 301 (1965), 439, 442

*Landau* v. *Fording*, 389 U.S. 889 (1967), 499

*Lane* v. *Brown*, 372 U.S. 477 (1963), 642

*Lane* v. *Wilson*, 307 U.S. 268 (1939), 748

*Lanzetta* v. *New Jersey*, 306 U.S. 451 (1939), 640

*Lassiter* v. *Northampton County Board of Elections*, 360 U.S. 45 (1959), 749

*Lauf* v. *E. G. Shinner and Co.*, 303 U.S. 315 (1938), 121

*Laura, The*, 114 U.S. 411 (1885), 349

*Leach* v. *Carlile*, 258 U.S. 138 (1922), 439

*Lee* v. *Washington*, 389 U.S. 967 (1968), 728

*Leeper* v. *Charlotte Park Cmsn.*, 350 U.S. 983 (1956), 717

*Legal Tender Cases* (*Knox* v. *Lee* and *Parker* v. *Davis*), 12 Wall. 457 (1871), 249–250

*Leisy* v. *Hardin,* 135 U.S. 100 (1890), 293

*Leloup* v. *Port of Mobile,* 127 U.S. 640 (1888), 300

*Lem Moon Sing* v. *United States,* 158 U.S. 538 (1895), 771

*Leng May Ma* v. *Barber,* 357 U.S. 185 (1958), 772

*Lerner* v. *Casey,* 357 U.S. 468 (1958), 542

*Leser* v. *Garnett,* 258 U.S. 130 (1922), 36, 40

*Levitt, Ex parte,* 302 U.S. 633 (1937), 189

*Levy* v. *Corcoran,* 387 U.S. 915 (1967), 383

*Lewis* v. *United States,* 385 U.S. 206 (1966), 607

*Lewis Publishing Co.* v. *Morgan,* 229 U.S. 228 (1913), 440

*Leyra* v. *Denno,* 347 U.S. 556 (1954), 624

*License Cases,* 5 How. 504 (1847), 255, 282–283, 286, 296

*License Tax Cases,* 5 Wall. 462 (1867), 233

*Lichter* v. *United States,* 334 U.S. 742 (1948), 202, 374

*Liggett Co.* v. *Baldridge,* 278 U.S. 105 (1928), 661

   v. *Lee,* 288 U.S. 517 (1933), 706

*Lincoln Federal Labor Union* v. *Northwestern Iron & Metal Co.,* 335 U.S. 525 (1949), 680

*Lincoln National Life Insurance Co.* v. *Read,* 325 U.S. 673 (1945), 706

*Linkletter* v. *Walker,* 381 U.S. 618 (1965), 612, 621, 629

*Linn* v. *United Plant Guard Workers,* 383 U.S. 53 (1966), 517

*Lisenba* v. *California,* 314 U.S. 219 (1941), 624

*Local 167 I.B.T.* v. *United States,* 291 U.S. 293 (1934), 267

*Local Union No. 10* v. *Graham,* 345 U.S. 192 (1953), 462

*Lochner* v. *New York,* 198 U.S. 45 (1905), 54, 420, 672–673, 679

*Lockerty* v. *Phillips,* 319 U.S. 182 (1943), 121

*Loewe* v. *Lawlor,* 208 U.S. 274 (1908), 266

*Lombard* v. *Louisiana,* 373 U.S. 267 (1963), 482, 735

*Long* v. *Rockwood,* 277 U.S. 142 (1928), 242–243

*Lopez* v. *United States,* 373 U.S. 427 (1963), 614

*Lorain Journal Co.* v. *United States,* 342 U.S. 143 (1951), 434

*Lottery Case, The* (see *Champion* v. *Ames*)

*Louisiana* v. *McAdoo,* 234 U.S. 627 (1914), 145

*Louisiana ex rel. Francis* v. *Resweber,* 329 U.S. 459 (1947), 647

*Louisiana Financial Assistance Committee* v. *Poindexter,* 389 U.S. 571 (1968), 727

*Louisville Joint Stock Land Bank Co.* v. *Radford,* 295 U.S. 555 (1935), 697

*Louisville, New Orleans & Texas R. Co.* v. *Mississippi,* 133 U.S. 587 (1890), 718

*Lovell* v. *Griffin,* 303 U.S. 444 (1938), 436, 554

*Loving* v. *Virginia,* 388 U.S. 1 (1967), 732

*Lucas* v. *Rhodes,* 389 U.S. 212 (1967), 91

*Ludecke* v. *Watkins,* 335 U.S. 160 (1948), 375, 377, 778

*Luther* v. *Borden,* 7 How. 1 (1849), 82–83, 85, 176, 379

*Lynch* v. *United States,* 189 F. 2d 476 (1951), 733–734

*McCabe* v. *Atchison, Topeka & Santa Fe,* 235 U.S. 151 (1914), 719

*Macallen* v. *Massachusetts,* 279 U.S. 620 (1929), 242–243

*McCardle, Ex parte,* 7 Wall. 506 (1869), 130–131

*McCarroll* v. *Dixie Greyhound Lines,* 309 U.S. 176 (1940), 304

*McCollum* v. *Board of Education,* 333 U.S. 203 (1948), 572–575

*McConnell, In re,* 370 U.S. 230 (1962), 118

*McCray* v. *Illinois,* 386 U.S. 300 (1967), 603

*McCray* v. *United States,* 195 U.S. 27 (1904), 238

*McCulloch* v. *Maryland,* 4 Wheat. 316 (1819), 50, 52, 71–72, 197, 233, 240–241, 248, 374

*MacDougall* v. *Green,* 335 U.S. 281 (1948), 185

McElroy v. Guagliardo, 361 U.S. 281 (1960), 386

McGoldrick v. Berwind-White Coal Mining Co., 309 U.S. 33 (1940), 299

McGrain v. Daugherty, 273 U.S. 135 (1927), 216, 220, 231

MacKenzie v. Hare, 239 U.S. 299 (1915), 766

McKim v. Voorhies, 7 Cr. 279 (1812), 154

McLaughlin v. Florida, 379 U.S. 184 (1964), 731–732

McLaurin v. Oklahoma State Regents, 339 U.S. 637 (1950), 722

McLeod v. Dilworth Co., 322 U.S. 327 (1944), 299

McNabb v. United States, 318 U.S. 332 (1943), 598, 623

Madsen v. Kinsella, 343 U.S. 341 (1952), 377

Magoun v. Illinois Trust and Savings Bank, 170 U.S. 283 (1898), 705

Mahler v. Eby, 264 U.S. 32 (1924), 602

Mahon v. Justice, 127 U.S. 700 (1888), 107

Maine v. Grand Trunk Railway Co., 142 U.S. 217 (1891), 300–302

Maisenberg v. United States, 356 U.S. 670 (1958), 532, 764

Malinski v. New York, 324 U.S. 401 (1945), 624

Mallory v. United States, 354 U.S. 449 (1957), 623

Malloy v. Hogan, 378 U.S. 1 (1964), 621, 653

Manigault v. Springs, 199 U.S. 473 (1905), 696

Manual Enterprises, Inc. v. Day, 370 U.S. 478 (1962), 439, 495–496, 502

Mapp v. Ohio, 367 U.S. 643 (1961), 608, 611–612, 621, 653

Marbury v. Madison, 1 Cr. 137 (1803), 45, 48, 52, 121, 129, 163–165

Marchetti v. United States, 390 U.S. 39 (1968), 240, 620

Marcus v. Search Warrant, 367 U.S. 717 (1961), 504–505

Marino v. Ragen, 332 U.S. 561 (1947), 628

Marks v. Esperdy, 377 U.S. 214 (1964), 767

Marsh v. Alabama, 326 U.S. 501 (1946), 471

Martin v. City of Struthers, 319 U.S. 141 (1943), 471

Martin v. Hunter's Lessee, 1 Wheat, 304 (1816), 74, 152

Martin v. Mott, 12 Wheat. 19 (1827), 379

Martino v. Michigan Window Cleaning Co., 327 U.S. 173 (1946), 273

Maryland v. Baltimore Radio Show, 338 U.S. 912 (1950), 132, 445

Massachusetts v. Mellon, 262 U.S. 447 (1923), 147, 170, 173–174, 246, 579
    v. Missouri, 308 U.S. 1 (1939), 110

Masses Publishing Co. v. Patten, 244 Fed. 535 (1917), 415, 441

Massiah v. United States, 377 U.S. 201 (1964), 630

Maxwell v. Bishop, 385 U.S. 650 (1967), 651

Maxwell v. Dow, 176 U.S. 581 (1900), 593–594, 636

Mayflower Farms v. Ten Eyck, 297 U.S. 266 (1936), 683

Mayor of Baltimore v. Dawson, 220 F. 2d 386, 350 U.S. 877 (1955), 728

Mempa v. Rhay, 389 U.S. 128 (1967), 633

Memphis Natural Gas Co. v. Stone, 335 U.S. 80 (1948), 301

Merryman, Ex parte, 17 Fed. Cases 9487 (1861), 380

Metcalf v. Mitchell, 269 U.S. 514 (1926), 242

Meyer v. Nebraska, 262 U.S. 390 (1923), 418, 420

Michigan-Wisconsin Pipe Line Co. v. Calvert, 347 U.S. 157 (1954), 302

Miles v. Graham, 268 U.S. 501 (1925), 139

Miles v. Illinois Central Railroad, 315 U.S. 698 (1942), 99

Milk Wagon Drivers Union v. Meadowmoor Dairies, 312 U.S. 287 (1941), 461

Miller v. Pate, 386 U.S. 1 (1967), 641

Miller v. United States, 357 U.S. 301 (1958), 606

Miller v. United States, 389 U.S. 930 (1967), 464

Miller Bros. Co. v. Maryland, 347 U.S. 340 (1954), 299

Milligan, Ex parte, 4 Wall. 2 (1866), 130, 380–381, 387, 634

Mills v. Alabama, 384 U.S. 214 (1966), 434–435

Mills v. Duryee, 7 Cr. 481 (1813), 101

Milwaukee Publishing Co. v. Burleson, 255 U.S. 407 (1921), 441, 453

Minersville School District v. Gobitis, 310 U.S. 586 (1940), 558

Minnesota v. Wisconsin, 252 U.S. 273 (1920), 110

Minor v. Happersett, 21 Wall. 162 (1875), 746–747

Miranda v. Arizona, 384 U.S. 436 (1966), 383, 622, 625, 631–632

Mishkin v. New York, 383 U.S. 502 (1966), 498, 500

Mississippi v. Johnson, 4 Wall. 475 (1867), 175

Missouri v. Holland, 252 U.S. 416 (1920), 50, 363, 365

Missouri ex rel. Gaines v. Canada, 305 U.S. 337 (1938), 722

Mitchell v. United States, 313 U.S. 80 (1941), 719

Mitchell v. United States, 386 U.S. 972 (1967), 374

M'Naghten's Case, 8 Eng. Rep. 718 (H. L. 1843), 645

Monaco v. Mississippi, 292 U.S. 313 (1934), 150

Monongahela Nav. Co. v. United States, 148 U.S. 312 (1893), 698

Monroe v. Pape, 365 U.S. 176 (1961), 612, 742

Montgomery Ward and Co. v. United States, 326 U.S. 690 (1945), 389

Mooney v. Holohan, 294 U.S. 103 (1935), 641

Moore v. Dempsey, 261 U.S. 86 (1923), 643

Moore v. Michigan, 355 U.S. 155 (1957), 628

Mora v. McNamara, 389 U.S. 934 (1967), 203, 374

Morehead v. Tipaldo, 298 U.S. 587 (1936), 675, 679

Morey v. Doud, 354 U.S. 457 (1957), 684

Morgan v. Devine, 237 U.S. 632 (1915), 646

Morgan v. Tennessee Valley Authority, 312 U.S. 701 (1941), 347

Morgan v. Virginia, 328 U.S. 373 (1946), 290, 719

Morris v. Rockwell, 368 U.S. 913 (1961), 457

Motor Coach Employees v. Missouri, 374 U.S. 74 (1963), 291

Mouton v. International Shoe Co., 379 U.S. 902 (1964), 304

Mugler v. Kansas, 123 U.S. 623 (1887), 660, 664–665

Mulford v. Smith, 307 U.S. 38 (1939), 247, 274

Mulkey v. Reitman, 413 F. 2d 825 (1966), 737

Mullane v. Central Hanover Bank and Trust Co., 339 U.S. 306 (1950), 592

Mullaney v. Anderson, 342 U.S. 415 (1952), 100

Muller v. Dows, 94 U.S. 444 (1877), 147

Muller v. Oregon, 208 U.S. 412 (1908), 670, 674

Munn v. Illinois, 94 U.S. 113 (1877), 54, 658–659, 664, 670–671, 676, 680

Murchison, In re, 349 U.S. 133 (1955), 642

Murdock v. Pennsylvania, 319 U.S. 105 (1943), 422, 555, 559–561, 563–564

Murphy v. Waterfront Commission of New York Harbor, 378 U.S. 52 (1964), 622

Murray v. Goldstein, 385 U.S. 816 (1966), 581

Murray's Lessee v. Hoboken Land and Improvement Co., 18 How. 272 (1856), 404, 588–589, 593, 656

Muskrat v. United States, 219 U.S. 346 (1911), 169

Mutual Film Corp. v. Industrial Commission of Ohio, 236 U.S. 230 (1915), 505

Mutual Life Insurance Co. v. Johnson, 293 U.S. 335 (1934), 149

Myers v. United States, 272 U.S. 52 (1926), 334, 344–346


Naim v. Naim, 87 S.E. 2d 749 (1955), 731

Nardone v. United States, 302 U.S. 379 (1937), 613

Nardone v. United States, 308 U.S. 338 (1939), 613

NAACP v. Alabama, 357 U.S. 449 (1958), 229, 521, 548–549, 686; 377 U.S. 288 (1964), 549

*NAACP* v. *Button,* 371 U.S. 415 (1963), 454, 549

*National Bellas Hess, Inc.* v. *Illinois,* 386 U.S. 753 (1967), 299

*National Labor Relations Board* v. *Fainblatt,* 306 U.S. 601 (1939), 271

v. *Friedman-Harry Marks Clothing Co.,* 301 U.S. 58 (1937), 271

v. *Fruehauf Trailer Co.,* 301 U.S. 49 (1937), 271

v. *Jones and Laughlin Corp.,* 301 U.S. 1 (1937), 269–271

v. *Reliance Fuel Oil Corp.,* 371 U.S. 224 (1963), 271

*National Prohibition Cases,* 253 U.S. 350 (1920), 36

*Neagle, In re,* 135 U.S. 1 (1890), 336–337

*Near* v. *Minnesota,* 283 U.S. 697 (1931), 432–433, 490, 503–504, 509

*Nebbia* v. *New York,* 291 U.S. 502 (1934), 678–679

*Nelson* v. *County of Los Angeles,* 362 U.S. 1 (1960), 542

*Nelson* v. *Montgomery Ward & Co.,* 312 U.S. 373 (1941), 299

*Nelson* v. *Sears, Roebuck & Co.,* 312 U.S. 359 (1941), 299

*New Hampshire* v. *Louisiana,* 108 U.S. 76 (1883), 109, 146

*New Jersey* v. *Wilson,* 7 Cr. 164 (1812), 690, 692, 694

*New Orleans City Park Improvement Assn.* v. *Detiege,* 252 F. 2d 122 (1958), 728

*New State Ice Co.* v. *Liebman,* 285 U.S. 262 (1932), 677

*New York* v. *New Jersey,* 256 U.S. 296 (1921), 110

v. *O'Neill,* 359 U.S. 1 (1959), 100

v. *United States,* 326 U.S. 572 (1946), 244

*New York ex rel. Rogers* v. *Graves,* 299 U.S. 401 (1937), 243

*New York Central Ry. Co.* v. *White,* 243 U.S. 188 (1917), 671, 696

*New York Times Co.* v. *Sullivan,* 376 U.S. 254 (1964), 414, 435, 511–514, 516–517, 591

*Newberry* v. *United States,* 256 U.S. 232 (1921), 750–752

*Ng Fung Ho* v. *White,* 259 U.S. 276 (1922), 777

*Niemotko* v. *Maryland,* 340 U.S. 268 (1951), 456, 465, 474, 554

*Nippert* v. *City of Richmond,* 327 U.S. 416 (1946), 298

*Nishimura Ekiu* v. *United States,* 142 U.S. 651 (1892), 771

*Niukkanen* v. *McAlexander,* 362 U.S. 390 (1960), 777

*Nixon* v. *Condon,* 286 U.S. 73 (1932), 751

*Nixon* v. *Herndon,* 273 U.S. 536 (1927), 751

*Norman* v. *Baltimore and Ohio Railroad Co.,* 294 U.S. 240 (1935), 250

*Norris* v. *Alabama,* 294 U.S. 587 (1935), 636–637

*North American Co.* v. *SEC,* 327 U.S. 686 (1946), 279

*Northwest Airlines* v. *Minnesota,* 322 U.S. 292 (1944), 303–304

*Northwestern States Portland Cement Co.* v. *Minnesota,* 358 U.S. 450 (1959), 302, 304

*Noto* v. *United States,* 367 U.S. 290 (1961), 533

*Nowak* v. *United States,* 356 U.S. 660 (1958), 532, 764

*Nye* v. *United States,* 313 U.S. 33 (1941), 443

*O'Brien* v. *United States,* 376 F. 2d 538 (1967), 464

*O'Donoghue* v. *United States,* 289 U.S. 516 (1933), 134

*Offutt* v. *United States,* 348 U.S. 11 (1954), 118

*Ogden* v. *Saunders,* 12 Wheat. 213 (1827), 695

*Oklahoma ex rel. Phillips* v. *Guy Atkinson Co.,* 313 U.S. 508 (1941), 276

*Oklahoma Press Publishing Co.* v. *Walling,* 327 U.S. 186 (1946), 434

*Old Dominion S. S. Co.* v. *Virginia,* 198 U.S. 299 (1905), 303

*Oliver, In re,* 333 U.S. 257 (1948), 640–641

*Oliver Iron Mining Co.* v. *Lord,* 262 U.S. 172 (1923), 257

*Olmstead* v. *United States,* 277 U.S. 438 (1928), 612–616

*Olsen* v. *Nebraska,* 313 U.S. 236 (1941), 679–680, 687

*O'Malley* v. *Woodrough,* 307 U.S. 277 (1939), 139

*On Lee* v. *United States,* 343 U.S. 747 (1952), 614

*One 1958 Plymouth Sedan* v. *Pennsylvania,* 380 U.S. 693 (1965), 608

*Opp Cotton Mills* v. *Administrator of Wage and Hour Division,* 312 U.S. 126 (1941), 201

*Orient Insurance Co.* v. *Daggs,* 172 U.S. 557 (1899), 683

*Orleans Parish* v. *Bush,* 242 F. 2d 156 (1957), 726

*Osborn* v. *United States,* 385 U.S. 323 (1966), 616

*Osborn* v. *United States Bank,* 9 Wheat. 738 (1824), 147, 154, 241, 726

*Otis Co.* v. *Ludlow Mfg. Co.,* 201 U.S. 140 (1906), 698

*Ott* v. *Mississippi Barge Line Co.,* 336 U.S. 169 (1949), 303

*Oyama* v. *California,* 332 U.S. 631 (1948), 715


*Pace* v. *Alabama,* 106 U.S. 583 (1882), 731

*Pacific Employers Insurance Co.* v. *Industrial Accident Commission,* 306 U.S. 493 (1939), 105

*Pacific States Telephone and Telegraph Co.* v. *Oregon,* 223 U.S. 118 (1912), 83

*Pacific Telephone and Telegraph Co.* v. *Tax Commission,* 297 U.S. 403 (1936), 300

*Packer Corp.* v. *Utah,* 285 U.S. 105 (1932), 666

*Palko* v. *Connecticut,* 302 U.S. 319 (1937), 421, 594–596, 647, 652

*Panama Refining Co.* v. *Ryan,* 293 U.S. 388 (1935), 200–201

*Panhandle Oil Company* v. *Mississippi,* 277 U.S. 218 (1928), 242, 243

*Pappadio* v. *United States,* 384 U.S. 364 (1966), 120

*Parker* v. *Davis* (*Legal Tender Cases*), 12 Wall. 461 (1871), 249

*Parker* v. *Gladden,* 385 U.S. 363 (1966), 640

*Passenger Cases,* 7 How. 283 (1849), 255, 282, 283

*Pate* v. *Robinson,* 383 U.S. 375 (1966), 645

*Patton* v. *United States,* 281 U.S. 276 (1930), 634

*Paul* v. *Virginia,* 8 Wall. 168 (1869), 276, 300

*Pauling* v. *News Syndicate Co.,* 335 F. 2d 659 (1964), 516

*Penhallow* v. *Doane,* 3 Dall. 54 (1795), 373

*Pennekamp* v. *Florida,* 328 U.S. 331 (1946), 423, 444

*Pennoyer* v. *Neff,* 95 U.S. 714 (1878), 590

*Pennsylvania* v. *Board of City Trusts of Philadelphia,* 353 U.S. 230 (1957), 733

   v. *Nelson,* 350 U.S. 497 (1956), 71, 72, 292

   v. *Wheeling Bridge Co.,* 13 How. 518 (1852), 304

*Pennsylvania Hospital* v. *Philadelphia,* 245 U.S. 21 (1917), 694

*Pensacola Telegraph Co.* v. *Western Union Telegraph Co.,* 96 U.S. 1 (1878), 256

*People* v. *Woody,* 394 P. 2d 813 (1964), 561

*Perez* v. *Brownell,* 356 U.S. 44 (1958), 767–768

*Perez* v. *Lippold,* 198 P. 2d 17 (1948), 731

*Perkins* v. *Elg,* 307 U.S. 325 (1939), 766

*Perkins* v. *Lukens Steel Co.,* 310 U.S. 13 (1940), 173

*Perry* v. *United States,* 294 U.S. 330 (1935), 250–251

*Peters* v. *Hobby,* 349 U.S. 331 (1955), 544

*Peters* v. *New York,* 389 U.S. 950 (1968), 612

*Petersen Baking Co.* v. *Bryan,* 290 U.S. 570 (1934), 677

*Peterson* v. *Greenville,* 373 U.S. 244 (1963), 482, 734–735

*Petite* v. *United States,* 361 U.S. 529 (1960), 647

*Philadelphia Fire Assn.* v. *New York,* 119 U.S. 110 (1886), 706

*Phillips* v. *United States,* 312 U.S. 246 (1941), 126

*Pierce* v. *Society of Sisters,* 268 U.S. 510 (1925), 171, 418, 554, 580

*Pierce* v. *United States,* 252 U.S. 239 (1920), 417

*Pierson* v. *Ray,* 386 U.S. 547 (1967), 139, 742

*Pipe Line Cases,* 234 U.S. 548 (1914), 255

*Piqua Branch of the State Bank* v. *Knoop,* 16 How. 369 (1853), 694

*Plessy* v. *Ferguson,* 163 U.S. 537 (1896), 717–718

*Pocket Veto Case,* 279 U.S. 655 (1929), 333

*Poe* v. *Ullman,* 367 U.S. 497 (1961), 687

*Pointer* v. *Texas,* 380 U.S. 400 (1965), 640

*Polish Alliance* v. *Labor Board,* 322 U.S. 643 (1944), 271

*Pollard* v. *United States,* 352 U.S. 354 (1957), 639

*Pollock* v. *Farmers' Loan and Trust Co.,* 157 U.S. 429, 158 U.S. 601 (1895), 35, 168, 235, 242

*Pollock* v. *Williams,* 322 U.S. 4 (1944), 404

*Pope* v. *Williams,* 193 U.S. 621 (1904), 747

*Popovici* v. *Agler,* 280 U.S. 379 (1930), 151

*Poulos* v. *New Hampshire,* 345 U.S. 395 (1953), 456, 465–467

*Powell* v. *Alabama,* 287 U.S. 45 (1932), 626–628

*Powell* v. *McCormack,* 266 F. Supp. 354 (1967), 190

*Powell* v. *Pennsylvania,* 127 U.S. 678 (1888), 661

*Powell* v. *Texas,* 389 U.S. 810 (1967), 651

*Preston* v. *United States,* 376 U.S. 364 (1964), 608

*Prigg* v. *Pennsylvania,* 16 Pet. 539 (1842), 152

*Prince* v. *Massachusetts,* 321 U.S. 158 (1944), 556–557

*Prize Cases,* 2 Bl. 635 (1863), 376

*Providence Bank* v. *Billings,* 4 Pet. 514 (1830), 694

*Prudential Insurance Co.* v. *Benjamin,* 328 U.S. 408 (1946), 277, 287

v. *Cheek,* 259 U.S. 530 (1922), 418

*Public Affairs Associates* v. *Rickover,* 369 U.S. 111 (1962), 168

*Public Clearing House* v. *Coyne,* 194 U.S. 497 (1904), 437–439

*Pullman's Palace Car Co.* v. *Pennsylvania,* 141 U.S. 18 (1891), 301

*Purity Extract & Tonic Co.* v. *Lynch,* 226 U.S. 192 (1912), 665

*Quaker City Cab Co.* v. *Pennsylvania,* 277 U.S. 389 (1928), 706

*Quantity of Copies of Books* v. *Kansas,* 378 U.S. 205 (1964), 505

*Queen* v. *Boyes,* 1 B. & S. 311 (1861), 617

*Queen* v. *Hicklin,* Law Reports, 3 Queen's Bench 360 (1868), 491–493

*Quick Bear* v. *Leupp,* 210 U.S. 50 (1908), 569

*Quinn* v. *United States,* 349 U.S. 155 (1955), 219

*Quirin, Ex parte,* 317 U.S. 1 (1942), 127, 387

*Quong Wing* v. *Kirkendall,* 223 U.S. 59 (1912), 706

*Rabinowitz* v. *United States,* 366 F. 2d 34 (1966), 635

*Rahrer, In re,* 140 U.S. 545 (1891), 293

*Railroad Commission* v. *Rowan & Nichols Oil Co.,* 311 U.S. 570, 614 (1941), 154

*Railroad Commission of Texas* v. *Pullman Co.,* 312 U.S. 496 (1941), 153

*Railroad Transfer Service* v. *Chicago,* 386 U.S. 351 (1967), 292

*Railway Employees Department* v. *Hanson,* 351 U.S. 225 (1956), 292

*Railway Express Agency* v. *New York,* 336 U.S. 106 (1949), 684

*Railway Express Agency, Inc.* v. *Virginia,* 358 U.S. 434 (1959), 301

*Rapier, In re,* 143 U.S. 110 (1892), 260, 438

*Rathbun* v. *United States,* 355 U.S. 107 (1957), 613

*Ray* v. *Blair,* 343 U.S. 214 (1952), 315

*Redrup* v. *New York,* 386 U.S. 767 (1967), 499–500

*Reed* v. *Gardner,* 261 F. Supp. 87 (1966), 539, 547

*Reid* v. *Covert,* 351 U.S. 487 (1956), 386

Reid v. Covert, 354 U.S. 1 (1957), 365, 386

Reitman v. Mulkey, 387 U.S. 369 (1967), 737

Reynolds v. Sims, 377 U.S. 533 (1964), 37, 87–90

Reynolds v. United States, 98 U.S. 145 (1879), 556

Ribnik v. McBride, 277 U.S. 350 (1928), 677, 679

Rice v. Elmore, 333 U.S. 875 (1948), 752

Rice v. Olson, 324 U.S. 786 (1945), 628

Rice v. Rice, 336 U.S. 674 (1949), 102, 104

Rideau v. Louisiana, 373 U.S. 723 (1963), 446

Rinaldi v. Yeager, 384 U.S. 305 (1966), 642

Robbins v. Shelby County Taxing District, 120 U.S. 489 (1887), 298

Robertson v. Baldwin, 165 U.S. 275 (1897), 405, 413, 415

Robertson v. California, 328 U.S. 440 (1946), 277

Robinson v. California, 370 U.S. 660 (1962), 650–651

Rochin v. California, 342 U.S. 165 (1952), 609–610, 687

Rockefeller v. Wells, 389 U.S. 421 (1967), 91

Rogers v. Quan, 357 U.S. 193 (1958), 772

Rogers v. Richmond, 365 U.S. 534 (1961), 624

Rogers v. United States, 340 U.S. 367 (1951), 219, 618

Rosenberg v. Fleuti, 374 U.S. 449 (1963), 776

Rosenblatt v. Baer, 383 U.S. 75 (1966), 512, 514–515

Ross, In re, 140 U.S. 453 (1891), 386

Roth v. United States, 354 U.S. 476 (1957), 493–496, 500–502

Rowoldt v. Perfetto, 354 U.S. 934 (1957), 777

Rudolph v. Alabama, 152 So. 2d 662, cert. den. 375 U.S. 889 (1963), 651

Rugendorf v. United States, 376 U.S. 529 (1964), 603

Rusk v. Cort, 372 U.S. 144 (1963), 768

Russell v. United States, 369 U.S. 749 (1962), 228

Sacher v. United States, 343 U.S. 1 (1952), 118

Sacher v. United States, 356 U.S. 576 (1958), 228

Saia v. New York, 334 U.S. 558 (1948), 458, 554

Sailors v. Board of Education of Kent County, 387 U.S. 105 (1967), 91

San Diego Unions v. Garmon, 353 U.S. 26 (1957), 359 U.S. 236 (1959), 291

San Mateo County v. Southern Pacific R. Co., 116 U.S. 138 (1885), 669

Santa Clara County v. Southern Pacific R. Co., 118 U.S. 394 (1886), 669

Santa Cruz Fruit Packing Co. v. NLRB, 303 U.S. 453 (1938), 271

Santiago v. Nogueras, 214 U.S. 260 (1909), 378

Savio v. California, 388 U.S. 460 (1967), 485

Savorgnan v. United States, 338 U.S. 491 (1950), 766

Scales v. United States, 367 U.S. 203 (1961), 532–533, 546

Schaefer v. United States, 251 U.S. 466 (1920), 417

Schechter Poultry Corp. v. United States, 295 U.S. 495 (1935), 169, 201, 267–268

Schenck v. United States, 249 U.S. 47 (1919), 416–417

Schiro v. Bynum, 375 U.S. 395 (1964), 728

Schmerber v. California, 384 U.S. 757 (1966), 611, 622, 687

Schneider v. Irvington, 308 U.S. 147 (1939), 422, 436–437

Schneider v. Rusk, 377 U.S. 163 (1964), 765, 767

Schneider v. Smith, 390 U.S. 17 (1968), 536

Schneiderman v. United States, 320 U.S. 118 (1943), 526, 762, 764

School District of Abington Township v. Schempp, 374 U.S. 203 (1963), 46, 173, 553, 577–580

School of Magnetic Healing v. McAnulty, 187 U.S. 94 (1902), 439

Schowgurow v. State, 213 A. 2d 475 (1965), 564

Schware v. New Mexico Board of Bar Examiners, 353 U.S. 232 (1957), 122, 544, 687

Scott v. Germano, 381 U.S. 407 (1965), 91

Scott v. Sandford (see Dred Scott v. Sandford)

Screws v. United States, 325 U.S. 91 (1945), 732–733, 740

Scull v. Virginia, 359 U.S. 344 (1959), 228

Secombe, Ex parte, 19 How. 9 (1857), 122

Second Employers' Liability Cases, 223 U.S. 1 (1912), 152

See v. Seattle, 387 U.S. 541 (1967), 612

Selective Draft Law Cases, 245 U.S. 366 (1918), 374, 405

Semler v. Oregon State Board of Dental Examiners, 294 U.S. 608 (1935), 661, 683

Senn v. Tile Layers Protective Union, 301 U.S. 468 (1937), 460

Service v. Dulles, 354 U.S. 363 (1957), 544

Schachtman v. Dulles, 225 F. 2d 938 (1955), 368

Shapiro v. Thompson, 389 U.S. 1032 (1968), 290

Shapiro v. United States, 335 U.S. 1 (1948), 620

Shaughnessy v. United States ex rel Mezei, 345 U.S. 206 (1953), 773

Shelden v. Sill, 8 How. 441 (1850), 142

Sheldon v. Fannin, 221 F. Supp. 766 (1963), 561

Shelley v. Kraemer, 334 U.S. 1 (1948), 716, 736–737

Shelton v. Tucker, 364 U.S. 479 (1960), 542–543, 549

Shepherd v. Florida, 341 U.S. 50 (1951), 445

Sheppard v. Maxwell, 384 U.S. 333 (1966), 447–449

Sherbert v. Verner, 374 U.S. 398 (1963), 560–561

Sherrer v. Sherrer, 334 U.S. 343 (1948), 103

Shillitani v. United States, 384 U.S. 364 (1966), 120

Short v. Ness Produce Co., 385 U.S. 537 (1967), 291

Shreveport Rate Case, 234 U.S. 342 (1914), 264–265

Shuttlesworth v. Birmingham, 382 U.S. 87 (1965), 469

Shuttlesworth v. Birmingham Board of Education, 358 U.S. 101 (1958), 726

Sibron v. New York, 389 U.S. 950 (1968), 612

Silverman v. United States, 365 U.S. 505 (1961), 614

Simms v. Simms, 175 U.S. 162 (1899), 93

Simons v. Miami Beach First National Bank, 381 U.S. 81 (1965), 104

Sims v. Baggett, 247 F. Supp. 96 (1965), 91

Sims v. Georgia, 385 U.S. 538 (1967), 624

Singer v. United States, 380 U.S. 24 (1965), 634

Sipuel v. Board of Regents of the University of Oklahoma, 332 U.S. 631 (1948), 722

Skaneateles Water Works Co. v. Skaneateles, 184 U.S. 354 (1902), 694

Skinner v. Oklahoma, 316 U.S. 535 (1942), 685

Slagle v. Ohio, 366 U.S. 259 (1961), 228

Slaughterhouse Cases, 16 Wall. 36 (1873), 53, 99, 592, 658–659, 681–682, 713, 760

Slochower v. Board of Higher Education of New York City, 350 U.S. 551 (1956), 541–542

Smith v. Allwright, 321 U.S. 649 (1944), 752

Smith v. Cahoon, 283 U.S. 553 (1931), 683

Smith v. California, 361 U.S. 147 (1959), 424, 502–503

Smith v. Illinois, 390 U.S. 129 (1968), 640

Smith v. Kansas City Title and Trust Co., 255 U.S. 180 (1921), 168

Smith v. Texas, 311 U.S. 128 (1940), 637

Smyth v. Ames, 169 U.S. 466 (1898), 678, 680

Snyder v. Massachusetts, 291 U.S. 97 (1934), 591

Sonnenborn Bros. v. Cureton, 262 U.S. 506 (1923), 297

Sonzinsky v. United States, 300 U.S. 506 (1937), 240

South v. Peters, 339 U.S. 276 (1950), 185

South Carolina v. Katzenbach, 383 U.S. 301 (1966), 741, 756–757

v. United States, 199 U.S. 437 (1905), 242, 244

*South Carolina Highway Department* v. *Barnwell Brothers*, 303 U.S. 177 (1938), 289

*South Dakota* v. *North Carolina*, 192 U.S. 286 (1904), 110, 146

*Southern Pacific Co.* v. *Arizona*, 325 U.S. 761 (1945), 289

*Southern Railway Co.* v. *United States*, 222 U.S. 20 (1911), 263

*Spahn* v. *Julian Messner*, 221 N.E. 2d 543 (1966), 435

*Spalding & Brothers* v. *Edwards*, 262 U.S. 66 (1923), 296

*Spano* v. *New York*, 360 U.S. 315 (1959), 630

*Spector Motor Service* v. *O'Connor*, 340 U.S. 602 (1951), 300

*Speiser* v. *Randall*, 357 U.S. 513 (1958), 539

*Spevack* v. *Klein*, 385 U.S. 511 (1967), 621

*Spiro* v. *United States*, 88 S. Ct. 1028 (1968), 566

*Springer* v. *United States*, 102 U.S. 586 (1881), 234

*Springfield School Committee* v. *Barksdale*, 348 F. 2d 261 (1965), 730

*Sproles* v. *Binford*, 286 U.S. 374 (1932), 666

*Stack* v. *Boyle*, 342 U.S. 1 (1951), 649

*Stafford* v. *Wallace*, 258 U.S. 495 (1922), 264

*Stamler* v. *Willis*, 371 F. 2d 413 (1966), 229

*Stanard* v. *Oleson*, 74 S. Ct. 768 (1954), 438

*Stanford* v. *Texas*, 379 U.S. 476 (1965), 604

*State* v. *Keeran*, 5 R.I. 497 (1858), 657

*State* v. *Paul*, 5 R.I. 185 (1858), 657

*State Athletic Commission* v. *Dorsey*, 359 U.S. 533 (1959), 728

*State Board of Tax Commissioners* v. *Jackson*, 283 U.S. 527 (1931), 706

*State Freight Tax Case* (*Reading R.R.* v. *Pennsylvania*), 15 Wall. 232 (1873), 297

*State Tax Commission of Utah* v. *Aldrich*, 316 U.S. 174 (1942), 704

*Stearns* v. *Minnesota*, 179 U.S. 223 (1900), 79

*Steel Seizure Case* (see *Youngstown Sheet & Tube Co.* v. *Sawyer*)

*Stein* v. *New York*, 346 U.S. 156 (1953), 624, 653–654

*Stettler* v. *O'Hara*, 243 U.S. 629 (1917), 670

*Steward Machine Co.* v. *Davis*, 301 U.S. 548 (1937), 247

*Stewart Dry Goods Co.* v. *Lewis*, 294 U.S. 550 (1935), 706

*Stone* v. *Mississippi*, 101 U.S. 814 (1880), 695

*Stoner* v. *California*, 376 U.S. 483 (1964), 611

*Strauder* v. *West Virginia*, 100 U.S. 303 (1880), 636

*Strawbridge* v. *Curtiss*, 3 Cr. 267 (1806), 147

*Strickley* v. *Highland Boy Gold Mining Co.*, 200 U.S. 527 (1906), 698

*Stroble* v. *California*, 343 U.S. 181 (1952), 445, 625

*Stromberg* v. *California*, 283 U.S. 359 (1931), 524–526

*Stuart* v. *Laird*, 1 Cr. 299 (1903), 138

*Sturges* v. *Crowninshield*, 4 Wheat. 122 (1819), 690, 695

*Sugar Trust Case* (see *United States* v. *E. C. Knight Co.*)

*Summerfield* v. *Sunshine Book Co.*, 349 U.S. 921 (1955), 440

*Summers, In re*, 325 U.S. 561 (1945), 122

*Sunday Closing Cases*, 366 U.S. 420 (1961), 560

*Sunshine Anthracite Coal Co.* v. *Adkins*, 310 U.S. 381 (1940), 238, 679

*Superior Films* v. *Ohio Dept. of Education*, 346 U.S. 587 (1954), 506

*Swann* v. *Adams*, 385 U.S. 440 (1967), 91

*Swart* v. *School District*, 167 A. 2d 514 (1961), 572

*Sweatt* v. *Painter*, 339 U.S. 629 (1950), 722–723

*Sweet Briar Institute* v. *Button*, 387 U.S. 423 (1967), 733

*Sweezy* v. *New Hampshire*, 354 U.S. 234 (1957), 221–222, 225, 686

*Swenson* v. *Bosler*, 386 U.S. 258 (1967), 642

*Swift* v. *Tyson*, 16 Pet. 1 (1842), 148–149

*Swift and Co.* v. *United States*, 196 U.S. 375 (1905), 264, 266

v. *Wickham*, 382 U.S. 111 (1965), 126

*Takahashi* v. *Fish and Game Commission,* 334 U.S. 410 (1948), 715

*Talley* v. *California,* 362 U.S. 60 (1960), 437, 686

*Tarble's Case* (*United States* v. *Tarble*), 13 Wall. 397 (1872), 155

*Taylor* v. *McElroy,* 360 U.S. 709 (1959), 544

*Teamsters Union* v. *Oliver,* 358 U.S. 283 (1959), 291

*Tehan* v. *Shott,* 382 U.S. 406 (1966), 621

*Teitel Film Corp.* v. *Cusack,* 390 U.S. 139 (1968), 507

*10 East 40th Street Building* v. *Callus,* 325 U.S. 578 (1945), 272

*Tennessee* v. *Davis,* 100 U.S. 257 (1880), 156

*Tennessee Electric Power Co.* v. *TVA,* 306 U.S. 118 (1939), 276

*Tenney* v. *Brandhove,* 341 U.S. 367 (1951), 193

*Terminiello* v. *Chicago,* 337 U.S. 1 (1949), 476–477, 514

*Terrace* v. *Thompson,* 263 U.S. 197 (1923), 714, 761

*Terral* v. *Burke Construction Co.,* 257 U.S. 529 (1922), 151

*Terry* v. *Adams,* 345 U.S. 461 (1953), 734, 752

*Terry* v. *Ohio,* 387 U.S. 929 (1967), 612

*Testa* v. *Katt,* 330 U.S. 386 (1947), 152

*Texas* v. *White,* 7 Wall. 700 (1869), 69

*Textile Workers Union* v. *Lincoln Mills,* 353 U.S. 448 (1957), 150

*Thiel* v. *Southern Pacific Co.,* 328 U.S. 217 (1946), 635

*Thomas* v. *Collins,* 323 U.S. 516 (1945), 422–423, 471–472

*Thompson* v. *City of Louisville,* 362 U.S. 199 (1960), 142, 641

*Thornhill* v. *Alabama,* 310 U.S. 88 (1940), 454–455, 460, 463, 465

*Tigner* v. *Texas,* 310 U.S. 141 (1940), 683

*Time, Inc.* v. *Hill,* 385 U.S. 374 (1967), 435, 686

*Times Film Corp.* v. *Chicago,* 244 F. 2d 432 (1957), 506; 365 U.S. 43 (1961), 506–507

*Tod* v. *Waldman,* 266 U.S. 113 (1924), 772

*Toledo Newspaper Co.* v. *United States,* 247 U.S. 402 (1918), 443

*Tomkins* v. *Missouri,* 323 U.S. 485 (1945), 628

*Toolson* v. *New York Yankees,* 346 U.S. 356 (1953), 277

*Toomer* v. *Witsell,* 334 U.S. 385 (1948), 100

*Torcaso* v. *Watkins,* 367 U.S. 488 (1961), 564

*Tot* v. *United States,* 319 U.S. 463 (1943), 641

*Townsend* v. *Burke,* 334 U.S. 736 (1948), 628

*Townsend* v. *Yoemans,* 301 U.S. 441 (1937), 671, 679

*Travelers Health Assn.* v. *Virginia,* 339 U.S. 643 (1950), 591

*Travis* v. *United States,* 385 U.S. 491 (1967), 370

*Trebilcock* v. *Wilson,* 12 Wall. 687 (1872), 250

*Trop* v. *Dulles,* 356 U.S. 86 (1958), 650, 768

*Truax* v. *Corrigan,* 257 U.S. 312 (1921), 709

*Truax* v. *Raich,* 239 U.S. 33 (1915), 171–172, 714–715

*Trupiano* v. *United States,* 334 U.S. 699 (1948), 604–605

*Tucker* v. *Texas,* 326 U.S. 517 (1946), 471

*Tumey* v. *Ohio,* 273 U.S. 510 (1927), 642

*Turner* v. *Bank of North America,* 4 Dall. 8 (1799), 142

*Turner* v. *Louisiana,* 379 U.S. 466 (1965), 640

*Turner* v. *Memphis,* 369 U.S. 350 (1962), 728

*Turner* v. *New York,* 386 U.S. 773 (1967), 469

*Turner* v. *Pennsylvania,* 338 U.S. 62 (1949), 624

*Turner* v. *Williams,* 194 U.S. 279 (1904), 770

*Tutun* v. *United States,* 270 U.S. 568 (1926), 761

*Twining* v. *New Jersey,* 211 U.S. 78 (1908), 403, 594, 620, 623

*Tyson & Brother* v. *Banton,* 273 U.S. 418 (1927), 676, 679

*Ullmann* v. *United States,* 350 U.S. 422 (1956), 619

*Ungar* v. *Sarafite,* 376 U.S. 575 (1964), 118

*Union Refrigerator Transit Co.* v. *Kentucky,* 199 U.S. 194 (1905), 703

*United Artists Corp.* v. *Dallas,* 387 U.S. 903 (1967), 507

*United Automobile Workers* v. *Wisconsin Employment Relations Board,* 351 U.S. 266 (1956), 292

*United Mine Workers* v. *Coronado Co.,* 259 U.S. 344 (1922), 257

v. *Illinois State Bar Assn.,* 389 U.S. 217 (1967), 550

*United Public Workers* v. *Mitchell,* 330 U.S. 75 (1947), 173, 348, 472–473

*United States* v. *Allegheny County,* 322 U.S. 174 (1944), 244–245

v. *Appalachian Electric Power Co.,* 311 U.S. 377 (1940), 275

v. *Ball,* 163 U.S. 662 (1896), 646

v. *Ballin,* 144 U.S. 1 (1892), 212

v. *Barnett,* 376 U.S. 681 (1964), 119–120, 634

v. *Belmont,* 301 U.S. 324 (1937), 359

v. *Bevans,* 3 Wheat. 336 (1818), 144

v. *Bland,* 283 U.S. 636 (1931), 566

v. *Brown,* 381 U.S. 437 (1965), 539, 547, 602

v. *Burr,* 4 Cr. 470 (1807), 600

v. *Butler,* 297 U.S. 1 (1936), 246–247, 273

v. *California,* 332 U.S. 19 (1947), 79

v. *Carolene Products Co.,* 304 U.S. 144 (1938), 421

v. *Causby,* 328 U.S. 256 (1946), 699

v. *Central Eureka Mining Co.,* 357 U.S. 155 (1958), 700

v. *Chandler-Dunbar Water Co.,* 229 U.S. 53 (1913), 699

v. *C.I.O.,* 335 U.S. 106 (1948), 169

v. *Classic,* 313 U.S. 299 (1941), 732, 752

v. *Commodities Trading Corp.,* 339 U.S. 121 (1950), 701

v. *Commodore Park, Inc.,* 324 U.S. 386 (1945), 700

v. *Constantine,* 296 U.S. 287 (1935), 239

v. *Cors,* 337 U.S. 325 (1949), 701

v. *Cress,* 243 U.S. 316 (1917), 699

v. *Cruikshank,* 92 U.S. 542 (1876), 397, 746

*United States* v. *Currens,* 290 F. 2d 751 (1961), 645

v. *Curtiss-Wright Export Corporation,* 299 U.S. 304 (1936), 354, 356, 374

v. *Darby Lumber Co.,* 312 U.S. 100 (1941), 73, 239, 272, 680

v. *Dennett,* 39 F. 2d 564 (1930), 492

v. *Dickinson,* 331 U.S. 745 (1947), 699

v. *Doremus,* 249 U.S. 86 (1919), 238

v. *E. C. Knight Co.,* 156 U.S. 1 (1895), 235, 257, 265

v. *Ewell,* 383 U.S. 116 (1966), 639, 646

v. *Felin & Co.,* 334 U.S. 624 (1948), 701

v. *Grimaud,* 220 U.S. 506 (1911), 199

v. *Guest,* 383 U.S. 745 (1966), 740–742

v. *Guy W. Capps, Inc.,* 348 U.S. 296 (1955), 359

v. *Hudson and Goodwin,* 7 Cr. 32 (1812), 142–143, 599

v. *Jackson,* 387 U.S. 929 (1967), 634

v. *Johnson,* 383 U.S. 169 (1966), 192–193

v. *Josephson,* 165 F. 2d 82 (1947), 218

v. *Ju Toy,* 198 U.S. 253 (1905), 771–772

v. *Kahriger,* 345 U.S. 22 (1953), 239–240

v. *Kennerly,* 209 Fed. 119 (1913), 491–492

v. *Klein,* 13 Wall. 128 (1872), 349

v. *Lanza,* 260 U.S. 377 (1922), 648

v. *Lattimore,* 125 F. Supp. 295 (1954), 127 F. Supp. 405 (1955), 639

v. *Laub,* 385 U.S. 475 (1967), 370

v. *Lee,* 106 U.S. 196 (1882), 146

v. *Louisiana,* 339 U.S. 699 (1950), 79; 389 U.S. 155 (1967), 79

v. *Louisiana et al.,* 363 U.S. 1, 121 (1960), 79

v. *Lovett,* 328 U.S. 303 (1946), 248, 601

v. *Macintosh,* 283 U.S. 605 (1931), 566

v. *Midwest Oil Co.,* 236 U.S. 459 (1915), 336

v. *O'Brien,* 389 U.S. 814 (1967), 464

v. *One Book Entitled "Contraception,"* 51 F. 2d 525 (1931), 492

v. *One Book Entitled "Ulysses,"* 72 F. 2d 705 (1934), 491–493

v. *One Obscene Book Entitled "Married Love,"* 48 F. 2d 821 (1931), 492

*United States* v. *Paramount Pictures,* 334 U.S. 131 (1948), 505

v. *Perez,* 9 Wheat. 579 (1824), 646

v. *Peters,* 5 Cr. 115 (1809), 75

v. *Pink,* 315 U.S. 203 (1942), 359

v. *Price,* 383 U.S. 787 (1966), 740–741

v. *Provoo,* 17 F.R.D. 183 (1955), 639

v. *Rabinowitz,* 339 U.S. 56 (1950), 605

v. *Rebhuhn,* 109 F. 2d 512 (1940), 499

v. *Reese,* 92 U.S. 214 (1876), 746

v. *Robel,* 389 U.S. 258 (1967), 536

v. *Rock Royal Co-operative, Inc.,* 307 U.S. 533 (1939), 201, 274, 679

v. *Romano,* 382 U.S. 136 (1965), 641

v. *Rosenberg,* 344 U.S. 889 (1952), 601

v. *Roth,* 237 F. 2d 796 (1956), 491

v. *Rumley,* 345 U.S. 41 (1953), 220

v. *Schwimmer,* 279 U.S. 644 (1929), 566

v. *Seeger,* 380 U.S. 163 (1965), 565–566

v. *Sharpnack,* 355 U.S. 286 (1958), 203

v. *Smith,* 286 U.S. 6 (1932), 212, 343

v. *South-Eastern Underwriters Association,* 322 U.S. 533 (1944), 276

v. *States of Louisiana, Texas, Mississippi, Alabama, and Florida,* 363 U.S. 1 (1960), 79

v. *Sullivan,* 332 U.S. 689 (1948), 618

v. *Tempia,* 16 USCMA 629 (1967), 383

v. *Texas,* 339 U.S. 707 (1950), 79

v. *Township of Muskegon,* 355 U.S. 484 (1958), 245

v. *Twin City Power Co.,* 350 U.S. 222 (1956), 699

v. *United Mine Workers,* 330 U.S. 258 (1947), 117

v. *Ventresca,* 380 U.S. 102 (1965), 604

v. *Virginia Electric Co.,* 365 U.S. 624 (1961), 699

v. *Wade,* 388 U.S. 218 (1967), 632

v. *West Virginia,* 295 U.S. 463 (1935), 145

v. *Westinghouse Electric and Mfg. Co.,* 339 U.S. 261 (1950), 701

v. *White,* 322 U.S. 694 (1944), 620

v. *Williams,* 341 U.S. 70 (1951), 740

v. *Willow River Power Co.,* 324 U.S. 499 (1945), 699

v. *Wilson,* 7 Pet. 150 (1833), 349

v. *Witkovich,* 353 U.S. 194 (1957), 778

v. *Wong Kim Ark,* 169 U.S. 649 (1898), 760

*United States* v. *Wood,* 299 U.S. 123 (1936), 636

v. *Wrightwood Dairy Co.,* 315 U.S. 110 (1942), 274

v. *Yellow Cab Co.,* 332 U.S. 218 (1947), 258, 277

*United States and Borg-Warner* v. *City of Detroit,* 355 U.S. 466 (1958), 245

*United States ex rel. Hirshberg* v. *Cooke,* 336 U.S. 210 (1949), 384

*Knauff* v. *Shaughnessy,* 338 U.S. 537 (1950), 773

*Riggs* v. *Johnson County,* 6 Wall. 166 (1868), 154

*TVA* v. *Powelson,* 319 U.S. 266 (1943), 699, 701

*TVA* v. *Welch,* 327 U.S. 546 (1946), 698

*Toth* v. *Quarles,* 350 U.S. 11 (1955), 384, 386

*United States Gule Company* v. *Oak Creek,* 247 U.S. 321 (1918), 302

*University of Illinois* v. *United States,* 289 U.S. 48 (1933), 242

*Uphaus* v. *Wyman,* 364 U.S. 388 (1959), 225–226

*Utah Power and Light* v. *Pfost,* 286 U.S. 165 (1932), 257

*Valentine* v. *Chrestensen,* 316 U.S. 52 (1942), 437

*Vallandigham, Ex parte,* 1 Wall. 243 (1864), 381

*Vanderbilt* v. *Vanderbilt,* 354 U.S. 416 (1957), 104

*Veazie Bank* v. *Fenno,* 8 Wall. 533 (1869), 234, 238, 248

*Veterans of the Abraham Lincoln Brigade* v. *SACB,* 380 U.S. 513 (1965), 536

*Virginia, Ex parte,* 100 U.S. 339 (1880), 636, 732

*Virginia* v. *Rives,* 100 U.S. 313 (1880), 636

v. *Tennessee,* 148 U.S. 503 (1893), 108

v. *West Virginia,* 246 U.S. 565 (1918), 111

*Virtue Bros.* v. *County of Los Angeles,* 385 U.S. 820 (1966), 295

*Vitarelli* v. *Seaton,* 359 U.S. 535 (1959), 544

*Von Moltke* v. *Gillies,* 332 U.S. 708 (1948), 625

*Wabash Railway Co.* v. *Illinois,* 118 U.S. 557 (1886), 256

*Wade* v. *Hunter,* 336 U.S. 684 (1949), 383–384, 646

*Walker* v. *Birmingham,* 388 U.S. 307 (1967), 466–467

*Walker* v. *City of Hutchinson,* 352 U.S. 112 (1956), 592

*Wallace* v. *United States,* 385 U.S. 977 (1967), 729

*Walling* v. *Jacksonville Paper Co.,* 317 U.S. 564 (1943), 259

*Ward* v. *Maryland,* 12 Wall. 418 (1871), 99

*Warden* v. *Hayden,* 387 U.S. 294 (1967), 606–607

*Ware* v. *Hylton,* 3 Dall. 199 (1796), 52, 355

*Wartime Prohibition Cases,* 251 U.S. 146 (1919), 700

*Washington* v. *Oregon,* 214 U.S. 205 (1909), 110

v. *Texas,* 388 U.S. 14 (1967), 641

*Washington Ethical Society* v. *District of Columbia,* 249 F. 2d 127 (1957), 565

*Watkins* v. *United States,* 354 U.S. 178 (1957), 220–225, 231

*Watson* v. *Jones,* 13 Wall. 679 (1872), 566–567

*Watts* v. *Indiana,* 338 U.S. 49 (1949), 624

*Wayman* v. *Southard,* 10 Wheat. 1 (1825), 121, 199

*Weaver* v. *Palmer Brothers,* 270 U.S. 402 (1926), 661

*Weber* v. *Anheuser-Busch, Inc.,* 348 U.S. 468 (1955), 292

*Weeks* v. *United States,* 232 U.S. 383 (1914), 608

*Weems* v. *United States,* 217 U.S. 349 (1910), 650

*Weiss* v. *Gardner,* 386 U.S. 9 (1967), 539

*Weiss* v. *United States,* 308 U.S. 321 (1939), 613

*Welch* v. *Swasey,* 214 U.S. 91 (1909), 667

*Welton* v. *Missouri,* 91 U.S. 275 (1876), 298

*Wesberry* v. *Sanders,* 376 U.S. 1 (1964), 186–187

*West* v. *American Telephone & Telegraph Co.,* 311 U.S. 223 (1940), 150

*West Coast Hotel Co.* v. *Parrish,* 300 U.S. 379 (1937), 679–680

*West River Bridge Co.* v. *Dix,* 6 How. 507 (1848), 694

*West Virginia ex rel. Dyer* v. *Sims,* 341 U.S. 22 (1951), 109, 111

*West Virginia State Board of Education* v. *Barnette,* 319 U.S. 624 (1943), 422, 558–559

*Western Union Telegraph* v. *Kansas ex rel. Coleman,* 216 U.S. 1 (1910), 301

*Western Union Telegraph Co.* v. *Massachusetts,* 125 U.S. 530 (1888), 301

*Weston* v. *Charleston,* 2 Pet. 449 (1829), 241

*Wheeling Steel Corporation* v. *Glander,* 337 U.S. 562 (1949), 669, 707

*White* v. *Hart,* 13 Wall. 646 (1872), 36

*White* v. *Ragen,* 324 U.S. 760 (1945), 628

*Whitekill* v. *Elkins,* 389 U.S. 54 (1967), 537

*Whitfield* v. *Ohio,* 297 U.S. 431 (1936), 294

*Whitney* v. *California,* 274 U.S. 357 (1927), 418–419, 524

*Whitus* v. *Georgia,* 385 U.S. 545 (1967), 637

*Wickard* v. *Filburn,* 317 U.S. 111 (1942), 247, 274

*Wieman* v. *Updegraff,* 344 U.S. 183 (1952), 537

*Wiener* v. *United States,* 357 U.S. 349 (1958), 347–348

*Wilkinson* v. *United States,* 365 U.S. 399 (1961), 226

*Williams* v. *Mississippi,* 170 U.S. 213 (1898), 750

*Williams* v. *North Carolina,* 317 U.S. 287 (1942), 102–103

*Williams* v. *North Carolina,* 325 U.S. 226 (1945), 103

*Williams* v. *Standard Oil Co.,* 278 U.S. 235 (1929), 677

*Williams* v. *United States,* 289 U.S. 553 (1933), 133, 135

*Williams* v. *United States,* 341 U.S. 97 (1951), 740

*Williams* v. *Wallace,* 240 F. Supp. 100 (1965), 466

*Williams* v. *Zuckert,* 371 U.S. 531 (1963), 544

*Williamson* v. *Lee Optical of Oklahoma,* 348 U.S. 483 (1955), 681, 684, 687

*Williamson* v. *United States,* 207 U.S. 425 (1908), 192

*Willson* v. *Black-Bird Creek Marsh Co.,* 2 Pet. 245 (1829), 281, 283–284

*Wilson* v. *Girard,* 354 U.S. 524 (1957), 385

*Wilson* v. *New,* 243 U.S. 332 (1917), 260

*Wilson* v. *United States,* 221 U.S. 361 (1911), 620

*Winters* v. *New York,* 333 U.S. 507 (1948), 640

*Wiscart* v. *Dauchy,* 3 Dall. 321 (1796), 130

*Wisconsin* v. *J. C. Penney Co.,* 311 U.S. 435 (1940), 302

  v. *Milwaukee Braves, Inc.,* 385 U.S. 990 (1966), 277

  v. *Pelican Insurance Co.,* 127 U.S. 265 (1888), 147

*Witherspoon* v. *Illinois,* 389 U.S. 1035 (1968), 651

*Wolf* v. *Colorado,* 338 U.S. 25 (1949), 608–612, 652

*Wolff Packing Co.* v. *Court of Industrial Relations,* 262 U.S. 522 (1923), 677

*Wong Sun* v. *United States,* 371 U.S. 471 (1963), 606

*Wong Yang Sung* v. *McGrath,* 339 U.S. 33 (1950), 777

*Wood* v. *Broom,* 287 U.S. 1 (1932), 184

*Wood* v. *Georgia,* 370 U.S. 375 (1962), 445

*Woodby* v. *Immigration and Naturalization Service,* 385 U.S. 276 (1966), 779

*Woodruff* v. *Parham,* 8 Wall. 123 (1869), 296–297

*Woods* v. *Miller Co.,* 333 U.S. 138 (1948), 375

*Worthen Co.* v. *Kavanaugh,* 295 U.S. 56 (1935), 697

  v. *Thomas,* 292 U.S. 426 (1934), 697

*Worthy* v. *Herter,* 361 U.S. 918 (1959), 370

*Worthy* v. *United States,* 328 F. 2d 386 (1964), 370

*Wright* v. *Rockefeller,* 376 U.S. 52 (1964), 187

*Wynehamer* v. *New York,* 13 N.Y. 378 (1856), 657

*Yakus* v. *United States,* 321 U.S. 414 (1944), 202

*Yamashita, In re,* 327 U.S. 1 (1946), 387

*Yarbrough, Ex parte,* 110 U.S. 651 (1884), 747

*Yates* v. *United States,* 354 U.S. 298 (1957), 167, 530–532, 547, 764

*Yates* v. *United States,* 356 U.S. 363 (1958), 598

*Yellin* v. *United States,* 374 U.S. 109 (1963), 227

*Yick Wo* v. *Hopkins,* 118 U.S. 356 (1886), 684, 714

*Young, Ex parte,* 209 U.S. 123 (1908), 126, 154, 726

*Youngstown Sheet & Tube Co.* v. *Bowers,* 358 U.S. 534 (1959), 295

  v. *Sawyer,* 343 U.S. 579 (1952), 338–341, 359, 389

*Zemel* v. *Rusk,* 381 U.S. 1 (1965), 203, 369

*Zorach* v. *Clauson,* 343 U.S. 306 (1952), 573–575

*Zwickler* v. *Koota,* 389 U.S. 241 (1967), 153, 437

Absolutist interpretation of Constitution, 423–426, 429
Abstention, 153
Academic freedom, 473, 540–541
Adams, John, 9, 163, 309
Adams, John Quincy, 310, 322
Adams, Samuel, 9, 17
Administrative law, 597
Admiralty, 143–144
Advisory opinions, 36, 52, 167–168
Agricultural regulation, 201, 246–247, 273–275
Albany Plan, 5, 7, 10
Alcoholism, 651
Alfange, Dean, Jr., 427–428
Alien and Sedition Acts of 1798, 65, 67, 152, 375, 398, 414, 416, 774
Alien Registration Act of 1940 (*see* Smith Act)
Aliens, deportation of, 774–779
  discrimination against, 714–715
  exclusion of, 769–774

Ambassadors, 150
Amending process, appraisal of, 40–42
  in Constitutional Convention, 33–34
  political character of, 35–36
Amendments, constitutional, 34–35, 397
  proposing of, 36–39
  ratification of, 39–40
American Bar Association, 135, 448–449
American Civil Liberties Union, 231, 476, 486, 566, 635, 777
American Newspaper Publishers Association, 449
Appointing power of President, 341–343
Apportionment, in House, 182–183
  in taxation, 301–303
Arms, right to bear, 397
Arraignment, delay in, 623
Arrests in connection with searches, 605–608
Articles of Confederation, 10, 65, 98, 109, 401
  framework of government under, 11

Articles of Confederation, revision of, 14
  weaknesses of, 12–13
Association, freedom of, 521–550
  guilt by, 523–526
Attorney General, 123, 534, 613–614, 647,
    650, 729, 753–756, 772, 774, 776,
    778–779

Bail, excessive, 649–650
Balancing in interpretation of Constitution,
    426–429
Bank of North America, 11–12
Bankruptcy legislation, 696
Bar, admission to, 544–545, 687
Baseball, 277
Bayh, Birch, 316, 319
Beard, Charles A., 29, 162
Beck, Carl, 217, 230
Berger, Victor L., 190
Berns, Walter, 70, 663
Bible reading in public schools, 173, 575,
    577
Bicameral system, 21
  and legislative apportionment, 87–88
Bickel, Alexander M., 150
Bill of attainder, 122, 539, 601–602
Bill of Rights, adoption of, 34, 397–398
  in Constitutional Convention, 28–29,
    396
  and Fourteenth Amendment, 592–597,
    611, 621, 652–655
  Massachusetts, 8–9
  and states, 399–400
Bingham, John A., 401, 407–410, 708
Black, Charles L., Jr., 38, 738
Black, Hugo, 55, 92, 135, 153, 186, 224–
    226, 240, 244, 278, 340, 365, 376–
    377, 384, 423–424, 427, 435, 444,
    453, 461, 464, 468–469, 471, 473,
    483–484, 486–488, 498, 500–501, 513,
    515, 519, 529, 532–533, 538, 544,
    570–571, 573, 575–576, 578, 596, 602,
    614, 620, 622, 628–629, 645, 653, 669,
    681, 684, 687, 698, 715, 737, 754,
    757, 769
Black Muslims, 564
Blackstone, Sir William, 414, 431–432
Blood tests for drunkenness, 610–611, 622
Blount, William, 204
"Blue ribbon" juries, 638
Bond, Julian, 92–93
Borrowing power of Congress, 248–250

Bradley, Joseph P., 53, 241, 311, 658, 660,
    712
Brandeis, Louis D., 54, 136, 149, 168, 174,
    293, 417–418, 426, 439, 441, 460, 524,
    613, 666, 677, 777
Brandeis brief, 670
Breach of the peace, 475–489
Brennan, William J., Jr., 46, 56, 85–86,
    135, 155, 177, 225, 435, 467, 493–
    500, 502–503, 505, 510–514, 539, 541,
    553, 561, 578, 621–622, 653, 741, 768
Brewer, David J., 772, 775
Bricker Amendment, 39, 41, 364–366
Brown, Henry B., 437, 717
Budget and Accounting Act, 208, 346
Burr, Aaron, 34, 310, 600
Burton, Harold, 135, 202, 382
Business affected with public interest, 659,
    670–671, 677, 679
Butler, Pierce, 28
Butler, Pierce (Justice), 55, 432, 675

Cahn, Edmond, 426, 516
Calhoun, John C., 67–68, 511
Canvassing, constitutional status of, 470–
    471
Capital punishment, 651
Cardozo, Benjamin N., 55, 200, 269, 421,
    553, 595, 652
Carroll, Daniel, 28
Cases and controversies, 116–117, 142
Celler, Emanuel, 187
Censorship, of books, 503–505
  of motion pictures, 505–507
  of press, 431–449
  of speech, 451–473
Census, 182–183
Certiorari, writ of, 124, 131–132, 167
Chafee, Zechariah, Jr., 417, 426, 511
Chase, Salmon P., 53, 68, 249
Chase, Samuel, 52, 137
Chief Justice, role of, 128–129, 204
Child Labor Act of 1916, 239, 261
Child labor amendment, 35–36, 39, 170
Church, Frank, 188
Churches, liberty of, 566–567
Cigarette legislation, 259, 665–666
Circuit courts, 122, 124
  of appeals, 124, 127
Citizenship, diversity of, 125, 147–150
  loss of, 526, 765–769
  national, 408, 759–761

Citizenship, rights of, under privileges and immunities clause, 98–100, 400–401
  state, 759–760
Civil disobedience, 485–489
Civil rights, federal protection of, 738–743
Civil Rights Act, of 1866, 406–408, 710, 717, 732
  of 1871, 85, 712
  of 1875, 711–713, 717
  of 1957, 119, 739, 754
  of 1960, 739, 755
  of 1964, 119, 277–279, 483, 729, 736, 739, 742, 755
  of 1968, 739
Civil Rights Commission, 739, 758
Civil Rights Section, Department of Justice, 738, 752
Civil Service Commission, 472, 756
Clark, Ramsey, 56, 80, 615
Clark, Tom, 56, 89, 120, 156, 225, 228, 278, 446–448, 469, 480–481, 496, 499, 506, 517, 535, 541–542, 577–578, 610–611, 615, 653
Clarke, John H., 441
Class suits, 170
Clayton Act, 119, 266
Clear and present danger, 415–419, 426, 429, 444
Cleveland, Grover, 81, 337
Closed shop, 680
Cloture, 211–212
Cohen, Felix S., 429
Comity, 153
Commander in Chief, control of armed forces by, 378–379
  control of economy by, 388–390
  Lincoln's actions as, 372–373, 376
  martial law, 379–382
  military justice, 382–388
Commerce, and civil rights, 277–279, 736
  concurrent power theory, 282
  dormant power theory, 282–283
  "effect upon," concept of, 263–269
  interstate, 255–256, 258–259
  intrastate, 256–258
  mutual exclusiveness theory, 283–284
  power to regulate, by Congress, 259–263
    by states, 287–294
  racial equality in, 714–715
  selective exclusiveness theory, 284–286
  state taxation of, 296–303
  stream of, 264, 267

Commerce Court, 126; 133
Committee on Un-American Activities, 218–227, 230
Common law, federal, 143, 148–149
Communist Control Act of 1954, 545
Communist Party, 224, 369, 522–547, 604, 635, 649, 762–764, 776–777
  constitutional status of, 545–547
  legislation affecting, federal, 526–536, 538–540, 543–544
    state, 523–526, 537–538, 540–542, 544–545
  registration of, 533–536, 618
Concurrent resolutions, 330–331
Conference of Chief Justices, 57
Confessions, in absence of counsel, 630–632
  coerced, 623–625
Congress, adjournment of, 330
  administrative supervision by, 205–209
  convening of, 329–330
  elections to, 184–188
  members of, censure and expulsion, 190–191
    privileges and immunities, 192–193
  powers of, 22–24
    borrowing, 248–250
    contempt, 217–218
    delegation of, 198–203, 331
    implied, 197, 249
    investigatory, 214–232
    law-making, 195
    monetary, 250–251
    spending, 245–248
    taxing, 234–245
    war, 373–376
  procedures in, 209–212
  vacancies in, 191–192
Conscientious objectors, admission to bar, 122
  military service of, 565–566
  naturalization of, 566, 761–762
Constitution, interpretation of, 45–50
  meaning of, 3–4
  ratification of, 28–30
Constitutional Convention, committee, of detail, 18, 23, 25–27, 33
  of eleven, 26–27
  of style, 18
  major decisions of, 19–28
  membership of, 16–17
Constitutional courts, 133–135
Consuls, 150

Contempt, of Congress, 217–218
    of court, 117–120, 350–351, 443–445, 754
Continental Congress, 7, 10, 30
Contingent legislation, 200
Contract, freedom of, 668–676
Contract theory, 8–9
Contracts, protection of, 689–697
Conventions for amending Constitution, 37–38
Coolidge, Calvin, 54, 320, 350
Cooper, Joseph, 332
Corporations and Fourteenth Amendment, 669
Corwin, Edward S., 134, 144, 153, 175, 203, 308, 331, 356, 553, 678, 697
Council of State Governments, 37–39, 42
Counsel, right to, 625–632
    in pre-trial period, 629–632
Court of Claims, 132, 134, 145
Court of Customs and Patent Appeals, 132, 134
Court-packing plan, 55, 125, 138, 166
Courts of appeals, 124
Courts-martial, 382–385
Crimes against United States, 599–601
Crosskey, William W., 47, 162, 198, 246, 284, 334, 398, 400, 408, 709–710
Cruel and unusual punishment, 647, 650–651
Curse, right to, 475–476
Curtis, Benjamin R., 285–286, 588–589, 593, 657

Damnum absque injuria, 172
David, Paul T., 84
Davis, David, 381
Davis, Jefferson, 68
Day, William R., 72–73, 261–262
Debs, Eugene V., 54, 81, 416–417
Debtor moratorium legislation, 696–697
Decision of 1789, 334, 344
Declaration of Independence, 7–10, 406, 735
Declaratory judgment, 168
De facto segregation, 730
Defamation, 509–520
Delegation of legislative power, 198–203, 331, 356–357
Demonstrations, breach of peace by, 475–485
    constitutional status of, 463–465

Demonstrations, injunctions against, 466–467
    licensing of, 465–466
Denaturalization, 763–765
Deportation, 526, 602–603
Desegregation of public schools, 725–730
De Tocqueville, Alexis, 556
Diamond, Martin, 30
Dickinson, John, 8, 10, 17, 25
Direct action, 485–489
Dirksen, Everett M., 37, 278, 319
Dirksen amendment, on legislative apportionment, 37, 90
    on religion in public schools, 579
Disfranchisement of Negroes, 748–758
Disrict of Columbia, 94, 133
District courts, 122, 125–126
    three-judge, 126–127
Diversity of citizenship, 125, 147–150
Divorce, 101–104
Dodd, Thomas J., 191
Domestic violence, 80–82
Dorr's Rebellion, 82–83
Double jeopardy, 384, 645–648
Douglas, William O., 55, 72, 92, 104, 131, 135, 157, 193, 226, 229, 240, 244, 368, 370, 374–375, 391, 422, 438, 454, 458, 472–473, 476, 479, 483, 485, 494, 499, 514–515, 529, 532–533, 537, 540, 548, 559–560, 563–564, 566, 573–574, 613, 619, 630, 654, 668–669, 679–680, 686–687, 698, 720, 733, 735, 743, 765, 767, 776–778
Draft-card burning, 464
Draft evasion, loss of citizenship for, 768–769
Drug addiction, 650–651
Dual federalism, 72–73, 197, 239, 262
Due process, in Fifth Amendment, 403
    in Fourteenth Amendment, 592–599, 658–660
    in judicial proceedings, 589–592
    and legislation, 588–589
    procedural, 588–592
    substantive, 656–681, 684–688
    in taxation, 701–705

Eastland, James O., 192
Eighteenth Amendment, 25–26, 39–41
Eighth Amendment, cruel and unusual punishment, 647, 650–651
    excessive bail, 649–650

Eisenberg, Ralph, 84

Eisenhower, Dwight D., 39, 41, 56, 81, 117, 135, 137, 325–326, 348, 361, 382, 543, 725, 727

Elections, constitutional provisions on, 745–747

  county unit system, 86

  political-question doctrine, 85, 184–187

  primary, 750–753

  right to vote in, 746–747

Electoral college, 312–315

Electoral Commission, 311

Electors, presidential, 309–318

Electronic eavesdropping, 612–616

Elementary and Secondary Education Act, 173, 729

Eleventh Amendment, 34, 52, 75, 146

Ellsworth, Oliver, 17–18, 21, 24, 52, 164

Emergency Court of Appeals, 121, 133

Emergency powers, 696–697

Emergency Price Control Act, 121, 152, 202, 388

Emerson, Thomas I., 426–427

Eminent domain, 697–701

Employer-employee relations, 668–681

Enforcement Act of 1870, 746

Equal-footing doctrine, 78–79

Equal protection, 708–743

  and economic legislation, 681–684

  for indigents in criminal prosecutions, 641–642

  original understanding of, 709–714

  and racial discrimination, in commerce, 714–715

    in education, 720–730

    in housing, 715–717

    by private individuals, 736–738

    in public accommodations, 734–736

    in public transportation, 717–720

  and state taxation, 705–707

Ervin, Sam J., Jr., 37–40

Espionage Act of 1917, 416–417, 419, 440–441, 601

Establishment of religion, 567–581

Exclusionary rule, in federal trials, 608

  in state trials, 608–612

Executive agreements, 359, 366

Expatriation, 765–769

Exports, taxation of, 236–237

Ex post facto laws, 398, 602–603, 692

Extradition, 106–107

Fair Labor Standards Act, 201, 259, 271–273, 434, 680

Fair trial, 641–643

  and freedom of the press, 442–449

  in juvenile courts, 644–645

Fairman, Charles, 400, 408

Federal Communications Commission, 127, 199, 346

Federal Employers' Liability Act, 152

Federal Power Commission, 275, 343, 346

Federal questions, 142–143

Federal Radio Commission, 134

Federal Trade Commission, 346

Federalism, 63–64, 69

Federalist, The, 65, 115, 162, 164, 189, 307, 344, 354, 396, 633

Fellman, David, 557, 572, 586

Field, Stephen J., 53, 138, 336, 364–365, 436–438, 617–618, 658–660, 682, 694, 775

Fifteenth Amendment, 35–36, 404–405, 746–747, 755

Fifth Amendment, coerced confessions, 623–625

  double jeopardy, 645–648

  due process, 657–658

  grand jury indictment, 633

  self-incrimination, 218–219, 616–622

Fighting words, 428

Filibuster, 210–212

First Amendment, absolutist interpretation of, 423–426, 429

  and balancing, 426–429

  clear and present danger test, 415–419, 426, 429, 444

  and congressional investigations, 221

  preferred position of, 420–423, 429

  reasonable man interpretation of, 419–420, 429, 432, 680

  two-level theory, 428–429, 475, 493–496

Flag salute, 557–559

Food and drug regulation, 260

Foreign relations, Congress and, 360–362

  control of President over, 356–359

  nature of federal power over, 354–356

Foreign states and federal courts, 150

Fortas, Abe, 56, 92, 370, 435, 484, 499, 629, 644, 740

Fourteenth Amendment, 35–36, 182, 760

  drafting of, 404–410

Fourteenth Amendment, reduction of representation in House, 182, 746
  relation to Bill of Rights, 418, 592–597, 611, 621, 652–653
  validity of, 40
  (*See also* Due process; Equal protection; Privileges and immunities)
Fourth Amendment, 603–616
Franchise, 745–758
  state limitations on, 747–750
Franchise taxes, 300–301
Frank, Jerome, 491
Frank, John, 404
Frankfurter, Felix, 56, 70, 85–86, 103, 111, 118, 132, 137, 139, 149, 162, 169, 171, 177, 184–185, 193, 239, 244–245, 253, 272, 295, 304, 340–341, 348, 382, 415, 421, 423, 444–445, 458, 462–463, 465, 474, 492, 500, 502, 504, 519, 529, 534, 537, 543, 558–562, 567, 587, 596, 609–610, 619–620, 624, 636–637, 652, 654, 697, 740, 767, 778
Franklin, Benjamin, 5–7, 10, 17, 19, 22, 27
Frantz, Laurent B., 428
Freedom of contract, 668–676
Freedom of the press, 431–442
  and fair trial, 442–449
Freedom of speech, 412–413, 451–473
  and breach of peace, 475–489
  for civil servants, 472–473
  "pure speech," 454
  relation to free exercise of religion, 554–555
  "speech plus," 454–455
Freund, Paul A., 413
Frick, Henry Clay, 435
Friendly, Henry J., 150
Friendly suits, 168–169
Fugitive Slave Act, 76, 152
Full faith and credit, 100–105
Fuller, Melville W., 47, 53–54, 775

Gambling, taxation of, 239–240
Garfield, James A., 325
General welfare clause, 245
Georgia county unit system, 86
Gerry, Elbridge, 17–18, 24–25, 27–28
Gerrymandering, 184
  racial, 91, 187
Ginnane, Robert W., 208

Goldberg, Arthur J., 56, 120, 229, 369, 454–455, 464–465, 468–469, 481, 483, 487–488, 513, 516, 546, 630, 735–736, 768
Goldman, Sheldon, 135
Goldwin, Robert A., 30
Gorham, Nathaniel, 18, 24, 27–28
Government corporations, 145
Grand jury, indictment by, 633
  one-man, 640–641
Grant, Ulysses S., 570
Gray, Horace, 774–775
Grier, Robert C., 138, 376
Griswold, Erwin N., 617
Guam, 95
Guilt by association, 523–526, 532, 538, 540–542

Habeas corpus, 121, 155–157, 217, 387–388, 643
  suspension of, 379–380
Habeas Corpus Act of 1867, 155
Hamilton, Alexander, 13–14, 17–20, 29, 33, 45, 115, 162, 164, 189, 197, 234, 246, 307, 633
Hand, Augustus N., 492
Hand, Learned, 415, 491–492, 527–528
Handbills, 436–437
Harlan, John M. (1833–1911), 53, 138, 262–263, 593–594, 660–662, 664, 676, 712–713, 718
Harlan, John M. (1899–    ), 56, 90, 186–187, 222–223, 425–427, 454, 481–482, 494–496, 499–502, 505, 517, 530–531, 533, 549, 617, 621, 629, 653, 681, 686, 700, 733
Harris, Joseph P., 208, 332
Harris, Robert J., 682
Hartford Convention, 67
Hatch Act, 173, 472–473, 526
Hay, John, 358
Hayes-Tilden election, 310–311
Health and welfare legislation, 660–664
Hearings, alien exclusion, 772–773
  deportation, 777–778
  fair, 592
Henry, Patrick, 17
Heyman, Ira Michael, 488
Holmes, Oliver Wendell, 47–50, 54, 73, 136, 139, 148, 159, 243, 261–262, 264, 345, 350, 363, 412, 416–421, 423, 426, 439, 441, 443, 452–453,

Holmes, Oliver Wendell, 511, 604, 609, 613, 643, 662–664, 673–674, 676, 683, 703–704, 772
Hoover, Herbert, 55, 308, 343
Horn, Robert A., 269, 522
Hours legislation, 669–670, 672–673
House of Representatives, apportionment, 182–183
  censure, 190–191
  districting, 183–188
  expulsion, 190–191
  immunities of members, 192–193
  qualifications of members, 188–190
  reduction in representation in, 182–183
  terms, 188
  vacancies in, 191
Houston, William, 25
Howard, Jacob M., 409
Howe, Mark DeWolfe, 407
Hughes, Charles Evans, 54–55, 128, 136, 171, 176, 200, 256, 265, 267, 270–271, 294, 432, 490, 509, 525, 617, 623, 637, 666, 675, 679, 696, 702, 719, 722

Immigration and Nationality Act of 1952, 368, 370, 640, 761, 766, 770, 774–775, 778
Immunity, intergovernmental tax, 240–245
  judicial, 139
  legislative, 192–193, 425
  from prosecution for testimony, 618–619
  to suit, 145
Impeachment, 137–138, 203–205
Imports, taxes on, 258, 294–296
Imports-exports clause, 294–296
Income taxes, 234–236
Incorporation theory of Fourteenth Amendment, 592–597, 611, 621, 652–653
Indictment by grand jury, 633
Inherent power, of Congress, 197–198
  of President, 333–341
Inheritance taxes, 235–236
Injunction, 121, 153–155, 466–467
Insanity, legal tests for, 645
Insurance, regulation of, 276
Intention of Framers of Constitution, 45–46
Intergovernmental tax immunity, 240–245
Internal Security Act of 1950, 367, 771, 778
Interposition, 65–67, 77, 725–726

Interstate commerce, 255–259
  taxation of, 296–303
  (*See also* Commerce)
Interstate Commerce Act, 126, 252, 255, 260, 718–719
Interstate Commerce Commission, 126, 135, 199, 264–265, 345, 718, 720
Interstate compacts, 107–109
Intrastate commerce, 256–257
Invasion, guarantee against, 80
Investigations, congressional, 214–232
Involuntary servitude, 374, 404, 407
Israel, Jerold H., 629
Item veto, 333

Jackson, Andrew, 67–68, 116, 206–207, 310, 320
Jackson, Robert H., 102, 104, 156, 169, 176, 230, 274, 331, 340, 389, 422, 445, 452, 457–458, 477, 511, 519, 528, 546, 558, 562, 567, 573–574, 599–600, 610, 613, 638, 654, 685, 719, 773, 776–777
Jaffe, Louis L., 173, 445, 597
Japanese, discrimination against, 714–715
  evacuation in World War II, 390–392
Jay, John, 13, 17, 29, 51
Jefferson, Thomas, 7, 17, 34, 65–67, 93, 196, 309–310, 343, 511, 568, 774
Jehovah's Witnesses, 436–437, 456, 458, 465, 467, 471, 477, 544–559
Johnson, Andrew, 175, 204–205, 322, 344, 407
Johnson, Lyndon B., 39, 56, 80, 82–83, 94, 209, 278, 325–326, 361, 378, 580
Johnson, William (Justice), 53, 283
Johnson, William S., 18
Judicial review, 158–177
Judiciary, appointment of, 135–137
  compensation of, 139
  in Constitutional Convention, 27–28
  tenure of, 137–138
Judiciary Act, of 1789, 73, 120, 122–123, 129–130, 142–143, 148, 158, 163, 649
  of 1801, 123, 163
  of 1802, 123
  of 1925, 132
Juries, "blue ribbon," 638
  government employees on, 635–636
  selection of, 634–635
  racial discrimination in, 636–638

Jurisdiction, of federal courts, 142–157
   and judicial due process, 591
   in state taxation, 702–705
Jury trial, in contempt cases, 118–120
   in federal courts, 633–636
   in state courts, 636–638
Just compensation in eminent domain, 700–701
Justiciable questions, 167–174
Juvenile courts, due process in, 644–645

Kalven, Harry, Jr., 455, 463, 511, 519
Kamin, Alfred, 470
Kelly, Alfred H., 46–47
Kennedy, Edward M., 136
Kennedy, John F., 81, 135, 137, 317, 325–326, 576, 727–728
Kennedy, Robert F., 82, 189, 614
Kentucky Resolutions, 65–67, 774
Kidnap law and jury trial, 634
King, Martin Luther, Jr., 82, 466–467, 485–486, 739
King, Rufus, 17–18, 25, 234
Ku Klux (Second Enforcement) Act of 1871, 712
Ku Klux Klan, 523, 547, 550
Kurland, Philip B., 562

Labor Management Relations Act of 1947, 338–341
Labor regulation, 291–292
Labor unions, 675–676, 680
   and Sherman Act, 266–267
La Follette, Robert M., 41, 166
Lansing, Robert, 18–19, 22
Lee, Richard Henry, 7, 10, 17
Legislative courts, 133–134
Lend-Lease Act of 1941, 331
Lerner, Max, 51, 643
Levy, Leonard W., 511
Lewis, Anthony, 629
Libel, civil prosecution for, 510
   criminal prosecution for, 509
   group, 518–520
   in labor disputes, 517
   private defamation, 515–518
   by public officials, 515
   of public officials, 512–515
   seditious, 414, 510–512
License taxes and religious freedom, 559–560

Licensing, of labor union organizers, 291
   of parades, 465–466
   of public meetings, 456–458
Lincoln, Abraham, 69, 372–373, 376, 378, 380
Lippmann, Walter, 214
Liquor regulation, 293–294
Literacy tests, 749
Litigation and right of association, 549–550
Locke, John, 8, 160, 334, 336, 395
Lockhart, William, 497
Lodge-Gossett amendment, 160, 317, 334, 336
Loyalty oaths, 537–540
Loyalty-security programs, 543–544
Lynd, Staughton, 370–371

MacArthur, Douglas, 387
McCarran Act, 367, 533–536
McCarthy, Joseph, 218, 639
McCloskey, Robert G., 680, 687
McClure, Robert, 497
McIlwain, Charles H., 3, 395
McKenna, Joseph, 350, 751
McLean, John, 255
McReynolds, James C., 55, 242, 250, 422, 437, 460, 677
Madison, James, 12, 14, 17–18, 20–22, 25, 27–29, 33–34, 63–67, 75, 161, 163, 246, 286, 396–397, 568
Magna Carta, 395, 403, 588
Magrath, C. Peter, 498
Mandamus, 120, 163
Mann Act, 255, 261
Mann-Elkins Act, 126
Manwaring, David R., 556, 558
Marshall, John, 45–46, 48, 50, 52–53, 71, 73–75, 93, 121, 128, 133, 163–165, 175, 197, 199, 240–241, 253–256, 258, 281–286, 294, 296, 349, 356, 374, 399–400, 600, 635, 690–695, 761
Marshall, Thurgood, 56–57
Martial law, 379–382
Martin, Luther, 22
Mason, Alpheus T., 421
Mason, George, 17–18, 23, 25–28, 33, 65, 616
Matthews, Stanley, 590, 593
Mead, Margaret, 496
Medina, Harold R., 118, 449, 527, 635

Meetings, and breach of peace, 475–489
  public, 456–459
Meiklejohn, Alexander, 424–425, 511
Meiklejohn, Donald, 428
Mercer, John F., 24
Meredith, James H., 81, 120
Military trials, 382–388
Miller, Samuel, 53, 99, 296, 658–660, 681, 713
Minimum wage legislation, 670, 673–675, 679–680
Minton, Sherman, 540
Miscegenation, laws against, 730–732
Monetary powers of Congress, 250–251
Moody, William H., 594
Morals legislation, 664–666
Morgan, Arthur E., 347
Mormons, 556, 563
Morris, Gouverneur, 17–18, 22–23, 25–27, 34, 45
Morris, Robert, 12
Morrison, Stanley, 684–685
Motion-picture censorship, 505–507
Motor-vehicle taxation, 303
Multiple taxation, 703
Mundt amendment, 317
Murphy, Frank, 55–56, 387, 391, 426, 428, 460–461, 475, 490, 509, 557, 559, 561, 609, 738, 764–765
Murphy, Walter F., 57, 70, 131

National Association for the Advancement of Colored People, 82–83, 169, 228–229, 523, 548–549, 727
National Defense Education Act, 539, 579
National Industrial Recovery Act, 201, 267
National Labor Relations Board, 127, 269–271, 347
National Recovery Administration, 267
Nationality Act of 1940, 761–762, 764, 766
Natural law, 160
  and Justice Black, 687
Natural rights, 8
Naturalization, 761–763
Navigable waters, 275–276
Necessary and proper clause, 196–197
Negroes, discrimination against, in education, 720–730
  federal legislation on, 738–743
  in housing, 715–717, 736–738
  on juries, 636–637

Negroes, original intention of Fourteenth Amendment concerning, 709–714
  in public accommodations, 734–736
  in public transportation, 717–720
  in voting, 748–757
Nelson, Samuel, 241
Neutrality, 360
New Jersey Plan, 18–21, 27, 63
Newspaper tax, 433–434
Nineteenth Amendment, 35
Ninth Amendment, 374, 398, 686
Nixon, Richard M., 211, 317, 326, 534
Norris-La Guardia Act, 121
Northwest Ordinance of 1787, 11, 77–78
Notice and hearing, 592
Nullification, 67–68, 75–77

Oaths, loyalty, 537–538
  non-Communist, 538–540
Obscenity, 490–507
  exclusion from mail, 439–440
  and motion-picture censorship, 505–507
  tests for, contemporary community standards, 502
    pandering, 497–500
    patent offensiveness, 495
    prurient interest, 493
    redeeming social importance, 495
    subjective nature of, 500–502
  two-level theory of, 493–496
One man, one vote, 86–90, 92
  and local government, 91
Open occupancy laws, 736–738
Original package doctrine, 258–259, 294–295, 297
Osborne, George R., 549

Paine, Tom, 4, 7, 9, 17, 395, 436
Panama Canal Zone, 95
Parades, injunctions against, 466–467
  licensing of, 463–466
Pardoning power, 348–351
Parens patriae, 147
Parker, John J., 136
Passports, 366–371, 535
Paterson, William, 17, 19–21, 234
Patric, Gordon, 574
Pauling, Linus, 516, 518
Peckham, Rufus W., 672–673
Peltason, Jack W., 726
Peonage, 404

Permits (*see* Licensing)
Petition, right of, 480, 518
Pickering, John, 138
Picketing, of court houses, 469–470
  in labor disputes, 454–455, 459–463
  in public demonstrations, 463–470
  residential, 470
Pinckney, Charles, 17, 25
Pine, David A., 338–340
Pocket veto, 333
Police power, commerce power as, 260–261
  and freedom of contract, 668–676
  inalienability of, 694–695
  and public health, 660–666
Political questions, 85, 110, 176–177
  amending process, 36
  foreign relations, 353
  legislative districting and apportionment, 85–86, 184–186
Poll tax, 748–749, 753–754
Pollak, Louis H., 577, 737
Polygamy, 556, 563
Pornography, hard-core, 496–497
Post Office and freedom of press, 437–442
Powell, Adam Clayton, 190–191, 193
Powell, Thomas Reed, 49, 165, 287
Preamble, 64
Preemption, 71–72
Preferred-position argument, freedom of religion, 561–562
  freedom of speech, 420–423, 429
President, acting, 323
  in Constitutional Convention, 24–26
  election of, electors, 312–315
    by House, 315
    original plan for, 24–26, 309–310
    proposals for reform of, 41–42, 315–319
  inability of, 324–327
  powers of, appointing, 341–343
    armed forces, 378–379
    Commander in Chief, 372–373, 378–382
    foreign affairs, 353–366
    legislative, 329–332
    martial law, 379–382
    military justice, 382–388
    occupation of conquered territory, 377–378
    pardoning, 348–351
    removal, 334, 344–348
    seizure of industrial plants, 389
    signing of bills, 330–333

President, powers of, veto, 332–333
  qualifications, 308
  relation to courts, 175–176
  role in amending process, 38–39
  succession, 321–324
  theories of executive power, 333–341
  two-term tradition, 320
President pro tempore of Senate, 322–324
Presidential Succession Act, 323
Pre-trial publicity, 445–446
Previous restraint, of press, 431–449
  of religion, 555
  of speech, 451–470
Price fixing, 670–671, 676, 678–679
Primary elections, 750–753
Pringle, Henry F., 136
Prior restraint (*see* Previous restraint)
Pritchett, C. Herman, 57, 72, 131, 347
Privacy, right to, 435, 684–687
Privilege taxes, 300–301
Privileges and immunities, under Article IV, section 2, 98–100, 400–401, 403
  under Fourteenth Amendment, 592, 658
Prohibition, 350, 375, 664–665
Public accommodations and state action, 734–736
Public Accommodations Act of 1964, 736
Public education, and racial discrimination, 720–730
  and religious establishment, 570–581
Public employees, removal of, on Fifth Amendment grounds, 541–542
  on loyalty grounds, 540–541, 543–544
Public forum, access to, 452–470
Public meetings, 456–459
Public passages, obstruction of, 467–469
Public purpose, in eminent domain, 698
  in state taxation, 701–702
Puerto Rico, 94–95

Quorum, 210
Quota system for immigrants, 770

Racial discrimination, in commerce, 714–715
  in education, 720–730
  in housing, 715–717
  on juries, 636–637, 743
  on public transportation, 717–720
  in voting, 748–757

Randolph, Edmund, 17–20, 23–24, 27–28, 45, 106
Rate fixing, 671, 676–678, 680
Ratner, Leonard G., 131
Reapportionment, legislàtive, 84–92, 182–183
"Reasonable man" test, 419–420, 429, 432, 680
Recess appointments, 343
Reed, Stanley, 239–240, 423, 456, 458, 471–472, 559, 573, 596
Reitz, Curtis R., 155
Religion, definition of, 563–564
    establishment of, 567–581
        relation to free exercise of, 553
    free exercise of, 554–567
        alternative means test, 560–561
        preferred position for, 561–562
        secular regulation rule, 556–557, 560
    theism, 564
Religious education, public assistance to, 570, 579–580
    under Elementary and Secondary Education Act of 1965, 580
    pupil benefit theory, 570–572, 580
    in public schools, Bible reading, 173, 575, 577
        prayers, 575–577
        released-time programs, 572–575
Removal Act of 1875, 151
Removal from office, by congressional appropriations, 248
    of judges, 138
    under loyalty-security program, 543–544
    by President, 344–348
Rendition, 106–107
Reorganization acts, 208, 331–332
Representation, in Congress, 182–188
    in state legislatures, 84–93
Republican form of government, 82–83, 86, 92
Restrictive covenants, 715–717
Roberts, Owen J., 55, 136, 202, 247, 391, 422, 437, 453, 478, 525, 555–556, 627–628, 678
Roche, John P., 177
Rockwell, George Lincoln, 457, 466
Romney, George, 308
Roosevelt, Franklin D., 41, 44, 55–56, 109, 125, 166, 320, 332, 378
Roosevelt, Theodore, 54, 136, 320, 335, 357, 510, 770
Rossiter, Clinton, 373, 380

Rush, Dr. Benjamin, 13
Rutledge, John, 17–18, 27, 34, 52
Rutledge, Wiley B., 55–56, 85, 103, 185, 287, 298, 387, 422, 472, 555, 571, 764–765

Safety legislation, 666
Sales tax, 298–300
Samoa, 95
Sanford, Edward T., 415, 418–419, 716
Search and seizure, 603–616
    of automobiles, 607–608
    in connection with valid arrest, 605–607
    rules for, exclusionary, 608–612
        plain sight, 605
        silver platter, 608, 611
        state, 608–612
    warrant requirement for, 603–604
    wiretapping and electronic eavesdropping, 612–616
Search warrants, 604
Secession, 68–69
Second Amendment, 397
Second-class mailing privileges, 440–441
Secretary of State, 323
    control of passports by, 366–371
Sedition Act, of 1798, 509–511, 523, 527
    of 1918, 416
Seditious libel, 414, 510–512
Segregation, 714–720
    in public schools, 117, 720–730
Selective service, 374, 565
Self-incrimination, 240, 616–622
    before congressional committees, 218–219, 617
    in federal prosecutions and grand jury proceedings, 617–620
    in state prosecutions, 620–622
Self-restraint, judicial, 167–177
Senate, censure and expulsion by, 190–191
    confirmation of appointments by, 342–343
    as continuing body, 188
    immunities of members, 192–193
    indirect election, 181–182
    membership, 181
    qualifications, 188–190
    terms, 188
    vacancies, 191
"Separate but equal," 718, 724
Separation of powers, 9, 20, 174–177
Seventeenth Amendment, 35

Seventh Day Adventists, 560–561
Sexual sterilization, 662–664, 685
Shapiro, Martin, 231, 428–429, 511
Shays' Rebellion, 12, 20, 27–28
Sherman, Roger, 17, 23, 26–28, 34, 63, 397, 552
Sherman Act, 54, 126, 235, 257, 265–266, 276–277, 434
Shreveport doctrine, 264–265
Sidewalks, obstruction of, 467–469
Sit-ins, on private property, 481–483, 486–487, 734–735
  in public buildings, 483–485
Sixteenth Amendment, 35, 235
Sixth Amendment, compulsory process, 640–641
  confrontation with witnesses, 640
  counsel, 625–632
  information on accusation, 639–640
  jury trial, 633–638
  speedy and public trial, 638–639
Slander (see Libel)
Slavery, constitutional issues, 401–403
  constitutional provisions, 35, 182, 404, 407
Slum clearance, 668, 698
Smith, Frank L., 190
Smith Act, 56, 71, 118, 167, 526–533, 635
Social Security Act, 247–248
Sorauf, Frank J., 575
Sound trucks, 458–459
Speaker of House, 210, 322–324
Spending power, 245–248
Stamp Act, 6
Standing to sue, 170–174, 578
Stare decisis, 51
State action, under Fourteenth Amendment, 482, 732–738
  inaction of state officials, 733–734
States, admission of, 77–79
  disputes between, 109–111
  limits on powers of, 24
  suits against, 146–147
Stewart, Potter, 56, 89, 203, 226–228, 374, 464, 467, 481, 486, 494, 496–500, 515, 542, 560, 576–578, 611, 615–616, 731, 741, 743
Stockholders' suits, 168–169
Stone, Harlan F., 54–55, 73, 105, 121, 202, 243–244, 251, 272, 289, 421–422, 558, 675, 685, 703–704
Story, Joseph, 53, 74, 148, 246, 379
Submerged Lands Act, 79

Subsequent punishment for speech or assembly, 474–489
Subversive Activities Control Act of 1950, 771, 778
Subversive Activities Control Board, 534–536
Sumner, Charles, 708
Sunday closing laws, 560
Supremacy clause, 24, 70–71, 152, 282
Supreme Court, appellate jurisdiction, 130–131
  attacks on, 166
  history, 51–57
  methods of review, 131–132
  operation, 127–129
  original jurisdiction, 129–130, 163–164
  power to declare acts of Congress unconstitutional, 159, 163–166
  size, 123–124
Sutherland, Arthur E., Jr., 173, 667–668, 673–674, 676
Sutherland, George, 55, 147, 170, 268–269, 346–347, 354–357, 626–627
Swayne, Noah H., 658
Swisher, Carl B., 138

Taft, William Howard, 54, 79, 124, 136, 198, 264, 266, 293, 334–336, 344–347, 350, 642, 673–674, 721
Taft-Hartley Act, 338–341, 538–539, 546
Taney, Roger B., 47, 53, 72, 76, 82–83, 107, 122, 255, 283, 377, 379, 402–403, 657, 693–694, 760
Tariff, protective, 237
Tax Court, 127, 133
Tax exemption of churches, 580–581
Taxation, apportionment in, 301–303
  direct, 234–236
  equal protection in, 705–707
  of exports, 236–237
  of gambling, 239–240
  intergovernmental immunity, 240–245
  multiple, 703
  for nonrevenue purposes, 237–240
  state, due process in, 701–705
    imports-exports clause, 294–296
    on interstate commerce, 296–303
    public purpose in, 701–702
    on religion, 559–560, 580–581
  uniformity requirement in, 236
  (See also specific taxes)
Taxpayers' suits, 170, 174, 579

Tefft, Sheldon, 120
Television in trials, 446–447
Tennessee Valley Authority, 275–276
Tenth Amendment, 69–70, 72–73, 198, 363
Tenure of Office Act, 344
Territories, 93–95
Territory, acquisition of, 93
  occupation of, 377–378
Test cases, 169
Test Oath Act of 1862, 122, 189
Thirteenth Amendment, 35, 182, 404, 407
Three-judge courts, 126–127
Tidelands oil cases, 79
Travel, freedom to, 98–99
Treason, 599–601
Treaties, 143, 358–359, 362–366
Treaty of London, 374
Trespass, on private property, 481–483, 486–487
  on public property, 483–485
Trials, fairness of, 641–645
  speedy and public, 638–639
Truman, Harry S., 44, 135, 323, 333, 338–339, 389, 533, 543, 738
Trumbull, Lyman, 406–407
Twelfth Amendment, 34, 310–311, 321
Twentieth Amendment, 35, 322
Twenty-fifth Amendment, 35, 39, 322, 324, 326
Twenty-first Amendment, 35, 39, 293, 295
Twenty-fourth Amendment, 35, 42, 753
Twenty-second Amendment, 35, 41, 320
Twenty-third Amendment, 35, 94
Two-level theory, 428–429, 475, 493–496
Tyler, John, 322, 357

Unconstitutionality of acts of Congress, 159, 163–166
Uniform Code of Military Justice, 382–383, 386
Union, nature of, 64–69
Use taxes, 298–299

Vaccination, 557, 661–662
Van Alstyne, William W., 90
Van Devanter, Willis, 55, 216
Vare, William S., 190
Veto power, executive, 332–333
  judicial, 161
Vice President, 210
  in Constitutional Convention, 26–27

Vice President, role during inability of President, 325–327
  succession to presidency, 321–324
Vietnam war, 360–361, 377, 566
Vinson, Fred, 56, 338–339, 426, 479, 528, 538, 649, 715–716, 722, 778
Violence, expectation of, 478–481
Virgin Islands, 95
Virginia Plan, 18, 21–22, 24, 27–28, 33, 63–64
Virginia Resolutions, 65–67, 75
Vote, right to, constitutional provisions on, 745–747
  federal protection of, 753–758
  state limitations on, 747–750
Voting Rights Act of 1965, 145, 212, 755–758

Wages and Hours Act (see Fair Labor Standards Act)
Wages Legislation, 670, 673–675, 679–680
Wagner Act, 269–271, 291, 434
Waite, Morrison R., 53, 659–660, 664, 671
Walker, Edwin A., 517
Wallace, George, 82, 466
War, state of, 373–378
War Claims Commission, 347
Warrants, administrative, 606
  arrest, 603
  search, 603–606, 612
Warren, Charles, 74, 148
Warren, Earl, 56, 71, 87–88, 92, 219–221, 447, 497, 499, 501–502, 504, 517–518, 544, 560, 602, 632, 638, 648, 650, 723–724, 732, 768–769
Warren Court, attacks upon, 57
Washington, Bushrod, 99, 400–401, 409
Washington, George, 16–17, 30, 51–52, 167, 309, 357–358, 360, 378
Webster, Daniel, 253, 285, 403
Wechsler, Herbert, 728
Wellington, Harry H., 150
Westin, Alan F., 162
White, Byron R., 56, 468, 484, 487, 496, 499, 686, 731, 737
White, Edward D., 54, 111
White primary cases, 751–753
Whittaker, Charles E., 56
Willoughby, W. F., 207
Wilmerding, Lucius, Jr., 309
Wilson, James, 12, 17–18, 21–28, 52, 197

Wilson, Woodrow, 136, 211, 214, 325, 344,
    349, 357
Wire tapping, 612–616
Workmen's compensation, 105, 671–672
Worthy, William, 370
Wright, Benjamin F., 690
Wright, J. Skelly, 730

Yates, Robert, 18, 22
Yellow-dog contract, 675–676
Young, Roland, 184
Youngdahl, Luther W., 639

Zoning, 666–668